Foundations of
ECONOMICS
AP Edition

Robin Bade

Michael Parkin
University of Western Ontario

PEARSON
Addison
Wesley

Boston San Francisco New York
London Toronto Sydney Tokyo Singapore Madrid
Mexico City Munich Paris Cape Town Hong Kong Montreal

Editor-in-Chief	Denise Clinton
Senior Acquisitions Editor	Adrienne D'Ambrosio
Editorial Assistant	Jennifer Moquin
Senior Project Manager	Mary Clare McEwing
Supplements Editor	Marianne Groth
Senior Administrative Assistant	Dottie Dennis
Executive Media Producer	Michelle Neil
Senior Media Producer	Melissa Honig
Executive Marketing Manager	Stephen Frail
Marketing Assistant	Kate MacLean
Managing Editor	Nancy Fenton
Senior Design Manager	Charles Spaulding
Technical Illustrator	Richard Parkin
Senior Manufacturing Buyer	Carol Melville
Copy Editor	Barbara Willette
Project Management, Page Makeup	Elm Street Publishing Services, Inc.

School Edition ISBN: 0-13-196047-4

To Erin, Tessa, Jack, Abby, and Sophie

About the Authors

Robin Bade was an undergraduate at the University of Queensland, Australia, where she earned degrees in mathematics and economics. After a spell teaching high school math and physics, she enrolled in the Ph.D. program at the Australian National University, from which she graduated in 1970. She has held faculty appointments at the University of Edinburgh in Scotland, at Bond University in Australia, and at the Universities of Manitoba, Toronto, and Western Ontario in Canada. Her research on international capital flows appears in the *International Economic Review* and the *Economic Record*.

Robin first taught the principles of economics course in 1970 and has taught it (alongside intermediate macroeconomics and international trade and finance) most years since then. She developed many of the ideas found in this text while conducting tutorials with her students at the University of Western Ontario.

Michael Parkin studied economics in England and began his university teaching career immediately after graduating with a B.A. from the University of Leicester. He learned the subject on the job at the University of Essex, England's most exciting new university of the 1960s, and at the age of 30 became one of the youngest full professors. He is a past president of the Canadian Economics Association and has served on the editorial boards of the *American Economic Review* and the *Journal of Monetary Economics*. His research on macroeconomics, monetary economics, and international economics has resulted in more than 160 publications in journals and edited volumes, including the *American Economic Review*, the *Journal of Political Economy*, the *Review of Economic Studies*, the *Journal of Monetary Economics*, and the *Journal of Money, Credit, and Banking*. He is author of the best-selling textbook, *Economics* (Addison-Wesley), now entering its Seventh Edition.

Robin and Michael are a wife-and-husband duo. Their most notable joint research created the Bade-Parkin Index of central bank independence and spawned a vast amount of research on that topic. They don't claim credit for the independence of the new European Central Bank, but its constitution and the movement toward greater independence of central banks around the world were aided by their pioneering work. Their joint textbooks include *Macroeconomics* (Prentice-Hall), *Modern Macroeconomics* (Pearson Education Canada), and *Economics: Canada in the Global Environment*, the Canadian adaptation of Parkin, *Economics* (Addison-Wesley). They are dedicated to the challenge of explaining economics ever more clearly to an ever-growing body of students.

Music, the theater, art, walking on the beach, and five fast-growing grandchildren provide their relaxation and fun.

Economics

Brief Contents

Contents

PART 2   A CLOSER LOOK AT MARKETS   117

PART 4   A CLOSER LOOK AT DECISION MAKERS   **265**

PART 5   PRICES, PROFITS, AND INDUSTRY PERFORMANCE   323

PART 7   MONITORING THE MACROECONOMY   497

PART 8   THE REAL ECONOMY   **569**

Chapter 23 Potential GDP and the Natural Unemployment Rate   569

CHAPTER CHECKLIST   569

PART 10 ECONOMIC FLUCTUATIONS 725

PART 11 THE GLOBAL ECONOMY 857

For the AP* Student

The challenge for an economics AP student is to learn a new way of thinking and looking at the world around you. When you finish this course, you will understand the language of economics, and you will be able to integrate economic concepts into your everyday experiences. You will make more informed personal decisions, and you will better understand economic issues highlighted in the media. In short, you will see the world in a fresh perspective and new light.

Economics is a core competency for the responsible citizen and is a foundation for every type of career. *Foundations of Economics*, AP Edition, is inspired by the special place that economics occupies in every AP student's education. In order for AP students to see economics in the clearest possible light, this text:

- Focuses on core concepts;
- Steers a path between an overload of detail that swamps the AP student and a minimalist approach that leaves the AP student dangling with too much unsaid;
- Encourages learning-by-doing;
- Provides many learning tools for many learning styles.

HOW TO SUCCEED IN YOUR AP ECONOMICS COURSE

Any AP course demands a significant commitment of time, and one of your biggest challenges will be to allocate your time efficiently. By applying some analysis to this challenge, you will already be thinking like an economist!

Here are some key strategies for success in this course.

Keep up with the course material on a weekly basis. Skim the appropriate chapter in the textbook before it is covered in class to get a general understanding of

* *AP, Pre-AP, Advanced Placement, and Advanced Placement Program are registered trademarks of The College Entrance Examination Board, which was not involved in the production of, and does not endorse, this product.*

the basic concepts and issues. After class, work through the problems in the appropriate chapter of *The AP* Test Prep Workbook*, ISBN 0-13-173078-9. The key to success is repeated practice with your new economic tools.

Make the Checklist-Checkpoint structure work for you. To learn economics you have to do economics. The Checklist-Checkpoint system provides you with a structure for doing just that. To make it work for you, start by familiarizing yourself with the Checklist at the opening to each chapter: it tells you where you'll be heading. As you progress through the chapter, you'll see that each major section corresponds to one of the Checklist items. After studying each section, be sure to work the Checkpoint! That's the time to reinforce what you've just read—while it's still fresh in your mind. Don't jump to the next section until you feel you've mastered the Checkpoint of the section at hand. Then, when you reach the end of the chapter, review the Chapter Checklist. It corresponds seamlessly to the Checklist and the key points in the sections. This system is the glue that holds it all together. Used consistently and thoughtfully, it will help you attain success in mastering economics.

Tailor your learning style to the many study tools available. Do you work best interactively in an online environment? Are you a visual learner? Do you like to break tasks down into smaller, bite-sized pieces? Whatever your learning style, there is something for you in this fully integrated learning system. If you like to be in charge of your own learning, you'll find that MyEconLab is a powerful tool; you'll be able to complete Checkpoints and exercises online, work graphs, take Practice Tests, receive a customized Study Plan, and step through guided solutions—all at your own pace. If you're a visual learner, the graphs will be key to your understanding—color is used consistently to convey specific actions, numbered captions walk you step by step through key figures, and accompanying data tables show you the main plotting points. If you like patient explanation of concepts, *The AP* Test Prep Workbook* will amplify the material in the text for you and allow you to work additional problems.

Look for economics in the world around you. To give you some inspiration in this direction, read the "Eye On" features that will show you how the theory connects with the everyday world around you. Also, don't miss the Reality Check at the end of each chapter, which asks you to ponder how the economic concepts in a particular chapter actually have a real impact on your own life. You will finally have an answer to the perennial question, "What use is all this theory, anyway?"

The AP course description outline that follows on the subsequent pages provides the major topics included on the AP exam. Look closely at these topics and note how the textbook follows the sequence of ideas to be mastered.

■ Understanding the AP Economics Examinations

The AP Economics Examinations make use of a variety of question types and graphical analysis to assess the skill level of AP students. The AP examinations reflect the types of assessment that occur at the college level.

The AP Economics Examinations take two hours and 10 minutes to complete. In both the multiple-choice and free-response sections of the exams, AP students can expect to work with graphs, charts, and tables. Each examination consists of a 70-minute, multiple-choice section and a 60-minute free-response section that may require graphical analysis. The free-response section begins with a mandatory 10-minute reading period that can be used to read each of the questions, sketch graphs, make notes, and plan answers in the green insert. AP students then have 50 minutes to write the answers in the pink booklet.

■ Section I: Multiple-Choice Questions

The multiple-choice section of each exam contains 60 questions, with 70 minutes allotted for Section I. The multiple-choice section accounts for 2/3 of the AP student's examination grade. Each question has five choices and only one choice is judged correct. The questions are straightforward, and many require analysis and interpretation. Some will require analysis of a graph, chart, or table.

The AP Economics Examinations contain these distinct question types:

- **Definition or identification questions**
- **Graph or table questions**
- **Analysis or cause and effect questions**
- **Multiple-choice questions**

Hints on Grading: The multiple-choice section of each exam is worth 2/3 of the AP student's score. The questions are machine scored and determined by crediting one point for a correct answer and by deducting 1/4 of a point for an incorrect answer. No points are gained or lost for unanswered questions. If you have no idea what the correct answer is, leave the answer blank. But, if you can eliminate two or more of the five choices, you should make an educated guess.

■ Section II Free-Response Questions

The free-response section begins with a mandatory 10-minute reading period, during which AP students are encouraged to read the questions, sketch graphs, make notes, and plan answers in the green insert. AP students then have 50 minutes to write their answers in the pink booklet.

The free-response questions in Section II of each exam will require AP students to analyze a given economic situation and use economic principles to explain answers. Using explanatory diagrams that clarify the analysis and clearly explain the reasoning results in the greatest number of points. Sometimes a graph is given as part of the question and the AP student's task is to derive the answer from the graph data. Generally, the longer free-response questions require you to interrelate several content areas, while the two shorter free-response questions focus on a specific topic in a given content area.

Hints on Grading: This section of the exam is 1/3 of the score. The raw score for Section II is composed of the scores from the three questions and then apportioned according to value assigned to each (larger question—50% of score and two smaller questions each—25% of score).

■ Test Taking Strategies for the AP Economics Examinations

Section I: Strategies for Multiple-choice AP Economics Questions

- Remember to sort through the choices. Eliminate quickly those answer choices you know are incorrect.
- On a multiple-choice problem, there is a pattern to the types of questions. You will feel comfortable with the test format if you have studied the problems and exercises in this book.
- You have 70 minutes to answer 60 multiple-choice questions, so don't spend too much time on any one question. You don't need to get every multiple-choice question right to score well on the AP Economics exam.
- Make sure that you first answer all the questions that you know rather than answering the questions in consecutive order. Put a mark in the test booklet next to the questions that you cannot easily answer and return to them later. Remember that questions are random and disconnected.
- Practice all the "test type" assignments in this book and accompanying resources. That strategy will build your confidence on test day. With confidence, your mindset, approach, and score should benefit.

Section II: Strategies for Free-Response Questions

- A 10-minute reading period begins the free-response portion of the AP Economics exam. This time gives you an opportunity to read the questions and plan for the answers. You can sketch an answer in the test booklet (this is the page with the question); however, you cannot open your answer book (blank pages for your answer) and write the answer. When planning, pay attention to how the parts of a question might influence or be related to sequential subquestions. This might help you to confirm that you are answering a section completely or heading in the right direction.
- Remember that time may be an issue so allocate your time appropriately for the weighting of the questions asked. You have 25 minutes for the first essay and 12 minutes for each of the remaining two. If you used the 10-minute planning period well, you should have no problem finishing this section.
- Use correct terminology. Learn and use the correct language of economics.
- You may answer the questions in any order, but clearly indicate which question is being addressed. Use the same outline numbers or letters from the question in your answer, and answer them in the same order. The questions are divided into parts such as (a), (b), (c), and (d), with each part calling for a different response. Attempt to answer them all since points are earned independently. If the answer to a later part of a question depends on the answer to an earlier part, you may still be able to receive points for the later part, even if the earlier answer is wrong.
- If the question requires you to draw a graph, it is important, if asked, to explain what the graph shows. Label graphs clearly, correctly, and fully. Changes in curves should be indicated clearly with arrows or clear sequencing, such as showing a change in aggregate supply with AS and AS' or AS_1 and AS_2.

- Recall the terms used in your practice questions and exercises. All assertions, such as "the price increased," should explain the reason.
- If there is time, review your answers, always asking whether or not you have answered the question directly.

■ AP Economics Correlation Charts

This chart correlates the Advanced Placement Microeconomics topics as outlined by The College Board with the corresponding chapters and section numbers in *Foundations of Economics*, AP Edition.

AP Microeconomics Topics	Textbook Correlation
I. Basic Economic Concepts	Chapters 1, 2, 3
A. Scarcity, Choice, and Opportunity Costs	1.1, 1.2, 3.2, 12.1
B. Production Possibility Curve	3.1
C. Comparative Advantage, Specialization, and Trade	3.5, 34.2
D. Circular Flow	2.2, 20.1
E. Property Rights and Role of Incentives	1.2, 9.1
F. Marginal Analysis	1.2, 3.3
II. Nature and Functions of Product Markets	Chapters 4, 5, 6, 7, 8, 11, 12, 13, 14, 15, 16, 17
A. Supply and Demand	Chapter 4
1. Market equilibrium	4.3
2. Determinants of supply and demand	4.1, 4.2
3. Price and quantity controls	Chapter 7
a. Price ceiling	7.1
b. Price floor	7.2
c. Production quota	7.3
4. Elasticity	Chapter 5
a. Price elasticity of demand	5.1
b. Income and cross-price	5.3
c. Price elasticity of supply	5.2
5. Consumer surplus, producer surplus, and market efficiency	6.2, 6.3, 6.4
6. Tax incidence and deadweight loss	8.1
B. Theory of Consumer Choice	Chapter 11
1. Total utility and marginal utility	11.2
2. Utility maximization: equalizing marginal utility per dollar	11.2
3. Income and substitution effect	*The AP* Test Prep Workbook*
C. Production and Costs	Chapter 12
1. Production functions: short and long run	12.2
2. Marginal product and diminshing returns	12.2
3. Short-run costs	12.3
4. Long-run costs and economies of scale	12.4
5. Cost minimizing input combination	*The AP* Test Prep Workbook*

This chart correlates the Advanced Placement Macroeconomics topics as outlined by The College Board with the corresponding chapters and section numbers in *Foundations of Economics*, AP Edition.

AP Macroeconomics Topics	Textbook Correlation
I. Basic Economic Concepts	Chapters 1, 3, 4, 20, 21, 22
A. Scarcity, Choice, and Opportunity Cost	1.1, 1.2
B. Production Possibilities Curve	3.1
C. Comparative Advantage, Specialization, and Exchange	3.5, 34.2
D. Demand, Supply, and Market Equilibrium	4.1, 4.2, 4.3
E. Macroeconomic Issues: Business Cycle, Unemployment, Inflation, Growth	Chapters 20, 21, 22
II. Measurement of Economic Performance	
A. National Income Accounts	Chapter 20
1. Circular flow	2.2, 20.1
2. Gross domestic product	20.1, 20.2
3. Components of gross domestic product	20.1
4. Real versus nominal gross domestic product	20.3
B. Inflation Measurement and Adjustment	Chapters 22, 28
1. Price indices	22.1, 22.2
2. Nominal and real values	22.3
3. Costs of inflation	28.3
C. Unemployment	Chapter 21
1. Definition and measurement	21.1
2. Types of unemployment	21.3
3. Natural rate of unemployment	21.3, 23.1, 23.2
III. National Income and Price Determination	
A. Aggregate Demand	Chapter 29
1. Determinants of aggregate demand	29.3, 30.1, 30.2, 30.3, 30.4
2. Multiplier and crowding-out effects	24.3, 30.3
B. Aggregate Supply	Chapter 29
1. Short-run and long-run analyses	23.1, 30.1, 30.2, 32.1, 32.2
2. Sticky versus flexible wages and prices	32.1, 32.2
3. Determinants of aggregate supply	29.2
C. Macroeconomic Equilibrium	Chapters 21, 23, 29, 32
1. Real output and price level	29.4
2. Short and long run	32.1, 32.2
3. Actual versus full-employment output	21.3, 23.1, 29.4
4. Economic fluctuations	29.4
IV. Financial Sector	Chapters 24, 26, 27, 28
A. Money, Banking, and Financial Markets	Chapters 26, 27, 28
1. Definition of financial assets: money, stocks, bonds	24.1, 26.1
2. Time value of money (present and future value)	24.2, Chapter 24 Appendix

LOWERING THE BARRIERS TO ENTRY

Most of us want to teach a serious, analytical course that explains the core principles of our subject and helps AP students apply these principles in their lives and jobs. We are not content to teach "dumbed-down" economics or just teach to the AP Exam. But we know that most AP students drown rather than learn to swim when thrown into the deep end of the pool. In this book and its MyEconLab and in *The AP* Test Prep Workbook*, we make painstaking efforts to lower the barriers to learning and to reach out to the beginning AP student.

We focus on core concepts; provide a variety of learning tools to match diversity of learning styles; use diagrams in conjunction with captions that tell a complete story; and illustrate theory with examples and issues that AP students encounter in their lives.

■ Focus on Core Concepts

Each chapter of *Foundations* concentrates on a manageable number of main ideas (most commonly three or four) and reinforces each idea several times throughout the chapter. This patient, confidence-building approach guides AP students through unfamiliar terrain and helps them to focus their efforts on the most important tools and concepts of our discipline.

■ Many Learning Tools for Many Learning Styles

Foundations' integrated print and electronic package builds on the basic fact that AP students have a variety of learning styles. In MyEconLab AP students have a powerful tool at their fingertips—they can complete all Checkpoint exercises and end-of-chapter exercises online, work interactive graphs, assess their skills by taking Practice Tests, receive a customized Study Plan, and step through Guided Solutions.

■ Diagrams That Tell the Whole Story

We developed the style of our diagrams with extensive feedback from focus group participants and student reviewers. All figures make consistent use of color to show the direction of shifts and contain detailed, numbered captions designed to direct AP students' attention step by step through the action. Because AP students are often apprehensive about working with graphs, we have made a special effort to present material in as many as three ways—with graphs, words, and tables—in the same figure. And in an innovation that seems necessary but is to our knowledge unmatched, nearly all of the information supporting a figure appears on the same page as the figure itself. No more flipping pages back and forth!

■ Real-World Connections That Bring Theory to Life

AP students learn best when they can see the point of what they are studying. We have made a major effort to focus on the *why* behind the presentation. How often have AP teachers heard AP students ask, "What use is all this theory, anyway?" To answer this perennial question, we have added a feature entitled

Reality Check, which explores commonsense applications of economics in the everyday life of the AP student.

Current and recent events appear in Eye on the U.S. Economy boxes. We place our experience in global and historical perspectives with Eye on the Global Economy and Eye on the Past boxes. All our Eye On. . . boxes connect theory with reality.

PRACTICE MAKES PERFECT

Everyone agrees that the only way to learn economics is to do it! Reading and remembering don't work. Active involvement, working problems, repeated self-testing: These are the ingredients to AP Exam success. We have structured this text and its accompanying electronic and print tools to encourage learning by doing. The central device in the textbook that accomplishes this goal is a tightly knit learning system based on our innovative *Checklist-Checkpoints* structure.

■ Checklists

Each chapter opens with a *Chapter Checklist*—a list of (usually) three or four tasks the AP student will be able to perform after completing the chapter. Each Checklist item corresponds to a section of the chapter that engages the AP student with a conversational writing style, well-chosen examples, and carefully designed illustrations.

■ Checkpoints

The best time to review material is when it's fresh in AP students' minds. That's where Checkpoints come in. A full-page *Checkpoint*—containing a Practice Problem with solution and a parallel Exercise—immediately follows each chapter section. The Checkpoints serve as stopping points and encourage AP students to review the concept and to practice using it before moving on to new ideas. Diagrams and tables bring added clarity to the Checkpoint problems and solutions.

Each Checkpoint also contains a section reference to the corresponding material in MyEconLab.

■ Chapter Checkpoints

At the end of each chapter, a *Chapter Checkpoint* summarizes what the AP student has just learned with a set of key points and a list of key terms. It also contains a further set of questions divided into three groups: exercises, critical thinking, and Web exercises.

ORGANIZATION

Our text focuses on core topics with maximum flexibility. We cover all the standard topics of the principles of economics curriculum. And we do so in the order that is increasingly finding favor in the AP Economics course. We believe that a powerful case can be made for teaching the subject in the order in which we present it here.

We introduce and explain the core ideas about efficiency and fairness early and then cover major policy issues in a series of chapters that use only the tools of demand and supply and the ideas of marginal benefit, marginal cost, and consumer and producer surplus. Topics such as consumer choice and cost curves, which are more technical, are covered later.

Extensive reviewing suggests that most AP teachers agree with us. But we recognize that there is a range of opinion about sequencing, and we have structured our text so that it works equally well if other sequences are preferred.

Deciding the order in which to teach the components of microeconomics involves a tradeoff between building all the foundations and getting to policy issues early in the course. There is little disagreement that the place to begin is with production possibilities and demand and supply. We provide a carefully paced and thoroughly modern treatment of these topics.

Following the order of this text, the course quickly gets to interesting policy issues. Two further chapters lay the foundation: elasticity in Chapter 5 and a discussion of the efficiency and fairness of markets in Chapter 6. Introducing AP students to both efficiency and fairness (equity) issues early in the course enables a more complete and engaging discussion of topics such as price floors, price ceilings, production quotas, taxes, externalities, public goods, and common resources, all of which we cover in Chapters 7 through 10. Teaching this material early in the course maintains AP student interest, directly serves the role of the principles course as a foundation for citizenship, and provides an immediate payoff from learning the demand-supply and related tools. Only when these policy issues have been covered do we dig more deeply behind the consumption and production decisions.

AP teachers who prefer to cover policy issues later in the course can skip Chapters 6 through 10 and move straight from elasticity to consumer choice (Chapter 11) and then on to the economics of the firm. The policy-related chapters can be covered at any chosen point later in the course.

In the coverage of macroeconomics, the organizing device is the idea that at full employment, the real economy is influenced by only real variables and the price level is proportional to the quantity of money. This idea has been incredibly productive in advancing our understanding of both the full employment economy and the business cycle. By having a firm understanding of the forces that determine potential GDP, the AP student better appreciates the more complex interactions of real and monetary factors that bring economic fluctuations. Further, the AP student sees that the long-term trends in our economy play a larger role in determining our standard of living and cost of living than do the fluctuations around those trends.

The macro course divides naturally into three parts. The first explains the real economy at full employment (potential GDP, investment, saving, the real interest rate, and economic growth, including policies for achieving faster growth). The second explains the money economy (determining the interest rate in the short run and price level and inflation rate in the long run). The third explains economic fluctuations (interactions between the real and monetary sectors and stabilization policy issues).

Extensive reviewing suggests that most AP teachers agree with our view on how to organize the course. But we recognize that there is a range of opinion about sequencing, and we have structured our text so that it works equally well if other sequences are preferred. Some AP teachers want to follow the measurement material with the aggregate expenditure (fixed price level) model and aggregate demand and aggregate supply. Money and economic fluctuations come next. And the influences on potential GDP and economic growth either come last or are omitted. Our text supports this sequence. After Chapter 22, it is possible to jump to either Chapter 29 (*AS-AD* and the Business Cycle) or Chapter 30 (Aggregate Expenditure). The money chapters (26, 27, and 28) can be covered next followed by stabilization policy (Chapters 31, 32, and 33).

Flexibility charts on pp. xliv–xlv provide detailed information that enables you to rearrange the chapters in a variety of ways. And the alternative course charts on pp. xlvi–xlvii offer some suggestions of other possible paths through the book.

A RICH ARRAY OF SUPPORT MATERIALS FOR THE AP STUDENT

Foundations of Economics, AP Edition, is accompanied by the most comprehensive set of learning tools ever assembled. All the components of our package are organized by Checkpoint topic so that the AP student may move easily among the textbook, MyEconLab, and *The AP* Test Prep Workbook*, while mastering a single core concept.

The variety of tools that we provide enables AP students to select the path through the material that best suits their individual learning styles. The package is technology-enabled, not technology-dependent. Active learners can make extensive use of the MyEconLab personalized Study Plan and tutorial instruction and the animated graphics of textbook figures. Reflective learners may follow a print-only path if they prefer.

■ MyEconLab* (available through your AP teacher)

MyEconLab—the online homework and tutorial system—puts AP students in control of their own learning through a suite of study and practice tools correlated with the online, interactive version of the textbook and other media tools. Within MyEconLab's structured environment, AP students practice what they learn, test their understanding, and then pursue a Study Plan that MyEconLab generates for them based on their performance on practice tests.

At the core of MyEconLab are the following features:

- **Practice Tests**—Practice tests for every Checkpoint enable AP students to test their understanding and identify the areas in which they need to do further work. Practice Test questions based directly on the Practice Problem and Exercise in each Checkpoint and end-of-chapter problems ask AP students to work with graphs: interpreting them, manipulating them, and even drawing them. AP teachers can let AP students use the supplied pre-built tests or create their own tests.

---

* AP teachers will receive a pin code card with each revenue order that grants access for the entire class. AP teachers should send an e-mail to phwebaccess@pearsoned.com with questions about access.

- **Personalized Study Plan**—Based on an AP student's performance on practice or assigned tests, MyEconLab generates a Personalized Study Plan that shows where further study is needed. The correlation between the text and MyEconLab is perfect and seamless.

- **Additional Practice Exercises**—The Personalized Study Plans direct AP students to additional exercises for each topic. Additional practice exercises are keyed to each section of the textbook and link students to the eText with animated graphs.

- **Tutorial Instruction**—Launched from the additional practice exercises, tutorial instruction is provided in the form of solutions to problems, step-by-step explanations, and other media-based explanations.

- **Powerful Graphing Tool**—Integrated into the practice tests and additional practice exercises, the graphing tool lets AP students manipulate and even draw graphs so that they grasp how the concepts, numbers, and graphs are connected.

- **Three Types of Graphing Problems:**

  Draw Graphs—MyEconLab's Draw Graph problems automatically grade the graphs AP students draw.

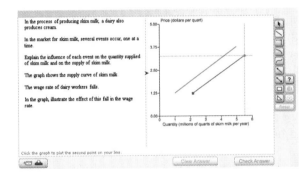

  Model-based Graphs—AP students can change data inputs and watch graphs shift. Multiple-choice, true/false, and short-answer questions quiz AP students on their interpretations of the graph.

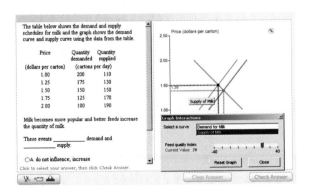

Data Graphs—AP students can plot up to five variables against each other, giving them a clear picture of how economic indicators relate to each other.

MyEconLab Study Plan links to the following resources:

- **eText**—Quick reference to specific pages of the textbook that correspond to each Study Plan exercise. (MyEconLab is also available in a version that contains a full, searchable online textbook. Ask your Pearson Prentice Hall representative for details.)
- **eStudy Guide**—The entire Study Guide in electronic format and printable.
- **Animated Figures**—Every figure from the textbook is presented in step-by-step animations with audio explanations of the action.
- **Glossary**—A searchable version of the textbook glossary with additional examples and links to related terms.

Additional MyEconLab Resources

- **Glossary Flashcards**—Every key term is available as a flashcard, allowing AP students to quiz themselves on vocabulary from one or more chapters at a time.
- **Economics in the News**—Updated most weekdays during the school year, news items with links to sources for further reading and discussion questions. Once per week, we post a quiz which AP teachers may assign to test AP student comprehension of the week's news.
- **eThemes of the Times**—Archived articles from *The New York Times*, correlated to each chapter of the textbook and paired with critical thinking questions.

▌ The AP* Test Prep Workbook

The guide is designed to give AP students the extra support they need to prepare for the AP Economics Exam. Each chapter includes an expanded Chapter Checklist, hints for taking the AP Economics Exam, and additional practice problems and self-test questions for the AP Economics Exam, consisting of true or false, multiple-choice, and short and long free-response questions. Margaret

Pride of St. Louis High School prepared the micro portion and Sandra Wright of Adlai E. Stevenson High School prepared the macro portion of *The AP* Test Prep Workbook*. Contributions to the guide were also prepared by Carl Coates of Homewood Flossmoor High School, Flossmoor, Illinois; Bruce L. Damasio of Liberty High School, Eldersburg, Maryland; Joy L. Joyce; Vanessa Lal of Adlai E. Stevenson High School, Lincolnshire, Illinois; Matt Pedlow of Jackson High School, Jackson, Michigan; and Amy Shrout.

A QUALITY-ASSURED SUPPORT SYSTEM FOR THE AP TEACHER

Our AP teacher resource tools are the most comprehensive, carefully developed, and accurate materials ever made available. MyEconLab, *The AP* Test Prep Workbook*, the PowerPoint lecture notes, the Instructor's Manual, and the Test Banks all key off the Checkpoints in the textbook. The entire package has a tight integrity. As the authors of the textbook, we have authored the MyEconLab content and PowerPoint notes. We have paid close attention to the design, structure, and organization of MyEconLab. And we have helped in the reviewing of the Instructor's Manual, and Test Banks, and *The AP* Test Prep Workbook* to ensure that every element of the package achieves the consistency that AP students and AP teachers need.

■ MyEconLab AP Teacher Resources

MyEconLab provides flexible tools that allow AP teachers to easily and effectively customize online course materials to suit their needs. AP teachers can create and assign tests, quizzes, or graded homework assignments. MyEconLab saves time by automatically grading all questions and tracking results—including AP student practice—in an online gradebook. MyEconLab can even grade assignments that require AP students to draw a graph.

After registering for MyEconLab, AP teachers have access to downloadable supplements such as AP Teacher's Manuals, PowerPoint lecture notes, and Test Banks. Test Banks can also be used within MyEconLab, giving AP teachers ample material from which they can create assignments.

To request Teacher Access to MyEconLab send an e-mail to phwebaccess@ pearsoned.com.

■ AP* Teacher's Manual

The AP Teacher's Manual contains chapter outlines and road maps, Lecture Launchers, answers to in-text exercises, additional exercises with solutions, and a virtual encyclopedia of suggestions on how to enrich class presentation and use class time efficiently. The micro portion has been written by Mark Rush, University of Florida; Carol Dole, State University of West Georgia; and Margaret Anne Shannon, Gordon College. The macro portion has been written by Mark Rush; Richard Gosselin, Houston Community College; and Rebecca Neumann, University of Wisconsin, Milwaukee.

■ Three Test Banks

Three separate Test Banks are available for *Foundations of Economics*, AP Edition, with more than 12,000 multiple-choice, numerical, fill-in-the-blank, short-answer, essay questions, and integrative questions that build on material from more than one Checkpoint or more than one chapter. The AP Edition features the addition of a fifth choice to all multiple-choice questions. Mark Rush reviewed and edited questions from seven dedicated principles instructors for microeconomics and six for macroeconomics and added all fifth choices to form one of the most comprehensive testing systems on the market. Our questions authors on the micro side are Seemi Ahmad (Dutchess Community College), Sue Bartlett (University of South Florida), Jack Chambless (Valencia Community College), Carol Dole (State University of West Georgia), Paul Harris (Camden County Community College), William Mosher (College of the Holy Cross), and Terry Sutton (Rogers State University). Our questions authors on the macro side are Ali Ataiifar (Delaware County Community College), Diego Mendez–Carbajo (Illinois Wesleyan University), William Mosher (College of the Holy Cross), Terry Sutton (Rogers State University), Cindy Tori (Valdosta State University), and Nora Underwood (University of Central Florida). These Test Bank authors also wrote questions for the Study Guide to ensure consistency.

■ PowerPoint Resources

We have created the PowerPoint resources based on our 10 years of experience using this tool in our own classrooms. Every figure and table—every single one, even those used in Checkpoint questions and solutions—is included in the PowerPoint lecture notes. Many of the figures and tables are animated so that you can build them gradually in the classroom. Key figures can be expanded to full-screen size or shrunk to make space for text explanations at a single mouse click during a lecture. We have determined the optimal build sequence for the animated figures and have produced them with the same degree of clarity and precision as the figures in the text.

The speaking notes sections of the PowerPoint files provide material from the AP Teacher's Manual on teaching tips and suggestions.

■ Overhead Transparencies

Full-color overhead transparencies of *all* figures from the text will improve the clarity of your lectures. They are available to qualified adopters of the text (contact your Pearson Prentice Hall sales representative).

■ AP Teacher's Resource Disk with ExamView Test Banks

This CD-ROM contains Computerized Test Bank files, Test Bank and AP Teacher's Manual files in Microsoft Word, and PowerPoint files. All three Test Banks are available in ExamView. Fully networkable, the CD-ROM is available for Windows and Macintosh. AP teachers can view, edit, and add questions; transfer questions to tests; and print different forms of tests. Tests can be formatted by varying fonts and styles, margins, and headers and footers, as in any word-processing document. Search and sort features let the AP teacher quickly locate questions and arrange them in a preferred order.

ACKNOWLEDGMENTS

Working on a project such as this generates many debts that can never be repaid. But they can be acknowledged, and it is a special pleasure to be able to do so here and to express our heartfelt thanks to each and every one of the following long list, without whose contributions we could not have produced *Foundations*.

Mark Rush coordinated, managed, and contributed to the AP Teacher's Manual, and Test Bank. He assembled, polished, wrote, and rewrote these materials to ensure their close consistency with the text. He and we were in constant contact as all the elements of our text and package came together. Mark also made many valuable suggestions for improving the text and the Checkpoints. His contribution went well beyond that of a reviewer. And his effervescent sense of humor kept us all in good spirits along the way.

Margaret Pride and Sandra Wright wrote *The AP* Test Prep Workbook*. They worked with and managed contributions from Carl Coates, Bruce L. Damasio, Joy Joyce, Vanessa Lal, Matt Pedlow, and Amy Shrout. Carol Dole, Richard Gosselin, Margaret Anne Shannon, and Rebecca Neumann wrote content for the AP Teacher's Manual. Maggy Shannon and Rebecca Neumann also inspired and energized us with their innovative ideas for chapter openers and Reality Check box content.

Seemi Ahmad, Ali Ataiifar, Sue Bartlett, Jack Chambless, Carol Dole, Paul Harris, Diego Mendez-Carbajo, William Mosher, Terry Sutton, Cindy Tori, and Nora Underwood provided questions for the Study Guide and Test Banks.

The ideas that ultimately became *Foundations* began to form over dinner at the Andover Inn in Andover, Massachusetts, with Denise Clinton and Sylvia Mallory. We gratefully acknowledge Sylvia's role not only at the birth of this project but also in managing its initial development team. Denise has been our ongoing inspiration for more than 10 years. She is the most knowledgeable economics editor in the business, and we are privileged to have the benefit of her enormous experience.

The success of *Foundations* owes much to its outstanding sponsoring editor, Adrienne D'Ambrosio. Adrienne's acute intelligence and sensitive understanding of the market have helped sharpen our vision of this text and package. Her value-added on this project is huge. It has been, and we hope it will for many future editions remain, a joy to work with her.

Mary Clare McEwing has been our indomitable development editor, ably assisted by Dottie Dennis. Mary Clare had rounded up the best group of reviewers we'd ever worked with. Perhaps we should stop being astounded! She has done it again. Mary Clare has steered *Foundations* along through several redrafts and polishes.

Charles Spaulding oversaw the impressive cover design and with Gina Kolenda converted the raw ideas of our brainstorms into an outstandingly designed text. Meredith Nightingale provided the detailed figure designs.

Marianne Groth did an excellent job as editor of our print supplements.

Michelle Neil, Executive Media Producer, and Melissa Honig, Senior Media Producer, have set a new standard for online learning and teaching resources. Michelle spearheaded the effort to set up MyEconLab, worked creatively to improve our technology systems, and worked with our editors and us to develop our media strategy. Melissa managed the building of MyEconLab. They have both been sources of high energy, good sense, and level-headed advice, and quickly found creative solutions to all our technology problems.

Nancy Fenton, our ever cheerful, never stressed production supervisor, worked with a talented team at Elm Street Publishing Services—project editor Ingrid Benson, typesetter Debbie Kubiak, art coordinators Angel Chavez and Angela Gelsomino, and the best proofreader we have ever encountered. Our photo researcher, Beth Anderson, provided us with an outstanding selection of images from which to choose.

Our marketing manager, Stephen Frail, has been a constant source of good judgment and sound advice on content and design issues ranging over the entire package from text to print and electronic supplements.

Our copy editor, Barbara Willette, and supplements copy editor, Kirsten Dickerson, gave our work a thorough review and helpful polish.

Richard Parkin, our technical illustrator, created the figures in the text, the dynamic figures in the eText, and the animated figures in the PowerPoint presentations and contributed many ideas to improve the clarity of our illustrations. Laurel Davies provided painstakingly careful work on MyEconLab questions and acted as one of its accuracy checkers.

Jeannie Gillmore, our personal assistant, worked closely with us in creating MyEconLab Exercises and Guided Solutions. She also served as a meticulous accuracy checker on the text, Study Guide, and AP Teacher's Manual. John Graham of Rutgers University and Constantin Ogloblin of Georgia Southern University provided careful accuracy reviews of the Test Banks.

Jane McAndrew, economics librarian at the University of Western Ontario, went the extra mile on many occasions to help us track down the data and references we needed.

Finally, our reviewers, whose names appear on the following pages, have made an enormous contribution to this text. Once again we find ourselves using superlatives. But they are called for. In the many texts that we've written, we've not seen reviewing of the quality that we enjoyed on this revision. It has been a pleasure (if at times a challenge) to respond constructively to their many excellent suggestions.

Robin Bade
Michael Parkin
London, Ontario, Canada
robin@econ100.com
michael.parkin@uwo.ca

AP Edition Reviewers

David A. Anderson, Centre College, Danville, Kentucky
Steve Bsharah, Delano High School, Delano, California
Bruce Damasio, Liberty High School, Eldersburg, Maryland
Paul Kasunich, Shaler Area High School, Shaler, Pennsylvania
John Lamb, Don Bosco Technical Institute, Rosemead, California
Chris McTanamy, Thomas S. Wootton High School, Rockville, Maryland
Margaret Pride, St. Louis High School, St. Louis, Missouri
James Spellicy, Lowell High School, San Francisco, California
Karen Wassman, Quince Orchard High School, Gaithersburg, Maryland
Sandra Wright, Adlai E. Stevenson High School, Lincolnshire, Illinois

Reviewers

Charles Aguilar, El Paso Community College
Seemi Ahmad, Dutchess Community College
William Aldridge, Shelton State Community College
Rashid B. Al-Hmoud, Texas Tech University
Ali Ataiifar, Delaware County Community College
John Baffoe-Bonnie, Pennsylvania State University, Delaware County Campus
A. Paul Ballantyne, University of Colorado
Sue Bartlett, University of South Florida
Klaus Becker, Texas Tech University
John Bethune, Barton College
Gautam Bhattacharya, University of Kansas
Gerald W. Bialka, University of North Florida
David Bivin, Indiana University–Purdue University at Indianapolis
Geoffrey Black, Boise State University
Carey Anne Borkoski, Arundel Community College
Barbara Brogan, Northern Virginia Community College
Christopher Brown, Arkansas State University
Donald Bumpass, Sam Houston State University
Seewoonundun Bunjun, East Stroudsburg University
Nancy Burnett, University of Wisconsin at Oshkosh
James L. Butkiewicz, University of Delaware
Barbara Caldwell, University of South Florida
Bruce Caldwell, University of North Carolina, Greensboro
Robert Carlsson, University of South Carolina
Shawn Carter, Jacksonville State University
Jack Chambless, Valencia Community College
Joni Charles, Southwest Texas State University

Robert Cherry, Brooklyn College
Chi-Young Choi, University of New Hampshire
Paul Cichello, Xavier University
Quentin Ciolfi, Brevard Community College
Jim Cobbe, Florida State University
John Cochran, Metropolitan State College
Ludovic Comeau, De Paul University
Carol Conrad, Cerro Coso Community College
Christopher Cornell, Fordham University
Richard Cornwall, University of California, Davis
Kevin Cotter, Wayne State University
Tom Creahan, Morehead State University
Elizabeth Crowell, University of Michigan at Dearborn
Susan Dadres, Southern Methodist University
Troy Davig, College of William and Mary
Jeffrey Davis, ITT Technical Institute (Utah)
Dennis Debrecht, Carroll College
Al DeCooke, Broward Community College
Vince DiMartino, University of Texas at San Antonio
Carol Dole, State University of West Georgia
Kathleen Dorsainvil, Winston-Salem University
John Dorsey, University of Maryland, College Park
Amrik Singh Dua, Mt. San Antonio College
Marie Duggan, Keene State College
David Eaton, Murray State University
Harold W. Elder, University of Alabama
Harry Ellis, University of North Texas
Stephen Ellis, North Central Texas College
Carl Enomoto, New Mexico State University
Chuen-mei Fan, Colorado State University

Gary Ferrier, University of Arkansas
Rudy Fichtenbaum, Wright State University
Kaya Ford, Northern Virginia Community College
Robert Francis, Shoreline Community College
Roger Frantz, San Diego State University
Arthur Friedberg, Mohawk Valley Community
  College
Julie Gallaway, Southwest Missouri State University
Byron Gangnes, University of Hawaii
Gay Garesché, Glendale Community College
Neil Garston, California State University at Los
  Angeles
Lisa Geib-Gunderson, University of Maryland
Linda Ghent, Eastern Illinois University
Kirk Gifford, Ricks College
Maria Giuili, Diablo Valley Community College
Mark Gius, Quinnipiac College
Randall Glover, Brevard Community College
Stephan Gohmann, University of Louisville
Richard Gosselin, Houston Community College
John Graham, Rutgers University
Warren Graham, Tulsa Community College
Jang-Ting Guo, University of California, Riverside
Dennis Hammett, University of Texas at El Paso
Leo Hardwick, Macomb Community College
Mehdi Haririan, Bloomsburg University
Paul Harris, Camden County Community College
Gus Herring, Brookhaven College
Michael Heslop, Northern Virginia Community
  College
Steven Hickerson, Mankato State University
Andy Howard, Rio Hondo College
Yu Hsing, Southeastern Louisiana University
Matthew Hyle, Winona State University
Todd Idson, Boston University
Harvey James, University of Hartford
Russell Janis, University of Massachusetts at Amherst
Ted Joyce, City University of New York, Baruch
  College
Arthur Kartman, San Diego State University
Chris Kauffman, University of Tennessee
Diane Keenan, Cerritos College
Brian Kench, University of Tampa
John Keith, Utah State University
Joe Kerkvliet, Oregon State University
Douglas Kinnear, Colorado State University
Morris Knapp, Miami Dade Community College
Steven Koch, Georgia Southern University
Kate Krause, University of New Mexico
Stephan Kroll, California State University—
  Sacramento

Joyce Lapping, University of Southern Maine
Tom Larson, California State University, Los Angeles
Robert Lemke, Florida International University
Tony Lima, California State University at Hayward
Kenneth Long, New River Community College
Marty Ludlum, Oklahoma City Community College
Roger Mack, De Anza College
Michael Magura, University of Toledo
Mark Maier, Glendale College
Paula Manns, Atlantic Cape Community College
Dan Marburger, Arkansas State University
Kathryn Marshall, Ohio State University
Drew E. Mattson, Anoka-Ramsey Community College
Stephen McCafferty, Ohio State University
Thomas McCaleb, Florida State University
Diego Mendez-Carbajo, Illinois Wesleyan University
Thomas Meyer, Patrick Henry Community College
Meghan Millea, Mississippi State University
Michael Milligan, Front Range Community College
Jenny Minier, University of Miami
David Mitchell, Valdosta State University
William Mosher, Clark University
Kevin Murphy, Oakland University
Ronald Nate, Brigham Young University, Idaho
Michael Nelson, Texas A&M University
Rebecca Neumann, University of Wisconsin—
  Milwaukee
Charles Newton, Houston Community College
  Southwest
Melinda Nish, Salt Lake Community College
Lee Nordgren, Indiana University at Bloomington
William C. O'Connor, Western Montana
  College–University of Montana
Fola Odebunmi, Cypress College
Charles Okeke, College of Southern Nevada
Sanjay Paul, Elizabethtown College
Ken Peterson, Furman University
Tim Petry, North Dakota State University
Charles Pflanz, Scottsdale Community College
Jonathon Phillips, North Carolina State University
Paul Poast, Ohio State University
Greg Pratt, Mesa Community College
Fernando Quijano, Dickinson State University
Ratha Ramoo, Diablo Valley College
Karen Reid, University of Wisconsin, Parkside
Mary Rigdon, University of Texas, Austin
Helen Roberts, University of Illinois, Chicago
Greg Rose, Sacramento City College
Barbara Ross, Kapi'olani Community College
Jeffrey Rous, University of North Texas
June Roux, Salem Community College

Foundations of Economics: Flexibility Chart

Core Principles

1. Getting Started

2. The U.S. and Global Economies
Not just a descriptive chapter. Defines the factors of production and introduces the circular flow model.

3. The Economic Problem
Carefully paced and complete first look at the fundamental economic problem. Includes explanation of efficiency and comparative advantage.

4. Demand and Supply
Carefully paced and complete explanation of this core topic.

5. Elasticities of Demand and Supply
A gentle explanation of elasticity with the emphasis on understanding and interpreting elasticity.

6. Efficiency and Fairness of Markets
A chapter that provides a description of the alternative methods of allocating resources and an explanation of the efficiency and fairness of market outcomes. The chapter unifies the micro chapters, and enables a wide range of policy applications to be studied early in the course.

12. Production and Cost

13. Perfect Competition

14. Monopoly

15. Monopolistic Competition

16. Oligopoly

Policy Applications

7. Government Influences on Markets
Explains the effects of price ceilings, price floors, and production quotas.

8. Taxes
Explains the incidence of taxes and discusses efficiency and equity issues. Chapters 3 through 6 are prerequisites.

9. Externalities
Describes full range of externalities, explains the Coase theorem, and the use of taxes, subsidies, and market solutions. Chapters 3 through 8 are prerequisites.

10. Public Goods and Common Resources
Describes the four types of goods and explains the free-rider problem and the problem of the commons. Chapters 3 through 8 are prerequisites.

Some or all of these chapters may be omitted. Chapter 12 is the foundation of the group and cannot be omitted if any of the others are to be covered. Chapters 15 and 16 build on both 13 and 14.

17. Regulation and Antitrust Law

19. Inequality and Poverty
Explains the sources of inequality and its trends and evaluates alternative redistribution methods.

Optional

1. Appendix: Making and Using Graphs
Good for students with a fear of graphs.

11. Consumer Choice and Demand
This optional chapter may be covered at any point after Chapter 3. Explains both marginal utility theory and (in an appendix) indifference curves.

18. Demand and Supply in Factor Markets
Enables you to cover all the factor market issues in a single chapter.

Four Alternative Micro Sequences

Four Alternative Macro Sequences

Getting Started

CHAPTER 1

CHAPTER CHECKLIST

When you have completed your study of this chapter,
you will be able to

1 Define economics and explain the kinds of questions that economists try to answer.

2 Explain the core ideas that define the economic way of thinking.

Natasha was earning $90,000 a year at Palm, the maker of hand-held PCs, when the firm sent her to train some of its workers in India. On her return to California, Natasha was laid off—replaced, she suspects, by one of the Indians she had trained. You probably think that it is totally unfair for Natasha to have to compete for a job with workers in poor countries who make only a few dollars a day. Yet because Palm is careful to control its costs, you can buy one of its hand-held PCs for $99. Should we pay more for our PCs so that Natasha can keep her job? Or should Natasha find another job?

Forbes magazine says that there are 691 billionaires in the world. Close to half of them live in the United States. At the top of the pile is Bill Gates, a co-founder of Microsoft, with $50 billion. At the other end of the scale are the 1 billion people who try to scrape by on a dollar a day or less. Isn't there way too much inequality in the world today?

Your economics course will help you to answer questions like the ones we've just asked. And it will help you to understand the powerful forces that shape our world and provide insights that will guide you in your everyday life and work.

1.1 DEFINITION AND QUESTIONS

All economic questions and problems arise because human wants exceed the resources available to satisfy them. We want good health and long lives. We want spacious and comfortable homes. We want a huge range of sports and recreational equipment from running shoes to jet skis. We want the time to enjoy our favorite sports, video games, novels, music, and movies; to travel to exotic places; and just to hang out with friends.

■ Scarcity

Scarcity
The condition that arises because wants exceed the ability of resources to satisfy them.

Our inability to satisfy all our wants is called **scarcity**. The ability of each of us to satisfy our wants is limited by the time we have, the incomes we earn, and the prices we pay for the things we buy. These limits mean that everyone has unsatisfied wants. The ability of all of us as a society to satisfy our wants is limited by the productive resources that exist. These resources include the gifts of nature, our labor and ingenuity, and tools and equipment that we have made.

Everyone, poor and rich alike, faces scarcity. A child wants a $1.00 can of soda and two 50¢ packs of gum but has only $1.00 in his pocket. He faces scarcity. A millionaire wants to spend the weekend playing golf and spend the same weekend at the office attending a business strategy meeting. She faces scarcity. The U.S. government wants to increase defense spending and cut taxes. It faces scarcity. An entire society wants improved health care, an Internet connection in every classroom, an ambitious space exploration program, clean lakes and rivers, and so on. Society faces scarcity.

Faced with scarcity, we must make choices. We must choose among the available alternatives. The child must choose the soda or the gum. The millionaire must choose the golf game or the meeting. The government must choose defense or tax cuts. And society must choose among health care, computers, space exploration, the environment, and so on. Even parrots face scarcity!

Not only do I want a cracker—we all want a cracker!

■ Economics Defined

Economics is the social science that studies the choices that individuals, businesses, governments, and entire societies make as they cope with *scarcity* and the *incentives* that influence and reconcile those choices.

The subject is extremely broad and touches all aspects of our lives. To get beyond this definition of economics, you need to understand the kinds of questions that economists try to answer and the way they think and go about seeking those answers.

We begin with some key economic questions. Although the scope of economics is broad and the range of questions that economists address is equally broad, two big questions provide a useful summary of the scope of economics:

- How do choices end up determining *what, how,* and *for whom* goods and services get produced?
- When do choices made in the pursuit of *self-interest* also promote the *social interest*?

■ What, How, and For Whom?

Goods and services are the objects and actions that people value and produce to satisfy human wants. Goods are objects that satisfy wants. Running shoes and ketchup are examples. Services are actions that satisfy wants. Haircuts and rock concerts are examples. We produce a dazzling array of goods and services that range from necessities such as food, houses, and health care to leisure items such as DVD players and roller coaster rides.

What?

What determines the quantities of corn we grow, homes we build, and DVD players we produce? Sixty years ago, 25 percent of Americans worked on a farm. That number has shrunk to less than 3 percent today. Over the same period, the number of people who produce goods—in mining, construction, and manufacturing—has also shrunk, from 30 percent to 20 percent. The decrease in farming and the production of goods is matched by an increase in the production of services. How will these quantities change in the future as ongoing changes in technology make an ever-wider array of goods and services available to us?

How?

How are goods and services produced? In a vineyard in France, basket-carrying workers pick the annual grape crop by hand. In a vineyard in California, a huge machine and a few workers do the same job that a hundred grape pickers in France do. Look around you and you will see many examples of this phenomenon—the same job being done in different ways. In some supermarkets, checkout clerks key in prices. In others, they use a laser scanner. One farmer keeps track of his livestock feeding schedules and inventories by using paper-and-pencil records, while another uses a personal computer. GM hires workers to weld auto bodies in some of its plants and uses robots to do the job in others.

Why do we use machines in some cases and people in others? Do mechanization and technological change destroy more jobs than they create? Do they make us better off or worse off?

Economics
The social science that studies the choices that we make as we cope with *scarcity* and the *incentives* that influence and reconcile our choices.

Goods and services
The objects (goods) and the actions (services) that people value and produce to satisfy human wants.

In a California vineyard a machine and a few workers do the same job as a hundred grape pickers in France.

A doctor gets more of the goods and services produced than a nurse or a medical assistant gets.

For Whom?

For whom are goods and services produced? The answer to this question depends on the incomes that people earn and the prices they pay for the goods and services they buy. At given prices, a person who has a high income is able to buy more goods and services than a person who has a low income. Doctors earn much higher incomes than do nurses and medical assistants. So doctors get more of the goods and services produced than nurses and medical assistants get.

You probably know about many other persistent differences in incomes. Men, on the average, earn more than women. Whites, on the average, earn more than minorities. College graduates, on the average, earn more than high school graduates. Americans, on the average, earn more than Europeans, who in turn earn more, on the average, than Asians and Africans. But there are some significant exceptions. The people of Japan and Hong Kong now earn an average income similar to that of Americans. And there is a lot of income inequality throughout the world.

What determines the incomes we earn? Why do doctors earn larger incomes than nurses? Why do white male college graduates earn more than minority female high school graduates? Why do Americans earn more, on the average, than Africans?

Economics explains how the choices that individuals, businesses, and governments make and the interactions of those choices end up determining *what, how,* and *for whom* goods and services get produced. In answering these questions, we have a deeper agenda in mind. We're not interesting in just knowing how many DVD players get produced, how they get produced, and who gets to enjoy them. We ultimately want to know the answer to the second big economic question that we'll now explore.

■ When Is the Pursuit of Self-Interest in the Social Interest?

Every day, you and 296 million other Americans, along with 6.1 billion people in the rest of the world, make economic choices that result in *"what," "how,"* and *"for whom"* goods and services get produced.

Are the goods and services produced, and the quantities in which they are produced, the right ones? Do the scarce resources get used in the best possible way? Do the goods and services that we produce go to the people who benefit most from them?

Self-Interest and the Social Interest

Self-interest
The choices that are best for the individual who makes them.

Social interest
The choices that are best for society as a whole.

Choices that are the best for the individual who makes them are choices made in the pursuit of **self-interest**. Choices that are the best for society as a whole are said to be in the **social interest**. The social interest has two dimensions: *efficiency* and *equity.* We'll explore these concepts in later chapters. For now, think of efficiency as being achieved by baking the biggest possible pie. And think of equity as being achieved by sharing the pie in the fairest possible way.

You know that your own choices are the best ones for you—or at least you *think* they're the best at the time that you make them. You use your time and other resources in the way that makes most sense to you. But you don't think much about how your choices affect other people. You order a home delivery pizza because you're hungry and want to eat. You don't order it thinking that the delivery person or the cook needs an income. You make choices that are in your self-interest—choices that you think are best for you.

When you act on your economic decisions, you come into contact with thousands of other people who produce and deliver the goods and services that you decide to buy or who buy the things that you sell. These people have made their own decisions—what to produce and how to produce it, whom to hire or whom to work for, and so on.

Like you, everyone else makes choices that they think are best for them. When the pizza delivery person shows up at your home, he's not doing you a favor. He's earning his income and hoping for a good tip.

Could it be possible that when each one of us makes choices that are in our own best interest—our self-interest—it turns out that these choices are also the best for society as a whole—in the social interest?

Much of the rest of this book helps you to learn what economists know about this question and its answer. To help you start thinking about the question, we're going to illustrate it with eight topics that generate heated discussion in today's world. You're already at least a little bit familiar with each one of them. They are

- Globalization and international outsourcing
- The new economy
- Disappearing tropical rainforests
- Water shortages
- Global warming
- Natural disasters
- Unemployment
- A Social Security time bomb

Globalization and International Outsourcing

Globalization and international outsourcing—the expansion of international trade and the production of components and services by firms in other countries—has been going on for centuries. But during the 1990s, its pace accelerated as advances in microchips, satellites, and fiber-optic cables lowered the cost of communication. A phone call, a video-conference, or a face-to-face meeting involving people who live 10,000 miles apart has become an everyday and easily affordable event.

Workers in Asia make our shoes.

This explosion of communication has globalized production decisions. When Nike produces more sports shoes, people in China, Indonesia, or Malaysia get more work. When Steven Spielberg wants an animation sequence for a new movie, programmers in New Zealand write the code. And when China Airlines wants a new airplane, Americans who work for Boeing build it.

The number of jobs in manufacturing and routine services is shrinking in the United States and Europe and expanding in India, China, and other Asian economies. And production is growing more rapidly in Asia than in the United States and Europe. China is already the world's second largest economy, and if the current trends continue, it will become the largest economy during the 2020s.

But globalization is leaving some people behind. The nations of Africa and parts of South America are not sharing in the prosperity that globalization is bringing to other parts of the world.

Is globalization in the social interest, or does it benefit some at the expense of others? The owners of multinational firms clearly benefit from lower production costs. So do the consumers of low-cost imported goods and services. But don't displaced American workers lose? And doesn't even the worker in Malaysia who sews your new running shoes for a few cents an hour also lose?

The New Economy

The 1980s and 1990s were years of extraordinary economic change that have been called the *Information Revolution*. This name suggests a parallel with the *Industrial Revolution* of the years around 1800 and the *Agricultural Revolution* of 12,000 years ago.

The changes that occurred during the last 25 years were based on one major technology: the microprocessor or computer chip. Moore's law predicted that the number of transistors that could be placed on one integrated chip would double every 18 months. This prediction turned out to be remarkably accurate.

The spin-offs from faster and cheaper computing have been widespread. Telecommunications became much faster and cheaper, music and movie recording became more realistic and cheaper, millions of routine tasks that previously required human decision and action were automated. You encounter these automated tasks every day when you check out at the supermarket, use an ATM, or call a government department or large business. All the new products and processes and the low-cost computing power that made them possible were produced by people who made choices in the pursuit of self-interest. They did not result from any grand design or government plan.

When Gordon Moore set up Intel and started making chips, no one had told him to do so, and he wasn't thinking how much easier it would be for you to turn in your essay on time if you had a faster PC. When Bill Gates quit Harvard to set up Microsoft, he wasn't trying to create the best operating system and improve people's computing experience. Moore and Gates and thousands of other entrepreneurs were in hot pursuit of the big payoffs that many of them achieved. Yet their actions did make many other people better off. They did advance the social interest.

But could more have been done? Were resources used in the best possible way during the information revolution? Did Intel make the best possible chips and sell them in the right quantities for the right prices? Or was the quality of the chips too low and the price too high? And what about Microsoft? Did Bill Gates have to be paid almost $50 billion to produce the successive generations of Windows and Word? Were these programs developed in the social interest?

The computer chip has transformed our lives.

Disappearing Tropical Rainforests

Tropical rainforests in South America, Africa, and Asia support the lives of 30 million species of plants, animals, and insects—approaching 50 percent of all species on the planet. The Amazon rainforest alone converts about 1 trillion pounds of carbon dioxide into oxygen each year. These rainforests also provide us with the ingredients for many goods including soaps, mouthwashes, shampoos, food preservatives, rubber, nuts, and fruits.

Yet tropical rainforests cover less than two percent of the earth's surface and are heading for extinction. Logging, cattle ranching, mining, oil extraction, hydroelectric dams, and subsistence farming are destroying the equivalent to two football fields every second, or an area larger than New York City every day. At the current rate of destruction, almost all the tropical rainforest ecosystems will be gone by 2030.

Each one of us makes economic choices that are in our self-interest to consume products, some of which are destroying our rainforests. Are our choices damaging the social interest? And if they are, what can be done to change the incentives we face and change our behavior?

Logging is destroying the world's rainforests.

Water Shortages

The world is awash with water—it is our most abundant resource. But 97 percent of it is seawater. Another 2 percent is frozen in glaciers and ice. The 1 percent of the earth's water that is available for human consumption would be sufficient if only it were in the right places. Finland, Canada, and a few other places have more water than they can use, but Australia, Africa, and California (and many other places) could use much more water than they can get.

Some people pay less for water than others. California farmers, for example, pay less than California households. Some of the highest prices for water are faced by people in the poorest countries who must either buy from a water dealer's truck or carry water in buckets over many miles.

In the United States, water is provided by public enterprises. In the United Kingdom, private companies deliver the water.

In India and Bangladesh, plenty of rain falls, but it falls during a short wet season and the rest of the year is dry. Dams could help to reduce the shortage in the dry season but too few have been built in those countries.

Are we managing our water resources properly? Are the decisions that each of us makes in our self-interest to use, conserve, and transport water also in the social interest?

Water is abundant but clean water is scarce.

Global Warming

The earth is getting hotter. Since the late nineteenth century, its surface temperature has increased about 1 degree Fahrenheit, and close to a half of that increase occurred over the past 25 years. While these changes are small, particularly when viewed against the temperature fluctuations associated with Ice Ages, they are large enough to have a lot of people worried.

Most climate scientists believe that the current warming has come at least in part from human economic activity—from self-interested choices—and that, if left unchecked, the warming will bring large future economic costs.

As part of an attempt to slow global warming, an international meeting in Japan in 1997 led to the Kyoto Protocol, an agreement that seeks legally binding emissions cuts for the industrialized nations. But the Protocol does not impose limits on the poorer developing nations. Almost the entire world signed onto Kyoto. But the United States and Australia refused to do so. They argue that the agreement does too little to address the global warming problem and that their own independent efforts will make a more effective contribution.

Are the choices that each of us makes to use energy damaging the social interest? What needs to be done to make our choices serve the social interest? Would the United States signing onto the Kyoto Protocol serve the social interest? What other measures must be introduced?

Human activity is raising the earth's temperature.

Natural Disasters

When Hurricane Katrina hit New Orleans on August 29, 2005, a thousand people died, tens of thousands lost everything they owned, and hundreds of thousands were forced from their homes. Much of the city was flooded and polluted, and posed a health risk for those who remained. Looting erupted as desperate people sought food and medicine and as others seized an opportunity to profit from tragedy and the temporary absence of law and order. Beyond the human tragedies, crude oil production and gasoline refining took a hit and one of the nation's busiest ports was silenced.

Katrina highlighted the tension between self-interest and the social interest.

But Katrina didn't only unleash devastation and disaster for the people of New Orleans. It also unleashed an economic response. The prices of oil and gasoline increased, which encouraged more careful use of these now less plentiful resources. The price of plywood needed to repair damaged homes jumped, which brought forth a greater quantity of this now more valued item.

Millions of individual Americans contributed money and thousands who work for organizations such as the Red Cross and the Salvation Army contributed time, energy, and effort to bring shelter, food, and comfort to the displaced. Governments also acted, but more slowly. Gradually levees were restored, streets were pumped dry, and the city slowly started to return to life.

The events that played out following Katrina provide a powerful illustration of the tension between self-interest and the social interest and raise questions about the ability of markets and governments to cope with major disasters.

Without government enforced laws, self-interest can be carried too far and damage the social interest. But can government do more? What is the best balance between government and private provision of services and aid to people struck down by natural disaster? And do price hikes that clearly serve the self-interest of producers and hurt the self-interest of consumers further the social interest?

Unemployment

During the 1930s, in a period called the *Great Depression,* more than 20 percent of the labor force was unemployed. One of the triumphs of economics is that we have developed policies that can stabilize the economy and avoid depressions. Yet even today, when only 5 percent of Americans are unemployed, more than 40 percent of African-American teenagers are unemployed. Why can't everyone who wants a job find one? If economic choices arise from scarcity, why are resources left unused?

During the 1930s, the longest lines were for jobs.

People get jobs because other people think they can earn a profit by hiring them. And people accept jobs when they think the pay and other conditions are good enough. So the number of people with jobs is determined by the self-interest of employers and workers. But is the number of jobs also in the social interest?

A Social Security Time Bomb

Every single day since September 30, 2004, the U.S. government has run a budget deficit of $2.21 billion, which means that the government's debt has increased each day by that amount. On March 2, 2005, the day these words were written, your personal share of the outstanding government debt was $26,094.

Also, during 2004, Americans bought goods and services from the rest of the world in excess of what foreigners bought from the United States to the tune of $600 billion. To pay for these goods and services, Americans borrowed from the rest of the world.

These large deficits are just the beginning of an even bigger problem. From about 2019 onwards, the retirement and health-care benefits to which older Americans are entitled are going to cost increasingly more than the current Social Security taxes can pay for. With no changes in taxes or benefit rates, the deficit and debt will swell ever higher.

Deficits and the debts they create cannot persist indefinitely, and debts must somehow be repaid. They will most likely be repaid by you, not by your parents. When we make our voter choices and our choices to buy from or sell to the rest of the world, we pursue our self-interest. Do our choices damage the social interest?

A social security time bomb is ticking as benefits grow faster than contributions.

CHECKPOINT I.I

I **Define economics and explain the kinds of questions that economists try to answer.**

Practice Problems I.I

1. Economics studies choices that arise from one fact. What is that fact?
2. Provide three examples of wants in the United States today that are especially pressing but not satisfied.
3. Which of the following headlines deals with *what, how,* and *for whom* questions?
   a. With more research, we will cure cancer.
   b. A good education is the right of every child.
   c. The government must trim its budget deficit.
4. Explain how the following headlines concern self-interest and social interest:
   a. Whole Foods, a U.S. supermarket, is opening in Britain and Starbucks is everywhere in China.
   b. Cigarette packs must carry a health warning.

Exercises I.I

1. Every day, we make many choices. Why can't we avoid having to make choices?
2. Look at today's newspaper and find an example of a want that is not satisfied.
3. Check the local media for headlines that ask two of the *what, how,* and *for whom* questions.
4. Which of the following headlines deals with *what, how,* and *for whom* questions?
   a. Major league baseball's turf keepers earn about $85,000, umpires earn about $350,000, and players make millions a year.
   b. Many full-service gas stations are switching to self-serve.
   c. Retail trends analysts make as much as $300,000 a year, while retail salespeople make less than $10 an hour.
5. Explain how the following headlines concern self-interest and social interest:
   a. President George W. Bush powers his Texas ranch with solar electricity.
   b. Today's upper-class traveler goes on safari in southern Africa or stays at eco-resorts that cost $1,000 a night but do not have electricity.

Solutions to Practice Problems I.I

1. The fact is scarcity—human wants exceed the resources available.
2. Security from international terrorism, cleaner air in our cities, better public schools. (You can perhaps think of some more.)
3a. More research is a *how* question, and a cure for cancer is a *what* question.
3b. Good education is a *what* question, and every child is a *for whom* question.
3c. Whether the government cuts expenditures or raises taxes, it is a *for whom* question and a *what* question.
4a. Decisions made by Whole Foods and Starbucks are in their self-interest.
4b. The health warning concerns the social interest, but the person who heeds it makes a decision in self-interest.

1.2 THE ECONOMIC WAY OF THINKING

The definition of economics and the kinds of questions that economists try to answer give you a flavor of the scope of economics. But they don't tell you how economists *think* about these questions and go about seeking answers to them. You're now going to see how economists approach their work.

We'll break this task into three parts. First, we'll explain the core ideas that economists constantly and repeatedly use to frame their view of the world. These ideas will soon have you thinking like an economist. Second, we'll explain the distinction between the micro and macro views of the economic world. Finally, we'll look at economics both as a social science and as a policy tool that governments, businesses, and *you* can use.

■ Core Economic Ideas

Five core ideas summarize the economic approach or economic way of thinking about the choices that must be made to cope with scarcity:

- People make *rational choices* by comparing costs and benefits.
- *Cost* is what you *must* give up to get something.
- *Benefit* is what you gain when you get something and is measured by what you *are willing to* give up to get it.
- A rational choice is made on the *margin.*
- Choices respond to *incentives.*

■ Rational Choice

The most basic idea of economics is that in making choices, people act rationally. A **rational choice** is one that uses the available resources to best achieve the objective of the person making the choice.

Only the wants and preferences of the person making a choice are relevant to determine its rationality. For example, you might like chocolate ice cream more than vanilla ice cream, but your friend prefers vanilla. So it is rational for you to choose chocolate and for your friend to choose vanilla.

A rational choice might turn out not to have been the best choice after the event. A farmer might decide to plant wheat rather than soybeans. Then, when the crop comes to market, the price of soybeans might be much higher than the price of wheat. The farmer's choice was rational when it was made, but subsequent events made it less profitable than the alternative choice.

The idea of rational choice provides an answer to the first question: What goods and services will get produced and in what quantities? The answer is: Those that people rationally choose to buy!

But how do people choose rationally? Why have most people chosen to buy Microsoft's Windows operating system rather than another? Why do more people today choose to drink bottled water and sports energy drinks than did in the past? Why has the U.S. government chosen to fund the building of an interstate highway system and not an interstate high-speed railroad system?

We make rational choices by comparing *costs* and *benefits.* But economists think about costs and benefits in a special and revealing way. Let's look at the economic concepts of cost and benefit.

Rational choice
A choice that uses the available resources to best achieve the objective of the person making the choice.

■ Cost: What You *Must* Give Up

Whatever you choose to do, you could have done something else instead. You could have done lots of things other than what you actually did. But one of these other things is the *best* alternative given up. The best thing that you must give up to get something is the **opportunity cost** of the thing that you get. The thing that you could have chosen—the highest-valued alternative forgone—is the opportunity cost of the thing that you did choose.

We use the term *opportunity cost* to emphasize that when we make a choice in the face of scarcity, we give up an opportunity to do something else. You can quit school right now, or you can remain in school. Suppose that if you quit school, the best job you can get is at Kinko's, where you can earn $10,000 during the year. The opportunity cost of remaining in school includes the things that you could have bought with this $10,000. The opportunity cost also includes the value of the leisure time that you must forgo to study.

Opportunity cost of the thing you get is *only* the alternative forgone. It does not include all the expenditures that you make. For example, your expenditure on tuition is part of the opportunity cost of being in school. But your meal plan and rent are not. Whether you're in school or working, you must eat and have somewhere to live. So the cost of your school meal plan and your rent are *not* part of the opportunity cost of being in school.

Also, past expenditures that cannot be reversed are not part of opportunity cost. Suppose you've paid your term's tuition and it is nonrefundable. If you now contemplate quitting school, the paid tuition is irrelevant. It is called a sunk cost. A **sunk cost** is a previously incurred and irreversible cost. Whether you remain in school or quit school, the tuition that you've paid is not part of the opportunity cost of remaining in school.

Opportunity cost
The opportunity cost of something is the best thing you *must* give up to get it.

Sunk cost
A previously incurred and irreversible cost.

■ Benefit: Gain Measured by What You *Are Willing* to Give Up

The **benefit** of something is the gain or pleasure that it brings. Benefit is how a person *feels* about something. For example, you might be anxious to get *Tekken 5*, a recently released video game. It will bring you a large benefit. And you might have almost no interest in a Yo Yo Ma CD of Vivaldi's cello concertos. It will bring you a small benefit.

Benefit
The benefit of something is the gain or pleasure that it brings.

For these students, the opportunity cost of being in school is worth bearing.

For the full-time fast-food worker, the opportunity cost of remaining in school is too high.

Economists measure the benefit of something by what a person *is willing to give up* to get it. You can buy CDs or magazines. The magazines that you are willing to give up to get a CD measure the benefit that you get from a CD.

■ On the Margin

Margin means "border" or "edge." So you can think of a choice on the margin as one that adjusts the borders or edges of a plan to determine the best course of action. Making a choice on the **margin** means comparing *all* the relevant alternatives systematically and incrementally.

For example, you must choose how to divide the next hour between studying and e-mailing your friends. To make this choice, you must evaluate the costs and benefits of the alternative possible allocations of your next hour. You choose on the margin by considering whether you will be better off or worse off if you spend an extra few minutes studying or an extra few minutes e-mailing.

The margin might involve a small change, as it does when you're deciding how to divide an hour between studying and e-mailing friends. Or it might involve a large change, as it does, for example, when you're deciding whether to remain in school for another year. Attending school for part of the year is no better (and might be worse) than not attending at all. So you likely will want to commit the entire year to school or to something else. But you still choose on the margin. It is just that the marginal change is now a change for one year rather than a change for a few minutes.

Marginal Cost

The opportunity cost of a one-unit increase in an activity is called **marginal cost**. Marginal cost is what you *must* give up to get *one more* unit of something. Think about your marginal cost of going to the movies for a third time in a week. Your marginal cost is what you must give up to see that one additional movie. It is *not* what you give up to see all three movies. The reason is that you've already given up something for two movies, so you don't count this cost as resulting from the decision to see the third movie.

The marginal cost of any activity increases as you do more of it. You know that going to the movies decreases your study time and lowers your grade. Suppose that seeing a second movie in a week lowers your grade by five percentage points. Seeing a third movie will lower your grade by more than five percentage points. Your marginal cost of moviegoing is increasing.

Marginal Benefit

The benefit of a one-unit increase in an activity is called **marginal benefit**. Marginal benefit is what you gain when you get *one more* unit of something. But the marginal benefit of something *is measured by* what you *are willing* to give up to get that one additional unit.

A fundamental feature of marginal benefit is that it diminishes. Think about your marginal benefit from movies. If you've been studying hard and haven't seen a movie this week, your marginal benefit from seeing your next movie is large. But if you've been on a movie binge this week, you now want a break and your marginal benefit is small.

Because the marginal benefit of a movie decreases as you see more movies, you are willing to give up less to see one more movie. For example, you know that going to the movies decreases your study time and lowers your grade. You pay

---

Margin
A choice on the margin is a choice that is made by comparing *all* the relevant alternatives systematically and incrementally.

Marginal cost
The opportunity cost that arises from a one-unit increase in an activity. The marginal cost of something is what you *must* give up to get *one additional* unit of it.

Marginal benefit
The benefit that arises from a one-unit increase in an activity. The marginal benefit of something is *measured* by what you are *willing to* give up to get *one additional* unit of it.

for seeing a movie with a lower grade. You might be willing to give up ten percentage points to see your first movie in a week. But you won't be willing to take such a big hit on your grade to see a second movie in a week. Your willingness to pay to see a movie is decreasing.

Making a Rational Choice

So will you go to the movies for that third time in a week? If the marginal cost is less than the marginal benefit, your rational choice will be to see the third movie. If the marginal cost exceeds the marginal benefit, your rational choice will be to spend the evening studying. We make a rational choice and use our scarce resources in the way that makes us as well off as possible when we take those actions for which marginal benefit exceeds or equals marginal cost.

■ Responding to Incentives

The choices we make depend on the incentives we face. An **incentive** is a reward or a penalty—a "carrot" or a "stick"—that encourages or discourages an action. We respond positively to "carrots" and negatively to "sticks." The carrots that we face are marginal benefits. The sticks are marginal costs. A change in marginal benefit or a change in marginal cost brings a change in the incentives that we face and leads us to change our actions.

Most students believe that the payoff from studying just before a test is greater than the payoff from studying a month before a test. In other words, as a test date approaches, the marginal benefit of studying increases and the incentive to study becomes stronger. For this reason, we observe an increase in study time and a decrease in leisure pursuits during the last few days before a test. And the more important the test, the greater is this effect.

A change in marginal cost changes incentives. For example, suppose that last week, you found your course work easy and scored 100 percent on your practice quizzes. The marginal cost of taking an evening off to enjoy a movie was low. Your grade on this week's test will not suffer, so you have a movie feast. But this week the going has gotten tough. You are just not getting it, and your practice test scores are low. If you take off even one evening, your grade on next week's test will suffer. The marginal cost of seeing a movie is higher this week than it was last week. So you decide to give the movies a miss.

A central idea of economics is that by observing changes in incentives, we can predict how choices will change.

Incentive
A reward or a penalty—a "carrot" or a "stick"—that encourages or discourages an action.

Changes in marginal benefit and marginal cost change the incentive to study or to enjoy a movie.

■ The Micro and Macro Views of the World

Just as doctors specialize in different branches of medicine, so economists specialize in different branches of economics. The major division of the subject is into two parts: microeconomics (or micro) and macroeconomics (or macro).

Microeconomics

Microeconomics
The study of the choices that individuals and businesses make and the way these choices interact and are influenced by governments.

Microeconomics is the study of the choices that individuals and businesses make and the way these choices interact and are influenced by governments. Some examples of microeconomic questions are: Will you buy a flat screen or traditional television? Will Sony sell more PlayStations if it cuts the price? Will a cut in the income tax rate encourage people to work longer hours? Will a hike in the gas tax lead to smaller automobiles? Are MP3 downloads killing CDs?

Macroeconomics

Macroeconomics
The study of the aggregate (or total) effects on the national economy and the global economy of the choices that individuals, businesses, and governments make.

Macroeconomics is the study of the aggregate (or total) effects on the national economy and the global economy of the choices that individuals, businesses, and governments make. Some examples of macroeconomic questions are: Why did production and jobs expand so slowly in the United States in the early 2000s? Why are incomes growing much faster in China and India than in the United States? Why are production and incomes stagnating in Japan? Why are Americans borrowing more than $2 billion a day from the rest of the world?

Micro and Macro Dimensions

All the issues that we reviewed earlier in this chapter—globalization and international outsourcing, the new economy, disappearing tropical rainforests, water shortages, global warming, natural disasters, unemployment, and the Social Security time bomb— have a micro and a macro dimension.

The effect of globalization and international outsourcing on the textile industry is a micro topic; its effect on average incomes in the United States and other countries is a macro topic. The influence of the Internet and online commerce is a micro topic; its influence on economy-wide production and jobs is a macro topic. The disappearing tropical rainforests, water shortages, global warming, and natural disasters affect individual industries and products, which are micro topics, but also affect total production, incomes, and jobs, which are macro topics. Unemployment in a region or industry is a micro topic; the national unemployment rate is a macro topic. And finally, Social Security arrangements affect the distribution of income, a micro topic, and the stability of the entire economy, a macro topic.

The distinction between microeconomics and macroeconomics is similar to the distinction between two views of a display of flags in an Olympic stadium. The micro view (left) is of a single participant and the actions he or she is taking. The macro view (right) is the patterns formed by the joint actions of all the people participating in the entire display.

■ Economics as Social Science

As social scientists, economists seek to discover how the economic world works. In pursuit of this goal, like all scientists, they distinguish between two types of statements:

- Positive statements
- Normative statements

Positive Statements

Positive statements are about what *is*. They say what is currently believed about the way the world operates. A positive statement might be right or wrong. But we can test a positive statement by checking it against the facts. "Our planet is warming because of the amount of coal that we're burning" is a positive statement. "A rise in the minimum wage will bring more teenage unemployment" is another positive statement. Each statement might be right or wrong, and it can be tested.

A central task of economists is to test positive statements about how the economic world works and to weed out those that are wrong. Economics first got off the ground in the late 1700s (see *Eye on the Past* on p. 17), so economics is a young subject compared with, for example, math and physics, and much remains to be discovered.

Normative Statements

Normative statements are statements about what *ought to be.* These statements depend on values and cannot be tested. The statement "We ought to cut back on our use of coal" is a normative statement. "The minimum wage should not be increased" is another normative statement. You may agree or disagree with either of these statements, but you can't test them. They express an opinion, but they don't assert a fact that can be checked. And they are not economics.

Unscrambling Cause and Effect

Economists are especially interested in positive statements about cause and effect. Are computers getting cheaper because people are buying them in greater quantities? Or are people buying computers in greater quantities because they are getting cheaper? Or is some third factor causing both the price of a computer to fall and the quantity of computers to increase? These are examples of positive statements that economists want to test. But doing so can be difficult.

The central idea that economists (and all scientists) use to unscramble cause and effect is *ceteris paribus*. **Ceteris paribus** is a Latin term (often abbreviated as *cet. par.*) that means "other things being equal" or "if all other relevant things remain the same." Ensuring that other things are equal is crucial in many activities, including athletic events, and all successful attempts to make scientific progress use this device. By changing one factor at a time and holding all the other relevant factors constant, we isolate the factor of interest and are able to investigate its effects in the clearest possible way.

In economics, we observe the outcomes of the simultaneous operation of many factors. Consequently, it is hard to sort out the effects of each individual factor and to compare the effects with what a model predicts. To cope with this problem, economists use natural experiments, statistical investigations, and economic experiments.

Ceteris paribus
Other things remaining the same (often abbreviated as *cet. par.*).

In track and field, other things are equal.

A natural experiment is a situation that arises in the ordinary course of economic life in which the one factor of interest is different and other things are equal (or similar). For example, Canada has higher unemployment benefits than the United States, but the people in the two nations are similar. So to study the effect of unemployment benefits on the unemployment rate, economists might compare the United States with Canada.

Correlation
The tendency for the values of two variables to move in a predictable and related way.

A statistical investigation looks for a **correlation**—a tendency for the values of two variables to move together (either in the same direction or in opposite directions) in a predictable and related way. For example, cigarette smoking and lung cancer are correlated. Sometimes a correlation shows a causal influence of one variable on the other. For example, smoking causes lung cancer. But sometimes the direction of causation is hard to determine.

An economic experiment puts people in a decision-making situation and varies the influence of one factor at a time to discover how they respond.

■ Economics as Policy Tool

Economics is useful. And you don't have to be an economist to think like one and to use the insights of economics as a policy tool. The subject provides a way of approaching problems in all aspects of our lives:

- Personal
- Business
- Government

Personal Economic Policy

Should you take out a student loan? Should you get a weekend job? Should you buy a used car or a new one? Should you rent an apartment or take out a loan and buy one? Should you pay off your credit card balance or make just the minimum payment? How should you allocate your time between study, working for a wage, caring for family members, and having fun? How should you allocate your time between studying economics and your other subjects? Should you quit school after getting a bachelor's degree or should you go for a masters or a professional qualification?

All these questions involve a marginal benefit and a marginal cost. And although some of the numbers might be hard to pin down, you will make more solid decisions if you approach these questions with the tools of economics.

Business Economic Policy

Should Sony make only flat panel televisions and stop making conventional ones? Should Texaco get more oil and gas from the Gulf of Mexico or from Alaska? Should Palm outsource its online customer services to India or run the operation from California? Should Miramax produce *Shrek 3*, a sequel to *Shrek 2*? Can Microsoft compete with Google in the search engine business? Can eBay compete with the surge of new Internet auction services? Is Manny Ramirez really worth $22,500,000 to the Boston Red Sox?

Like personal economic questions, these business questions involve the evaluation of a marginal benefit and a marginal cost. Some of the questions require a broader investigation of the interactions of individuals and firms. But again, by approaching these questions with the tools of economics and by hiring economists as advisers, businesses can make better decisions.

Adam Smith and the Birth of Economics as a Modern Social Science

Many people had written about economics before Adam Smith, but he made economics a social science.

Born in 1723 in Kirkcaldy, a small fishing town near Edinburgh, Scotland, Smith was the only child of the town's customs officer. Lured from his professorship (he was a full professor at 28) by a wealthy Scottish duke who gave him a pension of £300 a year—ten times the average income at that time—Smith devoted ten years to writing his masterpiece, *An Inquiry into the Nature and Causes of the Wealth of Nations,* published in 1776.

Why, Adam Smith asked in that book, are some nations wealthy while others are poor? He was pondering these questions at the height of the Industrial Revolution. During these years, new technologies were applied to the manufacture of textiles, iron, transportation, and agriculture.

Adam Smith answered his questions by emphasizing the role of the division of labor and free markets. To illustrate his argument, he used the example of a pin factory. He guessed that one person, using the hand tools available in the 1770s, might make 20 pins a day. Yet, he observed, by using those same hand tools but breaking the process into a number of individually small operations in which people specialize—by the division of labor—ten people could make a staggering 48,000 pins a day. One draws out the wire, another straightens it, a third cuts it, a fourth points it, a fifth grinds it. Three specialists make the head, and a fourth attaches it. Finally, the pin is polished and packaged.

But a large market is needed to support the division of labor: One factory employing ten workers would need to sell more than 15 million pins a year to stay in business!

Government Economic Policy

How can California balance its budget? Should the federal government cut taxes or raise them? How can the tax system be simplified? Should people be permitted to invest their Social Security money in stocks that they pick themselves? Should Medicaid and Medicare be extended to the entire population? Should there be a special tax to penalize corporations that send jobs overseas? Should cheap foreign imports of furniture and textiles be limited? Should the farms that grow tomatoes and sugar beets receive a subsidy? Should water be transported from Washington and Oregon to California?

These government policy questions call for decisions that involve the evaluation of a marginal benefit and a marginal cost and an investigation of the interactions of individuals and businesses. Yet again, by approaching these questions with the tools of economics, governments make better decisions.

Notice that all the policy questions we've just posed involve a blend of the positive and the normative. Economics can't help with the normative part—the objective. But for a given objective, economics provides a method of evaluating alternative solutions. That method is to evaluate the marginal benefits and marginal costs and to find the solution that brings the greatest available gain.

2 Explain the core ideas that define the economic way of thinking.

Practice Problems 1.2

1. Every week, Kate plays tennis for two hours, and her grade on each math test is 70 percent. Last week, after playing for two hours, Kate considered playing for another hour. She decided to play for another hour and cut her study time by one hour. But last week, her math grade fell to 60 percent.
    a. What was Kate's opportunity cost of the third hour of tennis?
    b. Given that Kate played the third hour, what can you conclude about her marginal benefit and marginal cost of the second hour of tennis?
    c. Was Kate's decision to play the third hour of tennis rational?
    d. Did Kate make her decision on the margin?

2. Check the local media and find an example of:
    a. A positive statement
    b. A normative statement

Exercises 1.2

1. Bill Gates gives away millions of dollars a year to universities, cancer research, a children's hospital, and the Seattle Symphony. Are his donations rational? In making these donations, might Bill Gates have responded to any incentive? Does he make his decision about his donations on the margin?

2. Tony is an engineering student, who is considering taking an extra course in history. What things might be part of his costs and benefits of the history course? Think of an incentive that might encourage him to take the course.

3. Check the local media and find three examples of:
    a. Macroeconomic issues and microeconomic issues
    b. Positive statements
    c. Normative statements
    d. Economics as a policy tool

Solutions to Practice Problems 1.2

1a. Kate's opportunity cost of the third hour of tennis was the ten-percentage point drop in her grade.

1b. The marginal benefit from the second hour of tennis must have exceeded the marginal cost of the second hour because Kate chose to play the third hour.

1c. If marginal benefit exceeded marginal cost, Kate's decision was rational.

1d. Kate made her decision on the margin because she considered the benefit and cost of one additional hour.

2a. "The Butterfly House must be kept near 80 degrees at all times, or butterflies won't fly." is a positive statement because it can be tested against the facts.

2b. "Flex-time, which allows employees to shift their work hours over a two-week period, will allow workers to better meet family needs." is a normative statement because it cannot be tested.

CHAPTER CHECKPOINT

Key Points

1 **Define economics and explain the kinds of questions that economists try to answer.**

- Economics is the social science that studies the choices that we make as we cope with scarcity and the incentives that influence and reconcile our choices.
- The first big question of economics is: How do the choices that people make end up determining *what, how,* and *for whom* goods and services get produced?
- The second big question is: When do choices made in the pursuit of *self-interest* also promote the *social interest*?

2 **Explain the core ideas that define the economic way of thinking.**

- Five core ideas define the economic way of thinking:
    1. People make *rational* choices by comparing costs and benefits.
    2. Cost is what you *must* give up to get something.
    3. Benefit is what you gain when you get something and is measured by what you *are willing to* give up to get it.
    4. A rational choice is made on the *margin*.
    5. Choices respond to *incentives*.
- Microeconomics is the study of individual choices and interactions, and macroeconomics is the study of the national economy and global economy.
- Economists try to understand how the economic world works by testing positive statements using natural experiments, statistical investigations, and economic experiments.
- Economics is a tool for personal, business, and government decisions.

Key Terms

Benefit, 11
Ceteris paribus, 15
Correlation, 16
Economics, 3
Goods and services, 3
Incentive, 13

Macroeconomics, 14
Margin, 12
Marginal benefit, 12
Marginal cost, 12
Microeconomics, 14
Opportunity cost, 11

Rational choice, 10
Scarcity, 2
Self-interest, 4
Social interest, 4
Sunk cost, 11

myeconlab **Exercises**

1. Provide three examples of scarcity that illustrate why even the 691 billionaires in the world face scarcity.

2. Think about the following news items and label each as involving a *what, how,* or *for whom* question:
   a. Today, most stores use computers to keep their inventory records, whereas 20 years ago most stores used paper records.
   b. Health-care professionals and drug companies say that Medicaid drug rebates should be available to everyone in need.
   c. A doubling of the gas tax might lead to a better public transit system.

3. Arnold Schwartzenegger chose politics over making a movie such as a sequel to *Terminator 3.* In making his decision to run for governor of California, did he make his choice at the margin? Was his choice rational? Did he face an opportunity cost? If so, what might have been some of the components of his opportunity cost?

4. Pam, Pru, and Pat are deciding how they will celebrate the New Year. Pam prefers to go on a cruise, is happy to go to Hawaii, but does not want to go skiing. Pru prefers to go skiing, is happy to go to Hawaii, but does not want to go on a cruise. Pat prefers to go to Hawaii or to take a cruise but does not want to go skiing. Their decision is to go to Hawaii. Is this decision rational? What is the opportunity cost of the trip to Hawaii for each of them? What is the benefit that each gets?

5. Your school has decided to increase the intake of new students next year. What economic concepts would your school consider in reaching its decision? Would the school make its decision at the margin?

6. Provide examples of two monetary and two non-monetary incentives, a carrot and a stick of each, that have influenced major government decisions during the past few years.

7. Think about the following news items and label each as involving a microeconomic or a macroeconomic issue:
   a. An increase in the tax on cigarettes will decrease teenage smoking.
   b. It would be better if the United States spent more on cleaning up the environment and less on space exploration.
   c. An increase in the number of police on inner-city streets will reduce the crime rate.
   d. The Congress will consider raising the minimum wage.

8. Label each of the following news items as a positive or a normative statement:
   a. The poor pay too much for housing.
   b. The number of farms has decreased over the last 50 years.
   c. The population in rural areas has remained constant over the past decade.

9. Explain why economists use the *ceteris paribus* assumption.

10. Find in the media one example of economics being used as a tool by each of a person, a business, and a government to make a decision.

Critical Thinking

11. Andrew Whittaker Jr. of West Virginia got a surprise present on Christmas Day 2002 when he won the $314.9 million jackpot of the Powerball lottery. This jackpot was the biggest ever won by a single person in U.S. history.
    a. Do the people who buy lottery tickets face scarcity?
    b. Do the winners of big prizes face scarcity after receiving their winners' checks?
    c. Do you think lotteries have both microeconomic effects and macroeconomic effects or only microeconomic effects? Explain.
    d. How do you think lotteries change what and for whom goods and services are produced?
    e. Think about the statement "Lotteries create more problems than they solve and should be banned." Which part of this statement is positive and how might it be tested? Which part of this statement is normative?
    f. Do people face a marginal cost and a marginal benefit when they decide to buy a lottery ticket?
    g. Does a person who buys a lottery ticket make a rational choice?
    h. Do the people who buy lottery tickets respond to incentives?
    i. How do you think the size of the jackpot affects the number of lottery tickets sold? What role do incentives play in this response?

12. *Shrek 2* was the most successful movie of 2004, with box office receipts of more than $346 million. Creating a successful movie brings pleasure to millions, generates work for thousands, and makes a few people rich.
    a. What contribution does a movie like *Shrek 2* make to coping with scarcity?
    b. Does the decision to make a blockbuster movie mean that some other more desirable activities get fewer resources than they deserve?
    c. Was your answer to part **b** a positive or a normative answer? Explain.
    d. Who decides whether a movie is going to be a blockbuster?
    e. How do you think the creation of a blockbuster movie influences what, how, and for whom goods and services are produced?
    f. What do you think are some of the marginal costs and marginal benefits that the producer of a movie faces?
    g. Suppose that Mike Myers had been offered a bigger and better part in another movie and that to hire him for *Shrek 2*, the producer had to double Mike Myers' pay. What incentives would have changed? How might the changed incentives have changed the choices that people made?

13. Think about each of the following situations and explain how they affect incentives and might change the choices that people make.
    a. A hurricane hits Central Florida.
    b. The World Series begins tonight but a thunderstorm warning is in effect for the area in which the stadium is located.
    c. The price of a personal computer falls to $50.
    d. Political instability in the Middle East cuts world oil production and sends the price of gasoline to $4 a gallon.
    e. Your school builds a new parking garage that increases the number of parking places available but doubles the price of parking on campus.

Web Exercises

If you haven't already done so, take a few minutes to visit MyEconLab, sign in, and obtain your username and password. Browse the Web site and become familiar with its structure and content. You'll soon appreciate that MyEconLab is a very useful and powerful learning tool. For each chapter, you will find sample tests, a study plan based on your test results, interactive tutorials and graphics, e-text with animations of your textbook figures, and much more. You will also find the links you need to work the Web exercises.

Use the links on MyEconLab to work the following exercises.

14. Visit the Show Us the Jobs Web site, click on "Your state" and read the Jobs Crisis report. Now visit the Bureau of Labor Statistics (BLS) Web site and check the data on jobs in your state. How does the official jobs situation for your state as reported by the BLS compare with the Jobs Crisis report?

15. Visit the Campaign for Tobacco-Free Kids. Obtain data on changes in state tobacco taxes and changes in state tobacco consumption.
    a. Calculate the percentage change in tobacco taxes in each of the states for which you have data.
    b. Make a graph that plots the percentage change in the tobacco tax on the *x*-axis and the percentage change in state tobacco consumption on the *y*-axis.
    c. Describe the relationship between these two variables. (Look at pp. 23, 24, and 25 if you need help with making and interpreting your graph.)
    d. How would you expect a rise in the tobacco tax to influence the incentive for a young person to smoke cigarettes?
    e. Do the data that you've obtained confirm what you expected or were you surprised by the data? Explain your answer.
    f. What can you infer about cause and effect in the data on tobacco taxes and tobacco consumption?
    g. What is the main obstacle to drawing a strong conclusion about the effect of tobacco taxes on tobacco consumption?

16. Visit the *Statistical Abstract of the United States* and obtain data on the levels of average annual pay and the percentage of persons with a bachelor's degree in each of the states.
    a. Which state has the highest average pay and which has the lowest?
    b. Where in the ranking of average pay does your state stand?
    c. Which state has the highest percentage of people with a bachelor's degree and which has the lowest?
    d. Where in the ranking of people with a bachelor's degree does your state stand?
    e. What do you think these numbers tell us about what, how, or for whom goods and services are produced?
    f. What is the difficulty in using these numbers to determine whether education levels influence pay levels?

17. Visit the Inflation Calculator. Then make this choice: You can have $11 and pay the prices of 1805, or you can have $100 and pay the prices of 2005. Which do you prefer and why?

When you have completed your study of this appendix, you will be able to

1 Interpret a scatter diagram, a time-series graph, and a cross-section graph.

2 Interpret the graphs used in economic models.

3 Define and calculate slope.

4 Graph relationships among more than two variables.

■ Basic Idea

A graph represents a quantity as a distance and enables us to visualize the relationship between two variables. To make a graph, we set two lines called *axes* perpendicular to each other, like those in Figure A1.1. The vertical line is called the *y*-axis, and the horizontal line is called the *x*-axis. The common zero point is called the *origin*. In Figure A1.1, the *x*-axis measures temperature in degrees Fahrenheit. A movement to the right shows an increase in temperature, and a movement to the left shows a decrease in temperature. The *y*-axis represents ice cream consumption, measured in gallons per day. To make a graph, we need a value of the variable on the *x*-axis and a corresponding value of the variable on the *y*-axis. For example, if the temperature is 40°F, ice cream consumption is 5 gallons a day at point *A* in the graph. If the temperature is 80°F, ice cream consumption is 20 gallons a day at point *B* in the graph. Graphs like that in Figure A1.1 can be used to show any type of quantitative data on two variables.

■ FIGURE A1.1

Making a Graph

All graphs have axes that measure quantities as distances.

❶ The horizontal axis (x-axis) measures temperature in degrees Fahrenheit. A movement to the right shows an increase in temperature.

❷ The vertical axis (y-axis) measures ice cream consumption in gallons per day. A movement upward shows an increase in ice cream consumption.

❸ Point *A* shows that 5 gallons of ice cream are consumed on a day when the temperature is 40°F.

❹ Point *B* shows that 20 gallons of ice cream are consumed on a day when the temperature is 80°F.

23

■ Interpreting Data Graphs

A **scatter diagram** is a graph of the value of one variable against the value of another variable. It is used to reveal whether a relationship exists between two variables and to describe the relationship. Figure A1.2 shows two examples.

Figure A1.2(a) shows the relationship between expenditure and income. Each point shows expenditure per person and income per person in the United States in a given year from 1995 to 2005. The points are "scattered" within the graph. The label on each point shows its year. The point marked 00 shows that in 2000, income per person was $25,500 and expenditure per person was $23,900. This scatter diagram reveals that as income increases, expenditure also increases.

Figure A1.2(b) shows the relationship between the number of minutes of international phone calls made from the United States and the average price per minute. This scatter diagram reveals that as the price per minute falls, the number of minutes called increases.

A **time-series graph** measures time (for example, months or years) on the x-axis and the variable or variables in which we are interested on the y-axis. Figure A1.2(c) shows an example. In this graph, time (on the x-axis) is measured in years, which run from 1980 to 2005. The variable that we are interested in is the price of coffee, and it is measured on the y-axis.

A time-series graph conveys an enormous amount of information quickly and easily, as this example illustrates. It shows when the value is

1. High or low. When the line is a long way from the x-axis, the price is high, as it was in 1997. When the line is close to the x-axis, the price is low, as it was in 1993.

2. Rising or falling. When the line slopes upward, as in 1988, the price is rising. When the line slopes downward, as in 2001, the price is falling.

3. Rising or falling quickly or slowly. If the line is steep, then the price is rising or falling quickly. If the line is not steep, the price is rising or falling slowly. For example, the price rose quickly in 1988 and slowly in 1984. The price fell quickly in 2001 and slowly in 2003.

A time-series graph also reveals whether the variable has a trend. A **trend** is a general tendency for the value of a variable to rise or fall. You can see that the price of coffee had a general tendency to rise from 1982 to the late 1990s. That is, although the price rose and fell, it had a general tendency to rise.

With a time-series graph, we can compare different periods quickly. Figure A1.2(c) shows that the 1990s were different from the 1980s. The price of coffee fluctuated more violently in the 1990s than it did in the 1980s. This graph conveys a wealth of information, and it does so in much less space than we have used to describe only some of its features.

A **cross-section graph** shows the values of an economic variable for different groups in a population at a point in time. Figure A1.2(d) is an example of a cross-section graph. It shows the percentage of people who participated in selected sports activities in the United States. This graph uses bars rather than dots and lines, and the length of each bar indicates the participation rate. Figure A1.2(d) enables you to compare the participation rates in these ten sporting activities. And you can do so much more quickly and clearly than by looking at a list of numbers.

FIGURE A1.2
Data Graphs

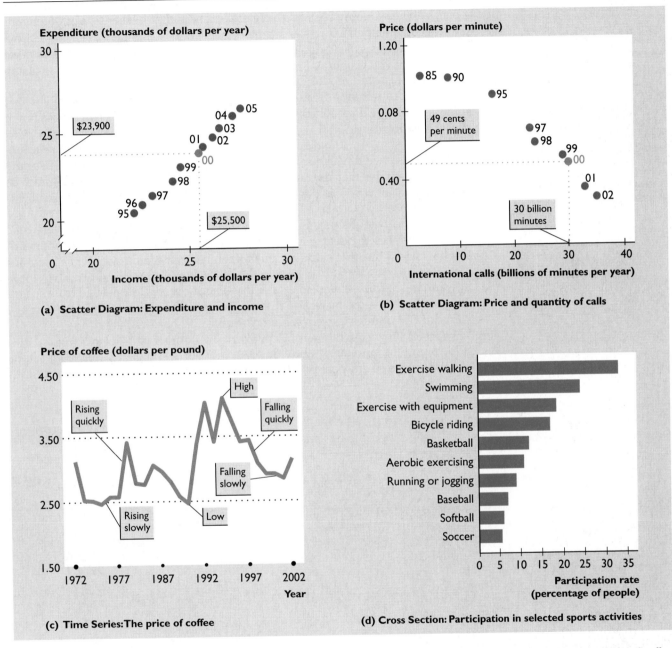

(a) Scatter Diagram: Expenditure and income

(b) Scatter Diagram: Price and quantity of calls

(c) Time Series: The price of coffee

(d) Cross Section: Participation in selected sports activities

A scatter diagram reveals the relationship between two variables. In part (a), as income increases, expenditure increases. In part (b), as the price per minute falls, the number of minutes called increases.

A time-series graph plots the value of a variable on the *y*-axis against time on the *x*-axis. Part (c) plots the price of coffee each

year from 1980 to 2005. The graph shows when the price of coffee was high and low, when it increased and decreased, and when it changed quickly and slowly.

A cross-section graph shows the value of a variable across the members of a population. Part (d) shows the participation rate in the United States in each of ten sporting activities.

■ Interpreting Graphs Used in Economic Models

We use graphs to show the relationships among the variables in an economic model. An *economic model* is a simplified description of the economy or of a component of the economy such as a business or a household. It consists of statements about economic behavior that can be expressed as equations or as curves in a graph. Economists use models to explore the effects of different policies or other influences on the economy in ways similar to those used to test model airplanes in wind tunnels and models of the climate.

Figure A1.3 shows graphs of the relationships between two variables that move in the same direction. Such a relationship is called a **positive relationship** or **direct relationship**.

Part (a) shows a straight-line relationship, which is called a **linear relationship**. The distance traveled in 5 hours increases as the speed increases. For example, point *A* shows that 200 miles are traveled in 5 hours at a speed of 40 miles an hour. And point *B* shows that the distance traveled increases to 300 miles if the speed increases to 60 miles an hour.

Part (b) shows the relationship between distance sprinted and recovery time (the time it takes the heart rate to return to its normal resting rate). An upward-sloping curved line that starts out quite flat but then becomes steeper as we move along the curve away from the origin describes this relationship. The curve slopes upward and becomes steeper because the extra recovery time needed from sprinting another 100 yards increases. It takes 5 minutes to recover from sprinting 100 yards but 15 minutes to recover from sprinting 200 yards.

Part (c) shows the relationship between the number of problems worked by a student and the amount of study time. An upward-sloping curved line that starts out quite steep and becomes flatter as we move away from the origin shows this

Positive relationship or direct relationship
A relationship between two variables that move in the same direction.

Linear relationship
A relationship that graphs as a straight line.

■ **FIGURE A1.3**
Positive (Direct) Relationships

Part (a) shows that as speed increases, the distance traveled increases along a straight line.

Part (b) shows that as the distance sprinted increases, recovery time increases along a curve that becomes steeper.

Part (c) shows that as study time increases, the number of problems worked increases along a curve that becomes less steep.

relationship. Study time becomes less effective as you increase the hours worked and become more tired.

Figure A1.4 shows relationships between two variables that move in opposite directions. Such a relationship is called a **negative relationship** or **inverse relationship**.

Part (a) shows the relationship between the number of hours for playing squash and the number of hours for playing tennis when the total number of hours available is five. One extra hour spent playing tennis means one hour less playing squash and vice versa. This relationship is negative and linear.

Part (b) shows the relationship between the cost per mile traveled and the length of a journey. The longer the journey, the lower is the cost per mile. But as the journey length increases, the cost per mile decreases, and the fall in the cost gets smaller. This feature of the relationship is shown by the fact that the curve slopes downward, starting out steep at a short journey length and then becoming flatter as the journey length increases. This relationship arises because some of the costs such as auto insurance are fixed, and the fixed costs are spread over a longer journey.

Part (c) shows the relationship between the amount of leisure time and the number of problems worked by a student. Increasing leisure time produces an increasingly large reduction in the number of problems worked. This relationship is a negative one that starts out with a gentle slope at a small number of leisure hours and becomes steeper as the number of leisure hours increases. This relationship is a different view of the idea shown in Figure A1.3(c).

Many relationships in economic models have a maximum or a minimum. For example, firms try to make the largest possible profit and to produce at the lowest possible cost. Figure A1.5 shows relationships that have a maximum or a minimum.

> **Negative relationship or inverse relationship**
> A relationship between two variables that move in opposite directions.

FIGURE A1.4 ⓧ myeconlab

Negative (Inverse) Relationships

(a) **Negative linear relationship**

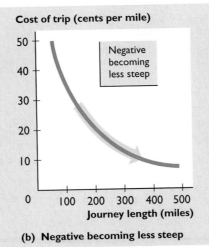

(b) **Negative becoming less steep**

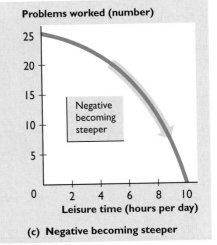

(c) **Negative becoming steeper**

Part (a) shows that as the time playing tennis increases, the time playing squash decreases along a straight line.

Part (b) shows that as the journey length increases, the cost of the trip falls along a curve that becomes less steep.

Part (c) shows that as leisure time increases, the number of problems worked decreases along a curve that becomes steeper.

■ FIGURE A1.5

Maximum and Minimum Points

In part (a), as the rainfall increases, the curve ❶ slopes upward as the yield per acre rises, ❷ is flat at point *A*, the maximum yield, and then ❸ slopes downward as the yield per acre falls.

In part (b), as the speed increases, the curve ❶ slopes downward as the cost per mile falls, ❷ is flat at the minimum point *B*, and then ❸ slopes upward as the cost per mile rises.

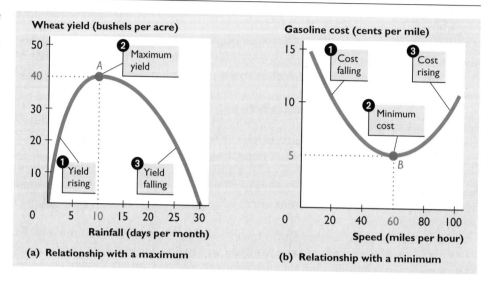

(a) Relationship with a maximum   (b) Relationship with a minimum

Part (a) shows the relationship that starts out sloping upward, reaches a maximum, and then slopes downward. Part (b) shows a relationship that begins sloping downward, falls to a minimum, and then slopes upward.

Finally, there are many situations in which, no matter what happens to the value of one variable, the other variable remains constant. Sometimes we want to show two variables that are unrelated in a graph. Figure A1.6 shows two graphs in which the variables are independent.

■ FIGURE A1.6

Variables That Are Unrelated

In part (a), as the price of bananas increases, the student's grade in economics remains at 75 percent. These variables are unrelated, and the curve is horizontal.

In part (b), the vineyards of France produce 3 billion gallons of wine no matter what the rainfall in California is. These variables are unrelated, and the curve is vertical.

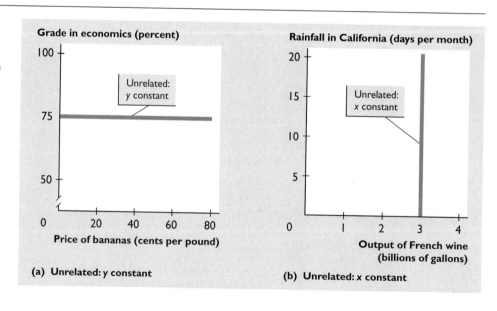

(a) Unrelated: y constant   (b) Unrelated: x constant

■ The Slope of a Relationship

We can measure the influence of one variable on another by the slope of the relationship. The **slope** of a relationship is the change in the value of the variable measured on the y-axis divided by the change in the value of the variable measured on the x-axis. We use the Greek letter Δ (delta) to represent "change in." So Δy means the change in the value of y, and Δx means the change in the value of x, and the slope of the relationship is

$$\Delta y \div \Delta x.$$

If a large change in y is associated with a small change in x, the slope is large and the curve is steep. If a small change in y is associated with a large change in x, the slope is small and the curve is flat.

Figure A1.7 shows you how to calculate slope. The slope of a straight line is the same regardless of where on the line you calculate it—the slope is constant. In part (a), when x increases from 2 to 6, y increases from 3 to 6. The change in x is 4—that is, Δx is 4. The change in y is 3—that is, Δy is 3. The slope of that line is 3/4. In part (b), when x increases from 2 to 6, y *decreases* from 6 to 3. The change in y is *minus* 3—that is, Δy is -3. The change in x is plus 4—that is, Δx is 4. The slope of the curve is $-3/4$.

In part (c), we calculate the slope at a point on a curve. To do so, place a ruler on the graph so that it touches point A and no other point on the curve, then draw a straight line along the edge of the ruler. The slope of this straight line is the slope of the curve at point A. This slope is 3/4.

Slope
The change in the value of the variable measured on the y-axis divided by the change in the value of the variable measured on the x-axis.

■ FIGURE A1.7

Calculating Slope

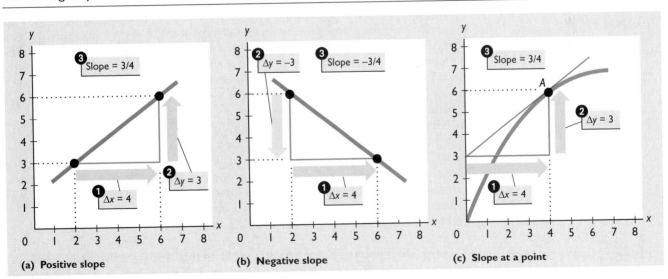

(a) Positive slope

(b) Negative slope

(c) Slope at a point

In part (a), ❶ when Δx is 4, ❷ Δy is 3, so ❸ the slope ($\Delta y \div \Delta x$) is 3/4.

In part (b), ❶ when Δx is 4, ❷ Δy is -3, so ❸ the slope ($\Delta y \div \Delta x$) is $-3/4$.

In part (c), the slope of the curve at point A equals the slope of the red line. ❶ When Δx is 4, ❷ Δy is 3, so ❸ the slope ($\Delta y \div \Delta x$) is 3/4.

■ Relationships Among More Than Two Variables

We have seen that we can graph the relationship between two variables as a point formed by the x and y values. But most of the relationships in economics involve relationships among many variables, not just two. For example, the amount of ice cream consumed depends on the price of ice cream and the temperature. If ice cream is expensive and the temperature is low, people eat much less ice cream than when ice cream is inexpensive and the temperature is high. For any given price of ice cream, the quantity consumed varies with the temperature; and for any given temperature, the quantity of ice cream consumed varies with its price.

Figure A1.8 shows a relationship among three variables. The table shows the number of gallons of ice cream consumed per day at various temperatures and ice cream prices. How can we graph these numbers?

To graph a relationship that involves more than two variables, we use the *ceteris paribus* assumption.

Ceteris Paribus

The Latin phrase *ceteris paribus* means "other things remaining the same." Every laboratory experiment is an attempt to create *ceteris paribus* and isolate the relationship of interest. We use the same method to make a graph.

Figure A1.8(a) shows an example. This graph shows what happens to the quantity of ice cream consumed when the price of ice cream varies while the temperature remains the same. The curve labeled 70°F shows the relationship between ice cream consumption and the price of ice cream if the temperature is 70°F. The numbers used to plot that curve are those in the first and fourth columns of the table in Figure A1.8. For example, if the temperature is 70°F, 10 gallons are consumed when the price is 60¢ a scoop and 18 gallons are consumed when the price is 30¢ a scoop. The curve labeled 90°F shows the relationship between consumption and the price when the temperature is 90°F.

We can also show the relationship between ice cream consumption and temperature while the price of ice cream remains constant, as shown in Figure A1.8(b). The curve labeled 60¢ shows how the consumption of ice cream varies with the temperature when the price of ice cream is 60¢ a scoop, and a second curve shows the relationship when the price of ice cream is 15¢ a scoop. For example, at 60¢ a scoop, 10 gallons are consumed when the temperature is 70°F and 20 gallons are consumed when the temperature is 90°F.

Figure A1.8(c) shows the combinations of temperature and price that result in a constant consumption of ice cream. One curve shows the combinations that result in 10 gallons a day being consumed, and the other shows the combinations that result in 7 gallons a day being consumed. A high price and a high temperature lead to the same consumption as a lower price and a lower temperature. For example, 10 gallons of ice cream are consumed at 90°F and 90¢ a scoop, at 70°F and 60¢ a scoop, and at 50°F and 45¢ a scoop.

With what you've learned about graphs in this Appendix, you can move forward with your study of economics. There are no graphs in this textbook that are more complicated than the ones you've studied here.

■ FIGURE A1.8

Graphing a Relationship Among Three Variables

Price (cents per scoop)	Ice cream consumption (gallons per day)			
	30°F	**50°F**	**70°F**	**90°F**
15	12	18	25	50
30	10	12	18	37
45	7	10	13	27
60	5	7	10	20
75	3	5	7	14
90	2	3	5	10
105	1	2	3	6

(a) Price and consumption at a given temperature

(b) Temperature and consumption at a given price

(c) Temperature and price at a given consumption

The table tells us how many gallons of ice cream are consumed each day at different prices and different temperatures. For example, if the price is 60¢ a scoop and the temperature is 70°F, 10 gallons of ice cream are consumed. This set of values is highlighted in the table and each part of the figure.

Part (a) shows the relationship between price and consumption when temperature is held constant. One curve holds temperature at 90°F, and the other at 70°F.

Part (b) shows the relationship between temperature and consumption when price is held constant. One curve holds the price at 60¢ a scoop, and the other at 15¢ a scoop.

Part (c) shows the relationship between temperature and price when consumption is held constant. One curve holds consumption at 10 gallons a day, and the other at 7 gallons a day.

Exercises

The spreadsheet provides data on the U.S. economy: Column A is the year; the other columns are actual and projected expenditures per person in dollars per year on recorded music (column B), Internet services (column C), and movies in theaters (column D). Use this spreadsheet to answer exercises 1, 2, 3, 4, and 5.

	A	B	C	D
1	1992	43	4	23
2	1993	47	5	24
3	1994	56	6	25
4	1995	57	11	25
5	1996	57	17	27
6	1997	55	26	29
7	1998	56	32	30
8	1999	58	37	31
9	2000	62	43	32
10	2001	66	48	33
11	2002	69	53	34
12	2003	73	57	36

1. Draw a scatter diagram to show the relationship between expenditure on recorded music and expenditure on Internet services. Describe the relationship.

2. Draw a scatter diagram to show the relationship between expenditure on Internet services and expenditure on movies in theaters. Describe the relationship.

3. Draw a scatter diagram to show the relationship between expenditure on recorded music and expenditure on movies in theaters. Describe the relationship.

4. Draw a time-series graph of expenditure on Internet services. Say in which year or years (a) expenditure was highest, (b) expenditure was lowest, (c) expenditure increased the most, and (d) expenditure increased the least. Also, say whether the data show a trend and describe its direction.

5. Draw a time-series graph of expenditure on recorded music. Say in which year or years (a) expenditure was highest, (b) expenditure was lowest, (c) expenditure increased the most, and (d) expenditure increased the least. Also, say whether the data show a trend and describe its direction.

6. Draw a graph to show the relationship between the two variables x and y:

x	0	1	2	3	4	5	6	7	8
y	0	1	4	9	16	25	36	49	64

   a. Is the relationship positive or negative?
   b. Calculate the slope of the relationship between x and y when x equals 2 and when x equals 4.
   c. How does the slope of the relationship change as the value of x increases?
   d. Think of some economic relationships that might be similar to this one.

7. Draw a graph to show the relationship between the two variables x and y:

x	0	1	2	3	4	5	6	7	8
y	60	49	39	30	22	15	9	4	0

   a. Is the relationship positive or negative?
   b. Calculate the slope of the relationship between x and y when x equals 2 and when x equals 4.
   c. How does the slope of the relationship change as the value of x increases?
   d. Think of some economic relationships that might be similar to this one.

Price (dollars per ride)	Balloon rides (number per day)		
	50°F	70°F	90°F
5	32	50	40
10	27	40	32
15	18	32	27
20	10	27	18

8. The table provides data on the price of a balloon ride, the temperature, and the number of rides a day. Draw graphs to show the relationship between:
   a. The price and the number of rides, holding the temperature constant.
   b. The number of rides and the temperature, holding the price constant.
   c. The temperature and the price, holding the number of rides constant.

The U.S. and Global Economies

CHAPTER 2

CHAPTER CHECKLIST

When you have completed your study of this chapter, you will be able to

1 Describe what, how, and for whom goods and services are produced in the United States.

2 Use the circular flow model to provide a picture of how households, firms, and governments interact.

3 Describe what, how, and for whom goods and services are produced in the global economy.

Scott Clark delivers mail around Virginia and earns more than he did at the job he lost when Viasystems, Inc. closed its Richmond plant. But Scott is working longer hours, and his benefits have gone. Yet Scott is better off than many of his friends. One of them, Raffael, now a guard in an armored car, has taken a big pay cut.

Half a world away, Chown Chong Chin and her husband have just got new jobs in a furniture factory in the Chinese province of Dong Guan. By leaving their rural life of farming and fishing, they have tripled their income.

Scott and Raffael are like many Americans who, in the face of ongoing changes in technology and international competition, are switching from manufacturing jobs to service jobs. And Chown Chong and her husband are like many Chinese who are switching from farming to factory jobs.

This chapter puts these lives and *your life* in a broad perspective by looking at the patterns and changes in *what, how,* and *for whom* goods and services are produced.

2.1 WHAT, HOW, AND FOR WHOM?

Walk around a shopping mall and pay close attention to the range of goods and services that are being offered for sale. Go inside some of the shops and look at the labels to see where various items are manufactured. The next time you travel on an interstate highway, look at the large trucks and pay attention to the names and products printed on their sides and the places in which the trucks are registered. Open the Yellow Pages and flip through a few sections. Notice the huge range of goods and services that businesses are offering.

You've just done a sampling of *what* goods and services are produced and consumed in the United States today.

■ What Do We Produce?

We divide the vast array of goods and services produced into four large groups:

- Consumption goods and services
- Capital goods
- Government goods and services
- Export goods and services

Consumption goods and services are items that are bought by individuals and used to provide personal enjoyment and contribute to a person's quality of life. They include items such as housing, SUVs, popcorn and fruit juice, movies and chocolate bars, microwave ovens and inline skates, and dental and dry cleaning services.

Capital goods are goods that are bought by businesses to increase their productive resources. They include items such as auto assembly lines, shopping malls, airplanes, and oil tankers.

Government goods and services are items that are bought by governments. Governments purchase missiles and weapons systems, travel services, Internet services, police protection, roads, and paper and paper clips.

Export goods and services are items that are produced in one country and sold in other countries. U.S. export goods and services include the airplanes produced by Boeing that Singapore Airlines buys, the computers produced by Dell that Europeans buy, and licenses sold by U.S. film companies to show U.S. movies in European movie theaters.

Figure 2.1(a) provides a snapshot of the division of total production in the United States in 2004 into these four groups. You can see that consumption goods and services have the largest share at 61 percent of the total. Investment goods account for 15 percent of total production. Goods and services bought by governments take another 15 percent of the total, and 9 percent is exported.

Figure 2.1(b) shows the production of the largest six services and four goods. Health services are the largest item and represent 13 percent of the value of total production. Real estate services comes next at 12 percent. The main component of this item is the services of rental and owner-occupied housing. Education is the next largest item, followed by retail and wholesale trades and transportation and storage.

The largest categories of goods—construction—accounts for less than 5 percent of the value of total production, and the next three—utilities, food, and chemicals— each accounts for 2 percent or less.

Consumption goods and services
Goods and services that are bought by individuals and used to provide personal enjoyment and contribute to a person's quality of life.

Capital goods
Goods that are bought by businesses to increase their productive resources.

Government goods and services
Goods and services that are bought by governments.

Export goods and services
Goods and services that are produced in one country and sold in other countries.

FIGURE 2.1

What We Produce

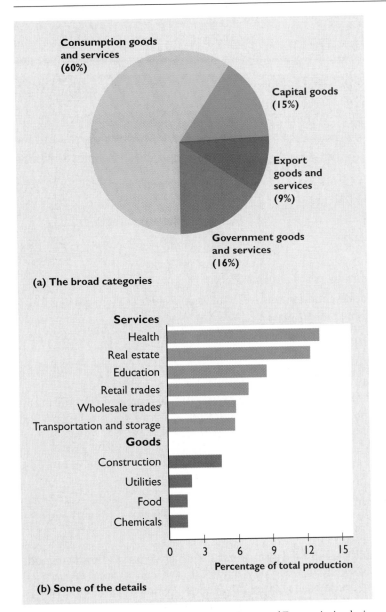

(a) The broad categories

Consumption goods and services (60%)

Capital goods (15%)

Export goods and services (9%)

Government goods and services (16%)

(b) Some of the details

SOURCE OF DATA: Bureau of Economic Analysis.

In 2005, consumption goods and services accounted for 60 percent of total production. Capital goods accounted for 15 percent, government goods and services accounted for 16 percent, and export goods and services accounted for 9 percent of total production.

Health and real estate services, education, retail and wholesale trades, and transportation and storage are the largest six services produced. Construction, utilities, food, and chemicals are the largest categories of goods produced. Services production greatly exceeds goods production and is growing faster.

Changes in What We Produce

Sixty-five years ago, one American in four worked on a farm. That number has shrunk to one in thirty-five. The number of people who produce goods—in mining, construction, and manufacturing—has also shrunk, from one in three to one in five. In contrast, the number of people who produce services has expanded from one in two to almost four in five. These changes in employment reflect changes in what we produce—services.

The story of Scott Clark and his friend Raffael (in the chapter opener) is just one example of the effects of this ongoing expansion of service jobs and shrinking of manufacturing jobs.

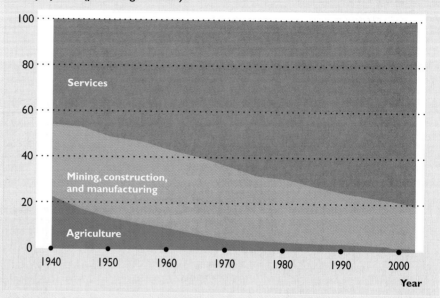

Employment (percentage of total)

SOURCE OF DATA: U.S. Census Bureau, *Statistical Abstract of the United States*, 1999 and 2004–2005.

This process is not new. You can see a similar trend over the past 60 years.

And that trend is likely to continue.

■ How Do We Produce?

Factors of production
The productive resources that are used to produce goods and services—land, labor, capital, and entrepreneurship.

Goods and services are produced by using productive resources. Economists call the productive resources **factors of production**. Factors of production are grouped into four categories:

- Land
- Labor
- Capital
- Entrepreneurship

Land

Land
The "gifts of nature," or *natural resources*, that we use to produce goods and services.

In economics, **land** includes all the "gifts of nature" that we use to produce goods and services. Land is what, in everyday language, we call *natural resources*. It includes land in the everyday sense, minerals, energy, water, air, and wild plants, animals, birds, and fish. Some of these resources are renewable, and some are non-renewable. The U.S. Geological Survey maintains a national inventory of the quantity and quality of natural resources and monitors changes to that inventory.

The United States covers almost 2 billion acres. About 45 percent of the land is forest, lakes, and national parks. In 2000, almost 50 percent of the land was used for agriculture and 5 percent was urban, but urban land use is growing and agricultural land use is shrinking.

Our land surface and water resources are renewable, and some of our mineral resources can be recycled. But many mineral resources can be used only once. They are nonrenewable resources. Of these, the United States has vast known reserves of coal but much smaller known reserves of oil and natural gas.

Labor

Labor is the work time and work effort that people devote to producing goods and services. It includes the physical and mental efforts of all the people who work on farms and construction sites and in factories, shops, and offices. The Census Bureau and Bureau of Labor Statistics measure the nation's labor force every month.

In the United States in May 2005, 148.9 million people had jobs or were available for work. Some worked full time, some worked part time, and some were unemployed but looking for an acceptable vacant job. The total amount of time worked during 2005 was about 240 billion hours.

The quantity of labor increases as the adult population increases. The quantity of labor also increases if a larger percentage of the population takes jobs. During the past 50 years, a larger proportion of women have taken paid work and this trend has increased the quantity of labor.

The quality of labor depends on how skilled people are. Economists use a special name for human skill: human capital. **Human capital** is the knowledge and skill that people obtain from education, on-the-job training, and work experience.

You are building your own human capital right now as you work on your economics course and other subjects. And your human capital will continue to grow when you get a full-time job and become better at it. Human capital improves the *quality* of labor.

Figure 2.2 shows that today 85 percent of the U.S. population has completed high school and 27 percent has a college or university degree.

Labor
The work time and work effort that people devote to producing goods and services.

Human capital
The knowledge and skill that people obtain from education, on-the-job training, and work experience.

■ **FIGURE 2.2**
Measures of Human Capital

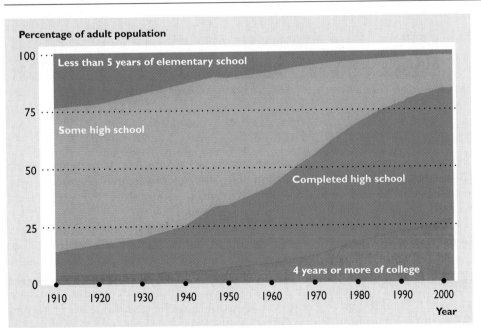

Percentage of adult population

Less than 5 years of elementary school

Some high school

Completed high school

4 years or more of college

Year

Human capital improves the quality of labor. And the level of education that people attain is a major influence on an economy's human capital.

In 2004, 27 percent of the U.S. population had 4 years or more of college education, up from 3 percent in 1910. An additional 58 percent had completed high school, up from 11 percent in 1910.

SOURCE OF DATA: U.S. Census Bureau, *Statistical Abstract of the United States*, 1999 and 2004–2005.

Changes in How We Produce in the New Economy

The new economy consists of the jobs and businesses that produce and use computers and equipment powered by computer chips. This new economy is highly visible in your daily life.

The pairs of images here remind you of two examples. In each pair, a new technology enables capital to replace labor.

The top pair of pictures illustrate the replacement of bank tellers (labor) with ATMs (capital). Although the ATM was invented almost 40 years ago, when it made its first appearance, it was located only inside banks and was not able to update customers' accounts. It is only in the last decade that ATMs have spread to corner stores and enable us to get cash and check our bank balance from almost anywhere in the world.

The bottom pair of pictures illustrate a more recent replacement of labor with capital. In the past few years, machines that enable passengers to do their own flight check-in and issue their own boarding pass have been springing up in our airports. For international flights, some of these machines now even check passport details.

The number of bank teller and airport check-in clerk jobs is shrinking. But these new technologies are creating a whole range of new jobs for people who make, program, install, and repair these machines.

Capital

Capital
Tools, instruments, machines, buildings, and other items that have been produced in the past and that businesses now use to produce goods and services.

In everyday language, we talk about money, stocks, and bonds as being capital. These items are *financial capital,* and they are not productive resources. They enable people to provide businesses with financial resources, but they are *not* used to produce goods and services. They are not capital.

Capital consists of the tools, instruments, machines, buildings, and other items that have been produced in the past and that businesses now use to produce goods and services. Capital includes hammers and screwdrivers, computers, auto assembly lines, office towers and warehouses, dams and power plants, airports and airplanes, shirt factories, and cookie shops. The Bureau of Economic Analysis in the U.S. Department of Commerce keeps track of the total value of capital and how it grows over time. In the United States today, it is around $35 trillion. The global value of capital is about $145 trillion.

Entrepreneurship

Entrepreneurship is the human resource that organizes labor, land, and capital. Entrepreneurs come up with new ideas about what and how to produce, make business decisions, and bear the risks that arise from these decisions.

The quantity of entrepreneurship is hard to describe or measure. At some periods, there appears to be a great deal of imaginative entrepreneurship around. People such as Sam Walton, who created Wal-Mart, one of the world's largest retailers; Bill Gates, who founded the Microsoft empire; and Michael Dell, who established Dell Computers, are examples of extraordinary entrepreneurial talent. But these highly visible entrepreneurs are just the tip of an iceberg that consists of hundreds of thousands of people who run businesses, large and small.

Entrepreneurship
The human resource that organizes labor, land, and capital.

■ For Whom Do We Produce?

Who gets the goods and services that are produced depends on the incomes that people earn and the goods and services that they choose to buy. A large income enables a person to buy large quantities of goods and services. A small income leaves a person with few options and small quantities of goods and services.

People earn their incomes by selling the services of the factors of production they own. **Rent** is paid for the use of land, **wages** are paid for the services of labor, **interest** is paid for the use of capital, and entrepreneurs receive a **profit** (or incur a **loss**) for running their businesses. What are the shares of these four factor incomes in the United States? Which factor receives the largest share?

Rent
Income paid for the use of land.

Wages
Income paid for the services of labor.

Interest
Income paid for the use of capital.

Profit (or loss)
Income earned by an entrepreneur for running a business.

FIGURE 2.3
For Whom?

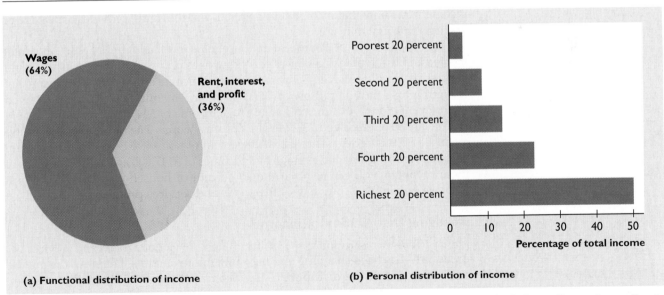

(a) Functional distribution of income   **(b) Personal distribution of income**

SOURCES OF DATA: Bureau of Economic Analysis and U.S. Census Bureau, *Income, Poverty, and Health Insurance in the United States: 2004,* Current Population Reports P60-229, 2005.

In 2005, wages (the income from labor) were 64 percent of total income. Rent, interest, and profit (the income from land, capital, and entrepreneurship) totaled the remaining 36 percent.

In 2004, the 20 percent of the population with the highest incomes received 50 percent of total income. The 20 percent with the lowest incomes received only 3.4 percent of total income.

Functional distribution of income
The distribution of income among the factors of production.

Functional Distribution of Income

The **functional distribution of income** is the distribution of income among the factors of production. Figure 2.3(a) shows that wages, the income from labor, were 64 percent of total income in 2005. The national accounts don't split the remaining income into rent, interest, and profit. Instead, they report the profits of corporations and of small businesses. These incomes are a mixture of rent, interest, and profit and were 36 percent of total income in 2005. These percentages remain remarkably constant over time.

The data in Figure 2.3(a) tell us how income is distributed among the factors of production. But the data don't tell us how income is distributed among individuals.

Personal Distribution of Income

You know of lots of people who earn very large incomes. Tiger Woods wins several million dollars a year in prize money and earns substantially more than this amount in endorsements. The average salary of major league baseball players in 2004 was almost $3 million, and some stars, such as Alex Rodriguez, Carlos Delgado, Derek Jeter, Barry Bonds, Pedro Martinez, Mo Vaughn, Shawn Green, and Mike Piazza earned more than $16 million. Manny Ramirez, the top earner in 2004, picked up a cool $22.5 million.

You know of even more people who earn very small incomes. Servers at McDonald's average around $6.50 an hour; checkout clerks, gas station attendants, and textile and leather workers earn less than $10 an hour.

Figure 2.3(b) shows the **personal distribution of income**—the distribution of income among households. Households (individuals or people living together) are divided into five groups, each of which represents 20 percent of all households. If incomes were equal, each 20 percent group would earn 20 percent of total income. You know that incomes are unequal, and the figure provides a measure of just how unequal they are.

In 2004, the poorest 20 percent of households received only 3.4 percent of total income and the average income of this group was only $10,000 a year. The second poorest 20 percent received 8.7 percent of total income and the average income of this group was still pretty low at $26,000 a year. The middle 20 percent received 14.7 percent of total income and an average income of $44,000 a year. The second richest 20 percent received 23.2 percent of total income. The incomes in this group averaged $70,000 a year. The richest 20 percent of households received 50 percent of total income and on the average had incomes of $147,000 a year. On the basis of these numbers, you can see that the 20 percent of households with the highest incomes can afford to buy half of the goods and services produced.

Changing Distribution of Income

The distribution of income in the United States—for whom goods and services get produced—has been changing and becoming more unequal. People in the middle and lower part of the distribution, like Scott and Raffael in the chapter opener, have lost out on the average. And people at the top end of the distribution have gained. The rich have become richer. But it isn't the case, on the whole, that the poor have become poorer. They just haven't become richer as fast as the rich have. There is also a lot of movement across the income distribution as some people fall on hard times and others enjoy successes.

Personal distribution of income
The distribution of income among households.

CHECKPOINT 2.1

1   **Describe what, how, and for whom goods and services are produced in the United States.**

Practice Problems 2.1

1. Name the four broad categories of goods and services that we use in economics, provide an example of each (different from those in the chapter), and say what percentage of total production each accounted for in 2005.

2. Name the four factors of production and the incomes they earn.

3. Distinguish between the functional distribution of income and the personal distribution of income.

4. In the United States, which factor of production earned the largest share of income in 2005 and what percentage did it earn?

Exercises 2.1

1. What is the distinction between consumption goods and services and investment goods? Which one of them brings an increase in productive resources?

2. Describe how the quality of the U.S. labor force, as measured by the level of education, changed during the last few decades.

3. If everyone in the United States were to consume an equal quantity of goods and services, what percentage of total income would the poorest 20 percent of households have to receive from higher-income groups? What percentage would the second poorest 20 percent have to receive?

4. Compare the percentage of total U.S. income that labor earns with the percentage earned by all the other factors of production combined.

Solutions to Practice Problems 2.1

1. The four categories are consumption goods and services, investment goods, government goods and services, and export goods and services. An example of a consumption good is a shirt and a consumption service is a haircut, of an investment good is an oil rig, of a government service is police protection, and of an export good is a computer chip sold to Ireland. Of total production, consumption goods and services were 60 percent; capital goods, 15 percent; government goods and services, 16 percent; and export goods and services, 9 percent.

2. The factors of production are land, labor, capital, and entrepreneurship. Land earns rent; labor earns wages; capital earns interest; and entrepreneurship earns profit or incurs a loss.

3. The functional distribution of income shows the percentage of total income received by each factor of production. The personal distribution of income shows the percentage of total income received by households.

4. Labor is the factor of production that earns the largest share of income in the United States. In 2005, labor earned 64 percent of total income.

2.2 THE CIRCULAR FLOWS

Circular flow model
A model of the economy that shows the circular flow of expenditures and incomes that result from decision makers' choices and the way those choices interact to determine what, how, and for whom goods and services are produced.

Households
Individuals or groups of people living together.

Firms
The institutions that organize the production of goods and services.

Market
Any arrangement that brings buyers and sellers together and enables them to get information and do business with each other.

Goods markets
Markets in which goods and services are bought and sold.

Factor markets
Markets in which factors of production are bought and sold.

We can organize the data you've just studied using the **circular flow model**—a model of the economy that shows the circular flow of expenditures and incomes that result from decision makers' choices and the way those choices interact to determine what, how, and for whom goods and services are produced. Figure 2.4 shows the circular flow model.

■ Households and Firms

Households are individuals or groups of people living together. The 112 million households in the United States own the factors of production—land, labor, capital, and entrepreneurship—and choose the quantities of these resources to provide to firms. Households also choose the quantities of goods and services to buy.

Firms are the institutions that organize the production of goods and services. The 20 million firms in the United States choose the quantities of the factors of production to hire and the quantities of goods and services to produce.

■ Markets

Households choose the quantities of the factors of production to provide to firms, and firms choose the quantities of the services of the factors of production to hire. Firms choose the quantities of goods and services to produce, and households choose the quantities of goods and services to buy. How are these choices coordinated and made compatible? The answer is: by markets.

A **market** is any arrangement that brings buyers and sellers together and enables them to get information and do business with each other. An example is the market in which oil is bought and sold—the world oil market. The world oil market is not a place. It is the network of oil producers, oil users, wholesalers, and brokers who buy and sell oil. In the world oil market, decision makers do not meet physically. They make deals by telephone, fax, and the Internet.

Figure 2.4 identifies two types of markets: goods markets and factor markets. **Goods markets** are markets in which goods and services are bought and sold. **Factor markets** are markets in which factors of production are bought and sold.

■ Real Flows and Money Flows

When households choose the quantities of land, labor, capital, and entrepreneurship to offer in factor markets, they respond to the incomes they receive—rent for land, wages for labor, interest for capital, and profit for entrepreneurship. When firms choose the quantities of factors to hire, they respond to the rent, wages, interest, and profits they must pay to households.

Similarly, when firms choose the quantities of goods and services to produce and offer for sale in goods markets, they respond to the amounts that they receive from the expenditures that households make. And when households choose the quantities of goods and services to buy, they respond to the amounts they must pay to firms.

Figure 2.4 shows the flows that result from these choices made by households and firms. The flows shown in orange are *real flows:* the flows of the factors of production that go from households through factor markets to firms and of the goods and services that go from firms through goods markets to households. The flows in the opposite direction are *money flows:* the flows of payments made in exchange for factors of production (shown in blue) and of expenditures on goods and services (shown in red).

Lying behind these real flows and money flows are millions of individual choices about what to consume, what to produce, and how to produce. These choices result in buying plans by households and selling plans by firms in goods markets. And the choices result in selling plans by households and buying plans by firms in factor markets. When these buying plans and selling plans are carried out, they determine the prices that people pay and the incomes they earn and so determine for whom goods and services are produced. You'll learn in Chapter 4 how markets coordinate the buying plans and selling plans of households and firms and make them compatible.

Firms produce most of the goods and services that we consume. But governments provide some of the services that we enjoy. And governments play a big role in modifying for whom goods and services are produced by changing the personal distribution of income. So we're now going to look at the role of governments in the U.S. economy and add them to the circular flow model.

◼ FIGURE 2.4
The Circular Flow Model

Rent, wages, interest, and profit

HOUSEHOLDS

Expenditures on goods and services

Land, labor, capital, and entrepreneurship supplied

Goods and services bought

FACTOR MARKETS

GOODS MARKETS

Land, labor, capital, and entrepreneurship hired

Goods and services supplied

FIRMS

Rent, wages, interest, and profit

Expenditures on goods and services

The orange flows are the factors of production that go from households through factor markets to firms and the goods and services that go from firms through goods markets to households. These flows are real flows.

The blue flow is the incomes earned by the factors of production, and the red flow is the expenditures on goods and services. These flows are money flows.

The choices that generate these real and money flows determine *what*, *how*, and *for whom* goods and services are produced.

■ Governments

More than 86,000 organizations operate as governments in the United States. Some are tiny like the Yuma, Arizona, school district and some are enormous like the U.S. federal government. We divide governments into two levels:

- Federal government
- State and local government

Federal Government

The federal government's major expenditures are to provide

1. Goods and services
2. Social security and welfare payments
3. Transfers to state and local governments

The goods and services provided by the federal government include the legal system, which defines property rights and enforces contracts, and national defense. Social security and welfare benefits, which include income for retired people and programs such as Medicare and Medicaid, are transfers from the federal government to households. Transfers to state and local governments are payments designed to provide more equality across the states and regions.

The federal government finances its expenditures by collecting a variety of taxes. The main taxes paid to the federal government are

1. Personal income taxes
2. Corporate (business) income taxes
3. Social security taxes

In 2005, the federal government spent $2.5 trillion—about 20 percent of the total value of all the goods and services produced in the United States in that year. The taxes they raised was less than this amount—the government had a deficit.

State and Local Government

The state and local governments' major expenditures are to provide

1. Goods and services
2. Welfare benefits

The goods and services provided by state and local governments include the state courts and law enforcement authorities, schools, roads, garbage collection and disposal, water supplies, and sewage management. Welfare benefits provided by state governments include unemployment benefits and other aid to low-income families.

State and local governments finance these expenditures by collecting taxes and receiving transfers from the federal government. The main taxes paid to state and local governments are

1. Sales taxes
2. Property taxes
3. State income taxes

In 2005, state and local governments spent $1.6 trillion—about 14 percent of the total value of all the goods and services produced in the United States in that year.

■ Governments in the Circular Flow

Figure 2.5 adds governments to the circular flow model. As you study this figure, first notice that the outer circle is the same as in Figure 2.4. In addition to these flows, governments buy goods and services from firms. The red arrows that run from governments through the goods markets to firms show this expenditure.

Households and firms pay taxes to governments. The green arrows running directly from households and firms to governments show these flows. Also, governments make money payments to households and firms. The green arrows running directly from governments to households and firms show these flows. Taxes and transfers are direct transactions with governments and do not go through the goods markets and factor markets.

Not part of the circular flow and not visible in Figure 2.5, governments provide the legal framework within which all transactions occur. For example, governments operate the courts and legal system that enable contracts to be written and enforced.

■ **FIGURE 2.5**
Governments in the Circular Flow

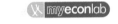

The green flows from households and firms to governments are taxes, and the green flows from governments to households and firms are money transfers.

The red flow from governments through goods markets to firms is the expenditures on goods and services by governments.

HOUSEHOLDS

Expenditures on goods and services

Rent, wages, interest, and profit

Transfers   Taxes

Expenditures on goods and services

FACTOR MARKETS

GOVERNMENTS

GOODS MARKETS

Transfers   Taxes

Expenditures on goods and services

Rent, wages, interest, and profit

Expenditures on goods and services

FIRMS

■ Federal Government Expenditures and Revenue

What are the main items of expenditures by the federal government on goods and services and transfers? And what are its main sources of tax revenue? Figure 2.6 answers these questions.

Three items of expenditure are similar in magnitude—and large. They are Social Security benefits, Medicare and Medicaid, and national defense and homeland security. The combined total of these items exceeds 60 percent of the government's expenditures. Other transfers to persons, which includes unemployment benefits, are also large. The "Others" category covers a wide range of items, which includes transfers to states, NASA's space program, and the National Science Foundation's funding of research in the universities.

The interest payment on the national debt is another significant item. The **national debt** is the total amount that the federal government has borrowed to make expenditures that exceed tax revenue—to run a government budget deficit. The national debt is a bit like a large credit card balance. And paying the interest on the national debt is like paying the minimum required monthly payment.

Most of the tax revenue of the federal government comes from personal income taxes and Social Security taxes. Corporate income taxes and other taxes are a small part of the federal government's revenue.

National debt

The total amount that the federal government has borrowed to make expenditures that exceed tax revenue—to run a government budget deficit.

■ FIGURE 2.6
Federal Government Expenditures and Revenue

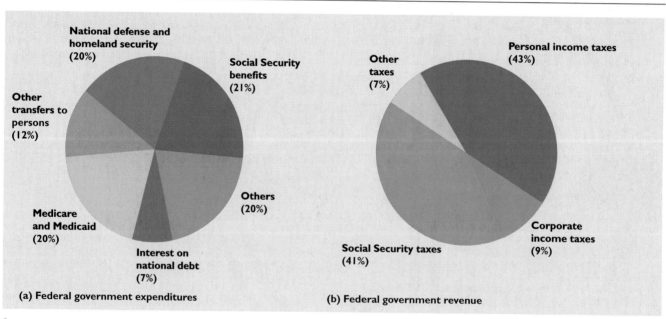

SOURCE OF DATA: Budget of the United States Government, Historical Tables, Table 2.1 and Table 3.1.

Social Security benefits, Medicare and Medicaid, and national defense and homeland security absorb more than 60 percent of the federal government's expenditures. Interest on the national debt is also a significant item.

Most of the federal government's revenue comes from personal income taxes and Social Security taxes. Corporate income taxes and other taxes are a small part of total revenue.

■ State and Local Government Expenditures and Revenue

What are the main items of expenditures by the state and local governments on goods and services and transfers? And what are the main sources of state and local government revenue? Figure 2.7 answers these questions.

You can see that education is by far the largest part of the expenditures of state and local governments. This item covers the cost of public schools, colleges, and universities. It absorbs 40 percent of total expenditures—approximately $560 billion, or $1,900 per person.

Welfare benefits are the second largest item and they take 20 percent of total expenditures. Highways are the next largest item, and they account for 8 percent of total expenditures. The remaining 32 percent is spent on other local public goods and services such as police services, garbage collection and disposal, sewage management, and water supplies.

Sales taxes and transfers from the federal government bring in similar amounts—about 25 percent and 23 percent of total revenue, respectively. Property taxes account for 21 percent of total revenue. Individual income taxes account for 15 percent, and corporate income taxes account for 3 percent. The remaining 13 percent comes from other taxes such as those on gasoline, cigarettes, and beer and wine.

■ **FIGURE 2.7**
State and Local Government Expenditures and Revenue

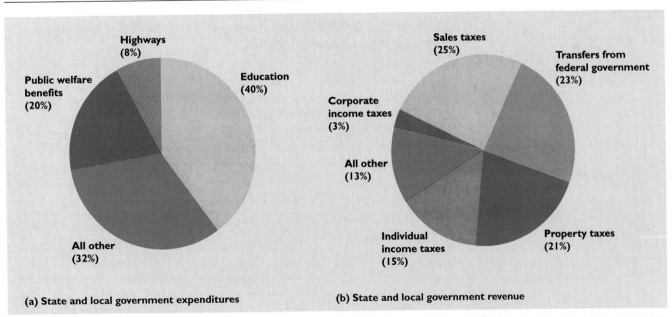

(a) State and local government expenditures   **(b) State and local government revenue**

SOURCES OF DATA: Bureau of Economic Analysis and *Statistical Abstract of the United States,* 2004–2005.

Education, public welfare benefits, and highways are the largest slices of state and local government expenditures.

Most of the state and local government revenue comes from sales taxes, property taxes, and transfers from the federal government.

EYE ON THE PAST

Growing Government

One hundred years ago, the federal government spent 2 cents out of each dollar earned. Today, it spends 20 cents. Government grew during the two world wars and during the 1960s and 1970s as social programs expanded.

Only during the 1980s and 1990s did big government begin to shrink in a process begun by Ronald Reagan and continued by Bill Clinton. But 9/11 saw the start of a new era of growing government.

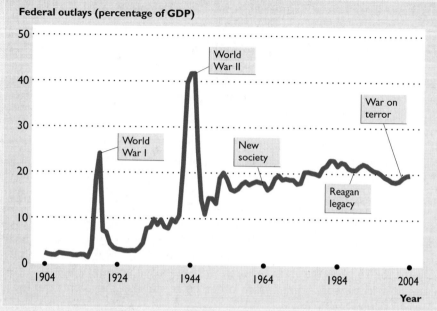

Federal outlays (percentage of GDP)

World War II

War on terror

World War I

New society

Reagan legacy

1904   1924   1944   1964   1984   2004

Year

SOURCE OF DATA: Budget of the United States Government, Historical Tables, Table 1.1.

CHECKPOINT 2.2

2 **Use the circular flow model to provide a picture of how households, firms, and governments interact.**

Practice Problem 2.2

1. What are the real flows and money flows that run between households, firms, and governments in the circular flow model?

Exercises 2.2

1. What are the choices made by households and firms that determine what, how, and for whom goods and services are produced? Where, in the circular flow model, do those choices appear?

2. How do the actions of governments modify what, how, and for whom goods and services are produced? Where, in the circular flow model, do those choices appear?

Solution to Practice Problem 2.2

1. The real flows are the services of factors of production that go from households to firms through factor markets and the goods and services that go from firms to households and from firms to governments through goods markets. The money flows are factor incomes, household and government expenditures on goods and services, taxes, and transfers.

2.3 THE GLOBAL ECONOMY

We're now going to look at *what, how,* and *for whom* goods and services get produced in the global economy. We'll begin with a brief overview of the people and countries that form the global economy.

■ The People

Visit the Web site of the U.S. Census Bureau and go to the population clocks to find out how many people there are today in both the United States and the entire world.

On the day these words were written, March 13, 2005, the U.S. clock recorded a population of 295,649,027. The world clock recorded a global population of 6,424,033,498. The U.S. clock ticks along showing a population increase of one person every 14 seconds. The world clock spins faster, adding 34 people in the same 14 seconds.

■ The Countries

The world's 6.42 billion (and rising) population lives in 175 countries, which the International Monetary Fund classifies into two broad groups of economies:

- Advanced economies
- Emerging market and developing economies

Advanced Economies

Advanced economies are the richest 29 countries (or areas). The United States, Japan, Italy, Germany, France, the United Kingdom, and Canada belong to this group. So do four new industrial Asian economies: Hong Kong, South Korea, Singapore, and Taiwan. The other advanced economies include Australia, New Zealand, and most of the rest of Western Europe. Almost 1 billion people (15 percent of the world's population) live in the advanced economies.

Emerging Market and Developing Economies

Emerging market economies are the 28 countries in Central and Eastern Europe and Asia that were, until the early 1990s, part of the Soviet Union or one of its satellites. Russia is the largest of these economies. Others include the Czech Republic, Hungary, Poland, Ukraine, and Mongolia.

Almost 500 million people live in these countries—only about half of the number in the advanced economies. But these countries are important because they are emerging (hence the name) from a system of state-owned production, central economic planning, and heavily regulated markets to a system of free enterprise and unregulated markets.

Developing economies are the 118 countries in Africa, Asia, the Middle East, Europe, and Central and South America that have not yet achieved high average incomes for their people. Average incomes in these economies vary a great deal, but in all cases, these average incomes are much lower than those in the advanced economies, and in some cases, they are extremely low. More than 5 billion people—almost four out of every five people—live in developing economies.

■ *What* in the Global Economy?

First, let's look at the big picture. Imagine that each year the global economy produces an enormous pie. In 2005, the pie was worth about $60 trillion! To give this number some meaning, if the pie were shared equally among the world's 6.5 billion people, each of us would get a slice worth a bit more than $9,000.

Where Is the Global Pie Baked?

Figure 2.8 shows us where in the world the pie is baked. The advanced economies produce 44 percent—18 percent in the United States and 26 percent in the other advanced economies. Another 16 percent comes from the emerging market economies. These economies, which produce 60 percent of the world's goods and services (by value) are home to only 23 percent of the world's population.

Most of the rest of the global pie comes from Asia. China produces 12 percent of the total and the rest of the developing Asian economies produce 13 percent. The developing countries of Africa and the Middle East produce 8 percent, and the Western Hemisphere—Mexico and South America—produces the rest.

The sizes of the slices in the global production pie are gradually changing—the U.S. share is shrinking and China's share is expanding.

Unlike the slices of an apple pie, those of the global pie have different fillings. Some slices have more oil and other energy-generating goods, some have more food and other agricultural products, some have more clothing, some have more housing services, some have more autos, and so on.

■ FIGURE 2.8
What in the World Economy in 2005

If we show the value of production in the world economy as a pie, the United States produces a slice that is 18 percent of the total. The other advanced economies produce 26 percent of the total. The next-biggest slice comes from the emerging market economies, with 16 percent of the total. This 60 percent of the world's production comes from 23 percent of the world's population.

Most of the rest of the global pie comes from Asia. China produces a 12 percent slice, and the rest of the developing Asian economies produce another 13 percent. The developing countries of Africa, the Middle East, and the Western Hemisphere produce the rest.

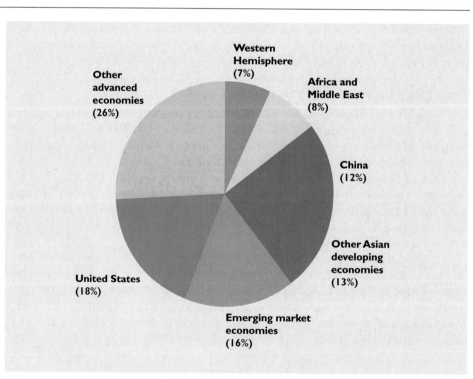

SOURCE OF DATA: International Monetary Fund, *World Economic Outlook Database*.

Let's take a quick look at some of these differences by looking at three broad groups:

- Energy
- Food
- Other goods and services

Energy

Land is the key resource for producing energy, and the location of oil, natural gas, and coal determines the sources of the world's energy. These resources are distributed unevenly across the globe.

No one knows exactly how much oil, natural gas, and coal is available. But we know what are called the "proven reserves." These are the quantities that have been detected and that can be extracted and used with existing technologies at current costs. Beyond the proven reserves are other reserves that are known but will need a new and more costly technology to extract them. And beyond these reserves are those that have yet to be discovered. China is the largest underexplored region where it is suspected large additional reserves will be found.

You can see in Figure 2.9 why the United States takes a strong interest in the stability of the Middle East. Two thirds of the world's oil reserves and two fifths of the natural gas reserves are located in the Middle East, and most of them in just three countries: Saudi Arabia, Iraq, and Iran. North America, in contrast, has only 5 percent of the world's oil reserves and 4 percent of the natural gas reserves. But the world's known coal reserves are distributed more in North America's favor, with a quarter of them in the United States. China also has large quantities of coal.

FIGURE 2.9

Energy Sources in the World Economy

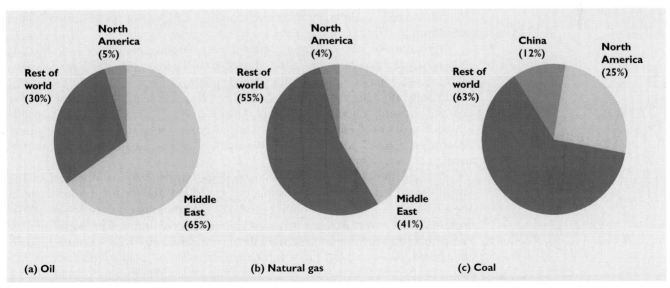

(a) Oil

(b) Natural gas

(c) Coal

SOURCE OF DATA: Energy Information Administration.

Most of the world's proven oil reserves are in the Middle East (Saudi Arabia, Iraq, and Iran). North America has 5 percent of these reserves. The Middle East also has the largest share of natural gas reserves. North America has only 4 percent of these reserves. Coal is abundant in North America and in China.

How Long Will It Last? We don't know how long our oil, natural gas, and coal will last. But we can calculate the number of years for which current proven reserves will last if they are used at the current rate. This number underestimates how long reserves will last because we will discover new sources and cheaper ways of extracting hard-to-reach reserves. And it overestimates how long reserves will last because the rate at which we're using these resources is increasing. But it provides a handy benchmark.

The world's oil reserves will last for about 40 years at the current rate of production. But this number has been *increasing*! We have been discovering more reserves than we've been using. The world's natural gas will last for about 60 years at the current rate of use, and coal will last for 200 years. So we're not going to run out of energy resources anytime soon. But we are going to run out one day. And oil will be the first to run dry.

What About the Wind and the Sun? Why don't we make more use of the wind and the sun and less of oil, gas, and coal? Part of the answer is that we are doing just that. Worldwide, the use of wind and solar power to generate electricity is increasing at twice the rate of other methods. But even after two decades of faster growth, the wind and sun provide only a tiny 2 percent of the world's electricity, way behind oil, natural gas, and coal at 64 percent and nuclear at 17 percent. Hydroelectric generation makes up the rest.

Another part of the answer is that everything has a cost—an opportunity cost—and with the technologies currently available, the cost of generating electricity is lower with coal, oil, or natural gas than with windmills or solar cells.

Food

You saw earlier in this chapter that agriculture is a small part of the U.S. economy. It is also a small part of the production of the other advanced economies. Total agricultural production in the United States is 1.4 percent of total production. The percentage is a bit higher in the European Union and a bit lower in Japan and the other advanced Asian economies and averages 1.8 percent for all 29 advanced economies.

Agriculture is a much larger part of the developing economies. In India, it is 23 percent of total production, and in Brazil, it is 10 percent. On the average across all the developing economies, agriculture is about 14 percent of total production.

Despite these large differences in the importance of agriculture, the advanced economies produce about one third of the world's food. How come? Because *total* production is much larger in the advanced economies than in the developing economies, a small percentage of a big number can be greater than a large percentage of a small number!

Why do the advanced economies produce such a large proportion of the world's food? Part of the answer is that large, efficient, and well-equipped farms in the advanced economies are highly productive. But another part of the answer is that the governments of many advanced economies pay farmers to enable them to compete against lower-cost food from developing economies. For example, in both the United States and the European Union, farmers are paid to grow sugar. But sugar can be grown in the Caribbean, Brazil, and Australia at a small fraction of the cost of producing it in the United States and Europe. This practice of paying farmers in rich countries deprives farmers in poor countries of global markets and is an example of the conflict between the pursuit of self-interest and the social interest.

Other Goods and Services

If you were to visit a shopping mall in Canada, England, Australia, Japan, or any of the other advanced economies, you would wonder whether you had left the United States. Of course, you would see McDonald's golden arches. You would see them in any of the 119 countries in which one or more of McDonald's 30,000 restaurants are located. But you'd also see Starbucks, Burger King, Pizza Hut, Domino's Pizza, KFC, Kmart, Wal-Mart, Target, the United Colors of Benetton, Gap, Tommy Hilfiger, Tie Rack, the upscale Louis Vuitton and Burberry's, and a host of other familiar names.

The similarities among the advanced economies goes beyond the view from the shopping mall. The structure of *what* is produced is similar in these economies. You've just seen that in all of them, agriculture is small. Manufacturing is also small and represents between a quarter and a third of the economy; and services are the major and fastest-growing part of the economy.

What is produced in the developing economies contrasts sharply with that of the advanced economies. Here, as you've just seen, agriculture remains a big part of the picture. But it is shrinking relative to the other parts of the economy. Manufacturing is the big story. Developing economies have relatively large and growing industries producing items such as textiles, footwear, sporting equipment, toys, electronic goods, furniture, steel, and even automobiles. The service industries in these economies are also important but not as large a proportion of the total economy as they are in the advanced economies.

The emerging market economies stand between the advanced and developing economies but most of them are closer to the advanced economies.

McDonald's in Shanghai.

■ *How* in the Global Economy?

Goods and services are produced by entrepreneurs using land, labor, and capital. Each country or region has its own blend of these resources. But there are some interesting common patterns and crucial differences between the advanced and developing economies that we'll now examine.

Starbucks in Paris.

Human Capital Differences

The quality of labor depends on human capital. And differences in human capital in advanced and developing economies are enormous. The proportion of the population with a college or university degree is tiny in developing economies. Even the proportion of the population that has completed high school is small. And in the poorest of the developing economies, many children even miss out on basic primary education. They just don't go to school at all.

On-the-job training and experience are also much more extensive in the advanced economies than in the developing economies.

A component of human capital that we tend to take for granted is our physical ability and state of health. Again, there is a huge contrast between the advanced and developing economies.

Physical Capital Differences

The major feature of an advanced economy that differentiates it from a developing economy is the amount of capital available for producing goods and services. The differences begin with the basic transportation system. In the advanced

Beijing has a highway system to match that of any advanced country. But away from the major cities, many of China's roads are unpaved and driving on them is slow and sometimes hazardous.

economies, a well-developed highway system connects all the major cities and points of production. You can see this difference most vividly by opening a road atlas of North America and contrasting the U.S. interstate highway system with the sparse highways of Mexico. You would see a similar contrast if you flipped through a road atlas of Western Europe and Africa.

But it isn't the case that the developing economies have no highways. In fact, some of them have the newest and the best. But the new and best are usually inside and around the major cities. The smaller centers and rural areas of developing economies often have some of the worst roads in the world.

The contrast in vehicles is perhaps even greater than that in highways. In an advanced economy, you're unlikely to run across a horse-drawn wagon. But in a developing economy, animal power can still be found, and trucks are often old and unreliable.

The contrasts in the transportation system are matched by those on farms and in factories. In general, the more advanced the economy, the greater are the amount and sophistication of the capital equipment used in production. But again, the contrast is not all black and white. Some factories in India, China, and other parts of Asia use the very latest technologies. Furniture manufacture is an example. To make furniture of a quality that Americans are willing to buy, firms in Asia use machines like those in the furniture factories of South Carolina.

Again, it is the extensiveness of the use of modern capital-intensive technologies that distinguishes a developing economy from an advanced economy. All the factories in the advanced economies are capital intensive. But only some in the developing economies are.

The differences in human and physical capital between advanced and developing economies have a big effect on who gets the goods and services.

■ *For Whom* in the Global Economy?

Who gets the world's goods and services depends on the incomes that people earn. So how are incomes distributed across the world?

Personal Distribution of Income

You saw earlier (on pp. 39–40) that in the United States, the lowest-paid 20 percent of the population receives 3.4 percent of total income and the highest-paid 20 percent receives 50 percent of total income. The personal distribution of income in the world economy is much more unequal. According to World Bank data, the lowest-paid 20 percent of the world's population receives 2 percent of world income, and the highest-paid 20 percent receives about 70 percent of world income.

International Distribution

Much of the greater inequality at the global level arises from differences in average incomes among countries. Figure 2.10 shows some of these differences. It shows the dollar value of what people can afford each day on the average. You can see that in the United States, that number is $108 a day—an average person in the United States can buy goods and services that cost $108. This amount is around five times the world average. Canada has an average income close to 90 percent of that in the United States. Japan, Germany, France, Italy, the United Kingdom, and the other advanced economies have average incomes around two thirds that of the United States. Income levels fall off quickly as we move farther down the graph, with Africa achieving average incomes of only $6 a day.

◼ FIGURE 2.10

For Whom in the Global Economy in 2005

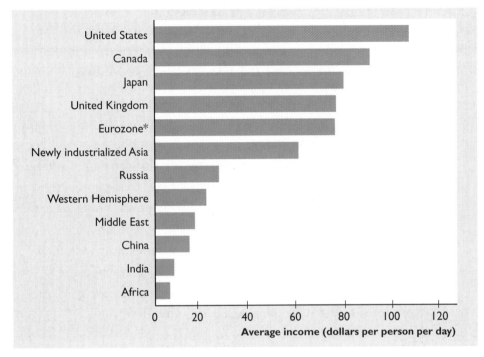

In 2005, the average income per day in the United States was $108. It was $90 in Canada and $80 in Japan. In advanced European economies such as the United Kingdom, it was about $75. The number falls off rapidly to about $27 in Russia, $14 in China, $8 in India, and $6 in Africa.

*The Eurozone is the countries of Europe that use the euro.

SOURCE OF DATA: International Monetary Fund, World Economic Outlook Database.

Changes in *For Whom* in the Global Economy

As people have lost well-paid manufacturing jobs and found lower-paid service jobs, inequality has increased in the United States and in most other advanced economies. In the developing economies, inequality is also increasing, but for a different reason. There, people who are willing to move, like Chown Chong and her husband, are enjoying rapidly rising incomes. But those who remain behind in the rural areas find their incomes either stagnating or falling.

A Happy Paradox and a Huge Challenge

Despite the increase in inequality inside most countries, inequality across the entire world has decreased during the past 20 years. And most important, according to Xavier Sala-i-Martin, an economics professor at Columbia University, extreme poverty has declined. Professor Sala-i-Martin estimates that between 1976 and 1998, the number of people who earn $1 a day or less fell by 235 million and the number who earn $2 a day or less fell by 450 million. This happy situation arises because in China and India, the two largest nations, incomes have increased rapidly and lifted millions from extreme poverty.

But between 1970 and 1998, the number of people in Africa who earn $1 a day or less rose by 175 million, and the number who earn $2 a day or less rose by 227 million. In 1960, 11 percent of the world's poor lived in Africa. In 1998, 66 percent did. Lifting Africa from poverty is one of today's biggest challenges.

REALITY CHECK

The U.S. and Global Economies in YOUR Life

You've encountered a lot of facts and trends about what, how, and for whom goods and services are produced in the U.S. economy and the global economy. How can you use this information? In two ways:

1. As you think about your future career, you are now better informed about some of the key trends. You know that a job in a manufacturing business is likely to be tough. A job in a service business is more likely to lead to success. Health care, education, communication, and entertainment are all likely to expand in the future and be sources of increasing employment and rising wages.

2. As you think about the stand you will take on the political question of protecting U.S. jobs, you are better informed about the basic facts and trends. But you have not yet learned the crucial bit of economics that will help you decide how to vote. That comes in the next chapter. So stay tuned!

 CHECKPOINT 2.3

3 **Describe what, how, and for whom goods and services are produced in the global economy.**

Practice Problem 2.3

1. Describe what, how, and for whom goods and services are produced in developing economies.

Exercise 2.3

1. Describe how inequality around the world has changed over the past few decades.

Solution to Practice Problem 2.3

1. In developing countries: agriculture is the largest percentage, manufacturing is an increasing percentage, and services are important but a small percentage of total production; most production does not use modern capital-intensive technologies, but some industries do; and people who are willing and can find jobs in factories experience increasing income while those working in rural industries are left behind.

CHAPTER CHECKPOINT

Key Points

1 **Describe what, how, and for whom goods and services are produced in the United States.**

- Consumption goods and services represent 61 percent of total production; investment goods represent 15 percent.
- Goods and services are produced by using the four factors of production: land, labor, capital, and entrepreneurship.
- The incomes people earn (rent for land, wages for labor, interest for capital, and profit for entrepreneurship) determine who gets what is produced.

2 **Use the circular flow model to provide a picture of how households, firms, and governments interact.**

- The circular flow model shows the real flows of factors of production and goods and the corresponding money flows of incomes and expenditures.
- Governments in the circular flow receive taxes, make transfers, and buy goods and services.
- Social Security, Medicare and Medicaid, and national defense and homeland security are large components of the federal government's expenditures. Interest on the national debt is also significant. Personal income taxes and Social Security taxes pay the largest share of these expenditures.
- Education, welfare benefits, and highways account for most of the expenditures of the state and local governments; and sales taxes, transfers from the federal government, and property taxes pay for these expenditures.

3 **Describe what, how, and for whom goods and services are produced in the global economy.**

- Sixty percent of the world's production (by value) comes from the advanced industrial countries and the emerging market economies.
- Production in the advanced economies uses more capital (both machines and human). But some parts of the developing economies use the latest capital and technologies.
- The global distribution of income is more unequal than the U.S. distribution. Poverty has fallen in Asia but has increased in Africa.

Key Terms

Capital, 38	Firms, 42	Land, 36
Capital goods, 34	Functional distribution of income, 40	Market, 42
Circular flow model, 42	Goods markets, 42	National debt, 46
Consumption goods and services, 34	Government goods and services, 34	Personal distribution of income, 40
Entrepreneurship, 39	Households, 42	Profit (or loss), 39
Export goods and services, 34	Human capital, 37	Rent, 39
Factor markets, 42	Interest, 39	Wages, 39
Factors of production, 36	Labor, 37	

Exercises

1. Which of the following items are *not* consumption goods and services and why?
    a. A chocolate bar
    b. A ski lift
    c. A golf ball
    d. An interstate highway
    e. An airplane
    f. A stealth bomber

2. Which of the following items are *not* investment goods and why?
    a. An auto assembly line
    b. A shopping mall
    c. A golf ball
    d. An interstate highway
    e. An oil tanker
    f. A construction worker

3. Which of the following items are *not* factors of production and why?
    a. Vans used by a baker to deliver bread
    b. 1,000 shares of Amazon.com stock
    c. Undiscovered oil
    d. A garbage truck
    e. A pack of bubble gum
    f. The President of the United States

4. On a graph of the circular flow model, indicate in which real or money flow the following belong:
    a. You pay your tuition.
    b. The University of Texas buys some Dell computers.
    c. A student works at Kinko's.
    d. Donald Trump rents a Manhattan building to a hotel.
    e. You pay your income tax.
    f. Raffael receives unemployment benefits.
    g. General Motors pays its workers wages.
    h. IBM pays a dividend to its stockholders.
    i. Bill Gates receives a profit from Microsoft.

5. Review the sources of government revenue and determine who pays most of the taxes: workers, businesses, or consumers. Do the same groups that pay most of the federal taxes also pay most of the state and local taxes?

6. Compare the scale of agricultural production in the advanced and developing economies. In which is the percentage higher? In which is the total amount produced greater? In which is the cost of production lower?

7. You've seen that the global distribution of income is unequal. Why do you think it is unequal?

8. Think about the trends in what and how goods and services are produced in the U.S. and global economies:
    a. Which jobs will grow fastest in the future? Explain your answer.
    b. What do you think will happen to the quality of labor over the next decade? Explain your answer.
    c. Do you think that at some future time, there will be no jobs in the United States and all the jobs will be in developing economies? Why or why not?

Critical Thinking

9. You saw in the chapter opener that Scott and Raffael, like many other Americans, lost their manufacturing jobs and found new service jobs. Why is the United States becoming a service-producing economy? You also saw that Chown Chong Chin and her husband, like many other Chinese, left their farm jobs to get manufacturing jobs. Why is China becoming a manufacturing economy?

   Reflecting on these trends, do you think that we should be concerned that most of our clothing, electronic goods, and other manufactured goods come from abroad? Organize your answer around the following four points:
   a. Who in the United States do you think benefits from the availability of cheap foreign-produced clothing, electronic goods, and other manufactured goods?
   b. Who in the United States do you think bears the cost of cheap foreign-produced goods?
   c. Who in the rest of the world do you think benefits from the United States buying foreign-produced goods?
   d. Who in the rest of the world do you think bears the cost of the United States buying cheap foreign-produced goods?

10. In the United States, urban areas use only a bit more than 100 million acres of the total 1,944 million acres of land. But urban use has increased by 35 million acres in just 20 years. In light of this change, do you think that we should be concerned that too much of our land is becoming urban? Organize your answer around the following five points:
    a. What type of land gets transferred to urban use?
    b. Who benefits from the transfer of an acre of farmland to an acre of suburban housing?
    c. Who bears the cost of the transfer of an acre of farmland to an acre of suburban housing?
    d. What steps could be taken to slow the transfer of farmland to urban use?
    e. Is there a case for not just slowing the transfer of farmland to urban use but either stopping it completely or even trying to reverse the trend?

11. "If the trends in schooling continue, at some point in the future, everyone will have a college degree and no one will be available to work as a janitor or garbage collector." Critically evaluate this statement.

12. "Income is unequally distributed, but because wages account for more than 70 percent of total income, any redistribution from the rich to the poor means taking from wage earners to give to others." What is wrong with the reasoning in this statement?

13. You've seen that all levels of government get only a small part of their revenues from taxing corporations. Why do you think corporations pay a small share of taxes? Would it be better if corporations paid more taxes and people paid less? Explain your answer.

14. How can it be that the distribution of income has become more unequal within most countries, yet the global distribution of income has become more equal? What problems remain despite the lessening of inequality at the global level?

Web Exercises

Use the links on MyEconLab to work the following exercises.

15. Visit washingtonpost.com and read the article about Scott Clark, Raffael, and others in the Richmond area and visit News-Record.com and read the article about Chown Chong Chin and her husband.
    a. What opportunity costs have these people borne?
    b. What benefits have they received?
    c. Can you think of anything that the U.S. government could have done to improve the lives of Scott and Raffael?
    d. Can you think of anything that the Chinese government could do to improve the lives of Chown Chong Chin and her husband?

16. Review the special "20th Century Statistics" section of the 1999 *Statistical Abstract of the United States* and find the table that describes trends in the characteristics of housing and the items that people own.
    a. Describe the trend in the ownership of homes. Do more people own or rent their homes today than the proportions in 1940?
    b. Describe the trend in the ownership of mobile homes and trailers.
    c. Describe the trend in plumbing facilities.
    d. Describe the trend in vehicle ownership.
    e. Describe the trend in telephone ownership.
    f. Can you explain the trends that you've found?

17. Review the special "20th Century Statistics" section of the 1999 *Statistical Abstract of the United States* and find the table that describes trends in transportation.
    a. Describe the trend in air travel.
    b. Describe the trend in the price of air travel.
    c. Can you explain the trends that you've found?
    d. How might these trends be influenced by the events of September 11, 2001?

18. Review the special "20th Century Statistics" section of the 1999 *Statistical Abstract of the United States* and find the table that describes trends in transportation.
    a. Describe the trend in road travel.
    b. Can you explain the trend that you've found?
    c. How might this trend be influenced by the events of September 11, 2001?

19. Visit the regional income pages of the Bureau of Economic Analysis at the U.S. Department of Commerce.
    a. Obtain data on per capita personal income for the states as a percentage of U.S. per capita personal income.
    b. Which state has the highest per capita income and which has the lowest?
    c. Where in the ranking does your state stand?
    d. Can you think of reasons for the ranking that you've found?
    e. Does the ranking change much from year to year? Why or why not?

20. Visit the University of Michigan's Statistical Resources on the Web.
    a. Find data that interest you and that provide information about what, how, and for whom goods and services are produced.
    b. Find data that tell you about the scale and trends in international trade.

The Economic Problem

When you have completed your study of this chapter, you will be able to

1 Use the production possibilities frontier to illustrate the economic problem.

2 Calculate opportunity cost.

3 Define efficiency and describe an efficient use of resources.

4 Explain what makes production possibilities expand.

5 Explain how people gain from specialization and trade.

If you enjoy music, you probably have an iPod or are thinking about getting one. Apple sold around 10 million of them in 2003 and 2004, and they are an increasingly common sight on campus and in the gym. The transition from the Walkman of the 1980s to the Discman of the 1990s to the iPod of today is an example of technological change expanding our consumption possibilities and changing the opportunity costs we face. Though our choices expand, we continue to face scarcity.

In this chapter, you will study an economic model of scarcity, choice, and opportunity cost that helps us to understand the choices that people and societies make. You will also learn about the central idea of economics: *efficiency*. And you will see what makes our production possibilities expand and how we gain by specializing and trading with each other.

3.1 PRODUCTION POSSIBILITIES

Every working day in the mines, factories, shops, and offices and on the farms and construction sites across the United States, we produce a vast array of goods and services. In the United States in 2005, 240 billion hours of labor equipped with $35 trillion worth of capital produced $12 trillion worth of goods and services.

Although our production capability is enormous, it is limited by our available resources and by technology. At any given time, we have fixed quantities of the factors of production and a fixed state of technology. Because our wants exceed our resources, we must make choices. We must rank our wants and decide which wants to satisfy and which to leave unsatisfied. In using our scarce resources, we make rational choices. And to make a rational choice, we must determine the costs and benefits of the alternatives.

Your first task in this chapter is to learn about an economic model of scarcity, choice, and opportunity cost—a model called the production possibilities frontier.

■ Production Possibilities Frontier

Production possibilities frontier
The boundary between the combinations of goods and services that can be produced and the combinations that cannot be produced, given the available factors of production and the state of technology.

The **production possibilities frontier** is the boundary between the combinations of goods and services that can be produced and the combinations that cannot be produced, given the available factors of production—land, labor, capital, and entrepreneurship—and the state of technology.

Although we produce millions of different goods and services, we can visualize the limits to production most easily if we imagine a simpler world that produces just two goods.

Imagine an economy that produces only bottled water and CDs. All the land, labor, capital, and entrepreneurship available gets used to produce these two goods.

Land can be used either for the water wells and springs and bottling plants that are required to make bottles of water or for space on which to build CD factories. Labor can be trained to work as water bottlers or as CD makers. Capital can be used for tapping springs and making water filtration plants or for the computers and lasers that make CDs. And entrepreneurs can put their creative talents to managing water resources and bottling factories or to running electronics businesses that make CDs. In every case, the more resources that get used to produce bottled water, the fewer are left for producing CDs.

We can illustrate the production possibilities frontier by using either a table or a graph. The table in Figure 3.1 describes six production possibilities for bottled water and CDs. These possibilities are alternative combinations of the quantities of the two goods that can be produced using all the economy's resources.

One possibility, A, is to allocate no factors of production to making bottled water, so bottled water production is zero. In this case, all the factors of production are used to make CDs and they can produce 15 million CDs a year. Another possibility, B, is to allocate the resources to bottled water production that are sufficient to produce 1 million bottles a year. But the resources that are being used in water-bottling plants must be taken from CD factories. So the economy can now produce only 14 million CDs a year. Possibilities C, D, E, and F show other combinations of the quantities of these two goods that the economy can produce. Possibility F uses all the resources to produce 5 million bottles of water a year and allocates no resources to producing CDs.

The graph in Figure 3.1 illustrates the production possibilities frontier, *PPF*, for bottled water and CDs. It is a graph of the production possibilities in the table. The *x*-axis shows the production of bottled water, and the *y*-axis shows the production of CDs. Each point on the graph labeled *A* through *F* represents the possibility in the table identified by the same letter. For example, point *B* represents the production of 1 million bottles of water and 14 million CDs. These quantities also appear in the table as possibility *B*.

The *PPF* is a valuable tool for illustrating the effects of scarcity and its consequences. The *PPF* puts three features of production possibilities in sharp focus. They are the distinctions between

- Attainable and unattainable combinations
- Efficient and inefficient production
- Tradeoffs and free lunches

FIGURE 3.1

The Production Possibilities Frontier

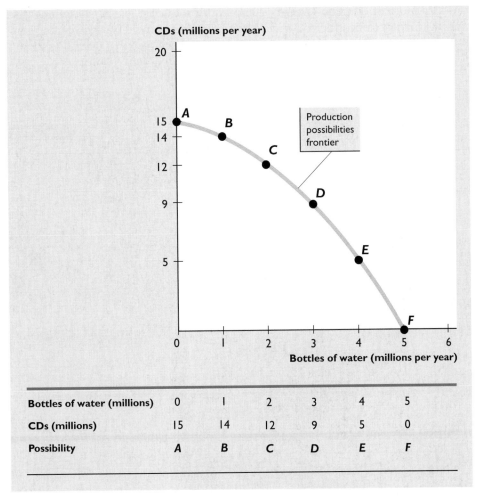

The table and the graph show the production possibilities frontier for bottled water and CDs.

Point *A* tells us that if the economy produces no bottled water, the maximum quantity of CDs it can produce is 15 million a year. Each point *A, B, C, D, E,* and *F* in the figure represents the possibility in the table identified by the same letter. The line passing through these points is the production possibilities frontier.

Bottles of water (millions)	0	1	2	3	4	5
CDs (millions)	15	14	12	9	5	0
Possibility	A	B	C	D	E	F

Attainable and Unattainable Combinations

Because the *PPF* shows the *limits* to production, it separates attainable combinations from unattainable ones. The economy can produce combinations of bottled water and CDs that are smaller than those on the *PPF*, and it can produce any of the combinations *on* the *PPF*. These combinations of bottled water and CDs are attainable. But it is impossible to produce combinations that are larger than those on the *PPF*. These combinations are unattainable.

Figure 3.2 emphasizes the attainable and unattainable combinations. Only the points on the *PPF* and inside it (in the orange area) are attainable. The combinations of bottled water and CDs beyond the *PPF* (in the white area), such as the combination at point *G*, are unattainable. These points illustrate combinations that cannot be produced with the current resources and technology. The *PPF* tells us that the economy can produce 4 million bottles of water and 5 million CDs at point *E or* 2 million bottles of water and 12 million CDs at point *C*. But the economy cannot produce 4 million bottles of water and 12 million CDs at point *G*.

Efficient and Inefficient Production

Production efficiency
A situation in which we cannot produce more of one good or service without producing less of something else.

Production is efficient when the economy is getting all that it can from its resources. More exactly, **production efficiency** occurs when it is not possible to produce more of one good or service without producing less of something else. For production to be efficient, there must be full employment—not just of labor but of all the available factors of production—and each resource must be assigned to the task that it performs comparatively better than other resources can.

■ **FIGURE 3.2**

Attainable and Unattainable Combinations

The production possibilities frontier, *PPF*, separates attainable combinations from unattainable ones. The economy can produce at any point *inside* the *PPF* (the orange area) or *on* the frontier. Any point outside the production possibilities frontier such as point *G* is unattainable.

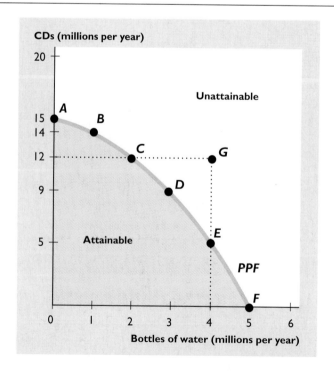

Figure 3.3 illustrates the distinction between efficient and inefficient production. With *inefficient* production, the economy might be at point *H*, where it produces 3 million bottles of water and 5 million CDs. With an *efficient* use of the economy's resources, it is possible to produce at a point on the *PPF* such as point *D* or *E*. At point *D*, there are more CDs and the same quantity of bottled water as at point *H*. And at point *E*, there are more bottles of water and the same quantity of CDs as at point *H*. At points *D* and *E*, production is efficient.

Tradeoffs and Free Lunches

A **tradeoff** is an exchange—giving up one thing to get something else. You trade off income for a better grade when you decide to cut back on the hours you spend on your weekend job and allocate the time to extra study. The Ford Motor Company faces a tradeoff when it cuts the production of trucks and uses the resources saved to produce more SUVs. The federal government faces a tradeoff when it cuts NASA's space exploration program and allocates more resources to homeland security. As a society, we face a tradeoff when we decide to cut down a forest and destroy the habitat of the spotted owl.

The production possibilities frontier illustrates the idea of a tradeoff. The *PPF* in Figure 3.3 shows how. If the economy produces at point *E* and people want to produce more CDs, they must forgo some bottled water. In the move from point *E* to point *D*, people trade off bottles of water for CDs.

Economists often express the central idea of economics—that choices involve tradeoffs—with the saying "There is no such thing as a free lunch." A **free lunch** is a gift—getting something without giving up something else. What does the

Tradeoff
An exchange—giving up one thing to get something else.

Free lunch
A gift—getting something without giving up something else.

■ **FIGURE 3.3**

Efficient and Inefficient Production, Tradeoffs, and Free Lunches

(X) myeconlab

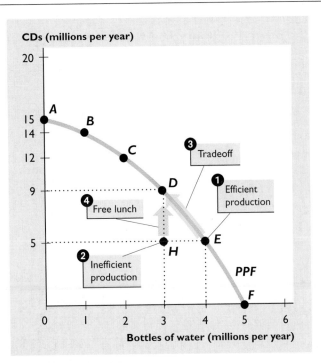

❶ When production occurs at a point on the *PPF*, such as point *E*, resources are used efficiently.

❷ When production occurs at a point inside the *PPF*, such as point *H*, resources are used inefficiently.

❸ When production is efficient— on the *PPF*—the economy faces a tradeoff. To move from point *E* to point *D* requires that some bottled water be given up for more CDs.

❹ When production is inefficient— inside the *PPF*—there is a free lunch. To move from point *H* to point *D* does not involve a tradeoff.

famous saying mean? Suppose some resources are not being used or are not being used efficiently. Isn't it then possible to avoid a tradeoff and get a free lunch?

The answer is yes. You can see why in Figure 3.3. If production is taking place *inside* the *PPF* at point *H,* then it is possible to move to point *D* and increase the production of CDs by using currently unused resources or by using resources in their most productive way. Nothing is forgone to increase production—there is a free lunch.

When production is efficient—at a point on the *PPF*—choosing to produce more of one good involves a tradeoff. But if production is inefficient—at a point inside the *PPF*—there is a free lunch. More of some goods and services can be produced without producing less of any others.

So "there is no such thing as a free lunch" means that when resources are used efficiently, every choice involves a tradeoff. Because economists view people as making rational choices, they expect that resources will be used efficiently. That is why they emphasize the tradeoff idea and deny the existence of free lunches. We might *sometimes* get a free lunch, but we *almost always* face tradeoffs.

REALITY CHECK

The *PPF* in YOUR Life

Think about your own production possibilities frontier. Two "goods" that concern you a great deal are your grade point average (GPA) and the amount of free time you have available to spend either working for an income or having fun.

The figure illustrates the *PPF* for a student who goes to class and studies for 48 hours each week and works or has fun (and sleeps) for the other 120 hours. The student is getting a GPA of 4.

■ How does *your PPF* compare with the one in the figure?

■ Show on this *PPF* what happens if you decide to go to a movie with friends instead of studying for your economics exam.

■ What is the tradeoff involved in your decision?

CHECKPOINT 3.1

1 Use the production possibilities frontier to illustrate the economic problem.

Practice Problem 3.1

1. Robinson Crusoe, a shipwrecked sailor, lived alone on a deserted island. His only resources were the land, which provided fish and fruit, and 8 hours a day of his labor, which he could allocate to catching fish or picking fruit. He varied the time spent on these two activities and kept a record of his production. Table 1 shows the numbers that Crusoe wrote in the sand.
   a. Use these numbers to make Crusoe's *PPF*.
   b. Which combinations (in pounds) are attainable and which are unattainable: (i) 10 fish and 30 fruit, (ii) 13 fish and 26 fruit, (iii) 16.5 fish and 21 fruit?
   c. Which combinations (in pounds) use all of Crusoe's 8 hours a day: (i) 15 fish and 21 fruit, (ii) 7 fish and 30 fruit, (iii) 18 fish and 0 fruit?
   d. Which combinations (in pounds) provide Crusoe with a free lunch and which confront him with a tradeoff when he increases fruit by 1: (i) 18 fish and 0 fruit, (ii) 15 fish and 15 fruit, (iii) 13 fish and 26 fruit?

TABLE 1

Hours	Fish (pounds)		Fruit (pounds)
0	0		0
1	4.0	or	8
2	7.5	or	15
3	10.5	or	21
4	13.0	or	26
5	15.0	or	30
6	16.5	or	33
7	17.5	or	35
8	18.0	or	36

Exercise 3.1

1. In the winter, Robinson Crusoe in practice problem 3.1 can work only 5 hours a day. Table 2 shows the quantities that Crusoe can produce in winter.
   a. Use these numbers to make Crusoe's *PPF* in winter.
   b. Which combinations (in pounds) are attainable and which are unattainable: (i) 7.5 fish and 11 fruit, (ii) 9 fish and 11 fruit, (iii) 5.5 fish and 14 fruit?
   c. Which combinations (in pounds) use all of Crusoe's 5 hours a day, which provide a free lunch, and which confront him with a tradeoff: (i) 10 fish and 0 fruit, (ii) 9 fish and 6 fruit, (iii) 3 fish and 16 fruit?

TABLE 2

Hours	Fish (pounds)		Fruit (pounds)
0	0		0
1	3.0	or	6
2	5.5	or	11
3	7.5	or	15
4	9.0	or	18
5	10.0	or	20

Solution to Practice Problem 3.1

1a. Table 3 sets out Crusoe's *PPF*. Crusoe can produce the fish and fruit that lie on his *PPF* if he uses a total of 8 hours a day. If he picks fruit for 8 hours, he picks 36 pounds and catches no fish (row *A*). If he picks fruit for 7 hours, he picks 35 pounds and has 1 hour for fishing in which he catches 4 pounds (row *B*). Check that you can construct the other rows of Table 3.

1b. (i) 10 fish and 30 fruit is attainable because Crusoe can produce 10.5 fish and 30 fruit (row *D* of Table 3). (ii) 13 fish and 26 fruit is attainable (row *E*). (iii) 16.5 fish and 21 fruit is unattainable because when Crusoe catches 16.5 fish he can pick only 15 fruit (row *G*).

1c. (i) 15 fish and 21 fruit uses all 8 hours—it is on his *PPF* (row *F*). (ii) 7 fish and 30 fruit does not use all 8 hours—it is inside his *PPF* (row *C*). (iii) 18 fish and 0 fruit uses all 8 hours—it is on his *PPF* (row *I*).

1d. (i) 18 fish and 0 fruit involves a tradeoff because it is on his *PPF*. (ii) 15 fish and 15 fruit provides a free lunch because it is inside his *PPF*. (iii) 13 fish and 26 fruit involves a tradeoff because it is on his *PPF*.

TABLE 3

Possibility	Fish (pounds)		Fruit (pounds)
A	0	and	36
B	4.0	and	35
C	7.5	and	33
D	10.5	and	30
E	13.0	and	26
F	15.0	and	21
G	16.5	and	15
H	17.5	and	8
I	18.0	and	0

3.2 OPPORTUNITY COST

You've seen that moving from one point to another on the *PPF* involves a trade-off. But what are the terms of the tradeoff? How much of one item must be forgone to obtain an additional unit of another item—a large amount or a small amount? The answer is given by opportunity cost—the best thing you must give up to get something (see p. 11). We can use the *PPF* to calculate opportunity cost.

■ The Opportunity Cost of a Bottle of Water

The opportunity cost of a bottle of water is the number of CDs forgone to get an additional bottle of water. It is calculated as the number of CDs forgone divided by the number of bottles of water gained.

Figure 3.4 illustrates the calculation. At point *A*, the quantities produced are zero water and 15 million CDs; and at point *B*, the quantities produced are 1 million bottles of water and 14 million CDs. To gain 1 million bottles of water by moving from point *A* to point *B*, 1 million CDs are forgone. So the opportunity cost of 1 bottle of water is 1 CD.

At point *C*, the quantities produced are 2 million bottles of water and 12 million CDs. To gain 1 million bottles of water by moving from point *B* to point *C*, 2 million CDs are forgone. So the opportunity cost of 1 bottle of water is 2 CDs.

If you repeat these calculations, moving from *C* to *D*, *D* to *E*, and *E* to *F*, you will obtain the opportunity costs shown in the table and the graph.

■ **FIGURE 3.4**

Calculating the Opportunity Cost of a Bottle of Water

Movement along *PPF*	Decrease in quantity of CDs	Increase in quantity of bottled water	Decrease in CDs divided by increase in bottled water
A to *B*	1 million	1 million	1 CD per bottle
B to *C*	2 million	1 million	2 CDs per bottle
C to *D*	3 million	1 million	3 CDs per bottle
D to *E*	4 million	1 million	4 CDs per bottle
E to *F*	5 million	1 million	5 CDs per bottle

Along the *PPF* from *A* to *F*, the opportunity cost of a bottle of water increases as the quantity of bottled water produced increases.

■ Increasing Opportunity Cost

Look at the numbers that we've just calculated for the opportunity cost of a bottle of water and notice that they follow a striking pattern. The opportunity cost of water increases as the quantity of water produced increases. Figure 3.5 shows this increasing opportunity cost.

■ Slope of the *PPF* and Opportunity Cost

The magnitude of the *slope* of the *PPF* measures opportunity cost. And because the *PPF* in Figure 3.4 is bowed outward, its slope changes and gets steeper as the quantity of water produced increases.

When a small quantity of water is produced—between points *A* and *B*—the *PPF* has a gentle slope and the opportunity cost of a bottle of water is low. A given increase in the quantity of water costs a small decrease in the quantity of CDs. When a large quantity of water is produced—between points *E* and *F*—the *PPF* is steep and the opportunity cost of a bottle of water is high. A given increase in the quantity of water costs a large decrease in the quantity of CDs.

Note that if the *PPF* were linear, it would have a constant slope and the opportunity cost of a bottle of water would be constant. The same quantity of CDs would be forgone for each bottle of water.

Why is the *PPF* not linear? Why is it bowed outward? The reason is that resources are not equally productive in all activities. When a small quantity of water is produced, the people who work at Aqua Springs are the best at bottling

---

■ **FIGURE 3.5**

The Opportunity Cost of a Bottle of Water

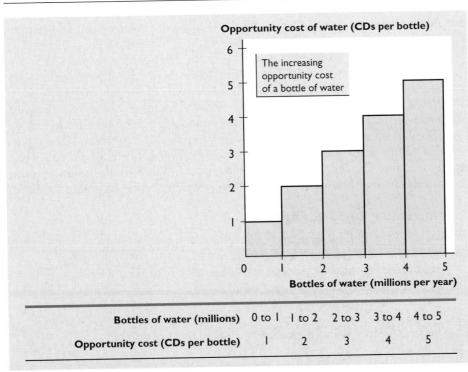

Because the *PPF* in Figure 3.4 is bowed outward, the opportunity cost of a bottle of water increases as the quantity of water produced increases.

Bottles of water (millions)	0 to 1	1 to 2	2 to 3	3 to 4	4 to 5
Opportunity cost (CDs per bottle)	1	2	3	4	5

water and the worst at making CDs. And some of the people who are working at Sony making CDs would be more productive at water bottling than they are at making CDs. In this situation, if workers move from Sony to Aqua Springs, a small quantity of CDs is forgone to get a given increase in the quantity of water.

But when a large quantity of water is produced, most people are working at Aqua Springs and the few people who work at Sony are the very best at making CDs and the worst at bottling water. In this situation, if workers move from Sony to Aqua Springs, a large quantity of CDs is forgone to get a given increase in the quantity of water.

■ Opportunity Cost Is a Ratio

You've seen that the opportunity cost of a bottle of water is the number of CDs forgone divided by the number of bottles of water gained—the *ratio* of CDs forgone to water gained.

Similarly, the opportunity cost of a CD is the number of bottles of water forgone divided by the number of CDs gained—the *ratio* of water forgone to CDs gained.

You saw that to gain 1 million bottles of water by moving along the *PPF* in Figure 3.4 from *C* to *D* costs 3 million CDs. So the opportunity cost of a bottle of water is 3 CDs.

By moving along the *PPF* in the opposite direction, from *D* to *C*, brings a gain of 3 million CDs at the cost of 1 million bottles of water. So the opportunity cost of a CD is 1/3 of a bottle of water.

Notice that the opportunity cost of a CD is equal to the inverse of the opportunity cost of a bottle of water. And just as in the case of water, the opportunity cost of a CD increases as the quantity of CDs produced increases.

■ Increasing Opportunity Costs Are Everywhere

Just about every activity that you can think of is one with an increasing opportunity cost. We allocate the most skillful farmers and the most fertile land to the production of food. And we allocate the best doctors and the least fertile land to the production of health-care services. If we shift fertile land and tractors away from farming to hospitals and ambulances and ask farmers to become hospital porters, the production of food drops drastically and the increase in the production of health-care services is small. The opportunity cost of a unit of health-care services rises. Similarly, if we shift our resources away from health care toward farming, we must use more doctors and nurses as farmers and more hospitals as hydroponic tomato factories. The decrease in the production of health-care services is large, but the increase in food production is small. The opportunity cost of a unit of food rises.

Your Increasing Opportunity Cost

Flip back to your *PPF* for time and GPA on p. 66 and think about its implications for your opportunity cost of a higher grade.

What is the opportunity cost of spending time with your friends in terms of the grade you might receive on your exam?

What is the opportunity cost of a higher grade in terms of the activities you give up to study?

Do you face increasing opportunity costs in these activities?

CHECKPOINT 3.2

2 **Calculate opportunity cost.**

Practice Problem 3.2

1. Table 1 shows Robinson Crusoe's production possibilities.
   a. Use the data in Table 1 to make a table that shows Crusoe's opportunity cost of a pound of fish as he increases the time he spends fishing and decreases the time that he spends picking fruit.
   b. If Crusoe increases his production of fruit from 21 pounds to 26 pounds and decreases his production of fish from 15 pounds to 13 pounds, what is his opportunity cost of a pound of fruit? Explain your answer.
   c. If Crusoe is producing 10 pounds of fish and 20 pounds of fruit, what is his opportunity cost of a pound of fruit and a pound of fish? Explain your answer.

Exercise 3.2

1. Table 2 shows Robinson Crusoe's production possibilities in winter.
   a. Use the data in Table 2 to make a table that shows Crusoe's opportunity cost of a pound of fruit as he increases the time he spends picking fruit and decreases the time he spends fishing.
   b. If Crusoe currently catches 5.5 pounds of fish and picks 11 pounds of fruit a day, calculate his opportunity cost of a pound of fruit and of a pound of fish. Explain your answer.
   c. If Crusoe increases the amount of fish caught from 5.5 to 7.5 pounds and decreases the amount of fruit picked from 15 to 11 pounds, what is his opportunity cost of a pound of fish? Explain your answer.
   d. Does Crusoe's opportunity cost of a pound of fruit increase as he spends more time picking fruit? Explain why or why not.

Solution to Practice Problem 3.2

1a. Crusoe's opportunity cost of a pound of fish is the fruit given up divided by the gain in fish as he moves along his *PPF*, increasing the time he spends fishing and decreasing the time he spends picking fruit. For example, when Crusoe spends no time fishing, he produces the quantities in row *A* in Table 1. When he spends more time fishing and moves to row *B* in Table 1, the gain in fish is 4 pounds and the fruit given up is 1 pound. So the opportunity cost of a pound of fish is 1/4 of a pound of fruit. Check that you can derive the other rows of Table 3.

1b. The opportunity cost of a pound of fruit is 2/5 of a pound of fish. To gain 5 pounds of fruit, he forgoes 2 pounds of fish. The opportunity cost of a pound of fruit is the 2 pounds of fish forgone divided by 5 pounds of fruit gained. This opportunity cost is the inverse of the opportunity cost of a pound of fish (Table 3, move from *E* to *F*).

1c. If Crusoe is producing 10 pounds of fish and 20 pounds of fruit, his opportunity cost of fruit and of fish is zero because to gain a pound of fruit and a pound of fish, he doesn't have to give up anything. He is producing a combination inside his *PPF*.

TABLE 1

Possibility	Fish (pounds)	Fruit (pounds)
A	0	36
B	4.0	35
C	7.5	33
D	10.5	30
E	13.0	26
F	15.0	21
G	16.5	15
H	17.5	8
I	18.0	0

TABLE 2

Possibility	Fish (pounds)	Fruit (pounds)
A	0	20
B	3.0	18
C	5.5	15
D	7.5	11
E	9.0	6
F	10.0	0

TABLE 3

Move from	Gain in fish (pounds)	Fruit given up (pounds)	Opportunity cost of fish (pounds of fruit)
A to B	4.0	1	0.25
B to C	3.5	2	0.57
C to D	3.0	3	1.00
D to E	2.5	4	1.60
E to F	2.0	5	2.50
F to G	1.5	6	4.00
G to H	1.0	7	7.00
H to I	0.5	8	16.00

3.3 USING RESOURCES EFFICIENTLY

Environmentalists say that we should expand the use of clean solar technologies and burn less oil and coal. They also say that we should create clean mass transit systems and decrease our reliance on the automobile. Political leaders of all parties say that we should hire more teachers to reduce class size and improve education. Many also want to spend more on prescription drug plans for seniors and improve health care for the uninsured. Some political leaders want to enter into a new phase of defense spending and create an effective antimissile defense system. All of these policy proposals and the political debates that surround them are about allocative efficiency.

Economists use the idea of allocative efficiency in a broad way that cuts to the heart of these debates. **Allocative efficiency** occurs when the quantities of goods and services produced are those that people value most highly. To put it another way, resources are *allocated efficiently* when we cannot produce more of a good or service without giving up some of another good or service that people *value more highly*.

If people value a pollution-free environment more highly than they value cheap electric power, it is efficient to use high-cost clean technologies to produce electricity. In this case, limiting the use of coal and oil and expanding the use of solar energy sources would be efficient. If people value the flexibility of being able to choose when and where to travel more highly than they value low-cost, low-pollution, safe transportation, it is efficient to use high-cost, polluting, accident-prone automobiles.

So just what is the efficient energy policy: one that favors clean-energy technologies or one that burns oil and coal? What is the efficient method of urban transportation: one that uses a clean mass transit system or a system of freeways and private automobiles? And what are the efficient quantities of education, health care, and national defense?

These are questions that have enormous consequences for human welfare, and they are difficult questions. But you can see the essence of the answers by thinking about the simpler question: What is the efficient quantity of bottled water to produce? The answer to this question provides the principles that underlie the answers to all questions about how to use our scarce resources.

Allocative efficiency
A situation in which the quantities of goods and services produced are those that people value most highly—it is not possible to produce more of a good or service without giving up some of another good that people value more highly.

■ Two Conditions for Allocative Efficiency

Allocative efficiency is achieved when two conditions are met:

- Production efficiency—producing on the *PPF*
- Producing at the highest-valued point on the *PPF*

Production Efficiency—Producing On the *PPF*

You've seen that *production efficiency* is achieved when it is not possible to produce more of one good or service without producing less of something else. When production is efficient, the economy is *on its PPF.* If production occurs *inside* the *PPF*, production is *inefficient.* Either some resources are unemployed or some resources are not being used in their most productive way. Putting unemployed resources to work and reallocating misused resources to their most productive use enables more to be produced.

When resources are unemployed or misused, it is possible to produce more of a good without incurring an opportunity cost. So production is not efficient. Only when all resources are fully employed and the economy is operating on the *PPF* is it impossible to produce more of one good or service without producing less of another good or service.

Producing at the Highest-Valued Point on the *PPF*

Allocative efficiency is achieved when the combination of goods and services produced on the *PPF* are those that are valued most highly. All the combinations of goods and services on the *PPF* achieve *production efficiency.* Each of these combinations is such that, to produce more of one good, the quantity produced of another good must decrease. But only one of these combinations achieves *allocative efficiency.* That is, only one combination is the most highly valued.

To find this combination, we need some additional information that is not contained in the *PPF*. The *PPF,* remember, tells us what it is *possible* to produce and provides information about opportunity cost. The *PPF* does not tell us the *value* of what we produce. To determine the value, we use the concept of marginal benefit.

■ Marginal Benefit

You learned in Chapter 1 (pp. 12–13) that the *benefit* of something is the gain or pleasure that it brings. Benefit is how a person *feels* about something. We defined *marginal benefit* as the benefit that a person receives from consuming one more unit of a good or service.

You also learned in Chapter 1 that economists measure the benefit of something by what a person *is willing to* give up to get it. So a person's *marginal* benefit of a good or service is what that person *is willing to* give up to get *one more* unit of it.

It is a general principle that the more we have of any good or service, the smaller is our marginal benefit from it—the principle of decreasing marginal benefit. To understand the principle of decreasing marginal benefit, think about your own marginal benefit from bottled water. If bottled water is very hard to come by and you can buy only one or two bottles a year, you will be very pleased to get one more bottle. The marginal benefit of that bottle of water is high. In this situation, you are willing to give up quite a lot of some other good or service to get one more bottle of water. But if there is plenty of bottled water around and you have as much as you can drink, you will get almost no benefit from one more bottle. So you are willing to give up almost nothing for that bottle of water.

The principle of diminishing marginal benefit applies to all goods and services. You get a lot of pleasure from one slice of pizza. A second slice is fine, too, but not quite as satisfying as the first one. But eat three, four, five, six, and more slices, and each additional slice is less enjoyable than the previous one. You get diminishing marginal benefit from pizza. So the more pizza you have, the less of some other good or service you would be willing to give up to get one more slice.

Although marginal benefit expresses a person's *feeling* toward a good or service, it is nonetheless a real, objective phenomenon. It is as real as the physical limits to production that we express in the *PPF*. The *PPF* shows what is *feasible.* Marginal benefit is an expression of what is *desirable.* And we need a way of describing marginal benefit that is as concrete as the *PPF*.

Let's see how economists describe marginal benefit.

Marginal Benefit Schedule and Curve

We describe marginal benefit by using either a marginal benefit schedule or a marginal benefit curve. Figure 3.6 illustrates these concepts, and we continue to use the same two goods as before: bottled water and CDs. The marginal benefit from a bottle of water can be expressed as the number of CDs that a person is willing to forgo to get one more bottle. This amount decreases as the quantity of bottled water available increases.

Begin by looking at the table below the graph. In possibility *A*, 1 million bottles of water are available, and at that quantity, people are willing to give up 4.5 CDs for a bottle of water. As the quantity of bottled water available increases, the amount that people are willing to give up for an additional bottle falls—3.5 CDs per bottle when 2 million bottles are available in possibility *B*, 2.5 CDs per bottle when 3 million bottles are available in possibility *C*, and 1.5 CDs per bottle when 4 million bottles are available in possibility *D*.

The marginal benefit curve is a graph of the marginal benefit schedule. The points *A*, *B*, *C*, and *D* on the marginal benefit curve correspond to the possibilities *A*, *B*, *C*, and *D* of the marginal benefit schedule.

The marginal benefit from a bottle of water and the opportunity cost of a bottle of water that you studied on p. 68 are both measured in CDs per bottle. But they are *not* the same concept. The opportunity cost of a bottle of water is the quantity of CDs that people *must forgo* to get another bottle. The marginal benefit from a bottle of water is the quantity of CDs that people are *willing to forgo* to get another bottle.

◼ FIGURE 3.6

Marginal Benefit of a Bottle of Water

The table and the graph show the marginal benefit of a bottle of water.

Point *A* tells us that if the quantity of water produced is 1 million bottles a year, the maximum quantity of CDs that people are willing to give up for an additional bottle of water is 4.5 CDs. Each point *A*, *B*, *C*, and *D* in the graph represents the possibility in the table identified by the same letter.

The line passing through these points is the marginal benefit curve. The marginal benefit of a bottle of water decreases as the quantity of bottled water available increases.

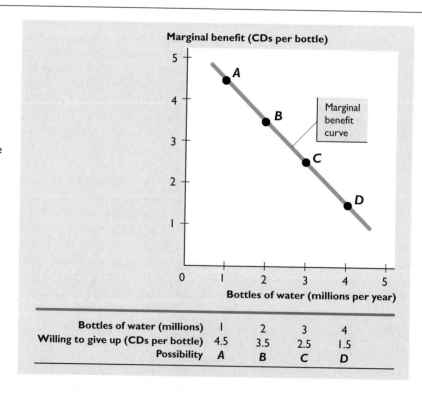

Bottles of water (millions)	1	2	3	4
Willing to give up (CDs per bottle)	4.5	3.5	2.5	1.5
Possibility	*A*	*B*	*C*	*D*

■ Marginal Cost

To achieve allocative efficiency, we must compare the marginal benefit of a bottle of water with its marginal cost. We defined *marginal cost* in Chapter 1 (p. 12) as the opportunity cost of producing one more unit of a good or service. You've seen how we can calculate opportunity cost as we move along the production possibilities frontier. We can calculate marginal cost in a similar way. The marginal cost of a bottle of water is the opportunity cost of one additional bottle—the quantity of CDs that must be given up to get one more bottle of water as we move along the *PPF*.

Figure 3.7 illustrates the marginal cost of a bottle of water based on the opportunity cost numbers that you've already calculated. The opportunity cost of the first 1 million bottles of water is 1 million CDs. So on the average over the range from zero to 1 million, 1 bottle of water costs 1 CD. Because this value is the average over a range, we graph it at the midpoint of the range—midway between zero and 1 million. The opportunity cost of the second 1 million bottles of water is 2 million CDs. So on the average over this range, 1 bottle of water costs 2 CDs. We graph this cost midway between 1 million and 2 million on the graph.

Figure 3.7 shows that the marginal cost curve of bottled water slopes upward. That is, as the quantity of bottled water produced increases, the marginal cost of bottled water increases. This increasing marginal cost occurs for the same reason the opportunity cost increases.

Let's use the concepts of marginal benefit and marginal cost to discover the efficient quantity of bottled water to produce.

▨ FIGURE 3.7

Marginal Cost of a Bottle of Water

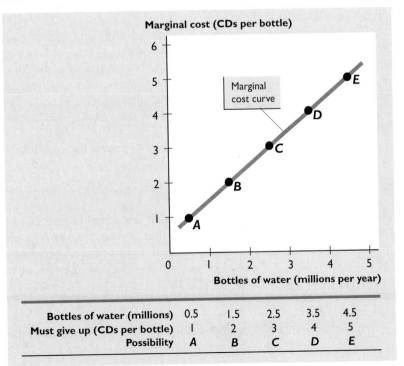

Bottles of water (millions)	0.5	1.5	2.5	3.5	4.5
Must give up (CDs per bottle)	1	2	3	4	5
Possibility	A	B	C	D	E

The table and the graph show the marginal cost of a bottle of water. Marginal cost is the opportunity cost of producing one more unit and is derived from the *PPF*.

Points *A*, *B*, *C*, *D*, and *E* in the graph represent the possibilities in the table. The marginal cost curve shows that the marginal cost of a bottle of water increases as the quantity of bottled water produced increases.

■ Efficient Use of Resources

Resource use is efficient when the goods and services that are produced are the ones that people value most highly. That is, when resources are allocated efficiently, it is not possible to produce more of any good without producing less of something else that is valued even more highly.

We can illustrate an efficient use of resources by continuing to use the example of bottled water and CDs. Figure 3.8(a) shows the production possibilities frontier (the same as in Figure 3.1 on p. 63). And Figure 3.8(b) shows the marginal cost (*MC*) and marginal benefit (*MB*) of a bottle of water.

Suppose that the quantity of water produced is 1.5 million bottles on the *PPF* in Figure 3.8(a). This quantity of water meets the condition for production efficiency because it is on the *PPF*. But does it meet the condition for allocative efficiency? To answer this question, we need to compare marginal benefit and marginal cost in Figure 3.8(b). At this quantity of water, the marginal benefit of water is 4 CDs per bottle, but the marginal cost of water is only 2 CDs per bottle. Because people value an additional bottle of water more highly than the cost to produce it, too little water is being produced (and too many CDs are being produced). Greater value can be obtained from the economy's resources by moving some of them out of CD production and into bottled water production.

Now suppose that the quantity of water produced is 3.5 million bottles on the *PPF* in Figure 3.8(a). Again, this point meets the condition for production efficiency because it is on the *PPF*. To check whether it meets the condition for allocative efficiency, we again need to compare marginal benefit and marginal cost. At this quantity of water, the marginal benefit of water is now 2 CDs per bottle, but the marginal cost of water is 4 CDs per bottle. Because people value an additional bottle of water less highly than the cost to produce it, too much water is being produced (and too few CDs are being produced). Greater value can now be obtained from the economy's resources by moving some of them out of bottled water production and into CD production.

Finally, suppose the quantity of water produced is 2.5 million bottles on the *PPF* in Figure 3.8(a). At this quantity, the marginal cost of water equals the marginal benefit. Both are 3 CDs per bottle. This quantity of bottled water (and CDs) is efficient. It is not possible to produce more bottled water without giving up some CDs that are valued more highly than the additional water. And it isn't possible to produce more CDs without giving up some water that is valued more highly than the additional CDs.

So 2.5 million bottles of water on the *PPF* meets the conditions for both production efficiency and allocative efficiency.

■ Efficiency in the U.S. Economy

Does the U.S. economy achieve an efficient use of resources? Do we have an efficient energy policy, or would a policy that favors clean-energy technologies be more efficient? Do we have an efficient method of urban transportation, or would more mass transit systems be more efficient? Do we have the efficient quantities of education and health care, or would an increase in the production of these items and a decrease in the production of some other goods and services be more efficient?

You will learn how to address these questions in Chapters 6 through 10.

FIGURE 3.8

The Efficient Quantity of Bottled Water

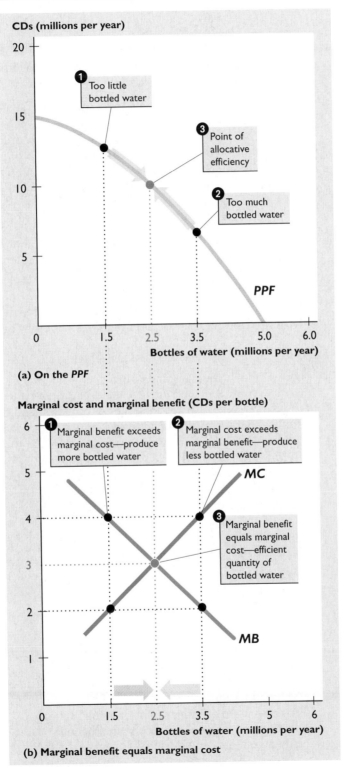

(a) On the PPF

(b) Marginal benefit equals marginal cost

Production efficiency occurs at all points on the *PPF*. But only one point meets the condition for allocative efficiency.

❶ When the quantity of water is 1.5 million bottles in part (a), too little bottled water is being produced because in part (b), the marginal benefit of water exceeds the marginal cost. It is efficient to produce more water.

❷ When the quantity of water is 3.5 million bottles in part (a), too much bottled water is being produced because in part (b), the marginal cost of water exceeds the marginal benefit. It is efficient to produce less water.

❸ When the quantity of water is 2.5 million bottles in part (a), the efficient quantity of bottled water is being produced because in part (b), the marginal cost of water equals the marginal benefit.

3 Define efficiency and describe an efficient use of resources.

Practice Problems 3.3

TABLE I

Possibility	Bananas (bunches)	Coffee (pounds)
A	70	40
B	50	100
C	30	140
D	10	160

1. Table 1 shows a nation's production possibilities of bananas and coffee. Use the table to calculate the nation's marginal cost of a bunch of bananas. Draw the marginal cost curve.

2. Use the following data to draw the nation's marginal benefit curve for a bunch of bananas:
   a. When 20 bunches of bananas are available, people are willing to give up 3 pounds of coffee to get an additional bunch of bananas.
   b. When 40 bunches of bananas are available, people are willing to give up 2 pounds of coffee to get an additional bunch of bananas.
   c. When 60 bunches of bananas are available, people are willing to give up 1 pound of coffee to get an additional bunch of bananas.

3. Use the data in practice problems 1 and 2 to calculate the efficient use of the nation's resources.

Exercise 3.3

1. Use the *PPF* shown in Figure 1(a) and the marginal benefit curve shown in Figure 1(b) to find the efficient quantities of yogurt and ice cream.

Solutions to Practice Problems 3.3

FIGURE I

(a) *PPF*

(b) Marginal benefit

1. Figure 2 shows the marginal cost curve. When the quantity of bananas increases from 10 to 30 bunches, the quantity of coffee decreases from 160 to 140 pounds. The gain in bananas is 20 bunches, and the coffee given up is 20 pounds. So the opportunity cost of 1 bunch of bananas is 1 pound of coffee. In the figure, marginal cost is 1 pound of coffee at the midpoint between 10 and 30 bunches, which is 20 bunches of bananas. When the quantity of bananas increases from 30 to 50 bunches, coffee decreases from 140 to 100 pounds. The gain in bananas is 20 bunches, and the coffee given up is 40 pounds. So the opportunity cost of 1 bunch of bananas is 2 pounds of coffee. In the figure, marginal cost is 2 pounds of coffee at the midpoint between 30 and 50 bunches, which is 40 bunches of bananas.

2. Figure 2 shows the marginal benefit curve, which slopes downward because as more bananas are available, the marginal benefit from an additional bunch of bananas decreases.

3. The nation uses its resources efficiently when it produces 40 bunches of bananas and (approximately) 120 pounds of coffee. When the nation produces this combination, production is on the *PPF* (production efficiency), and it is the highest-valued combination because marginal benefit equals marginal cost (allocative efficiency).

FIGURE 2

3.4 ECONOMIC GROWTH

Economic growth is the sustained expansion of production possibilities. Our economy grows when we develop better technologies for producing goods and services; improve the quality of labor by education, on-the-job training, and work experience; and get more machines to help us produce.

We can see how economic growth occurs by using the *PPF*. But to study economic growth, we must change the two goods. We need to look at the *PPF* for a consumption good and a capital good.

Figure 3.9 shows the *PPF* for bottled water—a consumption good—and water-bottling plants—a capital good. By using today's resources to produce bottling plants, the economy can expand its future production possibilities. The amount by which production possibilities expand depends on the quantity of capital—number of new bottling plants—produced. Producing no new plants (at point *L*) keeps the *PPF* in its original position. Decreasing the production of bottled water and producing 2 new bottling plants (at point *K*) increases production possibilities and shifts the *PPF* outward to the new *PPF*. The greater the production of new capital, the faster is the expansion of production possibilities.

But economic growth is not free. To make it happen, consumption must decrease. The move from *L* to *K* in Figure 3.9 means forgoing 2 million bottles of water now. The opportunity cost of producing more bottling plants is producing fewer bottles of water for consumption today.

Also, economic growth is no magic formula for abolishing scarcity. Economic growth shifts the *PPF* outward, but on the new *PPF*, we continue to face opportunity costs. To keep producing capital, current consumption must be less than its maximum possible level.

Economic growth
The sustained expansion of production possibilities.

■ FIGURE 3.9

Expanding Production Possibilities

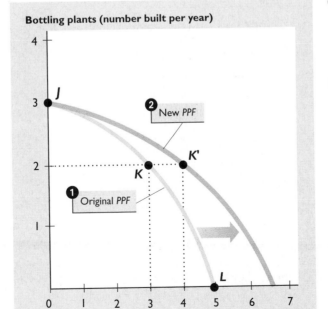

1 If firms allocate no resources to producing water-bottling plants and produce 5 million bottles of water a year at point *L*, the *PPF* doesn't change.

2 If firms decrease water production to 3 million bottles a year and produce 2 water-bottling plants, at point *K*, production possibilities will expand. After a year, the *PPF* shifts outward to the new *PPF* and production can move to point *K'*.

Hong Kong's Rapid Economic Growth

If Hong Kong continues to produce at a point such as *B*, it will grow more rapidly than the United States and its *PPF* will eventually move out beyond the U.S. *PPF*. But if Hong Kong produces at a point such as *D*, the pace of expansion of its *PPF* will slow.

Hong Kong's production possibilities per person were 25 percent of those of the United States in 1960. By 2000, they had grown to become 80 percent of U.S. production possibilities. Hong Kong grew faster than the United States because it allocated more of its resources to accumulating capital and less to consumption than the United States did.

In 1960, the United States and Hong Kong produced at point *A* on their respective *PPF*s. In 2000, Hong Kong was at point *B* and the United States was at point *C*.

CHECKPOINT 3.4

myeconlab

4 **Explain what makes production possibilities expand.**

Practice Problem 3.4

1. Table 1 shows an economy that produces education services and consumption goods. If the economy currently produces 500 graduates a year and 2,000 units of consumption goods, what is the opportunity cost of economic growth?

TABLE 1

Possibility	Education services (graduates)	Consumption goods (units)
A	1,000	0
B	750	1,000
C	500	2,000
D	0	3,000

Exercise 3.4

1. If the economy shown in Table 1 uses all its resources to produce consumption goods, at what rate will the economy grow? If the economy increases the number of graduates from 0 to 750, will the economy experience economic growth? Explain your answer.

Solution to Practice Problem 3.4

1. The opportunity cost of producing 500 graduates a year is 1,000 units (3,000 minus 2,000) of consumption goods forgone.

3.5 SPECIALIZATION AND TRADE

A person can produce several goods or can concentrate on producing one good and then trading some of that good for those produced by others. Concentrating on the production of only one good is called *specialization*. We are going to discover how people gain by specializing in the production of the good in which they have a *comparative advantage*.

■ Comparative Advantage

A person has a **comparative advantage** in an activity if that person can perform the activity at a lower opportunity cost than someone else. Let's explore the idea of comparative advantage by looking at two smoothie bars: one operated by Liz and the other operated by Joe.

Comparative advantage
The ability of a person to perform an activity or produce a good or service at a lower opportunity cost than someone else.

Liz's Smoothie Bar

Liz produces smoothies and salads. In Liz's high-tech bar, she can turn out *either* a smoothie *or* a salad every 90 seconds. If she spends all her time making smoothies, she produces 40 an hour. If she spends all her time making salads, she also produces 40 an hour. If she splits her time equally between the two, she can produce 20 smoothies *and* 20 salads an hour. For each additional smoothie Liz produces, she must decrease her production of salads by one, and for each additional salad Liz produces, she must decrease her production of smoothies by one. So

> **Liz's opportunity cost of producing 1 smoothie is 1 salad,**

and

> **Liz's opportunity cost of producing 1 salad is 1 smoothie.**

Liz's customers buy smoothies and salads in equal quantities, so Liz splits her time equally between the items and produces 20 smoothies and 20 salads an hour.

TABLE 3.1   LIZ'S PRODUCTION POSSIBILITIES

Item	Minutes to produce 1	Quantity per hour
Smoothies	1.5	40
Salads	1.5	40

Joe's Smoothie Bar

Joe also produces both smoothies and salads. But Joe's bar is smaller than Liz's. Also, Joe has only one blender, and it's a slow, old machine. Even if Joe uses all his resources to produce smoothies, he can produce only 6 an hour. But Joe is pretty good in the salad department, so if he uses all his resources to make salads, he can produce 30 an hour. Joe's ability to make smoothies and salads is the same regardless of how he splits an hour between the two tasks. He can make a salad in 2 minutes or a smoothie in 10 minutes. For each additional smoothie Joe produces, he must decrease his production of salads by 5. And for each additional salad Joe produces, he must decrease his production of smoothies by 1/5 of a smoothie. So

> **Joe's opportunity cost of producing 1 smoothie is 5 salads,**

and

> **Joe's opportunity cost of producing 1 salad is 1/5 of a smoothie.**

Joe's customers, like Liz's, buy smoothies and salads in equal quantities. So Joe spends 50 minutes of each hour making smoothies and 10 minutes of each hour making salads. With this division of his time, Joe produces 5 smoothies and 5 salads an hour.

TABLE 3.2   JOE'S PRODUCTION POSSIBILITIES

Item	Minutes to produce 1	Quantity per hour
Smoothies	10	6
Salads	2	30

Liz's Absolute Advantage

You can see from the numbers that describe the two smoothie bars that Liz is four times as productive as Joe—her 20 smoothies and 20 salads an hour are four times Joe's 5 smoothies and 5 salads. Liz has an **absolute advantage**—she is more productive than Joe in producing both smoothies and salads. But Liz has a comparative advantage in only one of the activities.

Liz's Comparative Advantage

In which of the two activities does Liz have a *comparative* advantage? Recall that comparative advantage is a situation in which one person's opportunity cost of producing a good is lower than another person's opportunity cost of producing that same good. Liz has a comparative advantage in producing smoothies. Her opportunity cost of a smoothie is 1 salad, whereas Joe's opportunity cost of a smoothie is 5 salads.

Joe's Comparative Advantage

If Liz has a comparative advantage in producing smoothies, Joe must have a comparative advantage in producing salads. His opportunity cost of a salad is 1/5 of a smoothie, while Liz's opportunity cost of a salad is 1 smoothie.

■ Achieving Gains from Trade

Liz and Joe run into each other one evening in a singles bar. After a few minutes of getting acquainted, Liz tells Joe about her amazingly profitable smoothie business that is selling 20 smoothies and 20 salads an hour. Her only problem, she tells Joe, is that she wishes she could produce more because potential customers leave when her lines get too long.

Joe isn't sure whether to risk spoiling his chances by telling Liz about his own struggling business. But he takes the risk. When he explains to Liz that he spends 50 minutes of every hour making 5 smoothies and 10 minutes making 5 salads, Liz's eyes pop. "Have I got a deal for you!" she exclaims.

Here's the deal that Liz sketches on a paper napkin. Joe stops making smoothies and allocates all his time to producing salads. And Liz increases her production of smoothies to 35 an hour and cuts her production of salads to 5 an hour—see Table 3.3(a). They then trade. Liz sells Joe 10 smoothies and Joe sells Liz 20 salads—the price of a smoothie is 2 salads—see Table 3.3(b).

After the trade, Joe has 10 salads—the 30 he produces minus the 20 he sells to Liz. And he has the 10 smoothies that he buys from Liz. So Joe doubles the quantities of smoothies and salads he can sell—see Table 3.3(c). Liz has 25 smoothies—the 35 she produces minus the 10 she sells to Joe. And she has 25 salads—the 5 she produces plus the 20 she buys from Joe—see Table 3.3(c). Both Liz and Joe gain 5 smoothies and 5 salads—see Table 3.3(d).

Liz draws a figure (Figure 3.10) to illustrate her suggestion. The red *PPF* is Joe's and the blue *PPF* is Liz's. They are each producing at the points marked *A*. Liz's proposal is that they each produce at the points marked *B*. They then trade—exchange—smoothies and salads at a price of 2 salads per smoothie, or 1/2 of a smoothie per salad. Liz gets salads for 1/2 a smoothie each, which is less than the 1 smoothie that it costs her to produce them. And Joe gets smoothies for 2 salads each, which is less than the 5 salads it costs him to produce them. Each moves to the points marked *C, outside* their respective *PPFs*.

Absolute advantage
When one person is more productive than another person in several or even all activities.

TABLE 3.3 LIZ AND JOE GAIN FROM TRADE

(a) Production	Liz	Joe
Smoothies	35	0
Salads	5	30

(b) Trade		
Smoothies	sell 10	buy 10
Salads	buy 20	sell 20

(c) After Trade		
Smoothies	25	10
Salads	25	10

(d) Gains from Trade		
Smoothies	+5	+5
Salads	+5	+5

FIGURE 3.10
The Gains from Specialization

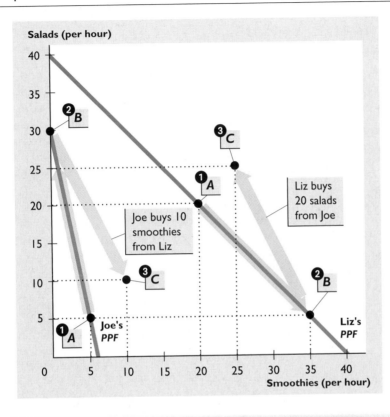

❶ Liz and Joe each produce at point A on their respective *PPFs*. Liz has a comparative advantage in smoothies, and Joe has a comparative advantage in salads.

❷ Joe specializes in salads and Liz increases her production of smoothies, so they each produce at point B on their respective *PPFs*.

❸ They exchange smoothies for salads at a price of 2 salads per smoothie. Each goes to C— a point outside their individual *PPFs*. They each gain 5 salads and 5 smoothies.

REALITY CHECK

Comparative Advantage in YOUR Life

What you have learned in this chapter has huge implications for the way you organize your life and for the position that you take on the political hot potato of global outsourcing.

1. Just as an economy expands its production possibilities by accumulating capital, so also you will expand your production possibilities by accumulating *human* capital.

2. By discovering *your* comparative advantage, you will be able to focus on producing the items that make you as well off as possible. Think hard about what you enjoy doing and that you do comparatively better than others.

3. Regardless of whether outsourcing is around the corner (like Liz and Joe) or around the globe (like the United States and India), both parties gain by exploiting their comparative advantage.

5 **Explain how people gain from specialization and trade.**

Practice Problem 3.5

TABLE 1 TONY'S PRODUCTION POSSIBILITIES

Snowboards (per week)		Skis (per week)
25	and	0
20	and	10
15	and	20
10	and	30
5	and	40
0	and	50

TABLE 2 PATTY'S PRODUCTION POSSIBILITIES

Snowboards (per week)		Skis (per week)
20	and	0
10	and	5
0	and	10

1. Tony and Patty produce skis and snowboards. Tables 1 and 2 show their production possibilities per week. Each week, Tony produces 5 snowboards and 40 skis and Patty produces 10 snowboards and 5 skis.
   a. Calculate Tony's opportunity cost of a snowboard.
   b. Calculate Patty's opportunity cost of a snowboard.
   c. Who has a comparative advantage in producing snowboards?
   d. Who has a comparative advantage in producing skis?
   e. If they specialize and trade 1 snowboard for 1 ski, who will gain?

Exercise 3.5

1. Sara and Sid produce boards and sails for windsurfing. Tables 3 and 4 show their production possibilities per week. Each week, Sara produces 6 boards and 6 sails, and Sid produces 24 boards and 24 sails.
   a. Calculate Sara's opportunity cost of a board.
   b. Calculate Sid's opportunity cost of a board.
   c. Who has a comparative advantage in producing boards?
   d. Who has a comparative advantage in producing sails?
   e. Can Sara and Sid gain by changing their production and trading 1 board for 1 sail? Explain why or why not.

TABLE 3 SARA'S PRODUCTION POSSIBILITIES

Boards (per week)		Sails (per week)
15	and	0
12	and	2
9	and	4
6	and	6
3	and	8
0	and	10

TABLE 4 SID'S PRODUCTION POSSIBILITIES

Boards (per week)		Sails (per week)
40	and	0
32	and	12
24	and	24
16	and	36
8	and	48
0	and	60

Solution to Practice Problem 3.5

1a. Tony's production possibilities show that to produce 5 more snowboards he must produce 10 fewer skis. So for Tony, the opportunity cost of producing a snowboard is 2 skis.

1b. Patty's production possibilities show that to produce 10 more snowboards, she must produce 5 fewer skis. So for Patty, the opportunity cost of producing a snowboard is 1/2 a ski.

1c. Patty has a comparative advantage in producing snowboards because her opportunity cost of producing a snowboard is less than Tony's.

1d. Tony has a comparative advantage in producing skis. For each ski produced, Tony gives up making 1/2 a snowboard. His opportunity cost of a ski is 1/2 a snowboard. For each ski that Patty produces, she must give up producing 2 snowboards. Her opportunity cost of a ski is 2 snowboards. So Tony's opportunity cost of a ski is lower than Patty's.

1e. Patty specializes in snowboards, and Tony specializes in skis. Patty produces 20 snowboards and Tony produces 50 skis. Before specializing, they produced 15 snowboards (10 by Patty and 5 by Tony) and 45 skis (40 by Tony and 5 by Patty). By specializing, they have increased their total output by 5 snowboards and 5 skis. They can share this gain by trading 1 ski for 1 snowboard. Patty can get skis from Tony for less than it costs her to produce them. Tony can buy snowboards from Patty for less than it cost him to produce them. Both Patty and Tony achieve gains from specialization and trade.

CHAPTER CHECKPOINT

Key Points

1   Use the production possibilities frontier to illustrate the economic problem.

- The production possibilities frontier, *PPF*, describes the limits to what can be produced by fully and efficiently using all the available resources.
- Points inside and on the *PPF* are attainable. Points outside the *PPF* are unattainable.
- Production at any point on the *PPF* achieves production efficiency. Production at a point inside the *PPF* is inefficient.
- When production is efficient—on the *PPF*—people face a tradeoff. If production is at a point inside the *PPF*, there is a free lunch.

2   Calculate opportunity cost.

- Along the *PPF*, the opportunity cost of *X* (the item on the *x*-axis) is the decrease in *Y* (the item on the *y*-axis) divided by the increase in *X*.
- The opportunity cost of *Y* is the inverse of the opportunity cost of *X*.
- The opportunity cost of producing a good increases as the quantity of the good produced increases.

3   Define efficiency and describe an efficient use of resources.

- Resource use is efficient when there is production efficiency and allocative efficiency.
- Production efficiency occurs at *all* points *on* the *PPF*.
- Allocative efficiency occurs at the *one* point on the *PPF* at which marginal benefit equals marginal cost.

4   Explain what makes production possibilities expand.

- Technological change and increases in capital and human capital expand production possibilities.
- The opportunity cost of economic growth is the decrease in current consumption.

5   Explain how people gain from specialization and trade.

- A person has a comparative advantage in an activity if he or she can perform that activity at a lower opportunity cost than someone else.
- People gain by increasing the production of the item in which they have a comparative advantage and trading.

Key Terms

Absolute advantage, 82	Economic growth, 79	Production possibilities frontier, 62
Allocative efficiency, 72	Free lunch, 65	Tradeoff, 65
Comparative advantage, 81	Production efficiency, 64	

myeconlab

Exercises

TABLE 1

Corn (bushels per year)		Beef (pounds per year)
1,000	and	0
800	and	900
600	and	1,200
400	and	1,400
200	and	1,450
0	and	1,500

TABLE 2

Entertainment (units)		Good food (units)
100	and	0
80	and	30
60	and	50
40	and	60
20	and	65
0	and	67

TABLE 3

Movies (per week)	Marginal cost	Marginal benefit
	(CDs per movie)	
1	2	8
2	4	6
3	6	4
4	8	2
5	10	0

TABLE 4

Robot services (units per year)		Consumption goods (units per year)
0	and	2,000
1	and	1,900
2	and	1,700
3	and	1,400
4	and	1,000
5	and	500

1. Table 1 shows the quantities of corn and beef that a farm can produce.
   a. Draw a graph of the farm's production possibilities frontier.
   b. Can the farm produce 500 bushels of corn and 500 pounds of beef a year?
   c. Can the farm produce 800 bushels of corn and 1,200 pounds of beef a year?
   d. What is the opportunity cost of the farm increasing beef production from 900 pounds to 1,200 pounds a year?
   e. If the farm produces 400 bushels of corn and 1,400 pounds of beef a year, is the farm using its resources efficiently? Explain your answer.

2. On Leisure Island, the only resources are 5 units of capital and 10 hours of labor a day. Table 2 shows the maximum quantities of entertainment and good food that Leisure Island can produce.
   a. Draw Leisure Island's production possibilities frontier.
   b. Is an output of 50 units of entertainment and 50 units of good food attainable? If so, is production efficient? What would be the opportunity cost of producing an additional unit of entertainment?
   c. Is an output of 40 units of entertainment and 60 units of good food attainable? If so, what would be the opportunity cost of producing an additional unit of entertainment? Do the people on Leisure Island face a tradeoff?
   d. What can you say about the opportunity cost of a unit of good food as the people on Leisure Island allocate more resources to producing good food?
   e. What is the marginal cost of a unit of entertainment when Leisure Island produces 60 units of entertainment and 50 units of good food?
   f. If the efficient quantity of entertainment is 40 units, what is the marginal benefit from entertainment?

3. Table 3 gives Taylor's marginal cost of and marginal benefit from a movie.
   a. If Taylor sees 2 movies a week, what must she give up to see a third movie?
   b. If Taylor sees 2 movies a week, what is she willing to give up to see a third movie?
   c. What is Taylor's efficient number of movies per week?

4. Tommy spends 5 hours per night playing chess online. He really enjoys playing chess, but over recent weeks, his economics grade has dropped. Tommy makes a rational decision to spend only 2 hours per night playing chess online. When Tommy spent 5 hours per night playing chess, did his marginal cost exceed his marginal benefit or did his marginal benefit exceed his marginal cost? Explain.

5. Table 4 shows the quantities of robots and consumption goods that the country Alpha can produce along its production possibilities frontier.
   a. If Alpha produces 2,000 units of consumption goods a year, will Alpha experience economic growth? Explain.
   b. If Alpha produces 1,100 units of consumption goods a year, will Alpha experience economic growth? Explain.
   c. If Alpha currently produces no robots and now decides to produce 1 robot a year, what is the cost of its economic growth?

6. People can now obtain music from Web sites such as iTunes and MP3.com.
   a. Have these Web sites changed the *PPF* for recorded music and other goods and services? If so, how has it changed?
   b. Is there still a tradeoff between recorded music and other goods and services, or is the opportunity cost of recorded music now zero?

7. AIDS has become an acute problem in Africa.
   a. How has the spread of AIDS influenced the *PPF* of the economies of Africa?
   b. Has the spread of AIDS increased the opportunity cost of some goods and services? Has it decreased the opportunity cost of anything?

8. A farm grows wheat and produces pigs. The marginal cost of producing each of these products increases as more of it is produced.
   a. Make a graph that illustrates the farm's *PPF*.
   b. The farm adopts a new technology, which allows the farm to use fewer resources to fatten pigs. Use your graph to illustrate the impact of the new technology on the farm's *PPF*.
   c. With the farm using the new technology in part **b**, has the opportunity cost of producing a ton of wheat changed? If so, how? If not, why not?

9. Explain how each of the following items might change the U.S. production possibilities frontier. In each case, is an opportunity cost incurred? If so, what is it? If not, why not?
   a. The government of California spends more on education.
   b. CNN hires more reporters to cover breaking news stories from around the world.
   c. Google announces a new intelligent search engine.
   d. A severe frost wipes out the Florida citrus crop.
   e. Wild brushfires sweep through large parts of California and Arizona.

10. Table 5 sets out Tom's production possibilities and Table 6 sets out Tessa's production possibilities. Tom allocates all his resources and produces 2 bats and 20 balls an hour. Tessa allocates all her resources and produces 2 bats and 40 balls an hour.
    a. Calculate Tom's opportunity cost of a ball.
    b. Calculate Tessa's opportunity cost of a ball.
    c. Who has a comparative advantage in producing balls?
    d. Who has a comparative advantage in producing bats?
    e. If Tom or Tessa specialized in producing the good in which he or she has a comparative advantage and they traded 1 bat for 15 balls, who would gain from the specialization and trade and why?

11. Mexico has 100 million workers, and each worker can produce 3 cars a year or 3 tons of steel a year. Canada has 25 million workers, and each worker in Canada can produce 10 cars a year or 6 tons of steel a year. Suppose that each country produces only cars and steel.
    a. Draw a graph of Canada's production possibilities frontier.
    b. Draw a graph of Mexico's production possibilities frontier.
    c. Calculate the opportunity cost of producing 1 ton of steel in each country.
    d. Calculate the opportunity cost of producing 1 car in each country.
    e. Does either country have an absolute advantage? If so, which one and why?
    f. In which country is the marginal cost of producing a car lower?

TABLE 5

Bats (per hour)		Balls (per hour)
0	and	40
1	and	30
2	and	20
3	and	10
4	and	0

TABLE 6

Bats (per hour)		Balls (per hour)
0	and	80
1	and	60
2	and	40
3	and	20
4	and	0

Critical Thinking

12. Think about the production of music and the effects of the technological changes that first brought the Walkman, then the Discman, and then the iPod.
    a. How might you go about finding the opportunity cost of listening to an hour of music using each of the technologies?
    b. How do you think each new technology changed the opportunity cost of listening to an hour of recorded music?
    c. Do you think any of the new technologies had an absolute advantage over its predecessor?
    d. Do you think any of the new technologies had a comparative advantage over its predecessor?

13. You have chosen to bear the opportunity cost of remaining in school to obtain a degree. Explain, using the concepts of rational choice, marginal cost, and marginal benefit:
    a. Why have you made this choice?
    b. Why did Bill Gates quit school before completing his degree?
    c. Why do so many people quit school at the end of grade 12?
    d. What can the government do to encourage more people to attend college?

14. The Kyoto agreement requires countries to achieve greenhouse gas reduction targets over the next ten years. The Canadian government has signed the Kyoto agreement, but the U.S. government will not sign it.
    a. As the Canadian government allocates more resources over the next ten years to reducing pollution, how will the Canadian *PPF* change?
    b. Do you think that Canadian economic growth will change by more than U.S. economic growth changes? Or will growth in neither country be affected? Explain your answer.
    c. Do you think that Canada will gain or lose some of its comparative advantage relative to the United States? Explain your answer.

Web Exercises

Use the links on MyEconLab to work the following exercises.

15. Visit the U.S. Census Bureau population clocks.
    a. What is the estimated population of the United States?
    b. What is the estimated population of the world?
    c. How fast is the U.S. population increasing? (Use the second timer on your computer clock to determine the pace of increase.)
    d. How fast is the world population increasing?
    e. What do the population increases that you've found imply about the U.S. *PPF* and the world *PPF*? Which is moving faster?

16. Review the article "Chicago School Tradeoff" on the New Republic Web site.
    a. What does the article report about opinion in the United States about outsourcing?
    b. How would you reconcile the reported views of people as producers and consumers?
    c. On the basis of what you have learned in this chapter, write a brief note that explains why you agree or disagree with the position taken by the author.

Demand and Supply

CHAPTER 4

CHAPTER CHECKLIST

When you have completed your study of this chapter, you will be able to

1 Distinguish between quantity demanded and demand and explain what determines demand.

2 Distinguish between quantity supplied and supply and explain what determines supply.

3 Explain how demand and supply determine price and quantity in a market and explain the effects of changes in demand and supply.

When gasoline prices are rising, many people blame greedy oil companies. But aren't the oil companies always greedy? Weren't they greedy when prices were low and stable? It isn't difficult to see that greedy oil companies are not the source of high or rising gas prices.

To explain rising prices, we need to point to some factor that has changed. And we need to understand the forces at work. Those forces are demand and supply. Economists use the demand and supply model to explain how markets work. Greed—or self-interest as economists prefer to call it—lies at the core of the model. The demand and supply model explains how the self-interested decisions of buyers and sellers end up being compatible and how they determine market prices. And it explains how those prices in turn influence what, how, and for whom goods and services get produced.

COMPETITIVE MARKETS

When you need a new pair of running shoes, want a bagel and a latte, or need to fly home for Thanksgiving, you must find a place where people sell those items or offer those services. The place in which you find them is a *market*.

You learned in Chapter 2 that a market is any arrangement that brings buyers and sellers together. A market has two sides: buyers (demanders) and sellers (suppliers). There are markets for *goods* such as apples and hiking boots, for *services* such as haircuts and tennis lessons, for *resources* such as computer programmers and tractors, and for other manufactured *inputs* such as memory chips and auto parts. There are also markets for money such as Japanese yen and for financial securities such as Yahoo! stock. Only imagination limits what can be traded in markets.

Some markets are physical places where buyers and sellers meet and where an auctioneer or a broker helps to determine the prices. Examples of this type of market are the New York Stock Exchange; wholesale fish, meat, and produce markets; and used car auctions.

Some markets are groups of people spread around the world who never meet and know little about each other but are connected through the Internet or by telephone. Examples of this type of market are the e-commerce markets, currency markets, and Internet auctions such as eBay.

But most markets are unorganized collections of buyers and sellers. You do most of your trading in this type of market. An example is the market for basketball shoes. The buyers in this $3-billion-a-year market are the 45 million Americans who play basketball (or who want to make a fashion statement) and are looking for a new pair of shoes. The sellers are the tens of thousands of retail sports equipment and footwear stores. Each buyer can visit several different stores, and each seller knows that the buyer has a choice of stores.

Markets vary in the intensity of competition that buyers and sellers face. In this chapter, we're going to study a *competitive market* that has so many buyers and so many sellers that no single buyer or seller can influence the price.

Markets for running shoes ...

coffee and bagel ...

and airline travel.

4.1 DEMAND

First, we'll study the behavior of buyers in a competitive market. The **quantity demanded** of any good, service, or resource is the amount that people are willing and able to buy during a specified period at a specified price. For example, when spring water costs $1 a bottle, you decide to buy 2 bottles a day. The 2 bottles a day is your quantity demanded of spring water.

The quantity demanded is measured as an amount *per unit of time*. For example, your quantity demanded of water is 2 bottles *per day*. We could express this quantity as 14 bottles per week or some other number per month or per year. But without a time dimension, a particular number of bottles has no meaning.

Many things influence buying plans, and one of them is price. We look first at the relationship between quantity demanded and price. To study this relationship, we keep all other influences on buying plans the same and we ask: How, other things remaining the same, does the quantity demanded of a good change as its price varies? The law of demand provides the answer.

■ The Law of Demand

The **law of demand** states

> **Other things remaining the same, if the price of a good rises, the quantity demanded of that good decreases; and if the price of a good falls, the quantity demanded of that good increases.**

So the law of demand states that when all else remains the same, if the price of a Palm Pilot falls, people will buy more Palm Pilots; or if the price of a baseball ticket rises, people will buy fewer baseball tickets.

Why does the quantity demanded increase if the price falls, all other things remaining the same?

The answer is that, faced with a limited budget, people always have an incentive to find the best deals they can. If the price of one item falls and the prices of all other items remain the same, the item with the lower price is a better deal than it was before. So people buy more of this item. Suppose, for example, that the price of bottled water fell from $1 a bottle to 25 cents a bottle while the price of Gatorade remained at $1 a bottle. Wouldn't some people switch from Gatorade to water? By doing so, they save 75 cents a bottle, which they can spend on other things they previously couldn't afford.

Think about the things that you buy and ask yourself: Which of these items does *not* obey the law of demand? If the price of a new textbook were lower, other things remaining the same (including the price of a used textbook), would you buy more new textbooks? Then think about all the things that you do not now buy but would if you could afford them. How cheap would a PC have to be for you to buy *both* a desktop and a laptop? There is a price that is low enough to entice you!

■ Demand Schedule and Demand Curve

Demand is the relationship between the quantity demanded and the price of a good when all other influences on buying plans remain the same. The quantity demanded is *one* quantity at *one* price. *Demand is a list of quantities at different prices* illustrated by a demand schedule and a demand curve.

Quantity demanded
The amount of any good, service, or resource that people are willing and able to buy during a specified period at a specified price.

Demand
The relationship between the quantity demanded and the price of a good when all other influences on buying plans remain the same.

Demand schedule
A list of the quantities demanded at each different price when all the other influences on buying plans remain the same.

Demand curve
A graph of the relationship between the quantity demanded of a good and its price when all the other influences on buying plans remain the same.

A **demand schedule** is a list of the quantities demanded at each different price when *all the other influences on buying plans remain the same*. The table in Figure 4.1 is one person's (Tina's) demand schedule for bottled water. It tells us that if the price of water is $2.00 a bottle, Tina buys no water. Her quantity demanded is 0 bottles a day. If the price of water is $1.50 a bottle, her quantity demanded is 1 bottle a day. Tina's quantity demanded increases to 2 bottles a day at a price of $1.00 a bottle and to 3 bottles a day at a price of 50 cents a bottle.

A **demand curve** is a graph of the relationship between the quantity demanded of a good and its price when all the other influences on buying plans remain the same. The points on the demand curve labeled *A* through *D* represent the rows *A* through *D* of the demand schedule. For example, point *B* on the graph represents row *B* of the demand schedule and shows that the quantity demanded is 1 bottle a day when the price is $1.50 a bottle. Point *C* on the demand curve represents row *C* of the demand schedule and shows that the quantity demanded is 2 bottles a day when the price is $1.00 a bottle.

The downward slope of the demand curve illustrates the law of demand. Along the demand curve, when the price of the good *falls*, the quantity demanded *increases*. For example, in Figure 4.1, when the price of a bottle of water falls from $1.00 to 50 cents, the quantity demanded increases from 2 bottles a day to 3 bottles a day. And when the price *rises*, the quantity demanded *decreases*. For example, when the price rises from $1.00 to $1.50 a bottle, the quantity demanded decreases from 2 bottles a day to 1 bottle a day.

■ **FIGURE 4.1**
Demand Schedule and Demand Curve

The table shows a demand schedule that lists the quantity of water demanded at each price if all other influences on buying plans remain the same. At a price of $1.50 a bottle, the quantity demanded is 1 bottle a day.

The demand curve shows the relationship between the quantity demanded and price, everything else remaining the same. The downward-sloping demand curve illustrates the law of demand. When the price falls, the quantity demanded increases; and when the price rises, the quantity demanded decreases.

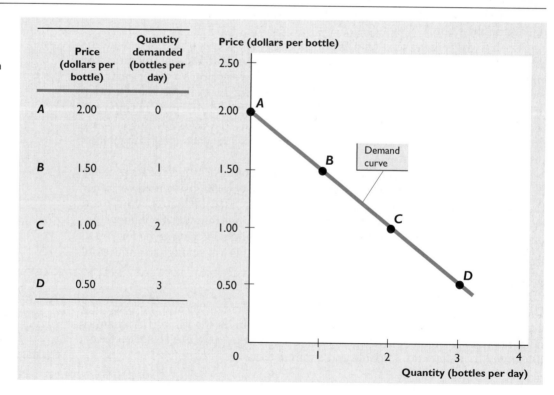

	Price (dollars per bottle)	Quantity demanded (bottles per day)
A	2.00	0
B	1.50	1
C	1.00	2
D	0.50	3

Individual Demand and Market Demand

The demand schedule and the demand curve that you've just studied are for one person. To study a market, we must determine the market demand.

Market demand is the sum of the demands of all the buyers in a market. To find the market demand, imagine a market in which there are only two buyers: Tina and Tim. The table in Figure 4.2 shows three demand schedules: Tina's, Tim's, and the market demand schedule. Tina's demand schedule is the same as before. It shows the quantity of water demanded by Tina at each different price. Tim's demand schedule tells us the quantity of water demanded by Tim at each price. To find the quantity of water demanded in the market, we sum the quantities demanded by Tina and Tim. For example, at a price of $1.00 a bottle, the quantity demanded by Tina is 2 bottles a day, the quantity demanded by Tim is 1 bottle a day, and so the quantity demanded in the market is 3 bottles a day.

Tina's demand curve in part (a) and Tim's demand curve in part (b) are graphs of the two individual demand schedules. The market demand curve in part (c) is a graph of the market demand schedule. At a given price, the quantity demanded on the market demand curve equals the horizontal sum of the quantities demanded on the individual demand curves.

Market demand
The sum of the demands of all the buyers in the market.

FIGURE 4.2
Individual Demand and Market Demand

Price (dollars per bottle)	Quantity demanded (bottles per day)		
	Tina	Tim	Market
2.00	0	0	0
1.50	1	0	1
1.00	2 +	1 =	3
0.50	3	2	5

The market demand schedule is the sum of the individual demand schedules, and the market demand curve is the horizontal sum of the individual demand curves.

At a price of $1 a bottle, the quantity demanded by Tina is 2 bottles a day and the quantity demanded by Tim is 1 bottle a day, so the total quantity demanded in the market is 3 bottles a day.

Price (dollars per bottle)

(a) Tina's demand

Price (dollars per bottle)

(b) Tim's demand

Price (dollars per bottle)

(c) Market demand

■ Changes in Demand

The demand curve shows how the quantity demanded changes when the price of the good changes but *all other influences on buying plans remain the same.* When any of these other influences on buying plans change, there is a **change in demand**, which means that there is a new demand schedule and new demand curve. *The demand curve shifts.*

Demand can either increase or decrease and Figure 4.3 illustrates the two cases. Initially, the demand curve is D_0. When demand decreases, the demand curve shifts leftward to D_1. On demand curve D_1, the quantity demanded at each price is smaller. And when demand increases, the demand curve shifts rightward to D_2. On demand curve D_2, the quantity demanded at each price is greater.

The main influences on buying plans that change demand are

- Prices of related goods
- Income
- Expectations
- Number of buyers
- Preferences

Prices of Related Goods

Every good has substitutes. A **substitute** for a good is another good that can be consumed in its place. Chocolate cake is a substitute for cheesecake, and bottled water is a substitute for Gatorade.

Many goods have complements. A **complement** of a good is another good that is consumed with it. Wrist guards are a complement of in-line skates, and bottled water is a complement of fitness center services.

Change in demand
A change in the quantity that people plan to buy when any influence on buying plans other than the price of the good changes.

Substitute
A good that can be consumed in place of another good.

Complement
A good that is consumed with another good.

▓ FIGURE 4.3
Changes in Demand

A change in any influence on buying plans, other than a change in the price of the good itself, changes demand and shifts the demand curve.

❶ When demand decreases, the demand curve shifts leftward from D_0 to D_1.

❷ When demand increases, the demand curve shifts rightward from D_0 to D_2.

A Change in the Price of a Substitute   The demand for a good *increases* if the price of one of its substitutes *rises;* and the demand for a good *decreases* if the price of one of its substitutes *falls.* That is, the demand for a good and the price of one of its substitutes move in the *same direction.* For example, the demand for cheesecake increases when the price of chocolate cake rises.

A Change in the Price of a Complement   The demand for a good *decreases* if the price of one of its complements *rises;* and the demand for a good *increases* if the price of one of its complements *falls.* That is, the demand for a good and the price of one of its complements move in *opposite directions.* For example, the demand for wrist guards decreases when the price of in-line skates rises.

Income

Faced with scarcity, people try to get the most out of their income. And when income increases, options expand. With a higher income, you might buy more of the things you're already buying or some things that you couldn't afford before. You might even stop buying some things and switch to something else.

A good is a **normal good** if a rise in income brings an increase in demand and a fall in income brings a decrease in demand. For example, if you buy more bottled water when your income increases, then bottled water is a normal good. Most goods are normal goods (hence the name).

A good is an **inferior good** if a rise in income brings a *decrease* in demand and a fall in income brings an *increase* in demand. For example, if when your income increases, you buy fewer plastic milk crates and more bookcases, then a plastic milk crate is an inferior good.

Normal good
A good for which demand increases when income increases and demand decreases when income decreases.

Inferior good
A good for which demand decreases when income increases and demand increases when income decreases.

Expectations

Expected future income and prices influence demand. For example, you are offered a well-paid summer job, so you go to Cancun during spring break. Your demand for vacation travel has increased. Or if you expect the price of ramen noodles to rise next week, you buy a big enough stockpile of it now to get you through the rest of the school year. Your demand for ramen noodles today has increased.

Number of Buyers

The greater the number of buyers in a market, the larger is demand. For example, the demand for parking spaces, movies, bottled water, or just about anything is greater in New York City than it is in Boise, Idaho.

Preferences

Tastes or *preferences,* as economists call them, influence demand. When preferences change, the demand for one item increases and the demand for another item (or items) decreases. For example, preferences have changed as people have become better informed about the health hazards of tobacco. This change in preferences has decreased the demand for cigarettes and has increased the demand for nicotine patches.

Preferences also change when new goods become available. For example, the development of MP3 technology has decreased the demand for CDs and has increased the demand for Internet service and MP3 players.

■ Change in Quantity Demanded Versus Change in Demand

The influences on buyers' plans you've just considered bring a *change in demand*. These are all the influences on buying plans *except for the price of the good*. To avoid confusion, when *the price of the good changes* and all other influences on buying plans remain the same, we say there has been a **change in the quantity demanded**.

The distinction between a change in demand and a change in the quantity demanded is crucial for figuring out how a market responds to the forces that hit it. Figure 4.4 illustrates and summarizes the distinction:

Change in the quantity demanded
A change in the quantity of a good that people plan to buy that results from a change in the price of the good with all other influences on buying plans remaining the same.

- If the price of bottled water *rises* when everything else remains the same, the quantity demanded of bottled water *decreases* and there is a *movement up* along the demand curve D_0. If the price *falls* when everything else remains the same, the quantity demanded *increases* and there is a *movement down* along the demand curve D_0.
- If some influence on buyers' plans other than the price of bottled water changes, there is a change in demand. When the demand for bottled water *decreases*, the demand curve *shifts leftward* to D_1. When the demand for bottled water *increases*, the demand curve *shifts rightward* to D_2.

When you are thinking about the influences on demand, try to get into the habit of asking: Does this influence change the quantity demanded or does it change demand? The test is: Did the price of the good change or did some other influence change? If the price changed, then quantity demanded changed. If some other influence changed and the price remained constant, then demand changed.

■ **FIGURE 4.4**

Change in Quantity Demanded Versus Change in Demand

❶ **A decrease in the quantity demanded**

If the price of a good rises, *cet. par.*, the quantity demanded decreases. There is a movement up along the demand curve D_0.

❷ **A decrease in demand**

Demand decreases and the demand curve shifts leftward (from D_0 to D_1) if

- The price of a substitute falls.
- The price of a complement rises.
- The price of the good is expected to fall or income is expected to fall in the future.
- Income decreases.*
- The number of buyers decreases.

* Bottled water is a normal good.

❸ **An increase in the quantity demanded**

If the price of a good falls, *cet. par.*, the quantity demanded increases. There is a movement down along the demand curve D_0.

❹ **An increase in demand**

Demand increases and the demand curve shifts rightward (from D_0 to D_2) if

- The price of a substitute rises.
- The price of a complement falls.
- The price of the good is expected to rise or income is expected to rise in the future.
- Income increases.*
- The number of buyers increases.

CHECKPOINT 4.1

1 Distinguish between quantity demanded and demand and explain what determines demand.

Practice Problem 4.1

1. In the market for cell phones, several events occur, one at a time. Explain the influence of each event on the quantity demanded of cell phones and on the demand for cell phones. Use a graph to illustrate the effects of each event. Does any event (or events) illustrate the law of demand? The events are
   a. The price of a cell phone falls.
   b. The price of a call made from a cell phone falls.
   c. After a public outcry against the ringing of cell phones, cities and towns ban cell phones from public places.
   d. Incomes increase.
   e. Rumor has it that the price of a cell phone will rise next month.
   f. With the introduction of camera phones, cell phones are more popular.

Exercise 4.1

1. In the market for Caribbean cruises, several events occur, one at a time. Explain the influence of each event on the quantity demanded of Caribbean cruises and the demand for Caribbean cruises. Use a graph to illustrate the effects of each event. Does any event illustrate the law of demand? The events are
   a. Caribbean cruises become more popular.
   b. The price of a Caribbean cruise rises.
   c. The price of a cruise to Asia falls.
   d. Celebrity Cruises launches its new "students only" Caribbean cruises.
   e. People expect the price of a Caribbean cruise to fall next season.
   f. Cruise companies increase the number of leading rock artists for their onboard entertainment.

FIGURE I

Solution to Practice Problem 4.1

1a. A fall in the price of a cell phone increases the quantity demanded of cell phones, shown by a movement down along the demand curve for cell phones (Figure 1) and is an example of the law of demand in action.

1b. A call made from a cell phone is a complement of a cell phone. So when the price of a call from a cell phone falls, the demand for cell phones increases. The demand curve shifts rightward (Figure 2).

1c. The ban on using cell phones in public places changes preferences and decreases the demand for cell phones. The demand curve shifts leftward (Figure 2).

1d. A cell phone is (likely) a normal good. So when income increases, the demand for cell phones increases. The demand curve for cell phones shifts rightward (Figure 2).

1e. A rise in the expected price of a cell phone increases the demand for cell phones now. The demand curve for cell phones shifts rightward (Figure 2).

1f. An increase in the number of buyers increases the demand for cell phones. The demand curve shifts rightward (Figure 2).

FIGURE 2

4.2 SUPPLY

A market has two sides. On one side are the buyers, or demanders, that we've just studied. On the other side of the market are the sellers, or suppliers. We now study the forces that determine suppliers' plans.

The **quantity supplied** of a good, service, or resource is the amount that people are willing and able to sell during a specified period at a specified price. For example, when the price of spring water is $1.50 a bottle, a spring owner decides to sell 2,000 bottles a day. The 2,000 bottles a day is the quantity supplied of spring water by this individual producer. (As in the case of demand, the quantity supplied is measured as an amount *per unit of time*.)

Quantity supplied
The amount of any good, service, or resource that people are willing and able to sell during a specified period at a specified price.

Many things influence selling plans, and one of them is the price. We look first at the relationship between quantity supplied of a good and its price. To study this relationship, we keep all other influences on selling plans the same. And we ask: How, other things remaining the same, does the quantity supplied of a good change as its price varies? The law of supply provides the answer.

■ The Law of Supply

The **law of supply** states

> **Other things remaining the same, if the price of a good rises, the quantity supplied of that good increases; and if the price of a good falls, the quantity supplied of that good decreases.**

So the law of supply states that when all else remains the same, if the price of bottled water rises, spring owners will offer more water for sale; if the price of a CD falls, Sony Corp. will offer fewer CDs for sale.

Why, other things remaining the same, does the quantity supplied increase if the price rises and decrease if the price falls? Part of the answer lies in the principle of increasing opportunity cost (see p. 70). Because factors of production are not equally productive in all activities, as more of a good is produced, the opportunity cost of producing it increases. A higher price provides the incentive to bear the higher opportunity cost of increased production. Another part of the answer is that for a given cost, the higher price brings a larger profit, so sellers have greater incentive to increase production.

Think about the resources that you own and can offer for sale to others and ask yourself: Which of these items does *not* obey the law of supply? If the wage rate for summer jobs increased, would you have an incentive to work longer hours and bear the higher opportunity cost of forgone leisure? If the bank offered a higher interest rate on deposits, would you have an incentive to save more and bear the higher opportunity cost of forgone consumption? If the used book dealer offered a higher price for last year's textbooks, would you have an incentive to sell that handy math text and bear the higher opportunity cost of visiting the library when you needed to check a formula?

■ Supply Schedule and Supply Curve

Supply
The relationship between the quantity supplied and the price of a good when all other influences on selling plans remain the same.

Supply is the relationship between the quantity supplied and the price of a good when all other influences on selling plans remain the same. The quantity supplied is *one* quantity at *one* price. *Supply* is a *list of quantities at different prices* illustrated by a supply schedule and a supply curve.

A **supply schedule** lists the quantities supplied at each different price when all the other influences on selling plans remain the same. The table in Figure 4.5 is one firm's (Agua's) supply schedule for bottled water. It tells us that if the price of water is 50 cents a bottle, Agua plans to sell no water. Its quantity supplied is 0 bottles a day. If the price of water is $1.00 a bottle, Agua's quantity supplied is 1,000 bottles a day. Agua's quantity supplied increases to 2,000 bottles a day at a price of $1.50 a bottle and to 3,000 bottles a day at a price of $2.00 a bottle.

A **supply curve** is a graph of the relationship between the quantity supplied of a good and its price when all the other influences on selling plans remain the same. The points on the supply curve labeled *A* through *D* represent the rows *A* through *D* of the supply schedule. For example, point *C* on the supply curve represents row *C* of the supply schedule and shows that the quantity supplied is 1,000 bottles a day when the price is $1.00 a bottle. Point *B* on the supply curve represents row *B* of the supply schedule and shows that the quantity supplied is 2,000 bottles a day when the price is $1.50 a bottle.

The upward slope of the supply curve illustrates the law of supply. Along the supply curve, when the price of the good *rises*, the quantity supplied *increases*. For example, in Figure 4.5, when the price of a bottle of water rises from $1.50 to $2.00, the quantity supplied increases from 2,000 bottles a day to 3,000 bottles a day. And when the price *falls*, the quantity supplied *decreases*. For example, when the price falls from $1.50 to $1.00 a bottle, the quantity supplied decreases from 2,000 bottles a day to 1,000 bottles a day.

Supply schedule
A list of the quantities supplied at each different price when all the other influences on selling plans remain the same.

Supply curve
A graph of the relationship between the quantity supplied of a good and its price when all the other influences on selling plans remain the same.

■ **FIGURE 4.5**

Supply Schedule and Supply Curve

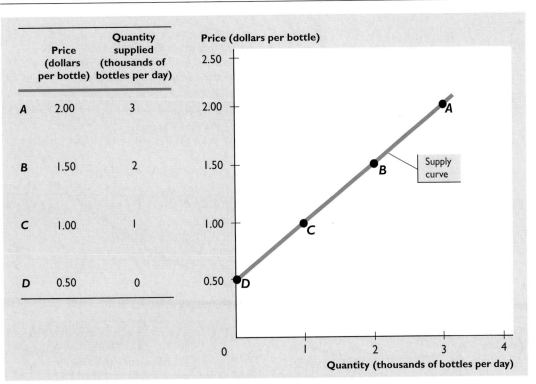

	Price (dollars per bottle)	Quantity supplied (thousands of bottles per day)
A	2.00	3
B	1.50	2
C	1.00	1
D	0.50	0

The table shows a supply schedule that lists the quantity of water supplied at each price if all other influences on selling plans remain the same. At a price of $1.50 a bottle, the quantity supplied is 2,000 bottles a day.

The supply curve shows the relationship between the quantity supplied and price, everything else remaining the same. The upward-sloping supply curve illustrates the law of supply. When the price rises, the quantity supplied increases; and when the price falls, the quantity supplied decreases.

Market supply
The sum of the supplies of all the sellers in the market.

■ Individual Supply and Market Supply

The supply schedule and the supply curve that you've just studied are for one seller. To study a market, we must determine the market supply.

Market supply is the sum of the supplies of all the sellers in the market. To find the market supply of water, imagine a market in which there are only two sellers: Agua and Prima. The table in Figure 4.6 shows three supply schedules: Agua's, Prima's, and the market supply schedule. Agua's supply schedule is the same as before. Prima's supply schedule tells us the quantity of water that Prima plans to sell at each price. To find the quantity of water supplied in the market, we sum the quantities supplied by Agua and Prima. For example, at a price of $1.00 a bottle, the quantity supplied by Agua is 1,000 bottles a day, the quantity supplied by Prima is 2,000 bottles a day, and the quantity supplied in the market is 3,000 bottles a day.

Agua's supply curve in part (a) and Prima's supply curve in part (b) are graphs of the two individual supply schedules. The market supply curve in part (c) is a graph of the market supply schedule. At a given price, the quantity supplied on the market supply curve equals the horizontal sum of the quantities supplied on the individual supply curves.

■ **FIGURE 4.6**
Individual Supply and Market Supply

Price (dollars per bottle)	Quantity supplied (thousands of bottles per day)		
	Agua	Prima	Market
2.00	3	4	7
1.50	2	3	5
1.00	1 +	2 =	3
0.50	0	0	0

The market supply schedule is the sum of the individual supply schedules, and the market supply curve is the horizontal sum of the individual supply curves.

At a price of $1 a bottle, the quantity supplied by Agua is 1,000 bottles a day and the quantity supplied by Prima is 2,000 bottles a day, so the total quantity supplied in the market is 3,000 bottles a day.

(a) Agua's supply

(b) Prima's supply

(c) Market supply

■ Changes in Supply

The supply curve shows how the quantity supplied changes when the price of the good changes but *all other influences on selling plans remain the same.* When any of these other influences on selling plans change, there is a **change in supply**, which means that there is a new supply schedule and new supply curve. *The supply curve shifts.*

Supply can either increase or decrease, and Figure 4.7 illustrates the two cases. Initially, the supply curve is S_0. When supply decreases, the supply curve shifts leftward to S_1. On supply curve S_1, the quantity supplied at each price is smaller. And when supply increases, the supply curve shifts rightward to S_2. On supply curve S_2, the quantity supplied at each price is greater.

The main influences on selling plans that change supply are

- Prices of related goods
- Prices of resources and other inputs
- Expectations
- Number of sellers
- Productivity

Change in supply
A change in the quantity that suppliers plan to sell when any influence on selling plans other than the price of the good changes.

Prices of Related Goods

Related goods are either substitutes *in production* or complements *in production.* A **substitute in production** for a good is another good that can be produced in its place. Button-fly jeans are substitutes in production for cargo pants in a clothing factory.

A **complement in production** of a good is another good that is produced along with it. Cream is a complement in production of skim milk in a dairy.

Substitute in production
A good that can be produced in place of another good.

Complement in production
A good that is produced along with another good.

■ FIGURE 4.7

Changes in Supply

A change in any influence on selling plans other than a change in the price of the good itself changes supply and shifts the supply curve.

❶ When supply decreases, the supply curve shifts leftward from S_0 to S_1.

❷ When supply increases, the supply curve shifts rightward from S_0 to S_2.

A Change in the Price of a Substitute in Production The supply of a good *decreases* if the price of one of its substitutes in production *rises;* and the supply of a good *increases* if the price of one of its substitutes in production *falls.* That is, the supply of a good and the price of one of its substitutes in production move in *opposite directions.* For example, a clothing factory can produce cargo pants or button-fly jeans, so these goods are substitutes in production. When the price of button-fly jeans rises, the clothing factory switches production from cargo pants to button-fly jeans, so the supply of cargo pants decreases.

A Change in the Price of a Complement in Production The supply of a good *increases* if the price of one of its complements in production *rises;* and the supply of a good *decreases* if the price of one of its complements in production *falls.* That is, the supply of a good and the price of one of its complements in production move in the *same direction.* For example, when a dairy produces skim milk, it also produces cream, so these goods are complements in production. When the price of skim milk rises, the dairy produces more skim milk, so the supply of cream increases.

Prices of Resources and Other Inputs

Supply changes when the price of a resource or other input used to produce the good changes. The reason is that resource and input prices influence the cost of production. And the more it costs to produce a good, the smaller is the quantity supplied of that good at each price (other things remaining the same). For example, if the wage rate of bottling-plant workers rises, it costs more to produce a bottle of water. So the supply of bottled water decreases.

Expectations

Expectations about future prices influence supply. For example, a severe frost that wipes out Florida's citrus crop doesn't change the production of orange juice today. But it will decrease production later in the year when the current crop would normally have been harvested. So people expect the price of orange juice to rise in the future. To get the higher future price, some firms will increase their inventory of frozen juice, and this action decreases the supply of juice today.

Number of Sellers

The greater the number of sellers in a market, the larger is the supply. For example, many new sellers have developed springs and water-bottling plants in the United States, and the supply of bottled water has increased.

Productivity

Productivity is output per unit of input. An increase in productivity lowers the cost of producing the good and increases its supply. A decrease in productivity has the opposite effect and decreases supply.

Technological change and the increased use of capital increase productivity. For example, advances in electronic technology have lowered the cost of producing a computer and increased the supply of computers. Technological change brings new goods such as the iPod, the supply of which was previously zero.

Natural events such as severe weather and earthquakes decrease productivity and decrease supply. For example, the Indian Ocean tsunami of 2004 decreased the supply of many agricultural products, fish, and seafood in many areas of Asia.

■ Change in Quantity Supplied Versus Change in Supply

The influences on sellers' plans you've just considered bring a *change in supply*. These are all the influences on sellers' plans *except the price of the good*. To avoid confusion, when the *price of the good changes* and all other influences on selling plans remain the same, we say there has been a **change in the quantity supplied**.

The distinction between a change in supply and a change in the quantity supplied is crucial for figuring out how a market responds to the forces that hit it. Figure 4.8 illustrates and summarizes the distinction:

- If the price of bottled water *falls* when other things remain the same, the quantity supplied of bottled water *decreases* and there is a *movement down* along the supply curve S_0. If the price *rises* when other things remain the same, the quantity supplied *increases* and there is a *movement up* along the supply curve S_0.
- If any influence on water bottlers' plans other than the price of bottled water changes, there is a change in the supply of bottled water. When the supply of bottled water *decreases*, the supply curve *shifts leftward* to S_1. When the supply of bottled water *increases*, the supply curve *shifts rightward* to S_2.

When you are thinking about the influences on supply, get into the habit of asking: Does this influence change the quantity supplied or does it change supply? The test is: Did the price change or did some other influence change? If the price of the good changed, then quantity supplied changed. If some other influence changed and the price of the good remained constant, then supply changed.

Change in the quantity supplied
A change in the quantity of a good that suppliers plan to sell that results from a change in the price of the good.

■ **FIGURE 4.8**
Change in Quantity Supplied Versus Change in Supply

❶ A decrease in the quantity supplied

If the price of a good falls, *cet. par.*, the quantity supplied decreases. There is a movement down along the demand curve S_0.

❷ A decrease in supply

Supply decreases and the supply curve shifts leftward (from S_0 to S_1) if

- The price of a substitute in production rises.
- The price of a complement in production falls.
- A resource price or other input price rises.
- The price of the good is expected to rise.
- The number of sellers decreases.
- Productivity decreases.

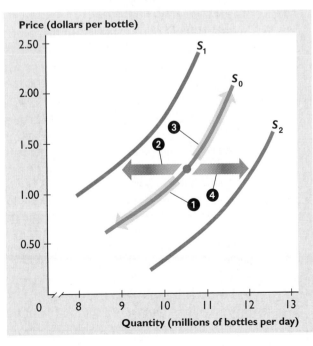

❸ An increase in the quantity supplied

If the price of a good rises, *cet. par.*, the quantity supplied increases. There is a movement up along the supply curve S_0.

❹ An increase in supply

Supply increases and the supply curve shifts rightward (from S_0 to S_2) if

- The price of a substitute in production falls.
- The price of a complement in production rises.
- A resource price or other input price falls.
- The price of the good is expected to fall.
- The number of sellers increases.
- Productivity increases.

2 **Distinguish between quantity supplied and supply and explain what determines supply.**

Practice Problem 4.2

1. Timber beams are made from logs, and in the process of making beams, the mill produces sawdust, which is made into pressed wood. In the market for timber beams, several events occur one at a time. Explain the influence of each event on the quantity supplied of timber beams and the supply of timber beams. Use a graph to illustrate the effects of each event. Does any event (or events) illustrate the law of supply? These events are
   a. The wage rate of sawmill workers rises.
   b. The price of sawdust rises.
   c. The price of a timber beam rises.
   d. The price of a timber beam is expected to rise next year.
   e. Environmentalists convince Congress to introduce a new law that reduces the amount of forest that can be cut for timber products.
   f. A new technology lowers the cost of producing timber beams.

Exercise 4.2

1. In the market for DVDs, several events occur one at a time. Explain the influence of each event on the quantity supplied of DVDs and the supply of DVDs. Use a graph to illustrate the effects of each event. Does any event (or events) illustrate the law of supply? These events are
   a. The price of a CD falls.
   b. A new robot technology lowers the cost of producing DVDs.
   c. The price of a DVD falls.
   d. The price of a DVD is expected to rise next year.
   e. The wage rate paid to DVD factory workers increases.

FIGURE I

Solution to Practice Problem 4.2

1a. A rise in the wage rate of sawmill workers decreases the supply of timber beams. The supply curve of timber beams shifts leftward (Figure 1).

1b. Sawdust and timber beams are complements in production. A rise in the price of sawdust increases the supply of timber beams. The supply curve of timber beams shifts rightward (Figure 1).

1c. A rise in the price of a timber beam increases the quantity supplied of timber beams, which is shown as a movement up along the supply curve of timber beams and is an example of the law of supply in action (Figure 2).

1d. The expected rise in the price of a timber beam decreases the supply of timber beams now. The supply curve of timber beams shifts leftward (Figure 1).

1e. The new law decreases the supply of timber beams. The supply curve of timber beams shifts leftward (Figure 1).

1f. The new technology increases the supply of timber beams and shifts the supply curve rightward (Figure 1).

FIGURE 2

4.3 MARKET EQUILIBRIUM

In everyday language, "equilibrium" means "opposing forces are in balance." Demand and supply are opposing forces. And **market equilibrium** occurs when the quantity demanded equals the quantity supplied—when buyers' and sellers' plans are in balance. At the **equilibrium price**, the quantity demanded equals the quantity supplied. The **equilibrium quantity** is the quantity bought and sold at the equilibrium price.

In the market for bottled water in Figure 4.9, equilibrium occurs where the demand curve and the supply curve intersect. The equilibrium price is $1.00 a bottle, and the equilibrium quantity is 10 million bottles a day.

■ Price: A Market's Automatic Regulator

When equilibrium is disturbed, market forces restore it. The **law of market forces** states

> **When there is a shortage, the price rises; and when there is a surplus, the price falls.**

A **shortage** or **excess demand** is a situation in which the quantity demanded exceeds the quantity supplied. If there is a shortage, buyers must pay a higher price to get more; and sellers are pleased to take the higher price. So the price rises. But a rising price is exactly what is needed to restore equilibrium because a shortage arises when the price is below the equilibrium price.

A **surplus** or **excess supply** is a situation in which the quantity supplied exceeds the quantity demanded. If there is a surplus, suppliers must cut the price to sell more; and buyers are pleased to take the lower price. So the price falls. But

Market equilibrium
When the quantity demanded equals the quantity supplied—buyers' and sellers' plans are in balance.

Equilibrium price
The price at which the quantity demanded equals the quantity supplied.

Equilibrium quantity
The quantity bought and sold at the equilibrium price.

Shortage or excess demand
A situation in which the quantity demanded exceeds the quantity supplied.

Surplus or excess supply
A situation in which the quantity supplied exceeds the quantity demanded.

■ **FIGURE 4.9**
Equilibrium Price and Equilibrium Quantity

myeconlab

① Market equilibrium occurs at the intersection of the demand curve and the supply curve.

② The equilibrium price is $1.00 a bottle.

③ At the equilibrium price, the quantity demanded and the quantity supplied are 10 million bottles a day, which is the equilibrium quantity.

a falling price is exactly what the market needs to restore equilibrium because a surplus arises when the the price is above the equilibrium price.

In Figure 4.10(a), at 75 cents a bottle, there is a shortage: The price rises, the quantity demanded decreases, the quantity supplied increases, and the shortage is eliminated at $1.00 a bottle. In Figure 4.10(b), at $1.50 a bottle, there is a surplus: The price falls, the quantity demanded increases, the quantity supplied decreases, and the surplus is eliminated at $1.00 a bottle.

■ Predicting Price Changes: Three Questions

Because price adjustments eliminate shortages and surpluses, markets are normally in equilibrium. And when an event disturbs an equilibrium, a new equilibrium soon emerges. So to explain and predict changes in prices and quantities, we need to consider only changes in the *equilibrium* price and the *equilibrium* quantity. We can work out the effects of an event on a market by answering three questions:

1. Does the event influence demand or supply?
2. Does the event *increase* or *decrease* demand or supply—shift the demand curve or the supply curve *rightward* or *leftward*?
3. What are the new *equilibrium* price and *equilibrium* quantity and how have they changed?

■ **FIGURE 4.10**

The Forces That Achieve Equilibrium

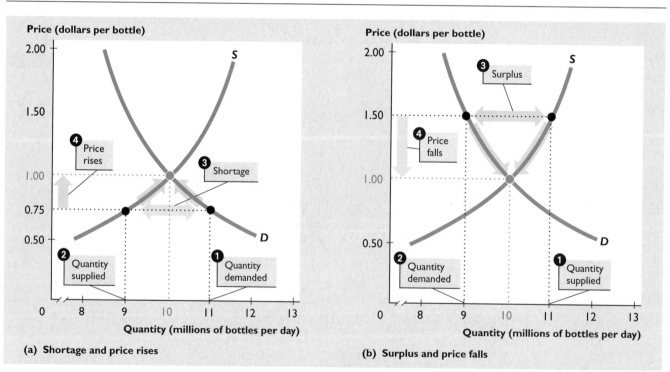

(a) Shortage and price rises

(b) Surplus and price falls

At 75 cents a bottle, ❶ the quantity demanded is 11 million bottles, ❷ the quantity supplied is 9 million bottles, ❸ the shortage is 2 million bottles, and ❹ the price rises.

At $1.50 a bottle, ❶ the quantity supplied is 11 million bottles, ❷ the quantity demanded is 9 million bottles, ❸ the surplus is 2 million bottles, and ❹ the price falls.

■ Effects of Changes in Demand

Let's practice answering the three questions by working out the effects of an event in the market for bottled water: A new study says that tap water is unsafe.

1. With tap water unsafe, the demand for bottled water changes.
2. The demand for bottled water *increases*, and the demand curve *shifts rightward*. Figure 4.11(a) shows the shift from D_0 to D_1.
3. There is now a *shortage* at \$1.00 a bottle. The *price rises* to \$1.50 a bottle, and the quantity increases to 11 million bottles.

Note that there is *no change in supply*. But the rise in price brings an *increase in the quantity supplied*—a movement along the supply curve.

Let's work out what happens if a new zero-calorie sports drink is invented.

1. The new drink is a substitute for bottled water, so the demand for bottled water changes.
2. The demand for bottled water *decreases*, and the demand curve *shifts leftward*. Figure 4.11(b) shows the shift from D_0 to D_2.
3. There is now a *surplus* at \$1.00 a bottle. The price *falls* to 75 cents a bottle, and the quantity decreases to 9 million bottles.

Note again that there is *no change in supply*. But the fall in price brings a *decrease in the quantity supplied*—a movement along the supply curve.

■ FIGURE 4.11

The Effects of a Change in Demand

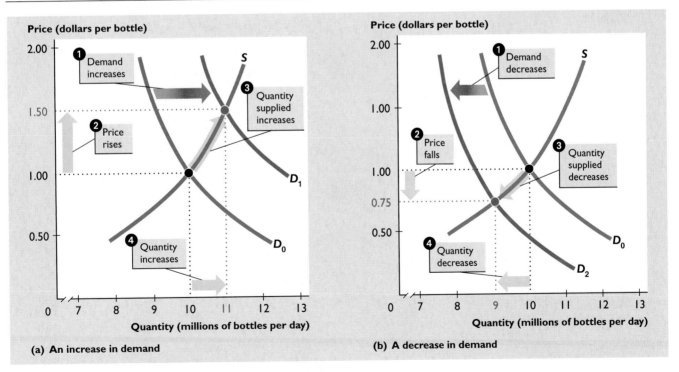

(a) An increase in demand

(b) A decrease in demand

❶ An increase in demand shifts the demand curve rightward to D_1 and creates a shortage. ❷ The price rises, ❸ the quantity supplied increases, and ❹ the equilibrium quantity increases.

❶ A decrease in demand shifts the demand curve leftward to D_2 and creates a surplus. ❷ The price falls, ❸ the quantity supplied decreases, and ❹ the equilibrium quantity decreases.

■ Effects of Changes in Supply

You can get more practice working out the effects of another event in the market for bottled water: European water bottlers buy springs and open new plants in the United States.

1. With more suppliers of bottled water, the supply changes.
2. The supply of bottled water *increases*, and the supply curve *shifts rightward*. Figure 4.12(a) shows the shift from S_0 to S_1.
3. There is now a *surplus* at $1.00 a bottle. The *price falls* to 75 cents a bottle, and the quantity increases to 11 million bottles.

Note that there is *no change in demand*. But the fall in price brings an *increase in the quantity demanded*—a movement along the demand curve.

What happens if a drought dries up some springs?

1. The drought changes the supply of water.
2. With fewer springs, the supply of bottled water *decreases*, and the supply curve *shifts leftward*. Figure 4.12(b) shows the shift from S_0 to S_2.
3. There is now a *shortage* at $1.00 a bottle. The *price rises* to $1.50 a bottle, and the quantity decreases to 9 million bottles.

Again, there is *no change in demand*. But the rise in price brings a *decrease in the quantity demanded*—a movement along the demand curve.

■ FIGURE 4.12
The Effects of a Change in Supply

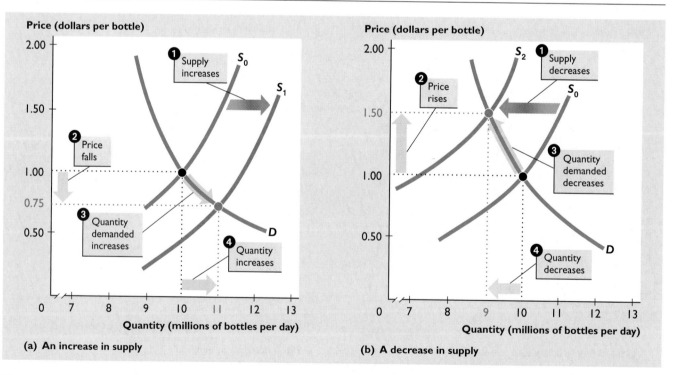

(a) An increase in supply

(b) A decrease in supply

❶ An increase in supply shifts the supply curve rightward to S_1 and creates a surplus. ❷ The price falls, ❸ the quantity demanded increases, and ❹ the equilibrium quantity increases.

❶ A decrease in supply shifts the supply curve leftward to S_2 and creates a shortage. ❷ The price rises, ❸ the quantity demanded decreases, and ❹ the equilibrium quantity decreases.

A Change in the Demand for Roses

Colombia and Ecuador grow most of the world's roses. On the average, the quantity of roses sold worldwide is around 6 million bunches a month. And the average price that consumers pay is around $40 a bunch.

But one month, February, is not a normal month. Each year, in February, the quantity of roses bought increases to four times that of any other month. The reason: Valentine's Day. And on Valentine's Day, the price of a bunch of roses doubles.

The demand-supply model explains these facts. The figure shows the supply curve of roses and two demand curves. The blue demand curve is the demand for roses in a normal month. This demand curve intersects the supply curve at an equilibrium price of $40 a bunch and an equilibrium quantity of 6 million bunches.

In February, the demand curve shifts rightward to the red curve. The equilibrium price rises to $80 a bunch and the equilibrium quantity increases to 24 million bunches.

A Change in the Supply of PCs

You can buy a pretty neat notebook computer for around $700 and a desktop machine for as little as $350. Just a few years ago, you would have paid double these price and have got much less computing power for your money.

Why has the price of a PC fallen so dramatically?

Higher incomes have probably brought an increase in the demand for PCs (not shown in the figure). If this were the only influence on the market, the price would have risen.

Events that have increased the supply of PCs have brought the lower prices. Ongoing advances in technology have lowered the costs of computer chips, hard drives, and, most of all, monitors—both conventional ones and flat panel displays.

With an increase in supply, the supply curve has shifted rightward. At the old prices, there would be a surplus, so the price has fallen.

The lower price has brought an increase in the quantity of PCs demanded—a movement along the demand curve.

■ Changes in Both Demand and Supply

When events occur that change *both* demand and supply, you can find the resulting change in the equilibrium price and equilibrium quantity by combining the cases you've just studied. Table 4.1 summarizes all the possible cases.

Increase in Both Demand and Supply

An increase in demand or an increase in supply increases the equilibrium quantity. So when demand and supply increase together, the quantity increases. But the price rises when demand increases and falls when supply increases. So when demand and supply increase together, we can't say what happens to the price unless we know the magnitudes of the changes. If demand increases by more than supply increases, the price rises. But if supply increases by more than demand increases, the price falls.

Decrease in Both Demand and Supply

A decrease in demand or a decrease in supply decreases the equilibrium quantity. So when demand and supply decrease together, the quantity decreases. But the price falls when demand decreases and rises when supply decreases. So when demand and supply decrease together, we can't say what happens to the price unless we know the magnitudes of the changes. If demand decreases by more than supply decreases, the price falls. But if supply decreases by more than demand decreases, the price rises.

Increase in Demand and Decrease in Supply

An increase in demand or a decrease in supply raises the equilibrium price, so combined, these changes raise the price. But an increase in demand increases the quantity, and a decrease in supply decreases the quantity. So when these changes occur together, we can't say what happens to the quantity unless we know the magnitudes of the changes. If demand increases by more than supply decreases, the quantity increases. But if supply decreases by more than demand increases, the quantity decreases.

Decrease in Demand and Increase in Supply

A decrease in demand or an increase in supply lowers the equilibrium price, so combined, these changes lower the price. But a decrease in demand decreases the quantity, and an increase in supply increases the quantity. So when these changes occur together, we can't say what happens to the quantity unless we know the magnitudes of the changes. If demand decreases by more than supply increases, the quantity decreases. But if supply increases by more than demand decreases, the quantity increases.

Table 4.1 lists all these effects. You can confirm them by revisiting Figures 4.11 and 4.12. Even better, by drawing your own demand-supply graphs, you can generate all these results. For the cases in which Table 4.1 lists "can't say" what happens to price or quantity, make some examples that go in each direction.

■ **TABLE 4.1**

How Price and Quantity Change When Demand or Supply Changes

Case	Change in demand	Change in supply	Effect on price	Effect on quantity	Illustrated in Figure
1.	Increase	None	Rise	Increase	4.11(a)
2.	Decrease	None	Fall	Decrease	4.11(b)
3.	None	Increase	Fall	Increase	4.12(a)
4.	None	Decrease	Rise	Decrease	4.12(b)
5.	Increase	Increase	Can't say	Increase	4.11(a) & 4.12(a)
6.	Decrease	Decrease	Can't say	Decrease	4.11(b) & 4.12(b)
7.	Increase	Decrease	Rise	Can't say	4.11(a) & 4.12(b)
8.	Decrease	Increase	Fall	Can't say	4.11(b) & 4.12(a)

REALITY CHECK

Demand and Supply in YOUR Life

The demand and supply model is going to be a big part of the rest of your life!

First, you will use it again and again during the rest of your economics course. The demand and supply model is one of your major tools. So having a firm grasp of this topic will bring an immediate practical payoff.

But second, and much more important, by understanding the laws of demand and supply and being aware of how prices adjust to balance these two opposing forces, you will have a much better appreciation of how *your* economic world works.

Every time you hear someone complaining about a price hike and blaming it on someone's greed, think about the law of market forces and the demand curve and the supply curve that intersect to determine that price.

As you shop for your favorite clothing, the latest music, and food items, try to describe the supply and demand influences on the prices of these goods and services.

3 Explain how demand and supply determine price and quantity in a market and explain the effects of changes in demand and supply.

TABLE 1

Price (dollars per carton)	Quantity demanded	Quantity supplied
	(cartons per day)	
1.00	200	110
1.25	175	130
1.50	150	150
1.75	125	170
2.00	100	190

TABLE 2

Price (dollars per roll)	Quantity demanded	Quantity supplied
	(rolls per week)	
2.00	3,000	1,000
3.00	2,500	1,500
4.00	2,000	2,000
5.00	1,500	2,500
6.00	1,000	3,000

FIGURE 1

FIGURE 2

Practice Problem 4.3

1. Table 1 shows the demand and supply schedules for milk.
   a. What is the equilibrium price and equilibrium quantity of milk?
   b. Describe the situation in the milk market if the price were $1.75 a carton and explain how the market reaches its new equilibrium.
   c. A drought decreases the quantity supplied by 45 cartons a day at each price. What is the new equilibrium and how does the market adjust to it?
   d. Milk becomes more popular and better feeds increase the quantity of milk. How do these events influence demand and supply? If there is no drought, do they create a shortage or a surplus at the equilibrium price in part **a**? Describe how the equilibrium price and equilibrium quantity change.

Exercise 4.3

1. Table 2 shows the demand and supply schedules for rolls of film.
   a. What is the market equilibrium?
   b. If the price of film is $3 a roll, describe the situation in the film market. Explain how market equilibrium is restored.
   c. A rise in income increases the quantity demanded by 1,000 rolls a week at each price. Explain how the film market adjusts to its new equilibrium.
   d. The number of film production lines increases, and at the same time, people switch to digital cameras. How do these events influence demand and supply? Do they create a shortage or a surplus at the equilibrium price in part **a**? Describe how the price and quantity change.

Solution to Practice Problem 4.3

1a. Equilibrium price is $1.50 a carton; equilibrium quantity is 150 cartons a day.

1b. At $1.75 a carton, the quantity demanded (125 cartons) is less than the quantity supplied (170 cartons), so there is a surplus of 45 cartons a day. The price begins to fall, and as it does, the quantity demanded increases, the quantity supplied decreases, and the surplus decreases. The price will fall until the surplus is eliminated. The price falls to $1.50 a carton.

1c. The supply curve shifts leftward by 45 cartons a day. At $1.50 a carton, the quantity demanded (150 cartons) exceeds the quantity supplied (105 cartons), so there is a shortage of milk. The price begins to rise, and as it does, the quantity demanded decreases, the quantity supplied increases, and the shortage decreases. The price will rise until the shortage is eliminated. The new equilibrium occurs at $1.75 a carton and 125 cartons a day (Figure 1).

1d. When milk becomes more popular, demand increases. With better feeds, supply increases. If supply increases by more than demand, there will be a surplus at $1.50 a carton. The price falls, and the quantity increases. (Figure 2 illustrates.) If demand increases by more than supply, there will be a shortage at $1.50 a carton. The price rises, and the quantity increases. But if demand and supply increase by the same amount, there is no shortage or surplus and the price remains at $1.50 a carton. The quantity increases.

CHAPTER CHECKPOINT

Key Points

1 **Distinguish between quantity demanded and demand and explain what determines demand.**

- Other things remaining the same, the quantity demanded increases as the price falls and decreases as the price rises—the law of demand.
- The demand for a good is influenced by the prices of related goods, income, expectations about future income and prices, the number of buyers, and preferences. A change in any of these influences changes the demand for the good.

2 **Distinguish between quantity supplied and supply and explain what determines supply.**

- Other things remaining the same, the quantity supplied increases as the price rises and decreases as the price falls—the law of supply.
- The supply of a good is influenced by the prices of related goods, prices of resources and other inputs, expectations about future prices, the number of sellers, and productivity. A change in any of these influences changes the supply of the good.

3 **Explain how demand and supply determine price and quantity in a market and explain the effects of changes in demand and supply.**

- The law of market forces brings market equilibrium—the equilibrium price and equilibrium quantity at which buyers and sellers trade.
- The price adjusts to maintain market equilibrium—to keep the quantity demanded equal to the quantity supplied. A surplus brings a fall in the price to restore market equilibrium; a shortage brings a rise in the price to restore market equilibrium.
- Market equilibrium responds to changes in demand and supply. An increase in demand increases both the price and the quantity; a decrease in demand decreases both the price and the quantity. An increase in supply increases the quantity but decreases the price; and a decrease in supply decreases the quantity but increases the price.

Key Terms

Change in demand, 94
Change in the quantity demanded, 96
Change in the quantity supplied, 103
Change in supply, 101
Complement, 94
Complement in production, 101
Demand, 91
Demand curve, 92
Demand schedule, 92
Equilibrium price, 105

Equilibrium quantity, 105
Inferior good, 95
Law of demand, 91
Law of market forces, 105
Law of supply, 98
Market demand, 93
Market equilibrium, 105
Market supply, 100
Normal good, 95
Quantity demanded, 91

Quantity supplied, 98
Shortage or excess demand, 105
Substitute, 94
Substitute in production, 101
Supply, 98
Supply curve, 99
Supply schedule, 99
Surplus or excess supply, 105

(myeconlab) Exercises

1. Explain how each of the following events changes the demand for or supply of air travel.
   a. Airfares tumble, while long-distance bus fares don't change.
   b. The price of jet fuel rises.
   c. Airlines reduce the number of flights each day.
   d. People expect airfares to increase next summer.
   e. As the winter turns very cold in New York, many people decide to take a midwinter break in Florida.
   f. With deep snow in the Rockies, many people flock to the ski slopes.
   g. The price of train travel falls.
   h. The price of a pound of air cargo increases.

2. Explain how each of the following events changes the demand for or supply of jeans.
   a. A new technology becomes available that cuts the time it takes to manufacture a pair of jeans by 50 percent.
   b. The price of the cloth (denim) used to make jeans falls.
   c. Jeans go out of fashion.
   d. The price of a pair of jeans falls.
   e. The wage rate paid to garment workers increases.
   f. Most baseball clubs start to sell their own brand of jeans.
   g. The price of a denim skirt doubles.
   h. People's income increase.

3. Use the laws of demand and supply to explain whether the following statements are true or false. In your explanation, distinguish between a change in demand and a change in the quantity demanded and between a change in supply and a change in the quantity supplied.
   a. The United States does not allow oranges from Brazil (the world's largest producer of oranges) to enter the United States. If Brazilian oranges were sold in the United States, oranges and orange juice would be cheaper.
   b. If soccer becomes more popular in the United States and basketball becomes less popular, the price of a pair of basketball shoes will rise.
   c. It is more expensive to ski in Aspen in the winter than in the spring.
   d. If the price of frozen yogurt falls, the quantity of ice cream consumed will decrease and the price of ice cream will rise.

4. What is the effect on the equilibrium price and quantity of orange juice of the following events if they occur one at a time?
   a. The price of apple juice decreases.
   b. The price of apple juice decreases, and the wage rate paid to orange grove workers increases.
   c. Orange juice becomes more popular, and a cheaper machine for picking oranges is used.
   d. Joggers switch from bottled water to orange juice.

5. Gasoline producers invent a new fuel that is cheaper and cleaner than gasoline. All new cars use the new fuel. Use a demand-supply graph to explain the effect of this new fuel on
   a. The price of gasoline and the quantity of gasoline bought.
   b. The price of a used car.

TABLE 1

Price (dollars per pad)	Quantity demanded	Quantity supplied
	(mouse pads per week)	
3.00	160	120
4.00	150	130
5.00	140	140
6.00	130	150
7.00	120	160
8.00	110	170

6. Table 1 shows the demand and supply schedules for mouse pads.
   a. What is the market equilibrium?
   b. If the price of a mouse pad is $7.00, describe the situation in the market. Explain how market equilibrium is restored.
   c. Explain what happens to the market equilibrium and how the market adjusts to its new equilibrium if a fall in the price of a computer changes the quantity demanded of mouse pads by 20 a week at each price.
   d. Explain what happens to the market equilibrium in part a if new voice-recognition software becomes popular and at the same time the cost of producing a mouse pad falls. Set out the three-step process of analysis and draw a graph to illustrate the adjustment process. Describe the change in the price and quantity of mouse pads.

7. "As more people buy computers, the demand for Internet service will increase and the price of an Internet service will decrease. The decrease in the price of an Internet service will decrease the supply of Internet services." Is this statement true or false? Explain your answer.

8. Oil prices in March 2005 were 32 percent higher than in 2004. The price of oil was $56 a barrel. Explain how each of the following events might have led to this large increase in the price of oil. Use a demand-supply graph to illustrate your answers.
   a. A very cold winter in the United States and Europe in the first three months of 2005.
   b. OPEC was expected to increase its production in March but the increase was very small.
   c. Supply disruptions in the Middle East.
   d. Oil traders expect the price of oil to move to $60 a barrel.
   e. Rapid growth in the use of petroleum in China.

9. During 2004, orange growers in Florida experienced three hurricanes. As a result, the amount of oranges harvested in Florida was expected to be smaller than usual.
   a. Draw a demand-supply graph to show the equilibrium in the U.S. orange market in a normal year.
   b. Use your graph to illustrate the effect of the smaller harvests in Florida, given that orange growers in other states experienced normal growing conditions.
   c. How do you think the price of oranges and the quantity bought and sold changed in early 2005?
   d. What do you predict happened to the price of frozen orange juice in early 2005?

10. The world price of coffee fell during the early 2000s, but in 2005, the price increased.
   a. Draw a demand-supply graph to show the equilibrium in the world coffee market in 2000.
   b. During the early 2000s, countries such as Vietnam started to produce coffee and coffee shops such as Starbucks started to spring up across Europe and Asia. Explain how these events have changed the demand for and supply of coffee.
   c. Why do you think the price of coffee fell in the early 2000s and then rose?

Critical Thinking

11. The *Wall Street Journal* reports that the five major recording companies think that music downloads are too cheap at 99 cents per song. They would like to see a price between $1.25 and $2.99 per song.
    a. What determines the price of a music download?
    b. What role does self-interest—of both the recording companies and the people who download songs—play in the market for music downloads?
    c. What do you predict would happen in the market for music downloads if the major recording companies tried to hike the price to $2.99 a song?

12. In 1995, 90 salmon farms operated in British Columbia. In 1995, the Canadian government banned the creation of any new salmon farms because the farms create pollution and might introduce disease into the wild salmon population. In September 2002, the Canadian government lifted this ban. The Heart and Stroke Foundation tells us that "salmon is one of the healthiest foods we can eat. There's no shortage of it. We're eating three times as much of it as we did just a few years ago."
    a. What do you predict happened to the price of farm-raised salmon and the quantity of farm-raised salmon grown from 1996 through 2001?
    b. What effect do you think the lifting of the ban will have on the price of farm-raised salmon and the quantity of farm-raised salmon bought?
    c. If disease breaks out in the salmon farms of British Columbia, describe what effects it will have on the market for wild Pacific salmon.

 ## Web Exercises

Use the links on MyEconLab to work the following exercises.

13. Obtain information about the history of the price of crude oil.
    a. What are the major changes that have occurred in the market for crude oil?
    b. On what three occasions did the price of oil rise by the largest amounts?
    c. What events occurred to trigger the price hikes that you've just described?
    d. Did the events that you've just described change the demand for crude oil, the supply, both, or neither? Explain your answer.
    e. Use the law of market forces and demand-supply graphs to explain the changes in the price and quantity of crude oil on the three occasions that you identified in part **b**.
    f. How do you think the price of crude oil influences the markets for coal and natural gas?
    g. How do you think the advances in technology that increased fuel efficiency in automobiles, airplanes, and home heating furnaces have influenced the world market for crude oil?

14. Visit eBay.
    a. What is eBay? Describe how eBay works.
    b. Do you think the prices of the items traded on eBay are determined by demand and supply or in some other way? Explain your answer.

Elasticities of Demand and Supply

CHAPTER **5**

CHAPTER CHECKLIST

When you have completed your study of this chapter, you will be able to

1 Define, explain the factors that influence, and calculate the price elasticity of demand.

2 Define, explain the factors that influence, and calculate the price elasticity of supply.

3 Define and explain the factors that influence the cross elasticity of demand and the income elasticity of demand.

What do you do when the price of gasoline rises? If you're like most people, you keep filling your tank, groan a bit, and cut back on something less essential so that you can afford to spend more on gas. But don't some people find that the higher price puts an automobile out of reach and forces them to ride the bus? Also, rising incomes, especially in China and other parts of Asia, are increasing the demand for oil, which is bringing higher fuel prices. Are you going to keep buying the same quantity of gasoline when the price hits $3 a gallon, $5, $10?

To answer questions such as these, we need to know how responsive buying plans and selling plans are to a change in prices. You're now going to discover a powerful tool for describing demand and supply and predicting the magnitudes of price and quantity changes when either demand or supply changes. That tool is *elasticity*—the elasticity of demand and the elasticity of supply.

117

5.1 THE PRICE ELASTICITY OF DEMAND

A decrease in supply of gasoline brings a large rise in its price and a small decrease in the quantity that people buy. The reason is that buying plans for gasoline are not very responsive to a change in price. But an increase in the supply of airline services brings a small decrease in its price and a large increase in the quantity of air travel. In the case of air travel, buying plans are highly sensitive to a change in price. By knowing how sensitive or responsive buying plans are to price changes, we can predict how a given change in supply will change price and quantity.

But we often want to go further and predict by how much a price will change when some event occurs in a market. To make more precise predictions about the magnitudes of price and quantity changes, we need to know quite a lot more about a demand curve than the fact that it slopes downward. We need to know how responsive the quantity demanded is to price. Elasticity provides this information.

Price elasticity of demand
A measure of the responsiveness of the quantity demanded of a good to a change in its price when all other influences on buyers' plans remain the same.

The **price elasticity of demand** is a measure of the responsiveness of the quantity demanded of a good* to a change in its price when all other influences on buyers' plans remain the same.

To determine the price elasticity of demand, we compare the percentage change in the quantity demanded with the percentage change in price. But we calculate percentage changes in a special way.

■ Percentage Change in Price

Suppose that Starbucks raises the price of a latte from $3 to $5 a cup. What is the percentage change in price? The change in price is the new price minus the initial price. And the percentage change is calculated as the change in price divided by the initial price, all multiplied by 100. The formula for the percentage change is

$$\text{Percentage change in price} = \left(\frac{\text{New price} - \text{Initial price}}{\text{Initial price}} \right) \times 100.$$

In this example, the initial price is $3 and the new price is $5, so

$$\text{Percentage change in price} = \left(\frac{\$5 - \$3}{\$3} \right) \times 100 = \left(\frac{\$2}{\$3} \right) \times 100 = 66.67 \text{ percent.}$$

Now suppose that Starbucks cuts the price of a latte from $5 to $3 a cup. What now is the percentage change in price? The initial price is now $5 and the new price is $3, so the percentage change in price is calculated as

$$\text{Percentage change in price} = \left(\frac{\$3 - \$5}{\$5} \right) \times 100 = \left(\frac{-\$2}{\$5} \right) \times 100 = -40 \text{ percent.}$$

The same price change, $2, over the same interval, $3 to $5, is a different percentage change depending on whether the price rises or falls.

Because elasticity compares the percentage change in the quantity demanded with the percentage change in price, we need a measure of percentage change that does not depend on the direction of the price change. The measure that economists use is called the *midpoint method*.

---

*What you learn in this chapter also applies to services and factors of production.

The Midpoint Method

To calculate the percentage change in price using the midpoint method, we divide the change in the price by the *average price*—the *average* of the new price and the initial price—and then multiply by 100. The average price is at the midpoint between the initial and the new price, hence the name *midpoint method*.

The formula for the percentage change using the midpoint method is

$$\text{Percentage change in price} = \left(\frac{\text{New price} - \text{Initial price}}{(\text{New price} + \text{Initial price}) \div 2} \right) \times 100.$$

In this formula, the numerator, (New price − Initial price), is the same as before. The denominator, (New price + Initial price) ÷ 2, is the average of the new price and the initial price.

To calculate the percentage change in the price of a Starbucks latte using the midpoint method, put $5 for new price and $3 for initial price in the formula:

$$\begin{array}{l} \text{Percentage} \\ \text{change in price} \end{array} = \left(\frac{\$5 - \$3}{(\$5 + \$3) \div 2} \right) \times 100 = \left(\frac{\$2}{\$8 \div 2} \right) \times 100$$

$$= \left(\frac{\$2}{\$4} \right) \times 100 = 50 \text{ percent.}$$

Because the average price is the same regardless of whether the price rises or falls, the percentage change in price calculated by the midpoint method is the same for a price rise and a price fall. In this example, it is 50 percent.

◼ Percentage Change in Quantity Demanded

Suppose that when the price of a latte rises from $3 to $5 a cup, the quantity demanded decreases from 15 cups to 5 cups an hour. The percentage change in the quantity demanded using the midpoint method is

$$\begin{array}{l} \text{Percentage change} \\ \text{in quantity} \end{array} = \left(\frac{\text{New quantity} - \text{Initial quantity}}{(\text{New quantity} + \text{Initial quantity}) \div 2} \right) \times 100$$

$$= \left(\frac{5 - 15}{(5 + 15) \div 2} \right) \times 100 = \left(\frac{-10}{20 \div 2} \right) \times 100$$

$$= \left(\frac{-10}{10} \right) \times 100 = -100 \text{ percent.}$$

When the price of a good *rises*, the quantity demanded of it *decreases*—a *positive* change in price brings a *negative* change in the quantity demanded. Similarly, when the price of a good *falls*, the quantity demanded of it *increases*—this time a *negative* change in price brings a *positive* change in the quantity demanded.

To compare the percentage change in the price and the percentage change in the quantity demanded, we use the absolute values or magnitudes of the percentage changes and we ignore the minus sign.

■ Elastic and Inelastic Demand

To determine the responsiveness of the quantity of Starbucks latte demanded to its price, we need to compare the two percentage changes we've just calculated. The percentage change in quantity is 100 and the percentage change in price is 50, so the percentage change in quantity demanded is twice the percentage change in price. If we collected data on the prices and quantities of a number of goods and services (and we were careful to check that other things had remained the same), we could calculate lots of percentage changes. Our calculations would fall into three groups: The percentage change in the quantity demanded might exceed the percentage change in price, equal the percentage change in price, or be less than the percentage change in price. These three possibilities give three cases for the price elasticity of demand:

- Demand is **elastic** if the percentage change in the quantity demanded exceeds the percentage change in price.
- Demand is **unit elastic** if the percentage change in the quantity demanded equals the percentage change in price.
- Demand is **inelastic** if the percentage change in the quantity demanded is less than the percentage change in price.

Figure 5.1 shows the different types of demand curves that illustrate the range of possible price elasticities of demand. Part (a) shows an extreme case of an elastic demand called a **perfectly elastic demand**—an almost zero percentage change in the price brings a very large percentage change in the quantity demanded. Consumers are willing to buy any quantity of the good at a given price but none at a higher price. Part (b) shows an elastic demand—the percentage change in the quantity demanded exceeds the percentage change in price. Part (c) shows a unit elastic demand—the percentage change in the quantity demanded equals the percentage change in price. Part (d) shows an inelastic demand—the percentage change in the quantity demanded is less than the percentage change in price. Finally, part (e) shows an extreme case of an inelastic demand called a **perfectly inelastic demand**—the percentage change in the quantity demanded is zero for any percentage change in price.

■ Influences on the Price Elasticity of Demand

What makes the demand for some things elastic and the demand for others inelastic? The influences on the price elasticity of demand fall into two groups:

- Availability of substitutes
- Proportion of income spent

Availability of Substitutes

The demand for a good is elastic if a substitute for it is easy to find. Soft drink containers can be made of either aluminum or plastic and it doesn't matter which, so the demand for aluminum is elastic.

The demand for a good is inelastic if a substitute for it is hard to find. Oil has poor substitutes (imagine a coal-fueled car), so the demand for oil is inelastic.

Three main factors influence the ability to find a substitute for a good: whether the good is a luxury or a necessity, how narrowly it is defined, and the amount of time available to find a substitute for it.

Elastic demand
When the percentage change in the quantity demanded exceeds the percentage change in price.

Unit elastic demand
When the percentage change in the quantity demanded equals the percentage change in price.

Inelastic demand
When the percentage change in the quantity demanded is less than the percentage change in price.

Perfectly elastic demand
When the quantity demanded changes by a very large percentage in response to an almost zero percentage change in price.

Perfectly inelastic demand
When the quantity demanded remains constant as the price changes.

■ **FIGURE 5.1**

The Range of Price Elasticities of Demand

(a) Perfectly elastic demand

Price (dollars per gallon)

① A close-to-zero percent price rise ...

② ... decreases the quantity demanded by a very large percentage

③ The demand for water from a single spring is perfectly elastic

(b) Elastic demand

Price (dollars per PlayStation)

① A 10 percent price rise ...

② ... decreases the quantity demanded by 20 percent

③ The demand for Sony PlayStations is elastic

(c) Unit elastic demand

Price (dollars per trip)

① A 10 percent price rise ...

② ... decreases the quantity demanded by 10 percent

③ The demand for transportation is unit elastic

(d) Inelastic demand

Price (cents per pack)

① A 20 percent price rise ...

② ... decreases the quantity demanded by 10 percent

③ The demand for chewing gum is inelastic

(e) Perfectly inelastic demand

Price (cents per dose)

① A price rise of any percentage ...

② ... decreases the quantity demanded by zero percent

③ The demand for insulin is perfectly inelastic over this price range

① A price rise brings **②** a decrease in the quantity demanded. The relationship between the percentage change in the quantity demanded and the percentage change in price determines **③** the price elasticity of demand, which ranges from perfectly elastic (part a) to perfectly inelastic (part e).

Luxury Versus Necessity   We call goods such as food and housing *necessities* and goods such as exotic vacations *luxuries*. A necessity has poor substitutes—you must eat—so the demand for a necessity is inelastic. A luxury has many substitutes—you don't absolutely have to go to Galapagos this summer—so the demand for a luxury is elastic.

Narrowness of Definition   The demand for a narrowly defined good is elastic. For example, the demand for a Starbucks latte is elastic because a New World latte is a good substitute for it. The demand for a broadly defined good is inelastic. For example, the demand for coffee is inelastic because tea is a poor substitute for it.

Time Elapsed Since Price Change   The longer the time that has elapsed since the price of a good changed, the more elastic is demand for the good. For example, when the price of gasoline increased steeply during the 1970s and 1980s, the quantity of gasoline demanded didn't change much because many people owned gas-guzzling automobiles—the demand for gasoline was inelastic. But eventually, fuel-efficient cars replaced gas guzzlers and the quantity of gasoline demanded decreased—the demand for gasoline became more elastic.

Proportion of Income Spent

A price rise, like a decrease in income, means that people cannot afford to buy the same quantities of goods and services as before. The greater the proportion of income spent on a good, the greater is the impact of a rise in its price on the quantity of that good that people can afford to buy and the more elastic is the demand for the good. For example, toothpaste takes a tiny proportion of your budget and housing takes a large proportion. If the price of toothpaste doubles, you buy almost as much toothpaste as before. Your demand for toothpaste is inelastic. If your apartment rent doubles, you shriek and look for more roommates. Your demand for housing is more elastic than is your demand for toothpaste.

■ Computing the Price Elasticity of Demand

To determine whether the demand for a good is elastic, unit elastic, or inelastic, we compute a numerical value for the price elasticity of demand by using the following formula:

$$\text{Price elasticity of demand} = \frac{\text{Percentage change in quantity demanded}}{\text{Percentage change in price}}.$$

- If the price elasticity of demand is greater than 1, demand is elastic.
- If the price elasticity of demand equals 1, demand is unit elastic.
- If the price elasticity of demand is less than 1, demand is inelastic.

Figure 5.2 illustrates and summarizes the calculation for the Starbucks latte example. Initially, the price is $3 a cup and 15 cups an hour are demanded—the initial point in the figure. Then the price rises to $5 a cup and the quantity demanded decreases to 5 cups an hour—the new point in the figure. The price rises by $2 a cup and the average (midpoint) price is $4 a cup, so the percentage change in price is 50. The quantity demanded decreases by 10 cups an hour and the average (midpoint) quantity is 10 cups an hour, so the percentage change in quantity demanded is 100.

FIGURE 5.2

Price Elasticity of Demand Calculation

❶ At the initial point, the price is $3 a cup and the quantity demanded is 15 cups an hour.

❷ At the new point, the price is $5 a cup and the quantity demanded is 5 cups an hour.

❸ The change in price is $2 a cup, and ❹ the change in the quantity demanded is 10 cups an hour.

❺ The average price is $4 a cup, and the ❻ average quantity demanded is 10 cups an hour.

The percentage change in quantity demanded is 100, the percentage change in price is 50, and ❼ the price elasticity of demand is 2.

Using the above formula, you can see that the price elasticity of demand for a Starbucks latte is

$$\text{Price elasticity of demand} = \frac{100 \text{ percent}}{50 \text{ percent}} = 2.$$

The price elasticity of demand is 2 at the midpoint between the initial price and the new price on the demand curve. Over this price range, the demand for a Starbucks latte is elastic.

■ Interpreting the Price Elasticity of Demand Number

The number we've just calculated for a Starbucks latte is only an example. We don't have real data on the price and quantity. But suppose we did have real data and we discovered that the price elasticity of demand for a Starbucks latte is 2. What does this number tell us?

It tells us three main things:

1. The demand for Starbucks latte is elastic. Being elastic, the good has plenty of convenient substitutes (such as other brands of latte) and takes only a small proportion of buyers' incomes.

2. Starbucks must be careful not to charge too high a price for its latte. Pushing the price up brings in more revenue per cup but wipes out a lot of potential business.

3. The flip side of the second point: Even a slightly lower price could end up bringing in a lot more revenue.

■ Elasticity Along a Linear Demand Curve

Slope measures responsiveness. But elasticity is *not* the same as *slope*. You can see the distinction most clearly by looking at the price elasticity of demand along a linear (straight-line) demand curve. The slope is constant, but the elasticity varies. Figure 5.3 shows the same demand curve for a Starbucks latte as that in Figure 5.2 but with the axes extended to show lower prices and larger quantities demanded.

Let's calculate the elasticity of demand at point *A*. If the price rises from $3 to $5 a cup, the quantity demanded decreases from 15 to 5 cups an hour. The average price is $4 a cup, and the average quantity is 10 cups—point *A*. The elasticity of demand at point *A* is 2, and demand is elastic.

Let's calculate the elasticity of demand at point *C*. If the price falls from $3 to $1 a cup, the quantity demanded increases from 15 to 25 cups an hour. The average price is $2 a cup, and the average quantity is 20 cups—point *C*. The elasticity of demand at point *C* is 0.5, and demand is inelastic.

Finally, let's calculate the elasticity of demand at point *B*, which is the midpoint of the demand curve. If the price rises from $2 to $4 a cup, the quantity demanded decreases from 20 to 10 cups an hour. The average price is $3 a cup, and the average quantity is 15 cups—point *B*. The elasticity of demand at point *B* is 1, and demand is unit elastic.

Along a linear demand curve,

- Demand is unit elastic at the midpoint of the curve.
- Demand is elastic at all points above the midpoint of the curve.
- Demand is inelastic at all points below the midpoint of the curve.

■ FIGURE 5.3

Elasticity Along a Linear Demand Curve

On a linear demand curve, the slope is constant but the elasticity decreases as the price falls and the quantity demanded increases.

❶ At point *A*, demand is elastic.

❷ At point *B*, which is the midpoint of the demand curve, demand is unit elastic.

❸ At point *C*, demand is inelastic.

Demand is elastic at all points above the midpoint of the demand curve and inelastic at all points below the midpoint of the demand curve.

Price Elasticities of Demand

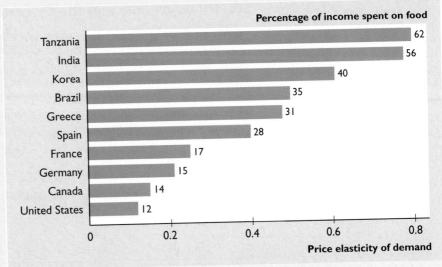

Percentage of income spent on food

Country	Value
Tanzania	62
India	56
Korea	40
Brazil	35
Greece	31
Spain	28
France	17
Germany	15
Canada	14
United States	12

(x-axis: 0 — 0.2 — 0.4 — 0.6 — 0.8)

Price elasticity of demand

A rich American student is casual about her food. It costs only a few dollars a day, and she's going to have her burger, even at double the price. But a poor Tanzanian boy takes his food with deadly seriousness. He has a tough time getting, preparing, and even defending his food. A rise in the price of food means that he must cut back and eat even less.

The figure shows the percentage of income spent on food and the price elasticity of demand for food in ten countries. The larger the proportion of income spent on food, the larger is the price elasticity of demand for food.

As the low-income countries become richer, the proportion of income they spend on food will decrease and their demand for food will become more inelastic. Consequently, the world's demand for food will become more inelastic.

Harvests fluctuate and bring fluctuations in the price of food. And as the world demand for food becomes more and more inelastic, the fluctuations in the prices of food items will become larger.

The table shows a few real-world price elasticities of demand. The numbers in the table range from 1.52 for metals to 0.12 for food. Metals have good substitutes, such as plastics, while food has virtually no substitutes. As we move down the list of items, they have fewer good substitutes and are more likely to be regarded as necessities.

Some Price Elasticities of Demand

Good or Service	Elasticity
Elastic Demand	
Metals	1.52
Electrical engineering products	1.39
Mechanical engineering products	1.30
Furniture	1.26
Motor vehicles	1.14
Instrument engineering products	1.10
Professional services	1.09
Transportation services	1.03
Inelastic Demand	
Gas, electricity, and water	0.92
Oil	0.91
Chemicals	0.89
Beverages (all types)	0.78
Clothing	0.64
Tobacco	0.61
Banking and insurance services	0.56
Housing services	0.55
Agricultural and fish products	0.42
Books, magazines, and newspapers	0.34
Food	0.12

SOURCES OF DATA: See p. C1.

125

■ Total Revenue and the Price Elasticity of Demand

Total revenue
The amount spent on a good and received by its seller and equals the price of the good multiplied by the quantity sold.

Total revenue is the amount spent on a good and received by its sellers and equals the price of the good multiplied by the quantity of the good sold. For example, suppose that the price of a Starbucks latte is $3 and that 15 cups an hour are sold. Then total revenue is $3 a cup multiplied by 15 cups an hour, which equals $45 an hour.

We can use the demand curve for Starbucks latte to illustrate total revenue. Figure 5.4(a) shows the total revenue from the sale of latte when the price is $3 a cup and the quantity of latte demanded is 15 cups an hour. Total revenue is shown by the blue rectangle, the area of which equals $3, its height, multiplied by 15, its length, which equals $45.

When the price changes, total revenue can change in the same direction, the opposite direction, or remain constant. Which of these outcomes occurs depends

---

■ FIGURE 5.4

Total Revenue and the Price Elasticity of Demand

Total revenue equals price multiplied by quantity. In part (a), when the price is $3 a cup, the quantity demanded is 15 cups an hour and total revenue equals $45 an hour. When the price rises to $5 a cup, the quantity demanded decreases to 5 cups an hour and total revenue decreases to $25 an hour. Demand is elastic.

In part (b), when the price is $50 a book, the quantity demanded is 5 million books a year and total revenue equals $250 million a year. When the price rises to $75 a book, the quantity demanded decreases to 4 million books a year and total revenue increases to $300 million a year. Demand is inelastic.

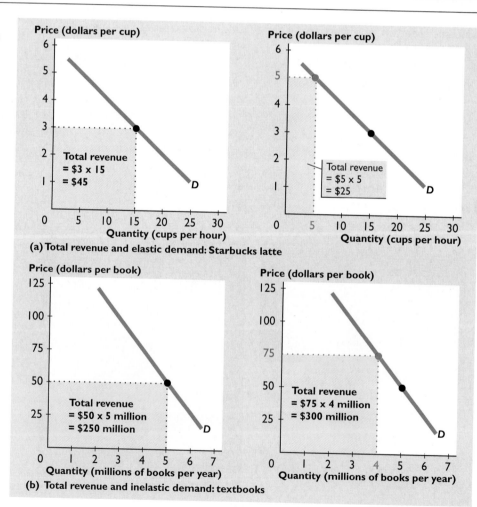

(a) Total revenue and elastic demand: Starbucks latte

(b) Total revenue and inelastic demand: textbooks

on the price elasticity of demand. By observing the change in total revenue that results from a price change (other things remaining the same), we can estimate the price elasticity of demand. This method of estimating the price elasticity of demand is called the **total revenue test**.

If demand is elastic, a given percentage rise in price brings a larger percentage decrease in the quantity demanded, so total revenue—price multiplied by quantity—decreases. Figure 5.4(a) shows this outcome. When the price of a latte is $3, the quantity demanded is 15 an hour and total revenue is $45 ($3 × 15). If the price of a latte rises to $5, the quantity demanded decreases to 5 an hour and total revenue *decreases* to $25 ($5 × 5).

If demand is inelastic, a given percentage rise in price brings a smaller percentage decrease in the quantity demanded, so total revenue increases. Figure 5.4(b) shows this outcome. When the price of a textbook is $50, the quantity demanded is 5 million a year and total revenue is $250 million ($50 × 5 million). If the price of a textbook rises to $75, the quantity demanded decreases to 4 million a year and total revenue *increases* to $300 million ($75 × 4 million).

The relationship between the price elasticity of demand and total revenue is

- If price and total revenue change in opposite directions, demand is elastic.
- If a price change leaves total revenue unchanged, demand is unit elastic.
- If price and total revenue change in the same direction, demand is inelastic.

Total revenue test
A method of estimating the price elasticity of demand by observing the change in total revenue that results from a price change (with all other influences on the quantity sold remaining unchanged).

REALITY CHECK

Elasticity in YOUR Life

Pay close attention the next time the price of something you buy rises. Did you spend more, the same, or less on this item?

Your expenditure on a good is its price multiplied by the quantity that you buy. So expenditure for the buyer is like total revenue for the seller. When the price of a good changes, the change in *your* expenditure on it depends on *your* elasticity of demand. When the price of a good *rises*, your demand for that good is

- Elastic if your expenditure on it decreases.

- Unit elastic if your expenditure on it remains constant.

- Inelastic if your expenditure on it increases.

Think about why your demand for a good is elastic or inelastic by checking back to the list of influences on the price elasticity of demand on p. 120.

■ Applications of the Price Elasticity of Demand

Does a frost in Florida bring a massive or a modest rise in the price of oranges? And does a smaller orange crop mean bad news or good news for orange growers? Knowledge of the price elasticity of demand for oranges enables us to answer these questions.

Orange Prices and Total Revenue

Economists have estimated the price elasticity of demand for agricultural products to be about 0.4—an inelastic demand. If this number applies to the demand for oranges, then

$$\text{Price elasticity of demand} = 0.4 = \frac{\text{Percentage change in quantity demanded}}{\text{Percentage change in price}}.$$

If supply changes and demand doesn't, the percentage change in the quantity demanded equals the percentage change in the equilibrium quantity. So if a frost in Florida decreases the orange harvest and decreases the equilibrium quantity of oranges by 1 percent, the price of oranges will rise by 2.5 percent. The percentage change in the quantity demanded (1 percent) divided by the percentage change in price (2.5 percent) equals the price elasticity of demand (0.4).

So the answer to the first question is that when the frost strikes, the price of oranges will rise by a larger percentage than the percentage decrease in the quantity of oranges. But what happens to the total revenue of the orange growers?

The answer is again provided by knowledge of the price elasticity of demand. Because the price rises by a larger percentage than the percentage decrease in quantity, total revenue increases. A frost is bad news for consumers and those growers who lose their crops but good news for growers who escape the frost.

A Florida frost is bad news for buyers of orange juice and for growers who lose their crops but good news for growers who escape the frost.

Addiction and Elasticity

We can gain important insights that might help to design potentially effective policies for dealing with addiction to drugs, whether legal (such as tobacco and alcohol) or illegal (such as crack cocaine or heroin). Nonusers' demand for addictive substances is elastic. A moderately higher price leads to a substantially smaller number of people trying a drug and so exposing themselves to the possibility of becoming addicted to it. But the existing users' demand for addictive substances is inelastic. Even a substantial price rise brings only a modest decrease in the quantity demanded.

These facts about the price elasticity of demand mean that high taxes on cigarettes and alcohol limit the number of young people who become habitual users of these products, but high taxes have only a modest effect on the quantities consumed by established users.

Similarly, effective policing of imports of an illegal drug that limits its supply leads to a large price rise and a substantial decrease in the number of new users but only a small decrease in the quantity consumed by addicts. Expenditure on the drug by addicts increases. Further, because many drug addicts finance their purchases with crime, the amount of theft and burglary increases.

Because the price elasticity of demand for drugs is low for addicts, any successful policy to decrease drug use will be one that focuses on the demand for drugs and attempts to change preferences through rehabilitation programs.

Cracking down on imports of illegal drugs limits supply, which leads to a large price increase. But it also increases the expenditure on drugs by addicts and increases the amount of crime that finances addiction.

CHECKPOINT 5.1

1 Define, explain the factors that influence, and calculate the price elasticity of demand.

Practice Problem 5.1

1. A 10 percent increase in the price of a good has led to a 2 percent decrease in the quantity demanded of that good.
   a. How would you describe the demand for this good?
   b. Are substitutes for this good easy to find or does it have poor substitutes?
   c. Is this good more likely to be a necessity or a luxury? Why?
   d. Is the good more likely to be narrowly or broadly defined? Why?
   e. Calculate the price elasticity of demand for this good.
   f. Explain how the total revenue from the sale of the good has changed.
   g. This good might be which of the following goods: orange juice, bread, toothpaste, theater tickets, clothing, blue jeans, Super Bowl tickets? Why?

Exercise 5.1

1. The price of Internet service rises from $24 to $26 a month, and the quantity demanded decreases from 204 million to 196 million subscribers.
   a. Calculate the percentage change in the price of Internet service.
   b. Calculate the percentage change in the quantity demanded of Internet services.
   c. Is the demand for Internet services elastic or inelastic?
   d. Would the demand for AOL service be more elastic or less elastic than the demand for Internet service? Why?
   e. Calculate the price elasticity of demand for Internet service.
   f. What is the change in the total revenue of Internet service providers?
   g. Explain why the concept of price elasticity of demand is useful.
   h. If the demand curve for Internet service is a straight line, is the price at which the demand for Internet service is unit elastic above or below $25 a month? Why?

Solution to Practice Problem 5.1

1a. Figure 1 illustrates a 10 percent increase in the price of a good that has led to a 2 percent decrease in the quantity demanded of it. The percentage change in the quantity demanded is less than the percentage change in the price, so the demand for the good is inelastic.

1b. Because the good has an inelastic demand, it usually has poor substitutes.

1c. Because the good has an inelastic demand, it is likely to be a necessity.

1d. Because the good has an inelastic demand, it is likely to be broadly defined.

1e. Price elasticity of demand equals the percentage change in the quantity demanded divided by the percentage change in price, which is $2 \div 10$ or 0.2.

1f. When demand is inelastic, a price rise increases total revenue.

1g. The good might be a necessity (bread), have poor substitutes (toothpaste), or be broadly defined (clothing).

FIGURE 1

5.2 THE PRICE ELASTICITY OF SUPPLY

You know that when demand increases, the equilibrium price rises and the equilibrium quantity increases. But does the price rise by a large amount and the quantity increase by a little? Or does the price barely rise and the quantity increase by a large amount? To answer this question, we need to know the price elasticity of supply.

The **price elasticity of supply** is a measure of the responsiveness of the quantity supplied of a good to a change in its price when all other influences on sellers' plans remain the same. We determine the price elasticity of supply by comparing the percentage change in the quantity supplied with the percentage change in price.

Elastic and Inelastic Supply

Supply might be

- Elastic
- Unit elastic
- Inelastic

Figure 5.5 illustrates the range of supply elasticities. Figure 5.5(a) shows the extreme case of a **perfectly elastic supply**—an almost zero percentage change in price brings a very large percentage change in the quantity supplied. Figure 5.5(b) shows an **elastic supply**—the percentage change in the quantity supplied exceeds the percentage change in price. Figure 5.5(c) shows a **unit elastic supply**—the percentage change in the quantity supplied equals the percentage change in price. Figure 5.5(d) shows an **inelastic supply**—the percentage change in the quantity supplied is less than the percentage change in price. And Figure 5.5(e) shows the extreme case of a **perfectly inelastic supply**—the percentage change in the quantity supplied is zero when the price changes.

Influences on the Price Elasticity of Supply

What makes the supply of some things elastic and the supply of others inelastic? The two main influences on the price elasticity of supply are

- Production possibilities
- Storage possibilities

Production Possibilities

Some goods can be produced at a constant (or very gently rising) opportunity cost. These goods have an elastic supply. The silicon in your computer chips is an example of such a good. Silicon is extracted from sand at a tiny and almost constant opportunity cost. So the supply of silicon is perfectly elastic.

Some goods can be produced in only a fixed quantity. These goods have a perfectly inelastic supply. A beachfront home in Santa Monica can be built only on a unique beachfront lot. So the supply of these homes is perfectly inelastic.

Hotel rooms in New York City can't easily be used as office accommodation and office space cannot easily be converted into hotel rooms, so the supply of hotel rooms in New York City is inelastic. Paper and printing presses can be used to produce textbooks or magazines, and the supplies of these goods are elastic.

Price elasticity of supply
A measure of the responsiveness of the quantity supplied of a good to a change in its price when all other influences on sellers' plans remain the same.

Perfectly elastic supply
When the quantity supplied changes by a very large percentage in response to an almost zero percentage change in price.

Elastic supply
When the percentage change in the quantity supplied exceeds the percentage change in price.

Unit elastic supply
When the percentage change in the quantity supplied equals the percentage change in price.

Inelastic supply
When the percentage change in the quantity supplied is less than the percentage change in price.

Perfectly inelastic supply
When the quantity supplied remains the same as the price changes.

The Range of Price Elasticities of Supply

(a) Perfectly elastic supply

(b) Elastic supply

(c) Unit elastic supply

(d) Inelastic supply

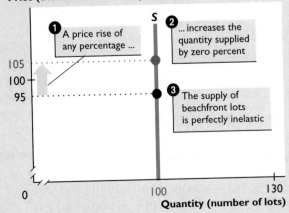

(e) Perfectly inelastic supply

❶ A price rise brings **❷** an increase in the quantity supplied. The relationship between the percentage change in the quantity supplied and the percentage change in price determines **❸** the price elasticity of supply, which ranges from perfectly elastic (part a) to perfectly inelastic (part e).

Time Elapsed Since Price Change As time passes after a price change, it becomes easier to change production plans and supply becomes more elastic. For some items—fruits and vegetables are examples—it is difficult or perhaps impossible to change the quantity supplied immediately after a price change. These goods have a perfectly inelastic supply on the day of a price change. The quantities supplied depend on crop-planting decisions that were made earlier. In the case of oranges, for example, planting decisions have to be made many years in advance of the crop being available.

Many manufactured goods also have an inelastic supply if production plans have had only a short period in which to change. For example, before it launched the PlayStation 2 in 2000, Sony made a forecast of demand, set a price, and made a production plan to supply the United States with the quantity that it believed people would be willing to buy. It turned out that demand outstripped Sony's earlier forecast. The price of a PlayStation 2 increased on eBay, an Internet auction market, to bring market equilibrium. At the high price that emerged, Sony would have liked to ship more PlayStations. But it could do nothing to increase the quantity supplied in the near term. The supply of the PlayStation 2 was inelastic.

As time passes, the elasticity of supply increases. After all the technologically possible ways of adjusting production have been exploited, supply is extremely elastic—perhaps perfectly elastic—for most manufactured items. By early 2001, Sony was able to step up the production rate of the PlayStation 2 and the price on eBay fell to the price at which Sony initially planned to sell the product. Over this longer time frame, the supply of the PlayStation 2 had become perfectly elastic.

Storage Possibilities

The elasticity of supply of a good that cannot be stored (for example, a perishable item such as fresh strawberries) or a service depends only on production possibilities. But the elasticity of supply of a good that can be stored depends on the decision to keep the good in storage or offer it for sale. A small price change can make a big difference to this decision, so the supply of a storable good is highly elastic. The cost of storage is the main influence on the elasticity of supply of a storable good. For example, rose growers in Colombia, anticipating a surge in demand on Valentine's Day in February, hold back supplies in late January and early February and increase their inventories of roses. They then release roses from inventory for Valentine's Day.

■ Computing the Price Elasticity of Supply

To determine whether the supply of a good is elastic, unit elastic, or inelastic, we compute a numerical value for the price elasticity of supply in a way similar to that used to calculate the price elasticity of demand. We use the formula:

$$\text{Price elasticity of supply} = \frac{\text{Percentage change in quantity supplied}}{\text{Percentage change in price}}$$

- If the price elasticity of supply is greater than 1, supply is elastic.
- If the price elasticity of supply equals 1, supply is unit elastic.
- If the price elasticity of supply is less than 1, supply is inelastic.

Let's calculate the price elasticity of supply of roses. We'll use the numbers that you saw in Chapter 4 on p. 109. Figure 5.6 illustrates and summarizes the calculation. In a normal month, the price of roses is $40 a bunch and 6 million bunches are supplied—the initial point in the figure. In February, the price rises to $80 a bunch and the quantity supplied increases to 24 million bunches—the new point in the figure. The price increases by $40 a bunch and the average, or midpoint, price is $60 a bunch, so the percentage change in the price is 66.67 percent. The quantity supplied increases by 18 million bunches and the average, or midpoint, quantity is 15 million bunches, so the percentage change in the quantity supplied is 120 percent.

Using the above formula, you can see that the price elasticity of supply of roses is

$$\text{Price elasticity of supply} = \frac{120 \text{ percent}}{66.67 \text{ percent}} = 1.8.$$

The price elasticity of supply is 1.8 at the midpoint between the initial point and the new point on the supply curve. In this example, over this price range, the supply of roses is elastic.

FIGURE 5.6

Price Elasticity of Supply Calculation

❶ At the initial point, the price is $40 a bunch and the quantity supplied is 6 million bunches a month.

❷ At the new point, the price is $80 a bunch and the quantity supplied is 24 million bunches a month.

❸ The change in price is $40 a bunch, and ❹ the change in the quantity supplied is 18 million bunches a month.

❺ The average price is $60 a bunch, and the ❻ average quantity supplied is 15 million bunches a month.

The percentage change in quantity supplied is 120, the percentage change in price is 66.67, and ❼ the price elasticity of supply is 1.8.

2 Define, explain the factors that influence, and calculate the price elasticity of supply.

Practice Problem 5.2

1. You are told that a 10 percent increase in the price of a good has led to a 1 percent increase in the quantity supplied of the good after one month. Use this information to answer the following questions.
   a. How would you describe the supply of this good?
   b. What can you say about the production possibilities of this good?
   c. Calculate the price elasticity of supply.
   d. If after one year, the quantity supplied has increased by 25 percent, describe how the supply has changed over the year.
   e. Calculate the elasticity of supply after one year.

Exercise 5.2

1. In 2002, the price of asparagus crashed from $45 a crate to $15 a crate. A typical Californian asparagus farmer would have supplied 2,000 crates a day at $45 a crate but at $15 a crate would plow the crop into the ground and supply nothing.
   a. How would you describe the Californian supply of asparagus?
   b. How do you think production possibilities and storage possibilities influence the price elasticity of supply of asparagus?
   c. Calculate the price elasticity of supply of Californian asparagus.
   d. If the price of asparagus remains at $15 a crate, do you think the elasticity of supply will change over the coming years? Explain your answer.
2. Use the data on the prices and quantities of roses in the *Eye on the Global Economy* on p. 109 to calculate the price elasticity of supply of roses.

Solution to Practice Problem 5.2

FIGURE I

1a. Figure 1 illustrates a 10 percent increase in the price of a good that has led to a 1 percent increase in the quantity supplied of it. The percentage change in the quantity supplied is less than the percentage change in the price of the good, so the supply of the good is inelastic.
1b. Because the quantity supplied increases by such a small percentage after one month, the factors of production that are used to produce this good are more likely to be unique or rare.
1c. The elasticity of supply equals the percentage change in the quantity supplied divided by the percentage change in the price, which is 1 ÷ 10 or 0.1.
1d. The supply of the good has become more elastic over the year since the price rise because other producers will have gradually started producing the good.
1e. The elasticity of supply equals the percentage change in the quantity supplied divided by the percentage change in the price. After one year, the elasticity of supply is 25 ÷ 10, which equals 2.5.

5.3 CROSS ELASTICITY AND INCOME ELASTICITY

Domino's Pizza in Chula Vista has a problem. Burger King has just cut its prices. Domino's manager, Pat, knows that pizzas and burgers are substitutes. He also knows that when the price of a substitute for pizza falls, the demand for pizza decreases. But by how much will the quantity of pizza bought decrease if Pat maintains his current price?

Pat also knows that pizza and soda are complements. He knows that if the price of a complement of pizza falls, the demand for pizza increases. So he wonders whether he might keep his customers by cutting the price he charges for soda. But he wants to know by how much he must cut the price of soda to keep selling the same quantity of pizza with cheaper burgers all around him.

To answer these questions, Pat needs to calculate the cross elasticity of demand. Let's examine this elasticity measure.

■ Cross Elasticity of Demand

The **cross elasticity of demand** is a measure of the responsiveness of the demand for a good to a change in the price of a substitute or complement when other things remain the same. It is calculated by using the formula:

$$\text{Cross elasticity of demand} = \frac{\text{Percentage change in quantity demanded of a good}}{\text{Percentage change in price of one of its substitutes or complements}}.$$

Cross elasticity of demand
A measure of the responsiveness of the demand for a good to a change in the price of a substitute or complement when other things remain the same.

Suppose that when the price of a burger falls by 10 percent, the quantity of pizza demanded decreases by 5 percent. The cross elasticity of demand for pizza with respect to the price of a burger is

$$\text{Cross elasticity of demand} = \frac{-5 \text{ percent}}{-10 \text{ percent}} = 0.5.$$

The cross elasticity of demand for a substitute is positive. A *fall* in the price of a substitute brings a *decrease* in the quantity demanded of the good. The quantity demanded of a good and the price of one of its substitutes change in the same direction.

Suppose that when the price of soda falls by 10 percent, the quantity of pizza demanded increases by 2 percent.* The cross elasticity of demand for pizza with respect to the price of soda is

$$\text{Cross elasticity of demand} = \frac{+2 \text{ percent}}{-10 \text{ percent}} = -0.2.$$

The cross elasticity of demand for a complement is negative. A *fall* in the price of a complement brings an *increase* in the quantity demanded of the good. The quantity demanded of a good and the price of one of its complements change in opposite directions.

---

*As before, these percentage changes are calculated by using the midpoint method.

■ FIGURE 5.7

Cross Elasticity of Demand

❶ A burger is a *substitute* for pizza. When the price of a burger falls, the demand curve for pizza shifts leftward from D_0 to D_1. At the fixed price of pizza, the quantity demanded of pizza decreases. The cross elasticity of the demand for pizza with respect to the price of a burger is *positive*.

❷ Soda is a *complement* of pizza. When the price of soda falls, the demand curve for pizza shifts rightward from D_0 to D_2. At the fixed price of pizza, the quantity demanded of pizza increases. The cross elasticity of the demand for pizza with respect to the price of soda is *negative*.

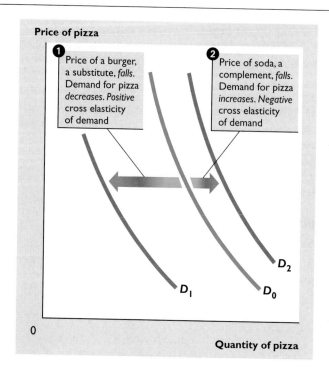

Figure 5.7 illustrates these two cross elasticities of demand for pizza. When the price of a burger falls, the demand for pizza decreases and the demand curve for pizza shifts leftward from D_0 to D_1. When the price of soda falls, the demand for pizza increases and the demand curve for pizza shifts rightward from D_0 to D_2. The magnitude of the cross elasticity determines how far the demand curve shifts.

■ Income Elasticity of Demand

The U.S. and global economies are expanding, and people are enjoying rising incomes. This increasing prosperity brings an increasing demand for most types of goods. But by how much will the demand for different items increase? Will the demand for some items increase so rapidly that we spend an increasing percentage of our incomes on them? And will the demand for some items decrease?

The answer depends on the income elasticity of demand. The **income elasticity of demand** is a measure of the responsiveness of the demand for a good to a change in income when other things remain the same. It is calculated by using the following formula:

Income elasticity of demand
A measure of the responsiveness of the demand for a good to a change in income when other things remain the same.

$$\text{Income elasticity of demand} = \frac{\text{Percentage change in quantity demanded}}{\text{Percentage change in income}}.$$

The income elasticity of demand falls into three ranges:

- Greater than 1 (normal good, income elastic)
- Between zero and 1 (normal good, income inelastic)
- Less than zero (inferior good)

As our incomes increase: items that have an income elastic demand take an increasing share of income; items that have an income inelastic demand take a decreasing share of income; and items that have a negative income elasticity of demand take an absolutely smaller amount of income.

You can make some strong predictions about how the world will change over the coming years by knowing the income elasticities of demand of different goods and services. *Eye on the Global Economy* (below) provides a sampling of numbers.

These estimated income elasticities of demand tell us that we can expect air travel—both domestic and international—to become hugely more important; watching movies, having meals in restaurants, and even our haircuts and auto-mobiles will take an increasing share of our incomes. Not shown in the table below, health care and education are two other prominent items the demand for which is income elastic. As our incomes grow, we can expect education and health care to take increasing shares of our incomes.

We'll be spending a decreasing percentage on clothing, phone calls, and food. The income elasticity of demand for food is less than one even for the poorest people. So we can predict a continuation of the trends of the past—shrinking agriculture and manufacturing and expanding services.

EYE ON THE GLOBAL ECONOMY

Income Elasticities of Demand

In the United States, necessities such as food and clothing are income inelastic; luxuries such as airline and foreign travel are income elastic.

The *level* of income has a big effect on income elasticities of demand. Using data for ten countries, the figure shows that the lower the income level, the more income elastic is the demand for food.

Some Income Elasticities of Demand

Good or Service	Elasticity
Income Elastic	
Airline travel	5.82
Movies	3.41
Foreign travel	3.08
Electricity	1.94
Restaurant meals	1.61
Local buses and trains	1.38
Haircuts	1.36
Cars	1.07
Income Inelastic	
Tobacco	0.86
Alcoholic beverages	0.62
Furniture	0.53
Clothing	0.51
Newspapers	0.38
Telephone	0.32
Food	0.14

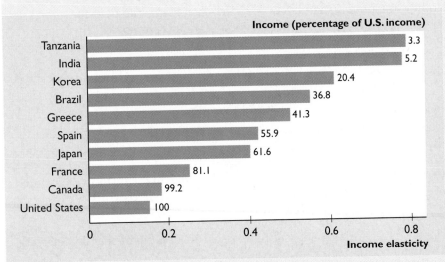

Income (percentage of U.S. income)

Tanzania	3.3
India	5.2
Korea	20.4
Brazil	36.8
Greece	41.3
Spain	55.9
Japan	61.6
France	81.1
Canada	99.2
United States	100

Income elasticity

Sources of data: See page C1.

3 Define and explain the factors that influence the cross elasticity of demand and the income elasticity of demand.

Practice Problems 5.3

1. If the quantity demanded of good *A* increases by 5 percent when the price of good *B* rises by 10 percent and other things remain the same,
   a. Are goods *A* and *B* complements or substitutes? Why?
   b. Describe how the demand for good *A* changes.
   c. Calculate the cross elasticity of demand.

2. If, when income rises by 5 percent and other things remain the same, the quantity demanded of good *C* increases by 1 percent,
   a. Is good *C* a normal good or an inferior good? Why?
   b. Describe how the demand for good *C* changes.
   c. Calculate the income elasticity of demand for good *C*.

Exercises 5.3

1. If, when the price of a pizza falls from $9 to $7 and other things remain the same, the quantity demanded of pizza increases from 100 to 200 an hour, the quantity demanded of burgers decreases from 200 to 100 an hour, and the quantity demanded of cola increases from 150 to 250 cans an hour,
   a. Are cola and pizza substitutes or complements? Why?
   b. Calculate the cross elasticity of demand for cola with respect to pizza.
   c. Are burgers and pizza substitutes or complements? Why?
   d. Calculate the cross elasticity of demand for burgers with respect to pizza.
   e. Of what use are these two cross elasticities of demand to the owner of a business that sells burgers and cola?

2. When incomes in Miami rise by 10 percent and other things remain the same, the quantity demanded of frozen fish cakes decreases by 5 percent and the quantity demanded of fresh fish increases by 15 percent.
   a. Are frozen fish cakes a normal good or an inferior good? Why?
   b. Calculate the income elasticity of demand for frozen fish cakes.
   c. Calculate the income elasticity of demand for fresh fish.
   d. How could a fish shop owner in Miami use these two income elasticities?

FIGURE I

Price of good *A*

D_0 D_1

0   Quantity of good *A*

FIGURE 2

Price of good *C*

D_0 D_1

0   Quantity of good *C*

Solutions to Practice Problems 5.3

1a. Goods *A* and *B* are substitutes because when the price of good *B* rises, the quantity demanded of good *A* increases. People switch from good *B* to good *A*.
1b. The demand for good *A* increases (Figure 1).
1c. Cross elasticity of demand = Percentage change in the quantity demanded of good *A* ÷ Percentage increase in the price of good *B*, which is 5 ÷ 10 or 0.5.

2a. Good *C* is a normal good; as income rises, the quantity demanded increases.
2b. The demand for good *C* increases (Figure 2).
2c. Income elasticity of demand = Percentage change in the quantity demanded of good *C* ÷ Percentage increase in income, which is 1 ÷ 5 or 0.2.

CHAPTER CHECKPOINT

Key Points

1 **Define, explain the factors that influence, and calculate the price elasticity of demand.**

- The demand for a good is elastic if when its price changes, the percentage change in the quantity demanded exceeds the percentage change in price.
- The demand for a good is inelastic if when its price changes, the percentage change in the quantity demanded is less than the percentage change in price.
- The price elasticity of demand for a good depends on how easy it is to find substitutes for the good and on the proportion of income spent on it.
- Price elasticity of demand equals the percentage change in the quantity demanded divided by the percentage change in price.
- If demand is elastic, a rise in price leads to a decrease in total revenue. If demand is unit elastic, a rise in price leaves total revenue unchanged. And if demand is inelastic, a rise in price leads to an increase in total revenue.

2 **Define, explain the factors that influence, and calculate the price elasticity of supply.**

- The supply of a good is elastic if when its price changes, the percentage change in the quantity supplied exceeds the percentage change in price.
- The supply of a good is inelastic if when its price changes, the percentage change in the quantity supplied is less than the percentage change in price.
- The main influences on the price elasticity of supply are the flexibility of production possibilities and storage possibilities.

3 **Define and explain the factors that influence the cross elasticity of demand and the income elasticity of demand.**

- Cross elasticity of demand shows how the demand for a good changes when the price of one of its substitutes or complements changes.
- Cross elasticity is positive for substitutes and negative for complements.
- Income elasticity of demand shows how the demand for a good changes when income changes. For a normal good, the income elasticity of demand is positive. For an inferior good, the income elasticity of demand is negative.

Key Terms

Cross elasticity of demand, 135
Elastic demand, 120
Elastic supply, 130
Income elasticity of demand, 136
Inelastic demand, 120
Inelastic supply, 130

Perfectly elastic demand, 120
Perfectly elastic supply, 130
Perfectly inelastic demand, 120
Perfectly inelastic supply, 130
Price elasticity of demand, 118
Price elasticity of supply, 130

Total revenue, 126
Total revenue test, 127
Unit elastic demand, 120
Unit elastic supply, 130

Exercises

1. One winter recently, the price of home heating oil increased by 20 percent and the quantity demanded decreased by 2 percent, and with no change in the price of wool sweaters, the quantity demanded of wool sweaters increased by 10 percent.
   a. How would you describe the demand for home heating oil?
   b. Is home heating oil more likely to be a necessity or a luxury good? Why?
   c. How did the total revenue from the sale of home heating oil change? Why?
   d. Calculate the cross elasticity of demand of wool sweaters with respect to the price of home heating oil.
   e. Are home heating oil and wool sweaters substitutes or complements? Why?

FIGURE 1

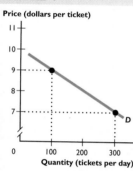

2. Figure 1 shows the demand for movie tickets.
   a. Is the demand for movie tickets elastic or inelastic over the price range $7 to $9 a ticket?
   b. If the price falls from $9 to $7 a ticket, will total revenue from the sale of movie tickets rise or fall? Explain.
   c. Calculate the price elasticity of demand for movie tickets.

3. The price elasticity of demand for Pete's chocolate chip cookies is 1.5. Pete wants to increase his total revenue. Would you recommend that Pete raise his price or lower his price of cookies? Explain your answer.

4. When heavy rain ruined the banana crop in Central America, the price of bananas rose from $1 a pound to $2 a pound. Banana sellers sold fewer bananas, but their total revenue remained unchanged.
   a. By how much did the quantity of bananas demanded change?
   b. Is the demand for bananas from Central America elastic or inelastic?

5. The price elasticity of demand for plane rides is 0.5. The price elasticity of demand for train rides is 0.2. The cross elasticity of demand for train rides with respect to the price of a plane ride is 0.4.
   a. If the price of a plane ride rises by 10 percent, what is the percentage change in the quantity demanded of plane rides?
   b. If the price of a plane ride rises by 10 percent, what is the percentage change in the quantity demanded of train rides?
   c. If the price of a train ride rises by 10 percent, what is the percentage change in the quantity demanded of train rides?
   d. When the price of a plane ride rises by 10 percent, what is the percentage change in the price of a train ride that will lead to no change in the quantity demanded of train rides?
   e. In part d, there is a movement along the demand curve for which ride and a shift of the demand curve for which ride?

6. When incomes increased by 10 percent, the quantity demanded of memberships in athletic clubs increased by 15 percent, the quantity of spring water demanded increased by 5 percent, and the quantity of sports drinks demanded decreased by 2 percent.
   a. Describe the demand for memberships in athletic clubs.
   b. Describe the demand for spring water.

   c. Describe the demand for sports drinks.
   d. The demand for which good is income elastic? Which is income inelastic?
   e. Which of the three goods are normal goods? Is any good an inferior good?

7. In Pioneer Ville, the price elasticity of demand for bus rides is 0.5, the income elasticity of demand for bus rides is −0.1, and the cross elasticity of demand for bus rides with respect to gasoline is 0.2.
   a. Is the demand for bus rides elastic or inelastic with respect to the price of a bus ride? Why?
   b. Would an increase in bus fares increase the bus company's total revenue? Explain your answer.
   c. Describe the relationship between bus rides and gasoline. Explain.
   d. If the price of gasoline increases by 10 percent with no change in the price of a bus ride, how will the number of bus rides change?
   e. If incomes in Pioneer Ville increase by 5 percent with no change in the price of a bus ride, how will the number of bus rides change?
   f. In Pioneer Ville, is a bus ride a normal good or an inferior good? Why?
   g. In Pioneer Ville, are bus rides and gasoline substitutes or complements? Why?

8. The income elasticity of demand for haircuts is 1.5, and the income elasticity of demand for food is 1.4. You take a weekend job, and the income you have to spend on food and haircuts doubles. If the prices of food and haircuts remain the same, will you double your expenditure on haircuts and double your expenditure on food? Explain why or why not.

9. Drought in many wheat-growing areas in 2002 cut the quantity of wheat grown by 2 percent. The price elasticity of demand for wheat is 0.5.
   a. By how much will the price of wheat rise?
   b. If pasta makers estimate that the change in the price of wheat in part **a** will increase the price of pasta by 25 percent and decrease the quantity demanded of pasta by 8 percent, what is the pasta makers' estimate of the price elasticity of demand for pasta?
   c. If pasta sauce makers estimate that, with the changes in part **b**, the quantity of pasta sauce demanded will decrease by 5 percent, what is the pasta sauce makers' estimate of the cross elasticity of demand for pasta sauce with respect to the price of pasta?

10. If textbooks became more expensive but no other prices changed and your income remained the same, do you think you would spend more, less, or the same as you now spend on textbooks? What does your answer tell you about *your* price elasticity of demand for textbooks?

Critical Thinking

11. How might the owners of the Houston Galleria shopping mall use the concept of cross elasticity of demand to determine the best combination of stores to operate in the Galleria?

12. "In a market in which demand is price inelastic, producers can gouge consumers and the government must set high standards of conduct for producers to ensure that consumers gets a fair deal." Do you agree or disagree with each part of this statement? Explain how you might go about testing the parts of the statement that are positive and lay bare the normative parts.

13. The Organization of the Petroleum Exporting Countries (OPEC) produces about 40 percent of the world's output of crude oil. OPEC knows that it can raise the world price of oil by cutting the total production of its member countries. OPEC also knows that the demand for crude oil is inelastic.
    a. Explain to the OPEC ministers, who are not economists, why it is not possible to conclude from these facts that OPEC's total revenue would increase if it were to cut its production.
    b. Does the elasticity of non-OPEC supply have any influence on how the price of crude oil changes when OPEC cuts production? Again, explain your answer in simple language that the OPEC ministers can understand.

14. Ron Gettelfinger, president of the United Auto Workers (UAW), wants your help. He has noticed that when he negotiates a pay increase for UAW members, the number of jobs available for them doesn't change at first, but then, over the next year or so, the number of jobs decreases. He has noticed that on the average, after a year, for every 1 percent rise in the wage rate, the number of jobs decreases by 1.5 percent.
    a. Describe the demand for UAW members' labor services.
    b. Calculate the price elasticity of demand for UAW members' labor services.
    c. How does the total wage bill of the employers of UAW members change immediately after a pay increase? Why?
    d. How does the total wage bill of the employers of UAW members change a year after a pay increase? Why?
    e. Can you think of any ways in which the UAW can make the demand for its members' labor services less elastic?
    f. Can you think of any ways in which the employers of UAW members can make the demand for labor services more elastic?

Web Exercises

Use the links on MyEconLab to work the following exercises.

15. Visit the Web site of the government of Canada and review the study of the price elasticity of demand for air travel.
    a. What are the six categories of air travel that the study used and why do you think it is necessary to break this service into several parts?
    b. Which category of air travel has the most inelastic demand? Why?
    c. Which category of air travel has the most elastic demand? Why?
    d. If the price of air travel falls, how will total expenditure on air travel change for each of the six categories in the study?
    e. How do you think an airline can use the information about the different price elasticities of demand? Hint: Think about the total revenue test.

16. Visit the Web sites of 3M and McDonald's. Think about the range of items each firm produces.
    a. Which firm do you think produces goods that have elastic demands? Why?
    b. If the demand for burgers is inelastic, does that mean that McDonald's can keep raising the price of a burger? Why or why not?
    c. If the demand for Post-it Notes is elastic, does that mean that 3M can be relied upon to keep the price of Post-it Notes low? Why or why not?

Efficiency and Fairness of Markets

CHAPTER 6

CHAPTER CHECKLIST

When you have completed your study of this chapter, you will be able to

1 Describe alternative methods of allocating scarce resources.

2 Distinguish between value and price and define consumer surplus.

3 Distinguish between cost and price and define producer surplus.

4 Evaluate the efficiency of the alternative methods of allocating scarce resources.

5 Explain the main ideas about fairness and evaluate the fairness of competitive markets and other allocation methods.

Markets make a lot of people unhappy! Unhappy because hard work doesn't always translate into a living wage. In the U.S. job markets, for example, around 12 million workers earn a wage of less than $6 an hour. Unhappy because where disaster strikes, price hikes seem to follow. A hurricane in Florida, a frost in Brazil, a tsunami in Asia—all send the prices of essential items sky high.

Do these examples show that markets are inefficient and unfair? Or are the outcomes just the result of markets making the best of it: allocating scarce resources efficiently and fairly in the social interest? These are the questions that we study in this chapter.

But if markets do a bad job, what are the alternatives? Can scarce resources be allocated more efficiently and fairly by means other than markets? We begin by reviewing alternative methods of allocating scarce resources.

6.1 RESOURCE ALLOCATION METHODS

The goal of this chapter is to evaluate the ability of markets to allocate resources in the social interest. The social interest has two dimensions: efficiency and fairness. So we must investigate whether the market is efficient and fair.

Because resources are scarce, they must be allocated somehow among their competing uses. But trading in markets isn't the only method. And to know whether the market does a good job, we need to compare it with its alternatives. So what are the alternatives?

Resources might be allocated by using any or some combination of the following methods:

- Market price
- Command
- Majority rule
- Contest
- First-come, first-served
- Sharing equally
- Lottery
- Personal characteristics
- Force

Let's see how each method works and look at an example of each.

■ Market Price

When a market price allocates a scarce resource, the people who get the resource are those who are willing and able to pay the market price. People who don't value the resource as highly as the market price leave it for others to buy and use.

Most of the scarce resources that you supply get allocated by market price. For example, you sell your labor services in a market. And you buy most of what you consume in markets.

Two kinds of people decide not to pay the market price: those who can afford to pay but choose not to buy and those who are too poor and simply can't afford to pay.

For many goods and services, distinguishing between those who choose not to buy and those who can't afford to pay doesn't matter. But for a few items, it does matter. For example, poor people can't afford to pay school fees and doctor's fees. The inability of poor people to buy items that most people consider to be essential is not handled well by the market price method and is usually dealt with by one of the other allocation methods.

But for most goods and services, the market turns out to do a good job. We'll examine just how good a job it does later in this chapter.

■ Command

Command system
A system that allocates resources by the order of someone in authority.

A **command system** allocates resources by the order (command) of someone in authority. Many resources get allocated by command. In the U.S. economy, the command system is used extensively inside firms and government bureaus. For example, if you have a job, most likely someone tells you what to do. Your labor time is allocated to specific tasks by a command.

Sometimes, a command system allocates the resources of an entire economy.

The former Soviet Union is an example. North Korea and Cuba are the only remaining command economies.

A command system works well in organizations in which the lines of authority and responsibility are clear and it is easy to monitor the activities being performed. But a command system works badly when applied to an entire economy. The range of activities to be monitored is just too large, and it is easy for people to fool those in authority. The system works so badly in North Korea that it fails even to deliver an adequate supply of food.

■ Majority Rule

Majority rule allocates resources in the way that a majority of voters choose. Societies use majority rule for some of their biggest decisions. For example, majority rule decides the tax rates that end up allocating scarce resources between private use and public use. And majority rule decides how tax dollars are allocated among competing uses such as national defense and health care for the aged.

Having 200 million people vote on every line in a nation's budget would be extremely costly. So instead of direct majority rule, the United States (and most other countries) use the system of representative government. Majority rule determines who will represent the people. And majority rule among the representatives decides the detailed allocation of scarce resources.

Majority rule works well when the decisions being made affect large numbers of people and self-interest must be suppressed to use resources most effectively.

■ Contest

A contest allocates resources to a winner (or a group of winners). The most obvious contests are sporting events. Serena Williams and Lindsay Davenport do battle on a tennis court, and the winner gets twice as much as the loser.

But contests are much more general than those in a sports arena, though we don't call them contests in ordinary speech. For example, Bill Gates won a big contest to provide the world's personal computer operating system, and Halle Berry won a type of contest to rise to the top of the movie-acting business.

Contests do a good job when the efforts of the "players" are hard to monitor and reward directly. By dangling the opportunity to win a big prize, people are motivated to work hard and try to become the "winner." Only a few people end up with a big prize, but many people work harder in the process of trying to win. So total production is much greater than it would be without the contest.

■ First-Come, First-Served

A first-come, first-served method allocates resources to those who are first in line. Most national parks allocate campsites in this way. Many casual restaurants won't accept reservations. They use first-come, first-served to allocate their scarce tables. The most visible example of first-come, first-served is the freeway. This scarce transportation resource gets allocated to the first to arrive at the on-ramp. If too many vehicles enter the freeway, the speed slows and people, in effect, wait in line for a bit of the "freeway" to become free!

First-come, first-served works best when, as in the above examples, a scarce resource can serve just one user at a time in a sequence. By serving the user who arrives first, this method minimizes the time spent waiting in line for the resource to become free.

■ Sharing Equally

When a resource is shared equally, everyone gets the same amount of it. You perhaps use this method to share dessert at a restaurant. People sometimes jointly own a vacation apartment and share its use equally.

To make equal shares work, people must be in agreement about its use and must make an arrangement to implement it. Sharing equally can work for small groups who share a set of common goals and ideals.

■ Lottery

Lotteries allocate resources to those who pick the winning number, draw the lucky cards, or come up lucky on some other gaming system. State lotteries and casinos reallocate millions of dollars worth of goods and services every year.

But lotteries are far more widespread than state jackpots and roulette wheels in casinos. They are used in a wide variety of situations to allocate scarce resources. The Federal Aviation Administration, for example, uses a lottery to allocate landing slots to airlines at New York City's LaGuardia airport.

Lotteries work well when there is no effective way to distinguish among potential users of a scarce resource.

■ Personal Characteristics

When resources are allocated on the basis of personal characteristics, people with the "right" characteristics get the resources. Some of the resources that matter most to you are allocated in this way. The people you like are the ones you spend the most time with. You try to avoid having to spend time with people you don't like. People choose marriage partners on the basis of personal characteristics. These uses of personal characteristics to allocate resources are regarded as completely natural and acceptable.

But this method also gets used in unacceptable ways. Allocating the best jobs to white, Anglo-Saxon males and discriminating against minorities and women is an example.

■ Force

Force plays a crucial role, for both good and ill, in allocating scarce resources. Let's start with the ill.

War, the use of military force by one nation against another, has played an enormous role historically in allocating resources. The economic supremacy of European settlers in the Americas and Australia owes much to the use of this method.

Theft, the taking of the property of others without their consent, also plays a large role. Both large-scale organized crime and small-scale petty crime collectively allocate billions of dollars worth of resources annually. A large amount of theft today is conducted by using sophisticated electronic methods that move resources from banks and thousands of innocent people.

But force plays a crucial positive role in allocating resources. It provides an effective method for the state to transfer wealth from the rich to the poor and the legal framework in which voluntary exchange in markets takes place.

Most income and wealth redistribution in modern societies occurs through a taxation and benefits system that is enforced by the power of the state. We vote for taxes and benefits—a majority vote allocation—but we use the power of the state to ensure that everyone complies with the rules and pays their allotted share.

A legal system is the foundation on which our market economy functions. Without courts to enforce contracts, it would not be possible to do business. But the courts could not enforce contracts without the ability to apply force if necessary. The state provides the ultimate force that enables the courts to do their work.

More broadly, the force of the state is essential to uphold the principle of the *rule of law.* This principle is the bedrock of civilized economic (and social and political) life. With the rule of law upheld, people can go about their daily economic lives with the assurance that their property will be protected—that they can sue for violations of their property (and be sued if they violate the property of others).

Free from the burden of protecting their property and confident in the knowledge that those with whom they trade will honor their agreements, people can get on with focusing on the activity at which they have a comparative advantage and trading for mutual gain.

In the next sections of this chapter, we're going to see how a market achieves an efficient use of resources, examine obstacles to efficiency, and see how sometimes, an alternative method might improve on the market. After looking at efficiency, we'll turn our attention to the more difficult issue of fairness.

CHECKPOINT 6.1

1 **Describe alternative methods of allocating scarce resources.**

Practice Problem 6.1

1. Which method is used to allocate the following scarce resources?
   a. Campus parking space between student areas and faculty areas
   b. A spot in a restricted student parking area
   c. Textbooks
   d. Host city for the Olympic Games

Exercise 6.1

1. Which method is used to allocate the following scarce resources?
   a. Airline tickets on the eve of Thanksgiving
   b. Goods at department stores in the January sales
   c. Presidency of the Students' Union
   d. The first serve in the final at the U.S. Open

Solution to Practice Problem 6.1

1a. A command system
1b. First-come, first served
1c. Market price (supplemented perhaps by sharing)
1d. Contest

6.2 VALUE, PRICE, AND CONSUMER SURPLUS

To investigate whether a market is efficient, we need to understand the connection between demand and marginal benefit and between supply and marginal cost.

■ Demand and Marginal Benefit

In everyday life, when we talk about "getting value for money," we're distinguishing between *value* and *price.* Value is what we get, and price is what we pay. In economics, the everyday idea of value is *marginal benefit,* which we measure as the maximum price that people are willing to pay for another unit of the good or service. The demand curve tells us this price. In Figure 6.1(a), the demand curve shows the quantity demanded at a given price—when the price is $10 a pizza, the quantity demanded is 10,000 pizzas a day. In Figure 6.1(b), the demand curve shows the maximum price that people are willing to pay when there is a given quantity—when 10,000 pizzas a day are available, the most that people are willing to pay for the 10,000th pizza is $10. The marginal benefit from the 10,000th pizza is $10.

> **A demand curve is a marginal benefit curve. The demand curve for pizza tells us the dollars' worth of other goods and services that people are willing to forgo to consume one more pizza.**

■ **FIGURE 6.1**

Demand, Willingness to Pay, and Marginal Benefit

(a) Price determines quantity demanded

(b) Quantity determines willingness to pay

❶ The demand curve for pizza, *D,* shows the quantity of pizza demanded at each price, other things remaining the same. At $10 a pizza, the quantity demanded is 10,000 pizzas a day.

❷ The demand curve shows the maximum price willingly paid if there is a given quantity. If 10,000 pizzas are available, the maximum price willingly paid for the 10,000th pizza is $10.

■ Consumer Surplus

We don't always have to pay as much as we're willing to pay. When people buy something for less than it is worth to them, they receive a consumer surplus. **Consumer surplus** is the marginal benefit from a good minus the price paid for it, summed over the quantity consumed.

Figure 6.2 illustrates consumer surplus. Lisa's demand curve for pizza tells us the quantity of pizza she plans to buy at each price and her marginal benefit from pizza at each quantity. If the price of pizza is $1.00 a slice, Lisa buys 20 slices a week. She spends $20 on pizza, which is shown by the area of the blue rectangle.

To calculate Lisa's consumer surplus, we must find her consumer surplus on each slice and add these consumer surpluses together. For the 20th slice, her marginal benefit equals $1 and she pays $1, so her consumer surplus on this slice is zero. For the 10th slice (highlighted in the figure), her marginal benefit is $1.50. So on this slice, she receives a consumer surplus of $1.50 minus $1.00, which is 50¢. For the first slice, Lisa's marginal benefit is almost $2, so on this slice, she receives a consumer surplus of almost $1.

Lisa's consumer surplus—the sum of the consumer surpluses on the 20 slices she buys—is $10 a week, which is shown by the area of the green triangle. (The base of the triangle is 20 slices a week and its height is $1, so its area is 20 × $1 ÷ 2 = $10.)

Lisa's *total benefit* is the amount she pays, $20 (blue rectangle), plus her consumer surplus, $10 (green triangle), and is $30. Because Lisa must pay $20 for the pizza she consumes, her net benefit is equal to her total benefit minus what she pays. Consumer surplus is the net benefit to the consumer.

Consumer surplus
The marginal benefit from a good or service minus the price paid for it, summed over the quantity consumed.

▦ FIGURE 6.2
A Consumer's Demand and Consumer Surplus

Price (dollars per slice)

❶ The market price of pizza is $1.00 a slice.

❷ At the market price, Lisa buys 20 slices a week and spends $20 on pizza—the blue rectangle.

❸ Lisa's demand curve tells us that she is willing to pay $1.50 for the 10th slice, so she receives a consumer surplus of 50¢ on the 10th slice.

❹ Lisa's consumer surplus from the 20 slices she buys is $10—the area of the green triangle. Lisa's total benefit from pizza is the $20 she pays for it plus the $10 consumer surplus she receives, or $30.

2 | **Distinguish between value and price and define consumer surplus.**

Practice Problem 6.2

FIGURE 1

1. Figure 1 shows the demand curve for CDs and the market price of a CD. Use the figure to answer the following questions.
   a. What is the value of the 10th CD?
   b. What is the willingness to pay for the 20th CD?
   c. What is the consumer surplus on the 10th CD?
   d. What are the quantity of CDs bought and the consumer surplus?
   e. What is the amount paid for the CDs in part **d**?
   f. What is the total benefit from the CDs bought in part **d**?
   g. If the price rises to $20, what is the change in consumer surplus?

Exercise 6.2

FIGURE 2

1. Figure 2 shows the demand curve for ice cream cones and the market price of an ice cream cone. Use the figure to answer the following questions.
   a. What is the value of the 15th cone?
   b. What is the willingness to pay for the 5th cone?
   c. What is the consumer surplus on the 5th cone?
   d. What are the quantity of ice cream cones bought and consumer surplus?
   e. What is the total expenditure on ice cream cones?
   f. What is the total benefit from ice cream cones?
   g. If demand doubles, what is the change in consumer surplus?

Solution to Practice Problem 6.2

FIGURE 3

1a. The value of the 10th CD is the marginal benefit from the 10th CD. Value is equal to the maximum price that someone is willing to pay for the 10th CD, which is $20 (Figure 3).

1b. The willingness to pay for the 20th CD is the maximum price that someone is willing to pay for the 20th CD, which is $15 (Figure 3).

1c. The consumer surplus on the 10th CD is its marginal benefit minus the price of a CD, which is $20 − $15 = $5 (the green arrow in Figure 3).

1d. The quantity of CDs bought is 20 a day, and the consumer surplus is ($25 − $15) × 20 ÷ 2 = $100 (the green triangle in Figure 3).

FIGURE 4

1e. The amount paid for CDs is price multiplied by quantity bought, which is $15 × 20 = $300 (the blue rectangle in Figure 3).

1f. The total benefit from CDs is the amount paid for CDs plus the consumer surplus from CDs, which is $300 + $100 = $400.

1g. If the price rises to $20, the quantity of CDs bought decreases to 10 a day. The consumer surplus from CDs decreases to ($25 − $20) × 10 ÷ 2 = $25 (the small green triangle in Figure 4).

6.3 COST, PRICE, AND PRODUCER SURPLUS

What you are now going to learn about cost, price, and producer surplus parallels what you've learned about value, price, and consumer surplus.

■ Supply and Marginal Cost

Just as buyers distinguish between *value* and *price*, so sellers distinguish between *cost* and *price*. Cost is what a seller must give up to produce the good, and price is what a seller receives when the good is sold. The cost of producing one more unit of a good or service is its *marginal cost*. It is just worth producing one more unit of a good or service if the price for which it can be sold equals marginal cost. But the supply curve tells us this price. In Figure 6.3(a), the supply curve shows the quantity supplied at a given price—when the price of a pizza is $10, the quantity supplied is 10,000 pizzas a day. In Figure 6.3(b), the supply curve shows the minimum price that producers must receive to supply a given quantity—to supply 10,000 pizzas a day, producers must be able to get at least $10 for the 10,000th pizza. The marginal cost of the 10,000th pizza is $10. So:

> **A supply curve is a marginal cost curve. The supply curve of pizza tells us the dollars' worth of other goods and services that people must forgo if firms produce one more pizza.**

■ FIGURE 6.3
Supply, Minimum Supply Price, and Marginal Cost

(a) Price determines quantity supplied

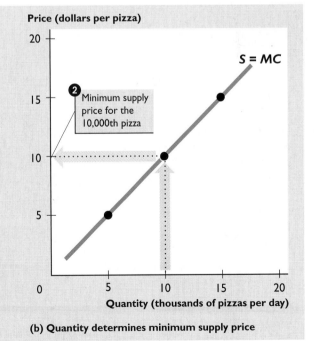

(b) Quantity determines minimum supply price

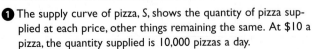 ❶ The supply curve of pizza, S, shows the quantity of pizza supplied at each price, other things remaining the same. At $10 a pizza, the quantity supplied is 10,000 pizzas a day.

❷ The supply curve shows the minimum price that firms must be offered to supply a given quantity. The minimum supply price for the 10,000th pizza is $10.

Producer surplus
The price of a good minus the marginal cost of producing it, summed over the quantity produced.

■ Producer Surplus

When the price exceeds marginal cost, the firm obtains a producer surplus. **Producer surplus** is the price of a good minus the marginal cost of producing it, summed over the quantity produced.

Figure 6.4 illustrates producer surplus. Max can produce pizza or bake bread. The more pizza he bakes, the less bread he can bake. His marginal cost (opportunity cost) of pizza is the value of the bread he must forgo. The marginal cost of pizza increases as Max produces more pizza.

Max's supply curve of pizza tells us the quantity of pizza that Max plans to sell at each price and his marginal cost of producing at each quantity. If the price of a pizza is $10, Max produces 100 pizzas a day. Max's total revenue is $1,000 a day ($10 × 100 = $1,000).

To calculate Max's producer surplus, we must find the producer surplus on each pizza and add these producer surpluses together. The marginal cost of the 100th pizza is $10 and equals the $10 Max can sell it for, so his producer surplus on this pizza is zero. For the 50th pizza (highlighted in the figure), his marginal cost is $6. So on this pizza, he receives a producer surplus of $10 minus $6, which is $4. For the first pizza produced, Max's marginal cost is a bit more than $2, so on this pizza, he receives a producer surplus of almost $8.

Max's producer surplus—the sum of the producer surpluses on the 100 pizzas he sells—is $400 a day, which is shown by the blue triangle. (The base of the triangle is 100 pizzas a day and its height is $8, so its area is 100 × $8 ÷ 2 = $400.)

The red area shows Max's cost of producing 100 pizzas a day, which is $600. This amount equals Max's total revenue of $1,000 a day minus his producer surplus of $400 a day.

■ FIGURE 6.4

A Producer's Supply and Producer Surplus

❶ The market price of a pizza is $10. At this price, Max sells 100 pizzas a day and receives a total revenue of $1,000 a day.

❷ Max's supply curve shows that the minimum that he must be offered for the 50th pizza a day is $6, so he receives a producer surplus of $4 on the 50th pizza.

❸ Max's producer surplus from the 100 pizzas he sells is $400 a day— the area of the blue triangle.

❹ Max's cost of producing 100 pizzas a day is the red area beneath the marginal cost curve. It equals Max's total revenue of $1,000 minus his producer surplus of $400 and is $600 a day.

CHECKPOINT 6.3

3 **Distinguish between cost and price and define producer surplus.**

Practice Problem 6.3

1. Figure 1 shows the supply curve of CDs and the market price of a CD. Use the figure to answer the following questions.
   a. What is the marginal cost of the 10th CD?
   b. What is the minimum supply price of the 20th CD?
   c. What is the producer surplus on the 10th CD?
   d. What are the quantity of CDs sold and producer surplus?
   e. What is the total revenue from the CDs sold in part **d**?
   f. What is the cost of producing the CDs sold in part **d**?
   g. If the price falls to $10, what is producer surplus?

FIGURE 1

Exercise 6.3

1. Figure 2 shows the supply curve of ice cream cones and the market price of an ice cream cone. Use the figure to answer the following questions.
   a. What is the opportunity cost of the 15th cone?
   b. What is the minimum supply price of the 5th cone?
   c. What is the producer surplus on the 5th cone?
   d. What are the quantity of ice cream cones sold and producer surplus?
   e. What is the total revenue from ice cream cones?
   f. What is the total cost of producing ice cream cones?
   g. If the price falls to $2.00 a cone, what is the change in producer surplus?

FIGURE 2

Solution to Practice Problem 6.3

1a. The marginal cost of the 10th CD is equal to the minimum supply price for the 10th CD, which is $10 (Figure 3).

1b. The minimum supply price of the 20th CD is the marginal cost of the 20th CD, which is $15 (Figure 3).

1c. The producer surplus on the 10th CD is its market price minus its marginal cost, which is $15 − $10 = $5 (the blue arrow in Figure 3).

1d. The quantity sold is 20 a day. Producer surplus = ($15 − $5) × 20 ÷ 2 = $100 (blue triangle in Figure 3).

1e. The total revenue is price multiplied by quantity sold. Total revenue is $15 × 20 = $300.

1f. The cost of producing CDs equals total revenue minus producer surplus, which is $300 − $100 = $200 (the red area in Figure 3).

1g. The quantity sold decreases to 10 a day. The producer surplus decreases to ($10 − $5) × 10 ÷ 2 = $25 (the small blue triangle in Figure 4).

FIGURE 3

FIGURE 4

Figure 6.5 shows the market for pizza. The demand curve is *D*, the supply curve is *S*, the equilibrium price is $10 a pizza, and the equilibrium quantity is 10,000 pizzas a day. The market forces that you studied in Chapter 4 (pp. 105–106) pull the pizza market to its equilibrium and coordinate the plans of buyers and sellers. But does this competitive equilibrium deliver the efficient quantity of pizza?

If the equilibrium is efficient, it does more than coordinate plans. It coordinates them in the best possible way. Resources are used to produce the quantity of pizza that people value most highly. It is not possible to produce more pizza without giving up some of another good or service that is valued more highly. And if a smaller quantity of pizza is produced, resources are used to produce some other good that is not valued as highly as the pizza that is forgone.

■ Marginal Benefit Equals Marginal Cost

To check whether the equilibrium in Figure 6.5 is efficient, recall the interpretation of the demand curve as a marginal benefit curve and the supply curve as a marginal cost curve. The demand curve tells us the marginal benefit from pizza. The supply curve tells us the marginal cost of pizza. So where the demand curve and the supply curve intersect, marginal benefit equals marginal cost.

■ FIGURE 6.5

An Efficient Market for Pizza

❶ Market equilibrium occurs at a price of $10 a pizza and a quantity of 10,000 pizzas a day.

❷ The supply curve is also the marginal cost curve.

❸ The demand curve is also the marginal benefit curve.

Because at the market equilibrium, marginal benefit equals marginal cost, the ❹ efficient quantity of pizza is produced. The sum of the ❺ consumer surplus and ❻ producer surplus is maximized.

But this condition—marginal benefit equals marginal cost—is the condition that delivers an efficient use of resources. It allocates resources to the activities that create the greatest possible value. So a competitive equilibrium is efficient.

■ Total Surplus Is Maximized

Another way of checking that the equilibrium is efficient is to look at the total surplus that it generates. **Total surplus** is the sum of producer surplus and consumer surplus. A price above the equilibrium might increase producer surplus, but it would decrease consumer surplus by more. And a price below the equilibrium price might increase consumer surplus, but it would decrease producer surplus by more. The competitive equilibrium price maximizes total surplus.

Total surplus
The sum of producer surplus and consumer surplus.

In Figure 6.5, if production is less than 10,000 pizzas a day, someone is willing to buy a pizza for more than it costs to produce. So buyers and sellers gain if production increases. If production exceeds 10,000 pizzas a day, it costs more to produce a pizza than anyone is willing to pay for it. So buyers and sellers gain if production decreases. Only when 10,000 pizzas a day are produced is there no unexploited gain from changing the quantity of pizza produced, and total surplus is maximized.

Buyers and sellers each attempt to do the best they can for themselves—they pursue their self-interest. No one plans for an efficient outcome for society as a whole. No one worries about the social interest. Buyers seek the lowest possible price, and sellers seek the highest possible price. But as buyers and sellers pursue their self-interest, this astonishing outcome occurs: The social interest is served.

■ The Invisible Hand

Writing in his *Wealth of Nations* in 1776, Adam Smith was the first to suggest that competitive markets send resources to the uses in which they have the highest value. Smith believed that each participant in a competitive market is "led by an invisible hand to promote an end [the efficient use of resources] which was no part of his intention."

You can see the effects of the invisible hand at work every day. Your campus bookstore is stuffed with texts at the start of each term. It has the quantities that it predicts students will buy. The coffee shop has the variety and quantities of drinks and snacks that people plan to buy. Your local clothing shop has the sweatpants and socks and other items that you plan to buy. Truckloads of textbooks, coffee and cookies, and sweatpants and socks roll along our highways and bring these items to where you and your friends want to buy them. Firms that don't know you anticipate your wants and work hard to help you satisfy them.

No government organizes all this production, and no government auditor monitors producers to ensure that they serve the public interest. The allocation of scarce resources is not planned. It happens because prices adjust to make buying plans and selling plans compatible. And it happens in a way that sends resources to the uses in which they have the highest value.

Adam Smith explained why all this amazing activity occurs. "It is not from the benevolence of the butcher, the brewer, or the baker that we expect our dinner," he wrote, "but from their regard to their own interest."

Publishing companies, coffee growers, garment manufacturers, and a host of other producers are led by their regard for their own interest to serve *your* interest.

The Invisible Hand and e-Commerce

You can see the influence of the invisible hand at work in the cartoon and in today's information economy.

The cold drinks vendor has both cold drinks and shade. He has an opportunity cost and a minimum supply price of each item. The park bench reader has a marginal benefit from a cold drink and from shade. The transaction that occurs tells us that the reader's marginal benefit from shade exceeds the vendor's marginal cost but the vendor's marginal cost of a cold drink exceeds the reader's marginal benefit. The transaction creates consumer surplus and producer surplus. The vendor obtains a producer surplus from selling the shade for more than its opportunity cost, and the reader obtains a consumer surplus from buying the shade for less than its marginal benefit. In the third frame of the cartoon, both the consumer and the producer are better off than they were in the first frame. The umbrella has moved to its highest-valued use.

The market economy relentlessly performs the activity illustrated in the cartoon to achieve an efficient allocation of resources. And rarely has the market been working as hard as it is today. Think about a few of the changes that are taking place in our economy and notice how the market is guiding resources toward their efficient use.

New technologies have cut the cost of producing computers. As these advances have occurred, the supply of computers has increased and the price of a computer has fallen. Lower prices have encouraged an increase in the quantity demanded of this now less costly tool. The marginal benefit from computers is brought to equality with their marginal cost.

During the past few years, hundreds of Web sites have been established that are dedicated to facilitating trading in all types of goods, services, and factors of production. One of these sites is Freeshop.com (http://www.freeshop.com/), which organizes access to hundreds of other sites that among them offer more than 1,000 "free and trial offers."

Another notable online market maker is the electronic auction site eBay (http://www.ebay.com/), where you can offer to buy or sell any of a huge variety of items.

These e-commerce innovations are increasing consumer surplus, increasing producer surplus, and achieving yet greater allocative efficiency.

■ Underproduction and Overproduction

Inefficiency can occur because either too little of an item is produced—underproduction—or too much is produced—overproduction.

Underproduction

In Figure 6.6(a), the quantity of pizza produced is 5,000 a day. At this quantity, consumers are willing to pay $15 for a pizza that costs only $6 to produce. The quantity produced is inefficient—there is underproduction.

A **deadweight loss**, which is the decrease in total surplus that results from an inefficient underproduction or overproduction, measures the scale of the inefficiency. The gray triangle in Figure 6.6(a) shows the deadweight loss.

Deadweight loss
The decrease in total surplus that results from an inefficient underproduction or overproduction.

Overproduction

In Figure 6.6(b), the quantity of pizza produced is 15,000 a day. At this quantity, consumers are willing to pay only $5 for a pizza that costs $14 to produce. By producing the 15,000th pizza, $9 is lost. Again, the gray triangle shows the deadweight loss. The total surplus is smaller than its maximum by the amount of deadweight loss. The deadweight loss is borne by the entire society. It is not a loss for the consumers and a gain for the producer. It is a *social* loss.

■ **FIGURE 6.6**

Underproduction and Overproduction

(a) Underproduction

(b) Overproduction

If pizza production is restricted to 5,000 a day, a deadweight loss (the gray triangle) arises. Total surplus is reduced by the amount of the deadweight loss triangle. Underproduction is inefficient.

If production increases to 15,000, a deadweight loss arises. Total surplus is reduced by the amount of the deadweight loss triangle. Overproduction is inefficient.

■ Obstacles to Efficiency

The obstacles to efficiency that bring underproduction or overproduction are

- Price and quantity regulations
- Taxes and subsidies
- Externalities
- Public goods and common resources
- Monopoly
- High transactions costs

Price and Quantity Regulations

Price regulations that put a cap on the rent a landlord is permitted to charge and laws that require employers to pay a minimum wage sometimes block the price adjustments that balance the quantity demanded and the quantity supplied and lead to underproduction. *Quantity regulations* that limit the amount that a farm is permitted to produce also lead to underproduction.

Taxes and Subsidies

Taxes increase the prices paid by buyers and lower the prices received by sellers. So taxes decrease the quantity produced and lead to underproduction. *Subsidies,* which are payments by the government to producers, decrease the prices paid by buyers and increase the prices received by sellers. So subsidies increase the quantity produced and lead to overproduction.

Externalities

An *externality* is a cost or a benefit that affects someone other than the seller and the buyer of a good. An electric utility creates an *external cost* by burning coal that brings acid rain and crop damage. The utility doesn't consider the cost of pollution when it decides how much power to produce. The result is overproduction.

An apartment owner would provide an *external benefit* if she installed a smoke detector. But she doesn't consider her neighbor's marginal benefit and decides to not install a smoke detector. There is underproduction.

Public Goods and Common Resources

A *public good* benefits everyone and no one can be excluded from its benefits. National defense is an example. It is in everyone's self-interest to avoid paying for a public good (called the *free-rider problem*), which leads to its underproduction.

A *common resource* is owned by no one but used by everyone. Atlantic salmon is an example. It is in everyone's self-interest to ignore the costs of their own use of a common resource that fall on others (called the *tragedy of the commons*), which leads to overproduction.

Monopoly

A *monopoly* is a firm that is the sole provider of a good or service. Local water supply and cable television are supplied by firms that are monopolies.

The self-interest of a monopoly is to maximize its profit. And because the monopoly has no competitors, it can set the price to achieve its self-interested goal. To achieve its goal, a monopoly produces too little and charges too high a price. It leads to underproduction.

High Transactions Costs

Stroll around a shopping mall and observe the retail markets in which you participate. You'll see that these markets employ enormous quantities of scarce labor and capital resources. It is costly to operate any market. Economists call the opportunity costs of making trades in a market **transactions costs**.

To use market prices as the allocators of scarce resources, its must be worth bearing the opportunity cost of establishing a market. Some markets are just too costly to operate. For example, when you want to play tennis on your local "free" court, you don't pay a market price for your slot on the court. You hang around until the court becomes vacant, and you "pay" with your waiting time.

When transactions costs are high, the market might underproduce.

Transactions costs
The opportunity costs of making trades in a market.

■ Alternatives to the Market

When a market is inefficient, can one of the alternative non-market methods that we described at the beginning of this chapter do a better job? Sometimes it can.

Table 6.1 summarizes the sources of market inefficiency and the possible remedies. Often, majority rule might be used, but majority rule has its own shortcomings. A group that pursues the self-interest of its members can become the majority. For example, price and quantity regulations that create deadweight loss are almost always the result of a self-interested group becoming the majority and imposing costs on the minority. Also, with majority rule, votes must be translated into actions by bureaucrats who have their own agendas.

Managers in firms issue commands and avoid the transactions costs that they would incur if they went to a market every time they needed a job done. First-come, first-served saves a lot of hassle in waiting lines. These lines could have markets in which people trade their place in the line—but someone would have to enforce the agreements. Can you imagine the hassle at a busy ATM if you had to buy your spot at the head of the line?

There is no one mechanism for allocating resources efficiently. But supplemented by majority rule, bypassed inside firms by command systems, and by occasionally using first-come, first-served, markets do an amazingly good job.

■ TABLE 6.1
Market Inefficiencies and Some Possible Remedies

Reason for inefficiency of market	Possible improvement over market
1. Price and quantity regulations	Remove regulation by majority rule
2. Taxes and subsidies	Minimize deadweight loss by majority rule
3. Externalities	Minimize deadweight loss by majority rule
4. Public goods	Allocate by majority rule
5. Common resources	Allocate by majority rule
6. Monopoly	Regulate by majority rule
7. High transactions costs	Command or first-come, first-served

4 Evaluate the efficiency of the alternative methods of allocating scarce resources.

Practice Problem 6.4

FIGURE 1

Price (dollars per ton)

Quantity (tons per day)

1. Figure 1 shows the market for paper.
   a. What are the equilibrium price and the equilibrium quantity of paper?
   b. In market equilibrium, what is consumer surplus?
   c. In market equilibrium, what is producer surplus?
   d. Is the market for paper efficient? Why or why not?
   e. If a news magazine lobbying group persuaded the government to pass a new law that requires producers to sell 50 tons of paper a day, would the market for paper be efficient? Why or why not?
   f. Shade the deadweight loss in part **e** on the figure.
   g. If an environmental lobbying group persuaded the government to pass a new law that limits the quantity of paper that producers sell to 20 tons a day, would the market for paper be efficient? Why or why not?
   h. In part **g**, what would be the deadweight loss?

Exercise 6.4

FIGURE 2

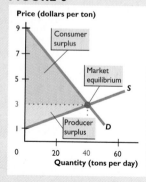

Price (dollars per cone)

Quantity (cones per day)

1. Figure 2 shows the market for ice cream cones.
   a. What are the equilibrium price and quantity of ice cream cones?
   b. In market equilibrium, what is consumer surplus?
   c. In market equilibrium, what is producer surplus?
   d. Is the market for ice cream cones efficient? Why or why not?
   e. If the government limits the quantity that producers can sell to 10 cones a day, would the market for ice cream cones be efficient? Explain.
   f. In part **e**, what would be the deadweight loss?
   g. If the government passed a law requiring producers to sell 20 ice cream cones a day, would the market for ice cream cones be efficient? Explain.
   h. In part **g**, what would be the deadweight loss?

Solution to Practice Problem 6.4

FIGURE 3

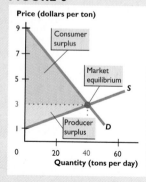

Price (dollars per ton)

Consumer surplus

Market equilibrium

Producer surplus

Quantity (tons per day)

1a. Market equilibrium is 40 tons a day at a price of $3 a ton (Figure 3).

1b. Consumer surplus = ($9 − $3) × 40 ÷ 2
= $120 (the green triangle in Figure 3).

1c. Producer surplus = ($3 − $1) × 40 ÷ 2 = $40 (the blue triangle in Figure 3).

1d. The market is efficient because marginal benefit equals marginal cost and the sum of consumer surplus and producer surplus is a maximum.

1e. This market is inefficient because marginal cost exceeds marginal benefit.

1f. Deadweight loss is the gray triangle 1 in Figure 4.

1g. This market is now inefficient because marginal benefit exceeds marginal cost.

1h. Deadweight loss is the gray triangle 2 in Figure 4.

FIGURE 4

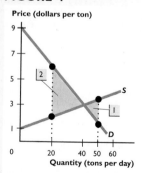

Price (dollars per ton)

Quantity (tons per day)

6.5 ARE MARKETS FAIR?

Is an efficient allocation of resources fair? Does the competitive market provide people with fair incomes for their work? And do people always pay a fair price for the things they buy? Do we need the government to step into some competitive markets to prevent the price from rising too high or falling too low?

When a natural disaster strikes, such as a severe winter storm or a hurricane, the prices of many essential items jump. The reason the prices jump is that some people have a greater demand and a greater willingness to pay while at the same time, the items are in limited supply. So the higher prices achieve an efficient allocation of scarce resources. News reports of these price hikes almost never talk about efficiency. Instead, they complain about unfairness. In Florida, there are even laws that prevent large price increases once a hurricane watch is in effect, and the state has set up an Anti-Gouging Hot Line.

Similarly, when low-skilled people work for a wage that is below what most would regard as a living wage, the media and politicians talk of employers taking unfair advantage of their workers.

How do we decide whether something is fair or unfair? You know when *you* think something is unfair. But how do you know? What are the *principles* of fairness?

Economists have a clear definition of efficiency: making the economic pie as large as possible and baking it at the lowest possible cost. But economists do not have a similarly clear definition of fairness—of what are fair shares of the economic pie for all the people who make it. A big reason for the lack of clarity is that ideas about fairness are not exclusively economic ideas. They also involve the study of ethics.

Think of economic life as a game—a serious game. A game has an outcome or result, and it has rules. All the players face the same rules, but they don't all get the same score. The equality of the rules and inequality of outcomes lies at the heart of discussions about fairness in economics. Two broad and generally conflicting approaches to fairness are

- It's not fair if the *result* isn't fair.
- It's not fair if the *rules* aren't fair.

■ It's Not Fair If the *Result* Isn't Fair

The earliest efforts to establish a principle of fairness were based on the view that the result is what matters. And the general idea was that it is unfair if people's incomes are too unequal. It is unfair that bank presidents earn millions of dollars a year while bank tellers earn only thousands of dollars a year. It is unfair that a store owner enjoys a larger profit and her customers pay higher prices in the aftermath of a winter storm.

But what is "too unequal"? Is it fair for some people to receive twice as much as others but not ten times as much or a hundred times as much? Or is all that matters that the poorest people shouldn't be "too poor"?

There was a lot of excitement during the nineteenth century when economists thought they had made an incredible discovery that answered these questions. And the answer was that *any* inequality is too much! Further, inequality brings inefficiency! This idea turns out to be wrong, but there is a lesson in the reason that it is wrong. So this idea is worth a closer look.

Utilitarianism

Utilitarianism
A principle that states that we should strive to achieve "the greatest happiness for the greatest number."

The nineteenth century idea that only equality brings efficiency is an extreme version of utilitarianism. **Utilitarianism** is a principle that states that we should strive to achieve "the greatest happiness for the greatest number." The people who developed this idea were known as utilitarians. They included two of the most eminent thinkers: Jeremy Bentham and John Stuart Mill.

Some utilitarians argued that to achieve "the greatest happiness for the greatest number," income must be transferred from the rich to the poor up to the point of complete equality—to the point at which there are no rich and no poor.

They reasoned in the following way: First, everyone has the same basic wants and is similar in the capacity to enjoy life. In the technical language of economics that you've now learned to use, everyone has the same marginal benefit schedule or curve. Second, the greater a person's income, the smaller is the marginal benefit of a dollar's worth of goods and services. The millionth dollar spent by a rich person brings a smaller marginal benefit to that person than the marginal benefit of the thousandth dollar spent by a poorer person. So by transferring a dollar from the millionaire to the poorer person, more is gained than is lost, and the two people added together are better off.

But the same is true for every dollar transferred until there is no poor or rich person. Only when everyone's share of the economic pie is the same as everyone else's are we sharing resources in the most efficient way and bringing the greatest attainable total benefit. So complete equality is not only the fair outcome but also the only efficient outcome. It maximizes the value of society's scarce resources.

The Big Tradeoff

Big tradeoff
A tradeoff between efficiency and fairness that recognizes the cost of making income transfers.

One big problem with the utilitarian idea of complete equality is that it ignores the costs of making income transfers. Recognizing the costs of making income transfers leads to what is called the **big tradeoff**—a tradeoff between efficiency and fairness.

The big tradeoff is based on the following facts. Income can be transferred from people with high incomes to people with low incomes only by taxing high incomes. Taxing people's income from employment discourages work. It results in the quantity of labor being less than the efficient quantity. Taxing people's income from capital discourages saving. It results in the quantity of capital being less than the efficient quantity. With smaller quantities of both labor and capital, the quantity of goods and services produced is less than the efficient quantity. The economic pie shrinks.

Income redistribution creates a tradeoff between the size of the economic pie and the equality with which it is shared. The greater the scale of income redistribution through income taxes, the greater is the inefficiency—the smaller is the pie.

There is a second source of inefficiency: A dollar taken from a rich person does not end up as a dollar in the hands of a poorer person. Some of the dollar is spent on administration of the tax and transfer system. The cost of tax-collecting agencies, such as the IRS, and welfare-administering agencies, such as the Health Care Financing Administration, which administers Medicaid and Medicare, must be paid with some of the taxes collected. Also, taxpayers hire accountants, auditors, and lawyers to help them ensure that they pay the correct amount of tax. These activities use skilled labor and capital resources that could otherwise be used to produce other goods and services that people value.

You can see that when all these costs are taken into account, transferring a dollar from a rich person does not give a dollar to a poor person. It is even possible that with high taxes, those with low incomes end up being worse off. Suppose, for example, that highly taxed entrepreneurs decide to work less hard and shut down some of their businesses. Low-income workers get fired and must seek other, perhaps even lower-paid, work.

Because of the big tradeoff, those who say that fairness is equality propose a modified version of utilitarianism.

Make the Poorest as Well Off as Possible

Harvard philosopher John Rawls proposed a modified version of utilitarianism in a classic book, *A Theory of Justice*, published in 1971. Rawls said that, taking all the costs of income transfers into account, the fair distribution of the economic pie is the one that makes the poorest person as well off as possible. The incomes of rich people should be taxed and transferred to the poor. But the taxes must not be so high that they shrink the economic pie by so much that the poorest person ends up with a smaller piece. A bigger share of a smaller pie can be a smaller piece than a smaller share of a bigger pie. The goal is to make the piece enjoyed by the poorest person as big as possible. But this piece will not be an equal share.

The "fair results" ideas require a change in the results after the game is over. Some economists say that these changes are themselves unfair, and they propose a different way of thinking about fairness.

■ It's Not Fair If the *Rules* Aren't Fair

The idea that it's not fair if the rules aren't fair translates into *equality of opportunity*. Another Harvard philosopher, Robert Nozick, made this idea of fairness concrete in a book entitled *Anarchy, State, and Utopia*, published in 1974.

Equality of opportunity can arise only if two rules are followed:

- The state enforces laws that establish and protect private property.
- Private property may be transferred from one person to another only by voluntary exchange with everyone free to engage in such exchange.

The first rule says that everything that is valuable—all scarce resources and goods—must be owned by individuals and that the state must ensure that theft is prevented. The second rule says that the only legitimate way a person can acquire something is to buy it in exchange for something else that the person owns. If these rules are followed, regardless of what the result is, then the outcome is fair. It doesn't matter how unequally the economic pie is shared, provided that it is baked by people each one of whom voluntarily provides services in exchange for the share of the pie that is offered in compensation.

To see why the first rule is required for equality of opportunity, suppose that it is violated and that some resources are not owned. They are common property. Then everyone is free to participate in a grab to use them. The strongest will prevail. But when the strongest prevails, the strongest effectively *owns* the resources in question and can prevent others from enjoying them. The strong have greater opportunities than the weak. There is no equality of opportunity.

To see why the second rule is required for equality of opportunity, suppose that it is violated and we do not insist on voluntary exchange for transferring ownership of resources from one person to another. The alternative to voluntary exchange is *involuntary* transfer. In simple language, the alternative is theft.

Again, only the strong get what they want. The weak end up with only the resources and goods that the strong don't want.

In contrast, in Nozick's two rules, everyone—strong and weak—is treated in a similar way. Everyone is free to use their resources and human skills to create things that are valued by themselves and others and to exchange the fruits of their efforts with each other. This is the only set of arrangements that provides equality of opportunity.

No Big Tradeoff

In Nozick's view of fairness, there is no big tradeoff. If private property rights are enforced and if voluntary exchange takes place in a competitive market, then resources will be allocated efficiently. And the resulting distribution of income and wealth will be fair.

Involuntary transfers of income from the rich to the poor violate the principle of equality of opportunity. These transfers not only decrease the size of the economic pie by damaging incentives to work and save, but also unfairly restrict the opportunities of the current rich to enjoy the fruits of their efforts and restrict the opportunities of the current poor to become rich.

Let's illustrate Nozick's efficient and fair economy by thinking about what happens following a natural disaster.

A Price Hike in a Natural Disaster

Suppose that an earthquake breaks the pipes that deliver drinking water to a city and, in a competitive market for bottled water, the price jumps from $1 to $8. The marginal cost and marginal benefit of water is $8 a bottle.

The people who are willing and able to pay $8 get all the water that they want. And the people who are either unwilling or unable to pay $8 a bottle get no water. The people with water to sell make a gain, and the people who must buy water or go without water incur a loss. Because marginal benefit equals marginal cost, the water is being used *efficiently* and, says Nozick, it is also fair. You can see that water use is efficient. But it is less obvious that it is fair—that it provides equality of opportunity.

To see why the market provides equality of opportunity, suppose that the State directs the bottled water sellers to keep the price at $1 a bottle and to provide everyone with an equal share of the available water. Nothing has happened to change the equilibrium price of a bottle of water, so it remains at $8. Some of the people are willing to pay $8 to get more water. And at that price, some are willing to sell their "fair" share, which they bought for $1 a bottle. If voluntary exchange is permitted, people who value water at less than $8 a bottle will sell and people who are willing and able to pay $8 a bottle will buy. The water will be consumed by the same people as previously.

But there will now be a difference. The gainers are now the buyers for $1 a bottle. Some gain a consumer surplus from the share of water they get for $1 because they were willing to pay more. And some gain a producer surplus because they become sellers of water.

So different people gain in the two situations. But there is equality of opportunity only in the first situation. In the second situation, everyone except the shopowners is free to sell water at the market price. This arrangement discriminates against the water shopowners.

A Compromise

Most people, and probably most economists, have sympathy with the Nozick view but think it too extreme. They see a role for taxes and government income support schemes to transfer some income from the rich to the poor. Such transfers could be considered voluntary in the sense that they are decided by majority voting, and even those who vote against such transfers voluntarily participate in the political process.

Once we agree that using the tax system to make transfers from the rich to the poor is fair, we need to determine just what we mean by a fair tax. We'll look at this big question when we study the tax system in Chapter 8.

REALITY CHECK

Efficiency and Fairness in YOUR Life

You live in the national economy, your state economy, your regional economy, and your own household economy. The many decisions you must make affect efficiency and fairness at all these levels. But here, we'll focus on your own household economy.

Make a spreadsheet and on it identify all the factors of production that your household owns. Count all the person-hours available and any capital. Show how these resources are allocated.

By what methods are your household's scarce resources allocated? Identify those allocated by market price; by command; by first-come, first-served; and by equal shares. Are any resources allocated by majority vote?

Now the tough part: Are these resources allocated efficiently—meaning do the allocations maximize the household pie? To answer this question, think about how you can check whether marginal benefit equals marginal cost for each of your household's activities.

And now an even tougher question: Are the household's resources allocated fairly? To answer this question, think about how you can check whether there is equality of opportunity.

5 Explain the main ideas about fairness and evaluate the fairness of competitive markets and other allocation methods.

Practice Problem 6.5

1. A winter storm cuts the power supply and isolates a small town in the mountains. The people rush to buy candles from the town store, which is the only source of candles. The store owner decides to ration the candles to one per family but to keep the price of a candle unchanged.
   a. Who gets to use the candles?
   b. Who receives the consumer surplus on candles?
   c. Who receives the producer surplus on candles?
   d. Is the outcome efficient?
   e. Is the outcome fair according to the utilitarian principle?
   f. Is there equality of opportunity?

Exercise 6.5

1. An earthquake destroys the homes of a quarter of a city's population. People who are lucky enough to own one of the remaining homes offer rooms for rent at the highest amount that people are willing to pay.
   a. Who gets to occupy the available rooms?
   b. Who receives the consumer surplus on rooms?
   c. Who receives the producer surplus on rooms?
   d. Is the outcome efficient?
   e. Is this outcome fair or unfair?
   f. By what principle of fairness is the outcome fair or unfair?

Solution to Practice Problem 6.5

1a. The people who buy candles from the town store are not necessarily the people who use the candles. A buyer from the town store can sell a candle and will do so if he or she can get a price that exceeds his or her marginal benefit. The people who value the candles most—who are willing to pay the most—will use the candles.

1b. Only the people who are willing to pay the most for candles receive the consumer surplus on candles.

1c. The town store owner receives the same producer surplus as normal. People who sell the candles they buy from the store receive additional producer surplus.

1d. The outcome is efficient because the people who value the candles most use them.

1e. The outcome is unfair according to the utilitarian principle because candles are shared unequally.

1f. There is equality of opportunity because only voluntary exchanges occur.

CHAPTER CHECKPOINT

Key Points

1 **Describe alternative methods of allocating scarce resources.**

- Market price is one method of allocating scarce resources.
- Other methods are by command; majority rule; contest; first-come, first-served; sharing equally; lottery; personal characteristics; and force.
- All of the alternative methods are used and have benefits and costs.

2 **Distinguish between value and price and define consumer surplus.**

- Marginal benefit is measured by the maximum price that consumers are willing to pay for another unit of a good or service.
- A demand curve is a marginal benefit curve.
- Value is what people are *willing to* pay; price is what people *must* pay.
- Consumer surplus equals marginal benefit minus price, summed over the quantity consumed.

3 **Distinguish between cost and price and define producer surplus.**

- Marginal cost is measured by the minimum price producers must be offered to increase production by one unit.
- A supply curve is a marginal cost curve.
- Opportunity cost is what producers must pay; price is what producers receive.
- Producer surplus equals price minus marginal cost, summed over the quantity produced.

4 **Evaluate the efficiency of the alternative methods of allocating scarce resources.**

- In a competitive equilibrium, marginal benefit equals marginal cost and resource allocation is efficient.
- Price and quantity regulations, taxes, subsidies, externalities, public goods, common resources, monopoly, and high transactions costs lead to either underproduction or overproduction and create a deadweight loss.

5 **Explain the main ideas about fairness and evaluate the fairness of competitive markets and other allocation methods.**

- Ideas about fairness divide into two groups: fair *results* and fair *rules*.
- Fair results require income transfers from the rich to the poor.
- Fair rules require property rights and voluntary exchange.

Key Terms

Big tradeoff, 162
Command system, 144
Consumer surplus, 149

Deadweight loss, 157
Producer surplus, 152
Total surplus, 155

Transactions costs, 159
Utilitarianism, 162

TABLE 1

Price (dollars per sandwich)	Quantity demanded	Quantity supplied
	(sandwiches per hour)	
0	400	0
1	350	50
2	300	100
3	250	150
4	200	200
5	150	250
6	100	300
7	50	350
8	0	400

TABLE 2

Price (dollars per bag)	Quantity demanded before flood	Quantity demanded during flood	Quantity supplied
	(thousands of bags)		
0	40	70	0
1	35	65	5
2	30	60	10
3	25	55	15
4	20	50	20
5	15	45	25
6	10	40	30
7	5	35	35
8	0	30	40

Exercises

1. Table 1 shows the demand and supply schedules for sandwiches. Use the table to answer the following questions:
   a. What is the price of a sandwich and what is the consumer surplus?
   b. What is the producer surplus?
   c. What is the efficient quantity of sandwiches?
   d. If the quantity demanded of sandwiches decreases by 100 per hour at each price, what is the price of a sandwich and what is the change in total surplus?
   e. If the quantity supplied of sandwiches decreases by 100 per hour at each price, what is the price of a sandwich and what is the change in total surplus?

2. Table 1 shows the demand and supply schedules for sandwiches. Use the table to answer the following questions:
   a. If Sandwiches To Go, Inc. buys all the sandwich producers and cuts production to 100 sandwiches an hour, what is the deadweight loss that is created?
   b. If in part a, Sandwiches To Go, Inc. rations sandwiches to two per person, is this distribution of sandwiches fair? By what principle of fairness would the distribution be unfair?

3. Table 2 shows the demand and supply schedules for sandbags before and during a major flood. Use the table to answer the following questions:
   a. What happens to consumer surplus and producer surplus during the flood?
   b. Is the allocation of resources efficient (i) before the flood and (ii) during the flood?
   c. If, during the flood, the government allocated the available sandbags and gave all families an equal quantity of them, what would be the allocation method and how would consumer surplus, producer surplus, and the price of a sandbag change?
   d. Is the outcome described in part c more efficient than it would be if the government took no action? Explain.
   e. Is the outcome described in part c fairer than it would be if the government took no action? Explain.

4. In California, farmers pay a lower price for water than do city residents.
   a. What is this method of allocation of water resources?
   b. Is this allocation of water efficient? Explain why or why not.
   c. Is this use of water fair? Why or why not?

5. In California, farmers pay a lower price for water than do city residents. If farmers were charged the same price as city residents pay,
   a. Explain how the price of agricultural produce, the quantity of produce grown, consumer surplus, and producer surplus would change.
   b. What now is the method for allocating resources?
   c. Would the allocation of water now be more efficient? Why or why not?
   d. Would the use of water be fairer? Why or why not?

6. At the Metropolitan Museum of Art in New York, the regular admission price is $15 and the student price is $7.

    a. Is this arrangement efficient? Is it fair? Explain.

    b. When the museum puts on a special exhibition, the prices don't change but long lines develop. Would it be more efficient to increase the price that students pay? Explain why or why not.

    c. In part **c**, would the higher price for students be fairer? Explain why or why not.

7. Dan operates a one-person barbershop, and Zoe runs a large hairdressing salon. Table 3 shows the quantities of haircuts supplied by Dan and Zoe at various prices per haircut. Use the table to answer the following questions.

    a. If the price of a haircut is $15, who makes the larger producer surplus?

    b. If the price of a haircut is $10, who makes the larger producer surplus?

    c. Are both outcomes in parts **a** and **b** fair according to the utilitarian view of fairness? Explain why or why not.

    d. Are both outcomes in parts **a** and **b** fair according to John Rawls's view of fairness? Explain why or why not.

    e. Are both outcomes in parts **a** and **b** fair according to Robert Nozick's view of fairness? Explain why or why not.

TABLE 3

Price (dollars per haircut)	Quantity supplied	
	Dan	Zoe
	(haircuts per day)	
0	0	0
5	0	0
10	2	0
15	4	40
20	6	60
25	8	80
30	10	100

Critical Thinking

8. The winner of the men's tennis singles at the U.S. Open is paid much more than the runner-up, but it takes two to have a singles final. Is this compensation arrangement efficient? Is it fair? Explain why it might illustrate the big tradeoff.

9. In tennis, men play the best of five sets and women play the best of three sets, but the winner of the men's tennis singles at the U.S. Open is paid the same as the winner of the women's singles. In contrast, in golf, men and women play the same number of holes and rounds, but the winners of men's golf tournaments are paid much more than the winners of women's golf tournaments. Are these compensation arrangements efficient? Are they fair? Explain.

10. Is it fair that Roger Federer wins so many tennis championships? Suppose the following rule were adopted: After three wins in a season, a professional tennis player is not permitted to compete for the rest of the season. Would this rule be fair? Explain why or why not.

11. Two roommates, Ratna and Sara, decide to cut their expenditure by buying one copy of the required math textbook and sharing it.

    a. What allocation methods do you think they would consider as feasible?

    b. What allocation method do you think would be more efficient?

    c. Will the allocation method you selected in part **b** be fair? Explain why or why not.

    d. In the last week of the semester, as the final exam approaches, how do you think the agreed allocation method would work out?

12. Poor countries that join the World Trade Organization (the WTO) must agree to prevent the illegal production of generic drugs that violate the patents of multinational drug companies and the illegal copying of music CDs, software, and textbooks that violate copyrights.

    a. Do you think that it is efficient or inefficient if people in poor countries create cheap copies of drugs, music, software, and textbooks? Explain using the concepts of marginal benefit, marginal cost, total surplus, and deadweight loss.

b. Do you think that it is fair or unfair if people in poor countries create cheap copies of drugs, music, software, and textbooks? Which concept of fairness do you think is relevant for deciding this issue? Why?

c. Would it be efficient or inefficient, fair or unfair, to impose a large fine on a poor country that failed to prevent the illegal production of generic drugs or the illegal copying of music CDs, software, and textbooks? Use the concepts of marginal benefit, marginal cost, total surplus, and deadweight loss to explain your answer.

d. In part **c**, would it be fair or unfair to impose a large fine? Explain.

Web Exercises

Use the links on MyEconLab to work the following exercises.

13. Download and review the report "LaGuardia Airport: Can the Airport and the Community Co-exist?" by Congressman Joseph Crowley.
    a. What are the resource allocation problems at LaGuardia airport?
    b. How does the Federal Aviation Administration allocate landing slots at LaGuardia?
    c. Is the method of allocating landing slots efficient? Is it fair?
    d. Design a method of allocating landing slots at LaGuardia that is efficient.
    e. Design a method of allocating landing slots at LaGuardia that is fair.
    f. Do your allocation methods present a tradeoff between efficiency and fairness? If so, explain why. If not, explain why not.

14. Visit the Web site of the Hoover Institution and read the essay "Price Controls on Gasoline? Bad Idea" by David R. Henderson.
    a. How would price controls on gasoline influence the quantity of gasoline? Would it lead to overproduction or underproduction?
    b. How would price controls on gasoline influence the marginal cost, marginal benefit, producer surplus, consumer surplus, and deadweight loss in the market for gasoline.
    c. Would price controls on gasoline be fair or unfair? Which concept of fairness is relevant to make your decision?

15. Visit the Web site of the Goldwater Institute and read the report "Light Rail: Inefficient, Ineffective and Unfair."
    a. What are the scarce resources involved in the discussion of a light rail system for the Phoenix area?
    b. What methods of resource allocation are discussed in the report?
    c. Why does the report conclude that a light rail system would be inefficient? Can you figure out where the deadweight loss is?
    d. Why does the report conclude that a light rail system would be unfair? Who would win? Who would lose? Whose opportunities would be restricted unfairly? Who would gain an unfair advantage on others?
    e. How would you design an efficient and fair solution to the transportation problems of the Phoenix area?

PART 3

Government Influences on Markets

CHAPTER CHECKLIST

When you have completed your study of this chapter, you will be able to

1 Explain how a price ceiling works and show how a rent ceiling creates a housing shortage, inefficiency, and unfairness.

2 Explain how a price floor works and show how the minimum wage creates unemployment, inefficiency, and unfairness.

3 Explain how a price support in the market for an agricultural product creates a surplus, inefficiency, and unfairness.

Joe Calabrese likes high gasoline prices! Joe is the general manager of Cleveland's transit system and the high price of gas in 2005 brought a surge in the number of people riding his buses. But with the price of oil heading ever upward, how can the consumer be protected? Can the President wave a magic pen and sign an order that caps the price of oil?

Yoram lives in rental housing in Seattle. His rent is rising by 8 percent a year, but his wages are almost stagnant. Could the city impose rent controls to help people like Yoram? And could it provide more direct help by imposing a minimum wage law to keep Yoram's wage rising?

Jerry Henningfeld says his 900 acre farm in Wauconda, Illinois, isn't making him rich, and he is hoping prices will rise. Running a farm is like being a Cubs fan, he says: There's always next year! How can governments help Jerry and other farmers by keeping the prices of farm products high?

7.1 PRICE CEILINGS

Price ceiling or price cap
A government regulation that places an *upper* limit on the price at which a particular good, service, or factor of production may be traded.

A **price ceiling** (also called a **price cap**) is a government regulation that places an *upper* limit on the price at which a particular good, service, or factor of production may be traded. Trading at a higher price is illegal.

A price ceiling has been used in several markets. But the one that looms largest in everyone's budget is the housing market. The price of housing is the rent that people pay for a house or apartment. Demand and supply in the housing market determine the rent and the quantity of housing available.

Figure 7.1 illustrates the apartment rental market in Biloxi, Mississippi. The rent is $550 a month, and 4,000 apartments are rented.

Suppose that Biloxi apartment rents have increased by $100 a month in the past two years and that a Citizens' Action Group asks the mayor to roll rents back.

■ A Rent Ceiling

Rent ceiling
A regulation that makes it illegal to charge more than a specified rent for housing.

Responding to the demand, the mayor imposes a **rent ceiling**—a regulation that makes it illegal to charge more than a specified rent for housing.

The effect of a rent ceiling depends on whether it is imposed at a level above or below the equilibrium rent. In Figure 7.1, if the rent ceiling is set *above* $550 a month, nothing would change because people are already paying $550 a month.

But a rent ceiling that is set *below* the equilibrium rent has powerful effects on the market. The reason is that it attempts to prevent the rent from rising high enough to regulate the quantities demanded and supplied. The law and the market are in conflict, and one (or both) of them must yield.

■ FIGURE 7.1

A Housing Market

The figure shows the demand curve, *D*, and the supply curve, *S*, for rental housing.

❶ The market is in equilibrium when the quantity demanded equals the quantity supplied.

❷ The equilibrium price (rent) is $550 a month.

❸ The equilibrium quantity is 4,000 units of housing.

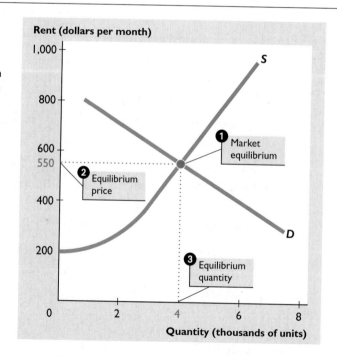

Rent (dollars per month)

❶ Market equilibrium

❷ Equilibrium price

❸ Equilibrium quantity

Quantity (thousands of units)

Figure 7.2 shows one effect of a rent ceiling that is set below the equilibrium rent. The rent ceiling is $400 a month. We've shaded the area *above* the rent ceiling because any rent in this region is illegal. At a rent of $400 a month, the quantity of housing supplied is 3,000 units and the quantity demanded is 6,000 units. So there is a shortage of 3,000 units of housing.

The first effect, then, of a rent ceiling is a housing shortage. People are seeking a larger amount of housing than builders and the owners of existing buildings have an incentive to make available.

But the story does not end here. The 3,000 units of housing that owners are willing to make available must somehow be allocated among people who are seeking 6,000 units. How is this allocation achieved? When a rent ceiling creates a housing shortage, two developments occur:

- A black market
- Increased search activity

A Black Market

A **black market** is an illegal market that operates alongside a government-regulated market. A rent ceiling sometimes creates a black market in housing as frustrated renters and landlords try to find ways of raising the rent above the legally imposed ceiling. Landlords want higher rents because they know that renters are willing to pay more for the existing quantity of housing. Renters are willing to pay more to jump to the head of the queue.

Because raising the rent is illegal, landlords and renters use creative tricks to get around the law. One of these tricks is for a new tenant to pay a high price for

Black market
An illegal market that operates alongside a government-regulated market.

■ FIGURE 7.2

A Rent Ceiling Creates a Shortage

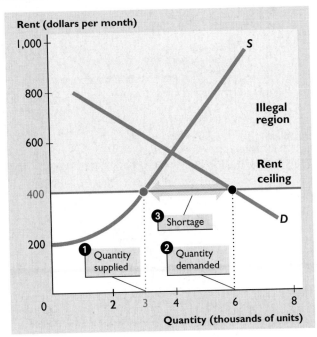

A rent ceiling is imposed below the equilibrium rent. In this example, the rent ceiling is $400 a month.

1 The quantity of housing supplied decreases to 3,000 units.

2 The quantity of housing demanded increases to 6,000 units.

3 A shortage of 3,000 units arises.

worthless fittings—perhaps paying $2,000 for threadbare drapes. Another is for the tenant to pay a high price for new locks and keys—called "key money."

Figure 7.3 shows how high the black market rent might go in Biloxi. With strict enforcement of the rent ceiling, the quantity of housing available is 3,000 units. But at this quantity, renters are willing to offer as much as $625 a month—the amount determined on the demand curve.

So a small number of landlords illegally offer housing for rents up to $625 a month. The black market rent might be at any level between the rent ceiling of $400 and the maximum that a renter is willing to pay of $625.

Increased Search Activity

Search activity
The time spent looking for someone with whom to do business.

The time spent looking for someone with whom to do business is called **search activity**. We spend some time in search activity almost every time we buy something. You want the latest CD, and you know four stores that stock it. But which store has the best deal? You spend a few minutes on the telephone or Internet finding out. In some markets, we spend a lot of time searching. An example is the used car market. People spend a lot of time checking out alternative dealers and cars.

But when a price ceiling creates a shortage of housing, search activity *increases*. In a rent-controlled housing market, frustrated would-be renters scan the newspapers, not only for housing ads but also for death notices! Any information about newly available housing is useful. And they race to be first on the scene when news of a possible apartment breaks.

The *opportunity cost* of a good is equal to its price *plus* the value of the search time spent finding the good. So the opportunity cost of housing is equal to the rent plus the value of the search time spent looking for an apartment. Search activity

---

◼ FIGURE 7.3

A Rent Ceiling Creates a Black Market and Housing Search

With a rent ceiling of $400 a month,

❶ 3,000 units of housing are available.

❷ Someone is willing to pay $625 a month for the 3,000th unit of housing.

❸ Black market rents might be as high as $625 a month and resources get used up in costly search activity.

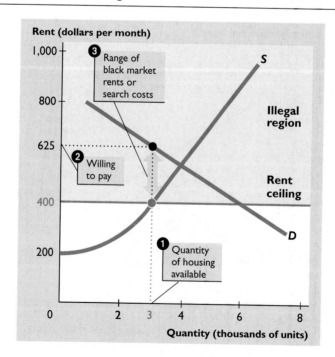

is costly. It uses time and other resources, such as telephones, automobiles, and gasoline that could have been used in other productive ways. In Figure 7.3, to find accommodation at $400 a month, someone who is willing to pay a rent of $625 a month would be willing to spend on search activity an amount that is equivalent to adding $225 a month to the rent. For a one-year lease, this amount is enormous.

A rent ceiling controls the rent portion of the cost of housing but not the search cost. So when the search cost is added to the rent, some people end up paying a higher opportunity cost for housing than they would if there were no rent ceiling.

EYE ON THE PAST

An Earthquake and a Rent Ceiling: A Tale of Two Eras in One City

Let's transport ourselves to San Francisco in April 1906, as the city is suffering from a massive earthquake and fire.

You can sense the enormity of San Francisco's problems from a headline in the *New York Times* on April 20, 1906, describing the first days of the crisis:

Army of Homeless Fleeing from Devastated City
200,000 Without Shelter and Facing Famine

The commander of federal troops in charge of the emergency described the magnitude of the problem:

Not a hotel of note or importance was left standing. The great apartment houses had vanished ... two-hundred-and-twenty-five thousand people were ... homeless.[1]

In a single day, more than half the people in a city of 400,000 had lost their homes. Temporary shelters and camps alleviated some of the problem, but the apartment buildings and houses left standing had to accommodate 40 percent more people than they had before the earthquake.

The *San Francisco Chronicle* was not published for more than a month after the earthquake. When it reappeared on May 24, 1906, the city's housing shortage—what would seem to be a major news item that would still be of grave importance—was not even mentioned. Milton Friedman and George Stigler describe the situation:

There is not a single mention of a housing shortage! The classified advertisements listed sixty-four offers of flats and houses for rent, and nineteen of houses for sale, against five advertisements of flats or houses wanted. Then and there-

---
[1] Milton Friedman and George J. Stigler, "Roofs or Ceilings? The Current Housing Problem," in *Popular Essays on Current Problems*, Vol. I, No. 2 (New York: Foundation for Economic Education, 1946), 3–159.

after a considerable number of all types of accommodation ... were offered for rent.[2]

How did San Francisco cope with such a devastating decrease in the supply of housing? The answer is that a free market brought a rise in the rent and an increase in the intensity of use of the buildings that remained. People rented out rooms that they had previously used themselves. The high rents were an incentive for owners to rebuild as quickly as possible.

At the end of World War II (in 1945), the population of San Francisco grew by 30 percent. At the same time, a large-scale building program increased the number of houses and apartments by 20 percent. So each dwelling unit had to accommodate 10 percent more people. San Francisco had a housing "problem" about a quarter of the magnitude of that following the 1906 earthquake. Yet in 1946, the city's housing shortage was a huge political problem. Newspaper advertisements seeking apartments outnumbered those offering apartments by more than seven to one. Why? San Francisco had rent ceilings in 1946. It had a free housing market in 1906.

---
[2] Friedman and Stigler, p. 3.

■ Are Rent Ceilings Efficient?

A housing market with no rent ceiling determines the rent at which the quantity demanded equals the quantity supplied. In this situation, scarce housing resources are allocated efficiently because the marginal cost of housing equals the marginal benefit. Figure 7.4(a) shows this efficient outcome in the Biloxi apartment rental market. In this efficient market, total surplus—the sum of *consumer surplus* (the green area) and *producer surplus* (the blue area)—is maximized at the equilibrium rent and quantity of housing (see Chapter 6, p. 155).

Figure 7.4(b) shows that with a rent ceiling, the outcome is inefficient. Marginal benefit exceeds marginal cost. Producer surplus and consumer surplus shrink, and a deadweight loss (the gray area) arises. This loss is borne by the people who can't find housing and by landlords who can't offer housing at the lower rent ceiling.

But the total loss exceeds the deadweight loss. Resources get used in costly search activity and in evading the law in the black market. The value of these resources might be as large as the red rectangle. There is yet a further loss: the cost of enforcing the rent ceiling law. This loss, which is borne by taxpayers, is not visible in the figure.

▨ FIGURE 7.4

The Inefficiency of a Rent Ceiling

(a) Efficient housing market

(b) Inefficient housing market

❶ The market equilibrium is efficient with marginal benefit equal to marginal cost. Total surplus, the sum of ❷ consumer surplus (green area) and ❸ producer surplus (blue area), is maximized.

A rent ceiling is inefficient. ❶ Consumer surplus and ❷ producer surplus shrink, a ❸ deadweight loss arises, and ❹ resources are lost in search activity and evading the rent ceiling law.

Although a rent ceiling causes inefficiency, not everyone loses. The people who live in apartments at the rent ceiling get an increase in consumer surplus, and landlords who charge a black market rent get an increase in producer surplus.

The costs of a rent ceiling that we've just considered are only the initial costs. With the rent below the market rent, landlords have no incentive to maintain their buildings in a good state of repair. So over time, the quality and quantity of housing supplied *decrease* and the loss arising from a rent ceiling increases.

The size of the loss from a rent ceiling depends on the elasticities of supply and demand. If supply is inelastic, a rent ceiling brings a small decrease in the quantity of housing supplied. And if demand is inelastic, a rent ceiling brings a small increase in the quantity of housing demanded. So the more inelastic the supply or the demand, the smaller is the shortage of housing and the smaller is the deadweight loss.

With rent ceilings, landlords have no incentive to maintain buildings, and the quality and quantity of housing supplied decrease.

■ Are Rent Ceilings Fair?

We've seen that rent ceilings prevent scarce resources from being allocated efficiently—resources do not flow to their highest-valued use. But don't they ensure that scarce housing resources are allocated more fairly?

You learned in Chapter 6 (pp. 157–161) that fairness is a complex idea about which there are two broad views: fair *results* versus fair *rules*. Rent controls violate the fair rules view of fairness because they block voluntary exchange. But do they deliver a fair result? Do rent ceilings ensure that scarce housing goes to the poor people whose need is greatest?

Blocking rent adjustments that bring the quantity of housing demanded into equality with the quantity supplied doesn't end scarcity. So when the law prevents the rent from adjusting and blocks the price mechanism from allocating scarce housing, some other allocation mechanism must be used. If that mechanism were one that provided the housing to the poorest, then the allocation might be regarded as fair.

But the mechanisms that get used do not usually achieve such an outcome. First-come, first-served is one allocation mechanism. Discrimination based on race, ethnicity, or sex is another. Discrimination against young newcomers and in favor of old established families is yet another. None of these mechanisms delivers a fair outcome.

Rent ceilings in New York City provide examples of these mechanisms at work. The main beneficiaries of rent ceilings in New York City are families that have lived in the city for a long time—including some rich and famous ones. These families enjoy low rents while newcomers pay high rents for hard-to-find apartments.

■ If Rent Ceilings Are So Bad, Why Do We Have Them?

The economic case against rent ceilings is now widely accepted, so *new* rent ceiling laws are rare. But when governments try to repeal rent control laws, as the New York City government did in 1999, current renters lobby politicians to maintain the ceilings. Also, people who are prevented from finding housing would be happy if they got lucky and managed to find a rent-controlled apartment. So there is plenty of political support for rent ceilings.

Apartment owners who oppose rent ceilings are a minority, so their views are not a powerful influence on politicians. Because more people support rent ceilings than oppose them, politicians are sometimes willing to support them too.

1 Explain how a price ceiling works and show how a rent ceiling creates a housing shortage, inefficiency, and unfairness.

Practice Problem 7.1

FIGURE 1

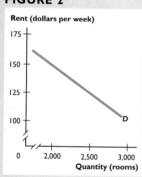

1. Figure 1 shows the rental market for apartments in Corsicana, Texas.
   a. What is the rent in this suburb and how many apartments are rented?
   b. If the city government imposes a rent ceiling of $900 a month, what is the rent and how many apartments are rented?
   c. If the city government imposes a rent ceiling of $600 a month, what is the rent and how many apartments are rented?
   d. With a strictly enforced rent ceiling of $600 a month, is the housing market efficient? Explain why or why not.
   e. If the city strictly enforces the rent ceiling of $600 a month, is the housing market fair? Explain why or why not.
   f. If a black market develops in part **d**, how high could the black market rent be? Explain your answer.

Exercise 7.1

FIGURE 2

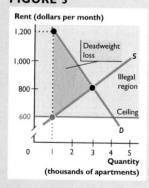

1. Figure 2 shows the demand for on-campus student housing at the University of Idaho, in Moscow, Idaho. The college has 2,000 rooms for rent.
   a. What is the equilibrium rent and how many rooms are rented?
   b. If the college sets a rent ceiling on on-campus housing of $125 a week, how would you describe the on-campus housing market? Would the allocation of housing be efficient? Would it be fair?
   c. If the rent ceiling of $125 a week were strictly enforced and there were no black market, who would gain and who would lose?
   d. If a black market developed as a result of the $125 a week rent ceiling, what range of rents would be offered for a room? Would the allocation of housing be efficient? Would it be fair? Explain.

Solution to Practice Problem 7.1

FIGURE 3

1a. The equilibrium rent is $800 a month, and 3,000 apartments are rented.
1b. A rent ceiling of $900 a month is above the equilibrium rent, so the outcome is the market equilibrium rent of $800 a month with 3,000 apartments rented.
1c. With the rent ceiling at $600 a month, the number of apartments rented is 1,000 and the rent is $600 a month (Figure 3).
1d. The housing market is not efficient. With 1,000 apartments rented, marginal benefit exceeds marginal cost and a deadweight loss arises (Figure 3).
1e. The rent ceiling makes the allocation of housing less fair in both views of fairness: It blocks voluntary transactions, and it does not provide more housing to those in most need.
1f. In a black market, some people are willing to rent an apartment for more than the rent ceiling. The highest rent that someone would offer is $1,200 a month. This rent equals someone's willingness to pay for the 1,000th apartment (Figure 3).

7.2 PRICE FLOORS

A **price floor** is a government regulation that places a *lower* limit on the price at which a particular good, service, or factor of production may be traded. Trading at a lower price is illegal.

> **Price floor**
> A government regulation that places a *lower* limit on the price at which a particular good, service, or factor of production may be traded.

Price floors are used in many markets. But the one that looms largest is the labor market. The price of labor is the wage rate that people earn. Demand and supply in the labor market determine the wage rate and the quantity of labor employed.

Figure 7.5 illustrates the market for fast-food servers in Yuma, Arizona. In this market, the demand for labor curve is *D*. On this demand curve, at a wage rate of $10 an hour, the quantity of fast-food servers demanded is zero. If A&W, Burger King, Taco Bell, McDonald's, Wendy's, and the other fast-food places had to pay servers $10 an hour, they wouldn't hire any. They would replace servers with vending machines! But at wage rates below $10 an hour, they would hire servers. At a wage rate of $5 an hour, firms would hire 5,000 servers.

On the supply side of the market, no one is willing to work for $2 an hour. To attract servers, firms must pay more than $2 an hour.

Equilibrium in this market occurs at a wage rate of $5 an hour with 5,000 people employed as servers.

Suppose that the government thinks that no one should have to work for a wage rate as low as $5 an hour and decides that it wants to increase the wage rate. Can the government improve conditions for these workers by passing a minimum wage law? Let's find out.

FIGURE 7.5
A Market for Fast-Food Servers

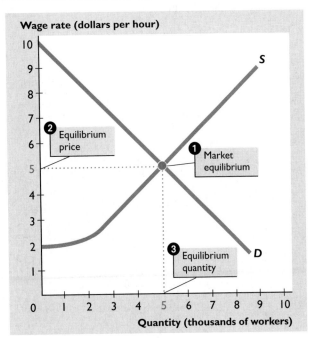

The figure shows the demand curve, *D*, and the supply curve, *S*, for fast-food servers.

❶ The market is in equilibrium when the quantity demanded equals the quantity supplied.

❷ The equilibrium price (wage rate) is $5 an hour.

❸ The equilibrium quantity is 5,000 servers.

■ The Minimum Wage

Minimum wage law
A government regulation that makes hiring labor for less than a specified wage illegal.

A **minimum wage law** is a government regulation that makes hiring labor for less than a specified wage illegal. Firms are free to pay a wage rate that exceeds the minimum wage but may not pay less than the minimum. A minimum wage is an example of a price floor.

The effect of a price floor depends on whether it is set below or above the equilibrium price. In Figure 7.5, the equilibrium wage rate is $5 an hour, and at this wage rate, firms hire 5,000 workers. If the government introduced a minimum wage below $5 an hour, nothing would change. The reason is that firms are already paying $5 an hour, and because this wage exceeds the minimum wage, the wage rate paid doesn't change. Firms continue to hire 5,000 workers.

But the aim of a minimum wage is to boost the incomes of low-wage earners. So in the markets for the lowest-paid labor, the minimum wage will exceed the equilibrium wage.

Suppose that the government introduces a minimum wage of $7 an hour. Figure 7.6 shows the effects of this law. Wage rates below $7 an hour are illegal, so we've shaded the illegal region *below* the minimum wage. Firms and workers are no longer permitted to operate at the equilibrium point in this market because it is in the illegal region. Market forces and political forces are in conflict.

The government can set a minimum wage. But it can't tell employers how many workers to hire. If firms must pay $7 an hour for labor, they will hire only 3,000 workers. At the equilibrium wage rate of $5 an hour, firms hired 5,000 workers. So when the minimum wage is introduced, firms fire 2,000 workers.

■ FIGURE 7.6
A Minimum Wage Creates Unemployment

A minimum wage is introduced above the equilibrium wage rate. In this example, the minimum wage rate is $7 an hour.

❶ The quantity of labor demanded decreases to 3,000 workers.

❷ The quantity of labor supplied increases to 7,000 people.

❸ 4,000 people are unemployed.

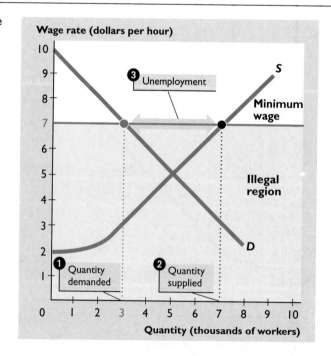

But at a wage rate of $7 an hour, another 2,000 people who didn't want to work for $5 an hour now try to find work as servers. So at $7 an hour, the quantity supplied is 7,000 people. With 2,000 workers fired and another 2,000 looking for work at the higher wage rate, 4,000 people who would like to work as servers are unemployed.

The 3,000 jobs available must somehow be allocated among the 7,000 people who are available for and willing to work. How is this allocation achieved? The answer is by increased job-search activity and illegal hiring.

Increased Job-Search Activity

People spend a great deal of time and resources finding a good job. But with a minimum wage, more people are looking for jobs than the number of jobs available. Frustrated unemployed people spend time and other resources searching for hard-to-find jobs. In Figure 7.7, to find a job at $7 an hour, someone who is willing to work for $3 an hour would be willing to spend on job-search activity an amount that is equivalent to subtracting $4 an hour from the wage rate. For a job that might last a year or more, this amount is large.

Illegal Hiring

With more people looking for work than the number of jobs available, some firms and workers might agree to do business at an illegal wage rate below the minimum wage in a black market.

FIGURE 7.7

A Minimum Wage Increases Job Search

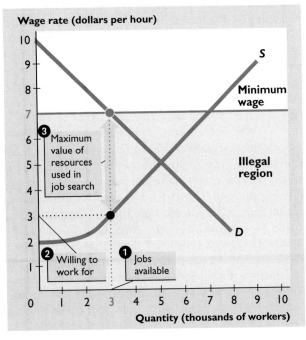

The minimum wage rate is set at $7 an hour:

❶ 3,000 jobs are available.

❷ The lowest wage rate for which someone is willing to work is $3 an hour.

❸ Illegal wage rates might range from just below the legal minimum of $7 an hour to the lowest wage rate that someone is willing to accept: $3 an hour.

The maximum that people are willing to spend on job search is an amount equivalent to subtracting $4 an hour—the $7 they would receive if they found a job minus the $3 they are willing to work for—from the wage rate.

The Federal Minimum Wage

The federal government's *Fair Labor Standards Act* sets the minimum wage, which was last changed in 1997, when it was raised to $5.15 an hour.

The minimum wage creates unemployment. But how much unemployment does it create? Until recently, most economists believed that a 10 percent increase in the minimum wage decreased teenage employment by between 1 and 3 percent.

David Card of the University of California at Berkeley and Alan Krueger of Princeton University have challenged this view. They claim that following a rise in the minimum wage in California, New Jersey, and Texas, the *employment* rate of low-income workers *increased*. They suggest three reasons why a rise in the wage rate might increase employment:

(1) Workers become more conscientious and productive.

(2) Workers are less likely to quit, so costly labor turnover is reduced.

(3) Managers make a firm's operations more efficient.

Most economists are skeptical about these ideas. They say that if higher wages make workers more productive and reduce labor turnover, firms will freely pay workers a higher wage. And they argue that there are other explanations for the employment increase that Card and Krueger found.

Daniel Hamermesh of the University of Texas at Austin says that they got the timing wrong. Firms *anticipated* the minimum wage rise and so cut employment *before* it occurred. Looking at employment changes *after* the minimum wage increased missed its main effect. Finis Welch of Texas A&M University and Kevin Murphy of the University of Chicago say that the employment effects that Card and Krueger found are caused by regional differences in economic growth, not changes in the minimum wage.

Also, looking only at employment misses the supply-side effect of the minimum wage. It brings an increase in the number of people who drop out of high school to look for work.

■ Is the Minimum Wage Efficient?

The efficient allocation of a factor of production is similar to that of a good or service, which you studied in Chapter 6. The demand for labor tells us about the marginal benefit of labor to the firms that hire it. Firms benefit because the labor they hire produces the goods or services that they sell. Firms are willing to pay a wage rate equal to the benefit they receive from an additional hour of labor. So in Figure 7.8(a), the demand curve for labor tells us the marginal benefit that the firms in Yuma receive from hiring fast-food servers. The marginal benefit minus the wage rate is a surplus for the firms.

The supply of labor tells us about the marginal cost of working. To work, people must forgo leisure or working in the home, activities that they value. The wage rate received minus the marginal cost of working is a surplus for workers.

An efficient allocation of labor occurs when the marginal benefit to firms equals the marginal cost borne by workers. Such an allocation occurs in the labor market in Figure 7.8(a). Firms enjoy a surplus (the blue area), and workers enjoy a surplus (the green area). The sum of these surpluses is maximized.

Figure 7.8(b) shows the loss from a minimum wage. With a minimum wage of $7 an hour, 3,000 workers are hired. Marginal benefit exceeds marginal cost. The firms' surplus and workers' surplus shrink, and a deadweight loss (the gray area) arises. This loss is borne by firms that cut back employment and by people who can't find jobs at the higher wage rate.

But the total loss exceeds the deadweight loss. Resources get used in costly job-search activity as each unemployed person keeps looking for a job—writing letters, making phone calls, going for interviews, and so on. The value of these resources might be as large as the red rectangle.

FIGURE 7.8

The Inefficiency of the Minimum Wage

(a) Efficient labor market

(b) Inefficient labor market

① The market equilibrium is efficient with marginal benefit equal to marginal cost. The sum of ② the firms' surplus (blue area) and ③ workers' surplus (green area) is maximized.

A minimum wage is inefficient. ① The firms' surplus and ② workers' surplus shrink, a ③ deadweight loss arises, and ④ resources are lost in job search.

Is the Minimum Wage Fair?

The minimum wage is unfair on both views of fairness: It delivers an unfair *result* and imposes unfair *rules*. The *result* is unfair because only those people who find jobs benefit. The unemployed end up worse off than they would be with no minimum wage. And those who get jobs are probably not the least well off. When the wage rate doesn't allocate jobs, discrimination, another source of unfairness, increases. The minimum wage imposes unfair *rules* because it blocks voluntary exchange. Firms are willing to hire more labor and people are willing to work more. But they are not permitted by the minimum wage law to do so.

If the Minimum Wage Is So Bad, Why Do We Have It?

Although the minimum wage is inefficient, not everyone loses from it. The people who find jobs at the minimum wage rate are better off. Other supporters of the minimum wage believe that the elasticities of demand and supply in the labor market are low, so not much unemployment results. Labor unions support the minimum wage because it puts upward pressure on all wage rates, including those of union workers. Nonunion labor is a substitute for union labor, so when the minimum wage rises, the demand for union labor increases.

Pizza delivery people gain from the minimum wage.

2 **Explain how a price floor works and show how the minimum wage creates unemployment, inefficiency, and unfairness.**

Practice Problem 7.2

FIGURE I

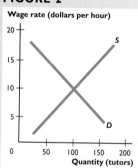

Wage rate (dollars per hour)

1. Figure 1 shows the market for tomato pickers in southern California.
   a. What is the equilibrium wage rate of tomato pickers and what is the equilibrium quantity of tomato pickers employed?
   b. Is the market for tomato pickers efficient?
   c. If California introduces a minimum wage for tomato pickers of $4 an hour, how many tomato pickers are employed and how many are unemployed?
   d. If California introduces a minimum wage for tomato pickers of $8 an hour, how many tomato pickers are employed and how many are unemployed?
   e. Is the minimum wage of $8 an hour efficient? Is it fair?
   f. Who gains and who loses from the minimum wage of $8 an hour?

Exercise 7.2

FIGURE 2

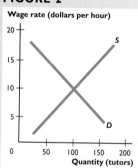

Wage rate (dollars per hour)

1. Figure 2 shows a market for private math tutors in College Station organized by the Students' Union.
   a. What is the wage rate that math tutors earn and how many are employed?
   b. If the Students' Union sets the minimum wage for private math tutors at $15 an hour, how many tutors are unemployed?
   c. If the Students' Union sets the minimum wage for private tutors at $8 an hour, how many tutors are unemployed?
   d. Is a minimum wage of $8 an hour efficient? Is it fair?
   e. Is a minimum wage of $15 an hour efficient? Is it fair?
   f. If a black market gets going, what wage rate might some tutors earn?

Solution to Practice Problem 7.2

1a. The equilibrium wage rate is $6 an hour, and 4,000 pickers are employed.

1b. The market for tomato pickers is efficient because the marginal benefit to tomato growers equals the marginal cost borne by the pickers.

1c. The minimum wage of $4 an hour is below the equilibrium wage rate, so 4,000 tomato pickers are employed and none are unemployed.

FIGURE 3

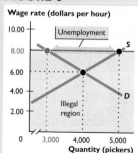

Wage rate (dollars per hour)

1d. The minimum wage of $8 an hour is above the equilibrium wage rate, so 3,000 pickers are employed (determined by the demand for tomato pickers) and 5,000 people would like to work as pickers for $8 an hour (determined by the supply curve), so 2,000 are unemployed (Figure 3).

1e. The minimum wage of $8 an hour is not efficient because it creates a deadweight loss—the marginal benefit to growers (on the demand curve) exceeds the marginal cost to pickers (on the supply curve). An additional loss arises as unemployed tomato pickers search for jobs. The minimum wage is unfair on both views of fairness.

1f. Tomato pickers who find work at $8 an hour gain. Tomato growers and unemployed pickers lose.

7.3 PRICE SUPPORTS IN AGRICULTURE

"The nation has got to eat," declared President George W. Bush when he asked Congress to spend $170 billion to support U.S. farmers. The United States is not alone among the advanced economies in spending billions of dollars each year on farm support. Governments in all the advanced economies do it, and none more than those of the European Union and Japan.

■ How Governments Intervene in Markets for Farm Products

The methods that governments use to support farms vary, but they almost always involve three elements:

- Isolate the domestic market from global competition
- Introduce a price floor
- Pay the farms a subsidy

Isolate Domestic Market

A government can't regulate a market price without first isolating the domestic market from global competition. If the cost of production in the rest of the world is lower than that in the domestic economy and if foreign producers are free to sell in the domestic market, the forces of demand and supply drive the price down and swamp any efforts by the government to influence the price.

To isolate the domestic market, the government restricts imports from the rest of the world.

Introduce a Price Floor

A price floor in an agricultural market is called a **price support**, because the floor is maintained by a government guarantee to buy any surplus output at that price. You saw that a price floor in the labor market—a minimum wage—creates a surplus of labor that shows up as unemployment. A price support in an agricultural market also generates a surplus. At the support price, the quantity supplied exceeds the quantity demanded. What happens to the surplus makes the effects of a price support different from those of a minimum wage. The government buys the surplus.

Price support
A price floor in an agricultural market maintained by a government guarantee to buy any surplus output at that price.

Subsidy

A **subsidy** is a payment by the government to a producer to cover part of the cost of production. When the government buys the surplus produced by farmers, it provides them with a subsidy. Without the subsidy, farmers could not cover their costs because they would not be able to sell the surplus.

Let's see how a price support works.

Subsidy
A payment by the government to a producer to cover part of the cost of production.

■ Price Support: An Illustration

To see the effects of a price support, we'll look at the market for sugar beets. Both the United States and the European Union have price supports for sugar beets.

Figure 7.9 shows the market. This market is isolated from rest-of-world influences. The demand curve, *D*, tells us the quantities demanded at each price in the domestic economy only. And the supply curve, *S*, tells us the quantities supplied at each price by domestic farmers.

Free Market Reference Point

With no price support, the equilibrium price is $25 a ton and the equilibrium quantity is 25 million tons a year. The market is efficient only if the price in the rest of the world is also $25 a ton. If the price in the rest of the world is less than $25 a ton, it is efficient for the domestic farmers to produce less and for some sugar beets to be imported at the lower price (and lower opportunity cost) available in the rest of the world. But if the price in the rest of the world exceeds $25 a ton, it is efficient for domestic farmers to increase production and export some of it.

Price Support and Subsidy

Suppose the government introduces a price support at $35 a ton. To make the price support work, the government agrees to pay farmers $35 for every ton of sugar beets they produce and can't sell on the market.

The farmers produce the quantity shown by the market supply curve. At a price of $35 a ton, the quantity supplied is 30 million tons a year, so production increases to this amount.

Domestic users of sugar beets cut back their purchases. At $35 a ton, the quantity demanded is 20 million tons a year, and purchases decrease to this amount.

Because farmers produce a greater quantity than domestic users are willing to buy, something must be done with the surplus. If the farmers just dumped the surplus on the market, you can see what would happen. The price would fall to that at which consumers are willing to pay for the quantity produced.

To make the price support work, the government buys the surplus. In this example, the government buys 10 million tons for $35 a ton and provides a subsidy to the farmers of $350 million.

■ FIGURE 7.9

The Domestic Market for Sugar Beets

The market for sugar beets is isolated from global competition.

❶ With no intervention, the competitive equilibrium price is $25 a ton and the equilibrium quantity is 25 million tons a year.

❷ The government intervenes in this market and sets a support price at $35 a ton.

❸ The quantity produced increases to 30 million tons a year.

❹ The quantity bought by domestic users decreases to 20 million tons a year.

❺ The government buys the surplus of 10 million tons a year and pays the farmers a subsidy.

❻ A deadweight loss arises.

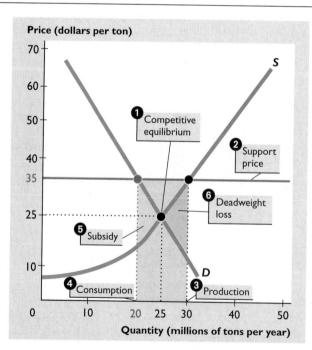

The price support increases farmers' total revenue. Without a subsidy, farmers would receive a total revenue of $625 billion ($25 a ton multiplied by 25 million tons). With a subsidy, they receive a total revenue of $1,050 billion ($35 a ton multiplied by 30 million tons).

The price support is inefficient because it creates a deadweight loss. Marginal cost exceeds marginal benefit. Farmers gain but buyers, who are also the taxpayers who end up paying the subsidy, lose. And buyers' losses exceed the farmers' gains by the amount of the deadweight loss.

Effects on the Rest of the World

The rest of the world receives a double-whammy from price supports. First, import restrictions in advanced economies deny developing economies access to the food markets of the advanced economies. The result is lower prices and smaller farm production in the developing economies.

Second, the surplus produced in the advanced economies gets sold in the rest of the world. So the price and the quantity produced in the rest of the world are depressed even further.

So the subsidies to U.S. farmers are paid not only by U.S. taxpayers and consumers but also by poor farmers in the developing economies.

REALITY CHECK

Price Ceilings and Price Floors in YOUR Life

Price ceilings and price floors play a role in *your* life in two ways:

1. They affect some of the markets in which you trade, and

2. They require you to take a stand as a voter.

The zero price you pay for using a freeway is a type of price ceiling. The next time you're stuck in traffic and moving at a crawl, think about how a free market in road use would allow you to zip along.

Think about your own (or a friend's) labor market experiences. Have you wanted a job and been willing and available to work, but unable to get hired? Would you have taken a job for a slightly lower wage if one had been available?

Develop your own considered view on price supports in agricultural markets. Do you think they are efficient? Do you think they are fair? Do you support them or oppose them?

3 **Explain how a price support in the market for an agricultural product creates a surplus, inefficiency, and unfairness.**

Practice Problem 7.3

FIGURE 1

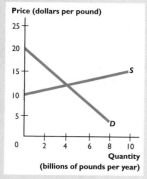

Price (dollars per pound)

Quantity
(billions of pounds per year)

1. Figure 1 shows the market for tomatoes.
   a. What are the equilibrium price and quantity of tomatoes?
   b. Is the market for tomatoes efficient?
   c. If the government introduces a price support for tomatoes at $8 per pound, what is the quantity of tomatoes produced and what is the surplus?
   d. If the government introduces a price support for tomatoes at $8 per pound, what is the subsidy received by tomato farmers?
   e. Is the price support efficient?
   f. Who gains and who loses from the price support and what is the deadweight loss?
   g. Could the price support be regarded as being fair?

Exercise 7.3

FIGURE 2

Price (dollars per pound)

Quantity
(billions of pounds per year)

1. Figure 2 shows the market for peanuts.
   a. What are the equilibrium price and quantity of peanuts?
   b. Is the market for peanuts efficient?
   c. If the government introduces a price support for peanuts at $15 per pound, what is the quantity of peanuts produced and what is the surplus?
   d. If the government introduces a price support for peanuts at $15 per pound, what is the subsidy paid to peanut farmers?
   e. Is the price support efficient?
   f. Who gains and who loses from the price support and what is the deadweight loss?
   g. Does the peanut price support redistribute more than the tomato price support in the practice problem? Explain.

Solution to Practice Problem 7.3

FIGURE 3

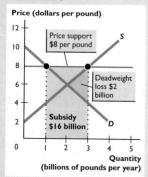

Price (dollars per pound)

Quantity
(billions of pounds per year)

1a. The equilibrium price is $6 a pound, and the equilibrium quantity is 2 billion pounds a year.

1b. The market for tomatoes is efficient—marginal benefit equals marginal cost.

1c. At a support price of $8 a pound, 3 billion pounds are produced and 1 billion pounds are demanded, so there is a surplus of 2 billion pounds (Figure 3).

1d. At a support price of $8 a pound, the subsidy is $8 per pound on 2 billion pounds, which is $16 billion (Figure 3).

1e. The price support is not efficient because it creates a deadweight loss—the marginal benefit (on the demand curve) is less than the marginal cost (on the supply curve).

1f. Consumers/taxpayers lose. They pay more for tomatoes and pay taxes to fund the subsidy. Farmers gain. The deadweight loss is $2 billion (the gray triangle.)

1g. The outcome is unfair on both views of fairness unless farmers are poorer than the consumers, in which case it might be fair to boost farmer's incomes.

CHAPTER CHECKPOINT

Key Points

1 **Explain how a price ceiling works and show how a rent ceiling creates a housing shortage, inefficiency, and unfairness.**

- A price ceiling set above the equilibrium price has no effects.
- A price ceiling set below the equilibrium price creates a shortage, increased search activity, and a black market.
- A price ceiling is inefficient and unfair.
- A rent ceiling is an example of a price ceiling.

2 **Explain how a price floor works and show how the minimum wage creates unemployment, inefficiency, and unfairness.**

- A price floor set below the equilibrium price has no effects.
- A price floor set above the equilibrium price creates a surplus, increased search activity, and illegal trading.
- A price floor is inefficient and unfair.
- A minimum wage is an example of a price floor.

3 **Explain how a price support in the market for an agricultural product creates a surplus, inefficiency, and unfairness.**

- A price support increases the quantity produced, decreases the quantity consumed, and creates a surplus.
- To maintain the support price, the government buys the surplus and subsidizes the producer.
- A price support benefits the producer but costs the consumer/taxpayer more than the producer gains—it creates a deadweight loss.
- A price support is inefficient and is usually unfair.

Key Terms

Black market, 173
Minimum wage law, 180
Price cap, 172

Price ceiling, 172
Price floor, 179
Price support, 185

Rent ceiling, 172
Search activity, 174
Subsidy, 185

TABLE 1

Rent (dollars per month)	Quantity demanded	Quantity supplied
	(rooms)	
500	2,500	2,000
550	2,250	2,000
600	2,000	2,000
650	1,750	2,000
700	1,500	2,000
750	1,250	2,000

Exercises

1. Table 1 shows the demand and supply schedules for on-campus housing.
   a. What are the equilibrium rent and number of rooms?
   b. If the college puts a rent ceiling on rooms of $650 a month, what is the rent and how many rooms are rented?
   c. If the college puts a rent ceiling on rooms of $550 a month, what is the rent and how many rooms are rented?
   d. If the college strictly enforces the rent ceiling of $550 a month, is the on-campus housing market efficient? Explain why or why not.
   e. If a black market develops, how high could the black market rent be? Explain.
   f. If a black market develops, is the housing market fair? Explain your answer.

2. During the 1996 Olympic Games, many residents of Atlanta left the city and rented out their homes. Despite the increase in the quantity of housing available, rents soared. If at the time of the 1996 Olympic Games, the city of Atlanta had imposed a rent ceiling, describe how the housing market would have functioned.

3. Concerned about the political fallout from rising gas prices, the government decides to impose a price ceiling on gasoline of $2.00 a gallon.
   a. Explain how the market for gasoline would react to this price ceiling if
      (i) The oil-producing nations increased production and drove the equilibrium price of gasoline to $1.50 cents a gallon.
      (ii) A global shortage of oil sent the equilibrium price of gasoline to $2.50 a gallon.
   b. Which of the situations in part a would result in an efficient use of resources? Explain.

4. Suppose the government introduced a ceiling on the fees that lawyers are permitted to charge.
   a. Explain the effects of such a ceiling on
      (i) The amount of work done by lawyers.
      (ii) The consumer surplus of people who hire lawyers.
      (iii) The producer surplus of law firms.
   b. Would this fee ceiling result in an efficient use of resources? Why or why not?

TABLE 2

Wage rate (dollars per hour)	Quantity demanded	Quantity supplied
	(student workers)	
5.00	600	300
5.50	500	350
6.00	400	400
6.50	300	450
7.00	200	500
7.50	100	550

5. Table 2 shows the demand and supply schedules for student workers at on-campus venues.
   a. What is the equilibrium wage rate of student workers and what is the equilibrium number of students employed?
   b. Is the market for student workers at on-campus venues efficient?
   c. If the college introduces a minimum wage of $5.50 an hour, how many students are employed at on-campus venues and how many are unemployed?
   d. If the college introduces a minimum wage of $6.50 an hour, how many students are employed at on-campus venues and how many are unemployed?
   e. Is the minimum wage of $6.50 an hour efficient? Is it fair?
   f. Who gains and who loses from the minimum wage of $6.50 an hour?

6. Bakers earn $15 an hour, gas pump attendants earn $6 an hour, and copy shop workers earn $7 an hour. If the government introduces a minimum wage of $7 an hour, explain how the markets for bakers, gas pump attendants, and copy shop workers will respond initially to the minimum wage.

7. The equilibrium price of beef falls to $2 a pound, a price at which cattle ranchers can't survive. To help the struggling ranchers, the government declares that it is illegal to buy beef for less than $5 a pound. But the government does not offer to buy the surplus and subsidize the ranchers. Instead, it appoints a large number of observers to keep a close watch on the beef market and ensure that the law is observed to the letter. Black market traders are effectively eliminated.
    a. Describe the situation in the beef market.
    b. Explain why the cattle ranchers want the government to abandon the price floor.

8. In exercise 7, the equilibrium price of beef falls to $2 a pound—a price at which cattle ranchers can't survive. Now the government introduces a price support and subsidy.
    a. Describe the situation in the beef market after the introduction of the price support and subsidy.
    b. Would you expect the cattle ranchers to be happier with this arrangement than they would be with a price floor and no subsidy? Explain.

9. Table 3 shows the demand and supply schedules for mushrooms.
    a. What are the equilibrium price and quantity of mushrooms?
    b. Is the market for mushrooms efficient?
    c. If the government introduces a price support for mushrooms of $4 per pound, what is the quantity of mushrooms produced and what is the surplus of mushrooms?
    d. Is there a deadweight loss from a price support of $4 a pound?
    e. If the government introduces a price support for mushrooms of $6 per pound, what is the quantity of mushrooms produced and what is the surplus?
    f. Is the price support of $6 a pound efficient?
    g. Who gains from a price support set at $6 a pound?
    h. Who loses from a price support set at $6 a pound?
    i. What is the deadweight loss if the price support is set at $6 a pound?

TABLE 3

Price (dollars per pound)	Quantity demanded	Quantity supplied
	(pounds per week)	
1.00	5,000	2,000
2.00	4,500	2,500
3.00	4,000	3,000
4.00	3,500	3,500
5.00	3,000	4,000
6.00	2,500	4,500

10. Table 4 shows the domestic demand and supply schedules of oranges.
    a. With no imported oranges, what are the equilibrium price and quantity of oranges?
    b. If the government introduces a price support of $250 per ton, what is the quantity of oranges produced and what is the surplus of oranges?
    c. What is the deadweight loss created by the price support and what is the subsidy the government must pay domestic producers?
    d. Is the domestic market for oranges fair?
    e. If the government sells the surplus of oranges on the world market for oranges, what changes will occur in the world market for oranges?

TABLE 4

Price (dollars per ton)	Quantity demanded	Quantity supplied
	(tons per year)	
50	16	10
100	15	11
150	14	12
200	13	13
250	12	14
300	11	15
350	10	16

Critical Thinking

11. The New York City Rent Guidelines Board is mandated to establish rent adjustments for the nearly one million apartments and houses that are subject to the city's Rent Stabilization Law. The board holds public hearings to consider testimony from owners, tenants, advocacy groups, and housing industry experts. Write a brief report to the New York City Rent Guidelines Board that explains why it is not possible to improve on permitting the market forces of supply and demand to determine rents at the levels that make the quantity demanded and quantity supplied equal.

12. Table 5 provides data on the minimum wage in the United States from 1995 to 2001. The table also provides data on the unemployment rate of all persons over 16 and of those aged 16 to 19. On the political campaign trail, a Republican presents these data and says that they support the view that the minimum wage causes unemployment among young people. A Democrat presents these same data and says they show that the minimum wage has no effect on the unemployment rate of any age groups.
    a. What claims can be made and cannot be made about the effects of the minimum wage on the unemployment rate?
    b. Do these data provide any evidence that bears on the issue? Explain why they do or do not help to resolve the issue.

13. A hurricane has destroyed most of the homes and cut off the drinking water, gas, and electricity in a city. Under these conditions, the mayor decides to impose rent ceilings and price ceilings on water, gas, and electricity.
    a. Predict the consequences of the mayor's decision in both the short run and the long run.
    b. Explain who will gain, who will lose, and whether you think the deadweight loss from the price regulations is worth bearing.

14. "Market prices might be fine in a rich country, but in a poor African nation where there are shortages of most items, without government control of prices everything would be too expensive." Do you agree or disagree with this statement? Use the concepts of efficiency and fairness to explain why.

TABLE 5

Year	Minimum wage (dollars per hour)	Unemployment rate (16 years and older)	Unemployment rate (aged 16 to 19)
1995	4.45	5.6	17.1
1996	4.75	5.3	16.2
1997	5.15	5.0	16.8
1998	5.15	4.5	15.0
1999	5.15	4.3	13.9
2000	5.15	4.0	11.9
2001	5.15	4.6	14.4

Web Exercises

Use the links on MyEconLab to work the following exercises.

15. Visit the Web site of the Harvard Living Wage Campaign.
    a. What is the campaign for a living wage?
    b. How would you distinguish the minimum wage from a living wage?
    c. If the Living Wage Campaign succeeds in getting wages increased above their equilibrium levels, what do you predict its effect will be?
    d. Would a living wage above the equilibrium wage be efficient?
    e. Who would gain and who would lose from a living wage above the equilibrium wage?
    f. Would a living wage above the equilibrium wage be fair?

16. Visit British Sugar to find information about the sugar market in Europe.
    a. Why do European nations subsidize the production of sugar?
    b. How do European sugar subsidies influence the price of sugar that consumers pay?
    c. How do European sugar subsidies influence the global sugar market?

Taxes

When you have completed your study of this chapter,
you will be able to

1 Explain how taxes change prices and quantities, are shared by buyers
and sellers, and create inefficiency.

2 Explain how income taxes and Social Security taxes change wage
rates and employment, are shared by employers and workers, and
create inefficiency.

3 Review ideas about the fairness of the tax system.

Jody is excited to be starting her new job at the
Bank of Alabama. She is now earning $47,000 a
year—more than $900 a week. She views her
first payslip with excitement—followed by dis-
may. Her $900 a week has become $660! She
stares at the numbers: Medicare $12.75, Federal
tax $102, Social Security $55, Alabama state tax
$30, Jefferson County tax $4.50, Birmingham
city tax $9—a tax bill of $213. Parking and other deductions
take another $27.

And when Jody spends her $660, she gets whacked with
a 4 percent sales tax and a 16 cent a gallon gas tax. She's
glad her good habits let her avoid Alabama's smoke and
drink taxes!

What are the effects of the taxes that governments
impose? Who bears the burden of these taxes? How do
taxes affect the efficiency of markets? Can Congress target
taxes at businesses so that workers pay less tax? Is the tax
system fair? This chapter answers these questions.

8.1 TAXES ON BUYERS AND SELLERS

Almost every time you buy something—a late-night order of chow mein, a plane ticket, a tank of gasoline—you pay a tax. On some items, you pay a sales tax that is added to the advertised price. On other items, you pay an excise tax—often at a high rate like the tax on gasoline—that is included in the advertised price.

But do you really pay these taxes? When a tax is added to the advertised price, isn't it obvious that *you* pay the tax? Isn't the price higher than it otherwise would be by an amount equal to the tax?

And what about a tax that is buried in the price, such as that on gasoline. Who pays that tax? Does the seller just pass on the full amount of the tax to you, the buyer? Or does the seller pay the tax by taking a lower price and leaving the price you pay unchanged?

To answer these questions, let's suppose that TIFS, the Tax Illegal File Sharing lobby, has persuaded the government to collect a $10 tax on every new MP3 player and use the tax revenue to compensate artists. But an argument is raging between those who claim that the buyer benefits and should pay the tax and those who claim that the seller profits and should pay the tax.

■ Tax Incidence

Tax incidence
The division of the burden of a tax between the buyer and the seller.

Tax incidence is the division of the burden of a tax between the buyer and the seller. We're going to find the incidence of a $10 tax on MP3 players with two different taxes: a tax on the buyer and a tax on the seller.

Figure 8.1 shows the market for MP3 players. With no tax, the equilibrium price is $100 and the equilibrium quantity is 5,000 players a week.

When a good is taxed, it has two prices: a price that excludes the tax and a price that includes the tax. Buyers respond only to the price that includes the tax, because that is the price they pay. Sellers respond only to the price that excludes the tax, because that is the price they receive. The tax is like a wedge between these two prices.

Figure 8.1(a) shows what happens if the government taxes the buyer. The tax doesn't change the buyer's willingness and ability to pay. But it changes how the amount paid is split between the seller and the government. The demand curve, *D*, tells us the *total* amount that buyers are willing and able to pay. And the red curve *D − tax* tells us what the buyers are willing to pay to the sellers, given that they must pay $10 to the government on each item bought. The red curve, *D − tax*, lies $10 below the blue demand curve.

Equilibrium occurs where the red *D − tax* curve intersects the supply curve, *S*. The buyer pays the equilibrium net-of-tax price $95 plus the $10 tax: $105. The seller receives the net-of-tax price $95. The government collects a tax revenue of $10 a player on 2,000 players, or $20,000 (shown by the purple rectangle).

Figure 8.1(b) shows what happens if the government taxes the seller. The tax acts like an increase in the suppliers' cost, so supply decreases and the supply curve shifts to the red curve labeled *S + tax*. This curve tells us what sellers are willing to accept, given that they must pay the government $10 on each item sold. The red curve, *S + tax*, lies $10 above the supply curve.

Equilibrium occurs where the red *S + tax* curve intersects the demand curve, *D*. The buyer pays the equilibrium market price $105. The seller receives the net-of-tax price $95. The government collects a tax revenue of $20,000.

FIGURE 8.1
A Tax on MP3 Players

(a) Government taxes buyer

(b) Government taxes seller

❶ With no tax, the price of an MP3 player is $100 and 5,000 players a week are bought. ❷ A $10 tax on buyers of MP3 players shifts the demand curve to *D − tax* in part (a). A $10 tax on sellers of MP3 players shifts the supply curve to *S + tax* in part (b). ❸ The price paid by buyers rises to $105—an increase of $5.

❹ The price received by sellers falls to $95—a decrease of $5. ❺ The quantity decreases to 2,000 players a week. ❻ The government collects tax revenue of $20,000 a week—the purple rectangle. The burden of the tax is split equally between the buyer and the seller—each pays $5 per player.

You can now see that the argument about making the buyer pay or the seller pay is futile. The buyer pays the same price, the seller receives the same price, and the government receives the same tax revenue on the same quantity regardless of whether the government taxes the buyer or the seller.

In this example, the buyer and the seller share the burden of the tax equally. But in most cases, the burden will be shared unequally and might even fall entirely on one side of the market. We'll explore what determines the incidence of a tax below. But first, let's see how a tax creates inefficiency.

■ Taxes and Efficiency

You've seen that resources are used efficiently when marginal benefit equals marginal cost. You've also seen that a tax places a wedge between the buyer's price and the seller's price. But the buyer's price equals marginal benefit and the seller's price equals marginal cost. So a tax puts a wedge between marginal benefit and marginal cost. The equilibrium quantity is less than the efficient quantity, and a deadweight loss arises.

Figure 8.2 shows the inefficiency of a tax. We'll assume that the government taxes the seller. In part (a), with no tax, marginal benefit equals marginal cost and the market is efficient. In part (b), with a tax, marginal benefit exceeds marginal cost. Consumer surplus and producer surplus shrink. Part of each surplus goes to the government as tax revenue—the purple area—and part of each surplus becomes a deadweight loss—the gray area.

Because a tax creates a deadweight loss, the burden of the tax exceeds the tax revenue. To remind us of this fact, we call the deadweight loss that arises from a tax the **excess burden** of the tax. But because the government uses the tax revenue to provide goods and services that people value, only the excess burden measures the inefficiency of the tax.

In this example, the excess burden is large. You can see how large by calculating the area of the deadweight loss triangle. This area is $15,000 ($10 × 3,000 ÷ 2). The tax revenue is $20,000, so the excess burden is 75 percent of the tax revenue.

■ Incidence, Inefficiency, and Elasticity

In the example of a $10 tax on MP3 players, the buyer and the seller split the tax equally and the excess burden is large. What determines how the tax is split and the size of its excess burden?

The incidence of a tax and its excess burden depend on the elasticities of demand and supply in the following ways:

Excess burden
The amount by which the burden of a tax exceeds the tax revenue received by the government—the deadweight loss from a tax.

■ **FIGURE 8.2**
Taxes and Efficiency

(a) **Efficient outcome**

(b) **Burden of tax**

❶ The market is efficient with marginal benefit equal to marginal cost. Total surplus—the sum of ❷ consumer surplus (green area) and ❸ producer surplus (blue area)—is at its maximum possible level.

A $10 tax drives a wedge between ❶ marginal benefit and ❷ marginal cost. ❸ Consumer surplus and ❹ producer surplus shrink by the amount of the ❺ tax revenue plus the ❻ deadweight loss. The deadweight loss is the excess burden of the tax.

- For a given elasticity of supply, the buyer pays a larger share of the tax the more inelastic is the demand for the good.
- For a given elasticity of demand, the seller pays a larger share of the tax the more inelastic is the supply of the good.
- The more inelastic is demand *or* supply, the smaller is the excess burden.

◼ Incidence, Inefficiency, and the Elasticity of Demand

To see how the division of a tax between the buyer and the seller and the size of the excess burden depend on the elasticity of demand, we'll look at two extremes.

Perfectly Inelastic Demand: Buyer Pays and Efficient

Figure 8.3(a) shows the market for insulin, a vital daily medication of diabetics. Demand is perfectly inelastic at 100,000 doses a week, as shown by the vertical demand curve. With no tax, the price is $2 a dose. A 20¢ a dose tax raises the price to $2.20, but the quantity does not change. The tax leaves the price received by the seller unchanged but raises the price paid by the buyer by the entire tax. The outcome is efficient (there is no deadweight loss) because marginal benefit equals marginal cost.

Perfectly Elastic Demand: Seller Pays and Inefficient

Figure 8.3(b) shows the market for pink marker pens. Demand is perfectly elastic at $1 a pen, as shown by the horizontal demand curve. If pink pens are less expensive than other pens, everyone uses pink. If pink pens are more expensive than other pens, no one uses a pink pen. With no tax, the price of a pink pen is $1 and the quantity is 4,000 pens a week. A 10¢ a pen tax leaves the price at $1 a pen, but the quantity decreases to 1,000 a week. The price paid by the buyer is unchanged and the seller pays the entire tax. The outcome is inefficient because marginal benefit exceeds marginal cost and a deadweight loss arises.

◼ **FIGURE 8.3**

Incidence, Inefficiency, and the Elasticity of Demand

(a) Inelastic demand

(b) Elastic demand

In part (a), the demand for insulin is perfectly inelastic. A tax of 20¢ a dose raises the price by 20¢, and the buyer pays all the tax. But marginal benefit still equals marginal cost, so the outcome is efficient.

In part (b), the demand for pink marker pens is perfectly elastic. A tax of 10¢ a pen lowers the price received by the seller by 10¢, and the seller pays all the tax. Marginal benefit exceeds marginal cost, so the outcome is inefficient. The deadweight loss is the excess burden of the tax and measures its inefficiency.

■ Incidence, Inefficiency, and the Elasticity of Supply

To see how the division of a tax between the buyer and the seller depends on the elasticity of supply, we'll again look at two extremes.

Perfectly Inelastic Supply: Seller Pays and Efficient

Figure 8.4(a) shows the market for spring water that flows at a constant rate that can't be controlled. Supply is perfectly inelastic at 100,000 bottles a week, as shown by the vertical supply curve. With no tax, the price is 50¢ a bottle and the 100,000 bottles that flow from the spring are bought. A tax of 5¢ a bottle leaves the quantity unchanged at 100,000 bottles a week. But buyers are willing to buy the 100,000 bottles only if the price is 50¢ a bottle. So the price remains at 50¢ a bottle. The tax lowers the price received by the seller by 5¢ a bottle. The seller pays the entire tax.

But marginal benefit equals marginal cost, so there is no deadweight loss and the outcome is efficient.

Perfectly Elastic Supply: Buyer Pays and Inefficient

Figure 8.4(b) shows the market for sand from which computer-chip makers extract silicon. Supply of this sand is perfectly elastic at a price of 10¢ a pound as shown by the horizontal supply curve. With no tax, the price is 10¢ a pound and 5,000 pounds a week are bought. A 1¢ a pound sand tax raises the price to 11¢, and the quantity decreases to 3,000 pounds a week. The buyer pays the entire tax.

Marginal benefit exceeds marginal cost, so a deadweight loss arises and the outcome is inefficient.

■ **FIGURE 8.4**

Incidence, Inefficiency, and the Elasticity of Supply

In part (a), the supply of a bottle of spring water is perfectly inelastic. A tax of 5¢ a bottle lowers the price received by the seller by 5¢ a bottle, and the seller pays all the tax. Marginal benefit equals marginal cost, so the outcome is efficient.

In part (b), the supply of sand is perfectly elastic. A tax of 1¢ a pound increases the price by 1¢ a pound, and the buyer pays all the tax. Marginal benefit exceeds marginal cost, so the outcome is inefficient. The deadweight loss is the excess burden of the tax and measures its inefficiency.

CHECKPOINT 8.1

1 Explain how taxes change prices and quantities, are shared by buyers and sellers, and create inefficiency.

Practice Problem 8.1

1. Figure 1 shows the market for softballs in which softballs are not taxed. Now softballs are taxed at 60 cents a ball.
    a. If buyers are taxed, what price do buyers pay?
    b. If sellers are taxed, what price do sellers receive?
    c. How many softballs are bought and sold?
    d. What is the tax revenue from sales of softballs?
    e. What is the excess burden of the tax on softballs?
    f. Which is more inelastic: the demand for or supply of softballs? Why?

FIGURE 1

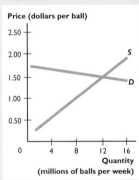

Exercises 8.1

1. With the increased popularity of cell phones, the government introduces a tax of $20 a cell phone and a tax of 10¢ a call on a cell phone. Suppose that the supply of cell phones is elastic, the demand for cell phones is inelastic, the supply of calls is perfectly elastic, and the demand for calls is elastic.
    a. Who pays more of the tax on a phone, the buyer or the seller?
    b. Who pays more of the tax on a call, the buyer or the seller?
    c. Would the taxes reduce the number of cell phones bought?
    d. Would the taxes reduce the number of calls made from cell phones?
    e. Which tax would raise more revenue for the government? Why?
    f. Which tax do you think would have the greater excess burden? Why?

2. The supply of apartments in New York City is inelastic, and the demand for apartments is elastic. The city introduces a tax on apartment rentals.
    a. Explain why landlords would pay more of the tax than renters.
    b. Explain why the government would collect a large revenue from this tax.

Solution to Practice Problem 8.1

1a. With a 60¢ tax on buyers, the demand curve shifts downward by 60¢. Buyers pay $1.60 a softball (Figure 2).

1b. With a 60¢ tax on sellers, the supply curve shifts upward by 60¢. Sellers receive $1.00 a softball (Figure 3).

1c. 8 million softballs a week (Figure 2 or 3).

1d. The tax revenue is $0.60 × 8 million, which is $4.8 million a week (the purple rectangle in Figure 2 or 3).

1e. The excess burden of the tax is $1.2 million. Excess burden equals the deadweight loss, illustrated by the gray triangle in Figure 2 or 3, which is (4 million balls × 60¢ a ball) ÷ 2 or $1.2 million.

1f. Supply is more inelastic because the seller pays the larger share of the tax.

FIGURE 2

FIGURE 3

8.2 INCOME TAX AND SOCIAL SECURITY TAX

Income taxes are paid on personal incomes and corporate profits. In 2004, personal income taxes raised more than $1 trillion for the federal government and another $300 billion for state and local governments. Corporation income taxes raised $250 billion for the federal government and $40 billion for the state governments. We'll look first at the effects of personal income taxes, then at corporation income taxes, and finally at Social Security taxes.

■ The Personal Income Tax

Taxable income

Total income minus a personal exemption and a standard exemption (or other allowable deductions).

The amount of income tax that a person pays depends on her or his **taxable income**, which equals total income minus a *personal exemption* and a *standard deduction* (or other allowable deductions). For the federal income tax in 2004, the personal exemption was $3,100 and the standard deduction was $4,850 for a single person. So for a single person, taxable income equals total income minus $7,950.

The tax rate depends on the income level, and Figure 8.5 shows how the tax rate for a single person increases with income. The percentages in the table are

EYE ON THE U.S. ECONOMY

Taxes in the United States Today

Federal, state, and local governments in the United States have five main revenue sources:
• Income taxes
• Social Security taxes
• Sales taxes
• Property taxes
• Excise taxes

The figure shows the relative amounts raised by these taxes in 2004. Personal income taxes are the biggest tax source at 36.2 percent of total tax revenues. Social Security taxes are the next biggest revenue source at 28.7 percent of tax revenues. Sales taxes and other indirect taxes raised 12.7 percent, state and local government property taxes raised 11.2 percent, income taxes on corporations raised

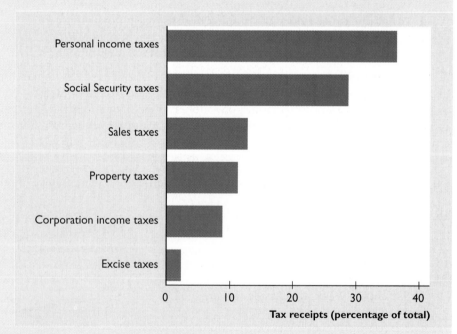

SOURCE OF DATA: *Economic Report of the President*, 2005.

8.8 percent, and excise taxes raised 2.3 percent. Although excise taxes

raise a small amount of revenue, they have big effects on some markets.

FIGURE 8.5

Marginal Tax Rates and Average Tax Rates

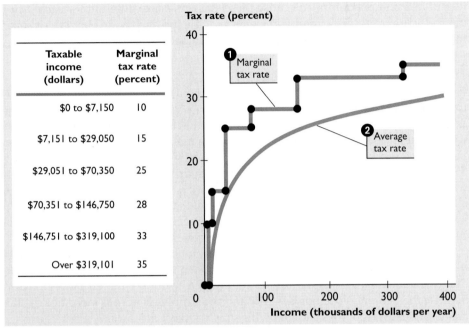

Taxable income (dollars)	Marginal tax rate (percent)
$0 to $7,150	10
$7,151 to $29,050	15
$29,051 to $70,350	25
$70,351 to $146,750	28
$146,751 to $319,100	33
Over $319,101	35

1 The marginal tax rate increases with income. The table provides the data for 2004.

2 The average tax rate increases with income, but the average rate is less than the marginal rate.

SOURCE OF DATA: Internal Revenue Service.

marginal tax rates. A **marginal tax rate** is the percentage of an additional dollar of income that is paid in tax. For example, if taxable income increases from $7,149 to $7,150, the tax paid on the additional dollar is 10 cents and the marginal tax rate is 10 percent. If taxable income increases from $319,100 to $319,101, the tax paid on the additional dollar is 35 cents and the marginal tax rate is 35 percent.

The **average tax rate** is the percentage of income that is paid in tax. The average tax rate is less than the marginal tax rate. For example, suppose a single person earns $50,000 in a year. Tax paid is zero on the first $7,950 plus $715 (10 percent) on the next $7,150 plus $3,285 (15 percent) on the next $21,900 plus $3,250 on the remaining $13,000. Total taxes equal $7,250, which is 14.5 percent of $50,000. The average tax rate is 14.5 percent.

If the average tax rate increases as income increases, the tax is a **progressive tax**. The personal income tax is a progressive tax. To see this feature of the income tax, calculate another average tax rate for someone whose income is $100,000 a year. Tax paid is zero on the first $7,950 plus $715 (10 percent) on the next $7,150 plus $3,285 (15 percent) on the next $21,900 plus $10,325 on the next $41,300 plus $6,076 on the remaining $21,700. Total taxes equal $20,401, which is 20.4 percent of $100,000. The average tax rate is 20.4 percent.

A progressive tax contrasts with a **proportional tax**, which has the same average tax rate at all income levels, and a **regressive tax**, which has a decreasing average tax rate as income increases.

Marginal tax rate
The percentage of an additional dollar of income that is paid in tax.

Average tax rate
The percentage of income that is paid in tax.

Progressive tax
A tax whose average rate increases as income increases.

Proportional tax
A tax whose average rate is constant at all income levels.

Regressive tax
A tax whose average rate decreases as income increases.

■ The Effects of the Income Tax

The income tax is a tax on sellers—the sellers of the services of labor, capital, and land. You know that the incidence and inefficiency of a tax depend on the elasticities of demand and supply. Because these elasticities are different for each factor of production, we must examine the effects of the income tax on each factor separately. Let's look first at the effects of the tax on labor income.

Tax on Labor Income

Figure 8.6 shows the demand curve, *LD,* and the supply curve, *LS,* in a competitive labor market. Firms can substitute machines for labor in many tasks, so the demand for labor is elastic. But most people have few good options other than to work for their income, so the supply of labor is inelastic. In this example, with no income tax, workers would earn $19 an hour and work 40 hours a week.

With a 20 percent income tax, the labor supply curve shifts to *LS + tax.* If workers are willing to supply the 40th hour a week for $19 with no tax, then with a 20 percent tax, they are willing to supply the 40th hour only if the wage is $23.75 an hour. That is, they want to get the $19 they received before plus $4.75 (20 percent of $23.75) that they now must pay to the government.

The equilibrium wage rate rises to $20 an hour, but the after-tax wage rate falls to $16 an hour—the tax is $4 an hour. Employment decreases to 35 hours a week. The worker pays most of the tax—$3 compared to the $1 the employer pays— because the demand for labor is elastic and the supply of labor is inelastic. The tax creates a deadweight loss shown by the gray triangle.

FIGURE 8.6

A Tax on Labor Income

With no income tax, workers would earn $19 an hour and work 40 hours a week.

❶ Workers face a 20 percent marginal income tax rate. The income tax decreases the supply of labor, raises the wage rate, and lowers the after-tax wage rate. Because the demand for labor is elastic and the supply of labor is inelastic, the tax ❷ paid by the employer is less than that ❸ paid by the worker. The quantity of labor employed is less than the efficient quantity, so ❹ a deadweight loss arises.

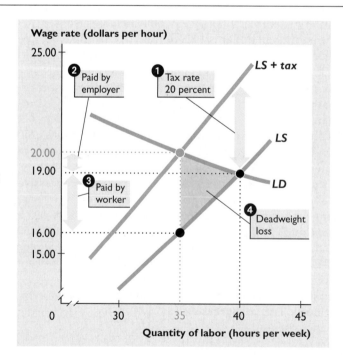

Tax on Capital Income

Capital income—interest on bonds and bank deposits and dividends on stocks—is taxed at the same rate as other sources of income. But dividends on stocks get taxed twice because corporations also pay a tax on the profits that are paid out as dividends. In his 2003 economic stimulus package, President Bush proposed the abolition of this double taxation of dividends.

Figure 8.7 shows the demand curve, *KD*, and the supply curve, *KS*, in a competitive capital market. Because firms can substitute machines for labor in many tasks, the demand for capital is elastic. Capital is internationally mobile, and its supply is highly elastic. In this example, firms can obtain all the capital they wish at an interest rate of 6 percent a year, so the supply of capital is perfectly elastic. With no income tax, firms use $40 billion worth of capital.

With a 40 percent tax on capital income, the supply curve shifts to *KS + tax*. Lenders want to receive an additional 4 percent interest to pay their capital income tax and are not willing to lend for less than 10 percent a year.

With the capital income tax, the quantity of capital decreases to $20 billion and the interest rate rises to 10 percent a year. Firms pay the entire capital income tax, and lenders receive the same after-tax interest rate as they receive in the absence of a capital income tax. The tax creates a deadweight loss shown by the gray triangle.

Tax on the Income from Land and Other Unique Resources

Each plot of land and reserve of mineral or other natural resource is unique, so its supply is perfectly inelastic. A fixed amount of the resource is supplied regardless of the rent offered for its use.

■ FIGURE 8.7
A Tax on Capital Income

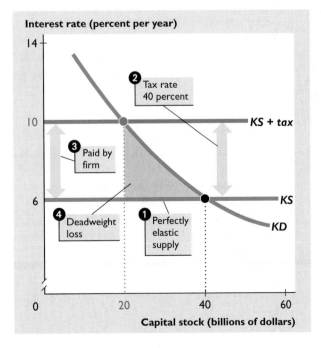

❶ The supply of capital is highly elastic (here perfectly elastic). With no tax on capital income, the interest rate is 6 percent a year and firms use $40 billion of capital.

With a ❷ 40 percent tax on income from capital, the supply curve becomes *KS + tax*. The interest rate rises to 10 percent a year, and ❸ firms pay the entire tax. The quantity of capital used is less than the efficient quantity, so ❹ a deadweight loss arises.

President Bush's Tax Cuts

In 2003, President Bush proposed a number of tax cuts to stimulate production and employment. The table lists the five major proposals and the size of the tax cut they would bring in 2003 and over the ten years to 2013.

Magnitude of Cuts

As a percentage of total personal income taxes, the proposed tax cut is large. In 2003 alone, total personal income tax payments fell from $1,006 billion to $908 billion, a cut of 9.7 percent.

But as a percentage of total personal income, the tax cut looks much more modest. In 2003, total personal income was about $9,400 billion. So a tax cut of $98 billion was only 1 percent of total personal income.

The average annual tax cut planned was $67 billion (one tenth of the ten-year total of $670 billion). This tax cut is 6.7 percent of the 2003 level of total personal income taxes and less than 1 percent of 2003 total personal income.

Who stands to benefit from these tax cuts? Will the tax cuts contribute to the efficiency of the economy? And are they fair?

Incidence of Tax Cuts

You can figure out who will benefit from the tax cuts—the incidence of the tax cuts—from what you've learned in this chapter.

Lower taxes on labor income will mainly benefit workers because the elasticity of demand for labor is much greater than the elasticity of supply of labor.

Lower taxes on capital income that result from the exclusion of dividends will have little effect on the after-tax income of savers. Because the supply of capital is highly elastic, the cost of capital to firms will fall and the quantity of capital will increase. Output and employment will also increase.

Efficiency of Tax Cuts

You can figure out how the tax cuts contribute to economic efficiency from what you've learned in this chapter.

Lower taxes on labor income will increase employment, but not by much because the supply of labor is inelastic. With the limited effect on employment, the deadweight loss from the labor income tax will decrease, but not by much.

Lower taxes on capital income will have a potentially large effect on efficiency. Because both the demand for capital and the supply of capital are elastic, a small tax cut brings a large increase in the quantity of capital and a large decrease in the deadweight loss from the tax on capital income.

Fairness of Tax Cuts

Whether the tax cuts are fair is controversial and depends on the criterion of fairness used. According to the U.S. Treasury, people who earn $200,000 a year or more will get 40 percent of the tax cuts and people who earn $30,000 a year or less will get less than 3 percent of the tax cuts.

But those with a high income pay most of the taxes, so it is not surprising that they benefit most from lower taxes.

If the tax cuts are expressed as percentages of taxes currently paid, the lower income groups benefit most. People with incomes of $30,000 a year or less get a tax cut of 17 percent, while people with incomes of $200,000 a year or more get a tax cut of 11 percent.

	2003	2003–2013
President Bush's Tax Cuts	**Billions of dollars**	
Accelerate income tax cuts	28	64
Exclude dividends from personal income tax	20	364
Accelerate reduction of marriage tax penalty	19	58
Accelerate child tax-credit increase	16	91
Accelerate expansion of 10 percent income tax bracket	5	48
Other measures	10	45
Total	98	670

SOURCE OF DATA: U.S. Treasury.

Figure 8.8(a) illustrates a tax on land income. In this example, a fixed 250 billion acres is supplied regardless of the rent. The equilibrium quantity of land is determined purely by supply and the equilibrium rent is determined by the demand for land. In this example, the equilibrium rent is $1,000 an acre.

When a 40 percent tax is imposed on rent income, landowners pay all of the tax. Their after-tax income falls to $600 an acre. This tax is efficient because the equilibrium quantity of land used is the same with the tax as without it. The tax generates no deadweight loss (excess burden) and is ideal from the perspective of efficiency.

The principle that applies to a tax on income from land also applies to the income from any unique resource that has a perfectly inelastic supply. Another example of such a resource is the talent of an outstanding movie star or television personality.

Figure 8.8(b) illustrates this case. Suppose that Barbara Walters is willing to do 24 big television interviews a year. Her supply of interview services is perfectly inelastic at that quantity. The networks compete for her services, and the demand curve reflects their willingness to pay for them. The equilibrium price is $250,000 per interview or $6 million a year. If Barbara Walters pays a 40 percent tax on this income, she receives an after-tax income of $150,000 per interview or $3.6 million a year. Barbara Walters pays the entire tax. The price paid by the networks is unaffected by this tax, and Barbara Walters performs the same number of interviews with the tax as without it. This tax creates no deadweight loss (excess burden).

■ FIGURE 8.8

A Tax on Land and Other Unique Resource Income

(a) Land tax

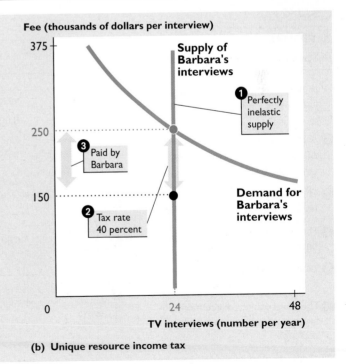

(b) Unique resource income tax

❶ In the markets for land and for interviews by Barbara Walters, supply is highly inelastic (here perfectly inelastic). With a **❷** 40 percent tax on income from these resources, the supply curve and the market price remain unchanged, and **❸** landowners and Barbara Walters pay the entire tax. The quantity of the resource used is unchanged and the tax is efficient.

■ The Social Security Tax

Social Security is never far from the headlines. And as the population gets older and more and more people begin to receive Social Security benefits, the cry to "fix Social Security" can only keep getting louder. The fundamental problem of ever-growing outlays must somehow be addressed.

One possible solution to the Social Security problem in the United States is to change the entitlements and cut the outlays. But this possibility is not popular and probably will not be the solution that is chosen. The other possibility is to increase the Social Security tax.

Currently, the law says that Social Security taxes fall equally on workers and employers. But does this outcome actually occur? If Congress decides to increase the Social Security tax, can Congress target employers and shield workers?

The Social Security tax is just like the other taxes you've studied in this chapter. Its incidence depends on the elasticities of demand and supply in the labor market and not on the wishes of Congress. Let's confirm this assertion by looking at two distinct arrangements: First, the tax is imposed only on workers, and second, the tax is imposed only on employers.

A Social Security Tax on Workers

Figure 8.9 shows the effects of a Social Security tax when the law says that workers must pay the entire tax. Without any taxes, the wage rate is $6 an hour and 4,000 people are employed. Now suppose that the government introduces a 20 percent Social Security tax on workers. If 4,000 people were willing to work for $6 an hour, this quantity of labor will now be supplied only if people can earn $6 an

---

■ **FIGURE 8.9**

A Social Security Tax on Workers

With no taxes, 4,000 people are employed at a wage rate of $6 an hour.

❶ A Social Security tax on workers of 20 percent shifts the supply curve to LS + tax.

❷ The wage rate rises to $6.25 an hour, an increase of 25¢ an hour.

❸ The quantity of labor employed decreases to 3,000 workers.

❹ Workers receive $5 an hour— a decrease of $1 an hour.

❺ The government collects tax revenue shown by the purple rectangle.

Workers pay most of the tax because the supply of labor is more inelastic than the demand for labor.

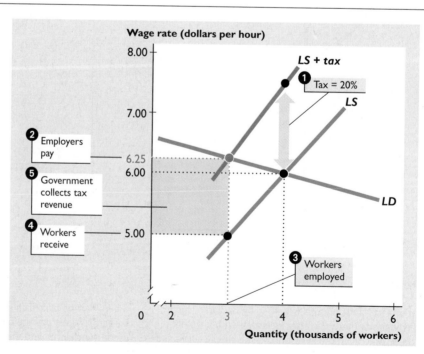

hour *after tax.* With a tax rate of 20 percent, the pre-tax wage rate will need to be $7.50 an hour to deliver an after-tax wage rate of $6 an hour. (Check that 20 percent of $7.50 is $1.50, so the wage rate after tax is $6.) The supply of labor curve shifts to the curve labeled *LS + tax*—a decrease in the supply of labor.

The wage rate rises to $6.25 an hour, and 3,000 workers are employed. With a wage rate of $6.25 an hour, employees *receive* that amount minus a 20 percent tax, which is $5 an hour. (Check that $1.25 equals 20 percent, or one fifth, of $6.25.)

So when the government puts a Social Security tax on workers, employers pay 25 cents and workers pay $1. This division of the burden of the tax arises because the demand for labor is more elastic than the supply of labor.

A Social Security Tax on Employers

Figure 8.10 shows the effects of a Social Security tax on employers. As before, with no taxes, the equilibrium wage rate is $6 an hour and 4,000 people are employed. With a $1.25 an hour tax, firms are no longer willing to hire 4,000 people at a $6 an hour wage rate. Because they must pay $1.25 an hour to the government, they will hire 4,000 people at a wage rate of $6 minus $1.25, which is $4.75 an hour.

The demand for labor decreases, and the demand curve shifts to *LD − tax*. The wage rate falls to $5 an hour, and 3,000 workers are employed. The total cost of labor to the firm is $6.25 an hour—the $5 an hour wage plus the $1.25 an hour tax.

The tax on employers delivers the same outcome as the tax on workers. Workers receive the same take-home wage, and firms pay the same total wage. Congress cannot decide who pays the Social Security tax. When the laws of Congress come into conflict with the laws of economics, economics wins. Congress can't repeal the laws of supply and demand!

FIGURE 8.10

myeconlab

A Social Security Tax on Employers

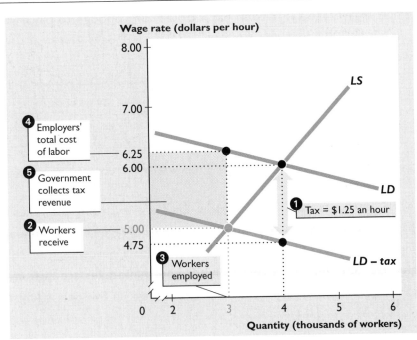

With no taxes, 4,000 people are employed at a wage rate of $6 an hour.

❶ A tax on employers of $1.25 an hour shifts the demand curve leftward to *LD − tax.*

❷ The wage rate falls to $5 an hour, a decrease of $1 an hour.

❸ The quantity of labor employed decreases to 3,000 workers.

❹ Employers' total cost of labor rises to $6.25 an hour—the wage rate of $5 an hour plus the $1.25 an hour tax.

❺ The government collects tax revenue shown by the purple rectangle.

EYE ON THE PAST

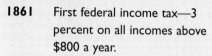

The Origins and History of the U.S. Income Tax

1861 First federal income tax—3 percent on all incomes above $800 a year.

1872 Income tax was repealed. (Tariffs on imports provided government revenue.)

1895 Income tax reestablished, but the Supreme Court ruled it unconstitutional.

1913 The 16th Amendment to the Constitution made the federal income tax legal.

1913–2004 Tax rates fluctuated, but the bottom rate remained

around 15 percent and the top rate was gradually lowered.

SOURCE OF DATA: Congressional Joint Committee on Taxation.

REALITY CHECK

Taxes in YOUR Life

The Tax Foundation has calculated "Tax Freedom Day"—the date by when an average U.S. citizen has worked long enough to pay a year's tax bill. In 2004, that day was April 17. The 107 days Americans must work to pay taxes break down this way:

    38 days to pay personal income taxes

    30 days to pay Social Security taxes

    16 days to pay sales and excise taxes

    11 days to pay property taxes

    9 days to pay corporate income taxes

    3 days for all other taxes

Work out your own "Tax Freedom Day" by recording the taxes you pay in a year. Express this number as a percentage of your annual income and then find the number of days (as a percentage of 365) that this amount of tax represents. If you think taxes are high in the United States, think again. "Tax Freedom Day" in Sweden is July 18!

CHECKPOINT 8.2

2 **Explain how income taxes and Social Security taxes change wage rates and employment, are shared by employers and workers, and create inefficiency.**

Practice Problems 8.2

1. Florida levies the following taxes: a 5.5 percent corporate income tax, a 6 percent sales tax, taxes of 4 cents a gallon on gasoline, 33.9 cents a pack on cigarettes, $0.48 a gallon on beer and $2.25 a gallon on wine, and property taxes that vary across the counties and range from 1.4 percent to 2.0 percent of property values. Classify Florida's taxes into progressive, proportional, and regressive taxes.

2. Explain why Tiger Woods pays his own Social Security tax and the PGA (the Professional Golf Association) pays none of it.

3. Which tax is more inefficient: a tax on land rent or a tax on capital income? Explain.

Exercise 8.2

1. California taxes personal incomes, and in 2004, there were six tax brackets that ranged from 1.0 percent on a taxable income of $6,146 to 9.3 percent on taxable incomes above $40,345. California has an 8.84 percent corporate income tax. California has a 7.25 percent sales tax. Other taxes are 18 cents a gallon on gasoline, 87 cents a pack on cigarettes, and $0.20 per gallon on beer and wine. Property taxes vary across the counties and range from 1 percent to 2 percent of property values.
   a. Classify California's taxes into progressive, proportional, and regressive taxes.
   b. Which of California's taxes creates the biggest excess burden? Explain.

Solutions to Practice Problems 8.2

1. If counties with the higher rates are those with high property values, then Florida's property taxes are progressive. The corporate income tax does not vary with income, so this tax is a proportional tax. Saving increases with income, so expenditure as a fraction of income decreases as income increases. So the sales tax, gasoline tax, cigarette tax, and beer tax are regressive taxes.

2. Tiger Woods pays his Social Security tax and the PGA pays none of it because the supply of Tiger Woods' services is (most likely) perfectly inelastic. The elasticities of demand and supply determine who pays the tax.

3. A tax on capital income is more inefficient than a tax on land rent. A tax on capital income has the larger effect on the quantities of factors of production employed than does a tax on land rent because the supply of land is perfectly inelastic while the supply of capital is highly (and perhaps perfectly) elastic. The larger the deadweight loss created by the tax (the excess burden of the tax), the more inefficient is the tax.

8.3 FAIRNESS AND THE BIG TRADEOFF

We've examined the incidence and the efficiency of different types of taxes. These topics have occupied most of this chapter because they are the issues about taxes that economics can address. But when political leaders debate tax issues, it is fairness, not just incidence and efficiency, that gets the most attention. Democrats complain that Republican tax cuts are unfair because they give the benefits of lower taxes to the rich. Republicans counter that because the rich pay most of the taxes, it is fair that they get most of the tax cuts. No easy answers are available to the questions about the fairness of taxes. And economists have proposed two conflicting principles of fairness to apply to a tax system:

- The benefits principle
- The ability-to-pay principle

■ The Benefits Principle

The **benefits principle** is the proposition that people should pay taxes equal to the benefits they receive from public goods and services. This arrangement is fair because it means that those who benefit most pay the most. It makes tax payments and the consumption of government-provided services similar to private consumption expenditures. If taxes are based on the benefits principle, the people who enjoy the largest benefits pay the most for them.

To implement the benefits principle, it would be necessary to have an objective method of measuring each individual's marginal benefit from government-provided goods. In the absence of such a method, the principle can be used to justify a wide range of different taxes.

For example, the benefits principle can justify high fuel taxes to pay for public highways. Here, the argument would be that those who value the highways most use them most and so should pay most of the cost of providing them. Similarly, the benefits principle can justify high taxes on alcoholic beverages and tobacco products. Here, the argument would be that those who drink and smoke the most place the largest burden on public health-care services and so should pay the greater part of the cost of those services.

The benefits principle can also be used to justify a progressive income tax. Here, the argument would be that the rich receive a disproportionately large share of the benefit from law and order and from living in a secure environment, so they should pay the largest share of providing these services.

■ The Ability-to-Pay Principle

The **ability-to-pay principle** is the proposition that people should pay taxes according to how easily they can bear the burden. A rich person can more easily bear the burden of providing public goods than a poor person can, so the rich should pay higher taxes than the poor. The ability-to-pay principle involves comparing people along two dimensions: horizontally and vertically.

Horizontal Equity

If taxes are based on ability to pay, taxpayers with the same ability to pay should pay the same taxes, a situation called **horizontal equity**. While horizontal equity is easy to agree with in principle, it is difficult to implement in practice. If two peo-

Benefits principle
The proposition that people should pay taxes equal to the benefits they receive from public goods and services.

Ability-to-pay principle
The proposition that people should pay taxes according to how easily they can bear the burden.

Horizontal equity
The requirement that taxpayers with the same ability to pay should pay the same taxes.

ple are identical in every respect, horizontal equity is easy to apply. But how do we compare people who are similar but not identical? The greatest difficulty arises in working out differences in ability to pay that arise from the state of a person's health and from a person's family responsibilities. The U.S. income tax has many special deductions and other rules that aim to achieve horizontal equity.

Vertical Equity

If horizontal comparisons are difficult, vertical comparisons are impossible. **Vertical equity** is the requirement that taxpayers with a greater ability to pay bear a greater share of the taxes. This proposition easily translates into the requirement that people with higher incomes should pay higher taxes. But it provides no help in determining how steeply taxes should increase as income increases. Should taxes be proportional to income? Should they be regressive? Should they be progressive? All of these arrangements have higher-income people paying higher taxes, so they all satisfy the basic idea of vertical equity. But most people have strong views that include the extent to which the rich should pay more.

You've seen that the U.S. tax code uses progressive income taxes—average tax rates that increase with income. Progressive taxes are justified as fair on the basis of the principle of vertical equity. But their use to achieve vertical equity produces a problem for the attainment of horizontal equity. The problem shows up most clearly in the U.S. tax code in its treatment of single people and married couples.

Vertical equity
The requirement that taxpayers with a greater ability to pay bear a greater share of the taxes.

■ The Marriage Tax Problem

Should a married couple (or two people living together) be treated as two individual taxpayers or as a single taxpayer? Until some changes were introduced in 2003, the U.S. tax code treated a married couple is a single taxpayer. This arrangement means that when a man and a woman get married, they stop paying income tax as two individuals and instead pay as one individual. To see the marriage tax problem, suppose the tax code (simpler than that in the United States) is as follows: no deductions or exemptions, incomes up to $20,000 a year bear no tax, and incomes in excess of $20,000 are taxed at 10 percent.

Now think about Al and Judy, two struggling young journalists, each of whom earns $20,000 a year and who get married. As single people, they paid no tax. Married, their income is $40,000, so they pay $2,000 a year in tax (10 percent of $20,000). Their marriage tax is $2,000 a year. (This example is *much* more severe than the marriage tax in the United States, but it serves to highlight the source of the problem.)

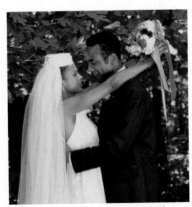

A married couple or two individuals?

We could make a simple change to the tax law to overcome this problem for Al and Judy: Tax married couples as two single persons. That is what is done in most countries and what some economists say should be done in the United States. If we make this change in the tax law, Al and Judy pay no tax after their marriage just as before. We've solved the marriage tax problem.

Before we conclude that this small change to the tax code would clean up a source of unfairness, let's think about its effect on Denise and Frank. Frank is a painter whose work just doesn't sell. He has no income. Denise is a successful artist whose work is in steady demand and earns her $40,000 a year. As two single artists, Frank pays no tax and Denise pays $2,000 a year (10 percent of $20,000). If they marry, under the arrangement that taxes a married couple as a single taxpayer, they still pay $2,000 in tax.

Now compare Frank and Denise with Al and Judy. If we tax married couples as a single taxpayer, both couples earn $40,000 a year and both pay income tax of $2,000 a year. But if we tax them as single persons, Frank and Denise pay $2,000 a year and Al and Judy pay nothing. So which is fair?

Horizontal equity requires Frank and Denise to be treated like Al and Judy. Taxing them as couples rather than as individuals achieves this outcome. But it taxes marriage, which seems unfair.

This problem arises from the progressive tax. It would not arise if taxes were proportional. Because horizontal equity conflicts with progressive taxes, some people say that only proportional taxes are fair.

■ The Big Tradeoff

Questions about the fairness of taxes conflict with efficiency questions and create the *big tradeoff* that you met in Chapter 6. The taxes that generate the greatest deadweight loss are those on the income from capital. But most capital is owned by a relatively small number of people who have the greatest ability to pay taxes. So there is a conflict between efficiency and fairness. We want a tax system that is efficient, in the sense that it raises the revenue that the government needs to provide public goods and services, but we want a tax system that shares the burden of providing these goods and services fairly. Our tax system is an evolving compromise that juggles these two goals.

CHECKPOINT 8.3

3   **Review ideas about the fairness of the tax system.**

Practice Problem 8.3

1.   In Hong Kong, the marginal income tax rates range from 2 percent to 20 percent. Does Hong Kong place greater weight on the ability-to-pay principle than does the United States? Does Hong Kong place a greater weight on efficiency and a smaller weight on fairness than does the United States?

Exercise 8.3

1.   In Canada, the marginal income tax rates range from 22 percent to 40 percent. Does Canada place greater weight on the ability-to-pay principle than does the United States? Does Canada place a greater weight on efficiency and a smaller weight on fairness than does the United States?

Solution to Practice Problem 8.3

1.   Income tax rates are lower in Hong Kong than in the United States, so Hong Kong places less weight on the ability-to-pay principle than does the United States. With income tax rates in Hong Kong lower than in the United States, Hong Kong places a greater weight on efficiency and a smaller weight on fairness than does the United States.

CHAPTER CHECKPOINT

Key Points

1   **Explain how taxes change prices and quantities, are shared by buyers and sellers, and create inefficiency.**

* A tax on buyers has the same effect as a tax on sellers. It increases the price paid by the buyer and lowers the price received by the seller.
* A tax creates inefficiency by driving a wedge between marginal benefit and marginal cost and creating a deadweight loss.
* The less elastic the demand or the more elastic the supply, the greater is the price increase and the larger is the share of the tax paid by the buyer.
* If demand is perfectly elastic or supply is perfectly inelastic, the seller pays all the tax. And if demand is perfectly inelastic or supply is perfectly elastic, the buyer pays all the tax.
* If demand or supply is perfectly inelastic, the tax creates no deadweight loss and is efficient.

2   **Explain how income taxes and Social Security taxes change wage rates and employment, are shared by employers and workers, and create inefficiency.**

* Taxes can be progressive (the average tax rate rises with income), proportional (the average tax rate is constant), or regressive (the average tax rate falls with income).
* The U.S. income tax is progressive.
* The shares of the income tax paid by firms and households depend on the elasticity of demand and the elasticity of supply of the factors of production.
* The elasticities of demand and supply, not Congress, determine who pays the income tax and who pays the Social Security tax.
* The more elastic is either the demand or supply of a factor of production, the greater is the excess burden of an income tax.

3   **Review ideas about the fairness of the tax system.**

* The two main principles of fairness of taxes—the benefits principle and the ability-to-pay principle—do not deliver universally accepted standards of fairness, and vertical equity and horizontal equity can come into conflict.

Key Terms

Ability-to-pay principle, 210	Horizontal equity, 210	Regressive tax, 201
Average tax rate, 201	Marginal tax rate, 201	Taxable income, 200
Benefits principle, 210	Progressive tax, 201	Tax incidence, 194
Excess burden, 196	Proportional tax, 201	Vertical equity, 211

Exercises

1. In Florida, sunscreen and sunglasses are vital items. If the tax on sellers of these items is doubled from 5.5 percent to 11 percent, who will pay most of the tax increase: buyers or sellers? Will the tax increase halve the quantity of sunscreen and sunglasses bought?

2. Table 1 illustrates the market for Internet service. Use a demand-supply graph to answer the following questions.
    a. What is the market price of an Internet service?
    b. If the government taxes Internet service $15 a month, what price would the buyer of an Internet service pay?
    c. What price would the seller of the Internet service receive?
    d. Does the buyer or the seller pay more of the tax?
    e. What is the tax revenue collected by the government?
    f. What is the excess burden of the tax?

TABLE 1

Price (dollars per month)	Quantity demanded	Quantity supplied
	(units per month)	
0	30	0
10	25	10
20	20	20
30	15	30
40	10	40
50	5	50
60	0	60

3. The supply of luxury boats is perfectly elastic, and the demand for luxury boats is unit elastic. The government decides to tax luxury boats 20 percent. Before the tax is introduced, the price of a luxury boat is $1 million and 240 luxury boats a week are bought.
    a. What is the price that buyers of a luxury boat pay after the tax is imposed?
    b. How is the tax split between buyers and sellers?
    c. How much tax revenue will the government raise?
    d. Show in a graph the excess burden of this tax.
    e. Is this tax efficient? Explain your answer.
    f. Is this tax fair? Explain your answer.

TABLE 2

Price (dollars per tube)	Quantity demanded	Quantity supplied
	(thousands of tubes per week)	
0.00	11	6.5
0.50	10	7.0
1.00	9	7.5
1.50	8	8.0
2.00	7	8.5
2.50	6	9.0
3.00	5	9.5
3.50	4	10.0
4.00	3	10.5
4.50	2	11.0
5.00	1	11.5

4. Table 2 shows the demand schedule and the supply schedule of toothpaste. If the government decides to tax toothpaste $1.50 a tube:
    a. What price do buyers pay for toothpaste?
    b. What price do sellers receive?
    c. How much tax revenue does the government collect?
    d. What is the excess burden of the tax?

5. In exercise 4, suppose that when the government taxes toothpaste $1.50 a tube, all toothpaste manufacturers announce that to counteract the government's outrageous action, they will cut the price they charge by $1 a tube.
    a. Are the toothpaste manufacturers making a generous move to support oral hygiene or just seeking credit for market forces that are outside their control? Explain your answer using an appropriate graph.
    b. If the price charged by toothpaste makers fell by less than $1 a tube, would there be a shortage or a surplus of toothpaste? Explain your answer using an appropriate graph.

6. To encourage inner-city youths to spend more time playing sports, the government introduces a super income tax of 10 percent on professional basketball players and plans to use the revenue to improve inner-city sports facilities.
    a. Will the super income tax raise much revenue for the government?
    b. Who will pay most of the tax: the players or the team owners?
    c. Will the tax create a large or a small excess burden?

7. In an attempt to raise more revenue, the government decides to increase the tax on buyers of coffee.
   a. What will determine how much more Starbucks charges for a coffee?
   b. How will the quantity of coffee bought in coffee shops change?
   c. Will the government raise much revenue from the coffee tax?

8. Concerned about the political fallout from rising gas prices, the government decides to cut the tax on gasoline. Explain how the market for gasoline would react to this tax cut if
   a. The oil-producing nations increased production and drove the equilibrium price of gasoline down.
   b. A global shortage of oil sent the equilibrium price of gasoline up.

9. In 2002, New York State raised the cigarette tax by 39 cents to $1.50 a pack. Then New York City raised the tax from 8 cents to $1.50 a pack. These taxes raised the price of cigarettes to about $7.50 a pack—the highest in the nation.
   a. How will the $3 tax increase change the price buyers pay and the price sellers receive?
   b. Who will pay more of the tax increase? Buyers or sellers?
   c. Will these tax increases change the revenue collected by the government and the city? If so, will revenue increase or decrease? Explain why.
   d. How will these taxes change consumer surplus and producer surplus?
   e. Which of these tax hikes will have more excess burden?
   f. Everyone who buys cigarettes pays the $3 tax a pack. Is this tax a progressive, regressive, or proportional tax? Explain.

10. Larry earns $25,000 and pays $2,500 in tax, while Suzy earns $50,000 and pays $15,000 in tax. If Larry's income increases by $100, his tax increases by $12, but if Suzy's income increases by $100, her tax increases by $35.
    a. Calculate Larry's average tax rate and marginal tax rate.
    b. Calculate Suzy's average tax rate and marginal tax rate.
    c. Is the income tax fair? Explain.

11. Bakers earn $10 an hour, gas pump attendants earn $6 an hour, and copy shop workers earn $7 an hour.
    a. If the government introduces an income tax of $1 an hour, explain how the markets for bakers, gas pump attendants, and copy shop workers will respond.
    b. Calculate the marginal tax rates for bakers, gas pump attendants, and copy shop workers.
    c. Is this tax progressive, regressive, or proportional?

12. Figure 1 illustrates the labor market in a country that does not tax labor income.
    a. How many workers are employed and what is the wage rate they earn?
    b. If the government introduces a social security tax on workers of $2 per worker, what are the number of workers employed, the wage rate paid by employers, the wage rate received by workers, the number of workers no longer employed, and the tax revenue collected by the government?
    c. If the government splits the social security tax equally between workers and employers, what now are your answers to part **b**?
    d. Is the social security tax in part **b** or **c** fairer? Explain.

FIGURE I

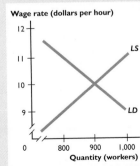

Critical Thinking

14. The government of the U.S. Virgin Islands seeks your help to evaluate two tax schemes. In scheme A, food is not taxed, luxury goods are taxed 10 percent, and all other goods are taxed at 5 percent. In scheme B, there is a flat 3 percent tax on all goods and services. The government asks you to explain what research must be undertaken and what features of the markets for food, luxury goods, and other goods will influence how the prices and quantities of food, luxury goods, and all other goods will differ under the two schemes.

15. In exercise 14, which tax would be more efficient if both schemes generated the same amount of tax revenue? The government asks you to explain what research must be undertaken and what features of the markets for food, luxury goods, and other goods will influence the excess burden of the taxes under the two schemes.

16. A study by Citizens for Tax Justice and the Children's Defense Fund says that the richest 1 percent of Americans will receive 50 percent of the benefit of the tax cuts that Congress enacted in 2001. Debate this assessment. What assumptions about the elasticities of demand and supply for high-wage labor and capital might be consistent with this assessment? What other facts about demand and supply and market outcomes would you need to know? If the assessment is correct, is such an outcome likely to be efficient? Is such an outcome fair on any of the standard principles of fairness?

Web Exercises

Use the links on MyEconLab to work the following exercises.

17. Obtain data on the sales tax rates in each state.
    a. Which states have the highest sales tax rate and which states have the lowest?
    b. Compare the sales taxes in your state with those in the neighboring states. Of these states, which do you think has the biggest excess burden of these taxes?
    c. Compare California with the nearby states of Nevada and Washington. In which state do you think consumer surplus and producer surplus (per person) is greatest? Why?

18. Learn about the poll tax introduced in Great Britain during the 1980s.
    a. What is a poll tax? Is a poll tax a progressive, regressive, or proportional tax?
    b. How do you think the effects of a poll tax differ from those of a sales tax?
    c. Why do you think a poll tax generates anger and rioting?
    d. Despite its problems, do you think a poll tax is efficient? Explain why.

19. Visit *Slate* and read the article by Steven Landsburg entitled "Bush's Tax Cuts Are Unfair..."
    a. To whom are the Bush tax cuts unfair?
    b. Do you agree with Steven Landsburg? Explain why or why not.

Externalities

CHAPTER CHECKLIST

When you have completed your study of this chapter,
you will be able to

1 Explain why negative externalities lead to inefficient overproduction and how property rights, pollution charges, and taxes can achieve a more efficient outcome.

2 Explain why positive externalities lead to inefficient underproduction and how public provision, subsidies, vouchers, and patents can achieve a more efficient outcome.

Paul J. Evanson is Chairman, President, and Chief Executive Officer of Allegheny Electric, a power utility that operates the Fort Martin Power Station in Maidsville, West Virginia. Mr. Evanson is a good man and a respected, accomplished, well-paid manager. But Fort Martin is the dirtiest coal-fired power plant in the United States. How can governments create incentives—sticks or carrots—that align the self-interest of Mr. Evanson, his stockholders, and his customers with the social interest?

Rob Goldston is director of the Princeton Plasma Physics Laboratory, a group of physicists, engineers, and technicians who are trying to make fusion energy a reality. Fusion would provide abundant low-cost energy with no air pollution. If this scientific breakthrough can be achieved everyone on the planet will enjoy enormous benefits. How can governments provide the incentives to ensure that the scale of research that brings advances in technology is in the social interest?

These are the questions that we study in this chapter.

EXTERNALITIES IN OUR DAILY LIVES

Externality
A cost or a benefit that arises from production that falls on someone other than the producer or a cost or benefit that arises from consumption that falls on someone other than the consumer.

Negative externality
A production or consumption activity that creates an external cost.

Positive externality
A production or consumption activity that creates an external benefit.

An **externality** is a cost or a benefit that arises from production that falls on someone other than the producer or a cost or a benefit that arises from consumption that falls on someone other than the consumer. Before we embark on the two main tasks of this chapter, we're going to review the range of externalities, classify them, and give some everyday examples.

First, an externality can arise from either a production activity or a consumption activity. Second, it can be either a **negative externality**, which imposes an external cost, or a **positive externality**, which provides an external benefit. So there are four types of externalities:

- Negative production externalities
- Positive production externalities
- Negative consumption externalities
- Positive consumption externalities

■ Negative Production Externalities

When the U.S. Open tennis tournament is being played at Flushing Meadows, players, spectators, and television viewers around the world share a negative production externality that many New Yorkers experience every day: the noise of airplanes taking off from LaGuardia Airport. Aircraft noise imposes a large cost on millions of people who live under the flight paths to airports in every major city.

Logging and the clearing of forests are sources of another negative production externality. These activities destroy the habitat of wildlife and influence the amount of carbon dioxide in the atmosphere, which has a long-term effect on temperature. So these external costs are borne by everyone and by future generations.

Pollution, which we examine in more detail in the next section, is a major example of this type of externality.

■ Positive Production Externalities

To produce orange blossom honey, Honey Run Honey of Chico, California, locates beehives next to an orange orchard. The honeybees collect pollen and nectar from the orange blossoms to make the honey. At the same time, they transfer pollen

Negative production externality.

Positive production externality.

between the blossoms, which helps to fertilize the blossoms. Two positive production externalities are present in this example. Honey Run Honey gets a positive production externality from the owner of the orange orchard; and the orange grower gets a positive production externality from Honey Run.

■ Negative Consumption Externalities

Negative consumption externalities are a source of irritation for most of us. Smoking tobacco in a confined space creates fumes that many people find unpleasant and that pose a health risk. So smoking in restaurants and on airplanes generates a negative externality. To avoid this negative externality, many restaurants and all airlines ban smoking. But while a smoking ban avoids a negative consumption externality for most people, it imposes a negative external cost on smokers who would prefer to enjoy the consumption of tobacco while dining or taking a plane trip.

Noisy parties and outdoor rock concerts are other examples of negative consumption externalities. They are also examples of the fact that a simple ban on an activity is not a solution. Banning noisy parties avoids the external cost on sleep-seeking neighbors, but it results in the sleepers imposing an external cost on the fun-seeking partygoers.

Permitting dandelions to grow in lawns, not picking up leaves in the fall, allowing a dog to bark loudly or to foul a neighbor's lawn, and letting a cell phone ring in class are other examples of negative consumption externalities.

■ Positive Consumption Externalities

When you get a flu vaccination, you lower your risk of being infected. If you avoid the flu, your neighbor, who didn't get vaccinated, has a better chance of remaining healthy. Flu vaccinations generate positive consumption externalities.

When the owner of a historic building restores it, everyone who sees the building gets pleasure from it. Similarly, when someone erects a spectacular home—such as those built by Frank Lloyd Wright during the 1920s and 1930s—or other exciting building—such as the Chrysler and Empire State Buildings in New York or the Wrigley Building in Chicago—an external consumption benefit flows to everyone who has an opportunity to view it.

Education, which we examine in more detail in this chapter, is a major example of this type of externality.

Negative consumption externality.

Positive consumption externality.

9.1 NEGATIVE EXTERNALITIES: POLLUTION

You've just seen that pollution is an example of a negative externality. Both production and consumption activities create pollution. But here, we'll focus on pollution as a negative production externality. When a chemical factory dumps waste into a river, the people who live by the river and use it for fishing and boating bear the cost of the pollution. The chemical factory does not consider the cost of pollution when it decides the quantity of chemicals to produce. The factory's supply curve is based on its own costs, not on the costs that it inflicts on others. You're going to discover that when external costs are present, we produce more output than the efficient quantity and we get more pollution than the efficient quantity.

Pollution and other environmental problems are not new. Preindustrial towns and cities in Europe had severe sewage disposal problems that created cholera epidemics and plagues that killed millions. Nor is the desire to find solutions to environmental problems new. The development in the fourteenth century of a pure water supply and the hygienic disposal of garbage and sewage are examples of early contributions to improving the quality of the environment.

Popular discussions about pollution and the environment often pay little attention to economics. They focus on physical aspects of the environment, not on costs and benefits. A common assumption is that activities that damage the environment are normally wrong and must cease. In contrast, an economic study of the environment emphasizes costs and benefits. Economists talk about the efficient amount of pollution or environmental damage. This emphasis on costs and benefits does not mean that economists, as citizens, don't have the same goals as others and value a healthy environment. Nor does it mean that economists have the right answers and everyone else has the wrong ones. Rather, economics provides a set of tools and principles that help to clarify the issues.

The starting point for an economic analysis of the environment is the distinction between private costs and social costs.

■ Private Costs and Social Costs

Marginal private cost
The cost of producing an additional unit of a good or service that is borne by the producer of that good or service.

Marginal external cost
The cost of producing an additional unit of a good or service that falls on people other than the producer.

Marginal social cost
The marginal cost incurred by the entire society—by the producer and by everyone else on whom the cost falls. It is the sum of marginal private cost and marginal external cost.

A *private cost* of production is a cost that is borne by the producer of a good or service. *Marginal cost* is the cost of producing an *additional unit* of a good or service. So **marginal private cost** (MC) is the cost of producing an additional unit of a good or service that is borne by the producer of that good or service.

You've seen that an *external cost* is a cost of producing a good or service that is *not* borne by the producer but borne by other people. A **marginal external cost** is the cost of producing an additional unit of a good or service that falls on people other than the producer.

Marginal social cost (MSC) is the marginal cost incurred by the entire society—by the producer and by everyone else on whom the cost falls—and is the sum of marginal private cost and marginal external cost. That is,

$$MSC = MC + \text{Marginal external cost.}$$

We express costs in dollars. But we must always remember that a cost is an opportunity cost—the best thing we give up to get something. A marginal external cost is what someone other than the producer of a good or service must give up when the producer makes one more unit of the item. Something real that people value, such as a clean river or clean air, is given up.

Valuing an External Cost

Economists use market prices to put a dollar value on the cost of pollution. For example, suppose that there are two similar rivers, one polluted and the other clean. Five hundred identical homes are built along the side of each river. The homes on the clean river rent for $2,500 a month, and those on the polluted river rent for $1,500 a month. If the pollution is the only detectable difference between the two rivers and the two locations, the rent decrease of $1,000 per month is the cost of the pollution. For the 500 homes, the external cost is $500,000 a month.

External Cost and Output

Figure 9.1 shows an example of the relationship between output and cost in a chemical industry that pollutes. The marginal cost curve, *MC*, describes the private marginal cost borne by the firms that produce the chemical. Marginal cost increases as the quantity of the chemical produced increases. If the firms dump waste into a river, they impose an external cost that increases with the amount of the chemical produced. The marginal social cost curve, *MSC*, is the sum of marginal private cost and marginal external cost. For example, when firms produce 4,000 tons of chemical a month, marginal private cost is $100 a ton, marginal external cost is $125 a ton, and marginal social cost is $225 a ton.

In Figure 9.1, as the quantity of the chemical produced increases, the amount of pollution increases and the external cost of pollution increases. The quantity of the chemical produced and the pollution created depend on how the market for the chemical operates. First, we'll see what happens when the industry is free to pollute.

FIGURE 9.1
An External Cost

The *MC* curve shows the private marginal cost borne by the factories that produce a chemical. The *MSC* curve shows the sum of marginal private cost and marginal external cost.

When the quantity of chemical produced is 4,000 tons a month, ❶ marginal private cost is $100 a ton, ❷ marginal external cost is $125 a ton, and ❸ marginal social cost is $225 a ton.

■ Production and Pollution: How Much?

When an industry is unregulated, the amount of pollution it creates depends on the market equilibrium price and quantity of the good produced. Figure 9.2 illustrates the outcome in the market for a pollution-creating chemical.

The demand curve for the chemical is *D*. This curve also measures the marginal benefit, *MB*, to the buyers of the chemical (see Chapter 6, p. 148). The supply curve is *S*. This curve also measures the marginal private cost, *MC*, of the producers (see Chapter 6, p. 151). The supply curve is the marginal private cost curve because when firms make their production and supply decisions, they consider only the costs that they will bear. Market equilibrium occurs at a price of $100 a ton and a quantity of 4,000 tons of chemical a month.

This equilibrium is inefficient. You learned in Chapter 6 that the allocation of resources is efficient when marginal benefit equals marginal cost. But we must count all the costs—private and external—when we compare marginal benefit and marginal cost. So with an external cost, the allocation is efficient when marginal benefit equals marginal *social* cost. This outcome occurs when the quantity of the chemical produced is 2,000 tons a month. The market equilibrium *overproduces* by 2,000 tons a month and creates a deadweight loss, the gray triangle.

How can the people who live by the polluted river get the chemical factories to decrease their output of the chemical and create less pollution? If some method can be found to achieve this outcome, everyone—the owners of the factories and the residents of the riverside homes—can gain. Let's explore some solutions.

▨ FIGURE 9.2

Inefficiency with an External Cost

The market supply curve is the marginal private cost curve, *S* = *MC*. The demand curve is the marginal benefit curve, *D* = *MB*. The marginal social cost curve is *MSC*.

❶ Market equilibrium at a price of $100 a ton and 4,000 tons of chemical a month is inefficient because ❷ marginal social cost exceeds ❸ marginal benefit.

❹ The efficient quantity of chemical is 2,000 tons a month where marginal benefit equals marginal social cost.

❺ The gray triangle shows the deadweight loss created by the pollution externality.

■ Property Rights

Sometimes it is possible to reduce the inefficiency arising from an externality by establishing a property right where one does not currently exist. **Property rights** are legally established titles to the ownership, use, and disposal of factors of production and goods and services that are enforceable in the courts.

Suppose that the chemical factories own the river and the 500 homes alongside it. The rent that people are willing to pay depends on the amount of pollution. Using the earlier example, people are willing to pay $2,500 a month to live alongside a pollution-free river but only $1,500 a month to live with the pollution created by 4,000 tons of chemical a month. If the factories produce this quantity, they lose $1,000 a month for each home and a total of $500,000 a month.

The chemical factories are now confronted with the cost of their pollution decision. They might still decide to pollute, but if they do, they face the opportunity cost of their actions—forgone rent from the people who live by the river.

Figure 9.3 illustrates the outcome. With property rights in place, the marginal cost curve in Figure 9.2 no longer measures all the factories' costs of producing the chemical. It excludes the pollution cost that they must now bear. The former *MSC* curve now becomes the marginal private cost curve *MC*. The market supply curve is based on all the marginal costs and is the curve labeled $S = MC$.

Market equilibrium now occurs at a price of $150 a ton and a quantity of 2,000 tons a month. This outcome is efficient. The factories still produce some pollution, but it is the efficient quantity.

Property rights
Legally established titles to the ownership, use, and disposal of factors of production and goods and services that are enforceable in the courts.

■ FIGURE 9.3
Property Rights Achieve an Efficient Outcome

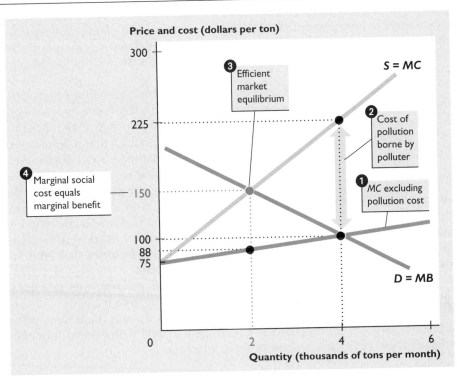

❶ With property rights, the marginal cost curve that excludes the cost of pollution shows only part of the producers' marginal cost.

The marginal private cost curve includes ❷ the cost of pollution, so the supply curve is $S = MC$.

❸ Market equilibrium is at a price of $150 a ton and a quantity of 2,000 tons of chemical a month and is efficient because ❹ marginal social cost equals marginal benefit.

■ The Coase Theorem

Does it matter how property rights are assigned? Does it matter whether the polluter or the victim of the pollution owns the resource that might be polluted? Until 1960, everyone—including economists who had thought long and hard about the problem—thought that it did matter. But in 1960, Ronald Coase had a remarkable insight, now called the Coase theorem.

The **Coase theorem** is the proposition that if property rights exist, only a small number of parties are involved, and transactions costs are low, then private transactions are efficient. There are no externalities because the transacting parties take all the costs and benefits into account. Furthermore, it doesn't matter who has the property rights.

Application of the Coase Theorem

Let's apply the Coase theorem to the polluted river. In the example that we've just studied, the factories own both the river and the homes. Suppose that instead, the residents own both their homes and the river. Now the factories must pay a fee to the homeowners for the right to dump their waste. The greater the quantity of waste dumped into the river, the more the factories must pay. So again, the factories face the opportunity cost of the pollution they create. The quantity of chemical produced and the amount of waste dumped are the same, whoever owns the homes and the river. If the factories own them, they bear the cost of pollution because they receive a lower income from home rents. And if the residents own the homes and the river, the factories bear the cost of pollution because they must pay a fee to the homeowners. In both cases, the factories bear the cost of their pollution and dump the efficient amount of waste into the river.

The Coase solution works only when transactions costs are low. **Transactions costs** are the opportunity costs of conducting a transaction. For example, when you buy a house, you incur a series of transactions costs. You might pay a real estate agent to help you find the best place and a financial planner to help you get the best loan, and you pay a lawyer to run checks that assure you that the seller owns the property and that after you've paid for it, the ownership has been properly transferred to you.

In the example of the homes alongside a river, the transactions costs that are incurred by a small number of chemical factories and a few homeowners might be low enough to enable them to negotiate the deals that produce an efficient outcome. But in many situations, transactions costs are so high that it would be inefficient to incur them. In these situations, the Coase solution is not available.

Suppose, for example, that everyone owns the airspace above their homes up to, say, 10 miles. If someone pollutes your airspace, you can charge a fee. But to collect the fee, you must identify who is polluting your airspace and persuade them to pay you. Imagine the cost to you and the 50 million people who live in your part of the United States (and perhaps in Canada or Mexico) of negotiating and enforcing agreements with the several thousand factories that emit sulfur dioxide and create acid rain that falls on your property!

In this situation, we use public choices through governments to cope with externalities. But the transactions costs that prevent us from using the Coase solution are opportunity costs, and governments can't wave a magician's wand to eliminate them. So attempts by the government to deal with externalities offer no easy solution. Let's look at some of these attempts.

Coase theorem
The proposition that if property rights exist, only a small number of parties are involved, and transactions costs are low, then private transactions are efficient and the outcome is not affected by who is assigned the property right.

Transactions costs
The opportunity costs of conducting a transaction.

■ Government Actions in the Face of External Costs

The three main methods that governments use to cope with externalities are

- Emission charges
- Marketable permits
- Taxes

Emission Charges

Emission charges confront a polluter with the external cost of pollution and provide an incentive to seek new technologies that are less polluting. In the United States, the Environmental Protection Agency (EPA) sets emission charges, which are, in effect, a price per unit of pollution. The more pollution a firm creates, the more it pays in emission charges. This method of dealing with environmental externalities has been used only modestly in the United States, but it is common in Europe. For example, in France, Germany, and the Netherlands, water polluters pay a waste disposal charge.

To work out the emission charge that achieves efficiency, the regulator must determine the marginal external cost of pollution at different levels of output and levy a charge on polluters that equals that cost. The polluter then incurs a marginal cost that includes both private and external costs. But to achieve the efficient outcome, the regulator needs a lot of information about the polluting industry that, in practice, is not available.

Another way of overcoming excess pollution is to issue firms with pollution quotas that they can buy and sell—with marketable permits. Let's look at this alternative.

Marketable Permits

An alternative to an emission charge is to assign each polluter an emission limit. Provided that the marginal benefit and marginal cost are assessed correctly, the same efficient outcome can be achieved with emission limits as with emission charges. But in the case of emission limits, a cap must be set for each polluter.

Marketable permits are a clever way of overcoming the need for the regulator to know every firm's marginal cost schedule. The government issues an emissions permit to each firm, and firms can buy and sell these permits. Firms with a low marginal cost of reducing pollution sell permits and firms with a high marginal cost of reducing pollution buy permits. The market in permits determines the price at which firms trade permits. And firms buy or sell permits until their marginal cost of pollution equals the market price.

The 1990 Clear Air Act and the 1994 Regional Clean Air Incentives Market (RECLAIM) in the Los Angeles basin successfully use this method of dealing with pollution. The method provides an even stronger incentive than do emission charges to find technologies that pollute less because the price of a permit to pollute rises as the demand for permits increases.

Taxes

The government can use taxes as an incentive for producers to cut back on an activity that creates an external cost. By setting the tax rate equal to the marginal external cost, firms can be made to behave in the same way as they would if they bore the cost of the externality directly.

Pollution Trends

Air quality in the United States is getting better. Lead has been almost eliminated, and sulfur dioxide, carbon monoxide, and suspended particulates have been reduced substantially. But nitrogen dioxide and ozone have persisted at close to their 1975 levels.

The earth's average temperature has increased over the past 100 years, and most of the increase occurred before 1940. No one knows why this temperature increase has occurred, but some scientists believe the cause to be carbon dioxide emissions from road transportation and electric utilities, methane created by cows and other livestock, nitrous oxide emissions of electric utilities and from fertilizers, and chlorofluorocarbons (CFCs) from refrigeration equipment and (in the past) aerosols.

The ozone layer in the earth's atmosphere protects us from cancer-causing ultraviolet rays from the sun. A hole in the ozone layer over Antarctica is getting bigger. How our industrial activity influences the ozone layer is not well understood, but some scientists think that CFCs are one source of ozone layer depletion.

The largest sources of water pollution are the dumping of industrial waste and treated sewage in lakes and rivers and the runoff from fertilizers. A more dramatic source is the accidental spilling of crude oil into the oceans such as the *Exxon Valdez* spill in Alaska in 1989 and an even larger spill from the *Prestige* off Spain in 2002. The most frightening is the dumping of nuclear waste into the ocean by the former Soviet Union.

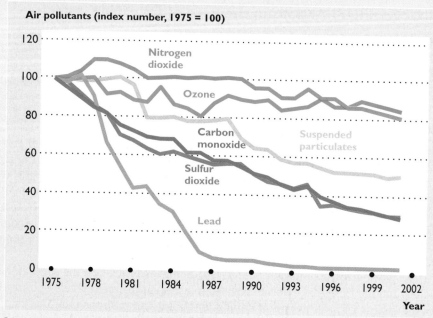

Air pollutants (index number, 1975 = 100)

Nitrogen dioxide · Ozone · Carbon monoxide · Suspended particulates · Sulfur dioxide · Lead

SOURCE OF DATA: Environmental Protection Agency, *National Air Quality: 2001 Status and Trends*, 2002.

Land pollution arises from dumping toxic waste products. Ordinary household garbage does not pose a pollution problem unless dumped garbage seeps into the water supply. This possibility increases as less suitable landfill sites are used. It is estimated that 80 percent of existing landfills in the United States will be full by 2010.

Some densely populated regions (such as New York and New Jersey) and densely populated countries (such as Japan and the Netherlands), where land costs are high, are seeking less costly alternatives to landfill, such as recycling and incineration. Recycling is an apparently attractive alternative, but it requires an investment in new technologies to be effective. Incineration is a high-cost alternative to landfill, and it produces air pollution. These alternatives become efficient only when the cost of using landfills is high, as it is in densely populated regions and countries.

Effects of Government Actions

To see how government actions can change market outcomes in the face of externalities, let's return to the example of the chemical factories and houses alongside the river.

Assume that the government has assessed the marginal external cost of pollution accurately and imposes a tax on the chemical factories that exactly equals this external cost.

Figure 9.4 illustrates the effects of this pollution tax. The demand curve and marginal benefit curve $D = MB$ and the firms' marginal cost curve MC are the same as those in Figure 9.2. The pollution tax equals the marginal external cost of the pollution. We add this tax to marginal cost to find the market supply curve. This curve is the one labeled $S = MC + tax = MSC$. This curve is the market supply curve because it tells us the quantity of chemical supplied at each price given the firms' marginal cost and the pollution tax they must pay. This curve is also the marginal social cost curve because the pollution tax has been set equal to the marginal external cost.

Demand and supply now determine the market equilibrium price at $150 a ton and the equilibrium quantity at 2,000 tons of chemical a month. At this scale of chemical production, the marginal social cost is $150 a ton and the marginal benefit is $150 a ton, so the outcome is efficient. The firms incur a marginal cost of $88 a ton and pay a tax of $62 a ton. The government collects tax revenue of $124,000 a month.

FIGURE 9.4

A Pollution Tax

❶ A pollution tax is imposed that is equal to the marginal external cost of pollution. The supply curve becomes the marginal private cost curve, *MC*, plus the tax—the curve labeled $S = MC + tax$.

Because the pollution tax equals the marginal external cost, the supply curve is also the marginal social cost curve *MSC*.

❷ Market equilibrium is at a price of $150 a ton and a quantity of 2,000 tons a month and is efficient because ❸ marginal social cost equals marginal benefit.

❹ The government collects tax revenue shown by the purple rectangle.

A Carbon Fuel Tax?

The gasoline tax in the United Kingdom and in most other countries is much higher than that in the United States. Why don't we have a higher gas tax to encourage a large reduction in emissions?

Part of the reason is that many people don't accept the scientific evidence that emissions produce global warming. Climatologists are uncertain about how carbon emissions translate into atmospheric concentrations. And economists are uncertain about how a temperature increase translates into economic costs and benefits.

Another factor weighing against a large change in fuel use is that the costs are certain and would be borne now, while the benefits, if any, would come many years in the future.

A final factor working against a large change in fuel use is the international pattern and trend. Today, carbon pollution comes in equal doses from industrial and developing economies. But by 2050, three quarters of carbon pollution will come from the developing economies (if the trends persist).

SOURCES OF DATA: Energy Information Administration and Automobile Association.

REALITY CHECK

Externalities in YOUR Life

Think about the negative and positive externalities that play a huge part in *your* life. And think about the sticks and carrots that attempt to align your self-interest with the social interest.

You respond to the stick of the gasoline tax by buying a little bit less gas than you otherwise would. This stick is small in comparison to that in most other countries. With a bigger gas tax, such as that in the United Kingdom, for example, traffic on our roads and highways would be lighter.

You are responding to the huge carrot of subsidized tuition by being in school. Faced with full-cost tuition, many people would quit school. Without subsidized college education (as you'll see in the next section), fewer people would have a degree and the benefits we all receive from living in a well-educated society would be smaller.

Think about your attitude as a citizen-voter to these two externalities. Have our politicians set the right incentives? Should the gas tax be higher? Should tuition be even lower?

CHECKPOINT 9.1

1 Explain why negative externalities lead to inefficient overproduction and how property rights, pollution charges, and taxes can achieve a more efficient outcome.

Practice Problem 9.1

1. Figure 1 illustrates the unregulated market for pesticide. When the factories produce pesticide, they also create waste, which they dump into a lake on the outskirts of the town. If the marginal external cost of the dumped waste is equal to the marginal private cost of producing the pesticide, then the marginal social cost of producing the pesticide is double the marginal private cost.
   a. What is the quantity of pesticide produced if no one owns the lake?
   b. What is the efficient quantity of pesticide?
   c. If the residents of the town own the lake, what is the quantity of pesticide produced and how much do the pesticide factories pay to residents of the town?
   d. If the pesticide factories own the lake, how much pesticide is produced?
   e. Suppose that no one owns the lake but that the government levies a pollution tax. What is the tax per ton of pesticide that will achieve the efficient outcome?

FIGURE 1

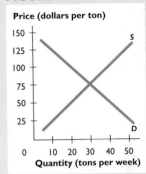

Exercise 9.1

1. Suppose that, in practice problem 9.1, the marginal external cost increases to twice the marginal private cost, so the marginal social cost of producing the pesticide is three times the marginal private cost. With no property rights, the government issues enough marketable permits to the town's residents to enable the factory to produce the efficient output of pesticide.
   a. How much pesticide gets produced?
   b. What is the price of a permit?
   c. How, if at all, would the outcome change if the government allocated the permits to the factories instead of to the town's residents?

Solution to Practice Problem 9.1

1a. The quantity of pesticide produced is 30 tons a week (Figure 2).
1b. The efficient quantity of pesticide is 20 tons a week. At the efficient quantity, the marginal benefit to the factories equals the marginal social cost, which is the sum of the marginal private cost and the marginal external cost. When the factories produce 20 tons a week, the marginal social cost is $100 a ton and the marginal benefit is $100 a ton.
1c. The quantity of pesticide produced is the efficient quantity, 20 tons a week, and the factories pay the townspeople the marginal external cost of $50 a ton.
1d. The factories produce the efficient quantity: 20 tons a week.
1e. A tax of $50 a ton will achieve the efficient quantity of pesticide produced.

FIGURE 2

9.2 POSITIVE EXTERNALITIES: KNOWLEDGE

Knowledge comes from education and research. To study the economics of knowledge, we must distinguish between private benefits and social benefits.

■ Private Benefits and Social Benefits

Marginal private benefit
The benefit from an additional unit of a good or service that the consumer of that good or service receives.

Marginal external benefit
The benefit from an additional unit of a good or service that people other than the consumer of the good or service enjoy.

Marginal social benefit
The marginal benefit enjoyed by society—by the consumers of a good or service and by everyone else who benefit from it. It is the sum of marginal private benefit and marginal external benefit.

A *private benefit* is a benefit that the consumer of a good or service receives. So **marginal private benefit** (*MB*) is the benefit from an additional unit of a good or service that the consumer of that good or service receives.

An *external benefit* is a benefit from a good or service that someone other than the consumer receives. A **marginal external benefit** is the benefit from an additional unit of a good or service that people other than the consumer enjoy.

Marginal social benefit (*MSB*) is the marginal benefit enjoyed by society—by the consumers of a good or service (marginal private benefit) and by others who benefit from it (the marginal external benefit). That is,

$$MSB = MB + \text{Marginal external benefit.}$$

Figure 9.5 shows an example of the relationship between marginal private benefit, marginal external benefit, and marginal social benefit. The marginal benefit curve, *MB*, describes the marginal private benefit—such as expanded job opportunities and higher incomes—enjoyed by college graduates. Marginal private benefit decreases as the quantity of education increases.

■ FIGURE 9.5

An External Benefit

The *MB* curve shows the marginal private benefit enjoyed by the people who receive a college education. The *MSB* curve shows the sum of marginal private benefit and marginal external benefit.

When 15 million students attend college, ❶ marginal private benefit is $10,000 per student, ❷ marginal external benefit is $15,000 per student, and ❸ marginal social benefit is $25,000 per student.

But college graduates generate external benefits. On the average, college graduates communicate more effectively with others and tend to be better citizens. Their crime rates are lower, and they are more tolerant of the views of others. And a society with a large number of college graduates can support activities such as high-quality music, theater, and other organized social activities.

In the example in Figure 9.5, the marginal external benefit is $15,000 per student per year when 15 million students enroll in college. The marginal social benefit curve, *MSB*, is the sum of marginal private benefit and marginal external benefit. For example, when 15 million students a year enroll in college, the marginal private benefit is $10,000 per student and the marginal external benefit is $15,000 per student, so the marginal social benefit is $25,000 per student.

When people make decisions about how much schooling to undertake, they ignore its external benefits and consider only its private benefits. The result is that if education were provided by private schools that charged full-cost tuition, we would produce too few college graduates.

Figure 9.6 illustrates the underproduction if the government left education to the private market. The supply curve is the marginal cost curve of the private schools, *S = MC*. The demand curve is the marginal private benefit curve, *D = MB*. Market equilibrium is at a tuition of $15,000 per student per year and 7.5 million students per year. At this equilibrium, marginal social benefit is $38,000 per student, which exceeds marginal cost by $23,000. Too few students enroll in college. The efficient number is 15 million, where marginal social benefit equals marginal cost. The gray triangle shows the deadweight loss created by the underproduction.

FIGURE 9.6

Inefficiency with an External Benefit

The market demand curve is the marginal private benefit curve, *D = MB*. The supply curve is the marginal cost curve, *S = MC*.

❶ Market equilibrium is at a tuition of $15,000 a year and 7.5 million students and is inefficient because ❷ marginal social benefit exceeds ❸ marginal cost.

❹ The marginal social benefit curve is *MSB*, so the efficient number of students is 15 million a year.

❺ The gray triangle shows the deadweight loss created because too few students enroll in college.

Underproduction similar to that in Figure 9.6 would occur at other levels of education—grade school and high school—if an unregulated market produced it. When children learn basic reading, writing, and number skills, they receive the private benefit of increased earning power. But even these basic skills bring the external benefit of developing better citizens.

External benefits also arise from research that leads to the discovery of new knowledge. When Isaac Newton worked out the formulas for calculating the rate of response of one variable to another—calculus—everyone was free to use his method. When a spreadsheet program called VisiCalc was invented, Lotus Corporation and Microsoft were free to copy the basic idea and create 1-2-3 and Excel. When the first shopping mall was built and found to be a successful way of arranging retailing, everyone was free to copy the idea, and malls spread like mushrooms.

Once someone has discovered how to do something, others can copy the basic idea. They do have to work to copy an idea, so they face an opportunity cost. But they do not usually have to pay the person who made the discovery to use it. When people make decisions about how much research to undertake, they ignore its external benefits and consider only its private benefits.

When people make decisions about the quantity of education or the amount of research to undertake, they balance the marginal private cost against the marginal private benefit. They ignore the external benefit. As a result, if we left education and research to unregulated market forces, we would get too little of these activities.

To get closer to producing the efficient quantity of a good or service that generates an external benefit, we make public choices, through governments, to modify the market outcome.

■ Government Actions in the Face of External Benefits

Four devices that governments can use to achieve a more efficient allocation of resources in the presence of external benefits, such as those that arise from education and research, are

- Public provision
- Private subsidies
- Vouchers
- Patents and copyrights

Public Provision

Public provision
The production of a good or service by a public authority that receives most of its revenue from the government.

Public provision is the production of a good or service by a public authority that receives most of its revenue from the government. Education services produced by the public universities, colleges, and schools are examples of public provision.

Figure 9.7(a) shows how public provision might overcome the underproduction that arises in Figure 9.6. Public provision cannot lower the cost of production, so marginal cost is the same as before. Marginal private benefit and marginal external benefit are also the same as before.

The efficient quantity occurs where marginal social benefit equals marginal cost. In Figure 9.7(a), this quantity is 15 million students per year. Tuition is set to ensure that the efficient number of students enrolls. That is, tuition is set at the level that equals the marginal private benefit at the efficient quantity. In Figure 9.7(a), tuition is $10,000 a year. The rest of the cost of the public university is borne by the taxpayers and, in this example, is $15,000 per student per year.

Private Subsidies

A **subsidy** is a payment by the government to a producer to cover part of the costs of production. By giving producers a subsidy, the government can induce private decision makers to consider external benefits when they make their choices.

Figure 9.7(b) shows how a subsidy to private colleges works. In the absence of a subsidy, the marginal cost curve is the market supply curve of private college education, $S = MC$. The marginal benefit is the demand curve, $D = MB$. In this example, the government provides a subsidy to colleges of $15,000 per student per year. We must subtract the subsidy from the marginal cost of education to find the colleges' supply curve. That curve is $S = MC - subsidy$ in the figure. The equilibrium tuition (market price) is $10,000 a year, and the equilibrium quantity is 15 million students. To educate 15 million students, colleges incur a marginal cost of $25,000 a year. The marginal social benefit is also $25,000 a year. So with marginal cost equal to marginal social benefit, the subsidy has achieved an efficient outcome. The tuition and the subsidy just cover the colleges' marginal cost.

Whether a public school operating on government-provided funds or a private school receiving a subsidy does a better job is a difficult question to resolve.

Subsidy
A payment by the government to a producer to cover part of the costs of production.

FIGURE 9.7

Public Provision or Private Subsidy to Achieve an Efficient Outcome

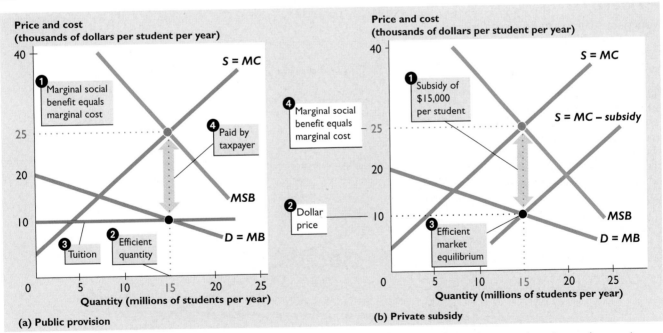

(a) Public provision

(b) Private subsidy

❶ Marginal social benefit equals marginal cost with 15 million students enrolled in college, the ❷ efficient quantity.

❸ Tuition is set at $10,000 per year, and ❹ the taxpayers cover the remaining $15,000 of marginal cost per student.

With a ❶ subsidy of $15,000 per student, the supply curve is $S = MC - subsidy$. ❷ The equilibrium price is $10,000, and ❸ the market equilibrium is efficient with 15 million students enrolled in college. ❹ Marginal social benefit equals marginal cost.

It turns on the efficiency of alternative mechanisms for monitoring school performance and on the strength of the incentives that school boards and private school operators have to deliver a high-quality service.

Vouchers

Voucher
A token that the government provides to households that can be used to buy specified goods or services.

A **voucher** is a token that the government provides to households, which they can use to buy specified goods or services. Food stamps that the U.S. Department of Agriculture provides under a federal Food Stamp Program are examples of vouchers. The vouchers (stamps) can be spent only on food and are designed to improve the diet and health of extremely poor families.

School vouchers have been advocated as a means of improving the quality of education and have been used in Cleveland and Milwaukee, though a proposition to introduce school vouchers in Michigan was defeated in the 2000 election.

A school voucher allows parents to choose the school their children will attend and to use the voucher to pay part of the cost. The school cashes the vouchers to pay its bills. A voucher could be provided to a college student in a similar way, and although technically not a voucher, a federal Pell Grant has a similar effect.

Because vouchers can be spent only on a specified item, they increase the willingness to pay for that item and so increase the demand for it. Figure 9.8 shows how a voucher system works. The government provides vouchers worth $15,000 per student per year. Parents (or students) use these vouchers to supplement the dollars they pay for college education. The market equilibrium occurs at a price of

FIGURE 9.8

Vouchers Achieve an Efficient Outcome

With vouchers, buyers are willing to pay MB plus the value of the voucher.

❶ With a voucher worth $15,000, ❷ the market equilibrium is efficient. With 15 million students enrolled in college, ❸ marginal social benefit equals marginal cost. The tuition, ❹ the dollar price, is $10,000 and the school collects $15,000 from the government.

$25,000 per student per year and 15 million students attend college. Each student pays $10,000 tuition, and schools collect an additional $15,000 per student from the voucher.

If the government estimates the value of the external benefit correctly and makes the value of the voucher equal the marginal external benefit, the outcome from the voucher scheme is efficient. Marginal cost equals marginal social benefit, and the deadweight loss is eliminated.

Vouchers are similar to subsidies, but they provide the consumer rather than the producer with the financial resources. Advocates of vouchers say that they offer a more efficient outcome than subsidies do because the consumer can monitor school performance more effectively than the government can.

Patents and Copyrights

Every inventor benefits from previous inventions. Some inventions are so fundamental that they benefit many subsequent inventors. Some examples are calculus, invented by Newton and Leibniz, and the structure of DNA discovered by Crick and Watson. *Basic research* is the activity that leads to the development of these fundamental tools.

Research and development efforts build on the fruits of basic research to refine and improve on earlier advances. For example, each advance in knowledge about how to design and manufacture a processor chip for a PC has brought ever-larger increments in performance and productivity. Similarly, each advance in knowledge about how to design and build an airplane has brought ever larger increments in performance: Orville and Wilbur Wright's "Flyer 1" was a one-seat plane that could hop a farmer's field. The Lockheed Constellation could fly 120 passengers from New York to London, with two refueling stops, not much space, and a lot of noise and vibration. The latest Boeing 747 can carry 450 people nonstop from Los Angeles to Sydney or New York to Tokyo (flights of 7,500 miles that take 14 hours). Examples of the cumulative fruits of research and development efforts such as these can be found in fields as diverse as agriculture, biogenetics, communications, entertainment, medicine, and publishing.

Because discoveries build on previous discoveries, research generates external benefits. So it is necessary to use public policies to ensure that those who develop new ideas have incentives to encourage an efficient level of effort. The main way of providing the right incentives uses the central idea of the Coase theorem and assigns property rights—called **intellectual property rights**—to creators. The legal device for establishing intellectual property rights is the patent or copyright. A **patent** or **copyright** is a government-sanctioned exclusive right granted to the inventor of a good, service, or productive process to produce, use, and sell the invention for a given number of years. A patent enables the developer of a new idea to prevent others from benefiting freely from an invention for a limited number of years. But to obtain the protection of the law, an inventor must make knowledge of the invention public.

Although patents encourage invention and innovation, they do so at an economic cost. While a patent is in place, its holder has a monopoly. And monopoly is another source of inefficiency (which is explained in Chapter 14). But without patents, the effort to develop new goods, services, or processes is diminished and the flow of new inventions is slowed. So the efficient outcome is a compromise that balances the benefits of more inventions against the cost of temporary monopoly in newly invented activities.

Intellectual property rights
The property rights of the creators of knowledge and other discoveries.

Patent or copyright
A government-sanctioned exclusive right granted to the inventor of a good, service, or productive process to produce, use, and sell the invention for a given number of years.

2 Explain why positive externalities lead to inefficient underproduction and how public provision, subsidies, vouchers, and patents can achieve a more efficient outcome.

Practice Problem 9.2

FIGURE 1

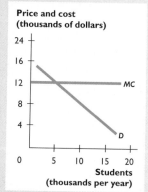

1. Figure 1 shows the marginal private benefit from college education. The marginal cost of a college education is a constant $6,000 a year. The marginal external benefit from a college education is $4,000 per student per year.
   a. If colleges are private and government has no involvement in college education, how many people will undertake a college education and what will be the tuition?
   b. What is the efficient number of students?
   c. If the government decides to provide public colleges, what tuition will these colleges charge to achieve the efficient number of students? How much will taxpayers have to pay?
   d. If the government decides to subsidize private colleges, what subsidy will achieve the efficient number of college students?
   e. If the government offers vouchers to those who enroll at a college and no subsidy, what is the value of the voucher that will achieve the efficient number of students?

Exercise 9.2

FIGURE 2

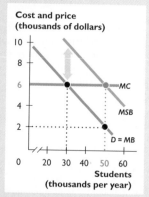

1. Figure 2 shows the marginal private benefit from a law degree and the marginal cost of obtaining a law degree. The marginal external benefit is $8,000 per law graduate per year.
   a. If colleges are private and the government is not involved in educating lawyers, how many people enroll in law school and what is the tuition?
   b. What is the efficient number of law students?
   c. If the government decides to provide public law schools, what tuition will the public schools charge to achieve the efficient number of students?
   d. If the government decides to subsidize private law schools, what subsidy will achieve the efficient number of students?
   e. If the government offers vouchers to law students, what is the value of the voucher that will achieve the efficient number of students?

Solution to Practice Problem 9.2

FIGURE 3

1a. The tuition will be $6,000 a year, and 30,000 students will enroll—the intersection of the *MB* and *MC* curves (Figure 3).

1b. The efficient number of students is 50,000 a year—the intersection of the *MSB* and *MC* curves (Figure 3).

1c. To enroll 50,000 students, public colleges would charge $2,000 per student and taxpayers would pay $4,000 per student (Figure 3).

1d. The subsidy would be $4,000 per student, which is equal to the marginal external benefit.

1e. The value of the voucher will be $4,000. Enrollment will be 50,000 if the tuition is $2,000. But the private college tuition is $6,000, so to get 50,000 students to enroll, the value of the voucher will have to be $4,000.

CHAPTER CHECKPOINT

Key Points

1 **Explain why negative externalities lead to inefficient overproduction and how property rights, pollution charges, and taxes can achieve a more efficient outcome.**

- External costs are costs of production that fall on people other than the producer of a good or service. Marginal social cost equals marginal private cost plus marginal external cost.
- Producers take account only of marginal private cost and produce more than the efficient quantity when there is a marginal external cost.
- Sometimes it is possible to overcome a negative externality by assigning a property right.
- When property rights cannot be assigned, governments might overcome a negative externality by using emission charges, marketable permits, or taxes.

2 **Explain why positive externalities lead to inefficient underproduction and how public provision, subsidies, vouchers, and patents can achieve a more efficient outcome.**

- External benefits are benefits that are received by people other than the consumer of a good or service. Marginal social benefit equals marginal private benefit plus marginal external benefit.
- External benefits from education arise because better-educated people are better citizens, commit fewer crimes, and support social activities.
- External benefits from research arise because once someone has worked out a basic idea, others can copy.
- Vouchers or subsidies to private schools or the provision of public education below cost can achieve a more efficient provision of education.
- Patents and copyrights create intellectual property rights and an incentive to innovate. But they do so by creating a temporary monopoly, the cost of which must be balanced against the benefit of more inventive activity.

Key Terms

Coase theorem, 224
Copyright, 235
Externality, 218
Intellectual property rights, 235
Marginal external benefit, 230
Marginal external cost, 220

Marginal private benefit, 230
Marginal private cost, 220
Marginal social benefit, 230
Marginal social cost, 220
Negative externality, 218
Patent, 235

Positive externality, 218
Property rights, 223
Public provision, 232
Subsidy, 233
Transactions costs, 224
Voucher, 234

Exercises

TABLE 1

Pollution cut (percentage)	Property taxes willingly paid (dollars per day)	Total cost of pollution cut (dollars per day)
0	0	0
10	150	10
20	285	25
30	405	45
40	510	70
50	600	100
60	675	135
70	735	175
80	780	220
90	810	270

1. A city borders on a polluting steel mill. Table 1 shows the cost of cutting the pollution and the property taxes that people are willing to pay at different levels of pollution. Assume that the property taxes willingly paid measure the total benefit from cleaner air that results from the percentage cut in pollution.
   a. With no pollution control, how much pollution will there be?
   b. What is the efficient percentage decrease in pollution?
   c. If the city owns the steel mill, how much pollution will there be?
   d. If the city is a company town owned by the steel mill, how much pollution will there be?

2. Tom and Larry are working on a project that requires them to spend a day together. Tom likes to smoke, and his marginal benefit from one cigar a day is $20. The price of a cigar is $2. Larry dislikes cigar smoke, and his marginal benefit from a smoke-free environment is $25 a day. What is the outcome if
   a. They meet at Tom's home?
   b. They meet at Larry's home?

3. If in exercise 2, Tom's marginal benefit from one cigar a day is $25 and Larry's marginal benefit from a smoke-free environment is $20 a day, what is the outcome if they:
   a. Meet at Tom's home?
   b. Meet at Larry's home?

TABLE 2

Students (millions per year)	Marginal private benefit (dollars per student per year)
1	5,000
2	3,000
3	2,000
4	1,500
5	1,200
6	1,000
7	800
8	500

4. The marginal cost of educating a college student is $5,000 a year. Table 2 shows the marginal private benefit schedule from a college education. The marginal external benefit for college education is $2,000 per student per year.
   a. With no public colleges and no government involvement in college education, how many students will enroll and what is the tuition?
   b. If the government subsidizes private colleges and sets the subsidy so that the efficient number of students will enroll in college, what is the subsidy per student? How many students will enroll?
   c. If the government offers vouchers to students (but no subsidy to private colleges) and values the vouchers so that the efficient number of students will enroll in college, what is the value of the voucher? How many students will enroll?

5. For many people, distance education has cut the cost of a college education. If in exercise 4, an Internet course cuts the cost to $3,500 a year and increases the marginal external benefit to $3,000 per student per year, what now are your answers to exercise 4?

6. Suppose that researchers could not obtain patents for their discoveries.
   a. What do you think would happen to the pace of technological change?
   b. Would consumers' or producers' interests be damaged by a lack of patent protection?
   c. Would anyone gain?

7. Suppose that popular singers could not obtain copyrights for their recordings.
   a. What do you think would happen to the quantity and quality of recorded music?
   b. Would consumers be better off because they could buy cheaper CDs? Explain why or why not.

Critical Thinking

8. The Kyoto Protocol on greenhouse gas emissions was adopted at the United Nations Framework Convention on Climate Change in 1997. The major provision of the protocol is a set of national targets, with dates, for the reduction of greenhouse gas emissions. Countries with large amounts of emissions (of which the United States is one) have the most severe targets. The United States has steadfastly refused to ratify the Kyoto Protocol, but the European Union has ratified it.
   a. Why might the United States be reluctant to ratify the Kyoto Protocol?
   b. Why do you think the European Union was willing to ratify it?
   c. In light of the principles you've learned in this chapter, what types of data would you need to collect if you were to determine whether the emission target for the United States laid out in the Kyoto Protocol is efficient?
   d. What is your own view on whether the United States should ratify the Kyoto Protocol and why?

9. The price of gasoline in Europe is much higher than that in the United States, and the reason is that the gas tax is much higher in Europe than in the United States.
   a. What is the range of externalities that arise from automobiles?
   b. In light of the principles you've learned in this chapter, what is the case *for* increasing the gas tax in the United States to the European level?
   c. In light of the principles you've learned in this chapter, what is the case *against* increasing the gas tax in the United States to the European level?
   d. What is your view on whether the United States should raise the gas tax to the European level and why?

10. The debate over school vouchers often creates more heat than light.
    a. Why do you think that school vouchers are controversial?
    b. In light of the principles you've learned in this chapter, what is the case *for* replacing the existing school funding arrangements with vouchers?
    c. In light of the principles you've learned in this chapter, what is the case *against* replacing the existing school funding arrangements with vouchers?

11. It has been estimated that developing new technologies and figuring out how to use them account for more than half of economic growth—the expansion of production possibilities. In light of this fact:
    a. Do you think that the government should subsidize research and development?
    b. Do you think that the government should subsidize basic research?
    c. Do you think it would be a good idea to award prizes to firms for the successful development of a new technology?
    d. Do you think that firms should be given tax breaks for the successful development of a new technology?
    e. Do you think the patent laws should be strengthened so that the inventor of a new technology can be protected from competition for longer than is currently the case?
    f. Provide your own ranking of the alternatives in parts **a** through **e** along with the further alternative of leaving research and development to unregulated market forces. Explain your ranking, being explicit about your assumptions about the efficiency of each approach.

Web Exercises

Use the links on MyEconLab to work the following exercises.

12. Visit the EPA "Search Your Community" page. Enter your zip code in the box provided and press the "Submit" button.
    a. Obtain information about a negative production externality in your neighborhood.
    b. Explain which, if any, of the tools reviewed in this chapter the government is using to address this externality.
    c. Explain how the government's action will work or why you think it will not work. Use the concepts of marginal private cost, marginal external cost, marginal social cost, and efficiency in your explanation.
    d. If you think the current measures for dealing with this externality are not working or are not working well enough, what do you think needs to be done? Again, use the concepts of marginal private cost, marginal external cost, marginal social cost, and efficiency in your analysis.

13. Visit the EPA "Ground Water and Drinking Water" page.
    a. What types of externalities arise in the production of safe drinking water?
    b. Review and summarize the elements of the cost-benefit analysis that the EPA is undertaking on this issue.
    c. What do you think are the main outstanding issues to be resolved in ensuring the provision of safe drinking water in the United States? Use the concepts of marginal private cost, marginal external cost, marginal social cost, and efficiency in your analysis.

14. Visit the *Cape Cod Times* and read the article about wind farms off the New England coast.
    a. What types of externalities arise in the production of electricity using wind technologies?
    b. Comparing the externalities from wind technologies with those from burning coal and oil, which do you think are the more widespread and affect more people?
    c. How do you think the external costs of using wind technologies should be dealt with? Compare all the alternative methods suggested by the range of solutions considered in this chapter.
    d. Can you think of reasons why, despite the lower external costs, a campaign against the use of wind technology might be more successful than a campaign against the use of coal or oil?

15. Learn about the destruction of the habitat of the northern spotted owl.
    a. What production activity is creating problems for the northern spotted owl?
    b. What type of externalities arise from this production activity?
    c. How would you set about designing a method for dealing with this externality?

16. Visit the Global Policy site and read about the idea of introducing a carbon tax. Explain how a carbon tax might work. How would a carbon tax change the choices of Allegheny Electric and its customers? Who would bear the costs of the tax and who would enjoy the benefits?

Public Goods and Common Resources

CHAPTER CHECKLIST

When you have completed your study of this chapter,
you will be able to

1 Distinguish among private goods, public goods, and common resources.

2 Explain the free-rider problem and how public provision might help to overcome that problem.

3 Explain the tragedy of the commons and review the possible solutions to that problem.

Zanab has just finished loading her MP3 player with a bunch of tunes that she got from her friend Saacha. She doesn't know how Saacha gets so many great tunes, but he's always got the latest and shares them freely. But Zanab is worried. What if Saacha gets his files illegally and is sharing them with lots of people? That's not only illegal—it deprives artists and recording companies of incomes, and it might even dry up the supply of new tunes! Zanab is worrying about a "free-rider problem."

Tammy McCorkle loves her job as a Ranger Supervisor at the South Mountain Recreation Area on the Appalachian Trail. But Tammy is concerned about the state of the Annapolis Rock, a spot that towers above Cumberland Valley and offers breathtaking views. The repeated erection of tents and the incessant trampling of feet have left the rock totally devoid of plant life. And past camp fires and trash litter the cliffs. Tammy is worrying about a "tragedy of the commons."

You will study these two problems in this chapter.

10.1 CLASSIFYING GOODS AND RESOURCES

What's the difference between the services provided by the city police department and those provided by Brinks, a private security firm that loads ATMs for banks? What's the difference between fish in the Pacific Ocean and fish produced by East Point Seafood Company, a Seattle fish farm? What's the difference between a live Kelly Clarkson concert and a concert on network television? You will have several answers for these questions based on differences in your perceived quality of the items. But if we ignore such differences, a general answer is the same for each question: Each pair differs in the extent to which people can be *excluded* from consuming them and in the extent to which one person's consumption *rivals* the consumption of others.

■ Excludable

Excludable
A good, service, or resource is excludable if it is possible to prevent someone from enjoying its benefits.

A good, service, or resource is **excludable** if it is possible to prevent someone from enjoying its benefits. Brinks's security services, East Point Seafood's fish, and Kelly Clarkson concerts are examples. You must pay to consume them.

A good, service, or resource is **nonexcludable** if it is impossible (or extremely costly) to prevent someone from benefiting from it. The services of the city police department, fish in the Pacific Ocean, and a concert on network television are examples. When a police cruiser slows the traffic on a highway to the speed limit, it lowers the risk of an accident to all the road users. It can't exclude some road users from the lower risk. Anyone with a boat can try to catch the fish in the ocean. And anyone with a TV can watch a network broadcast.

Nonexcludable
A good, service, or resource is nonexcludable if it is impossible to prevent someone from benefiting from it.

■ Rival

Rival
A good, service, or resource is rival if its use by one person decreases the quantity available to someone else.

A good, service, or resource is **rival** if its use by one person decreases the quantity available for someone else. Brinks might work for two banks, but one truck can't deliver cash to two banks at the same time. A fish, whether in the ocean or on a fish farm, can be consumed only once. And one seat at a concert can hold only one person at a time. These items are rival.

A good, service, or resource is **nonrival** if its use by one person does not decrease the quantity available for someone else. The services of the city police department and a concert on network television are nonrival. The arrival of one more person in a neighborhood doesn't lower the level of police protection enjoyed by the community. And when one additional person switches on the TV, no other viewer is affected.

Nonrival
A good, service, or resource is nonrival if its use by one person does not decrease the quantity available to someone else.

■ A Fourfold Classification

Figure 10.1 classifies goods, services, and resources into four types using the two criteria that we've just considered.

Private Goods

Private good
A good or service that can be consumed by only one person at a time and only by the person who has bought it or owns it.

A good or service that is both rival and excludable (top left of Figure 10.1) is a **private good**: It can be consumed by only one person at a time and only by the person who has bought it or owns it. A can of Coke is an example of a private good. Only one person enjoys the benefits of a single can of Coke, and everyone except the person who bought the can is excluded from consuming it. The fish on East Point Seafood's farm are another example of a private good.

Public Goods

A good or service that is both nonrival and nonexcludable (bottom right of Figure 10.1) is a **public good**: It can be consumed simultaneously by everyone, and no one can be excluded from enjoying its benefits. A flood-control levee is an example of a public good. Everyone who lives in a protected flood plain enjoys the benefits, and no one can be excluded from receiving those benefits. The system of law and order provided by the courts and the body of laws is another example.

Public good
A good or service that can be consumed simultaneously by everyone and from which no one can be excluded.

Common Resources

A resource that is rival and nonexcludable (top right of Figure 10.1) is a **common resource**: A unit of it can be used only once, but no one can be prevented from using what is available. Ocean fish and the earth's atmosphere are examples of common resources. Ocean fish are rival because a fish taken by one person is not available for anyone else, and they are nonexcludable because it is difficult to prevent people from catching them. The earth's atmosphere is rival because oxygen used by one person is not available for anyone else, and it is nonexcludable because we can't prevent people from breathing!

Common resource
A resource that can be used only once, but no one can be prevented from using what is available.

Natural Monopolies

A good that is nonrival but excludable (bottom left of Figure 10.1) is a good produced by a *natural monopoly.* We define natural monopoly in Chapter 14, p. 350. A natural monopoly is a firm that can produce at a lower cost than two or more firms can. Examples are the Internet, cable television, and a bridge or tunnel. One more user doesn't decrease the enjoyment of the other users, and people can be excluded with user codes, scramblers, and tollgates.

FIGURE 10.1
Fourfold Classification of Goods

	Private goods	Common resources
Rival	Food and drink Car House	Fish in ocean Atmosphere National parks
	Natural monopolies	Public goods
Nonrival	Internet Cable television Bridge or tunnel	National defense The law Flood-control levees
	Excludable	**Nonexcludable**

Goods that are rival and excludable are private goods (top left).

Goods that are nonrival and nonexcludable are public goods (bottom right).

Goods and resources that are rival but nonexcludable are common resources (top right).

Goods that are nonrival but excludable are goods produced by a natural monopoly (bottom left).

SOURCE OF DATA: Adapted from and inspired by E. S. Savas, *Privatizing the Public Sector,* Chatham House Publishers, Inc., Chatham, NJ, 1982, p. 34.

EYE ON THE PAST

Is a Lighthouse a Public Good?

One of the great classical economists, John Stuart Mill, used the lighthouse as an example of a public good. And economists used Mill's example for two centuries, until it was challenged in 1974 by Ronald Coase (see p. 224). Coase discovered that before the nineteenth century, lighthouses in England were built and operated by private companies that earned profits by charging tolls on ships docking at nearby ports. A ship that refused to pay the lighthouse toll was excluded from using the port. So even the ser-vices of a lighthouse, when it is near a port, are excludable! Such a lighthouse is an example of a natural monopoly, not a public good.

CHECKPOINT 10.1

1   **Distinguish among private goods, public goods, and common resources.**

Practice Problem 10.1

1. Classify each of the following as a public good, a private good, or a common resource:
   a. Fire protection
   b. A Big Mac
   c. The Mississippi River

Exercise 10.1

1. Classify each of the following as a public good, a private good, or a common resource:
   a. The Grand Canyon
   b. Street lighting in urban areas
   c. Flood control in the Mississippi watershed
   d. A CD

Solution to Practice Problem 10.1

1a. Fire protection is a public good.
1b. A Big Mac is a private good.
1c. The Mississippi River is a common resource.

10.2 PUBLIC GOODS AND THE FREE-RIDER PROBLEM

Why does the U.S. government provide our national defense and district court system? Why do the state governments provide flood-control levees? Why do our city governments provide fire and police services? Why don't we buy our national defense from North Pole Protection, Inc., a private firm that competes for our dollars in the marketplace in the same way that McDonald's does? Why don't private engineering firms provide levees? Why don't we buy our policing and fire services from Brinks and other private firms? The answer is that all of these goods are public goods—goods that are nonexcludable and nonrival—and such goods create a free-rider problem.

■ The Free-Rider Problem

A **free rider** is a person who enjoys the benefits of a good or service without paying for it. Because everyone consumes the same quantity of a public good and no one can be excluded from enjoying its benefits, no one has an incentive to pay for it. Everyone has an incentive to free ride. The free-rider problem is that the private market, left on its own, would provide too small a quantity of a public good. To produce the efficient quantity, government action is required.

To see how a private market would provide too little of a public good and how government might provide the efficient quantity, we need to consider the marginal benefit and the marginal cost of a public good. The marginal benefit of a public good is a bit different from that of a private good, so we'll begin on the benefit side of the calculation.

Free rider
A person who enjoys the benefits of a good or service without paying for it.

Some public goods.

■ The Marginal Benefit of a Public Good

To learn about the marginal benefit of a public good, think about a concrete example. Lisa and Max share a common parking area that has no security lighting. Both of them would like some lights. But how many lights? What is the value or benefit of just one light, of adding a second, and perhaps of adding a third light? To answer this question, we must somehow combine the value of lights to both Lisa and Max and find the marginal benefit of different quantities of lights—the marginal benefit curve of lights.

For a private good, the marginal benefit curve is the market demand curve. But everyone pays the same market price for a private good and each person chooses the quantity they wish to buy at that price. In contrast, for a public good, everyone must consume the same quantity. But each person puts a different private value on that quantity. So how are we to find the equivalent of the demand curve for a public good? Figure 10.2 answers this question and illustrates the calculation of marginal benefit and the marginal benefit curve.

Lisa and Max know their own marginal benefit from different levels of security lighting. The tables in parts (a) and (b) of Figure 10.2 show these marginal benefits. The curves MB_L and MB_M are Lisa's and Max's marginal benefit curves. Each person's marginal benefit from a public good diminishes as the quantity of the good increases—just as it does for a private good. For Lisa, the marginal benefit from the first light is $80, and from the second it is $60. By the time 5 lights are installed, Lisa's marginal benefit is zero. For Max, the marginal benefit from the first light is $50, and from the second it is $40. By the time 5 lights are installed, Max perceives only $10 worth of marginal benefit.

The table in part (c) of Figure 10.2 shows the marginal benefit for the entire economy. We obtain this curve by summing the individual marginal benefits at each quantity. For example, with 3 lights, the marginal benefit is $70 ($40 for Lisa plus $30 for Max) and with 4 lights, the marginal benefit is $40 ($20 for Lisa plus $20 for Max). The curve MB is the marginal benefit curve.

Because we find the marginal benefit of a public good by summing the marginal benefits of all individuals at each *quantity*—we find the marginal benefit curve by summing the individual marginal benefit curves *vertically*. In contrast, to obtain the MB curve for a private good—which is also the market demand curve—we sum the quantities demanded by all individuals at each *price*—we sum the individual demand curves *horizontally* (see Chapter 4, p. 93).

Notice that the marginal benefit curve for a public good is both a marginal private benefit curve and marginal social benefit curve. A public good doesn't have external benefits (see Chapter 9, p. 230). Everyone consumes a public good in equal quantities, and everyone benefits from it. So the marginal benefit curve includes all the benefits. We could call it the marginal social benefit curve.

The principle that we've learned in this example of security lights for Lisa and Max applies to the marginal benefit of a public good such as national defense in our economy with its 290 million people. The marginal benefit of national defense is the sum of the marginal benefits of all 290 million people.

■ The Marginal Cost of a Public Good

The marginal cost of a public good is determined in exactly the same way as that of a private good. The principle of *increasing marginal cost* that you learned in Chapter 3 and Chapter 6 applies to the marginal cost of a public good. So the marginal cost curve of a public good slopes upward.

FIGURE 10.2

Marginal Benefit of a Public Good

(a) Lisa's marginal benefit

(b) Max's marginal benefit

The marginal benefit curves for a public good are MB_L for Lisa and MB_M for Max. The marginal benefit of the public good for the economy is the sum of the marginal benefits of all individuals at each quantity. The marginal benefit curve for the economy is MB.

Quantity of lights	0	1	2	3	4	5
Lisa's MB (dollars per light)		80	60	40	20	0

Quantity of lights	0	1	2	3	4	5
Max's MB (dollars per light)		50	40	30	20	10

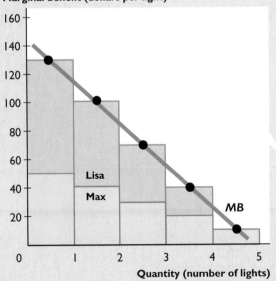

(c) Economy's marginal benefit

Quantity of lights	0	1	2	3	4	5
Lisa's MB (dollars per light)		80	60	40	20	0
Max's MB (dollars per light)		50	40	30	20	10
Economy's MB (dollars per light)		130	100	70	40	10

■ The Efficient Quantity of a Public Good

To determine the efficient quantity, we use exactly the same principles that you first learned in Chapter 6 and that you've used repeatedly in Chapters 7 and 8. We find the quantity at which marginal benefit equals marginal cost.

Figure 10.3 shows the marginal benefit curve *MB* and marginal cost curve *MC* of surveillance satellites that provide national defense services. The *MB* curve is based on the same principle that determines the marginal benefit of the two-person (Lisa and Max) economy for security lights. If marginal benefit exceeds marginal cost, resources can be used more efficiently by increasing the quantity produced. If marginal cost exceeds marginal benefit, resources can be used more efficiently by decreasing the quantity produced. And if marginal benefit equals marginal cost, resources are being used efficiently. In this example, marginal benefit equals marginal cost with 200 satellites.

■ Private Provision: Underproduction

Could a private firm—say, North Pole Protection, Inc.—deliver the efficient quantity of satellites? Most likely, it couldn't because no one would have an incentive to buy his or her share of the satellite system. Everyone would reason as follows: "The number of satellites provided by North Pole Protection, Inc., is not affected by my decision to pay my share or not. But my own private consumption will be greater if I free ride and do not pay my share of the cost of the satellite system. If I do not pay, I enjoy the same level of security and I can buy more private goods. I will spend my money on private goods and free ride on the public good." Such reasoning is the free-rider problem. If everyone reasons the same way, North Pole Protection, Inc., has no revenue and so provides no satellites.

▦ FIGURE 10.3

The Efficient Quantity and Private Underproduction of a Public Good

❶ With fewer than 200 satellites, marginal benefit *MB* exceeds marginal cost *MC*. An increase in the quantity will make resource use more efficient.

❷ With more than 200 satellites, marginal cost exceeds marginal benefit. A decrease in the quantity will make resource use more efficient.

❸ With 200 satellites, marginal benefit *MB* equals marginal cost *MC*. Resource use is efficient.

❹ The efficient quantity is 200 satellites.

❺ Private provision leads to underproduction—in the extreme, to zero production.

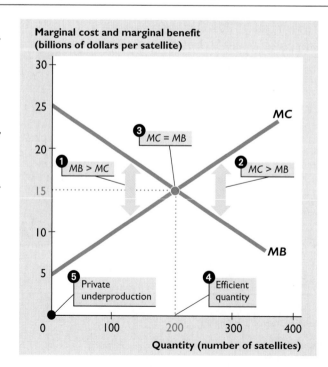

Public Provision: Efficient Production

The political process might be efficient or inefficient. We look first at an efficient outcome. There are two political parties, the Hawks and the Doves, which agree on all issues except for the quantity of defense satellites. The Hawks want 300 satellites, and the Doves want 100 satellites. But both parties want to get elected, so they run a voter survey and discover the marginal benefit curve of Figure 10.4. They also consult with satellite producers to establish the marginal cost schedule. The parties then do a "what-if" analysis. If the Hawks propose 300 satellites and the Doves propose 100 satellites, the voters will be equally unhappy with both parties. Compared to the efficient quantity, the Doves want an underprovision of 100 satellites and the Hawks want an overprovision of 100 satellites. The dead-weight losses are equal. So the election would be too close to call.

Contemplating this outcome, the Hawks realize that they are too hawkish to get elected. They figure that if they scale back to 250 satellites, they will win the election if the Doves propose 100 satellites. The Doves reason in a similar way and figure that if they increase the number of satellites to 150, they can win the election if the Hawks propose 300 satellites. But each party knows how the other is reasoning. And they each realize that they must provide 200 satellites, or they will lose the election. So they both propose 200 satellites. The voters are indifferent between the parties, and each party receives 50 percent of the vote.

■ **FIGURE 10.4**
An Efficient Political Outcome

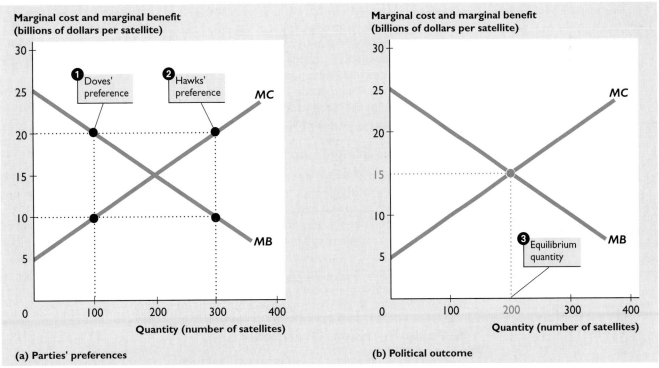

(a) Parties' preferences

(b) Political outcome

❶ The Doves would like to provide 100 satellites. ❷ The Hawks would like to provide 300 satellites.

❸ The political outcome is 200 satellites because unless each party proposes 200 satellites, the other party can beat it in an election.

Defense Spending

Following the terrorist attacks of September 11, 2001, defense spending increased yet again. But the increase was much smaller than those of the 1960s and 1980s.

The marginal benefit of national defense changes as global events change the demands placed on the military.

During the Vietnam War, U.S. defense spending increased to more than 9 percent of total income. During the early 1970s, successive administrations pursued dialog with China and arms reduction agreements with the Soviet Union and U.S. defense spending as a percentage of total income decreased.

During the early 1980s, the Reagan administration increased the pressure on the Soviet Union and increased defense spending.

The end of the Cold War brought further defense spending cuts during the 1990s.

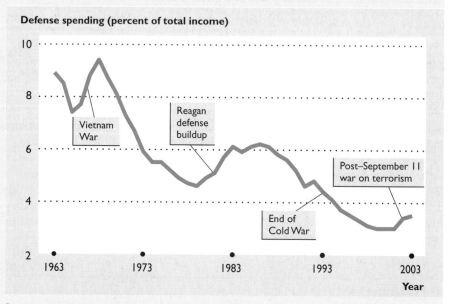

SOURCE OF DATA: *Economic Report of the President*, 2005.

Regardless of which party wins the election, 200 satellites are provided. And this quantity is efficient. In this example, competition in the political marketplace results in the efficient provision of a public good.

For this outcome to occur, voters must be well informed, evaluate the alternatives, and vote in the election. Political parties must be well informed about voter preferences. As you will see, we can't expect to achieve this outcome.

The Principle of Minimum Differentiation

Principle of minimum differentiation
The tendency for competitors to make themselves identical to appeal to the maximum number of clients or voters.

In the example that we've just studied, the two parties propose identical policies. This tendency toward identical policies is an example of the **principle of minimum differentiation**: To appeal to the maximum number of clients or voters, competitors tend to make themselves identical. This principle not only describes the behavior of political parties but also explains why fast-food restaurants cluster in the same block and even why new car models have similar features. If McDonald's opens a restaurant in a new location, it is more likely that Burger King will open next door to McDonald's rather than a mile down the road. If Chrysler designs a new van with a sliding door on the driver's side, most likely Ford will too.

■ Public Provision: Overproduction

If competition between two political parties is to deliver the efficient quantity of satellites, the Defense Department—the Pentagon—must cooperate and help to achieve this outcome.

Objective of Bureaucrats

A bureau head wants to maximize her or his department's budget. A bigger budget brings greater status and power. So the Pentagon's objective is to maximize the defense budget.

Figure 10.5 shows the outcome if the Pentagon is successful in the pursuit of its goal. The Pentagon might try to persuade the politicians that 200 satellites cost more than the originally budgeted amount; or the Pentagon might press its position more strongly and argue for more than 200 satellites. In Figure 10.5, the Pentagon persuades the politicians to go for 300 satellites.

Why don't the politicians block the Pentagon? Won't overproducing satellites cost future votes? It will if voters are well informed and know what is best for them. But voters might not be well informed. And well-informed interest groups might enable the Pentagon to achieve its objective and overcome the objections of the politicians.

Rational Ignorance

Rational choice balances marginal benefit and marginal cost. An implication of rational choice is that it is rational for a voter to be ignorant about an issue unless that issue has a perceptible effect on the voter's well-being. **Rational ignorance** is the decision not to acquire information because the marginal cost of doing so exceeds the marginal benefit. For example, each voter in the United States knows that he or she can make virtually no difference to the defense policy of the U.S. government. Each voter also knows that it would take an enormous amount of

Rational ignorance
The decision not to acquire information because the marginal cost of doing so exceeds the marginal benefit.

■ **FIGURE 10.5**

Inefficient Bureaucratic Overproduction

[myeconlab]

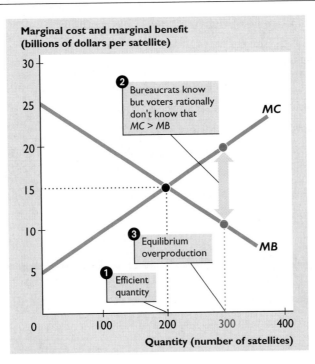

❶ The efficient quantity is 200 satellites with marginal benefit *MB* equal to marginal cost *MC*.

❷ Bureaucrats are well-informed and voters are rationally ignorant, so bureaucrats are able to increase production (and their budget) to a level at which marginal cost *MC* exceeds marginal benefit *MB*.

❸ With 300 satellites, marginal cost exceeds marginal benefit. Inefficient overproduction occurs.

time and effort to become even moderately well informed about alternative defense technologies. So voters remain relatively uninformed about the technicalities of defense issues. (Although we are using defense policy as an example, the same principle applies to all aspects of government economic activity.)

All voters benefit from national defense. But not all voters produce national defense—only a small number work in the defense industry. Voters who own or work for firms that produce satellites have a direct personal interest in defense because it affects their incomes. These voters have an incentive to become well informed about defense issues and to lobby politicians to further their own interests. In collaboration with the defense bureaucracy, these voters exert a larger influence on public policy than do the relatively uninformed voters who only benefit from this public good.

Why Government Is Large

Now that you know how the quantity of a public good is determined, you can explain part of the reason why government is large: inefficient overproduction of public goods. Once a bureaucracy gets established, its goal of budget maximization combined with voters' rational ignorance explains why the government takes a large proportion of total income.

REALITY CHECK

A Free-Rider Problem in YOUR Life

We've studied a free-rider problem for which public provision is a solution. But what about Zanab's free-rider problem (and possibly yours) that arises from sharing music files?

The legal right to copy an MP3 file is restricted by the copyright laws. But these files are nonrival because they can be illegally copied and shared at the click of a mouse.

An MP3 file isn't as nonexcludable as national defense, but it is costly to exclude anyone who wants to copy a file. So MP3 files create a free-rider problem.

Should we try to solve this problem by having the government provide our pop, jazz, rock, and classical music? Not a good idea! Can you imagine Donald Rumsfeld telling Alicia Keys what her next record will be?

The government could make everyone who buys an MP3 player pay a tax and use the revenue to compensate artists and recording companies. But the best solution is for the government to uphold property rights so that recording companies can pursue illegal file sharers and hit them with large penalties.

CHECKPOINT 10.2

2 **Explain the free-rider problem and how public provision might help to overcome that problem.**

Practice Problems 10.2

1. For each of the following goods, explain whether there is a free-rider problem. If there is no such problem, how is it avoided?
    a. Fire protection
    b. July 4th fireworks display
    c. Interstate 80 in rural Wyoming

2. Table 1 provides information about a mosquito control program.
    a. What quantity of spraying would a private mosquito control program provide?
    b. What is the efficient quantity of spraying?
    c. In a single-issue election on the quantity of spraying, what quantity would the winner of the election provide?

TABLE 1

Quantity (square miles sprayed per day)	Marginal cost (dollars per day)	Marginal benefit (dollars per day)
0	0	0
1	1,000	5,000
2	2,000	4,000
3	3,000	3,000
4	4,000	2,000
5	5,000	1,000

Exercises 10.2

1. For each of the following goods, explain whether there is a free-rider problem. If there is no such problem, how is it avoided?
    a. The Grand Canyon
    b. Street lighting in urban areas
    c. Flood control in the Mississippi watershed
    d. The beach at Santa Monica

2. Table 2 provides information about fire protection in Amarillo, Texas.
    a. What quantity of fire protection would a private company provide?
    b. What is the efficient quantity of fire protection?
    c. In a single-issue election on the quantity of fire protection, what quantity would the winner of the election provide?

TABLE 2

Quantity (number of fire stations)	Marginal cost (cents per $100 of property per year)	Marginal benefit (cents per $100 of property per year)
0	0	0
1	2.08	60.00
2	3.04	30.00
3	4.00	10.00
4	4.06	4.06
5	5.12	3.00

Solutions to Practice Problems 10.2

1a. Fire protection is a public good.
1b. July 4th fireworks display is a public good.
In parts **a** and **b**, the free-rider problem is avoided by public provision and financing through taxes.
1c. Interstate 80 in rural Wyoming is a public good. The public good creates a free-rider problem that is avoided because governments collect various taxes via the tax on gas and the vehicle registration fee.

2a. A private mosquito control program would provide zero spraying because the free-rider problem would prevail.
2b. The efficient quantity is 3 square miles a day—the quantity at which the marginal benefit equals the marginal cost.
2c. The winner will provide the efficient quantity: 3 square miles sprayed a day.

Atlantic Ocean cod stocks have been declining since the 1950s, and some marine biologists fear that this species is in danger of becoming extinct in some regions. The whale population of the South Pacific has been declining also, and some groups are lobbying to establish a whale sanctuary in the waters around Australia and New Zealand to regenerate the population. Since the start of the Industrial Revolution in 1750, the concentration of carbon dioxide in the atmosphere has steadily increased. It is estimated that it is about 30 percent higher today than it was in 1750.

These situations involve common property, and the problem that we have identified is called the "tragedy of the commons."

■ The Tragedy of the Commons

Tragedy of the commons
The absence of incentives to prevent the overuse and depletion of a commonly owned resource.

The **tragedy of the commons** is the absence of incentives to prevent the overuse and depletion of a commonly owned resource. If no one owns a resource, no one considers the effects of her or his use of the resource on others. To appreciate the tragedy of the commons, we'll look at a concrete example: fishing for cod in the North Atlantic Ocean.

Figure 10.6 illustrates the relationship between the number of boats and the sustainable quantity of fish caught. As the number of boats increases from zero to 5,000, the sustainable catch increases to a maximum of 250,000 tons a month. As the number of boats increases above 5,000, the sustainable catch begins to

---

■ FIGURE 10.6

Sustainable Production of Fish

myeconlab

As the number of boats increases, the quantity of fish caught increases, but only up to some maximum sustainable catch. Beyond that level, more boats mean a diminished stock of fish and a smaller sustainable catch.

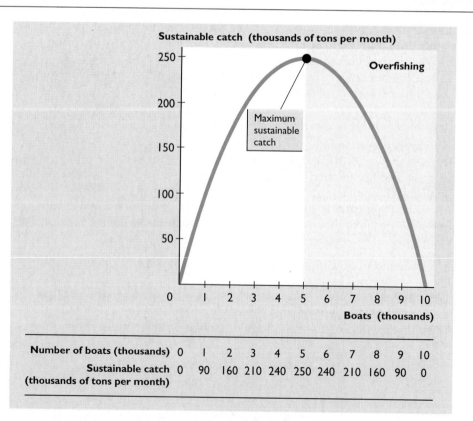

Number of boats (thousands)	0	1	2	3	4	5	6	7	8	9	10
Sustainable catch (thousands of tons per month)	0	90	160	210	240	250	240	210	160	90	0

decrease. By the time 10,000 boats are fishing, the fish stock is depleted to the point at which no fish are available. In the region above 5,000 boats, there is overfishing. Overfishing arises if the number of boats increases to the point at which the fish stock begins to decrease so the remaining fish are harder to find and catch.

Why would overfishing occur? Why isn't the maximum number of boats that take to the sea 5,000, the number that maximizes the sustainable catch? To answer this question, we need to look at the marginal cost and marginal benefit to an individual fisher: marginal private benefit.

Suppose that the marginal cost of a fishing boat is the equivalent of 20 tons of fish per month. That is, if a fishing boat can catch at least 20 tons a month, the boat owner earns a producer surplus and is willing to go fishing. Figure 10.7 shows the marginal cost curve labeled *MC*.

The marginal private benefit is the quantity of fish that one boat can catch in a month. This quantity depends on the number of boats being used. To calculate it, we divide the total catch by the number of boats. The table in Figure 10.7 shows this calculation. One boat catches 100 tons a month. With 1,000 boats, the total catch is 90,000 tons and the catch per boat is 90 tons. With 2,000 boats, the total catch is 160,000 tons and the catch per boat is 80 tons. As more boats take to the ocean, the catch per boat decreases. By the time there are 8,000 boats, each boat is catching just 20 tons a month. Figure 10.7 shows the marginal private benefit curve, *MPB*.

You can see in Figure 10.7 that with fewer than 8,000 boats, each boat catches more fish than it costs to catch them. Because boat owners can gain from fishing, the number of boats increases to 8,000 and there is an overfishing equilibrium.

FIGURE 10.7

Why Overfishing Occurs

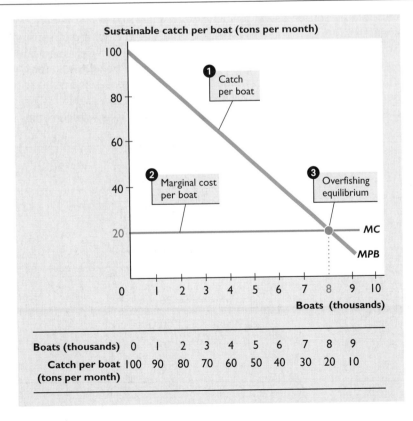

❶ The catch per boat (total catch divided by number of boats) decreases as the number of boats increases. The catch per boat is the marginal private benefit, *MPB*, of a boat.

❷ The marginal cost of a boat is equivalent to 20 tons of fish a month, shown by the curve *MC*.

❸ The equilibrium quantity of boats is 8,000, which means there is an overfishing equilibrium.

Boats (thousands)	0	1	2	3	4	5	6	7	8	9
Catch per boat (tons per month)	100	90	80	70	60	50	40	30	20	10

■ The Efficient Use of the Commons

The quantity of fish caught by each boat decreases as additional boats are introduced. But when individual boat owners are deciding whether to fish, they ignore this decrease. Only the marginal *private* benefit is considered. The result is an *inefficient* overuse of the resource. What is the efficient use of the resource? To answer this question, we need to know the marginal *social* benefit of a boat.

Marginal Social Benefit

The marginal social benefit of a boat is the increase in the total fish catch that results from an additional boat, not the catch per boat. Table 10.1 summarizes the calculation of marginal social benefit. The marginal social benefit is the change in the total catch divided by the change in the number of boats. For example, in rows *C* and *D* of the table, when the number of boats increases by 1,000, the catch increases by 50,000 tons, so the increase in the catch per boat equals 50 tons. In the table, we place this amount midway between the two rows because it is the marginal social benefit at 2,500 boats, midway between the two levels that we used to calculate it. The other numbers in the table are calculated in a similar way.

Figure 10.8 shows marginal social benefit as the *MSB* curve and the marginal private benefit curve, *MPB*. Notice that at any given number of boats, marginal social benefit is less than marginal private benefit. Each boat benefits privately from the average catch, but the addition of one more boat *decreases* the catch of every boat, and this decrease must be subtracted from the catch of the additional boat to determine the social benefit from the additional boat.

Efficient Use

Figure 10.8 also shows the marginal cost curve, *MC*, and the efficient use of the resource. Resource use is efficient when marginal social benefit equals marginal cost. This outcome occurs with 4,000 boats, each catching 60 tons of fish a month. You can see in Table 10.1 that when the number of boats increases from 3,000 to 4,000 (3,500 being the midpoint), marginal social benefit is 30 tons, which exceeds marginal cost. When the number of boats increases from 4,000 to 5,000 (4,500 being the midpoint), marginal social benefit is 10 tons, which is less than marginal cost. At 4,000 boats, marginal social benefit is 20 tons, which equals marginal cost.

■ **TABLE 10.1**

Marginal Social Benefit of a Common Resource

The marginal social benefit of a fishing boat is the change in total benefit that results from an additional boat. For example, when the number of boats increases from 1,000 to 2,000 (row B to row C), the total catch increases from 90,000 to 160,000 tons a month, an increase of 70,000 tons a month, so the marginal social benefit of one boat is 70 tons of fish.

	Boats (thousands)	Total catch (thousands of tons)	Marginal social benefit (tons per boat)
A	0	0	
			90
B	1	90	
			70
C	2	160	
			50
D	3	210	
			30
E	4	240	
			10
F	5	250	

■ FIGURE 10.8
Efficient Use of a Common Resource

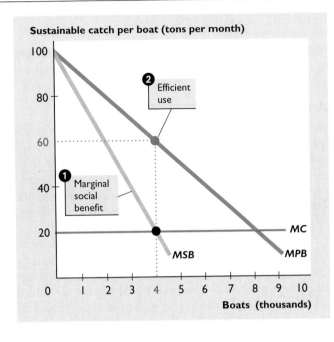

① The marginal *social* benefit, *MSB,* of a boat (increase in total catch divided by increase in number of boats) decreases as the number of boats increases. For any quantity of boats, the marginal social benefit of a boat is *less* than the marginal private benefit, *MPB.*

② The efficient quantity of boats is 4,000, and the sustainable catch is 60 tons per boat.

EYE ON THE PAST

The Commons of England's Middle Ages

The term "the tragedy of the commons" comes from fourteenth century England, where areas of rough grassland surrounded villages. The commons were open to all and were used for grazing cows and sheep owned by the villagers.

Because the commons were open to all, no one had an incentive to ensure that the land was not overgrazed. The result was an overgrazing situation similar to that of overfishing in some of today's oceans.

During the sixteenth century, when the price of wool increased, England became a wool exporter to the world.

Sheep farming became profitable, and sheep owners needed better control of the land they used. So the commons were gradually enclosed and privatized. Overgrazing ended, and land use became more efficient.

■ Achieving an Efficient Outcome

Defining the conditions under which a common resource is used efficiently is easier than bringing those conditions about. To use a common resource efficiently, three main methods might be used:

- Property rights
- Quotas
- Individual transferable quotas (ITQs)

Property Rights

A common resource that no one owns and that anyone is free to use contrasts with *private property*, which is a resource that *someone* owns and has an incentive to use in the way that maximizes its value. One way of overcoming the tragedy of the commons is to remove the commons and make it private property. By assigning private property rights, each owner faces the same conditions as society faces. The *MSB* curve of Figure 10.8 becomes the marginal *private* benefit curve, and the use of the resource is efficient.

The private property solution to the tragedy of the commons *is* available in some cases—see *Eye on the Past* on p. 257. A modern example is the airwaves that we use to carry our cell phone messages. The right to use this space—called the frequency spectrum—has been auctioned by governments to the highest bidders, and the owner of a particular part of the spectrum is the only one who is permitted to use it (or license someone else to use it).

But this solution is not always available. It would be difficult, for example, to assign private property rights to the oceans. It would not be impossible, but the cost of enforcing private property rights over thousands of square miles of ocean would be high. And it would be even harder to assign and protect private property rights to the atmosphere. When private property rights are too costly to assign and enforce, some form of government intervention is used, and quotas are the simplest.

Quotas

A *quota* is an upper limit to the quantity of a good that may legally be produced in a specified period. If a quota is set below the efficient output level, it drives a wedge between marginal benefit and marginal cost and is inefficient. But in the case of the use of common property, the market is inefficient because it is overproducing. So a quota that limits production can bring a move toward a more efficient outcome.

Figure 10.9(a) shows a quota that achieves an efficient use of a common resource. A quota is set for total production at the quantity at which marginal social benefit equals marginal cost. Here, that quantity is what 4,000 boats can produce. Individual boat owners are assigned their own share of the total permitted catch. If everyone sticks to the assigned quota, the outcome is efficient.

But everyone has an incentive to cheat on the assigned quota. The reason is that marginal private benefit exceeds marginal cost. So by catching more than the allocated quota, each boat owner gets a higher income. If everyone breaks the quota, overproduction returns and the tragedy of the commons remains. A simple quota can work only if the production of each person can be monitored. Where producers are hard to monitor, the quota breaks down.

Individual Transferable Quotas

Where producers are hard to monitor, a more sophisticated quota system can be used. An **individual transferable quota (ITQ)** is a production limit that is assigned to an individual, who is free to transfer the quota to someone else. A market in ITQs emerges, and ITQs are transferred at their market price.

Figure 10.9(b) shows how ITQs work. In the market for ITQs, the price is the highest price that an ITQ is worth. If the number of ITQs issued equals the efficient production level, that price will equal the amount shown in the figure. This price equals the marginal private benefit at the quota quantity minus the private marginal cost of using a boat. The price rises to this level because people who don't have a quota would be willing to pay this amount to acquire the right to fish. And people who do own a quota could sell it for this price, so to not sell it is to incur an opportunity cost. The result is that the marginal cost, which now includes the cost of the ITQ, rises from MC_0 to MC_1. The equilibrium is efficient.

ITQs have been used extensively by New Zealand and Australia to conserve fish stocks in the South Pacific Ocean, and they have a good record. People still have an incentive to cheat and produce more than the amount for which they have a quota. But such cheating is rare because the ITQs are well policed from the air.

> **Individual transferable quota (ITQ)**
> A production limit that is assigned to an individual, who is free to transfer the quota to someone else.

■ FIGURE 10.9

Two Ways of Coping with the Tragedy of the Commons

(a) A quota to achieve efficiency

(b) An individual transferable quota

❶ A quota is set at the efficient quantity, which makes the number of boats equal to the quantity at which marginal social benefit, *MSB*, equals marginal cost, *MC*. ❷ If the quota is not broken, the outcome is efficient.

ITQs are issued on a scale that keeps output at the efficient level and ❸ the market price of an ITQ equals the marginal private benefit minus marginal cost. ❹ The outcome is efficient.

3 **Explain the tragedy of the commons and review the possible solutions to that problem.**

TABLE I

Number of cows	Milk output (gallons per day)
100	300
200	500
300	600
400	600
500	500
600	300
700	0

Practice Problem 10.3

1. In an English village in 1375, cows graze on common pasture and can produce milk in the amounts shown in Table 1. The marginal private cost of a cow is zero.
   a. What is the marginal private benefit at each quantity of cows?
   b. What is the equilibrium number of cows?
   c. What is the marginal social benefit at each quantity of cows?
   d. What are the efficient number of cows and quantity of milk to produce?
   e. If the common pasture were converted to private land and fenced off, how many cows would the landowner keep?
   f. If ITQs were issued for the efficient quantity of milk production, what would be the market price of an ITQ?

Exercise 10.3

TABLE 2

Number of wells	Oil output (gallons per day)
0	0
2	12
4	22
6	30
8	36
10	40
12	42
14	42

1. An oil reserve runs under plots of land owned by seven people. Each person has the right to sink a well on her or his land and take oil from the reserve. The amount of oil that is produced depends on the number of wells sunk and is shown in Table 2. The marginal private cost of a well is 4 gallons a day.
   a. What is the marginal private benefit at each quantity of wells?
   b. What are the equilibrium number of wells and quantity of oil produced?
   c. What is the marginal social benefit at each quantity of wells?
   d. What are the efficient number of wells and quantity of oil to produce?
   e. If the common reserve were owned by only one person, how many wells would be sunk and how much oil would be produced?
   f. How much would someone offer the seven owners to rent the rights to all the oil in the common reserve? (Use gallons of oil as the units.)

Solution to Practice Problem 10.3

TABLE 3

Number of cows	Milk output (gallons per day)	MSB (gallons per cow)	MPB (gallons per cow)
0	0		—
		3	
100	300		3.0
		2	
200	500		2.5
		1	
300	600		2.0
		0	
400	600		1.5
		−1	
500	500		1.0
		−2	
600	300		0.5
		−3	
700	0		0

1a. Table 3 shows the marginal private benefit per cow.
1b. The equilibrium number of cows is 700, and no milk is produced.
1c. Table 3 shows the marginal social benefit at each quantity of cows.
1d. The efficient number of cows is the number at which marginal social benefit is zero and equals marginal cost. This number of cows is 350 (midway between 300 and 400 cows in the table). The efficient quantity of milk is the milk output of 350 cows, which is 600 gallons a day.
1e. If the common pasture were converted to private land and fenced off, the landowner would keep 350 cows because the milk output is maximized at this number of cows.
1f. The market price of an ITQ would be 1.75 gallons of milk (midway between 2.0 and 1.5 gallons per cow in the table). This price is the marginal private benefit at the efficient quantity minus marginal cost, which is zero.

CHAPTER CHECKPOINT

Key Points

1 **Distinguish among private goods, public goods, and common resources.**

- A private good is a good or service that is rival and excludable.
- A public good is a good or service that is nonrival and nonexcludable.
- A common resource is a resource that is rival but nonexcludable.

2 **Explain the free-rider problem and how public provision might help to overcome that problem.**

- A public good creates a free-rider problem—no one has a private incentive to pay her or his share of the cost of providing a public good.
- The efficient level of provision of a public good is that at which marginal benefit equals marginal cost.
- Competition between political parties, each of which tries to appeal to the maximum number of voters, can lead to the efficient scale of provision of a public good and to both parties proposing the same policies—the principle of minimum differentiation.
- Bureaucrats try to maximize their budgets, and if voters are rationally ignorant, they might vote to support taxes that provide public goods in quantities that exceed the efficient quantity.

3 **Explain the tragedy of the commons and review the possible solutions to that problem.**

- Common resources create the tragedy of the commons—no one has a private incentive to conserve the resource and use it at an efficient rate.
- A common resource is used to the point at which the marginal private benefit equals the marginal cost.
- The efficient use of a common resource is the point at which marginal social benefit equals marginal cost.
- A common resource might be used efficiently by creating a private property right, setting a quota, or issuing individual transferable quotas.

Key Terms

(X) **myeconlab**   Exercises

1. Classify each of the following items as a private good, a public good, or a common resource. With each public good, is there a free-rider problem? If not, how is the free-rider problem avoided? With each common resource, is there a tragedy of the commons? If not, how is the tragedy of the commons avoided?
    a. New Year's Eve celebrations in Times Square, New York
    b. The Santa Monica freeway on a Friday afternoon
    c. A sewer system
    d. The railway network
    e. A skateboard
    f. Niagara Falls

2. Make a list with three examples that are different from those in Figure 10.1 and different from those in exercise 1 of a private good, a public good, and a common resource.
    a. Which of the items you've listed are likely to leave people with a smaller quantity than they are willing to buy?
    b. Which of the items you've listed are likely to make people concerned that the quantity exceeds what they would like to buy?
    c. Which of the items you've listed are unlikely to be either in short supply or too abundant?

3. Figure 1 shows the marginal benefit and marginal cost of a waste disposal system in a city of 1 million people.
    a. What is the efficient capacity of the waste disposal system?
    b. How much would each person have to pay in taxes if the city installed the efficient capacity?
    c. If voters are well informed about the costs and benefits of the waste disposal system, what capacity will voters choose in a referendum?
    d. If voters are rationally ignorant, will bureaucrats install the efficient capacity? Explain your answer.

FIGURE I

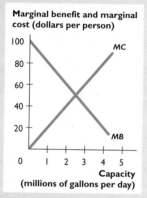

Marginal benefit and marginal cost (dollars per person)

Capacity (millions of gallons per day)

TABLE I

Number of fishing boats	Value of cod caught (thousands of dollars per month)	Value placed on cod stock by concerned citizens (thousands of dollars per month)
0	0	10,000
10	2,000	9,000
20	3,500	8,000
30	4,500	7,000
40	4,800	6,000
50	5,000	5,000
60	4,800	4,000
70	4,200	3,000
80	2,400	2,000

4. Table 1 shows the value of cod caught in the Atlantic Ocean by European and North American fishing boats. It also shows the value that concerned citizens of Europe and North America place on the Atlantic cod stock. The marginal cost of operating a cod fishing boat is $70,000 a month.
    a. What is the marginal private benefit of each fishing boat?
    b. What is the marginal social cost of each fishing boat?
    c. With no regulation of cod fishing, what is the equilibrium number of boats and the approximate value of cod caught?
    d. Is the equilibrium in part c an overfishing outcome?
    e. What is the marginal social benefit of each fishing boat?
    f. What is the efficient number of boats?
    g. What is the efficient value of cod to catch?
    h. Do you think that the concerned citizens of Europe and North America and the fishing industry will agree about how much cod should be caught?
    i. If the United States, Canada, and the European Union issued ITQs to fishing boats to limit the cod catch to the efficient quantity, what would be the price of an ITQ?

Critical Thinking

5. If hikers and others were required to pay a fee to use the Appalachian Trail, would the use of this common resource be more efficient? Would it be even more efficient if the most popular spots such as Annapolis Rock had more highly priced access? Why do you think we don't see more market solutions to the tragedy of the commons?

6. "Creating private property rights to the ocean and its fish, even if only through transferable quotas, is immoral." Do you think that relying on the morality and public spirit of the fishing industry is a potentially effective way of avoiding overfishing? Provide reasons.

7. Although the scientific evidence is not firm, most people agree that global warming is a real phenomenon and that the increase in carbon dioxide that has resulted from burning coal and oil is a significant contributor to the average temperature of the atmosphere. If we could measure the marginal social cost of global warming and the marginal social benefit of controlling it, how could we use those measurements to achieve an efficient use of our common atmospheric resources? What special problems arise, if any, from the fact that there is no global central authority but, instead, 200 or so independent nations?

8. "The tragedy of the commons is a problem only because people don't think about the consequences of their actions. If people were educated to see the damage they do to the environment, there would be no problem." Do you think education is a potentially viable solution to the tragedy of the commons? Provide reasons.

9. To produce the efficient quantity of a public good, we need to know the marginal cost of producing it and its marginal benefit.
    a. Do you think that we could get a better measure of marginal benefit if people were offered the opportunity to vote for each public good as a single issue rather than, as now, for an entire package of public goods?
    b. What would be some of the negative consequences of voting for each public good as a single issue?

10. Almost every day, you read about or hear complaints that the government isn't doing enough to address a perceived problem. And almost always, the issue comes down to spending more tax revenue on a particular public good. It might be medical research, cheap drugs for the poor or aged, a better-equipped military, better public schools and universities, and so on.
    a. On the basis of what you've learned about public goods, why do you think people complain in these ways?
    b. Is the volume of lobbying a sign that the political system delivers too little? Or does it deliver too much despite the complaining?

11. Can you think of any public goods that are provided privately with people paying for them voluntarily? How is the free-rider problem solved in this case? Could the solution be applied more widely? Why or why not?

Web Exercises

Use the links on MyEconLab to work the following exercises.

12. Visit Mark Skousen and read his essay on the private provision of public goods.
    a. Are the examples that he uses actually public goods?
    b. Could you use his proposed solution for national defense? Why or why not?
    c. Could you use his proposed solution for the court system? Why or why not?

13. Review the key points in the Kyoto Protocol on global warming.
    a. What are the common resources that the Kyoto Protocol seeks to conserve?
    b. What special difficulties lie in the path of conserving these resources?
    c. Can you think of an international solution to the problem of global warming?

14. Review Chapter 1 of Bjorn Lomborg's book *The Skeptical Environmentalist*.
    a. Summarize Lomborg's views and contrast them with the views that led to the Kyoto Protocol.
    b. If Lomborg is correct, does that mean that the environment can be left to the market?
    c. Can you think of an international solution to the problem of global warming?

15. Review the discussion of the case for private jails.
    a. What is the case for private rather than public jails?
    b. How does a private jail overcome the free-rider problem?
    c. Are there any general lessons to be learned from private jails?

16. Find information about the top defense contractors—the firms that supply the U.S. military with its equipment.
    a. Why do private firms produce the equipment that provides national defense, a public good?
    b. What is the difference between a private defense contractor and a private jail?
    c. Think about and comment on the distinction between the public production of a public good and the public consumption of a public good.

17. Find information about the budget of the U.S. government.
    a. How much of what the U.S. government spends is on public goods?
    b. How much of what the U.S. government spends is just redistributing income from one group to another? Is redistribution a public good? Explain why or why not.

18. Find information about spending by the U.S. government and by governments in other major countries.
    a. Does the U.S. government spend a greater, smaller, or about the same percentage of income as most other countries?
    b. What might your answer to part **a** suggest about the marginal benefit and marginal cost of public goods in the countries for which you have data?
    c. What other possible reasons can you think of for international differences in government spending on public goods?

Consumer Choice and Demand

CHAPTER CHECKLIST

When you have completed your study of this chapter, you will be able to

1 Calculate and graph a budget line that shows the limits to a person's consumption possibilities.

2 Explain marginal utility theory and use it to derive a consumer's demand curve.

3 Use marginal utility theory to explain the paradox of value: why water is vital but cheap while diamonds are relatively useless but expensive.

As Amy settled into her back-of-the-plane seat, she was surprised by the familiar face of the person sitting next to her. "Excuse me sir," she said, "but you look awfully like Steve Forbes." "I hope I do," came the reply. "I *am* Steve Forbes.

Steve Forbes, owner of *Forbes Magazine*, said to be worth around half a billion dollars, owner of an island in Fiji, a Boeing 727, and a chateau in France, sometimes travels coach!

You're not likely to run into Tiger Woods at the back of a plane. Like most top golfers, Tiger does most of his traveling in his private jet.

Why can Steve Forbes sometimes be seen traveling coach and Tiger Woods never? What determines the way in which people choose to spend their income—whether a large amount or a small one?

This chapter explains a model of consumer choice that helps us to understand and even predict the choices that people make.

11.1 CONSUMPTION POSSIBILITIES

We begin our study of consumption choices by learning about the limits to what a person can afford to buy. Your consumption choices are limited by your income and by the prices that you must pay. We summarize these influences on buying plans in a budget line.

■ The Budget Line

Budget line
A line that describes the limits to consumption possibilities and that depends on a consumer's budget and the prices of goods and services.

A **budget line** describes the limits to consumption possibilities. Tina has already committed most of her income to renting an apartment, buying textbooks, paying her campus meal plan, and saving a few dollars each month. Having made these decisions, Tina has a remaining budget of $4 a day, which she spends on two goods: bottled water and chewing gum. The price of water is $1 a bottle, and the price of gum is 50¢ a pack. If Tina spends all of her available budget, she reaches the limits of her consumption of bottled water and gum.

Figure 11.1 illustrates Tina's budget line. Rows *A* through *E* in the table show five possible ways of spending $4 on these two goods. If Tina spends all of her $4 on gum, she can buy 8 packs a day. In this case, she has nothing available to spend on bottled water. Row *A* shows this possibility. At the other extreme, if Tina spends her entire $4 on bottled water, she can buy 4 bottles a day and no gum. Row *E* shows this possibility. Rows *B, C,* and *D* show three other possible combinations that Tina can afford.

■ FIGURE 11.1
Consumption Possibilities

Tina's budget line shows the boundary between what she can and cannot afford. The rows of the table list Tina's affordable combinations of bottled water and chewing gum when her budget is $4 a day, the price of water is $1 a bottle, and the price of chewing gum is 50¢ a pack. For example, row *A* tells us that Tina exhausts her $4 budget when she buys 8 packs of gum and no water.

The figure graphs Tina's budget line. Points *A* through *E* on the graph represent the rows of the table.

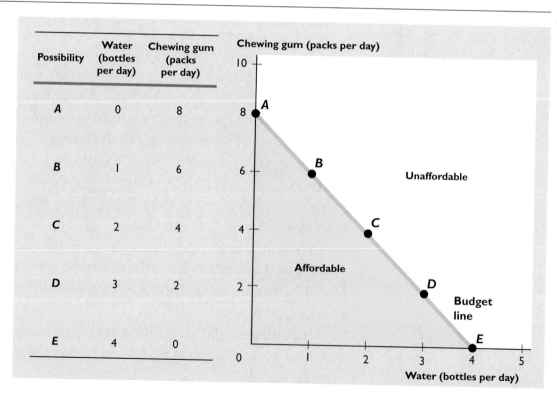

Possibility	Water (bottles per day)	Chewing gum (packs per day)
A	0	8
B	1	6
C	2	4
D	3	2
E	4	0

Points *A* through *E* in the figure graph the possibilities in the table. The line passing through these points is Tina's budget line, which marks the boundary between what she can and cannot afford. She can afford any combination on the budget line and inside it (in the orange area). She cannot afford any combination outside the budget line (in the white area).

The budget line in Figure 11.1 is similar to the *production possibilities frontier*, or *PPF*, in Chapter 3 (pp. 62–63). Both curves show a limit to what is feasible. But the *PPF* is a technological limit that changes only when technology changes. The budget line depends on the consumer's budget and on prices, so it changes when the budget or prices change.

■ A Change in the Budget

Figure 11.2 shows the effect of a change in Tina's budget on her consumption possibilities. When Tina's budget increases, her consumption possibilities expand, and her budget line shifts outward. When her budget decreases, her consumption possibilities shrink and her budget line shifts inward.

On the initial budget line (the same as in Figure 11.1), Tina's budget is $4. On a day on which Tina loses her purse with $2 in it, she has only $2 to spend. Her new budget line in Figure 11.2 shows how much she can consume with a budget of $2. She can buy any of the combinations on the $2 budget line.

On a day on which Tina sells an old CD for $2, she has $6 available and her budget line shifts rightward. She can now buy any of the combinations on the $6 budget line.

■ **FIGURE 11.2**

Changes in a Consumer's Budget

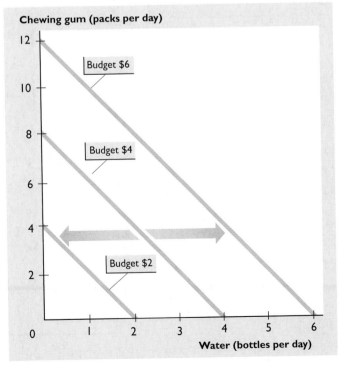

A decrease in the budget shifts the budget line leftward, and an increase in the budget shifts the budget line rightward.

■ Changes in Prices

If the price of one good rises when the prices of other goods and the budget remain the same, consumption possibilities shrink. If the price of one good falls when the prices of other goods and the budget remain the same, consumption possibilities expand. To see these changes in consumption possibilities, let's see what happens to Tina's budget line when the price of a bottle of water changes.

A Fall in the Price of Water

Figure 11.3 shows the effect on Tina's budget line of a fall in the price of a bottle of water from $1 to 50¢ when the price of gum and her budget remain unchanged. If Tina spends all her budget on bottled water, she can now afford 8 bottles a day. Her consumption possibilities have expanded. But because the price of gum is unchanged, if she spends all her budget on gum, she can still afford only 8 packs of gum a day. Her budget line has rotated outward.

A Rise in the Price of Water

Figure 11.4 shows the effect on Tina's budget line of a rise in the price of a bottle of water from $1 to $2 when the price of gum and her budget remain unchanged. If Tina spends all of her budget on bottled water, she can now afford only 2 bottles a day. Tina's consumption possibilities have shrunk. But again, because the price of gum is unchanged, if Tina spends all her budget on gum, she can still afford 8 packs of gum a day. Her budget line has rotated inward.

■ FIGURE 11.3

A Fall in the Price of Water

When the price of water falls from $1 a bottle to 50¢ a bottle, the budget line rotates outward and becomes less steep.

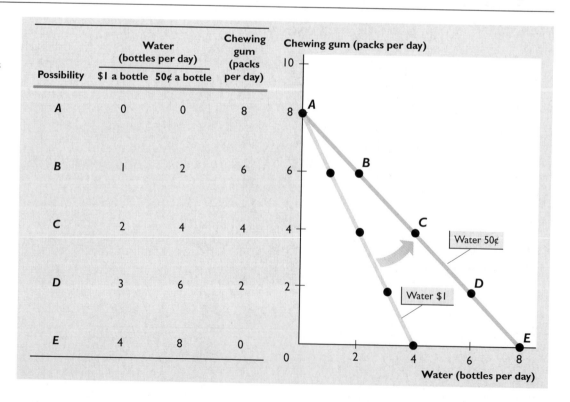

Possibility	Water (bottles per day) $1 a bottle	Water (bottles per day) 50¢ a bottle	Chewing gum (packs per day)
A	0	0	8
B	1	2	6
C	2	4	4
D	3	6	2
E	4	8	0

■ Prices and the Slope of the Budget Line

Notice that when the price of bottled water changes and the price of gum remains unchanged, the slope of the budget line changes. In Figure 11.3, when the price of bottled water falls, the budget line becomes less steep. In Figure 11.4, when the price of a bottle of water rises, the budget line becomes steeper.

Recall that "slope equals rise over run." The rise is an *increase* in the quantity of gum, and the run is a *decrease* in the quantity of bottled water. The slope of the budget line is negative, which means that there is a tradeoff between the two goods. Along the budget line, consuming more of one good implies consuming less of the other good. The slope of the budget line is an *opportunity cost*. It tells us what the consumer must give up to get one more unit of a good.

Let's calculate the slopes of the three budget lines in Figures 11.3 and 11.4:

- When the price of water is $1 a bottle, the slope of the budget line is 8 packs of gum divided by 4 bottles of water, which equals 2 packs of gum per bottle.
- When the price of water is 50¢ a bottle, the slope of the budget line is 8 packs of gum divided by 8 bottles water, which equals 1 pack of gum per bottle.
- When the price of water is $2 a bottle, the slope of the budget line is 8 packs of gum divided by 2 bottles of water, which equals 4 packs of gum per bottle.

A Rise in the Price of Water

Possibility	Water (bottles per day) $2 a bottle	Water (bottles per day) $1 a bottle	Chewing gum (packs per day)
A	0	0	8
		1	6
B	1	2	4
		3	2
C	2	4	0

When the price of water rises from $1 a bottle to $2 a bottle, the budget line rotates inward and becomes steeper.

Think about what these slopes mean as opportunity costs. When the price of water is $1 a bottle and the price of gum is 50¢ a pack, it costs 2 packs of gum to buy a bottle of water. When the price of water is 50¢ a bottle and the price of gum is 50¢ a pack, it costs 1 pack of gum to buy a bottle of water. And when the price of water is $2 a bottle and the price of gum is 50¢ a pack, it costs 4 packs of gum to buy a bottle of water.

Another name for an opportunity cost is a relative price. A **relative price** is the price of one good in terms of another good. If the price of gum is 50¢ a pack and the price of water is $1 a bottle, the relative price of water is 2 packs of gum per bottle. It is calculated as the price of water divided by the price of gum ($1 a bottle ÷ 50¢ a pack = 2 packs per bottle).

When the price of the good plotted on the *x*-axis falls, other things remaining the same, the budget line becomes less steep, and the opportunity cost and relative price of the good on the *x*-axis fall.

Relative price
The price of one good in terms of another good—an opportunity cost. It equals the price of one good divided by the price of another good.

EYE ON THE U.S. ECONOMY

Relative Prices on the Move

Over a number of years, relative prices change a great deal. Some of the most dramatic changes occur in high-technology products such as computers. But many other relative prices change, and many fall.

The figure shows the price changes between 1995 and 2005 of 16 items that featured in most student's budgets.

Gasoline and college books and supplies have had some of the largest relative price increases.

The price of a personal computer has fallen by 90 percent. Other large relative price declines have been in coffee and long-distance phone calls. But bananas, electricity, and a host of other items have relatively lower prices today than they did 10 years ago.

These changes in relative prices change people's consumption possibilities and change the choices that they make. Lower prices provide an incen-

tive to buy greater quantities, and higher prices provide an incentive to

find substitutes and buy smaller quantities.

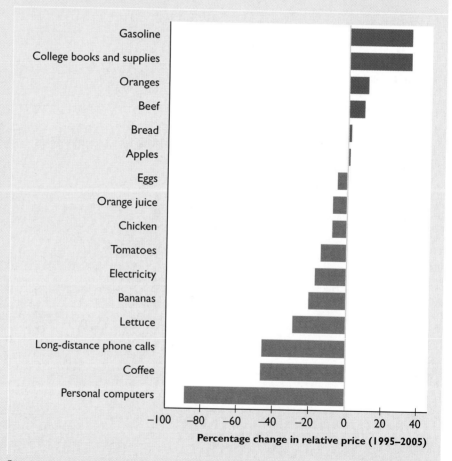

Percentage change in relative price (1995–2005)

SOURCE OF DATA: Bureau of Labor Statistics.

CHECKPOINT 11.1

1 Calculate and graph a budget line that shows the limits to a person's consumption possibilities.

Practice Problem 11.1

1. Jerry's burger and magazine budget is $12 a week. The price of a burger is $2, and the price of a magazine is $4.
   a. List the combinations of burgers and magazines that Jerry can afford.
   b. Draw a graph of Jerry's budget line with the quantity of burgers plotted on the x-axis.
   c. What is the relative price of a magazine? Explain your answer.
   d. Describe how the budget line in part **b** changes if, other things remaining the same, the following changes occur one at a time:
      • The price of a magazine falls.
      • Jerry's budget for burgers and magazines increases.

Exercise 11.1

1. Jenny's burger and salad budget is $36 a week. The price of a burger is $3, and the price of a salad is $2.
   a. List the combinations of burgers and salads that Jenny can afford.
   b. Draw a graph of Jenny's budget line with the quantity of burgers plotted on the x-axis.
   c. Describe how Jenny's budget line in part **b** changes if, other things remaining the same, the following changes occur one at a time:
      • The price of a burger falls.
      • Jenny's burger and salad budget decreases.
   d. How does the relative price of a salad change if the price of a burger halves? Explain your answer.

FIGURE 1

Solution to Practice Problem 11.1

1a. Jerry can afford the combinations that cost the $12 in his budget: 3 magazines and no burgers; 2 magazines and 2 burgers; 1 magazine and 4 burgers; no magazines and 6 burgers.

1b. The budget line is a straight line from 3 magazines on the y-axis to 6 burgers on the x-axis (Figure 1).

1c. The relative price of a magazine is the number of burgers that Jerry must forgo to get 1 magazine, which equals the price of a magazine divided by the price of a burger, or 2 burgers per magazine.

1d. With a lower price of a magazine, the number of magazines that Jerry can buy with $12 increases. The budget line rotates outward (Figure 2). With a bigger budget, Jerry can buy more of both magazines and burgers. The budget line shifts outward (Figure 3).

FIGURE 2

FIGURE 3

11.2 MARGINAL UTILITY THEORY

The budget line tells us about consumption *possibilities*, but it doesn't tell us a person's consumption *choice*. The quantities of goods and services that people choose depend on consumption possibilities and *preferences*. Economists use the concept of utility* to describe preferences. You are going to learn how economists use the concept of utility to explain the quantities that people choose to buy and predict how those quantities change when prices change. You will see how economists derive a consumer's demand curve from utility-maximizing choices.

■ Utility

Utility

The benefit or satisfaction that a person gets from the consumption of a good or service.

The benefit or satisfaction that a person gets from the consumption of a good or service is called **utility**. In everyday language, "utility" means "usefulness." In economics, it is an index of how much a person wants something. Utility is a bit like temperature. It is a useful but abstract concept measured in arbitrary units.

Temperature: An Analogy

You know when you feel hot, and you know when you feel cold. But you can't *observe* temperature itself. It is an abstract concept. You can observe water turning to steam if it is hot enough or turning to ice if it is cold enough. And you can use a thermometer to predict when such changes will occur.

The scale on the thermometer is what we call temperature. But the units in which we measure temperature are arbitrary. For example, we can accurately predict that when a Celsius thermometer shows a temperature of 0, water will turn to ice. But the units of measurement do not matter because this same event also occurs when a Fahrenheit thermometer shows a temperature of 32. Similarly, when a Celsius thermometer shows a temperature of 100, water will boil. But this same event also occurs when a Fahrenheit thermometer shows a temperature of 212.

The concept of utility helps us to make predictions about consumption choices in much the same way that the concept of temperature helps us to make predictions about physical phenomena. But marginal utility theory is not as precise as the theory that enables us to predict when water will turn to ice or steam. The main reason is that people's preferences sometimes change.

Let's now see how we can use the concept of utility to describe preferences.

■ Total Utility

Total utility

The total benefit that a person gets from the consumption of a good or service. Total utility generally increases as the quantity consumed of a good increases.

Total utility is the total benefit that a person gets from the consumption of a good or service. Total utility depends on the quantity of the good consumed—more consumption generally gives more total utility. Table 11.1 shows Tina's total utility from bottled water and chewing gum. If she consumes no bottled water and no gum, she gets no utility. If she consumes 1 bottle of water a day, she gets 15 units of utility. If she consumes 1 pack of gum a day, it provides her with 32 units of utility. As Tina increases the quantity of bottled water and packs of gum she consumes, her total utility from each increases.

---

*Economists also use an alternative method of describing preferences called *indifference curves*, which are described in the optional appendix to this chapter.

Tina's total utility numbers tell us that she gets a lot of pleasure from chewing gum. The first pack a day gives her more than twice the utility that her first bottle of water provides. But by the time Tina has consumed 7 packs of gum in a day, the 8th pack gives her no more utility. An 8th bottle of water, on the other hand, does increase her total utility.

■ Marginal Utility

Marginal utility is the change in total utility that results from a one-unit increase in the quantity of a good consumed. Table 11.1 shows the calculation of Tina's marginal utility from bottled water and chewing gum. Let's find Tina's marginal utility from a 3rd bottle of water a day (highlighted in the table). Her total utility from 3 bottles is 36 units, and her total utility from 2 bottles is 27 units. So for Tina, the marginal utility from drinking a 3rd bottle of water each day is

Marginal utility of 3rd bottle = 36 units − 27 units = 9 units.

In the table, marginal utility appears midway between the quantities because the *change* in consumption produces the *marginal* utility. The table displays the marginal utility for each quantity of water and gum consumed.

Notice that Tina's marginal utility decreases as her consumption of water and gum increases. For example, her marginal utility from bottled water decreases from 15 units for the first bottle to 12 units from the second and 9 units from the third. Similarly, her marginal utility from chewing gum decreases from 32 units for the first pack to 16 units for the second and 8 units for the third. We call this decrease in marginal utility as the quantity of a good consumed increases the principle of **diminishing marginal utility**.

To see why marginal utility diminishes, think about the following situations: In one, you've been studying all day and have had nothing to drink. Someone offers you a bottle of water. The marginal utility you get from that water is large.

Marginal utility
The change in total utility that results from a one-unit increase in the quantity of a good consumed.

Diminishing marginal utility
The general tendency for marginal utility to decrease as the quantity of a good consumed increases.

■ TABLE 11.1

Tina's Total Utility and Marginal Utility

Bottled water			Chewing gum		
Quantity (bottles per day)	Total utility	Marginal utility	Quantity (packs per day)	Total utility	Marginal utility
0	0		0	0	
		15			32
1	15		1	32	
		12			16
2	27		2	48	
		9			8
3	36		3	56	
		6			6
4	42		4	62	
		5			4
5	47		5	66	
		4			2
6	51		6	68	
		3			1
7	54		7	69	
		2			0
8	56		8	69	

The table shows Tina's total utility and marginal utility for bottled water and chewing gum. Marginal utility is the change in total utility when the quantity consumed increases by one unit. When Tina's consumption of bottled water increases from 2 bottles a day to 3 bottles per day, her total utility from bottled water increases from 27 units to 36 units. So Tina's marginal utility of the 3rd bottle a day is 9 units. Total utility increases and marginal utility diminishes as the quantity consumed increases.

With Tina's numbers, it provides 15 units of utility. In the second situation, you've been on a bottled water binge. You've drunk 7 bottles during the day. Now someone offers you another bottle of water, and you say thanks very much and sip it slowly. You enjoy the 8th bottle of the day, but the marginal utility from the 8th bottle is only 2 units.

Similarly, suppose you've been unable to buy a pack of gum for more than a day. A friend offers you a pack. Relief! You chew and receive 32 units of utility. On another day, you've chewed until your jaws ache and have gone through 7 packs. You're offered an 8th, and this time you say thanks very much but I'll pass on that one. You know that the 8th pack of gum would bring you no marginal utility.

For Tina, the marginal utility of gum diminishes more rapidly than does the marginal utility of bottled water.

We can illustrate the features of a consumer's preferences that we've just described with a total utility curve and a marginal utility curve. Figure 11.5 shows Tina's total utility and marginal utility from bottled water. You can see the principle of diminishing marginal utility in this figure. Part (a) shows us that as Tina drinks more bottled water, her total utility from it increases. It also shows that total utility increases at a decreasing rate. You can see diminishing marginal utility in part (a) because the step increases in utility get smaller as the quantity of water consumed increases.

Part (b) graphs Tina's marginal utility. The steps in part (a) are placed side by side in part (b). We've enlarged the scale of the *y*-axis in part (b) to emphasize the diminishing marginal utility. The curve that passes through the midpoints of the bars in part (b) is Tina's marginal utility curve.

The numbers in Table 11.1 and the graphs in Figure 11.5 describe Tina's preferences and, along with her budget line, enable us to predict the choices that she makes. That is our next task.

EYE ON THE PAST

Jeremy Bentham, William Stanley Jevons, and the Birth of Utility

The concept of utility was revolutionary when Jeremy Bentham (1748–1832) proposed it in the early 1800s. He used the idea to advance his then radical support for free education, free medical care, and social security. It took another fifty years before William Stanley Jevons (1835–1882) developed the concept of *marginal* utility and used it to pre- dict people's consumption choices. Jevons's main claim to fame in his own day was his suggestion—wrong as it turned out—that sunspots cause business cycles. But his lasting legacy is the marginal utility theory.

Jeremy Bentham

William Stanley Jevons

FIGURE 11.5

Total Utility and Marginal Utility

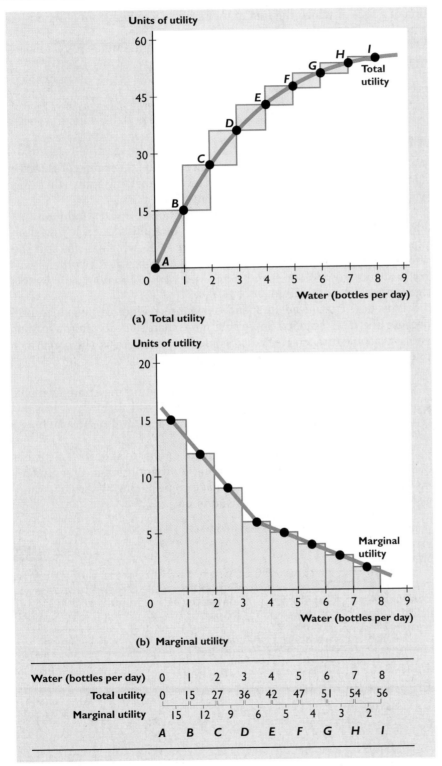

(a) Total utility

(b) Marginal utility

Water (bottles per day)	0	1	2	3	4	5	6	7	8
Total utility	0	15	27	36	42	47	51	54	56
Marginal utility		15	12	9	6	5	4	3	2	
	A	B	C	D	E	F	G	H	I

Part (a) graphs Tina's total utility from bottled water. It also shows as a bar the extra total utility she gains from each additional bottle of water—her marginal utility—as the steps along the total utility curve.

Part (b) shows how Tina's marginal utility from bottled water diminishes by placing the bars shown in part (a) side by side as a series of declining steps.

■ Maximizing Total Utility

The consumer's goal is to allocate the available budget in the way that maximizes total utility. The consumer achieves this goal by choosing the affordable combination of goods at which the *sum* of the utilities obtained from all goods consumed is as large as possible.

We can find a consumer's best budget allocation by using a two-step **utility-maximizing rule**:

1. Allocate the entire available budget.
2. Make the marginal utility per dollar equal for all goods.

Allocate the Available Budget

We're going to see how the two-step utility-maximizing rule works for Tina as she allocates $4 a day between bottled water and chewing gum when the price of water is $1 a bottle and the price of gum is 50¢ a pack.

The first step is to establish the combinations of water and gum that cost $4. Table 11.2 shows these combinations. The quantities in each row describe one point that is on Tina's budget line (in Figure 11.1), which means that she can just afford to buy each combination. For example, if she buys 1 bottle of water and 6 packs of gum (row *B*), she spends $1 on water and $3 on gum, and her total expenditure equals her entire budget of $4.

Why does Tina need to spend her entire budget to maximize utility? It is because she faces scarcity. She wants more than she can afford, so she uses the entire available budget. If she had some budget left over, she could increase her total utility by buying more of either good.

A Side Note on Saving and Other Goods Spending the entire available budget doesn't necessarily mean not saving anything. The available budget is the amount remaining after choosing how much to save and, in Tina's case, how much to spend on some other goods.

The principles that explain Tina's choice of how to allocate her currently available budget between water and chewing gum apply more broadly and explain how a consumer allocates her or his total income among all the goods and services available and saving for future consumption.

Utility-maximizing rule
The rule that leads to the greatest total utility from all the goods and services consumed. The rule is
1. Allocate the entire available budget.
2. Make the marginal utility per dollar equal for all goods.

■ TABLE 11.2

Tina's Affordable Combinations of Water and Gum
myeconlab

The rows of the table show Tina's affordable combinations of water and gum when she has $4 to spend on these two items, the price of water is $1 a bottle, and the price of gum is 50¢ a pack. Each combination *A* through *E* is a point on Tina's budget line in Figure 11.1.

	Quantity of water (bottles per day)	Quantity of gum (packs per day)	Expenditure on water at $1 per bottle	Expenditure on gum at 50¢ per pack	Total expenditure
			(dollars per day)		
A	0	8	0	4	4
B	1	6	1	3	4
C	2	4	2	2	4
D	3	2	3	1	4
E	4	0	4	0	4

Equalize the Marginal Utility Per Dollar

The second step to finding a consumer's best budget allocation is to establish the affordable combination that makes the marginal utility per dollar equal for both goods. The **marginal utility per dollar** is the marginal utility from a good relative to the price of the good.

Calculating the Marginal Utility per Dollar   To calculate the marginal utility per dollar, we divide the marginal utility from a good by the price of the good. For example, if Tina buys 1 pack of gum a day, her marginal utility from the 1 pack is 32 units. The price of a pack of gum is 50¢, so the marginal utility per dollar from gum is 32 units divided by 50¢, which equals 64 units of utility per dollar. If Tina buys 1 bottle of water a day, her marginal utility from the 1 bottle of water is 15 units. The price of a bottle of water is $1, so Tina's marginal utility per dollar from bottled water is 15 units divided by $1, which equals 15 units of utility per dollar.

Why Equal Marginal Utility per Dollar Maximizes Total Utility   Suppose that Tina can get more utility by shifting a dollar of expenditure from water to gum. What do you know about the marginal utility per dollar from water and gum? You know that the gain in utility from the extra gum must be greater than the loss of utility from the smaller quantity of water. So the marginal utility per dollar from gum must have been greater than the marginal utility per dollar from water. The top balance scale in Figure 11.6 illustrates this situation.

But as Tina buys more gum, the marginal utility from gum decreases and so does the marginal utility per dollar from gum. And as she buys less water, the marginal utility per dollar from water increases.

When the marginal utility per dollar from gum is equal to the marginal utility per dollar from water, Tina cannot get more utility by shifting a dollar from one good to the other. If Tina did buy more gum, the gain in utility from more gum would be less than the loss in utility from less water. The bottom balance scale in Figure 11.6 illustrates this situation.

Marginal utility per dollar
The marginal utility from a good relative to the price paid for the good.

■ FIGURE 11.6

Utility-Maximizing Balancing Act

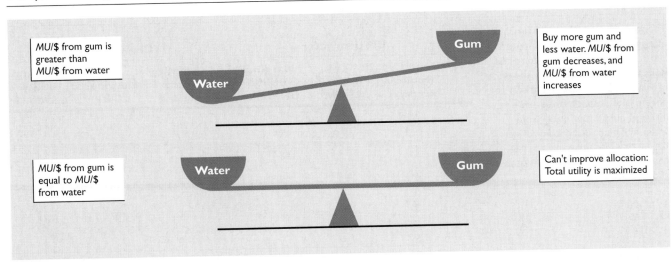

Finding Tina's Utility-Maximizing Choice To find Tina's utility-maximizing choice, we need to calculate the marginal utility per dollar for only the affordable combinations that exhaust her budget. Other combinations are irrelevant. Either they are not affordable or they waste some of the budget.

Table 11.3 shows Tina's marginal utilities per dollar from water and gum for all the affordable combinations that exhaust her budget.

Begin by checking that you can calculate the marginal utilities per dollar. Let's do a sample calculation on row *D*. In this row of the table, Tina buys 3 bottles of water and 2 packs of gum. Her marginal utility from water is 9 units, and because the price of water is $1 a bottle, her marginal utility per dollar from water is 9 divided by $1, which is 9 units per dollar. Her marginal utility from gum is 16 units and because the price of gum is 50¢ a pack, her marginal utility per dollar from gum is 16 divided by 50¢, which is 32 units per dollar.

You can see in the table that the combination that equalizes the marginal utilities per dollar is 2 bottles of water and 4 packs of gum—in row *C*.

Suppose that Tina were to move from row *C* to row *D* and buy 3 bottles of water and only 2 packs of gum. You can see that with this allocation of her budget, Tina's marginal utility per dollar from water is 9 units of utility per dollar and her marginal utility per dollar from gum is 32 units per dollar.

Making this move, Tina would gain 9 units per dollar from the extra water and she would lose 12 units per dollar from the forgone gum. Tina would be worse off with this combination.

Now suppose that Tina were to move from row *C* to row *B* and buy 1 bottle of water and 6 packs of gum. You can see that with this allocation of her budget, Tina's marginal utility per dollar from water is 15 units per dollar and her marginal utility per dollar from gum is 4 units per dollar.

Making this move, Tina would gain 4 units per dollar from the extra gum but she would lose 12 units per dollar from the forgone water. Again, Tina would be worse off with this combination.

Tina can do no better than to buy 2 bottles of water and 4 packs of gum.

■ **TABLE 11.3**

Tina's Marginal Utilities per Dollar: Water $1 a Bottle and Gum 50¢ a Pack   ⓧ myeconlab

The rows of the table show Tina's marginal utility per dollar from water and gum for the affordable combinations when her budget is $4, the price of water is $1 a bottle, and the price of gum is 50¢ a pack. By equalizing the marginal utilities per dollar from water and gum, Tina maximizes her total utility. Her utility-maximizing choice is to buy 2 bottles of water and 4 packs of gum.

	Bottled water			Chewing gum		
	Quantity (bottles per day)	Marginal utility	Marginal utility per dollar	Quantity (packs per day)	Marginal utility	Marginal utility per dollar
A	0			8	0	0
				7	1	2
B	1	15	15	6	2	4
				5	4	8
C	2	12	12	4	6	12
				3	8	16
D	3	9	9	2	16	32
				1	32	64
E	4	6	6	0		

■ Finding an Individual Demand Curve

We can use marginal utility theory to find a person's demand schedule and demand curve. In fact, we've just found one entry in Tina's demand schedule and one point on her demand curve for bottled water: When the price of bottled water is $1 and other things remain the same (the price of gum is 50¢ and her budget is $4 a day), the quantity of water that Tina buys is 2 bottles a day (row C in Table 11.3).

Let's find a second entry in Tina's demand schedule and point on her demand curve for water—the quantity of water that Tina buys when the price of water falls to 50¢ a bottle and other things remain the same.

You know right away that Tina will buy more bottled water. Why? With the fall in the price of water, the marginal utility per dollar from water increases and must now exceed the marginal utility per dollar from gum. Also, with a lower price of water, Tina can afford to buy more water each day.

If Tina continued to consume 2 bottles of water and 4 packs of gum when the price of water halved, her marginal utility per dollar from bottled water would double to 24 units per dollar, which is twice the marginal utility per dollar from gum. Also, Tina would be spending only $3, so she would have another $1 available. Suppose that she spent the spare $1 on bottled water. She would then be consuming 4 bottles of water a day.

Table 11.4 shows some of Tina's new affordable combinations and the marginal utility per dollar from each good. Row E shows that when Tina spends all her $4 and consumes 4 bottles of water and 4 packs of gum a day, her marginal utility per dollar from bottled water is 12 and her marginal utility per dollar from gum is 12. So this combination is Tina's new choice.

You've now found a second entry in Tina's demand schedule and point on her demand curve for bottled water: When the price of bottled water is 50¢ (other things remaining the same), Tina buys 4 bottles of water a day.

In this example, Tina increases the quantity of water consumed and does not change her consumption of gum. This outcome is special to this numerical example and doesn't usually happen.

Figure 11.7 shows Tina's demand curve that we've just derived.

■ **TABLE 11.4**

myeconlab

Tina's Marginal Utilities per Dollar: Water 50¢ a Bottle and Gum 50¢ a Pack

	Bottled water			Chewing gum		
	Quantity (bottles per day)	Marginal utility	Marginal utility per dollar	Quantity (packs per day)	Marginal utility	Marginal utility per dollar
D	3	9	18	5	4	8
E	4	6	12	4	6	12
F	5	5	10	3	8	16

The rows of the table show Tina's marginal utility per dollar from water and gum for the affordable combinations when her budget is $4, the price of water is 50¢ a bottle, and the price of gum is 50¢ a pack. By equalizing the marginal utilities per dollar from water and gum, Tina maximizes her total utility. Her utility-maximizing choice is to buy 4 bottles of water and 4 packs of gum.

FIGURE 11.7

Tina's Demand for Bottled Water

When the price of water is $1 a bottle (and her budget is $4 and the price of a pack of gum is 50¢), Tina buys 2 bottles of water and 4 packs of gum a day. She is at point *C* on her demand curve for water.

When the price of water falls to 50¢ a bottle and other things remain the same, Tina buys 4 bottles of water and 4 packs of gum a day and moves to point *E* on her demand curve for bottled water.

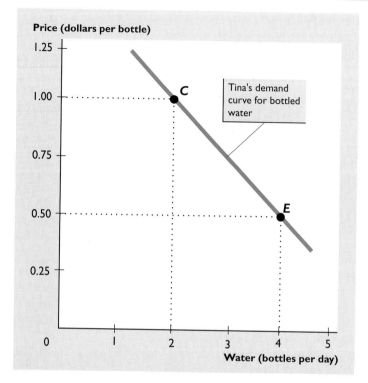

The Power of Marginal Analysis

The method that we've used to find Tina's utility-maximizing choice of bottled water and gum is an example of the power of marginal analysis. By comparing the marginal gain from having more of one good with the marginal loss from having less of another good, Tina gets the maximum attainable utility.

More generally, if the marginal gain from an action exceeds the marginal loss, take the action. You have met this principle before, and you will meet it time and again in your study of economics. Soon, you will find yourself using it when you make your own choices, especially when you must make a big decision.

Units of Utility

In calculating Tina's utility-maximizing choice, we didn't use the concept of *total* utility. All our calculations use *marginal utility* and *price*. By making the marginal utility per dollar from each good equal, we know that Tina maximizes her total utility.

This way of viewing maximum utility is important: It means that the units in which utility is measured do not matter. We could double or halve all the numbers measuring utility or multiply them by any other positive number. None of these changes in the units used to measure utility makes any difference to the outcome. Just as changing from degrees Celsius to degrees Fahrenheit doesn't affect a prediction about the freezing point of water, so changing the units of utility doesn't affect our prediction about the consumption choice that maximizes total utility.

CHECKPOINT 11.2

2 Explain marginal utility theory and use it to derive a consumer's demand curve.

Practice Problem 11.2

1. Table 1 shows Jerry's total utility from burgers and magazines.
   a. Calculate Jerry's marginal utility from the second burger in the week.
   b. If the price of a burger is $2, calculate the marginal utility per dollar from burgers when Jerry buys 2 burgers a week.
   c. Calculate Jerry's marginal utility from the second magazine in the week.
   d. If the price of a magazine is $4, calculate the marginal utility per dollar from magazines when Jerry buys 2 magazines.
   e. When the price of a burger is $2, the price of a magazine is $4, and Jerry has $12 a week to spend, Jerry buys 2 burgers and 2 magazines. Does he maximize his total utility? Explain your answer.

TABLE 1

Burgers		Magazines	
Quantity per week	Total utility	Quantity per week	Total utility
0	0	0	0
1	14	1	100
2	24	2	120
3	32	3	134
4	38	4	144

Exercise 11.2

1. Table 2 shows Wanda's total utility for juice and pasta. The price of a can of juice is $1, the price of a dish of pasta is $4, and Wanda has $11 a week to spend on these two items.
   a. Calculate Wanda's marginal utility from the third dish of pasta a week.
   b. Calculate the marginal utility per dollar from pasta when Wanda has 3 dishes of pasta a week.
   c. Calculate Wanda's marginal utility from the fourth can of juice in a week.
   d. Calculate the marginal utility per dollar from juice when Wanda buys 2 cans of juice a week.
   e. If Wanda buys 2 cans of juice and 2 dishes of pasta a week, is she maximizing her total utility? If Wanda is not maximizing her total utility, explain how she would adjust her consumption choice to do so.

TABLE 2

Juice		Pasta	
Cans per week	Total utility	Dishes per week	Total utility
0	0	0	0
1	22	1	64
2	40	2	120
3	54	3	168
4	60	4	208
5	62	5	240
6	62	6	264

Solution to Practice Problem 11.2

1a. The marginal utility from the second burger equals the total utility from 2 burgers minus the total utility from 1 burger, which is 24 − 14 or 10 units.

1b. When Jerry buys 2 burgers, the marginal utility per dollar from burgers equals the marginal utility of the second burger (10) divided by the price of a burger ($2), which equals 5.

1c. The marginal utility from the second magazine equals the total utility from 2 magazines minus the total utility from 1 magazine, which is 120 − 100 or 20 units.

1d. When Jerry buys 2 magazines, the marginal utility per dollar from magazines equals the marginal utility of the second magazine (20) divided by the price of a magazine ($4), which equals 5.

1e. When a burger costs $2 and a magazine costs $4, Jerry buys 2 burgers and 2 magazines. Jerry has $12 to spend, so he spends his entire budget. The marginal utility per dollar from burgers (5, answer **b**) equals the marginal utility per dollar from magazines (5, answer **d**), so Jerry maximizes his total utility.

11.3 EFFICIENCY, PRICE, AND VALUE

Marginal utility theory helps us to deepen our understanding of the concept of efficiency and to see more clearly the distinction between *value* and *price*. Let's see how.

■ Consumer Efficiency

When Tina allocates her limited budget to maximize total utility, she is using her resources efficiently. Any other allocation of her budget would leave her able to attain a higher level of total utility.

But when Tina has allocated her budget to maximize total utility, she is *on* her demand curve for each good. A demand curve describes the quantity demanded at each price *when total utility is maximized*. When we studied efficiency in Chapter 6, we learned that a demand curve is also a willingness-to-pay curve. It tells us a consumer's *marginal benefit*—the benefit from consuming an additional unit of a good. You can now give the idea of marginal benefit a deeper meaning.

> **Marginal benefit is the maximum price a consumer is willing to pay for an extra unit of a good or service when total utility is maximized.**

■ The Paradox of Value

For centuries, philosophers were puzzled by the paradox of value. Water is more valuable than a diamond because water is essential to life itself. Yet water is much cheaper than a diamond. Why? Adam Smith tried to solve this paradox, but it was not until marginal utility theory had been developed that anyone could give a satisfactory answer.

You can solve this puzzle by distinguishing between *total* utility and *marginal* utility. Total utility tells us about relative value; marginal utility tells us about relative price. The total utility from water is enormous. But remember, the more we consume of something, the smaller is its marginal utility. We use so much water that its marginal utility—the benefit we get from one more glass of water—diminishes to a small value. Diamonds, on the other hand, have a small total utility relative to water, but because we buy few diamonds, they have a large marginal utility. When a household has maximized its total utility, it has allocated its budget so that the marginal utility per dollar is equal for all goods. Diamonds have a high price and a high marginal utility. Water has a low price and a low marginal utility. When the high marginal utility of diamonds is divided by the high price of a diamond, the result is a marginal utility per dollar that equals the low marginal utility of water divided by the low price of water. The marginal utility per dollar is the same for diamonds as for water.

Consumer Surplus

Consumer surplus measures value in excess of the amount paid. In Figure 11.8, the demand for and supply of water in part (a) determine the price of water P_W and the quantity of water consumed Q_W. The demand for and supply of diamonds in part (b) determine the price of a diamond P_D and the quantity of diamonds Q_D. Water is cheap but provides a large consumer surplus, while diamonds are expensive but provide a small consumer surplus.

FIGURE 11.8

The Paradox of Value

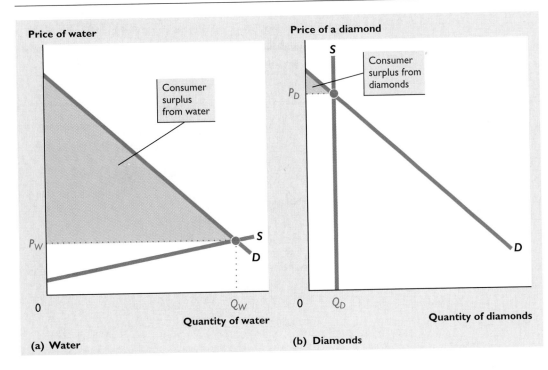

(a) Water

(b) Diamonds

Part (a) shows the demand for water, D, and the supply of water, S. Demand and supply determine the price of water at P_W and the quantity at Q_W. The consumer surplus from water is the large green triangle.

Part (b) shows the demand for diamonds, D, and the supply of diamonds. S. Demand and supply determine the price of a diamond at P_D and the quantity at Q_D. The consumer surplus from diamonds is the small green triangle.

Water is valuable—has a large consumer surplus—but cheap. Diamonds are less valuable than water—have a smaller consumer surplus—but are expensive.

CHECKPOINT 11.3

3 Use marginal utility theory to explain the paradox of value: why water is vital but cheap while diamonds are relatively useless but expensive.

Practice Problem 11.3

1. In a year, Tony rents 500 videos at $3 each and buys 10,000 gallons of tap water, for which he pays $50. Tony is maximizing total utility. If Tony's marginal utility from water is 0.5 unit per gallon, what is his marginal utility from a video rental? Which good is the more valuable to Tony: water or videos? Why?

Exercise 11.3

1. Which good is more valuable to you: water or your economics text?

Solution to Practice Problem 11.3

1. Marginal utility of a video rental ÷ $3 = Marginal utility of a gallon of water ÷ 0.5¢. So the marginal utility of a video rental is 600 times the marginal utility of a gallon of water, which is 600 × 0.5 or 300 units. Most likely, the total utility from water is larger, so Tony values water more than videos.

Maximizing Utility in Beverage Markets

The figure shows how the quantities of bottled water, soda, and beer consumed in the United States changed during the 1990s. You can understand these changes by using marginal utility theory.

To maximize total utility, people make the marginal utility per dollar equal for all goods. So people buy bottled water, soda, and beer in quantities that make the marginal utilities per dollar from them equal.

The price of bottled water fell as more firms entered the market and increased supply. The price of soda also fell.

The true price of beer, or opportunity cost of beer, increased. The money price of beer didn't change much, but improved policing and stiffer penalties for drunk driving increased the cost of drinking beer.

These changes in what people drink are the responses to changes in prices and the attempt to make the marginal utilities per dollar equal for them.

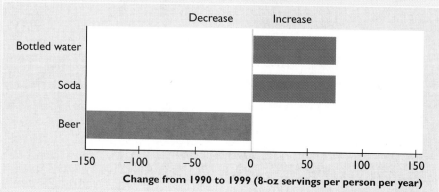

Change from 1990 to 1999 (8-oz servings per person per year)

SOURCE OF DATA: *Detroit News.*

REALITY CHECK

Marginal Utility in YOUR Life

You're probably thinking that this marginal utility stuff is pretty unreal! You know that you don't go around the mall with a marginal utility calculator in hand. You just buy what you can afford and want, and that's all there is to it.

Well, marginal utility theory isn't about *how* people make their choices. It's about *what* choices people make. It's a tool that enables economists to explain people's choices.

You see lots of examples of people juggling their purchases to equalize marginal utilities per dollar. The next time you're in a supermarket, note the items that someone had second thoughts about and stuffed into the magazine rack by the checkout. When the crunch came to pay, the marginal utility per dollar was just not high enough.

You'll even find yourself actually using marginal utility to make your own decisions. It clarifies the options, and it helps to make the value of the alternatives explicit.

CHAPTER CHECKPOINT

Key Points

1 **Calculate and graph a budget line that shows the limits to a person's consumption possibilities.**

- Consumption possibilities and preferences determine consumption choices.
- Consumption possibilities are constrained by the budget and prices. Some combinations of goods are affordable, and some are not affordable.
- The budget line is the boundary between what a person can and cannot afford with a given budget and given prices.
- The slope of the budget line determines the relative price of the good measured on the *x*-axis in terms of the good measured on the *y*-axis.
- A change in one price changes the slope of the budget line. A change in the budget shifts the budget line but does not change its slope.

2 **Explain marginal utility theory and use it to derive a consumer's demand curve.**

- Total utility is maximized when the entire budget is spent and marginal utility per dollar is equal for all goods.
- If the marginal utility per dollar from good *A* exceeds that on good *B*, total utility increases if the quantity purchased of good *A* increases and the quantity purchased of good *B* decreases.
- Marginal utility theory implies the law of demand. That is, other things remaining the same, the higher the price of a good, the smaller is the quantity demanded of that good.

3 **Use marginal utility theory to explain the paradox of value: why water is vital but cheap while diamonds are relatively useless but expensive.**

- When consumers maximize total utility, they use resources efficiently.
- Marginal utility theory resolves the paradox of value.
- When we talk loosely about value, we are thinking of *total* utility or consumer surplus. But price is related to *marginal* utility.
- Water, which we consume in large amounts, has a high total utility and a large consumer surplus but a low price and low marginal utility.
- Diamonds, which we consume in small amounts, have a low total utility and a small consumer surplus but a high price and a high marginal utility.

Key Terms

Budget line, 266
Diminishing marginal utility, 273
Marginal utility, 273

Marginal utility per dollar, 277
Relative price, 270
Total utility, 272

Utility, 272
Utility-maximizing rule, 276

Exercises

1. Amy has $12 a week to spend on coffee and soda. The price of coffee is $2 a cup, and the price of soda is $1 a can.
   a. Make a table that shows Amy's consumption possibilities.
   b. Draw a graph of Amy's budget line.
   c. Can Amy afford to buy 7 cans of soda and 2 cups of coffee a week?
   d. Can Amy afford to buy 7 cups of coffee and 2 cans of soda a week?
   e. What is the relative price of a cup of coffee?
   f. What is the relative price of a can of soda?

2. Amy, in exercise 1, has $12 a week to spend on coffee and soda and the price of soda remains at $1 a can but the price of coffee rises to $3 a cup.
   a. Make a table that shows Amy's new consumption possibilities.
   b. Draw Amy's new budget line on the graph that you made to answer exercise 1b.
   c. If Amy buys 6 cans of soda, what is the maximum number of cups of coffee she can buy in a month?
   d. What now is the relative price of coffee?
   e. Has the relative price of soda changed? If so, has it increased or decreased?

3. Table 1 shows Ben's utility from orange juice.
   a. Calculate the values of A, B, C, and D.
   b. Why, given these numbers, would Ben ever want to buy more than one carton of orange juice a day?
   c. Why, given these numbers, would Ben ever want to buy no orange juice?
   d. Does the principle of diminishing marginal utility apply to Ben's consumption of orange juice? How do you know?

4. Use the numbers in Table 11.1 on p. 273 to make graphs of Tina's total utility and marginal utility from chewing gum.
   a. Compare Tina's marginal utility from chewing gum with that from bottled water. Which diminishes more rapidly?
   b. The price of gum is 25¢ a pack and the price of water is 50¢ a bottle. If Tina is spending all her budget by consuming 4 packs of gum and 4 bottles of water, is she maximizing total utility?
   c. If in the situation described in part b, Tina is not maximizing total utility, can she increase her total utility by consuming more water or more gum? Explain your answer.

5. Tina is maximizing her utility. If her budget increases, will she buy more bottled water or more chewing gum? Why? (Hint: Use her marginal utility for bottled water and chewing gum in Table 11.1 on p. 273.)

6. Tina is maximizing her utility. If her budget increases and at the same time, the price of a bottle of water rises, what can you say about how Tina's consumption of bottled water and chewing gum will change? (Hint: Use her marginal utility for bottled water and chewing gum in Table 11.1 on p. 273.)

7. Table 2 shows Martha's total utility from cake and pasta.
   a. Calculate Martha's total utility when she buys 3 cakes and 2 dishes of pasta a week.

TABLE 1

Orange juice (cartons per day)	Total utility	Marginal utility
0	0	
		7
1	7	
		5
2	A	
		B
3	15	
		2
4	C	
		D
5	18	

b. Calculate Martha's marginal utility from the third cake in a week.

c. If the price of a cake is $4, calculate the marginal utility per dollar from cake when Martha buys 3 cakes a week.

d. Calculate Martha's marginal utility from the second dish of pasta in a week.

e. If the price of pasta is $8 a dish, calculate the marginal utility per dollar from pasta when Martha buys 2 dishes a week.

f. When the price of a cake is $4, the price of pasta is $8 a dish, and Martha has $24 a week to spend, she buys 2 cakes and 2 dishes of pasta. Does she maximize her total utility? Explain your answer.

TABLE 2

Cake		Pasta	
Quantity per week	Total utility	Dishes per week	Total utility
0	0	0	0
1	10	1	20
2	18	2	36
3	25	3	48
4	31	4	56
5	36	5	60
6	40	6	60

8. Use the information in Table 2 to answer the following questions:

   a. When the price of a cake is $4, Martha has $24 to spend, and the price of pasta falls from $8 to $4 a dish, what quantities of cake and pasta does Martha buy?

   b. What are two points on Martha's demand curve for pasta?

   c. Is Martha's demand for pasta elastic or inelastic?

   d. When the price of a cake is $4, the price of pasta is $8 a dish, and Martha's available income increases to $40 a week, what quantities of cake and pasta does Martha buy?

9. Tim buys 2 pizzas and sees 1 movie a week when he has $16 to spend, a movie ticket is $8, and the price of a pizza is $4.

   a. What is the relative price of a movie ticket?

   b. If the price of a movie ticket falls to $4,

      i. How will Tim's consumption possibilities change? Explain.

      ii. Will Tim change what he buys with his $16? Explain your answer.

      iii. How will Tim's consumption of pizza change?

10. Every day, Josie buys 2 cups of coffee and 1 sandwich for lunch. The price of a cup of coffee is $2 and the price of a sandwich is $5. Josie's choice of lunch maximizes her total utility, and she spends only $9 on lunch.

    a. Compare Josie's marginal utility from coffee with her marginal utility from the sandwich.

    b. Is Josie's allocation of her $9 efficient? Explain.

11. Adrienne loves riding her horse every weekend. She pays $500 a month to the stable to care for her horse, but she tells a friend that she thinks she's getting a real bargain and would willingly pay twice the price for the great service she gets from the stable and the fun she gets every weekend. Adrienne's only other significant expense is her apartment rent, which is $1,000 a month. Unlike the stable, she doesn't think the deal she gets from her landlord is all that good, and she is on the verge of looking for something better for the same price.

    a. From which does Adrienne get the greater marginal utility: her horse or her apartment?

    b. From which does Adrienne get the greater total utility: her horse or her apartment?

    c. How does Adrienne's consumption of horse-riding and housing explain the paradox of value?

Critical Thinking

12. Some students buy a college meal plan, and some pay for each meal as they consume it.
    a. Why would a student decide to buy a meal plan rather than pay for each meal as it is consumed? Explain using marginal utility theory.
    b. What does marginal utility theory predict about the demand for lunches by the two groups?
    c. Who gets the greater marginal utility from lunch: someone who buys a meal plan or someone who pays for each lunch as it is consumed?
    d. Suppose the price of a lunch increases and all other relevant factors remain unchanged. What does marginal utility theory predict will happen to the quantity of lunches demanded by each group?

13. In a bid to attract new customers to public transportation, the Maryland Transit Authority had a free-ride day.
    a. Why would some people who don't normally use public transportation use it on a free-ride day?
    b. Why would some people who don't normally use public transportation still not use it on a free-ride day? (Hint: Think about the opportunity cost of a trip.)
    c. What does marginal utility theory predict about the demand for public transportation on the day after the free-ride day? Do you think the theory is correct?

14. Why do you think the percentage of income spent on food has decreased while the percentage of income spent on cars has increased during the past 50 years? Use the marginal utility theory to explain these trends.

 ## Web Exercises

Use the links on MyEconLab to work the following exercises.

15. Visit the Maryland Transit Authority Web site and get information about fares and passes.
    a. Show the effects of the different ticket options on the consumer's consumption possibilities.
    b. How would a person decide whether to pay for each trip, to buy a day pass, or to buy a pass for a longer period? Use marginal utility theory to answer this question.
    c. How do you think the number of riders would change if the price of a single trip fell and the price of a day pass increased?

16. Work this exercise with a friend or in a group. Visit Dick's Sporting Goods.
    a. Imagine that each of you has been given a $500 voucher to spend only at Dick's Sporting Goods. Select the items that maximize your total utility.
    b. Compare the choices that each member of your group has made and use the ideas of marginal utility theory to explain the differences.
    c. How would your choices have changed if your voucher had been worth $1,000 and all the prices were doubled? Explain with reference to your budget line.

17. Visit Shopper.com. Look up the prices at the different stores listed on the Web site of an iPod that excites you. If you were going to buy this item, from which store would you buy it and why? Explain your answer using the ideas of marginal utility theory.

You are going to discover a neat idea—that of drawing a map of a person's preferences. A preference map is based on the intuitively appealing assumption that people can sort all the possible combinations of goods into three groups: preferred, not preferred, and indifferent. To make this idea concrete, let's ask Tina to tell us how she ranks combinations of bottled water and chewing gum.

■ An Indifference Curve

Figure A11.1(a) shows part of Tina's answer. She tells us that she currently consumes 2 bottles of water and 4 packs of gum a day at point *C*. She then lists all the combinations of bottled water and chewing gum that she says are as acceptable to her as her current consumption. When we plot these combinations of water and gum, we get the green curve. This curve is the key element in a map of preferences and is called an indifference curve.

An **indifference curve** is a line that shows combinations of goods among which a consumer is *indifferent*. The indifference curve in Figure A11.1(a) tells us that Tina is just as happy to consume 2 bottles of water and 4 packs of gum a day at point *C* as to consume the combination of water and gum at any other point along the indifference curve. Tina also says that she prefers all the combinations of bottled water and gum above the indifference curve—the yellow area—to those on the indifference curve. These combinations contain more water, more gum, or more of both. She also prefers any combination on the indifference curve to any

Indifference curve
A line that shows combinations of goods among which a consumer is *indifferent*.

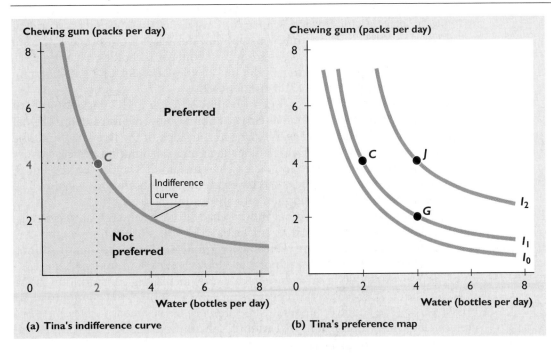

(a) Tina's indifference curve

(b) Tina's preference map

In part (a), Tina consumes 2 bottles of water and 4 packs of chewing gum a day at point *C*. She is indifferent between all the points on the green indifference curve. She prefers any point above the indifference curve (yellow area) to any point on it, and she prefers any point on the indifference curve to any point below it (gray area).

Part (b) shows three indifference curves of Tina's preference map. She prefers point *J* to point *C* or *G*, so she prefers any point on I_2 to any point on I_1.

combination in the gray area below the indifference curve. These combinations contain less water, less gum, or less of both.

The indifference curve in Figure A11.1(a) is just one of a whole family of such curves. This indifference curve appears again in Figure A11.1(b) labeled I_1. The curves labeled I_0 and I_2 are two other indifference curves. Tina prefers any point on indifference curve I_2, such as point J, to any point on indifference curve I_1, such as points C or G. She prefers any point on I_1 to any point on I_0. We refer to I_2 as being a higher indifference curve than I_1 and to I_1 as being higher than I_0.

A preference map is a series of indifference curves that resemble the contour lines on a map. By looking at the shape of the contour lines on a map, we can draw conclusions about the terrain. Similarly, by looking at the shape of the indifference curves, we can draw conclusions about a person's preferences.

■ Marginal Rate of Substitution

Marginal rate of substitution
The rate at which a person will give up good y (the good measured on the y-axis) to get more of good x (the good measured on the x-axis) and at the same time remain on the same indifference curve.

The concept of the marginal rate of substitution is the key to "reading" a preference map. The **marginal rate of substitution** (*MRS*) is the rate at which a person will give up good y (the good measured on the y-axis) to get more of good x (the good measured on the x-axis) and at the same time remain indifferent (remain on the same indifference curve). The marginal rate of substitution is measured by the magnitude of the slope of an indifference curve.

If the indifference curve is *steep*, the marginal rate of substitution is *high*. The person is willing to give up a large quantity of good y to get a small quantity of good x while remaining indifferent. But if the indifference curve is *flat*, the marginal rate of substitution is *low*. The person is willing to give up only a small amount of good y to get a large amount of good x to remain indifferent.

Figure A11.2 shows you how to calculate the marginal rate of substitution. Suppose that Tina consumes 2 bottles of water and 4 packs of gum at point C on indifference curve I_1. We calculate her marginal rate of substitution by measuring the magnitude of the slope of the indifference curve at point C. To measure this magnitude, place a straight line against, or tangent to, the indifference curve at point C. Along that line, as gum consumption decreases from 8 packs to zero packs, water consumption increases from zero bottles to 4 bottles. So at point C, Tina is willing to give up 8 packs of gum for 4 bottles of water, or 2 packs of gum per bottle. Her marginal rate of substitution is 2.

Now suppose that Tina consumes 4 bottles of water and 2 packs of gum at point G. The slope of the indifference curve at point G now measures her marginal rate of substitution. That slope is the same as the slope of the line tangent to the indifference curve at point G. Here, as chewing gum consumption decreases from 4 packs to zero, water consumption increases from zero to 8 bottles. So at point G, Tina is willing to give up 4 packs of chewing gum for 8 bottles of water, or 1/2 pack of gum per bottle. Her marginal rate of substitution is 1/2.

Diminishing marginal rate of substitution
The general tendency for the marginal rate of substitution to decrease as the consumer moves down along the indifference curve, increasing consumption of the good measured on the x-axis and decreasing consumption of the good measured on the y-axis.

As Tina moves down along her indifference curve, her marginal rate of substitution diminishes. Diminishing marginal rate of substitution is the key assumption of consumer theory. **Diminishing marginal rate of substitution** is the general tendency for the marginal rate of substitution to diminish as the consumer moves down along an indifference curve, increasing consumption of the good measured on the x-axis and decreasing consumption of the good measured on the y-axis. The shape of a person's indifference curves incorporates the principle of the diminishing marginal rate of substitution because the curves are bowed toward the origin.

■ FIGURE A11.2
The Marginal Rate of Substitution

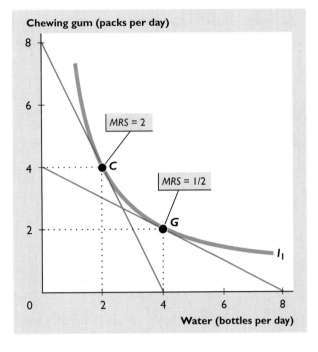

The magnitude of the slope of an indifference curve is called the marginal rate of substitution (*MRS*).

The red line at point *C* tells us that Tina is willing to give up 8 packs of gum to consume 4 bottles of water. Her marginal rate of substitution at point *C* is 8 divided by 4, which equals 2.

The red line at point *G* tells us that Tina is willing to give up 4 packs of gum to get 8 bottles of water. Her marginal rate of substitution at point *G* is 4 divided by 8, which equals 1/2.

■ Consumer Equilibrium

The consumer's goal is to buy the affordable quantities of goods that make the consumer as well off as possible. The indifference curves describe the consumer's preferences, and they tell us that the higher the indifference curve, the better off is the consumer. So the consumer's goal can be restated as being to allocate his or her budget in such a way as to get onto the highest attainable indifference curve.

The consumer's budget and the prices of the goods limit the consumer's choices. The budget line illustrated in Figure 11.1 (p. 266) summarizes the limits on the consumer's choice. We combine the indifference curves of Figure A11.1(b) with the budget line of Figure 11.1 to work out the consumer's choice and find the consumer equilibrium.

Figure A11.3 shows Tina's budget line from Figure 11.1 and her indifference curves from Figure A11.1(b). Tina's best affordable point is 2 bottles of water and 4 packs of gum—at point *C*. Here, Tina

- Is on her budget line
- Is on her highest attainable indifference curve
- Has a marginal rate of substitution between water and gum equal to the relative price of water and gum.

For every point inside the budget line, such as point *L*, there are points *on* the budget line that Tina prefers. For example, she prefers any point on the budget line between *F* and *H* to point *L*. So she chooses a point on the budget line.

FIGURE A11.3
Consumer Equilibrium

Tina's best affordable point is *C*. At that point, she is on her budget line and also on the highest attainable indifference curve.

At a point such as *H*, Tina is willing to give up more bottled water in exchange for chewing gum than she has to. She can move to point *L*, which is just as good as point *H*, and have some unspent budget. She can spend that budget and move to *C*, a point that she prefers to point *L*.

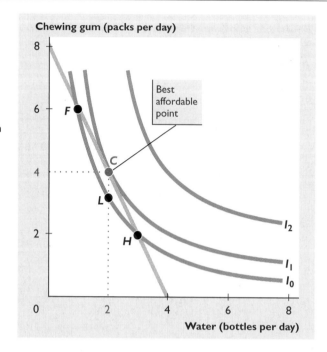

Every point on the budget line lies on an indifference curve. For example, point *H* lies on the indifference curve I_0. At point *H*, Tina's marginal rate of substitution (the magnitude of the slope of the indifference curve I_0) is less than the relative price (the magnitude of the slope of the budget line). Tina is willing to give up more bottled water in exchange for chewing gum than the budget line says she must. So she moves along her budget line from *H* toward *C*. As she does so, she passes through a number of indifference curves (not shown in the figure) located between indifference curves I_0 and I_1. All of these indifference curves are higher than I_0, so Tina prefers any point on them to point *H*. But when Tina gets to point *C*, she is on the highest attainable indifference curve. If she keeps moving along the budget line, she starts to encounter indifference curves that are lower than I_1. So Tina chooses point *C*—her best affordable point.

At the chosen point, the marginal rate of substitution (the magnitude of the slope of the indifference curve) equals the relative price (the magnitude of the slope of the budget line).

We can now use this model of consumer choice to predict the effect of a change in the price of water on the quantity of water demanded. That is, we can use this model to generate the demand curve for bottled water.

■ Deriving the Demand Curve

To derive Tina's demand curve for bottled water, we change the price of water, shift the budget line, and work out the new best affordable point. Figure A11.4(a) shows the change in the budget line and the change in consumer equilibrium when the price of water falls from $1 a bottle to 50¢ a bottle.

Initially, when the price of water is $1 a bottle, Tina consumes at point *C* in part (a). When the price of a bottle of water falls from $1 to 50¢, her budget line rotates outward and she can now get onto a higher indifference curve. Her best affordable point is now point *K*. Tina increases the quantity of water she buys from 2 to 4 bottles a day. She continues to buy 4 packs of gum a day.

Figure A11.4(b) shows Tina's demand curve for bottled water. When the price of water is $1 a bottle, she buys 2 bottles a day, at point *A*. When the price of water falls to 50¢ a bottle, she buys 4 bottles a day, at point *B*. Tina's demand curve traces out her best affordable quantity of water as the price of a bottle of water varies.

■ **FIGURE A11.4**

Deriving Tina's Demand Curve

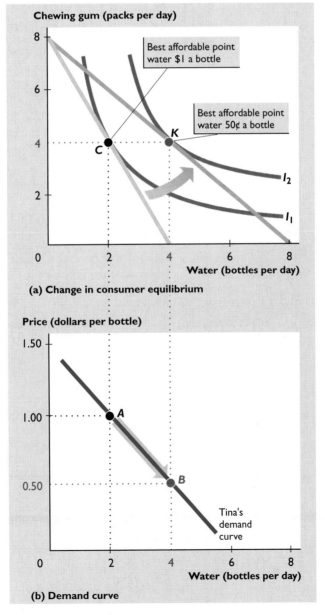

(a) **Change in consumer equilibrium**

(b) **Demand curve**

In part (a), Tina initially consumes at point *C*. When the price of water falls from $1 to 50¢ a bottle, she consumes at point *K*.

In part (b), when the price of water falls from $1 to 50¢ a bottle, Tina moves along her demand curve for bottled water from point *A* to point *B*.

Exercises

FIGURE I

FIGURE 2

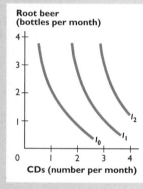

1. Sara has a budget of $12 a week. Popcorn costs $3 a bag, and cola costs $3 a can. Figure 1 illustrates Sara's preferences.
   a. What is the relative price of cola in terms of popcorn?
   b. What is the opportunity cost of a can of cola?
   c. Draw a graph of Sara's budget line with cola on the *x*-axis.
   d. What are the quantities of popcorn and cola that Sara buys?
   e. What is Sara's marginal rate of substitution of popcorn for cola at the point at which she consumes?

2. Suppose that in the situation described in exercise 1, the price of cola falls to $1.50 a can and the price of popcorn and Sara's budget remain constant.
   a. Find the new quantities of cola and popcorn that Sara buys.
   b. Find two points on Sara's demand curve for cola.

3. Marc has a budget of $20 a month. Root beer costs $5 a bottle, and CDs cost $10 each. Figure 2 illustrates his preferences.
   a. What is the relative price of root beer in terms of CDs?
   b. What is the opportunity cost of a bottle of root beer?
   c. Draw a graph of Marc's budget line with CDs on the *x*-axis.
   d. What quantities of root beer and CDs does Marc buy?
   e. Calculate Marc's marginal rate of substitution of CDs for root beer at the point at which he consumes.

4. Now suppose that in the situation described in exercise 3, the price of a CD falls to $5 and the price of root beer and Marc's budget remain constant.
   a. Find the new quantities of root beer and CDs that Marc buys.
   b. Find two points on Marc's demand curve for CDs.

5. In most states, there is no sales tax on food. Some people say that a consumption tax, a tax that is paid on all goods and services, would be better. If we replaced the sales tax with a consumption tax,
   a. What would happen to the relative price of food and haircuts?
   b. What would happen to the budget line showing the quantities of food and haircuts you can afford to buy?
   c. How would you change your purchases of food and haircuts?
   d. Which type of tax is best for the consumer and why?

6. Jim spends all his income on apartment rent, food, clothing, and vacations. He gets a pay raise from $3,000 a month to $4,000 a month. At the same time, airfares and other vacation-related costs increase by 50 percent.
   a. How do you think Jim will change his spending pattern as a result of the changes in his income and prices?
   b. Can you say whether Jim is better off or worse off in his new situation?
   c. If all prices rise by 50 percent, how does Jim change his purchases? Can you now say whether he is better off or worse off?
   d. Show in a graph the changes in Jim's choices that the change in income and changes in prices induce.

Production and Cost

CHAPTER CHECKLIST

When you have completed your study of this chapter, you will be able to

1 Explain how economists measure a firm's cost of production and profit.

2 Explain the relationship between a firm's output and labor employed in the short run.

3 Explain the relationship between a firm's output and costs in the short run.

4 Derive and explain a firm's long-run average cost curve.

Samantha is beaming. Her business plan impressed the bank, she got the loan she needed, and Sam's Smoothies has just ended its first year of operations on a high. But Samantha made some tough decisions to keep her business efficient and profitable. She was careful to hire exactly the amount of labor she needed and operate the right number of blenders and other equipment.

In this chapter, you're going to see the principles that guided Samantha to make decisions that minimized her production cost.

You will use what you learn in this chapter again and again in the three chapters that follow, so it is very important that you thoroughly understand the content of this chapter before moving forward to Chapter 13.

12.1 ECONOMIC COST AND PROFIT

The 20 million firms in the United States differ in size and in what they produce. But they all perform the same basic economic function: They hire factors of production and organize them to produce and sell goods and services. To understand the behavior of a firm, we need to know its goals.

■ The Firm's Goal

If you asked a group of entrepreneurs what they are trying to achieve, you would get many different answers. Some would talk about making a high-quality product, others about business growth, others about market share, and others about job satisfaction of the work force. All of these goals might be pursued, but they are not the fundamental goal. They are a means to a deeper goal.

The firm's goal is to *maximize profit*. A firm that does not seek to maximize profit is either eliminated or bought by firms that *do* seek to achieve that goal. To calculate a firm's profit, we must determine its total revenue and total cost. Economists have a special way of defining and measuring cost and profit, which we'll explain and illustrate by looking at Sam's Smoothies, a firm that is owned and operated by Samantha.

■ Accounting Cost and Profit

In 2004, Sam's Smoothies' total revenue from the sale of smoothies was $150,000. The firm paid $20,000 for fruit, yogurt, and honey; $22,000 in wages for the labor it hired; and $3,000 in interest to the bank. These expenses totaled $45,000.

Sam's accountant said that the depreciation of the firm's blenders, refrigerators, and shop during 2004 was $10,000. Depreciation is the fall in the value of the firm's capital, and accountants calculate it by using the Internal Revenue Service's rules, which are based on standards set by the Financial Accounting Standards Board. So the accountant reported Sam's Smoothies' total cost for 2004 as $55,000 and the firm's profit as $95,000—$150,000 of total revenue minus $55,000 of total costs.

Sam's accountant measures cost and profit to ensure that the firm pays the correct amount of income tax and to show the bank how Sam's has used its bank loan. Economists have a different purpose: to predict the decisions that a firm makes to maximize its profit. These decisions respond to *opportunity cost* and *economic profit*.

■ Opportunity Cost

To produce its output, a firm employs factors of production: land, labor, capital, and entrepreneurship. Another firm could have used these same resources to produce other goods or services. In Chapter 3 (pp. 68–70), resources can be used to produce either bottled water or CDs, so the opportunity cost of producing a bottle of water is the number of CDs forgone. Pilots who fly passengers for United Airlines can't at the same time fly freight for FedEx. Construction workers who are building an office high-rise can't simultaneously build apartments. A communications satellite operating at peak capacity can carry television signals or e-mail messages but not both at the same time. A journalist writing for the *New York Times* can't at the same time create Web news reports for CNN. And Samantha can't simultaneously run her smoothies business and a flower shop.

The highest-valued alternative forgone is the opportunity cost of a firm's production. From the viewpoint of the firm, this opportunity cost is the amount that the firm must pay the owners of the factors of production it employs to attract them from their best alternative use. So a firm's opportunity cost of production is the cost of the factors of production it employs.

To determine these costs, let's return to Sam's and look at the opportunity cost of producing smoothies.

Explicit Costs and Implicit Costs

The amount that a firm pays to attract resources from their best alternative use is either an explicit cost or an implicit cost. A cost paid in money is an **explicit cost**. Because the amount spent could have been spent on something else, an explicit cost is an opportunity cost. The wages that Samantha pays labor, the interest she pays the bank, and her expenditure on fruit, yogurt, and honey are explicit costs.

A firm incurs an **implicit cost** when it uses a factor of production but does not make a direct money payment for its use. The two categories of implicit cost are economic depreciation and the cost of the resources of the firm's owner.

Economic depreciation is the opportunity cost of the firm using capital that it owns. It is measured as the change in the *market value* of capital—the market price of the capital at the beginning of a period minus its market price at the end of a period. Suppose that Samantha could have sold her blenders, refrigerators, and shop on December 31, 2003, for $250,000. If she can sell the same capital on December 31, 2004, for $246,000, her economic depreciation during 2004 is $4,000. This is the opportunity cost of using her capital during 2004, not the $10,000 depreciation calculated by Sam's accountant.

Interest is another cost of capital. When the firm's owner provides the funds used to buy capital, the opportunity cost of those funds is the interest income forgone by not using them in the best alternative way. If Sam loaned her firm funds that could have earned her $1,000 in interest, this amount is an implicit cost of producing smoothies.

When a firm's owner supplies labor, the opportunity cost of the owner's time spent working for the firm is the wage income forgone by not working in the best alternative job. For example, instead of working at her next best job that pays $34,000 a year, Sam supplies labor to her smoothies business. This implicit cost of $34,000 is part of the opportunity cost of producing smoothies.

Finally, a firm's owner often supplies entrepreneurship, the factor of production that organizes the business and bears the risk of running it. The return to entrepreneurship is **normal profit**. Normal profit is part of a firm's opportunity cost because it is the cost of a forgone alternative—running another firm. Instead of running Sam's Smoothies, Sam could earn $16,000 a year running a flower shop. This amount is an implicit cost of production at Sam's Smoothies.

■ Economic Profit

A firm's **economic profit** equals total revenue minus total cost. Total revenue is the amount received from the sale of the product. It is the price of the output multiplied by the quantity sold. Total cost is the sum of the explicit costs and implicit costs and is the opportunity cost of production.

Explicit cost
A cost paid in money.

Implicit cost
An opportunity cost incurred by a firm when it uses a factor of production for which it does not make a direct money payment.

Economic depreciation
An opportunity cost of a firm using capital that it owns—measured as the change in the *market value* of capital over a given period.

Normal profit
The return to entrepreneurship. Normal profit is part of a firm's opportunity cost because it is the cost of not running another firm.

Economic profit
A firm's total revenue minus total cost.

■ **TABLE 12.1**

Economic Accounting

Item		
Total Revenue		**$150,000**
Explicit Costs		
Cost of fruit, yogurt, and honey	$20,000	
Wages	$22,000	
Interest	$3,000	
Implicit Costs		
Samantha's forgone wages	$34,000	
Samantha's forgone interest	$1,000	
Economic depreciation	$4,000	
Normal profit	$16,000	
Opportunity Cost		**$100,000**
Economic Profit		**$50,000**

Because one of the firm's implicit costs is *normal profit*, the return to the entrepreneur equals normal profit plus economic profit. If a firm incurs an economic loss, the entrepreneur receives less than normal profit.

Table 12.1 summarizes the economic cost concepts, and Figure 12.1 compares the economic view and the accounting view of cost and profit. The total revenue received by Sam's Smoothies is $150,000; the opportunity cost of the resources that Sam uses is $100,000; and Sam's economic profit is $50,000.

■ **FIGURE 12.1**

Two Views of Cost and Profit

Economists measure economic profit as total revenue minus opportunity cost. Opportunity cost includes explicit costs and implicit costs. Normal profit is an implicit cost. Accountants measure profit as total revenue minus explicit costs—costs paid in money—and depreciation.

CHECKPOINT 12.1

1 Explain how economists measure a firm's cost of production and profit.

Practice Problem 12.1

1. Lee is a computer programmer who earned $35,000 in 2003. But Lee loves water sports, and in 2004, he opened a body board manufacturing business. At the end of the first year of operation, he submitted the following information to his accountant:
    i.   He stopped renting out his cottage for $3,500 a year and used it as his factory. The market value of the cottage increased from $70,000 to $71,000.
    ii. He spent $50,000 on materials, phone, utilities, etc.
    iii. He leased machines for $10,000 a year.
    iv. He paid $15,000 in wages.
    v.   He used $10,000 from his savings account, which earns 5 percent a year interest.
    vi. He borrowed $40,000 at 10 percent a year from the bank.
    vii. He sold $160,000 worth of body boards.
    viii. Normal profit is $25,000 a year.

    a. Calculate Lee's explicit costs and implicit costs.
    b. Calculate Lee's economic profit.
    c. Lee's accountant recorded the depreciation on Lee's cottage during 2004 as $7,000. What did the accountant say Lee's profit or loss was?

Exercise 12.1

1. In 2003, Toni taught music and earned $20,000. She also earned $4,000 by renting out her basement. On January 1, 2004, she quit teaching, stopped renting out her basement, and began to use it as the office for her new Web site design business. She took $2,000 from her savings account to buy a computer. During 2004, she paid $1,500 for the lease of a Web server and $1,750 for high-speed Internet service. She received a total revenue from Web site designing of $45,000 and earned interest at 5 percent a year on her savings account balance. Normal profit is $55,000 a year. At the end of 2004, Toni could have sold her computer for $500.
    a. Calculate Toni's explicit costs and implicit costs in 2004.
    b. Calculate Toni's economic profit in 2004.

Solution to Practice Problem 12.1

1a. Explicit costs are costs paid with money: items (ii), (iii), (iv), and (vi). Explicit costs are $50,000 + $10,000 + $15,000 + $4,000, or $79,000. Implicit costs are the wages forgone and items (i), (v), and (viii) minus the increase in the market value of the cottage. That is, implicit costs are $35,000 + $3,500 + $500 + $25,000 − $1,000, or $63,000.

1b. Economic profit equals total revenue minus total cost. Total cost is the sum of explicit costs plus implicit costs: $79,000 + $63,000, or $142,000. So Lee's economic profit is $160,000 − $142,000, or $18,000.

1c. The accountant measures Lee's profit as total revenue minus explicit costs minus depreciation: $160,000 − $79,000 − $7,000, or $74,000.

SHORT RUN AND LONG RUN

The main goal of this chapter is to explore the influences on a firm's cost. The key influence on cost is the quantity of output that the firm produces per period. The greater the output rate, the higher is the total cost of production. But the effect of a change in production on cost depends on how soon the firm wants to act. A firm that plans to change its output rate tomorrow has fewer options than does a firm that plans ahead and intends to change its production six months from now.

To study the relationship between a firm's output decision and its costs, we distinguish between two decision time frames:

- The short run
- The long run

The Short Run: Fixed Plant

Short run
The time frame in which the quantities of some resources are fixed. In the short run, a firm can usually change the quantity of labor it uses but not its technology and quantity of capital.

The **short run** is the time frame in which the quantities of some resources are fixed. For most firms, the fixed resources are the firm's technology and capital—its equipment and buildings. The management organization is also fixed in the short run. The fixed resources that a firm uses are its *fixed factors of production* and the resources that it can vary are its *variable factors of production*. The collection of fixed resources is the firm's *plant*. So in the short run, a firm's plant is fixed.

Sam's Smoothies' plant is its blenders, refrigerators, and shop. Sam's cannot change these inputs in the short run. An electric power utility can't change the number of generators it uses in the short run. An airport can't change the number of runways, terminal buildings, and traffic control facilities in the short run.

To increase output in the short run, a firm must increase the quantity of variable factors it uses. Labor is usually the variable factor of production. To produce more smoothies, Sam must hire more labor. Similarly, to increase the production of electricity, a utility must hire more engineers and run its generators for longer hours. To increase the volume of traffic it handles, an airport must hire more check-in clerks, cargo handlers, and air-traffic controllers.

Short-run decisions are easily reversed. A firm can increase or decrease output in the short run by increasing or decreasing the number of labor hours it hires.

The Long Run: Variable Plant

Long run
The time frame in which the quantities of *all* resources can be varied.

The **long run** is the time frame in which the quantities of *all* resources can be varied. That is, the long run is a period in which the firm can change its *plant*.

To increase output in the long run, a firm can increase the size of its plant. Sam's Smoothies can install more blenders and refrigerators and increase the size of its shop. An electric power utility can install more generators. And an airport can build more runways, terminals, and traffic-control facilities.

Long-run decisions are *not* easily reversed. Once a firm buys a new plant, its resale value is usually much less than the amount the firm paid for it. The difference between the cost of the plant and its resale value is a *sunk cost*. A sunk cost is irrelevant to the firm's decisions (see Chapter 1, p. 14). The only costs that influence the firm's decisions are the short-run cost of changing its labor inputs and the long-run cost of changing its plant.

We're going to study costs in the short run and the long run. We begin with the short run and describe the limits to the firm's production possibilities.

12.2 SHORT-RUN PRODUCTION

To increase the output of a fixed plant, a firm must increase the quantity of labor it employs. We describe the relationship between output and the quantity of labor employed by using three related concepts:

- Total product
- Marginal product
- Average product

■ Total Product

Total product (*TP*) is the total quantity of a good produced in a given period. Total product is an output *rate*—the number of units produced per unit of time (for example, per hour, day, or week). Total product increases as the quantity of labor employed increases, and we illustrate this relationship as a total product schedule and total product curve like those in Figure 12.2. The total product schedule (the table below the graph) lists the maximum quantities of smoothies per hour that Sam can produce with her existing plant at each quantity of labor. Points *A* through *H* on the *TP* curve correspond to the columns in the table.

Total product
The total quantity of a good produced in a given period.

■ FIGURE 12.2
Total Product Schedule and Total Product Curve

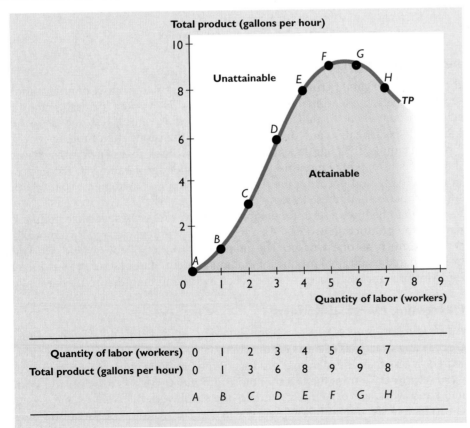

Quantity of labor (workers)	0	1	2	3	4	5	6	7
Total product (gallons per hour)	0	1	3	6	8	9	9	8
	A	*B*	*C*	*D*	*E*	*F*	*G*	*H*

The total product schedule shows how the quantity of smoothies that Sam's can produce changes as the quantity of labor employed changes. In column *C*, Sam's employs 2 workers and can produce 3 gallons of smoothies an hour.

The total product curve, *TP*, graphs the data in the table. Points *A* through *H* on the curve correspond to the columns of the table. The total product curve separates attainable outputs from unattainable outputs. Points below the *TP* curve are inefficient. Points on the *TP* curve are efficient.

Like the *production possibilities frontier* (see Chapter 3, p. 62), the total product curve separates attainable outputs from unattainable outputs. All the points that lie above the curve are unattainable. Points that lie below the curve, in the orange area, are attainable. But they are inefficient: They use more labor than is necessary to produce a given output. Only the points *on* the total product curve are efficient.

■ Marginal Product

Marginal product (*MP*) is the change in total product that results from a one-unit increase in the quantity of labor employed. It tells us the contribution to total product of adding one additional worker. When the quantity of labor increases by more (or less) than one worker, we calculate marginal product as

Marginal product = Change in total product ÷ Change in quantity of labor.

Figure 12.3 shows Sam's Smoothies' marginal product curve, *MP*, and its relationship with the total product curve. You can see that as the quantity of labor increases from 1 to 3 workers, marginal product increases. But as yet more workers are employed, marginal product decreases. When the seventh worker is employed, marginal product is negative.

Notice that the steeper the slope of the total product curve in part (a), the greater is marginal product in part (b). And when the total product curve turns downward in part (a), marginal product is negative in part (b).

The total product curve and marginal product curve in Figure 12.3 incorporate a feature that is shared by all production processes in firms as different as the Ford Motor Company, Jim's Barber Shop, and Sam's Smoothies:

- Increasing marginal returns initially
- Decreasing marginal returns eventually

Increasing Marginal Returns

Increasing marginal returns occur when the marginal product of an additional worker exceeds the marginal product of the previous worker. Increasing marginal returns occur when a small number of workers are employed and arise from increased specialization and division of labor in the production process.

For example, if Samantha employs just one worker, that person must learn all the aspects of making smoothies: running the blender, cleaning it, fixing breakdowns, buying and checking the fruit, and serving the customers. That one person must perform all these tasks.

If Samantha hires a second person, the two workers can specialize in different parts of the production process. As a result, two workers can produce more than twice as much as one worker. The marginal product of the second worker is greater than the marginal product of the first worker. Marginal returns are increasing. Most production processes experience increasing marginal returns initially.

Decreasing Marginal Returns

All production processes eventually reach a point of *decreasing* marginal returns. **Decreasing marginal returns** occur when the marginal product of an additional worker is less than the marginal product of the previous worker. Decreasing marginal returns arise from the fact that more and more workers use the same equipment and work space. As more workers are employed, there is less and less that is productive for the additional worker to do. For example, if Samantha hires a

FIGURE 12.3

Total Product and Marginal Product

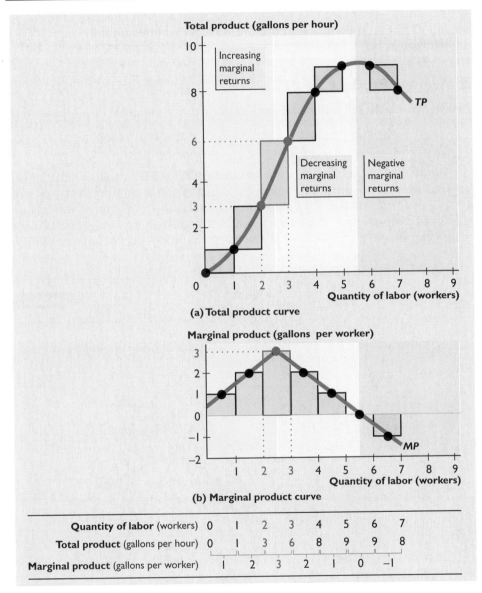

(a) Total product curve

(b) Marginal product curve

The table calculates marginal product, and the orange bars illustrate it. When labor increases from 2 to 3 workers, total product increases from 3 gallons to 6 gallons an hour. So marginal product is the orange bar whose height is 3 gallons (in both parts of the figure).

In part (b), marginal product is graphed midway between the labor inputs to emphasize that it is the result of *changing* inputs. Marginal product increases to a maximum (when 3 workers are employed in this example) and then declines—diminishing marginal product.

Quantity of labor (workers)	0	1	2	3	4	5	6	7
Total product (gallons per hour)	0	1	3	6	8	9	9	8
Marginal product (gallons per worker)		1	2	3	2	1	0	−1

fourth worker, output increases but not by as much as it did when she hired the third worker. In this case, three workers exhaust all the possible gains from specialization and the division of labor. By hiring a fourth worker, Sam's produces more smoothies per hour, but the equipment is being operated closer to its limits. Sometimes the fourth worker has nothing to do because the machines are running without the need for further attention.

Hiring yet more workers continues to increase output but by successively smaller amounts until Samantha hires the sixth worker, at which point total product stops rising. Add a seventh worker, and the workplace is so congested that the workers get in each other's way and total product falls.

Decreasing marginal returns are so pervasive that they qualify for the status of a law: the **law of decreasing returns**, which states that

> **As a firm uses more of a variable input, with a given quantity of fixed inputs, the marginal product of the variable input eventually decreases.**

Average product
Total product divided by the quantity of an input. The average product of labor is total product divided by the quantity of labor employed.

■ Average Product

Average product (*AP*) is the total product per worker employed. It is calculated as

$$\text{Average product} = \text{Total product} \div \text{Quantity of labor.}$$

Another name for average product is *productivity*.

Figure 12.4 shows the average product of labor, *AP*, and the relationship between average product and marginal product. Average product increases from 1 to 3 workers (its maximum value) but then decreases as yet more workers are employed. Notice also that average product is largest when average product and marginal product are equal. That is, the marginal product curve cuts the average

---

■ FIGURE 12.4
Average Product and Marginal Product

The table calculates average product. For example, when the quantity of labor is 3 workers, total product is 6 gallons an hour, so average product is 6 gallons ÷ 3 workers = 2 gallons a worker.

The average product curve is *AP*. When marginal product exceeds average product, average product is increasing. When marginal product is less than average product, average product is decreasing.

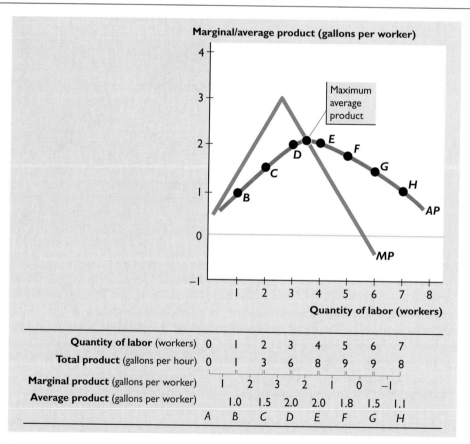

Quantity of labor (workers)	0		1		2		3		4		5		6		7
Total product (gallons per hour)	0		1		3		6		8		9		9		8
Marginal product (gallons per worker)		1		2		3		2		1		0		−1	
Average product (gallons per worker)			1.0		1.5		2.0		2.0		1.8		1.5		1.1
			A		*B*		*C*		*D*		*E*		*F*		*G*	*H*

product curve at the point of maximum average product. For employment levels at which marginal product exceeds average product, the average product curve slopes upward and average product increases as more labor is employed. For employment levels at which marginal product is less than average product, the average product curve slopes downward and average product decreases as more labor is employed.

The relationship between average product and marginal product is a general feature of the relationship between the average value and the marginal value of any variable. Let's look at a familiar example.

REALITY CHECK

Marginal and Average Values in YOUR Life

Jen, a part-time student, takes one course each semester over five semesters. In the first semester, she takes calculus and her grade is a C (2). This grade is her marginal grade. It is also her average grade—her GPA.

In the next semester, Jen takes French and gets a B (3)—her new marginal grade. Because her marginal grade exceeds her average grade, the marginal grade pulls her average up. Her GPA rises to 2.5.

In the third semester, Jen takes economics and gets an A (4). Again her marginal grade exceeds her average, so the marginal grade pulls her average up. Jen's GPA is now 3—the average of 2, 3, and 4.

In the fourth semester, she takes history and gets a B (3). Now her marginal grade equals her average, so her average doesn't change. It remains at 3.

In the fifth semester, Jen takes English and gets a C (2). Because her marginal grade, 2, is below her average of 3, the marginal grade pulls the average down. Her GPA falls.

This everyday relationship between average and marginal grades is similar to the relationship between average and marginal product.

2 **Explain the relationship between a firm's output and labor employed in the short run.**

Practice Problem 12.2

TABLE 1

Labor (students)	Total product (pineapples per day)
0	0
1	100
2	220
3	300
4	360
5	400
6	420
7	430

1. Tom leases a farmer's field and grows pineapples. Tom hires students to pick and pack the pineapples. Table 1 sets out Tom's total product schedule.
   a. Calculate the marginal product of the third student.
   b. Calculate the average product of three students.
   c. Over what numbers of students does marginal product increase?
   d. When marginal product increases, compare average product and marginal product.

Exercise 12.2

TABLE 2

Labor (students)	Total product (houses painted per week)
0	0
1	2
2	5
3	9
4	12
5	14
6	15

1. Lizzie hires students in the summer to paint houses. Table 2 sets out her total product schedule.
   a. Calculate the marginal product of the fourth student.
   b. Calculate the average product of four students.
   c. Over what numbers of students does marginal product decrease?
   d. When marginal product decreases, compare average product and marginal product.

Solution to Practice Problem 12.2

1a. Marginal product of the third student is the change in total product that results from hiring the third student. When Tom hires 2 students, total product is 220 pineapples a day. When Tom hires 3 students, total product is 300 pineapples a day. Marginal product of the third student is the total product of 3 students minus the total product of 2 students, which is 300 pineapples − 220 pineapples a day, or 80 pineapples a day.

1b. Average product equals total product divided by the number of students. When Tom hires 3 students, total product is 300 pineapples a day, so average product is 300 pineapples a day ÷ 3 students, which equals 100 pineapples a day.

1c. Marginal product of the first student is 100 pineapples a day, that of the second student is 120 pineapples a day, and that of the third student is 80 pineapples a day. So marginal product increases when Tom hires the first and second students.

1d. When Tom hires 1 student, marginal product is 100 pineapples per student and average product is 100 pineapples per student. When Tom hires 2 students, marginal product is 120 pineapples per student and average product is 110 pineapples per student. That is, when Tom hires the second student, marginal product exceeds average product.

12.3 SHORT-RUN COST

To produce more output (total product) in the short run, a firm must employ more labor, which means that it must increase its costs. We describe the relationship between output and cost using three cost concepts:

- Total cost
- Marginal cost
- Average cost

◼ Total Cost

A firm's **total cost** (*TC*) is the cost of all the factors of production used by the firm. Total cost divides into two parts: total fixed cost and total variable cost. **Total fixed cost** (*TFC*) is the cost of a firm's fixed factors of production: land, capital, and entrepreneurship. Because in the short run, the quantities of these inputs don't change as output changes, total fixed cost doesn't change as output changes. **Total variable cost** (*TVC*) is the cost of a firm's variable factor of production—labor. To change its output in the short run, a firm must change the quantity of labor it employs, so total variable cost changes as output changes.

Total cost is the sum of total fixed cost and total variable cost. That is,

$$TC = TFC + TVC.$$

Table 12.2 shows Sam's Smoothies' total costs. Sam's fixed costs are $10 an hour regardless of whether it operates or not—*TFC* is $10 an hour. To produce smoothies, Samantha hires labor, which costs $6 an hour. *TVC*, which increases as output increases, equals the number of workers per hour multiplied by $6. For example, to produce 6 gallons an hour, Samantha hires 3 workers, so *TVC* is $18 an hour. *TC* is the sum of *TFC* and *TVC*. So to produce 6 gallons an hour, *TC* is $28. Check the calculation in each row and note that to produce some quantities—2 gallons an hour, for example—Sam hires a worker for only part of the hour.

Total cost
The cost of all the factors of production used by a firm.

Total fixed cost
The cost of the firm's fixed factors of production—the cost of land, capital, and entrepreneurship.

Total variable cost
The cost of the firm's variable factor of production—the cost of labor.

◼ **TABLE 12.2**
Sam's Smoothies' Total Costs

Labor (workers per hour)	Output (gallons per hour)	Total fixed cost	Total variable cost	Total cost
			(dollars per hour)	
0	0	10	0.00	10.00
1.00	1	10	6.00	16.00
1.60	2	10	9.60	19.60
2.00	3	10	12.00	22.00
2.35	4	10	14.10	24.10
2.70	5	10	16.20	26.20
3.00	6	10	18.00	28.00
3.40	7	10	20.40	30.40
4.00	8	10	24.00	34.00
5.00	9	10	30.00	40.00

Figure 12.5 illustrates Sam's total cost curves. The green total fixed cost curve (*TFC*) is horizontal because total fixed cost does not change when output changes. It is a constant at $10 an hour. The purple total variable cost curve (*TVC*) and the blue total cost curve (*TC*) both slope upward because variable cost increases as output increases. The arrows highlight total fixed cost as the vertical distance between the *TVC* and *TC* curve.

Let's now look at Sam's Smoothies' marginal cost.

■ Marginal Cost

In Figure 12.5, total variable cost and total cost increase at a decreasing rate at small levels of output and then begin to increase at an increasing rate as output increases. To understand these patterns in the changes in total cost, we need to use the concept of *marginal cost*.

Marginal cost
The change in total cost that results from a one-unit increase in output.

A firm's **marginal cost** is the change in total cost the results from a one-unit increase in output. Table 12.3 calculates the marginal cost for Sam's Smoothies. When, for example, output increases from 5 gallons to 6 gallons an hour, total cost increases from $26.20 to $28. So the marginal cost of this gallon of smoothie is $1.80 ($28 − $26.20).

Marginal cost tells us how total cost changes as output changes. The final cost concept tells us what it costs, on the average, to produce a unit of output. Let's now look at Sam's average costs.

■ FIGURE 12.5

Total Cost Curves at Sam's Smoothies

Total fixed cost (*TFC*) is constant—it graphs as a horizontal line—and total variable cost (*TVC*) increases as output increases. Total cost (*TC*) also increases as output increases. The vertical distance between the total cost curve and the total variable cost curve is total fixed cost, as illustrated by the two arrows.

■ Average Cost

There are three average cost concepts:

- Average fixed cost
- Average variable cost
- Average total cost

Average fixed cost (*AFC*) is total fixed cost per unit of output. **Average variable cost** (*AVC*) is total variable cost per unit of output. **Average total cost** (*ATC*) is total cost per unit of output. The average cost concepts are calculated from the total cost concepts as follows:

$$TC = TFC + TVC.$$

Divide each total cost term by the quantity produced, *Q*, to give

$$\frac{TC}{Q} = \frac{TFC}{Q} + \frac{TVC}{Q}$$

or

$$ATC = AFC + AVC.$$

Table 12.3 shows these average costs. For example, when output is 3 gallons an hour, average fixed cost is ($10 ÷ 3), which equals $3.33; average variable cost is ($12 ÷ 3), which equals $4.00; and average total cost is ($22 ÷ 3), which equals $7.33. Note that average total cost ($7.33) equals average fixed cost ($3.33) plus average variable cost ($4.00).

Average fixed cost
Total fixed cost per unit of output.

Average variable cost
Total variable cost per unit of output.

Average total cost
Total cost per unit of output, which equals average fixed cost plus average variable cost.

■ **TABLE 12.3**

Sam's Smoothies' Marginal Cost and Average Cost

Output (gallons per hour)	Total cost (dollars per hour)	Marginal cost (dollars per gallon)	Average fixed cost	Average variable cost	Average total cost
				(dollars per gallon)	
0	10.00		—	—	—
		6.00			
1	16.00		10.00	6.00	16.00
		3.60			
2	19.60		5.00	4.80	9.80
		2.40			
3	22.00		3.33	4.00	7.33
		2.10			
4	24.10		2.50	3.53	6.03
		2.10			
5	26.20		2.00	3.24	5.24
		1.80			
6	28.00		1.67	3.00	4.67
		2.40			
7	30.40		1.43	2.91	4.34
		3.60			
8	34.00		1.25	3.00	4.25
		6.00			
9	40.00		1.11	3.33	4.44

Figure 12.6 graphs the marginal cost and average cost data in Table 12.3. The red marginal cost curve (*MC*) is U-shaped because of the way in which marginal product changes. Recall that when Samantha hires a second or a third worker, marginal product increases and output increases to 6 gallons an hour (Figure 12.3 on p. 303). Over this output range, marginal cost decreases as output increases. When Samantha hires a fourth or more workers, marginal product decreases but output increases up to 9 gallons an hour (Figure 12.3). Over this output range, marginal cost increases as output increases.

The green average fixed cost curve (*AFC*) slopes downward. As output increases, the same constant total fixed cost is spread over a larger output. The blue average total cost curve (*ATC*) and the purple average variable cost curve (*AVC*) are U-shaped. The vertical distance between the average total cost and average variable cost curves is equal to average fixed cost—as indicated by the two arrows. That distance shrinks as output increases because average fixed cost decreases with increasing output.

The marginal cost curve intersects the average variable cost curve and the average total cost curve at their minimum points. That is, when marginal cost is less than average cost, average cost is decreasing; and when marginal cost exceeds average cost, average cost is increasing. This relationship holds for both the *ATC* curve and the *AVC* curve and is another example of the relationship you saw in Figure 12.4 for average product and marginal product.

◼ FIGURE 12.6

Average Cost Curves and Marginal Cost Curve at Sam's Smoothies

Average fixed cost (*AFC*) decreases as output increases. The average total cost curve (*ATC*) and average variable cost curve (*AVC*) are U-shaped. The vertical distance between these two curves is equal to average fixed cost, as illustrated by the two arrows.

Marginal cost is the change in total cost when output increases by one unit. The marginal cost curve (*MC*) is U-shaped and intersects the average variable cost curve and the average total cost curve at their minimum points.

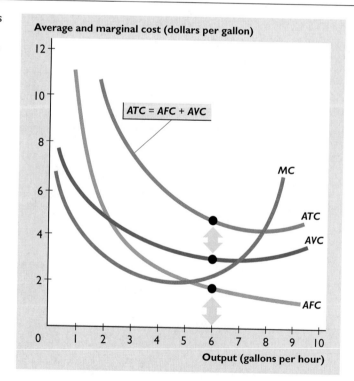

■ Why the Average Total Cost Curve Is U-Shaped

Average total cost, *ATC*, is the sum of average fixed cost, *AFC*, and average variable cost, *AVC*. So the shape of the *ATC* curve combines the shapes of the *AFC* and *AVC* curves. The U-shape of the average total cost curve arises from the influence of two opposing forces:

- Spreading total fixed cost over a larger output
- Decreasing marginal returns

When output increases, the firm spreads its total fixed costs over a larger output and its average fixed cost decreases—its average fixed cost curve slopes downward.

Decreasing marginal returns means that as output increases, ever larger amounts of labor are needed to produce an additional unit of output. So average variable cost eventually increases, and the *AVC* curve eventually slopes upward.

The shape of the average total cost curve combines these two effects. Initially, as output increases, both average fixed cost and average variable cost decrease, so average total cost decreases and the *ATC* curve slopes downward. But as output increases further and decreasing marginal returns set in, average variable cost begins to increase. Eventually, average variable cost increases more quickly than average fixed cost decreases, so average total cost increases and the *ATC* curve slopes upward.

All the short-run cost concepts that you've met are summarized in Table 12.4.

■ TABLE 12.4
A Compact Glossary of Costs

Term	Symbol	Definition	Equation
Fixed cost		The cost of a fixed factor of production that is independent of the quantity produced	
Variable cost		The cost of a variable factor of production that varies with the quantity produced	
Total fixed cost	*TFC*	Cost of the fixed factors of production	
Total variable cost	*TVC*	Cost of the variable factor of production	
Total cost	*TC*	Cost of all factors of production	$TC = TFC + TVC$
Marginal cost	*MC*	Change in total cost resulting from a one-unit increase in output (Q)	$MC = \Delta TC \div \Delta Q^*$
Average fixed cost	*AFC*	Total fixed cost per unit of output	$AFC = TFC \div Q$
Average variable cost	*AVC*	Total variable cost per unit of output	$AVC = TVC \div Q$
Average total cost	*ATC*	Total cost per unit of output	$ATC = AFC + AVC$

*In this equation, the Greek letter delta (Δ) stands for "change in."

■ Cost Curves and Product Curves

A firm's cost curves and product curves are linked, and Figure 12.7 shows how. The top figure shows the average product curve and the marginal product curve. The bottom figure shows the average variable cost curve and the marginal cost curve.

The figure highlights the links between the product and cost curves. At low levels of employment and output, as the firm hires more labor, marginal product and average product rise and output increases faster than costs. So marginal cost and average variable cost fall. Then, at the point of maximum marginal product, marginal cost is a minimum. As the firm hires more labor, marginal product decreases and marginal cost increases. But average product continues to rise, and average variable cost continues to fall. Then, at the point of maximum average product, average variable cost is a minimum. As the firm hires even more labor, average product decreases and average variable cost increases.

■ Shifts in the Cost Curves

The position of a firm's short-run cost curves in Figures 12.5 and 12.6 depend on two factors:

- Technology
- Prices of factors of production

Technology

A technological change that increases productivity shifts the total product curve upward. It also shifts the marginal product curve and the average product curve upward. With a better technology, the same inputs can produce more output, so an advance in technology lowers the average and marginal costs and shifts the short-run cost curves downward.

For example, advances in robotic technology have increased productivity in the automobile industry. As a result, the product curves of DaimlerChrysler, Ford, and GM have shifted upward, and their average and marginal cost curves have shifted downward. But the relationships between their product curves and cost curves have not changed. The curves are still linked, as in Figure 12.7.

Often a technological advance results in a firm using more capital, a fixed input, and less labor, a variable input. For example, today telephone companies use computers to connect long-distance calls instead of the human operators they used in the 1980s. When a telephone company makes this change, total variable cost decreases and total cost decreases, but total fixed cost increases. This change in the mix of fixed cost and variable cost means that at small output levels, average total cost might increase, but at large output levels, average total cost decreases.

Prices of Factors of Production

An increase in the price of a factor of production increases costs and shifts the cost curves. But how the curves shift depends on which resource price changes. An increase in rent or some other component of *fixed* cost shifts the fixed cost curves (*TFC* and *AFC*) upward and shifts the total cost curve (*TC*) upward but leaves the variable cost curves (*AVC* and *TVC*) and the marginal cost curve (*MC*) unchanged.

FIGURE 12.7

Product Curves and Cost Curves

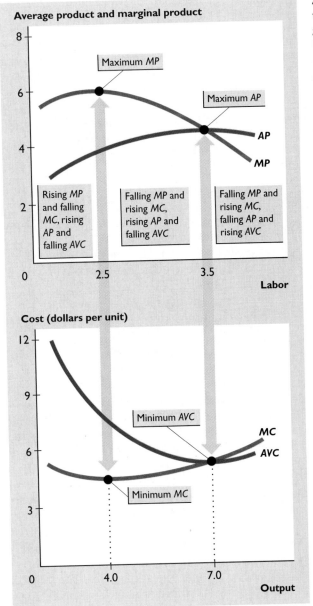

A firm's marginal cost curve is linked to its marginal product curve. If marginal product rises, marginal cost falls. If marginal product is a maximum, marginal cost is a minimum. If marginal product diminishes, marginal cost rises.

A firm's average variable cost curve is linked to its average product curve. If average product rises, average variable cost falls. If average product is a maximum, average variable cost is a minimum. If average product diminishes, average variable cost rises.

An increase in wage rates or some other component of *variable* cost shifts the variable cost curves (*TVC* and *AVC*) and the marginal cost curve (*MC*) upward but leaves the fixed cost curves (*AFC* and *TFC*) unchanged. So, for example, if the interest expense paid by a trucking company increases, the fixed cost of transportation services increases, but if the wage rate paid to truck drivers increases, the variable cost and marginal cost of transportation services increase.

3 **Explain the relationship between a firm's output and costs in the short run.**

Practice Problem 12.3

TABLE 1

Labor (students)	Output (pineapples per day)
0	0
1	100
2	220
3	300
4	360
5	400
6	420
7	430

1. Tom leases a farmer's field for $120 a day and grows pineapples. Tom pays students $100 a day to pick and pack the pineapples. Tom leases capital at $80 a day. Table 1 gives the daily output.
   a. Construct the total cost schedule.
   b. Construct the average total cost schedule.
   c. Construct the marginal cost schedule.
   d. At what output is Tom's average total cost a minimum?

Exercise 12.3

TABLE 2

Labor (students)	Output (pineapples per day)
0	0
1	2
2	5
3	9
4	12
5	14
6	15

1. Lizzie hires students at $50 a day to paint houses. She leases equipment that costs her $100 a day. Table 2 shows her total product schedule.
   a. Construct the total variable cost and total cost schedules.
   b. Construct the average fixed cost, average variable cost, and average total cost schedules.
   c. Construct the marginal cost schedule.
   d. Check that the gap between total cost and total variable cost is the same at all outputs. Explain why.

Solution to Practice Problem 12.3

TABLE 3

Labor	TP	TC	MC	ATC
0	0	200		–
			1.00	
1	100	300		3.00
			0.83	
2	220	400		1.82
			1.25	
3	300	500		1.67
			1.67	
4	360	600		1.67
			2.50	
5	400	700		1.75
			5.00	
6	420	800		1.90
			10.00	
7	430	900		2.09

1a. Total cost is the sum of total fixed cost and total variable cost. Tom leases the farmer's field for $120 a day and leases capital for $80 a day, so Tom's total fixed cost is $200 a day. Total variable cost is the wages of the students. For example, when Tom hires 3 students, the total variable cost is $300 a day. So when Tom hires 3 students, total cost is $500 a day. The *TC* column of Table 3 shows the total cost schedule.

1b. Average total cost is the total cost divided by total product. For example, when Tom hires 3 students, they pick and pack 300 pineapples a day, and Tom's total cost is $500 a day. Average total cost is $1.67 a pineapple. The *ATC* column of Table 3 shows the average total cost schedule.

1c. Marginal cost is the increase in total cost that results from picking and packing one additional pineapple a day. The total cost (from Table 3) of picking and packing 100 pineapples a day is $300. The total cost of picking and packing 220 pineapples a day is $400. The increase in the number of pineapples is 120, and the increase in total cost is $100. So the marginal cost is the increase in total cost divided by the increase in the number of pineapples. Marginal cost equals $100 ÷ 120 pineapples, which is $0.83 a pineapple. The *MC* column of Table 3 shows the marginal cost schedule.

1d. At the minimum of average total cost, average total cost equals marginal cost. Minimum average total cost is $1.67 a pineapple at 330 pineapples a day—midpoint between 300 and 360 pineapples.

12.4 LONG-RUN COST

In the long run, a firm can vary both the quantity of labor and the quantity of capital. A small firm, such as Sam's Smoothies, can increase its plant size by moving into a larger building and installing more machines. A big firm such as General Motors can decrease its plant size by closing down some production lines.

We are now going to see how costs vary in the long run when a firm varies its plant—the quantity of capital it uses—along with the quantity of labor it uses.

The first thing that happens is that the distinction between fixed cost and variable cost disappears. All costs are variable in the long run.

■ Plant Size and Cost

When a firm changes its plant size, its cost of producing a given output changes. In Table 12.3 and Figure 12.6, the lowest average total cost that Samantha can achieve is $4.25 a gallon, which occurs when she produces 8 gallons of smoothie an hour. Samantha wonders what would happen to her average total cost if she increased the size of her plant by renting a bigger building and installing a larger number of blenders and refrigerators. Will the average total cost of producing a gallon of smoothie fall, rise, or remain the same?

Each of these three outcomes is possible, and they arise because when a firm changes the size of its plant, it might experience

- Economies of scale
- Diseconomies of scale
- Constant returns to scale

Economies of Scale

If when a firm increases its plant size and labor employed by the same percentage, its output increases by a larger percentage, the firm's average total cost decreases. The firm experiences **economies of scale**. The main source of economies of scale is greater specialization of both labor and capital.

Economies of scale
A condition in which, when a firm increases its plant size and labor employed by the same percentage, its output increases by a larger percentage and its average total cost decreases.

Specialization of Labor   If GM produced 100 cars a week, each production line worker would have to perform many different tasks. But if GM produces 10,000 cars a week, each worker can specialize in a small number of tasks and become highly proficient at them. The result is that the average product of labor increases and the average total cost of producing a car falls.

Specialization also occurs off the production line. For example, a small firm usually does not have a specialist sales manager, personnel manager, and production manager. One person covers all these activities. But when a firm is large enough, specialists perform these activities. Average product increases, and the average total cost falls.

Specialization of Capital   At a small output rate, firms often must employ general-purpose machines and tools. For example, with an output of a few gallons an hour, Sam's Smoothies uses regular blenders like the one in your kitchen. But if Sam's produces hundreds of gallons an hour, it uses custom blenders that fill, empty, and clean themselves. The result is that the output rate is larger and the average total cost of producing a gallon of smoothie is lower.

Dieconomies of scale
A condition in which, when a firm increases its plant size and labor employed by the same percentage, its output increases by a smaller percentage and its average total cost increases.

Constant returns to scale
A condition in which, when a firm increases its plant size and labor employed by the same percentage, its output increases by the same percentage and its average total cost remains constant.

Long-run average cost curve
A curve that shows the lowest average cost at which it is possible to produce each output when the firm has had sufficient time to change both its plant size and labor employed.

Diseconomies of Scale

If when a firm increases its plant size and labor employed by the same percentage, output increases by a smaller percentage, the firm's average total cost increases. The firm experiences **diseconomies of scale**. Diseconomies of scale arise from the difficulty of coordinating and controlling a large enterprise. The larger the firm, the greater is the cost of communicating both up and down the management hierarchy and among managers. Eventually, management complexity brings rising average cost. Diseconomies of scale occur in all production processes but in some perhaps only at a very large output rate.

Constant Returns to Scale

If when a firm increases its plant size and labor employed by the same percentage, output increases by that same percentage, the firm's average total cost remains constant. The firm experiences **constant returns to scale**. Constant returns to scale occur when a firm is able to replicate its existing production facility including its management system. For example, General Motors might double its production of Cavaliers by doubling its production facility for those cars. It can build an identical production line and hire an identical number of workers. With the two identical production lines, GM produces exactly twice as many cars. The average cost of producing a Cavalier is identical in the two plants. So when production increases, average total cost remains constant.

■ The Long-Run Average Cost Curve

The **long-run average cost curve** shows the lowest average cost at which it is possible to produce each output when the firm has had sufficient time to change both its plant size and its labor force.

Figure 12.8 shows Sam's Smoothies' long-run average cost curve LRAC. This long-run average cost curve is derived from the short-run average total cost curves for different possible plant sizes.

With its current small plant, Sam's Smoothies operates on the average total cost curve ATC_1 in Figure 12.8. The other three average total cost curves are for successively bigger plants. In this example, for outputs up to 5 gallons an hour, the existing plant with average total cost curve ATC_1 produces smoothies at the lowest attainable average cost. For outputs between 5 and 10 gallons an hour, average total cost is lowest on ATC_2. For outputs between 10 and 15 gallons an hour, average total cost is lowest on ATC_3. And for outputs in excess of 15 gallons an hour, average total cost is lowest on ATC_4.

The segment of each of the four average total cost curves for which that plant has the lowest average total cost is highlighted in dark blue in Figure 12.8. The scallop-shaped curve made up of these four segments is Sam's Smoothies' long-run average cost curve.

Economies and Diseconomies of Scale

When economies of scale are present, the LRAC curve slopes downward. The LRAC curve in Figure 12.8 shows that Sam's Smoothies experiences economies of scale for output rates up to 9 gallons an hour. At output rates between 9 and 12 gallons an hour, the firm experiences constant returns to scale. And at output rates that exceed 12 gallons an hour, the firm experiences diseconomies of scale.

FIGURE 12.8

Long-run Average Cost Curve

In the long run, Samantha can vary both capital and labor inputs. The long-run average cost curve traces the lowest attainable average total cost of producing each output.

Sam's experiences economies of scale as output increases to 9 gallons an hour, constant returns to scale for outputs between 9 gallons and 12 gallons an hour, and diseconomics of scale for outputs that exceed 12 gallons an hour.

EYE ON THE U.S. ECONOMY

The ATM and the Cost of Getting Cash

Most banks use automated teller machines—ATMs—to dispense cash. But small credit unions don't have ATMs. Instead, they employ tellers.

Gemini Consulting of Morristown, New Jersey, estimates that the average total cost of a transaction is $1.07 for a teller and 27¢ for an ATM. Given these numbers, why don't small credit unions install ATMs and lay off their tellers?

The answer is scale. At a small number of transactions per month, it costs less to use a teller than an ATM. In the figure, the average total cost curve for transactions done with a teller is ATC_T. The average total cost

curve for transactions done with an ATM is ATC_A. You can see that if the number of transactions is Q a month, the average total cost per transaction is the same for both methods. For a bank that does more than Q transac-

tions per month, the least-cost method is the ATM. For a credit union that does fewer than Q transactions a month, its least-cost method is the teller. More technology is not always more efficient.

4 Derive and explain a firm's long-run average cost curve.

Practice Problem 12.4

TABLE 1

Labor (students per day)	Output with 1 field	Output with 2 fields
	(pineapples per day)	
0	0	0
1	100	220
2	220	460
3	300	620
4	360	740
5	400	820
6	420	860
7	430	880

1. Tom grows pineapples. He leases a farmer's field for $120 a day and capital for $80 a day. He hires students at $100 a day. Suppose that Tom now leases two fields for $240 a day and twice as much capital for $160 a day. Tom discovers that his output is the numbers in the third column of Table 1. The numbers in the second column are his output with one field and the original amount of capital.
   a. Find Tom's average total cost curve schedule when he farms two fields.
   b. Make a graph of Tom's average total cost curves using one field and two fields, and show on the graph Tom's long-run average cost curve.
   c. Over what output range will Tom operate with one field and at what output rate will he operate with two fields?
   d. What happens to Tom's average total cost curve if he farms two fields and doubles his capital?
   e. Does Tom experience economies of scale or diseconomies of scale?

Exercise 12.4

1. Lizzie hires students at $50 a day to paint houses. She leases equipment that costs her $100 a day. Suppose that Lizzie doubles the number of students she hires and doubles the amount of equipment that she leases. If Lizzie experiences diseconomies of scale,
   a. Explain what has happened to her average total cost curve.
   b. Explain what might be the source of those diseconomies of scale.

Solution to Practice Problem 12.4

TABLE 2

TP (1 field)	ATC (1 field)	TP (2 fields)	ATC (2 fields)
100	3.00	220	2.27
220	1.82	460	1.30
300	1.67	620	1.13
360	1.67	740	1.08
400	1.75	820	1.10
420	1.90	860	1.16
430	2.09	880	1.25

1a. Total cost is fixed cost of $400 a day plus $100 a day for each student hired. Average total cost is the total cost divided by output. The "ATC (2 fields)" column of Table 2 shows Tom's average total cost schedule.

1b. Figure 1 shows Tom's average total cost curves using one field as ATC_1. This curve graphs the data on ATC and TP in Table 3 on p. 314. Using two fields, the average total cost curve is ATC_2. Tom's long-run average cost curve is the lower segments of these two ATC curves, highlighted in Figure 1.

1c. If Tom produces up to 300 pineapples a day, he will operate with one field. If he produces more than 300 pineapples a day, he will operate with two fields.

1d. When Tom farms two fields and doubles his capital, average total cost increases at low outputs (up to 300 a day) and decreases at high outputs (greater than 300 a day).

1e. Tom experiences economies of scale up to an output of 740 pineapples a day because as he increases his plant and produces up to 740 pineapples a day, the average total cost of picking and packing a pineapple decreases.

FIGURE 1

Average total cost (dollars per pineapple)

ATC₁, ATC₂, LRAC

Output (pineapples per day)

CHAPTER CHECKPOINT

Key Points

1 **Explain how economists measure a firm's cost of production and profit.**

- Firms seek to maximize economic profit, which is total revenue minus total cost.
- Total cost equals opportunity cost—the sum of explicit costs plus implicit costs and includes normal profit.

2 **Explain the relationship between a firm's output and labor employed in the short run.**

- In the short run, the firm can change the output it produces by changing labor only.
- A total product curve shows the limits to the output that the firm can produce with a given quantity of capital and different quantities of labor.
- As the quantity of labor increases, the marginal product of labor increases initially but eventually decreases—the law of decreasing returns.

3 **Explain the relationship between a firm's output and costs in the short run.**

- As total product increases, total fixed cost is constant, and total variable cost and total cost increase.
- As total product increases, average fixed cost decreases and average variable cost, average total cost, and marginal cost decrease at small outputs and increase at large outputs. Their curves are U-shaped.

4 **Derive and explain a firm's long-run average cost curve.**

- In the long run, the firm can change the size of its plant.
- Long-run cost is the cost of production when all inputs have been adjusted to produce at the lowest attainable cost.
- The long-run average cost curve traces out the lowest attainable average total cost at each output when both capital and labor inputs can be varied.
- The long-run average cost curve slopes downward with economies of scale and upward with diseconomies of scale.

Key Terms

Average fixed cost, 309
Average product, 304
Average total cost, 309
Average variable cost, 309
Constant returns to scale, 316
Decreasing marginal returns, 302
Diseconomies of scale, 316
Economic depreciation, 297

Economic profit, 297
Economies of scale, 315
Explicit cost, 297
Implicit cost, 297
Increasing marginal returns, 302
Law of decreasing returns, 304
Long run, 300
Long-run average cost curve, 316

Marginal cost, 308
Marginal product, 302
Normal profit, 297
Short run, 300
Total cost, 307
Total fixed cost, 307
Total product, 301
Total variable cost, 307

Exercises
(X) myeconlab

1. Joe runs a shoeshine stand at the airport. With no skills and no job experience, Joe has no alternative employment. The other shoeshine stand operators that Joe knows earn $10,000 a year. Joe pays the airport $2,000 a year for the space he uses, and his total revenue from shining shoes is $15,000 a year. He spent $1,000 on a chair, polish, and brushes and paid for these items using his credit card. The interest on his credit card balance is 20 percent a year. At the end of the year, Joe was offered $500 for his business and all its equipment. Calculate Joe's
   a. Explicit costs.
   b. Implicit costs.
   c. Economic profit.

2. Sonya used to sell real estate and earn $25,000 a year, but she now sells greeting cards. Normal profit for the retailers of greeting cards is $14,000. Over the past year, Sonya bought $10,000 worth of cards from manufacturers of cards. She sold these cards for $58,000. Sonya rents a shop for $5,000 a year and spends $1,000 on utilities and office expenses. Sonya owns a cash register, which she bought for $2,000 with her savings account. Her bank pays 3 percent a year on savings accounts. At the end of the year, Sonya was offered $1,600 for her cash register. Calculate Sonya's
   a. Explicit costs.
   b. Implicit costs.
   c. Economic profit.

3. Len's body board factory rents equipment for shaping boards and hires students. Table 1 sets out Len's total product schedule.
   a. Construct Len's marginal product and average product schedules.
   b. Over what range of workers do marginal returns increase?
   c. After how many workers employed do marginal returns decrease?

4. Yolanda runs a bullfrog farm in Yuma, Arizona. When Yolanda employed one person, she produced 1,000 bullfrogs a week. When she hired a second worker, her total product doubled. Her total product doubled again when she hired a third worker. When she hired a fourth worker, her total product increased but by only 1,000 bullfrogs.
   a. Construct Yolanda's marginal product and average product schedules.
   b. Over what range of workers do marginal returns increase?
   c. After how many workers employed do marginal returns decrease?

5. Len, in exercise 3, pays $300 a week for equipment and $1,000 a week to each student he hires. Given his total product schedule in Table 1,
   a. Construct Len's total variable cost and total cost schedules.
   b. Calculate total cost minus total variable cost at each output rate. What does this quantity equal? Why?
   c. Construct the average fixed cost, average variable cost, and average total cost schedules.
   d. Construct the marginal cost schedule.
   e. Calculate the output at which Len's average total cost is a minimum.
   f. Calculate the output at which Len's average variable cost is a minimum.
   g. Explain why the output at which average variable cost is a minimum is smaller than the output at which average total cost is a minimum.

TABLE 1

Labor (workers per day)	Total product (body boards per day)
0	0
1	20
2	44
3	60
4	72
5	80
6	84
7	86

6. Yolanda, in exercise 4, pays $1,000 a week for equipment and $500 a week to each worker she hires. Given her description of how her total product changes as she hires more labor,
   a. Construct Yolanda's total variable cost and total cost schedules.
   b. Calculate total cost minus total variable cost at each output rate. What does this quantity equal? Why?
   c. Construct the average fixed cost, average variable cost, and average total cost schedules.
   d. Construct the marginal cost schedule.
   e. Calculate the output at which Yolanda's average total cost is a minimum.
   f. Calculate the output at which Yolanda's average variable cost is a minimum.
   g. Explain why the output at which average total cost is a minimum is larger than the output at which average variable cost is a minimum.

7. Table 2 shows the costs incurred at Pete's peanut farm. Complete the table.

TABLE 2

L	TP	TVC	TC	AFC	AVC	ATC	MC
0	0	0	100				
1	10	35					
2	24	70					
3	38	105					
4	44	140					
5	47	175					

8. Table 3 shows some of the costs incurred at Bill's Bakery. Calculate the values of A, B, C, D, and E. Show your work.

TABLE 3

L	TP	TVC	TC	AFC	AVC	ATC	MC
1	100	350	850	C	3.50	D	2.50
2	240	700	B	2.08	2.92	5.00	E
3	380	A	1,550	1.32	2.76	4.08	5.83
4	440	1,400	1,900	1.14	3.18	4.32	11.67
5	470	1,750	2,250	1.06	3.72	4.79	

9. Explain what the long-run average cost curve shows and how it is derived.

10. Can a firm that produces at the lowest possible average cost lower its average cost further by increasing production? Explain, using the long-run average cost curve.

11. Explain the sources of economies of scale and diseconomies of scale and illustrate these two situations in a graph.

12. Provide examples of industries in which you think economies of scale exist and explain why you think they are present in these industries.

13. Provide examples of industries in which you think diseconomies of scale exist and explain why you think they are present in these industries.

Critical Thinking

14. WorldCom, a global communications company, spent billions of dollars laying fiber-optic cables under the oceans. Is the cost of this communications network a short-run cost or a long-run cost? Is it a sunk cost or an opportunity cost? Explain your answer.

15. Study *Eye on the U.S. Economy* on p. 317 and then answer the following questions:
    a. What is the main difference, from a cost point of view, between human tellers and ATMs?
    b. Why do you think ATMs have become so popular?
    c. Would it ever make sense for a bank in the United States not to use ATMs?
    d. Do you think that ATMs are as common in China as they are in the United States? Explain why or why not.

16. Suppose the government put a tax on banks for each ATM transaction but did not put a similar tax on human teller transactions.
    a. How would the tax affect a bank's costs and cost curves?
    b. Would the tax change the number of ATMs and the number of tellers that banks hire? If so, explain how. If not, why not?

 ## Web Exercises

Use the links on MyEconLab to work the following exercises.

17. Visit the Web site of Bullfrogs.louisiana and check out the prices of bullfrogs of various sizes. Assume that prices reflect the cost of production and answer the following questions:
    a. Does farming bullfrogs appear to display increasing marginal cost? Explain why or why not.
    b. Does farming bullfrogs appear to display decreasing marginal returns? Explain why or why not.
    c. Why might someone pay $20 for a large (6 inches plus) bullfrog when the price of a smaller (4 to 6 inch) bullfrog is only $12?

18. Visit the Federal Reserve Bank of St. Louis and read the article "Do Economies of Scale Exist in the Banking Industry?"
    a. What is the survivor technique for identifying whether the firms in an industry experience economies of scale?
    b. Why does the survivor technique work?
    c. What does the survivor technique imply about economies of scale in the banking industry?
    d. Sketch the long-run average cost curve of a bank that is consistent with what the survivor technique implies about economies of scale.

19. Obtain information about the cost of producing pumpkins.
    a. List all the costs referred to on the Web site.
    b. For each item, classify it as a fixed cost, a variable cost, or perhaps a combination of the two.
    c. Make some assumptions and sketch the average cost curves (AFC, AVC, and ATC) and the marginal cost curve.
    d. Identify the minimum points of the AVC and ATC curves in your graph.

Perfect Competition

CHAPTER CHECKLIST

**When you have completed your study of this chapter,
you will be able to**

1 Explain a perfectly competitive firm's profit-maximizing choices and derive its supply curve.

2 Explain how output, price, and profit are determined in the short run.

3 Explain how output, price, and profit are determined in the long run and explain why perfect competition is efficient.

The sun is not yet up on a dark February morning as Don Harlow climbs into his truck. After a bumpy ride on unpaved forest tracks, he reaches a tank into which a few hundred gallons of maple sap have flowed from the 11,000 taps and 40 miles of plastic tubing that he has set up. Don carts the sap to a sugaring house, where he boils it down to become syrup. Don and his forebears have produced maple syrup for more than 100 years.

But Don faces tough competition from 10,000 other farms that produce maple syrup—the real thing, not the Aunt Jemima synthetic variety.

You're going to see how a firm in a highly competitive market operates. You'll see how the principles of rational choice, balancing costs and benefits at the margin, and responding to incentives enable us to understand and predict the decisions that Don and entrepreneurs like him make when the competitive environment is fierce.

MARKET TYPES

The four market types are

- Perfect competition
- Monopoly
- Monopolistic competition
- Oligopoly

■ Perfect Competition

Perfect competition
A market in which there are many firms, each selling an identical product; many buyers; no restrictions on the entry of new firms into the industry; no advantage to established firms; and buyers and sellers are well informed about prices.

Perfect competition exists when

- Many firms sell an identical product to many buyers.
- There are no restrictions on entry into (or exit from) the market.
- Established firms have no advantage over new firms.
- Sellers and buyers are well informed about prices.

These conditions that define perfect competition arise when the market demand for the product is large relative to the output of a single producer. And this situation arises when economies of scale are absent so the efficient scale of each firm is small. But a large market and the absence of economies of scale are not sufficient to create perfect competition. In addition, each firm must produce a good or service that has no characteristics that are unique to that firm so that consumers don't care from which firm they buy. Firms in perfect competition all look the same to the buyer.

Wheat farming, fishing, wood pulping and paper milling, the manufacture of paper cups and plastic shopping bags, lawn service, dry cleaning, and the provision of laundry services are all examples of highly competitive industries.

■ Other Market Types

Monopoly
A market for a good or service that has no close substitutes and in which there is one supplier that is protected from competition by a barrier preventing the entry of new firms.

Monopoly arises when one firm sells a good or service that has no close substitutes and a barrier blocks the entry of new firms. In some places, the phone, gas, electricity, and water suppliers are local monopolies—monopolies that are restricted to a given location. For many years, a global firm called DeBeers had a near international monopoly in diamonds.

Monopolistic competition
A market in which a large number of firms compete by making similar but slightly different products.

Monopolistic competition arises when a large number of firms compete by making similar but slightly different products. Each firm is the sole producer of the particular version of the good in question. For example, in the market for running shoes, Nike, Reebok, Fila, Asics, New Balance, and many others make their own versions of the perfect shoe. The term "monopolistic competition" reminds us that each firm has a monopoly on a particular brand of shoe but the firms compete with each other.

Oligopoly
A market in which a small number of firms compete.

Oligopoly arises when a small number of firms compete. Airplane manufacture is an example of oligopoly. Oligopolies might produce almost identical products, such as Kodak and Fuji film. Or they might produce differentiated products, such as the colas produced by Coke and Pepsi.

We study perfect competition in this chapter, monopoly in Chapter 14, monopolistic competition in Chapter 15, and oligopoly in Chapter 16.

13.1 A FIRM'S PROFIT-MAXIMIZING CHOICES

A firm's objective is to maximize *economic profit,* which is equal to *total revenue* minus the *total cost* of production. *Normal profit,* the return that the firm's entrepreneur can obtain in the best alternative business, is part of the firm's cost.

In the short run, a firm achieves its objective by deciding the quantity to produce. This quantity influences the firm's total revenue, total cost, and economic profit. In the long run, a firm achieves its objective by deciding whether to enter or exit a market.

These are the key decisions that a firm in perfect competition makes. Such a firm does *not* choose the price at which to sell its output. The firm in perfect competition is a **price taker**—it cannot influence the price of its product.

Price taker
A firm that cannot influence the price of the good or service that it produces.

■ Price Taker

To see why a firm in perfect competition is a price taker, imagine that you are a wheat farmer in Kansas. You have a thousand acres under cultivation—which sounds like a lot. But then you go on a drive through Colorado, Oklahoma, Texas, and back up to Nebraska and the Dakotas. You find unbroken stretches of wheat covering millions of acres. And you know that there are similar vistas in Canada, Argentina, Australia, and Ukraine. Your thousand acres are a drop in the ocean. Nothing makes your wheat any better than any other farmer's, and all the buyers of wheat know the price they must pay. If the going price of wheat is $4 a bushel, you are stuck with that price. You can't get a higher price than $4, and you have no incentive to offer it for less than $4 because you can sell your entire output at that price.

The producers of most agricultural products are price takers. We'll illustrate perfect competition with another agriculture example: the market for maple syrup. The next time you pour syrup on your pancakes, think about the competitive market that gets this product from the sap of the maple tree to your table!

Dave's Maple Syrup is one of the more than 11,000 similar firms in the maple syrup market of North America. Dave is a price taker. Like the Kansas wheat farmer, he can sell any quantity he chooses at the going price but none above that price. Dave faces a *perfectly elastic* demand. The demand for Dave's syrup is perfectly elastic because syrup from Don Harlow, Casper Sugar Shack, and all the other maple farms in North America are *perfect substitutes* for Dave's syrup.

We'll explore Dave's decisions and their implications for the way a competitive market works. We begin by defining some revenue concepts.

Wheat farmers and maple syrup farmers are price takers.

■ Revenue Concepts

In perfect competition, market demand and market supply determine the price. A firm's *total revenue* equals this given price multiplied by the quantity sold. A firm's **marginal revenue** is the change in total revenue that results from a one-unit increase in the quantity sold. In perfect competition, marginal revenue equals price. The reason is that the firm can sell any quantity it chooses at the going market price. So if the firm sells one more unit, it sells it for the market price and total revenue increases by that amount. But this increase in total revenue is marginal revenue. So marginal revenue equals price.

The table in Figure 13.1 illustrates the equality of marginal revenue and price. The price of syrup is $8 a can. Total revenue is equal to the price multiplied by the

Marginal revenue
The change in total revenue that results from a one-unit increase in the quantity sold.

quantity sold. So if Dave sells 10 cans, his total revenue is $10 \times \$8 = \$80$. If the quantity sold increases from 10 cans to 11 cans, total revenue increases from $80 to $88, so marginal revenue is $8 a can, the same as the price.

Figure 13.1 illustrates price determination and revenue in the perfectly competitive market. Market demand and market supply in part (a) determine the market price. Dave is a price taker, so he sells his syrup for the market price. The demand curve for Dave's syrup is the horizontal line at the market price in part (b). Because price equals marginal revenue, the demand curve for Dave's syrup is Dave's marginal revenue curve (*MR*). The total revenue curve (*TR*), in part (c), shows the total revenue at each quantity sold. Because he sells each can for the market price, the total revenue curve is an upward-sloping straight line.

■ Profit-Maximizing Output

As output increases, total revenue increases. But total cost also increases. And because of *decreasing marginal returns* (see pp. 302–304), total cost eventually increases faster than total revenue. There is one output level that maximizes economic profit, and a perfectly competitive firm chooses this output level.

■ FIGURE 13.1

Demand, Price, and Revenue in Perfect Competition

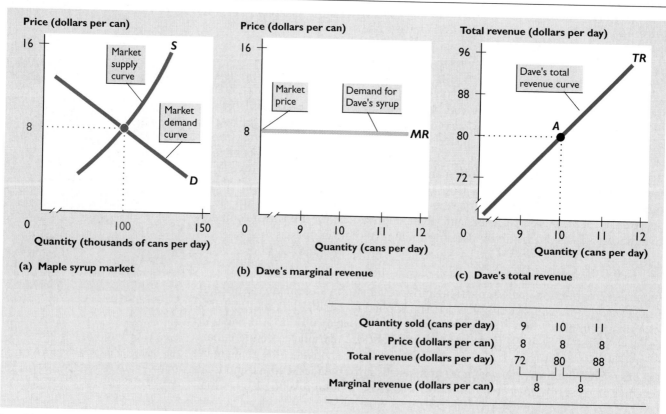

Quantity sold (cans per day)	9	10	11
Price (dollars per can)	8	8	8
Total revenue (dollars per day)	72	80	88
Marginal revenue (dollars per can)		8	8

Part (a) shows the market for maple syrup. The market price is $8 a can. The table calculates total revenue and marginal revenue.

Part (b) shows the demand curve for Dave's syrup, which is Dave's marginal revenue curve (*MR*).

Part (c) shows Dave's total revenue curve (*TR*). Point *A* corresponds to the second column of the table.

One way to find the profit-maximizing output is to use a firm's total revenue and total cost curves. Profit is maximized at the output level at which total revenue exceeds total cost by the largest amount. Figure 13.2 shows how to do this for Dave's Maple Syrup.

The table lists Dave's total revenue, total cost, and economic profit at different output levels. Figure 13.2(a) shows the total revenue and total cost curves. These curves are graphs of the numbers shown in the first three columns of the table. The total revenue curve (*TR*) is the same as that in Figure 13.1(c). The total cost curve (*TC*) is similar to the one that you met in Chapter 12 (p. 308). Figure 13.2(b) is an economic profit curve.

Dave makes an economic profit on outputs between 4 and 13 cans a day. At outputs of fewer than 4 cans a day and more than 13 cans a day, he incurs an economic loss. At outputs of 4 cans and 13 cans a day, total cost equals total revenue and Dave's economic profit is zero—Dave's *break-even points*.

The profit curve is at its highest when the vertical distance between the *TR* and *TC* curves is greatest. In this example, profit maximization occurs at an output of 10 cans a day. At this output, Dave's economic profit is $29 a day.

FIGURE 13.2

Total Revenue, Total Cost, and Economic Profit

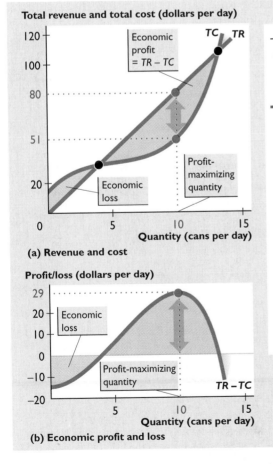

(a) Revenue and cost

(b) Economic profit and loss

Quantity (Q) (cans per day)	Total revenue (TR)	Total cost (TC)	Economic profit (TR – TC)
	(dollars per day)		
0	0	15	–15
1	8	22	–14
2	16	27	–11
3	24	30	–6
4	32	32	0
5	40	33	7
6	48	34	14
7	56	36	20
8	64	39	25
9	72	44	28
10	80	51	29
11	88	60	28
12	96	76	20
13	104	104	0
14	112	144	–32

In part (a), economic profit is the vertical distance between the total cost and total revenue curves. Dave's maximum economic profit is $29 a day ($80 – $51) when output is 10 cans a day.

In part (b), economic profit is the height of the profit curve.

■ Marginal Analysis and the Supply Decision

Another way to find the profit-maximizing output is to use *marginal analysis,* which compares marginal revenue, *MR,* with marginal cost, *MC.* As output increases, marginal revenue is constant but marginal cost eventually increases.

If marginal revenue exceeds marginal cost (if *MR* > *MC*), then the extra revenue from selling one more unit exceeds the extra cost incurred to produce it. Economic profit increases if output *increases.* If marginal revenue is less than marginal cost (if *MR* < *MC*), then the extra revenue from selling one more unit is less than the extra cost incurred to produce it. Economic profit increases if output *decreases.* If marginal revenue equals marginal cost (if *MR* = *MC*), economic profit is maximized. The rule *MR* = *MC* is a prime example of marginal analysis.

Figure 13.3 illustrates these propositions. The table records Dave's marginal revenue and marginal cost. If Dave increases output from 9 cans to 10 cans a day, marginal revenue is $8 and marginal cost is $7. Because marginal revenue exceeds marginal cost, economic profit increases. The last column of the table shows that economic profit increases from $28 to $29. The blue area in the figure shows this economic profit from the tenth can.

If Dave increases output from 10 cans to 11 cans a day, marginal revenue is still $8 but marginal cost is $9. Because marginal revenue is less than marginal cost, economic profit decreases. The last column of the table shows that economic profit decreases from $29 to $28. The red area in the figure shows this economic loss from the eleventh can.

Dave maximizes economic profit by producing 10 cans a day, the quantity at which marginal revenue equals marginal cost.

FIGURE 13.3
Profit-Maximizing Output

Quantity (Q) (cans per day)	Total revenue (TR) (dollars per day)	Marginal revenue (MR) (dollars per can)	Total cost (TC) (dollars per day)	Marginal cost (MC) (dollars per can)	Economic profit (TR − TC) (dollars per day)
8	64		39		25
		8		5	
9	72		44		28
		8		7	
10	80		51		29
		8		9	
11	88		60		28
		8		16	
12	96		76		20

❶ Profit is maximized when marginal revenue equals marginal cost at 10 cans a day. **❷** If output increases from 9 to 10 cans a day, marginal cost is $7, which is less than the marginal revenue of $8, and profit increases. **❸** If output increases from 10 to 11 cans a day, marginal cost is $9, which exceeds the marginal revenue of $8, and profit decreases.

In the example that we've just worked through, Dave's profit-maximizing output is 10 cans a day. This quantity is Dave's *quantity supplied* at a price of $8 a can. If the price were higher than $8 a can, he would increase production. If the price were lower than $8 a can, he would decrease production. These profit-maximizing responses to different prices are the foundation of the law of supply: *Other things remaining the same, the higher the price of a good, the greater is the quantity supplied of that good.*

Exit and Temporary Shutdown Decisions

Sometimes, the price falls so low that a firm cannot cover its costs. What does the firm do in such a situation? The answer depends on whether the firm expects the low price to be permanent or temporary.

If a firm is incurring an economic loss that it believes is permanent and sees no prospect of ending, the firm exits the market. We'll study the consequences of this action later in this chapter where we look at the long run (pp. 338–339).

If a firm is incurring an economic loss that it believes is temporary, it will remain in the market, and it might produce some output or temporarily shut down. To decide whether to produce or to shut down, the firm compares the loss it would incur in the two situations.

If the firm shuts down, it incurs an economic loss equal to total fixed cost. If the firm produces some output, it incurs an economic loss equal to total fixed cost *plus* total variable cost *minus* total revenue. If total revenue exceeds total variable cost, the firm's economic loss is less than total fixed cost. So it pays the firm to produce. But if total revenue were less than total variable cost, the firm's economic loss would exceed total fixed cost. So the firm would shut down temporarily. Total fixed cost is the largest economic loss that the firm will incur.

The firm's economic loss equals total fixed cost when price equals average variable cost. So the firm produces if price exceeds average variable cost and shuts down if average variable cost exceeds price.

The Firm's Short-Run Supply Curve

A perfectly competitive firm's short-run supply curve shows how the firm's profit-maximizing output varies as the price varies, other things remaining the same. This supply curve is based on the marginal analysis and shutdown decision that we've just explored.

Figure 13.4 derives Dave's supply curve. Part (a) shows the marginal cost and average variable cost curves, and part (b) shows the supply curve. There is a direct link between the marginal cost and average variable cost curves and the supply curve. Let's see what that link is.

If the price is above minimum average variable cost, Dave maximizes profit by producing the output at which marginal cost equals price. We can determine the quantity produced at each price from the marginal cost curve. At a price of $8 a can, the marginal revenue curve is MR_1 and Dave maximizes profit by producing 10 cans a day. If the price rises to $12 a can, the marginal revenue curve is MR_2 and Dave increases production to 11 cans a day.

The firm shuts down if the price falls below minimum average variable cost. The **shutdown point** is the output and price at which the firm just covers its total variable cost. In Figure 13.4(a), if the price is $3 a can, the marginal revenue curve is MR_0, and the profit-maximizing output is 7 cans a day at the shutdown point.

Shutdown point
The output and price at which the firm just covers its total variable cost.

But both price and average variable cost equal $3 a can, so total revenue equals total variable cost and Dave incurs an economic loss equal to total fixed cost. At a price below $3 a can, if Dave produces any positive quantity, average *variable* cost exceeds price and the firm's loss exceeds total fixed cost. So at a price below $3 a can, Dave shuts down and produces nothing.

Dave's short-run supply curve, shown in Figure 13.4(b), has two separate parts: First, at prices that exceed minimum average variable cost, the supply curve is the same as the marginal cost curve above the shutdown point (T). Second, at prices below minimum average variable cost, Dave shuts down and produces nothing. His supply curve runs along the vertical axis. At a price of $3 a can, Dave is indifferent between shutting down and producing 7 cans a day. Either way, he incurs a loss of $15 a day, which equals his total fixed cost.

So far, we have studied one firm in isolation. We have seen that the firm's profit-maximizing actions depend on the price, which the firm takes as given. In the next section, you'll learn how market supply is determined.

■ **FIGURE 13.4**

Dave's Supply Curve

Part (a) shows that at $8 a can, Dave produces 10 cans a day; at $12 a can, he produces 11 cans a day; and at $3 a can, he produces either 7 cans a day or nothing. At any price below $3 a can, Dave produces nothing. The minimum average variable cost is the shutdown point.

Part (b) shows Dave's supply curve, which is made up of the marginal cost curve (part a) at all points *above* the shutdown point T (minimum average variable cost) and the vertical axis at all prices *below* the shutdown point.

(a) Marginal cost and average variable cost

(b) Dave's supply curve

CHECKPOINT 13.1

1 Explain a perfectly competitive firm's profit-maximizing choices and derive its supply curve.

Practice Problems 13.1

1. Sarah's Salmon Farm produces 1,000 fish a week. The marginal cost is $30 a fish, average variable cost is $20 a fish, and the market price is $25 a fish. Is Sarah maximizing profit? If Sarah is not maximizing profit, to do so, will she increase or decrease the number of fish she produces in a week?

2. Trout farming is a perfectly competitive industry, and all trout farms have the same cost curves. The market price is $25 a fish. To maximize profit, each farm produces 200 fish a week. Average total cost is $20 a fish, and average variable cost is $15 a fish. Minimum average variable cost is $12 a fish.
   a. If the price falls to $20 a fish, will a trout farm continue to produce 200 fish a week? Explain why or why not.
   b. If the price falls to $12 a fish, what will the trout farmer do?
   c. What is one point on the trout farm's supply curve?

Exercise 13.1

1. Paula is an asparagus farmer, and the world asparagus market is perfectly competitive. The market price is $15 a box. Paula sells 800 boxes a week, and her marginal cost is $18 a box.
   a. Calculate Paula's total revenue.
   b. Calculate Paula's marginal revenue.
   c. Is Paula maximizing profit? Explain your answer.
   d. The price falls to $12 a box, and Paula cuts her output to 500 boxes a week. Her average variable cost and marginal cost fall to $12 a box. Is Paula maximizing profit? Is she making an economic profit or a loss?
   e. What is one point on Paula's supply curve?

Solutions to Practice Problems 13.1

1. Profit is maximized when marginal cost equals marginal revenue. In perfect competition, marginal revenue equals the market price and is $25 a fish. Because marginal cost exceeds marginal revenue, Sarah is not maximizing profit. To maximize profit, Sarah will decrease her output until marginal cost falls to $25 a fish (Figure 1).

2a. The farm will produce fewer than 200 fish a week. The marginal cost increases as the farm produces more fish. So to reduce its marginal cost from $25 to $20, the farm cuts production.

2b. If the price falls to $12 a fish, farms cut production to the quantity at which marginal cost equals $12. But because $12 is minimum average variable cost, this price puts farms at the shutdown point. Farms will be indifferent between producing the profit-maximizing output and producing nothing. Either way, each farm incurs an economic loss equal to total fixed cost.

2c. At $25 a fish, the quantity supplied is 200 fish; at $12 a fish, the quantity supplied might be zero; at a price below $12 a fish, the quantity supplied is zero.

FIGURE 1

Price and cost (dollars per fish)

13.2 OUTPUT, PRICE, AND PROFIT IN THE SHORT RUN

To determine the price and quantity in a perfectly competitive market, we need to know how market demand and supply interact. We begin by studying a perfectly competitive market in the short run when the number of firms is fixed.

■ Market Supply in the Short Run

The market supply curve in the short run shows the quantity supplied at each price by a fixed number of firms. The quantity supplied at a given price is the sum of the quantities supplied by all firms at that price.

Figure 13.5 shows the supply curve for the competitive syrup market. In this example, the market consists of 10,000 firms exactly like Dave's Maple Syrup. The table shows how the market supply schedule is constructed. At prices below $3, every firm in the market shuts down; the quantity supplied is zero. At a price of $3, each firm is indifferent between shutting down and producing nothing or operating and producing 7 cans a day. The quantity supplied by each firm is *either* 0 or 7 cans, and the quantity supplied in the market is *between* 0 (all firms shut down) and 70,000 (all firms produce 7 cans a day each). At prices above $3, we sum the quantities supplied by the 10,000 firms, so the quantity supplied in the market is 10,000 times the quantity supplied by one firm.

At prices below $3, the market supply curve runs along the price axis. Supply is perfectly inelastic. At a price of $3, the market supply curve is horizontal. Supply is perfectly elastic. At prices above $3, the supply curve is upward sloping.

■ **FIGURE 13.5**

The Market Supply Curve

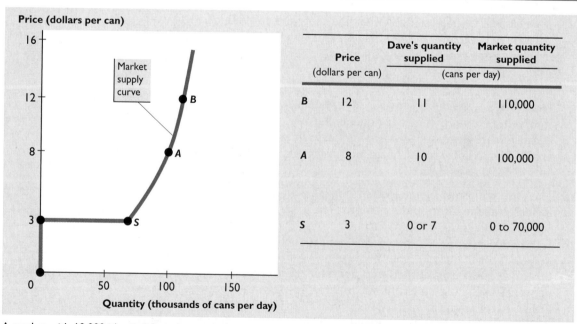

	Price	Dave's quantity supplied	Market quantity supplied
	(dollars per can)	(cans per day)	
B	12	11	110,000
A	8	10	100,000
S	3	0 or 7	0 to 70,000

A market with 10,000 identical firms has a supply schedule similar to that of the individual firm, but the quantity supplied is 10,000 times greater. At the shutdown price of $3 a can, each firm produces either 0 or 7 cans a day, but the market supply curve is perfectly elastic at that price.

■ Short-Run Equilibrium in Good Times

Market demand and market supply determine the price and quantity bought and sold. Figure 13.6(a) shows a short-run equilibrium in the syrup market. The supply curve S is the same as that in Figure 13.5.

If the demand curve D_1 shows market demand, the equilibrium price is $8 a can. Although market demand and market supply determine this price, each firm takes the price as given and produces its profit-maximizing output, which is 10 cans a day. Because the market has 10,000 firms, market output is 100,000 cans a day.

Figure 13.6(b) shows the situation that Dave faces. The price is $8 a can, so Dave's marginal revenue is constant at $8 a can. Dave maximizes profit by producing 10 cans a day.

Figure 13.6(b) also shows Dave's average total cost curve (*ATC*). Recall that average total cost is the cost per unit produced. It equals total cost divided by the quantity of output produced.

Here, when Dave produces 10 cans a day, his average total cost is $5.10 a can. So the price of $8 a can exceeds average total cost by $2.90 a can. This amount is Dave's economic profit per can.

If we multiply the economic profit per can of $2.90 by the number of cans, 10 a day, we arrive at Dave's economic profit, which is $29 a day.

The blue rectangle shows this economic profit. The height of that rectangle is the profit per can, $2.90, and the length is the quantity of cans, 10 a day, so the area of the rectangle (height × length) measures Dave's economic profit of $29 a day.

FIGURE 13.6
Economic Profit in the Short Run

(a) Syrup market

(b) Dave's syrup

In part (a), with market demand curve D_1 and market supply curve S, the equilibrium market price is $8 a can.

In part (b), Dave's marginal revenue is $8 a can, so he produces 10 cans a day. At this quantity, price ($8) exceeds average total cost ($5.10), so Dave makes an economic profit shown by the blue rectangle.

■ Short-Run Equilibrium in Bad Times

In the short-run equilibrium that we've just examined, Dave is enjoying an economic profit. But such an outcome is not inevitable. Figure 13.7 shows the syrup market in a less happy state. The market demand curve is now D_2. The market still has 10,000 firms, and the costs of these firms are the same as before. So the market supply curve, S, is the same as before.

With the demand and supply curves shown in Figure 13.7(a), the equilibrium price of syrup is $3 a can and the equilibrium quantity is 70,000 cans a day.

Figure 13.7(b) shows the situation that Dave faces. The price is $3 a can, so Dave's marginal revenue is constant at $3 a can. Dave maximizes profit by producing 7 cans a day.

Figure 13.7(b) also shows Dave's average total cost curve (ATC), and you can see that when Dave produces 7 cans a day, his average total cost is $5.14 a can. So the price of $3 a can is less than average total cost by $2.14 a can. This amount is Dave's economic loss per can.

If we multiply the economic loss per can of $2.14 by the number of cans, 7 a day, we arrive at Dave's economic loss, which is $14.98 a day.

The red rectangle shows this economic loss. The height of that rectangle is the loss per can, $2.14, and the length is the quantity of cans, 7 a day, so the area of the rectangle measures Dave's economic loss of $14.98 a day.

■ FIGURE 13.7
Economic Loss in the Short Run

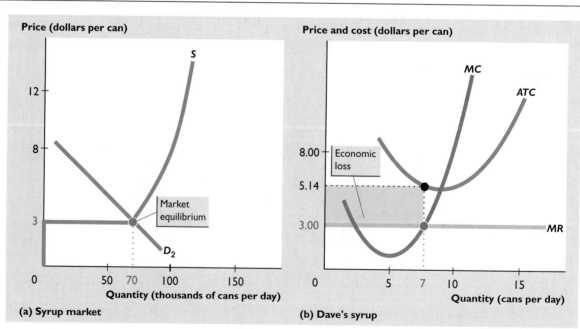

(a) Syrup market

(b) Dave's syrup

In part (a), with market demand curve D_2 and market supply curve S, the equilibrium market price is $3 a can.

In part (b), Dave's marginal revenue is $3 a can, so he produces 7 cans a day. At this quantity, price ($3) is less than average total cost ($5.14), so Dave incurs an economic loss shown by the red rectangle.

CHECKPOINT 13.2

2 **Explain how output, price, and profit are determined in the short run.**

Practice Problem 13.2

1. Tulip growing is a perfectly competitive industry, and all tulip growers have the same cost curves. The market price of tulips is $25 a bunch, and each grower maximizes profit by producing 2,000 bunches a week. The average total cost of producing tulips is $20 a bunch, and the average variable cost is $15 a bunch. Minimum average variable cost is $12 a bunch.
   a. What is the economic profit that each grower is making in the short run?
   b. What is the price at the grower's shutdown point?
   c. What is each grower's profit at the shutdown point?

Exercises 13.2

1. Tom's Tattoos is a tattooing business in a perfectly competitive market in Miami. The market price of a tattoo is $20. Table 1 shows Tom's total costs.
   a. How many tattoos an hour does Tom's Tattoos sell?
   b. What is Tom's Tattoos' economic profit in the short run?

2. In exercise 1, if the market price of a tattoo falls to $15,
   a. How many tattoos an hour does Tom's Tattoos sell?
   b. What is Tom's Tattoos' economic profit in the short run?

3. In exercise 1,
   a. At what market price will Tom's Tattoos shut down?
   b. At the shutdown point, what is Tom's Tattoos' economic loss?

TABLE 1

Quantity (tattoos per hour)	Total cost (dollars per hour)
0	30
1	50
2	65
3	75
4	90
5	110
6	140

Solution to Practice Problem 13.2

1a. The market price ($25) exceeds the average total cost ($20), so tulip growers are making an economic profit of $5 a bunch. Each grower produces 2,000 bunches a week, so each grower makes an economic profit of $10,000 a week (Figure 1).

1b. The price at which a grower will shut down is equal to minimum average variable cost—$12 a bunch (Figure 1).

1c. At the shutdown point, the grower incurs an economic loss equal to total fixed cost. $ATC = AFC + AVC$. When 2,000 bunches a week are grown, ATC is $20 a bunch and AVC is $15 a bunch, so AFC is $5 a bunch. Total fixed cost equals $10,000 a week—$5 a bunch × 2,000 bunches a week. So at the shutdown point, the grower incurs an economic loss equal to $10,000 a week.

FIGURE 1

13.3 OUTPUT, PRICE, AND PROFIT IN THE LONG RUN

Neither good times nor bad times last forever in perfect competition. In the long run, a firm in perfect competition earns normal profit. It earns zero economic profit and incurs no economic loss.

Figure 13.8 shows the syrup market in a long-run equilibrium. The market demand curve is now D_3. The market still has 10,000 firms, and the costs of these firms are the same as before. So the market supply curve, S, is the same as before.

With the demand and supply curves shown in Figure 13.8(a), the equilibrium price of syrup is $5 a can and the equilibrium quantity is 90,000 cans a day.

Figure 13.8(b) shows the situation that Dave faces. The price is $5 a can, so Dave's marginal revenue is constant at $5 a can and Dave maximizes profit by producing 9 cans a day.

Figure 13.8(b) also shows Dave's average total cost curve (*ATC*), and you can see that when Dave produces 9 cans a day, his average total cost is $5 a can, which is also the minimum average total cost. That is, Dave can't produce syrup at an average total cost that is less than $5 a can no matter what his output is.

The price of $5 a can equals average total cost, so Dave has neither an economic profit nor an economic loss. He breaks even. But because his average total cost includes normal profit, Dave earns normal profit.

■ **FIGURE 13.8**

Long-run Equilibrium

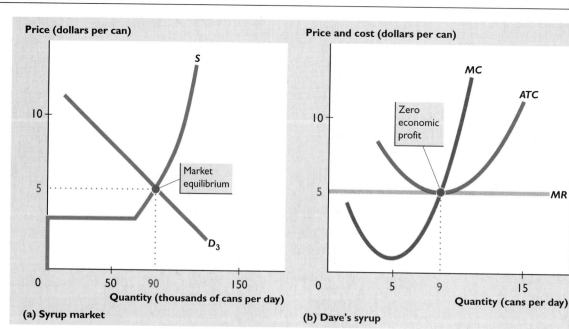

(a) Syrup market

(b) Dave's syrup

In part (a), with market demand curve D_3 and market supply curve, S, the equilibrium market price is $5 a can.

In part (b), Dave's marginal revenue is $5 a can, so he produces 9 cans a day, where marginal cost equals marginal revenue. At this profit-maximizing quantity, price equals average total cost ($5), so Dave earns no economic profit. He earns normal profit.

■ Entry and Exit

In the short run, a perfectly competitive firm might make an economic profit (Figure 13.6) or incur an economic loss (Figure 13.7). But in the long run, a firm earns normal profit (Figure 13.8).

In the long run, firms respond to economic profit and economic loss by either entering or exiting a market. New firms enter a market in which the existing firms are making an economic profit. And existing firms exit a market in which they are incurring an economic loss. Temporary economic profit or temporary economic loss, like a win or loss at a casino, does not trigger entry and exit. But the prospect of persistent economic profit or loss does.

Entry and exit influence price, the quantity produced, and economic profit. The immediate effect of the decision to enter or exit is to shift the market supply curve. If more firms enter a market, supply increases and the market supply curve shifts rightward. If firms exit a market, supply decreases and the market supply curve shifts leftward.

Let's see what happens when new firms enter a market.

The Effects of Entry

Figure 13.9 shows the effects of entry. Initially, the market is in long-run equilibrium. Demand is D_0, supply is S_0, the price is $5 a can, and the quantity is 90,000 cans a day. A surge in the popularity of syrup increases demand, and the demand curve shifts to D_1. The price rises to $8 a can, and the firms in the syrup market increase output to 100,000 cans a day and make an economic profit.

Times are good for syrup producers like Dave, so other potential syrup producers want some of the action. New firms begin to enter the market. As they do so, supply increases and the market supply curve shifts rightward to S_1. With the

---

■ FIGURE 13.9
The Effects of Entry

Starting in long-run equilibrium, ❶ demand increases and the demand curve shifts from D_0 to D_1. The price rises from $5 to $8 a can.

Economic profit brings entry. ❷ As firms enter the market, the supply curve shifts rightward, from S_0 to S_1. The equilibrium price falls from $8 to $5 a can, and the quantity produced increases from 100,000 to 140,000 cans a day.

greater supply and unchanged demand, the price falls from $8 to $5 a can and the quantity increases to 140,000 cans a day.

Market output increases, but because the price falls, Dave and the other producers decrease output, back to its original level. But because the number of firms in the market increases, the market as a whole produces more.

As the price falls, each firm's economic profit decreases. When the price falls to $5, economic profit disappears and each firm makes a normal profit. The entry process stops, and the market is again in long-run equilibrium.

You have just discovered a key proposition:

Economic profit is an incentive for new firms to enter a market, but as they do so, the price falls and the economic profit of each existing firm decreases.

The Effects of Exit

Figure 13.10 shows the effects of exit. Again we begin on demand curve D_0 and supply curve S_0 in long-run equilibrium. Now suppose that the development of a new high-nutrition, low-fat breakfast food decreases the demand for pancakes, and as a result, the demand for maple syrup decreases. The demand curve shifts from D_0 to D_2. Firms' costs are the same as before, so the market supply curve is S_0.

With demand at D_2 and supply at S_0, the price falls to $3 a can and 70,000 cans a day are produced. The firms in the syrup market incur economic losses.

Times are tough for syrup producers, and Dave must seriously think about leaving his dream business and finding some other way of making a living. But other producers are in the same situation as Dave. And some start to exit the market while Dave is still thinking through his options.

■ **FIGURE 13.10**

The Effects of Exit

Starting in long-run equilibrium, ❶ demand decreases and the demand curve shifts from D_0 to D_2. The price falls from $5 to $3 a can.

Economic loss brings exit. ❷ As firms exit the market, the supply curve shifts leftward, from S_0 to S_2. The equilibrium price rises from $3 to $5 a can, and the quantity produced decreases from 70,000 to 40,000 cans a day.

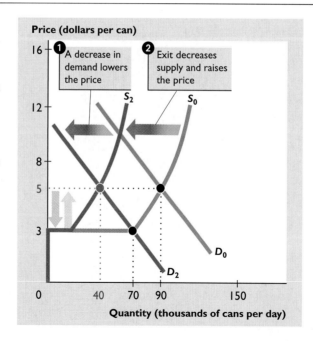

As firms exit, the market supply curve shifts leftward to S_2. With the decrease in supply, output decreases from 70,000 to 40,000 cans and the price rises from $3 to $5 a can.

As the price rises, Dave and each other firm that remains in the market move up along their supply curves and increase output. That is, for each firm that remains in the market, the profit-maximizing output *increases*. As the price rises and each firm sells more, economic loss decreases. When the price rises to $5, each firm makes a normal profit. Dave is happy that he can still make a living producing syrup.

You have just discovered a second key proposition:

Economic loss is an incentive for firms to exit a market, but as they do so, the price rises and the economic loss of each remaining firm decreases.

EYE ON THE U.S. ECONOMY

Entry in Personal Computers, Exit in Farm Machines

An example of entry and falling prices occurred during the 1980s and 1990s in the personal computer market. When IBM introduced its first PC in 1981, there was little competition; the price was $7,000 (a bit more than $14,000 in today's money), and IBM earned a large economic profit on the new machine. But new firms such as Compaq, NEC, Dell, and a host of others entered the market with machines that were technologically identical to IBM's. In fact, they were so similar that they came to be called "clones." The massive wave of entry into the personal computer market shifted the supply curve rightward and lowered the price and the economic profit for all firms. Today, a $1,000 computer is much more powerful than its 1981 ancestor that cost 14 times as much.

An example of a firm leaving a market is International Harvester, a manufacturer of farm equipment. For decades, people associated the name "International Harvester" with tractors, combines, and other farm machines. But International Harvester wasn't the only maker of farm equipment. The market became intensely competitive, and the firm began to incur an economic loss. Now the company has a new name, Navistar International, and it doesn't make tractors any more. After years of economic losses and shrinking revenues, it got out of the farm-machine business in 1985 and started to make trucks.

International Harvester exited because it was incurring an economic loss. Its exit decreased supply and made it possible for the remaining firms in the market to earn a normal profit.

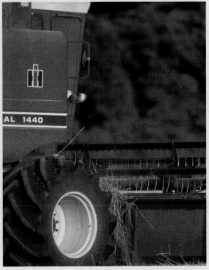

■ Change in Demand

A competitive market is in long-run equilibrium and the firms are earning normal profit (zero economic profit). Then demand increases, the price rises, firms increase production to keep marginal cost equal to price, and firms are earning an economic profit. The market is now in short-run equilibrium but not in long-run equilibrium.

Economic profit is an incentive for new firms to enter the market. As firms enter, market supply increases and the price falls. With a lower price, firms decrease output to keep marginal cost equal to price.

Notice that as firms enter the market, market output increases, but each firm's output decreases. Eventually, enough firms enter to eliminate economic profit and the market is again in long-run equilibrium.

The key difference between the initial long-run equilibrium and the new long-run equilibrium is the number of firms. A permanent increase in demand increases the number of firms. Each firm produces the same output in the new long-run equilibrium as initially and earns normal profit. In the process of moving from the initial equilibrium to the new one, firms earn economic profits.

The demand for airline travel in the world economy increased during the 1990s, and the deregulation of the airlines freed up firms to seek profit opportunities in this market. The result was a massive rate of entry of new airlines. The process of competition and change in the airline market were similar to what we have just studied.

A decrease in demand triggers a similar response, except in the opposite direction. The decrease in demand brings a lower price, economic loss, and exit. Exit decreases market supply, raises the price, and eliminates the economic loss.

■ Technological Change

Firms are constantly discovering lower-cost techniques of production. For example, the cost of producing personal computers has tumbled. So have the cost of MP3 players and most other electronic products. Most cost-saving production techniques can be implemented only by investing in a new plant. Consequently, it takes time for a technological advance to spread through an industry. Firms whose plants are on the verge of being replaced are quick to adopt the new technology, while firms whose plants have recently been replaced continue to operate an old technology until they can no longer cover their average variable cost. Once average variable cost cannot be covered, a firm scraps even a relatively new plant (embodying an old technology) in favor of a plant with a new technology.

New technology lowers cost. So as firms adopt a new technology, their cost curves shift downward. With lower costs, firms are willing to supply a given quantity at a lower price, or, equivalently, they are willing to supply a larger quantity at a given price. In other words, market supply increases, and the market supply curve shifts rightward. With a given demand, the quantity produced increases and the price falls.

Firms that adopt the new technology make an economic profit, so new-technology firms enter. Firms that stick with the old technology incur economic losses, so they either exit or switch to the new technology. As new-technology firms enter and old-technology firms exit, the price falls and the quantity produced increases. Eventually, the market arrives at a long-run equilibrium in which all the firms use the new technology and each firm makes zero economic profit (a normal profit).

Because competition eliminates economic profit in the long run, technological change brings only temporary gains to firms. But the lower prices and better products that technological advances bring are permanent gains for consumers.

The process that we've just described is one in which some firms experience economic profits and others experience economic losses—a period of dynamic change for a market. Some firms do well, and others do badly. Often, the process has a geographical dimension—the expanding new-technology firms bring prosperity to what was once the boondocks, and with old-technology firms going out of business, traditional industrial regions decline. Sometimes, the new-technology firms are in a foreign country, while the old-technology firms are in the domestic economy. The information revolution of the 1990s produced many examples of changes like these. Commercial banking (a competitive but less than perfectly competitive industry), traditionally concentrated in New York, San Francisco, and

EYE ON THE GLOBAL ECONOMY

The North American Market in Maple Syrup

North American maple syrup production runs at about 8 million gallons a year. Most of this syrup is produced in Canada, but farms in Vermont, New York, Maine, Wisconsin, New Hampshire, Ohio, and Michigan together produce close to 20 percent of the total output.

The number of firms that produce maple syrup can only be estimated, because some are tiny and sell their output to a small local market. But there are around 9,500 producers in Canada and approaching 2,000 in the United States.

The syrup of each producer is not quite identical. And at the retail level, people have preferences about brands and sources of supply. But at the wholesale level, the market is highly competitive and a good example of perfect competition.

All of the events that can occur in a perfectly competitive market and that we've studied in this chapter have actually occurred in the maple syrup market over the past 20 years.

During the 1980s, the technology for extracting sap advanced as more taps that use a plastic tube vacuum technology were installed. During this period, farms exited the market and the average farm increased in scale. In 1980, the average farm had 1,400 taps; by 1990, this number was 2,000; and

by 1996, the number of taps had increased to 2,400.

During the 1990s, with a steady growth in the demand for maple syrup, new farms entered the market.

Through the past 20 years, total production has increased and the price has held remarkably stable at around $8 per half-gallon can. So increasing demand has brought economic profit, which in turn has brought entry and an increase in supply.

other large cities, now flourishes in Charlotte, North Carolina, which has become the nation's number three commercial banking city. Television shows and movies, traditionally made in Los Angeles and New York, are now made in large numbers in Orlando and Toronto.

Technological advances are not confined to the information and entertainment market. Food production has seen major technological change, and today, genetic engineering is fueling that change.

■ Is Perfect Competition Efficient?

Perfect competition is efficient. To see why, first recall the conditions for an efficient allocation of resources. Resources are used efficiently when it is not possible to get more of one good without giving up something that is valued more highly. To achieve this outcome, marginal benefit must equal marginal cost. That is what perfect competition achieves.

We derive a firm's supply curve in perfect competition from its marginal cost curve. The supply curve is the marginal cost curve at all points above the minimum of average variable cost (the shutdown price). Because the market supply curve is found by summing the quantities supplied by all the firms at each price, the market supply curve is the entire market's marginal cost curve.

The demand curve is the marginal benefit curve. And because the supply curve and demand curve intersect at the equilibrium price, that price equals both marginal cost and marginal benefit.

Figure 13.11 illustrates the efficiency of perfect competition. We've labeled the demand curve $D = MB$ and the supply curve $S = MC$ to remind you that these curves are also the marginal benefit (MB) and marginal cost (MC) curves.

▓ FIGURE 13.11
The Efficiency of Perfect Competition

❶ Market equilibrium occurs at a price of $5 a can and a quantity of 90 cans a day.

❷ The supply curve is also the marginal cost curve.

❸ The demand curve is also the marginal benefit curve.

Because at the market equilibrium, marginal benefit equals marginal cost, the ❹ efficient quantity of syrup is produced. ❺ Total surplus (consumer surplus plus producer surplus) is maximized.

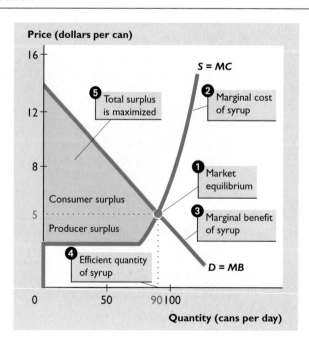

These curves intersect at the equilibrium price and quantity. The price equals marginal benefit and marginal cost. And the equilibrium quantity is efficient. The total surplus, which is the sum of consumer surplus and producer surplus, is maximized. Any departure from this outcome is inferior to it and brings an avoidable deadweight loss.

▇ Is Perfect Competition Fair?

Perfect competition places no restrictions on anyone's actions. Everyone is free to try to earn an economic profit. And the process of competition eliminates economic profit and brings maximum attainable benefit to the consumer.

Fairness as equality of opportunity and fairness as equality of outcomes are achieved in perfect competition in long-run equilibrium.

But in the short run, economic profit and economic loss arise. So there are unequal outcomes in the short run. These inequalities might sometimes seem unfair.

REALITY CHECK

Perfect Competition in YOUR Life

You don't run into *perfect* competition very often. But you do see many markets that are highly competitive and almost perfectly competitive. And your entire life is influenced by and benefits immeasurably from the forces of competition. Adam Smith's invisible hand might be hidden from view, but it is enormously powerful.

Just about every good or service that you consume and take for granted is available because of the forces of competition. Your home, your food, your clothing, your books, your CDs, your MP3 files, your computer, your bike, your car, ..., the list is endless.

No one organizes all the magic that enables you to consume this vast array of products. But competitive markets and entrepreneurs striving to earn the largest possible profit make it happen.

When either demand or technology changes and makes the current allocation of resources the wrong one, the market swiftly and silently acts. It sends signals to entrepreneurs that bring entry and exit and a new and efficient use of scarce resources.

3 Explain how output, price, and profit are determined in the long run and explain why perfect competition is efficient.

Practice Problem 13.3

1. Tulip growing is a perfectly competitive industry, and all tulip growers have the same cost curves. The market price of tulips is $15 a bunch, and each grower maximizes profit by producing 1,500 bunches a week. The average total cost of producing tulips is $21 a bunch. Minimum average variable cost is $12 a bunch, and the minimum average total cost is $18 a bunch.
   a. What is a tulip grower's economic profit in the short run?
   b. How does the number of tulip growers change in the long run?
   c. What is the price in the long run?
   d. What is a tulip grower's economic profit in the long run?

Exercise 13.3

TABLE 1

Quantity (tattoos per hour)	Total cost (dollars per hour)
0	30
1	50
2	65
3	75
4	90
5	110
6	140

1. Tom's Tattoos is a tattooing business in a perfectly competitive market in Miami. Table 1 shows Tom's total costs.
   a. If the market price is $20 per tattoo, what is Tom's economic profit?
   b. If the market price is $20 per tattoo, do new firms enter or do existing firms exit the industry in the long run?
   c. What is the price of a tattoo in the long run?
   d. How many tattoos per hour does Tom sell in the long run?
   e. What is Tom's economic profit in the long run?

Solution to Practice Problem 13.3

FIGURE 1

Price and cost (dollars per bunch)

1a. The price is less than average total cost, so the tulip grower is incurring an economic loss in the short run. Because the price exceeds minimum average variable cost, the tulip grower continues to produce. The economic loss equals the loss per bunch ($21 minus $15) multiplied by the number of bunches (1,500), which equals $9,000 (Figure 1).

1b. Because firms in the industry are incurring a loss, some firms will exit in the long run. So the number of tulip growers will decrease.

1c. The price in the long run will be such that economic profit is zero. That is, as tulip growers exit, the price will rise until it equals minimum average total cost. The long-run price will be $18 a bunch (Figure 2).

1d. A tulip grower's economic profit in the long run will be zero because average total cost equals price. Each tulip grower will make a normal profit (Figure 2).

FIGURE 2

Price and cost (dollars per bunch)

CHAPTER CHECKPOINT

Key Points

1   **Explain a perfectly competitive firm's profit-maximizing choices and derive its supply curve.**

- A perfectly competitive firm is a price taker.
- Marginal revenue equals price.
- The firm produces the output at which price equals marginal cost.
- If price is less than minimum average variable cost, the firm temporarily shuts down.
- A firm's supply curve is the upward-sloping part of its marginal cost curve above minimum average variable cost and the vertical axis at all prices below minimum average variable cost.

2   **Explain how output, price, and profit are determined in the short run.**

- Market demand and market supply determine price.
- Firms choose the quantity to produce that maximizes profit, which is the quantity at which marginal cost equals price.
- In short-run equilibrium, a firm can make an economic profit or incur an economic loss.

3   **Explain how output, price, and profit are determined in the long run and explain why perfect competition is efficient.**

- Economic profit induces entry, which increases market supply and lowers price and profit. Economic loss induces exit, which decreases market supply, raises price, and lowers the losses.
- In the long run, economic profit is zero and there is no entry or exit.
- An increase in demand increases the number of firms and increases the equilibrium quantity.
- An advance in technology that lowers cost increases market supply, lowers the price, and increases the quantity.
- Perfect competition is efficient because it makes marginal benefit equal marginal cost, and it is fair in the sense that it provides equal opportunity for profit.

Key Terms

Marginal revenue, 325
Monopolistic competition, 324
Monopoly, 324
Oligopoly, 324

Perfect competition, 324
Price taker, 325
Shutdown point, 329

Exercises

1. In what type of market is each of the following goods and services sold? Explain your answers.
   a. Wheat
   b. Jeans
   c. Camera film
   d. Toothpaste
   e. Taxi rides in a town with one taxi company

2. Explain why in a perfectly competitive market, the firm is a price taker. Why can't the firm choose the price at which it sells its good?

3. Table 1 shows the demand schedule for Lin's Fortune Cookies.
   a. In what type of market does Lin's Fortune Cookies operate? How can you tell?
   b. Calculate Lin's marginal revenue for each quantity demanded.
   c. Why does Lin's marginal revenue equal price?

4. Table 2 shows some cost data for Lin's Fortune Cookies, which operates in the market described in exercise 3. To answer these questions, draw Lin's short-run cost curves.

TABLE I

Price (dollars per batch)	Quantity demanded (batches of fortune cookies per day)
50	0
50	1
50	2
50	3
50	4
50	5
50	6

TABLE 2

Total product (batches of cookies per day)	Average fixed cost	Average variable cost	Average total cost	Marginal cost
		(dollars per batch)		
1	84.0	51.00	135	
				37
2	42.0	44.00	86	
				29
3	28.0	39.00	67	
				27
4	21.0	36.00	57	
				32
5	16.8	35.20	52	
				40
6	14.0	36.00	50	
				57
7	12.0	39.00	51	
				83
8	10.5	44.50	55	

   a. At a price of $50 per batch of cookies, what quantity does Lin produce and what is the firm's economic profit? Do firms enter or exit the industry?
   b. At a price of $35.20 per batch, what quantity does Lin produce and what is the firm's economic profit? Do firms enter or exit the industry?
   c. At a price of $83 per batch, what quantity does Lin produce and what is the firm's economic profit? Do firms enter or exit the industry?

5. Use the data in Table 2 to create Lin's short-run supply schedule and make a graph of Lin's short-run supply curve.

6. Explain why Lin's supply curve is only part of his marginal cost curve. Why will Lin never consider producing two batches of fortune cookies a day?

7. Suppose there are 1,000 fortune cookie producers that are exactly like Lin's Fortune Cookies. Table 3 shows the demand schedule for fortune cookies.
   a. What is the short-run equilibrium price of fortune cookies?
   b. What is the short-run equilibrium quantity of fortune cookies?
   c. What is the economic profit earned or loss incurred by each firm?
   d. Do firms enter or exit the industry? Why?
   e. What is the price in long-run equilibrium?
   f. Approximately how many firms are in the industry in long-run equilibrium?

8. Suppose that the restaurant industry is perfectly competitive. Joe's Diner is always packed in the evening but rarely has a customer at lunchtime. Why doesn't Joe's Diner close—temporarily shut down—at lunchtime?

9. 3M created the sticky note, which 3M called the Post-it note. Soon many other firms entered the sticky note market and started to produce sticky notes.
   a. What was the incentive for these firms to enter the sticky note market?
   b. As time goes by, do you expect more firms to enter this market? Explain why or why not.
   c. Can you think of any reason why any of these firms might exit the sticky note market?

10. In 1969, when Rod Laver completed his tennis grand slam, all tennis rackets were made of wood. Today, tennis players use graphite rackets.
    a. Draw two graphs of the market for wooden tennis rackets in 1969: one that shows the market as a whole and one that shows an individual producer of rackets.
    b. Show in the graphs the effect of a permanent decrease in the demand for wooden rackets.
    c. How did the economic profit from producing wooden rackets change and what effects did the change in profit have on the number of producers of wooden rackets?

11. During the 1980s and 1990s, the cost of producing a personal computer decreased.
    a. Draw two graphs of the market for personal computers: one that shows the market as a whole and one that shows an individual producer.
    b. Show in the graphs the effect of a decrease in the cost of producing a computer on the price of a computer, the quantity of computers bought, and the economic profit of producers in the short run and in the long run.

12. Small aluminum scooters became popular during 2000. Sketch the cost and revenue curves of a typical firm in the scooter industry when
    a. The scooter fashion began.
    b. The scooter fashion was two years old.
    c. The scooter fashion faded.

TABLE 3

Price (dollars per batch)	Quantity demanded (batches per day)
92	4,000
85	4,500
78	5,000
71	5,500
64	6,000
57	6,500
50	7,000
43	7,500
36	8,000

Critical Thinking

13. Airport security was stepped up after the attacks on September 11, 2001, and much of the additional security service was provided by private firms that operate in a competitive market. Use the perfect competition model to answer the following questions.
    a. Do you think that airport security providers earned an economic profit or incurred an economic loss during 2002? Explain your answer.
    b. Would you expect the price of airport security services to have increased or decreased in 2003 and 2004? Why?

14. Review *Eye on the Global Economy* on p. 341.
    a. List the features of the maple syrup market that make it an example of perfect competition.
    b. Draw a graph to describe the maple syrup market and the cost and revenue of an individual firm in 1980, assuming that the industry was in long-run equilibrium.
    c. Use your answer to part **b** to explain the effects of the technological changes in maple syrup farming during the 1980s.
    d. Suppose that Aunt Jemima invents a new maple-flavored syrup that no one can distinguish, in a blind test, from the real thing and can produce it for $5 a gallon. What effect would this invention have on the market for real maple syrup? Illustrate the effects graphically.

15. The combination of the DVD player, the flat plasma screen, and surround sound has revolutionized watching a movie at home. At the same time, advances in technology in the movie theater have raised the standard that the home entertainment alternative must achieve. Think about the effects of these technological changes on competitive markets for goods and services that are influenced by movie going and home movie watching. Identify the market for one related good or service that will expand and one that will contract. Describe in detail the sequence of events as the two markets you've identified respond to the new technologies.

 ## Web Exercise

Use the links on MyEconLab to work the following exercise.

16. Open the spreadsheet that provides information about the world market for wheat and then answer the following questions:
    a. Is the world market for wheat perfectly competitive? Why or why not?
    b. What happened to the price of wheat during the 1990s?
    c. What happened to the quantity of wheat produced during the 1990s?
    d. What do you think were the main influences on the demand for wheat during the 1990s?
    e. What do you think were the main influences on the supply of wheat during the 1990s?
    f. Do you think farmers entered or exited the wheat market during the 1990s? Explain your answer.

Monopoly

CHAPTER CHECKLIST

When you have completed your study of this chapter, you will be able to

1 Explain how monopoly arises and distinguish between single-price monopoly and price-discriminating monopoly.

2 Explain how a single-price monopoly determines its output and price.

3 Compare the performance of a single-price monopoly with that of perfect competition.

4 Explain how price discrimination increases profit.

5 Explain why monopoly can sometimes achieve a better allocation of resources than competition can.

From Boston to Baton Rouge to Sacramento, cable TV customers are fuming. AT&T Broadband rates are up 8 percent, Cox Communications rates are up 7 percent, Comcast standard rates are up 6.2 percent, and rates for premium packages are up by as much as 21 percent. But what can an angry customer do when there's no effective alternative to cable? Switch to satellite perhaps. But the switch isn't hassle-free.

The providers of cable TV services face little competition. They are the sole suppliers of these services in the regions they serve—they are monopolies. How does a monopoly choose the quantity to produce and the price at which to sell it? Does a monopoly charge too much?

In this chapter, we study monopolies such as your cable TV provider. We learn how a monopoly behaves, and we discover whether it is efficient and fair.

349

14.1 MONOPOLY AND HOW IT ARISES

The market for diamonds is close to being a monopoly.

A *monopoly* is a market with a single supplier of a good or service that has no close substitutes and in which a barrier to entry prevents competition from new firms.

Markets for local telephone service, gas, electricity, and water are examples of local monopoly. GlaxoSmithKline has a monopoly on AZT, a drug that is used to treat AIDS. DeBeers, a South African firm, controls 80 percent of the world's production of raw diamonds—close to being a monopoly but not quite one.

■ How Monopoly Arises

Monopoly arises when there are

- No close substitutes
- A barrier to entry

No Close Substitutes

If a good has a close substitute, even though only one firm produces it, that firm effectively faces competition from the producers of substitutes. Water supplied by a local public utility is an example of a good that does not have close substitutes. While it does have a close substitute for drinking—bottled spring water—it has no effective substitutes for doing the laundry, taking a shower, or washing a car.

The availability of close substitutes isn't static. Technological change can create substitutes and weaken a monopoly. For example, the creation of courier services such as UPS and the development of the fax machine and e-mail provide close substitutes for the mail-carrying services provided by the U.S. Postal Service and have weakened its monopoly. Broadband fiber-optic phone lines and satellite dishes have weakened the monopoly of cable television companies.

The arrival of a new product can also create a monopoly. For example, the IBM PC of the early 1980s provided an opportunity for Microsoft to become the monopoly supplier of DOS and Windows.

A Barrier to Entry

Anything that protects a firm from the arrival of new competitors is a **barrier to entry**. There are three types of barrier to entry:

- Natural
- Ownership
- Legal

Barrier to entry
A natural or legal constraint that protects a firm from competitors.

Natural monopoly
A monopoly that arises because one firm can meet the entire market demand at a lower average total cost than two or more firms could.

Natural Barrier to Entry A **natural monopoly** exists when the technology for producing a good or service enables one firm to meet the entire market demand at a lower average total cost than two or more firms could. One electric power distributor can meet the market demand for electricity at a lower cost than two or more firms could. Imagine two or more sets of wires running to your home so that you could choose your electric power supplier.

Figure 14.1 illustrates a natural monopoly in the distribution of electric power. Here, the demand curve for electric power is *D*, and the long-run average cost curve is *LRAC*. Economies of scale prevail over the entire length of this *LRAC* curve, indicated by the fact that the curve slopes downward. One firm can produce 4 million kilowatt-hours at 5 cents a kilowatt-hour. At this price, the quan-

FIGURE 14.1
Natural Monopoly

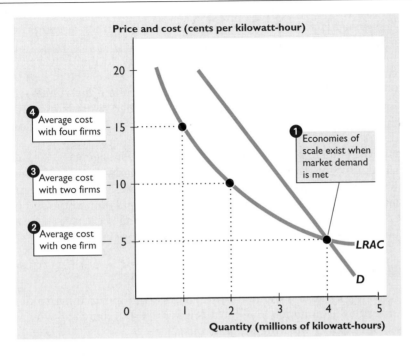

The demand curve for electric power is *D*, and the long-run average cost curve is *LRAC*.

❶ Economies of scale exist over the entire *LRAC* curve. One firm can distribute 4 million kilowatt-hours at a **❷** cost of 5 cents a kilowatt-hour. This same total output **❸** costs 10 cents a kilowatt-hour with two firms and **❹** 15 cents a kilowatt-hour with four firms. So one firm can meet the market demand at a lower cost than two or more firms can, and the market is a natural monopoly.

tity demanded is 4 million kilowatt-hours. So if the price was 5 cents, one firm could supply the entire market. If two or more firms shared the market, average total cost would be higher.

In Chapter 10 (p. 243), we said that a good that is nonrival but excludable is produced by a natural monopoly. You can now see why. If a good is nonrival, one more person can use it without any additional cost being incurred. The costs of producing the good are fixed costs, and the cost of supplying an additional user is zero. So for a nonrival good, the average total cost curve slopes downward like that in Figure 14.1. If the good is excludable as well as nonrival, it will be produced by a natural monopoly.

Ownership Barrier to Entry   A monopoly can arise in a market in which competition and entry are restricted by the concentration of ownership of a natural resource. DeBeers, which controls more than 80 percent of the world's production of raw diamonds, is an example of this type of monopoly. There is no natural barrier to entry in diamonds. Even though the diamond is a relatively rare mineral, its sources of supply could have many owners who compete in a global competitive auction market. Only by buying control over most of the world's diamonds was DeBeers able to prevent entry and competition.

Legal Barrier to Entry   A legal barrier to entry creates a legal monopoly. A **legal monopoly** is a market in which competition and entry are restricted by the granting of a public franchise, government license, patent, or copyright.

A *public franchise* is an exclusive right granted to a firm to supply a good or service, an example of which is the U.S. Postal Service's exclusive right to deliver

Legal monopoly
A market in which competition and entry are restricted by granting of a public franchise, government license, patent, or copyright.

first-class mail. A *government license* controls entry into particular occupations, professions, and industries. An example is Michael's Texaco in Charleston, Rhode Island, which is the only firm in the area licensed to test for vehicle emissions.

A *patent* is an exclusive right granted to the inventor of a product or service. A *copyright* is an exclusive right granted to the author or composer of a literary, musical, dramatic, or artistic work. Patents and copyrights are valid for a limited time period that varies from country to country. In the United States, a patent is valid for 20 years. Patents are designed to encourage the *invention* of new products and production methods. They also stimulate *innovation*—the use of new inventions—by encouraging inventors to publicize their discoveries and offer them for use under license. Patents have stimulated innovations in areas as diverse as soybean seeds, pharmaceuticals, memory chips, and video games.

Most monopolies are regulated by government agencies. We can better understand why governments regulate monopolies and what effects regulations have if we know how an unregulated monopoly behaves. So we'll first study an unregulated monopoly and then look at monopoly regulation at the end of this chapter.

A monopoly sets its own price, but in doing so, it faces a market constraint. Let's see how the market limits a monopoly's pricing choices.

■ Monopoly Price-Setting Strategies

A monopoly faces a tradeoff between price and the quantity sold. To sell a larger quantity, the monopoly must set a lower price. But there are two price-setting possibilities that create different tradeoffs:

- Single price
- Price discrimination

Single Price

Single-price monopoly
A monopoly that must sell each unit of its output for the same price to all its customers.

A **single-price monopoly** is a firm that must sell each unit of its output for the same price to all its customers. DeBeers sells diamonds (of a given size and quality) for the same price to all its customers. If it tried to sell at a higher price to some customers than to others, only the low-price customers would buy from DeBeers. Others would buy from DeBeers's low-price customers. So DeBeers is a *single-price* monopoly.

Price Discrimination

Price-discriminating monopoly
A monopoly that is able to sell different units of a good or service for different prices.

A **price-discriminating monopoly** is a firm that is able to sell different units of a good or service for different prices. Many firms price discriminate. Airlines offer a dizzying array of different prices for the same trip. Pizza producers charge one price for a single pizza and almost give away a second one. Different customers might pay different prices (like airfares), or one customer might pay different prices for different quantities bought (like the bargain price for a second pizza).

When a firm price discriminates, it appears to be doing its customers a favor. In fact, it is charging each group of customers the highest price it can get them to pay and is increasing its profit.

Not all monopolies can price discriminate. The main obstacle to the practice of price discrimination is resale by the customers who buy for a low price. Because of resale possibilities, price discrimination is limited to monopolies that sell services that cannot be resold.

CHECKPOINT 14.1

1 **Explain how monopoly arises and distinguish between single-price monopoly and price-discriminating monopoly.**

Practice Problems 14.1

1. Monopoly arises in which of the following situations?
   a. Coca-Cola cuts its price below that of Pepsi-Cola in an attempt to increase its market share.
   b. A single firm, protected by a barrier to entry, produces a personal service that has no close substitutes.
   c. A barrier to entry exists, but some close substitutes for the good exist.
   d. A firm offers discounts to students and seniors.
   e. A firm can sell any quantity it chooses at the going price.
   f. The government issues Tiger Woods, Inc. an exclusive license to produce golf balls.
   g. A firm experiences economies of scale even when it produces the quantity that meets the entire market demand.

2. Which of the cases **a** to **f** in practice problem 1 are natural monopolies and which are legal monopolies? Which can price discriminate, which cannot, and why?

Exercises 14.1

1. Which of the following are monopolies?
   a. A large shopping mall in downtown Houston
   b. Tiffany, the upscale jeweler
   c. Wal-Mart
   d. The Grand Canyon mule train
   e. The only shoe-shine stand licensed to operate in an airport
   f. The U.S. Postal Service

2. Which of the monopolies in exercise 1 are natural monopolies and which are legal monopolies? Which can price discriminate, which cannot, and why?

Solutions to Practice Problems 14.1

1. Monopoly arises when a single firm produces a good or service that has no close substitutes and a barrier to entry exists. Monopoly arises in **b**, **f**, and **g**. In **a**, there is more than one firm. In **c**, the good has some close substitutes. In **d**, a monopoly might be able to price discriminate, but other types of firms (for example, pizza producers and art museums) price discriminate and they are not monopolies. In **e**, the demand for the good that the firm produces is perfectly elastic and there is no limit to what the firm could sell if it wished. Such a firm is in perfect competition.

2. Natural monopoly exists when one firm can meet the entire market demand at a lower price than two or more firms could. So **g** is a natural monopoly, but **b** could be also. Legal monopoly exists when the granting of a right creates a barrier to entry. So **f** is a legal monopoly, but **b** could be also. Monopoly **b** could price discriminate because a personal service cannot be resold.

14.2 SINGLE-PRICE MONOPOLY

To understand how a single-price monopoly makes its output and price decisions, we must first study the link between price and marginal revenue.

■ Price and Marginal Revenue

Because in a monopoly there is only one firm, the demand for the firm's output is the market demand. Let's look at Bobbie's Barbershop, the sole supplier of haircuts in Cairo, Nebraska. The table in Figure 14.2 shows the demand schedule for Bobbie's haircuts. For example, at $12, consumers demand 4 haircuts an hour (row E).

Total revenue is the price multiplied by the quantity sold. For example, in row D, Bobbie sells 3 haircuts at $14 each, so total revenue is $42. *Marginal revenue* is the change in total revenue resulting from a one-unit increase in the quantity sold. For example, if the price falls from $16 (row C) to $14 (row D), the quantity sold increases from 2 to 3 haircuts. Total revenue rises from $32 to $42, so the change in total revenue is $10. Because the quantity sold increases by 1 haircut, marginal revenue equals the change in total revenue and is $10. Marginal revenue is placed between the two rows to emphasize that marginal revenue relates to the *change* in the quantity sold.

Figure 14.2 shows the market demand curve and Bobbie's marginal revenue curve (*MR*) and also illustrates the calculation that we've just made. Notice that at each output, marginal revenue is less than price—the marginal revenue curve lies below the demand curve. Why is marginal revenue less than price? It is because when the price is lowered to sell one more unit, two opposing forces affect total

---

FIGURE 14.2

Demand and Marginal Revenue

The table shows the market demand schedule and Bobbie's total revenue and marginal revenue schedules.

If the price falls from $16 to $14, the quantity sold increases from 2 to 3. ❶ Total revenue lost on 2 haircuts is $4; ❷ total revenue gained on 1 haircut is $14; and ❸ marginal revenue is $10.

	Price (dollars per haircut)	Quantity demanded (haircuts per hour)	Total revenue (dollars per hour)	Marginal revenue (dollars per haircut)
A	20	0	0	
				18
B	18	1	18	
				14
C	16	2	32	
				10
D	14	3	42	
				6
E	12	4	48	
				2
F	10	5	50	

revenue. The lower price results in a revenue loss, and the increased quantity sold results in a revenue gain. For example, at a price of $16, Bobbie sells 2 haircuts (point C). If she lowers the price to $14 a haircut, she sells 3 haircuts and has a revenue gain of $14 on the third haircut. But she now receives only $14 a haircut on the first two—$2 a haircut less than before. So she loses $4 of revenue on the first 2 haircuts. To calculate marginal revenue, she must deduct this amount from the revenue gain of $14. So her marginal revenue is $10, which is less than the price.

■ Marginal Revenue and Elasticity

In Chapter 5 (p. 126), you learned about the *total revenue test,* which determines whether demand is elastic or inelastic. Recall that if a price fall increases total revenue, demand is elastic, but if it decreases total revenue, demand is inelastic.

We can use the total revenue test to see the relationship between marginal revenue and elasticity. Figure 14.3 illustrates this relationship. As the price falls from $20 to $10, the quantity demanded increases from 0 to 5 an hour. Total revenue increases (part b), so demand is elastic and marginal revenue is positive (part a). As the price falls from $10 to $0, the quantity demanded increases from 5 to 10 an hour. Total revenue decreases (part b), so demand is inelastic and marginal revenue is

FIGURE 14.3

Marginal Revenue and Elasticity

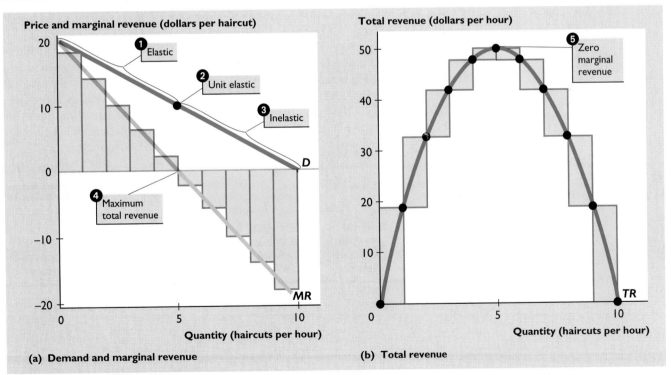

(a) Demand and marginal revenue

(b) Total revenue

Over the range from 0 to 5 haircuts an hour, marginal revenue is positive and ❶ demand is elastic. At 5 haircuts an hour, marginal revenue is zero and ❷ demand is unit elastic. Over the range 5 to 10 haircuts an hour, marginal revenue is negative and ❸ demand is

inelastic. At zero marginal revenue in part (a), ❹ total revenue is maximized. And at maximum total revenue in part (b), ❺ marginal revenue is zero.

negative (part a). When the price is $10, total revenue is at a maximum, demand is unit elastic, and marginal revenue is zero.

The relationship between marginal revenue and elasticity implies that a monopoly never profitably produces an output in the inelastic range of its demand curve. It could charge a higher price, produce a smaller quantity, and increase its profit. Let's look at a monopoly's output and price decision.

■ Output and Price Decision

To determine the output level and price that maximize a monopoly's profit, we study the behavior of both revenue and costs as output varies.

Table 14.1 summarizes the information we need about Bobbie's revenue, costs, and economic profit. Economic profit, which equals total revenue minus total cost, is maximized at $12 an hour when Bobbie sells 3 haircuts an hour for $14 each. If she sold 2 haircuts for $16 each, her economic profit would be only $9. And if she sold 4 haircuts for $12 each, her economic profit would be only $8.

You can see why 3 haircuts is Bobbie's profit-maximizing output by looking at the marginal revenue and marginal cost. When Bobbie increases output from 2 to 3 haircuts, her marginal revenue is $10 and her marginal cost is $7. Profit increases by the difference, $3 an hour. If Bobbie increases output yet further, from 3 to 4 haircuts, her marginal revenue is $6 and her marginal cost is $10. In this case, marginal cost exceeds marginal revenue by $4, so profit decreases by $4 an hour.

Figure 14.4 shows the information contained in Table 14.1 graphically. Part (a) shows Bobbie's total revenue curve (*TR*) and her total cost curve (*TC*). It also shows Bobbie's economic profit as the vertical distance between the *TR* and *TC* curves. Bobbie maximizes her profit at 3 haircuts an hour and earns an economic profit of $12 an hour ($42 of total revenue minus $30 of total cost).

Figure 14.4(b) shows the market demand curve (*D*) and Bobbie's marginal revenue curve (*MR*) along with her marginal cost curve (*MC*) and average total cost curve (*ATC*). Bobbie maximizes profit by producing the output at which marginal cost equals marginal revenue—3 haircuts an hour. But what price does she charge for a haircut? To set the price, the monopoly uses the demand curve and finds the highest price at which it can sell the profit-maximizing output. In Bobbie's case, the highest price at which she can sell 3 haircuts an hour is $14 a haircut.

■ TABLE 14.1

A Monopoly's Output and Price Decision

	Price (dollars per haircut)	Quantity demanded (haircuts per hour)	Total revenue (dollars per hour)	Marginal revenue (dollars per haircut)	Total cost (dollars per hour)	Marginal cost (dollars per haircut)	Profit (dollars per hour)
A	20	0	0		12		−12
				18		5	
B	18	1	18		17		1
				14		6	
C	16	2	32		23		9
				10		7	
D	14	3	42		30		12
				6		10	
E	12	4	48		40		8
				2		15	
F	10	5	50		55		−5

When Bobbie produces 3 haircuts an hour, her average total cost is $10 (read from the *ATC* curve) and her price is $14 (read from the *D* curve). Her profit per haircut is $4 ($14 minus $10). Bobbie's economic profit is shown by the blue rectangle, which equals the profit per haircut ($4) multiplied by the number of haircuts (3 an hour), for a total of $12 an hour.

A positive economic profit is an incentive for firms to enter a market. But barriers to entry prevent that from happening in a monopoly. So in a monopoly, the firm can make a positive economic profit and continue to do so indefinitely.

A monopoly charges a price that exceeds marginal cost, but does it always make an economic profit? The answer is no! Bobbie makes a positive economic profit in Figure 14.4. But suppose that Bobbie's landlord increases the rent she pays for her barbershop. If Bobbie pays an additional $12 an hour in shop rent, her fixed cost increases by that amount. Her marginal cost and marginal revenue don't change, so her profit-maximizing output remains at 3 haircuts an hour. Her profit decreases by $12 an hour to zero. If Bobbie pays more than an additional $12 an hour for her shop rent, she incurs an economic loss. If this situation were permanent, Bobbie would go out of business. But monopoly entrepreneurs are creative, and Bobbie might find another shop at a lower rent.

▇ **FIGURE 14.4**

A Monopoly's Profit-Maximizing Output and Price

(a) Total revenue and total cost

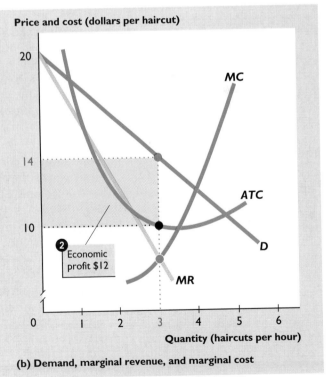

(b) Demand, marginal revenue, and marginal cost

In part (a), economic profit is maximized when total revenue (*TR*) minus total cost (*TC*) is greatest. ❶ Economic profit, the vertical distance between *TR* and *TC*, is $12 an hour at 3 haircuts an hour.

In part (b), economic profit is maximized when marginal cost (*MC*) equals marginal revenue (*MR*). The price is determined by the demand curve (*D*) and is $14. ❷ Economic profit, the blue rectangle, is $12—the profit per haircut ($4) multiplied by 3 haircuts.

2 Explain how a single-price monopoly determines its output and price.

Practice Problem 14.2

TABLE 1

Price (dollars per bottle)	Quantity (bottles per hour)	Total cost (dollars per hour)
10	0	1.0
9	1	1.5
8	2	2.5
7	3	5.5
6	4	10.5
5	5	17.5

1. Minnie's Mineral Springs is a single-price monopoly. The first two columns of Table 1 show the demand schedule for Minnie's spring water, and the middle and third columns show the firm's total cost schedule.
   a. Calculate Minnie's total revenue and marginal revenue schedules.
   b. Sketch the demand curve and Minnie's marginal revenue curve.
   c. Calculate Minnie's profit-maximizing output, price, and economic profit.
   d. If the owner of the water source that Minnie's uses increases the fee that Minnie's pays by $15.50 an hour, what are Minnie's new profit-maximizing output, price, and economic profit?
   e. If instead of increasing the fee that Minnie's pays by $15.50 an hour, the owner of the water source increases the fee that Minnie pays by $4 a bottle, what are Minnie's new profit-maximizing output, price, and economic profit?

Exercise 14.2

TABLE 2

Price (thousands of dollars per ride)	Quantity (rides per month)	Total cost (thousands of dollars per month)
220	0	80
200	1	160
180	2	260
160	3	380
140	4	520
120	5	680

1. Fossett's Round-the-World Balloon Rides is a single-price monopoly. The first two columns of Table 2 show the demand schedule for Fossett's rides, and the middle and third columns show the firm's total cost schedule.
   a. Calculate Fossett's total revenue and marginal revenue schedules.
   b. Sketch the demand curve and Fossett's marginal revenue curve.
   c. Calculate Fossett's profit-maximizing output, price, and economic profit.
   d. If the government places a fixed tax on Fossett's of $60,000 a month, what are the new profit-maximizing output, price, and economic profit?
   e. If instead of imposing a fixed tax on Fossett's, the government taxes Fossett's by $30,000 per ride, what are the new profit-maximizing output, price, and economic profit?

Solution to Practice Problem 14.2

TABLE 3

Quantity (bottles per hour)	Total revenue (dollars per hour)	Marginal revenue (dollars per bottle)
0	0	
1	9	9
2	16	7
3	21	5
4	24	3
5	25	1

1a. Total revenue equals price multiplied by quantity sold, and marginal revenue equals the change in total revenue when the quantity sold increases by one unit (Table 3).

1b. Figure 1 shows the demand curve and Minnie's marginal revenue curve.

1c. The profit-maximizing output is 3 bottles an hour, the quantity at which marginal revenue equals marginal cost. Marginal cost is the change in total cost when the quantity produced increases by 1 bottle. Minnie's profit-maximizing price is $7 a bottle, and its economic profit is $15.50 an hour.

1d. If the fee that Minnie's pays increases by $15.50 an hour, Minnie's fixed cost increases but its marginal cost doesn't change. Its profit-maximizing output and price are unchanged, but it now earns no economic profit.

1e. If Minnie's pays an extra $4 a bottle, its marginal cost increases by this amount. Its new profit-maximizing output is 2 bottles an hour; the price is $8 a bottle; and economic profit is $5.50 an hour.

FIGURE 1

Price and costs (dollars per bottle)

14.3 MONOPOLY AND COMPETITION COMPARED

Imagine a market in which many small firms operate in perfect competition. Then a single firm buys out all these small firms and creates a monopoly. What happens in this market to the quantity produced, the price, and efficiency?

■ Output and Price

Figure 14.5 shows the market that we'll study. The market demand curve is D. Initially, with many small firms in the market, the market supply curve is S, which is the sum of the supply curves—and marginal cost curves—of the firms. The equilibrium price is P_C, which makes the quantity demanded equal the quantity supplied. The equilibrium quantity is Q_C. Each firm takes the price P_C and maximizes its profit by producing the output at which its own marginal cost equals the price.

A single firm now buys all the firms in this market. Consumers don't change, so the demand curve doesn't change. But the monopoly recognizes this demand curve as a constraint on its sales and knows that its marginal revenue curve is MR.

The market supply curve in perfect competition is the sum of the marginal cost curves of the firms in the industry. So the monopoly's marginal cost curve is the market supply curve of perfect competition—labeled $S = MC$. The monopoly maximizes profit by producing the quantity at which marginal revenue equals marginal cost, which is Q_M. This output is smaller than the competitive output, Q_C. And the monopoly charges the price P_M, which is higher than P_C. So

Compared to perfect competition, a single-price monopoly produces a smaller output and charges a higher price.

■ **FIGURE 14.5**
Monopoly's Smaller Output and Higher Price

❶ A competitive industry produces the quantity Q_C at price P_C.

❷ A single-price monopoly produces the quantity Q_M at which marginal revenue equals marginal cost and sells that quantity for the price P_M. Compared to perfect competition, a single-price monopoly restricts output and raises the price.

■ Is Monopoly Efficient?

You learned in Chapter 6 that resources are used efficiently when marginal benefit equals marginal cost. Figure 14.6(a) shows that perfect competition achieves this efficient use of resources. The demand curve ($D = MB$) shows the marginal benefit to consumers. The supply curve ($S = MC$) shows the marginal cost (opportunity cost) to producers. At the competitive equilibrium, the price is P_C and the quantity is Q_C. Marginal benefit equals marginal cost, and resource use is efficient. Total surplus (Chapter 6, p. 154), the sum of *consumer surplus*, the green triangle, and *producer surplus*, the blue area, is maximized.

Figure 14.6(b) shows that monopoly is inefficient. Monopoly output is Q_M and price is P_M. Price (marginal benefit) exceeds marginal cost and the underproduction creates a *deadweight loss* (Chapter 6, p. 157), which is shown by the gray area. Consumers lose partly by getting less of the good, shown by the gray triangle above P_C, and partly by paying more for the good. Consumer surplus shrinks to the smaller green triangle. Producers lose by selling less of the good, shown by the part of the gray area below P_C, but gain by selling their output for a higher price, shown by the dark blue rectangle. Producer surplus expands and is larger in monopoly than in perfect competition.

■ **FIGURE 14.6**

The Inefficiency of Monopoly

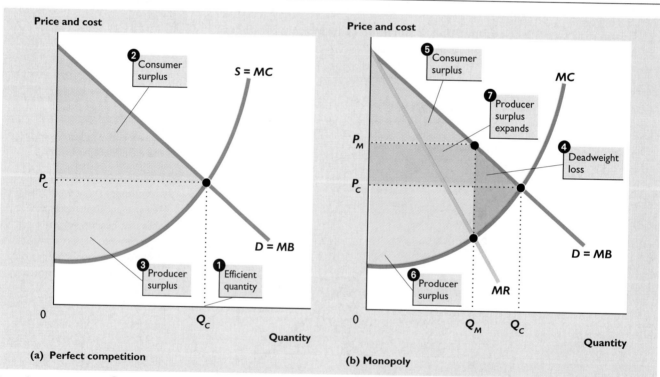

(a) **Perfect competition**

(b) **Monopoly**

In perfect competition, ❶ the equilibrium quantity is the efficient quantity, Q_C, because at that quantity, the price, P_C, equals marginal benefit and marginal cost. The sum of ❷ consumer surplus and ❸ producer surplus is maximized.

In a single-price monopoly, the equilibrium quantity, Q_M, is inefficient because the price, P_M, which equals marginal benefit, exceeds marginal cost. Underproduction creates a ❹ deadweight loss. ❺ Consumer surplus shrinks, and ❻ producer surplus ❼ expands.

■ Is Monopoly Fair?

Monopoly is inefficient because it creates a deadweight loss. But monopoly also *redistributes* consumer surplus. The producer gains, and the consumers lose.

Figure 14.6 shows this redistribution. The monopoly gets the difference between the higher price, P_M, and the competitive price, P_C, on the quantity sold, Q_M. So the dark blue rectangle shows the part of the consumer surplus taken by the monopoly. This portion of the loss of consumer surplus is not a loss to society. It is redistribution from consumers to the monopoly producer.

Are the gain for the monopoly and loss for consumers fair? You learned about two standards of fairness in Chapter 6: fair *results* and fair *rules*. Redistribution from the rich to the poor is consistent with the fair results view. So on this view of fairness, whether monopoly redistribution is fair or unfair depends on who is richer: the monopoly or the consumers of its product. It might be either. Whether the *rules* are fair depends on whether the monopoly has benefited from a protected position that is not available to anyone else. If everyone is free to acquire the monopoly, then the rules are fair. So monopoly is inefficient and it might be, but is not always, unfair.

The pursuit of monopoly profit leads to an additional costly activity that we'll now describe: rent seeking.

■ Rent Seeking

Rent seeking is the act of obtaining special treatment by the government to create economic profit or to divert consumer surplus or producer surplus away from others. ("Rent" is a general term in economics that includes all forms of surplus such as consumer surplus, producer surplus, and economic profit.) Rent seeking does not always create a monopoly, but it always restricts competition and often creates a monopoly.

Scarce resources can be used to produce the goods and services that people value or they can be used in rent seeking. Rent seeking is potentially profitable for the rent seeker but costly to society because it uses scarce resources purely to transfer wealth from one person or group to another person or group rather than to produce the things that people value.

To see why rent seeking occurs, think about the two ways in which a person might become the owner of a monopoly:

- Buy a monopoly
- Create a monopoly by rent seeking

Buy a Monopoly

A person might try to earn a monopoly profit by buying a firm (or a right) that is protected by a barrier to entry. Buying a taxicab medallion in New York is an example. The number of medallions is restricted, so their owners are protected from unlimited entry into the industry. A person who wants to operate a taxi must buy a medallion from someone who already has one. But anyone is free to enter the bidding for a medallion. So competition among buyers drives the price up to the point at which they earn only normal profit. For example, competition for the right to operate a taxi in New York City has led to a price of more than $165,000 for a taxi medallion, which is sufficiently high to eliminate economic profit for taxi operators and leave them with normal profit.

Rent seeking
The act of obtaining special treatment by the government to create economic profit or to divert consumer surplus or producer surplus away from others.

Create a Monopoly by Rent Seeking

Because buying a monopoly means paying a price that soaks up the economic profit, creating a monopoly by rent seeking is an attractive alternative to buying one. Rent seeking is a political activity. It takes the form of lobbying and trying to influence the political process to get laws that create legal barriers to entry. Such influence might be sought by making campaign contributions in exchange for legislative support or by indirectly seeking to influence political outcomes through publicity in the media or by direct contacts with politicians and bureaucrats. An example of a rent created in this way is the law that restricts the quantities of textiles that can be imported into the United States. Another is a law that limits the quantity of tomatoes that can be imported into the United States. These laws restrict competition, which decreases the quantity for sale and increases prices.

Rent-Seeking Equilibrium

Rent seeking is a competitive activity. If an economic profit is available, a rent seeker will try to get some of it. Competition among rent seekers pushes up the cost of rent seeking until it leaves the monopoly earning only a normal profit after paying the rent-seeking costs.

Figure 14.7 shows a rent-seeking equilibrium. The cost of rent seeking is a fixed cost that must be added to a monopoly's other costs. The average total cost curve, which includes the fixed cost of rent seeking, shifts upward until it just touches the demand curve. Consumer surplus is unaffected. But the deadweight loss of monopoly now includes the original deadweight loss triangle plus the economic profit consumed by rent seeking, which the enlarged gray area shows.

▮ FIGURE 14.7
Rent-Seeking Equilibrium

❶ Rent-seeking costs exhaust economic profit. The firm's rent-seeking costs are fixed costs. They add to total fixed cost and to average total cost. The ATC curve shifts upward until, at the profit-maximizing price, the firm breaks even.

❷ Consumer surplus shrinks.

❸ The deadweight loss increases.

CHECKPOINT 14.3

3 Compare the performance of a single-price monopoly with that of perfect competition.

Practice Problem 14.3

1. Township is a small isolated community served by one newspaper that can meet the market demand at a lower cost than two or more newspapers could. There is no local radio or TV station and no Internet access. The *Township Gazette* is the only source of news. Figure 1 shows the marginal cost of printing the *Township Gazette* and the demand for it. The *Township Gazette* is a profit-maximizing, single-price monopoly.
   a. How many copies of the *Township Gazette* are printed each day?
   b. What is the price of the *Township Gazette*?
   c. What is the efficient number of copies of the *Township Gazette*?
   d. What is the price at which the efficient number of copies could be sold?
   e. Is the number of copies printed the efficient quantity? Explain why or why not.
   f. On the graph, show the consumer surplus that is redistributed from consumers to the *Township Gazette*.
   g. On the graph, show the deadweight loss that arises from the monopoly of the *Township Gazette*.

FIGURE 1

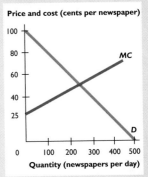

Exercise 14.3

1. Is Bobbie's Barbershop in Cairo, Nebraska, (on pp. 354–355) efficient? What is the consumer surplus that is transferred to Bobbie? What is the deadweight loss that she generates? How much would someone be willing to pay to buy Bobbie's monopoly?

Solution to Practice Problem 14.3

1a. The profit-maximizing quantity of newspapers for the *Township Gazette* is 150 a day, where marginal revenue equals marginal cost (Figure 2).
1b. The price is 70¢ a copy (Figure 2).
1c. The efficient quantity of copies is 250, where demand (marginal benefit) equals marginal cost (Figure 2).
1d. The efficient quantity would be bought at 50¢ a copy (Figure 2).
1e. The number of copies printed is not efficient because the marginal benefit of the 150th copy exceeds its marginal cost (Figure 2).
1f. The blue rectangle ❶ in Figure 2 shows the consumer surplus transferred from the consumers to the *Township Gazette*.
1g. The gray triangle ❷ in Figure 2 shows the deadweight loss.

FIGURE 2

14.4 PRICE DISCRIMINATION

Price discrimination—selling a good or service at a number of different prices—is widespread. You encounter it when you travel, go to the movies, get your hair cut, buy pizza, or visit an art museum. At first sight, it appears that price discrimination contradicts the assumption of profit maximization. Why would a movie operator allow children to see movies at half price? Why would a hairdresser charge students and senior citizens less? Aren't these firms losing profit by being nice to their customers?

Deeper investigation shows that far from lowering profit, price discriminators make a bigger profit than they would otherwise. So a monopoly has an incentive to find ways of discriminating and charging each buyer the highest possible price. Some people pay less with price discrimination, but others pay more.

Most price discriminators are *not* monopolies, but monopolies do price discriminate when they can. To be able to price discriminate, a firm must

- Identify and separate different types of buyers.
- Sell a product that cannot be resold.

Price discrimination is charging different prices for a single good or service because the willingness to pay varies across buyers. Not all price *differences* are price *discrimination*. Some goods that are similar but not identical have different prices because they have different production costs. For example, the cost of producing electricity depends on time of day. If an electric power company charges a higher price for consumption between 7:00 and 9:00 in the morning and between 4:00 and 7:00 in the evening than it does at other times of the day, the company is not price discriminating.

■ Price Discrimination and Consumer Surplus

The key idea behind price discrimination is to convert consumer surplus into economic profit. To extract every dollar of consumer surplus from every buyer, the monopoly would have to offer each individual customer a separate price schedule based on that customer's own willingness to pay. Such price discrimination cannot be carried out in practice because a firm does not have enough information about each consumer's demand curve. But firms try to extract as much consumer surplus as possible, and to do so, they discriminate in two broad ways:

- Among groups of buyers
- Among units of a good

Discriminating Among Groups of Buyers

To price discriminate among groups of buyers, the firm offers different prices to different types of buyers, based on things such as age, employment status, or some other easily distinguished characteristic. This type of price discrimination works when each group has a different average willingness to pay for the good or service.

For example, a face-to-face sales meeting with a customer might bring a large and profitable order. For salespeople and other business travelers, the marginal benefit from an airplane trip is large and the price that such a traveler will pay for a trip is high. In contrast, for a vacation traveler, any of several different trips or even no vacation trip are options. So for vacation travelers, the marginal benefit of a trip is small and the price that such a traveler will pay for a trip is low. Because business travelers are willing to pay more than vacation travelers are, it is possible for an airline to profit by price discriminating between these two groups.

Discriminating Among Units of a Good

To price discriminate among units of a good, the firm charges the same prices to all its customers but offers a lower price per unit for a larger number of units bought. When Pizza Hut charges $10 for one home-delivered pizza and $14 for two, it is using this type of price discrimination. In this example, the price of the second pizza is only $4.

Let's see how an airline exploits the differences in demand by business and vacation travelers and increases its profit by price discriminating.

■ Profiting by Price Discriminating

Global Air has a monopoly on an exotic route. Figure 14.8 shows the demand curve (*D*) for travel on this route and Global Air's marginal revenue curve (*MR*). It also shows Global Air's marginal cost (*MC*) and average total cost (*ATC*) curves.

Initially, Global is a single-price monopoly and maximizes its profit by producing 8,000 trips a year (the quantity at which *MR* equals *MC*). The price is $1,200 a trip. The average total cost of a trip is $600, so economic profit is $600 a trip. On 8,000 trips, Global's economic profit is $4.8 million a year, shown by the blue rectangle. Global's customers enjoy a consumer surplus shown by the green triangle.

■ FIGURE 14.8
A Single Price of Air Travel

Global Air has a monopoly on an air route. The demand curve for travel on this route is *D*, and Global's marginal revenue curve is *MR*. Its marginal cost curve is *MC*, and its average total cost curve is *ATC*.

As a single-price monopoly, Global maximizes profit by selling 8,000 trips a year at $1,200 a trip. ❶ Global's customers enjoy a consumer surplus—the green triangle—and ❷ Global's economic profit is $4.8 million a year—the blue rectangle.

Global is struck by the fact that many of its customers are business travelers, and Global suspects that they are willing to pay more than $1,200 a trip. So Global does some market research, which tells Global that some business travelers are willing to pay as much as $1,800 a trip. Also, these customers almost always make their travel plans at the last moment. Another group of business travelers is willing to pay $1,600. These customers know a week ahead when they will travel, and they never want to stay over a weekend. Yet another group is willing to pay up to $1,400. These travelers know two weeks ahead when they will travel, and they don't want to stay away over a weekend.

So Global announces a new fare schedule. No restrictions, $1,800; 7-day advance purchase, non-refundable, $1,600; 14-day advance purchase, non-refundable, $1,400; 14-day advance purchase, must stay over weekend, $1,200.

Figure 14.9 shows the outcome with this new fare structure and also shows why Global is pleased with its new fares. It sells 2,000 trips at each of its four prices. Global's economic profit increases by the blue steps in the figure. Its economic profit is now its original $4.8 million a year plus an additional $2.4 million from its new higher fares. Consumer surplus has shrunk to the smaller green area.

■ Perfect Price Discrimination

Perfect price discrimination
Price discrimination that extracts the entire consumer surplus by charging the highest price that consumers are willing to pay for each unit.

But Global reckons that it can do even better. It plans to achieve **perfect price discrimination**, which extracts the entire consumer surplus by charging the highest price that consumers are willing to pay for each unit. To do so, Global must get creative and come up with a host of additional business fares ranging between $2,000 and $1,200, each one of which appeals to a small segment of the business market.

■ FIGURE 14.9
Price Discrimination

myeconlab

Global revises its fare structure. It now offers no restrictions at $1,800, 7-day advance purchase, non-refundable at $1,600, 14-day advance purchase, non-refundable at $1,400, and 14-day advance purchase, must stay over the weekend, at $1,200.

Global sells 2,000 units at each of its four new fares. Its economic profit increases by $2.4 million a year to $7.2 million a year, which is shown by the original blue rectangle plus the blue steps. Global's customers' consumer surplus shrinks.

Once Global is discriminating finely between different customers and getting from each customer the maximum he or she is willing to pay, something special happens to marginal revenue. Recall that for the single-price monopoly, marginal revenue is less than price. The reason is that when the price is cut to sell a larger quantity, the price is lower on all units sold. But with perfect price discrimination, Global sells only the marginal seat at the lower price. All the other customers continue to buy for the highest price they are willing to pay. So for the perfect price discriminator, marginal revenue equals price and the demand curve becomes the marginal revenue curve.

With marginal revenue equal to price, Global can obtain yet greater profit by increasing output up to the point at which price (and marginal revenue) is equal to marginal cost.

So Global now seeks additional travelers who will not pay as much as $1,200 a trip but who will pay more than marginal cost. More creative pricing comes up with vacation specials and other fares that have combinations of advance reservation, minimum stay, and other restrictions that make these fares unattractive to Global's existing customers but attractive to a further group of travelers. With all these fares and specials, Global extracts the entire consumer surplus and maximizes economic profit.

Figure 14.10 shows the outcome with perfect price discrimination. The dozens of fares paid by the original travelers who are willing to pay between $1,200 and $2,000 have extracted the entire consumer surplus from this group and converted it into economic profit for Global. The new fares between $900 and $1,200 have attracted 3,000 additional travelers but have taken their entire consumer surplus also. Global is earning an economic profit of more than $9 million a year.

■ FIGURE 14.10

Perfect Price Discrimination

With perfect price discrimination, the demand curve becomes Global's marginal revenue curve. Economic profit is maximized when the lowest price equals marginal cost.

❶ Output increases to 11,000 passengers a year, and **❷** Global's economic profit increases to $9.35 million a year.

EYE ON THE U.S. ECONOMY

Airline Price Discrimination

The normal coach fare from San Francisco to Washington, D.C. is $1,400. Book 14 days in advance, and this fare is $550. On a typical flight, passengers might be paying as many as 20 different fares.

The airlines sort their customers according to their willingness to pay by offering a maze of advance-purchase and stayover restrictions that attract price-sensitive leisure travelers but don't get bought by business travelers.

Despite the sophistication of the airlines' pricing schemes, about 30 percent of seats fly empty. The marginal cost of filling an empty seat is close to

zero, so a ticket sold at a few dollars would be profitable.

Extremely low prices are now feasible, thanks to Priceline.com. Priceline's Web site gets 1.5 million hits a week. Shopping around airlines with bids from travelers, Priceline brokers several thousand tickets a day and gets the lowest possible fares for its customers.

Would it bother you to hear how little I paid for this flight?

From William Hamilton, "Voodoo Economics," © 1992 by the Chronicle Publishing Company, p. 3. Reprinted with permission of Chronicle Books.

■ Price Discrimination and Efficiency

With perfect price discrimination, the monopoly increases output to the point at which price equals marginal cost. This output is identical to that of perfect competition. Perfect price discrimination pushes consumer surplus to zero but increases producer surplus to equal the sum of consumer surplus and producer surplus in perfect competition. Deadweight loss with perfect price discrimination is zero. So perfect price discrimination produces the efficient quantity.

But there are two differences between perfect competition and perfect price discrimination. First, the distribution of the total surplus is different. It is shared by consumers and producers in perfect competition while the producer gets it all with perfect price discrimination. Second, because the producer grabs all the total surplus, rent seeking becomes profitable.

Rent seekers use resources in pursuit of monopoly, and the bigger the rents, the greater is the incentive to use resources to pursue those rents. With free entry into rent seeking, the long-run equilibrium outcome is that rent seekers use up the entire producer surplus.

CHECKPOINT 14.4

4 Explain how price discrimination increases profit.

Practice Problem 14.4

1. Village, a small isolated town, has one doctor. For a 30-minute consultation, the doctor charges a rich person twice as much as a poor person.
   a. Does the doctor practice price discrimination?
   b. Does the doctor's pricing system redistribute consumer surplus? If so, explain how.
   c. Is the doctor using resources efficiently? Explain your answer.
   d. If the doctor decided to charge everyone the maximum price that he or she would be willing to pay, what would be the consumer surplus?
   e. In part **d**, is the market for medical service in Village efficient?

Exercises 14.4

1. Under what conditions is price discrimination possible?

2. Which of the following is *not* an example of price discrimination?
   a. A diner offers senior citizens a discount on Tuesday lunches.
   b. An airline offers stand-by fares at a 75 percent discount.
   c. An airline offers a 25 percent discount on a round-trip ticket for a week-end stay.
   d. A supermarket sells water for $2 a bottle or $18 for a box of 12 bottles.
   e. A bank charges a higher interest rate on a loan to buy a motorcycle than the rate it charges the same person on a student loan.
   f. A California car wash pays a higher price for water than a California farmer pays.
   g. A cell phone company offers free calls on the weekend.
   h. A museum offers discounts to students and senior citizens.
   i. A power utility charges a steel smelter a higher price for electricity between 6:00 A.M. and 9:00 A.M. than it charges between midnight and 6:00 A.M.

Solution to Practice Problem 14.4

1a. The doctor practices price discrimination because rich people and poor people pay a different price for the same service: a 30-minute consultation.
1b. With price discrimination, the doctor takes some of the consumer surplus. So yes, consumer surplus is reduced and redistributed to the doctor as economic profit.
1c. No, the doctor creates a deadweight loss and so is not using resources efficiently.
1d. The doctor now practices perfect price discrimination. To maximize profit, the doctor increases the number of consultations to make the lowest price charged equal to marginal cost. The doctor takes the entire consumer surplus. So consumer surplus is zero.
1e. The doctor no longer creates a deadweight loss, so resources are being used efficiently.

14.5 MONOPOLY POLICY ISSUES

A single-price monopoly produces too little with marginal benefit greater than marginal cost. A price discriminating monopoly might produce the efficient quantity, but if it does so it converts the entire consumer surplus into economic profit. And all monopolies waste resources through rent seeking. If monopoly is so bad, why do we put up with it? Why don't we have laws that crack down on monopoly so hard that it never rears its head? We do indeed have laws that limit monopoly and regulate the prices that monopolies are permitted to charge. We explain the regulation of monopoly in Chapter 17.

But monopoly also brings some benefits. So society faces a tradeoff between these benefits and the inefficiency (and perhaps unfairness) that monopoly brings. We begin this review of monopoly policy issues by looking at the benefits of monopoly.

■ Benefits of Monopoly

Monopoly has two potential benefits over competition. Monopoly can lower the cost of production by enabling a firm to capture economies of scale. And by enabling a firm to earn an economic profit, monopoly provides an incentive to firms to innovate either by developing new products or by seeking lower-cost methods of production.

Capturing Economies of Scale

Economies of scale can lead to *natural monopoly*—a situation in which a single firm can produce at a lower average total cost than a larger number of smaller firms can. Examples of industries in which economies of scale are so significant that they lead to a natural monopoly include the distribution of electric power and natural gas, cable television, and water.

If a natural monopoly were broken into a number of competing firms, resources would be wasted. The cost of running not one but several cables through every neighborhood and to every home to deliver competitive television would be large. The cost of running several water pipes and gas pipes to bring competition to those industries would be even greater.

So here is the dilemma: Where economies of scale can be enjoyed only with a single producer, should we take the economies of scale and put up with monopoly, or should we forgo the economies of scale and make the industry competitive?

Breaking up a natural monopoly to create competition is almost never a good idea and is almost impossible to accomplish. It is a bad idea because it increases cost. It is hard to accomplish because each firm has an incentive to expand and try to take the entire market.

So the choice that most societies make is to operate natural monopolies but try to regulate them so that they operate at an efficient price and output level. You can study the regulation of natural monopoly in Chapter 17.

Strengthening the Incentive to Innovate

We take it for granted that every year will bring new and better products. Flat-screen television is gradually replacing the bulky old TV set. Pocket-sized MP3 players are replacing the Discman and a case of CDs. Ever faster and more powerful computer games keep appearing. Drug companies frequently announce yet another breakthrough in the treatment of some dreaded disease. Chemical companies routinely discover new compounds. Seed and fertilizer makers provide farmers with new products that lower the cost of food production.

But the process of invention and innovation that brings all these new goods and lower-cost technologies is not free. Firms spend billions of dollars in pursuit of the blockbuster product that will make their stockholders and managers rich.

Most (perhaps all) of these innovations bring greater benefits than they cost. Which type of market is likely to lead to more innovation: monopoly or competition? The answer is monopoly. If a firm can capture some economic profit from investing in a new product, it has an incentive to undertake the investment. But if a firm knows that competition will drive its economic profit to zero, it has a weak incentive to innovate.

So here's another dilemma: Where innovations can be enjoyed only with monopoly, should we take the innovations and put up with monopoly, or should we forgo the innovations and make markets competitive?

REALITY CHECK

Monopoly in YOUR Life

When Bill Gates decided to quit Harvard in 1975, he realized that PCs would need an operating system and applications programs to interact with the computer's hardware. He also knew that whoever owned the copyright on these programs would have a license to print money. And he wanted to be that person.

In less than 30 years, Bill Gates became the world's richest person. Such is the power of the right monopoly.

You, along with millions of other PC users, have willingly paid the monopoly price for Windows and Microsoft Office. Sure, the marginal cost of a copy of these programs is close to zero, so the quantity sold is way too few. There is a big deadweight loss.

Compared with the alternative of no Windows, you're better off. But are you better off than you would be if there were many alternatives to Windows competing for your attention? To answer this question, think about the applications—spreadsheets, word processing, and so on—that you need to make your computer useful. With lots of operating systems, what would happen to the cost of developing applications? Would you have more or less choice?

Patent law is the main tool that governments use to resolve this dilemma and to choose the point on the tradeoff between the gains from innovation and the efficiency loss from monopoly.

By granting a firm a patent, the law creates a legal monopoly and the innovator is able to earn an ongoing economic profit. But the patent eventually expires, and the market for the product then becomes competitive.

■ U.S. Patent Law

In the United States, the inventor of a new product or process may patent the invention and enjoy exclusive use of it for 20 years. At the end of 20 years, the patent expires and everyone is free to copy the original invention.

There is no deep economic science behind the 20-year time limit for a patent. The intent is to make the period long enough to provide a strong incentive to the innovator and short enough to avoid the deadweight loss from monopoly to persist for too long.

Although a patent expires after 20 years, patent holders sometimes try to extend their patent protection. One method of doing so is to make a small change to a patented product or process so that a new patent can by applied for. This activity is a form of rent seeking and, like other forms of rent seeking, it uses scarce resources and is a further source of inefficiency.

There is no neat bottom line on monopoly versus competition. Where competition is possible, it is more efficient. But often, the choice is between monopoly and nothing. Then monopoly might be better.

CHECKPOINT 14.5

5   **Explain why monopoly can sometimes achieve a better allocation of resources than competition can.**

Practice Problem 14.5

1. Major league baseball is a monopoly.
   a. Is it a natural monopoly?
   b. Can you think of a justification for baseball being a monopoly on the basis of either economies of scale or the incentive to innovate?

Exercise 14.5

1. The distribution of water is undertaken by a monopoly.
   a. Is water distribution a natural monopoly? Explain why or why not.
   b. Could water be distributed more efficiently by competitive water companies? Why or why not?

Solution to Practice Problem 14.5

1a. Major league baseball is a legal monopoly, not a natural monopoly.
1b. There is no justification for major league baseball being given monopoly status. It doesn't have economies of scale, and the rules of the game make innovation and product development irrelevant.

CHAPTER CHECKPOINT

Key Points

1 **Explain how monopoly arises and distinguish between single-price monopoly and price-discriminating monopoly.**

- A monopoly is a market with a single supplier of a good or service that has no close substitutes and in which legal or natural barriers to entry prevent competition.
- A monopoly can price discriminate when there is no resale possibility.
- Where resale is possible, a firm charges a single price.

2 **Explain how a single-price monopoly determines its output and price.**

- The demand for a monopoly's output is the market demand, and a single-price monopoly's marginal revenue is less than price.
- A monopoly maximizes profit by producing the output at which marginal revenue equals marginal cost and by charging the maximum price that consumers are willing to pay for that output.

3 **Compare the performance of a single-price monopoly with that of perfect competition.**

- A single-price monopoly charges a higher price and produces a smaller quantity than does a perfectly competitive market and creates a deadweight loss.
- Monopoly imposes a loss on society that equals its deadweight loss plus the cost of the resources devoted to rent seeking.

4 **Explain how price discrimination increases profit.**

- Perfect price discrimination charges a different price for each unit sold, obtains the maximum price that each consumer is willing to pay for each unit, and redistributes the entire consumer surplus to the monopoly.
- With perfect price discrimination, the monopoly produces the same output as would a perfectly competitive market, but rent seeking uses some of the surplus.

5 **Explain why monopoly can sometimes achieve a better allocation of resources than competition can.**

- A natural monopoly can produce at a lower price than competitive firms can, and monopoly strengthens the incentive to innovate.
- The U.S. patent law provides the creators of new products and technologies with a 20-year temporary monopoly.

Key Terms

Barrier to entry, 350
Legal monopoly, 351
Natural monopoly, 350

Perfect price discrimination, 366
Price-discriminating monopoly, 352

Rent seeking, 361
Single-price monopoly, 352

Exercises

1. What are the three types of barrier to entry that can create a monopoly? Provide an example of each type. Why can't barriers to entry simply be torn down so that all markets become competitive?

2. Technological change is constantly creating and destroying barriers to entry and is changing the competitive and monopoly landscapes.
   a. Provide three examples of technological changes that have occurred during the past 20 years that have created a new barrier to entry and resulted in monopoly.
   b. Provide three examples of technological changes that have occurred during the past 20 years that have destroyed a barrier to entry and resulted in competition where previously monopoly was present.

3. Why isn't the demand for the good or service produced by a monopoly perfectly elastic like the demand for the good or service produced by a firm in perfect competition?

4. What is price discrimination? Can any monopoly choose to price discriminate? Why or why not?

5. Explain why the marginal revenue curve of a single-price monopoly is downward sloping.

6. Elixir Spring produces a unique and highly prized mineral water. The firm's total fixed cost is $5,000 a day, and its marginal cost is zero. Table 1 shows the demand schedule for Elixir water.
   a. Construct Elixir's total revenue schedule and marginal revenue schedule and make a graph of the demand and marginal revenue curves.
   b. Calculate and illustrate in a graph Elixir's profit-maximizing price, output, and economic profit.
   c. Compare Elixir's profit-maximizing price with the marginal cost of producing the profit-maximizing output.
   d. What is the elasticity of demand for Elixir water at the profit-maximizing quantity?

7. The Blue Rose Company is the only flower grower to have cracked the secret of making a blue rose. The first two columns of Table 2 show the demand schedule for blue roses, and the middle and third columns show the total cost schedule for producing them.
   a. Construct Blue Rose's total revenue and marginal revenue schedule and make a graph of the demand and marginal revenue curves.
   b. Calculate Blue Rose's marginal cost schedule and add it to your graph.
   c. Calculate Blue Rose's profit-maximizing price, output, and economic profit.

8. Use the demand schedule for Elixir water in Table 1. Suppose that there are 1,000 springs, all able to produce this water at zero marginal cost. Suppose that for these firms, total fixed cost is also zero.
   a. What are the equilibrium price and quantity of Elixir water?
   b. Compare this equilibrium with the monopoly equilibrium in exercise 6.

TABLE 1

Price (dollars per bottle)	Quantity (bottles per day)
10	0
9	1,000
8	2,000
7	3,000
6	4,000
5	5,000
4	6,000
3	7,000
2	8,000
1	9,000
0	10,000

TABLE 2

Price (dollars per bunch)	Quantity (bunches per day)	Total cost (dollars per day)
80	0	80
72	1	82
64	2	88
56	3	100
48	4	124
40	5	160
32	6	208
24	7	268
16	8	340

c. What is the consumer surplus if Elixir water is produced in perfect competition?

d. What is the producer surplus if Elixir water is produced in perfect competition?

e. What are the consumer surplus and producer surplus from Elixir water if a monopoly produces it?

f. When the Elixir monopoly maximizes profit, what is the deadweight loss?

9. Suppose that 1,000 competitive firms produce Elixir water and that one of these firms begins quietly to buy the others.

   a. What is the most that a firm would be willing to pay to obtain a monopoly in Elixir water?

   b. Illustrate this maximum amount in a graph.

   c. If a firm pays the maximum amount it is willing to pay for a monopoly in Elixir water, what is the firm's economic profit? Explain.

10. Bobbie's Hair Care is a natural monopoly in a small isolated town. The first two columns of Table 3 show the demand schedule for Bobbie's haircuts, and the middle and third columns show Bobbie's total cost. Bobbie has done a survey and discovered that she gets four types of customer each hour: one woman who is willing to pay $18, one senior citizen who is willing to pay $16, one student who is willing to pay $14, and one boy who is willing to pay $12. If Bobbie price discriminates among the four types of customer,

   a. What is the price she charges to each type of customer?

   b. How many haircuts an hour does Bobbie sell?

   c. What is Bobbie's economic profit?

   d. Is the quantity of haircuts efficient? Explain why or why not.

   e. What are the consumer surplus and producer surplus?

   f. Who benefits from Bobbie's price discrimination?

TABLE 3

Price (dollars per haircut)	Quantity (haircuts per hour)	Total cost (dollars per hour)
20	0	20
18	1	21
16	2	24
14	3	30
12	4	40
10	5	54

11. A city art museum, which is a local monopoly, is worried that it is not generating enough revenue to cover its costs, and the city government is cutting the museum's budget. The museum charges $1 admission and $5 for special exhibitions. The museum director asks you to help him solve his problem. Can you suggest a pricing scheme that will bring in more revenue? At the same time, can you help the museum get even more people to visit it?

12. Big Top is the only circus in the nation. Table 4 sets out the demand schedule for circus tickets and the cost schedule for producing the circus.

   a. Calculate Big Top's total revenue and marginal revenue.

   b. Calculate Big Top's profit-maximizing price, output, and economic profit if it charges a single price for all tickets.

   c. In part **b**, what is the consumer surplus and producer surplus?

   d. When Big Top maximizes profit in part **b**, is the circus efficient? Explain why or why not.

   e. If the circus industry were perfectly competitive, how many tickets would be sold and what would be the price of a ticket?

   f. Big Top offers children a discount of 50 percent. How will this discount change the consumer surplus and producer surplus? Will Big Top be more efficient?

TABLE 4

Price (dollars per ticket)	Quantity (tickets per show)	Total cost (dollars per show)
20	0	1,000
18	100	1,600
16	200	2,200
14	300	2,800
12	400	3,400
10	500	4,000
8	600	4,600
6	700	5,200
4	800	5,800

Critical Thinking

13. The National Collegiate Athletic Association (NCAA) controls the market for college athletes. It sets the amounts paid to these athletes below what they would be in a competitive market and ensures that colleges do not violate the rules that it lays down.
    a. Is the NCAA a natural monopoly, a legal monopoly, or neither? Explain.
    b. Who benefits and who loses from the NCAA's control of the market for college athletes?
    c. Is the system operated by the NCAA efficient?

14. Major league baseball is exempt from laws designed to limit market power and operates as a monopoly.
    a. How might competition be introduced into the market for baseball?
    b. If the baseball market became competitive, what do you predict would happen to the number of teams and the economic profit of a team?
    c. If the baseball market became competitive, what do you predict would happen to the number of players and their average salaries?
    d. All things considered, would you favor or oppose the introduction of competition among leagues in baseball?

15. Before 1991, the eight Ivy League colleges (Brown, Columbia, Cornell, Dartmouth, Harvard, Princeton, the University of Pennsylvania, and Yale), along with MIT, shared information and agreed on rules for setting their prices of education (price equals tuition minus scholarship). Since 1991, these schools have set their prices in competition with each other. Compare the market for an Ivy League education before and after 1991. Predict what has happened to the efficiency of the market, to the distribution of producer and consumer surplus, and to deadweight loss.

Web Exercises

Use the links on MyEconLab to work the following exercises.

16. Visit the Web site of Robert Barro and read his article on competition and monopoly in the hi-tech sector.
    a. What is Robert Barro's central argument?
    b. Explain why you agree or disagree with Barro.
    c. What are the main implications of Barro's view for government policy toward monopoly?

17. Visit the Web site of the Department of Justice and review the information on the case of the United States versus Microsoft.
    a. Did the courts find Microsoft to be a monopoly?
    b. What are the main factors that the courts considered in reaching their conclusions about Microsoft?
    c. What remedies did the court propose?
    d. Compare the court's findings with Barro's views (in exercise 16).

18. Visit the Web site of United Airlines and get some prices for a trip from the major airport nearest you to anywhere in the world that interests you. Get the best fare possible and establish the restrictions on its use. Compare it with the normal fare. Explain how the restrictions increase United Airlines' total revenue.

Monopolistic Competition

CHAPTER CHECKLIST

When you have completed your study of this chapter,
you will be able to

1 Describe and identify monopolistic competition.

2 Explain how a firm in monopolistic competition determines its output
and price in the short run and the long run.

3 Explain why advertising costs are high and why firms use brand names
in monopolistic competition.

Raymond's end-of-term party had to be run on a
a tight budget. But he knew that he'd be able to
keep his costs down by using the coupons he'd
saved from this week's papers. He would need to
spend a bit of time running around Albertsons,
Kroger, Safeway, Winn-Dixie, and Shop 'n Save to
get each of their weekly "specials" and pay the
lowest prices. But time was what he now had,
and money was what he was short of.

The supermarkets that Raymond visited for his party
shopping compete. But they are not like the firms in perfect
competition that you studied in Chapter 13. There are no
best deals, fliers, or specials in perfect competition. There is
no gain from advertising or price cutting when you sell a
product identical to that of your competitors.

To understand fliers, coupons, and the competition that
we witness every day in the markets in which we buy, we
need the model of monopolistic competition that is
explained in this chapter.

15.1 WHAT IS MONOPOLISTIC COMPETITION?

Most real-world markets lie between the extremes of perfect competition in Chapter 13 and monopoly in Chapter 14. Most firms possess some power to set their prices as monopolies do, and they face competition from the entry of new firms as the firms in perfect competition do. We call the markets in which such firms operate *monopolistic competition*. (Another market that lies between perfect competition and monopoly is *oligopoly*, which we study in Chapter 16.)

Monopolistic competition is a market structure in which

- A large number of firms compete.
- Each firm produces a differentiated product.
- Firms compete on price, product quality, and marketing.
- Firms are free to enter and exit.

■ Large Number of Firms

In monopolistic competition, as in perfect competition, the industry consists of a large number of firms. The presence of a large number of firms has three implications for the firms in the industry.

Small Market Share

Each firm supplies a small part of the market. Consequently, while each firm can influence the price of its own product, it has little power to influence the average market price.

No Market Dominance

Each firm must be sensitive to the average market price of the product. But it does not pay attention to any one individual competitor. Because all the firms are relatively small, no single firm can dictate market conditions, so no one firm's actions directly affect the actions of the other firms.

Collusion Impossible

Firms sometimes try to profit from illegal agreements—collusion—with other firms to fix prices and not undercut each other. Collusion is impossible when the market has a large number of firms, as it does in monopolistic competition.

■ Product Differentiation

Product differentiation

Making a product that is slightly different from the products of competing firms.

Product differentiation is making a product that is slightly different from the products of competing firms. A differentiated product has close substitutes but does not have perfect substitutes. Some people will pay more for one variety of the product, so when its price rises, the quantity demanded decreases. For example, Adidas, Asics, Diadora, Etonic, Fila, New Balance, Nike, Puma, and Reebok all make differentiated running shoes. Other things remaining the same, if the price of Adidas running shoes rises and the prices of the other shoes remain constant, Adidas sells fewer shoes.

■ Competing on Quality, Price, and Marketing

Product differentiation enables a firm to compete with other firms in three areas: quality, price, and marketing.

Quality

The quality of a product is the physical attributes that make it different from the products of other firms. Quality includes design, reliability, the service provided to the buyer, and the buyer's ease of access to the product. Quality lies on a spectrum that runs from high to low. Go to the J.D. Power Consumer Center at jdpower.com, and you'll see the many dimensions on which this rating agency describes the quality of autos, boats, financial services, travel and accommodation services, telecommunication services, and new homes—all examples of products that have a large range of quality variety.

Price

Because of product differentiation, a firm in monopolistic competition faces a downward-sloping demand curve. So, like a monopoly, the firm can set both its price and its output. But there is a tradeoff between the product's quality and price. A firm that makes a high-quality product can charge a higher price than what a firm that makes a low-quality product can.

Marketing

Because of product differentiation, a firm in monopolistic competition must market its product. Marketing takes two main forms: advertising and packaging. A firm that produces a high-quality product wants to sell it for a suitably high price. To be able to do so, it must advertise and package its product in a way that convinces buyers that they are getting the higher quality for which they are paying. For example, drug companies advertise and package their brand-name drugs to persuade buyers that these items are superior to the lower-priced generic alternatives. Similarly, a low-quality producer uses advertising and packaging to persuade buyers that although the quality is low, the low price more than compensates for this fact.

■ Entry and Exit

In monopolistic competition, there are no barriers to entry. Consequently, a firm cannot make an economic profit in the long run. When firms make economic profits, new firms enter the industry. This entry lowers prices and eventually eliminates economic profits. When economic losses are incurred, some firms leave the industry. This exit increases prices and profits of the remaining firms and eventually eliminates the economic losses. In long-run equilibrium, firms neither enter nor leave the industry and the firms in the industry make zero economic profit.

■ Identifying Monopolistic Competition

Several factors must be considered to identify monopolistic competition and distinguish it from perfect competition on the one side and oligopoly and monopoly on the other side. One of these factors is the extent to which a market is dominated by a small number of firms. To measure this feature of markets, economists use two indexes called measures of concentration. These indexes are

- The four-firm concentration ratio
- The Herfindahl-Hirschman Index

The Four-Firm Concentration Ratio

Four-firm concentration ratio
The percentage of the total revenue in an industry accounted for by the four largest firms in an industry.

The **four-firm concentration ratio** is the percentage of the total revenue of the industry accounted for by the four largest firms in the industry. The range of the concentration ratio is from almost zero for perfect competition to 100 percent for monopoly. This ratio is the main measure used to assess market structure.

Table 15.1 shows two calculations of the four-firm concentration ratio: one for tire makers and one for printers. In this example, 14 firms produce tires. The largest four firms have 80 percent of the industry's total revenue, so the four-firm concentration ratio is 80 percent. In the printing industry, with 1,004 firms, the largest four firms have only 0.5 percent of the industry's total revenue, so the four-firm concentration ratio is 0.5 percent.

A low concentration ratio indicates a high degree of competition, and a high concentration ratio indicates an absence of competition. A monopoly has a concentration ratio of 100 percent—the largest (and only) firm has 100 percent of the total revenue. A four-firm concentration ratio that exceeds 60 percent is regarded as an indication of a market that is highly concentrated and dominated by a few firms in an oligopoly. A ratio of less than 40 percent is regarded as an indication of a competitive market—monopolistic competition.

■ **TABLE 15.1**

Concentration Ratio Calculations

(a) Firms' total revenue

Tire makers		Printers	
Firm	**(millions of dollars)**	**Firm**	**(millions of dollars)**
Top, Inc.	200	Fran's	4
ABC, Inc.	250	Ned's	3
Big, Inc.	150	Tom's	2
XYZ, Inc.	100	Jill's	1
Largest 4 firms	700	Largest 4 firms	10
Other 10 firms	175	Other 1,000 firms	1,990
Industry	**875**	Industry	**2,000**

(b) Four-firm concentration ratios

Tire makers		Printers	
Total revenue of largest 4 firms	700	Total revenue of largest 4 firms	10
Industry's total revenue	875	Industry's total revenue	2,000

Four-firm concentration ratio

$$\frac{700}{875} \times 100 = 80 \text{ percent}$$

Four-firm concentration ratio

$$\frac{10}{2,000} \times 100 = 0.5 \text{ percent}$$

The Herfindahl-Hirschman Index

The **Herfindahl-Hirschman Index**—also called the HHI—is the square of the percentage market share of each firm summed over the largest 50 firms (or summed over all the firms if there are fewer than 50) in a market. For example, if there are four firms in a market and the market shares of the firms are 50 percent, 25 percent, 15 percent, and 10 percent, the Herfindahl-Hirschman Index is

$$HHI = 50^2 + 25^2 + 15^2 + 10^2 = 3,450.$$

In perfect competition, the HHI is small. For example, if each of the largest 50 firms in an industry has a market share of 0.1 percent, the HHI is $0.1^2 \times 50 = 0.5$. In a monopoly, the HHI is 10,000—the firm has 100 percent of the market: $100^2 = 10,000$.

The HHI became a popular measure of the degree of competition during the 1980s, when the Justice Department used it to classify markets. A market in which the HHI is less than 1,000 is regarded as being competitive and an example of monopolistic competition. A market in which the HHI lies between 1,000 and 1,800 is regarded as being moderately competitive. It probably is an example of monopolistic competition. But a market in which the HHI exceeds 1,800 is regarded as being uncompetitive. The Justice Department scrutinizes any merger of firms in a market in which the HHI exceeds 1,000 and is likely to challenge a merger if the HHI exceeds 1,800.

Concentration measures are a useful indicator of the degree of competition in a market. But they must be supplemented by other information to determine a market's structure. Table 15.2 summarizes the range of other information, along with the measures of concentration that determine which market structure describes a particular real-world market.

Herfindahl-Hirschman Index
The square of the percentage market share of each firm summed over the largest 50 firms (or summed over all the firms if there are fewer than 50) in a market.

■ **TABLE 15.2**
Market Structure

Characteristics	Perfect competition	Monopolistic competition	Oligopoly	Monopoly
Number of firms in industry	Many	Many	Few	One
Product	Identical	Differentiated	Identical or differentiated	No close substitutes or regulated
Barriers to entry	None	None	Moderate	High
Firm's control over price	None	Some	Considerable	Considerable
Concentration ratio	0	Low	High	100
HHI	Close to 0	Less than 1,800	More than 1,800	10,000
Examples	Wheat, corn	Food, clothing	Cereals	Local water supply

Limitations of Concentration Measures

The two main limitations of concentration measures alone as determinants of market structure are their failure to take proper account of

- The geographical scope of the market
- Barriers to entry and firm turnover

Geographical Scope of the Market Concentration measures take a national view of the market. Many goods are sold in a *national* market, but some are sold in a *regional* market and some in a *global* one. The ready-mix concrete industry consists of local markets. The four-firm concentration ratio for ready-mix concrete is 6.2, and the HHI is 26. These numbers suggest a market that is close to perfect competition. But there is a high degree of concentration in the ready-mix concrete industry in most cities, so this industry is not competitive despite its low measured concentration. The four-firm concentration ratio for automobiles is 87, and the HHI is 2,725. These numbers suggest a highly concentrated market. But competition from imports gives the auto market many of the features of monopolistic competition.

Barriers to Entry and Firm Turnover Concentration measures don't measure barriers to entry. Some industries are highly concentrated but have easy entry and an enormous amount of turnover of firms. For example, many small towns have few restaurants, but there are no restrictions on opening a restaurant and many firms attempt to do so.

A market with a high concentration ratio or HHI might nonetheless be competitive because low barriers to entry create *potential competition*. The few firms in a market face competition from many firms that can easily enter the market and will do so if economic profits are available.

EYE ON THE U.S. ECONOMY

Examples of Monopolistic Competition

These ten industries are all examples of monopolistic competition. They have a large number of firms, shown in parentheses after the name of the industry. The bars measure the percentage of industry total revenue received by the 20 largest firms. The number on the right is the Herfindahl-Hirschman Index.

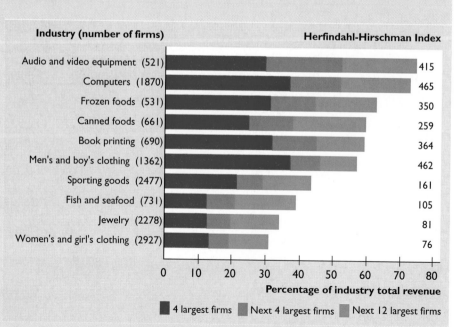

SOURCE OF DATA: U.S. Census Bureau.

CHECKPOINT 15.1

1 **Describe and identify monopolistic competition.**

Practice Problems 15.1

1. Table 1 shows the total revenue of the 50 firms in the tattoo industry.
    a. Calculate the four-firm concentration ratio.
    b. Calculate the HHI.
    c. What is the structure of the tattoo industry?
    d. How would your answer to part **c** change if the 50 firms in the tattoo industry operated in different cities spread across the nation?
    e. What additional information would you need about the tattoo industry to be sure that it is an example of monopolistic competition?

2. Suppose that a new tattoo technology makes it easier for anyone to enter the tattoo industry. How might the market structure of the tattoo industry change?

TABLE 1

Firm	Total revenue (dollars)
Bright Spots	450
Freckles	325
Love Galore	250
Native Birds	200
Next 16 firms (each)	50
Next 30 firms (each)	20
Total total revenue	2,625

Exercises 15.1

1. Table 2 shows the total revenue of the six firms that make fine chocolates.
    a. Calculate the four-firm concentration ratio.
    b. Calculate the HHI.
    c. What is the structure of the chocolate industry?
    d. Suppose that the firms in the chocolate industry face fierce competition from foreign suppliers. How does this information affect your answer to part **c**?
    e. What additional information would you need about the chocolate industry to be sure that it is an example of monopolistic competition?

2. Suppose that a new chocolate-making technology enables anyone with a kitchen to produce outstanding chocolates. How might the market structure of the chocolate industry change?

TABLE 2

Firm	Total revenue (dollars)
Mayfair	30
Bond	40
Magic	10
All Nature	30
Truffles	60
Gold	30
Total total revenue	200

Solution to Practice Problems 15.1

1a. The four-firm concentration ratio is 46.6. The market shares of the four largest firms are 17.1, 12.4, 9.5, and 7.6.
1b. The HHI is 671.14. The market shares from largest to smallest are 17.1, 12.4, 9.5, 7.6, 1.9, and 0.8 percent. Square these numbers to get $292.41 + 153.76 + 90.25 + 57.76 + (3.61 \times 16) + (0.64 \times 30) = 671.14$.
1c. The four-firm concentration ratio and the HHI suggest that the tattoo industry is an example of monopolistic competition unless there are other reasons that would make the concentration measures unreliable guides.
1d. If each of the 50 firms in the tattoo industry operates in different cities spread across the nation, each firm is effectively without competition. The market might be a series of monopolies.
1e. We would want to know about product differentiation; to observe competition on price, quality, and marketing; and to see evidence of low barriers to the entry of new firms.

2. This new tattoo technology would most likely lead to the entry of more firms, greater product differentiation, and more competition.

15.2 OUTPUT AND PRICE DECISIONS

Think about the decisions that Tommy Hilfiger must make about Tommy jeans. First, the firm must decide on the design and quality of its jeans and on its marketing program. We'll suppose that Tommy Hilfiger has already made these decisions so that we can concentrate on the firm's output and pricing decision. But we'll study quality and marketing decisions in the next section.

For a given quality of jeans and a given amount of marketing activity, Tommy Hilfiger faces given costs and market conditions. How, given its costs and the demand for its jeans, does Tommy Hilfiger decide the quantity of jeans to produce and the price at which to sell them?

■ The Firm's Profit-Maximizing Decision

A firm in monopolistic competition makes its output and price decision just as a monopoly firm does. Figure 15.1 illustrates this decision for Tommy jeans. The demand curve for Tommy jeans is *D*. The *MR* curve shows the marginal revenue curve associated with this demand curve and is derived just like the marginal revenue curve of a single-price monopoly in Chapter 14. The *ATC* curve shows the average total cost of producing Tommy jeans, and *MC* is the marginal cost curve.

Tommy Hilfiger maximizes profit by producing the output at which marginal revenue equals marginal cost. In Figure 15.1, this output is 125 pairs of jeans a day. Tommy Hilfiger charges the price that buyers are willing to pay for this quantity, which is determined by the demand curve. This price is $75 a pair. When it produces 125 pairs of jeans a day, Tommy Hilfiger's average total cost is $25 a pair and it makes an economic profit of $6,250 a day ($50 a pair multiplied by 125 pairs a day). The blue rectangle shows Tommy Hilfiger's economic profit.

▨ FIGURE 15.1

Output and Price in Monopolistic Competition

❶ Profit is maximized where marginal revenue equals marginal cost.

❷ The profit-maximizing quantity is 125 pairs of Tommy jeans a day.

❸ The price of $75 a pair exceeds the average total cost of $25 a pair, so the firm makes an economic profit of $50 a pair.

❹ The blue rectangle illustrates economic profit, which equals $6,250 a day ($50 a pair multiplied by 125 pairs).

■ Profit Maximizing Might Be Loss Minimizing

Tommy Hilfiger in Figure 15.1 is earning a healthy economic profit. But such an outcome is not inevitable. The demand for a firm's product might be too low for it to earn an economic profit. Excite@Home was such a firm. Offering high-speed Internet service over the same cable that provides television, Excite@Home hoped to capture a large share of the Internet portal market in competition with AOL, MSN, and a host of other providers.

Figure 15.2 illustrates the situation facing Excite@Home in 2001. The demand curve for its portal service is *D*, the marginal revenue curve is *MR*, the average total cost curve is *ATC*, and the marginal cost curve is *MC*. Excite@Home maximizes profit—equivalently, it minimizes its loss—by producing the output at which marginal revenue equals marginal cost. In Figure 15.2, this output is 40,000 customers. Excite@Home charges the price that buyers are willing to pay for this quantity, which is determined by the demand curve and which is $40 a month. With 40,000 customers, Excite@Home's average total cost is $50 a customer, so Excite@Home incurs an economic loss of $400,000 a month ($10 a customer multiplied by 40,000 customers). The red rectangle shows the firm's economic loss.

The largest loss that a firm will incur is equal to total fixed cost. The reason is that if the profit-maximizing (loss-minimizing) price is less than average variable cost, the firm will shut down temporarily and produce nothing (just like a firm in perfect competition—see p. 329)

So far, the firm in monopolistic competition looks like a single-price monopoly. It produces the quantity at which marginal revenue equals marginal cost and then charges the highest price that buyers are willing to pay for that quantity. The difference between monopoly and monopolistic competition lies in what happens when firms either earn an economic profit or incur an economic loss.

■ FIGURE 15.2
Economic Loss in the Short Run

❶ Profit is maximized and loss is minimized where marginal revenue equals marginal cost.

❷ The loss-minimizing quantity is 40,000 customers connected.

❸ The price of $40 a month is less than average total cost of $50 a month, so the firm incurs an economic loss of $10 a customer.

❹ The red rectangle illustrates economic loss, which equals $400,000 a month ($10 a customer multiplied by 40,000 customers).

■ Long Run: Zero Economic Profit

A firm like Excite@Home is not going to incur an economic loss for long. Eventually, it goes out of business. Also, there is no restriction on entry in monopolistic competition, so if firms in an industry are making an economic profit, other firms have an incentive to enter that industry.

As the Gap and Calvin Klein start to make jeans similar to Tommy jeans, the demand for Tommy jeans decreases. The demand curve for Tommy jeans and the marginal revenue curve start to shift leftward. At each point in time, the firm maximizes its profit by producing the quantity at which marginal revenue equals marginal cost and by charging the highest price that buyers are willing to pay for this quantity. But as the demand curve shifts leftward, the profit-maximizing quantity and price fall.

Figure 15.3 shows the long-run equilibrium. The demand curve for Tommy jeans and the marginal revenue curve have shifted leftward. The firm produces 75 pairs of jeans a day and sells them for $50 each. At this output level, average total cost is also $50 a pair. So Tommy Hilfiger is making zero economic profit on its jeans. When all the firms in the industry are earning zero economic profit, there is no incentive for new firms to enter.

If demand is so low relative to costs that firms incur economic losses, exit will occur. As firms leave an industry, the demand for the products of the remaining firms increases and their demand curves shift rightward. The exit process ends when all the firms in the industry are making zero economic profit.

■ FIGURE 15.3

Output and Price in the Long Run

myeconlab

Economic profit encourages entry, which decreases the demand for each firm's product. Economic loss encourages exit, which increases the demand for each remaining firm's product.

When the demand curve touches the average total cost curve at the quantity at which marginal revenue equals marginal cost, the market is in long-run equilibrium. ❶ The output that maximizes profit is 75 pairs of Tommy jeans a day, and ❷ the price, $50 a pair, equals average total cost. ❸ Economic profit is zero.

■ Monopolistic Competition and Perfect Competition

Figure 15.4 compares monopolistic competition and perfect competition and highlights two key differences between them: excess capacity and markup.

Excess Capacity

A firm has **excess capacity** if it produces below its **efficient scale**, which is the quantity at which average total cost is a minimum—the quantity at the bottom of the U-shaped *ATC* curve. In Figure 15.4(a), Tommy Hilfiger has *excess capacity*. Because the demand curve for Tommy jeans is downward sloping, zero profit occurs only where the average total cost curve is also downward sloping. In Figure 15.4(b), a firm in perfect competition has no excess capacity. Because the demand curve for a perfectly competitive firm's jeans is horizontal, zero profit occurs where the average total cost is a minimum.

Excess capacity
When the quantity that a firm produces is less than the quantity at which average total cost is a minimum.

Efficient scale
The quantity at which average total cost is a minimum.

Markup

A firm's **markup** is the amount by which price exceeds marginal cost. Figure 15.4(a) shows Tommy's markup. Figure 15.4(b) shows the zero markup of perfect competition. Buyers pay a higher price in monopolistic competition than in perfect competition and pay more than marginal cost.

Markup
The amount by which price exceeds marginal cost.

■ **FIGURE 15.4**
Excess Capacity and Markup

(a) Monopolistic competition

(b) Perfect competition

❶ The efficient scale is 100 pairs a day. In monopolistic competition in the long run, the firm has ❷ excess capacity. ❸ Price exceeds ❹ marginal cost by the amount of the ❺ markup and ❻ creates a deadweight loss.

In contrast, because in perfect competition demand for the firm's output is perfectly elastic, ❶ the quantity produced equals the efficient scale and ❷ price equals marginal cost.

■ Is Monopolistic Competition Efficient?

You've learned that resources are used efficiently when marginal benefit equals marginal cost. You've also learned that price measures marginal benefit. So if the price of a pair of Tommy jeans exceeds the marginal cost of producing them, the quantity of Tommy jeans produced is less than the efficient quantity. And you've just seen that in long-run equilibrium in monopolistic competition, price *does* exceed marginal cost.

Deadweight Loss

Because price exceeds marginal cost, monopolistic competition creates deadweight loss, just like monopoly. Figure 15.4(a) shows this deadweight loss. But is monopolistic competition less efficient than perfect competition?

Making the Relevant Comparison

Two economists meet in the street, and one asks the other how her husband is. "Compared to what?" is the quick reply. This bit of economic wit illustrates a key point: Before we can conclude that something needs fixing, we must check out the available alternatives.

The markup that drives a gap between price and marginal cost in monopolistic competition arises from product differentiation. It is because Tommy jeans are not quite the same as jeans from Banana Republic, CK, Diesel, DKNY, Earl Jeans, Gap, Levi, Ralph Lauren, or any of the other dozens of producers of jeans that the demand for Tommy jeans is not perfectly elastic. The only way in which the demand for jeans from Tommy Hilfiger might be perfectly elastic is if there were only one kind of jeans and Tommy along with every other firm made them. In this situation, Tommy jeans would be indistinguishable from all other jeans. They wouldn't even have identifying labels.

If there was only one kind of jeans, the marginal benefit of jeans would almost certainly be less than it is with variety. People value variety. And people value variety not only because it enables each person to select what he or she likes best but also because it provides an external benefit. Most of us enjoy seeing variety in the choices of others. Contrast a scene from the China of the 1960s when everyone wore a Mao tunic with the China of today when everyone wears the clothes of their own choosing. Or contrast a scene from the Germany of the 1930s when almost everyone who could afford a car owned a first-generation Volkswagen Beetle with the world of today with its variety of styles and types of automobiles.

If people value variety, why don't we see infinite variety? The answer is that variety is costly. Each different variety of any product must be designed, and then customers must be informed about it. These initial costs of design and marketing—called setup costs—mean that some varieties that are too close to others already available are just not worth creating.

The Bottom Line

Product variety is both valued and costly. The efficient degree of product variety is the one for which the marginal benefit of product variety equals its marginal cost. The loss that arises because the marginal benefit of one more unit of a given variety exceeds marginal cost is offset by a gain that arises from having an efficient degree of product variety. So compared to the alternative—complete product uniformity—monopolistic competition is efficient.

CHECKPOINT 15.2

2 **Explain how a firm in monopolistic competition determines its output and price in the short run and the long run.**

Practice Problem 15.2

1. Natti is a dot.com entrepreneur who has established a Web site at which people can design and buy a pair of way-cool sunglasses. Natti pays $4,000 a month for her Web server and Internet connection. The glasses that her customers design are made to order by another firm, and Natti pays this firm $50 a pair. Natti has no other costs. Table 1 shows the demand schedule for Natti's sunglasses.
   a. Calculate Natti's profit-maximizing output, price, and economic profit.
   b. Do you expect other firms to enter the Web sunglasses business and compete with Natti?
   c. What happens to the demand for Natti's sunglasses in the long run?
   d. What happens to Natti's economic profit in the long run?

TABLE 1

Price (dollars per pair)	Quantity (pairs per month)
250	0
200	50
150	100
100	150
50	200
0	250

Exercise 15.2

1. Lorie restrings tennis racquets. Her fixed costs are $1,000 a month, and it costs her $15 of labor to string one racquet. Table 2 shows the demand schedule for Lorie's restringing services.
   a. Calculate Lorie's profit-maximizing output, price, and economic profit.
   b. Do you expect other firms to enter the tennis racquet restringing business and compete with Lorie?
   c. What happens to the demand for Lorie's restringing services in the long run?
   d. What happens to Lorie's economic profit in the long run?

TABLE 2

Price (dollars per racquet)	Quantity (racquets per month)
25	0
20	10
15	20
10	30
5	40
0	50

Solution to Practice Problem 15.2

1a. Marginal cost, MC, is $50 a pair—the price that Natti pays her supplier of glasses. To find marginal revenue, calculate the change in total revenue when the quantity increases by 1 pair of sunglasses. Figure 1 shows the demand curve, the marginal revenue curve, and the marginal cost curve. Profit is maximized when $MC = MR$ and Natti sells 100 pairs a month. The price is $150, and average total cost, ATC, is $90—the sum of $50 marginal (and average variable) cost and $40 average fixed cost. Economic profit is $60 a pair on 100 pairs a month, so it is $6,000 a month.

1b. Because Natti is making an economic profit, other firms have an incentive to enter and will do so.

1c. Because firms will enter the market, the demand for Natti's sunglasses will decrease and the demand curve for Natti's sunglasses will shift leftward.

1d. As the demand for Natti's sunglasses decreases, her economic profit also decreases. In the long run, she will earn zero economic profit.

FIGURE 1

Price and cost (dollars per pair)

15.3 PRODUCT DEVELOPMENT AND MARKETING

When we studied a firm's output and price decisions, we supposed that the firm had already made its product quality and marketing decisions. We're now going to study these decisions and the impact they have on the firm's output, price, and economic profit.

■ Innovation and Product Development

To enjoy economic profits, firms in monopolistic competition must be continually developing new products because whenever economic profits are earned, imitators emerge and set up business. So to maintain its economic profit, a firm must seek out new products that will provide it with a competitive edge, even if only temporarily. A firm that manages to introduce a new and differentiated product will temporarily face a less elastic demand and will be able to increase its price temporarily. The firm will make an economic profit. Eventually, new firms that make close substitutes for the innovative product will enter and compete away the economic profit. So to restore economic profit, the firm must again innovate.

Cost Versus Benefit of Product Innovation

The decision to innovate is based on the same type of profit-maximizing calculation that you've already studied. Innovation and product development are costly activities, but they also bring in additional revenues. The firm must balance the cost and benefit at the margin. At a low level of product development, the marginal revenue from a better product exceeds the marginal cost. When the marginal dollar of product development expenditure (the marginal cost of product development) brings in a dollar of additional revenue (the marginal benefit from product development), the firm is spending the profit-maximizing amount on product development.

For example, when Eidos Interactive released "Lara Croft Tomb Raider: The Angel of Darkness," it was probably not the best game that Eidos could have created. But it was a game with features whose marginal benefit—and consumers' willingness to pay—equaled the marginal cost of those features.

Efficiency and Product Innovation

Is product innovation an efficient activity? Does it benefit the consumer? There are two views about the answers to these questions. One view is that monopolistic competition brings to market many improved products that bring great benefits to the consumer. Clothing, kitchen and other household appliances, computers, computer programs, cars, and many other products keep getting better every year, and the consumer benefits from these improved products.

But many so-called improvements amount to little more than changing the appearance of a product or giving a different look to the packaging. In these cases, there is little objective benefit to the consumer.

But regardless of whether a product improvement is real or imagined, its value to the consumer is its marginal benefit, which equals the amount the consumer is willing to pay. In other words, the value of product improvements is the increase in price that the consumer is willing to pay. The marginal benefit to the producer is marginal revenue, which in equilibrium equals marginal cost. Because price exceeds marginal cost in monopolistic competition, product improvement is not pushed to its efficient level.

■ Advertising

Firms differentiate their products by designing and developing features that are actually different from those of the other firms. But firms also attempt to create a consumer perception of product differentiation even when actual differences are small. Advertising and packaging are the principal means firms use to achieve this end. An American Express card is a different product from a Visa card. But the actual differences are not the main ones that American Express emphasizes in its marketing. The deeper message is that if you use an American Express card, you can be like Tiger Woods (or some other high-profile successful person).

Advertising Expenditures

Firms incur huge costs to ensure that buyers appreciate and value the differences between their own products and those of their competitors. So a large proportion of the prices that we pay cover the cost of selling a good. And this proportion is increasing. Advertising in newspapers and magazines and on radio, television, and the Internet is the main selling cost. But it is not the only one. Selling costs include the cost of shopping malls that look like movie sets; glossy catalogs and brochures; and the salaries, airfares, and hotel bills of salespeople.

The total scale of advertising costs is hard to estimate, but some components can be measured. A survey conducted by a commercial agency suggests that for liquor and real estate agents, around 15 percent of the price is spent on advertising. Figure 15.5 shows estimates for a wide range of goods and services.

■ FIGURE 15.5
Advertising Expenditures

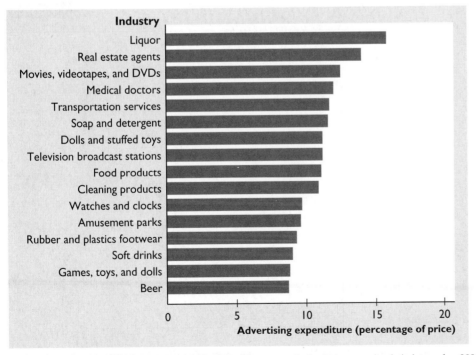

Advertising expenditures are about 15 percent of the price of liquor and real estate service and more than 10 percent of the price of movies, videotapes, DVDs, soap, detergents, and food products.

SOURCE OF DATA: Marketing Today, reported at http://www.marketingtoday.com/tools/ad_to_sales_2004.html.

For the U.S. economy as a whole, there are some 20,000 advertising agencies, which employ more than 200,000 people and have total revenue of $45 billion. But these numbers are only part of the total cost of advertising because many firms have their own internal advertising departments, the costs of which we can only guess.

Advertising expenditures and other selling costs affect firms' profits in two ways: They increase costs and they change demand. Let's look at these effects.

■ Selling Costs and Total Costs

Selling costs such as advertising expenditures increase the costs of a monopolistically competitive firm above those of a perfectly competitive firm or a monopoly. Advertising costs and other selling costs are fixed costs. They do not vary as total output varies. So, just like fixed production costs, advertising costs per unit decrease as production increases.

Figure 15.6 shows how selling costs and advertising expenditures change a firm's average total cost. The blue curve shows the average total cost of production. The red curve shows the firm's average total cost of production plus advertising. The height of the red area between the two curves shows the average fixed cost of advertising. The *total* cost of advertising is fixed. But the *average* cost of advertising decreases as output increases.

Figure 15.6 shows that if advertising increases the quantity sold by a large enough amount, it can lower average total cost. For example, if the quantity sold increases from 25 pairs of jeans a day with no advertising to 100 pairs of jeans a day with advertising, average total cost falls from $60 a pair to $40 a pair. The reason is that although the *total* fixed cost has increased, the greater fixed cost is spread over a greater output, so average total cost decreases.

■ **FIGURE 15.6**

Selling Costs and Total Costs

Selling costs such as the cost of advertising are fixed costs. ❶ When advertising costs are added to ❷ the average total cost of production, ❸ average total cost increases by more at small outputs than at large outputs.

❹ If advertising enables the quantity sold to increase from 25 pairs of jeans a day to 100 pairs a day, it *lowers* average total cost from $60 a pair to $40 a pair.

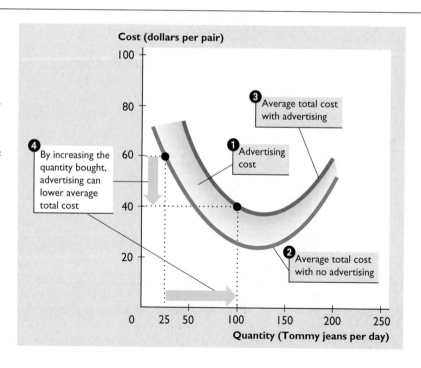

Selling Costs and Demand

Advertising and other selling efforts change the demand for a firm's product. But how? Does demand increase or does it decrease? The most natural answer is that advertising increases demand. By informing people about the quality of its products or by persuading people to switch from the products of other firms, a firm might expect to increase the demand for its own products.

But all firms in monopolistic competition advertise. And all seek to persuade customers that they have the best deal. If advertising enables a firm to survive, it might increase the number of firms in the market. And to the extent that it increases the number of firms, it *decreases* the demand for any one firm's products. It also makes the demand for any one firm's product more elastic. So advertising can end up not only lowering average total cost but also lowering the markup and the price.

Figure 15.7 illustrates this possible effect of advertising. In part (a), with no advertising, the demand for Tommy jeans is not very elastic. Profit is maximized at 75 pairs of jeans a day, and the markup is large. In part (b), advertising, which is a fixed cost, increases average total cost and shifts the average total cost curve upward from ATC_0 to ATC_1 but leaves the marginal cost curve unchanged at MC. Demand becomes much more elastic, the profit-maximizing quantity increases, and the markup shrinks.

FIGURE 15.7
Advertising and the Markup

① With no firms advertising, demand is low and not very elastic, so the **②** markup is large.

③ Advertising shifts the average total cost curve upward from ATC_0 to ATC_1 and makes demand more elastic. **④** With all firms advertising, the price falls and the markup shrinks.

Selling Costs in YOUR Life

When you buy a new pair of running shoes, you're buying materials that cost $9, production costs of $8, a U.S. import duty of $3, and selling costs of $50.

Running shoes are not unusual. Almost everything that you buy includes a selling cost component that exceeds one half of the total cost.

The table provides a detailed breakdown of the cost of a pair of shoes.

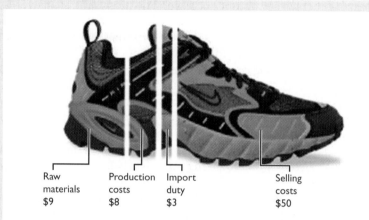

| Raw materials $9 | Production costs $8 | Import duty $3 | Selling costs $50 |

Manufacturer (Asia)		Nike (Beaverton, Oregon)		Retailer (your town)	
Materials	$9.00				
Cost of labor	$2.75	Cost of shoe to Nike	$20.00	Cost of shoe to retailer	$35.50
Cost of capital	$3.00	Sales, distribution, and administration	$5.00	Sales clerk's wages	$9.50
Profit	$1.75	Advertising	$4.00	Shop rent	$9.00
Shipping	$0.50	Research & development	$0.25	Retailer's other costs	$7.00
Import duty	$3.00	Nike's profit	$6.25	Retailer's profit	$9.00
Nike's cost	**$20.00**	**Retailer's cost**	**$35.50**	**Price paid by you**	**$70.00**

■ Using Advertising to Signal Quality

Some advertising, like the Tiger Woods' American Express card ads on television and in glossy magazines or the huge number of dollars that Coke and Pepsi spend, seems hard to understand. There doesn't seem to be any concrete information about a credit card in the glistening smile of a golfer. And surely everyone knows about Coke and Pepsi. What is the gain from pouring millions of dollars a month into advertising a well-known cola?

One answer is that advertising is a signal to the consumer of a high-quality product. A **signal** is an action taken by an informed person (or firm) to send a message to uninformed people. Think about two colas: Coke and Oke.

Oke knows that its cola is not very good and that its taste varies a lot depending on which cheap batch of unsold cola it happens to buy each week. So Oke knows that while it could get a lot of people to try Oke by advertising, they would all quickly discover what a poor product it is and switch back to the cola they bought before. The amount that Oke spent on advertising would exceed the revenue that came in.

Coke, in contrast, knows that its product has a high-quality consistent taste and that once someone has tried it, there is a good chance that they'll never drink

Signal
An action taken by an informed person (or firm) to send a message to uninformed people.

anything but Coke. If Coke ran a costly advertising campaign, more people would try Coke and most would stick with it. The revenue earned would exceed the cost of the advertising campaign.

On the basis of this reasoning, Oke doesn't advertise but Coke does. And Coke spends a lot of money to make a big splash.

Cola drinkers who see Coke's splashy ads believe that the firm would not spend so much money advertising if its product were not truly good. So the cola drinker reasons that Coke is indeed a really good product. The flashy expensive ad has signaled that Coke is really good without saying anything about Coke.

Notice that if advertising is a signal, it doesn't need any specific product information. It just needs to be expensive and hard to miss. That's what a lot of advertising looks like. So the signaling theory of advertising predicts much of the advertising that we see.

■ Brand Names

Many firms create a brand name and spend a lot of money promoting it. Why? What benefit does a brand name bring to justify the sometimes high cost of establishing it? The basic answer is that a brand name provides consumers with information about the quality of a product and the producer with an incentive to achieve a high and consistent quality standard.

To see how a brand name helps the consumer, think about how you use brand names to get information about quality. You're on a road trip, and it is time to find a place to spend the night. You see roadside advertisements for Holiday Inn and Embassy Suites and for Joe's Motel and Annie's Driver's Stop. You know about Holiday Inn and Embassy Suites because you've stayed in them before. And you've seen their advertisements. You know what to expect from them. You have no information at all about Joe's and Annie's. They might be better than the lodging you do know about, but without that knowledge, you're not going to chance them. You use the brand name as information and stay at Holiday Inn.

This same story explains why a brand name provides an incentive to the producer to achieve high and consistent quality. Because no one would know whether they were offering a high standard of service, Joe's and Annie's have no incentive to do so. But equally, because everyone expects a given standard of service from Holiday Inn, a failure to meet a customer's expectation would almost surely lose that customer to a competitor. So Holiday Inn has a strong incentive to deliver what it promises in the advertising that creates its brand name.

■ Efficiency of Advertising and Brand Names

To the extent that advertising and brand names provide consumers with information about the precise nature of product differences and about product quality, they benefit the consumer and enable a better product choice to be made. But the opportunity cost of the additional information must be weighed against the gain to the consumer.

The final verdict on the efficiency of monopolistic competition is ambiguous. In some cases, the gains from extra product variety unquestionably offset the selling costs and the extra cost arising from excess capacity. The tremendous varieties of books and magazines, clothing, food, and drinks are examples of such gains. It is less easy to see the gains from being able to buy brand-name drugs that have a chemical composition identical to that of a generic alternative. But many people do willingly pay more for the brand-name alternative.

3 **Explain why advertising costs are high and why firms use brand names in monopolistic competition.**

Practice Problem 15.3

1. Bianca bakes delicious cookies. Her total fixed cost is $40 a day, and her average variable cost is $1 a bag. Few people know about Bianca's Cookies, and she is maximizing her profit by selling 10 bags a day for $5 a bag. Bianca thinks that if she spends $50 a day on advertising, she can increase her market and sell 25 bags a day for $5 a bag. If Bianca's belief about the effect of advertising is correct,
   a. Can she increase her economic profit by advertising?
   b. If she advertises, will her average total cost increase or decrease at the quantity produced?
   c. If she advertises, will she continue to sell her cookies for $5 a bag or will she raise her price or lower her price?

Exercise 15.3

1. Bianca—the same Bianca as in the practice problem—changes the recipe that she uses and now bakes even more delicious cookies. Bianca's costs don't change, but people love her new cookies and think that they are much better than those of the other cookie producers.
   a. How will the change described here affect Bianca's price, quantity produced, and economic profit?
   b. Can she still increase her economic profit by advertising?

Solution to Practice Problem 15.3

1a. With no advertising, Bianca's total revenue is $50 (10 bags at $5 a bag) and her total cost is $50 (the sum of $40 total fixed cost and $10 total variable cost). So her economic profit is zero. With $50 a day advertising expenditure, Bianca has a total revenue of $125 (25 bags at $5 a bag) and total cost of $115 (total fixed cost is now $90, and total variable cost is now $25). Her economic profit with no price change is $10. So Bianca can increase her economic profit by advertising.

1b. If Bianca advertises, her average total cost will decrease. With no advertising, her average total cost is $5 a bag ($50 ÷ 10). With advertising, her average total cost is $4.60 a bag ($115 ÷ 25).

1c. We can't say if she will continue to sell her cookies for $5 a bag. It depends on how her demand curve shifts. Advertising costs are fixed costs, so they don't change marginal cost, which remains at $1 a bag. She will sell the profit-maximizing quantity (the quantity at which marginal revenue equals marginal cost) for the highest price she can charge for the quantity produced.

CHAPTER CHECKPOINT

Key Points

1 Describe and identify monopolistic competition.

- Monopolistic competition is a market structure in which a large number of firms compete; each firm produces a product that is slightly different from the products of its competitors; firms compete on price, quality, and marketing; and new firms are free to enter the industry.
- Monopolistic competition is identified by a low degree of concentration measured by either the four-firm concentration ratio or the HHI.

2 Explain how a firm in monopolistic competition determines its output and price in the short run and the long run.

- Firms in monopolistic competition face downward-sloping demand curves and produce the quantity at which marginal revenue equals marginal cost.
- Entry and exit result in zero economic profit and excess capacity in long-run equilibrium.

3 Explain why advertising costs are high and why firms use brand names in monopolistic competition.

- Firms in monopolistic competition innovate and develop new products to maintain economic profit.
- Advertising expenditures increase total cost, but they might lower average total cost if they increase the quantity sold by enough.
- Advertising expenditures might increase demand, but they might also decrease the demand facing a firm by increasing competition.
- Whether monopolistic competition is inefficient depends on the value people place on product variety.

Key Terms

Efficient scale, 387
Excess capacity, 387
Four-firm concentration ratio, 380
Herfindahl-Hirschman Index, 381

Markup, 387
Product differentiation, 378
Signal, 394

Exercises

1. Which of the following goods and services are sold by firms in monopolistic competition?
   a. Cable television service
   b. Wheat
   c. Athletic shoes
   d. Soda
   e. Shaving cream
   f. Toothbrushes
   g. Ready-mix concrete
   Explain your selections.

FIGURE 1

2. The four-firm concentration ratio for audio equipment makers is 30, and that for electric lamp makers is 89. The HHI for audio equipment makers is 415, and that for electric lamp makers is 2,850. Which of these markets is an example of monopolistic competition?

3. Figure 1 shows the demand curve, marginal revenue curve, and cost curves of Lite and Kool, Inc., a producer of running shoes in monopolistic competition.
   a. What quantity does Lite and Kool produce?
   b. What price does it charge?
   c. What is Lite and Kool's markup?
   d. How much profit does Lite and Kool make?
   e. Do firms in monopolistic competition always have excess capacity?
   f. Explain why Lite and Kool does or does not have excess capacity.
   g. Do you expect firms to enter the running shoes market or exit from that market in the long run? Explain your answer.

FIGURE 2

4. Figure 2 shows the demand curve, marginal revenue curve, and cost curves of Stiff Shirt, Inc., a producer of shirts in monopolistic competition.
   a. Show on the graph the quantity that Stiff Shirt produces.
   b. Show on the graph the price that Stiff Shirt charges.
   c. Show on the graph Stiff Shirt's markup.
   d. Show on the graph Stiff Shirt's profit.
   e. Does Stiff Shirt have excess capacity?
   f. If Stiff Shirt increased output, would its average total cost fall or rise?
   g. In light of your answer to part **f**, why doesn't Stiff Shirt increase its output?
   h. Do you expect firms to enter the shirt market or exit from that market in the long run? Explain your answer.
   i. Do you expect the price of a shirt to rise or fall in the long run? Explain your answer.

FIGURE 3

5. Figure 3 shows the demand curve, marginal revenue curve, and cost curves of La Bella Pizza, a firm in monopolistic competition.
   a. Show on the graph the quantity La Bella produces.
   b. Show on the graph the price La Bella charges.
   c. Show on the graph La Bella's economic profit.

    d. Does La Bella have excess capacity? Explain why or why not.

    e. Does La Bella have a price markup? Explain why or why not.

    f. Do you expect firms to enter the pizza market or exit from that market in the long run? Explain your answer.

    g. Do you expect the price of pizza to rise or fall in the long run?

6. Figure 4 shows the demand curve, marginal revenue curve, and cost curves of Bob's Best Burgers, a firm in monopolistic competition.

    a. What quantity of burgers does Bob produce?

    b. What price does Bob charge?

    c. What is Bob's economic profit?

    d. Do you expect other firms to enter the burger business and compete with Bob? Why or why not?

    e. Does Bob have excess capacity? Explain why or why not.

    f. Does Bob have a price markup? Explain why or why not.

7. Jeb and George are discussing their respective businesses. Jeb says that there is no way he could lower his average total cost. He wouldn't be able to hold his costs to their current level if he either increased or decreased his production. George says that he is frustrated by the level of demand for his product and that he could cut his costs if only he could sell more. One of these people runs a diner, and the other is a wheat farmer.

    a. Who is which and why?

    b. What does this conversation imply about the efficiency of wheat farms and diners?

    c. What does this conversation imply about the economic profit earned by wheat farms and diners?

8. Mike's, a firm in monopolistic competition, produces running shoes. With no advertising, Mike's profit-maximizing output is 500 pairs a day and the price is $100 a pair. But the firms in this market begin to advertise, and so does Mike's. With advertising, Mike's profit-maximizing output increases to 1,000 pairs a day, but the price falls to $50 a pair.

    a. Sketch a demand curve, marginal revenue curve, average total cost curve, and marginal cost curve that are consistent with the no-advertising situation described.

    b. Sketch a demand curve, marginal revenue curve, average total cost curve, and marginal cost curve that are consistent with the advertising situation described.

    c. In which situation does Mike's have the larger markup?

    d. In which situation does Mike's have the larger excess capacity?

9. Some people happily pay more for Coke or Pepsi than they are willing to pay for a nonbranded cola. And some people happily pay more for Tylenol than they are willing to pay for generic acetaminophen.

    a. Does this behavior mean that such people are irrational?

    b. How do brand names help consumers?

    c. How do brand names change the behavior of producers?

    d. Why would it not be efficient to ban brand names?

FIGURE 4

Critical Thinking

10. "Advertising and brand names are a social waste. We would be better off if brand names were not protected and if advertising were banned." Discuss these assertions, and in doing so, use the analysis of the effects of advertising and brand names presented in this chapter.

11. What is your favorite television advertisement?
    a. Describe the advertisement.
    b. Is this advertisement a signal?
    c. How do you think this advertisement increases the profits of the producer?
    d. How do you think this advertisement benefits the consumer?
    e. In what ways do you think this advertisement creates deadweight loss?

12. The Xerox brand of photocopiers has become so common that people often use the name Xerox as a common noun (a xerox) and a verb (to xerox). Xerox launched an expensive campaign urging the public to use "Xerox" only as a proper noun (the Xerox brand photocopiers).
    a. Why is Xerox so concerned about the use of its brand name as a common noun or verb?
    b. Do consumers benefit if "Xerox" is not used as an everyday noun and verb?

 ## Web Exercises

Use the links on MyEconLab to work the following exercises.

13. Go to the U.S. Census Bureau and get the latest (1997) data on concentration ratios in manufacturing.
    a. Find the four-firm concentration ratio and HHI for six consumer items that are examples of monopolistic competition.
    b. Find the four-firm concentration ratio and HHI for six consumer items that are too concentrated to be examples of monopolistic competition.
    c. Explain your selections.

14. Go to pricescan.com and check the prices of an item that interests you.
    a. What is the lowest price for which the item is available?
    b. What is the highest price for which the item is available?
    c. What is the high-price source offering that the low-price source isn't?
    d. If you were buying this item, from which source would you buy it and why?

15. Go to Brand Names Education Forum and read the article "Be a Smart Shopper."
    a. Summarize the article in about 100 words.
    b. Does the article correctly identify the benefits of brand names? Explain why or why not.
    c. Does the advice on being a smart shopper correctly identify the benefits to the consumer of using brand name information? Explain why or why not.

16. See what the Brand-naming Service at yourDictionary.com offers. On the basis of the economics of brand names explained in the chapter, do you think that the specific name chosen for a brand matters much? Explain why or why not.

CHAPTER 16

Oligopoly

When you have completed your study of this chapter,
you will be able to

1 Describe and identify oligopoly and explain how it arises.

2 Explore the range of alternative price and quantity outcomes and describe the dilemma faced by firms in oligopoly.

3 Use game theory to explain how price and quantity are determined in oligopoly.

When you go shopping for a softball bat, you buy an Anderson, a DeMarini, an Easton, a Louisville Slugger, a Miken, or a Worth. When PC makers go shopping for chips, their choice is narrower. They buy from one of two firms: Intel or Advanced Micro Devices (AMD). And when the world's airlines go shopping for a large passenger jet, they buy a Boeing or an Airbus. In all of these markets, there is competition. But the competition is unlike perfect competition or monopolistic competition. It is unlike perfect competition because the producers of softball bats, computer chips, and airplanes are not price takers. They can influence their prices. It is unlike monopolistic competition because each firm is so big that its actions influence the profits of all the other firms, so it must consider how the other firms might react to its own decisions. To understand how the prices and quantities of softball bats, computer chips, and airplanes are determined, we need the models of oligopoly explained in this chapter.

16.1 WHAT IS OLIGOPOLY?

Oligopoly, like monopolistic competition, is a type of market that lies between perfect competition and monopoly. The firms in oligopoly might produce an identical product and compete only on price, or they might produce a differentiated product and compete on price, product quality, and marketing. The distinguishing features of oligopoly are that

- A small number of firms compete.
- Natural or legal barriers prevent the entry of new firms.

■ Small Number of Firms

In contrast to monopolistic competition and perfect competition, an oligopoly consists of a small number of firms. Each firm has a large share of the market, the firms are interdependent, and they face a temptation to collude.

Interdependence

With a small number of firms in a market, each firm's actions influence the profits of the other firms. To see how, suppose you run one of the three gas stations in a small town. If you cut your price, your market share increases, and your profits might increase too. But the market share and profits of the other two firms fall. In this situation, the other firms will most likely cut their prices too. If they do cut their prices, your market share and profit take a tumble. So before deciding to cut your price, you must predict how the other firms will react and take into account the effects of those reactions on your own profit. Your profit depends on the actions of the other firms, and their profit depends on your actions. You and the other two firms are interdependent.

Temptation to Collude

When a small number of firms share a market, they can increase their profits by forming a cartel and acting like a monopoly. A **cartel** is a group of firms acting together—colluding—to limit output, raise price, and increase economic profit. Cartels are illegal in the United States (and most other countries), but even when there is no formal cartel, firms might try to operate like a cartel. Also, international cartels can operate legally (see *Eye on the Global Economy* on p. 409).

For reasons that you'll discover in this chapter, cartels tend to be unstable and eventually break down.

■ Barriers to Entry

Either natural or legal barriers to entry can create oligopoly. You saw in Chapter 14 how economies of scale and demand form a natural barrier to entry that can create a *natural monopoly*. These same factors can create a natural oligopoly.

Like natural monopoly, a natural oligopoly arises from the interaction of the demand for a good or service and the extent of economies of scale in its production. Figure 16.1 illustrates two natural oligopolies.

The demand curve, D (in both parts of the figure), shows the demand for taxi rides in a town. If the average total cost curve of a taxi company is ATC_1 in part (a), the market is a natural **duopoly**—a market with only two firms. You can prob-

Cartel
A group of firms acting together to limit output, raise price, and increase economic profit.

Duopoly
A market with only two firms.

■ FIGURE 16.1

Natural Oligopoly

(a) Natural duopoly

(b) Natural oligopoly with three firms

❶ The lowest possible price is $10 a ride, which is the minimum average total cost. **❷** When a firm produces 30 rides a day, the efficient scale, **❸** two firms can satisfy the market demand. This natural oligopoly has two firms—a natural duopoly.

❹ When the efficient scale of one firm is 20 rides a day, **❺** three firms can satisfy the market demand at the lowest possible price. This natural oligopoly has three firms.

ably see some examples of duopoly where you live. Some cities have only two suppliers of milk, two local newspapers, two taxi companies, two car rental firms, two copy centers, or two college bookstores.

Notice in part (a) that the efficient scale of one firm is 30 rides a day. The lowest price at which the firm would remain in business is $10 a ride. At that price, the quantity of rides demanded is 60 a day, the quantity that can be provided by just two firms. There is no room in this market for three firms. To sell more than 60 rides a day, the price would have to fall below $10 a ride. But then the firms would incur an economic loss, and one of them would exit. If there were only one firm, it would earn an economic profit and a second firm would enter to take some of the business and economic profit.

If the average total cost curve of a taxi company is ATC_2 in part (b), the efficient scale of one firm is 20 rides a day. This market is large enough for three firms. But it is not large enough for a fourth firm. Economies of scale limit the market to three because firms would incur a loss if there were four of them. And this market will not operate with two firms because with only two, economic profit would encourage the entry of a third firm.

A legal oligopoly arises when a legal barrier to entry protects the small number of firms in a market. A city might license two taxi firms or two bus companies, for example, even though the combination of demand and economies of scale leaves room for more than two firms.

When barriers to entry create an oligopoly, firms can make an economic profit in the long run without fear of triggering the entry of additional firms.

■ Identifying Oligopoly

Identifying oligopoly is the flip side of identifying monopolistic competition. But the borderline between the two market types is hard to pin down. We need to know whether a market is an oligopoly or monopolistic competition for two reasons. First, we want to be able to make predictions about how the market operates and how price and quantity will respond to such factors as a change in demand or a change in costs. Second, we want to know whether the firms in a market are delivering an efficient outcome that serves the public interest.

The key features of a market that we need to identify are whether the firms are so few that they recognize the interdependencies among them and whether they are acting in a similar way to a monopoly.

As a practical matter, we try to identify oligopoly by looking at the four-firm concentration ratio and the Herfindahl-Hirschman Index, qualified with other information about the geographical scope of the market and barriers to entry.

As we noted in Chapter 15, a market in which the HHI lies between 1,000 and 1,800 is usually an example of monopolistic competition. And a market in which the HHI exceeds 1,800 is usually an example of oligopoly.

E Y E ON THE U. S. ECONOMY

Examples of Oligopoly

You're pretty familiar with some of the industries shown in the figure. You probably know, for example, that Kellogg's makes most of the breakfast cereals consumed in the United States. It is said that Kellogg's does more business before eight o'clock in the morning than most firms do all day!

You probably also know that Phillip Morris and RJ Reynolds make most of the cigarettes sold in the United States. You also know that you see Duracell, Energizer, and not much else when you go shopping for a battery. And the washing machine and dryer in

your home were most likely made by General Electric, Maytag, or Whirlpool.

Some of these industries are less familiar, but you see a lot of their products without recognizing them. One of these industries is the manufacture of glass bottles and jars. When you buy anything that comes in glass, there's a good chance that the container was made in Toledo, Ohio, by Owens-Illinois, the world's largest glass packaging manufacturer.

There isn't much room for hesitation about identifying the first seven industries shown in the figure as oligopolies. They have a small number of firms, a high four-firm concentration

ratio, and an HHI that exceeds 2,000. All of these industries are ones in which the largest firms pay serious attention to each other and think hard about the impact of their decisions on their competitors and the repercussion they may themselves face from their competitors' reactions. The last three industries in the figure are less easily classified. They might be considered borderline between oligopoly and monopolistic competition. The four-firm concentration ratio and HHI are high. But there are many firms in these industries. And while a few of the firms are very large, they face tough competition from the many others.

CHECKPOINT 16.1

■ Describe and identify oligopoly and explain how it arises.

Practice Problems 16.1

1. What are the distinguishing features of oligopoly?

2. Why are breakfast cereals made by firms in oligopoly? Why isn't there monopolistic competition in that industry?

Exercises 16.1

1. Identify an oligopoly market in which you have bought something recently.

2. Why are the firms that make boxes of chocolates on the borderline between oligopoly and monopolistic competition?

Solution to Practice Problems 16.1

1. The distinguishing features of oligopoly are a small number of interdependent firms competing behind natural or legal barriers to entry.

2. Breakfast cereals are made by firms in oligopoly because economies of scale and demand limit the number of firms that can earn a profit in that market.

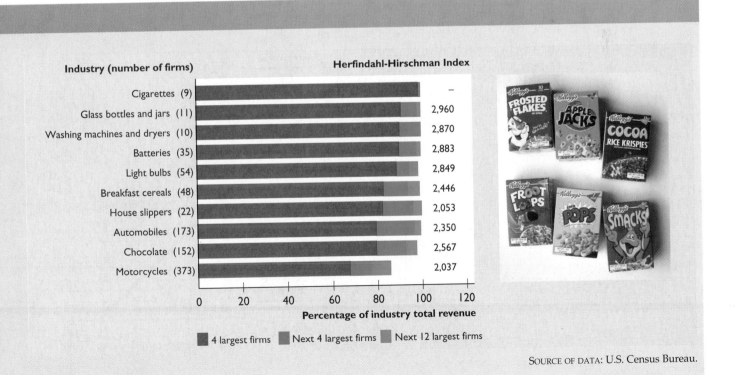

Industry (number of firms)	Herfindahl-Hirschman Index
Cigarettes (9)	—
Glass bottles and jars (11)	2,960
Washing machines and dryers (10)	2,870
Batteries (35)	2,883
Light bulbs (54)	2,849
Breakfast cereals (48)	2,446
House slippers (22)	2,053
Automobiles (173)	2,350
Chocolate (152)	2,567
Motorcycles (373)	2,037

Percentage of industry total revenue

■ 4 largest firms ■ Next 4 largest firms ■ Next 12 largest firms

SOURCE OF DATA: U.S. Census Bureau.

16.2 ALTERNATIVE OLIGOPOLY OUTCOMES

Oligopoly might operate like monopoly, like perfect competition, or somewhere between these two extremes. To see these alternative possible outcomes, we'll study duopoly in the market for airplanes. Airbus and Boeing are the only makers of large commercial jet aircraft. Suppose that they have identical costs. To keep the numbers simple, assume that total fixed cost is zero and that regardless of the rate of production, the marginal cost of an airplane is $1 million.

Figure 16.2 shows the market demand schedule and demand curve for airplanes. Airbus and Boeing share this market. The total quantity sold and the quantities sold by each firm depend on the price of an airplane.

■ Monopoly Outcome

If this industry had only one firm operating as a single-price monopoly, its marginal revenue curve would be the one shown in Figure 16.2. Marginal revenue equals marginal cost when 6 airplanes a week are produced and the price is $13 million an airplane. Total cost would be $6 million and total revenue would be $78 million, so economic profit would be $72 million a week.

■ **FIGURE 16.2**

A Market for Airplanes

Quantity (airplanes per week)	Price	Total revenue	Marginal revenue
	(millions of dollars per airplane)		
0	25	0	
			25
			23
1	23	23	
			21
			19
2	21	42	
			17
			15
3	19	57	
			13
			11
4	17	68	
			9
			7
5	15	75	
			5
			3
6	13	78	
			1
			−1
7	11	77	
8	9	72	
9	7	63	
10	5	50	
11	3	33	
12	1	12	

Price and cost (millions of dollars per airplane)

❶ Market demand curve

❷ Marginal revenue of a single-price monopoly

❻ Range of possible quantities for oligopoly

❺ Perfect competition equilibrium quantity

❸ Marginal cost

❹ Monopoly equilibrium price

❻ Range of possible prices for oligopoly

❹ Monopoly equilibrium quantity

❺ Perfect competition equilibrium price

Quantity (airplanes per week)

Cartel to Achieve Monopoly Outcome

Can the two firms achieve the monopoly outcome that we've just found and maximize their joint profit? They can attempt to do so by forming a cartel.

Suppose that Airbus and Boeing agreed to limit the total production of airplanes to 6 a week. The market demand curve tells us that the price would be $13 million per airplane and economic profit would be $72 million a week. Suppose that the two firms also agree to split the market evenly and each produce 3 airplanes a week. They would each make an economic profit of $36 million a week—see Table 16.1.

Would it be in the self-interest of Airbus and Boeing to stick to their agreement and limit production to 3 aircraft a week each?

To begin answering this question, notice that with the price of an airplane exceeding marginal cost, if one firm increased production, it would increase its profit. But if both firms increased output whenever price exceeded marginal cost, the end of the process would be the same as perfect competition.

■ Perfect Competition Outcome

You can see the perfect competition outcome in Figure 16.2. The equilibrium is where the industry supply curve, which is the marginal cost curve, intersects the demand curve. The quantity is 12 million airplanes a week, and the price is the same as marginal cost—$1 million per airplane.

■ Other Possible Cartel Breakdowns

Because price exceeds marginal cost, a cartel is likely to break down. But a cartel might not unravel all the way to perfect competition. In *Eye on the Global Economy* on p. 409, you can see the brief history of a sometimes successful and sometimes unsuccessful cartel in the global market for oil. You can see why a cartel breaks down but not all the way to perfect competition by looking at some alternative outcomes in the airplane industry example.

Boeing Increases Output to 4 Airplanes a Week

Suppose that starting from a cartel that achieves the monopoly outcome, Boeing increases output by 1 airplane a week. Table 16.2 keeps track of the data. With Boeing producing 4 airplanes a week and Airbus producing 3 airplanes a week, total output is 7 airplanes a week. To sell 7 airplanes a week, the price must fall. The demand schedule in Figure 16.2 tells us that the quantity demanded is 7 airplanes a week when the price is $11 million an airplane.

Market total revenue would now be $77 million, total cost would be $7 million, and economic profit would fall to $70 million. But the distribution of this economic profit is now unequal. Boeing would gain, and Airbus would lose.

Boeing would now receive $44 million a week in total revenue, have a total cost of $4 million, and earn an economic profit of $40 million. Airbus would receive $33 million a week in total revenue, incur a total cost of $3 million, and earn an economic profit of $30 million.

So by increasing its output by 1 airplane a week, Boeing can increase its economic profit by $4 million and cause the economic profit of Airbus to fall by $6 million.

Because the two firms in this example are identical, we could rerun the above story with Airbus increasing production by 1 airplane a week and Boeing holding

TABLE 16.1 MONOPOLY OUTCOME

	Boeing	Airbus	Market total
Quantity (airplanes a week)	3	3	6
Price ($ million per airplane)	13	13	13
Total revenue ($ million)	39	39	78
Total cost ($ million)	3	3	6
Economic profit ($ million)	36	36	72

TABLE 16.2 BOEING INCREASES OUTPUT TO 4 AIRPLANES A WEEK

	Boeing	Airbus	Market total
Quantity (airplanes a week)	4	3	7
Price ($ million per airplane)	11	11	11
Total revenue ($ million)	44	33	77
Total cost ($ million)	4	3	7
Economic profit ($ million)	40	30	70

output at 3 a week. In this case, Airbus would earn $40 million a week and Boeing would earn $30 million a week.

Boeing is better off producing 4 airplanes a week if Airbus sticks with 3 a week. But is it in Airbus's interest to hold its output at 3 airplanes a week? To answer this question, we need to compare the economic profit Airbus makes if it maintains its output at 3 airplanes a week with the profit it makes if it produces 4 airplanes a week. How much economic profit does Airbus make if it produces 4 airplanes a week with Boeing also producing 4 airplanes a week?

Airbus Increases Output to 4 Airplanes a Week

With both firms producing 4 airplanes a week, total output is 8 airplanes a week. To sell 8 airplanes a week, the price must fall further. The demand schedule in Figure 16.2 tells us that the quantity demanded is 8 airplanes a week when the price is $9 million an airplane.

Table 16.3 keeps track of the data. Market total revenue would now be $72 million, total cost would be $8 million, and economic profit would fall to $64 million. With both firms producing the same output, the distribution of this economic profit is now equal.

Both firms would now receive $36 million a week in total revenue, have a total cost of $4 million, and earn an economic profit of $32 million. For Airbus, this outcome is an improvement on the previous one by $2 million a week. For Boeing, this outcome is worse than the previous one by $8 million.

This outcome is better for Airbus, but would Boeing go along with it? You know that Boeing would be worse off if it decreased its output to 3 airplanes a week because it would get the outcome that Airbus has in Table 16.2—an economic profit of only $30 million a week. But would Boeing be better off if it increased output to 5 airplanes a week?

Boeing Increases Output to 5 Airplanes a Week

Suppose now that Airbus maintains its output at 4 airplanes a week and Boeing increases output to 5 a week. Table 16.4 keeps track of the data. Total output is now 9 airplanes a week. To sell this quantity, the price must fall to $7 million an airplane. Market total revenue is $63 million and total cost is $9 million, so economic profit for the two firms is $54 million. The distribution of this economic profit is again unequal. But now both firms would lose.

Boeing would now receive $35 million a week in total revenue, have a total cost of $5 million, and earn an economic profit of $30 million—$2 million less than it would earn if it maintained its output at 4 airplanes a week. Airbus would receive $28 million a week in total revenue, incur a total cost of $4 million, and earn an economic profit of $24 million—$8 million less than before. So neither firm gains by increasing total output beyond 8 airplanes a week.

■ The Oligopoly Cartel Dilemma

With a cartel, both firms make the maximum available economic profit. If both increase production, both see their profit fall. If only one firm increases production, that firm makes a larger economic profit while the other makes a lower economic profit. So what will the firms do? We can speculate about what they will do. But to work out the answer, we need some game theory. That's our next task.

TABLE 16.3 AIRBUS INCREASES OUTPUT TO 4 AIRPLANES A WEEK

	Boeing	Airbus	Market total
Quantity (airplanes a week)	4	4	8
Price ($ million per airplane)	9	9	9
Total revenue ($ million)	36	36	72
Total cost ($ million)	4	4	8
Economic profit ($ million)	32	32	64

TABLE 16.4 BOEING INCREASES OUTPUT TO 5 AIRPLANES A WEEK

	Boeing	Airbus	Market total
Quantity (airplanes a week)	5	4	9
Price ($ million per airplane)	7	7	7
Total revenue ($ million)	35	28	63
Total cost ($ million)	5	4	9
Economic profit ($ million)	30	24	54

The OPEC Global Oil Cartel

The Organization of the Petroleum Exporting Countries (OPEC) is an international cartel of oil-producing nations. OPEC was created in 1960 by the governments of Iran, Iraq, Kuwait, Saudi Arabia, and Venezuela. Six other nations are now members of the organization: Qatar, Indonesia, Libya, United Arab Emirates, Algeria, and Nigeria.

OPEC describes its objective as being "to co-ordinate and unify petroleum policies among member countries in order to secure fair and stable prices, . . . an efficient, economic and regular supply of petroleum to consuming nations; and a fair return on capital to those investing in the industry." These words can be interpreted as being code for "restricting the production of oil to keep its price high."

During the 1960s, OPEC quietly built its organization and prepared the ground for its push to dominate the global oil market. Its first opportunity came in 1973 when, with an Arab-Israeli war raging, it was able to organize an embargo on oil shipments to the United States and Europe and drive the price of oil to four times its previous level.

OPEC's second opportunity came with a revolution in Iran in 1979 when the price of oil more than doubled.

The figure shows these two price hikes. To make the prices mean the same in terms of the value of money, the graph shows the price of oil in terms of the value of the dollar in 2000. You can see that the price went from about $7 a barrel in 1970 to more than $55 a barrel by 1981.

OPEC ministers meeting in Vienna

During the 1980s, many new sources of oil supply opened up and the OPEC cartel lost control of the global market. The cartel broke down, and the price of oil fell.

The price of oil remained remarkably stable during the 1990s, and the power of OPEC was countered by a large supply of oil from other sources.

But during 2004 and 2005, when the global demand for oil increased dramatically, with much of the increased demand coming from China and other developing Asian economies, OPEC was again able to dominate the market, restrict its own production, and raise the world price.

Price of oil (2000 dollars per barrel)

SOURCE OF DATA: OPEC and Bureau of Economic Analysis.

2 Explore the range of possible price and quantity outcomes and describe the dilemma faced by firms in oligopoly.

Practice Problem 16.2

TABLE 1

Price (dollars per unit)	Quantity demanded (units per day)
12	0
11	1
10	2
9	3
8	4
7	5
6	6
5	7
4	8
3	9
2	10
1	11
0	12

TABLE 2

Quantity (units per day)	Total revenue (dollars per day)	Marginal revenue (dollars per unit)
0	0	
1	11	11
2	20	9
3	27	7
4	32	5
5	35	3
6	36	1
7	35	−1
8	32	−3
9	27	−5
10	20	−7
11	11	−9
12	0	−11

1. Isolated Island has two natural gas wells, one owned by Tom and the other owned by Jerry. Each well has a valve that controls the rate of flow of gas, and the marginal cost of producing gas is zero. Table 1 gives the demand schedule for gas on this island. What will the price of gas be on Isolated Island if Tom and Jerry
   a. Form a cartel and maximize their joint profit?
   b. Are forced to sell at the perfectly competitive price?
   c. Compete as duopolists?

Exercises 16.2

1. A third gas well is discovered on Isolated Island, and Joey owns it. There is no change in the demand for gas, and Joey's cost of production is zero, like Tom's and Jerry's costs. Now what is the price of gas on Isolated Island if Tom, Jerry, and Joey
   a. Form a cartel and maximize their joint profit?
   b. Are forced to sell at the perfectly competitive price?

2. Kodak and Fuji are the only major producers of high-speed photo film. Each company has developed a fast-speed film and aggressively advertises it. The two firms are locked in a duopolists' dilemma.
   a. Describe the dilemma facing Kodak and Fuji.
   b. Suppose that Kodak and Fuji were to secretly form a cartel. What do you predict would
      i. Happen to the price of film?
      ii. Be the change in the two firms' advertising and research and development budgets?

Solution to Practice Problem 16.2

1a. If Tom and Jerry form a cartel and maximize their joint profit, they will charge the monopoly price. This price is the highest price the market will bear when the quantity produced makes marginal revenue equal to marginal cost. Marginal cost is zero, so we need to find the price at which marginal revenue is zero. Marginal revenue is zero when total revenue is a maximum, which occurs when output is 6 units a day (Table 2) and price is $6 a unit (see the demand schedule in Table 1).

1b. The perfectly competitive price equals marginal cost, which is zero. In this case, output is 12 units a day.

1c. If Tom and Jerry compete as duopolists, they will increase production above the monopoly level, but they will not drive the price down to zero.

16.3 GAME THEORY

Game theory is the main tool that economists use to analyze *strategic behavior*—behavior that recognizes mutual interdependence and takes account of the expected behavior of others. John von Neumann invented game theory in 1937, and today it is a major research field in economics.

Game theory helps us to understand oligopoly and many other forms of economic, political, social, and even biological rivalries. We will begin our study of game theory and its application to the behavior of firms by thinking about familiar games that we play for fun.

Game theory
The tool that economists use to analyze *strategic behavior*—behavior that recognizes mutual interdependence and takes account of the expected behavior of others.

■ What Is a Game?

What is a game? At first thought, the question seems silly. After all, there are many different games. There are ball games and parlor games, games of chance and games of skill. But what is it about all these different activities that make them games? What do all these games have in common? All games share three features:

- Rules
- Strategies
- Payoffs

Let's see how these common features of games apply to a game called "the prisoners' dilemma." The **prisoners' dilemma** is a game between two prisoners that shows why it is hard to cooperate even when it would be beneficial to both players to do so. This game captures the essential feature of the duopolists' dilemma that we've just been studying. The prisoners' dilemma also provides a good illustration of how game theory works and how it generates predictions.

Prisoners' dilemma
A game between two prisoners that shows why it is hard to cooperate even when it would be beneficial to both players to do so.

■ The Prisoners' Dilemma

Art and Bob have been caught red-handed, stealing a car. During the district attorney's interviews with the prisoners, he begins to suspect that he has stumbled on the two people who committed a multimillion-dollar bank robbery some months earlier. But this is just a suspicion. The district attorney has no evidence on which he can convict them of the greater crime unless he can get them to confess. He makes the prisoners play a game with the following rules.

Rules

Each prisoner (player) is placed in a separate room and cannot communicate with the other player. Each is told that he is suspected of having carried out the bank robbery and that

- If both of them confess to the larger crime, each will receive a reduced sentence of 3 years for both crimes.
- If he alone confesses and his accomplice does not, he will receive an even shorter sentence of 1 year, while his accomplice will receive a 10-year sentence.
- If neither of them confesses to the larger crime, each will receive a 2-year sentence for car theft.

Strategies
All the possible actions of each player in a game.

Payoff matrix
A table that shows the payoffs for each player for every possible combination of actions by the players.

TABLE 16.5 PRISONERS' DILEMMA PAYOFF MATRIX

Each square shows the payoffs for the two players, Art and Bob, for each possible pair of actions. In each square, the red triangle shows Art's payoff and the blue triangle shows Bob's. For example, if both confess, the payoffs are in the top left square.

Nash equilibrium
An equilibrium in which each player takes the best possible action given the action of the other player.

Strategies

In game theory, **strategies** are all the possible actions of each player. Art and Bob each have two possible strategies:

- Confess to the bank robbery.
- Deny having committed the bank robbery.

Payoffs

Because there are two players, each with two strategies, there are four possible outcomes:

- Both confess.
- Both deny.
- Art confesses and Bob denies.
- Bob confesses and Art denies.

Each prisoner can work out exactly what happens to him—his *payoff*—in each of these four situations. We can tabulate the four possible payoffs for each of the prisoners in what is called a payoff matrix for the game. A **payoff matrix** is a table that shows the payoffs for every possible action by each player given every possible action by the other player.

Table 16.5 shows a payoff matrix for Art and Bob. The squares show the payoffs for each prisoner—the red triangle in each square shows Art's, and the blue triangle shows Bob's. If both prisoners confess (top left), each gets a prison term of 3 years. If Bob confesses but Art denies (top right), Art gets a 10-year sentence and Bob gets a 1-year sentence. If Art confesses and Bob denies (bottom left), Art gets a 1-year sentence and Bob gets a 10-year sentence. Finally, if both of them deny (bottom right), neither can be convicted of the bank robbery charge but both are sentenced for the car theft—a 2-year sentence.

Equilibrium

The equilibrium of a game occurs when each player takes the best possible action given the action of the other player. This equilibrium concept is called **Nash equilibrium**. It is so named because John Nash of Princeton University, who received the Nobel Prize for Economic Science in 1994, proposed it. (The same John Nash was portrayed in the popular movie *A Beautiful Mind*.)

In the case of the prisoners' dilemma, equilibrium occurs when Art makes his best choice given Bob's choice and when Bob makes his best choice given Art's choice. Let's find the equilibrium.

First, look at the situation from Art's point of view. If Bob confesses, it pays Art to confess because in that case, he is sentenced to 3 years rather than 10 years. If Bob does not confess, it still pays Art to confess because in that case, he receives 1 year rather than 2 years. So no matter what Bob does, Art's best action is to confess.

Second, look at the situation from Bob's point of view. If Art confesses, it pays Bob to confess because in that case, he is sentenced to 3 years rather than 10 years. If Art does not confess, it still pays Bob to confess because in that case, he receives 1 year rather than 2 years. So no matter what Art does, Bob's best action is to confess.

Because each player's best action is to confess, each does confess, each gets a 3-year prison term, and the district attorney has solved the bank robbery. This is the equilibrium of the game.

Not the Best Outcome

The equilibrium of the prisoners' dilemma game is not the best outcome for the prisoners. Isn't there some way in which they can cooperate and get the smaller 2-year prison term? There is not, because the players cannot communicate with each other. Each player can put himself in the other player's place and can figure out what the other will do. The prisoners are in a dilemma. Each knows that he can serve only 2 years if he can trust the other to deny. But each also knows that it is not in the best interest of the other to deny. So each prisoner knows that he must confess, thereby delivering a bad outcome for both.

Let's now see how we can use the ideas we've just developed to understand the behavior of firms in oligopoly. We'll start by returning to the duopolists' dilemma.

■ The Duopolist's Dilemma

The dilemma of Airbus and Boeing is similar to that of Art and Bob. Each firm has two strategies. It can produce airplanes at the rate of

- 3 a week
- 4 a week

Because each firm has two strategies, there are four possible combinations of actions for the two firms:

- Both firms produce 3 a week (monopoly outcome).
- Both firms produce 4 a week.
- Airbus produces 3 a week and Boeing produces 4 a week.
- Boeing produces 3 a week and Airbus produces 4 a week.

The Payoff Matrix

Table 16.6 sets out the payoff matrix for this game. It is constructed in exactly the same way as the payoff matrix for the prisoners' dilemma in Table 16.5. The squares show the payoffs for Airbus and Boeing. In this case, the payoffs are economic profits. (In the case of the prisoners' dilemma, the payoffs were losses.)

The table shows that if both firms produce 4 a week (top left), each firm makes an economic profit of $32 million. If both firms produce 3 a week (bottom right), they make the monopoly profit, and each firm earns an economic profit of $36 million. The top right and bottom left squares show what happens if one firm produces 4 a week while the other produces 3 a week. The firm that increases production makes an economic profit of $40 million, and the one that keeps production at the monopoly quantity makes an economic profit of $30 million.

Equilibrium of the Duopolist's Dilemma

What do the firms do? To answer this question, we must find the equilibrium of the duopoly game.

TABLE 16.6 DUOPOLISTS' DILEMMA PAYOFF MATRIX

Each square shows the payoffs from a pair of actions. For example, if both firms produce 3 airplanes a week, the payoffs are recorded in the bottom right square. The red triangle shows Airbus's payoff, and the blue triangle shows Boeing's.

TABLE 16.7 THE NASH EQUILIBRIUM

The Nash equilibrium is for each firm to produce 4 airplanes a week.

Using the information in Table 16.7, look at things from Airbus's point of view. Airbus reasons as follows: Suppose that Boeing produces 4 a week. If I produce 3 a week, I will make an economic profit of $30 million. If I also produce 4 a week, I will make an economic profit of $32 million. So I'm better off producing 4 a week. Airbus continues to reason: Now suppose Boeing produces 3 a week. If I produce 4 a week, I will make an economic profit of $40 million, and if I produce 3 a week, I will make an economic profit of $36 million. An economic profit of $40 million is better than an economic profit of $36 million, so I'm better off if I produce 4 a week. So regardless of whether Boeing produces 4 a week or 3 a week, it pays Airbus to produce 4 a week.

Because the two firms face identical situations, Boeing comes to the same conclusion as Airbus. So both firms produce 4 a week. The equilibrium of the duopoly game is that both firms produce 4 airplanes a week.

Collusion Is Profitable but Difficult to Achieve

In the duopolists' dilemma that you've just studied, Airbus and Boeing end up in a situation that is similar to that of the prisoners in the prisoners' dilemma game. They don't achieve the best joint outcome. Because each produces 4 airplanes a week, each earns an economic profit of $32 million a week.

If firms were able to collude, they would agree to limit their production to 3 airplanes a week each and they would each earn the monopoly profit of $36 million a week.

The outcome of the duopolists' dilemma shows why it is difficult for firms to collude. Even if collusion were a legal activity, firms in duopoly would find it difficult to implement an agreement to restrict output. Like the players of the prisoners' dilemma game, the duopolists would reach a Nash equilibrium in which they produce more than the joint profit-maximizing quantity.

If two firms have difficulty maintaining a collusive agreement, oligopolies with more than two firms have an even harder time. The operation of OPEC (see *Eye on the Global Economy* on p. 409) illustrates this difficulty. To raise the price of oil, OPEC must limit global oil production. The members of this cartel meet from time to time and set a production limit for each member nation. Almost always, within a few months of a decision to restrict production, some (usually smaller) members of the cartel break their quotas, production increases, and the price sags below the cartel's desired target. The OPEC cartel plays an oligopoly dilemma game similar to the prisoners' dilemma. Only in 1973, 1979–1980, and 2005 did OPEC manage to keep its members' production under control and raise the price of oil.

■ Advertising and Research Games in Oligopoly

Every month, Coke and Pepsi, Kodak and Fuji, Xerox and Canon, Nike and Reebok, Procter & Gamble and Kimberly-Clark, and hundreds of other pairs of big firms locked in fierce competition spend millions of dollars on advertising campaigns and on research and development (R&D). They make decisions about whether to increase or cut the advertising budget or whether to undertake a large R&D effort aimed at making the product more reliable (usually, the more reliable a product, the more expensive it is to produce but the more people are willing to pay for it) or at lowering production costs. These choices can be analyzed as games. Let's look at some examples of these types of games.

Advertising Game

A key to success in the soft drink industry is to run huge advertising campaigns. These campaigns affect market share but are costly to run. Table 16.8 shows some hypothetical numbers for the advertising game that Pepsi and Coke play. Each firm has two strategies: Advertise or don't advertise. If neither firm advertises, they each make $50 million (bottom right of the payoff matrix). If each firm advertises, each firm's profit is lower by the amount spent on advertising (top left square of the payoff matrix). If Pepsi advertises but Coke does not, Pepsi gains and Coke loses (top right square of the payoff matrix). Finally, if Coke advertises and Pepsi does not, Coke gains and Pepsi loses (bottom left square).

Pepsi reasons as follows: Regardless of whether Coke advertises, we're better off advertising. Coke reasons similarly: Regardless of whether Pepsi advertises, we're better off advertising. Because advertising is the best strategy for both players, it is the Nash equilibrium. The outcome of this game is that both firms advertise and make less profit than they would if they could collude to achieve the cooperative outcome of no advertising.

Research and Development Game

A key to success in the disposable diaper industry is to design a product that people value highly relative to the cost of producing it. The firm that develops the most highly valued product and also develops the least-cost technology for producing it gains a competitive edge, undercutting the rest of the market, increasing its market share, and increasing its profit. But the R&D that must be undertaken to achieve product improvements and cost reductions is costly. So the cost of R&D must be deducted from the profit resulting from the increased market share that lower costs achieve. If no firm does R&D, every firm can be better off, but if one firm initiates the R&D activity, all must follow.

Table 16.9 illustrates the dilemma (with hypothetical numbers) for the R&D game that Kimberly-Clark and Procter & Gamble play. Each firm has two strategies: Do R&D or do no R&D. If neither firm does R&D, Kimberly-Clark makes $30 million and Procter & Gamble makes $70 million (bottom right of the payoff matrix). If each firm does R&D, each firm's profit is lower by the amount spent on R&D (top left square of the payoff matrix). If Kimberly-Clark does R&D but Procter & Gamble does not, Kimberly-Clark gains and Procter & Gamble loses (top right square of the payoff matrix). Finally, if Procter & Gamble conducts R&D and Kimberly-Clark does not, Procter & Gamble gains and Kimberly-Clark loses (bottom left square).

Kimberly-Clark reasons as follows: Regardless of whether Procter & Gamble undertakes R&D, we're better off doing R&D. Procter & Gamble reasons similarly: Regardless of whether Kimberly-Clark does R&D, we're better off doing R&D.

Because R&D is the best strategy for both players, it is the Nash equilibrium. The outcome of this game is that both firms conduct R&D. They make less profit than they would if they could collude to achieve the cooperative outcome of no R&D.

The real-world situation has more players than Kimberly-Clark and Procter & Gamble. A large number of other firms strive to capture market share from Procter & Gamble and Kimberly-Clark. So the R&D effort by these two firms not only serves the purpose of maintaining shares in their own battle but also helps to keep barriers to entry high enough to preserve their joint market share.

TABLE 16.8 THE ADVERTISING GAME PAYOFF MATRIX

The red triangle shows Coke's payoff, and the blue triangle shows Pepsi's. If both firms advertise they earn less than if neither firm advertises. But each firm is better off advertising if the other doesn't advertise. The Nash equilibrium for this prisoners' dilemma advertising game is for both firms to advertise.

TABLE 16.9 THE R&D GAME PAYOFF MATRIX

The red triangle shows Procter & Gamble's payoff, and the blue triangle shows Kimberly-Clark's. If both firms do R&D, they earn less than if neither firm undertakes R&D. But each firm is better off doing R&D if the other does no R&D. The Nash equilibrium for this prisoners' dilemma R&D game is for both firms to do R&D.

■ Repeated Games

The games that we've studied are played just once. In contrast, most real-world games get played repeatedly. This fact suggests that real-world duopolists might find some way of learning to cooperate so that they can enjoy a monopoly profit. If a game is played repeatedly, one player has the opportunity to penalize the other player for previous "bad" behavior. If Airbus produces 4 airplanes this week, perhaps Boeing will produce 4 next week. Before Airbus produces 4 this week, won't it take account of the possibility of Boeing producing 4 next week? What is the equilibrium of this more complicated dilemma game when it is repeated indefinitely?

The monopoly equilibrium might occur if each firm knows that the other will punish overproduction with overproduction, "tit for tat." Let's see why.

Table 16.10 keeps track of the numbers. Suppose that Boeing contemplates producing 4 airplanes in week 1. This move will bring it an economic profit of $40 million and will cut the economic profit of Airbus to $30 million. In week 2, Airbus will punish Boeing and produce 4 airplanes. But Boeing must go back to 3 airplanes to induce Airbus to cooperate again in week 3. So in week 2, Airbus makes an economic profit of $40 million, and Boeing makes an economic profit of $30 million. Adding up the profits over these two weeks of play, Boeing would have made $72 million by cooperating (2 × $36 million) compared with $70 million from producing 4 airplanes in week 1 and generating Airbus's tit-for-tat response.

What is true for Boeing is also true for Airbus. Because each firm makes a larger profit by sticking to the monopoly output, both firms do so and the monopoly price, quantity, and profit prevail.

In reality, whether a duopoly (or more generally an oligopoly) works like a one-play game or a repeated game depends primarily on the number of players and the ease of detecting and punishing overproduction. The larger the number of players, the harder it is to maintain the monopoly outcome.

TABLE 16.10 PAYOFFS WITH PUNISHMENT

Period of play	Cooperate		Overproduce	
	Boeing profit	Airbus profit	Boeing profit	Airbus profit
	(millions of dollars)			
1	36	36	40	30
2	36	36	30	40

■ Is Oligopoly Efficient?

The quantity produced of any good or service is the efficient quantity if the price (which measures marginal benefit) equals marginal cost. Does oligopoly produce efficient quantities of goods and services?

You've seen that if firms in oligopoly play a repeated prisoners' dilemma game, they can end up restricting output to the monopoly level and earning the same economic profit as a monopoly would earn. You've also seen that even when the firms don't cooperate, they don't necessarily drive the price down to marginal cost. So generally, oligopoly is not efficient. It suffers from the same source of inefficiency as monopoly.

Also, firms in oligopoly might end up operating at a higher average total cost than the lowest attainable cost because their advertising and research budgets are higher than the socially efficient level.

Because oligopoly creates inefficiency, antitrust laws and regulations are established that seek to reduce market power and move the outcome closer to that of competition and efficiency. We study these laws and regulations in Chapter 17.

Duopoly in CPUs

The CPU in your computer or your game box—the brainpower of the machine—is made either by Intel Corporation or by Advanced Micro Devices, Inc. (AMD). Intel dominates this market, as the pie charts show.

The graph in part (c) shows the prices of some of the most popular CPU chips in May 2005. Notice that at comparable clock speeds, AMD chips are higher priced than Intel chips but Intel makes the fastest chips.

Competition between Intel and AMD is like the duopolists' dilemma that you've studied in this chapter. The game is played on both price and product design and quality and across a range of differentiated products.

SOURCE OF DATA: sharkyextreme.com.

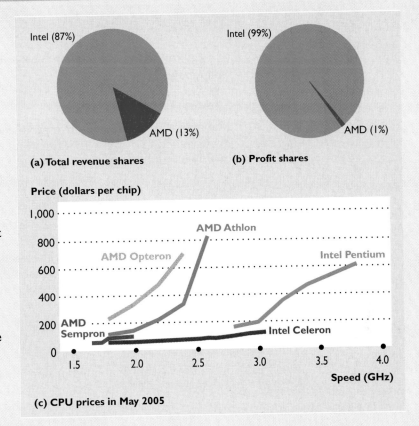

(a) Total revenue shares   (b) Profit shares

(c) CPU prices in May 2005

REALITY CHECK

A Game in YOUR Life

The payoff matrix here describes a game that might be familiar to you. But it isn't a prisoners' dilemma. It's a lovers' dilemma. Jane and Jim like to do things together. But Jane likes the movies more than the ball game, and Jim likes the ball game more than the movies. The payoff matrix describes how much they like the various outcomes (measured in units of utility). What do they do?

You can figure out that Jim never goes to the movies alone and Jane never goes to the ball game alone. You can also figure out that Jim doesn't go to the ball game alone and Jane doesn't go to the movies alone. So they go out together. But do they do the movies or the ball game? This game has no unique equilibrium. The payoffs tell you that they might go to either the game or the movies. In a repeated game, they'll probably alternate between the two!

Payoffs are in units of utility

3 Use game theory to explain how price and quantity are determined in oligopoly.

Practice Problem 16.3

1. Bud and Wise are the only two producers of aniseed beer, a New Age product designed to displace root beer. Bud and Wise are trying to figure out how much of this new beer to produce. They know that if they both limit production to 10,000 gallons a day, they will make the maximum attainable joint profit of $200,000 a day—$100,000 a day each. They also know that if either of them produces 20,000 gallons a day while the other produces 10,000 a day, the one that produces 20,000 gallons will make an economic profit of $150,000 and the one that sticks with 10,000 gallons will incur an economic loss of $50,000. They also each know that if they both increase production to 20,000 gallons a day, they will both earn zero economic profit.
   a. Construct a payoff matrix for the game that Bud and Wise must play.
   b. Find the Nash equilibrium.
   c. What is the equilibrium if this game is played repeatedly?

Exercise 16.3

1. Bud and Wise are racing to develop a new brand of coconut milk that they both believe will be the next big soft drink. Bud and Wise know that if they both develop the new product, they will earn zero economic profit; if only one of them develops the new product, that firm will make an economic profit of $2 million a week and the other will incur an economic loss of $1 million a week; and if neither of them develops the new product, both will earn zero economic profit.
   a. Construct a payoff matrix for this game.
   b. Find the Nash equilibrium.
   c. Is there any chance of cooperation in this research and development game?

Solution to Practice Problem 16.3

1a. Table 1 shows the payoff matrix for the game that Bud and Wise must play.

1b. The Nash equilibrium is for both to produce 20,000 gallons. To see why, notice that regardless of the quantity that Bud produces, Wise makes more profit by producing 20,000 gallons. The same is true for Bud. So Bud and Wise each produce 20,000 gallons a day.

1c. If this game is played repeatedly, both Bud and Wise produce 10,000 gallons a day and earn maximum economic profit. They can achieve this outcome by playing a tit-for-tat strategy.

TABLE 1

Payoffs are in thousands of dollars

CHAPTER CHECKPOINT

Key Points

1 Describe and identify oligopoly and explain how it arises.

- Oligopoly is a market type in which a small number of interdependent firms compete behind a barrier to entry.
- The barriers to entry that create oligopoly are both natural (economies of scale and demand) and legal.

2 Explore the range of possible price and quantity outcomes and describe the dilemma faced by firms in oligopoly.

- Firms in oligopoly would make the same economic profit as a monopoly if they could act together to restrict output to the monopoly level.
- Each firm can make a larger profit by increasing production, but this action damages the economic profit of other firms.

3 Use game theory to explain how price and quantity are determined in oligopoly.

- Game theory is a method of analyzing strategic behavior.
- In a prisoners' dilemma, two prisoners acting in their own interests harm their joint interest.
- An oligopoly (duopoly) game is like the prisoners' dilemma.
- The firms might cooperate to produce the monopoly output or overproduce.
- In a one-play game, both firms overproduce and the price and economic profit are less than they would be in monopoly.
- Advertising and research and development create a prisoners' dilemma for firms in oligopoly.
- In a repeated game, a punishment strategy can produce a monopoly output, price, and economic profit.
- Oligopoly is usually inefficient because the price (marginal benefit) exceeds marginal cost and cost might not be the lowest attainable.

Key Terms

Cartel, 402
Duopoly, 402
Game theory, 411
Nash equilibrium, 412

Payoff matrix, 412
Prisoners' dilemma, 411
Strategies, 412

Exercises

1. When the first automobiles were built in 1901, they were manufactured by skilled workers using hand tools. Later, in 1913, Henry Ford introduced the moving assembly line, which lowered costs and speeded production. Over the years, the production line has become ever more mechanized, and today robots have replaced people in many operations.
   a. Sketch the average total cost curve and the demand curve for automobiles in 1901.
   b. Sketch the average total cost curve and the demand curve for automobiles in 1913.
   c. Sketch the average total cost curve and the demand curve for automobiles in 2006.
   d. Describe the changing barriers to entry in the automobile industry and explain how the combination of demand and economies of scale has changed the structure of the industry over the past 100 years.

FIGURE 1

Price and cost (dollars per ride)

2. Isolated Island has two taxi companies, one owned by Ann and the other owned by Zack. Figure 1 shows the demand curve for taxi rides, D, and the average total cost curve of one of the firms, ATC.
   a. If Ann and Zack produce the same quantity of rides as would be produced in perfect competition, what are the quantity of rides, the price of a ride, and the economic profit of Ann and Zack?
   b. If Ann and Zack form a cartel and produce the same quantity of rides as would be produced in monopoly, what are the quantity of rides, the price of a ride, and the economic profit of Ann and Zack?
   c. Would Ann and Zack have an incentive to break the cartel agreement and cut their price to increase the number of rides? Explain why or why not.

3. Use the information about the market for taxi rides on Isolated Island provided in exercise 2. Suppose that Ann and Zack have two strategies: collude, fix the monopoly price, and limit the number of rides or break the collusion, cut the price, and produce more rides.
   a. Create a payoff matrix for the game that Ann and Zack play.
   b. Find the Nash equilibrium for this game if it is played just once.
   c. Do the people of Isolated Island get the efficient quantity of taxi rides from Ann and Zack in the situation in part b?
   d. Find the Nash equilibrium for this game if it is played repeatedly and Ann and Zack use a tit-for-tat punishment strategy.
   e. Do the people of Isolated Island get the efficient quantity of taxi rides from Ann and Zack in the situation in part d?

4. Jenny loves the movies (payoff of +100) and hates the ball game (payoff of −100). Joe loves the ball game (payoff of +100) and hates the movies (payoff of −100). But both Jenny and Joe prefer to go out together (bonus payoff of +100 each in addition to the payoff from the activity they choose). If they go out separately, they get no bonus payoff.
   a. Make a payoff matrix of the game that Jenny and Joe play.
   b. Is this game similar to the prisoners' dilemma or different in some way?
   c. What is the Nash equilibrium? What do Jenny and Joe do? Does it make a difference if the game is repeated many times?
   d. Do Jenny and Joe get the best outcome for each of them?

5. The United States claims that Canada subsidizes the production of softwood lumber and that imports of Canadian lumber damage the interests of U.S. producers. The United States has imposed a high tariff on Canadian imports to counter the subsidy. Canada is thinking of retaliating by refusing to export water to California. Table 1 shows a payoff matrix for the game that the United States and Canada are playing.
   a. What is the United States' best strategy?
   b. What is Canada's best strategy?
   c. What is the outcome of this game? Explain.
   d. Is this game like a prisoners' dilemma or different in some crucial way? Explain.
   e. Which country would benefit more from a free trade agreement?

6. Agile Airlines is earning $10 million a year economic profit on a route on which it has a monopoly. Wanabe Airlines is considering entering the market and operating on this route. Agile warns Wanabe to stay out and threatens to cut the price to the point at which Wanabe will make no profit if it enters. Wanabe does some research and determines that the payoff matrix for the game in which it is engaged with Agile is that shown in Table 2.
   a. Does Wanabe believe Agile's assertion?
   b. Does Wanabe enter or not? Explain.

7. Coke and Pepsi know that they are spending millions of dollars on advertising just to counter each other's ads. The marketing managers of the two firms spend a weekend on the golf course plotting a collaboration that will cut the costs of both firms by $100 million a year. When they get back to the office on Monday morning, they begin to sell their scheme to their chief financial officers (CFOs), who have studied some economics. The CFOs tell the marketing managers that they are dreaming and that their plan has no chance of working.
   a. Why are the CFOs so sure?
   b. Sketch a payoff matrix that describes the advertising game played by Coke and Pepsi that supports the CFOs.
   c. Find and describe the Nash equilibrium for the game in part **b**.
   d. Sketch a payoff matrix that describes an advertising game played by Coke and Pepsi that does not support the CFOs and that makes the sales managers' plan possible.
   e. Find and describe the Nash equilibrium for the game in part **d**.

Critical Thinking

8. Adam Smith wrote in *The Wealth of Nations*, published in 1776, "People of the same trade seldom meet together, even for merriment and diversion, but the conversation ends in a conspiracy against the public, or in some contrivance to raise prices." What do you think this quotation implies about the predominant market structure in Adam Smith's world of the late 1700s? Why?

9. Dental care is big business and three firms, Procter & Gamble (which now owns Gillette), Colgate, and GlaxoKlineSmith, are the dominant players. Check the dental care products in the supermarket. Describe how these firms differentiate their dental products. Do you think these firms are locked in an R&D game or an advertising game in dental products? Why?

TABLE 1

TABLE 2

10. Do you think the market for word-processing software such as Microsoft Word, Lotus WordPro, and WordPerfect is an example of oligopoly or monopolistic competition?
    a. Would consumers benefit from greater cooperation between software developers so that instead of having to choose among Microsoft Word, Lotus WordPro, and WordPerfect, they could buy just one word processor?
    b. What benefits do consumers enjoy with competition among software developers that would be lost from cooperation?
    c. Why (aside from the fact that it is illegal) is it impossible for software producers to collude and earn a larger economic profit?

11. Suppose that Netscape and Microsoft develop their own versions of an amazing new Web browser that allows advertisers to target consumers with great precision. Advertisers would pay Netscape or Microsoft a fee for providing this service. The new browser is easier and more fun to use than existing browsers. Each firm is trying to decide whether to sell the browser or to give it away.
    a. What are the possible benefits from each action?
    b. Sketch the payoff matrix for the game that Netscape and Microsoft must play.
    c. On the basis of the payoff matrix you've constructed, what do Netscape and Microsoft do?

 ## Web Exercises

Use the links on MyEconLab to work the following exercises.

12. Visit the BBC and read the article on OPEC. Also visit OPEC and review the "About OPEC" pages.
    a. Is OPEC a cartel?
    b. What do you think OPEC's main objective is?
    c. What actions can OPEC take to achieve its main objective?
    d. What are the obstacles that OPEC must overcome?
    e. Use the ideas of the prisoners' dilemma to analyze the decisions of OPEC and its member countries.
    f. Use the ideas of the prisoners' dilemma to analyze the decisions of non-OPEC oil producers.
    g. Do you think the global market in crude oil is efficient or inefficient? Provide reasons.

13. Visit EV World and read the article on ethanol price fixing by Archer Daniels Midland.
    a. Would you describe the market for ethanol as an oligopoly?
    b. What does the news article claim about the price of ethanol?
    c. Use the ideas of the prisoners' dilemma to analyze the decisions of Archer Daniels Midland and other producers of ethanol.
    d. Do you think the market for ethanol is efficient or inefficient? Provide reasons.

Regulation and Antitrust Law

CHAPTER CHECKLIST

**When you have completed your study of this chapter,
you will be able to**

1 Explain the effects of regulation of natural monopoly and oligopoly.

2 Describe U.S. antitrust law and explain three antitrust policy debates.

When you consume water or use the local telephone service, you are buying from a regulated monopoly. Why are the industries that produce these items regulated? How are they regulated? Do the regulations work in the public interest— the interest of all consumers and producers—or do they serve special interests—the interests of particular groups of consumers or producers?

The U.S. Department of Justice has accused Microsoft of violating the antitrust laws. What are the antitrust laws? How have they evolved over the years? How are they used today?

This chapter studies government regulation of monopolies and U.S. antitrust law that restricts the behavior of monopolies and oligopolies.

The chapter draws several threads together. It uses what you've learned about how markets work and your knowledge of consumer surplus and producer surplus. It shows how consumers and producers can redistribute these surpluses in the political marketplace, and it identifies who stands to win and who stands to lose from government regulation.

17.1 REGULATION

You learned in Chapter 6 and saw again in Chapter 13 that a competitive market produces the quantity at which marginal benefit equals marginal cost and is efficient. Because it is efficient, a competitive market doesn't need any government intervention. It is self-regulating. You also saw in Chapter 6 that underproduction creates a deadweight loss. In your detailed look at monopoly and oligopoly in Chapters 14 and 16, you saw that profit-maximizing firms in these types of markets chose to produce less than the efficient quantity. For this reason, governments regulate monopoly and oligopoly.

Regulation consists of rules administered by a government agency to influence economic activity by determining prices, product standards and types, and the conditions under which new firms may enter an industry. To implement its regulations, the government establishes agencies to oversee the regulations and ensure their enforcement.

Regulation
Rules administered by a government agency to influence economic activity by determining prices, product standards and types, and the conditions under which new firms may enter an industry.

The past 120 years have seen big changes in the way the U.S. economy is regulated. We're going to begin by examining these changes. Next, we'll turn to the regulatory process and examine how regulators control prices and other aspects of market behavior. Finally, we'll tackle the more difficult and controversial questions: Why do we regulate some things but not others? Who benefits from the regulations that we have: consumers or producers?

■ The Changing Scope of Regulation

The first national regulatory agency to be set up in the United States was the Interstate Commerce Commission (ICC), established in 1887. Its task was to control prices, routes, and the quality of service of interstate railroads. Its scope later expanded to cover trucking lines, bus lines, water carriers, and oil pipelines. Following the establishment of the ICC, the federal regulatory environment remained static until the years of the Great Depression. Then, during the 1930s, more agencies were established: the Federal Power Commission, the Federal Communications Commission, the Securities and Exchange Commission, the Federal Maritime Commission, the Federal Deposit Insurance Corporation, and, in 1938, the Civil Aeronautical Agency, which was replaced in 1940 by the Civil Aeronautics Board. There was a further lull until the establishment during the 1970s of the Copyright Royalty Tribunal and the Federal Energy Regulatory Commission. In addition to these, there are many state and local regulatory commissions.

Regulation peaked during the 1970s when almost a quarter of the nation's output was produced by regulated industries. Regulation applied to banking and financial services; telecommunications; gas and electric utilities; railroads, trucking, airlines, and buses; many agricultural products; and even haircutting and braiding. Since the late 1970s, there has been a tendency to deregulate the U.S. economy.

Deregulation
The process of removing restrictions on prices, product standards and types, and entry conditions.

Deregulation is the process of removing restrictions on prices, product standards and types, and entry conditions. During the past 25 years, deregulation has occurred in domestic air transportation, telephone service, interstate trucking, and banking and financial services. Cable TV was deregulated in 1984, re-regulated in 1992, and deregulated again in 1996.

What exactly do regulatory agencies do? How do they regulate?

■ The Regulatory Process

Though regulatory agencies vary in size and scope and in the detailed aspects of economic life that they control, all agencies have features in common.

First, the Administration, Congress, and state and local governments appoint the people who run the regulatory agencies. In addition, all agencies have a permanent bureaucracy made up of experts in the industry being regulated and often recruited from regulated firms. Agencies have budgets, voted by Congress or state or local legislatures, to cover the costs of their operations.

Second, each agency adopts a set of practices or operating rules for controlling prices and other aspects of economic performance. These rules and practices are based on well-defined physical and financial accounting procedures, but they are extremely complicated and, in practice, hard to administer.

In a regulated industry, individual firms are usually free to determine their production technology. But they are not free to determine the prices to charge, the quantities to produce, or the markets to serve. The regulatory agency certifies a company to serve a particular market and produce a particular line of goods and services, and it determines the prices that may be charged. In some cases, the agency also determines the scale of output permitted.

■ Economic Theory of Regulation

Two broad economic theories of regulation are

- Public interest theory
- Capture theory

Public Interest Theory

The **public interest theory** is that regulation seeks an efficient use of resources. Public interest theory assumes that the political process relentlessly seeks out deadweight loss and introduces regulations that eliminate it. For example, where monopoly exists, the political process will introduce price regulations to ensure that output increases and price falls to its competitive level.

Public interest theory
The theory that regulation seeks an efficient use of resources.

Capture Theory

The **capture theory** is that a regulated firm captures the regulator and makes a monopoly profit. Capture theory assumes that the cost of regulation is high and only those regulations that increase the surplus of small, easily identified groups and that have low organization costs are supplied by the political process. Because of rational ignorance (see Chapter 10, p. 251), even though these regulations impose costs on others, if the costs are spread thinly, they do not decrease votes.

Capture theory
The theory that a regulated firm captures the regulator and makes a monopoly profit.

The predictions of the capture theory are less clear-cut than those of the public interest theory. The capture theory predicts that regulations benefit cohesive interest groups, bring large and visible benefits to each member of the interest group, and impose a small cost on everyone else. The cost per person is so small that no one finds it worthwhile to incur the cost of organizing an interest group to avoid it.

Which theory of regulation best explains real-world regulations? Which regulations are in the public interest and which are in the interest of producers? To answer these questions, it is convenient to distinguish between the regulation of a natural monopoly and the regulation of a cartel. Let's begin with the regulation of a natural monopoly.

■ Natural Monopoly

We defined *natural monopoly* in Chapter 14 (pp. 350–351) as an industry in which one firm can supply the entire market at a lower price than two or more firms can. Examples of natural monopoly include local distribution of water, electricity and gas, and urban rail services. For these activities, most of the costs are fixed, so the larger the output, the lower is its average total cost. It is much more expensive to have two or more sets of pipes, wires, and train lines serving every neighborhood than it is to have a single set. What industry or market is a natural monopoly changes over time as technology changes. With the introduction of fiber-optic cables, both telephone companies and cable television companies can compete in urban areas that have a sufficiently dense population. So what were once natural monopolies are becoming more competitive industries. Direct satellite TV is a substitute, but not a close substitute, for cable TV, and in many parts of the country, cable TV remains a natural monopoly.

Figure 17.1 shows the market for cable TV in the 20 states served by Cox Communications based in Atlanta. The demand curve for cable TV is *D*. Cox's marginal cost curve is *MC*. That marginal cost curve is (assumed to be) horizontal at $10 per household per month—that is, the cost of providing each additional household with a month of cable programming is $10. Cox Communications has invested heavily in satellite receiving dishes, cables, and control equipment and so has large fixed costs. These fixed costs are part of the company's average total cost curve, shown as *ATC*. The average total cost curve slopes downward because

---

■ FIGURE 17.1

Natural Monopoly: Marginal Cost Pricing

A cable TV operator faces the demand curve *D*. Its marginal cost *MC* is a constant $10 per household per month. Its fixed cost is large, and the average total cost curve, which includes average fixed cost, is *ATC*.

❶ Price is set equal to marginal cost at $10 a month.

At this price, ❷ the efficient quantity (8 million households) is served.

❸ Consumer surplus is maximized as shown by the green triangle.

❹ The firm incurs a loss on each household, shown by the red arrow.

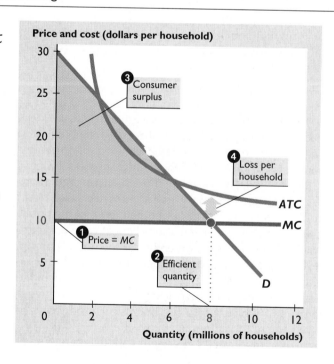

as the number of households served increases, the fixed cost is spread over a larger number of households. (If you need to refresh your memory on the average total cost curve, take a quick look back at Chapter 12, pp. 309–311.)

■ Public Interest or Private Interest Regulation?

According to public interest theory, regulation achieves an efficient use of resources, which occurs if marginal cost equals marginal benefit, which also equals price. A **marginal cost pricing rule**, which sets price equal to marginal cost, achieves an efficient output in a regulated industry.

Marginal cost pricing rule
A rule that sets price equal to marginal cost to achieve an efficient output in a regulated industry.

Marginal Cost Pricing

Figure 17.1 illustrates the marginal cost pricing rule. The efficient outcome occurs if the price is regulated at $10 per household per month and if 8 million households are served.

A natural monopoly that follows the marginal cost pricing rule incurs an economic loss. Because the average total cost curve of a natural monopoly is downward sloping, marginal cost is less than average total cost. Because price equals marginal cost, price is less than average total cost. Average total cost minus price is the loss per unit produced. It's pretty obvious that a cable TV company that is required to use a marginal cost pricing rule will not stay in business for long. How can a company cover its costs and, at the same time, obey a marginal cost pricing rule?

One possibility is price discrimination (see Chapter 14, pp. 364–368). Another possibility is to use a two-part price (called a *two-part tariff*). For example, local telephone companies charge consumers a monthly fee for being connected to the telephone system and then charge a price equal to marginal cost (zero) for each local call. A cable TV operator charges a one-time connection fee that covers its fixed cost and then charges a monthly fee equal to marginal cost.

But a natural monopoly cannot always cover its costs in these ways. If the price that a natural monopoly can charge its customers does not cover its total cost and if the government wants it to follow a marginal cost pricing rule, the government must subsidize the firm and raise the revenue for the subsidy by taxing some other activity. But as we saw in Chapter 8, taxes themselves generate deadweight loss. So the deadweight loss that results from additional taxes must be subtracted from the efficiency gained by forcing the natural monopoly to adopt a marginal cost pricing rule. As a result, it might be more efficient to permit the natural monopoly to charge a price that is higher than marginal cost. Doing so avoids taxing other parts of the economy to subsidize the natural monopoly and avoids creating deadweight loss in those parts of the economy.

Average Cost Pricing

For a natural monopoly to cover its total cost, its price must equal average total cost. And the pricing rule that delivers this outcome is called the **average cost pricing rule**, a rule that sets price equal to average total cost. Because average total cost exceeds marginal cost for a natural monopoly, when price equals average total cost, the quantity is less than the efficient quantity and a deadweight loss arises. Figure 17.2 illustrates the outcome for Cox Communications.

Average cost pricing rule
A rule that sets price equal to average total cost to enable a regulated firm to cover its costs.

■ **FIGURE 17.2**

Natural Monopoly: Average Cost Pricing

❶ Price is set equal to average total cost at $15 a month.

At this price, ❷ the quantity served (6 million households) is less than the efficient quantity (8 million households).

❸ Consumer surplus shrinks to the smaller green triangle.

❹ A producer surplus enables the firm to pay its fixed cost and break even.

❺ A deadweight loss, shown by the gray triangle, arises.

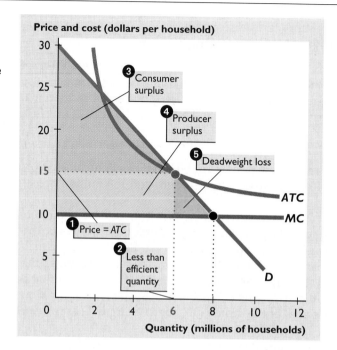

In Figure 17.2, to cover its costs, Cox charges $15 a month and serves 6 million households. A deadweight loss arises, which is shown by the gray triangle in the figure. This outcome is in the public interest—is efficient—if this deadweight loss is smaller than the deadweight loss from collecting the taxes to finance a subsidy under marginal cost pricing.

Implementing the pricing rules that we've just examined is difficult because the regulator does not directly observe the firm's costs and doesn't know how hard the firm is trying to minimize cost. So regulators use one of two practical rules:

- Rate of return regulation
- Price cap regulation

Let's see whether these practical rules deliver an outcome that is in the public interest or the private interest.

Rate of Return Regulation

Rate of return regulation
A regulation that sets the price at a level that enables a regulated firm to earn a specified target percent return on its capital.

Under **rate of return regulation**, a regulated firm must justify its price by showing that the price enables it to earn a specified target percent return on its capital. The target rate of return is determined with reference to what is normal in competitive industries. This rate of return is part of the opportunity cost of the natural monopoly and part of the firm's average total cost.

If the regulator were able to observe the firm's total cost and also know that the firm had minimized total cost, it would accept only a price proposal from the firm that was equivalent to average cost pricing.

The outcome would be like that in Figure 17.2, in which the regulated price is $15 a month and 6 million households are served. In this case, rate of return regulation would result in a price that favors the consumer and prevents the producer from making monopoly profit. The special interest group will have failed to capture the regulator, and the outcome will be closer to that predicted by the public interest theory of regulation.

But the managers of a regulated firm might not minimize cost. And if the firm is regulated to achieve a target rate of return, the managers have an incentive to inflate costs and raise price. One way to inflate the firm's costs is to spend on inputs that are not strictly required for the production of the good. On-the-job luxury in the form of sumptuous office suites, limousines, free baseball tickets (disguised as public relations expenses), company jets, lavish international travel, and entertainment are all ways in which managers can inflate costs.

Managers also have an incentive to use more capital than the efficient amount because the more capital they use, the larger is the total return they are permitted to earn. And they have an incentive to make larger-than-required charges for depreciation and losses from bad debts.

If the cable TV operator in our example persuades the regulator that its true costs are higher than the *ATC* curve in Figure 17.2, then rate of return regulation will raise the price and decrease the quantity and might end up enabling the firm to operate at the same price and quantity as those that would occur if the monopoly were unregulated.

EYE ON THE U.S. ECONOMY

Airline Deregulation

U.S. airline deregulation in 1979 lowered fares by an estimated 18 percent.

And fares have continued to fall in recent years with the arrival of new low-cost airlines such as AirTran, ATA, America West, Frontier, JetBlue, Southwest, and Spirit, which has put the traditional carriers under competitive pressure.

Fares were falling during 2001 well before 9/11 decreased the demand for air travel. And fares continued to fall through 2004.

The figure shows the average (inflation-adjusted) fare of a flight that cost $100 in the first quarter of 1985.

But air fares could be even lower. The reason is that the airline industry operates with barriers to entry that arise from the allocation of slots at major airports and legal restrictions on foreign airlines. Air fares would fall if these barriers to entry were lowered.

SOURCE OF DATA: Bureau of Transportation Statistic and the Bureau of Economic Analysis.

Price Cap Regulation

Price cap regulation

A rule that specifies the highest price that a firm is permitted to set—a price ceiling.

For the reason that we've just examined, rate of return regulation is increasingly being replaced by price cap regulation. A **price cap regulation** is a price ceiling—a rule that specifies the highest price the firm is permitted to set. This type of regulation gives a firm an incentive to operate efficiently and keep costs under control. Price cap regulation has become common for the electricity and telecommunications industries and is replacing rate of return regulation.

To see how a price cap works, let's suppose that the cable TV operator is subject to this type of regulation. Figure 17.3 shows that without regulation, the firm maximizes profit by serving 4 million households and charging a price of $20 a month. If a price cap is set at $15 a month, the firm is permitted to sell any quantity it chooses at that price or at a lower price. At 4 million households, the firm now incurs an economic loss. It can decrease the loss by *increasing* output to 6 million households. To increase output above 6 million households, the firm would have to lower the price and again it would incur a loss. So the profit-maximizing quantity is 6 million households—the same as with average cost pricing.

Notice that a price cap lowers the price and increases output. This outcome is in sharp contrast to the effect of a price ceiling in a competitive market that you studied in Chapter 7 (pp. 172–177). The reason is that in a monopoly, the unregulated equilibrium output is less than the competitive equilibrium output and the price cap regulation replicates the conditions of a competitive market.

Earnings sharing regulation

A regulation that requires firms to make refunds to customers when profits rise above a target level.

In Figure 17.3, the price cap delivers average cost pricing. In practice, the regulator might set the cap too high. For this reason, price cap regulation is often combined with **earnings sharing regulation**—a regulation that requires firms to make refunds to customers when profits rise above a target level.

■ **FIGURE 17.3**

Natural Monopoly: Price Cap Regulation

❶ With no regulation, a cable TV operator serves 4 million households at a price of $20 a month.

❷ A price cap regulation sets the maximum price at $15 a month.

❸ Only when 6 million households are served can the firm break even and earn a normal rate of return. (When fewer than 6 million households are served or more than 6 million households are served, the firm incurs an economic loss.) The firm has an incentive to keep costs as low as possible and to produce the quantity demanded at the price cap.

❹ The price cap regulation lowers the price and increases the quantity.

■ Oligopoly Regulation

A *cartel* is a collusive agreement among a number of firms that is designed to restrict output and achieve a higher profit for its members. Cartels are illegal in the United States and in most other countries. But international cartels can sometimes operate legally, such as the international cartel of oil producers known as OPEC (Organization of the Petroleum Exporting Countries).

Illegal cartels can arise in oligopoly. You saw in Chapter 16 that if firms in oligopoly can collude and behave like a monopoly, they will set the same price and sell the same total quantity as a monopoly firm would. But we also discovered that in such a situation, each firm is tempted to cheat, increasing its own output and profit at the expense of the other firms. Such cheating unravels the monopoly equilibrium and leads to a higher output rate, lower price, and smaller economic profit. Such an outcome benefits consumers at the expense of producers.

How is oligopoly regulated? Does regulation prevent monopoly practices or does it encourage those practices?

According to the public interest theory, oligopoly is regulated to ensure a competitive outcome. Consider, for example, the market for trucking tomatoes from the San Joaquin Valley to Los Angeles, illustrated in Figure 17.4. The market demand curve for trips is *D*. The industry marginal cost curve—and the competitive supply curve—is *MC*. Public interest regulation will regulate the price of a trip at $20, and there will be 300 trips a week.

How would this industry be regulated according to the capture theory? Regulation that is in the producer interest will maximize profit. To find the outcome in this case, we need to determine the price and quantity when marginal

---

FIGURE 17.4

Collusive Oligopoly

Ten trucking firms transport tomatoes from the San Joaquin Valley to Los Angeles. The demand curve is *D*, and the industry marginal cost curve is *MC*. Under competition, the *MC* curve is the industry supply curve.

❶ Public interest regulation will achieve the efficient competitive outcome: a price of $20 a trip and 300 trips a week.

❷ Producer interest regulation will limit output to 200 trips a week (where industry marginal revenue, *MR*, is equal to industry marginal cost, *MC*), and the price will be $30 a trip.

cost equals marginal revenue. The marginal revenue curve is *MR*. So marginal cost equals marginal revenue at 200 trips a week. The price of a trip is $30.

One way of achieving this outcome is to place an output limit on each firm in the industry. If there are 10 trucking companies, an output limit of 20 trips per company ensures that the total number of trips in a week is 200. Penalties can be imposed to ensure that no single producer exceeds its output limit.

All the firms in the industry would support this type of regulation because it helps to prevent cheating and maintain a monopoly outcome. Each firm knows that without effectively enforced production quotas, every firm has an incentive to increase output. (For each firm, price exceeds marginal cost, so a greater output brings a larger profit.) So each firm wants a method of preventing output from increasing above the industry profit-maximizing output, and the quotas enforced by regulation achieve this end. With this type of cartel regulation, the regulator enables a cartel to operate legally and in its own best interest.

Cartel-like behavior occurs in many regulated activities when the *purpose* of regulation is quality control but the *effect* of regulation is monopoly profit. One example is citrus fruit production in California and Florida, where the state citrus boards, whose purpose is to regulate the size and quality of fruit, also regulate the weekly sales of the producers. Another example is the provision of physicians' services. Regulation of the quality of doctors ends up regulating entry and achieving a monopoly price for their services.

EYE ON THE U.S. ECONOMY

Regulatory Roller Coaster

You are paying much more than marginal cost for your cable TV services. And until effective competition arrives from an improved wireless technology, it is difficult to see lower cable TV prices coming.

Cable television has been on a regulatory roller coaster. When cable first arrived, its prices were regulated. They were deregulated in 1984, but profits soared and in 1992, prices were again regulated. Congress passed yet another deregulation law in 1996 and set March 31, 1999, as the date when the Federal Communications

Commission (FCC) would stop regulating most cable TV prices. Federal price controls were removed from packages that include popular channels, such as CNN, Discovery, ESPN, and MTV.

Before the 1999 deregulation, consumers paid an average of $31 a month for cable TV services.

Back in 1996, when Congress set the date of March 31, 1999, it expected to see effective competition among cable companies, but competition did not develop.

When the 1992 regulated prices took effect in 1993, prices fell. But in 1994, the FCC loosened the rules and prices began to rise. In mid-1996, cable

rates increased sharply. Prices have continued to increase but the range and quality of service have improved as well.

CHECKPOINT 17.1

1 **Explain the effects of regulation of natural monopoly and oligopoly.**

Practice Problem 17.1

1. An unregulated natural monopoly bottles Elixir, a unique health product that has no substitutes. The monopoly's total fixed cost is $150,000, and its marginal cost is 10 cents a bottle. Figure 1 illustrates the demand for Elixir.
   a. How many bottles of Elixir does the monopoly sell?
   b. What is the price of a bottle of Elixir?
   c. Is the monopoly's use of resources efficient?
   d. How might the government regulate the monopoly in the public interest?
   e. If the government introduces a marginal cost pricing rule, what will be the price of a bottle of Elixir, the quantity of Elixir sold, and the monopoly's profit?

FIGURE 1

Exercise 17.1

1. An unregulated natural monopoly cans Mt. McKinley air, unique clean air that has no substitutes. The monopoly's total fixed cost is $30,000, and its marginal cost is 10 cents a can. Figure 2 illustrates the demand for Mt. McKinley air.
   a. How many cans of Mt. McKinley air does the monopoly sell?
   b. What is the price of a can of Mt. McKinley air?
   c. If the monopoly captures the regulator, how might the monopoly be regulated?
   d. If the monopoly can mislead the regulator about its costs, what is the maximum excess average total cost that it would claim?
   e. Would the regulated monopoly use resources efficiently?

FIGURE 2

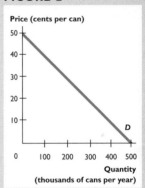

Solution to Practice Problem 17.1

1a. The monopoly will produce 1 million bottles a year—the quantity at which marginal revenue equals marginal cost (Figure 3).

1b. The price is 30 cents a bottle—the highest price at which the monopoly can sell the 1 million bottles a year (Figure 3).

1c. The monopoly's use of resources is inefficient. If resource use were efficient, the monopoly would produce the quantity at which price equals marginal cost: 2 million bottles a year.

1d. The government might use a marginal cost pricing rule or an average cost pricing rule to regulate the monopoly.

1e. With a marginal cost pricing rule, the price would be 10 cents a bottle and the monopoly would produce 2 million bottles a year. The monopoly would make an economic loss of $150,000 a year. The monopoly would need a subsidy from the government to keep it in business.

FIGURE 3

17.2 ANTITRUST LAW

Antitrust law
A law that regulates and prohibits certain kinds of market behavior, such as monopoly and monopolistic practices.

Antitrust law is the body of law that regulates and prohibits certain kinds of market behavior, such as monopoly and monopolistic practices. Antitrust law is enacted by Congress and enforced through the judicial system. Lawsuits under the antitrust laws may be initiated either by government agencies or by injured private parties. The main thrust of antitrust law is the prohibition of monopoly practices of restricting output to achieve higher prices and profits.

■ The Antitrust Laws

The U.S. antitrust laws are easily summarized. The first antitrust law, the Sherman Act, was passed in 1890 in an atmosphere of outrage and disgust at the actions and practices of J. P. Morgan, John D. Rockefeller, and W. H. Vanderbilt—the so-called "robber barons." Ironically, the most lurid stories of the actions of these great American capitalists are not of their monopolization and exploitation of consumers but of their sharp practices against each other. Nevertheless, monopolies did emerge—for example, the spectacular control of the oil industry by John D. Rockefeller.

A wave of mergers at the turn of the twentieth century produced stronger antitrust laws. The Clayton Act of 1914 supplemented the Sherman Act, and the Federal Trade Commission, an agency charged with enforcing the antitrust laws, was created.

Table 17.1 summarizes the two main provisions of the Sherman Act. Section 1 of the act is precise. Conspiring with others to restrict competition is illegal. But section 2 is general and imprecise. Just what is an "attempt to monopolize"? The Clayton Act and its two amendments, the Robinson-Patman Act of 1936 and Celler-Kefauver Act of 1950, which outlaw specific practices, answers this question. Table 17.2 describes these practices and summarizes the main provisions of these three acts.

■ **TABLE 17.1**

The Sherman Act, 1890

Section 1:

Every contract, combination in the form of trust or otherwise, or conspiracy, in restraint of trade or commerce among the several States, or with foreign nations, is hereby declared to be illegal.

Section 2:

Every person who shall monopolize, or attempt to monopolize, or combine or conspire with any other person or persons, to monopolize any part of the trade or commerce among the several States, or with foreign nations, shall be deemed guilty of a felony.

■ TABLE 17.2

The Clayton Act and Its Amendments

Clayton Act   1914

Robinson-Patman Act 1936

Celler-Kefauver Act   1950

These acts prohibit the following practices only if they substantially lessen competition or create monopoly:

1. Price discrimination.
2. Contracts that require other goods to be bought from the same firm (called tying arrangements).
3. Contracts that require a firm to buy all its requirements of a particular item from a single firm (called requirements contracts).
4. Contracts that prevent a firm from selling competing items (called exclusive dealing).
5. Contracts that prevent a buyer from reselling a product outside a specified area (called territorial confinement).
6. Acquiring a competitor's shares or assets.
7. Becoming a director of a competing firm.

■ Three Antitrust Policy Debates

Price fixing is *always* a violation of the antitrust law. If the Justice Department can prove the existence of price fixing, a defendant can offer no acceptable excuse. But other practices are more controversial and generate debate among antitrust lawyers and economists. We'll examine three of these practices:

- Resale price maintenance
- Tying arrangements
- Predatory pricing

Resale Price Maintenance

Most manufacturers sell their products to the final consumer indirectly through a wholesale and retail distribution system. **Resale price maintenance** occurs when a manufacturer agrees with a distributor on the price at which the product will be resold.

Resale price maintenance (also called vertical price fixing) *agreements* are illegal under the Sherman Act. But it isn't illegal for a manufacturer to refuse to supply a retailer who doesn't accept the manufacturer's guidance on what the price should be.

Attorneys general in 41 states alleged that Universal, Sony, Warner, Bertelsmann, and EMI kept CD prices artificially high between 1995 and 2000 with a practice called "minimum-advertised pricing." The companies denied the allegation but made a large payment to settle the case.

Resale price maintenance
An agreement between a manufacturer and a distributor on the price at which a product will be resold.

Does resale price maintenance create an inefficient or efficient use of resources? Economists can be found on both sides of this question.

Inefficient Resale Price Maintenance Resale price maintenance is inefficient if it enables dealers to charge the monopoly price. By setting and enforcing the resale price, the manufacturer might be able to ensure that retailers don't try to undercut each other.

Efficient Resale Price Maintenance Resale price maintenance might be efficient if it enables a manufacturer to induce dealers to provide the efficient standard of service. Suppose that SilkySkin wants shops to demonstrate the use of its new unbelievable moisturizing cream in an inviting space. With resale price maintenance, SilkySkin can offer all the retailers the same incentive and compensation. Without resale price maintenance, a cut-price drug store might offer SilkySkin products at a low price. Buyers would then have an incentive to visit a high-price shop and get the product demonstrated and then buy from the low-price shop. The low-price shop would be a free rider (like the consumer of a public good in Chapter 10, p. 245), and an inefficient level of service would be provided.

SilkySkin could pay a fee to retailers that provide good service and leave the resale price to be determined by the competitive forces of supply and demand. But it might be too costly for SilkySkin to monitor shops and ensure that they provided the desired level of service.

Tying Arrangements

Tying arrangement
An agreement to sell one product only if the buyer agrees to buy another, different product.

A **tying arrangement** is an agreement to sell one product only if the buyer agrees to buy another, different product. With tying, the only way the buyer can get the one product is to buy the other product at the same time. Microsoft has been accused of tying Internet Explorer and Windows (see next page). Textbook publishers sometimes tie a Web site and a textbook and force students to buy both. (You can't buy the book you're now reading, new, without the Web site. But you can buy the Web site access without the book, so these products are not tied.)

Could publishers of textbooks make more money by tying a book and access to a Web site? The answer is sometimes but not always. Think about what you are willing to pay for a book and access to a Web site. To keep the numbers simple, suppose that you and other students are willing to pay $40 for a book and $10 for access to a Web site. The publisher can sell these items separately for these prices or bundled for $50. There is no gain to the publisher from bundling.

But now suppose that you and only half of the students are willing to pay $40 for a book and $10 for a Web site. And suppose that the other half of the students are willing to pay $40 for a Web site and $10 for a book. Now if the two items are sold separately, the publisher can charge $40 for the book and $40 for the Web site. Half the students buy the book but not the Web site, and the other half buy the Web site but not the book. But if the book and Web site are bundled for $50, everyone buys the bundle and the publisher makes an extra $10 per student. In this case, bundling has enabled the publisher to price discriminate.

There is no simple, clear-cut test of whether a firm is engaging in tying or whether, by doing so, it has increased its market power and profit and created inefficiency.

Predatory Pricing

Predatory pricing is setting a low price to drive competitors out of business with the intention of setting a monopoly price when the competition has gone. John D. Rockefeller's Standard Oil Company was the first to be accused of this practice in the 1890s, and it has been claimed often in antitrust cases since then.

It is easy to see that predatory pricing is an idea, not a reality. Economists are skeptical that predatory pricing occurs. They point out that a firm that cuts its price below the profit-maximizing level loses during the low-price period. Even if the firm succeeds in driving its competitors out of business, new competitors will enter as soon as the price is increased. So any potential gain from a monopoly position is temporary. A high and certain loss is a poor exchange for a temporary and uncertain gain. No case of predatory pricing has been definitively found.

Predatory pricing
Setting a low price to drive competitors out of business with the intention of setting a monopoly price when the competition has gone.

■ A Recent Antitrust Showcase: The United States Versus Microsoft

In 1998, the U.S. Department of Justice along with a number of states charged Microsoft, the world's largest producer of software for personal computers, with violations of both sections of the Sherman Act. A 78-day trial followed that pitched two prominent MIT economics professors against each other (Franklin Fisher for the government and Richard Schmalensee for Microsoft).

The Case Against Microsoft

The claims against Microsoft were that it

- Possessed monopoly power in the market for PC operating systems.
- Used *predatory pricing* and *tying arrangements* to achieve a monopoly in the market for Web browsers.
- Used other anticompetitive practices to strengthen its monopoly in these two markets.

It was claimed that with 80 percent of the market for PC operating systems, Microsoft had excessive monopoly power. This monopoly power arose from two barriers to entry: economies of scale and network economies. Microsoft's average total cost falls as production increases (economies of scale) because the fixed cost of developing an operating system like Windows is large while the marginal cost of producing one copy of Windows is small. Further, as the number of Windows users increases, the range of Windows applications expands (network economies), so a potential competitor would need to produce not only a competing operating system but also an entire range of supporting applications.

When Microsoft entered the Web browser market with its Internet Explorer (IE), it offered the browser for a zero price. This price was viewed as *predatory pricing*. Microsoft integrated IE with Windows so that anyone who uses this operating system would not need a separate browser such as Netscape Communicator. Microsoft's competitors claimed that this practice was an illegal *tying arrangement*.

Microsoft's Response

Microsoft challenged all these claims. It said that although Windows was the dominant operating system, it was vulnerable to competition from other operating systems such as Linux and Apple's Mac OS and that there was a permanent threat of competition from new entrants.

Microsoft claimed that integrating Internet Explorer with Windows provided a single, unified product of greater consumer value. Instead of tying, Microsoft said, the browser and operating system constituted a single product. It was like a refrigerator with a chilled water dispenser or an automobile with a stereo player.

The Outcome

The court agreed that Microsoft was in violation of the Sherman Act and ordered that it be broken into two firms: an operating systems producer and an applications producer. Microsoft successfully appealed this order. But in the final judgment, Microsoft was ordered to disclose details about how its operating system works to other software developers so that they could compete effectively against Microsoft. In the summer of 2002, Microsoft began to comply with this order.

We end this chapter by examining the rules that guide merger decisions.

■ Merger Rules

The Department of Justice uses guidelines to determine which mergers it will examine and possibly block on the basis of the Herfindahl-Hirschman index (HHI), which is explained in Chapter 15 (p. 382). A market in which the HHI is less than 1,000 is regarded as competitive. An index between 1,000 and 1,800 indicates a moderately concentrated market, and a merger in this market that would increase the index by 100 points is challenged by the Department of Justice. An index above 1,800 indicates a concentrated market, and a merger in this market that would increase the index by 50 points is challenged. Figure 17.5(a) summarizes these guidelines.

The Department of Justice used these guidelines to analyze two proposed mergers in the market for soft drinks in 1986. First, PepsiCo announced its intention to buy 7-Up for $380 million. A month later, Coca-Cola said that it would buy Dr Pepper for $470 million. Whether this market is concentrated depends on how it is defined. The market for all soft drinks, which includes carbonated drinks marketed by these four companies plus fruit juices and bottled water, has an HHI of 120, so it is highly competitive. But the market for carbonated soft drinks is highly concentrated. Coca-Cola has a 39 percent share, PepsiCo has 28 percent, Dr Pepper is next with 7 percent, then comes 7-Up with 6 percent. One other producer, RJR, has a 5 percent market share. So the five largest firms in this market have an 85 percent market share. If we assume that the other 15 percent of the market consists of 15 firms, each with a 1 percent market share, the Herfindahl-Hirschman index is

$$\text{HHI} = 39^2 + 28^2 + 7^2 + 6^2 + 5^2 + 15 = 2,430.$$

With an HHI of this magnitude, a merger that increases the index by 50 points is examined by the Department of Justice. Figure 17.5(b) shows how the HHI would have changed with the mergers. The PepsiCo and 7-Up merger would have increased the index by more than 300 points, the Coca-Cola and Dr Pepper merger would have increased it by more than 500 points, and both mergers together would have increased the index by almost 800 points. The Justice Department decided to define the market narrowly and, with increases of these magnitudes, blocked the mergers.

◾ FIGURE 17.5
The HHI Merger Guidelines

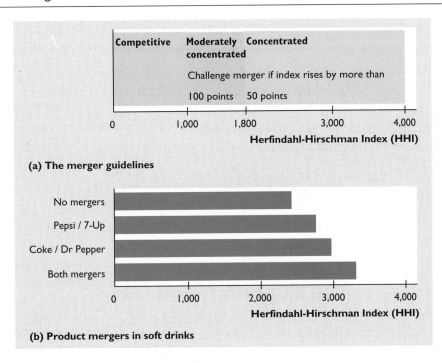

(a) The merger guidelines

(b) Product mergers in soft drinks

The Department of Justice scrutinizes proposed mergers if the HHI exceeds 1,000. Proposed mergers between producers of carbonated soft drinks were blocked in 1986 by application of these guidelines.

REALITY CHECK

Regulation in YOUR Life

Regulation and deregulation touch *your* life at many points. We have noted some of them already in this chapter.

Pay attention as you go about your everyday affairs and think about the regulation that you encounter. Before you open your eyes, you are awakened by an alarm clock that uses regulated electric power; you turn on the regulated cable news channel; you go to school on a regulated commuter train; you write your term paper on a laptop that runs Windows produced by a firm that has been pulled through the antitrust courts. It is hard to get away from regulation and laws designed to limit monopoly power.

Think hard about who benefits from and who bears the cost of the regulation that you encounter. Do we really need all the regulation we've got? And do we need more regulation in some areas?

2 **Describe U.S. antitrust law and explain three antitrust policy debates.**

Practice Problems 17.2

1. Since 1987, hundreds of hospital mergers have taken place in the United States. Rarely has the Federal Trade Commission (FTC) challenged a hospital merger. Use the link on MyEconLab to find out why the FTC decided not to challenge hospital mergers under U.S. antitrust law.

2. Explain each of the following terms:
   a. Attempt to monopolize
   b. Price fixing
   c. Predatory pricing
   d. Tying arrangements

Exercises 17.2

1. The FTC approved the $27 billion merger of BP Amoco PLC and ARCO only after it met the U.S. Federal Trade Commission's demands for substantial divestitures. Use the link on MyEconLab to find what some of the required divestitures were and why the FTC insisted on them.

2. In 1911, Standard Oil Company was found guilty under the Sherman Act and was ordered to divest itself. Some of the oil companies that were created as a result of the 1911 order have now merged to form large companies. Why do you think Standard Oil Company was found guilty under the Sherman Act while recent oil company mergers have been approved?

Solutions to Practice Problems 17.2

1. The FTC will not challenge a hospital merger if the merger will not substantially lessen competition. Such a situation arises if (1) the merger would not increase the likelihood of market power either because strong competitors exist or because the merging hospitals were sufficiently differentiated; (2) the merger would allow the hospitals to reduce cost; or (3) the merger would eliminate a hospital that otherwise would probably have failed and left the market.

2a. An attempt to monopolize is an attempt by a company to drive out its competitors so that it can operate as a monopoly.

2b. Price fixing is making an agreement with competitors to set a specified price and not to vary it.

2c. Predatory pricing is the attempt to drive out competitors by charging a price that is too low for anyone to earn a profit. (Economists think the practice is unlikely to be used.)

2d. Tying arrangements exist when a company does not offer a buyer the opportunity to buy one item without at the same time buying another item.

CHAPTER CHECKPOINT

Key Points

1 **Explain the effects of regulation of natural monopoly and oligopoly.**

- The Interstate Commerce Commission, established in 1887, was the first national regulatory agency.
- At the peak of regulation, in the late 1970s, almost a quarter of U.S. output was produced by regulated industries.
- Public interest theory predicts that regulation achieves an efficient use of resources. Capture theory predicts that regulation helps producers to maximize economic profit.
- A natural monopoly is efficient if its price equals marginal cost.
- A natural monopoly maximizes its profit if its marginal revenue equals marginal cost and price exceeds marginal cost.
- Rate of return regulation makes price equal to average cost.
- Price cap regulation motivates a firm to earn an economic profit by keeping costs under control.

2 **Describe U.S. antitrust law and explain three antitrust policy debates.**

- Antitrust law is used to control monopoly and monopolistic practices.
- The first U.S. antitrust law, the Sherman Act, was passed in 1890, and the law was strengthened in 1914 when the Clayton Act was passed and the Federal Trade Commission was created.
- All price-fixing agreements are in violation of the Sherman Act.
- Resale price maintenance might be efficient if it enables a producer to ensure the efficient level of service by distributors.
- Tying arrangements can enable a monopoly to price discriminate and increase profit, but in many cases, tying would not increase profit.
- Predatory pricing is unlikely to occur because it brings losses and only temporary potential gains.
- The Federal Trade Commission uses guidelines to determine which mergers to examine and possibly block on the basis of the Herfindahl-Hirschman Index.

Key Terms

Antitrust law, 434
Average cost pricing rule, 427
Capture theory, 425
Deregulation, 424
Earnings sharing regulation, 430

Marginal cost pricing rule, 427
Predatory pricing, 437
Price cap regulation, 430
Public interest theory, 425
Rate of return regulation, 428

Regulation, 424
Resale price maintenance, 435
Tying arrangement, 436

Exercises

1. When were the antitrust laws introduced? Why were they introduced? What practices do the laws make illegal? And why are these practices illegal?

2. What charges might be brought under the antitrust law in each of the following situations? And why, if at all, might a firm or firms want to take the actions described?
   a. The owners of the only two ready-mix concrete producers in a city are discovered holding secret meetings to fix their prices.
   b. Amazon.com proposes to buy Barnes & Noble and other major book retailers.
   c. A pharmaceutical manufacturer opens a chain of drug stores.
   d. Ford Motor Company installs a small refrigerator in all its cars, and GM accuses Ford of a tying arrangement.
   e. A video rental store requires customers to rent a B movie with every A movie they rent.

3. Hawaii Cable Television is a natural monopoly. Sketch a demand curve, a marginal revenue curve, an average total cost curve, and a marginal cost curve that illustrate Hawaii Cable's situation.

4. If Hawaii Cable (in exercise 3) is unregulated and maximizes profit, show in your graph the price, quantity, economic profit, consumer surplus, and deadweight loss.

5. If Hawaii Cable (in exercise 3) is regulated in the public interest, show in your graph the price, quantity, economic profit, consumer surplus, and deadweight loss.

6. If Hawaii Cable (in exercise 3) is subject to a price cap regulation that enables it to earn normal profit, show in your graph the price, quantity, economic profit, consumer surplus, and deadweight loss.

7. What would happen if the regulator set the price cap for Hawaii Cable (in exercise 3) too low for the firm to earn normal profit?

FIGURE 1

8. Land Line and Cellular City are the only two phone companies that offer local calls in an area. Figure 1 illustrates the market demand for calls and the marginal cost and average total cost of a call for each firm.
   a. If these firms behave as a cartel, show on the graph the price they charge for a call and the quantity of calls made.
   b. If the phone companies are regulated in the public interest, show on the graph the price of a call and the quantity of calls made.
   c. Show on the graph the price of a call and the quantity of calls if the phone companies capture the regulator.
   d. Show on the graph the deadweight loss that arises in part c.

9. Using the information in exercise 8,
   a. What regulation would lead to resource use being efficient?
   b. Would the firms incur an economic loss with efficient regulation? Why or why not?

    c. Show on the graph the price and quantity of calls if the firms were subject to an efficient price cap regulation.

    d. Show on the graph the deadweight loss that arises in part **c**.

10. In the market for local phone calls in which Land Line and Cellular City operate in exercise 8, suppose that the market is unregulated but that the price has been driven down to the competitive level because the firms are unable to form an effective cartel. Land Line would like to drive Cellular City out of business and considers practicing predatory pricing. Could Land Line succeed in eliminating competition in the short run and in the long run?

11. Explain why, during the 1980s, the antitrust authorities blocked a proposed merger between PepsiCo and 7-Up and between Coca-Cola and Dr Pepper. What do you predict would have happened to the price and quantity of soda if the mergers had occurred?

12. The Organization of the Petroleum Exporting Countries (OPEC) is an international cartel headquartered in Vienna, Austria, and operates outside the scope of the U.S. antitrust laws. OPEC controls about 40 percent of the world's crude oil production but owns about 75 percent of the world's known crude oil reserves. OPEC routinely meets to fix production quotas that are designed to change—usually to raise—the world price of oil.

    a. If the U.S antitrust laws could be extended to cover OPEC, would OPEC be in violation of the law? If so, explain which part of the law it would violate. If not, explain why not.

    b. What do you think would happen to the world price of oil and the quantity of oil consumed if OPEC were made to operate under antitrust laws like those of the United States?

13. Suppose that in the market for local phone calls described in exercise 8, Land Line and Cellular City propose a merger to create Land and Cell, Inc.

    a. What would happen to the price and quantity of local calls?

    b. What would happen to the consumer surplus, producer surplus, and deadweight loss in the market for local calls?

    c. Why would the antitrust authorities block this merger?

14. Suppose that Burger King, McDonald's, and Wendy's proposed a merger into a single Super Burger Chain.

    a. Do you think such a merger would be in the public interest? Explain.

    b. What do you think would happen to the price of a burger? Explain.

    c. What do you think would happen to consumer surplus, producer surplus, and deadweight loss if such a merger occurred?

    d. Would the antitrust authorities block such a merger? Why or why not?

    e. What is the main reason that, in reality, a merger would be in the interest of any of these firms?

Critical Thinking

15. Governments talk about regulating the Internet and taxing e-commerce. From what you know about how the Internet works and what e-commerce is,
    a. What problems might governments encounter in regulating the Internet?
    b. What difficulties do you think governments would have taxing e-commerce?
    c. Do you think that the arrival of the Internet has created more problems for the antitrust laws to solve or lessened the problems of monopoly?
    d. What parts of antitrust law do you think will be hard to enforce on companies that trade on the Internet?

16. Thinking about the Microsoft antitrust case,
    a. Do you agree that Microsoft attempted to monopolize the market for PC operating systems? Explain.
    b. Do you agree that Microsoft engaged in predatory pricing of Internet Explorer? Explain.
    c. Do you agree that Microsoft engaged in an illegal tying arrangement by bundling Internet Explorer with Windows? Explain.
    d. Do you think that the court's direction to Microsoft to share its code is an adequate way of achieving an efficient use of resources in the software market? Explain.

Web Exercises

Use the links on MyEconLab to work the following exercises.

17. Visit the Federal Trade Commission, where you can obtain information about Intel, the computer chip maker.
    a. Is Intel a natural monopoly?
    b. What was the problem that the FTC had with Intel?
    c. What did Intel agree to do?
    d. Explain how Intel's agreement will influence the price, quantity, consumer surplus, and producer surplus in the market for computer chips.

18. Visit the CNN Special on the California Electricity market.
    a. Describe how electricity utilities were regulated in California before 1996.
    b. Describe the changes in regulations that occurred in 1996.
    c. Identify at least three areas in which the electricity industry in California remained regulated after "deregulation."
    d. Explain the probable effects of the price cap on electricity generated in California.
    e. How do you think the situation in California would be different if, instead of a price cap, the state had introduced an earnings sharing plan?

19. Visit the U.S. Department of Justice Antitrust Division and look at the long list of antitrust cases listed on that Web site.
    a. Select a case that interests you.
    b. Describe the alleged violation of the antitrust laws.
    c. Explain the likely effects of the violation on price, quantity, producer surplus, consumer surplus, and deadweight loss.
    d. Describe the outcome of the case.
    e. Explain the likely effects of the settlement of the case on price, quantity, producer surplus, consumer surplus, and deadweight loss.

Demand and Supply in Factor Markets

CHAPTER CHECKLIST

When you have completed your study of this chapter, you will be able to

1 Describe the anatomy of the markets for labor, capital, and land.

2 Explain how the value of marginal product determines the demand for a factor of production.

3 Explain how wage rates and employment are determined.

4 Explain how interest rates, borrowing, and lending are determined.

5 Explain how rents and natural resource prices are determined.

Bobby Stoops makes $2.2 million a year coaching the Sooners, the University of Oklahoma's football team. Deborah Watson, a Harvard Ph.D. physicist, is one of the University of Oklahoma's female professors who on the average earn $62,000 a year. What is going on? How can a football coach earn 37 times what a professor earns? You will learn in this chapter how factor markets answer these questions.

First, we'll describe the anatomy of the labor, capital, and land markets. Then we'll learn what determines the demand for a factor of production. We'll go on to study demand, supply, and equilibrium in factor markets. These markets determine the quantities of factors of production that are used to produce goods and services, which determine the prices and incomes of the factors of production and determine *for whom* goods and services get produced.

445

18.1 THE ANATOMY OF FACTOR MARKETS

The four factors of production that produce goods and services are

- Labor
- Capital
- Land
- Entrepreneurship

The first three factors—labor, capital, and land—are traded in markets that work like the markets for goods and services that you studied in Chapter 4. What a factor of production is paid—a **factor price**—is determined in a *factor market*. Entrepreneurship is different. Entrepreneurs create firms and hire labor, capital, and land in factor markets. The income of an entrepreneur is a profit (or a loss).

We'll begin by looking at the anatomy of the factor markets.

Factor price
The price of a factor of production. The wage rate is the price of labor, the interest rate is the price of capital, and rent is the price of land.

■ Labor Markets

Whether you're looking for a summer job or a permanent job after you graduate, you'll find it by searching in a labor market. Similarly, if you're running a business and want to hire some workers, you'll go to a labor market.

Labor consists of the work effort of people. And a **labor market** is a collection of people and firms who are trading labor services. Some labor is traded day by day, called casual labor. People who pick fruit and vegetables often just show up at a farm and take whatever work is available that day. But most labor is traded on a contract, called a **job**.

Labor market
A collection of people and firms who are trading labor services.

Job
A contract between a firm and a household to provide labor services.

Labor is supplied in combination with *human capital*—the skills obtained from education, on-the-job training, and work experience. Each person has a fixed (and equal) amount of time, but individual ability and human capital vary. Also, productivity depends on how well the skills of a worker match the skills required by an employer. For these reasons, a large amount of search activity takes place in labor markets. People search for the best job they can find, and firms search for the best person to fill a particular job.

People find jobs by using a variety of search devices, such as leads from friends and family members, help wanted advertisements, job centers, and job-clearing Web sites such as NationJob.com.

The price of labor is a wage rate, which is expressed as dollars per unit of time—dollars per hour, day, week, month, or year.

People find jobs from help wanted advertisements, at job centers, and on job-clearing Web sites.

■ Financial Markets

Capital consists of the tools, instruments, machines, buildings, and other constructions that have been produced in the past and that businesses now use to produce goods and services. These physical objects are themselves goods—*capital goods*—and are traded in markets, just as bottled water and toothpaste are. There are markets for earth-moving equipment, cranes, printing presses, Internet servers, and so on. The prices and quantities of capital goods are determined in markets just like those that you studied in Chapter 4.

Financial capital consists of the funds that firms use to buy and operate capital. The financial market is where firms get the funds that they use to buy capital. Firms are the demanders in the financial market. On the other side of a financial market are the people who have savings to lend.

A **financial market** is the collection of people and firms who are lending and borrowing to finance the purchase of physical capital. The price of financial capital, which is determined in the financial markets, is expressed as an interest rate (percent per year).

The two main types of financial market are

- Stock market
- Bond market

Stock Market

A **stock market** is a market in which shares in the stocks of companies are traded. A share in the stock of a company is an entitlement to a share in the profits of the company. The New York Stock Exchange and NASDAQ (the National Association of Security Dealers Automated Quotation System) are examples of stock markets. You can visit the Web sites of these stock markets and see the prices and the quantities of shares that are being traded minute by minute throughout the business day.

The growth of the Internet has created many new methods of participating in the stock market, and dozens of new firms offer services that enable anyone who is connected to the Internet to trade online.

Bond Market

A **bond market** is a market in which bonds issued by firms and governments are traded. A **bond** is a promise to pay specified sums of money on specified dates. To learn more about bond markets and how they are organized, you might visit the Bond Market Web site.

Financial capital
The funds that firms use to buy and operate physical capital.

Financial market
A collection of people and firms who are lending and borrowing to finance the purchase of physical capital.

Stock market
A market in which shares in the stocks of companies are traded.

Bond market
A market in which bonds issued by firms and governments are traded.

Bond
A promise to pay specified sums of money on specified dates.

Closing bell at the New York Stock Exchange.

■ Land Markets

Land consists of all the gifts of nature. So there are many different objects in this category of the factors of production. What we call *land* in everyday speech is just one of these. Raw materials that we dig or pump from beneath the ground or ocean, such as metal ores, coal, oil, and natural gas, are also called *land.*

The market for land as a factor of production is the market for the services of land (of all types). These services are rented, and the price that is determined in a land market is a rent expressed as dollars per unit. The market for a raw material is called a **commodity market**.

Commodity market
A market in which raw materials are traded.

■ Competitive Factor Markets

Factor markets vary in many ways. But most factor markets have one thing in common: many buyers and sellers. These markets are competitive markets.

In competitive factor markets, buyers and sellers are price takers—wage rate, interest rate, and rental rate takers—and market forces determine factor prices. We study competitive factor markets in this chapter.

CHECKPOINT 18.1

1 Describe the anatomy of the markets for labor, capital, and land.

Practice Problem 18.1

1. To stage the 2004 Olympic Games, the Athens Organizing Committee
   a. Borrowed money and sold sponsorships.
   b. Built an Olympic Village and other venues.
   c. Hired and trained several thousand volunteers and security guards.
   d. Sold more than 7 million tickets.
   e. Built environmentally friendly water- and waste-recycling plants in the Olympic facilities.
   f. Set up an Internet site, which was able to receive 1 million hits a day.

   Which of these items are not factors of production? Divide those that are factors of production into land, labor, physical capital, human capital, financial capital, and entrepreneurship.

Exercise 18.1

1. Visit the Web site of the 2006 Winter Olympics: Torino 2006. What are some of the factors of production that the organizers are using to stage the 2006 Winter Olympic Games?

Solution to Practice Problem 18.1

1. The tickets sold are not a factor of production. The other items are factors of production. *Land* includes sites on which housing and facilities are built. *Labor* includes volunteers and guards. *Physical capital* includes Olympic Village, other venues, recycling plants, and Internet site. *Human capital* includes the skill of the security guards and the trained volunteers. *Financial capital* includes money borrowed and sponsorships sold. *Entrepreneurship* includes the Athens Organizing Committee.

18.2 THE DEMAND FOR A FACTOR OF PRODUCTION

The demand for a factor of production is a **derived demand**—it is derived from the demand for the goods and services that it is used to produce. You've seen, in Chapters 13 through 16, how a firm determines its profit-maximizing output. The quantities of factors of production demanded are a direct consequence of firms' output decisions. Firms hire the quantities of factors of production that maximize profit.

To decide the quantity of a factor of production to hire, a firm compares the cost of hiring an additional unit of the factor with its value to the firm. The cost of hiring an additional unit of a factor of production is the factor price. The value to the firm of hiring one more unit of a factor of production is called the factor's **value of marginal product**, which equals the price of a unit of output multiplied by the marginal product of the factor of production. To study the demand for a factor of production, we'll examine the demand for labor.

Derived demand
The demand for a factor of production, which is derived from the demand for the goods and services it is used to produce.

■ Value of Marginal Product

Table 18.1 shows you how to calculate the value of the marginal product of labor at Max's Wash 'n' Wax car wash service. The first two columns show Max's *total product* schedule—the number of car washes per hour that each quantity of labor can produce. The third column shows the *marginal product* of labor—the change in total product that results from a one-unit increase in the quantity of labor employed. (See Chapter 12, pp. 297–301 for a refresher on product schedules.) Max can sell car washes at the going market price of $3 a wash. Given this information, we can calculate the value of marginal product (fourth column). It equals price multiplied by marginal product. For example, the marginal product of hiring the second worker is 4 car washes an hour. Each wash brings in $3, so the value of the marginal product of the second worker is $12 (4 washes at $3 each).

Value of marginal product
The value to a firm of hiring one more unit of a factor of production, which equals price of a unit of output multiplied by the marginal product of the factor of production.

■ **TABLE 18.1**

Calculating the Value of Marginal Product

	Quantity of labor (workers)	Total product (car washes per hour)	Marginal product (washes per additional worker)	Value of marginal product (dollars per additional worker)
A	0	0		
			5	15
B	1	5		
			4	12
C	2	9		
			3	9
D	3	12		
			2	6
E	4	14		
			1	3
F	5	15		

The price of a car wash is $3. The value of the marginal product of labor equals the price of the product multiplied by marginal product of labor (column 3). The marginal product of the second worker is 4 washes, so the value of the marginal product of the second worker (in column 4) is $3 a wash multiplied by 4 washes, which is $12.

The Value of Marginal Product Curve

Figure 18.1 graphs the value of the marginal product of labor at Max's Wash 'n' Wax as the number of workers that Max hires changes. The blue bars that show the value of the marginal product of labor correspond to the numbers in Table 18.1. The curve labeled *VMP* is Max's value of marginal product curve.

■ A Firm's Demand for Labor

The value of the marginal product of labor and the wage rate determine the quantity of labor demanded by a firm. The value of the marginal product of labor tells us the additional revenue the firm earns by hiring one more worker. The wage rate tells us the additional cost the firm incurs by hiring one more worker.

Because the value of marginal product decreases as the quantity of labor employed increases, there is a simple rule for maximizing profit: Hire labor up to the point at which the value of marginal product equals the wage rate. If the value of marginal product of labor exceeds the wage rate, a firm can increase its profit by employing one more worker. If the wage rate exceeds the value of marginal product of labor, a firm can increase its profit by employing one fewer worker. But if the wage rate equals the value of the marginal product of labor, the firm cannot increase its profit by changing the number of workers it employs. The firm is making the maximum possible profit.

So the quantity of labor demanded by a firm is the quantity at which the wage rate equals the value of the marginal product of labor.

■ **FIGURE 18.1**

The Value of the Marginal Product at Max's Wash 'n' Wax

The blue bars show the value of the marginal product of the labor that Max hires based on the numbers in Table 18.1. The orange line is the firm's value of the marginal product of labor curve.

	Quantity of labor (workers)	Value of marginal product (dollars per additional worker)
A	1	15
B	2	12
C	3	9
D	4	6
E	5	3

A Firm's Demand for Labor Curve

A firm's demand for labor curve is also its value of marginal product curve. If the wage rate falls and other things remain the same, a firm hires more workers. Figure 18.2 shows Max's value of marginal product curve in part (a) and demand for labor curve in part (b). The x-axis measures the number of workers hired in both parts. The y-axis measures the value of marginal product in part (a) and the wage rate—dollars per hour—in part (b).

Suppose the wage rate is $10.50 an hour. You can see in part (a) that if Max hires 1 worker, the value of the marginal product of labor is $15 an hour. Because this 1 worker costs Max only $10.50 an hour, he makes a profit of $4.50 an hour. If Max hires 2 workers, the value of the marginal product of the second worker is $12 an hour. So on this second worker, Max makes a profit of $1.50 an hour. Max's total profit per hour on the first two workers is $6 an hour—$4.50 on the first worker plus $1.50 on the second worker.

If Max hired 3 workers, his profit would fall. The third worker generates a marginal product of only $9 an hour but costs $10.50 an hour, so Max does not hire

---

FIGURE 18.2

The Demand for Labor at Max's Wash 'n' Wax

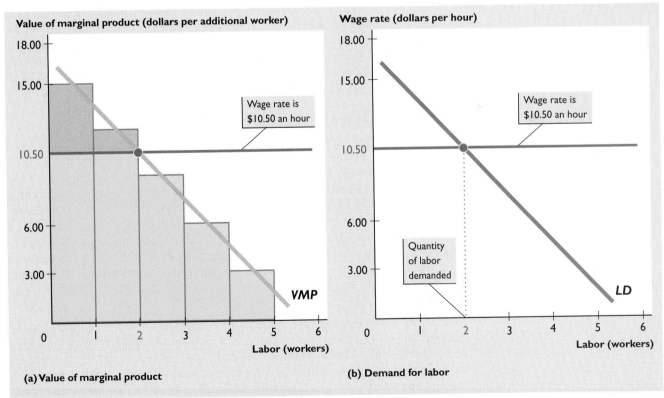

(a) Value of marginal product

(b) Demand for labor

At a wage rate of $10.50 an hour, Max makes a profit on the first 2 workers but would incur a loss on the third worker (part a), so the quantity of labor demanded is 2 workers (part b). Max's demand for labor curve in part (b) is the same as the value of

marginal product curve. The demand for labor curve slopes downward because the value of the marginal product of labor diminishes as the quantity of labor employed increases.

3 workers. The quantity of labor demanded by Max when the wage rate is $10.50 an hour is 2 workers, which is a point on Max's demand for labor curve, *LD,* in Figure 18.2(b).

If the wage rate increased to $12.50 an hour, Max would decrease the quantity of labor demanded to 1 worker. If the wage rate decreased to $7.50 an hour, Max would increase the quantity of labor demanded to 3 workers.

A change in the wage rate brings a change in the quantity of labor demanded and a movement along the demand curve. A change in any other influence on a firm's labor-hiring plans changes the demand for labor and shifts the demand for labor curve.

■ Changes in the Demand for Labor

The demand for labor depends on

- The price of the firm's output
- The prices of other factors of production
- Technology

The Price of the Firm's Output

The higher the price of a firm's output, the greater is its demand for labor. The price of output affects the demand for labor through its influence on the value of marginal product. A higher price for the firm's output increases the value of the marginal product of labor. A change in the price of a firm's output leads to a shift in the firm's demand for labor curve. If the price of the firm's output increases, the demand for labor increases and the demand for labor curve shifts rightward.

For example, if the price of a car wash increased to $4, the value of the marginal product of Max's third worker would increase from $9 an hour to $12 an hour. At a wage rate of $10.50, Max would now hire 3 workers instead of 2.

The Prices of Other Factors of Production

If the price of using capital decreases relative to the wage rate, a firm substitutes capital for labor and increases the quantity of capital it uses. Usually, the demand for labor will decrease when the price of using capital falls. For example, if the price of a car wash machine falls, Max might decide to install an additional machine and lay off a worker. But the demand for labor could increase if the lower price of capital led to a sufficiently large increase in the scale of production. For example, with cheaper capital equipment available, Max might install an additional car wash machine and hire more labor to operate it. These types of factor substitution occur in the *long run* when the firm can change the scale of its plant.

Technology

New technologies decrease the demand for some types of labor and increase the demand for other types. For example, if a new automated car wash machine becomes available, Max might install one of these machines and fire most of his work force—a decrease in the demand for car wash workers. But the firms that manufacture and service automatic car wash machines hire more labor—an increase in the demand for these types of labor. During the 1980s and 1990s, the electronic telephone exchange decreased the demand for telephone operators and increased the demand for computer programmers and electronics engineers.

CHECKPOINT 18.2

2 **Explain how the value of marginal product determines the demand for a factor of production.**

Practice Problem 18.2

1. Kaiser's Ice Cream Parlor hires workers to produce smoothies. The market for smoothies is perfectly competitive, and smoothies sell for $4.00 each. The labor market is competitive, and the wage rate is $40 a day. Table 1 shows the workers' total product schedule.
   a. Calculate the marginal product of hiring the fourth worker.
   b. Calculate the value of the marginal product of the fourth worker.
   c. How many workers will Kaiser's hire to maximize its profit?
   d. How many smoothies a day will Kaiser's produce to maximize its profit?
   e. If the price rises to $5 a smoothie, how many workers will Kaiser's hire?
   f. Kaiser's installs a new soda fountain that increases the productivity of workers by 50 percent. If the price remains at $4 a smoothie and the wage rises to $48 a day, how many workers does Kaiser's hire?

TABLE 1

Workers	Smoothies per day
1	7
2	21
3	33
4	43
5	51
6	55

Exercise 18.2

1. Greg's Grooming hires workers to groom dogs. The market for dog grooming is perfectly competitive, and the price of a grooming is $20. The labor market is competitive, and the wage rate is $40 a day. Table 2 shows the workers' total product schedule.
   a. Calculate the marginal product of hiring the third worker.
   b. Calculate the value of the marginal product of the third worker.
   c. How many workers will Greg's hire to maximize its profit?
   d. How many dogs a day will Greg's groom to maximize its profit?
   e. If the wage rate rises to $60 a day, how many workers will Greg's hire?
   f. If Greg installs a machine that doubles the productivity of workers and the price of a grooming falls to $10, how many workers will Greg's hire at $40 a day?

TABLE 2

Workers	Groomings per day
1	4
2	7
3	11
4	16
5	20
6	23
7	25

Solution to Practice Problem 18.2

1a. The *MP* of hiring the fourth worker equals the *TP* of 4 workers (43 smoothies) minus the *TP* of 3 workers (33 smoothies), which is 10 smoothies.

1b. The *VMP* of the fourth worker equals the *MP* of the fourth worker (10 smoothies) multiplied by the price of a smoothie ($4), which is $40.

1c. Kaiser's maximizes profit by hiring the number of workers that makes *VMP* equal to the wage rate ($40 a day). Kaiser's hires 4 workers.

1d. Kaiser's hires 4 workers, and they produce 43 smoothies. When Kaiser's hires 4 workers, the *MP* of labor is 10 smoothies. The cost of a worker is $40 a day, so the *MC* of a smoothie is $40 ÷ 10 smoothies a day, which is $4 a smoothie. Kaiser's *MC* equals the price of a smoothie ($4 a smoothie) when Kaiser's produces 43 smoothies a day.

1e. Kaiser's maximizes its profit by hiring 5 workers.

1f. Kaiser's maximizes its profit by hiring 5 workers.

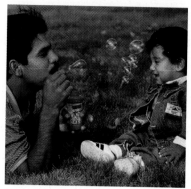

18.3 WAGES AND EMPLOYMENT

For most of us, the labor market is our only source of income. We work and earn a wage. What determines the amount of labor that we supply?

■ The Supply of Labor

People supply labor to earn an income. Many factors influence the quantity of labor that a person plans to provide, but a key factor is the wage rate.

To see how the wage rate influences the quantity of labor supplied, think about Larry's labor supply decision, which Figure 18.3 illustrates. Larry enjoys his leisure time, and he would be pleased if he didn't have to spend his evenings and weekends working at Max's Wash 'n' Wax. But Max pays him $10.50 an hour, and at that wage rate, Larry chooses to work 30 hours a week. The reason is that he is offered a wage rate that is high enough to make him regard this use of his time as the best available to him. If he were offered a lower wage rate, Larry would not be willing to give up so much leisure. If he were offered a higher wage rate, Larry would want to work even longer hours, but only up to a point. Offer Larry $25 an hour, and he would be willing to work a 40-hour week (and earn $1,000). With the goods and services that Larry can buy for $1,000, his priority would be a bit more leisure time if the wage rate increased further. If the wage rate increased above $25 an hour, Larry would cut back on his work hours and take more leisure. Larry's labor supply curve eventually bends backward.

■ FIGURE 18.3

An Individual's Labor Supply Curve

ⓍⓂⓎeconlab

❶ At a wage rate of $10.50 an hour, ❷ Larry is willing to supply 30 hours a week of labor.

❸ Larry's quantity of labor supplied ❹ increases as the wage rate increases up to ❺ a maximum, and then further increases in the wage rate ❻ bring a decrease in the quantity of labor supplied. Larry's labor supply curve eventually bends backward.

	Wage rate (dollars per hour)	Quantity of labor (hours per week)
A	40.00	30
B	35.00	35
C	30.00	38
D	25.00	40
E	20.00	38
F	15.00	35
G	10.50	30
H	5.00	0

Market Supply Curve

Larry's supply curve shows the quantity of labor supplied by one person as that person's wage rate changes. Most people behave like Larry. But different people have different wage rates at which they are willing to work and at which their labor supply curve bends backward. A market supply curve shows the quantity of labor supplied by all households in a particular job. It is found by adding together the quantities supplied by all households at each wage rate. Also, along a market supply curve, the wage rates available in other jobs remain the same. So, for example, along the supply curve of car wash workers, we hold constant the wage rates of car salespeople, mechanics, and all other types of labor.

Offer Larry more for car washing than for oil changing, and he will supply more of his labor to car washing. So the market supply curve in a given job slopes upward like the one in Figure 18.4, which shows the market supply curve for car wash workers in a large city.

■ Influences on the Supply of Labor

The supply of labor changes when influences other than the wage rate change. The key factors that change the supply of labor are

- Adult population
- Preferences
- Time in school and training

FIGURE 18.4

The Supply of Car Wash Workers

	Wage rate (dollars per hour)	Quantity of labor (workers)
A	20.00	400
B	15.00	350
C	10.50	300
D	7.00	200
E	3.50	100

The supply curve of car wash workers shows how the quantity supplied changes when the wage rate changes, other things remaining the same. In a market for a specific type of labor, the quantity supplied increases as the wage rate increases, other things remaining the same.

Adult Population

An increase in the adult population increases the supply of labor. Such an increase might occur because the birth rate exceeds the death rate. Or it might occur because of migration. Historically, the population of the United States has been strongly influenced by migration.

Preferences

In 1960, 34 percent of women had jobs. In 2005, 56 percent of women had jobs and the percentage was still rising. Many factors contributed to this change, which economists classify as a change in preferences. The result has been a large increase in the supply of female labor. At the same time, the percentage of men with jobs has shrunk, from 80 percent in 1960 to 73 percent in 2005.

Time in School and Training

The more people who remain in school for full-time education and training, the smaller is the supply of low-skilled labor. Today in the United States, almost everyone completes high school and more than 50 percent of high-school graduates enroll in college or university. Although many students work part time, the supply of labor by students is less than it would be if they were full-time workers. So when more people pursue higher education, other things remaining the same, the supply of low-skilled labor decreases. But time spent in school and training converts low-skilled labor into high-skilled labor. So the greater the proportion of people who receive a higher education, the greater is the supply of high-skilled labor.

When the amount of work that people want to do at a given wage rate changes, the supply of labor changes. So an increase in the adult population or an increase in the percentage of women with jobs increases the supply of labor. An increase in college enrollment decreases the supply of low-skilled labor. Later, it increases the supply of high-skilled labor. Changes in the supply of labor shift the supply of labor curve, just like the shifts of the supply curves that you studied in Chapter 4 (p. 101).

■ Labor Market Equilibrium

Labor market equilibrium determines the wage rate and employment. In Figure 18.5, the market demand curve for car wash workers is *LD*. Here, if the wage rate is $10.50 an hour, the quantity of labor demanded is 300 workers. If the wage rate rises to $14 an hour, the quantity demanded decreases to 200. And if the wage rate falls to $9 an hour, the quantity demanded increases to 350. Figure 18.5 also shows the supply curve of car wash workers, *LS*, which is the same as that in Figure 18.4.

Figure 18.5 also shows equilibrium in the labor market. The equilibrium wage rate is $10.50 an hour, and the equilibrium quantity is 300 car wash workers. If the wage rate exceeded $10.50 an hour, there would be a surplus of car wash workers. More people would be looking for car wash jobs than firms were willing to hire.

In such a situation, the wage rate would fall as firms found it easy to hire people at a lower wage rate. If the wage rate were less than $10.50 an hour, there would be a shortage of car wash workers. Firms would not be able to fill all the jobs they had available. In this situation, the wage rate would rise as firms found it necessary to offer higher wages to attract labor. Only at a wage rate of $10.50 an hour are there no forces operating to change the wage rate.

Reallocating Labor

Technological change destroys some jobs and creates others. But it creates more jobs than it destroys, and *on the average*, the new jobs pay more than the old ones did. But to benefit from technological change, people must acquire new skills and change their jobs. Between 2002 and 2012, the number of jobs in clothing manufacturing, tobacco, metal ore mining, and coal mining are expected to decline. But the number of jobs in services industries, especially in computer and data services, is expected to expand.

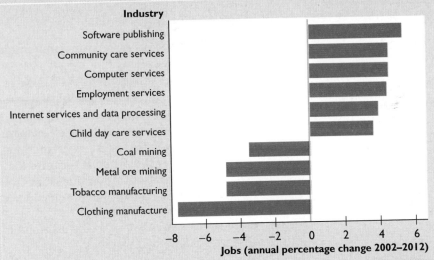

SOURCE OF DATA: *Statistical Abstract of the United States*, 2004–2005, Table 602.

Changes in demand and supply in these labor markets will change employment and the equilibrium wage rates.

FIGURE 18.5

Labor Market Equilibrium

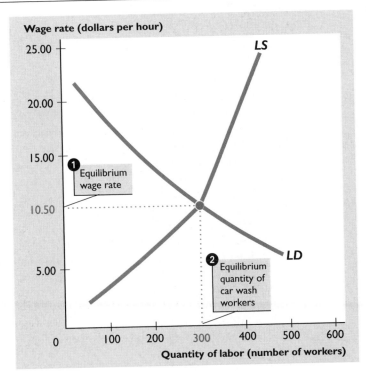

The labor market coordinates firms' demand for labor and households' supply of labor plans by changing the wage rate. The market is in equilibrium—the quantity of labor demanded equals the quantity supplied. ❶ The equilibrium wage rate is $10.50 an hour and ❷ the equilibrium quantity of labor is 300 workers.

If the wage rate exceeds $10.50 an hour, the quantity supplied exceeds the quantity demanded and the wage rate falls. If the wage rate is below $10.50 an hour, the quantity demanded exceeds the quantity supplied and the wage rate rises.

3 **Explain how wage rates and employment are determined.**

Practice Problem 18.3

1. Fast-food outlets in Greenville hire teenagers and retirees. In Greenville, the following events occur one at a time and other things remain the same. Explain the influence of each event on the market for fast-food workers.
   a. A new theme park opens and hires teenagers to sell tickets for its rides.
   b. The new theme park becomes the hottest tourist attraction in the state.
   c. Retirees from around the state flock to Greenville and make it their home.
   d. The demand for hamburgers decreases, and as a result, the price of a hamburger decreases.
   e. New technology in the fast-food industry decreases the marginal product of fast-food workers.

Exercises 18.3

1. Ski instructors are skilled workers. Consider the market for ski instructors in the greater Salt Lake City region and explain how that market would change if
   a. Ski holidays became more popular.
   b. New skis were invented that were much easier to use than the current ones.

2. What do you think the effect of Internet commerce has been on the markets for truck drivers, couriers, and sales clerks?

3. More and more people use the Internet. What are three types of labor for which the demand will continue to increase and three types for which the demand will continue to decrease? Explain your answer.

4. As more people go to college, what changes do you predict will occur in the markets for college graduates and low-skilled workers?

Solution to Practice Problem 18.3

1a. Some teenagers prefer to work as ticket sellers, so the supply of labor in the fast-food market decreases. The supply curve shifts from S_0 to S_1 (Figure 1). The wage rate rises, and the number of fast-food workers employed decreases.

1b. The number of visitors to Greenville increases. The demand for fast food increases, so the demand for fast-food workers increases. The demand curve shifts from D_0 to D_1 (Figure 2). The wage rate increases, and the number of fast-food workers employed increases.

1c. An increase in the number of retirees increases the supply of fast-food labor. The supply curve shifts from S_0 to S_2 (Figure 1). The wage rate falls, and the number of fast-food workers employed increases.

1d. A decrease in the price of fast food decreases the demand for fast-food workers. The demand curve shifts from D_0 to D_2 (Figure 2). The wage rate decreases, and the number of fast-food workers employed decreases.

1e. A decrease in the marginal product of fast-food workers decreases the demand for fast-food workers. The demand curve shifts from D_0 to D_2 (Figure 2). The wage rate falls, and the number of fast-food workers employed decreases.

FIGURE 1

Wage rate (dollars per hour)

Quantity of labor (workers)

FIGURE 2

Wage rate (dollars per hour)

Quantity of labor (workers)

18.4 FINANCIAL MARKETS

Financial markets are the channels through which firms borrow financial resources to buy capital. These financial resources come from saving. The price of financial capital, which adjusts to make the quantity of capital supplied equal to the quantity demanded, is the interest rate.

For most of us, financial markets are where we make our biggest-ticket transactions. We borrow in a financial market to buy a home. And we lend in financial markets to build up a fund on which to live when we retire.

Let's look at demand and supply in financial markets.

■ The Demand for Financial Capital

A firm's demand for *financial* capital stems from its demand for *physical* capital to produce goods and services. And the quantity of *physical* capital that a firm plans to use depends on the price of *financial* capital—the interest rate.

Other things remaining the same, the higher the interest rate, the smaller is the quantity of capital demanded. The quantity of capital demanded decreases if the interest rate rises, other things remaining the same, because the marginal product of capital diminishes as the quantity of capital employed by a firm increases.

For example, suppose that the interest rate is 4 percent a year and Amazon.com is planning to build a $100 million warehouse. The cost of this capital is 4 percent of $100 million, or $4 million a year. Amazon reckons that the value of the marginal product of this warehouse is enough to earn the $4 million a year that the capital will cost. Now suppose that the interest rate rises to 6 percent a year while all other prices remain constant. If Amazon goes ahead with its plan, it will now incur a cost of $6 million a year. In this situation, Amazon scales back its warehouse plans and borrows less.

Two main factors that change the demand for capital are

- Population growth
- Technological change

As the population grows, the demand for all goods and services increases, so the demand for the physical capital that produces them increases. Advances in technology increase the demand for some types of physical capital and decrease the demand for other types. For example, the development of desktop computers increased the demand for office computing equipment, decreased the demand for electric typewriters, and increased the overall demand for capital in the office. So the demand for financial capital increased.

■ The Supply of Financial Capital

The quantity of financial capital supplied results from people's saving decisions. Other things remaining the same, the higher the interest rate, the greater is the quantity of saving supplied.

A dollar saved today grows into a dollar plus interest tomorrow. The higher the interest rate, the greater is the amount that a dollar saved today becomes in the future. Other things remaining the same, if the interest rate rises, the opportunity cost of current consumption increases, so people cut their consumption and increase their saving.

The supply of saving changes if the amount that people want to save at a given interest rate changes. The main influences on the supply of saving are

- Population
- Average income
- Expected future income

An increase in the population increases the supply of saving because it increases the number of potential savers.

Saving converts *current* income into *future* consumption potential. For example, saving can pay for a child's future college education or for consumption during retirement. The higher a household's income, the more it consumes both now and in the future. But to increase *future* consumption, the household must save. So other things remaining the same, the higher a household's income, the more it saves. Most households save a roughly constant proportion of their income. So as income increases, the supply of capital also increases.

Over their lives, most people try to achieve a level of consumption that fluctuates less than their income—that is, they try to smooth out the effects of income fluctuations on consumption. So the amount that a household saves depends not only on its current income but also on its *expected future income*. If a household's current income is high and its expected future income is low, the household will have a high level of saving. But if the household's current income is low and its expected future income is high, the household's saving will be low (perhaps even negative).

EYE ON THE U.S. ECONOMY

Interest Rate Fluctuations

The figure shows the *real interest rate*—which is the interest rate that people *really* earn and pay after adjusting for the fact that inflation lowers the value of money—earned in the stock market and in the bond market in the United States since 1964.

Interest rates fluctuate a lot because the demand for capital fluctuates much more than does the supply of capital. When rapid technological change brings an increase in the demand for capital, the real interest rate rises, as it did during the 1990s. When the demand for capital grows slowly or decreases temporarily, the real interest rate falls, as it did in 1975.

SOURCE OF DATA: *Economic Report of the President,* 2005 and the Bureau of Economic Analysis.

The real interest rate earned on stocks is more volatile than that on bonds, but the average real interest rate on stocks is higher.

Young people (especially students) usually have low current incomes compared with their expected future incomes. They often consume more than they earn and go into debt. In middle age, most people's incomes reach a peak. At this stage in life, their current income is large and their expected future income is small because they anticipate stopping full-time work during their sixties. At this stage of life, saving is at a maximum. After retirement, people spend part of the wealth they have accumulated during their working lives, so saving falls again.

■ Financial Market Equilibrium and the Interest Rate

Figure 18.6 illustrates financial market equilibrium. The demand curve, *KD*, shows the relationship between the total quantity of financial capital demanded and the interest rate, other things remaining the same. And the supply curve, *KS*, shows the relationship between the quantity of financial capital supplied and the interest rate, other things remaining the same. Here, the equilibrium interest rate is 6 percent a year, and the quantity of capital is $200 billion.

Over time, the demand for capital and the supply of capital increase and the demand curve and the supply curve shift rightward. Population growth increases the demand for capital. And as the increased population earns a larger income, the supply of capital increases. Technological advances increase the demand for capital and bring higher incomes, which in turn increase the supply of capital. Because both the demand for capital and the supply of capital increase over time, the quantity of capital increases but the interest rate does not persistently increase or decrease (see *Eye on the U.S. Economy* on p. 460).

■ FIGURE 18.6

Financial Market Equilibrium

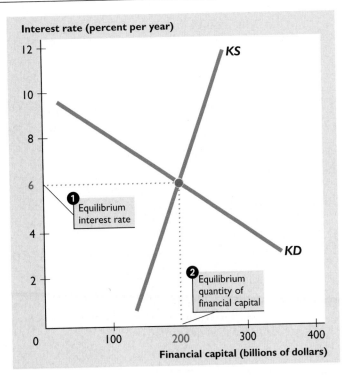

The demand for financial capital is *KD*, and the supply of financial capital is *KS*. Market equilibrium occurs at **1** an interest rate of 6 percent a year with a **2** quantity of financial capital of $200 billion.

4 Explain how interest rates, borrowing, and lending are determined.

Practice Problem 18.4

1. Wendy plans to open a Starbucks coffee shop. To do so, she will need $50,000 to buy the franchise and $20,000 to outfit the coffee shop. Wendy has $15,000 in her bank account, and the current interest rate is 5 percent a year.
   a. What is Wendy's opportunity cost of opening the coffee shop?
   b. What is the quantity of financial capital that Wendy plans to get from the financial market?
   c. What is the quantity of financial capital that Wendy plans to provide herself?
   d. If demand for financial capital increases just when Wendy plans to go to the financial market, what will happen to her opportunity cost of the coffee shop? Explain your answer.
   e. If the supply of financial capital increases just when Wendy plans to go to the financial market, what will happen to her opportunity cost of the coffee shop? Explain your answer.

Exercise 18.4

1. Lou operates an avocado orchard. He plans to buy trees that will cost $20,000. He also plans to hire some workers to help run the orchard. The wage rate for orchard workers is currently $8 an hour, and he will need to hire 100 hours of labor a week. The interest rate is 3 percent a year. Lou has no savings.
   a. What is the cost of the capital in Lou's orchard?
   b. Lou predicts that in the first 50 weeks, he will harvest no avocados. How much financial capital is Lou planning to get from the financial market?
   c. If an avocado-picking machine becomes available that allows Lou to replace the workers and that costs $10,000, how much financial capital will Lou now need to get from the financial market?

Solution to Practice Problem 18.4

1a. Wendy's opportunity cost is 5 percent of the cost of the coffee shop, which is 5 percent of $70,000 or $3,500 a year.
1b. Wendy needs $70,000 but has $15,000, so the quantity of financial capital that she requires is $55,000 ($70,000 minus $15,000).
1c. Wendy plans to provide $15,000 herself.
1d. An increase in the demand for capital will increase the interest rate. The interest rate that Wendy has to pay will exceed 5 percent a year and increase the opportunity cost of her coffee shop.
1e. An increase in the supply of capital will decrease the interest rate. Wendy will pay less than 5 percent a year for her financial capital and decrease the opportunity cost of her coffee shop.

18.5 LAND AND NATURAL RESOURCE MARKETS

All natural resources are called *land*, and they fall into two categories:

* Renewable
* Nonrenewable

Renewable natural resources are natural resources that can be used repeatedly such as forestland—land in its everyday sense. **Nonrenewable natural resources** are resources that can be used only once and that cannot be replaced once they have been used. Examples are coal, natural gas, and oil—called hydrocarbon fuels.

Let's look first at the market for a renewable natural resource.

Renewable natural resources
Natural resources that can be used repeatedly.

Nonrenewable natural resources
Natural resources that can be used only once and that cannot be replaced once they have been used.

■ The Market for Land (Renewable Natural Resources)

The demand for land is based on the same factors as the demand for labor and the demand for capital. The lower the rent, other things remaining the same, the greater is the quantity of land demanded.

But the supply of land is special: The quantity is fixed, so the quantity supplied cannot be changed by people's decisions. People can vary the amount of land they own. But when one person buys some land, another person sells it. The aggregate quantity of land supplied of a particular type and in a particular location is fixed. This fact means that the supply of each particular block of land is *perfectly inelastic*. Figure 18.7 illustrates the supply of a 10-acre block on Chicago's "Magnificent Mile." The quantity supplied is 10 acres regardless of the rent.

■ FIGURE 18.7

A Market for Land

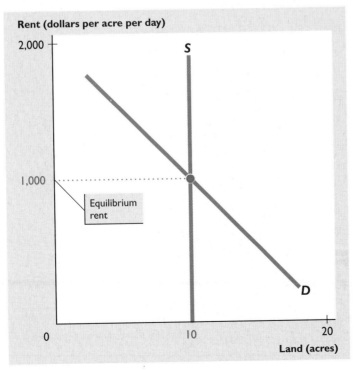

The demand curve for a 10-acre block of land is *D*, and the supply curve is *S*. Equilibrium occurs at a rent of $1,000 an acre per day.

Because the quantity of land supplied is fixed, the rent is determined by demand. In Figure 18.7, the demand curve is D and the equilibrium price (rent) is $1,000 an acre per day. The greater the demand, the higher is the rent.

■ Economic Rent and Opportunity Cost

Rent is a special kind of income because the resource that receives a rent would be available even if the rent were zero. Low demand would make the rent low, and high demand would make the rent high. But the quantity of land wouldn't change.

Land is not the only resource that is in fixed supply. Some human resources are too. There is only one Tiger Woods. This extraordinary golfer earns a large income because he has a high value of marginal product. A large part of Tiger Woods's income is called "economic rent." **Economic rent** is the income received by *any* factor of production over and above the amount required to induce a given quantity of the factor to be supplied. The income that is required to induce the supply of a given quantity of a factor of production is its *opportunity cost*—the value of the factor of production in its next best use.

Figure 18.8 illustrates the economic rent and opportunity cost components of a factor's income. Suppose that the demand curve for Tiger's time were D and his supply curve were S. The wage rate would be $50,000 an hour, and Tiger would work 40 hours a week. His income is the sum of the red and green areas. The red area below the supply curve measures opportunity cost, and the green area above the supply curve but below the resource price measures economic rent.

Economic rent
The income received by *any* factor of production over and above the amount required to induce a given quantity of the factor to be supplied.

■ **FIGURE 18.8**
Economic Rent and Opportunity Cost

myeconlab

Part of the income of a factor of production is ❶ opportunity cost (the red area), and part is ❷ economic rent (the green area). The figure shows the market for Tiger Woods's labor. At $50,000 an hour, Tiger is willing to work 40 hours a week. Tiger earns a large economic rent.

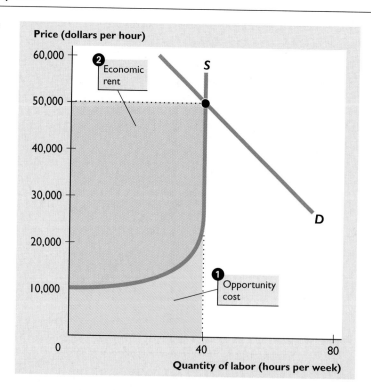

■ The Supply of a Nonrenewable Natural Resource

At a given time, the quantity of any natural resource is fixed and is independent of its price. Over time, the quantity of a nonrenewable natural resource decreases as it is used up. But the *known* quantity of a natural resource increases because advances in technology enable ever less accessible sources of the resource to be discovered.

Using a natural resource decreases its supply, which causes its price to rise. But new technologies that lead to the discovery of previously unknown reserves increase supply, which causes the price to fall. Also, new technologies that enable a more efficient use of a nonrenewable natural resource decrease demand, which causes the price to fall.

Historically, the forces that bring lower prices have outweighed those that bring higher prices and natural resource prices have fallen. Adjusted for inflation, the prices of metals, for example, fell by more than 50 percent between 1970 and 2005. Again, adjusted for inflation, even the price of crude oil was lower in 2005 than it had been at its peak in 1980.

You've now seen how competitive factor markets work. In the next chapter, we look more closely at the labor market and the reasons for earnings differences.

REALITY CHECK

Factor Markets in YOUR Life

Would you like to be a millionaire? If you would, it is in factor markets that you are going to make it happen.

You might come up with a $1 million idea that you develop with your entrepreneurial skills. In this case, you'll be hiring factors of production—borrowing to finance capital expenditures and hiring labor.

But the surest way of becoming a millionaire is by saving. If starting at age 25 you save $66 a week and earn an interest rate of 8 percent a year (which is less than the average of the past 30 years), how long do you think it will take you to accumulate $1 million? The answer is 40 years.

You will have saved $137,000—that is $66 multiplied by 2080 weeks—and you will have earned almost $870,000 in interest on your savings (and interest on your interest).

With a bit of financial planning, you can probably manage to save more than $66 a week, and much more if your earnings rise as you get older. By making the capital market work for you, you can grow a few dollars a week into $1 million.

5 Explain how rents and natural resource prices are determined.

Practice Problem 18.5

1. Which of the following items are nonrenewable natural resources, which are renewable natural resources, and which are not natural resources? Explain your answers.
   a. Beaches in Florida
   b. Lake Powell
   c. The Empire State Building
   d. Silver mines in Arizona
   e. The Great Lakes
   f. National parks
   g. Redwood forests
   h. The Statue of Liberty

Exercises 18.5

1. New technology has allowed oil to be pumped from much deeper offshore oil fields than before. For example, 28 deep ocean rigs operate in the deep waters of the Gulf of Mexico. What effect do you think deep ocean sources have had on the world oil price? Who will benefit from drilling for oil in the Gulf of Mexico? Explain your answer.

2. Water is a natural resource that is plentiful in Canada but not plentiful in Arizona and southern California. If Canadians start to export bulk water to Arizona and southern California, what do you predict will be the effect on the price of bulk water? Will Canada eventually run out of water?

3. In the 1970s, few people drank bottled spring water and the major producers of bottled spring water were in Europe. Today, lots of people drink bottled spring water. How has this increase in the demand for spring water been satisfied? Will this increase in demand lead to some springs running dry?

4. As cities grow, good farmland is being replaced by urban sprawl. Why do farmers sell their land to urban developers?

Solution to Practice Problem 18.5

1. Natural resources include all the gifts of nature. A nonrenewable natural resource is one that once used cannot be used again. A renewable natural resource is one that can be used repeatedly.

   Nonrenewable natural resources include silver mines in Arizona.

   Renewable natural resources include beaches in Florida, Lake Powell, the Great Lakes, national parks, and redwood forests.

   The Empire State Building and the Statue of Liberty are national landmarks, but they are not natural resources. Labor and capital were used to build the Empire State Building. The Statue of Liberty was a gift from France and not a gift of nature.

CHAPTER CHECKPOINT

Key Points

1 **Describe the anatomy of the markets for labor, capital, and land.**

- Labor is traded on job contracts.
- Financial markets provide the funds that are used to buy physical capital.
- Natural resources are traded in land markets and commodity markets.

2 **Explain how the value of marginal product determines the demand for a factor of production.**

- The demand for a factor of production is a derived demand—it is derived from the demand for the goods and services that the factor of production is used to produce.
- The quantity of a factor of production that is demanded depends on its price and the value of its marginal product, which equals the price of the product multiplied by marginal product.

3 **Explain how wage rates and employment are determined.**

- Wage rates are determined by demand and supply in labor markets.
- Changes in technology bring changes in the allocation of labor.

4 **Explain how interest rates, borrowing, and lending are determined.**

- Interest rates are determined by demand and supply in financial markets.
- Real interest rates on stocks are higher on the average but fluctuate by more than those on bonds.

5 **Explain how rents and natural resource prices are determined.**

- Rents and natural resource prices are determined by demand and supply in land and commodity markets.
- Nonrenewable natural resource prices have fallen because technological change has led to the discovery of new sources and made the use of natural resources more productive.

Key Terms

Bond, 447
Bond market, 447
Commodity market, 448
Derived demand, 449
Economic rent, 464

Factor price, 446
Financial capital, 447
Financial market, 447
Job, 446
Labor market, 446

Nonrenewable natural resources, 463
Renewable natural resources, 463
Stock market, 447
Value of marginal product, 449

Exercises

1. Through the 1990s, the percentage of high school students who decided to go to college increased. What effect do you predict that this increase has had on the market for
   a. College graduates? Draw a demand-supply graph to illustrate your answer.
   b. College professors? Explain your answer.
   c. High school graduates? Draw a demand-supply graph to illustrate your answer.

2. If your college switched to online delivery of its courses, what changes do you predict would occur in the factor markets in the town where your college is located?

3. A California asparagus farmer is maximizing profit. The price of asparagus is $2 a box, a farm worker's wage rate is $12 an hour, and the asparagus farm employs six workers.
   a. What is the marginal product of the sixth farm worker?
   b. Is the marginal product of the fifth worker greater or less than the marginal product of the sixth?
   c. If, when the price of asparagus rises to $3 a box, the farm hires eight workers, what is the marginal product of the eighth worker?

4. Suppose that Palm Island is the world's largest grower of coconuts and the interest rate on Palm Island is 3 percent a year. The following events occur, one at a time:
   a. Palm Island plans to build a $100 million airport on 100 acres—its first airport.
   b. Palm Island plans to double its population in 3 years by hiring well-educated people from the United States.
   c. The world price of coconuts is expected to increase by 200 percent next year and remain high for the next decade.
   d. Palm Island is short of entrepreneurs and plans to allow anyone with $1 million to immigrate to Palm Island.

   Explain the influence of each event on Palm Island's financial market and land market.

5. Use the laws of demand and supply in factor markets to explain whether the following statements are true or false:
   a. New technology enables tomato growers to pick and pack tomatoes by machine. Tomato growers will now hire fewer workers and will be able to hire these workers at a lower wage rate than before.
   b. If soccer becomes more popular in the United States and basketball becomes less popular, basketball players will earn more than they do today.
   c. A recent new discovery of diamonds in the Yukon in Canada will lower the world price of diamonds and lower the wage rate paid to diamond workers in South Africa.
   d. As cars become more and more fuel efficient, the price of gasoline at the pump will fall.

6. Suppose that a tax is imposed on college and university tuition and the revenue generated is spent on making payments to firms that provide on-the-job training for low-skilled labor. Draw diagrams to show what happens to the demand for labor, the supply of labor, and the equilibrium wage rate in the markets for
   a. College graduates.
   b. Industrial workers with skills acquired on the job.
   c. College professors.
   d. Skilled industrial workers.

7. The personal saving rate has fallen in recent years in the United States.
   a. What are some of the factors that might have contributed to the fall?
   b. Of the factors that you identified in part **a,** which have changed the quantity of saving supplied and which have changed the supply of saving?
   c. How do you expect the fall in the saving rate to have affected the real interest rate?

8. During the years after World War II, there was a big increase in the birth rate that created the so-called baby boom generation. That generation is fast approaching retirement age.
   a. What do you predict will happen to the saving rate when the baby boom generation retires?
   b. How will the real interest rate be affected?
   c. Do you expect production to become more capital intensive?

9. Since 1983, the United States has borrowed $4 trillion from the rest of the world that has financed capital expenditures.
   a. Draw a demand-supply graph of the U.S. capital market to show the effects of this inflow of funds from abroad on the quantity of capital, the real interest rate, and the amount of domestic saving.
   b. Draw a graph of the U.S. labor market to show the effects of this inflow of funds from abroad on the quantity of labor employed and the real wage rate.
   c. Show the effects in your demand-supply graph of the U.S. capital market if the government restricted the amount that firms were permitted to borrow from abroad.
   d. Show the effects in your demand-supply graph of the U.S. labor market if the government restricted the amount that firms were permitted to borrow from abroad.

10. Hong Kong is much more densely populated than the United States is. How do you think the rent on land compares in Hong Kong with that in Chicago? Can you explain why the percentage of commercial buildings that are new in downtown Chicago is less than in Hong Kong?

11. "As more people buy Internet service, the price of Internet service will fall. The fall in the price of Internet service will lead to a fall in the wage rate paid to Web page designers." Is this statement true or false? Explain your answer.

12. Draw demand-supply graphs of the U.S. labor markets and capital markets to show the effects of the increased provision of airport security following the September 11, 2001, attacks.

Critical Thinking

13. In 1811, in England, the real wage rate of young, unskilled mill workers was cut. The workers, led by Ned Ludd and known as Luddites, broke into factories at night and destroyed the new machines that their employers were using.
    a. If technological change increases productivity, why didn't the development of new cotton and wool milling technologies at the beginning of the 1800s increase rather than decrease the wage rate of mill workers?
    b. Do you think any workers benefited from the advance in technology in the cotton and wool industries of the early 1800s?
    c. How do you think the actions of the Luddites affected the wage rate of unskilled mill workers?
    d. Write a note to Ned Ludd explaining why he would or would not be wise to encourage people to destroy machines. (Ignore the fact that the actions of the Luddites were illegal.)

14. What parallels can you see between the introduction of machines in the cotton mills and wool mills of the early 1800s and the introduction of computers in the telecommunications industry at the end of the 1900s? Consider the effects on the demand for labor in all the markets affected.

15. Explain why you think that technological changes that lower wage rates justify or do not justify minimum wage laws.

 ## Web Exercises

Use the links on MyEconLab to work the following exercises.

16. Visit the Web site of monster.com.
    a. Create your free user account.
    b. Search for a job that interests you.
    c. Are there any jobs that match your interests?
    d. Who pays for monster.com?

17. Visit the Web site of the New York Stock Exchange.
    a. What happened to the prices of stocks on the average over this day?
    b. Find the price of the stock of a company that interests you.
    c. Is the stock of the company you've chosen performing better or worse than average? Why do you think that might be?

18. Visit the Web site of the U.S. Open tennis tournament and look at the prize money lists for men's and women's singles, doubles, and mixed doubles. Also visit the PGA to check the prize money for the 2005 PGA championship and the LPGA to check the prize money for the LPGA.
    a. What main differences and similarities do you notice between the earnings of women and men in tennis and golf?
    b. How might you use the theory of the labor market that you've learned in this chapter to explain the differences and similarities?
    c. In particular, why do you think women earn the same as men in tennis but much less than men in golf? (Note that in tennis, men play longer matches than women but in golf, both sexes play the same type of course.)

Inequality and Poverty

CHAPTER CHECKLIST

When you have completed your study of this chapter,
you will be able to

1 Describe the economic inequality and poverty in the **United States.**

2 Explain how economic inequality and poverty arise.

3 Explain why governments redistribute income and describe the effects
of redistribution on economic inequality and poverty.

Billionaires Michael Bloomberg (New York City mayor) and Rupert Murdoch (CEO of News Corp, which owns Fox News and movie studios) are watching the sun setting across the Hudson River and the city skyline beyond from a penthouse high above Central Park. The temperature is falling and on the street below this mansion in the sky, a small group of men and women huddle in a shop doorway to escape the biting wind. Tonight, they will sleep in cardboard boxes and seek warmth from subway grates. They are frostbitten, hungry, and lonely. They have neither jobs, homes, nor hope.

Why are some people exceedingly rich while others are very poor? Are the rich getting richer and the poor getting poorer? How do taxes, social security, welfare, and health-care programs influence economic inequality?

The goal of this chapter is to examine these emotion-charged questions using the dispassionate tools of economics. You will learn how we measure economic inequality, how it arises, and how government actions influence it.

19.1 ECONOMIC INEQUALITY IN THE UNITED STATES

We measure economic inequality by looking at the distributions of income and wealth. A household's *income* is the amount that it receives in a given period. A household's *wealth* is the value of the things it owns at a point in time.

Imagine the population of the United States lined up from the lowest to the highest income earner. Now divide the line into five equal-sized groups, each with 20 percent of the population. Then share out total income among these groups so that the shares represent the U.S. income distribution. Table 19.1(a) lists the percentages received by each group. The lowest 20 percent receives 3.4 percent of total income, while the richest 20 percent receives 50 percent.

Next share out the pie of total wealth. Table 19.1(b) shows the percentages owned by each of seven groups. The poorest 40 percent owns 0.2 percent of total wealth, while the richest 1 percent owns 38.1 percent.

■ Lorenz Curves

Lorenz curve

A curve that graphs the cumulative percentage of income (or wealth) against the cumulative percentage of households.

A **Lorenz curve** graphs the cumulative percentage of income (or wealth) on the *y*-axis against the cumulative percentage of households on the *x*-axis. Figure 19.1 shows the Lorenz curves for income and wealth in the United States. Graphing the cumulative percentage of income against the cumulative percentage of households makes the Lorenz curve for income and the points *A* to *D* on the graph correspond to the rows identified by those letters in the table. For example, row *B* and point *B* show that the 40 percent of households with the lowest incomes received 12.1 percent of total income—3.4 percent plus 8.7 percent from Table 19.1(a).

■ TABLE 19.1

The Income Distribution and Wealth Distribution in the United States

(a) Income distribution in 2004: median household income $44,389

	Households		Income	
	Percentage	Cumulative percentage	Percentage	Cumulative percentage
A	Lowest 20	20	3.4	3.4
B	Second 20	40	8.7	12.1
C	Third 20	60	14.7	26.8
D	Fourth 20	80	23.2	50.0
E	Highest 20	100	50.0	100.0

(b) Wealth distribution in 1998: median household wealth $60,700

	Households		Wealth	
	Percentage	Cumulative percentage	Percentage	Cumulative percentage
A'	Lowest 40	40	0.2	0.2
B'	Next 20	60	4.5	4.7
C'	Next 20	80	11.9	16.6
D'	Next 10	90	12.5	29.1
E'	Next 5	95	11.5	40.6
F'	Next 4	99	21.3	61.9
G'	Highest 1	100	38.1	100.0

SOURCES OF DATA: DeNavas-Walt, Carmen, Bernadette D. Proctor, and Cheryl Hill Lee, U.S. Census Bureau, Current Population Reports, P60–229, *Income, Poverty, and Health Insurance Coverage in the United States: 2004*, U.S. Government Printing Office, Washington, DC, 2005, and Edward N. Wolff, "Recent Trends in Wealth Ownership, 1983–1998," Jerome Levy Economics Institute Working Paper No. 300, April 2000.

FIGURE 19.1

Lorenz Curves for Income and Wealth in the United States

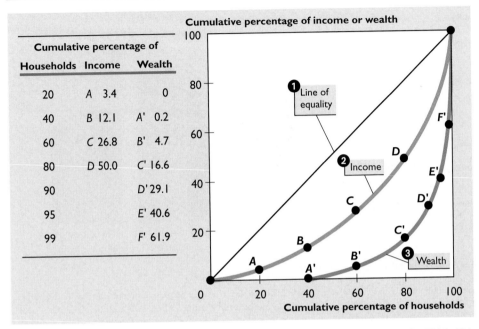

Cumulative percentage of		
Households	Income	Wealth
20	A 3.4	0
40	B 12.1	A' 0.2
60	C 26.8	B' 4.7
80	D 50.0	C' 16.6
90		D' 29.1
95		E' 40.6
99		F' 61.9

① If income and wealth were distributed equally, the Lorenz curve would lie along the straight line labeled "Line of equality."

② The income Lorenz curve shows the cumulative percentage of income graphed against the cumulative percentage of households. The 20 percent of households with the lowest incomes received 3.4 percent of total income, and the 20 percent of households with the highest incomes received 50 percent.

③ The wealth Lorenz curve shows the cumulative percentage of wealth graphed against the cumulative percentage of households. The poorest 40 percent of households owned 0.2 percent of total wealth, and the richest 1 percent owned 38.1 percent.

SOURCES OF DATA: See Table 19.1.

Graphing the cumulative percentage of wealth against the cumulative percentage of households makes the Lorenz curve for wealth and the points A' to F' on the graph correspond to the rows identified by those letters in the table of Figure 19.1. For example, row C' and point C' show that the poorest 80 percent of households owned 16.6 percent of total wealth—0.2 percent plus 4.5 percent plus 11.9 percent from Table 19.1(b).

If income (or wealth) were distributed equally, each 1 percent of households would receive 1 percent of total income (or own 1 percent of total wealth), and the cumulative percentage of income received (or wealth owned) by a given cumulative percentage of households would fall along the straight line labeled "Line of equality." The Lorenz curve is always below this line, and the closer the Lorenz curve is to the line of equality, the more equal is the distribution. You can see that the Lorenz curve for wealth is much farther away from the line of equality than is the Lorenz curve for income. The distribution of wealth is much more unequal than is the distribution of income.

■ Inequality over Time

Has U.S. income inequality increased or decreased over the past few decades? It has increased. The highest incomes have increased much faster than the lower incomes and the gap between the rich and the poor has widened.

Figure 19.2(a) shows this widening gap by looking at the average incomes of each 20 percent (or quintile) group between 1967 and 2004. The numbers are expressed in 2004 dollars, which means that the effects of rising prices have been removed from the data. These numbers show us the changes in the real volumes of goods and services that people can afford to buy.

■ **FIGURE 19.2**

Trends in the Distribution of Income and Economic Mobility

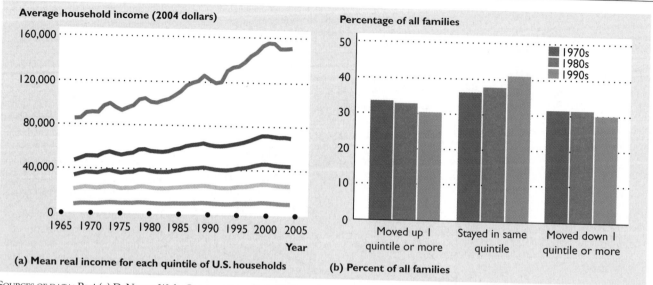

(a) Mean real income for each quintile of U.S. households

(b) Percent of all families

SOURCES OF DATA: Part (a) DeNavas-Walt, Carmen, Bernadette D. Proctor, and Cheryl Hill Lee, U.S. Census Bureau, Current Population Reports, P60-229, *Income, Poverty, and Health Insurance Coverage in the United States: 2004*, U.S. Government Printing Office, Washington, DC, 2005; part (b) Katharine Bradbury and Jane Katz, "Are lifetime incomes becoming more unequal? Looking at new evidence on family income mobility," *Regional Review*, Federal Reserve Bank of Boston, Volume 12, Number 4, Quarter 4 2002, pp. 2–5.

In part (a), the average income of the highest 20 percent group increased from $85,000 a year in 1967 to $152,000 a year in 2004, a 77 percent increase. The average income of the lowest 20 percent group increased from $7,700 a year in 1967 to $10,300 a year in 2004, a 34 percent increase. The average income of the three middle groups also increased by 34 percent between 1967 and 2004.

In part (b), over a ten-year period, about 30 percent of families move up a quintile or more and a similar percentage move down a quintile or more. Between 35 and 40 percent of families remain in the same quintile. Mobility through the quintiles has decreased over the 1980s and 1990s.

You can see that the highest quintile have seen their incomes grow from about $85,000 a year in 1967 to $152,000 a year in 2004, a 77 percent increase. In contrast, the lowest quintile have seen their incomes grow from about $7,700 a year in 1967 to $10,300 a year in 2004, a 34 percent increase. The three middle quintiles have seen their incomes increase by a similar percentage to that of the lowest quintile.

■ **Economic Mobility**

Economic mobility is the movement of a family up or down the income ladder and through the income quintiles. If there were no economic mobility, a family would be stuck at a given point in the income distribution and be persistently poor, or rich, or somewhere in the middle. Also, in such a situation, the data on annual income distribution would be a good indicator of life-time inequality.

But if there is economic mobility, families move upward or downward through the income distribution and life-time inequality is not as severe as the inequality apparent in the data for a single year. How much economic mobility is there?

Katharine Bradbury and Jane Katz, economists at the Federal Reserve Bank of Boston, have provided an answer to this question and Figure 19.2(b) shows what they found. The figure shows the percentages of families that moved up or down the income ladder by one quintile or more over a ten-year period. It also shows the percentage of families that remained in the same quintile.

You can see from Figure 19.2(b) that there is quite a lot of economic mobility. About 30 percent of families move up by a quintile or more during a decade and a slightly smaller percentage move down by a quintile or more. Between 35 percent and 40 percent of families remain in the same quintile.

What is the source of economic mobility? Much of it arises from normal changes over a family's life cycle. Most families start out with a low income and are in one of the bottom three quintiles. Many of these families experience income growth as their workers become more skilled and experienced and in some cases, income grows by enough to move the family up a quintile or more. As a family continues to get older and its workers retire, its income falls. At this stage, some families move down a quintile or more.

So if we look at three households that have identical lifetime incomes—that are *economically equal*—but one is young, one is middle-aged, and one is old, we will see a great deal of inequality. Inequality of annual incomes overstates the degree of lifetime inequality.

You've seen that income inequality is increasing. But is economic mobility also increasing? The data in Figure 19.2(b) answer this question. And they show a

EYE ON THE GLOBAL ECONOMY

Global Inequality

Global incomes are rising and by some estimates, inequality is decreasing. But other estimates suggest that global inequality, like U.S. inequality, is increasing. Better data are needed to settle this issue.

There is much more income inequality in the global economy than in the United States. The Lorenz curves in this figure provide a comparative picture. You can see that the global Lorenz curve lies much farther from the line of equality than does the U.S. Lorenz curve.

Numbers that highlight the comparison are the percentages of families that get a half (50 percent) of the income. In the United States, the top 20 percent of families get a half of the income and the remaining 80 percent share the other half. In the global economy the top 10 percent of families get a half of the income and the remaining 90 percent share the other half.

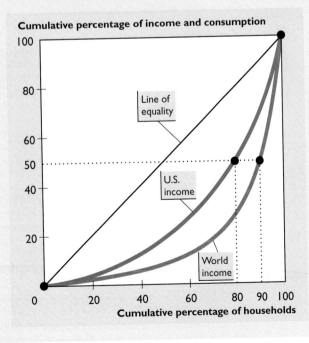

SOURCES OF DATA: U.S. see Figure 19.1. World, Branko Milanovic, "True World Income Distribution, 1988 and 1993: First Calculation Based on Household Surveys Alone", *Economic Journal*, 112, 2002.

trend toward less economic mobility, not more. A decreasing percentage of families is moving either up or down a quintile or more and an increasing percentage of families is remaining in the same quintile. Why economic mobility has decreased remains a question for future research.

■ Who Are the Rich and the Poor?

The lowest-income household in the United States today is likely to consist of a black woman over 65 years of age who lives alone somewhere in the South and has fewer than nine years of elementary school education. The highest-income household in the United States today is likely to consist of a college-educated white married couple between 45 and 54 years of age living together with two children somewhere in the Northeast or the West.

These snapshot profiles are the extremes in Figure 19.3. That figure illustrates the importance of education, size of household, marital status, age of householder, race, and region of residence in influencing the size of a household's income. The range arising from education differences is the largest—from $18,800 a year for people with less than grade 9 to $76,000 a year for people with a bachelor's degree or higher. Household size, marital status, and age are also important. Race and region of residence have much smaller effects than do these first four factors.

■ FIGURE 19.3

The Distribution of Income by Selected Household Characteristics in 2004

Education is the single biggest factor affecting the distribution of household income, but size of household, marital status, and age of householder are also important. Race and region of residence also play a role.

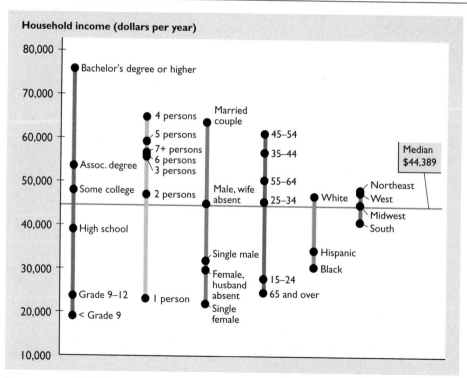

SOURCE OF DATA: U.S. Bureau of the Census, Current Population Reports, P60–218, 2001; P60–229, 2004 (see Table 19.1 for details.)

■ Poverty

Households with very low incomes are so poor that they are considered to be living in poverty. What is poverty? How do we measure it, how much is there, and is the amount of poverty decreasing or increasing?

Poverty Defined

Poverty is a state in which a household's income is too low to be able to buy the quantities of food, shelter, and clothing that are deemed necessary. Poverty is a *relative* concept. Millions of people living in Africa and Asia survive on incomes of less than $400 a year. Almost no one in the United States experiences this degree of poverty. But there are some very poor people in the United States compared with the average.

Measurement, Incidence, and Trends

To measure the degree of poverty, the Census Bureau considers a household to be living in poverty if its income is less than some defined level. The level varies with household size and is updated each year. In 2004, the poverty level for a household with 2 adults and 2 children was an income of $19,157. In that year, 37 million or 12.7 percent of Americans lived in households that had incomes below the poverty level.

   Figure 19.4 shows the level, trends in, and distribution by race of poverty in the United States. Black and Hispanic households are more than twice as likely to be poor as are white households. In 2004, the poverty rates were 10.8 percent for whites, 24.7 percent for blacks, and 21.9 percent for Hispanics.

Poverty
A state in which a household's income is too low to be able to buy the quantities of food, shelter, and clothing that are deemed necessary.

■ **FIGURE 19.4**

Poverty Rates in the United States

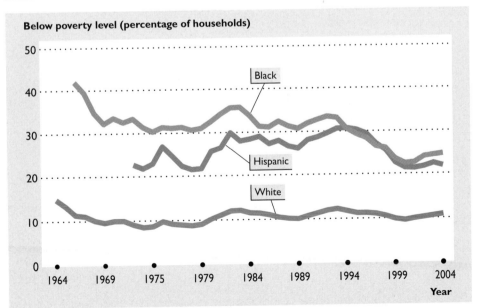

Poverty rates for blacks and Hispanics were about double those for whites in 2004. The poverty rate of black households has fallen in two waves: the late 1960s and the late 1990s. The poverty rate of Hispanics also fell during the late 1990s, but it had previously increased. The poverty rate of whites fell during the 1960s but then remained fairly steady.

SOURCE OF DATA: U.S. Bureau of the Census, *Income, Poverty, and Health Insurance Coverage in the United States: 2004*, Current Population Reports, P60–229.

The trends in poverty have been downward—and strikingly so during the late 1990s for black and Hispanic households. The poverty rate of black households had also fallen during the late 1960s. So between 1965 and 2004, the poverty rate for blacks halved. The fall in the poverty rate of Hispanic households during the late 1990s came after a previous increase, so the poverty rate of this group was the same in 2004 as it had been 30 years earlier.

Poverty Duration

Another dimension of poverty is its duration. If a household is in poverty for a few months it faces serious hardship during those months, but it faces a less serious problem than it would if its poverty persisted for several months or, worse yet, for several years.

Because the duration of poverty is an important additional indicator of the hardship that poverty brings, the Census Bureau has provided measures of duration for the years 1996 to 1999. Figure 19.5 shows these data.

It turns out that more than 50 percent of poverty lasts for between 2 and 4 months. So for about a half of poor families, their most severe problems are not persistent. But almost 30 percent of poverty lasts for more than 9 months. So a seriously large number of households experience chronic poverty.

In the next sections, we look at the sources of inequality and poverty and the policies that aim to redistribute income and lift the living standard of the poor.

■ FIGURE 19.5

The Duration of Poverty Spells in the United States

More than 50 percent of the people who fall below the poverty level remain in that state for 2 to 4 months. Almost 30 percent of the people who fall below the poverty level remain in that state for more than 9 months.

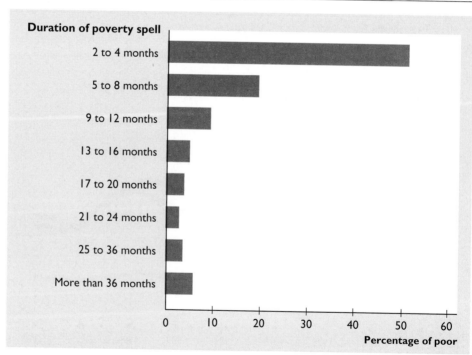

SOURCE OF DATA: U.S. Bureau of the Census, *Dynamics of Economic Well-Being: Poverty 1996–1999,* Current Population Reports, P70–91.

CHECKPOINT 19.1

 Describe the economic inequality and poverty in the United States.

Practice Problem 19.1

1. Table 19.1(a) on page 472 shows the distribution of income in the United States. Table 1 shows the distribution of income in Canada:
   a. Create a table that shows the cumulative percentages of households and income in Canada.
   b. Draw the Lorenz curves for Canada and the United States.
   c. Compare the distribution of income in Canada with that in the United States. Which distribution is more unequal?

TABLE 1

Households	Income (percentage)
Lowest 20 percent	7.4
Second 20 percent	13.2
Third 20 percent	18.1
Fourth 20 percent	24.9
Highest 20 percent	36.4

Exercise 19.1

1. Table 19.1(a) on page 472 shows the distribution of income in the United States, the table in the practice problem above shows the distribution of income in Canada, and Table 2 shows the distribution of income in the United Kingdom:
   a. Create a table that shows the cumulative percentages of households and income in the United Kingdom.
   b. Draw the Lorenz curves for the United Kingdom, Canada, and the United States.
   c. Compare the distribution of income in the United Kingdom with that in the United States. Which distribution is more unequal?
   d. Compare the distribution of income in the United Kingdom with that in Canada. Which distribution is more unequal?

TABLE 2

Households	Income (percentage)
Lowest 20 percent	3
Second 20 percent	5
Third 20 percent	14
Fourth 20 percent	25
Highest 20 percent	53

Solution to Practice Problem 19.1

1a. The following table shows the cumulative percentages of households and income.

Households	Income (percentage)	Cumulative percentage of Households	Income
Lowest 20 percent	7.4	Lowest 20	7.4
Second 20 percent	13.2	Lowest 40	20.6
Third 20 percent	18.1	Lowest 60	38.7
Fourth 20 percent	24.9	Lowest 80	63.6
Highest 20 percent	36.4	100	100.0

1b. Lorenz curve plots the cumulative percentage of income against the cumulative percentage of households. The blue curve in Figure 1 plots these data.

1c. The line of equality shows an equal distribution. The Canadian Lorenz curve lies closer to the line of equality than does the U.S. Lorenz curve, so the distribution of income in the United States is more unequal than that in Canada.

FIGURE 1

19.2 HOW INEQUALITY AND POVERTY ARISE

Economic inequality and poverty arise from a wide variety of factors. The five key ones that we'll examine here are

- Human capital
- Discrimination
- Financial and physical capital
- Entrepreneurial ability
- Personal and family characteristics

■ Human Capital

Human capital is the accumulated skill and knowledge of human beings. To see how human capital differences affect economic inequality, we'll study an economy with two levels of human capital, which we'll call *high-skilled labor* and *low-skilled labor*. Low-skilled labor might be law clerks, hospital orderlies, or bank tellers, and high-skilled labor might be attorneys, surgeons, or bank CEOs.

The Demand for High-Skilled and Low-Skilled Labor

High-skilled workers can perform tasks that low-skilled workers would perform badly or couldn't even perform at all. Imagine an untrained person doing surgery or piloting an airplane. High-skilled workers have a higher value of marginal product (*VMP*) than low-skilled workers do. As we learned in Chapter 18, a firm's demand for labor curve is derived from and is the same as the firm's value of marginal product of labor curve.

Figure 19.6(a) shows the demand curves for high-skilled and low-skilled labor. At any given employment level, firms are willing to pay a higher wage rate to a high-skilled worker than to a low-skilled worker. The gap between the two wage rates measures the value of marginal product of skill—for example, at an employment level of 2,000 hours, firms are willing to pay a high-skilled worker $25 an hour and a low-skilled worker only $10 an hour, a difference of $15 an hour. Thus the value of marginal product of skill is $15 an hour.

The Supply of High-Skilled and Low-Skilled Labor

Skills are costly to acquire. The opportunity cost of acquiring a skill includes actual expenditures, such as tuition, and costs in the form of lost or reduced earnings while the skill is being acquired. When a person goes to school full time, that cost is the total earnings forgone. But some people acquire skills on the job. Such skill acquisition is called on-the-job training. Usually, a worker who is undergoing on-the-job training is paid a lower wage rate than one who is doing a comparable job but not undergoing training. In such a case, the cost of acquiring the skill is equal to the wage paid to a person not being trained minus the wage paid to a person being trained.

Because skills are costly to acquire, a high-skilled person is not willing to work for the same wage that a low-skilled person is willing to accept. The position of the supply curve of high-skilled workers reflects the cost of acquiring the skill. Figure 19.6(b) shows two supply curves: one of high-skilled workers and the other of low-skilled workers. The supply curve of high-skilled workers is S_H, and that of low-skilled workers is S_L.

FIGURE 19.6
Skill Differentials

In part (a), D_L is the demand curve for low-skilled labor and D_H is the demand curve for high-skilled labor. **❶** The vertical distance between these two curves is the value of marginal product of the skill.

In part (b), S_L is the supply curve of low-skilled workers and S_H is the supply curve of high-skilled workers. **❷** The vertical distance

between these two curves is the required compensation for the cost of acquiring a skill.

In part (c), in equilibrium, low-skilled workers earn a wage rate of $10 an hour and high-skilled workers earn a wage rate of $20 an hour. **❸** The $10 wage differential is the equilibrium effect of acquiring skill.

The high-skilled worker's supply curve lies above the low-skilled worker's supply curve. The vertical distance between the two supply curves is the compensation that high-skilled workers require for the cost of acquiring the skill. For example, suppose that the quantity of low-skilled labor supplied is 2,000 hours at a wage rate of $10 an hour. This wage rate compensates the low-skilled workers mainly for their time on the job. Consider next the supply of high-skilled workers. To induce high-skilled labor to supply 2,000 hours, firms must pay a wage rate of $17 an hour. This wage rate for high-skilled labor is higher than that for low-skilled labor because high-skilled labor must be compensated not only for the time on the job but also for the time and other costs of acquiring the skill.

Wage Rates of High-Skilled and Low-Skilled Labor

To work out the wage rates of high-skilled and low-skilled labor, we have to bring together the effects of skill on the demand for and supply of labor.

Figure 19.6(c) shows the demand curves and the supply curves for high-skilled and low-skilled labor. These curves are the same as those plotted in parts (a) and (b). Equilibrium occurs in the market for low-skilled labor where the supply and demand curves for low-skilled labor intersect. The equilibrium wage rate is $10 an hour, and the quantity of low-skilled labor employed is 2,000 hours. Equilibrium in the market for high-skilled workers occurs where the supply and demand curves for high-skilled workers intersect. The equilibrium wage rate is $20 an hour, and the quantity of high-skilled labor employed is 3,000 hours.

As you can see in Figure 19.6(c), the equilibrium wage rate of high-skilled labor is higher than that of low-skilled labor. There are two reasons why this occurs: First, high-skilled labor has a higher value of marginal product than does low-skilled labor, so at a given wage rate, the quantity of high-skilled labor demanded exceeds that of low-skilled labor. Second, skills are costly to acquire, so at a given wage rate, the quantity of high-skilled labor supplied is less than that of low-skilled labor. The wage differential (in this case, $10 an hour) depends on both the value of marginal product of the skill and the cost of acquiring it. The higher the value of marginal product of the skill, the larger is the vertical distance between the demand curves. The more costly it is to acquire a skill, the larger is the vertical distance between the supply curves. The higher the value of marginal product of the skill and the more costly it is to acquire, the larger is the wage differential between high-skilled and low-skilled workers.

Education and on-the-job training enable people to acquire skills and move up through the income distribution. But education is the most important contributor to a higher income, as you can see in *Eye on the U.S. Economy* below.

Discrimination, which we examine next, is another possible source of economic inequality.

EYE ON THE U.S. ECONOMY

Does Education Pay?

The figure shows that there are large differences in earnings based on the degree of education.

Rates of return on high school and college education have been estimated to be in the range of 5 to 10 percent a year after allowing for inflation, which suggests that a college degree is a better investment than almost any other that a person can undertake.

The gain from graduating from high school is a bit more than $12,000 a year. But the gain from going to college or university and getting a bachelor's degree is greater and brings in an additional $18,000 a year.

Remaining at the university to complete a master's degree (usually one more year of study) brings in an extra

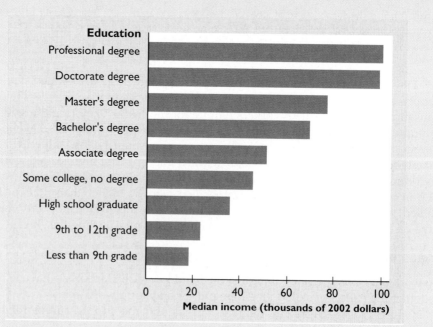

SOURCE OF DATA: U.S. Bureau of the Census, *Statistical Abstract of the United States*, 2004, Table 667.

$7,000 a year, and working for a professional degree or doctorate increases income by more than $22,000 a year.

■ Discrimination

Large and persistent earnings differences exist between women and men and among the races. You can see them in *Eye on the U.S. Economy* below. Does discrimination contribute to these differences? It might. But economists do not yet have the ability to isolate and measure the effect of discrimination, so we can't say exactly whether or by how much the differences arise from this source.

For discrimination to bring persistent wage differences, people must be willing to pay to indulge their prejudices. If they are not willing to pay, then any wage difference would encourage people who are prejudiced to hire (or buy from) the people against whom they are prejudiced. This force would eliminate the wage differences.

But if people are willing to pay to indulge their prejudices, wage differences can persist. For example, suppose that black women and white men have identical abilities as investment advisors. With everyone free of prejudice about race and sex, the two groups have the same value of marginal product, face the same demand curve for their services, and earn the same wage. But if some people are so prejudiced that they are not willing to pay as much for the investment advice of a black woman as they are for that of a white man, then the value of marginal product of black women is lower than that of white men. And the demand for investment advice from black women is lower than that from white men. The result is a lower equilibrium wage rate (and fewer high-paying jobs) for black women than for white men.

EYE ON THE U.S. ECONOMY

Sex and Race Earnings Differences

The figure shows the earnings of different race and sex groups expressed as a percentage of the earnings of white men.

In 2003, white women earned, on the average, 79 percent of what white men earned. Black men earned 78 percent, and black women earned 69 percent. The lowest-income groups, men and women of Hispanic origin, earned only 65 percent and 57 percent, respectively, of white men's wages.

These earnings differentials have persisted over many years, and only those of women have begun to narrow in a significant way

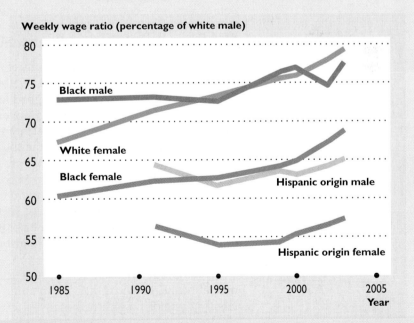

SOURCE OF DATA: U.S. Bureau of the Census, *Statistical Abstract of the United States: 2000*, Table 696 and 2004, Table 623.

■ Financial and Physical Capital

The people with the highest incomes are usually those who own large amounts of financial capital and physical capital. These people receive incomes in the form of interest and dividend payments and from capital gains—increases in the stock market value.

Families with a large amount of capital tend to become even more wealthy across generations for two reasons. First, they bequeath wealth to their children and second, rich people marry rich partners (on the average).

Saving, and the wealth accumulation that it brings, is not inevitably a source of increased inequality and can even be a source of increased equality. When a household saves to redistribute an uneven income over the life cycle, it enjoys more equal consumption. Also, if a lucky generation that has a high income saves a large amount and makes a bequest to a generation that is unlucky, this act of saving also decreases the degree of inequality.

■ Entrepreneurial Ability

Some of the most spectacularly rich people have benefited from unusual entrepreneurial talent. Household names such as Bill Gates (Microsoft), Michael Dell (Dell Computers), and Sam Walton (Wal-Mart) are examples of people who began life with modest amounts of wealth and modest incomes and through a combination of hard work, good luck, and outstanding entrepreneurship have become extremely rich.

But some very poor people, and some who fall below the poverty level, have also tried their hands at being entrepreneurs. We don't hear much about these people. They are not in the headlines. But they have put together a business plan, borrowed heavily, and through a combination of hard work, bad luck, and in some cases poor decisions have become extremely poor.

■ Personal and Family Characteristics

Each individual's personal and family characteristics play a crucial role, for either good or ill, in influencing economic well-being.

People who are exceptionally good looking and talented with stable and creative families enjoy huge advantages over the average person. Many movie stars, entertainers, and extraordinarily talented athletes are in this category. These people enjoy some of the highest incomes because their personal or family characteristics make the value of the marginal product of their labor very large.

Success often breeds yet further success. A large income can generate a large amount of saving, which in turn generates yet more interest income.

Adverse personal circumstances, such as chronic physical or mental illness, drug abuse, or an unstable home life possibly arising from the absence of a parent or from an abusive parent, place a huge burden on many people and result in low incomes and even poverty.

A tough life, just like its opposite, can be self-reinforcing. Weak physical or mental health makes it difficult to study and obtain a skill and results in a low labor income or no income because a job is just too hard to hold down. And the children of the poorest people find it hard to get into college and university and so find it difficult to break the cycle of poverty.

CHECKPOINT 19.2

2 **Explain how economic inequality and poverty arise.**

Practice Problem 19.2

1. In the United States in 2000, 30 million people had full-time managerial and professional jobs that paid an average of $800 a week. At the same time, 10 million people had full-time sales positions that paid an average of $530 a week.
   a. Explain why managers and professionals are paid more than salespeople.
   b. Explain why, despite the higher weekly wage, more people are employed as managers and professionals than as salespeople.
   c. Shopping online has become popular and more and more firms offer their goods and services for sale online. If this trend continues, how do you think the market for salespeople will change in coming years?

Exercises 19.2

1. In the United States in 2000, 2 million people worked full-time in protective services and were paid an average of $600 a week. At the same time, 7 million people worked as full-time machine operators and were paid an average of $450 a week.
   a. Explain why people who are employed in protective services are paid more than machine operators.
   b. Explain why fewer people are employed in protective services than as machine operators.

2. In Canada and Australia, the manager of a manufacturing plant earns 20 times what the factory floor worker earns. In Hong Kong and Malaysia, such a manager earns 40 times what the factory floor worker earns. Can you explain this difference?

Solution to Practice Problem 19.2

1a. A typical manager or professional has incurred a higher cost of education and on-the-job training than has the typical salesperson. The supply curve of managers and professionals, S_H, lies above that of salespeople, S_L (Figure 1). The better education and more on-the-job training result in managers and professionals having more human capital and a higher value of marginal product than that of a salesperson. The demand curve for managers and professionals, D_H, is greater than the demand for salespeople, D_L. Figure 1 shows that the combination of demand and supply leads to a higher wage rate for managers and professionals than for salespeople.

1b. Figure 1 shows that the demand and supply for each type of labor leads to a greater employment for managers and professionals than for salespeople.

1c. As shopping online continues to grow, firms will hire fewer salespeople. The demand for salespeople will decrease, and fewer people will work in sales. What will happen to their wage rate will depend on how the supply of salespeople will change.

FIGURE 1

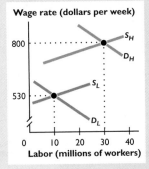

19.3 INCOME REDISTRIBUTION

We've described the distribution of income and wealth in the United States and examined the five main sources of economic inequality and poverty. Our task in the final section of this chapter is to study the *redistribution* of income by government.

How do governments redistribute income? What is the scale of redistribution? Why do we vote for policies that redistribute income? What are the challenges in designing policies that achieve a fair and efficient distribution of income and reduction of poverty?

■ How Governments Redistribute Income

The three main ways in which governments in the United States redistribute income are

- Income taxes
- Income maintenance programs
- Subsidized services

Income Taxes

Income taxes may be progressive, regressive, or proportional (see Chapter 8, p. 201). A *progressive income tax* is one that taxes income at an average rate that increases with the level of income. A *regressive income tax* is one that taxes income at an average rate that decreases with the level of income. A *proportional income tax* (also called a *flat-rate income tax*) is one that taxes income at a constant rate, regardless of the level of income.

The income tax rates that apply in the United States are composed of two parts: federal and state taxes. Some cities, such as New York City, also have an income tax. There is variety in the detailed tax arrangements in the individual states, but the tax system, at both the federal and state levels, is progressive. The poorest working households receive money from the government through an earned income tax credit. The middle-income households pay 15 percent of each additional dollar they earn, and successively richer households pay 25 percent, 28 percent, 33 percent, and 35 percent of each additional dollar earned.

Income Maintenance Programs

Three main types of programs redistribute income by making direct payments (in cash, services, or vouchers) to people in the lower part of the income distribution. They are

- Social Security programs
- Unemployment compensation
- Welfare programs

Social Security Programs   Social Security is a public insurance system paid for by compulsory payroll taxes on employers and employees. Social Security has two main components: Old Age, Survivors, Disability, and Health Insurance or OASDHI, which provides monthly cash payments to retired or disabled workers or their surviving spouses and children; and Medicare, which provides hospital and health insurance for the elderly and disabled. In 2005, Social Security supported 48 million people, who received average monthly checks of $874.

Unemployment Compensation   To provide an income to unemployed workers, every state has established an unemployment compensation program. Under these programs, a tax is paid that is based on the income of each covered worker and such a worker receives a benefit when he or she becomes unemployed. The details of the benefits vary from state to state.

Welfare Programs   The purpose of welfare programs is to provide incomes for people who do not qualify for Social Security or unemployment compensation. The programs are

1. Supplementary Security Income (SSI) program, which is designed to help the neediest elderly, disabled, and blind people

2. Temporary Assistance for Needy Families (TANF) program, which is designed to help families that have inadequate financial resources

3. Food Stamp program, which is designed to help the poorest households obtain a basic diet

4. Medicaid, which is designed to cover the costs of medical care for households that receive help under the SSI and TANF programs

Subsidized Services

A great deal of redistribution takes place in the United States through the provision of subsidized services—services provided by the government at prices far below the cost of production. The taxpayers who consume these goods and services receive a transfer in kind from the taxpayers who do not consume them. The two most important areas in which this form of redistribution takes place are education—both kindergarten through grade 12 and college and university—and health care. But neither necessarily redistributes from the rich to the poor.

In 2005–2006, students who were enrolled in the University of California system who were not residents of California paid a tuition of $12,627 per semester. This amount is probably close to the cost of providing a semester's education at UCLA or Berkeley. But California residents paid tuition of only $3,717. So California households with a member enrolled at the University of California received a benefit from the government of almost $9,000 a semester. Many of these households have above-average incomes.

Government provision of health-care services has grown to equal the scale of private provision. Medicaid provides high-quality and high-cost health care to millions of people who earn too little to buy such services themselves. Medicaid redistributes from the rich to the poor. Medicare, which is available to all over 65 years of age, is not targeted at the poor.

■ The Scale of Income Redistribution

A household's income in the absence of government redistribution is called **market income.** We can measure the scale of income redistribution by calculating the percentage of market income paid in taxes minus the percentage received in benefits at each income level. The available data include redistribution through taxes and cash and noncash benefits to welfare recipients. The data do not include the value of subsidized services such as a college education, which might decrease the total scale of redistribution from the rich to the poor.

Figure 19.7 shows how government actions change the distribution of income. The blue Lorenz curve describes the market distribution of income. It is not the

Market income
A household's income earned from the markets for factors of production and with no government redistribution.

Money income
Market income plus money benefits paid by the government.

same as that in Figure 19.1, which is based on money income. **Money income** is market income plus money benefits paid by the government. The green Lorenz curve shows the income distribution based on this measure. The orange Lorenz curve shows the distribution of income after all taxes and benefits, including Medicaid and Medicare benefits. The distribution after taxes and benefits is more equal than the market distribution of income.

Figure 19.7(b) shows that redistribution increases the share received by the lowest 60 percent of households and decreases the share received by the highest 40 percent of households.

The sources of income at different income levels provide another measure of the scale of redistribution. The poorest 20 percent of households receive 80 percent of their income from the government. The second 20 percent receive around 33 percent of their income from the government. In contrast, the richest 20 percent receive almost nothing from the government but receive a third of their income from capital—interest and dividends from financial assets.

■ **FIGURE 19.7**

The Scale of Income Redistribution

Ⓧ myeconlab

Taxes and income maintenance programs reduce the degree of inequality that the market generates. In part (a), the Lorenz curve moves closer to the line of inequality.

Part (b) shows the redistribution in 2001 (the most recent year for which this type of income distribution data are available). The 20 percent of households with the lowest incomes received net benefits that increased their share of total income from 0.9 percent to 4.5 percent. The 20 percent of households with the highest incomes paid taxes that decreased their share of total income from 55.7 percent to 46.6 percent of total income.

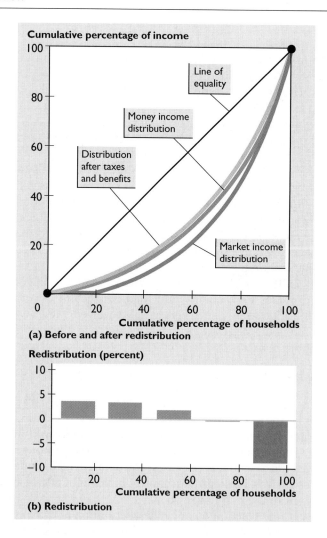

SOURCE OF DATA: U.S. Bureau of the Census, *Money Income in the United States: 2001*, Current Population Reports, P60–218.

■ Why We Redistribute Income

Why do we vote for government polices that redistribute income? Why don't we leave everyone to make voluntary contributions to charities that help the poor?

There are two ways of approaching these questions: normative and positive. The normative approach discusses why we *should* compel everyone to help the poor and looks for principles to guide the appropriate scale of redistribution. The positive approach seeks reasons why we *do* compel everyone to help the poor and tries to explain the actual scale of redistribution.

Normative Theories of Income Redistribution

Philosophy and politics, not economics, are the subjects that consider the normative theories of redistribution. And not surprisingly, there are several different points of view on whether income should be redistributed and, if so, on what scale.

Utilitarianism points to the ideal distribution being one of equality. But efficiency is also desirable. And greater equality can be achieved only at the cost of greater inefficiency—the *big tradeoff* (defined in Chapter 6, p. 162). The redistribution of income creates the big tradeoff because it uses scarce resources and weakens incentives, which decreases the total size of the economic pie to be shared.

A dollar collected from a rich person does not translate into a dollar received by a poor person. Some of it gets used up in the process of redistribution. Tax-collecting agencies such as the Internal Revenue Service and welfare-administering agencies (as well as tax accountants and lawyers) use skilled labor, computers, and other scarce resources to do their work. The bigger the scale of redistribution, the greater is the opportunity cost of administering it.

But the cost of collecting taxes and making welfare payments is a small part of the total cost of redistribution. A bigger cost arises from the inefficiency—*excess burden*—of taxes and benefits (see Chapter 8, p. 196). Greater equality can be achieved only by taxing productive activities such as work and saving. Taxing people's income from their work and saving lowers the after-tax income they receive. This lower income makes them work and save less, which in turn results in smaller output and less consumption not only for the rich who pay the taxes but also for the poor who receive the benefits.

Benefit recipients as well as taxpayers face weaker incentives. In fact, under the welfare arrangements that prevailed before the 1996 reforms, the weakest incentives to work were those faced by households that benefited from welfare. When a welfare recipient got a job, benefits were withdrawn and eligibility for programs such as Medicaid ended, so the household in effect paid a tax of more than 100 percent on its earnings. This arrangement locked poor households in a welfare trap.

Recognizing the tension between equality and efficiency, John Rawls proposed the principle that income should be redistributed to the point at which it maximizes the size of the slice of the economic pie received by the person with the smallest slice (see Chapter 6, p. 163).

Libertarian philosophers such as Robert Nozick say that any redistribution is wrong because it violates the sanctity of private property and voluntary exchange. (see Chapter 6, p. 163).

Modern political parties stand in the center of the extremes that we've just described. Some favor a bit more redistribution than others, but the major political parties are broadly happy with the prevailing scale of redistribution.

Median voter theory
The theory that governments pursue policies that make the median voter as well off as possible.

Positive Theories of Income Redistribution

A good positive theory of income redistribution would explain why some countries have more redistribution than others and why redistribution has increased over the past 200 years. We don't have such a theory. But economists have proposed a promising idea called the median voter theory. The **median voter theory** is that the policies that governments pursue are those that make the median voter as well off as possible. If a proposal can be made that improves the well-being of the median voter, a political party that makes the proposal can improve its standing in an election.

The median voter theory arises from thinking about how a democratic political system such as that of the United States works. In this system, governments must propose policies that appeal to enough voters to get them elected. And in a majority voting system, the voter whose views carry the most weight is the one in the middle—the median voter.

The median voter wants income to be redistributed to the point at which her or his own after-tax income is as large as possible. Taxing the rich by too much would weaken their incentives to create businesses and jobs and lower the median voter's after-tax income. But taxing the rich by too little would leave some money on the table that could be transferred to the median voter.

The median voter might be concerned about the poor and want to reduce poverty. Unselfishly, the median voter might simply be concerned about the plight of the poor and want to help them. Self-interestedly, the median voter might believe that if there is too much poverty, there will be too much crime and some of it will touch her or his life.

If for either reason the median voter wants to help the poor, the political process will deliver a greater scale of redistribution to reflect this voter preference.

■ The Major Welfare Challenge

Among the poorest people in the United States (see p. 476) are young women who have not completed high school, have a child (or children), live without a partner, and are more likely to be black or Hispanic than white. These young women and their children present the major welfare challenge.

There are about 10 million single mothers, and a quarter of them receive no support from their children's fathers. The long-term solution to the problem of these women is education and job training—acquiring human capital. The short-term solution is welfare. But welfare must be designed in ways that strengthen the incentive to pursue the long-term solution. And a change in the U.S. welfare programs introduced during the 1990s pursues this approach.

The Current Approach: TANF

Passed in 1996, the Personal Responsibility and Work Opportunities Reconciliation Act created the Temporary Assistance for Needy Families (TANF) program. TANF is a block grant that is paid to the states, which administer payments to individuals. It is not an open-ended entitlement program. An adult member of a household receiving assistance must either work or perform community service. And there is a five-year limit for assistance.

These measures go a long way toward removing one of the most serious poverty problems while being sensitive to the potential inefficiency of welfare. But some economists want to go further and introduce a negative income tax.

Negative Income Tax

The negative income tax is not on the political agenda. But it is popular among economists, and it is the subject of several real-world experiments. A **negative income tax** provides every household with a guaranteed minimum annual income and taxes all earned income above the guaranteed minimum at a fixed rate. Suppose the guaranteed minimum annual income is $10,000 and the tax rate is 25 percent. A household with no earned income receives the $10,000 guaranteed minimum income from the government. This household "pays" income tax of *minus* $10,000, hence the name "negative income tax."

A household that earns $40,000 a year pays $10,000—25 percent of its earnings—to the government. But this household also receives from the government the $10,000 guaranteed minimum income, so it pays no income tax. It has the break-even income. Households that earn between zero and $40,000 a year receive more from the government than they pay to the government. They "pay" a negative income tax.

A household that earns $60,000 a year pays $15,000—25 percent of its earnings—to the government. But this household receives from the government the $10,000 guaranteed minimum income, so it pays an income tax of $5,000. All households that earn more than $40,000 a year pay more to the government than they receive from it. They pay a positive amount of tax.

A negative income tax doesn't eliminate the excess burden of taxation. But it improves the incentives to work and save at all levels of income.

Negative income tax
A tax and redistribution scheme that provides every household with a guaranteed minimum annual income and taxes all earned income above the guaranteed minimum at a fixed rate.

REALITY CHECK

Redistribution in YOUR Life

You are on both sides of the redistribution equation. But what's your bottom line? Are you a net receiver or a net payer? Try to figure out which.

First work out how much tax you're paying. If you have a job, your payslip shows the amount of income tax you're paying. You can calculate the sales taxes you pay by keeping a note for a week every time you buy something. You can work out how much gas, tobacco, and alcohol tax you pay by checking the scale of these taxes in your state at www.taxadmin.org.

Now for the benefits. If you're receiving any direct cash payments such as unemployment benefits, these are easy to identify. But most likely, you don't receive any money from the government. You do, though, receive the benefits of services provided by government. Your education costs more than the tuition you're paying. One estimate of the value of your education is the tuition paid by an out-of-state student minus the tuition paid by a state resident. Try to estimate what all the government-provided services are worth to you and then work out your bottom line.

3 Explain why governments redistribute income and describe the effects of redistribution on economic inequality and poverty.

Practice Problem 19.3

1. Table 1 shows the distribution of market income in an economy. The government redistributes income by collecting income taxes and paying benefits shown in Table 2.
   a. Calculate the income shares of each 20 percent of households after tax and redistribution.
   b. Draw this economy's Lorenz curve before and after taxes and benefits.

Exercises 19.3

1. In the economy in the practice problem, the government lowers the tax rate on the third 20 percent to 15 percent, on the fourth 20 percent to 25 percent, and on the highest 20 percent to 30 percent but benefits are unchanged.
   a. Calculate the income shares of each 20 percent of households after tax and redistribution.
   b. Draw this economy's Lorenz curve before and after taxes and benefits.

2. In the economy in the practice problem, the government increases the benefits paid to the lowest 20 percent to $12 million, to the second 20 percent to $10 million, and to the third 20 percent to $5 million but keeps the tax rates unchanged. Calculate the income shares of each 20 percent of households after tax and redistribution.

Solution to Practice Problem 19.3

1a. To find the distribution of income, multiply the market incomes by the tax rates, subtract the taxes paid, and add the benefits received to obtain the income after tax and benefits. Then calculate each group's income as a percentage of total income. The following table summarizes the calculations.

TABLE 1

Households	Income (millions of dollars per year)
Lowest 20 percent	5
Second 20 percent	10
Third 20 percent	18
Fourth 20 percent	28
Highest 20 percent	39

TABLE 2

Households	Income tax (percent)	Benefits (millions of dollars)
Lowest 20 percent	0	10
Second 20 percent	10	8
Third 20 percent	18	3
Fourth 20 percent	28	0
Highest 20 percent	39	0

Households	Market Income (millions of dollars)	Tax paid (millions of dollars)	Benefits received (millions of dollars)	Income after tax and benefits (millions of dollars)	Income (percentage)
Lowest 20 percent	5	0.0	10	15.0	16.0
Second 20 percent	10	1.0	8	17.0	18.1
Third 20 percent	18	3.2	3	17.8	19.0
Fourth 20 percent	28	7.8	0	20.2	21.5
Highest 20 percent	39	15.2	0	23.8	25.4

1b. To draw the Lorenz curves, calculate the cumulative shares. For example, before taxes and benefits, the lowest 20 percent have 5 percent of total income and the lowest 40 percent have 15 percent (5 + 10) of total income. After taxes and benefits, the lowest 20 percent have 16 percent of total income and the lowest 40 percent have 34.1 percent (16 + 18.1) of total income. Figure 1 plots the Lorenz curves.

FIGURE 1

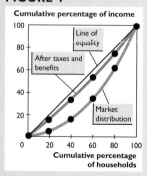

CHAPTER CHECKPOINT

Key Points

1 **Describe the economic inequality and poverty in the United States.**

- The richest 1 percent of Americans own almost one third of the total wealth in the country.

- Income is distributed less unevenly than wealth. Throughout the 1970s and 1980s, inequality increased.

- The poorest people in the United States are single black women over 65 years of age with less than nine years of schooling who live in the South. The richest people live in the West and are college-educated, middle-aged, white families in which husband and wife live together.

- The distribution of wealth exaggerates the degree of inequality because it excludes human capital.

- The distribution of annual income exaggerates lifetime inequality.

2 **Explain how economic inequality and poverty arise.**

- Economic inequality arises from inequality of labor market outcomes, ownership of capital, entrepreneurial ability, and personal and family characteristics.

- In labor markets, skill differences result in earnings differences. Discrimination might also contribute to earnings differences.

- Inherited capital, unusual entrepreneurial talent, and personal or family good fortune or misfortune widen the gaps between rich and poor.

3 **Explain why governments redistribute income and describe the effects of redistribution on economic inequality and poverty.**

- Governments redistribute income through progressive income taxes, income maintenance programs, and provision of subsidized services.

- Normative theories of redistribution recognize the tension between equality and efficiency—the big tradeoff—and seek principles to guide the political debate.

- The main positive theory of redistribution is the median voter theory.

- The negative income tax is a proposal for addressing the big tradeoff.

Key Terms

Lorenz curve, 472
Market income, 487
Median voter theory, 490

Money income, 488
Negative income tax, 491
Poverty, 477

Exercises

TABLE 1

Households	Income (percentage)
Lowest 20 percent	1
Second 20 percent	3
Third 20 percent	15
Fourth 20 percent	26
Highest 20 percent	55

TABLE 2

Professional golfers	Income (percentage)
Lowest 20 percent	15
Second 20 percent	16
Third 20 percent	18
Fourth 20 percent	20
Highest 20 percent	31

FIGURE 1

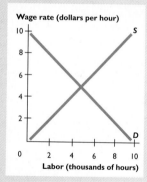

TABLE 3

Households	Income (percentage)
Lowest 20 percent	5
Second 20 percent	9
Third 20 percent	20
Fourth 20 percent	30
Highest 20 percent	36

1. Table 1 shows the distribution of income in Australia.
   a. Create a pie chart to illustrate the distribution of income in Australia.
   b. Calculate the cumulative distribution of income for Australia.
   c. Draw the Lorenz curve for Australian income.
   d. Compare the distribution of income in Australia with that in the United States.
   e. Which distribution is more unequal?

2. Table 2 shows the distribution of prize money among the top 20 professional golfers.
   a. Create a pie chart to illustrate the distribution of income of these golfers.
   b. Calculate the cumulative distribution of income of these golfers.
   c. Draw the prize money distribution Lorenz curve of these golfers.
   d. Compare the distribution of income of these golfers with that in the United States as a whole.
   e. Which distribution is more unequal?
   f. Which distribution is more desirable? Why?

3. Figure 1 shows the market for low-skilled workers. With on-the-job training, low-skilled workers can become high-skilled workers. The value of the marginal product of high-skilled workers at each employment level is twice the value of the marginal product of low-skilled workers. But the cost of acquiring the skill adds $2 an hour to the wage rate that will attract high-skilled labor. What is the equilibrium
   a. Wage rate of low-skilled labor.
   b. Number of low-skilled workers employed.
   c. Wage rate of high-skilled labor.
   d. Number of high-skilled workers employed.

4. Suppose the cost of acquiring a skill increases and the value of the marginal product of skill increases. Draw demand-supply graphs of the labor markets for high-skilled and low-skilled labor to explain what happens to the equilibrium
   a. Wage rate of low-skilled labor.
   b. Number of low-skilled workers employed.
   c. Wage rate of high-skilled labor.
   d. Number of high-skilled workers employed.

5. Table 3 shows the distribution of market income in an economy. If the government redistributes income by taxing the 60 percent of households with the highest incomes 10 percent; and paying the tax collected as benefits to the 40 percent of the population with the lowest market income,
   a. Calculate the distribution of income after taxes and benefits.
   b. Draw the Lorenz curve before and after taxes and benefits.
   c. If the cost of administrating the redistribution scheme takes 50 percent of the taxes collected, calculate the new distribution of income.
   d. If the people whose incomes are taxed cut their work hours and their incomes fall by 10 percent, what now is the distribution of income? (Ignore the cost of administrating the redistribution scheme.)

6. In the United States in 2002, 130,000 aircraft mechanics and services technicians earned an average of $20 an hour, while 30,000 elevator installers and
   repairers earned an average of $25 an hour. The skill and training for these
   two jobs are very similar.
   a. Draw the demand and supply curves for these two types of labor.
   b. Describe the feature of your graph that accounts for the differences in the
      wage rates of these two groups.
   c. Describe the feature of your graph that accounts for the differences in the
      quantities of labor employed of these two groups.
   d. Why do you think these demand for labor curves differ?
   e. Why do you think these supply of labor curves differ?
   f. Suppose that a government law required both groups to be paid $22.50 an
      hour. What would happen in the two markets?

Critical Thinking

7. Why do economists think that discrimination in the labor market based on
   prejudice against visible minorities or women is an unlikely explanation for
   the persistent inequality in earnings of these two groups compared to white
   males?

8. How do you think the minimum wage influences the distribution of
   income?

9. What is the big tradeoff? How does the 1996 Personal Responsibility and
   Work Opportunities Reconciliation Act address the big tradeoff and how
   might a negative income address it?

10. What were the features of U.S. redistribution prior to 1996 that created
    weaker incentives for benefit recipients and taxpayers? What does it mean to
    say that the scheme "locked poor people in a welfare trap"?

11. Do you think the distributions of income and wealth in the United States
    today are too unequal, too equal, or about right? Provide a detailed justifica-
    tion for your opinion using the ideas of economic efficiency, the two views
    of fairness explained in Chapter 6, the concept of the big tradeoff, and the
    data presented in the tables in this chapter.

12. What practical changes would you suggest to the government actions that
    redistribute income and wealth in the United States today? Provide a
    detailed justification for your suggestions using the ideas of economic effi-
    ciency, the two views of fairness explained in Chapter 6, the concept of the
    big tradeoff, and the data presented in the tables in this chapter.

13. "The distribution of income within a country is only a small part of the story
    of economic inequality. The truly disturbing inequality is that among
    nations. The rich countries must do much more to help the poor ones."
    Appraise this statement. Do you agree or disagree with it? Provide a
    detailed justification for your opinion using the ideas of economic efficiency,
    the two views of fairness explained in Chapter 6, the concept of the big
    tradeoff, and the data presented in the tables in this chapter.

Web Exercises

Use the links on MyEconLab to work the following exercises.

14. Obtain data on the salaries of the major league baseball players or download the spreadsheet.
    a. Calculate the cumulative distribution of income for the major league players.
    b. Is the distribution of income among the major league players more unequal or less unequal than that for the United States?
    c. Which distribution of income, the major league players or the United States, is better? Why?

15. Visit the Economic Policy Institute's page on the living wage.
    a. What is the concept of the living wage?
    b. How does the concept of the living wage relate to the concept of poverty that you've studied in this chapter?
    c. How does the concept of the living wage relate to the concept of the minimum wage that you studied in Chapter 7?
    d. Do you think that the living wage solves the problem of low income?

16. Visit the Center on Budget and Policy Priorities and other sites and obtain information on President George W. Bush's tax cut proposals.
    a. What are the main elements in the President's tax plan?
    b. How do you think the President's proposals would change the Lorenz curve? Explain in detail.

17. Read the article "Reengineering Social Security in the New Economy" by Thomas F. Siems, an economist at the Dallas Federal Reserve.
    a. What does Dr. Siems say is wrong with Social Security?
    b. How does he suggest that the problems with Social Security be fixed?
    c. How would Dr. Siems's suggestions influence the distribution of income?

GDP and the Standard of Living

CHAPTER CHECKLIST

When you have completed your study of this chapter, you will be able to

1 Define GDP and explain why the value of production, income, and expenditure are the same for an economy.

2 Describe how economic statisticians measure GDP in the United States.

3 Distinguish between nominal GDP and real GDP and define the GDP deflator.

4 Describe and explain the limitations of real GDP as a measure of the standard of living.

Jesse lives in Chicago, and his income is equal to the average U.S. income. Chen lives in Beijing, and his income is equal to the average income in China. Is Jesse better off than Chen? If so, by how much? How can we measure average incomes and compare them?

Jesse's grandparents also live in Chicago, but they were born in the 1930s. Jesse is better off than his grandparents were when they were young. But by how much? How can we compare how well off people are across generations?

To answer these questions, we need a measure of income and of the value of the goods and services produced. In this chapter, you will find out how economic statisticians arrive at such measures and how they are used to compare the economic well-being of people at different times and in different places.

20.1 GDP, INCOME, AND EXPENDITURE

Standard of living
The level of consumption of goods and services that people enjoy, *on the average*, measured by average income per person.

When we ask who is better off: you or a college student in Beijing, China, and you today or your grandparents when they were young, we are comparing standards of living. A nation's **standard of living** is the level of consumption of goods and services that its people enjoy, *on the average,* measured by average income per person. So to answer the questions we've just posed, you might try to discover who has the higher income: you today or your grandparents in the 1940s, and you or a college student in China.

But it is the quantities of goods and services consumed that determine how well off people are. For goods and services to be consumed, they must be produced. So another way to answer the questions posed is to discover who produces the greater total value of goods and services. Do we produce more goods and services per person today than our grandparents' generation did in the 1940s, and do we produce more goods and services per person than the people of China produce? To answer these questions, we need to measure total production.

Gross domestic product, or GDP, measures the total value of production. And as you're about to discover, it also measures total income.

■ GDP Defined

Gross domestic product (GDP)
The market value of all the final goods and services produced within a country in a given time period.

We measure total production as **gross domestic product**, or **GDP**, which is the market value of all the final goods and services produced within a country in a given time period. This definition has four parts, which we'll examine in turn.

Value Produced

To measure total production, we must add together the production of apples and oranges, bats and balls. Just counting the items doesn't get us very far. Which is the greater total production: 100 apples and 50 oranges or 50 oranges and 100 apples? GDP answers this question by valuing items at their *market value*—at the prices at which the items are traded in markets.

If the price of an apple is 10 cents and the price of an orange is 20 cents, the market value of 100 apples plus 50 oranges is $20 and the market value of 50 apples and 100 oranges is $25. So by using market prices to value production, we can add the apples and oranges together.

What Produced

Final good or service
A good or service that is produced for its final user and not as a component of another good or service.

Intermediate good or service
A good or service that is produced by one firm, bought by another firm, and used as a component of a final good or service.

To calculate GDP, we value all the *final goods and services.* A **final good or service** is a good or service that is produced for its final user and not as a component of another good or service. It contrasts with an **intermediate good or service**, which is a good or service that is produced by one firm, bought by another firm, and used as a component of a final good or service. For example, a Ford SUV is a final good, but a Firestone tire on the SUV is an intermediate good.

GDP aims to be a full count of the value of everything that is produced. In practice, with one exception, GDP includes only those items that are traded in markets. It does not include the market value of goods and services that people produce for their own use. For example, GDP includes the value of a car wash that is bought but excludes the value of washing your own car. The exception is the market value of homes that people own. GDP puts a rental value on such homes and pretends that the owners rent their homes to themselves.

Where Produced

Only goods and services that are produced *within a country* count as part of that country's GDP. Nike Corporation, a U.S. firm, produces sneakers in Vietnam, and the market value of those shoes is part of Vietnam's GDP, not part of U.S. GDP. Toyota, a Japanese firm, produces automobiles in Georgetown, Kentucky, and the value of this production is part of U.S. GDP, not part of Japan's GDP.

When Produced

GDP measures the value of production *during a given time period*. This time period is either a quarter of a year—called the quarterly GDP data—or a year—called the annual GDP data. The Federal Reserve and others use the quarterly GDP data to keep track of the short-term evolution of the economy, and economists use the annual GDP data to examine long-term trends.

GDP measures not only the value of total production but also total income and total expenditure. The circular flow model that you studied in Chapter 2 explains why.

■ Circular Flows in the U.S. Economy

Four groups buy the final goods and services produced: households, firms, governments, and the rest of the world. Four types of expenditure correspond to these groups:

- Consumption expenditure
- Investment
- Government expenditure on goods and services
- Net exports of goods and services

Consumption Expenditure

Consumption expenditure is the expenditure by households on consumption goods and services. It includes expenditures on *nondurables* such as orange juice and pizza, *durables* such as microwave ovens and DVD players, and *services* such as rock concerts and haircuts. Consumption expenditure also includes house and apartment rents, including the rental value of owner-occupied housing.

Consumption expenditure
The expenditure by households on consumption goods and services.

Investment

Investment is the purchase of new *capital goods* (tools, instruments, machines, buildings, and other items) and additions to inventories. Investment includes capital goods produced by one firm and bought by another. Examples are PCs produced by Dell and bought by General Motors, and airplanes produced by Boeing and bought by United Airlines. Investment also includes the purchase of new homes by households.

At the end of a year, some of a firm's output might remain unsold. For example, if GM produces 4 million cars and sells 3.9 million of them, the other 0.1 million (100,000) cars remain unsold. In this case, GM's inventory of cars increases by 100,000. When a firm adds unsold output to inventory, we count those items as part of investment.

It is important to note that investment does *not* include the purchase of stocks and bonds. In macroeconomics, we reserve the term "investment" for the purchase of new capital goods and the additions to inventories.

Investment
The purchase of new *capital goods* (tools, instruments, machines, buildings, and other items) and additions to inventories.

Government Expenditure on Goods and Services

Government expenditure on goods and services
The expenditure by all levels of government on goods and services.

Government expenditure on goods and services is expenditure by all levels of government on goods and services. Governments buy a wide range of goods and services. For example, the U.S. Defense Department buys missiles and other weapons systems, the State Department buys travel services, the White House buys Internet services, and state and local governments buy cruisers for law enforcement officers.

Net Exports of Goods and Services

Net exports of goods and services
The value of exports of goods and services minus the value of imports of goods and services.

Exports of goods and services
Items that firms in the United States produce and sell to the rest of the world.

Imports of goods and services
Items that households, firms, and governments in the United States buy from the rest of the world.

Net exports of goods and services is the value of exports of goods and services minus the value of imports of goods and services. **Exports of goods and services** are items that firms in the United States produce and sell to the rest of the world. **Imports of goods and services** are items that households, firms, and governments in the United States buy from the rest of the world. Imports are produced in other countries, so expenditure on imports is not included in expenditure on U.S.-produced goods and services. If exports exceed imports, net exports are positive and increase expenditure on U.S.-produced goods and services. If imports exceed exports, net exports are negative and decrease expenditure on U.S.-produced goods and services.

Total Expenditure

Total expenditure on goods and services produced in the United States is the sum of the four items that you've just examined. We call consumption expenditure C, investment I, government expenditure on goods and services G, and net exports of goods and services NX. So total expenditure, which is also the total amount received by the producers of final goods and services, is

$$\text{Total expenditure} = C + I + G + NX.$$

Income

Labor earns wages, capital earns interest, land earns rent, and entrepreneurship earns profits. Households receive these incomes. Some part of total income, called *undistributed profit,* is a combination of interest and profit that is not paid out to households. But from an economic viewpoint, undistributed profit is income paid to households and then loaned to firms.

■ Expenditure Equals Income

Figure 20.1 shows the circular flows of income and expenditure that we've just described. The figure is based on Figures 2.4 and 2.5 (on p. 43 and p. 45), but it includes some more details and additional flows.

We call total income Y and show it by the blue flow from firms to households. When households receive their incomes, they pay some in taxes and save some. Some households receive benefits from governments. *Net taxes* equal taxes paid minus benefits received and are the green flow from households to governments labeled NT. Saving flows from households to financial markets and is the green flow labeled S. These two green flows are not expenditures on goods and services. They are just flows of money.

The red flows show the four expenditure flows described above: consumption expenditure from households to firms, government expenditure from governments to firms, and net exports from the rest of the world to firms. Investment flows from the financial markets, where firms borrow, to the firms that produce capital goods.

Because firms pay out everything they receive as incomes to the factors of production, total expenditure equals total income. That is,

$$Y = C + I + G + NX.$$

From the viewpoint of firms, the value of production is the cost of production, which equals income. From the viewpoint of purchasers of goods and services, the value of production is the cost of buying it, which equals expenditure. So

The value of production equals income equals expenditure.

The circular flow and the equality of income and expenditure provide two approaches to measuring GDP that we'll study in the next section.

FIGURE 20.1

The Circular Flow of Income and Expenditure

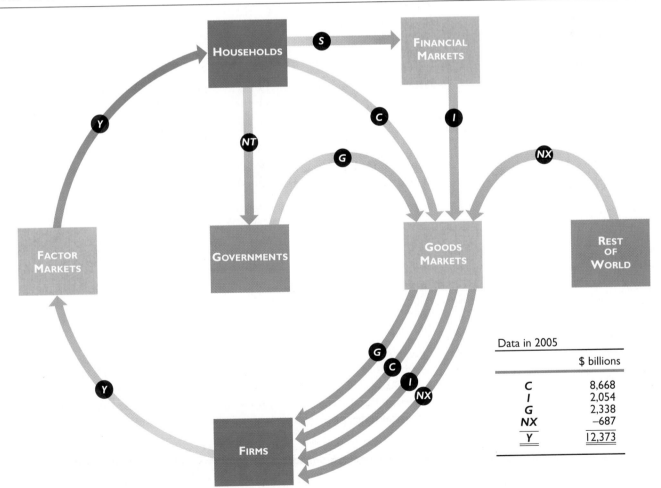

Data in 2005	
	$ billions
C	8,668
I	2,054
G	2,338
NX	−687
Y	12,373

In the circular flow, the blue flow (Y) is income and the red flows (C, I, G, and NX) are expenditures on goods and services. The green flows are flows of money: Households pay net taxes (NT) to governments and save (S) some of their income. Firms borrow in financial markets to buy goods (I) from other firms. Expenditure equals income and equals the value of production.

I **Define GDP and explain why the value of production, income, and expenditure are the same for an economy.**

Practice Problems 20.1

1. Classify each of the following items as a final good or service or an intermediate good or service:
   a. Banking services bought by a student.
   b. New cars bought by Hertz, the car rental firm.
   c. Newsprint bought by *USA Today* from International Paper.
   d. Ice cream bought by a diner and used to produce sundaes.

2. During 2004 on Lotus Island, net taxes were $10 billion; consumption expenditure was $30 billion; government expenditure on goods and services was $12 billion; investment was $15 billion; and net exports were $3 billion. Calculate
   a. Total expenditure.
   b. Total income.
   c. Value of production.

Exercises 20.1

1. Classify each of the following items as a final good or an intermediate good and classify expenditure on each final good as consumption expenditure or investment:
   a. The fertilizer bought by a Florida tomato grower.
   b. The ringtone you bought today.
   c. New computers bought by PepsiCo.
   d. The aircraft bought by Southwest Airlines.

2. During 2005 on Lotus Island, households spent $60 million of their income on goods and services, saved $20 million, and paid the rest of their income in net taxes; government expenditure on goods and services was $15 million; investment was $25 million; and net exports were zero. Calculate
   a. Total expenditure.
   b. Total income.
   c. Net taxes.

Solutions to Practice Problems 20.1

1a. A final service—The student is the final user.
1b. Final goods—The new cars that Hertz buys are additions to its capital, so these cars are part of Hertz's investment.
1c. An intermediate good—Newsprint is a component of the newspaper.
1d. An intermediate good—Ice cream is a component of sundaes.

2a. Total expenditure is $60 billion. Total expenditure = $C + I + G + NX$. That is, Total expenditure = $(30 + 15 + 12 + 3)$ billion = $60 billion.
2b. Total income = Total expenditure = $60 billion.
2c. Value of production = Total expenditure = $60 billion.

20.2 MEASURING U.S. GDP

U.S. GDP is the market value of all the final goods and services produced within the United States during a year. In 2005, U.S. GDP exceeded $12 trillion. The Bureau of Economic Analysis in the U.S. Department of Commerce measures GDP by using two approaches:

- Expenditure approach
- Income approach

■ The Expenditure Approach

The expenditure approach measures GDP by using data on consumption expenditure, investment, government expenditure on goods and services, and net exports. This approach is like attaching a meter to the circular flow diagram on all the flows running through the goods markets to firms and measuring the magnitudes of those flows. Table 20.1 shows this approach. The first column gives the terms used in the U.S. National Income and Product Accounts. The next column gives the symbols we used in the previous section.

Using the expenditure approach, GDP is the sum of consumption expenditure on goods and services (C), investment (I), government expenditure on goods and services (G), and net exports of goods and services (NX). The third column gives the expenditures in 2005. GDP measured by the expenditure approach was $12,373 billion.

Net exports were negative in 2005 because imports exceeded exports. Imports were $1,991 billion and exports were $1,304 billion, so net exports—exports minus imports—were −$687 as shown in the table.

The fourth column in Table 20.1 shows the relative magnitudes of the expenditures. Consumption expenditure is by far the largest component of total expenditure; investment and government expenditure are a similar size; and net exports is the smallest component. In 2005, consumption expenditure was 70 percent, investment was 16.6 percent, government expenditure was 18.9 percent, and net exports were a negative 5.5 percent of GDP.

■ TABLE 20.1

GDP: The Expenditure Approach

Item	Symbol	Amount in 2005 (second quarter) (billions of dollars)	Percentage of GDP
Consumption expenditure	C	8,668	70.0
Investment	I	2,054	16.6
Government expenditure	G	2,338	18.9
Net exports	NX	−687	−5.5
GDP	Y	12,373	100.0

SOURCE OF DATA: U.S. Department of Commerce, Bureau of Economic Analysis.

The expenditure approach measures GDP by adding together consumption expenditure (C), investment (I), government expenditure (G), and net exports (NX).

In 2005, GDP measured by the expenditure approach was $12,373 billion.

Expenditures Not in GDP

Total expenditure (and GDP) does not include all the things that people and businesses buy. GDP is the value of *final goods and services,* so spending that is *not* on final goods and services is not part of GDP. Spending on intermediate goods and services is not part of GDP, although it is not always obvious whether an item is an intermediate good or a final good (see *Eye on the U.S. Economy*). Also, we do not count as part of GDP spending on

- Used goods
- Financial assets

Used Goods Expenditure on used goods is not part of GDP because these goods were part of GDP in the period in which they were produced and during which time they were new goods. For example, a 2002 automobile was part of GDP in 2002. If the car is traded on the used car market in 2005, the amount paid for the car is not part of GDP in 2005.

Financial Assets When households buy financial assets such as bonds and stocks, they are making loans, not buying goods and services. The expenditure on newly produced capital goods is part of GDP, but the purchase of financial assets is not.

EYE ON THE U.S. ECONOMY

Is a Computer Program an Intermediate Good or a Final Good?

When American Airlines buys a new reservations software package, is that like General Motors buying tires? If it is, then software is an *intermediate good* and it is not counted as part of GDP. Airline ticket sales, like GM cars, are part of GDP, but the intermediate goods that are used to produce air transportation or cars are *not* part of GDP.

Or when American Airlines buys new software, is that like General Motors buying a new assembly-line robot? If it is, then the software is a capital good and its purchase is the purchase of a final good. In this case, the software purchase is an *investment* and it *is* counted as part of GDP.

Brent Moulton is a government economist who works in the Bureau of Economic Analysis (BEA). Moulton's job was to oversee periodic adjustments to the GDP estimates to incorporate new data and new ideas about the economy.

The biggest change was in how the purchase of computer software by firms is classified. Before 1999, it was regarded as an *intermediate good.* But since 1999, it has been treated as an *investment.*

How big a deal is this? When the BEA recalculated the 1996 GDP, the change increased the estimate of the 1996 GDP by $115 billion. That is a lot of money. To put it in perspective, GDP in 1996 was $7,662 billion. So the adjustment was 1.5 percent of GDP.

This change is a nice example of the ongoing effort by the BEA to keep the GDP measure as accurate as possible.

■ The Income Approach

To measure GDP using the income approach the Bureau of Economic Analysis uses data collected by the Internal Revenue Service and other agencies on the incomes that firms pay households for the services of the factors of production they hire—wages for labor services, interest for the use of capital, rent for the use of land, and profits for entrepreneurship—and sums those incomes. This approach is like attaching a meter to the circular flow diagram on all the flows running through factor markets from firms to households and measuring the magnitudes of those flows. Let's see how the income approach works.

The U.S. National Income and Product Accounts divide incomes into two big categories:

• Wages
• Interest, rent, and profit

Wages

Wages, called *compensation of employees* in the national accounts, is the payment for labor services. It includes net wages and salaries plus fringe benefits paid by employers such as health care insurance, social security contributions, and pension fund contributions.

Interest, Rent, and Profit

Interest, rent, and profit, called *net operating surplus* in the national accounts, is the sum of the incomes earned by capital, land, and entrepreneurship.

Interest income is the interest that households receive on the loans they make minus the interest households pay on their own borrowing.

Rent includes payments for the use of land and other rented inputs. It includes payments for rented housing and imputed rent for owner-occupied housing. (Imputed rent is an estimate of what homeowners would pay to rent the housing they own and use themselves. By including this item in the national accounts, we measure the total value of housing services, whether they are owned or rented.)

Profit includes the profits of corporations and the incomes of proprietors who run their own businesses. These incomes are a mixture of interest and profit.

Table 20.2 shows these two components of incomes and their relative magnitudes. The sum of wages, interest, rent, and profit is **net domestic product at factor cost**.

Net domestic product at factor cost is not GDP, and we must make two further adjustments to get to GDP: one from factor cost to market prices and another from net product to gross product.

Net domestic product at factor cost
The sum of the wages, interest, rent, and profit.

From Factor Cost to Market Price

The expenditure approach values goods and services at market prices, and the income approach values them at factor cost—the cost of the factors of production used to produce them. Indirect taxes (such as sales taxes) and subsidies (payments by government to firms) make these two values differ. Sales taxes make market prices exceed factor cost, and subsidies make factor cost exceed market prices. To convert the value at factor cost to the value at market prices, we must add indirect taxes and subtract subsidies.

■ **TABLE 20.2**

GDP: The Income Approach

The sum of all incomes equals net domestic product at factor cost. GDP equals net domestic product at factor cost plus indirect taxes less subsidies plus depreciation (capital consumption).

In 2005, GDP measured by the income approach was $12,367 billion. This amount is $6 billion less than GDP measured by the expenditure approach—a statistical discrepancy of $6 billion.

Wages are by far the largest part of total income.

Item	Amount in 2005 (second quarter)	
	(billions of dollars)	Percentage of GDP
Wages (compensation of employees)	7,111	57.5
Interest, rent, and profit (net operating surplus)	2,953	23.9
Net domestic product at factor cost	10,064	81.4
Indirect taxes less subsidies	847	6.8
Depreciation (capital consumption)	1,456	11.8
GDP (income approach)	12,367	100.0
Statistical discrepancy	6	0
GDP (expenditure approach)	12,373	100.0

SOURCE OF DATA: U.S. Department of Commerce, Bureau of Economic Analysis.

Depreciation
The decrease in the value of capital that results from its use and from obsolescence.

From Gross to Net

The expenditure approach measures *gross* product, and the income approach measures *net* product. The difference is **depreciation**, the decrease in the value of capital that results from its use and from obsolescence. Firms' profits, which are included in the income approach, are net of depreciation, so the income approach gives a *net* measure. Investment, which is included in the expenditure approach, includes the purchase of capital to replace worn out or obsolete capital, so the expenditure approach gives a *gross* measure. To get *gross* domestic product from the income approach, we must add depreciation to total income.

Table 20.2 summarizes these adjustments and shows that the income approach gives almost the same estimate of GDP as the expenditure approach.

Statistical Discrepancy

The expenditure approach and income approach do not deliver exactly the same estimate of GDP. If a taxi driver doesn't report all his tips, they get missed in the income approach. But they get caught by the expenditure approach when he spends his income. So the sum of expenditures might exceed the sum of incomes. But most income gets reported to the Internal Revenue Service on tax returns while many items of expenditure are not recorded and must be estimated. So the sum of incomes might exceed the sum of estimated expenditures.

Statistical discrepancy
The discrepancy between the expenditure approach and the income approach estimates of GDP, calculated as the GDP expenditure total minus the GDP income total.

The discrepancy between the expenditure approach and the income approach is called the **statistical discrepancy**, and it is calculated as the GDP expenditure total minus the GDP income total.

The two measures of GDP provide a check on the accuracy of the numbers. If the two are wildly different, we will want to know what mistakes we've made. Have we omitted some item? Have we counted something twice? The fact that the two estimates are close gives some confidence that they are reasonably accurate. But the expenditure total is regarded as the more reliable estimate of GDP, so the discrepancy is added to or subtracted from income to reconcile the two estimates.

■ GDP and Related Measures of Production and Income

Although GDP is the main measure of total production, you will sometimes encounter another: gross *national* product or GNP.

Gross National Product

A country's **gross national product**, or **GNP**, is the market value of all the final goods and services produced anywhere in the world in a given time period by the factors of production supplied by the residents of that country. For example, when Nike produces shoes in its factory in Vietnam, Nike's income from the capital that it supplies is part of U.S. GNP but not part of U.S. GDP. It is part of Vietnam's GDP. Similarly, when Toyota produces cars in its Kentucky plant, Toyota's income on its capital is part of U.S. GDP but not part of U.S. GNP. It is part of Japan's GNP.

U.S. GNP equals U.S. GDP plus net factor income from abroad—income received from factors supplied in other countries minus income paid for factors of production supplied by foreigners in the United States. The difference between U.S. GDP and GNP is tiny, as you can see in Figure 20.2.

Gross national product (GNP)
The market value of all the final goods and services produced anywhere in the world in a given time period by the factors of production supplied by the residents of the country.

Disposable Personal Income

You've seen that consumption expenditure is the largest component of aggregate expenditure. One of the main influences on consumption expenditure is **disposable personal income**, which is the income received by households minus personal income taxes. Because disposable personal income plays an important role in influencing spending, the national accounts measure this item along with a number of intermediate totals that you can see in Figure 20.2. This figure shows how disposable personal income is calculated and how it relates to GDP and GNP.

Disposable personal income
Income received by households minus personal income taxes paid.

▮ FIGURE 20.2
GDP and Related Product and Income Measures

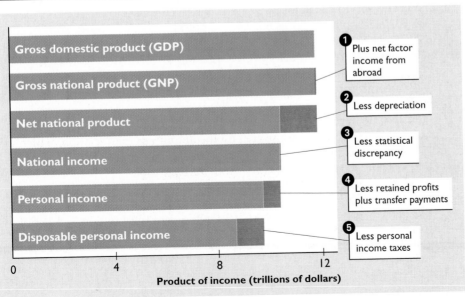

The green bars show six related product and income measures and the relationship among them.

❶ Starting with GDP, we add net factor income from abroad to get GNP. ❷ Subtract depreciation from GNP to get net national product. ❸ Subtract the statistical discrepancy between the expenditure and income measures (almost invisible in the figure because it is tiny) to get national income. ❹ Subtract business profits retained by firms and add transfer payments by governments to get personal income. ❺ Finally, subtract personal income taxes to get disposable personal income.

SOURCE OF DATA: U.S. Department of Commerce, Bureau of Economic Analysis.

2 **Describe how economic statisticians measure GDP in the United States.**

Practice Problem 20.2

TABLE 1

Item	Amount (billions of dollars)
Consumption expenditure	7,761
Government expenditure	2,076
Indirect taxes less subsidies	630
Depreciation	1,354
Net factor income from abroad	55
Investment	1,665
Net exports	−498
Statistical discrepancy	26

TABLE 2

Item	Amount (billions of dollars)
Wages	6,075
Government expenditure	1,957
Interest, rent, and profit	2,399
Consumption expenditure	7,376
Investment	1,579
Net exports	−425
Indirect taxes less subsidies	724
Retained profits plus transfer payments	347
Personal income taxes	1,051
GNP	10,514
Depreciation	1,304

1. Table 1 shows some of the items in the U.S. National Income and Product Accounts in 2003.
   a. Use the expenditure approach to calculate U.S. GDP in 2003.
   b. What was U.S. GDP as measured by the income approach in 2003?
   c. By how much did gross product and net product differ in 2003?
   d. Calculate U.S. GNP in 2003.
   e. Calculate U.S. national income in 2003.

Exercise 20.2

1. Table 2 shows some of the items in the U.S. National Income and Product Accounts in 2002.
   a. Use the expenditure approach to calculate U.S. GDP in 2003.
   b. Use the income approach to calculate net domestic product at factor cost.
   c. Calculate the statistical discrepancy.
   d. Calculate the difference between GDP and GNP. What determines this magnitude?
   e. Calculate U.S. national income.
   f. Calculate disposable personal income.
   g. What percentage of U.S. total income is disposable personal income?
   h. What percentage of disposable personal income is consumption expenditure?

Solution to Practice Problem 20.2

1a. The expenditure approach to measuring GDP sums the expenditure on final goods and services. That is, GDP = C + I + G + NX.
In 2003, GDP (in billions) = $7,761 + $1,665 + $2,076 − $498. So U.S. GDP in 2003 was $11,004 billion.

1b. GDP (expenditure approach) = GDP (income approach) + Statistical discrepancy. So rearranging this equation
GDP (income approach) = GDP (expenditure approach) − Statistical discrepancy.
GDP (income approach) = $11,004 billion − $26 billion = $10,978 billion.

1c. Gross product exceeds net product by the amount of depreciation, which in 2003 was $1,354 billion.

1d. GNP = GDP + Net factor income from abroad.
So in 2003, GNP = $11,004 billion + $55 billion, which was $11,059 billion.

1e. National income = GNP − Depreciation − Statistical discrepancy.
So in 2003, National income = $11,059 billion − $1,354 billion − $26 billion. National income in 2003 was $9,679 billion.

20.3 NOMINAL GDP VERSUS REAL GDP

You've seen that GDP measures total expenditure on final goods and services in a given period. In 2003, GDP was $11,004 billion. In 2004, GDP was $11,735 billion. Because GDP was greater in 2004 than in 2003, we know that one or two things must have happened during that period:

- We produced more goods and services.
- We paid higher prices for our goods and services.

Producing more goods and services contributes to an improvement in our standard of living. Paying higher prices means that our cost of living has increased but our standard of living has not. So it matters a great deal why GDP has increased.

You're going to learn how economists at the Bureau of Economic Analysis split the increase in GDP into two parts. One part, called *real GDP*, tells us the amount of production; the other part, called the *GDP deflator*, tells us the prices. Let's see how these numbers are calculated.

■ Calculating Real GDP

Real GDP is the value of the final goods and services produced in a given year expressed in the prices of a *base year*. Real GDP contrasts with **nominal GDP**, which is the value of the final goods and services produced in a given year expressed in the prices of that same year. Nominal GDP is just a more precise name for GDP that we use when we want to emphasize that we're not talking about real GDP.

The method used for calculating real GDP has changed in recent years. We will describe both methods, beginning with the traditional (and simpler) one.

Real GDP
The value of the final goods and services produced in a given year expressed in the prices of a *base year*.

Nominal GDP
The value of the final goods and services produced in a given year expressed in the prices of that same year.

Traditional Method of Calculating Real GDP

To focus on the principles and keep the numbers easy to work with, we'll calculate real GDP for an economy that produces only apples and oranges. We'll use 2006 as the *current year* and 2000 as the *base year*. (The base year is 2000 in the United States today.)

Table 20.3 shows the quantities produced and prices in 2000. Because 2000 is the base year, nominal GDP and real GDP are the same. To calculate real GDP in 2000, sum the values of apples and oranges produced in 2000 using the prices of 2000 (Table 20.3) as follows:

Value of apples	= 60 apples × $0.50	= $30.
Value of oranges	= 80 oranges × $0.25	= $20.
Real GDP in 2000	= $30 + $20	= $50.

Table 20.4 shows the quantities and prices for 2006. To calculate real GDP in 2006, sum the values of apples and oranges produced in 2006 *using the prices of 2000* (Table 20.3) as follows:

Value of apples	= 160 apples × $0.50	= $80.
Value of oranges	= 220 oranges × $0.25	= $55.
Real GDP in 2006	= $80 + $55	= $135.

We refer to real GDP as a "constant dollars" or "2000 dollars" measure.

TABLE 20.3 GDP DATA FOR 2000

Item	Quantity	Price
Apples	60	$0.50
Oranges	80	$0.25

TABLE 20.4 GDP DATA FOR 2006

Item	Quantity	Price
Apples	160	$1.00
Oranges	220	$2.00

TABLE 20.5 DATA FOR CHAINED INDEX CALCULATIONS

A. QUANTITIES AND PRICES IN 2005

	Apples	Oranges
Quantities	100	200
Prices	$1.50	$0.75
Value	$150	$150

Nominal GDP in 2005: $300

B. 2006 QUANTITIES AT 2005 PRICES

	Apples	Oranges
Quantities	160	220
Prices	$1.50	$0.75
Value	$240	$165

2006 Q at 2005 P: $405

C. 2005 QUANTITIES AT 2006 PRICES

	Apples	Oranges
Quantities	100	200
Prices	$1.00	$2.00
Value	$100	$400

2005 Q at 2006 P: $500

D. QUANTITIES AND PRICES IN 2006

	Apples	Oranges
Quantities	160	220
Prices	$1.00	$2.00
Value	$160	$440

Nominal GDP in 2006: $600

GDP deflator

An average of current prices expressed as a percentage of base-year prices.

Chained-Dollar Method of Calculating Real GDP

The traditional method of calculating real GDP uses base-year prices. In 2000 (the base year), the price of an apple is twice the price of an orange, so an apple contributes twice as much as an orange to real GDP. But by 2006, the price of an orange was twice the price of an apple. The chained-dollar method uses the prices of the current year and the preceding year. The calculation has five steps.

Step 1: Calculate the value of production in both 2005 and 2006 at the prices of 2005. Table 20.5 part A shows the value of 2005 production at 2005 prices, which is nominal GDP in 2005. Table 20.5 part B shows the value of the 2006 quantities at 2005 prices. Now calculate the percentage change in production valued at 2005 prices. Table 20.6 (p. 511) shows the numbers. The value of production increased from $300 to $405, an increase of $105 or 35 percent.

Step 2: Calculate the value of production in both 2005 and 2006 at the prices of 2006. Table 20.5 part C shows the value of the 2005 quantities at 2006 prices. Table 20.5 part D shows the value of 2006 production at 2006 prices, which is nominal GDP in 2006. Now calculate the percentage change in production valued at 2006 prices. Table 20.6 shows the numbers. The value of production increased from $500 to $600, an increase of $100 or 20 percent.

We've now calculated two percentage changes in the value of production from 2005 to 2006, one valued at 2005 prices and one valued at 2006 prices, and we're ready to take the next step.

Step 3: Calculate the average of the two percentage changes in the value of production. In Table 20.6, you can see that the average of 35 percent (the increase at 2005 prices) and 20 percent (the increase at 2006 prices) is 27.5 percent. This percentage change is our estimate of real GDP growth between 2005 and 2006.

Step 4: Repeat the calculations that we've just described for each year going back to the base year so that we have an estimate of the growth rate of real GDP each year starting from the base year. Table 20.6 shows an example of a sequence of percentage changes going back to 2000, the base year for real GDP.

Step 5: Starting with nominal GDP in the base year, apply the calculated percentage changes to obtain chained dollar estimates of real GDP in 2000 dollars. For example, in 2000 (the base year) real GDP is $50. In 2001, real GDP increases by 20 percent, so real GDP in 2001 is $60. Using the percentage changes in Table 20.6, by 2005, real GDP is $114 and the 27.5 percent increase in 2006 takes it to $145.

■ Calculating the GDP Deflator

The **GDP deflator** is an average of current prices expressed as a percentage of base-year prices. The GDP deflator measures the price level. We calculate the GDP deflator by using nominal GDP and real GDP in the following formula:

$$\text{GDP deflator} = (\text{Nominal GDP} \div \text{Real GDP}) \times 100.$$

You can see why the GDP deflator is a measure of the price level. If nominal GDP rises but real GDP remains unchanged, it must be that prices have risen. The formula would deliver that result in the form of a higher GDP deflator. The larger the nominal GDP for a given real GDP, the higher are prices and the larger is the GDP deflator.

Let's calculate the GDP deflator for 2006 with 2000 as the base year using the numbers in Table 20.6. In 2006, nominal GDP is $600 and real GDP $145, so the GDP deflator is ($600 ÷ $145) × 100, which equals 414.

■ TABLE 20.6

Calculating the Chained-Dollar Measure of Real GDP

		Increase	Percentage increase	Average percentage increase
Valued at 2005 prices				
2005 quantities	$300			
2006 quantities	$405	$105	35.0	
Valued at 2006 prices				27.5
2005 quantities	$500			
2006 quantities	$600	$100	20.0	

(a) Percentage change in real GDP

Year	2000	2001	2002	2003	2004	2005	2006
Percentage increase		20	25	16	14	15	27.5
Real GDP	$50	$60	$75	$87	$99	$114	$145

(b) Chain linking

In part (a), at 2005 prices, the value of production increased from $300 to $405—a 35 percent increase. At 2006 prices, the value of production increased from $500 to $600—a 20 percent increase. The average of these two changes is a 27.5 percent. Real GDP growth in 2006 is 27.5.

In part (b), the real GDP growth rates are chained together to create a time series. Starting with real GDP in 2000, apply the calculated growth rates to obtain the chained-dollar estimates of real GDP for each year.

EYE ON THE U.S. ECONOMY

Deflating the GDP Balloon

Nominal GDP increased every year between 1995 and 2005. Part of the increase reflects increased production, and part of it reflects rising prices.

You can think of GDP as a balloon that is blown up by growing production and rising prices. In the figure, the GDP deflator lets the inflation air— the contribution of rising prices—out of the nominal GDP balloon so that we can see what has happened to real GDP. The red balloon for 1995 shows real GDP in that year. The green balloon shows nominal GDP in 2005. The red balloon for 2005 shows real GDP for that year. To see real GDP in 2005,

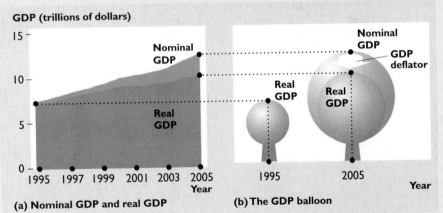

(a) Nominal GDP and real GDP

(b) The GDP balloon

SOURCE OF DATA: Bureau of Economic Analysis.

we use the GDP deflator to deflate nominal GDP.

With the inflation air removed, real GDP shows how the total value of production has changed. Production

grew from 1995 through 2005, but in 2001, real GDP shrank. Over the 10 years, real GDP grew by 3.3 percent a year, and in 2005, it was 39 percent higher than it was in 1995.

3 **Distinguish between nominal GDP and real GDP and define the GDP deflator.**

Practice Problem 20.3

1. An island economy produces only bananas and coconuts. Table 1 gives the quantities produced and prices in 2004, and Table 2 gives the quantities produced and prices in 2005. The base year is 2004. Calculate
   a. Nominal GDP in 2004.
   b. Nominal GDP in 2005.
   c. The value of 2005 production in 2004 prices.
   d. The percentage increase in production when valued at 2004 prices.
   e. The value of 2004 production in 2005 prices.
   f. The percentage increase in production when valued at 2005 prices.
   g. Real GDP in 2004 and 2005 (use the chained-dollar method).
   h. The GDP deflator in 2005.

TABLE 1

In 2004:

Item	Quantity	Price
Bananas	100	$10 a bunch
Coconuts	50	$12 a bag

TABLE 2

In 2005:

Item	Quantity	Price
Bananas	110	$15 a bunch
Coconuts	60	$10 a bag

Exercise 20.3

1. An island economy produces only lobsters and crabs. Table 3 gives the quantities produced and the prices in 2004, and Table 4 gives the quantities produced and the prices in 2005. The base year is 2004. Calculate
   a. Nominal GDP in 2004.
   b. Nominal GDP in 2005.
   c. The value of 2005 production in 2004 prices.
   d. The percentage increase in production when valued at 2004 prices.
   e. The value of 2004 production in 2005 prices.
   f. The percentage increase in production when valued at 2005 prices.
   g. Real GDP in 2004 and 2005 (use the chained-dollar method).
   h. The GDP deflator in 2005.

TABLE 3

In 2004:

Item	Quantity	Price
Lobsters	90	$15 each
Crabs	20	$20 each

TABLE 4

In 2005:

Item	Quantity	Price
Lobsters	100	$20 each
Crabs	25	$20 each

Solution to Practice Problem 20.3

1a. Nominal GDP in 2004 is $1,600—expenditure is $1,000 on bananas and $600 on coconuts (Table 1).

1b. Nominal GDP in 2005 is $2,250—expenditure is $1,650 on bananas and $600 on coconuts (Table 2).

1c. The value of 2005 production in 2004 prices is $1,820 (Table 5).

1d. In 2004 prices, the value of production increased from $1,600 to $1,820, an increase of $220. The percentage increase is $(220 \div 1,600) \times 100$, or 13.75 percent.

1e. The value of 2004 production in 2005 prices is $2,000 (Table 6).

1f. In 2005 prices, the value of production increased from $2,000 to $2,250, an increase of $250. The percentage increase is $(250 \div 2,000) \times 100$, or 12.5 percent.

1g. Real GDP in 2004 is $1,600. The average percentage increase in production is $(13.75 + 12.5) \div 2$, which is 13.125 percent. Real GDP in 2005 is 13.125 percent greater than $1,600, which is $1,810.

1h. The GDP deflator in 2005 is (nominal GDP ÷ real GDP) × 100, which is 124.3.

TABLE 5

2005 quantities and 2004 prices

Item	Quantity	Price	Expenditure
Bananas	110	$10	$1,100
Coconuts	60	$12	$720
Value in 2004 prices: $1,820			

TABLE 6

2004 quantities and 2005 prices

Item	Quantity	Price	Expenditure
Bananas	100	$15	$1,500
Coconuts	50	$10	$500
Value in 2005 prices: $2,000			

20.4 THE USE AND LIMITATIONS OF REAL GDP

We use estimates of real GDP for two main purposes:

- To compare the standard of living over time
- To compare the standard of living among countries

■ The Standard of Living Over Time

One method of comparing the standard of living over time is to calculate real GDP per person in different years. **Real GDP per person** is real GDP divided by the population. Real GDP per person tells us the value of goods and services that the average person can enjoy. And by using *real* GDP, we remove any influence that rising prices and a rising cost of living might have had on our comparison.

Table 20.8 summarizes two calculations for the United States: one for 1965 and the other for 2005. In 1965, real GDP was $3,191 billion and the population was 194 million. Dividing $3,191 billion by 194 million, we arrive at $16,448 as the value of real GDP per person in 1965. Doing a similar calculation for 2005, we get real GDP per person of $37,337 in that year.

Most years, the standard of living rises, but sometimes it stands still and occasionally it falls. Let's look at the trends and cycles in the U.S. standard of living.

Real GDP per person
Real GDP divided by the population.

TABLE 20.8 CALCULATING REAL GDP PER PERSON

Year	1965	2005
Real GDP (billions)	$3,191	$11,089
Population (millions)	194	297
Real GDP per person	$16,448	$37,337

Long-Term Trend

A handy way of comparing real GDP per person over time is to express it as a ratio of some reference year. For example, real GDP per person in 2005 is 2.3 times its 1965 level—that is, $37,337 ÷ $16,448 = 2.3.

Figure 20.3 shows the entire 40 years of real GDP per person from 1965 to 2005 expressed as a ratio of the 1965 level. You can see that real GDP per person has increased and that it doubled in the 33 years from 1965 to 1998. Real GDP per person has doubled roughly every 30 years for the past 100 years or more.

Doubling in 30 years means that each generation is about twice as well off as its predecessor. Your generation is twice as well off as your parent's generation and four times as well off as your grandparent's generation. But remember that there is a lot of variation around the average, so individual families don't share the same experience as the average.

Short-Term Fluctuations

We call the fluctuations in the pace of expansion of real GDP the business cycle. A **business cycle** is a periodic but irregular up-and-down movement of total production and other measures of economic activity.

The business cycle isn't a regular, predictable, and repeating cycle like the phases of the moon. The timing and the intensity of the business cycle vary a lot. But every cycle can be described in terms of four stages:

Business cycle
A periodic but irregular up-and-down movement of total production and other measures of economic activity.

1. Expansion
2. Peak
3. Recession
4. Trough

The *expansion* stage of the business cycle is the usual condition of the economy. It is a period during which real GDP is rising. An expansion ends when the

■ **FIGURE 20.3**

Real GDP Per Person in the United States: 1965–2005

Real GDP per person is expressed as a ratio of its level in 1965. When the ratio is 2, as it was in 1998, real GDP per person has doubled—reached twice its 1965 level.

In 2005, real GDP per person was 2.3 times its 1965 level.

The shaded periods are recessions.

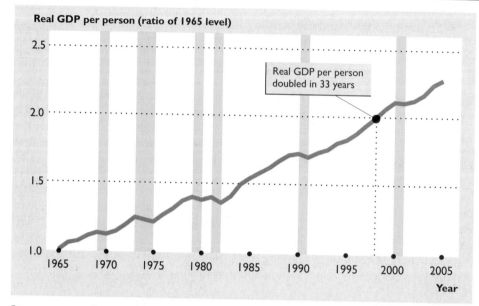

SOURCES OF DATA: Bureau of Economic Analysis, the U.S. Census Bureau, and the National Bureau of Economic Research.

economy reaches a peak. A *peak* is the highest level of real GDP that has been attained up to that time. A peak is followed by a *recession*—defined as a period of falling production that lasts for at least six months. During a recession, incomes are falling, people get laid off from their jobs, and new jobs are harder to find. A recession ends at a *trough,* when real GDP reaches a temporary low point and from which the next expansion begins.

Figure 20.3 highlights the six U.S. recessions of the past 40 years. You can see that there were fewer recessions during the 1990s and 2000s than in earlier years. And you can see that the most recent recession in 2001 was the least intense.

Let's now leave comparisons of the standard of living over time and take a brief look at comparisons among countries.

■ The Standard of Living Among Countries

To use real GDP per person to compare the standard of living among countries, we must convert the numbers for other countries into U.S. dollars. We must also calculate real GDP using a common set of prices—called *purchasing power parity prices*—for all countries. The International Monetary Fund performs these calculations and Figure 2.10 on p. 55 uses this type of data, which tell us, for example, that Jesse, an average American in Chicago, is almost 8 times as well off as Chen, an average Chinese in Beijing.

We've seen how real GDP is used to make standard of living comparisons. But real GDP doesn't include *all* the goods and services produced. Also, real GDP has nothing to say about factors other than the goods and services that affect the standard of living. Let's explore these limitations of real GDP.

■ Goods and Services Omitted from GDP

GDP measures the value of goods and services that are bought in markets. But it excludes

- Household production
- Underground production
- Leisure time
- Environment quality

Household Production

An enormous amount of production takes place every day in our homes. We prepare meals, clean the kitchen, change a light bulb, cut the grass, wash the car, and help a student with homework. These are all examples of production. But because these items are not bought in markets, they are not counted as part of GDP and GDP underestimates the value of the production.

But market production is increasingly replacing household production. Today, 66 percent of people have jobs outside the home, compared with 59 percent in 1965. And many items that were traditionally produced at home are now bought in the market. For example, more families now eat in fast-food restaurants—one of the fastest-growing industries in the United States—and use day-care services. These trends mean that food preparation and child-care services that were once part of household production are now measured as part of GDP. So real GDP grows more rapidly than does real GDP plus home production.

Underground Production

The underground economy is the part of the economy that is hidden from the view of the government either because people want to avoid taxes and regulations or because their actions are illegal. Because underground economic activity is unreported, it is omitted from GDP.

The underground economy includes the production and distribution of illegal drugs, production that uses illegal workers who are paid less than the minimum wage, and jobs that are done for cash to avoid paying income taxes. This last category might be quite large and includes tips earned by cab drivers, hairdressers, and hotel and restaurant workers.

Edgar L. Feige, an economist at the University of Wisconsin, estimates that the U.S. underground economy peaked at 20 percent of GDP in 1987 and decreased to about 16 percent of GDP during the early 1990s. The underground economy is larger than this in many countries and much larger in most developing countries.

Leisure Time

Leisure time is an economic good. Other things remaining the same, the more leisure we have, the better off we are. Our working time is valued as part of GDP, but our leisure time is not. Yet that leisure time must be at least as valuable to us as the wage we earn for working. If it were not, we would work instead. Over the years, leisure time has steadily increased. The workweek has become shorter, more people take early retirement, and the number of vacation days has increased. These improvements in our standard of living are not measured in real GDP.

Environment Quality

An industrial society produces more pollution than an agricultural society does. For example, an industrial society burns more coal, oil, and gas. And it depletes resources, clears forests, and pollutes lakes and rivers.

But industrial activity increases wealth, and wealthy people value a clean environment and are better able to devote resources to protecting it. So pollution does not necessarily increase when production increases. For example, pollution in low-income eastern Germany is much worse than in high-income western Germany.

The value of goods and services produced to protect the environment are included in GDP. For example, the value of catalytic converters that help to protect the atmosphere from automobile emissions is part of GDP. But pollution is not subtracted from GDP. If we didn't produce catalytic converters but instead polluted the atmosphere, we would not count the deteriorating atmosphere as a negative part of GDP. So if our standard of living is adversely affected by pollution, our GDP measure does not show this fact.

■ Other Influences on the Standard of Living

The quantity of goods and services consumed is a major influence on the standard of living. But other influences are

- Health and life expectancy
- Political freedom and social justice

REALITY CHECK

GDP in YOUR Life

As you read the newspaper or business magazine or you listen to the news on TV, look for references to GDP. How is GDP used in daily life? Can you tell whether the reporter is referring to *nominal* GDP or *real* GDP? Are the terms being used accurately or is the news article misusing them?

Using U.S. GDP per person, how does your income compare to the average income?

How do you think your standard of living compares to that of a student who lives in France, or Canada, or China?

Think about your own production of goods and services. Do you produce more market goods than nonmarket goods? How would you go about valuing the nonmarket goods and services that you produce? How is your production counted in the nation's output? Think about the expenditure approach and the income approach as you try to answer this question.

Health and Life Expectancy

Good health and a long life—the hopes of everyone—do not show up directly in real GDP. A higher real GDP enables us to spend more on medical research, health care, a good diet, and exercise equipment. And as real GDP has increased, our life expectancy has lengthened—from 70 years at the end of World War II to nearly 80 years today. Infant deaths and death in childbirth, two scourges of the nineteenth century, have almost been eliminated in the United States.

But we face new health and life expectancy problems every year. Diseases such as AIDS and drug abuse are taking young lives at a rate that causes serious concern. When we take these negative influences into account, real GDP growth overstates the improvements in the standard of living.

Political Freedom and Social Justice

A country might have a very large real GDP per person but have limited political freedom and social justice. For example, a small elite might enjoy political liberty and extreme wealth while the majority of people have limited freedom and live in poverty. Such an economy would generally be regarded as having a lower standard of living than one that had the same amount of real GDP but in which everyone enjoyed political freedom. Today, China has rapid real GDP growth but limited political freedom, while Russia has slower real GDP growth and an emerging democratic political system.

Because of the limitations of real GDP, other measures such as the Human Development Index have been proposed (see *Eye on the Global Economy* below).

EYE ON THE GLOBAL ECONOMY

The Human Development Index

The limitations of real GDP that we've reviewed in this chapter affect the standard of living of every country. So to make international comparisons of the standard of living, we must look at real GDP and other indicators. Nonetheless, real GDP per person is a major component of international comparisons.

The United Nations has constructed a broader measure called the Human Development Index, or HDI, which combines real GDP, life expectancy and health, and education.

The figure shows the relationship between real GDP per person and the HDI. Each dot represents a country. The United States has the third highest real GDP per person but the eighth highest HDI. The small African nation of Sierra Leone has the lowest HDI and the second lowest real GDP per person.

Why is the United States not ranked higher on the HDI?

It is because people who live in the seven countries that have a higher HDI live longer and have slightly better access to health care and education than do people in the United States.

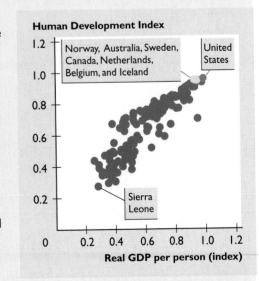

SOURCE OF DATA: *United Nations Human Development Report*, 2004, http://www.undp.org/hdro

4 Describe and explain the limitations of real GDP as a measure of the standard of living.

Practice Problem 20.4

1. The United Nations Human Development Report gives the following data for real GDP per person in 2002: China, $4,580; Russia, $8,230; Canada, $29,480; United States, $35,750. Other information suggests that household production is similar in Canada and the United States and smaller in these two countries than in the other two. The underground economy is largest in Russia and China and a similar proportion of these economies. Canadians and Americans enjoy more leisure hours than do the Chinese and Russians. Canada and the United States spend significantly more to protect the environment, so air, water, and land pollution is less in these countries than in China and Russia. Given this information and ignoring any other influences
   a. In which pair (or pairs) of these four countries is it easiest to compare the standard of living? Why?
   b. In which pair (or pairs) of these four countries is it most difficult to compare the standard of living? Why?
   c. What additional information would we need to be able to make an accurate assessment of the relative standard of living in these four countries?
   d. Do you think that differences in real GDP per person correctly rank the standard of living in these four countries?

Exercise 20.4

1. Life expectancy at birth is 79.3 in Canada, 77.0 in the United States, 70.5 in China, and 66.7 in Russia. Freedom House rates political freedom each year, and its ratings are as follows: Canada and the United States, 1.1 (1.0 is the most free); Russia, 4.5; and China, 7.6 (ratings in the 7+ range are the least free). How do these facts change the relative ranking of living standards indicated by differences in real GDP per person?

Solution to Practice Problem 20.4

1a. Two pairs—Canada and the United States, and China and Russia—are easy to compare because household production, the underground economy, leisure hours, and the environment are similar in the two countries in each pair.

1b. Canada and the United States are the most difficult to compare with China and Russia because household production and the underground economy narrow the differences and leisure hours and the environment widen them.

1c. We would need more detailed information on the value of household production, the underground economy, the value of leisure, and the value of environmental differences.

1d. Differences in real GDP per person probably correctly rank the standard of living in these four countries because where the gap is small (Canada and the United States), other factors are similar, and where other factors differ, the gaps are huge.

CHAPTER CHECKPOINT

Key Points

1 **Define GDP and explain why the value of production, income, and expenditure are the same for an economy.**

- GDP is the market value of all final goods and services produced within a country in a given time period.
- We can value goods and services either by what they cost to produce (incomes) or by what people are willing to pay (expenditures).
- The value of production equals income equals expenditure.

2 **Describe how economic statisticians measure GDP in the United States.**

- We measure GDP by summing expenditures and by summing incomes, and with no errors of measurement the two totals are the same, but in practice, a small statistical discrepancy arises.
- GNP is similar to GDP but GNP is the value of production by factors of production supplied by the residents of a country.

3 **Distinguish between nominal GDP and real GDP and define the GDP deflator.**

- Nominal GDP is the value of production using the prices of the current year and the quantities produced in the current year.
- Real GDP is the value of production using the prices of a base year and the quantities in a current year.
- The GDP deflator is the ratio of nominal GDP to real GDP (multiplied by 100).

4 **Describe and explain the limitations of real GDP as a measure of the standard of living.**

- Real GDP per person is a major indicator of the standard of living.
- Real GDP omits some goods and services and ignores some factors that influence the standard of living.
- The Human Development Index takes some other factors into account.

Key Terms

Business cycle, 513
Consumption expenditure, 499
Depreciation, 506
Disposable personal income, 507
Exports of goods and services, 500
Final good or service, 498
GDP deflator, 510
Government expenditure on goods and services, 500

Gross domestic product (GDP), 498
Gross national product (GNP), 507
Imports of goods and services, 500
Intermediate good or service, 498
Investment, 499
Net domestic product at factor cost, 505
Net exports of goods and services, 500

Nominal GDP, 509
Real GDP, 509
Real GDP per person, 513
Standard of living, 498
Statistical discrepancy, 506

Exercises

FIGURE I

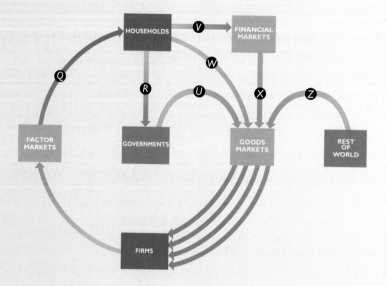

1. In Figure 1, name each of the flows labeled Q, R, U, V, W, X, and Z.

2. You are provided with the following data on the economy of Iberia: GDP was $100 billion, net taxes were $18 billion, government expenditure on goods and services were $20 billion, household saving was $15 billion, consumption expenditure was $67 billion, investment was $21 billion, and exports of goods and services were $30 billion.
    a. Find Iberia's net exports.
    b. Find the value of Iberia's import goods and services.
    c. Label all the items in Figure 1 with their values in Iberia.

3. The values of some of the flows shown in Figure 1 in the U.S. economy in 2002 were U = $1,957 billion, W = $7,376 billion, X = $1,579 billion, and Z = −$424 billion. Calculate
    a. Q.
    b. $R + V$.
    c. GDP.

4. The values of some of the flows shown in Figure 1 in the Canadian economy in 2001 were Q = $1,092 billion, U = $231 billion, W = $621 billion, and Z = $56 billion. Calculate
    a. X.
    b. GDP.

5. The national accounts of Parchment Paradise are kept on (you guessed it) parchment. A fire destroyed the national statistics office, and the national income and product accounts are now incomplete. But they contain the following information for 2005: GDP (income approach) was $2,900; consump-

tion expenditure was $2,000; indirect taxes less subsidies were $100; interest, rental, and profit were $500; investment was $800; government expenditure on goods and services was $400; wages were $2,000; net factor income from abroad was $50; and net exports were −$200. You've been hired as an economist to reconstruct the missing numbers by calculating for 2005

a. GDP (expenditure approach).
b. Depreciation.
c. Net domestic product at factor cost.
d. Statistical discrepancy.
e. GNP.

6. Nominal GDP in the United States in 2004 was $11,734.3 billion, and real GDP (in 2000 dollars) was $10,755.7 billion. Real GDP in 2000 (in 2000 dollars) was $9,817 billion.
   a. Calculate the GDP deflator in 2004.
   b. What was the GDP deflator in 2000?
   c. By what percentage did the price level rise between 2000 and 2004?
   d. By what percentage did real GDP increase between 2000 and 2004?
   e. By what percentage did nominal GDP increase between 2000 and 2004?

7. The GDP deflator in the United States in 1990 was 81.6, and real GDP in 1990 (in 2000 dollars) was $7,112.5 billion. The GDP deflator in the United States in 2004 was 109.1, and real GDP in 2004 (in 2000 dollars) was $10,755.7 billion.
   a. Calculate nominal GDP in 1990.
   b. Calculate nominal GDP in 2004.
   c. What was the percentage increase in the nominal GDP between 1990 and 2004?
   d. What was the percentage increase in production between 1990 and 2004?
   e. By what percentage did the cost of living rise between 1990 and 2004?

8. Use the information in Table 1 and a base year of 2005 to calculate
   a. Nominal GDP in 2005.
   b. Nominal GDP in 2006.
   c. Real GDP in 2006 by using the traditional method.
   d. Real GDP in 2006 by using the chained-dollar method.
   e. The GDP deflator in 2006.
   f. Comment on the percentage increase in production in 2006.

9. Use the information in Tables 1 and 2 and a base year of 2005 to calculate
   a. Nominal GDP in 2007.
   b. Nominal GDP in 2008.
   c. Real GDP in 2007 by using the traditional method.
   d. Real GDP in 2008 by using the traditional method.
   e. Real GDP in 2007 by using the chained-dollar method.
   f. Real GDP in 2008 by using the chained-dollar method.
   g. The GDP deflator in 2007 and 2008.
   h. Comment on the percentage increase in production between 2006 and 2008.
   i. Comment on the change in the cost of living between 2006 and 2008.

TABLE 1

(a) In 2005:

Item	Quantity	Price
Fun	40	$2
Food	60	$3

(b) In 2006:

Item	Quantity	Price
Fun	44	$3
Food	72	$2

TABLE 2

(a) In 2007:

Item	Quantity	Price
Fun	50	$3
Food	72	$3

(b) In 2008:

Item	Quantity	Price
Fun	51	$4
Food	80	$6

Critical Thinking

10. Boeing plans to outsource the production of its new 787 airliner to Japan. At the same time, Toyota outsources the manufacture of cars to Kentucky.
    a. Explain how Boeing's outsourcing decision affects U.S. GDP, U.S. GNP, and real GDP per person in the United States.
    b. Explain how Toyota's outsourcing decision affects U.S. GDP, U.S. GNP, and real GDP per person in the United States.

11. How do underground economic activities affect the usefulness of the national accounts for comparing the value of production over time and across countries? What underground economic activities do the national accounts miss? Do these activities contribute to the standard of living? Do you think that it would be worth expanding the scope of the accounts to include estimates of the value of underground activities?

12. The United Nations Index of Human Development is based on the levels of GDP per person, life expectancy at birth, and indicators of the quality and quantity of education. Do you think the United Nations should expand its index to include items such as pollution, resource depletion, and political freedom? Are there any other factors that influence the standard of living that you think should be included in a comprehensive measure?

 ## Web Exercises

Use the links on MyEconLab to work the following exercises.

13. Visit the Bureau of Economic Analysis Web site and obtain the most recently released National Income and Product Account data for the United States. For the most recently available quarter,
    a. What are the values of consumption expenditure, investment, government expenditure, and net exports?
    b. Check that when you sum the items in part **a**, the total equals GDP.
    c. Find the GDP deflator with the base year of 2000.
    d. Calculate real GDP.
    e. Was the cost of living higher in the most recent quarter than in 2000? Explain your answer.

14. Visit the Bureau of Economic Analysis Web site and obtain the most recently released real GDP data—Gross State Product—for the state in which you live. Visit the Census Bureau Web site and obtain data on the population of your state.
    a. Calculate Gross State Product per person in your state. Compare this number with the U.S. average for the same time period.
    b. Which industries in your state contribute most to your state's production?

15. Visit the International Monetary Fund World Economic Outlook Web site and obtain data for 1980 and the current year for the United States and Japan that enable you to answer the following questions.
    a. Which country had the greater increase in real GDP per person?
    b. What is the GDP of each country as a percentage of world GDP?
    c. What is the level of real GDP per person in Japan as a percentage of that in the United States?
    d. What do you learn from your answers to parts **a**, **b**, and **c** about the standard of living in Japan and the United States?

Jobs and Unemployment

CHAPTER CHECKLIST

When you have completed your study of this chapter, you will be able to

1 Define the unemployment rate and other labor market indicators.

2 Describe the trends and fluctuations in the indicators of labor market performance in the United States.

3 Describe the sources and types of unemployment, define full employment, and explain the link between unemployment and real GDP.

What kind of job market will you encounter when you graduate? How long will it take you to find the right job? Will well-paid and interesting jobs be hard to find? Or will you have lots of choice with employers competing to hire you and trying to outbid each other?

The answers to these questions depend on a large number of personal factors. Among them are the subject in which you've majored, your grades, and your ability to convince a potential employer that you're focused and hardworking. They also depend on the general health of the labor market.

In this chapter, you will learn how economists track the labor market. We'll describe a monthly survey that discovers the labor market status of the population—the raw material for job market statistics. We'll describe the trends and fluctuations in the indicators of labor market performance. And we'll look at the sources and types of unemployment and learn what we mean by "full employment."

21.1 LABOR MARKET INDICATORS

Every month, 1,600 field interviewers and supervisors working on a joint project between the Bureau of Labor Statistics (or BLS) and the Bureau of the Census survey 60,000 households and ask a series of questions about the age and labor market status of its members. This survey is called the Current Population Survey. Let's look at the types of data collected by this survey.

■ Current Population Survey

Figure 21.1 shows the categories into which the BLS divides the population. It also shows the relationships among the categories. The first category divides the population into two groups: the working-age population and others. The **working-age population** is the total number of people aged 16 years and over who are not in jail, hospital, or some other form of institutional care or in the U.S. Armed Forces. In May 2005, the estimated population of the United States was 296.1 million. In May 2005, the working-age population was 225.7 million and 70.4 million people were under 16 years of age, in the military, or living in institutions.

The second category divides the working-age population into two groups: those in the labor force and those not in the labor force. The **labor force** is the number of people employed plus the number unemployed. In May 2005, the U.S. labor force was 148.9 million and 76.8 million were not in the labor force. Most of those not in the labor force were in school full time or had retired from work.

The third category divides the labor force into two groups: the employed and the unemployed. In May 2005 in the United States, 141.6 million were employed and 7.3 million were unemployed.

■ Population Survey Criteria

The survey counts as employed all persons who, during the week before the survey, either

1. Worked at least 1 hour as paid employees or worked 15 hours or more as unpaid workers in their family business or
2. Were not working but had jobs or businesses from which they were temporarily absent.

The survey counts as unemployed all persons who, during the week before the survey,

1. Had no employment,
2. Were available for work,

and either

1. Had made specific efforts to find employment some time during the previous four weeks or
2. Were waiting to be recalled to a job from which they had been laid off.

People in the working-age population who by the above criteria are neither employed nor unemployed are classified as not in the labor force.

Working-age population
The total number of people aged 16 years and over who are not in jail, hospital, or some other form of institutional care or in the U.S. Armed Forces.

Labor force
The number of people employed plus the number unemployed.

FIGURE 21.1

Population Labor Force Categories

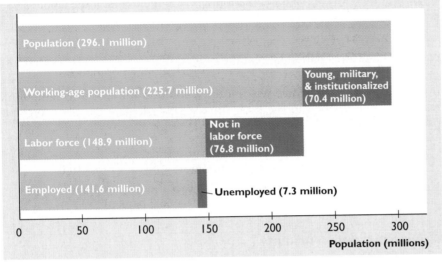

The U.S. population is divided into the working-age population and the young, military, and institutionalized. The working-age population is divided into the labor force and those not in the labor force. The labor force is divided into the employed and the unemployed. The figure shows the data for May 2005.

SOURCE OF DATA: Bureau of Labor Statistics.

■ Two Main Labor Market Indicators

Using the numbers from the Current Population Survey, the BLS calculates several indicators of the state of the labor market. The two main labor market indicators are

- The unemployment rate
- The labor force participation rate

The Unemployment Rate

The amount of unemployment is an indicator of the extent to which people who want jobs can't find them. It tells us the amount of slack in the labor market. The **unemployment rate** is the percentage of the people in the labor force who are unemployed. That is,

Unemployment rate
The percentage of the people in the labor force who are unemployed.

$$\text{Unemployment rate} = \frac{\text{Number of people employed}}{\text{Labor force}} \times 100.$$

In May 2005, the number of people unemployed was 7.3 million and the labor force was 148.9 million. We can use these numbers to calculate the unemployment rate in May 2005, which is

$$\text{Unemployment rate} = \frac{7.3 \text{ million}}{148.9 \text{ million}} \times 100$$

$$= 4.9 \text{ percent.}$$

The Labor Force Participation Rate

Labor force participation rate
The percentage of the working-age population who are members of the labor force.

The number of people in the labor force is an indicator of the willingness of people of working age to take jobs. The **labor force participation rate** is the percentage of the working-age population who are members of the labor force. That is

$$\text{Labor force participation rate} = \frac{\text{Labor force}}{\text{Working-age population}} \times 100.$$

In May 2005, the labor force was 148.9 million and the working-age population was 225.7 million. We can use these numbers to calculate the labor force participation rate in May 2005, which is

$$\text{Labor force participation rate} = \frac{148.9 \text{ million}}{225.7 \text{ million}} \times 100$$

$$= 66.0 \text{ percent.}$$

■ Discouraged Workers

Discouraged worker
A person who does not have a job, is available and willing to work, but has not made specific efforts to find a job within the previous four weeks.

A **discouraged worker** is a person who does not have a job, is available and willing to work, but has not made specific efforts to find a job within the previous four weeks. Neither the unemployment rate nor the labor force participation rate includes discouraged workers. In May 2005, 300,000 people who were not in the labor force wanted jobs. If we add this group to the labor force and the number unemployed, the unemployment rate becomes 5.1 percent—only slightly higher than the standard definition of the unemployment rate.

■ Part-Time Workers

Full-time workers
People who usually work 35 hours or more a week.

Part-time workers
People who usually work less than 35 hours a week.

Involuntary part-time workers
People who work 1 to 34 hours per week but who are looking for full-time work.

The Current Population Survey measures the number of full-time workers and part-time workers. **Full-time workers** are those who usually work 35 hours or more a week. **Part-time workers** are those who usually work less than 35 hours a week. Part-time workers are divided into two groups: part time for economic reasons and part time for noneconomic reasons.

Part-time workers for economic reasons, also called **involuntary part-time workers**, are people who work 1 to 34 hours but who are looking for full-time work. These people are unable to find full-time work because of unfavorable business conditions or because of seasonal decreases in the availability of full-time work.

Part-time workers for noneconomic reasons do not want to work full time and are not available for such work. This group includes people with health problems, family or personal responsibilities, or education commitments that limit their availability for work.

The Bureau of Labor Statistics uses the data on full-time and part-time status to calculate the full-time labor force and the part-time labor force as well as the full-time unemployment rate and the part-time unemployment rate.

In May 2005, when the labor force was 148.9 million, the full-time labor force was 117.5 million and the part-time labor force was 24.1 million. An estimated 4.2 million involuntary part-time workers, or 17 percent of part-time workers, were looking for full-time work.

The Current Population Survey

The Bureau of Labor Statistics and the Bureau of the Census go to great lengths to collect accurate labor force data. They constantly train and retrain around 1,600 field interviewers and supervisors. Each month, each field interviewer contacts 37 households and asks basic demographic questions about all persons living at the address and detailed labor force questions about persons aged 15 or over.

Once a household has been selected for the survey, it is questioned for four consecutive months and then again for the same four months a year later. Each month, the addresses that have been in the panel eight times are removed and 6,250

new addresses are added. The rotation and overlap of households provide very reliable information about month-to-month and year-to-year changes in the labor market.

The first time that a household is in the panel, an interviewer, armed with a laptop computer, visits it. If the household has a telephone, most of

the subsequent interviews are conducted by phone, many of them from one of the three telephone interviewing centers in Hagerstown, Maryland; Jeffersonville, Indiana; and Tucson, Arizona.

For more information about the Current Population Survey, visit http://www.bls.gov/cps/cps_faq.htm.

■ Aggregate Hours

The labor market indicators that we've just examined are useful signs of the health of the economy and directly measure what matters to most people: jobs and whether those jobs are full time or part time. But they don't tell us the *quantity of labor* employed.

The reason the number of people employed does not measure the quantity of labor employed is that jobs are not all the same. You've seen that people in part-time jobs work between 1 and 34 hours a week and people in full-time jobs work 35 or more hours a week. A Starbucks coffee shop might hire six students who work for three hours a day each. Another Starbucks might hire two full-time workers who work nine hours a day each. The total number of people employed is eight, but the total hours worked by six part-time workers is the same as the total hours worked by the two full-time workers.

To determine the total amount of labor employed, we measure labor in hours rather than in jobs. **Aggregate hours** are the total number of hours worked by all the people employed, both full time and part time, during a year and equal the number of people employed multiplied by the average work hours per person.

In May 2005, 141.6 million people worked an average of 33.9 hours per week. With 50 workweeks per year, aggregate hours were

$$\text{Aggregate hours} = 141.6 \text{ million} \times 33.9 \times 50 = 240 \text{ billion.}$$

The measurement of aggregate hours is not very precise. But the estimation of the percentage change in aggregate hours from one month to another is more precise. For this reason, the Bureau of Labor Statistics publishes aggregate hours data as an index number rather than as a number of hours.

Aggregate hours
The total number of hours worked by all the people employed, both full time and part time, during a year.

I **Define the unemployment rate and other labor market indicators.**

Practice Problem 21.1

1. The Bureau of Labor Statistics reported that in January 2000, the labor force was 140.9 million, employment was 135.2 million, and the working-age population was 208.6 million. Average weekly hours were 34.5. Calculate for that month the
   a. Unemployment rate.
   b. Labor force participation rate.
   c. Aggregate hours worked in a week.

Exercises 21.1

1. The Bureau of Labor Statistics reported that in July 2002, the labor force was 143.9 million; employment was 135.3 million; and the working-age population was 214 million. Calculate for that month the
   a. Unemployment rate.
   b. Labor force participation rate.

2. Statistics Canada reported that in January 2002, the Canadian labor force was 16.2 million, employment was 14.8 million, and the working-age population was 24.8 million. Calculate for that month the Canadian
   a. Unemployment rate.
   b. Labor force participation rate.

3. Given the data in exercises 1 and 2, do you think jobs are harder to find in Canada or in the United States? Why?

4. Use the link on the Foundations Web site to obtain data on the labor force, employment, unemployment, and the working-age population for your own state in the most recent month for which data are available. For that month,
   a. Calculate your state's unemployment rate.
   b. Calculate your state's labor force participation rate.
   c. Compare the labor market indicators in your state with the U.S. averages.

Solution to Practice Problem 21.1

1a. The unemployment rate is 4.0 percent. The labor force is the sum of the number employed plus the number unemployed. So the number unemployed equals the labor force minus the number employed, which equals 140.9 million − 135.2 million = 5.7 million. The unemployment rate is the number unemployed as a percentage of the labor force, which is (5.7 million ÷ 140.9 million) × 100 = 4.0 percent.

1b. The labor force participation rate is 67.5 percent. The labor force participation rate is the percentage of the working-age population who are in the labor force, which equals (140.9 million ÷ 208.6 million) × 100 = 67.5 percent.

1c. Aggregate hours worked in a week are 4,664.4 million. In January 2000, average weekly hours were 34.5 and employment was 135.2 million. So the aggregate hours worked in a week were 34.5 × 135.2 million = 4,664.4 million.

21.2 LABOR MARKET TRENDS AND FLUCTUATIONS

What do we learn about the U.S. labor market from changes in the unemployment rate, the labor force participation rate, part-time employment, and hours worked? Let's explore the trends and fluctuations in these indicators.

■ Unemployment

Figure 21.2 shows the U.S. unemployment rate over the 40 years from 1965 to 2005. Over these years, the average U.S. unemployment rate was 5.9 percent—a bit higher than the 2005 unemployment rate. The 1960s and the late 1990s were years of below-average unemployment, and the 1970s and 1980s were years of above-average unemployment.

During the 1960s, the unemployment rate fell to 3.5 percent. These years saw a rapid rate of job creation partly from the demands placed on the economy by the growth of defense production during the Vietnam War and partly from an expansion of consumer spending encouraged by an expansion of social programs. Another burst of rapid job creation driven by the "new economy"—the high-technology sector driven by the expansion of the Internet—took the unemployment rate below average between 1995 and 2000.

In contrast to the 1960s and 1990s, the 1970s and 1980s were years of above-average unemployment, a consequence of massive hikes in the world oil price. The unemployment rate peaked at almost 10 percent during the 1982 recession.

In 2001 and 2002, the unemployment rate increased as the U.S. economy went into a recession. But the unemployment rate peaked at its 40-year average level. The expansion of 2003–2005 pushed the unemployment rate below average again but the pace of job creation was slow so the fall in unemployment was modest.

▨ FIGURE 21.2

The U.S. Unemployment Rate: 1965–2005

The average unemployment rate from 1965 to 2005 was 5.9 percent. The unemployment rate increases in recessions and decreases in expansions. Unemployment fell to an unusually low rate during the expansion of the 1990s and increased during the 2001 recession.

Source of data: Bureau of Labor Statistics.

The Labor Market in the Great Depression

The Great Depression was a period of prolonged and extreme economic hardship that lasted from 1929 until the end of the 1930s.

By 1933, the worst of the Depression years, real GDP had fallen by a huge 30 percent. And, as the figure shows, one in four of the people who wanted jobs couldn't find them.

The horrors of the Great Depression led to the New Deal and shaped political attitudes that persist today.

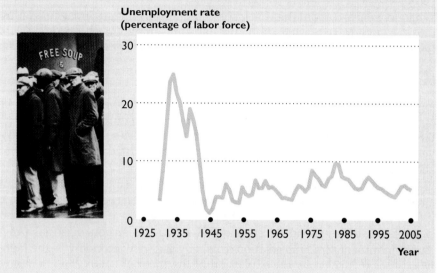

SOURCE OF DATA: Bureau of Labor Statistics.

■ The Participation Rate

Figure 21.3 shows the labor force participation rate, which increased from 59 percent during the 1960s to 67 percent in 2000. Since 2000, the participation rate has fallen slightly. The cyclical fluctuations in the participation rate are mild and result

---

■ FIGURE 21.3

The Changing Face of the Labor Market: 1965–2005

〤 myeconlab

During the past 40 years, the labor force participation rate has increased. The labor force participation rate of men has decreased, and that of women has increased.

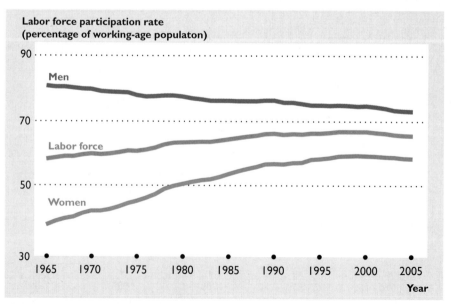

SOURCE OF DATA: Bureau of Labor Statistics.

Unemployment Around the World

In 1995, France, Germany, Italy, and Canada had the highest unemployment rates and Japan had the lowest. The United Kingdom and the United States were in the middle of the pack.

Through the 1990s, unemployment rates fell in the United States, the United Kingdom, and Canada but increased in Japan.

By 2005, the unemployment rates of the United States, the United Kingdom, and Japan had converged.

The average unemployment rate of France, Germany, and Italy, as well as Canada, remained high. All of these countries have higher unemployment benefits than the United States. Also, labor unions and regulations make the European labor markets less flexible than the U.S. labor market.

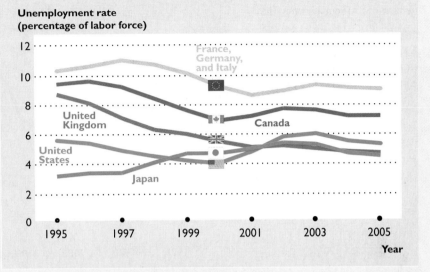

SOURCE OF DATA: International Monetary Fund, *World Economic Outlook*, May 2005.

from unsuccessful job seekers becoming discouraged workers—people who leave the labor force in a recession and reenter in an expansion.

Why has the labor force participation rate increased? The main reason is an increase in the number of women who have entered the labor force. Figure 21.3 shows this increase. Between 1965 and 1999, the participation rate of women increased from 39 percent to 60 percent. This increase is spread across women of all age groups and occurred for four main reasons. First, more women pursued a college education and so increased their earning power. Second, technological change in the workplace created a large number of white-collar jobs with flexible work hours that many women found attractive. Third, technological change in the home increased the time available for paid employment. And fourth, families looked increasingly to a second income to balance tight budgets.

Figure 21.3 also shows another remarkable trend in the U.S. labor force: The participation rate of men *decreased* from 81 percent in 1965 to 73 percent in 2005. As in the case of women, this decrease is spread across all age groups. Some of the decrease occurred because older men decided to retire earlier. During the 1990s, some of this earlier retirement was made possible by an increase in wealth. But some arose from job loss at an age at which finding a new job was difficult. For other men, mainly those in their teens and twenties, decreased labor force participation occurred because more remained in full-time education.

■ Part-Time Workers

A part-time job is attractive to many workers because it enables them to balance family and other commitments with work. Part-time jobs are attractive to employers because they don't have to pay benefits to part-time workers and are

531

■ FIGURE 21.4
Part-time Workers: 1975–2005

Part-time workers are a steady 16 to 17 percent of total employment. The percentage of workers who are part time barely fluctuates with the business cycle. But the percentage of part-time workers who would like full-time work increases in a recession and decreases in an expansion.

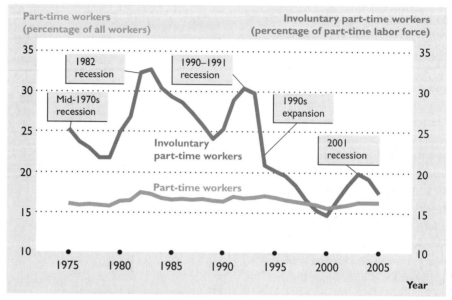

SOURCE OF DATA: Bureau of Labor Statistics.

less constrained by government regulations. Figure 21.4 shows some interesting facts about part-time workers. First, the percentage of workers who are part time has stayed remarkably steady at between 16 and 17 percent of total employment, and that percentage barely fluctuates with the business cycle. Even in the 1982 recession, the part-time percentage reached only 17.4 percent, and in the 1990–1991 recession, it reached 18.1 percent. During the expansion years after 1994, it declined.

Second, the involuntary part-time rate has averaged 24 percent but has experienced large swings. In the 1982 recession, the rate climbed to approach 33 percent of part-time work. And in the 1990–1991 recession, it climbed to 30 percent. During the 1990s expansion, the involuntary part-time rate decreased rapidly, and even after rising again in the 2001 recession, it stood below its 1975 level.

■ Aggregate and Average Hours

Figure 21.5(a) shows aggregate hours in the U.S. economy from 1965 to 2005. Aggregate hours have an upward trend, but they have not grown as quickly as have the number of people employed. Between 1965 and 2005, the number of people employed in the U.S. economy doubled—an increase of 100 percent. During that same period, aggregate hours increased by 75 percent. Why the difference? Because average hours per worker decreased.

Figure 21.5(b) shows average hours per worker. Starting out at 38.5 hours a week in 1965, average hours per worker decreased to just below 34 hours a week in 2005. This shortening of the average workweek occurred almost entirely because the average hours worked by full-time workers decreased. The number of part-time jobs as a percentage of full-time jobs was basically constant.

Fluctuations in aggregate hours and average hours per worker line up with the business cycle. Figure 21.5 identifies the four recessions, during which aggregate hours decreased and average hours per worker decreased faster than trend.

FIGURE 21.5

Aggregate and Average Hours: 1965–2005

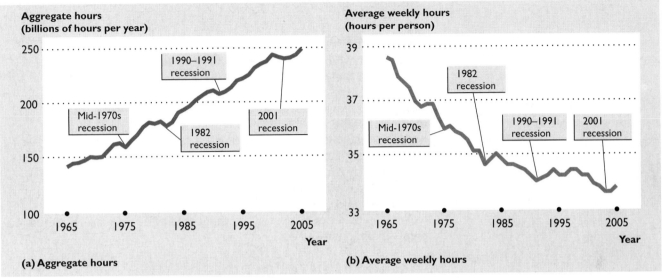

(a) Aggregate hours

(b) Average weekly hours

SOURCE OF DATA: Bureau of Labor Statistics.

In part (a), between 1965 and 2005, aggregate hours increased by 75 percent a year. Fluctuations in aggregate hours coincide with business cycle fluctuations.

In part (b), average weekly hours decreased and also, like aggregate hours, fluctuated with the business cycle.

EYE ON THE GLOBAL ECONOMY

Women in the Labor Force

The participation rate of women in the U.S. labor force increased from 40 percent in 1965 to 60 percent in 2000 and has remained at that level. This upward trend is found in most of the world's rich advanced nations.

But the *level* of women's participation in the labor force varies a great deal around the world. Here, we compare seven other countries—Australia, Canada, France, Japan, Spain, Sweden, and the United Kingdom—with the United States.

Among these countries, Sweden's labor force has the largest participa-

tion rate of women and the United States comes second. Spain and Japan have the lowest rates.

Cultural factors play a role in determining national differences in

women's work choices. But economic factors such as the percentage of women with a college degree will ultimately dominate cultural influences and bring a convergence of outcomes.

SOURCE OF DATA: OECD.

2 **Describe the trends and fluctuations in the indicators of labor market performance in the United States.**

Practice Problem 21.2

1. Use the link on MyEconLab and view the data for Figures 21.2, 21.3, 21.4, and 21.5. Then answer the following questions:
   a. In which decade—the 1960s, 1970s, 1980s, or 1990s—was the unemployment rate the lowest? What brought low unemployment in that decade?
   b. In which decade was the unemployment rate the highest? What brought high unemployment in that decade?
   c. Describe the trends in the participation rates of men and women and all workers. Why did these trends occur?
   d. Describe the trends and fluctuations in part-time work. Why is part-time work on the increase?
   e. Do aggregate hours increase at the same rate as the increase in employment? Explain why or why not.

Exercise 21.2

1. Use the link on MyEconLab and view the data for Figures 21.2, 21.3, 21.4, and 21.5. Then answer the following questions:
   a. During which decade—the 1960s, 1970s, 1980s, or 1990s—did the labor force participation rate of women increase most? Suggest some reasons why this rapid increase occurred during that decade.
   b. In which decade did the labor force participation rate of men decrease most? Why do you think this rapid decrease occurred in that decade?
   c. Describe the trends in the unemployment rate, the labor force participation rates of men and women, part-time workers, involuntary part-time workers, and aggregate hours since 1994. Why did these trends occur?

Solution to Practice Problem 21.2

1a. The average unemployment rates in each decade were: 1960s, 4.8 percent; 1970s, 6.2 percent; 1980s, 7.3 percent; 1990s, 5.7 percent. The unemployment rate was lowest during the 1960s. Unemployment was low during the 1960s because defense spending on the Vietnam War and an expansion of social programs brought about a rapidly expanding economy.

1b. The unemployment rate was highest during the 1980s. A deep recession in 1982 sent the unemployment rate to a peak of almost 10 percent.

1c. The participation rate of women increased because (1) better-educated women earn more, (2) more white-collar jobs with flexible work hours were created, (3) people have more time for paid employment, and (4) families increasingly needed two incomes to balance their budgets. The participation rate of men decreased because more men remained in school and some men took early retirement. The overall participation rate increased.

1d. Part-time work has increased because it provides flexible hours for workers and cuts costs for firms.

1e. Aggregate hours increase more slowly than employment because average hours per worker fall.

21.3 THE SOURCES AND TYPES OF UNEMPLOYMENT

Why do people become unemployed, how long do they remain unemployed, and who is at greatest risk of becoming unemployed? Let's begin to answer these questions by looking at the events that move people into and out of the labor market and into and out of jobs.

■ Sources of Unemployment

The labor market is constantly churning. New jobs are created, and old ones are destroyed; and some people move into the labor force, and some move out of it. An astonishing 4.8 million people start a new job every month and a similar but normally slightly smaller number lose or leave their job every month. This churning creates unemployment. People become unemployed if they are

1. Job losers
2. Job leavers
3. Entrants or reentrants

Job Losers

A *job loser* is someone who is fired or laid off from a job, either permanently or temporarily. People lose their jobs for many reasons. Some people are just not a good match for the job they're doing. Firms fail, or a new technology destroys some types of jobs. Offshore outsourcing also takes some jobs—but fewer than 2 million a year are lost for this reason (less than a half of a month's job turnover).

A job loser has two choices: Either look for another job or withdraw from the labor force. A job loser who decides to look for a new job remains in the labor force and becomes unemployed. A job loser who decides to withdraw from the labor force is classified as "not in the labor force." Most job losers decide to look for a new job, and some of them take a long time to find one.

Job Leavers

A *job leaver* is someone who voluntarily quits a job. Most people who leave their jobs do so for one of two reasons: Either they've gotten a better job or they've decided to withdraw from the labor force. Neither of these types of job leavers becomes unemployed. But a few people quit their jobs because they want to spend time looking for a better one. These job leavers become unemployed.

Entrants and Reentrants

An *entrant* is someone who has just left school and is looking for a job. Some entrants get a job right away and are never unemployed. But many entrants spend time searching for their first job, and during this period, they are unemployed.

A *reentrant* is someone who has previously had a job, has then quit and left the labor force, and has now decided to look for a job again. Some reentrants are people who have been out of the labor force rearing children, but most are discouraged workers—people who gave up searching for jobs because they were not able to find suitable ones and who have now decided to look again.

Figure 21.6 shows the magnitudes of the three sources of unemployment. Most unemployed people are job losers. Also, their number fluctuates most.

FIGURE 21.6

Unemployment by Reasons: 1975–2005

Everyone who is unemployed is a job loser, a job leaver, or an entrant or reentrant into the labor force. Job losers are the biggest group, and their number fluctuates most. Entrants and reentrants are the second biggest group. Their number also fluctuates. Job leavers are the smallest group and their number fluctuates least.

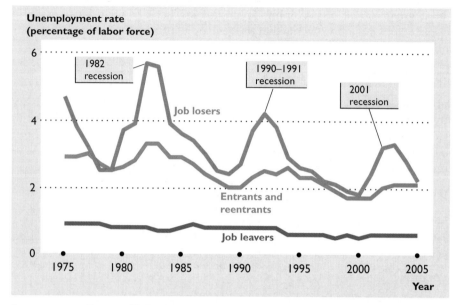

SOURCE OF DATA: Bureau of Labor Statistics.

Entrants and reentrants are also a large component, and their number also fluctuates. Job leavers are the smallest and most stable source of unemployment.

People who end a period of unemployment are either

1. Hires and recalls or
2. Withdrawals

Hires and Recalls

A *hire* is someone who has been unemployed and has started a new job. And a *recall* is someone who has been temporarily laid off and has started work again. Firms are constantly hiring and recalling workers, so there are always people moving from unemployment to employment.

Withdrawals

A *withdrawal* is someone who has been unemployed and has decided to stop looking for a job. Most of these people are *discouraged workers*. They will most likely reenter the labor force later when they think that job prospects have improved.

■ Types of Unemployment

Unemployment is classified into four types:

- Frictional
- Structural
- Seasonal
- Cyclical

Frictional Unemployment

Frictional unemployment is the unemployment that arises from normal labor turnover—from people entering and leaving the labor force and from the ongoing creation and destruction of jobs. Frictional unemployment is a permanent and healthy phenomenon in a dynamic, growing economy.

The unending flow of people into and out of the labor force and the processes of job creation and job destruction create the need for people to search for jobs and the need for businesses to search for workers. There are always some businesses with unfilled jobs and some people seeking jobs.

Look in your local newspaper, and you will see that there are always jobs being advertised. Businesses don't usually hire the first person who applies for a job, and unemployed people don't usually take the first job that comes their way. Instead, both firms and workers spend time searching out what they believe will be the best attainable match. By this search process, people can match their own skills and interests with the available jobs and find a satisfying job and income. While these unemployed people are searching, they are frictionally unemployed.

The amount of frictional unemployment depends on the rate at which people enter and reenter the labor force and on the rate at which jobs are created and destroyed. During the 1970s, the amount of frictional unemployment increased because of the postwar baby boom that began during the 1940s. By the late 1970s, the baby boom created a bulge in the number of people leaving school. As these people entered the labor force, the amount of frictional unemployment increased. Frictional unemployment remained high until the information-age expansion of the mid-1990s. Since 1994, frictional unemployment has decreased.

The amount of frictional unemployment is also influenced by unemployment compensation. The greater the number of unemployed people eligible for benefits and the more generous those benefits, the longer is the average time taken in job search and the greater is the amount of frictional unemployment. Unemployment benefits in Canada and Western Europe exceed those in the United States, and these economies have higher unemployment rates.

Structural Unemployment

Structural unemployment is the unemployment that arises when changes in technology or international competition change the skills needed to perform jobs or change the locations of jobs. Structural unemployment usually lasts longer than frictional unemployment because workers must retrain and possibly relocate to find a job. For example, when a telephone exchange in Gary, Indiana, is automated, some jobs in that city are destroyed. Meanwhile, new jobs for life-insurance salespeople and retail clerks are created in Chicago, Indianapolis, and other cities. The former telephone operators remain unemployed for several months until they move, retrain, and get one of these jobs. Structural unemployment is painful, especially for older workers for whom the best available option might be to retire early but with a lower income than they had expected.

Sometimes, the amount of structural unemployment is modest. At other times, it is large, and at such times, structural unemployment can become a serious long-term problem. It was especially large during the late 1970s and early

Frictional unemployment
The unemployment that arises from normal labor turnover—from people entering and leaving the labor force and from the ongoing creation and destruction of jobs.

A new graduate interviews for a job.

Structural unemployment
The unemployment that arises when changes in technology or international competition change the skills needed to perform jobs or change the locations of jobs.

A job lost to computer technology.

1980s. During those years, oil price hikes and an increasingly competitive international environment destroyed jobs in traditional U.S. industries, such as auto and steel making, and created jobs in new industries, such as information processing, electronics, and bioengineering. Structural unemployment was also present during the early 1990s as many businesses and governments downsized.

Seasonal Unemployment

Seasonal unemployment The unemployment that arises because of seasonal weather patterns.

Seasonal unemployment is the unemployment that arises because of seasonal weather patterns. Seasonal unemployment increases during the winter months and decreases during the spring and summer. A fruit picker who is laid off after the fall harvest and who gets rehired the following summer experiences seasonal unemployment. A construction worker who gets laid off during the winter and rehired in the spring also experiences seasonal unemployment.

Cyclical Unemployment

Cyclical unemployment The fluctuating unemployment over the business cycle that increases during a recession and decreases during an expansion.

Cyclical unemployment is the fluctuating unemployment over the business cycle. Cyclical unemployment increases during a recession and decreases during an expansion. An autoworker who is laid off because the economy is in a recession and who gets rehired some months later when the expansion begins has experienced cyclical unemployment.

■ Duration and Demographics of Unemployment

Some people are unemployed for a week or two and others for a year or more. The longer the period of unemployment, the greater is the personal cost to the unemployed. The average duration of unemployment varies over the business cycle. In a recession, the average duration increases, and during an expansion, the average duration decreases.

In 2000, the economy was in a strong expansion and the unemployment rate was low. In that year the average unemployment spell lasted for 6 weeks and 77 percent of the unemployed found jobs in less than 14 weeks. About 11 percent of the unemployed took longer than 27 weeks to find a job. In 1983, the economy was recovering from a deep recession and the unemployment rate was high. In that year the average unemployment spell lasted for 10 weeks and only 60 percent of the unemployed found jobs in less than 14 weeks. Almost 25 percent of the unemployed took longer than 27 weeks to find a job.

Unemployment does not affect all demographic groups in the same way. The differences between the groups that are most and least affected by unemployment are large. Figure 21.7 shows some averages between 1995 and 2005. During this period, black teenagers had the highest unemployment rates, which averaged more than 30 percent. Whites aged 20 years and over had the lowest unemployment rates, which averaged about 4 percent. Women have lower unemployment rates than men.

Why are teenage unemployment rates so high? There are two reasons. First, young people are still discovering what they are good at and trying different lines of work, so they leave their jobs more frequently than older workers do. Second, firms often hire teenagers on a short-term or trial basis, so the rate of job loss is higher for teenagers than for older workers.

You've seen that there is always *some* unemployment—someone looking for a job or laid off and waiting to be recalled. Yet one of the goals of economic policy is to achieve full employment. What do we mean by *full employment*?

■ FIGURE 21.7

Unemployment Demographics

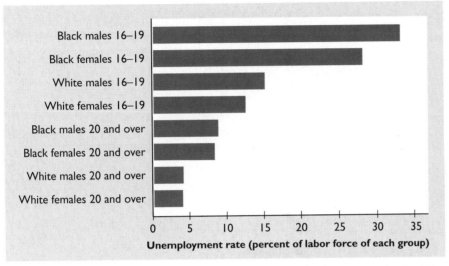

On the average during the ten years from 1995 to 2005, blacks experienced more than twice the unemployment of whites, and teenagers experienced more than three times the unemployment of workers aged 20 and over. Women have lower unemployment rates than men.

SOURCE OF DATA: Bureau of Labor Statistics.

■ Full Employment

There can be a lot of unemployment at full employment, and the term "full employment" is an example of a technical economic term that does not correspond with everyday language. **Full employment** occurs when there is no cyclical unemployment or, equivalently, when **all** the unemployment is frictional, structural, and seasonal. The divergence of the unemployment rate from full employment is cyclical unemployment. The unemployment rate when the economy is at full employment is called the **natural unemployment rate**. The term "natural unemployment rate" is another example of a technical economic term that does not correspond with everyday language.

Why do economists call a situation with a lot of unemployment one of full employment? And why is the unemployment rate at full employment called the "natural" unemployment rate? The reason is that the U.S. economy is a complex mechanism that undergoes constant change in its players, structure, and direction. For example, in 2002, around 3 million people retired and more than 3 million new workers entered the labor force. Thousands of businesses (including new startups) expanded and created jobs while thousands of others downsized or failed and destroyed jobs. This process of change creates frictions and dislocations that are unavoidable—that are natural. And they create unemployment.

Full employment
When there is no cyclical unemployment or, equivalently, when all the unemployment is frictional, structural, and seasonal.

Natural unemployment rate
The unemployment rate when the economy is at full employment.

■ Unemployment and Real GDP

Cyclical unemployment is the fluctuating unemployment over the business cycle—unemployment that increases during a recession and decreases during an expansion. At full employment, there is *no* cyclical unemployment. At a business cycle trough, cyclical unemployment is *positive* and at a business cycle peak, cyclical unemployment is *negative*.

Figure 21.8(a) shows the unemployment rate in the United States between 1975 and 2005. It also shows the natural unemployment rate and cyclical unemployment.

◼ **FIGURE 21.8**

The Relationship Between Unemployment and Real GDP

As the unemployment rate fluctuates around the natural unemployment rate in part (a), real GDP fluctuates around potential GDP in part (b).

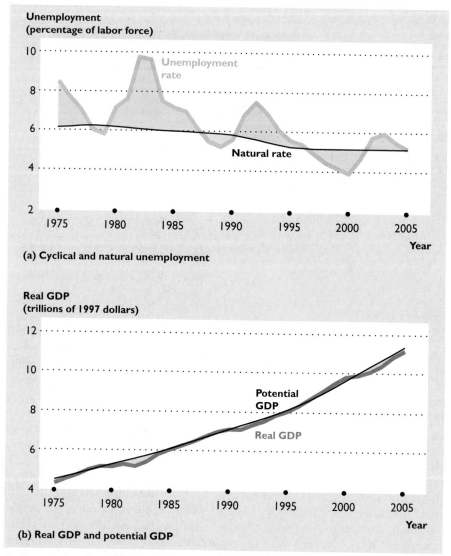

(a) Cyclical and natural unemployment

(b) Real GDP and potential GDP

SOURCES OF DATA: Bureau of Economic Analysis, Bureau of Labor Statistics, and Congressional Budget Office.

The natural unemployment rate in this figure was estimated by the Congressional Budget Office (CBO).

Most economists believe that the natural unemployment rate changes slowly and would accept the CBO estimate as a reasonable one. But an increasing number of economists think that the natural unemployment rate experiences short-term fluctuations and that when major changes in technology bring a rise in structural unemployment, or when rapid demographic change brings a rise in frictional unemployment, the natural unemployment rate can be high.

The true natural unemployment rate is unknown and is estimated with a margin of uncertainty. You will learn more about the uncertain value of the natural rate of unemployment in Chapters 23 and 32.

Figure 21.8(a) shows that during most of the 1980s and the early 1990s unemployment was above the natural unemployment rate, so cyclical unemployment was positive (shaded red) and that during the late 1980s and between 1997 and 2001 unemployment was below the natural unemployment rate, so cyclical unemployment was negative (shaded blue).

Figure 21.8(b) shows real GDP in the United States from 1975 to 2005. The figure also shows **potential GDP**, which is the level of real GDP that the economy would produce if it were at full employment. Because the unemployment rate fluctuates around the natural unemployment rate, real GDP fluctuates around potential GDP. When the unemployment rate is above the natural unemployment rate (in part a), real GDP is below potential GDP (in part b); when the unemployment rate is below the natural unemployment rate, real GDP is above potential GDP; and when the unemployment rate equals the natural unemployment rate, real GDP equals potential GDP.

You will learn what determines potential GDP and the natural unemployment rate in Chapter 23. And you'll learn what brings the fluctuations around potential GDP and cyclical unemployment in Chapters 29 and 30.

Potential GDP
The level of real GDP that the economy would produce if it were at full employment.

REALITY CHECK

The Labor Market in YOUR Life

Think about yourself and some of your friends. Classify your labor market status.

Are you in the labor force or not?
Are you employed or unemployed?
Are you a part-time or a full-time worker?

Think about someone you know who is unemployed. Is this person experiencing frictional, structural, seasonal, or cyclical unemployment? How can you tell?

Think about someone you know who has been unemployed but is now back at work. Did this person experience frictional, structural, seasonal, or cyclical unemployment? How long did it take this person to find a job?

Visit the Web site of the BLS (www.bls.gov) and get data on the unemployment rate for a number of cities or regions in which you either live or would like to live. In which city or region do you think you would you have the hardest time finding a job? In which city or region would you have the easiest time?

3 Describe the sources and types of unemployment, define full employment, and explain the link between unemployment and real GDP.

Practice Problem 21.3

1. A labor force survey on a Polynesian island records the following data for December 31, 2002: employed, 13,500; unemployed, 1,500; not in the labor force, 7,500. The survey also recorded during 2003: hires and recalls, 1,000; job losers, 750; job leavers 300; entrants, 150; reentrants, 450; withdrawals, 500. The working-age population increased during 2003 by 100. (All the job losers, entrants, and reentrants became unemployed.) Calculate for the end of 2003,
   a. The unemployment rate.
   b. The labor force participation rate.

Exercise 21.3

1. The Polynesian island labor force survey provides the following information about labor market flows during 2004: hires and recalls, 1,500; job losers, 550; job leavers, 300; entrants, 200; reentrants, 500; withdrawals, 450. The working-age population increased during 2004 by 150. Starting with the situation at the end of 2003 in the practice problem, calculate for the end of 2004,
   a. The unemployment rate.
   b. The labor force participation rate.

Solution to Practice Problem 21.3

1a. The number of people unemployed at the end of 2003 equals the number unemployed at the end of 2002, which is 1,500, plus the number of job losers (750), job leavers (300), entrants (150), and reentrants (450) minus the number of hires and recalls (1,000) and withdrawals (500). That is,

$$1,500 + 750 + 300 + 150 + 450 - 1,000 - 500 = 1,650.$$

The number of people employed at the end of 2003 equals the number employed at the end of 2002, which is 13,500, plus the number of hires and recalls (1,000) minus the number of job losers (750) and the number of job leavers (300). That is,

$$13,500 + 1,000 - 750 - 300 = 13,450$$

Next calculate the labor force, which is the sum of the number unemployed and the number employed, which equals 1,650 + 13,450 = 15,100.
   The unemployment rate is the percentage of the labor force who are unemployed, which is (1,650 ÷ 15,100) × 100 = 10.9 percent.

1b. The labor force participation rate is the percentage of the working-age population who are in the labor force. The working-age population at the end of 2002 is the sum of number employed (13,500), number unemployed (1,500), and the number not in the labor force (7,500), which equals 22,500.
   The working-age population increased during 2003 by 100, so at the end of 2003, the working-age population was 22,600.
   The labor force participation rate is (15,100 ÷ 22,600) × 100 = 66.8 percent.

CHAPTER CHECKPOINT

Key Points

1 **Define the unemployment rate and other labor market indicators.**

- The unemployment rate is the number of people unemployed as a percentage of the labor force, and the labor force is the sum of the number of people employed and the number unemployed.
- The labor force participation rate is the labor force as a percentage of the working-age population.

2 **Describe the trends and fluctuations in the indicators of labor market performance in the United States.**

- The unemployment rate fluctuates with the business cycle.
- The female labor force participation rate has increased, and the male labor force participation rate has decreased.
- Aggregate hours trend upward more slowly than employment because average hours decrease. Aggregate hours and average hours fluctuate with the business cycle.

3 **Describe the sources and types of unemployment, define full employment, and explain the link between unemployment and real GDP.**

- Unemployment arises from the process of job creation and job destruction and from the movement of people into and out of the labor force.
- Unemployment can be frictional, structural, seasonal, or cyclical.
- The duration of unemployment fluctuates over the business cycle.
- Young people and minorities have the highest unemployment rates.
- Full employment occurs when there is no cyclical unemployment; the unemployment rate equals the natural unemployment rate.
- As the unemployment rate fluctuates around the natural unemployment rate, real GDP fluctuates around potential GDP.

Key Terms

Aggregate hours, 527
Cyclical unemployment, 538
Discouraged worker, 526
Frictional unemployment, 537
Full employment, 539
Full-time workers, 526
Involuntary part-time workers, 526
Labor force, 524

Labor force participation rate, 526
Natural unemployment rate, 539
Part-time workers, 526
Potential GDP, 541
Seasonal unemployment, 538
Structural unemployment, 537
Unemployment rate, 525
Working-age population, 524

ⓧ myeconlab Exercises

1. A BLS labor market survey interviewer visited four households.

   In the first household, Candy reported that she worked for 20 hours last week trying to get her Internet shopping business up and running. The rest of the week, she filled out application forms and attended two job interviews. Candy's husband Jerry worked for 40 hours at his job at General Motors. Candy and Jerry's 17-year-old daughter, who is still in high school, worked for 10 hours at her weekend convenience store job.

   In the second household, Joey, who works full time in a bank, reported that he was on his annual vacation. Joey's wife, Serena, who wants a full-time job, worked for 10 hours as a part-time checkout clerk.

   In the third household, Ari reported that he had no work last week but was going to be recalled to his regular farm job at the end of the month. Ari's housemate Kosta said that after months of search, he hasn't been able to find a job, so he has stopped looking and is now planning to go back to school.

   In the fourth household, Mimi and Henry reported that they are now senior citizens and are enjoying a well-earned retirement. Hank, their bachelor son who lives with them and is a professional artist, reported that he painted for 12 hours last week and sold one picture.

   a. Classify each of the ten people in these four households by the categories into which the BLS divides the population.
   b. Which of the people are part-time workers and which are full-time workers?
   c. Of the part-time workers, which are involuntary part-time workers?
   d. Calculate for these 10 people the
      i. Unemployment rate.
      ii. Labor force participation rate.
   e. Compare the unemployment rate and labor force participation rate of these four households with the U.S. data. How do these households differ from the average U.S. household?

2. The BLS survey found the following numbers in a small community:

   Total number of persons—320.

   Worked at least 1 hour as paid employees or worked 15 hours or more as unpaid workers in their family business—200.

   Were not working but had jobs or businesses from which they were temporarily absent—20.

   Had no employment—40.

   Were available for work and had made specific efforts to find employment some time during the previous 4 weeks—10.

   Were available for work and were waiting to be recalled to a job from which they had been laid off—6.
   a. Calculate for this community the
      i. Unemployment rate.
      ii. Labor force participation rate.

b. Compare the unemployment rate and labor force participation rate of this community with that for the households in exercise 1 and with the U.S. data. How does this community differ from the average U.S. household?

3. Describe the trends and fluctuations in the unemployment rate in the United States from 1962 through 2002. In which periods was the unemployment rate above average and in which periods was it below average?

4. Describe the trends and fluctuations in the labor force participation rate in the United States from 1965 through 2005, and contrast and explain the different trends for women and men.

5. What are the labor market flows that create and end a spell of unemployment? Of these flows, which fluctuate most and account for fluctuations in the unemployment rate?

6. Distinguish among the four types of unemployment: frictional, structural, seasonal, and cyclical. Provide an example of each type of unemployment in the United States today.

7. Describe the relationship between the unemployment rate and the natural unemployment rate as real GDP fluctuates around potential GDP. In which periods was real GDP below potential GDP?

Critical Thinking

8. The official measure of the unemployment rate omits many people who don't have a job but would like one. Do you think the omissions make the official unemployment rate an unhelpful indicator of the state of the economy? Or do you think that despite the omissions, the official measure provides useful information? Take a position on this issue and support your argument with examples.

9. If aggregate hours worked provides a more accurate measure of the quantity of labor employed than does the number of persons employed, why doesn't aggregate hours *not worked* provide a more accurate measure of the quantity of unemployment? (Hint: Think about the definition of unemployment.)

10. "Economics is supposed to be about scarcity. But if some labor is always unemployed, how can there be scarcity? All we need to do to produce more goods and services is employ the unemployed people."
    a. Do you agree or disagree with this statement? Why?
    b. Explain why scarcity and unemployment are not incompatible.

11. Most discussion and concern about unemployment arise from unemployed labor. Unemployed capital and land don't generate as much passion. But there is probably much more unemployment of capital and land than of labor.
    a. Provide some examples of unemployed capital and land.
    b. Explain why the unemployment of capital and land does not mean that scarcity isn't a problem.
    c. Can you think of benefits of unemployment that make some unemployment of all factors of production desirable?

Web Exercises

Use the links on MyEconLab to work the following exercises.

12. Visit the Bureau of Labor Statistics Web site and find the following labor market data for the United States in the most recent month and for the same month one year ago: the labor force, the number employed, the number unemployed, and the working-age population.
    a. Calculate for the two months the
       i.   Unemployment rate.
       ii. Labor force participation rate.
    b. Describe the change in the labor market over the past year.

13. Visit the Bureau of Economic Analysis Web site and find the data on real GDP for the past year through the most recent quarter.
    a. Describe the change in real GDP over the past year.
    b. Explain how the change in real GDP relates to the changes in the labor market that you described in part **b** of exercise 12.

14. Visit the Bureau of Labor Statistics Web site and find labor market data for your own state.
    a. What have been the trends in employment, unemployment, and labor force participation in your own state during the past two years?
    b. On the basis of what you know about your own region, how would you set about explaining these trends?
    c. Try to identify the industries that have expanded most and those that have shrunk.
    d. What are the problems with your own regional labor market that you think need state government action to resolve?
    e. What actions do you think your state government must take to resolve them? Answer this question by using the demand and supply model of the labor market and predict the effects of the actions you prescribe.
    f. Compare the labor market performance of your own state with that of the nation as a whole.
    g. If your state is performing better than the national average, to what do you attribute the success? If your region is performing worse than the national average, to what do you attribute its problems?

15. Visit the Statistics Canada Web site and obtain labor market data for Canada.
    a. What have been the trends in employment, unemployment, and labor force participation in Canada during the past two years?
    b. Compare and contrast Canadian and U.S. labor market trends during these years.
    c. On the basis of what you've learned in this chapter about the types of unemployment, which types of unemployment do you think Canada has more of than the United States? Why?
    d. Is the natural unemployment rate in Canada higher or lower than that in the United States?
    e. To what do you attribute the difference in the natural unemployment rate in the two countries?

The CPI and the Cost of Living

CHAPTER CHECKLIST

When you have completed your study of this chapter, you will be able to

1. Explain what the Consumer Price Index (CPI) is and how it is calculated.

2. Explain the limitations of the CPI as a measure of the cost of living.

3. Adjust money values for inflation and calculate real wage rates and real interest rates.

It is the fall of 2006, and Gus is about to begin a four-year law degree program. He plans to take out a student loan that will accumulate to $80,000 when he starts making repayments at the end of the maximum 5-year grace period. So Gus plans to make his first repayment in the fall of 2015. How much will $80,000 of today's money be worth in 2015 when Gus begins his loan repayment? The answer depends on the CPI in 2015.

The Consumer Price Index, or CPI, is the main measure of the cost of living. The Department of Labor publishes new CPI figures each month, and analysts in newspapers and on TV quickly leap to conclusions about the causes of recent changes in prices and the implications of the latest numbers for interest rate actions by the Federal Reserve.

How does the government determine the CPI? How well does the CPI measure the cost of living and the inflation rate? You will find the answers in this chapter. You will also learn how we use price index numbers to strip away the veil of money and dollar values to see the real values that they represent—like the real value of Gus's $80,000 student loan.

22.1 THE CONSUMER PRICE INDEX

Consumer Price Index
A measure of the average of the prices paid by urban consumers for a fixed market basket of consumption goods and services.

The **Consumer Price Index** (CPI) is a measure of the average of the prices paid by urban consumers for a fixed market basket of consumption goods and services. The Bureau of Labor Statistics (BLS) calculates the CPI every month, and we can use these numbers to compare what the fixed market basket costs this month with what it cost in some previous month or other period.

■ Reading the CPI Numbers

Reference base period
A period for which the CPI is defined to equal 100. Currently, the reference base period is 1982–1984.

The CPI is defined to equal 100 for a period called the **reference base period**. Currently, the reference base period is 1982–1984. That is, the CPI equals 100 on the average over the 36 months from January 1982 through December 1984.

In May 2005, the CPI was 194.4. This number tells us that the average of the prices paid by urban consumers for a fixed market basket of consumption goods and services was 94.4 percent higher in May 2005 than it was on the average during 1982–1984.

In April 2005, the CPI was 194.6. Comparing the May CPI with the April CPI tells us that the average of the prices paid by urban consumers for a fixed market basket of consumption goods and services *decreased* by 0.2 of a percentage point in May 2005.

■ Constructing the CPI

Constructing the CPI is a huge operation that costs millions of dollars and involves three stages:

- Selecting the CPI market basket
- Conducting the monthly price survey
- Calculating the CPI

■ The CPI Market Basket

The first stage in constructing the CPI is to determine the *CPI market basket*. This "basket" contains the goods and services represented in the index and the relative importance, or weight, attached to each of them. The idea is to make the weight of the items in the CPI basket the same as in the budget of an average urban household. For example, if the average household spends 1.1 percent of its income on public transportation, then the CPI places a 1.1 percent weight on the prices of bus, subway, and other transit system rides.

Although the CPI is calculated every month, the CPI market basket isn't updated every month. The information used to determine the CPI market basket comes from a survey, called the Consumer Expenditure Survey, that discovers what people actually buy. This survey is an ongoing activity, and the CPI market basket in 2005 was based on a survey conducted during 2001 and 2002. More than 30,000 individuals and families contributed information. Some of them were interviewed every three months, and others kept detailed diaries for two weeks in which they listed absolutely everything they bought. (Before 1999, the Consumer Expenditure Survey was conducted much less frequently.)

The reference base period for the CPI has been fixed at 1982–1984 for about 20 years and doesn't change when the market basket is updated by a new Consumer Expenditure Survey.

Figure 22.1 shows the CPI market basket at the end of 2004. The basket contains around 80,000 goods and services arranged in the eight large groups shown in the figure. The most important item in a household's budget is housing, which accounts for 42 percent of total expenditure. Transportation comes next at 17 percent. Third in relative importance is food and beverages at 15 percent. These three groups account for almost three quarters of the average household budget. Medical care, recreation, and education and communication take 6 percent, and apparel (clothing and footwear) takes 4 percent. Another 4 percent is spent on other goods and services.

The BLS breaks down each of these categories into smaller ones. For example, education and communication breaks down into textbooks and supplies, tuition, telephone services, and personal computer services.

As you look at these relatively important numbers, remember that they apply to the average household. Each individual household is spread around the average. Think about your own expenditure and compare it with the average.

■ The Monthly Price Survey

Each month, BLS employees check the prices of the 80,000 goods and services in the CPI market basket in 30 metropolitan areas. Because the CPI aims to measure price changes, it is important that the prices recorded each month refer to exactly the same items. For example, suppose the price of a box of jelly beans has increased but a box now contains more beans. Has the price of a jelly bean increased? The BLS employee must record the details of changes in quality, size, weight, or packaging so that price changes can be isolated from other changes.

Once the raw price data are in hand, the next task is to calculate the CPI.

■ FIGURE 22.1

The CPI Market Basket

This shopping cart is filled with the items that an average household buys. Housing (42 percent), transportation (17 percent), and food and beverages (15 percent) take 74 percent of household income.

SOURCE OF DATA: Bureau of Labor Statistics.

■ Calculating the CPI

The CPI calculation has three steps:

- Find the cost of the CPI market basket at base period prices.
- Find the cost of the CPI market basket at current period prices.
- Calculate the CPI for the base period and the current period.

We'll work through these three steps for a simple example. Suppose the CPI market basket contains only two goods and services: oranges and haircuts. We'll construct an annual CPI rather than a monthly CPI with the reference base period 2000 and the current period 2003.

Table 22.1 shows the quantities in the CPI market basket and the prices in the base period and the current period. Part (a) contains the data for the base period. In that period, consumers bought 10 oranges at $1 each and 5 haircuts at $8 each. To find the cost of the CPI market basket in the base period prices, multiply the quantities in the CPI market basket by the base period prices. The cost of oranges is $10 (10 at $1 each), and the cost of haircuts is $40 (5 at $8 each). So total expenditure in the base period on the CPI market basket is $50 ($10 + $40).

Part (b) contains the price data for the current period. The price of an orange increased from $1 to $2, which is a 100 percent increase ($1 ÷ $1 × 100 = 100 percent). The price of a haircut increased from $8 to $10, which is a 25 percent increase ($2 ÷ $8 × 100 = 25 percent).

The CPI provides a way of averaging these price increases by comparing the cost of the basket rather than the price of each item. To find the cost of the CPI market basket in the current period, 2003, multiply the quantities in the basket by their 2003 prices. The cost of oranges is $20 (10 at $2 each), and the cost of haircuts is $50 (5 at $10 each). So total expenditure on the fixed CPI market basket at current period prices is $70 ($20 + $50).

■ TABLE 22.1

The Consumer Price Index: A Simplified CPI Calculation

(a) The cost of the CPI basket at base period prices: 2000

| CPI market basket | | | Cost of |
Item	Quantity	Price	CPI basket
Oranges	10	$1 each	$10
Haircuts	5	$8 each	$40
Cost of CPI market basket at base period prices			$50

(b) The cost of the CPI basket at current period prices: 2003

| CPI market basket | | | Cost of |
Item	Quantity	Price	CPI basket
Oranges	10	$2 each	$20
Haircuts	5	$10 each	$50
Cost of CPI market basket at current period prices			$70

You've now taken the first two steps toward calculating the CPI. The third step uses the numbers you've just calculated to find the CPI for 2000 and 2003. The formula for the CPI is

$$\text{CPI} = \frac{\text{Cost of CPI basket at current period prices}}{\text{Cost of CPI basket at base period prices}} \times 100.$$

In Table 22.1, you established that in 2000, the cost of the CPI market basket was $50 and in 2003, it was $70. If we use these numbers in the CPI formula, we can find the CPI for 2000 and 2003. The base period is 2000, so for 2000,

$$\text{CPI in 2000} = \frac{\$50}{\$50} \times 100 = 100.$$

For 2003,

$$\text{CPI in 2003} = \frac{\$70}{\$50} \times 100 = 140.$$

The principles that you've applied in this simplified CPI calculation apply to the more complex calculations performed every month by the BLS.

Figure 22.2(a) shows the CPI in the United States during the 30 years between 1975 and 2005. The CPI increased every year during this period. During the late 1970s and in 1980, the CPI was increasing rapidly, but since the early 1980s, the rate of increase has slowed.

◼ Measuring Inflation

A major purpose of the CPI is to measure *changes* in the cost of living and in the value of money. To measure these changes, we calculate the **inflation rate**, which is the percentage change in the price level from one year to the next. To calculate the inflation rate, we use the formula

Inflation rate
The percentage change in the price level from one year to the next.

$$\text{Inflation rate} = \frac{(\text{CPI in current year} - \text{CPI in previous year})}{\text{CPI in previous year}} \times 100.$$

Suppose that the current year is 2003 and the CPI for 2003 is 140. And suppose that in the previous year, 2002, the CPI was 120. Then in 2003,

$$\text{Inflation rate} = \frac{(140 - 120)}{120} \times 100 = 16.7 \text{ percent.}$$

This inflation rate is very high—much higher than anything that we experience in the United States. You can check the latest inflation rate by visiting the BLS Web site. Let's calculate a recent U.S. inflation rate. In April 2005, the CPI was 194.4, and in April 2004, it was 189.1. So during the year to April 2005,

$$\text{Inflation rate} = \frac{(194.4 - 189.1)}{189.1} \times 100 = 2.8 \text{ percent.}$$

Figure 22.2(b) shows the inflation rate between 1975 and 2005. The two parts of Figure 22.2 are related. When the price *level* in part (a) rises rapidly, the inflation rate in part (b) is high, and when the price level in part (a) rises slowly, the inflation rate in part (b) is low.

700 Years of Inflation and Deflation

These extraordinary data show that inflation became a persistent problem only after 1900. During the preceding 600 years, inflation was almost unknown. Inflation increased slightly during the sixteenth century after Europeans discovered gold in America. But this inflation barely reached 2 percent a year—less than we have today—and eventually subsided. The Industrial Revolution saw a temporary burst of inflation.

SOURCES OF DATA: E.H. Phelps Brown and Sheila V. Hopkins, *Economica*, 1955 and Robert Sahr, http://oregonstate.edu/dept/pol_sci/fac/sahr/sahr.htm.

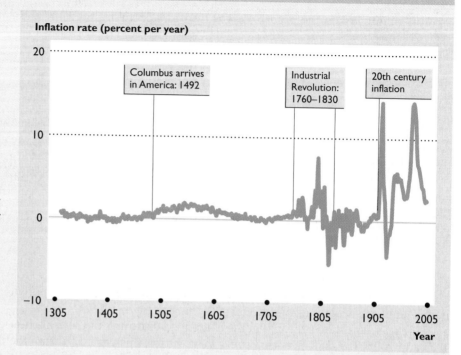

FIGURE 22.2

The CPI and the Inflation Rate: 1975–2005

(a) CPI: 1975–2005

(b) CPI inflation rate: 1975–2005

SOURCE OF DATA: Bureau of Labor Statistics.

In part (a), the CPI (the price *level*) has increased every year. In part (b), the inflation rate has averaged 5 percent a year. During the 1970s and early 1980s, it exceeded 10 percent a year, but since the early 1980s, it has been around 3 percent a year.

CHECKPOINT 22.1

1   Explain what the Consumer Price Index (CPI) is and how it is calculated.

Practice Problems 22.1

1. A Consumer Expenditure Survey in Sparta shows that people buy only juice and cloth. In 2006, the year of the Consumer Expenditure Survey and also the reference base year, the average household spent $40 on juice and $25 on cloth. The price of juice in 2006 was $4 a bottle, and the price of cloth was $5 a yard. In the current year, 2007, juice is $4 a bottle and cloth is $6 a yard. Calculate
    a. The CPI market basket.
    b. The percentage of household budget spent on juice in the base year.
    c. The CPI in 2007.

2. Table 1 shows the CPI in Russia. Calculate Russia's inflation rate in 2001 and 2002. Did the price level rise or fall in 2002? Did the inflation rate increase or decrease in 2002?

TABLE 1

Year	CPI
2000	225
2001	274
2002	310

Exercise 22.1

1. A Consumer Expenditure Survey in the city of Firestorm shows that people buy only firecrackers and bandages. In 2005, the year of the Consumer Expenditure Survey and also the reference base year, the average household spent $150 on firecrackers and $15 on bandages. The price of a firecracker in 2005 was $2, and the price of bandages was $1 a pack. In the current year, 2006, firecrackers are $3 each and bandages are $1.25 a pack. Calculate
    a. The CPI market basket.
    b. The percentage of a household's budget spent on firecrackers in the base year.
    c. The CPI in 2006.
    d. The inflation rate in 2006.

Solutions to Practice Problems 22.1

1a. The CPI market basket is the quantities bought during the Consumer Expenditure Survey year, 2006. Households spent $40 on juice at $4 a bottle, so the quantity of juice bought was 10 bottles. Households spent $25 on cloth at $5 a yard, so the quantity of cloth bought was 5 yards. The CPI market basket is 10 bottles of juice and 5 yards of cloth.

1b. In the reference base year, expenditure on juice was $40 and expenditure on cloth was $25, so the household budget was $65. Expenditure on juice was 61.5 percent of the household budget: ($40 ÷ $65) × 100 = 61.5 percent.

1c. To calculate the CPI in 2007, find the cost of the CPI basket in 2006 and 2007. In 2006, the CPI basket costs $65 ($40 for juice + $25 for cloth). In 2007, the CPI basket costs $70 (10 bottles of juice at $4 a bottle + 5 yards of cloth at $6 a yard). The CPI in 2007 is ($70 ÷ $65) × 100 = 107.7.

2. The inflation rate in 2001 is [(274 − 225) ÷ 225] × 100 = 21.8 percent. The inflation rate in 2002 is [(310 − 274) ÷ 274] × 100 = 13.1 percent. In 2002, the price level increased and the inflation rate decreased.

22.2 THE CPI AND THE COST OF LIVING

Cost of living index
A measure of changes in the amount of money that people would need to spend to achieve a given standard of living.

The CPI is sometimes called a cost of living index. The purpose of a **cost of living index** is to measure changes in the amount of money that people would need to spend to achieve a given standard of living. The CPI does not measure the cost of living for two broad reasons.

First, the CPI does not try to measure all the components of the cost of living. For example, a severe winter might cause people to buy more natural gas and electricity to heat their homes. An increase in the prices of these items would increase the CPI, but the increased quantities bought would not change the CPI because the CPI market basket is fixed. So part of this increase in spending, which is an increase in the cost of maintaining a given standard of living, would not show up as an increase in the CPI.

Second, even those components of the cost of living that are measured by the CPI are not always measured accurately. The result is that the CPI is possibly a biased measure of changes in the cost of living. Let's look at some of the problems faced by the BLS that could lead to bias in the CPI.

■ Sources of Bias in the CPI

The potential sources of bias in the CPI are

- New goods bias
- Quality change bias
- Commodity substitution bias
- Outlet substitution bias

New Goods Bias

New goods keep replacing old ones. For example, the PC has replaced the typewriter. The DVD player is gradually replacing the videocassette player. The digital camera is replacing the film camera. These are just a few examples of a very long list of new goods to which you can easily add.

If you want to compare the price level in 2005 with that in 1995, you must somehow compare the price of a DVD player today with that of a videocassette player in 1995. Because DVD players do a better job than videocassette players, you are better off with the new technology if the prices were the same. But a DVD player is more expensive than a videocassette player. How much of the higher price is a sign of the higher quality?

The BLS does its best to answer this type of question and employs many experts to help get the correct answer. But there is no sure way of making the necessary adjustment, and most likely, the arrival of new goods puts an upward bias into the CPI and its measure of the inflation rate.

Quality Change Bias

Cars, CD players, and many other items get better every year. For example, central locking, airbags, and antilock braking systems all add to the quality of a car. But they also add to the cost. Is the improvement in quality greater than the increase in cost? Or do car prices rise by more than can be accounted for by quality improvements? To the extent that a price rise is a payment for improved quality, it is not inflation. Again, the BLS does the best job it can to estimate the effects of quality improvements on price changes. But the CPI probably counts too much of any price rise as inflation and so overstates inflation.

Commodity Substitution Bias

Changes in relative prices lead consumers to change the items they buy. People cut back on items that become relatively more costly and increase their consumption of items that become relatively less costly. For example, suppose the price of beef rises while the price of chicken remains constant. Now that beef is more costly relative to chicken, you might decide to buy more chicken and less beef. Suppose that you switch from beef to chicken, spend the same amount on meat as before, and get the same enjoyment as before. Your cost of meat has not changed. But the CPI says that the price of meat has increased because it ignores your substitution between goods in the CPI market basket.

Outlet Substitution Bias

When confronted with higher prices, people use discount stores more frequently and convenience stores less frequently. This phenomenon is called *outlet substitution*. Suppose, for example, that gas prices rise by 10 cents a gallon. Instead of buying from your nearby gas station for $2.20 a gallon, you now drive farther to a gas station that charges $2.10 a gallon. Your cost of gas has increased because you must factor in the cost of your time and the gas that you use driving several blocks down the road. But your cost has not increased by as much as the 10 cents a gallon increase in the pump price. However, the CPI says that the price of gas has increased by 10 cents a gallon because it does not measure outlet substitutions.

The growth of online shopping in recent years has provided an alternative to discount stores that makes outlet substitution even easier and potentially makes this source of bias more serious.

■ The Magnitude of the Bias

You have reviewed the sources of bias in the CPI. But how big is the bias? When this question was tackled in 1996 by a Congressional Advisory Commission chaired by Michael Boskin, an economics professor at Stanford University, the answer was that the CPI overstated inflation by 1.1 percentage points a year. That is, if the CPI reports that inflation is 3.1 percent a year, most likely inflation is actually 2 percent a year.

In the period since the Boskin Commission reported, the BLS has taken steps to reduce the CPI bias. The more frequent Consumer Expenditure Survey that we described earlier in this chapter is one of these steps. Beyond that, the BLS uses ever more sophisticated models and methods to try to eliminate the sources of bias and make the CPI as accurate as possible.

■ Two Consequences of the CPI Bias

Avoiding bias in the CPI is important for two main reasons. Bias

- Distorts private contracts.
- Increases government outlays.

Distortion of Private Contracts

Many wage contracts contain a cost of living adjustment. For example, the United Auto Workers Union (UAW) and General Motors Corporation (GM) might agree on a wage rate of $30 an hour initially that increases over three years at the same rate as the cost of living increases. The idea is that both the union and the employer want a contract in "real" terms. As the cost of living rises, the firm wants to pay the workers the number of dollars per hour that buys a given market basket of goods and services. And the firm is happy to pay the higher wage because it can sell its output for a higher price.

Suppose that over the three years of a UAW and GM contract, the CPI increases by 5 percent each year. Then the wage rate will increase to $31.50 in the second year and $33.08 in the third year.

But suppose that the CPI is biased and the true price increase is 3 percent a year. The workers' cost of living increases by this amount, so in the second year, $30.90 rather than $31.50 is the intended wage. In the third year, a wage rate of $31.83 and not $33.08 compensates for the higher cost of living. So in the second year, the workers gain 60 cents an hour, or $21 for a 35-hour workweek. And in the third year, they gain $1.25 an hour, or $43.75 for a 35-hour workweek.

The workers' gain is GM's loss. With a work force of a few thousand, the loss amounts to several thousand dollars a week and a few million dollars over the life of a 3-year wage contract.

If the CPI bias was common knowledge and large, the CPI would not be used without some adjustment in contracts. Unions and employers would seek agreement on the extent of the bias and make an appropriate adjustment to their contract. But for a small bias, the cost of negotiating a more complicated agreement might be too large.

Increases in Government Outlays

Because rising prices decrease the buying power of the dollar, the CPI is used to adjust the incomes of the 48 million Social Security beneficiaries, 22 million food stamp recipients, and 4 million retired former military personnel and federal civil servants (and their surviving spouses) and the budget for 27 million school lunches.

Close to a third of federal government outlays are linked directly to the CPI. If the CPI has a 1.1 percentage point bias, all of these expenditures increase by more than required to compensate for the fall in the buying power of the dollar and, although a bias of 1.1 percent a year seems small, accumulated over a decade, it adds up to almost a trillion dollars of additional government outlays.

■ The GDP Deflator: A Better Measure?

In Chapter 20, you learned about another measure of average prices: the *GDP deflator*. When we calculate the GDP deflator, we compare the current year's prices with the previous year's prices using the current year's and a previous year's baskets of goods and services. Because the GDP deflator uses current year quantities, it includes new goods and quality improvements and even allows for substitution effects of both commodities and retail outlets. So in principle, the GDP deflator is not subject to the biases of the CPI.

But in practice, the GDP deflator suffers from some of the CPI's problems. To arrive at its estimate of real GDP, the Commerce Department does not directly measure the physical quantities that are produced. Instead, it estimates quantities by dividing expenditures by price indexes. And one of these price indexes is the CPI. So the biased CPI injects a bias into the GDP deflator.

Also, the GDP deflator is broader than the CPI. GDP is the sum of expenditures on all final goods and services, not just consumption expenditures. So the GDP deflator reflects the prices of such items as paper mills bought by 3M to make Post-it Notes, nuclear submarines bought by the Defense Department, and Boeing 747s bought by British Airways. So the GDP deflator is not an alternative to the CPI as a measure of the cost of living.

Figure 22.3(a) shows the CPI and the GDP deflator measures of inflation. The two measures move up and down in similar ways, but the CPI measure exceeds the GDP deflator measure and in Figure 22.3(b) they gradually get farther apart.

■ **FIGURE 22.3**
Two Measures of Inflation and the Price Level

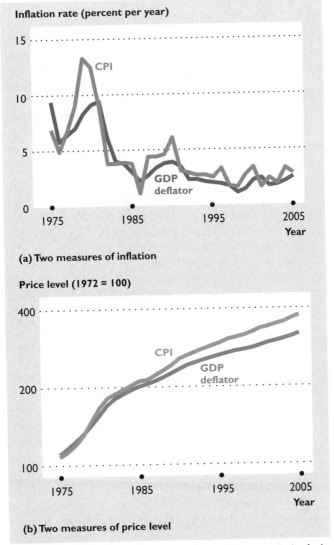

(a) Two measures of inflation

(b) Two measures of price level

The two measures of the inflation rate in part (a) fluctuate together, but the CPI measure rises more rapidly than the GDP deflator measure, and in part (b), the two price levels get farther apart. Both measures probably overstate the inflation rate.

SOURCES OF DATA: Bureau of Labor Statistics and Bureau of Economic Analysis.

2 Explain the limitations of the CPI as a measure of the cost of living.

Practice Problem 22.2

1. Economists in the Statistics Bureau decide to check the substitution bias in the CPI. To do so, they conduct a Consumer Expenditure Survey in both 2005 and 2006. Table 1 shows the results of the survey. It shows the items that consumers buy and their prices. The Statistics Bureau fixes the reference base year as 2005 and asks you to
   a. Calculate the CPI in 2006 using the 2005 CPI market basket.
   b. Calculate the CPI in 2006 using the 2006 CPI market basket.
   c. Explain whether there is any substitution bias in the CPI that uses the 2005 basket.

Exercise 22.2

1. In Virtual Reality, time travel became possible only in 3006. Economists in the Statistics Bureau decided to conduct a Consumer Expenditure Survey in both 3005 and 3006 to check the substitution bias of the CPI. Table 2 shows the results of the survey. It shows the items that consumers buy and their prices. The Statistics Bureau fixes the reference base year as 3005 and asks you to
   a. Calculate the CPI in 3006 using the 3005 CPI market basket.
   b. Calculate the CPI in 3006 using the 3006 CPI market basket.
   c. Explain whether there is any substitution bias in the CPI that uses the 3005 basket.

Solution to Practice Problem 22.2

1a. Table 3 shows the calculation of the CPI in 2006 using the 2005 basket. The cost of the 2005 basket at 2005 prices is $60, and the cost of the 2005 basket at 2006 prices is $90. So the CPI in 2006 using the 2005 basket is ($90 ÷ $60) × 100 = 150.

1b. Table 4 shows the calculation of the CPI in 2006 using the 2006 basket. The cost of the 2006 basket at 2005 prices is $65, and the cost of the 2006 basket at 2006 prices is $85. So the CPI in 2006 using the 2006 basket is ($85 ÷ $65) × 100 = 131.

1c. There is some substitution bias in the CPI that uses the 2005 basket. The price of broccoli remains constant, but the price of carrots rises by 100 percent. So consumers cut the quantity of carrots consumed and increase the quantity of broccoli consumed. They end up spending $85 on vegetables. But they would have spent $90 if they had not substituted the now relatively less costly broccoli. The cost of vegetables does not rise by 50 percent as shown by the CPI. Instead, because of substitution, the cost of vegetables increases by only 42 percent ($85 is 42 percent greater than $60). When we calculate the increase in the price of vegetables using the 2006 CPI market basket, the increase is only 31 percent ($85 compared with $65). So the CPI is biased upward because it ignores the substitutions that people make in response to changes in the price of one item relative to the price of another.

TABLE 1

Item	2005 Quantity	2005 Price	2006 Quantity	2006 Price
Broccoli	10	$3.00	15	$3.00
Carrots	15	$2.00	10	$4.00

TABLE 2

Item	3005 Quantity	3005 Price	3006 Quantity	3006 Price
Games	20	$60	10	$70
Time travel	0	–	20	$8,000

TABLE 3

Item	2005 basket at 2005 prices	2005 basket at 2006 prices
Broccoli	$30	$30
Carrots	$30	$60
Total	$60	$90

TABLE 4

Item	2006 basket at 2005 prices	2006 basket at 2006 prices
Broccoli	$45	$45
Carrots	$20	$40
Total	$65	$85

22.3 NOMINAL AND REAL VALUES

In 2005, it cost 37 cents to mail a first-class letter. One hundred years earlier, in 1905, that same letter would have cost 2 cents to mail. Does it *really* cost you 18.5 times the amount that it cost your great-great-grandmother to mail a letter?

You know that it does not. You know that a dollar today buys less than what a dollar bought in 1905, so the cost of a stamp has not really increased to 18.5 times its 1905 level. But has it increased at all? Did it really cost you any more to mail a letter in 2005 than it cost your great-great-grandmother in 1905?

The CPI can be used to answer questions like these. In fact, that is one of the main reasons for constructing a price index. Let's see how we can compare the price of a stamp in 1905 and the price of a stamp in 2005.

■ Dollars and Cents at Different Dates

To compare dollar amounts at different dates, we need to know the CPI at those dates. Currently, the CPI has a base of 100 for 1982–1984. That is, the average of the CPI in 1982, 1983, and 1984 is 100. (The numbers for the three years are 96.4, 99.6, and 103.9, respectively. Calculate the average of these numbers and check that it is indeed 100.)

In 2005, the CPI was 195.6, and in 1905, it was 9.4. By using these two numbers, we can calculate the relative value of the dollar in 1905 and 2005. To do so, we divide the 2005 CPI by the 1905 CPI. That ratio is 195.6 ÷ 9.4 = 20.8. That is, prices on the average were 20.8 times higher in 2005 than in 1905.

We can use this ratio to convert the price of a 2-cent stamp in 1905 into its 2005 equivalent. The formula for this calculation is

$$\text{Price of stamp in 2005 dollars} = \text{Price of stamp in 1905 dollars} \times \frac{\text{CPI in 2005}}{\text{CPI in 1905}}$$

$$= 2 \text{ cents} \times \frac{195.6}{9.4} = 42 \text{ cents}.$$

So your great-great-grandmother had a raw deal! It *really* cost her more to mail that first-class letter than it cost you in 2005. She paid the equivalent of 42 cents, and you paid 37 cents.

The calculation that we've just done is an example of converting a *nominal* value into a *real* value. A nominal value is one that is expressed in current dollars. A real value is one that is expressed in the dollars of a given year.

■ Nominal and Real Values in Macroeconomics

Macroeconomics makes a big issue of the distinction between nominal and real values. You saw that distinction in Chapter 20, where you learned the difference between nominal GDP and real GDP. To calculate real GDP, we use the same idea that you've just used to calculate the real price of a postage stamp but we use the GDP deflator rather than the CPI as our measure of the price level. The reason is that we are dealing with economy totals, of which consumer spending is just one part. So real GDP is equal to nominal GDP divided by the GDP deflator and *not* nominal GDP divided by the CPI. But we might use the CPI if we're trying to compare personal living standards over time.

EYE ON THE PAST

The Nominal and Real Price of a First-Class Letter

The figure shows the cost of a first-class letter since 1905. The green line is the nominal price—the actual price of a stamp in the dollars (cents) of the year in question. The red line is the real price—the price in terms of the 2005 dollar. You can see that the nominal price has gradually increased, but the real price has fluctuated, sometimes rising and sometimes falling. The highest real price, 45 cents, occurred in 1933, and the lowest real price, 19 cents, occurred in 1920.

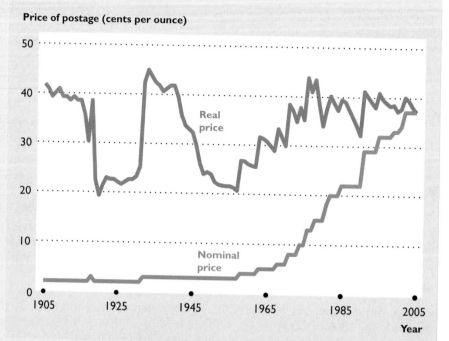

SOURCE OF DATA: Robert Sahr, Oregon State University, http://www.orst.edu/dept/pol_sci/fac/sahr/stamp.htm.

Two other nominal–real distinctions play a big role in macroeconomics—and in your life. They are the distinctions between

- The nominal wage rate and the real wage rate
- The nominal interest rate and the real interest rate

Let's study these vital distinctions.

■ Nominal and Real Wage Rates

Nominal wage rate
The average hourly wage rate measured in *current* dollars.

Real wage rate
The average hourly wage rate measured in the dollars of a given reference base year.

The price of labor is the wage rate—the income that an hour of labor earns. In macroeconomics, we are interested in economy-wide performance, so we focus on the *average* hourly wage rate. The **nominal wage rate** is the average hourly wage rate measured in *current* dollars. The **real wage rate** is the average hourly wage rate measured in the dollars of a given reference base year.

To calculate the real wage rate, we divide the nominal wage rate by the CPI and multiply by 100. That is,

$$\text{Real wage rate in 2002} = \frac{\text{Nominal wage rate in 2002}}{\text{CPI in 2002}} \times 100.$$

In June 2002, the nominal wage rate (average hourly wage rate) of production workers was $14.68 and the CPI was 179.9, so

$$\text{Real wage rate in June 2002} = \frac{\$14.68}{179.9} \times 100 = \$8.16.$$

Because we measure the real wage rate in constant base year dollars, a change in the real wage rate measures the change in the quantity of goods and services that an hour's work can buy. In contrast, a change in the nominal wage rate measures a combination of a change in the quantity of goods and services that an hour's work can buy and a change in the price level. So the real wage rate takes the effects of inflation out of changes in the nominal wage rate.

The real wage rate is a significant economic variable because it measures the real reward for labor, which is a major determinant of the standard of living. The real wage rate is also significant because it measures the real cost of labor, which influences the quantity of labor that firms are willing to hire.

Figure 22.4 shows what has happened to the nominal wage rate and the real wage rate in the United States between 1975 and 2005. The nominal wage rate is the average hourly earnings of production workers. This measure is just one of the several different measures of average hourly earnings that we might have used.

The nominal wage rate increased from $4.73 an hour in 1975 to $15.68 an hour in 2004. But the real wage rate decreased. In 1982–1984 dollars (the CPI base period dollars), the real wage rate was $8.48 in 1975 and $8.24 in 2004.

The real wage rate decreased as the nominal wage rate increased because the nominal wage rate didn't keep up with inflation. When the effects of inflation are removed from the nominal wage rate, we can see what is happening to the buying power of the average wage rate.

You can also see that the real wage rate has fluctuated. During the late 1970s, the real wage rate increased briefly. It then decreased until the mid-1990s, after which it increased slightly.

■ **FIGURE 22.4**

Nominal and Real Wage Rates: 1975–2005

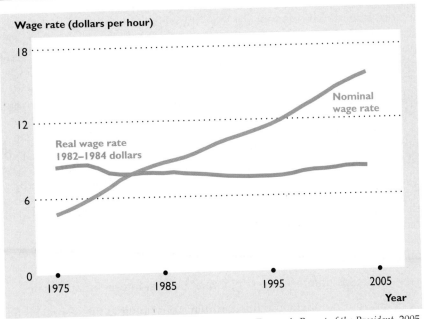

The nominal wage rate has increased every year since 1975. The real wage rate increased briefly during the late 1970s and then decreased through the mid-1990s, after which it increased slightly again. Over the entire 30-year period, the real wage rate decreased.

SOURCE OF DATA: *Economic Report of the President*, 2005.

EYE ON THE PAST

The Nominal and Real Wage Rates of Presidents of the United States

Who earned more, George W. Bush in 2005 or George Washington in 1789? George Washington's pay was $25,000 (on the green line) but in 2005 dollars (on the red line), it was $521,000. George W. Bush was paid $400,000 in 2005.

But the White House is more comfortable today, and presidential travel arrangements are a breeze compared to earlier times. So adding in the perks of the job, George W. Bush doesn't get such a raw deal.

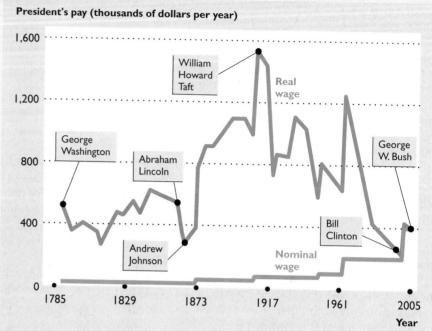

President's pay (thousands of dollars per year)

SOURCE OF DATA: Robert Sahr, Oregon State University, http://www.orst.edu/dept/pol_sci/fac/sahr/sahr.htm.

■ Nominal and Real Interest Rates

You've just seen that we can calculate real values from nominal values by deflating them using the CPI. And you've seen that to make this calculation, we *divide* the nominal value by a price index. Converting a nominal interest rate to a real interest rate is a bit different. To see why, we'll start with their definitions.

A **nominal interest rate** is the percentage return on a loan, calculated by using dollars. For example, if you deposit $100 in a savings account on which the bank pays a nominal interest of 5 percent a year, you will receive $5 on your deposit.

A **real interest rate** is the percentage return on a loan, calculated by using purchasing power. That is, the real interest rate is the nominal interest rate adjusted for the effects of inflation.

Suppose that you have $100 in a bank account and that after one year, you take your money out of the bank. The bank pays you the $100 that you deposited plus the $5 interest that you've earned (at 5 percent a year). But suppose that during the year, prices have increased by 3 percent. You've now got $105, but you need $103 just to buy what $100 would have bought when you put your money in the bank. So how much interest have you really earned? You've earned $2, or a real interest rate of 2 percent a year.

To convert a nominal interest rate to a real interest rate, we *subtract* the *inflation rate*. That is,

Real interest rate = Nominal interest rate − Inflation rate.

Plug your numbers into this formula. Your nominal interest rate is 5 percent a year, the inflation rate is 3 percent a year, and your real interest rate is 5 percent minus 3 percent, which equals 2 percent a year.

Nominal interest rate
The percentage return on a loan, calculated by using dollars.

Real interest rate
The percentage return on a loan, calculated by using purchasing power—the nominal interest rate adjusted for the effects of inflation.

■ **FIGURE 22.5**

Nominal and Real Interest Rates: 1965–2005

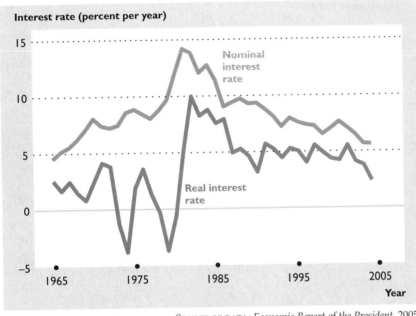

The real interest rate equals the nominal interest rate minus the inflation rate. During the 1970s, the real interest rate became negative.

SOURCE OF DATA: *Economic Report of the President*, 2005.

Figure 22.5 shows the nominal interest rate and the real interest rate in the United States between 1965 and 2005. When the inflation rate was high, during the 1970s and 1980s, the gap between the real interest rate and the nominal interest rate was large. The real interest rate was even negative in the mid-1970s. When the real interest rate is negative, the lender pays the borrower!

REALITY CHECK

The CPI in YOUR Life

Think about your student loan—or if you don't have one, think about Gus's $80,000 loan. Suppose that the CPI rises by 3 percent a year each year from now through 2025. Also suppose that the nominal interest rate on your loan is fixed at 8 percent a year.

How much will a $100 repayment cost you, in 2005 dollars, when you start to pay off your loan in 2015?

How much will a $100 repayment cost you, in 2005 dollars, when you make your final payment in 2025?

What is the real interest rate that you will have paid?

Would you be better off or worse off if the CPI began to rise at a rate of 5 percent a year?

3 Adjust money values for inflation and calculate real wage rates and real interest rates.

Practice Problems 22.3

TABLE 1

Year	Price of gasoline (cents per gallon)	CPI
1971	36	40.5
1981	138	90.9
1991	114	136.2
2001	146	176.6

1. Table 1 shows some gas prices and the CPI for four years. The reference base period is 1982–1984.
   a. Calculate the real price of gasoline in each year in 1982–1984 dollars.
   b. In which year was gasoline the most costly in real terms?
   c. In which year was gasoline the least costly in real terms?

2. Amazon.com agreed to pay its workers $20 an hour in 1999 and $22 an hour in 2001. The CPI for these years was 166 in 1999 and 180 in 2001.
   a. Calculate the real wage rate in each year.
   b. Did these workers really get a pay raise between 1999 and 2001?

3. Sally worked hard all year so that she could go to school full time the following year. She put her savings into a mutual fund that paid a nominal interest rate of 7 percent a year. The CPI was 165 at the beginning of the year and 177 at the end of the year. What was the real interest rate that Sally earned?

Exercise 22.3

TABLE 2

Year	Nominal interest rate	Inflation rate
	(percent per year)	
1992	4.6	1.7
1993	3.0	1.2
1994	2.1	0.7
1995	1.2	−0.1
1996	0.4	0.1
1997	0.4	1.7
1998	0.4	0.6
1999	0.1	−0.3
2000	0.1	−0.6
2001	0.1	−0.7
2002	0.1	−0.7

1. Table 2 shows the nominal interest rate and inflation rate in Japan for several years.
   a. Calculate the real interest rate for each year.
   b. In which year was the real interest rate the highest?
   c. In which year was the real interest rate the lowest?
   d. Was the real interest rate in Japan negative in any year?

Solutions to Practice Problems 22.3

1a. To calculate the real price of gasoline in 1982–1984 dollars, multiply the nominal price by 100 and divide by the CPI. Table 3 shows the calculations.

1b. Gasoline was the most costly in real terms in 1981, when it was 152 cents (1982–1984 cents) per gallon.

1c. Gasoline was the least costly in real terms in 2001, when it was 83 cents (1982–1984 cents) per gallon.

TABLE 3

Year	Price of gasoline (cents per gallon)	CPI	Price of gasoline (1982–1984 cents per gallon)
1971	36	40.5	89
1981	138	90.9	152
1991	114	136.2	84
2001	146	176.6	83

2a. The real wage rate in 1999, expressed in dollars of the reference base year, was ($20 ÷ 166) × 100 = $12.05. The real wage rate in 2001, expressed in dollars of the reference base year, was ($22 ÷ 180) × 100 = $12.22 an hour.

2b. The real wage of these workers increased between 1999 and 2001.

3. The inflation rate during the year that Sally was working was (177 − 165) ÷ 165 × 100 = 7.3 percent. On the savings that Sally had in the mutual fund for the full year, she earned a real interest rate equal to the nominal interest rate minus the inflation rate, which is 7 − 7.3 = −0.3. Sally's real interest rate was negative. (Sally would have been even worse off if she had just kept her saving in cash. Her nominal interest rate would then have been zero, and her real interest rate would have been −7.3 percent.)

CHAPTER CHECKPOINT

Key Points

1 **Explain what the Consumer Price Index (CPI) is and how it is calculated.**

- The Consumer Price Index (CPI) is a measure of the average prices of the goods and services that a typical urban household buys.
- The CPI is calculated by dividing the cost of the CPI market basket in the current period by its cost in the base period and then multiplying by 100.

2 **Explain the limitations of the CPI as a measure of the cost of living.**

- The CPI does not include all the items that contribute to the cost of living.
- The CPI cannot provide an accurate measure of price changes because of new goods, quality improvements, and substitutions that consumers make when relative prices change.

3 **Adjust money values for inflation and calculate real wage rates and real interest rates.**

- To adjust a money value (also called a nominal value) for inflation, we express the value in terms of the dollar of a given year.
- To convert a dollar value of year B to the dollars of year A, multiply the value in year B by the price level in year A and divide by the price level in year B.
- The real wage rate equals the nominal wage rate divided by the CPI and multiplied by 100.
- The real interest rate equals the nominal interest rate minus the inflation rate.

Key Terms

Consumer Price Index, 548
Cost of living index, 554
Inflation rate, 551
Nominal interest rate, 562

Nominal wage rate, 560
Real interest rate, 562
Real wage rate, 560
Reference base period, 548

myeconlab **Exercises**

1. Looking at some travel magazines, you read that the CPI in Turkey in 2002 was 6,912 and in Russia, it was 670. You do some further investigating and discover that the reference base period in Turkey is 1994 and in Russia it is 1995. The CPI in Russia in 1994 was 34.
   a. By what percentage did prices rise in Turkey between 1994 and 2002?
   b. By what percentage did prices rise in Russia between 1995 and 2002?
   c. By what percentage did prices rise in Russia between 1994 and 1995?
   d. By what percentage did prices rise in Russia between 1994 and 2002?
   e. In which of these two countries did prices rise more between 1994 and 2002?

2. Two countries, Sahara and Arctica, conduct consumer surveys. In Sahara, consumers buy 70 units of bottled water, 20 units of food, and 10 units of housing. In Arctica, consumers buy no bottled water (they suck icicles, which are free), 80 units of housing, and 20 units of food. Both countries use dollars, and prices in these two countries are the same. In the reference base years, water costs $1 a unit, food costs $5 a unit, and housing costs $10 a unit. In the current year, water costs $2 a unit, food costs $6 a unit, and housing costs $11 a unit.
   a. What is the CPI in Sahara in the current year?
   b. What is the CPI in Arctica in the current year?
   c. In which of these two countries did the CPI rise faster?
   d. Why did the CPI rise faster in one country?

3. In Brazil, the reference base period for the CPI is December 1993. In September 2000, prices had risen by 1,565.93 percent since the base period. The inflation rate in Brazil during the year ending September 2001 was 6.46 percent, and during the year ending September 2002, the inflation rate was 7.93 percent.
   a. What is the CPI in Brazil for December 1993?
   b. Calculate Brazil's CPI in September 2000.
   c. Calculate Brazil's CPI in September 2001.
   d. Calculate Brazil's CPI in September 2002.
   e. Is the price level in Brazil rising or falling?
   f. Did Brazil's inflation rate increase or decrease in 2001 and in 2002?
   g. Was the inflation rate in Brazil between 2000 and 2002 greater or less than the inflation rate in the United States?

4. Keep a careful record of your own expenditures during a two-week period. Keep separate data for week 1 and week 2. In particular, record the items that you buy, their prices, and the quantities that you buy. Use these records to calculate
   a. Your own CPI market basket based on your week 1 expenditures.
   b. The percentage of your expenditures on each item.
   c. The cost of your CPI market basket in week 1.
   d. The cost of your CPI market basket in week 2.
   e. Your personal CPI for week 2.
   f. Your personal inflation rate in week 2.

5. On the basis of your observations of your own expenditures in weeks 1 and 2 (recorded in your answer to exercise 4), explain and discuss the way in which your personal CPI is influenced by
   a. New goods
   b. Quality changes
   c. Commodity substitution
   d. Outlet substitution

6. Visit a local supermarket on two days a month apart. Select 10 items of standard products that the shop always sells. Record the prices of these 10 items on the two dates. Assuming that a consumer buys one of each item in the basket you've chosen, calculate
   a. The cost of the basket in the first month.
   b. The cost of the basket in the second month.
   c. A price index for the second month.
   d. The inflation rate of these 10 prices over the month.

7. On the basis of the price observations recorded in your answer to exercise 6, explain and discuss the way in which commodity substitution and outlet substitution might occur and the effects that these substitutions might have on the inflation rate in your area during the month of observation.

8. In 2002, Annie, an 80-year-old, is telling her granddaughter Suzie about the good old days. Annie says that in 1932, when she was a child, you could buy a nice house for $15,000 and a jacket for $5. Suzie looks up some current prices and finds that a house that costs $200,000 and a jacket that costs $50 are today's equivalent of the ones that Annie says cost so little when she was a child. Suzie, an economics student, looks up the CPI for 1932 and discovers that it is 13.7. The reference base is 1982–1984. The CPI for 2002 is 180.3.
   a. What is the 2002 price that is equivalent to $15,000 in 1932?
   b. Which is the lower cost: $15,000 in 1932 or $200,000 in 2002?
   c. Which is the lower cost: $5 in 1932 or $50 in 2002?
   d. Is Annie correct about the good old days?

9. Annie and Suzie of exercise 8 continue their conversation. But the subject now changes to wages. Suzie points out that when houses and jackets were cheap, wages were low. Annie recalls that her mother earned 55¢ an hour in 1932, which was the average wage at that time. Suzie seizes on this number and says that the good old days don't sound so good compared to 2002, when the average hourly wage rate was $14.76. Use the information about the CPI provided in exercise 8.
   a. What is the 2002 wage rate that is equivalent to 55¢ in 1932?
   b. Which is the higher wage rate: 55¢ in 1932 or $14.76 in 2002?
   c. How do the calculations in parts **a** and **b** along with those in exercise 8 help to determine whether the good old days were better or worse than today?

10. In 2002, the interest rate was 19 percent a year in Argentina and 0.01 percent a year in Japan. The inflation rate was 39 percent a year in Argentina and −0.9 percent a year in Japan.
    a. What was the real interest rate in Argentina in 2002?
    b. What was the real interest rate in Japan in 2002?

Critical Thinking

11. Imagine that you are given $1,000 to spend and told that you must spend it all buying items from a Sears catalog. But you do have a choice of catalog. You may select from the 1903 catalog or from Sears.com today. You will pay the prices quoted in the catalog that you choose.
    a. Why might you lean toward choosing the 1903 catalog?
    b. Why might you lean toward choosing sears.com?
    c. The bottom line: What is your choice and why? Refer to any biases in the CPI that might be relevant to your choice.

12. "The CPI is too political to be left to governments to calculate. It should be calculated by an independent agency." Argue both sides of this proposition.

Web Exercises

Use the links on MyEconLab to work the following exercises.

13. Visit the Web site of the Bureau of Labor Statistics and find the CPI data for the U.S. city and for the region of the country or metropolitan area in which you live.
    a. Is your local CPI higher or lower than the national average?
    b. Explain the deviation of your regional CPI from the national average.

14. Visit the Web site of the Bureau of Labor Statistics and find data on the CPI-U and the CPI-W.
    a. How do these two versions of the CPI differ?
    b. Which version of the CPI showed the faster inflation rate during 2002?
    c. Which of the two CPI measures do you think more closely matches your personal inflation experience?

15. Visit the Web site of the U.S. Senate and find data on the pay of senators in 1900, 1950, and 2000. Also obtain the CPI for those years.
    a. Calculate the real pay of senators in 1900 and 1950 in terms of 2000 dollars.
    b. In which of these years did senators receive the highest real earnings?
    c. In which of these years did senators receive the lowest real earnings?

16. Download the Excel spreadsheet that provides data on nominal interest rates and inflation rates for the United States and Italy during the 1990s.
    a. Calculate the real interest rate for each country and each year.
    b. In which year and country was the real interest rate higher on the average?
    c. Describe the similarities, if any, and the differences between the real and nominal interest rates for the two countries.

Potential GDP and the Natural Unemployment Rate

CHAPTER **23**

CHAPTER CHECKLIST

When you have completed your study of this chapter, you will be able to

1 Explain the forces that determine potential **GDP** and the real wage rate and employment at full employment.

2 Explain the forces that determine the natural unemployment rate.

Pierre lives in Paris, France. He works an average of 28 hours a week and earns the equivalent of $14.50 an hour. Peter lives in New York, works 34 hours a week, and earns $15.50 an hour.

When Pierre finished school, he entered a labor market with several million unemployed and took more than three months to find a job. Peter entered a labor market with little unemployment and had a job to start the day he graduated.

Pierre and Peter are representative of their fellow Europeans and Americans. They are both average in their economic regions. Why does the average American work longer hours, earn a bit more per hour, and face a labor market with less unemployment than the average European?

This chapter explains the forces that determine an economy's employment, real wage rate, production potential, and natural unemployment rate.

But we begin with a bit of macroeconomic perspective.

MACROECONOMIC APPROACHES AND PATHWAYS

In the three previous chapters, you learned how economists define and measure the variables that describe macroeconomic performance. Your task in this chapter and those that follow is to become familiar with the *theories* of macroeconomics that *explain* macroeconomic performance and with the *policies* that might improve it.

Before you embark on this task, we want to give you an overview of the alternative approaches to macroeconomics and the one that we'll take. We also want to give you a taste of the path that you will follow as you learn more about macroeconomics. We hope that this overview will help you to be aware of some of the main ideas that have come together to create the modern approach to macroeconomics that you will learn in this book.

■ The Two Main Schools of Thought

There are two main approaches to macroeconomics based on two schools of thought:

- Classical macroeconomics
- Keynesian macroeconomics

Classical Macroeconomics

Classical macroeconomics is a body of theory about how a market economy works and why it experiences economic growth and fluctuations. The first classical macroeconomists included Adam Smith, David Ricardo, and John Stuart Mill, all of whom worked in the 18th and 19th centuries.

The classical view is that markets work well and deliver the best available macroeconomic performance. The economy will fluctuate, and growth will slow down from time to time. But no remedy by government can improve on the performance of the market.

Classical macroeconomics fell into disrepute during the 1930s, which was a decade of high unemployment and stagnant production throughout the world economy known as the **Great Depression**. In the depression's worst year, 1933, the production of U.S. farms, factories, shops, and offices was only 70 percent of its 1929 level and 25 percent of the labor force was unemployed. These were years of human misery on a scale that is hard to imagine today. They were also years of extreme pessimism about the ability of the market economy to work properly. Many people believed that private ownership, free markets, and democratic political institutions could not survive. And the major alternative economic system of state ownership of capital and central planning seemed increasingly attractive to many people.

Classical macroeconomics predicted that the Great Depression would eventually end but offered no method for ending it more quickly.

Keynesian Macroeconomics

Keynesian macroeconomics is a body of theory about how a market economy works that stresses its inherent instability and the need for active government intervention to achieve full employment and sustained economic growth. One person, John Maynard Keynes, and his book *The General Theory of Employment, Interest, and Money,* published in 1936, began this school of thought.

Classical macroeconomics
A body of theory about how a market economy works and why it experiences economic growth and fluctuations.

Great Depression
A decade (the 1930s) of high unemployment and stagnant production throughout the world economy.

Keynesian macroeconomics
A body of theory about how a market economy works that stresses its inherent instability and the need for active government intervention to achieve full employment and sustained economic growth.

Keynes' theory was that depression and high unemployment occur when households don't spend enough on consumer goods and services and businesses don't spend enough investing in new capital. That is, too little *private* spending is the cause of depression (and recession). To counter the problem of too little private spending, *government* spending must rise.

This Keynesian view picked up many followers, and by the 1950s, Keynesian macroeconomics was mainstream macroeconomics.

But Keynes believed that after his cure for depression had restored full employment, two long-term problems would arise. One of these is a slow rate of increase in real GDP—a slow pace of improvement in the standard of living. The other long-term problem is persistent inflation—a persistently rising cost of living. And Keynes suspected that his cure for depression, increased government spending, might bring both inflation and a lower growth rate of real GDP. With a lower growth rate of real GDP, the pace of job creation would also slow. So a policy aimed at lowering unemployment in the *short term* might end up increasing it in the *long term.*

By the late 1960s and through the 1970s, Keynes' predictions became a reality. Inflation increased during the 1960s and exploded in the 1970s. Real GDP growth slowed, and the unemployment rate increased.

Keynes focused on the short term. He wanted to cure the immediate problem of depression regardless of the long-term consequences of the cure. "In the long run," said Keynes, "we're all dead." In the 1970s, Keynes was dead, but others were alive and well but living with the long-term consequences of Keynes' advice!

It was time for another challenge to the mainstream, and a new generation of classical economists, led by Robert E. Lucas, Jr. of the University of Chicago, was up to the challenge.

■ The New Macroeconomics

The **new macroeconomics** is a body of theory about how the economy works that is based on the view that macro outcomes depend on micro choices—the choices of rational individuals and firms interacting in markets. *New classical* macroeconomics incorporates the ideas of the classical economists that markets work well and a more recent *new Keynesian* macroeconomics incorporates the ideas of Keynes that markets adjust slowly to shocks. The key difference between the two new schools is in their views about how quickly prices and wages adjust in the face of excess demand or excess supply. But this difference is tiny, and a consensus is emerging in macroeconomics.

Part of that consensus is the view shared by all macroeconomists that the *long-term* problem of economic growth is vastly more important than the still very important *short-term* problem of economic fluctuations. If you turn the page and take a look at *Eye on the U.S. Economy,* you will see why. Even a small slowdown in economic growth brings a huge cost that dominates the cost of economic fluctuations.

New macroeconomics
A body of theory about how the economy works that is based on the view that macro outcomes depend on micro choices—the choices of rational individuals and firms interacting in markets.

■ The Road Ahead

This book organizes its tour of macroeconomics on the basis of the new consensus. The book begins in this chapter and the two that follow with an explanation of the forces that determine real GDP at full employment and the pace at which real GDP grows over time. It then moves to study money and the forces that bring inflation. Finally, it explains how real and monetary forces interact to bring about the business cycle. It also reviews an ongoing debate about how the government and the Federal Reserve can use policies to improve economic performance.

EYE ON THE U.S. ECONOMY

The Lucas Wedge and the Okun Gap

During the 1960s, U.S. real GDP expanded at a rate of 4.6 percent a year. The black line in part (a) shows the track that would have been followed if this growth rate had been maintained. The red line in part (a) shows the actual course of U.S. real GDP. The wedge-shaped shaded area between the black and red lines illustrates the lost output—called the Lucas wedge because University of Chicago economist Robert E. Lucas, Jr. drew attention to it. The Lucas wedge is equivalent to 10 years' real GDP.

The red line in part (b) shows the output gap—the percentage deviation of real GDP from potential GDP. When real GDP is below potential GDP, output is lost and the gap is negative. A negative output gap is called the Okun gap because Brookings Institution economist Arthur B. Okun drew attention to it. The Okun gaps since the end of the 1960s are equivalent to about 4 months' real GDP.

Smoothing the business cycle has a small payoff compared to the potentially huge payoff from restoring real GDP growth to its 1960s rate.

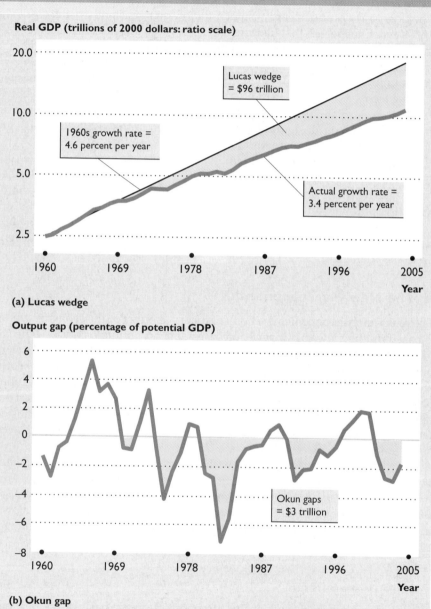

Real GDP (trillions of 2000 dollars: ratio scale)

Lucas wedge = $96 trillion

1960s growth rate = 4.6 percent per year

Actual growth rate = 3.4 percent per year

(a) Lucas wedge

Output gap (percentage of potential GDP)

Okun gaps = $3 trillion

(b) Okun gap

SOURCES OF DATA: Bureau of Economic Analysis and Congressional Budget Office.

23.1 POTENTIAL GDP

Potential GDP is the level of real GDP that the economy would produce if it were at full employment (see Chapter 21, p. 541). It is vital to understand the forces that determine potential GDP for three reasons. First, when the economy is *at full employment*, real GDP equals potential GDP; so actual real GDP is determined by the same factors that determine potential GDP. Second, real GDP can exceed potential GDP only temporarily as it approaches and then recedes from a business cycle peak. So potential GDP is the *sustainable* upper limit of production. Third, real GDP fluctuates around potential GDP, which means that on the average over the business cycle, real GDP equals potential GDP.

We produce the goods and services that make up real GDP by using the *factors of production:* labor and human capital, physical capital, land (and natural resources), and entrepreneurship. At any given time, the quantities of capital, land, and entrepreneurship and the state of technology are fixed. But the quantity of labor is not fixed. It depends on the choices that people make about the allocation of time between work and leisure. So with fixed quantities of capital, land, and entrepreneurship and fixed technology, real GDP depends on the quantity of labor employed. To describe this relationship between real GDP and the quantity of labor employed, we use a relationship that is similar to the production possibilities frontier, which is called the production function.

Potential GDP
The level of real GDP that the economy would produce if it were at full employment.

EYE ON THE GLOBAL ECONOMY

Potential GDP in the United States and the European Union

The population of the United States is a bit smaller than that of the European Union—290 million versus 310 million.

But the United States produces a much greater volume of goods and services than Europe produces. The top graph shows the numbers for real GDP. The United States produces 65 percent more than Europe.

Despite this enormous difference in real GDP, the real rate in Europe is not very different from that in the United States. You can see in the middle graph that the average hourly wage rate is only $1 an hour greater

in the United States than it is in Europe.

So how can production be so much lower in Europe? Part of the answer is that Europeans work shorter hours than Americans (shown in the bottom graph.)

Europeans take longer vacations, have more sick days, and end up working the equivalent of only 28 hours a week compared to the 34 hours that an average American works.

Another part of the answer is that Americans produce more per hour than Europeans produce.

This chapter will enable you to understand the deeper sources of these differences.

SOURCES OF DATA: Bureau of Economic Analysis and Eurostat.

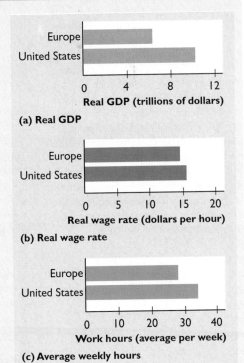

(a) Real GDP

(b) Real wage rate

(c) Average weekly hours

Production function
A relationship that shows the maximum quantity of real GDP that can be produced as the quantity of labor employed changes and all other influences on production remain the same.

Diminishing returns
The tendency for each additional hour of labor employed to produce a successively smaller additional amount of real GDP.

■ The Production Function

The **production function** is a relationship that shows the maximum quantity of real GDP that can be produced as the quantity of labor employed changes and all other influences on production remain the same. Figure 23.1 shows a production function, which is the curve labeled *PF*.

In Figure 23.1, when 100 billion labor hours are employed, real GDP is $6 trillion (at point *A*). When 200 billion labor hours are employed, real GDP is $10 trillion (at point *B*). And when 300 billion labor hours are employed, real GDP is $12 trillion (at point *C*).

The production function shares a feature of the *production possibilities frontier* that you studied in Chapter 3 (p. 62). Like the *PPF*, the production function is a boundary between the attainable and the unattainable. It is possible to produce at any point along the production function and beneath it in the shaded area. But it is not possible to produce at points above the production function. Those points are unattainable.

The production function displays **diminishing returns**—each additional hour of labor employed produces a successively smaller additional amount of real GDP. The first 100 billion hours of labor produces $6 trillion of real GDP. The second 100 billion hours of labor increases real GDP to $10 trillion and so produces only an

---

■ FIGURE 23.1

The Production Function

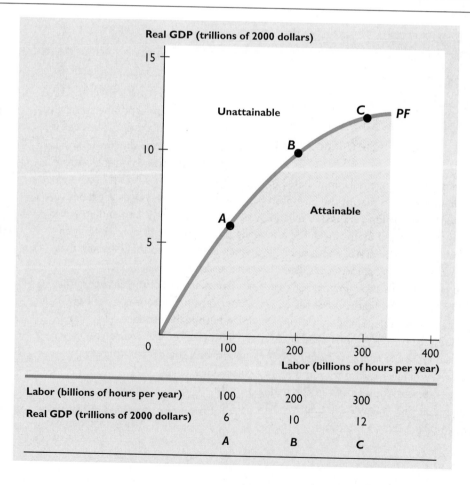

The production function shows the maximum quantity of real GDP that can be produced as the quantity of labor employed changes and all other influences on production remain the same. In this example, 100 billion hours of labor can produce $6 trillion of real GDP at point A, 200 billion hours of labor can produce $10 trillion of real GDP at point B, and 300 billion hours of labor can produce $12 trillion of real GDP at point C.

The production function separates attainable combinations of labor hours and real GDP from unattainable combinations and displays diminishing returns: Each additional hour of labor produces a successively smaller additional amount of real GDP.

Labor (billions of hours per year)	100	200	300
Real GDP (trillions of 2000 dollars)	6	10	12
	A	B	C

additional $4 trillion of real GDP. The third 100 billion hours of labor increases real GDP to $12 trillion and so produces only an additional $2 trillion of real GDP.

Diminishing returns arise because the quantity of capital (and other factors of production) is fixed. As more labor is hired, the additional output produced decreases because the extra workers have less capital to work with. For example, a forest service has three chain saws and an axe and hires three workers to clear roads and trails of fallen trees and debris during the spring thaw. Hiring a fourth worker will contribute less to the amount cleared than the amount that the third worker added, and hiring a fifth worker will add even less.

Because real GDP depends on the quantity of labor employed, potential GDP depends on the point on the production function at which the economy operates. To find that point, we must understand what determines the quantity of labor employed.

■ The Labor Market

You've already studied the tool that we use to determine the quantity of labor employed: demand and supply. In macroeconomics, we apply the concepts of demand, supply, and market equilibrium to economy-wide markets. Here, we apply these concepts to the economy-wide labor market.

The quantity of labor employed depends on firms' decisions about how much labor to hire (the demand for labor). It also depends on households' decisions about how to allocate time between employment and other activities (the supply of labor). And it depends on how the labor market coordinates the decisions of firms and households (labor market equilibrium). So we will study

- The demand for labor
- The supply of labor
- Labor market equilibrium

The Demand for Labor

The **quantity of labor demanded** is the total labor hours that all the firms in the economy plan to hire during a given time period at a given real wage rate. The **demand for labor** is the relationship between the quantity of labor demanded and the real wage rate when all other influences on firms' hiring plans remain the same. The lower the real wage rate, the greater is the quantity of labor demanded.

The real wage rate is the *nominal wage rate* (the dollars per hour that people earn on the average) divided by the price level (see Chapter 22, p. 560). We express the real wage rate in constant dollars—today in 2000 dollars. Think about the real wage rate as the quantity of real GDP that an hour of labor earns.

The lower the real wage rate, the greater is the quantity of labor that firms find it profitable to hire. The real wage rate influences the quantity of labor demanded because what matters to firms is not the number of dollars they pay for an hour of labor (the nominal wage rate) but how much output they must sell to earn those dollars. So firms compare the extra output that an hour of labor can produce with the real wage rate.

Firms are in business to maximize profit. So they hire labor as long as each additional hour hired produces at least as much additional output as the real wage rate. When a small quantity of labor is hired, an extra hour of labor produces more output than the real wage rate. But each additional hour of labor produces less additional output than the previous hour. As a firm hires more labor, eventually the extra output from an extra hour of labor exactly equals the real wage rate. This equality determines the quantity of labor demanded at the real wage rate.

Quantity of labor demanded
The total labor hours that all the firms in the economy plan to hire during a given time period at a given real wage rate.

Demand for labor
The relationship between the quantity of labor demanded and real wage rate when all other influences on firms' hiring plans remain the same.

The Demand for Labor in a Soda Factory You can understand the demand for labor better by thinking about a single firm rather than the economy as a whole. Suppose that the money wage rate is $15 an hour. And suppose that the price of a bottle of soda is $1.50. For the soda factory, the real wage rate is a number of bottles of soda. To find the soda factory's real wage rate, divide the money wage rate by the price of its output—$15 an hour ÷ $1.50 a bottle = 10 bottles of soda an hour. It costs the soda factory 10 bottles of soda to hire an hour of labor. As long as the soda factory can hire labor that produces more than 10 additional bottles of soda an hour, it is profitable to hire more labor. Only when the extra output produced by an extra hour of labor falls to 10 bottles an hour has the factory reached the profit-maximizing quantity of labor.

Labor Demand Schedule and Labor Demand Curve We can represent the demand for labor as either a demand schedule or a demand curve. The table in Figure 23.2 shows part of a demand for labor schedule. It tells us the quantity of labor demanded at three different real wage rates. For example, if the real wage rate is $30 an hour (row *B*), the quantity of labor demanded is 200 billion hours a year. If the real wage rate rises to $50 an hour (row *A*), the quantity of labor demanded decreases to 100 billion hours a year. And if the real wage rate falls to $10 an hour (row *C*), the quantity of labor demanded increases to 300 billion hours a year.

Figure 23.2 shows the demand for labor curve. Points *A*, *B*, and *C* on the demand curve correspond to rows *A*, *B*, and *C* of the demand schedule.

FIGURE 23.2

The Demand for Labor

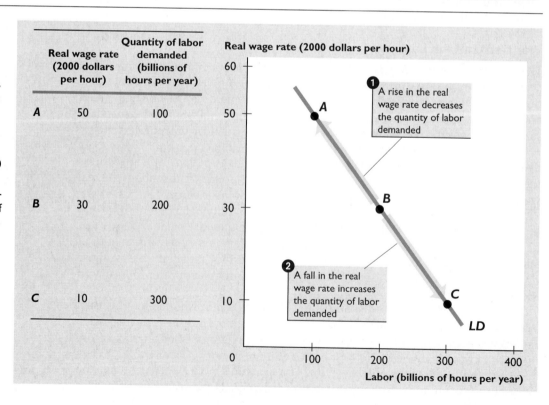

Firms are willing to hire labor only if it produces more than the real wage rate it costs. So the lower the real wage rate, the more labor firms can profitably hire and the greater is the quantity of labor demanded.

At a real wage rate of $30 an hour, the quantity of labor demanded is 200 billion hours at point B. **1** If the real wage rate rises to $50 an hour, the quantity of labor demanded decreases to 100 billion hours at point A. **2** If the real wage rate falls to $10 an hour, the quantity of labor demanded increases to 300 billion hours at point C.

	Real wage rate (2000 dollars per hour)	Quantity of labor demanded (billions of hours per year)
A	50	100
B	30	200
C	10	300

1 A rise in the real wage rate decreases the quantity of labor demanded

2 A fall in the real wage rate increases the quantity of labor demanded

The Supply of Labor

The **quantity of labor supplied** is the number of labor hours that all the households in the economy plan to work during a given time period at a given real wage rate. The **supply of labor** is the relationship between the quantity of labor supplied and the real wage rate when all other influences on work plans remain the same.

We can represent the supply of labor as either a supply schedule or a supply curve. The table in Figure 23.3 shows a supply of labor schedule. It tells us the quantity of labor supplied at three different real wage rates. For example, if the real wage rate is $30 an hour (row B), the quantity of labor supplied is 200 billion hours a year. If the real wage rate falls to $15 an hour (row A), the quantity of labor supplied decreases to 100 billion hours a year. And if the real wage rate rises to $50 an hour (row C), the quantity of labor supplied increases to 300 billion hours a year.

Figure 23.3 shows the supply of labor curve. It corresponds to the supply schedule, and the points A, B, and C on the curve correspond to the rows A, B, and C of the supply schedule.

The real wage rate influences the quantity of labor supplied because what matters to people is not the number of dollars they earn but what those dollars will buy.

The quantity of labor supplied increases as the real wage rate increases for two reasons:

- Hours per person increase.
- Labor force participation increases.

Quantity of labor supplied
The number of labor hours that all the households in the economy plan to work during a given time period at a given real wage rate.

Supply of labor
The relationship between the quantity of labor supplied and the real wage rate when all other influences on work plans remain the same.

FIGURE 23.3
The Supply of Labor

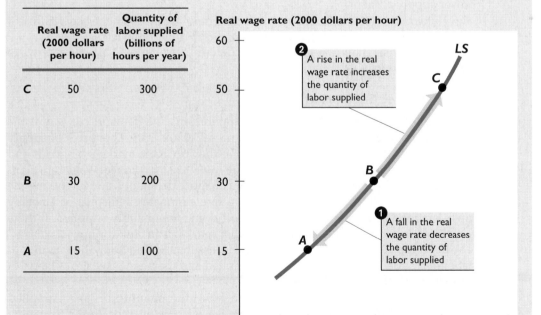

Real wage rate (2000 dollars per hour)	Quantity of labor supplied (billions of hours per year)
C 50	300
B 30	200
A 15	100

2 A rise in the real wage rate increases the quantity of labor supplied

1 A fall in the real wage rate decreases the quantity of labor supplied

Households are willing to supply labor only if the real wage rate is high enough to attract them from other activities. The higher the real wage rate, the greater is the quantity of labor supplied.

At a real wage rate of $30 an hour, the quantity of labor supplied is 200 billion hours at point B. **1** If the real wage rate falls to $15 an hour, the quantity of labor supplied decreases to 100 billion hours at point A. **2** If the real wage rate rises to $50 an hour, the quantity of labor supplied increases to 300 billion hours at point C.

Hours per Person The real wage rate is the opportunity cost of taking leisure and not working. And as the opportunity cost of taking leisure rises, other things remaining the same, households choose to work more. But other things don't remain the same. A higher real wage rate brings a higher income, which increases the demand for leisure and encourages less work.

So a rise in the real wage rate has two opposing effects. But for most households, the opportunity cost effect is stronger than the income effect. So a rise in the real wage rate brings an increase in the quantity of labor supplied.

Labor Force Participation Most people have productive opportunities outside the labor force and choose to work only if the real wage rate exceeds the value of other productive activities. For example, a parent might spend time caring for her or his child. The alternative is day care. The parent will choose to work only if he or she can earn enough per hour to pay the cost of day care and have enough left to make the work effort worthwhile. The higher the real wage rate, the more likely it is that a parent will choose to work and so the greater is the labor force participation rate.

Other Influences on Labor Supply Decisions Many factors other than the real wage rate influence labor supply decisions and influence the position of the labor supply curve. Income taxes and unemployment benefits are two of these factors.

The work-leisure decision depends on the *after-tax* wage rate—the wage rate actually received by the household. So, for a given wage rate, the income tax decreases the after-tax wage rate and the quantity of labor supplied decreases. The result is a lower supply of labor. (The income tax rate doesn't change the demand for labor because for the employer, the cost of labor is the before-tax wage rate.)

Unemployment benefits lower the cost of searching for a job and encourage unemployed workers to take longer to find the best job available. The result is a lower supply of labor.

Higher income tax rates and more generous unemployment benefits lower supply of labor—a labor supply curve that lies further to the left.

Let's now see how the labor market determines employment, the real wage rate, and potential GDP.

Labor Market Equilibrium

Figure 23.4(a) shows the labor market equilibrium. The demand curve and the supply curve are the same as those in Figures 23.2 and 23.3. The forces of supply and demand operate in labor markets just as they do in the markets for goods and services. The price of labor is the real wage rate. A rise in the real wage rate eliminates a shortage of labor by decreasing the quantity demanded and increasing the quantity supplied. A fall in the real wage rate eliminates a surplus of labor by increasing the quantity demanded and decreasing the quantity supplied. If there is neither a shortage nor a surplus, the labor market is in equilibrium.

In Figure 23.4(a), if the real wage rate is less than $30 an hour, the quantity of labor demanded exceeds the quantity supplied and there is a shortage of labor. In this situation, the real wage rate rises.

If the real wage rate exceeds $30 an hour, the quantity of labor supplied exceeds the quantity demanded and there is a surplus of labor. In this situation, the real wage rate falls.

If the real wage rate is $30 an hour, the quantity of labor demanded equals the quantity supplied and there is neither a shortage nor a surplus of labor. In this

FIGURE 23.4

Labor Market Equilibrium and Potential GDP

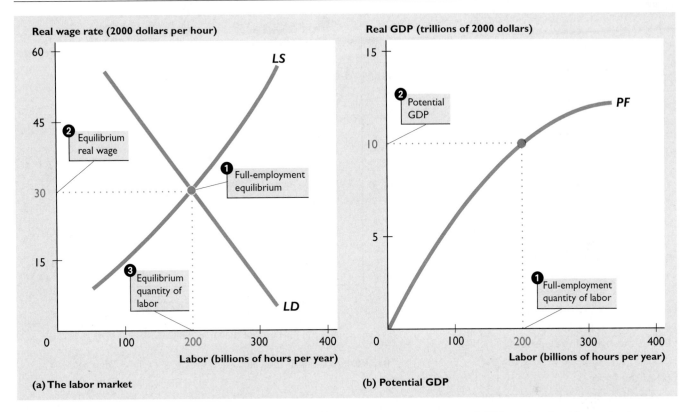

(a) The labor market

(b) Potential GDP

❶ Full employment occurs when the quantity of labor demanded equals the quantity of labor supplied. **❷** The equilibrium real wage rate is $30 an hour, and **❸** equilibrium employment is 200 billion hours a year.

Potential GDP is the real GDP produced on the production function by the full-employment quantity of labor. **❶** The full-employment quantity of labor, 200 billion hours a year, produces a **❷** potential GDP of $10 trillion.

situation, the labor market is in equilibrium and the real wage rate remains constant. The equilibrium quantity of labor is 200 billion hours a year. When the equilibrium quantity of labor is employed, the economy is at full employment. So the full-employment quantity of labor is 200 billion hours a year.

Full Employment and Potential GDP

You've seen that the quantity of real GDP depends on the quantity of labor employed. The production function tells us how much real GDP a given amount of employment can produce. Now that we've determined the full-employment quantity of labor, we can find potential GDP.

Figure 23.4(b) shows the relationship between labor market equilibrium and potential GDP. The equilibrium quantity of labor employed in Figure 23.4(a) is 200 billion hours. The production function in Figure 23.4(b) tells us that 200 billion hours of labor produces $10 trillion of real GDP. This quantity of real GDP is potential GDP.

When the labor market is in equilibrium, the economy is at full employment and real GDP equals potential GDP.

Explaining the Differences Between the United States and Europe

The quantity of capital per worker is greater in the United States than in Europe, and U.S. technology, on the average, is more productive than European technology.

These differences between the United States and Europe mean that U.S. labor is more productive than European labor.

Because U.S. labor is more productive than European labor, U.S. employers are willing to pay more for a given quantity of labor than European employers are. So the demand for labor curve in the United States, LD_{US}, lies to the right of the European demand for labor curve, LD_{EU}, in part (a) of the figure.

This difference in labor productivities also means that the U.S. production function, PF_{US}, lies above the European production function, PF_{EU}, in part (b) of the figure.

Higher income taxes and unemployment benefits in Europe mean that to induce a person to take a job, a firm in Europe must offer a higher wage rate than the one that a firm in the United States has to offer. So the European labor supply curve, LS_{EU}, lies to the left of the U.S. labor supply curve, LS_{US}.

The equilibrium real wage rates are similar in the two economies but equilibrium employment and potential GDP are much lower in Europe than in the United States.

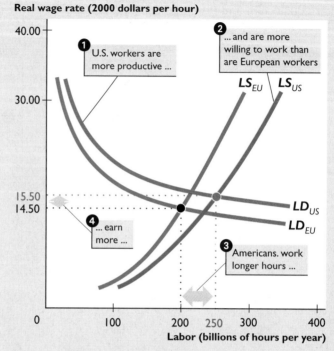

(a) Labor market in Europe and the United States

(b) Production function in Europe and the United States

CHECKPOINT 23.1

1 **Explain the forces that determine potential GDP and the real wage rate and employment at full employment.**

Practice Problem 23.1

1. Table 1 describes an economy's production function and demand for labor

TABLE 1

Quantity of labor demanded (billions of hours per year)	0	1	2	3	4
Real GDP (billions of 2000 dollars)	0	40	70	90	100
Real wage rate (2000 dollars per hour)	50	40	30	20	10

Table 2 describes the supply of labor in this economy.

TABLE 2

Quantity of labor supplied (billions of hours per year)	0	1	2	3	4
Real wage rate (2000 dollars per hour)	10	20	30	40	50

a. Make graphs of the labor market and production function.
b. Find the equilibrium employment, real wage rate, and potential GDP.

Exercise 23.1

1. Table 3 describes an economy's production function and demand for labor.

TABLE 3

Quantity of labor demanded (billions of hours per year)	0	1	2	3	4	5
Real GDP (billions of 2000 dollars)	0	5	9	12	14	15
Real wage rate (2000 dollars per hour)		5	4	3	2	1

Table 4 describes the supply of labor in this economy.

TABLE 4

Quantity of labor supplied (billions of hours per year)	0	1	2	3	4	5
Real wage rate (2000 dollars per hour)		1.50	2.00	2.50	3.00	3.50	4.00

a. Make graphs of the labor market and the production function.
b. Find the equilibrium employment, real wage rate, and potential GDP.

Solution to Practice Problem 23.1

1a. The demand for labor is a graph of the first and last row of Table 1 and the supply of labor is a graph of the data in Table 2 (Figure 1). The production function is a graph of the first two rows of Table 1 (Figure 2).

1b. Labor market equilibrium occurs when the real wage rate is $30 an hour and 2 billion hours of labor are employed (Figure 1). Potential GDP is the real GDP produced by the equilibrium quantity of labor (2 billion hours in Figure 1). Potential GDP is $70 billion (Figure 2).

FIGURE 1

FIGURE 2

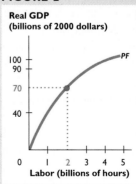

23.2 THE NATURAL UNEMPLOYMENT RATE

So far, we've focused on the forces that determine the real wage rate, the quantity of labor employed, and real GDP at full employment. We're now going to bring unemployment into the picture.

You learned in Chapter 21 how unemployment is measured. And you learned how people become unemployed by losing or leaving their jobs and by entering or reentering the labor force. You also learned how we classify unemployment as frictional, structural, seasonal, or cyclical. Finally, you learned that the unemployment rate when the economy is at full employment, which consists of frictional, structural, and seasonal unemployment, is called the *natural unemployment rate*.

Measuring, describing, and classifying unemployment tell us a lot about it. But these activities do not *explain* the amount of unemployment that exists or why its rate changes over time and varies across economies.

Many forces interact to determine the unemployment rate. Understanding these forces is a challenging task. Economists approach this task in two steps. The first step is to understand what determines the natural unemployment rate—the unemployment rate when the economy is at full employment. The second step is to understand what makes unemployment fluctuate around the natural unemployment rate. In this chapter, we take the first of these steps. We take the second step in Chapters 29–33 when we study economic fluctuations.

 EYE ON THE **PAST**

Average Unemployment Rates over Six Decades

saw the average unemployment rate fall but not quite back to the rate of the 1950s and 1960s.

You will be a member of the labor force of the 2000s. And the average unemployment rate of the first decade of the 2000s will have a big effect on your job market success.

If we look back at the U.S. economy decade by decade, we can see through the ups and downs of the business cycle and focus on the broad trends. By looking at the average unemployment rates across the decades, we get an estimate of movements in the natural unemployment rate.

The figure shows these averages. During the 1950s and 1960s, the unemployment rate averaged less than 5 percent. During the 1970s, the average unemployment rate climbed to 6 percent, and in the 1980s, it climbed to more than 7 percent. The 1990s

Unemployment rate (percentage of labor force)

SOURCE OF DATA: Bureau of Labor Statistics.

To understand the amount of frictional and structural unemployment that exists at the natural unemployment rate, economists focus on two fundamental causes of unemployment that cut across the frictional-structural classification. These two fundamental causes of unemployment are

- Job search
- Job rationing

■ Job Search

Job search is the activity of looking for an acceptable vacant job. Because the labor market is in a constant state of change, there are always some people who have not yet found suitable jobs and who are actively searching. The failure of businesses destroys jobs. The expansion of businesses and the startup of new businesses create jobs. As people pass through different stages of life, some enter or reenter the labor market, others leave their jobs to look for better ones, and others retire. This constant churning in the labor market means that there are always some people looking for jobs, and these people are part of the unemployed.

The amount of job search depends on a number of factors that change over time. The main ones are

- Demographic change
- Unemployment benefits
- Structural change

Job search
The activity of looking for an acceptable vacant job.

Demographic Change

An increase in the proportion of the population that is of working age brings an increase in the entry rate into the labor force and an increase in the unemployment rate. This factor was important in the U.S. labor market during the 1970s. The bulge in the birth rate that occurred in the late 1940s and early 1950s increased the proportion of new entrants into the labor force during the 1970s and brought an increase in the unemployment rate.

As the birth rate declined, the bulge moved into higher age groups and the proportion of new entrants declined during the 1980s. During this period, the unemployment rate decreased.

Another source of demographic change has been an increase in the number of households with two incomes. When unemployment comes to one of these workers, it is possible, with income still flowing in, to take longer to find a new job. This factor might have increased frictional unemployment.

Unemployment Benefits

The opportunity cost of job search influences the length of time that an unemployed person spends searching for a job. With no unemployment benefits, the opportunity cost of job search is high, and a person is likely to accept a job that is found quickly. With generous unemployment benefits, the opportunity cost of job search is low, and a person is likely to spend a considerable time searching for the ideal job.

Generous unemployment benefits are a large part of the story of high unemployment rates in Europe and some other countries such as Canada—see *Eye on the Global Economy* on p. 584.

Unemployment Benefits and the Natural Unemployment Rate

The natural unemployment rate in Europe is higher than in the United States. And Europe has much higher unemployment benefits than the United States. But are unemployment benefits the source of the difference?

To isolate the effects of unemployment benefits, we need to keep other things the same. Canada provides an experiment in which other things are very similar.

The natural unemployment rate in Canada equalled that in the United States until 1980 but then it increased. Why?

The key change in the 1980s was an increase in Canadian unemploy-

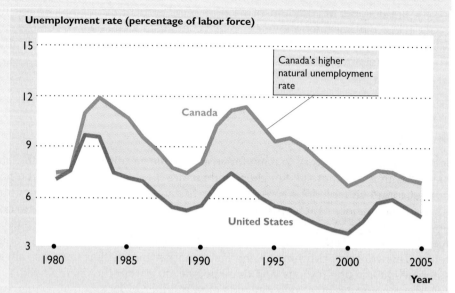

Unemployment rate (percentage of labor force)

Canada's higher natural unemployment rate

Canada

United States

Year

SOURCES OF DATA: Bureau of Labor Statistics and Statistics Canada.

ment benefits. Close to 100 percent of Canada's unemployed receive generous benefits compared to 38 percent in the United States.

The level of unemployment benefits appears to have a large effect on the natural unemployment rate.

Structural Change

Technological change influences unemployment. Sometimes it brings a structural slump, a condition in which some industries and even regions contract while other industries and regions flourish. When these events occur, labor turnover is high, job search increases, and the natural unemployment rate rises.

At other times, technological change brings a structural boom. It creates new jobs that are a good match for the people who are losing their jobs. When these events occur, labor turnover might be high, but job search decreases because new jobs are found quickly, and the natural unemployment rate falls. The Internet economy of the 1990s is an example of a structural boom. Lots of new jobs were created in every major population center, and these jobs were a good match for the skills available. So the natural unemployment rate decreased.

■ Job Rationing

Job rationing
A situation that arises when the real wage rate is above the full-employment equilibrium level.

Job rationing occurs when the real wage rate is above the full-employment equilibrium level. You have learned that markets allocate scarce resources by adjusting the market price to bring buying plans and selling plans into balance. You can think of the market as *rationing* scarce resources. In the labor market, the real wage rate rations employment and therefore rations jobs. Changes in the real wage rate keep the number of people seeking work and the number of jobs available in balance. But the real wage rate is not the only possible instrument for rationing jobs. And in some industries, the real wage rate is set above the full-employment equilibrium level, which brings a surplus of labor. So in these labor markets, jobs are rationed by some other means.

The real wage rate might be set above the full-employment equilibrium level for three reasons:

- Efficiency wage
- Minimum wage
- Union wage

Efficiency Wage

An **efficiency wage** is a real wage rate that is set above the full-employment equilibrium wage rate to induce a greater work effort. The idea is that if a firm pays only the going market average wage, employees have no incentive to work hard because they know that even if they are fired for shirking, they can find a job with another firm at a similar wage rate. But if a firm pays *more* than the going market average wage, employees have an incentive to work hard because they know that if they are fired, they *cannot* expect to find a job with another firm at a similar wage rate.

Further, by paying an efficiency wage, a firm can attract the most productive workers. Also, its workers are less likely to quit their jobs, so the firm faces a lower rate of labor turnover and lower training costs. Finally, the firm's recruiting costs are lower because it always faces a steady stream of available new workers.

Paying an efficiency wage is costly, so only those firms that can't directly monitor the work effort of their employees use this device. But if enough firms pay an efficiency wage, the average real wage rate will exceed the full-employment equilibrium level.

The Minimum Wage

A *minimum wage law* is a government regulation that makes hiring labor for less than a specified wage illegal. If the minimum wage is set below the equilibrium wage, the minimum wage has no effect. The minimum wage law and market forces are not in conflict. But if a minimum wage is set above the equilibrium wage, the minimum wage is in conflict with market forces and unemployment arises.

The current federal minimum wage is $5.15 an hour, and the minimum wage has a major effect in the markets for low-skilled labor. Because skill grows with work experience, teenage labor is particularly affected by the minimum wage.

Union Wage

A **union wage** is a wage rate that results from collective bargaining between a labor union and a firm. Because a union represents a group of workers, it can usually achieve a wage rate that exceeds the level that would prevail in a competitive labor market.

For the United States, it is estimated that, on the average, union wage rates are 30 percent higher than nonunion wage rates. But this estimate probably overstates the true effects of labor unions on the wage rate. In some industries, union wages are higher than nonunion wages because union members do jobs that require greater skill than nonunion jobs. In these cases, even without a union, those workers would earn a higher wage.

One way to calculate the effects of unions is to examine the wages of union and nonunion workers who do nearly identical work. For workers with similar skill levels, the union-nonunion wage difference is between 10 percent and 25 percent. For example, airline pilots who are members of the Air Line Pilots

Efficiency wage
A real wage rate that is set above the full-employment equilibrium wage rate to induce greater work effort.

Union wage
A wage rate that results from collective bargaining between a labor union and a firm.

Association earn about 25 percent more than what nonunion pilots with the same level of skill earn.

Labor unions are much more influential in Europe than in the United States. In Europe, unions not only achieve wage rates above those of a competitive market but also have broad political influence on labor market conditions.

Job Rationing and Unemployment

Whether because of efficiency wages, a minimum wage law, or the actions of labor unions, if the real wage rate is above the full-employment equilibrium level, the natural unemployment rate increases. The above-equilibrium real wage rate decreases the quantity of labor demanded and increases the quantity of labor supplied.

Figure 23.5 illustrates job rationing and the frictional and structural unemployment it creates. The full-employment equilibrium real wage rate is $30 an hour, and the equilibrium quantity of labor is 200 billion hours a year. The existence of efficiency wages, the minimum wage, and union wages raises the economy's average real wage rate to $40 an hour. At this wage rate, the quantity of labor demanded decreases to 150 billion hours and the quantity of labor supplied increases to 250 billion hours. Firms ration jobs and choose the workers to hire on the basis of criteria such as education and previous job experience. The labor market is like a game of musical chairs in which a large number of chairs have been removed. So the quantity of labor supplied persistently exceeds the quantity demanded, and additional unemployment arises from job rationing.

■ FIGURE 23.5

Job Rationing Increases the Natural Unemployment Rate

The full-employment equilibrium real wage rate is $30 an hour. Efficiency wages, the minimum wage, and union wages put the average real wage rate above the full-employment equilibrium level—at $40 an hour.

❶ The quantity of labor demanded decreases to 150 billion hours.

❷ The quantity of labor supplied increases to 250 billion hours.

❸ A surplus of labor arises and increases the natural unemployment rate.

The Federal Minimum Wage

The Fair Labor Standards Act of 1938 set the federal minimum wage in the United States at 25¢ an hour. Over the years, the minimum wage has increased, and in 2005, it was $5.15 an hour. Although the minimum has increased, it hasn't kept up with the rising cost of living.

The figure shows the real minimum wage rate in 2000 dollars. You can see that during the 1960s, the minimum wage in 2000 dollars was $8 an hour. It decreased during the 1970s and 1980s and has been roughly constant at around $5 an hour since the mid-1980s.

SOURCE OF DATA: Bureau of Labor Statistics.

REALITY CHECK

Natural Unemployment in YOUR Life

You will encounter natural unemployment at many points in your life.

If you now have a job, you probably went through a spell of natural unemployment as you searched for that job. And when you graduate and look for a full-time job, you might spend some more time searching for the best match for your skills and location preferences. You might know an older worker who has recently lost a job and is going through the agony of figuring out what to do next.

Although natural unemployment can be painful for people who experience it, from a social perspective, it is productive. Natural unemployment enables scarce resources to be *re*-allocated to their most valuable uses.

2 **Explain the forces that determine the natural unemployment rate.**

Practice Problem 23.2

1. The economy of Singapore has seen huge changes during the past 50 years. It has experienced rapid population growth and has restructured its economy several times to remain at the forefront of the latest technology. Singapore has modest unemployment benefits, no minimum wage, and weak labor unions.
   a. Does the unemployment that Singapore experiences arise primarily from job search or job rationing?
   b. Which factors mentioned above suggest that Singapore has a higher natural unemployment rate than the United States?
   c. Which factors mentioned above suggest that Singapore has a lower natural unemployment rate than the United States?

Exercise 23.2

1. The economy of Sweden has seen changes during the past 50 years, but the change has been steady and population growth has been modest. Sweden has high unemployment benefits, a high minimum wage, and strong labor unions.
   a. Does the unemployment that Sweden experiences arise primarily from job search or job rationing?
   b. Which factors mentioned above suggest that Sweden has a higher natural unemployment rate than the United States?
   c. Which factors mentioned above suggest that Sweden has a lower natural unemployment rate than the United States?

Solution to Practice Problem 23.2

1a. Singapore's unemployment is likely to arise primarily from job search. Of the sources of job rationing (efficiency wages, minimum wages, and union wages) only efficiency wages applies.

1b. The factors mentioned above that point toward a higher natural unemployment rate in Singapore than in the United States are rapid population growth and restructuring to remain at the forefront of new technologies, both of which will create a large amount of job search, other things remaining the same.

1c. The factors mentioned above that point toward a lower natural unemployment rate in Singapore than in the United States are modest unemployment benefits, which will limit the amount of job search, and the absence of a minimum wage and weak labor unions, which will limit the amount of job rationing.

CHAPTER CHECKPOINT

Key Points

1 **Explain the forces that determine potential GDP and the real wage rate and employment at full employment.**

- Potential GDP is the quantity of real GDP that the full-employment quantity of labor produces.
- The production function describes the relationship between real GDP and the quantity of labor employed when all other influences on production remain the same. As the quantity of labor increases, real GDP increases.
- The quantity of labor demanded increases as the real wage rate falls, other things remaining the same.
- The quantity of labor supplied increases as the real wage rate rises, other things remaining the same.
- At full-employment equilibrium, the real wage rate makes the quantity of labor demanded equal the quantity of labor supplied.

2 **Explain the forces that determine the natural unemployment rate.**

- The unemployment rate at full employment is the natural unemployment rate.
- Unemployment is always present because of job search and job rationing.
- Job search is influenced by demographic change, unemployment benefits, and structural change.
- Job rationing arises from an efficiency wage, the minimum wage, and a union wage.

Key Terms

Classical macroeconomics, 570
Demand for labor, 575
Diminishing returns, 574
Efficiency wage, 585
Great Depression, 570

Job rationing, 584
Job search, 583
Keynesian macroeconomics, 570
New macroeconomics, 571
Potential GDP, 573

Production function, 574
Quantity of labor demanded, 575
Quantity of labor supplied, 577
Supply of labor, 577
Union wage, 585

Exercises

1. Sort the items in the following list of events into four groups: those that change the production function, those that change the demand for labor, those that change the supply of labor, and those that do not change the production function, the demand for labor, or the supply of labor in the United States. Say in which direction any changes occur.
   a. Dell introduces a new supercomputer that everyone can afford.
   b. A major hurricane hits Florida.
   c. More teenagers go to college.
   d. The CPI rises.
   e. An economic slump in the rest of the world decreases U.S. exports.
   f. An oil embargo in the Middle East cuts supplies of oil to the United States.
   g. The Anaheim Angels win the World Series.
   h. U.S. labor unions negotiate wage hikes that affect all workers.
   i. A huge scientific breakthrough doubles U.S. labor productivity.
   j. Migration to the United States increases the working-age population.

2. Which of the events in exercise 1 increase the equilibrium quantity of labor?

3. Which of the events in exercise 1 decrease the equilibrium quantity of labor?

4. Which of the events in exercise 1 raise the real wage rate?

5. Which of the events in exercise 1 lower the real wage rate?

6. Which of the events in exercise 1 increase potential GDP?

7. Which of the events in exercise 1 decrease potential GDP?

8. The following tables set out information about the economy of Athabasca:

Labor hours (millions per year)	Real GDP (millions of dollars)	Real wage rate (dollars per hour)	Quantity of labor demanded (millions of hours per year)	Quantity of labor supplied (millions of hours per year)
0	0			
1	10	10	5	1
2	19	9	4	2
3	27	8	3	3
4	34	7	2	4
5	40	6	1	5

In Athabasca, what is
a. The quantity of labor employed?
b. Potential GDP?
c. The real wage rate?
d. Total labor income?

9. In the economy of Athabasca described in exercise 8, the population increases. In what directions do potential GDP, employment, and the real wage rate change?

10. In the economy of Athabasca described in exercise 8, the labor productivity increases. In what directions do potential GDP, employment, and the real wage rate change?

11. The people of Nautica can work a maximum of 100 hours in total every day. The first 10 hours of work can produce $10 of real GDP. The second 10 hours a day can produce an additional $9 of real GDP. The third 10 hours a day produce an additional $8 of real GDP. Each additional 10 hours of work a day produces additional GDP of $1 a day less than the previous 10 hours. Make a table and a graph of Nautica's production function.

12. Use the information provided in exercise 11 about the economy of Nautica. Also use the information that the firms in Nautica are willing to hire 10 hours of labor a day for a real wage rate of $1 an hour, 20 hours a day for 90¢ an hour, and an additional 10 hours a day for each 10¢ cut in the real wage rate. The people of Nautica are willing to work 10 hours a day for a real wage rate of 10¢ an hour. And for each 10¢ an hour increase in the real wage, they are willing to work an additional 10 hours a day.
    a. Make a table that shows Nautica's demand for labor schedule and draw Nautica's demand for labor curve.
    b. Make a table that shows Nautica's supply of labor schedule and draw Nautica's supply of labor curve.
    c. Find the full-employment equilibrium real wage rate and quantity of labor in Nautica's economy.
    d. Find Nautica's potential GDP.

13. Two island economies, Cocoa Island and Plantation Island, are identical in every respect except one. A survey tells us that at full employment, people on Cocoa Island spend 1,000 hours a day in job search, while the people on Plantation Island spend 2,000 hours a day in job search.
    a. Which economy has the greater level of potential GDP?
    b. Which economy has the higher real wage rate?
    c. Which economy has the higher natural unemployment rate?

14. On Cocoa Island described in exercise 13, the government introduces a minimum wage that creates an additional 1,000 hours a day of unemployment. On Plantation Island, nothing changes from the situation described in exercise 13.
    a. Which economy now has the greater level of potential GDP?
    b. Which economy now has the higher real wage rate?
    c. Which economy now has the higher natural unemployment rate?
    d. How much unemployment in these two economies results from job search and how much from job rationing?

Critical Thinking

15. In the figure in *Eye on the Global Economy* on page 573, we compare the United States and Europe. Speculate by looking 40 years ahead. Do you think the comparison of the United States and Europe in the 2040s will be similar or different in some significant ways? Provide reasons for your speculation.

16. If the minimum wage were abolished, what do you predict would happen to potential GDP, employment, and the equilibrium real wage rate? Would you favor or oppose the abolition of the minimum wage? Why?

17. How do you think real GDP and potential GDP would change if the United States adopted the level of unemployment benefits that Canada has? Refer to *Eye on the Global Economy* on page 584 for information on the comparison between Canada and the United States. Would you favor or oppose such a change in arrangements?

Web Exercises

Use the links on MyEconLab to work the following exercises.

18. Visit the Web site of the Bureau of Economic Analysis and obtain the data on real GDP in the United States going back to 1929. Assuming that potential GDP increased between 1929 and 1940 at a constant rate and that both those years were at full employment, how much output was lost during the Great Depression years? Does that amount of lost output change the comparison between the Lucas wedge and the Okun gap in the figure on page 572?

19. Use the Web site described in exercise 18 and figure out what happened to the production function and to the demand for labor and supply of labor in the United States from 1990 through 2005.

20. Visit some or all of the following Web sites to obtain information about the economy of Russia since 1990:

    CIA World Factbook 2000, Russia section
    IMF World Economic Outlook October 2000, Focus on Transition Economies
    IMF World Economic Outlook October 2005, Data Appendix
    Hoover Institution material on the Russian economy
    Article by the American Enterprise Institute on the Russian economy

    Use the production function and labor market model to organize a description of the influences on and the course of the Russian economy since 1990. Pay special attention to the changes in labor productivity and the demand for and supply of labor.

    Do you think Russia was at full employment during these years?

21. Use your answers to exercises 19 and 20 to compare and contrast the macroeconomic performances of the United States and Russia during the 1990s and 2000s.

Investment and Saving

CHAPTER CHECKLIST

When you have completed your study of this chapter,
you will be able to

1 Define and explain the relationships among capital, investment,
wealth, and saving.

2 Explain how investment and saving decisions are made and how these
decisions interact in financial markets to determine the real interest
rate and the amount of investment and saving.

3 Explain how government influences the real interest rate, investment,
and saving.

With a click of your mouse, you begin a download from your favorite music site. In the next few minutes, as files pour into your computer, you're using some of the most expensive equipment ever created. The satellite that is beaming in your data cost $500 million. And Intelsat, the firm that owns the satellite, has another 20 of them for which it paid almost $5 billion. How can a firm afford to spend such a huge amount?

The answer is by borrowing. But where do the funds that Intelsat borrows come from? The answer is the savings of millions of individuals all over the world.

In this chapter, you are going to learn about the choices that businesses and households make that determine the quantity of saving and investment in new capital. You're going to see how financial markets coordinate these choices to determine the quantity of capital and the real interest rate. You'll also learn how governments influence these markets.

24.1 CAPITAL, INVESTMENT, WEALTH, AND SAVING

Physical capital
The tools, instruments, machines, buildings, and other items that have been produced in the past and that are used to produce goods and services.

Financial capital
The funds that firms use to buy and operate physical capital.

Capital, or **physical capital**, is the tools, instruments, machines, buildings, and other items that have been produced in the past and that are used to produce goods and services. Inventories of raw materials, semifinished goods, and components are part of physical capital. When economists use the term *capital*, they mean physical capital. **Financial capital** is the funds that firms use to buy and operate physical capital.

Along the *production function* in Chapter 23, the quantity of capital is fixed. An increase in the quantity of capital increases production possibilities and shifts the production function upward. You're now going to see how spending, saving, borrowing, and lending decisions influence the quantity of capital. We begin by describing the links between capital and investment.

■ Investment and Capital

Gross investment
The total amount spent on new capital goods.

Net investment
The change in the quantity of capital—equals gross investment minus depreciation.

Investment and depreciation change the quantity of capital. *Investment* (Chapter 20, p. 499) increases the quantity of capital and *depreciation* (Chapter 20, p. 506) decreases it. The total amount spent on new capital goods is called **gross investment**. The change in the quantity of capital is called **net investment**. Net investment equals gross investment minus depreciation.

Figure 24.1 illustrates these concepts. On January 1, 2006, Tom's DVD Burning, Inc. had DVD-recording machines worth $30,000—Tom's initial capital. During 2006, the market value of Tom's machines fell by 67 percent—$20,000. After this depreciation, Tom's machines were valued at $10,000. During 2006, Tom spent $30,000 on new machines. This amount is Tom's gross investment. By December 31, 2006, Tom had capital valued at $40,000, so his capital had increased by $10,000. This amount is Tom's net investment. Tom's net investment equals his gross investment of $30,000 minus depreciation of $20,000.

▩ FIGURE 24.1
Capital and Investment

On January 1, 2006, Tom's DVD Burning, Inc. had DVD-recording machines valued at $30,000. During 2006, the value of Tom's machines fell by $20,000—depreciation—and he spent $30,000 on new machines—gross investment. Tom's net investment was $10,000, so at the end of 2006, Tom had capital valued at $40,000.

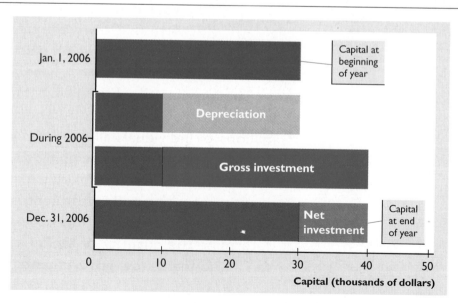

EYE ON THE U.S. ECONOMY

Investment and Capital, 1975–2005

Each nation's capital and investment work just like the example of Tom's DVD-recording shop on page 594. A nation's capital today equals its capital a year ago plus its net investment during the past year. And a nation's net investment during the past year equals its gross investment minus depreciation.

Here, we look at U.S. investment and capital growth from 1975 to 2005.

Gross investment, shown in part (a) of the figure, increases in most years and increased rapidly during the booming 1990s. But it decreases in recession years (highlighted in the figure).

Depreciation, also shown in part (a), increases in most years, but it fluctuates less than gross investment.

Gross investment minus depreciation is net investment. You can see net investment in part (a) as the gap between the two curves.

Part (b) of the figure provides a sharper view of net investment. You can see that it fluctuates a great deal and decreases sharply during a recession.

Like gross investment, net investment increased rapidly during the 1990s expansion.

Although net investment fluctuates, it rarely (and never during the 30 years shown here) becomes negative. Negative net investment would mean that the quantity of capital was shrinking. Because net investment is always positive, the quantity of capital, shown in part (c) of the figure, increases each year.

The quantity of capital grows steadily despite huge swings in net investment. The reason is that net investment is tiny in comparison to the quantity of capital.

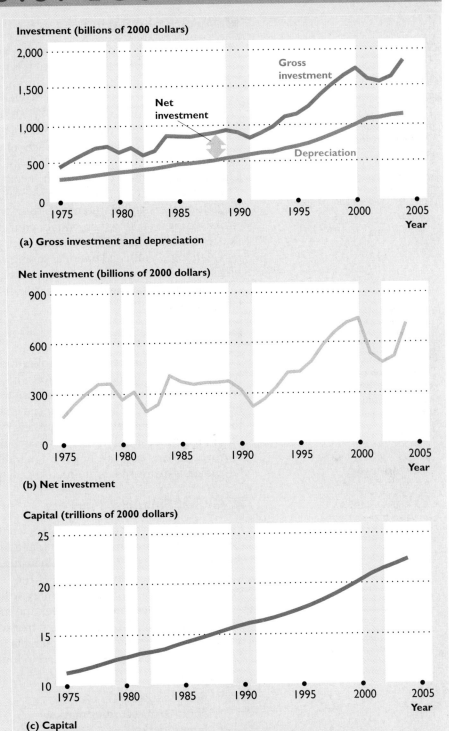

(a) Gross investment and depreciation

(b) Net investment

(c) Capital

SOURCE OF DATA: Bureau of Economic Analysis.

Between 1975 and 2005, net investment averaged less than 3 percent of the quantity of capital.

595

■ Wealth and Saving

Wealth
The value of all the things that a person owns.

A person's **wealth** is the value of all the things that the person owns. What people *own* is related to what they *earn*. But it is not the same thing. People *earn* an *income*, which is the amount they receive during a given time period from supplying the services of the resources they own. **Saving** is the amount of income that is not paid in taxes or spent on consumption goods and services, and saving adds to wealth. Wealth also increases when the value of assets rises—called *capital gains*.

Saving
The amount of income that is not paid in taxes or spent on consumption goods and services; saving adds to wealth.

Suppose that at the end of the school year, you have $250 in a savings account and some textbooks that are worth $300. That's all you own. Your wealth is $550. During the summer, you earn an income (after tax) of $5,000. You spend only $1,000 through the summer on consumption. At the end of the summer, you have $4,250 in your savings account. Your wealth is now $4,550. Your wealth has increased by $4,000, which equals your saving of $4,000. Your saving of $4,000 equals your income of $5,000 minus your consumption expenditure of $1,000.

National wealth and national saving work just like this personal example. The wealth of a nation at the start of a year equals its wealth at the start of the previous year plus its saving during the year. Its saving equals its income minus its consumption expenditure.

■ Financial Markets

Financial markets
The collection of households, firms, governments, banks, and other financial institutions that lend and borrow.

The **financial markets** are the collections of households, firms, governments, banks, and other financial institutions that lend and borrow. Financial markets are where firms get the funds that they use to buy capital. Firms are demanders and households are suppliers in financial markets. Governments are demanders if they have a budget deficit and suppliers if they have a budget surplus. Banks and other financial institutions help to match the lending plans of households and the borrowing plans of firms. Financial markets determine the price of financial capital, which is expressed as an interest rate (percent per year).

■ Global Financial Markets

Financial markets are global. Lenders want to earn the highest possible real interest rate. If, for equal risk, they can get a higher real interest rate in Japan than in the United States, they will move their funds to Japan. Borrowers want to pay the lowest possible real interest rate. If they can borrow at a lower interest rate in Europe than in the United States, they will borrow in Europe.

Because lenders are free to seek the highest possible real interest rate in any country and because borrowers are free to seek the lowest possible real interest rate in any country, the financial markets form a single global market.

Financial markets are organized in four groups:

- Stock markets
- Bond markets
- Short-term securities markets
- Loans markets

Stock Markets

Stock
A certificate of ownership and claim to the profits that a firm makes.

When Boeing wanted to raise funds to expand its airplane building business, it issued stock. A **stock** is a certificate of ownership and claim to the profits that a firm makes. Boeing has issued about 900 million shares of its stock. So if you owned 900 Boeing shares, you would own one millionth of Boeing and be entitled to receive one millionth of the company's profits.

A **stock market** is a financial market in which shares in companies' stocks are traded. An example of a stock market is the New York Stock Exchange. The London Stock Exchange (in England) and the Frankfurt Stock Exchange (in Germany) are the main stock markets in Europe. In Asia, the Tokyo and Hong Kong stock exchanges are the dominant ones. You can visit the Web sites of stock markets and see the prices and the quantities of shares that are being traded minute by minute throughout the business day.

If you buy some Boeing stock today, you pay the current owner of the stock, not Boeing. Boeing received the value of the stock when it first issued it.

Demand and supply in stock markets determine the prices of the individual stocks and the returns on them. The return on a stock is the dividend that the firm pays plus the change in the market value of the stock—the capital gain or loss.

Stock market
A financial market in which shares of companies' stocks are traded.

Bond Markets

When Wal-Mart Stores, Inc. planned to expand its business, instead of issuing stock it raised the funds it needed by selling bonds. A **bond** is a promise to pay specified sums of money on specified dates and is a debt for the issuer of the bond. For example, a Wal-Mart bond is a promise to pay $3.4375 every May and October until 2009 and then pay $100 in October 2009. Governments—federal, state, and municipal—also issue bonds. The buyer of a bond from Wal-Mart made a loan to the company and is entitled only to the payments promised by the bond. A bond-holder differs from a stockholder and is not a part owner of the firm. When a person buys a newly issued bond, he or she may hold the bond until the borrower repays the amount borrowed or sell it to someone else. The **bond market** is a financial market in which bonds issued by firms and governments are traded. Demand and supply in the bond market determine the prices of bonds and the interest rates on them.

Bond
A promise to pay specified sums of money on specified dates; it is a debt for the issuer.

Bond market
A financial market in which bonds issued by firms and governments are traded.

Short-Term Securities Markets

When General Motors sells $100 million of railway locomotives to Union Pacific, GM wants to be paid as soon as the items are shipped. But Union Pacific doesn't want to pay until the locomotives are operating and earning an income. In this situation, GM might issue a short-term security called a commercial bill. Each bill would be a promise by GM to pay $100 on a date three months in the future. A bank would be willing to buy these bills for an amount less than $100, and the difference between the price paid and $100 would be the interest on the bill. The U.S. Treasury also issues bills of this type, called Treasury bills.

Demand and supply in the short-term securities market determine the price and interest rate on commercial bills and Treasury bills.

Loans Markets

Many businesses finance their short-term capital, such as inventories, with a loan from a bank. Banks and other financial institutions lower the cost of financing firms' capital expenditures by accepting short-term deposits and making longer-term loans. They enable the small savings of millions of individuals to be pooled to finance investment. (You will study banks in some detail in Chapter 26.)

1 Define and explain the relationships among capital, investment, wealth, and saving.

Practice Problems 24.1

1. Michael is an Internet service provider. On December 31, 2004, he bought an existing business with servers and a building worth $400,000. During his first year of operation, his business grew and he bought new servers for $500,000. The market value of some of his older servers fell by $100,000. What was Michael's
   a. Gross investment during 2005?
   b. Depreciation during 2005?
   c. Net investment during 2005?
   d. Capital at the end of 2005?

2. Lori is a student who teaches golf on the weekend and in a year earns $20,000 in fees after paying her taxes. At the beginning of 2004, Lori owned $1,000 worth of books, CDs, and golf clubs and she had $5,000 in a savings account at the bank. During 2004, the interest on her savings account was $300 and she spent a total of $15,300 on consumption goods and services. There was no change in the market values of her books, CDs, and golf clubs.
   a. How much did Lori save in 2004?
   b. What was Lori's wealth at the end of 2004?

Exercises 24.1

1. Annie runs a fitness center. On December 31, 2004, she bought an existing business with exercise equipment and a building worth $300,000. During her first year of operation, business was poor. She sold some of her equipment to a competitor for $100,000. What was
   a. Annie's gross investment during 2005?
   b. Annie's depreciation during 2005?
   c. Annie's net investment during 2005?
   d. The value of Annie's capital at the end of 2005?

2. Karrie is a golf pro, and after she paid taxes, her income from golf and from stocks and bonds was $1,500,000 in 2005. At the beginning of 2005, she owned $900,000 worth of stocks and bonds. At the end of 2005, Karrie's stocks and bonds were worth $1,900,000. How much did Karrie save during 2005 and how much did she spend on consumption goods and services?

Solutions to Practice Problems 24.1

1a. Michael's gross investment during 2005 was $500,000.
1b. Michael's depreciation during 2005 was $100,000.
1c. Michael's net investment during 2005 was $400,000 ($500,000 − $100,000).
1d. At the end of 2005, Michael's capital was $800,000.

2a. Lori's saving equals her income (after tax) minus the amount she spent. That is, her saving equaled $20,300 minus $15,300, or $5,000.
2b. Lori's wealth at the end of 2004 was $11,000—the sum of her wealth at the start of 2004 ($6,000) plus her saving during 2004 ($5,000).

24.2 INVESTMENT, SAVING, AND INTEREST

Firms' investment decisions (investment demand) and households' consumption and saving decisions (saving supply) are coordinated in a global financial market to determine the quantity of capital and the real interest rate (financial market equilibrium). You learned how we define and measure the real interest rate in Chapter 22 (p. 562). We're now going to learn how the forces of demand and supply in the global financial market determine the real interest rate. We will study

- Investment demand
- Saving supply
- Financial market equilibrium

■ Investment Demand

How does Amazon.com decide whether to invest in a new warehouse? How does Chrysler decide whether to build a new car assembly plant? Many details influence business investment decisions such as these, but we can summarize them in two factors: the expected rate of profit and the real interest rate.

The real interest rate is the opportunity cost of the funds used to finance the purchase of capital, and firms compare the real interest rate with the rate of profit they expect to earn on their new capital. Firms invest only when they expect to earn a rate of profit that exceeds the real interest rate. Fewer projects are profitable at a high real interest rate than at a low real interest rate. So as the real interest rate rises, the amount of investment demanded decreases.

> **Other things remaining the same, the higher the real interest rate, the smaller is the quantity of investment demanded; and the lower the real interest rate, the greater is the quantity of investment demanded.**

Suppose that Amazon.com expects to earn $5 million (before paying its interest costs) if it builds a new $100 million warehouse. If the real interest rate is 4 percent a year, Amazon's interest bill for this warehouse is $4 million a year, so the investment earns $1 million a year. But if the real interest rate is 6 percent a year (other things remaining the same), Amazon's interest bill is $6 million a year, so the investment incurs a loss of $1 million a year. Amazon invests in the warehouse at a real interest rate of 4 percent a year but not at 6 percent a year.

To finance investment, a firm either borrows or uses its own funds (retained earnings). The opportunity cost of both sources of funds is the real interest rate because the firm *pays* this interest rate and *forgoes* this interest rate by buying new capital rather than by making a loan.

We summarize the influences on investment decisions in an investment demand curve.

Investment Demand Curve

The relationship between the quantity of investment demanded and the real interest rate, other things remaining the same, is called **investment demand**. If the real interest rate rises, other things remaining the same, the quantity of investment demanded decreases. The table in Figure 24.2 shows an example of this relationship.

Investment demand
The relationship between the quantity of investment demanded and the real interest rate, other things remaining the same.

■ FIGURE 24.2

Investment Demand

The table shows the quantity of investment demanded at five real interest rates. The graph shows the investment demand curve, *ID*. Points *A* through *E* correspond to the rows of the table.

At a real interest rate of 6 percent a year, the quantity of investment demanded is $10 trillion at point *C*.

❶ If the real interest rate rises to 8 percent a year, the quantity of investment demanded decreases to $9 trillion at point *B*.

❷ If the real interest rate falls to 4 percent a year, the quantity of investment demanded increases to $11 trillion at point *D*.

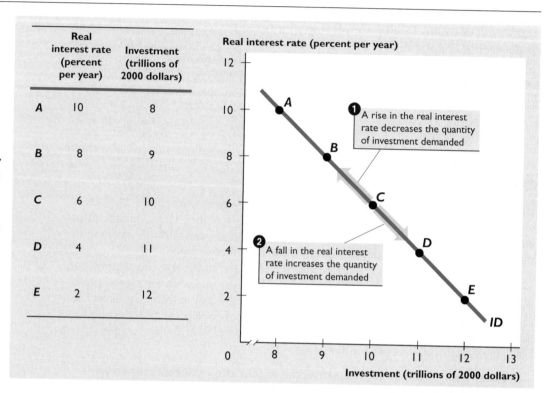

	Real interest rate (percent per year)	Investment (trillions of 2000 dollars)
A	10	8
B	8	9
C	6	10
D	4	11
E	2	12

❶ A rise in the real interest rate decreases the quantity of investment demanded

❷ A fall in the real interest rate increases the quantity of investment demanded

Figure 24.2 shows an investment demand curve. Each point (*A* through *E*) corresponds to a row in the table. If the real interest rate is 6 percent a year, the quantity of investment demanded is $10 trillion. A change in the real interest rate brings a movement along the investment demand curve. If the real interest rate rises to 8 percent a year, the quantity of investment demanded decreases to $9 trillion; there is a movement up the investment demand curve. If the real interest rate falls to 4 percent a year, the quantity of investment demanded increases to $11 trillion; there is a movement down the investment demand curve.

Changes in Investment Demand

When the expected rate of profit changes, investment demand changes. Other things remaining the same, the greater the expected rate of profit from new capital, the greater is the amount of investment. The many influences on expected profit can be placed in three groups:

- Objective influences such as the phase of the business cycle, technological change, and population growth
- Subjective influences summarized in the phrase "animal spirits"
- Contagion effects summarized in the phrase "irrational exuberance"

The expected rate of profit rises in an expansion and falls in a recession and so brings swings in investment demand over the business cycle. For example, investment soared during the information-based expansion of the late 1990s and sagged during the recession of the early 1990s.

Technological change lowers costs and creates new and profitable products. But to take advantage of new technologies, firms must invest in the equipment that employs them. For example, to produce a new generation of enormously profitable computer chips, Intel Corporation must invest several billion dollars in chip-making equipment that incorporates the latest technology.

Population growth brings a steady increase in the demand for all goods. Greater demand leads to greater profits. But to meet the increased demand and earn the profits available, firms must invest in additional capital.

Because investment decisions are forward looking, they are based on subjective feelings about the future. Keynes called these feelings "animal spirits." Sometimes people are optimistic and sometimes they are pessimistic, and swings of mood bring swings in investment demand.

Also, mood swings can be contagious. Federal Reserve chairman Alan Greenspan called the contagious optimism of the 1990s "irrational exuberance."

Shifts of the Investment Demand Curve

When investment demand changes, the investment demand curve shifts. Figure 24.3 shows how the investment demand curve depends on the expected rate of profit. When firms expect an average rate of profit, the investment demand curve is ID_0, which is the same investment demand curve as the one in Figure 24.2

When the expected rate of profit increases, investment demand increases and the investment demand curve shifts rightward to ID_1. When the expected rate of profit decreases, investment demand decreases and the investment demand curve shifts leftward to ID_2.

■ **FIGURE 24.3**

Changes in Investment Demand

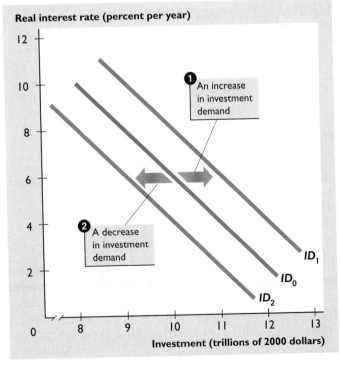

A change in profit expectations shifts the investment demand curve.

❶ An increase in the expected rate of profit increases investment demand and shifts the investment demand curve rightward to ID_1.

❷ A decrease in the expected rate of profit decreases investment demand and shifts the investment demand curve leftward to ID_2.

■ Saving Supply

You've graduated and landed a great job that pays you $50,000 a year. How do you decide how much of your income to spend on consumption goods and how much to save? Your decision would be influenced by many factors that we'll now review. But we'll begin by focusing on one of them: the real interest rate.

> **Other things remaining the same, the higher the real interest rate, the greater is the quantity of saving supplied; and the lower the real interest rate, the smaller is the quantity of saving supplied.**

The real interest rate is the *opportunity cost* of consumption expenditure. A dollar spent is a dollar not saved, so the interest that could have been earned on that saving is forgone. This opportunity cost arises regardless of whether a person is a lender or a borrower. For a lender, saving less this year means receiving less interest next year. For a borrower, saving less this year means paying less off a loan this year and paying more interest next year.

By thinking about student loans, you can see why the real interest rate influences saving. If the real interest rate on student loans jumped to 20 percent a year, graduates would save more (buying cheaper food and finding lower-rent accommodations) to pay off their loans as quickly as possible and avoid, as much as possible, paying the higher interest cost of their loan. If the real interest rate on student loans fell to 1 percent a year, graduates would save less and take longer to pay off their loans because the interest burden was easier to bear.

Saving Supply Curve

The relationship between the quantity of saving supplied and the real interest rate, other things remaining the same, is called **saving supply**.

Figure 24.4 illustrates saving supply. The points *A* through *E* on the saving supply curve correspond to the rows of the table. For example, point *C* shows that when the real interest rate is 6 percent a year, the quantity of saving supplied is $10 trillion. If the real interest rate rises from 6 percent a year to 8 percent a year, the quantity of saving supplied increases from $10 trillion to $11 trillion and there is a movement along the saving supply curve from *C* to *B*. If the real interest rate falls from 6 percent a year to 4 percent a year, the quantity of saving supplied decreases from $10 trillion to $9 trillion and there is a movement along the saving supply curve from *C* to *D*.

Changes in Saving Supply

When any influence on saving other than the real interest rate changes, saving supply changes. The three main factors that influence saving supply are

- Disposable income
- The buying power of net assets
- Expected future disposable income

Disposable Income   A household's **disposable income** is the income earned minus net taxes. The greater a household's disposable income, other things remaining the same, the greater is its saving. For example, a student works part time and earns a disposable income of $10,000. She spends the entire $10,000 on consumption and saves nothing. When she graduates as an economics major, her disposable income increases to $35,000 a year. She now saves $10,000 and spends

FIGURE 24.4

Saving Supply

Real interest rate (percent per year)	Saving (trillions of 2000 dollars)	
A	10	12
B	8	11
C	6	10
D	4	9
E	2	8

Real interest rate (percent per year)

① A rise in the real interest rate increases the quantiy of saving supplied

② A fall in the real interest rate decreases the quantity of saving supplied

Saving (trillions of 2000 dollars)

The table shows the quantity of saving supplied at five real interest rates. The graph shows the saving supply curve, SS. Points A through E correspond to the rows of the table.

At a real interest rate of 6 percent a year, the quantity of saving supplied is $10 trillion at point C.

① If the real interest rate rises to 8 percent a year, the quantity of saving supplied increases to $11 trillion at point B.

② If the real interest rate falls to 4 percent a year, the quantity of saving supplied decreases to $9 trillion at point D.

$25,000 on consumption. The increase in disposable income of $25,000 has increased saving by $10,000.

Buying Power of Net Assets   A household's net assets are what it owns minus the debts that it owes. The buying power of a household's net assets is the quantity of goods and services that its net assets can buy. The greater the buying power of the net assets a household has accumulated, other things remaining the same, the less it will save.

Patty is a department store executive who earns $50,000 a year. She has been saving $5,000 a year and now has $15,000 in the bank and no debts. With $15,000 in the bank, Patty decides to spend $5,000 on a vacation and save nothing this year. Tony is another department store executive who earns $50,000. He has saved nothing and has an outstanding balance of $10,000 on his credit card. With nothing in the bank and a big debt, Tony feels financially insecure, so he decides to cut his consumption and start saving.

Expected Future Disposable Income   The higher a household's expected future disposable income, other things remaining the same, the smaller is its saving today. That is, if two households have the same disposable income in the current year, the household with the larger expected future disposable income will spend a larger portion of current disposable income on consumption goods and services and so save less today.

Look at Patty and Tony again. Patty has just been promoted and will receive a $10,000 pay raise next year. Tony has just been told that he will be fired at the end of the year. On receiving this news, Patty buys a new car—increases her consumption expenditure and cuts her saving—and Tony sells his car and takes the bus—decreases his consumption expenditure and increases his saving.

Most young households expect to have a higher future income for some years and then to have a lower income during retirement. Because of this pattern of income over the life cycle, young people save a small amount, middle-aged people save a lot, and retired people gradually spend their accumulated savings.

Shifts of the Saving Supply Curve

Along the saving supply curve, all the influences on saving other than the real interest rate remain the same. A change in any of these influences on saving changes saving supply and shifts the saving supply curve. An increase in disposable income, a decrease in the buying power of net assets, or a decrease in expected future disposable income increases saving supply. Figure 24.5 shows the effect of this change on the saving supply curve.

Initially, the saving supply curve is SS_0. Then disposable income increases, the buying power of net assets decreases, or expected future disposable income decreases. Saving supply increases, and the saving supply curve shifts rightward from SS_0 to SS_1. Changes in these factors in the opposite direction decrease saving supply and shift the saving supply curve leftward from SS_0 to SS_2.

■ FIGURE 24.5

Changes in Saving Supply

❶ An increase in disposable income, a decrease in the buying power of net assets, or a decrease in expected future disposable income increases saving and shifts the saving supply curve rightward from SS_0 to SS_1.

❷ A decrease in disposable income, an increase in the buying power of net assets, or an increase in expected future disposable income decreases saving and shifts the saving supply curve leftward from SS_0 to SS_2.

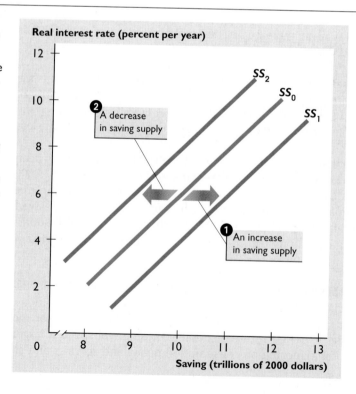

Saving (trillions of 2000 dollars)

■ Financial Market Equilibrium

Earlier in this chapter, we described the four groups of financial markets: stock, bond, short-term securities, and loans. Each of those market types determines a large number of interest rates. But interest rates in one financial market quickly spill over to another, so all the interest rates move up and down together. We will imagine that just one big financial market embraces the entire economy. The *interest rate* is an average of all the interest rates in the different types of financial markets.

Figure 24.6 shows how this average real interest rate is determined. The *ID* curve is the investment demand curve, the *SS* curve is the saving supply curve, and the equilibrium real interest rate is 6 percent a year. When the real interest rate exceeds 6 percent a year, the quantity of saving supplied exceeds the quantity of investment demanded. There is a surplus of funds. Borrowers have an easy time finding the loans they want, but lenders are unable to lend all the funds they have available. The real interest rate falls, and as it does so, the quantity of investment demanded increases and the quantity of saving supplied decreases.

Alternatively, when the interest rate is less than 6 percent a year, the quantity of saving supplied is less than the quantity of investment demanded. There is a shortage of funds. Borrowers can't find the loans they want, but lenders are able to lend all the funds they have available. So the real interest rate rises, and as it does so, the quantity of investment demanded decreases and the quantity of saving supplied increases.

■ FIGURE 24.6

Financial Market Equilibrium

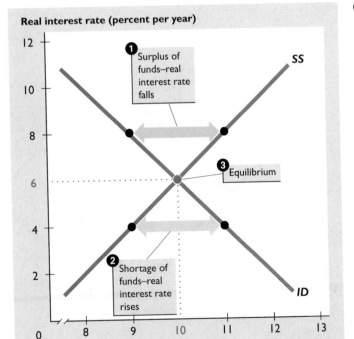

❶ If the real interest rate is 8 percent a year, the quantity of investment demanded is less than the quantity of saving supplied. There is a surplus of funds, and the real interest rate falls.

❷ If the real interest rate is 4 percent a year, the quantity of investment demanded exceeds the quantity of saving supplied. There is a shortage of funds, and the real interest rate rises.

❸ When the real interest rate is 6 percent a year, the quantity of investment demanded equals the quantity of saving supplied. There is neither a shortage nor a surplus of funds, and the real interest rate is at its equilibrium level.

Regardless of whether there is a surplus or a shortage of funds, the real inter-est rate changes and is pulled toward an equilibrium level. In Figure 24.6, this equilibrium is 6 percent a year. At this real interest rate, there is neither a surplus nor a shortage of funds. Investors can get the funds they demand, and savers can lend all the funds they have available. The plans of savers and investors are con-sistent with each other.

■ Changes in Investment and Saving

Fluctuations in either investment demand or saving supply bring fluctuations in the real interest rate and in the amount of saving and investment. Here we'll illus-trate the effects of an increase in each.

If the inducement to invest increases, the investment demand curve shifts rightward. In Figure 24.7(a), the *ID* curve shifts from ID_0 to ID_1. With no change in saving supply, there is a shortage of funds at a real interest rate of 6 percent a year. So the real interest rate rises. At a rate of 8 percent a year, equilibrium is restored. Investment and saving increase.

If the inducement to save increases, the saving supply curve shifts rightward. In Figure 24.7(b), the *SS* curve shifts from SS_0 to SS_1. With no change in invest-ment, there is a surplus of funds at a real interest rate of 6 percent a year. So the real interest rate falls. At a rate of 4 percent a year, equilibrium is restored. Investment and saving increase.

Over time, both investment demand and saving supply fluctuate and the real interest rate rises and falls. Both saving supply and investment demand tend to increase over time, and on the average, they increase at a similar pace. So although saving and investment trend upward, the real interest rate has no trend. It fluctu-ates around a constant average level.

■ **FIGURE 24.7**

Changes in Investment and Saving

❶ If investment demand increases and saving supply remains the same, the real interest rate rises and invest-ment and saving increase.

❷ If saving supply increases and investment demand remains the same, the real interest rate falls and invest-ment and saving increase.

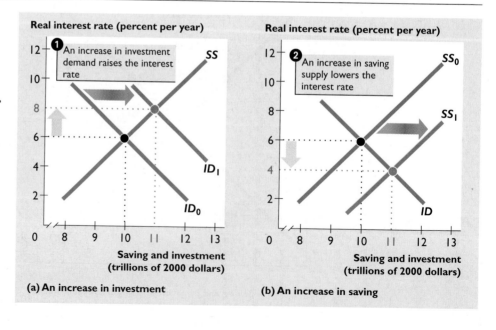

(a) An increase in investment

(b) An increase in saving

CHECKPOINT 24.2

2 Explain how investment and saving decisions are made and how these decisions interact in financial markets to determine the real interest rate and the amount of investment and saving.

Practice Problems 24.2

1. First Call, Inc. is a cellular phone company. It plans to build an assembly plant that costs $10 million if the real interest rate is 6 percent a year. If the real interest rate is 5 percent a year, First Call will build a larger plant that costs $12 million. And if the real interest rate is 7 percent a year, First Call will build a smaller plant that costs $8 million.
   a. Draw a graph of First Call's investment demand curve.
   b. First Call expects its profit from the sale of cellular phones to double next year. If everything else remains the same, explain how this increase in expected profit influences First Call's investment demand.

2. Draw graphs that illustrate how an increase in saving supply and a decrease in investment demand can lower the real interest rate and leave the equilibrium quantity of saving and investment unchanged.

Exercises 24.2

1. In 2004, the Lee family had a disposable income of $80,000, assets of $140,000, and an expected future disposable income of $80,000 a year. At a real interest rate of 4 percent a year, the Lee family saves $15,000 a year; at a real interest rate of 6 percent a year, they save $20,000 a year; and at a real interest rate of 8 percent, they save $25,000 a year.
   a. Draw a graph of the Lee family's saving supply curve.
   b. In 2005, the stock market crashes and the Lee family's assets decrease by 50 percent. Explain how this decrease in assets influences the Lee family's saving supply curve.

2. Draw graphs that illustrate the effect of an increase in investment demand and an even larger increase in saving supply on the real interest rate and the equilibrium quantity of saving and investment.

Solutions to Practice Problems 24.2

1a. The investment demand curve is the downward-sloping curve ID_0 and passes through the points highlighted in Figure 1.

1b. An increase in the expected profit increases the amount of investment at each real interest rate. First Call's investment demand increases, and the investment demand curve shifts rightward to ID_1 (Figure 1).

2. The increase in saving supply shifts the saving supply curve rightward. The decrease in investment demand shifts the investment demand curve leftward. The real interest rate falls. If the shifts are of the same magnitude, the equilibrium quantity of saving and investment remains unchanged (Figure 2). If the shift of the saving supply curve is greater (less) than that of the investment demand curve, then saving and investment increase (decrease).

FIGURE 1

FIGURE 2

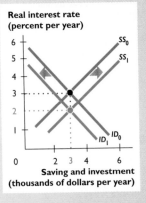

24.3 GOVERNMENT IN THE FINANCIAL MARKET

Part of each nation's saving is government saving, and part of global saving is saving by governments around the world. So government actions that change the saving supply influence the real interest rate which changes the quantity of investment. To complete our study of the forces that determine the quantity of capital and the real interest rate, we investigate the role played by government saving.

■ Government Budget and Government Saving

You learned in Chapter 20 (pp. 500–501) that GDP, Y, equals the sum of consumption expenditure, C; investment, I; government expenditure, G; and net exports, NX. Table 24.1 shows data on these variables for 2005. Because we are studying the global financial market, we focus on the global economy, in which net exports are zero. So for the world as a whole,

$$Y = C + I + G.$$

GDP equals total income, which is the sum of consumption expenditure; saving, S; and net taxes, NT. That is,

$$Y = C + S + NT.$$

By combining these two ways of looking at GDP, you can see that

$$C + I + G = C + S + NT.$$

Because consumption expenditure, C, is on both sides of this equation, we can subtract C and simplify the equation to

$$I + G = S + NT.$$

Now subtract government expenditure, G, from both sides of this equation to obtain

$$I = S + (NT - G).$$

This equation tells us that investment, I, is financed by private saving, S, and government saving, $NT - G$. Government saving, $NT - G$, is also the government budget surplus. Table 24.2 shows that data for the global economy in 2005.

Total saving equals private saving plus government saving. So when the government has a budget surplus, it contributes toward financing investment. But when the government has a budget deficit, it competes with businesses for private saving and decreases the funds available for investment. Let's study the effects of government saving.

■ Effect of Government Saving

A government budget surplus increases total saving supply. To find total saving supply, we must add the government budget surplus to the private saving supply. An increase in total saving supply brings a lower interest rate, which decreases the quantity of private saving supplied and increases the quantity of investment.

Figure 24.8 shows these effects of government saving. The private saving supply curve, PS, shows the relationship between private saving and the real interest rate. The saving supply curve, SS, shows the sum of private saving and government saving. Here, government saving is a constant $2 trillion at each real interest rate, so the saving supply curve lies $2 trillion to the right of the private saving

TABLE 24.1 INCOME AND EXPENDITURE IN THE GLOBAL ECONOMY

	Y	$=$ C	$+$ I	$+$ G	$+$ NX
		(trillions of dollars)			
United States	12.2	8.5	2.1	2.3	−0.7
Rest of world	47.4	27.3	11.0	8.4	0.7
Global economy	59.6	35.8	13.1	10.7	0

SOURCES OF DATA: Bureau of Economic Analysis, International Monetary Fund, and authors' assumptions and calculations.

TABLE 24.2 INVESTMENT AND SAVING IN THE GLOBAL ECONOMY

	I	$=$ S	$+(NT - G)$	$-$ NX
		(trillions of dollars)		
United States	2.1	1.8	−0.4	−0.7
Rest of world	11.0	11.9	−0.2	0.7
Global economy	13.1	13.7	−0.6	0

SOURCES OF DATA: Bureau of Economic Analysis, International Monetary Fund, and authors' assumptions and calculations.

supply curve. That is, the horizontal distance between the private saving curve and the saving supply curve is government saving.

With no government saving, the real interest rate would be 6 percent a year and saving and investment would be $10 trillion a year. But with the government saving $2 trillion a year, the equilibrium real interest rate falls to 4 percent a year. Investment increases to $11 trillion. Private saving decreases to $9 trillion. Private saving plus government saving equals investment.

So government saving—a government budget surplus—lowers the real interest rate and increases investment.

■ Government Deficit and Crowding Out

A government budget deficit works in the opposite way to the surplus that we've just examined. A government budget deficit decreases total saving—total saving equals private saving minus the government budget deficit. But a decrease in saving raises the real interest rate, which increases the quantity of private saving supplied. So to work out the effects of government saving, we need to find its effects on the real interest rate.

Figure 24.9 illustrates. The private saving supply curve is *PS*, and the investment demand curve is *ID*. The horizontal distance between the private saving curve and the saving supply curve *SS* is the government budget deficit. In this example, government saving is a negative $2 trillion—a budget deficit of $2 trillion. The effect of government negative saving (also called *dissaving*) is to decrease total saving supply and increase the real interest rate. Investment decreases.

■ **FIGURE 24.8**
Government Saving

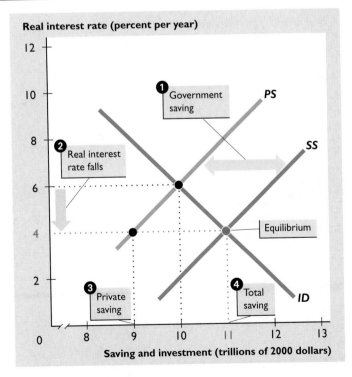

The investment demand curve is *ID*, and the private saving supply curve is *PS*. With a balanced government budget, the real interest rate is 6 percent a year and investment equals saving at $10 trillion a year.

❶ A government budget surplus of $2 trillion is added to private saving to determine the saving supply curve *SS*.

❷ The real interest rate falls to 4 percent a year, ❸ private saving decreases to $9 trillion, and ❹ total saving and investment increase to $11 trillion.

In Figure 24.9, with a government budget deficit of $2 trillion, the saving supply curve lies $2 trillion to the left of the private saving curve. The real interest rate rises from 6 percent a year to 8 percent a year. Total saving and investment decrease from $10 trillion to $9 trillion. By raising the real interest rate, the government budget deficit crowds out investment. The tendency for a government budget deficit to decrease investment is called the **crowding-out effect**.

Crowding-out effect
The tendency for a government budget deficit to decrease investment.

Investment does not decrease by the full amount of the government budget deficit because the higher real interest rate induces an increase in private saving. In this example, private saving increases by $1 trillion to $11 trillion.

The Ricardo-Barro Effect

First suggested by the English economist David Ricardo in the eighteenth century and refined by Robert J. Barro of Harvard University during the 1980s, the Ricardo-Barro effect holds that the effects we've just shown are wrong and that the government budget deficit has no effect on the real interest rate or investment. Barro says that rational taxpayers can see that a deficit today means that future taxes will be higher and future disposable incomes will be smaller. With smaller expected future disposable incomes, saving increases. Private saving supply increases to offset the government dissaving, so the total saving supply remains at *PS*.

Most economists regard this view as extreme. But there is probably some partial change in private saving supply that goes in the direction suggested by the Ricardo-Barro effect that lessens the influence of the government budget on the real interest rate and investment.

■ FIGURE 24.9
A Crowding-Out Effect

The investment demand curve is *ID*, and the private saving supply curve is *PS*. With a balanced government budget, the real interest rate is 6 percent a year and investment equals saving at $10 trillion a year.

❶ A government budget deficit of $2 trillion is subtracted from private saving to determine the saving supply curve *SS*.

❷ The real interest rate rises to 8 percent a year, ❸ private saving increases to $11 trillion, and ❹ total saving and investment decrease to $9 trillion. Investment is crowded out.

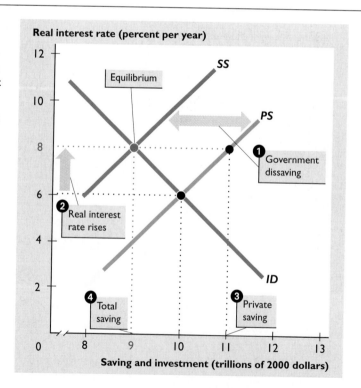

Interest Rate Puzzle

The real interest rate paid by big corporations fell from 5.5 percent in 2001 to 2.5 percent in 2005. Alan Greenspan said he was puzzled that the real interest rate was falling at a time when the U.S. government budget deficit was increasing.

Why did the real interest rate fall? The answer lies in the global capital market. Global saving supply increased. The figure illustrates. Saving supply increased from SS_{01} in 2001 to SS_{05} in 2005. (Investment demand might have increased, but here we assume that it didn't.)

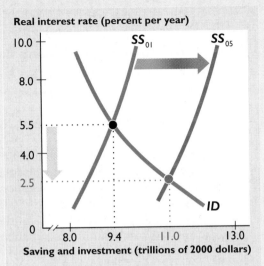

Real interest rate (percent per year)

Saving and investment (trillions of 2000 dollars)

SOURCES OF DATA: Federal Reserve, Bureau of Labor Statistics, International Monetary Fund World Economic Outlook database, Penn World Tables.

U.S. saving decreased and U.S. borrowing from the rest of the world increased during these years.

Alan Greenspan

Saving supply increased because Asian and European saving increased strongly. The Chinese, Japanese, and Germans all have much higher saving rates than Americans do.

The interest rate puzzle illustrates the important fact that the capital market is a global market, not a national market.

REALITY CHECK

Saving and Investment in YOUR Life

Think about the amount of saving that you do. How much of your disposable income do you save? What do you do with your savings? Do you put them in a bank, in the stock market, in bonds, or under your mattress at home?

How do you think your saving will change when you graduate and get a better-paying job?

Also think about the amount of investment you do. You are investing in your human capital by being in school. How are you financing this investment? What is it costing you?

You might decide to invest in an apartment or a house rather than paying rent. How would you make such a decision? Would it be smart to borrow $200,000 to finance the purchase of a home? How would the interest rate influence that decision?

3 Explain how government influences the real interest rate, investment, and saving.

Practice Problem 24.3

TABLE I

Real interest rate (percent per year)	Investment	Private saving
	(trillions of 2000 dollars per year)	
4	8.5	5.5
5	8.0	6.0
6	7.5	6.5
7	7.0	7.0
8	6.5	7.5
9	6.0	8.0
10	5.5	8.5

1. Table 1 shows the investment demand schedule and the supply schedule of private saving.
   a. If the government budget surplus is $1 trillion, what are the real interest rate, the quantity of investment, and the quantity of private saving? Is there any crowding out in this situation?
   b. If the government budget deficit is $1 trillion, what are the real interest rate, the quantity of investment, and the quantity of private saving? Is there any crowding out in this situation?
   c. If the Ricardo-Barro effect occurs, how do your answers to part **b** change?

Exercise 24.3

1. Starting from the situation in Table 1, investment demand increases by $1 trillion at each real interest rate and the supply of private saving increases by $2 trillion at each interest rate.
   a. If the government budget has neither a surplus nor a deficit, what are the real interest rate, the quantity of investment, and the quantity of private saving? Is there any crowding out in this situation?
   b. If the government budget deficit is $1 trillion, what are the real interest rate, the quantity of investment, and the quantity of private saving? Is there any crowding out in this situation?
   c. If governments want to stimulate the quantity of investment and increase it to $9 trillion, what must they do?

Solution to Practice Problem 24.3

FIGURE I

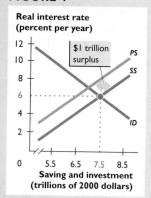

Real interest rate (percent per year)

$1 trillion surplus

PS
SS
ID

Saving and investment (trillions of 2000 dollars)

FIGURE 2

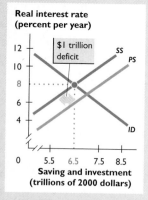

Real interest rate (percent per year)

$1 trillion deficit

SS
PS
ID

Saving and investment (trillions of 2000 dollars)

1a. If the government budget surplus is $1 trillion, the equilibrium real interest rate is 6 percent a year, the quantity of investment is $7.5 trillion, and the quantity of private saving is $6.5 trillion. There is no crowding out in this situation (Figure 1).

1b. If the government budget deficit is $1 trillion, the equilibrium real interest rate is 8 percent a year, the quantity of investment is $6.5 trillion, and the quantity of private saving is $7.5 trillion. There is crowding out in this situation because the deficit increases the real interest rate, which decreases the quantity of investment demanded (Figure 2).

1c. If the Ricardo-Barro effect occurs, private saving changes to offset the budget deficit, the equilibrium real interest rate remains at 7 percent a year, and the equilibrium quantity of investment is $7 trillion. There is no crowding out because the government dissaving has no effect on the real interest rate and the quantity of investment.

CHAPTER CHECKPOINT

Key Points

1 **Define and explain the relationships among capital, investment, wealth, and saving.**

- Firms use financial capital to buy and operate physical capital.
- Gross investment is the total amount spent on physical capital in a given period. Net investment equals gross investment minus depreciation.
- Wealth is the value of what people own; saving is the amount of income that is not spent, and it adds to wealth.
- A financial market is the collection of households, firms, government, banks, and other financial institutions that lend and borrow to finance the purchase of physical capital.

2 **Explain how investment and saving decisions are made and how these decisions interact in financial markets to determine the real interest rate and the amount of investment and saving.**

- Other things remaining the same, the lower the real interest rate or the higher the expected profit rate, the greater is the amount of investment.
- Investment demand changes when the expected profit rate changes.
- Other things remaining the same, the higher the real interest rate, the greater is saving.
- Saving supply changes when disposable income, the buying power of net assets, or expected future disposable income changes.
- Because capital is free to move internationally to seek the highest possible real rate of return, the real interest rate is determined in a global market.
- The equilibrium real interest rate makes global saving equal to global investment.

3 **Explain how government influences the real interest rate, investment, and saving.**

- Total saving equals private saving plus government saving.
- Government saving equals net taxes minus government purchases.
- A government budget deficit might increase the real interest rate and crowd out private investment.
- A government budget deficit might also increase private saving supply because it decreases expected future disposable income.

Key Terms

Bond, 597	Financial markets, 596	Saving, 596
Bond market, 597	Gross investment, 594	Saving supply, 602
Crowding-out effect, 610	Investment demand, 599	Stock, 596
Disposable income, 602	Net investment, 594	Stock market, 597
Financial capital, 594	Physical capital, 594	Wealth, 596

Exercises

1. On January 1, 2006 Terry's Towing Service owned 4 tow trucks valued at $300,000. During 2006, Terry's bought 2 new trucks that cost a total of $180,000, and at the end of the year, the market value of all the firm's trucks was $400,000.
   a. What was Terry's gross investment during 2006?
   b. What was its depreciation?
   c. What was its net investment?

2. The Bureau of Economic Analysis reported that the U.S. capital stock (in 1996 dollars) was $23,087 billion at the end of 1999, $23,801 billion at the end of 2000, and $24,390 billion at the end of 2001. Depreciation in 2000 was $1,049 billion, and gross investment during 2001 was $1,575 billion (all in 1996 dollars).
   a. What was U.S. net investment during 2000 and 2001?
   b. What was the amount of gross investment during 2000?
   c. What was the amount of depreciation during 2001?
   d. Compare the net investment, gross investment, depreciation, and capital in 2000 and 2001. What do you think these numbers tell us was happening in the U.S. economy during 2001?

3. Mike takes a summer job washing cars. During the summer, he earns an after-tax income of $3,000 and he spends $1,000 on goods and services.
   a. What was Mike's saving during the summer?
   b. What was the change, if any, to Mike's wealth?

TABLE 1 HOUSEHOLDS AND NONPROFIT ORGANIZATIONS

Year	Net worth (billions of 1996 dollars)	Saving (billions of 1996 dollars)
1991	24,342	415
1992	24,695	450
1993	25,340	373
1994	25,487	329
1995	27,700	308
1996	29,713	272
1997	32,854	248
1998	35,681	292
1999	39,810	154
2000	38,353	63
2001	36,450	108

4. The numbers in the second column of Table 1 are the Federal Reserve's estimates of the net worth of households and nonprofit organizations at the end of each year. The numbers in the third column are the Bureau of Economic Analysis's estimates of personal saving—disposable income minus consumption expenditure—each year.
   a. In which years did the change in wealth exceed saving?
   b. In which years did saving exceed the change in wealth?
   c. Given the definitions of saving and wealth, how can the change in wealth differ from saving?
   d. What would you estimate was the total value of capital gains during 1997?
   e. What would you estimate was the total value of capital gains during 2001?

5. What is a financial market? What gets traded in a financial market? What is the price that a financial market determines?

6. Explain why when the real interest rate rises, investment demand does not change but the quantity of investment demanded decreases.

7. A new technology is developed that increases firms' expected profits and creates an increase in investment demand.
   a. Draw a graph to show the effect of this development on the investment demand curve.

   b. Show on a graph the effect of this development on the equilibrium real interest rate.

   c. Show on a graph the effect of this development on the amount of saving and investment.

8. Explain why each of the following items changes the private saving supply:

   a. An increase in the buying power of assets.

   b. An increase in expected future disposable income.

   c. A cut in current income taxes.

9. Consider the effects of two developments that occurred during the 1990s:

   i. The invention and use of fiber-optic technologies that required billions of dollars to be spent laying new cables under the oceans and launching communications satellites.

   ii. A stock market boom that increased the buying power of net assets by trillions of dollars.

   a. Draw a graph to illustrate investment demand, saving supply, and equilibrium in the global capital market before the two developments occurred.

   b. Show, on your graph, the effects of event **i.**

   c. Show, on your graph, the effects of event **ii.**

   d. Show, on your graph, the combined effects of the two events.

10. During the 1980s and most of the 1990s, governments around the world had large budget deficits. Around 2000, government budget deficits began to turn into surpluses.

   a. Draw a graph to illustrate the global capital market that distinguishes among private saving, government saving, and total saving.

   b. Show, on your graph, the effects of a switch from a government budget deficit to a government budget surplus if there is no Ricardo-Barro effect.

   c. Show, on your graph, the effects of a switch from a government budget deficit to a government budget surplus if there is a complete Ricardo-Barro effect.

   d. Show, on your graph, the effects of a switch from a government budget deficit to a government budget surplus if there is a partial Ricardo-Barro effect.

11. As global tension increased during 2001 and 2002, the defense budgets of the U.S. government and many other governments around the world brought an increase in overall government spending and a decrease in government budget surpluses.

   a. Draw a graph to illustrate the global capital market that distinguishes among private saving, government saving, and total saving.

   b. Show, on your graph, the effects of a decrease in government budget surpluses if there is no Ricardo-Barro effect.

   c. Show, on your graph, the effects of a decrease in government budget surpluses if there is a complete Ricardo-Barro effect.

   d. Show, on your graph, the effects of a decrease in government budget surpluses if there is a partial Ricardo-Barro effect.

Critical Thinking

12. Look at the data provided in *Eye on the U.S. Economy* on page 595.
    a. What fluctuates most and why: net investment, gross investment, depreciation, or capital?
    b. Why do you think net investment surged upward so strongly during the 1990s?
    c. How might you set about determining whether the swings in net investment were changes in investment demand or changes in the quantity of investment?
    d. Can you think of ways in which the fluctuations in investment might be smoothed?
    e. Do you think it would it be a good idea or a bad idea to smooth the fluctuations? Why?

13. China, India, and Indonesia account for about half the world's population and are expanding at a rapid rate. Do these countries lend to or borrow from the United States? As these countries become wealthier and more similar to the United States, how do you think they will affect the global capital market? Would you expect the real interest rate to rise, fall, or remain close to its current level? Why?

14. During 2001, the Commerce Department reported that the U.S. saving rate was negative. How can the saving rate be negative? Why might a negative saving rate be something to worry about? How do you think saving could be stimulated?

Web Exercises

Use the links on MyEconLab to work the following exercises.

15. Visit the Web sites of the New York Stock Exchange, the London Stock Exchange, and PACIFIC.
    a. Find a stock that trades on both exchanges and obtain its current price in New York and London.
    b. Find today's exchange rate between the U.S. dollar and the U.K. pound.
    c. Use today's exchange rate to convert the London price to U.S. dollars.
    d. What is the difference in the two prices? Could you earn a profit by buying in one market and selling in the other?
    e. Why do you think the prices are so similar in the two stock markets?

16. Open the file that provides data on saving rates in the United States and the new industrial economies of East Asia.
    a. Which of the countries has the highest saving rate and which has the lowest?
    b. Of the factors that influence saving, do you think the differences across these economies represent differences in the supply of saving or differences in the quantity of saving supplied? Explain your answer.
    c. Of the influences on the supply of saving, which do you think might account for the differences in saving rates that you've found?

APPENDIX: PRESENT VALUE

When you have completed your study of this appendix, you will be able to

1 Define present value, discounting, and compounding.

2 Calculate and interpret a present value.

When a firm decides whether to invest in some new capital, it must compare the present cost of the capital with the future revenue that the capital will generate. Similarly, when you make a saving decision, you must compare the present cost of less consumption with the future benefit you will enjoy when you spend your saving and the interest that it has earned.

To make these comparisons, we must convert future revenue or benefit to a present value. The **present value** of a future sum of money is the amount that will earn enough interest to grow to that future sum. We calculate a present value by using a process called *discounting*. The easiest way to understand discounting is to begin with its opposite, *compounding*, which is converting a present sum of money to a future sum by earning interest on both the present sum and the interest that it earns.

Present value
The present value of a future sum of money is the amount that will earn enough interest to grow to that future sum.

■ Compounding and Future Value

A future sum of money is equal to the present sum (present value) plus the interest it will accumulate in the future. Suppose that you put $100 in a savings account that earns an interest rate of 10 percent a year. How much will you have in your savings account after one year? How much will you have after two years? How much will you have after any given number of years?

You can see right away that your $100 accumulates to $110 after one year: the original $100 plus $10 interest. So after one year, you have $110 in the bank. You now start earning interest on $110: the original $100 plus $10 interest earned in the first year. So you earn $11 interest in the second year: $10 interest on the original $100 plus $1 interest on the $10 interest earned in the first year. So at the end of the second year, you have $121: the original $100 plus $10 interest earned in the first year plus $11 interest earned in the second year.

You now have $121 in your savings account, so you will receive $12.10 interest in the third year.

You can see that your interest earnings are growing: $10, $11, and $12.10 in the first three years. If you leave your $100 plus the interest that it earns in your savings account for ten years, you will have $259.37 at the end of the tenth year and you'll earn $25.94 interest in the eleventh year!

Future Value Formula

It is useful to describe the calculations that we've just done using equations. To do so, we need to express the interest rate as a decimal rather than as a percentage. So instead of saying that the interest rate is 10 percent a year, we say that it is one tenth or 0.1 per year. Let's call the interest rate expressed in this way r with $r = 0.1$ in our example. We can now describe how your $100 accumulates as follows:

After 1 year: $\$100 \times (1 + r) = \$100 \times 1.1 = \$110$.
After 2 years: $\$100 \times (1 + r) \times (1 + r) = \$100 \times (1 + r)^2 = \$100 \times 1.21 = \$121$.
After N years: $\$100 \times (1 + r)^N$

■ Discounting and Present Value

Now think about this question: If the interest rate is 10 percent a year ($r = 0.1$) and you can have either $110 one year from now or a different amount today, what is the amount that you'd accept today?

The answer is that you'd accept the present value of $110. The present value of a future sum of money is the sum that, if invested today, will grow to be as large as that future sum when the interest it will earn is taken into account.

You can see that the present value of $110 one year from now is $100. That is, $100 is the present sum that, if invested at an interest rate of 10 percent a year, will grow to $110 after one year.

Similarly, the present value of $121 two years from now is $100. That is, $100 is the present sum that, if invested at an interest rate of 10 percent a year, will grow to $121 after two years.

And the present value of $259.37 ten years from now is $100. That is, $100 is the present sum that, if invested at an interest rate of 10 percent a year, will grow to $259.37 after ten years.

Present Value Formula

The equations that we have just used to calculate future sums can be used to calculate the present value.

Present value = Sum 1 year later ÷ $(1 + r)$ = $110 ÷ 1.1 = $100.
Present value = Sum 2 years later ÷ $(1 + r)^2$ = $121 ÷ 1.21 = $100.
Present value = Sum N years later ÷ $(1 + r)^N$.

The Crucial Role of Time and the Interest Rate

The present value of a future sum depends on two things: how far in the future the money is received or paid and the interest rate. Both factors have a powerful effect that increases exponentially: Shifting the time farther into the future lowers the present value, and raising the interest rate lowers the present value.

So other things remaining the same, the farther in the future that an investment starts to generate revenue, the less attractive is that investment. When Boeing plans to introduce a new airplane, it makes a multibillion dollar investment but doesn't start to receive revenue from the sale of the new airplane for several years. The longer it takes Boeing to develop a new plane, the larger is the number of planes that it must sell to make the investment worthwhile.

Also, other things remaining the same, the higher the interest rate, the less attractive is an investment. If the interest rate becomes high enough, the present value might become so small that an investment is just not worth making. It is for this reason that the investment demand curve sloped downward. Fewer investment projects are profitable at a higher interest rate than at a lower interest rate.

Present Values in Your Decisions

You make many decisions, some small and some large, that turn on a present value calculation: how much of your credit card balance to pay off; how big a student loan to take out and when to begin the repayments; whether to rent or buy an apartment; whether to lease or buy a car.

Try to get into the habit of thinking in terms of present values when you make these decisions!

Economic Growth

CHAPTER CHECKLIST

When you have completed your study of this chapter,
you will be able to

1 Define and calculate the economic growth rate, and explain the
implications of sustained growth.

2 Identify the main sources of economic growth.

3 Review the theories of economic growth that explain why growth
rates vary over time and across countries.

4 Describe policies that might speed economic growth.

Bob Geldof has done a lot to bring African
poverty to the top of the political agenda with
his Live 8 concerts. Geldof understands that to
rid Africa of extreme poverty, the standard of
living of its people must rise.

Why is real GDP per person in most of
Africa so low and what must be done to raise
the standard of living of Africans?

A continent away, in India and China, people are on the
move. The standard of living in these countries is rising
rapidly and lifting millions from poverty every year.

Why are some Asian economies expanding rapidly while
many African economies are stagnating?

These questions are hard ones to answer. But this chapter
lays the foundation for the answers. It combines the lessons
of the two preceding chapters and explains how capital accumulation and technological change bring sustained growth in
real GDP and the standard of living.

25.1 THE BASICS OF ECONOMIC GROWTH

Economic growth is a sustained expansion of production possibilities measured as the increase in real GDP over a given period. Rapid economic growth maintained over a number of years can transform a poor nation into a rich one. Such has been the experience of Hong Kong, South Korea, Taiwan, and some other Asian economies. Slow economic growth or the absence of growth can condemn a nation to devastating poverty. Such has been the fate of Sierra Leone, Somalia, Zambia, and much of the rest of Africa.

The main goal of this chapter is to help you to understand why some economies expand rapidly and others stagnate. We'll begin by learning how to calculate the economic growth rate and by discovering the magic of sustained growth.

■ Calculating Growth Rates

Economic growth rate
The annual percentage change of real GDP.

We express the **economic growth rate** as the annual percentage change of real GDP. To calculate this growth rate, we use the formula:

$$\text{Growth rate of real GDP} = \frac{\begin{array}{c}\text{Real GDP} \\ \text{in current year}\end{array} - \begin{array}{c}\text{Real GDP} \\ \text{in previous year}\end{array}}{\text{Real GDP in previous year}} \times 100.$$

For example, if real GDP in the current year is $8.4 trillion and if real GDP in the previous year was $8.0 trillion, then

$$\text{Growth rate of real GDP} = \frac{\$8.4 \text{ trillion} - \$8.0 \text{ trillion}}{\$8.0 \text{ trillion}} \times 100 = 5 \text{ percent.}$$

The growth rate of real GDP tells us how rapidly the total economy is expanding. This measure is useful for telling us about potential changes in the balance of economic power among nations. But it does not tell us about changes in the standard of living.

Real GDP per person
Real GDP divided by the population.

The standard of living depends on **real GDP per person** (also called *per capita real GDP*), which is real GDP divided by the population. So the contribution of real GDP growth to the change in the *standard of living* depends on the growth rate of real GDP per person. We use the above formula to calculate this growth rate, replacing real GDP with real GDP per person.

Suppose, for example, that in the current year, when real GDP is $8.4 trillion, the population is 202 million. Then real GDP per person is $8.4 trillion divided by 202 million, which equals $41,584. And suppose that in the previous year, when real GDP was $8.0 trillion, the population was 200 million. Then real GDP per person in that year was $8.0 trillion divided by 200 million, which equals $40,000.

Use these two real GDP per person values with the growth formula to calculate the growth rate of real GDP per person. That is,

$$\text{Growth rate of real GDP per person} = \frac{\$41,584 - \$40,000}{\$40,000} \times 100 = 4 \text{ percent.}$$

The growth rate of real GDP per person can also be calculated by using the formula:

$$\text{Growth rate of real GDP per person} = \text{Growth rate of real GDP} - \text{Growth rate of population.}$$

In the example you've just worked through, the growth rate of real GDP is 5 percent. The population changes from 200 million to 202 million, so

$$\text{Growth rate of population} = \frac{202 \text{ million} - 200 \text{ million}}{200 \text{ million}} \times 100 = 1 \text{ percent}$$

and

$$\text{Growth rate of real GDP per person} = 5 \text{ percent} - 1 \text{ percent} = 4 \text{ percent.}$$

This formula makes it clear that real GDP per person grows only if real GDP grows faster than the population grows. If the growth rate of the population exceeds the growth of real GDP, real GDP per person falls.

■ The Magic of Sustained Growth

Sustained growth of real GDP per person can transform a poor society into a wealthy one. The reason is that economic growth is like compound interest (see pp. 619–620). Suppose that you put $100 in the bank and earn 5 percent a year interest on it. After one year, you have $105. If you leave that money in the bank for another year, you earn 5 percent interest on the original $100 and on the $5 interest that you earned last year. You are now earning interest on interest! The next year, things get even better. Then you earn 5 percent on the original $100 and on the interest earned in the first year and the second year. Your money in the bank is *growing* at a rate of 5 percent a year. Before too many years have passed, you'll have $200 in the bank. But after *how many* years?

The answer is provided by a powerful and general formula known as the **Rule of 70,** which states that the number of years it takes for the level of any variable to double is approximately 70 divided by the annual percentage growth rate of the variable. Using the Rule of 70, you can now calculate how many years it takes your $100 to become $200. It is 70 divided by 5, which is 14 years.

The Rule of 70 applies to any variable, so it applies to real GDP per person. Table 25.1 shows the doubling time for a selection of other growth rates. You can see that real GDP per person doubles in 70 years (70 divided by 1)—an average human life span—if the growth rate is 1 percent a year. It doubles in 35 years if the growth rate is 2 percent a year and in just 10 years if the growth rate is 7 percent a year.

We can use the Rule of 70 to answer other questions about economic growth. For example, in 2000, U.S. real GDP per person was approximately 8 times that of China. China's recent growth rate of real GDP per person was 7 percent a year. If this growth rate were maintained, how long would it take China's real GDP per person to reach that of the United States in 2000? The answer, provided by the Rule of 70, is 30 years. China's real GDP per person doubles in 10 (70 divided by 7) years. It doubles again to 4 times its current level in another 10 years. And it doubles yet again to 8 times its current level in another 10 years. So after 30 years of growth at 7 percent a year, China's real GDP per person is 8 times its current level and equals that of the United States in 2000.

Rule of 70
The number of years it takes for the level of any variable to double is approximately 70 divided by the annual percentage growth rate of the variable.

TABLE 25.1 GROWTH RATES

Growth rate (percent per year)	Years for level to double
1	70
2	35
3	23
4	18
5	14
6	12
7	10
8	9
9	8
10	7

How Fast Has Real GDP per Person Grown?

Professor Michael Kremer of Harvard University and Professor J. Bradford DeLong of the University of California, Berkeley, have constructed an extraordinary picture of real GDP in the global economy going back one million years. According to their numbers, human societies lived for a million years with no economic growth.

The top figure shows the numbers using the value of the dollar in 2000 as the measuring rod. Real GDP per person hovered around $100 per year from 1,000,000 BC until 1350! There were some wiggles and wobbles along the way. When Aristotle and Plato were teaching in Athens, around 500 BC, real GDP per person climbed to $175. But it slipped back over the next thousand years, and as the Roman Empire collapsed around 400 AD, it was $120. Even when the Pilgrim Fathers began to arrive in America in the 1620s, real GDP per person was similar to that of Ancient Greece!

Then, beginning around 1750, first in England and then in Europe and the United States, an astonishing change known as the Industrial Revolution occurred. Real GDP per person began to increase, apparently without limit. By 1850, real GDP per person was twice its 1650 level. By 1950, it was more than five times its 1850 level, and by 2000, it was four times its 1950 level.

The bottom figure gives you a close-up view of U.S. real GDP per person over the past 100 years. In 2005, real GDP per person was almost eight times its level in 1905. It has grown by 2 percent a year. But the growth rate

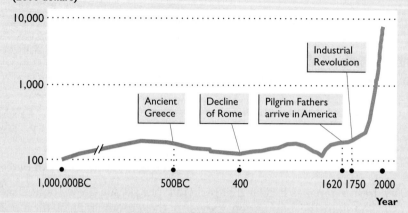

Real GDP per person (2000 dollars)

SOURCE OF DATA: J. Bradford DeLong, *"Estimating World GDP, One Million B.C.—Present."*

has been uneven. The 1930s saw almost no growth, and the 1940s saw the fastest growth. Measured decade by decade, growth has been slowing since the 1960s.

But if we divide the 1990s into two periods, before and after the Internet

(1994), we see a speedup in the growth rate after 1994. Some people think that in the current information age, we are at the beginning of a new increase in economic growth similar to that of the Industrial Revolution. No one knows yet whether this view is correct.

(a) Real GDP per person

(b) Growth rate of real GDP per person

SOURCES OF DATA: Bureau of Economic Analysis and Bureau of Labor Statistics.

CHECKPOINT 25.1

1 Define and calculate the economic growth rate, and explain the implications of sustained growth.

Practice Problem 25.1

1. Mexico's real GDP was 1,448 billion pesos in 1998 and 1,501 billion pesos in 1999. Mexico's population growth rate in 1999 was 1.8 percent. Calculate
   a. Mexico's economic growth rate in 1999.
   b. The growth rate of real GDP per person in Mexico in 1999.
   c. The approximate number of years it takes for real GDP per person in Mexico to double if the 1999 economic growth rate and population growth rate are maintained.
   d. The approximate number of years it takes for real GDP per person in Mexico to double if the 1999 economic growth rate is maintained but the population growth rate slows to 1 percent a year.

Exercise 25.1

1. In Canada, real GDP was $1,012 billion in 2000 and $1,028 billion in 2001. The population was 30.8 million in 2000 and 31.1 million in 2001. Calculate
   a. Canada's economic growth rate in 2001.
   b. The growth rate of real GDP per person in Canada in 2001.
   c. The approximate number of years it takes for real GDP per person in Canada to double if the 2001 economic growth rate and population growth rate are maintained.
   d. The approximate number of years it takes for real GDP per person in Canada to double if the economic growth rate rises to 6 percent a year but the population growth rate remains the same as it was in 2001.

Solution to Practice Problem 25.1

1a. Mexico's economic growth rate in 1999 was 3.7 percent. The economic growth rate equals the percentage change in real GDP:
[(Real GDP in 1999 − Real GDP in 1998) ÷ Real GDP in 1998] × 100. When we substitute the numbers, Mexico's economic growth rate equals [(1,501 billion − 1,448 billion) ÷ 1,448 billion] × 100, which is 3.7 percent.

1b. The growth rate of real GDP per person in Mexico in 1999 was 1.9 percent. Growth rate of real GDP per person equals the growth rate of real GDP minus the population growth rate. When we substitute the numbers, Growth rate of real GDP per person = 3.7 percent − 1.8 percent, which is 1.9 percent.

1c. It will take approximately 37 years for real GDP per person to double. The Rule of 70 tells us that the level of a variable that grows at 1.9 percent a year will double in 70 ÷ 1.9 years, which is approximately 37 years.

1d. If Mexico's population growth rate falls to 1.0 percent a year, real GDP per person in Mexico will increase to 2.7 percent a year. The Rule of 70 tells us that real GDP in Mexico will double in 70 ÷ 2.7 years, which is approximately 26 years.

25.2 THE SOURCES OF ECONOMIC GROWTH

Real GDP grows when the quantities of the factors of production grow or when persistent advances in technology make them increasingly productive. To understand what determines the growth rate of real GDP, we must understand what determines the growth rates of the factors of production and rate of increase in their productivity. We've already seen that saving and investment determine the growth rate of physical capital. We're now going to see how the growth of physical capital and human capital and advances in technology interact to determine the economic growth rate.

We are interested in real GDP growth because it contributes to improvements in our standard of living. But our standard of living improves only if we produce more goods and services with each hour of labor. So our main concern is to understand the forces that make our labor more productive. For this reason, we begin by dividing all the influences on real GDP growth into those that increase

- Aggregate hours
- Labor productivity

■ Aggregate Hours

Over time, aggregate hours increase. This growth in aggregate hours comes from growth in the labor force rather than from growth in average hours per worker. As you saw in Chapter 21 (pp. 532–533), average hours per worker have *decreased* over the past decades. This decrease—and an associated *increase* in average leisure hours—is one of the benefits of economic growth.

The labor force depends on the population and the *labor force participation rate* (see Chapter 21, p. 526). While the participation rate has increased over the past few decades, it has an upper limit, and most of the growth of aggregate hours comes from population growth. So population growth is the only source of growth in aggregate labor hours that can be sustained over long periods.

Population growth brings economic growth, but it does not bring growth in real GDP per person unless labor becomes more productive.

■ Labor Productivity

Labor productivity
The quantity of real GDP produced by one hour of labor.

The quantity of real GDP produced by one hour of labor is called **labor productivity.** It is calculated by using the formula:

$$\text{Labor productivity} = \frac{\text{Real GDP}}{\text{Aggregate hours}}$$

For example, if real GDP is $8,000 billion and if aggregate hours are 200 billion, then we can calculate labor productivity as

$$\text{Labor productivity} = \frac{\$8,000 \text{ billion}}{200 \text{ billion hours}} = \$40 \text{ per hour.}$$

You can turn this formula around and see that

$$\text{Real GDP} = \text{Aggregate hours} \times \text{Labor productivity.}$$

When labor productivity grows, real GDP per person grows. So the growth in labor productivity is the basis of rising living standards. The growth of labor productivity depends on three things:

- Saving and investment in physical capital
- Expansion of human capital
- Discovery of new technologies

These three sources of growth in labor productivity interact and are the primary sources of the extraordinary growth in productivity during the past 200 years. Let's look at each in turn.

Saving and Investment in Physical Capital

Saving and investment in physical capital increase the amount of capital per worker and increase labor productivity. Labor productivity took a dramatic upturn when the amount of capital per worker increased during the Industrial Revolution. Production processes that use hand tools can create beautiful objects, but production methods that use large amounts of capital per worker, such as auto plant assembly lines, enable workers to be much more productive. The accumulation of capital on farms, in textile factories, in iron foundries and steel mills, in coal mines, on building sites, in chemical plants, in auto plants, in banks, and in insurance companies has added incredibly to the productivity of our labor.

A strong and experienced farm worker of 1830, using a scythe, could harvest 3 acres of wheat in a day. A farm worker of 1831, using a mechanical reaper, could harvest 15 acres in a day. And a farm worker of today, using a combine harvester, can harvest and thresh 100 acres a day.

The next time you see a movie set in the old West, look carefully at the small amount of capital around. Try to imagine how productive you would be in such circumstances compared with your productivity today.

Expansion of Human Capital

Human capital—the accumulated skill and knowledge of people—comes from two sources:

- Education and training
- Job experience

A hundred years ago, most people attended school for around eight years. A hundred years before that, most people had no formal education at all. Today, 90 percent of Americans complete high school and more than 60 percent go to college or university. Our ability to read, write, and communicate effectively contributes enormously to our productivity.

While formal education is productive, school is not the only place where people acquire human capital. We also learn from on-the-job experience—from *learning by doing*. One carefully studied example illustrates the importance of learning by doing. Between 1941 and 1944 (during World War II), U.S. shipyards produced 2,500 Liberty Ships—cargo ships built to a standardized design. In 1941, it took 1.2 million person-hours to build a ship. By 1942, it took 600,000, and by 1943, it took only 500,000. Not much change occurred in the physical capital employed during these years. But an enormous amount of human capital was accumulated. Thousands of workers and managers learned from experience and more than doubled their productivity in two years.

Production using 1950s technology.

Production using 2000s technology.

The expansion of human capital is the most fundamental source of economic growth because it directly increases labor productivity and is the source of the discovery of new technologies.

Discovery of New Technologies

The growth of physical capital and human capital has made a large contribution to economic growth. But the discovery and application of new technologies have made an even greater contribution.

The development of writing, one of the most basic human skills, was the source of some of the earliest productivity gains. The ability to keep written records made it possible to reap ever-larger gains from specialization and trade. Imagine how hard it would be to do any kind of business if all the accounts, invoices, and agreements existed only in people's memories.

Later, the development of mathematics laid the foundation for the eventual extension of knowledge in physics, chemistry, and biology. This base of scientific knowledge was the foundation for the technological advances of the Industrial Revolution 200 years ago and of today's Information Revolution.

Since the Industrial Revolution, technological change has become a part of everyday life. Firms routinely conduct research to develop technologies that are more productive, and partnerships between business and the universities are commonplace in fields such as biotechnology and electronics.

To reap the benefits of technological change, capital must increase. Some of the most powerful and far-reaching technologies are embodied in human capital—for example, language, writing, and mathematics. But most technologies are embodied in physical capital. For example, to reap the benefits of the internal combustion engine, millions of horse-drawn carriages had to be replaced by automobiles and trucks; more recently, to reap the benefits of computerized word processing, millions of typewriters had to be replaced by PCs and printers.

◼ Sources of Growth: A Summary

Figure 25.1 summarizes the sources of economic growth. Your next task is to learn how these sources combine and how we identify the separate contributions of capital growth and the other influences on labor productivity.

◼ FIGURE 25.1

The Sources of Economic Growth

Real GDP depends on aggregate labor hours and labor productivity. Labor productivity depends on the amount of physical capital and human capital and the state of technology. Growth in aggregate hours and growth in labor productivity bring real GDP growth.

U.S. Labor Productivity Growth since 1960

The top figure shows labor productivity growth (red line) and its changing trends (black line). Rapid growth during the 1960s was followed by slower growth after 1969 and even slower growth after 1974. It is this productivity slowdown that brought the enormous $96 trillion Lucas wedge that we described in Chapter 23; see p. 572.

Why does labor productivity growth fluctuate? The bottom figure provides a summary of the answer. Using a method developed by MIT economist Robert Solow, we've separated the contribution of capital accumulation from those of human capital growth and technological change.

You can see that the 1960s were years of rapid human capital growth and technological change. Spillover effects from World War II, plastics, and the transistor were some of the key sources of this rapid growth.

The contribution of human capital growth and technological change slowed during the 1970s for several reasons.

First, oil price hikes in 1973–1974 and 1979–1980 diverted technological change toward saving energy rather than increasing labor productivity. (For example, airplanes became more fuel efficient, but they didn't operate with smaller crews.)

Second, taxes and government regulation increased during the late 1960s and 1970s, so incentives were weakened and labor productivity growth slowed.

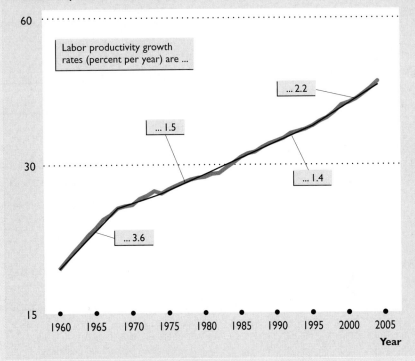

Real GDP per hour of labor (2000 dollars, ratio scale)

SOURCES OF DATA: Bureau of Economic Analysis and Bureau of Labor Statistics.

Third, rapid inflation distorted saving and investment decisions and shortened the horizon over which firms made their borrowing and lending plans.

The contribution of human capital growth and technological change remained low until the new economy era of the 1990s, when computer and information technology kicked in to bring faster labor productivity growth again.

SOURCES OF DATA: Bureau of Economic Analysis and Bureau of Labor Statistics.

627

2 Identify the main sources of economic growth.

Practice Problem 25.2

1. The table provides some data on the Canadian economy in 2001 and 2002.

Item	2001	2002
Aggregate hours (billions)	27.0	27.3
Real GDP (billions of 1997 dollars)	1,028	1,074
Capital per hour of labor (1997 dollars)	96.21	97.40

a. Calculate the growth rate of real GDP in 2002.
b. Calculate labor productivity in 2001 and 2002.
c. Calculate the growth rate of labor productivity in 2002.

Exercise 25.2

1. The table provides some data on the U.S. economy in 2002 and 2003.

Item	2002	2003
Aggregate hours (billions)	240.7	242.3
Real GDP (billions of 2000 dollars)	9,440	9,629
Capital per hour of labor (2000 dollars)	104.85	106.23

a. Calculate the growth rate of real GDP in 2003
b. Calculate labor productivity in 2002 and 2003.
c. Calculate the growth rate of labor productivity in 2003.

Solution to Practice Problem 25.2

1a. The growth rate of real GDP in 2002 was
[($1,074 billion − $1,028 billion) ÷ $1,028 billion] × 100, which equals 4.51 percent.
1b. Labor productivity equals real GDP per hour of labor. In 2001, labor productivity was $1,028 billion ÷ 27.0 billion, which equals $38.12 per hour of labor. In 2002, labor productivity was $1,074 billion ÷ 27.3 billion hours, which equals $39.31 per hour of labor.
1c. The growth rate of labor productivity in 2002 was
[($39.31 − $38.12) ÷ $38.12] × 100, which equals 3.14 percent.

25.3 THEORIES OF ECONOMIC GROWTH

You've seen that real GDP grows when the quantity of labor—aggregate hours—grows and when labor productivity grows. And you've seen that labor productivity grows when saving and investment increase physical capital, education and on-the-job training expand human capital, and research leads to the discovery of new technologies.

But what is cause and what is effect? Do all of the sources of economic growth—aggregate hours growth, saving and investment, the expansion of human capital, and the discovery of new technologies—*cause* economic growth? They might. But there are other possibilities. One of these factors might be the cause of real GDP growth, and the others might be the effects.

Governments want to be able to influence the pace at which the standard of living advances, so they want to influence the growth rate of real GDP per person and achieve faster sustained growth. But to do so, economists must develop policies based on an understanding of how the influences on economic growth interact with each other. What makes some economies grow quickly and others grow slowly? Why do growth rates sometimes speed up and sometimes slow down?

We're now going to study the interactions among the sources of economic growth by reviewing the theories of growth.

Economists have been trying to understand why and how poor countries become rich and rich countries become richer since the time of Adam Smith in the eighteenth century. Three main theories have been proposed. They are

- Classical growth theory
- Neoclassical growth theory
- New growth theory

■ Classical Growth Theory

Classical growth theory predicts that the clash between an exploding population and limited resources will eventually bring economic growth to an end. According to classical growth theory, labor productivity growth is temporary. When labor productivity rises and lifts real GDP per person above the subsistence level, which is the minimum real income needed to maintain life, a population explosion occurs. Eventually, the population grows so large that labor productivity falls and returns real GDP per person back to the subsistence level.

Adam Smith, Thomas Robert Malthus, and David Ricardo, the leading economists of the late eighteenth and early nineteenth centuries, proposed this theory, but the view is most closely associated with Malthus and is sometimes called the **Malthusian theory.** It is also sometimes called the Doomsday theory.

Many people today are Malthusians. They say that if today's global population of 6.3 billion explodes to 11 billion by 2200, we will run out of resources and return to a primitive standard of living. We must act, say the Malthusians, to contain the population growth.

The Basic Idea

To understand the basic idea of classical growth theory, let's transport ourselves back to the world of 1776. Adam Smith's *Wealth of Nations* has just been published, the Industrial Revolution is under way in England, and the United States of

Classical growth theory
The theory that the clash between an exploding population and limited resources will eventually bring economic growth to an end.

Malthusian theory
Another name for classical growth theory—named for Thomas Robert Malthus.

America has not yet been born. Most of the 2.5 million people who live in the not yet independent United States of America work on farms or on their own land and perform their tasks using simple tools and animal power. They earn an average of 2 shillings (a bit less than 12 dollars in today's money) for working a ten-hour day.

Then advances in farming technology bring new types of plows and seeds that increase farm productivity. As farm productivity increases, farm production increases and some farm workers move from the land to the cities, where they get work producing and selling the expanding range of farm equipment. Real GDP per person rises, and people are prospering. But will the prosperity last? Classical growth theory says that it will not. The prosperity will induce a population explosion. And the population explosion will decrease real GDP per person.

Classical Theory of Population Growth

When the classical economists were developing their ideas about population growth, an unprecedented population explosion was under way. In England and other Western European countries, improvements in diet and hygiene had lowered the death rate while the birth rate remained unchanged. For several decades, population growth was extremely rapid.

For example, after being relatively stable for several centuries, the population of England increased by 40 percent between 1750 and 1800 and by another 50 percent between 1800 and 1830. At the same time, an estimated 1 million people (about 20 percent of the 1750 population) left England for America and Australia before 1800, and outward migration continued on a similar scale through the nineteenth century. This historical population explosion was the basis for the classical theory of population growth.

To explain the high rate of population growth, the classical economists used the idea of a subsistence real income. If the actual real income is less than the subsistence real income, some people cannot survive and the population decreases. In classical theory, when real income exceeds the subsistence real income, the population grows. But the increasing population decreases the amount of capital per hour of labor. So labor productivity and real GDP per person eventually decrease. And no matter how much technological change occurs, real GDP per person is always pushed back toward the subsistence level. This dismal implication led to economics being called the dismal science.

Illustrating the Classical Growth Theory

Figure 25.2 illustrates the classical growth theory using the model of the full-employment economy that you met in Chapter 23. Part (a) shows the labor market, and part (b) shows the production function.

The subsistence real wage rate is $25 an hour but the current wage exceeds the subsistence wage and is $35 an hour, where the demand for labor, LD, equals the supply of labor, LS_0 in part (a). In part (b), the production function, PF, shows that with 200 billion hours of labor employed, real GDP is $10 trillion.

Because the real wage rate exceeds the subsistence wage rate, the population increases. And the increase in population increases the supply of labor and shifts the labor supply curve rightward. The population and labor supply keep increasing as long as the real wage rate exceeds the subsistence level. So the labor supply curve keeps shifting rightward until it reaches LS_1. At this labor supply, the real wage rate has fallen to the subsistence level of $25 an hour.

In the new equilibrium, the quantity of labor employed is 300 billion hours a year and real GDP is $12 trillion.

■ FIGURE 25.2

The Effects of an Increase in Population

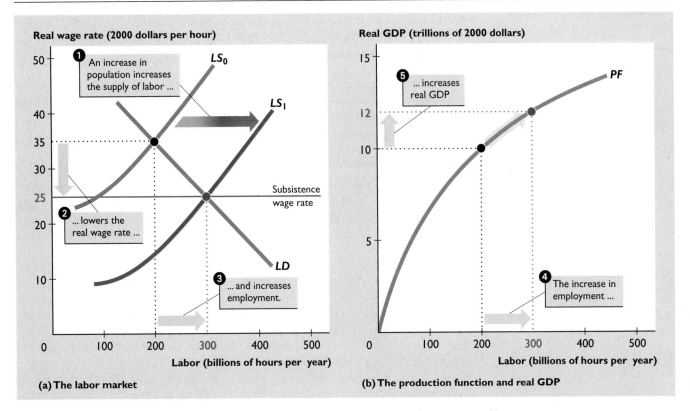

(a) The labor market

(b) The production function and real GDP

The subsistence real wage rate is $25 an hour. Initially, with demand for labor *LD* and supply of labor, LS_0, the equilibrium wage rate is $35 an hour and is above the subsistence wage rate.

1 Because the wage rate is above its subsistence level, the population increases and the labor supply curve shifts rightward. The population and the labor supply keep increasing until the wage rate has fallen to the subsistence wage rate.

2 When the supply of labor has increased to LS_1, the real wage rate has fallen to the subsistence level. **3** Labor hours have increased and **4** the increased labor hours bring **5** an increase in real GDP.

You can see that the increase in population increases employment and real GDP and lowers the real wage rate. The increase in population also decreases real GDP per hour of work.

You can calculate real GDP per hour of work by dividing real GDP by total labor hours. Initially, with real GDP at $10 trillion and labor hours at 200 billion, real GDP per hour of work was $50. With the increase in population, real GDP is $12 trillion and labor hours are 300 billion, so real GDP per hour of work is $40.

Diminishing returns—the tendency for each additional hour of labor employed to produce a successively smaller additional amount of output—is the source of the decrease in real GDP per hour of work (see Chapter 23, p. 574).

So if for some reason the real wage rate exceeds the subsistence real wage rate, according to the classical theory, population growth brings a fall in the real wage rate and a fall in real GDP per hour of work (and per person).

■ Neoclassical Growth Theory

Neoclassical growth theory (developed by Robert Solow of MIT during the 1960s) predicts that real GDP per person will increase as long as technology keeps advancing. Real GDP will grow at a rate equal to the population growth rate plus the labor productivity growth rate induced by technological change and the expansion of human capital. So according to the neoclassical theory, growth will persist.

Neoclassical growth theory asserts that population growth and the pace of technological change determine, but are not themselves influenced by, the growth rate of real GDP. Let's examine the neoclassical view of population growth and technological change.

Population Growth

The population explosion of eighteenth century Europe that created the classical theory eventually ended. The birth rate fell, and the population growth rate slowed. This slowdown in population growth seemed to make the classical theory increasingly less relevant. And the slowdown in population growth eventually led to the development of a new economic theory of population growth.

Economists began to realize that although the population growth rate is influenced by economic factors, that influence is not the one identified by the classical economists. Key among the economic influences on population growth is the opportunity cost of a woman's time. As women's wage rates rise and their job opportunities expand, the opportunity cost of having children increases. Faced with a higher opportunity cost, families choose to have fewer children and the birth rate falls.

A second economic influence lowers the death rate. The technological advances that increase labor productivity also bring advances in health care that extend lives.

So two opposing economic forces influence population growth. As incomes increase, the birth rate decreases and the death rate decreases. It turns out that these opposing forces are offsetting, so the rate of population growth is independent of the economic growth rate.

The historical population trends contradict the views of the classical economists and call into question the contemporary Doomsday conclusion that one day we will be swamped with too many people for the planet to feed.

Technological Change

In the neoclassical theory, the pace of technological change influences the economic growth rate, but the economic growth does not influence the pace of technological change. Technological change results from chance. When we get lucky, we have rapid technological change; and when bad luck strikes, the pace of technological advance slows.

The Basic Idea

To understand the basic idea of neoclassical growth theory, imagine the world of the mid-1950s. Americans are enjoying post–World War II prosperity. Real GDP per person is around $12,000 a year in today's money. The population is growing at about 1 percent a year, and people are saving and investing enough to make capital grow at a similar rate. So real GDP per person is not growing much.

Then technology advances at a more rapid pace across a range of activities. The transistor revolutionizes an emerging electronics industry. New plastics revolutionize the manufacture of household appliances. Jet airliners start to replace piston engine airplanes and speed transportation. And Elvis and the Beatles change the face of popular music!

These technological advances bring new profit opportunities. Businesses expand, and new businesses are created to exploit the new technologies. Investment and saving increase, so capital per hour of labor increases. The economy enjoys increased prosperity and economic growth. But will the prosperity last? And will the growth last? Neoclassical growth theory says that the prosperity will last but the growth will not unless technology keeps advancing.

The prosperity persists because no population explosion occurs to lower real GDP per person. But economic growth stops if technology stops advancing because capital accumulation brings diminishing returns, which slows the growth rate of real GDP and reduces saving and investment. Eventually, the growth rate of capital slows to that of the population, and real GDP per person stops growing.

A Problem with Neoclassical Growth Theory

Neoclassical growth theory predicts that real GDP per person will grow at a rate that is determined by the pace of technological change. But the theory does not explain what determines technological change. In the neoclassical theory, technological change is like the weather—it rains down on us at a pace that we must simply accept. In reality, the pace of technological change results from choices. The new growth theory, which we'll now study, emphasizes the role of these choices.

■ New Growth Theory

New growth theory predicts that our unlimited wants will lead us to ever greater productivity and perpetual economic growth. According to new growth theory, real GDP per person grows because of the choices people make in the pursuit of profit. Paul Romer of Stanford University developed this theory during the 1980s, but the new growth theory builds on ideas developed by Joseph Schumpeter during the 1930s and 1940s.

New growth theory
The theory that our unlimited wants will lead us to ever greater productivity and perpetual economic growth.

Choices and Innovation

The new growth theory emphasizes three facts about market economies:

- Human capital expands because of choices.
- Discoveries result from choices.
- Discoveries bring profit, and competition destroys profit.

Human Capital Expansion and Choices People decide how long to remain in school, what to study, and how hard to study. And when they graduate from school, people make more choices about job training and on-the-job learning. All these choices govern the speed at which human capital expands.

Discoveries and Choices When people discover a new product or technique, they consider themselves lucky. They are right. But the pace at which new discoveries are made—and at which technology advances—is not determined by chance. It depends on how many people are looking for a new technology and how intensively they are looking.

Discoveries and Profits   Profit is the spur to technological change. The forces of competition squeeze profits, so to increase profit, people constantly seek either lower-cost methods of production or new and better products for which people are willing to pay a higher price. Inventors can maintain a profit for several years by taking out a patent or copyright. But eventually, a new discovery is copied, and profits disappear.

Two other facts play a key role in the new growth theory:

- Many people can use discoveries at the same time.
- Physical activities can be replicated.

Discoveries Used by All   Once a profitable new discovery has been made, everyone can use it. For example, when Marc Andreeson created Mosaic, the Web browser that led to the creation of Netscape Navigator and Microsoft's Internet Explorer, everyone who was interested in navigating the Internet had access to a new and more efficient tool. One person's use of a Web browser does not prevent others from using it. This fact means that as the benefits of a new discovery spread, socially free resources become available. These resources are free because nothing is given up when an additional person uses them. They have a zero opportunity cost.

Replicating Activities   Production activities can be replicated. For example, there might be 2, 3, or 53 identical firms making fiber-optic cable by using an identical assembly line and production technique. If one firm increases its capital and output, that *firm* experiences diminishing returns. But the economy can increase its capital and output by adding another identical fiber cable factory, and the *economy* does not experience diminishing returns.

The assumption that capital does not experience diminishing returns is the central novel proposition of the new growth theory. And the implication of this simple and appealing idea is astonishing. As capital accumulates, labor productivity grows indefinitely as long as people devote resources to expanding human capital and introducing new technologies.

■ Analyzing the Effects of Labor Productivity Growth

Figure 25.3 shows the effects of an increase in labor productivity that results from an increase in capital or an advance in technology. Part (a) shows the production function, which initially is PF_0. Part (b) shows the labor market. The demand for labor initially is LD_0, and the supply of labor is LS. The real wage rate is $15 an hour, and full employment is 200 billion hours a year. With 200 billion hours of labor employed, real GDP is $5 trillion in part (a).

Now an increase in physical capital or human capital or an advance in technology increases labor productivity. In Figure 25.3(a), the productivity of labor increase shifts the production function upward to PF_1. In Figure 25.3(b), the demand for labor increases and the demand curve shifts rightward to LD_1. At the original real wage rate of $15 an hour, there is now a shortage of labor. So the real wage rate rises. In this example, the real wage rate keeps rising until it reaches $25 an hour. At $25 an hour, the quantity of labor demanded equals the quantity of labor supplied and full employment increases to 300 billion hours a year.

Figure 25.3(a) shows the effects on real GDP of the increase in employment combined with the new production function. As full employment increases from 200 billion hours to 300 billion hours, real GDP increases from $5 trillion to $12 trillion. Real GDP per hour of work also increases. You can see this increase by

FIGURE 25.3

The Effects of an Increase in Labor Productivity

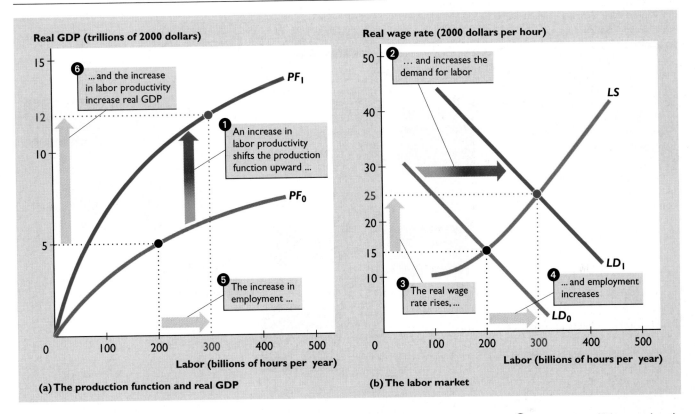

(a) The production function and real GDP

(b) The labor market

❶ An increase in labor productivity shifts the production function upward from PF_0 to PF_1 in part (a) and ❷ increases the demand for labor—shifts the demand for labor curve rightward from LD_0 to LD_1—in part (b).

❸ The real wage rate rises and ❹ the quantity of labor employed increases in part (b).

❺ The increase in employment and ❻ the increase in labor productivity increase real GDP in part (a).

dividing real GDP by total labor hours. Initially, with real GDP at $5 trillion and labor hours at 200 billion, real GDP per hour of work was $25. With the increase in labor productivity, real GDP is $12 trillion and labor hours are 300 billion, so real GDP per hour of work is $40.

We've just studied the effects of a one-shot increase in labor productivity. But the forces that bring it about are ongoing.

Perpetual Motion

Economic growth is like the perpetual motion machine in Figure 25.4. Growth is driven by insatiable wants that lead us to pursue profit and innovate. New and better products result from this process; new firms start up, and old firms go out of business. As firms start up and die, jobs are created and destroyed. New and better jobs lead to more leisure and more consumption. But our insatiable wants are still there, so the process continues—wants, profit incentives, innovation, and new products. The economic growth rate depends on the ability and the incentive to innovate.

■ **FIGURE 25.4**

A Perpetual Motion Machine

① ②econlab

① People want a higher standard of living and are spurred by **②** profit incentives to make the **③** innovations that lead to **④** new and better techniques and new and better products, which in turn lead to **⑤** the birth of new firms and the death of some old firms, **⑥** new and better jobs, and **⑦** more leisure and more consumption goods and services. The result is **⑧** a higher standard of living. But people want a yet higher standard of living, and the growth process continues.

Based on a similar figure in *These Are the Good Old Days: A Report on U.S. Living Standards,* Federal Reserve Bank of Dallas 1993 Annual Report.

② Incentives

③ Innovation

① Want a higher standard of living

④ New and better techniques

④ New and better products

⑤ New firms born and old firms die

⑧ Higher standard of living

⑦ More leisure

⑥ New and better jobs

⑦ More consumption goods and services

REALITY CHECK

Economic Growth in YOUR Life

Think about the choices that you have made to increase your human capital. What can you do to speed up the rate at which your human capital grows? Will you continue to expand your human capital when you finish school and get a job?

Think also about the choices that your local government officials have made to increase economic growth in your city or even in your own neighborhood. Do these choices create jobs? Do they create incentives for saving, investment, research, improved education?

What policies would you recommend to your local government officials to grow your local economy even faster?

Persistent Gaps or Convergence?

Growth rates of real GDP per person in Europe's Big 4 (France, Germany, Italy, and the United Kingdom) have been similar to that of the United States, so the gaps between these countries haven't changed much. (See part (a) of the figure.)

Central Europe, in a transition from Communism to operating a market economy, went through a depression during the early 1990s. But these countries started to grow faster than the United States in the late 1990s.

Africa and Central and South America have grown persistently more slowly than the United States, so the gaps between the United States and these regions have widened. Real GDP per person in East Asian economies (in part b) has converged toward that in the United States.

In 1960, real GDP per person in Hong Kong, Singapore, Taiwan, and South Korea ranged from 12 percent to 25 percent of that in the United States. By 2005, they ranged from 60 to 85 percent of that in the United States. China is also catching up, but from a very long way behind.

These Asian economies are like fast trains running on the same track at similar speeds and with roughly constant gaps between them. Hong Kong and Singapore are the lead trains and run about 15 years in front of Taiwan, 20 years in front of South Korea, and almost 40 years in front of China.

Between 1960 and 2005, Hong Kong and Singapore transformed

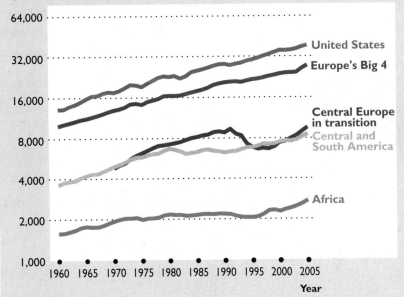

Real GDP per person
(2000 dollars: ratio scale)

(a) Persistent gaps

Real GDP per person
(2000 dollars: ratio scale)

(b) Convergence

SOURCES OF DATA: Alan Heston, Robert Summers and Bettina Aten, Penn World Table Version 6.1, Center for International Comparisons at the University of Pennsylvania (CICUP), October 2000 and International Monetary Fund *World Economic Outlook.*

themselves from poor developing countries to take their places among the world's richest countries. China is in the process of doing the same.

3 **Review the theories of economic growth that explain why growth rates vary over time and across countries.**

Practice Problems 25.3

1. What does classical growth theory say will eventually end economic growth?

2. What does neoclassical growth theory say about the source of persistent growth in real GDP per person?

3. What does neoclassical growth theory say is the process that will bring the growth of real GDP per person to a stop?

4. What is the driving force of economic growth according to new growth theory?

Exercises 25.3

1. Contrast the modern theory of population growth with the classical growth theory.

2. What is the main limitation of neoclassical growth theory?

3. What are the three facts about market economies that new growth theory emphasizes and how do those facts influence the economic growth rate? Provide examples of each.

4. Why don't diminishing returns limit growth in new growth theory?

5. Families in China are permitted to have only one child. Predict the effects of this policy on economic growth according to classical, neoclassical, and new growth theories.

Solutions to Practice Problems 25.3

1. Classical growth theory predicts that when the real income exceeds the subsistence real income, the population grows. With an increasing population, the supply of labor increases, the real wage rate falls and is pulled back toward subsistence level. Real GDP increases, but real GDP per person decreases.

2. Neoclassical growth theory says that technological advance is the source of persistent growth in real GDP per person.

3. If technology stops advancing, real GDP growth slows because capital accumulation brings diminishing returns. With real GDP growth slowing, saving and investment fall and the growth rate of capital decreases to the population growth rate. Real GDP per person stops growing.

4. The driving force of economic growth according to new growth theory is a persistent incentive to innovate and an absence of diminishing returns.

25.4 ACHIEVING FASTER GROWTH

Why did it take more than a million years of human life before economic growth began? Why are some countries even today still barely growing? Why don't *all* societies save and invest in new capital, expand human capital, and discover and apply new technologies on a scale that brings rapid economic growth? What actions can governments take to encourage growth?

■ Preconditions for Economic Growth

The key reason why economic growth is either absent or slow is that some societies lack the incentive system that encourages growth-producing activities. And economic freedom is the fundamental precondition for creating the incentives that lead to economic growth.

Economic Freedom

Economic freedom is present when people are able to make personal choices, their private property is protected, and they are free to buy and sell in markets. The rule of law, an efficient legal system, and the ability to enforce contracts are essential foundations for creating economic freedom. Impediments to economic freedom are corruption in the courts and government bureaucracy; barriers to trade, such as import bans; high tax rates; stringent regulations on business, such as health, safety, and environmental regulation; restrictions on banks; labor market regulations that limit a firm's ability to hire and fire workers; and illegal markets, such as those that violate intellectual property rights.

No unique political system is necessary to deliver economic freedom. Democratic systems do a good job. But the rule of law, not democracy, is the key requirement for creating economic freedom. Nondemocratic political systems that respect the rule of law do a good job too. Hong Kong is the best example of a place with little democracy but a lot of economic freedom—and a lot of economic growth. No country with a high level of economic freedom is economically poor. But many countries with low levels of economic freedom stagnate.

Economic freedom
A condition in which people are able to make personal choices, their private property is protected, and they are free to buy and sell in markets.

Property Rights

Economic freedom requires the protection of private property—the factors of production and goods that people own. The social arrangements that govern the protection of private property are called **property rights**. They include the rights to physical property (land, buildings, and capital equipment), to financial property (claims by one person against another), and to intellectual property (such as inventions). Clearly established and enforced property rights provide people with the incentive to work and save. If someone attempts to steal their property, a legal system will protect them. Such property rights also assure people that government itself will not confiscate their income or savings.

Property rights
The social arrangements that govern the protection of private property.

Markets

Economic freedom also requires free markets. Buyers and sellers get information and do business with each other in *markets*. And market prices send signals to buyers and sellers that create incentives to increase or decrease the quantities demanded and supplied. Markets enable people to trade and to save and invest. But markets cannot operate without property rights.

Property rights and markets create incentives for people to specialize and trade, to save and invest, to expand their human capital, and to discover and apply new technologies. Early human societies based on hunting and gathering did not experience economic growth because they lacked property rights and markets. Economic growth began when societies evolved the institutions that create incentives. But the presence of an incentive system and the institutions that create it do not guarantee that economic growth will occur. They permit economic growth but do not make it inevitable.

Growth begins when the appropriate incentive system exists because people can specialize in the activities at which they have a comparative advantage and trade with each other. You saw in Chapter 3 how everyone gains from such activity. By specializing and trading, everyone can acquire goods and services at the lowest possible cost. Consequently, people can obtain a greater volume of goods and services from their labor.

As an economy moves from one with little specialization to one that reaps the gains from specialization and trade, its production and consumption grow. Real GDP per person increases, and the standard of living rises.

But for growth to be persistent, people must face incentives that encourage them to pursue the three activities that generate *ongoing* economic growth: saving and investment, expansion of human capital, and the discovery and application of new technologies.

■ Policies to Achieve Faster Growth

To achieve faster economic growth, we must either increase the growth rate of capital per hour of labor or increase the growth rate of human capital or the pace of technological advance. The main actions that governments can take to achieve these objectives are

- Create incentive mechanisms.
- Encourage saving.
- Encourage research and development.
- Encourage international trade.
- Improve the quality of education.

Create Incentive Mechanisms

Economic growth occurs when the incentives to save, invest, and innovate are strong enough. And these incentives require property rights enforced by a well-functioning legal system. Property rights and a legal system are key missing ingredients in many societies. For example, they are absent throughout much of Africa. The first priority for growth policy is to establish these institutions so that incentives to save, invest, and innovate exist. Russia is a leading example of a country that is striving to take this step toward establishing the conditions in which economic growth can occur.

Encourage Saving

Saving finances investment, which brings capital accumulation. So encouraging saving can increase the growth of capital and stimulate economic growth. The East Asian economies have the highest saving rates and the highest growth rates. Some African economies have the lowest saving rates and the lowest growth rates.

Tax incentives can increase saving. Individual Retirement Accounts (IRAs) are an example of a tax incentive to save. Economists claim that a tax on consumption rather than on income provides the best incentive to save.

Encourage Research and Development

Everyone can use the fruits of basic research and development efforts. For example, all biotechnology firms can use advances in gene-splicing technology. Because basic inventions can be copied, the inventor's profit is limited and so the market allocates too few resources to this activity.

Governments can direct public funds toward financing basic research, but this solution is not foolproof. It requires a mechanism for allocating public funds to their highest-valued use. The National Science Foundation is one possibly efficient channel for allocating public funds to universities and public research facilities to finance and encourage basic research. Government programs such as national defense and space exploration also lead to innovations that have wide use. Laptop computers and Teflon coatings are two prominent examples of innovations that came from the U.S. space program.

Encourage International Trade

Free international trade stimulates economic growth by extracting all the available gains from specialization and trade. The fastest-growing nations today are those with the fastest-growing exports and imports. The creation of the North American Free Trade Agreement and the integration of the economies of Europe through the formation of the European Union are examples of successful actions that governments have taken to stimulate economic growth through trade.

Improve the Quality of Education

The free market would produce too little education because it brings social benefits beyond the benefits to the people who receive the education. By funding basic education and by ensuring high standards in skills such as language, mathematics, and science, governments can contribute enormously to a nation's growth potential. Education can also be expanded and improved by using tax incentives to encourage improved private provision. Singapore's Information Technology in Education program is one of the best examples of a successful attempt to stimulate growth through education.

■ How Much Difference Can Policy Make?

It is easy to make a list of policy actions that could increase a nation's economic growth rate. It is hard to convert that list into acceptable actions that make a big difference.

Societies are the way they are because they balance the interests of one group against the interests of another group. Change brings gains for some and losses for others. So change is slow. And even when change occurs, if the economic growth rate can be increased by even as much as half a percentage point, it takes many years for the full benefits to accrue.

A well-intentioned government cannot dial up a big increase in the economic growth rate. But it can pursue policies that will nudge the economic growth rate upward. And over time, the benefits from these policies will be large.

4 **Describe policies that might speed economic growth.**

Practice Problems 25.4

1. What are the preconditions for economic growth?

2. Why does much of Africa experience slow economic growth?

3. Why is economic freedom crucial for achieving economic growth?

4. What role do property rights play in encouraging economic growth?

5. Explain why, other things remaining the same, a country with a well-educated population has a faster economic growth rate than a country that has a poorly educated population.

Exercises 25.4

1. What is the key reason why economic growth is either absent or slow in some societies?

2. Is economic freedom the same as democracy? Can you think of a country that enjoys economic freedom and achieves rapid economic growth but does not have democracy?

3. Why are markets a necessary precondition for economic growth?

4. Explain why, other things remaining the same, a country or region that adopts free international trade (for example, Hong Kong) has a faster economic growth rate than a country that restricts international trade (for example, Myanmar).

Solutions to Practice Problems 25.4

1. The preconditions for economic growth are economic freedom, private property rights, and markets. Without these preconditions, people have little incentive to undertake the actions that lead to economic growth.

2. Some African countries experience slow economic growth because they lack economic freedom, private property rights are not enforced, and markets do not function well. People in these countries have little incentive to specialize and trade or to accumulate both physical and human capital.

3. Economic freedom is crucial for achieving economic growth because economic freedom allows people to make choices and gives them the incentives to pursue growth-producing activities.

4. Clearly defined private property rights and a legal system to enforce them give people the incentives to work, save, invest, and accumulate human capital.

5. A well-educated population has more skills and greater labor productivity than a poorly educated population. A well-educated population can contribute to the research and development that create new technology.

Key Points

1 **Define and calculate the economic growth rate, and explain the implications of sustained growth.**

- Economic growth is the sustained expansion of production possibilities. The annual percentage change in real GDP measures the economic growth rate.
- Real GDP per person must grow if the standard of living is to rise.
- Sustained economic growth transforms poor nations into rich ones.
- The Rule of 70 tells us the number of years in which real GDP doubles—70 divided by the percentage growth rate of real GDP.

2 **Identify the main sources of economic growth.**

- Real GDP grows when aggregate hours and labor productivity grow.
- Real GDP per person grows when labor productivity grows.
- Saving, investment in physical capital and human capital, and technological advance bring labor productivity growth.

3 **Review the theories of economic growth that explain why growth rates vary over time and across countries.**

- Classical growth theory predicts that economic growth will end because a population explosion will lower real GDP per person to its subsistence level.
- Neoclassical theory predicts that economic growth will persist at a rate that is determined by the pace of technological change.
- New growth theory predicts that capital accumulation, human capital growth, and technological change respond to incentives and can bring persistent growth in labor productivity.

4 **Describe policies that might speed economic growth.**

- Economic growth requires an incentive system created by economic freedom, property rights, and markets.
- It might be possible to achieve faster growth by encouraging saving, subsidizing research and education, and encouraging international trade.

Key Terms

Classical growth theory, 629
Economic freedom, 639
Economic growth rate, 620
Labor productivity, 624

Malthusian theory, 629
Neoclassical growth theory, 632
New growth theory, 633
Property rights, 639

Real GDP per person, 620
Rule of 70, 621

Exercises

1. Explain why sustained growth of real GDP per person can transform a poor country into a wealthy one.

2. In Ireland, the growth rate of real GDP per person averaged 10 percent a year during the 1990s. If this growth rate were to continue, in what year would real GDP per person be twice what it was in 2000?

3. Describe how U.S. real GDP per person has changed over the last 100 years.

4. Explain how the amount of physical capital increases, how human capital increases, and how technology advances.

5. What is the link between labor hours, labor productivity, and real GDP?

6. Explain how saving and investment in new capital, increases in human capital, and advances in technology change labor productivity. Use a graph to illustrate your answer.

7. Table 1 describes the labor market in the economy of Longland in 2005. Table 2 describes Longland's production function in 2005.
   a. What is the equilibrium real wage rate and the quantity of labor employed in 2005?
   b. What is the full-employment quantity of labor in 2005?
   c. What is potential GDP in 2005?
   d. What is real GDP per hour of labor in 2005?

8. The information in exercise 7 describes the economy of Longland in 2005. In 2006, the population increased and labor hours supplied increased by 10 at each real wage rate.
   a. What is the equilibrium real wage rate and the quantity of labor employed in 2006?
   b. What is the full-employment quantity of labor in 2006?
   c. What is potential GDP in 2006?
   d. What is real GDP per hour of labor in 2006?
   e. Does Longland's standard of living increase in 2006? Explain why or why not.
   f. If the subsistence real wage rate in Longland is $20 an hour, what, according to the classical growth theory, will happen to Longland's population?

TABLE I

Real wage rate (2000 dollars per hour)	Labor hours supplied	Labor hours demanded
80	45	5
70	40	10
60	35	15
50	30	20
40	25	25
30	20	30
20	15	35
10	10	40

TABLE 2

Labor (hours)	Real GDP (2000 dollars)
5	425
10	800
15	1,125
20	1,400
25	1,625
30	1,800
35	1,925
40	2,000

9. Table 3 describes Longland's labor market in 2007, and Table 4 describes Longland's production function in 2007.
   a. What is the equilibrium real wage rate and employment in 2007?
   b. What is full-employment quantity of labor hours in 2007?
   c. What is real GDP in 2007?
   d. What is potential GDP in 2007?
   e. What is real GDP per unit of labor in 2007?

10. Exercises 7, 8, and 9 describe the labor market and production function in the economy of Longland in 2005, 2006, and 2007.
    a. What has changed in Longland between 2005 and 2007?
    b. Use your solutions to exercises 7 and 8 to compare the economy of Longland in 2007 with that of 2005 and 2006.
    c. Has real GDP grown because the labor hours increased or because labor productivity increased? How can you tell?
    d. What has happened to potential GDP?
    e. What has happened to real GDP per unit of labor?
    f. Do you think the standard of living has improved in Longland?

11. List five actions that governments can take to encourage economic growth, and provide an example of each.

Critical Thinking

12. What do the classical, neoclassical, and new growth theories predict about growth in the global economy? Which theory do you think best fits the facts?

13. What can governments in Africa do to encourage economic growth and raise their living standards?

14. Why do you think the standard of living in Asian economies has increased in the last decade by so much more than the standard of living in the United States?

15. What are the ingredients of economic freedom and how does each ingredient make economic growth more likely? Provide examples of nations that do not enjoy political freedom and that have a low economic growth rate and examples of nations that do enjoy political freedom and have a high economic growth rate. Are there any notable examples that contradict the view that economic freedom and economic growth go together?

TABLE 3

Real wage rate (2000 dollars per hour)	Labor hours supplied	Labor hours demanded
80	55	15
70	50	20
60	45	25
50	40	30
40	35	35
30	30	40
20	25	45
10	20	50

TABLE 4

Labor (hours)	Real GDP (2000 dollars)
15	1,425
20	1,800
25	2,125
30	2,400
35	2,625
40	2,800
45	2,925
50	3,000

16. Why might high taxes hold back economic growth? Would you recommend any changes in the U.S. tax laws to encourage faster growth? How would the changes that you recommend work?

17. Critically evaluate the two following contradictory statements.

    (1) Economic growth results from technological change, which results from creative people responding to incentives. A larger population has more creative people, so it brings faster technological advance. So population growth brings faster growth of real GDP per person.

    (2) Economic growth can be sustained only if we conserve natural resources. A larger population places strain on natural resources. So population growth brings slower growth of real GDP per person.

18. An increasing number of Chinese citizens who are educated in the United States are returning to China to work. How do you think this development might influence economic growth in China? Do you think the Chinese government would be wise to adopt policies that encourage more of its students attending foreign universities to return to China when they have completed their studies?

Web Exercises

Use the links on MyEconLab to work the following exercises.

19. Visit the IMF's World Economic Outlook database and obtain data on growth rates of real GDP per person for the United States, China, South Africa, and Mexico since 1990.
    a. Draw a graph of the data.
    b. Which country has the lowest real GDP per person and which has the highest?
    c. Which country has experienced the fastest growth rate since 1990 and which has experienced the slowest?
    d. Explain why the growth rates in these four countries are ranked in the order you have discovered.

20. Visit the Web site of the Penn World Tables and obtain data for any four countries (but not those of the previous exercise) that interest you. Describe and explain the patterns that you find for these countries.

Money and the Monetary System

CHAPTER CHECKLIST

When you have completed your study of this chapter, you will be able to

1 Define money and describe its functions.

2 Describe the monetary system and explain the functions of banks and other monetary institutions.

3 Describe the functions of the Federal Reserve System.

It's spring break, and you decide to take a trip to the sun. You search the Web and find a good deal on a budget airline, so you enter your credit card details and buy a ticket. At the airport, you swipe your card in a machine, tap in your PIN, and get enough cash to see you through the week. A few weeks later, when you're back in class and refreshed from your vacation, your credit card statement arrives. You use Internet banking to pay the full balance and avoid a 20 percent interest charge.

Money and the monetary system that we study in this chapter make a huge contribution to your standard of living and are part of the economy's productive capital. Although we would be much less productive if we didn't have a well-functioning monetary system, the *quantity* of money does not influence the *standard* of living. It is the *cost* of living that the *quantity* of money influences.

This chapter explains what money is and describes the monetary system. The two following chapters explain how money gets created and why the cost of living rises when the quantity of money grows too quickly.

26.1 WHAT IS MONEY?

Money, like fire and the wheel, has been around for a very long time. An incredible array of items has served as money. North American Indians used wampum (beads made from shells), Fijians used whales' teeth, and early American colonists used tobacco. Cakes of salt served as money in Ethiopia and Tibet. What do wampum, whales' teeth, tobacco, and salt have in common? Why are they examples of money? Today, when we want to buy something, we use coins or notes (dollar bills), write a check, send an e-check, present a credit or debit card, or use a "smart card." Are all these things that we use today money? To answer these questions, we need a definition of money.

■ Definition of Money

Money is any commodity or token that is generally accepted as a *means of payment*. This definition has three bits that we'll examine in turn.

A Commodity or Token

Money is always something that can be recognized and that can be divided up into small parts. So money might be an actual commodity, such as a bar of silver or gold. But it might also be a token, such as a quarter or a $10 bill. Money might also be a virtual token, such as an electronic record in a bank's database (more about this type of money later).

Generally Accepted

Money is *generally* accepted, which means that it can be used to buy anything and everything. Some tokens can be used to buy some things but not others. For example, a phone card is accepted as payment for a phone call. But you can't use your phone card to buy toothpaste. So a phone card is not money. In contrast, you can use a $5 bill to buy either a phone call or toothpaste—or anything else that costs $5 or less. So a $5 bill is money.

Means of Payment

A **means of payment** is a method of settling a debt. When a payment has been made, the deal is complete. Suppose that Gus buys a car from his friend Ann. Gus doesn't have enough money to pay for the car right now, but he will have enough three months from now, when he gets paid. Ann agrees that Gus may pay for the car in three months' time. Gus buys the car with a loan from Ann and then pays off the loan. The loan isn't money. Money is what Gus uses to pay off the loan.

So what wampum, whales' teeth, tobacco, and salt have in common is that they have served as a generally accepted means of payment, and that is why they are examples of money.

■ The Functions of Money

Money performs three vital functions. It serves as a

- Medium of exchange
- Unit of account
- Store of value

Money
Any commodity or token that is generally accepted as a means of payment.

Means of payment
A method of settling a debt.

Medium of Exchange

A **medium of exchange** is an object that is generally accepted in return for goods and services. Money is a medium of exchange. Without money, you would have to exchange goods and services directly for other goods and services—an exchange called **barter**. Barter requires a *double coincidence of wants*. For example, if you want a soda and have only a paperback novel to offer in exchange for it, you must find someone who is selling soda and who also wants your paperback novel. Money guarantees that there is a double coincidence of wants because people with something to sell will always accept money in exchange for it. So money acts as a lubricant that smoothes the mechanism of exchange. It enables you to specialize in the activity in which you have a comparative advantage (see Chapter 3, pp. 81–82) instead of searching for a double coincidence of wants.

Medium of exchange
An object that is generally accepted in return for goods and services.

Barter
The direct exchange of goods and services for other goods and services, which requires a double coincidence of wants.

Unit of Account

A **unit of account** is an agreed-upon measure for stating the prices of goods and services. To get the most out of your budget, you have to figure out whether going to a rock concert is worth its opportunity cost. But that cost is not dollars and cents. It is the number of movies, cappuccinos, ice-cream cones, or local phone calls that you must give up to attend the concert. It's easy to do such calculations when all these goods have prices in terms of dollars and cents (see Table 26.1). If a rock concert costs $32 and a movie costs $8, you know right away that going to the concert costs you 4 movies. If a cappuccino costs $2, going to the concert costs 16 cappuccinos. You need only one calculation to figure out the opportunity cost of any pair of goods and services. For example, the opportunity cost of the rock concert is 128 local phone calls ($32.00 ÷ 25¢ = 128).

Now imagine how troublesome it would be if the rock concert ticket agent posted its price as 4 movies, and if the movie theater posted its price as 4 cappuccinos, and if the coffee shop posted the price of a cappuccino as 2 ice-cream cones, and if the ice-cream shop posted its price as 4 local phone calls! Now how much running around and calculating do you have to do to figure out how much that rock concert is going to cost you in terms of the movies, cappuccino, ice cream, or phone calls that you must give up to attend it? You get the answer for movies right away from the sign posted by the ticket agent. But for all the other goods, you're going to have to visit many different places to establish the price of each commodity in terms of another and then calculate prices in units that are relevant for your own decision. Cover up the column labeled "price in money units" in Table 26.1 and see how hard it is to figure out the number of local phone calls it costs to attend a rock concert. It's enough to make a person swear off rock! How much simpler it is using dollars and cents.

Unit of account
An agreed-upon measure for stating the prices of goods and services.

TABLE 26.1 A UNIT OF ACCOUNT SIMPLIFIES PRICE COMPARISONS

Good	Price in money units	Price in units of another good
Rock concert	$32.00	4 movies
Movie	$8.00	4 cappuccinos
Cappuccino	$2.00	2 ice-cream cones
Ice-cream cone	$1.00	4 local phone calls
Local phone call	$0.25	

Store of Value

Any commodity or token that can be held and exchanged later for goods and services is called a **store of value**. Money acts as a store of value. If it did not, it would not be accepted in exchange for goods and services. The more stable the value of a commodity or token, the better it can act as a store of value and the more useful it is as money. No store of value is completely stable. The value of a physical object, such as a house, a car, or a work of art, fluctuates over time. The value of the commodities and tokens that we use as money also fluctuates, and when there is inflation, money persistently falls in value.

Store of value
Any commodity or token that can be held and exchanged later for goods and services.

Fiat money
Objects that are money because the law decrees or orders them to be money.

Currency
Notes (dollar bills) and coins.

■ Money Today

Money in the world today is called **fiat money**. *Fiat* is a Latin word that means "Let it be done." The modern word "fiat" means decree or order. So today's money is money because the law decrees or orders it to be money. The objects that we use as money have little value as objects and are valued only because of their legal status as money.

Today's fiat money consists of

- Currency
- Deposits at banks and other financial institutions

Currency

The notes (dollar bills) and coins that we use in the United States today are known as **currency**. Notes are money because the government declares them to be with the words printed on every dollar bill, "This note is legal tender for all debts, public and private."

Deposits

Deposits at banks, credit unions, savings banks, and savings and loan associations are also money. Deposits are money because they can be used directly to make payments. You don't need to go to the bank to get currency to make a payment. You can tell your bank to move some money from your account to someone else's.

Currency in a Bank Is Not Money

Bank deposits are one form of money, and currency *held by individuals and businesses* is another form. Currency *inside* the banks is not money. When you get some cash from the ATM, you convert your bank deposit into currency. You change the form of your money, but there is no change in the quantity of money. Deposits decrease, and currency increases. If we counted both bank deposits and currency inside the banks as money, when you get cash at the ATM, the quantity of money would *appear* to decrease—your currency would increase, but *both* deposits *and* currency inside the banks would decrease. You can see that counting deposits *and* currency inside the banks as money would be double counting.

Deposits Are Money but Checks Are Not

Checks are not money. To see why, think about what happens when Colleen buys some inline skates from Rocky's Rollers. Colleen has $500 in her deposit account, and Rocky has $3,000 in his deposit account. Both of them bank at the Laser Bank. The total bank deposits of Colleen and Rocky are $3,500.

To pay for her skates, Colleen writes a check for $200. Rocky takes the check to the bank and deposits it. The Laser Bank now credits Rocky's account and debits Colleen's account. Rocky's deposit increases from $3,000 to $3,200, and Colleen's deposit decreases from $500 to $300. The total deposits of Colleen and Rocky are still the same as before: $3,500. Rocky now has $200 more, and Colleen has $200 less than before.

This transaction has transferred money from Colleen to Rocky. The check itself was never money. There wasn't an extra $200 worth of money while the check was in circulation. The check only instructs the bank to transfer money from Colleen to Rocky. Figure 26.1 shows these transactions in their bank statements.

FIGURE 26.1

Paying by Check

LASER BANK *123 Dakota Street, Andover, MA 01810 (508) 555-3937*

Date	Item	Debit	Credit	Balance
June 1 2006	Opening balance			$500.00
June 11 2006	Rocky's Rollers	$200.00		$300.00

(a) Colleen's account

LASER BANK *123 Dakota Street, Andover, MA 01810 (508) 555-3937*

Date	Item	Debit	Credit	Balance
June 1 2006	Opening balance			$3,000.00
June 11 2006	Colleen's check		$200.00	$3,200.00

(b) Rocky's Rollers's account

When you pay by check, you tell your bank to take some money from your deposit and put it into someone else's deposit. The deposit is money, but the check is not money.

Here, Colleen pays Rocky's Rollers $200 by check.

For Colleen in part (a), the $200 is a debit (a subtraction) and her bank balance falls by this amount.

For Rocky in part (b), the $200 is a credit (an addition) and his bank balance rises by this amount.

In the example, Colleen and Rocky use the same bank. The same story, but with additional steps, describes what happens if Colleen and Rocky use different banks. In that case, the check must be cleared and a payment made by Colleen's bank to Rocky's bank. But the principles are the same as when two people use the same bank. We explain the details of the process of check clearing in Chapter 27, pp. 677–678.

■ Credit Cards, Debit Cards, E-Checks, and E-Cash

We've seen that checks are not money, but what about credit cards? Are they money? And what about debit cards and some newer ways of making payments that use electronic technologies. Are they money?

Credit Cards

A credit card is not money. It is a special type of ID card. To see why, suppose that Colleen uses her credit card to buy her inline skates. Colleen signs a credit card slip and leaves the store with her new skates. But she has not yet *paid* for the skates. She has taken a loan from the bank that issued her credit card. Rocky's bank credits his account with $200 (minus the bank's charge) and sends a charge to the bank that issued Colleen's credit card. Colleen eventually gets her credit card bill, which she pays, using money.

If you pay by check, you are often asked to show your driver's license. Your driver's license is obviously not money. It's just an ID card. A credit card is also an ID card but one that enables you to get a loan at the instant you buy something.

So when you use a credit card to buy something, the bank that issued your credit card pays for the goods and you pay the bank back later. The credit card is not the means of payment, and it is not money.

Debit Cards

A debit card works like a paper check, only faster. And just as checks aren't money, so neither are debit cards. To see why a debit card works like a check, think about what happens if Colleen uses her debit card to buy her inline skates. When the sales clerk swipes Colleen's card in Rocky's store, the Laser Bank's computer gets a message: Take $200 from Colleen's account and put it in the account of Rocky's Rollers. The transactions shown in Figure 26.1 are done in a flash. But again, the bank deposits are the money and the debit card is the tool that causes money to move from Colleen to Rocky.

E-Checks

Electronic check (or e-check)
An electronic equivalent of a paper check.

An **electronic check** (or **e-check**) is an electronic equivalent of a paper check. A group of more than 90 banks and other financial institutions have formed the Financial Services Technology Consortium to collaborate on developing the electronic check. First Virtual offers an Internet e-check system via email. Like a paper check, an e-check is not money. The deposit transferred is money.

E-Cash

Electronic cash (or e-cash)
An electronic equivalent of paper notes and coins.

Electronic cash (or **e-cash**) is an electronic equivalent of paper notes (dollar bills) and coins. It is an electronic currency, and for people to be willing to use it, e-cash has to work like money. People use physical currency because it is portable, recognizable, transferable, untraceable, and anonymous and can be used to make change. The designers of e-cash aim to reproduce all of these features of notes and coins. Today's e-cash is portable, untraceable, and anonymous. But it has not yet reached the level of recognition that makes it universally accepted as a means of payment, so it doesn't meet the definition of money.

Like notes and coins, e-cash can be used in shops. It can also be used over the Internet. To use e-cash in a shop, the buyer uses a smart card that stores some e-cash and the shop uses a smart card reader. When a transaction is made, e-cash is transferred from the smart card directly to the shop's bank account. Users of smart cards receive their e-cash by withdrawing it from a bank account by using a special ATM or a special cell phone.

Several versions of e-cash in U.S. dollars, euros, and many other currencies are available on the Internet. The most popular and widely used e-cash system is PayPal, which is owned by eBay. Transactions using PayPal can be conducted in more than 50 countries between any pair of people as long as each of them has an e-mail address.

A handy advantage of e-cash over paper notes arises when you lose your wallet. If it is stuffed with dollar bills, you're out of luck. If it contains e-cash recorded on your smart card, your bank can cancel the e-cash stored in the card and issue you replacement e-cash.

Although e-cash is not yet widely accepted, it is likely that its use will grow and that it will gradually replace physical forms of currency.

■ Official Measures of Money: M1 and M2

Figure 26.2 shows the items that make up two official measures of money. **M1** consists of currency held by individuals and businesses and traveler's checks plus checkable deposits owned by individuals and businesses. M1 does not include currency inside the banks. **M2** consists of M1 plus savings deposits and small time deposits (less than $100,000), money market funds, and other deposits. Time deposits are deposits that can be withdrawn only after a fixed term. Money market funds are deposits that are invested in short-term securities that pay a higher interest rate than bank deposits.

M1
Currency held by individuals and businesses and traveler's checks plus checkable deposits owned by individuals and businesses.

M2
M1 plus savings deposits and small time deposits, money market funds, and other deposits.

Are M1 and M2 Means of Payment?

The test of whether something is money is whether it is a generally accepted means of payment. Currency passes the test. Checkable deposits also pass the test because they can be transferred from one person to another by writing a check. So all the components of M1 serve as means of payment.

But what about M2? Some of the savings deposits in M2 are just as much a means of payment as the checkable deposits in M1. You can use the ATM at the grocery store checkout or gas station to transfer funds directly from your savings account to pay for your purchase. But other savings deposits, time deposits, and money market funds are *not* means of payment.

▨ FIGURE 26.2

Two Measures of Money: July 2005

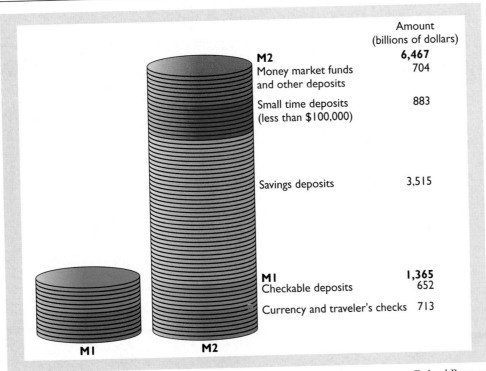

	Amount (billions of dollars)
M2	**6,467**
Money market funds and other deposits	704
Small time deposits (less than $100,000)	883
Savings deposits	3,515
M1	**1,365**
Checkable deposits	652
Currency and traveler's checks	713

M1 Currency held by individuals and businesses and traveler's checks plus checkable deposits owned by individuals and businesses.

M2 M1 plus savings deposits plus small time deposits plus money market funds and other deposits.

SOURCE OF DATA: Federal Reserve.

The U.S. Dollar Abroad

At the end of 2004, U.S. dollar bills worth $700 billion were in circulation. Of these, perhaps as much as $400 billion was circulating abroad. The figure shows the growth in this number.

U.S. dollars are used extensively in Russia and Argentina and throughout the Middle East and Asia.

Many, and perhaps most, of the U.S. dollar bills that go abroad get there as payments for illegal goods, especially drugs and weapons.

Counterfeit U.S. dollars are also in use but newly designed bills that are hard to forge have cut this illegal activity.

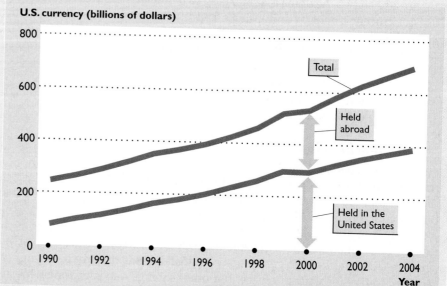

SOURCE OF DATA: U.S. Department of the Treasury, *The Use and Counterfeiting of United States Currency Abroad,* January 2000 and Part 2, March 2003.

Figure 26.3 shows the changing composition of money in the United States. Currency decreased in relative importance between 1960 and 1986 but became increasingly important during the 1990s. Checkable deposits decreased in relative importance but made a temporary comeback during the mid-1990s.

■ FIGURE 26.3

The Changing Face of Money in the United States

The proportion of money held as checkable deposits has been falling. The proportion of money held as currency fell slightly from 1960 through 1986 but then increased, mainly because the amount of U.S. currency abroad increased.

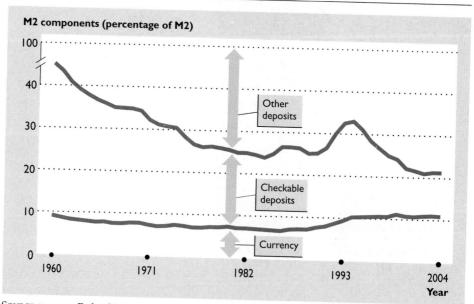

SOURCE OF DATA: Federal Reserve.

CHECKPOINT 26.1

I **Define money and describe its functions.**

Practice Problems 26.1

1. In the United States today, money includes which of the following items?
   a. Your Visa card
   b. The quarters inside public phones
   c. U.S. dollar bills in your wallet
   d. The check that you have just written to pay for your rent
   e. The loan you took out last August to pay for your school fees

2. In November 2004, currency held by individuals and businesses was $699.8 billion; traveler's checks were $7.6 billion; checkable deposits owned by individuals and businesses were $654.7 billion; savings deposits were $3,494.8 billion; small time deposits were $810.3 billion; and money market funds and other deposits were $713.3 billion.
   a. What was M1 in November 2004?
   b. What was M2 in November 2004?

Exercises 26.1

1. Which of the following items are money?
   a. Checkable deposits at First Boston Bank
   b. General Motors stock held by individuals
   c. A Sacagawea dollar coin
   d. U.S. government securities
   e. Money market funds

2. Sara withdraws $2,000 from her time deposit account at Bank of America, keeps $100 in cash, and deposits the balance in her checking account at Citibank. What is the immediate change in M1 and M2?

3. In March 2004, currency held by individuals and businesses was $666.8 billion; traveler's checks in circulation were $7.8 billion; checkable deposits owned by individuals and businesses were $651.1 billion; savings deposits were $3,279.1 billion; time deposits were $802.7 billion; and money market funds and other deposits were $760.5 billion.
   a. What was M1 in March 2004?
   b. What was M2 in March 2004?

Solutions to Practice Problems 26.1

1. Money is defined as a means of payment. Only items **b** and **c** (the quarters inside public phones and U.S. dollar bills in your wallet) are money.

2a. M1 is the sum of currency held by individuals and businesses, $699.8 billion; traveler's checks, $7.6 billion; and checkable deposits owned by individuals and businesses, $654.7 billion. M1 is $1,362.1 billion.

2b. M2 is the sum of M1 ($1,362.1 billion), savings deposits ($3,494.8 billion), small time deposits ($810.3 billion), and money market funds and other deposits ($713.3 billion). M2 is $6,380.5 billion.

26.2 THE MONETARY SYSTEM

Monetary system
The Federal Reserve and the banks and other institutions that accept deposits and provide the services that enable people and businesses to make and receive payments.

The **monetary system** consists of the Federal Reserve and the banks and other institutions that accept deposits and that provide the services that enable people and businesses to make and receive payments. Sitting at the top of the system (see Figure 26.4), the Federal Reserve (or Fed) sets the rules and regulates and influences the activities of the banks and other institutions. (We describe the Fed in greater detail in the next section). Three types of financial institutions accept the deposits that are part of the nation's money:

- Commercial banks
- Thrift institutions
- Money market funds

Here, we describe the functions of these institutions, and in the next section, we describe the structure and functions of the Fed.

■ Commercial Banks

Commercial bank
A firm that is chartered by the Comptroller of the Currency in the U.S. Treasury (or by a state agency) to accept deposits and make loans.

A **commercial bank** is a firm that is chartered by the Comptroller of the Currency in the U.S. Treasury (or by a state agency) to accept deposits and make loans. About 8,600 commercial banks operate in the United States today, down from 13,000 a few years ago. The number of banks has shrunk because in 1997, the rules under which banks operate were changed, permitting them to open branches in every state. A wave of mergers followed this change of rules.

Types of Deposit

A commercial bank accepts three broad types of deposit: checkable deposits, savings deposits, and time deposits. A bank pays a low interest rate (sometimes zero) on checkable deposits, and it pays the highest interest rate on time deposits.

■ FIGURE 26.4

The Institutions of the Monetary System

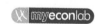

The Federal Reserve regulates and influences the activities of the commercial banks, thrift institutions, and money market funds, whose deposits make up the nation's money.

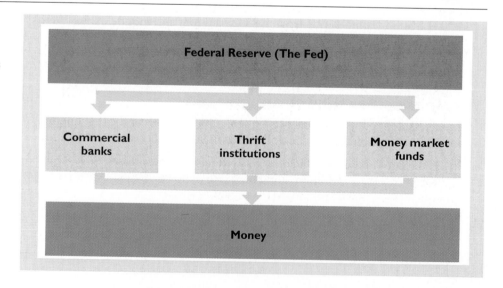

Profit and Prudence: A Balancing Act

The goal of a commercial bank is to maximize its stockholders' long-term wealth. To achieve this goal, a bank makes loans at a higher interest rate than the interest rate it pays on deposits. But lending is risky. The more a bank ties up its deposits in high-risk, high-interest rate loans, the bigger is the risk that it will not be able to pay its depositors when they want to withdraw funds. And if depositors perceive this risk, mass withdrawals—called a run on the bank—might create a crisis. So a bank must perform a balancing act. It must be prudent in the way it uses the depositors' funds and balance security for the depositors against profit for its stockholders. To achieve security for its depositors, a bank divides its assets into four parts: cash assets, interbank loans, securities, and loans.

Cash Assets

A bank's *cash assets* consist of its reserves and funds that are due from other banks as payments for checks that are being cleared. A bank's **reserves** consist of currency in its vaults plus the balance on its reserve account at a Federal Reserve Bank. The currency in a bank's vaults is a reserve to meet its depositors' withdrawals. A bank replenishes the ATM every time you and your friends have raided it for cash for a midnight pizza. A commercial bank's deposit at a Federal Reserve Bank is similar to your own bank deposit. The bank uses its reserve account at the Fed to receive and make payments to other banks and to obtain currency. The Fed requires banks to hold a minimum percentage of deposits as reserves, called the **required reserve ratio** (see Table 26.2 on p. 665). Reserves that exceed those needed to meet the required reserve ratio are called **excess reserves**.

Reserves
The currency in the bank's vaults plus the balance on its reserve account at a Federal Reserve Bank.

Required reserve ratio
The minimum percentage of deposits that banks and other financial institutions must hold in reserves.

Excess reserves
Bank reserves that exceed those needed to meet the required reserve ratio.

Interbank Loans

Banks that have excess reserves can lend them, and banks with a shortage of reserves can borrow them in an interbank loans market called the federal funds market. The interest rate in this market, called the **federal funds rate**, is the central target of the Fed's monetary policy actions.

Federal funds rate
The interest rate on interbank loans (loans made in the federal funds market).

Securities and Loans

Securities are bonds issued by the U.S. government and by other large, safe organizations. These bonds are traded every day on the bond market. A bank earns a moderate interest rate on securities, but it can sell them quickly if it needs cash to meet depositors' withdrawals. Loans are the provision of funds to businesses and individuals that earn the bank a high interest rate but that cannot be called in before the agreed date. A bank earns the highest interest rate on unpaid credit card balances, which are loans to its credit card holders.

Bank Deposits and Assets: The Relative Magnitudes

In 2005, checkable deposits at commercial banks (part of M1) were about 13 percent of total deposits. The other 87 percent of deposits were savings deposits and time deposits (part of M2). After performing their profit versus prudence balancing acts, the banks on the average kept about 6 percent of total deposits in cash assets and another 4 percent in interbank loans. The banks used 38 percent of total deposits to buy government bonds and 52 percent to make loans. Figure 26.5 summarizes the numbers in 2005.

FIGURE 26.5

Commercial Banks' Deposits and Assets

In 2005, commercial banks had $700 billion in checkable deposits and $4,800 billion in other deposits. They loaned $2,900 billion of these deposits, placed $2,000 billion in securities (bonds), and made $250 billion in interbank loans and kept $350 billion in cash assets.

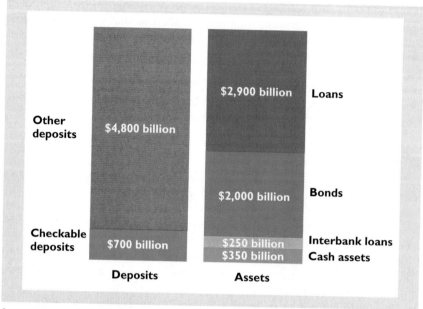

SOURCE OF DATA: Federal Reserve.

■ Thrift Institutions

The three types of thrift institutions are savings and loan associations, savings banks, and credit unions. A **savings and loan association** (S&L) is a financial institution that accepts checkable deposits and savings deposits and that makes personal, commercial, and home-purchase loans. A **savings bank** is a financial institution that accepts savings deposits and makes mostly consumer and home-purchase loans. The depositors own some savings banks (called mutual savings banks). A **credit union** is a financial institution owned by a social or economic group, such as a firm's employees, that accepts savings deposits and makes mostly consumer loans.

Like commercial banks, the thrift institutions hold reserves and must meet minimum reserve ratios set by the Fed.

The total deposits of thrift institutions in 2005 were $1,300 billion. Of these, $140 billion were checkable deposits included in M1 and $1,160 billion were savings deposits and time deposits included in M2.

■ Money Market Funds

A **money market fund** is a financial institution that obtains funds by selling shares and uses these funds to buy assets such as U.S. Treasury bills. Money market fund shares act like bank deposits. Shareholders can write checks on their money market fund accounts. But there are restrictions on most of these accounts.

Savings and loan association
A financial institution that accepts checkable deposits and savings deposits and that makes personal, commercial, and home-purchase loans.

Savings bank
A financial institution that accepts savings deposits and makes mostly consumer and home-purchase loans.

Credit union
A financial institution owned by a social or economic group such as a firm's employees, that accepts savings deposits and makes mostly consumer loans.

Money market fund
A financial institution that obtains funds by selling shares and uses these funds to buy assets such as U.S. Treasury bills.

For example, the minimum deposit accepted might be $2,500 and the smallest check a depositor is permitted to write might be $500.

In 2005, the value of money market funds included in M2 was $700 billion.

■ Relative Size of Monetary Institutions

Commercial banks provide most of the nation's bank deposits. In Figure 26.6, we show the relative contributions of commercial banks, thrift institutions, and money market funds. Part (a) shows that checkable deposits at commercial banks are 38 percent of M1, in contrast to the 10 percent of M1 at the thrift institutions. Currency represents 52 percent (more than one half) of M1.

Part (b) shows that M1 is 21 percent of M2. The savings deposits and time deposits at commercial banks are another 50 percent of M2. Money market funds and other deposits provide 11 percent of M2, and deposits at thrift institutions provide 18 percent.

On the basis of these numbers, you can see that commercial banks are the dominant financial institutions in the monetary system.

■ **FIGURE 26.6**
The Deposits Behind M1 and M2

(a) M1

(b) M2

Deposits in commercial banks account for a much larger percentage of the nation's money than do the deposits in thrift institutions and money market funds.

Source of data: Federal Reserve.

■ The Economic Functions of Monetary Institutions

The institutions of the monetary system earn their incomes by performing four economic functions that people and businesses value and are willing to pay for:

- Create liquidity
- Lower the costs of lending and borrowing
- Pool risks
- Make payments

Create Liquidity

Liquid asset
An asset that can be easily, and with certainty, converted into money—converted into the means of payment.

A **liquid asset** is an asset that can be easily and with certainty converted into money—converted into the means of payment. Some bank* deposits *are* means of payment. Other deposits can be converted into the means of payment instantly and safely—they are liquid assets.

A bank creates liquid assets by borrowing short and lending long. Borrowing short means accepting deposits and standing ready to repay them whenever the depositor requests the funds. Lending long means making loan commitments for a long term and not unexpectedly calling in a loan.

For example, a bank might have accepted $1 million in checkable deposits that could be withdrawn at any time and loaned $1 million to a startup Coffee Shop business for an agreed-upon 5 years. The bank earns part of its income by being able to charge a higher interest rate on a 5-year loan than the interest rate it must pay on a checkable account.

Lower Costs

Banks lower the costs of lending and borrowing funds. People with funds to lend can easily find a bank and make a deposit. Because banks offer a range of types of deposit, it is easy to find the type of deposit that best matches the plans of the depositor.

People who want to borrow can do so by using the facilities offered by banks. Business and personal loans can be tailored to match the cash flows of borrowers. And consumers can obtain instant loans by using credit card facilities.

Again, banks make profits because people are willing to make deposits at much lower interest rates than those available to the banks on their loans. Interest rates on credit card loans are especially high and so are profitable for the banks.

Pool Risks

Lending funds, as banks do, is risky. Some loans don't get repaid. By lending to a large number of businesses and individuals, a bank lowers the average risk it faces. The bank knows the odds of a loan not being repaid like a lottery operator knows the odds of having to pay out on a winning number. The lottery operator offers odds that ensure it ends up with a profit. Similarly, the market for bank loans determines an interest rate that ensures that the amount earned on the loans that do get repaid is sufficiently high to pay for the losses on the ones that don't get repaid.

---

*We'll use the term "bank" to mean any institution that accepts deposits when there is no gain from distinguishing among these institutions.

Make Payments

Bank deposits are money because they are a means of payment—they can be transferred from one person or business to another at low cost. The banks provide the payments system that enables these transfers of ownership to occur.

The check-clearing system is the main mechanism provided by the banks. Think of this system as a giant delivery service like FedEx that, instead of moving packages overnight to anywhere in the nation, moves checks and calculates the amounts that each bank must pay or receive based on the totals of the checks paid by and received by their customers. The banks collect a fee for these check-clearing activities.

The credit card payments system is another major payments mechanism operated by the banks. When you buy a new pair of jeans and the checkout clerk swipes your Visa card, a signal goes to the bank that issued your card to get approval for and place a hold on the amount that you are about to spend. Later that day, when the jeans store has some spare time, it transmits the accumulated day's credit card information from its card reader to its own bank and gets its account credited for the day's takings. At that same moment, a message goes from the jeans store's bank to your card-issuing bank (and the banks of all its other customers) that places the charge for your purchase on your credit card account (and likewise for the other customers). All these electronic transactions are performed automatically. The banks collect fees for all these credit card payment activities.

EYE ON THE GLOBAL ECONOMY

Big Banks

Before 1997, U.S. banks were not permitted to operate in more than one state. In 1997, that restriction was lifted, and since then, bank mergers and failures have decreased the number of banks from 13,000 to 8,100.

The largest U.S. banks are huge. But only one of them, Citigroup, made the world's top 10 list in 2004.

Japan has three of the top 10 and France has two. Switzerland, Germany, the United Kingdom, and Netherlands have one each.

Bar chart: Total assets (billions of U.S. dollars)

Bank	
Mizuho Financial Group, Japan	
Citigroup, United States	
UBS, Switzerland	
HSBC, United Kingdom	
Deutsche Bank, Germany	
Crédit Agricole, France	
Mitsubishi Tokyo Financial Group, Japan	
BNP Paribas, France	
ING Groep, Netherlands	
Sumitomo Mitsui Financial Group, Japan	

Total assets (billions of U.S. dollars)

SOURCE OF DATA: *Global Finance Magazine,* October 2004.

2 Describe the monetary system and explain the functions of banks and other monetary institutions.

Practice Problems 26.2

1. What are the institutions that make up the monetary system?

2. What is a bank's balancing act?

3. A bank has the following deposits and assets: $320 in checkable deposits, $896 in savings deposits, $840 in small time deposits, $990 in loans to businesses, $400 in outstanding credit card balances, $634 in government securities, $2 in currency, and $30 in its reserve account at the Fed. Calculate the bank's
   a. Total deposits
   b. Deposits that are part of M1
   c. Deposits that are part of M2
   d. Loans
   e. Securities
   f. Reserves

Exercises 26.2

1. Explain how a bank makes a profit.

2. A savings and loan association has $550 in checkable deposits, $1,600 in home loans, $900 in savings deposits, $600 in government securities, $800 in time deposits, $50 in currency, and no deposit at the Fed. Calculate

   a. Total deposits
   b. Deposits that are part of M1
   c. Deposits that are part of M2
   d. Loans
   e. Reserves

3. On which items does the S&L in exercise 2 pay interest (borrow short) and on which items does it receive interest (lend long)?

Solutions to Practice Problems 26.2

1. The institutions that make up the monetary system are the Fed, commercial banks, thrift institutions, and money market funds.

2. A bank makes a profit by borrowing from depositors at a low interest rate and lending at a higher interest rate. The bank earns no interest on reserves, but it must hold enough reserves to meet withdrawals. The bank's balancing act is to balance the risk of loans against the safety of reserves.

3a. Total deposits are $320 + $896 + $840 = $2,056.
3b. Deposits that are part of M1 are checkable deposits, $320.
3c. Deposits that are part of M2 include all deposits, $2,056.
3d. Loans are $990 + $400 = $1,390.
3e. Securities are $634.
3f. Reserves are $30 + $2 = $32.

26.3 THE FEDERAL RESERVE SYSTEM

The **Federal Reserve System**, which is organized into 12 Federal Reserve districts shown in Figure 26.7, is the central bank of the United States. A **central bank** is a public authority that provides banking services to banks and regulates financial institutions and markets. A central bank does not provide banking services to businesses and individual citizens. Its only customers are banks such as Bank of America and Citibank and the U.S. government.

The Fed conducts the nation's **monetary policy**, which means that it adjusts the quantity of money in the economy. The Fed's goals are to keep inflation in check, maintain full employment, moderate the business cycle, and contribute toward achieving economic growth. Complete success in the pursuit of these goals is impossible, and the Fed's more modest goal is to improve the performance of the economy and to move it closer to the goals than a hands-off approach would achieve. There is a range of opinion on whether the Fed succeeds in improving economic performance.

■ The Structure of the Federal Reserve

The key elements in the structure of the Federal Reserve are

- The Board of Governors
- The Regional Federal Reserve Banks
- The Federal Open Market Committee

Federal Reserve System
The central bank of the United States.

Central bank
A public authority that provides banking services to banks and regulates financial institutions and markets.

Monetary policy
Adjusting the quantity of money in the economy.

FIGURE 26.7

The Federal Reserve Districts

myeconlab

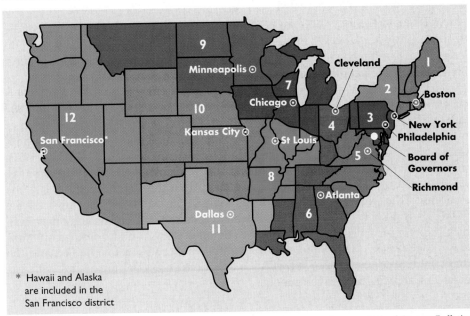

The nation is divided into 12 Federal Reserve districts, each having a Federal Reserve Bank. (Some of the larger districts also have branch banks.) The Board of Governors of the Federal Reserve System is located in Washington, D.C.

* Hawaii and Alaska
are included in the
San Francisco district

SOURCE: *Federal Reserve Bulletin.*

The Board of Governors

The Board of Governors has seven members, who are appointed by the President of the United States and confirmed by the Senate, each for a 14-year term. The terms are staggered so that one seat on the board becomes vacant every two years. The President appoints one of the board members as chairman for a term of four years, which is renewable.

The Regional Federal Reserve Banks

There are 12 regional Federal Reserve Banks, one for each of 12 Federal Reserve districts shown in Figure 26.7. Each regional Federal Reserve Bank has nine directors, three of whom are appointed by the Board of Governors and six of whom are elected by the commercial banks in the Federal Reserve district. The directors of the regional Federal Reserve Banks appoint the bank's president, and the Board of Governors approves this appointment.

The Federal Reserve Bank of New York (known as the New York Fed) occupies a special place because it implements some of the Fed's most important policy decisions.

The Federal Open Market Committee

Federal Open Market Committee
The Fed's main policy-making committee.

The **Federal Open Market Committee** (FOMC) is the Fed's main policy-making committee. The FOMC consists of the following twelve members:

- The chairman and the other six members of the Board of Governors
- The president of the Federal Reserve Bank of New York
- Four presidents of the other regional Federal Reserve Banks (on a yearly rotating basis)

The FOMC meets approximately every six weeks to review the state of the economy and to decide the actions to be carried out by the New York Fed.

■ The Fed's Power Center

Power in the Fed resides with the Board of Governors. But it is the chairman of the Board of Governors—today, Ben Bernanke, a former Princeton University economics professor—who has the largest influence on the Fed's monetary policy actions. Some remarkable people have preceded Ben Bernanke as Fed chairmen.

Alan Greenspan was chairman of the Board of Governors from 1987 to his retirement on January 31, 2006. He was appointed by President Reagan in 1987 and reappointed by each successive president. Alan Greenspan succeeded another influential chairman, Paul Volcker, who was appointed in 1979 by President Carter and reappointed in 1983 by President Reagan. Volcker ended the 1970s inflation but helped to create one of the most severe post–World War II recessions.

The chairman's power and influence stem from three sources. First, it is the chairman who controls the agenda and who dominates the meetings of the FOMC. Second, day-to-day contact with a large staff of economists and other technical experts provides the chairman with detailed background briefings on monetary policy issues. Third, the chairman is the spokesperson for the Fed and the main point of contact of the Fed with the President and government and with foreign central banks and governments.

FOMC meeting.

■ The Fed's Policy Tools

The Federal Reserve has many responsibilities, but we'll examine its single most important one: regulating the amount of money floating around in the United States. How does the Fed control the quantity of money? It does so by adjusting the reserves of the banking system. Also, by adjusting the reserves of the banking system and standing ready to make loans to banks, the Fed is able to prevent bank failures. The Fed uses three main policy tools to achieve its objectives:

- Required reserve ratios
- Discount rate
- Open market operations

Required Reserve Ratios

Banks hold reserves. These reserves are currency in the institutions' vaults and ATMs plus deposits held with other banks or with the Fed itself. Banks and thrifts are required to hold a minimum percentage of deposits as reserves. This minimum percentage is known as a *required reserve ratio*. The Fed determines a required reserve ratio for each type of deposit. In 2005, banks were required to hold minimum reserves equal to 3 percent of checkable deposits from $7.0 million to $47.6 million and 10 percent of these deposits in excess of this amount. The required reserves on other types of deposits were zero—see Table 26.2.

Discount Rate

The **discount rate** is the interest rate at which the Fed stands ready to lend reserves to commercial banks. A change in the discount rate begins with a proposal to the FOMC by at least one of the 12 Federal Reserve Banks. If the FOMC agrees that a change is required, it proposes the change to the Board of Governors for its approval.

TABLE 26.2 REQUIRED RESERVE RATIOS

Type of deposit	Percent
Checkable deposits from $7.0 million to $47.6 million	3
Checkable deposits above $47.6 million	10
All other deposits	0

SOURCE OF DATA: Federal Reserve.

Discount rate
The interest rate at which the Fed stands ready to lend reserves to commercial banks.

Open market operation
The purchase or sale of government securities—U.S. Treasury bills and bonds—by the Federal Reserve in the open market.

Open Market Operations

An **open market operation** is the purchase or sale of government securities—U.S. Treasury bills and bonds—by the Federal Reserve in the open market. When the Fed conducts an open market operation, it makes a transaction with a bank or some other business but it does not transact with the federal government.

To understand how the Fed's policy tools work, you need to know about the monetary base.

■ The Monetary Base

Monetary base
The sum of coins, Federal Reserve notes, and banks' reserves at the Fed.

The **monetary base** is the sum of coins, Federal Reserve notes, and banks' reserves at the Fed. The monetary base is so called because it acts like a base that supports the nation's money. The larger the monetary base, the greater is the quantity of money that it can support. Chapter 27 explains how a change in the monetary base leads to a change in the quantity of money.

In December 2004, the monetary base was $770 billion. Figure 26.8 shows how this amount was distributed among its three components: Coins were $35 billion; banks' deposits at the Fed were $25 billion; and the bulk of the monetary base, $710 billion, was made up of Federal Reserve notes.

Federal Reserve notes and banks' reserves at the Fed are *liabilities* of the Fed. The Fed's *assets* are

• Gold and deposits in other central banks
• U.S. government securities
• Loans to banks

■ FIGURE 26.8
The Monetary Base and Its Composition

The monetary base is the sum of banks' reserves at the Fed, coins, and Federal Reserve notes (bills). Most of the monetary base consists of Federal Reserve notes.

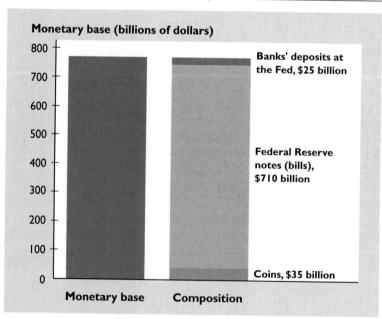

SOURCE OF DATA: Federal Reserve.

The Fed holds gold that it could sell if it needed or wished to. It also has deposits in other central banks such as the Bank of Japan and the Bank of England that it can withdraw if it needs to. The Fed holds U.S. government securities that it can sell. Finally, the Fed makes loans to banks, which it can call in. (These loans are usually very small). The Fed charges the banks the discount rate on these loans.

How the Fed's Policy Tools Work

The Fed's policy tools work by changing either the demand for or the supply of the monetary base, which in turn changes the interest rate.

By increasing the required reserve ratio, the Fed can force the banks to hold a larger quantity of monetary base. By raising the discount rate, the Fed can make it more costly for the banks to borrow reserves—borrow monetary base. And by selling securities in the open market, the Fed can decrease the monetary base. All of these actions lead to an increase in the interest rate.

Similarly, by decreasing the required reserve ratio, the Fed can permit the banks to hold a smaller quantity of monetary base. By lowering the discount rate, the Fed can make it less costly for the banks to borrow monetary base. And by buying securities in the open market, the Fed can increase the monetary base. All of these actions lead to a decrease in the interest rate.

Of these policy tools, open market operations are the most important and we learn more about how an open market operation works in the next chapter.

REALITY CHECK

Money in YOUR Life

Imagine a world without money in which you must barter for everything you buy. What kind of items would you have available for these trades? Would you keep some stocks of items that you know lots of people are willing to accept? Would you really be bartering, or would you be using a commodity as money? How much longer would it take you to conduct all the transactions of a normal day?

Now think about your own holdings of money today. How much money do you have in your pocket or purse? How much do you have in the bank? How does the money you hold change over the course of a month? Of the money you're holding, which items are part of M1 and which are part of M2? Are all the items that you hold in M2 means of payment?

3 **Describe the functions of the Federal Reserve System.**

Practice Problems 26.3

1. What is the Fed and what is the FOMC?

2. What is the Fed's power center and the Fed's main policy tools?

3. What is the monetary base?

4. Suppose that at the end of December 2007, the monetary base in the United States was $700 billion, Federal Reserve notes were $650 billion, and banks' reserves at the Fed were $20 billion. Calculate the quantity of coins.

Exercises 26.3

1. What is a central bank and what is the central bank in the United States?

2. Suppose that in September 2007, the monetary base in the United States was $750 billion, Federal Reserve notes were $630 billion, and the quantity of coins was $40 billion. What were the commercial banks' deposits at the Fed?

3. Suppose that in December 2007, the monetary base in Canada was $85 billion, Bank of Canada notes were $75 billion, and the quantity of coins was $3 billion. What were the reserve deposits of the Canadian banks at the Bank of Canada?

Solutions to Practice Problems 26.3

1. The Federal Reserve (Fed) is the central bank in the United States. The central bank in the United States is a public authority that provides banking services to banks and the U.S. government and that regulates the quantity of money and the monetary system. The FOMC is the Federal Open Market Committee. The FOMC is the Fed's main policy-making committee.

2. The Fed's power center is the chairman of the Board of Governors. In 2005, that chairman is Alan Greenspan. The Fed's main policy tools are required reserve ratios, the discount rate, and open market operations.

3. The monetary base is the sum of coins, Federal Reserve notes (dollar bills), and banks' reserves at the Fed.

4. To calculate the quantity of coins, we use the definition of the monetary base: coins plus Federal Reserve notes plus banks' reserves at the Fed.

   Quantity of coins = Monetary base − Federal Reserve notes − Banks' reserves at the Fed.

   So at the end of December 2005,

   Quantity of coins = $700 billion − $650 billion − $20 billion
                     = $30 billion.

CHAPTER CHECKPOINT

Key Points

1 **Define money and describe its functions.**

- Money is anything that serves as a generally accepted means of payment.
- Money serves as a medium of exchange, a unit of account, and a store of value.
- M1 consists of currency, travelers' checks, and checkable deposits. M2 consists of M1 plus savings deposits, small time deposits, and money market funds.

2 **Describe the monetary system and explain the functions of banks and other monetary institutions.**

- Commercial banks, S&Ls, savings banks, credit unions, and money market funds are financial institutions whose deposits are money.
- Banks borrow short term and lend long term and make a profit on the spread between the interest rates that they pay and receive.
- Banks lend most of the funds they receive as deposits and hold only a small amount as reserves.
- Banks can borrow and lend reserves in the federal funds market.

3 **Describe the functions of the Federal Reserve System.**

- The Federal Reserve is the central bank of the United States.
- The Fed influences the economy by setting the required reserve ratio for banks, by setting the discount rate, and by open market operations.

Key Terms

Barter, 649
Central bank, 663
Commercial bank, 656
Credit union, 658
Currency, 650
Discount rate, 665
Electronic cash (e-cash), 652
Electronic check (e-check), 652
Excess reserves, 657
Federal funds rate, 657

Federal Open Market Committee, 664
Federal Reserve System, 663
Fiat money, 650
Liquid asset, 660
M1, 653
M2, 653
Means of payment, 648
Medium of exchange, 649
Monetary base, 666
Monetary policy, 663

Monetary system, 656
Money, 648
Money market fund, 658
Open market operation, 666
Required reserve ratio, 657
Reserves, 657
Savings and loan association, 658
Savings bank, 658
Store of value, 649
Unit of account, 649

Exercises

1. What is money? Would you classify any of the following items as money?
   a. Store coupons for cat food
   b. A $100 Amazon.com gift certificate
   c. An S&L saving deposit
   d. Frequent Flier Miles
   e. Credit available on your Visa card
   f. The dollar coins that a coin collector owns
   g. Postage stamps issued to commemorate the 2002 Winter Olympic Games

2. What are the three vital functions that money performs? Which of the following items perform some but not all of these functions, and which perform all of these functions? Which of the items are money?
   a. A blank check
   b. A checkable deposit at the Bank of America
   c. A dime
   d. An antique clock
   e. Plastic sheets used to make Visa cards
   f. The coins in the Fed's museum
   g. Government bonds

3. Monica transfers $10,000 from her savings account at the Bank of Alaska to her money market fund. What is the immediate change in M1 and M2?

4. Naomi buys $1,000 worth of American Express travelers' checks and charges the purchase to her American Express card. What is the immediate change in M1 and M2?

5. Terry takes $100 from his checking account and deposits the $100 in his savings account. What is the immediate change in M1 and M2?

6. Vincenzo goes shopping. First, he visits an ATM, where he gets $200 from his savings account. Then he visits a clothing store, where he buys a shirt for $50 using his Visa card. At lunchtime, he meets Donna, his Italian girlfriend, who has just arrived from Rome and has only euros (the money of Italy) in her purse. Donna uses some of her euros to buy $100 from Vincenzo. Donna buys lunch and pays with the $100 that she got from Vincenzo. Did any of the transactions done by Vincenzo and Donna change the quantity of money?

7. In December 2002, banks in Australia had deposits of $500 billion, a required reserve ratio of 4 percent, and no excess reserves. The banks had $15 billion in currency. How much did the banks have in deposits at the Reserve Bank of Australia (the Australian central bank)?

8. Suppose that in December 2005, the Bank of Canada (the central bank of Canada) had
   Commercial banks' deposits at the Bank of Canada: $3 billion
   Government securities and other assets: $14 billion
   Currency outside the Bank of Canada: $11 billion

The Canadian commercial banks had
Checkable deposits: $400 billion
Savings deposits and time deposits: $600 billion
Currency in their vaults: $1 billion.
Calculate
a. The banks' reserves
b. The monetary base
c. M1
d. M2

9. In Mexico in January 2004, the Banco de México (the central bank of Mexico) reported that notes and coins held by individuals and businesses were 175 billion pesos. The Mexican banks had checkable deposits of 418 billion pesos and savings deposits and time deposits of 1,782 billion pesos. Currency inside the banks was 28 billion pesos. The Mexican banks had deposits at the Banco de México of 186 billion pesos. Calculate
a. The banks' reserves
b. The monetary base
c. M1
d. M2

10. What are the main differences and similarities among commercial banks, thrift institutions, and money market funds? How do these institutions earn a profit? What are the main risks they face? How do they manage their exposure to risk?

11. List the policy tools of the Fed and sketch the way in which each tool works to change the quantity of money.

Critical Thinking

12. The President of the United States has no formal authority over the Federal Reserve. In contrast, in some countries, the government directs the central bank and decides what its interest rate policy shall be. Provide some reasons why the central bank should be independent of the government as it is in the United States.

13. Suppose that e-cash issued by private online banks becomes so popular that it completely replaces physical cash and no one has any use for notes issued by the Fed and coins issued by the U.S. mint. What role do you think the Fed could play in such a world?

14. If banks are required to hold reserves at the Fed, doesn't that mean that the required reserves are not really reserves at all and that the only true reserves the banks hold are their excess reserves?

Web Exercises

Use the links on MyEconLab to work the following exercises.

15. Visit the Web site of the Federal Reserve. For the most recent week,
    a. What is M1?
    b. What is M2?
    c. What is the monetary base?
    d. What is the percentage increase in M1 over the past year?
    e. What is the percentage increase in M2 over the past year?
    f. What is the percentage increase in the monetary base over the past year?

16. Visit the page of the Federal Reserve Web site that provides data on the assets and liabilities of the commercial banks in the United States. For the most recent week and the same week a year earlier,
    a. What is the total amount of deposits?
    b. What is the total amount of cash assets?
    c. What is the total amount of loans?
    d. What is the percentage increase in deposits over the past year?
    e. What is the percentage increase in cash assets over the past year?
    f. What is the percentage increase in loans over the past year?

17. Visit the Web site of the Federal Reserve. For the most recent week,
    a. What is the total amount of reserves?
    b. What are the total borrowed reserves as a percentage of total reserves?
    c. What are excess reserves as a percentage of total reserves?

18. Visit the Open Market Operations page of the Federal Reserve Web site.
    a. What is the current target for the federal funds rate?
    b. How has the target for the federal funds rate changed over the past year?
    c. What do you think the Fed has been trying to do with the changes in the federal funds rate over the past year?

Money Creation and Control

CHAPTER CHECKLIST

When you have completed your study of this chapter,
you will be able to

1. Explain how banks create money by making loans.

2. Explain how the Fed influences the quantity of money.

During the Civil War, up to one half of the currency circulating in the United States was counterfeit. Counterfeiting U.S. dollars has again become a serious problem with the arrival of high-quality, low-cost color printers. The people who make imitation dollar bills are serious criminals, and the Counterfeit Division of the Secret Service works hard to detect and punish them.

Yet every day, banks create millions of dollars' worth of money. And their actions are perfectly legal. In this chapter, you're going to learn how banks create money by making loans.

You're going to see how money gets created and how the Fed influences its quantity. Understanding these processes is crucial to understanding how inflation occurs and how it can be kept under control. It is also crucial to understanding how the Fed tries to smooth the business cycle.

First, we'll study the links between the banks' reserves, the quantity of loans that banks make, and the quantity of deposits that they create. Then we'll learn how the Fed uses open market operations and other tools to influence the quantity of money.

27.1 HOW BANKS CREATE MONEY

Banks* create money out of thin air! But this doesn't mean that they have smoke-filled back rooms in which counterfeiters are busily working. Remember, most money is bank deposits, not currency. Banks create deposits, and they do so by making loans. But they cannot create any amount of money they wish. The amount of deposits they can create is limited by their reserves.

■ Creating a Bank

The easiest way to see how banks create money is to work through the process of creating a bank. Suppose that you and your friends decide to create the Virtual College Bank, an Internet bank that specializes in banking services for college students. You will need to go through the following eight steps:

- Obtain a charter to operate a commercial bank
- Raise some financial capital
- Buy some equipment and computer programs
- Accept deposits
- Establish a reserve account at a Federal Reserve Bank
- Clear checks
- Buy government securities
- Make loans

Obtaining a Charter

Your first task is to obtain a charter to operate a commercial bank. You apply to the Comptroller of the Currency for this charter and establish a federally chartered bank. (If you wanted to establish a state commercial bank, you would apply to your state treasurer's office.)

Raising Financial Capital

Balance sheet
A statement that summarizes assets (amounts owned) and liabilities (amounts owed).

Your next task is to get some funds. You figure that you can open your bank with $200,000, so Virtual College Bank creates 2,000 shares, each worth $100, and sells these shares in your local community. Your bank now has a **balance sheet**—a statement that summarizes its assets and liabilities. The bank's assets are what it owns, and its liabilities are the claims against it, or what it owes, and its owners' equity. Table 27.1 shows your new bank's first balance sheet.

■ **TABLE 27.1**
Virtual College Bank's Balance Sheet #1

Assets		Liabilities	
Cash	$200,000	Owners' equity	$200,000

You are now ready to take your third step.

---

*In this chapter, we'll use the term "bank" to include commercial banks and thrift institutions whose deposits are part of the money supply.

EYE ON THE PAST

The "Invention" of Banking

Goldsmiths and their customers stumbled upon a brilliant idea that led to the creation of the first banks. You will gain useful insights into modern banks and the way they create money by looking at these early banks.

Because gold is valuable and easy to steal, the goldsmiths of sixteenth century Europe had well-guarded safes in which to keep their own gold. They also rented space in their safes to artisans and others who wanted to put their gold in safekeeping. The goldsmiths issued a receipt to the owners of the gold entitling them to reclaim their "deposits" on demand. These receipts were similar to the coat check token you get at a theater or museum.

Isabella has a gold receipt that shows that she has deposited 100 ounces of gold with Samuel Goldsmith. She is going to use her gold to buy some land from Henry. Isabella can make this transaction in one of two ways: She can visit Samuel,

collect her gold, and hand the gold to Henry. Or she can give Henry her gold receipt, which will then enable Henry to claim the 100 ounces of gold from Samuel Goldsmith.

It is obviously much more convenient to pass the receipt to Henry. It is a simpler and safer transaction. When Henry wants to use the gold to buy something, he too can pass the receipt on to someone else.

So Samuel Goldsmith's gold receipt is circulating as a means of payment. It is money!

After some years, Samuel notices that the gold that people have placed in his safekeeping never leaves his vault. The receipts circulate, and the gold simply sits in the safe.

Samuel realizes that he can lend people gold receipts and charge them interest on the receipts. So he writes some receipts for gold that he doesn't have and lends these receipts.

After some further years, when many goldsmiths are doing what Samuel is doing, they begin to compete with each other for gold deposits, and instead of charging rent

to gold owners, they start to pay interest on gold deposits.

Samuel and his fellow goldsmiths have made the transition from being goldsmiths to being bankers.

As long as they don't issue too many gold receipts, they will always be able to honor requests from depositors who wish to reclaim their gold.

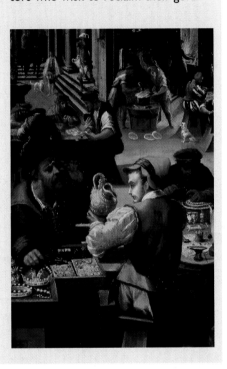

Buying Equipment

You buy some office equipment, a server, banking database software, and a high-speed Internet connection. These items cost you $200,000. Table 27.2 shows your bank's new balance sheet.

■ **TABLE 27.2**

Virtual College Bank's Balance Sheet #2

Assets		Liabilities	
Cash	$0		
Equipment	$200,000	Owners' equity	$200,000

Accepting Deposits

You are now ready to start accepting deposits. You pass the word around that you are offering the best terms available and the lowest charges on checkable deposits. Deposits begin to roll in. After a hectic day of business, you have accepted $120,000 of deposits. Table 27.3 shows Virtual College Bank's new balance sheet.

■ **TABLE 27.3**

Virtual College Bank's Balance Sheet #3

Assets		Liabilities	
Cash	$120,000	Checkable deposits	$120,000
Equipment	$200,000	Owners' equity	$200,000

The deposits at Virtual College Bank are now part of the money supply. But the quantity of money in the economy has not increased. People have deposited either currency or checks drawn on other banks. To keep the story simple, we'll suppose that all these deposits are currency. So currency outside the banks has decreased by $120,000, and checkable deposits have increased by $120,000.

Establishing a Reserve Account

Now that Virtual College Bank has deposits, it must establish a reserve account at its local Federal Reserve Bank. We'll suppose that your virtual bank is in College Station, Texas, in the Dallas Federal Reserve District. Virtual College Bank now opens an account at the Dallas Fed and deposits in that account all its cash. Table 27.4 shows Virtual College Bank's new balance sheet.

■ **TABLE 27.4**

Virtual College Bank's Balance Sheet #4

Assets		Liabilities	
Cash	$0		
Reserves at the Dallas Fed	$120,000	Checkable deposits	$120,000
Equipment	$200,000	Owners' equity	$200,000

Reserves: Actual and Required   You saw in Chapter 26 that banks don't keep $100 in bills for every $100 that people have deposited with them. In fact, a typical bank today has reserves of a bit less than $1 for every $100 of deposits. But there's no need for panic. These reserve levels are adequate for ordinary business needs.

The proportion of a bank's total deposits that are held in reserves is called the *reserve ratio*. Virtual College Bank's reserves are $120,000 and deposits are $120,000, so its reserve ratio is 100 percent.

The *required reserve ratio* is the ratio of reserves to deposits that banks are required, by regulation, to hold. We'll suppose that the required reserve ratio for virtual banks operated by college students is 25 percent, a much higher percentage than that for U.S. commercial banks (see Chapter 26, p. 665).

A bank's *required reserves* are equal to its deposits multiplied by the required reserve ratio. So Virtual College Bank's required reserves are

$$\text{Required reserves} = \$120,000 \times 25 \div 100 = \$30,000.$$

Actual reserves minus required reserves are *excess reserves*. Virtual College Bank's excess reserves are

$$\text{Excess reserves} = \$120,000 - \$30,000 = \$90,000.$$

Whenever banks have excess reserves, they are able to make loans. But before Virtual College Bank takes that step, it needs to learn how to clear checks.

Clearing Checks

Virtual College Bank's depositors want to be able to make and receive payments by check. So when Virtual College depositor Jay writes a check for $20,000 to buy some computers from Hal's PCs, which has a checkable deposit at the First American Bank, funds must move from Jay's account at your bank to Hal's account at First American. In the process, Virtual College loses reserves and First American gains reserves. Figure 27.1 tracks the balance sheet changes that occur.

When Hal's PCs banks Jay's check, First American sends an electronic image of the check to the Dallas Fed for collection. The Dallas Fed increases First American's reserves (blue arrow) and decreases Virtual College's reserves (red arrow) by $20,000—see Figure 27.1(a). First American now has an extra $20,000 in its reserves at the Dallas Fed, and it increases Hal's PCs' checkable deposit by $20,000. First American's assets and liabilities have both increased by $20,000 in Figure 27.1(b). The Dallas Fed sends an electronic image of the cleared check to Virtual College, which decreases Jay's checkable deposit by $20,000. Virtual College's assets and liabilities have both decreased by $20,000 in Figure 27.1(c).

■ FIGURE 27.1

Clearing a Check

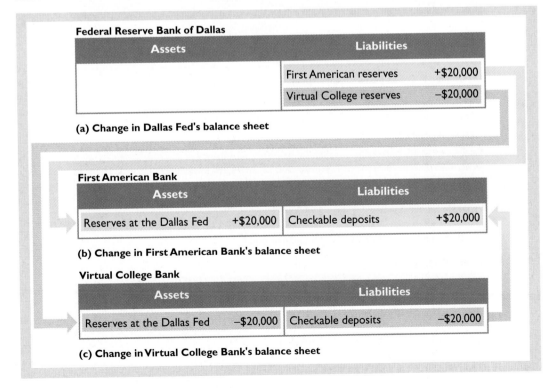

(a) First American sends a $20,000 check for collection to the Dallas Fed. The Dallas Fed increases First American's reserves by $20,000 and decreases Virtual College's reserves by $20,000.

(b) First American increases Hal's PCs' checkable deposit by $20,000. First American's assets and liabilities have both increased by $20,000.

(c) Virtual College decreases Jay's checkable deposit by $20,000. Virtual College's assets and liabilities have both decreased by $20,000.

The quantity of money is unaffected by these transactions. Checkable deposits have increased at First American and decreased at Virtual College, but total deposits are unchanged. Total bank reserves are also unaffected. First American's reserves have increased and Virtual College's reserves have decreased by the same amount.

Virtual College Bank is now ready to use some of its reserves to earn an income. It buys some government securities.

Buying Government Securities

Government securities provide Virtual College with an income and a safe asset that is easily converted back into reserves when necessary. Suppose that Virtual College decides to buy $60,000 worth of government securities. On the same day, First American decides to sell $60,000 of government securities to Virtual College. In reality, a bond broker will match the First American sale with Virtual College's purchase.

Figure 27.2 tracks the effects of this transaction on the balance sheets of the two banks and the Dallas Fed. Virtual College gives First American a check for $60,000, and First American transfers the government bonds to Virtual College (blue-to-red arrow). First American sends the check to the Dallas Fed for collection. The Dallas

---

FIGURE 27.2

Making Interbank Loans and Buying Government Securities

(a) Virtual College buys $60,000 worth of government securities from First American and pays by check. The Dallas Fed increases First American's reserves by $60,000 and decreases Virtual College's reserves by the same amount.

(b) First American's reserves have increased and its government securities have decreased by $60,000.

(c) Virtual College's reserves have decreased and its government securities have increased by the $60,000.

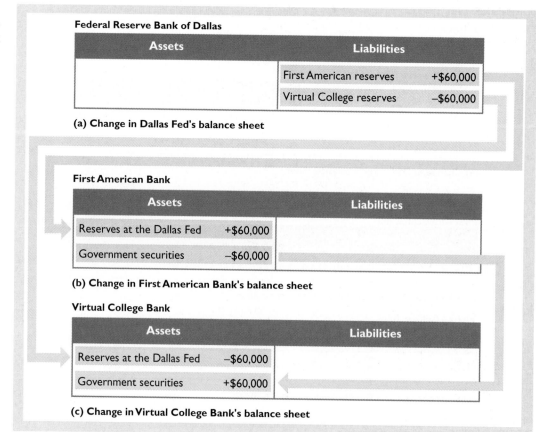

(a) Change in Dallas Fed's balance sheet

(b) Change in First American Bank's balance sheet

(c) Change in Virtual College Bank's balance sheet

Fed increases First American's reserves by $60,000 (blue arrow) and decreases Virtual College's reserves (red arrow) by the same amount in Figure 27.2(a).

First American's reserves have increased and its government securities have decreased by the same $60,000 in Figure 27.2(b). Virtual College's reserves have decreased and its government securities have increased by the same $60,000 in Figure 27.2(c).

After all the transactions we've just followed in Figures 27.1 and 27.2, Virtual College's balance sheet looks like that in Table 27.5.

TABLE 27.5

Virtual College Bank's Balance Sheet #5

Assets		Liabilities	
Reserves at the Dallas Fed	$40,000	Checkable deposits	$100,000
Government securities	$60,000	Owners' equity	$200,000
Equipment	$200,000		
Total assets	$300,000	Total liabilities	$300,000

With deposits of $100,000 and a required reserve ratio of 25 percent, Virtual College must hold a minimum of $25,000 in reserves. Because it currently has $40,000 in reserves, Virtual College can make some loans.

Making Loans

With reserves of $40,000 and required reserves of $25,000, Virtual College has excess reserves of $15,000. So the bank decides to make loans of this amount. Table 27.6 shows the bank's balance sheet on the day the bank makes these loans. Loans of $15,000 are added to the bank's assets. Loans are an asset to the bank because the borrower is committed to repaying the loan on an agreed-upon schedule. The bank places the $15,000 loaned in the checkable deposit accounts of the borrowers. So the bank's checkable deposits increase by $15,000 to $115,000.

TABLE 27.6

Virtual College Bank's Balance Sheet #6

Assets		Liabilities	
Reserves at the Dallas Fed	$40,000	Checkable deposits	$115,000
Government securities	$60,000	Owners' equity	$200,000
Loans	$15,000		
Equipment	$200,000		
Total assets	$315,000	Total liabilities	$315,000

The bank has now created some money. Checkable deposits have increased by the amount of the loans, so the quantity of money has increased by $15,000. And although Virtual College has made loans equal to its excess reserves of $15,000, it still has those reserves! Because its deposits have increased, its required reserves have also increased. They are now 25 percent of $115,000, or $28,750. So the bank now has excess reserves of $11,250.

Before you get too excited and decide to lend another $11,250, let's see what happens when the borrowers of the $15,000 that you've just loaned start to spend their loans.

Spending a Loan To spend their loans, the borrowers write checks on their checkable deposits. Let's assume that they spend the entire $15,000. Most likely, the people to whom these checks are paid do not bank at Virtual College. That's what we'll assume. So when these checks are cleared, transactions like those that we described above take place. The receiving banks send the checks to the Dallas Fed for collection. The Fed increases the reserves of the receiving banks by $15,000 and decreases the reserves of Virtual College by $15,000. Virtual College's balance sheet now looks like that in Table 27.7.

■ TABLE 27.7

Virtual College Bank's Balance Sheet #7

Assets		Liabilities	
Reserves at the Dallas Fed	$25,000	Checkable deposits	$100,000
Government securities	$60,000	Owners' equity	$200,000
Loans	$15,000		
Equipment	$200,000		
Total assets	$300,000	Total liabilities	$300,000

Both reserves and deposits have decreased by $15,000 because this amount has been paid to people with accounts in other banks. If some of the checks drawn were paid to customers of Virtual College, deposits and reserves would have fallen by less than the full $15,000 and the bank would still have some excess reserves. But in the situation shown in Table 27.7, the bank is fully loaned—its reserves are just sufficient to meet the required reserve ratio.

But the banks that received the deposits that Virtual College has lost have also received reserves. These banks now have excess reserves, so they can make some loans. And these loans will create some more money. Also, when Virtual College bought government securities from First American, the reserves of First American increased by $60,000. So other banks now have reserves of $75,000 that they did not have before that they could now lend. So yet more money can be created.

If you told the loan officer at your own bank that she creates money, she wouldn't believe you. People who work in banks see themselves as lending the money they receive from others, but (unless they've studied economics) they don't see the entire process, so they don't realize that they create money. But in fact, even though each bank lends only what it receives, the banking system creates money. To see how, let's see what happens in the entire banking system when one bank receives some new reserves.

■ The Limits to Money Creation

Figure 27.3 is going to keep track of what is happening in the process of money creation by a banking system in which each bank has a required reserve ratio of 25 percent. We'll start the process off with every bank holding exactly its required reserves. Then Al Capone, after years of shady dealing, decides to go to school. He takes $100,000 of notes from under his mattress and deposits them at Virtual College Bank. Virtual College now has $100,000 of new deposits and $100,000 of new reserves. With a required reserve ratio of 25 percent, the bank's required reserves are $25,000. So the bank makes a loan of $75,000 to Amy. Then Amy writes a check for $75,000 to buy a copy-shop franchise from Barb. At this point,

Virtual College has a new deposit of $100,000, a new loan of $75,000, and new reserves of $25,000. You can see this situation in Figure 27.3.

For Virtual College, that is the end of the story. But it's not the end of the story for the banking system. Barb deposits her check for $75,000 in First American, where deposits and reserves increase by $75,000. First American puts 25 percent of its increase in deposits ($18,750) into reserves and lends $56,250 to Bob. And Bob writes a check to Carl to pay off a business loan.

Figure 27.3 shows the state of play at the end of round 2. Total bank reserves have increased by $43,750 ($25,000 plus $18,750), total loans have increased by $131,250 ($75,000 plus $56,250), and total deposits have increased by $175,000 ($100,000 plus $75,000).

When Carl takes his check to Fleet PC, its deposits and reserves increase by $56,250. Fleet PC keeps $14,063 in reserves and lends $42,187. This process continues until there are no excess reserves in the banking system. But the process

---

■ **FIGURE 27.3**

The Multiple Creation of Bank Deposits

Round	The sequence		The running tally		
			Reserves	Loans	Deposits
1. Virtual College	Deposit $100,000 / Reserve $25,000 / Loan $75,000		$25,000	$75,000	$100,000
2. First American	Deposit $75,000 / Reserve $18,750 / Loan $56,250		$43,750	$131,250	$175,000
3. Fleet PC	Deposit $56,250 / Reserve $14,063 / Loan $42,187		$57,813	$173,437	$231,250
4. First e-bank	Deposit $42,187 / Reserve $10,547 / Loan $31,640		$68,360	$205,077	$273,437
	and so on ...		● ● ▼	● ● ▼	● ● ▼
			$100,000	$300,000	$400,000

When a bank receives a deposit, it keeps 25 percent in reserves and lends 75 percent. The amount loaned becomes a new deposit at another bank. The next bank in the sequence keeps 25 percent and lends 75 percent, and the process continues until the banking system has created enough deposits to eliminate its excess reserves. The running tally tells us the deposits and loans created at each stage. At the end of the process, an additional $100,000 of reserves creates an additional $400,000 of deposits.

takes many further steps. Figure 27.3 shows one additional step. The figure also shows the final tallies: Reserves increase by $100,000, loans increase by $300,000, and deposits increase by $400,000.

Why is the increase in deposits equal to 4 times the initial increase in reserves? It is because the required reserve ratio is 25 percent or 0.25. Once the banking system has additional reserves, banks keep on lending and creating deposits until all the new reserves are required. This outcome occurs when deposits have increased by $1/0.25 = 4$ times the initial increase in reserves.

Another way to work out the final tally is to sum the increase in each round of the process. You can see in Figure 27.3 that in each round, the new loan and deposit are 75 percent (0.75) of the previous loan and deposit. Call that proportion $L(L = 0.75)$. The complete sequence is

$$1 + L + L^2 + L^3 + L^4 + \cdots.$$

Because L is a fraction, the amount of new loans and new deposits gets smaller in each round of this sequence. The total increase in deposits when the process ends is the sum of the above sequence multiplied by the initial increase in reserves, which is

$$\frac{1}{1 - L} \times \text{Initial increase in reserves.}$$

If we use the numbers from the example, the total increase in deposits is

$$\$100,000 + 75,000 + 56,250 + 42,187 + \cdots$$

$$= \$100,000 \times (1 + 0.75 + 0.5625 + 0.42187 + \cdots)$$

$$= \$100,000 \times (1 + 0.75 + 0.75^2 + 0.75^3 + \cdots)$$

$$= \$100,000 \times \frac{1}{(1 - 0.75)}$$

$$= \$100,000 \times \frac{1}{0.25}$$

$$= \$400,000.$$

■ Real-World Reserve Changes

In the example that we've just worked through, the banking system's reserves changed because Al Capone moved $100,000 from under his mattress to a bank. If Al suddenly developed a distrust of banks and returned his funds to under his mattress, the reverse of the process we've just examined would occur and bank deposits would decrease by $400,000.

In the everyday life of the U.S. banking system, it is the Federal Reserve, not Al Capone, that has the biggest effect on the banking system's reserves.

In the next section, we're going to see how the actions of the Fed change reserves by changing the monetary base. And we're going to work out the multiplier effect of a change in the monetary base on the quantities of bank deposits, currency, and money.

CHECKPOINT 27.1

1 Explain how banks create money by making loans.

Practice Problems 27.1

1. How do banks create new deposits by making loans, and what factors limit the amount of deposits and loans they can create?

2. The required reserve ratio is 0.1, and banks have no excess reserves. Jamie deposits $100 in his bank. Calculate
   a. The bank's excess reserves as soon as Jamie makes the deposit.
   b. The maximum amount of loans that the banking system can make.
   c. The maximum amount of new money that the banking system can create.

Exercises 27.1

1. Your bank manager tells you that he does not create money. He just lends the money that people deposit in the bank. Explain to him how he does create money.

2. If the banking system receives new deposits of $200 million, what determines the maximum amount of new money that the banks can create?

3. If a multibank system has a required reserve ratio of 0.05 and Erin deposits $50 in her bank, calculate
   a. The bank's excess reserves as soon as Erin makes her deposit.
   b. The maximum amount of loans that the banking system can make.
   c. The maximum amount of new money that the banking system can create.

Solutions to Practice Problems 27.1

1. Banks can make loans when they have excess reserves—reserves in excess of those required. When a bank makes a loan, it creates a new deposit for the person who receives the loan. The bank uses its excess reserves to create new deposits. The amount of loans that the bank can make, and therefore the amount of new deposits that it can create, is limited by two things: the amount of excess reserves and the required reserve ratio.

2a. The bank's excess reserves are $90. When deposits increase by $100, the bank is required to keep 10 percent of the deposit as reserves. That is, required reserves increase by $10 and the bank has $90 of excess reserves.

2b. The maximum amount of loans that the banking system can make is $900. When reserves increase by $100, the deposit multiplier determines the maximum increase in deposits that the banking system can have. Deposits increase to make the bank's required reserves increase by $100. The deposit multiplier equals 1/Required reserve ratio, which is 1/0.1, or 10. With the $100 increase in reserves, deposits can increase to $1,000. Jamie deposited $100, so the banking system can create an additional $900 of deposits. It does so by making loans of $900.

2c. The maximum amount of new money that can be created is $900. When a bank makes loans, it creates new money. The maximum amount of new money created by the banking system equals the maximum amount of loans that it can make.

27.2 INFLUENCING THE QUANTITY OF MONEY

The Fed constantly takes actions that influence the quantity of money in the economy, and open market operations are the Fed's major policy tool. Let's see how an open market operation works.

■ How an Open Market Operation Works

When the Fed buys securities in an open market operation, it pays for them with newly created bank reserves and money. With more reserves in the banking system, the supply of interbank loans increases, the demand for interbank loans decreases, and the federal funds rate—the interest rate in the interbank loans market—falls.

Similarly, when the Fed sells securities in an open market operation, buyers pay for the securities with bank reserves and money. With smaller reserves in the banking system, the supply of interbank loans decreases, the demand for interbank loans increases, and the federal funds rate rises. The Fed sets a target for the federal funds rate and conducts open market operations on the scale needed to hit its target.

A change in the federal funds rate is only the first stage in an adjustment process that follows an open market operation. If banks' reserves increase, the banks can increase their lending and create even more money. If banks' reserves decrease, the banks must decrease their lending, which decreases the quantity of money. We'll study the effects of open market operations in some detail, beginning with an open market purchase.

The Fed Buys Securities

Suppose the Fed buys $100 million of U.S. government securities in the open market. There are two cases to consider, depending on who sells the securities. A bank might sell some of its securities, or a person or business that is not a commercial bank—the general public—might sell. The outcome is essentially the same in the two cases, but you might need to be convinced of this fact. So we'll study the two cases, starting with the simpler case in which a commercial bank sells securities. (The seller will be someone who thinks the Fed is offering a good price for securities and it is profitable to make the sale.)

A Commercial Bank Sells   When the Fed buys $100 million of securities from the Manhattan Commercial Bank, two things happen:

1. The Manhattan Commercial Bank has $100 million less in securities, and the Fed has $100 million more in securities.
2. To pay for the securities, the Fed increases the Manhattan Commercial Bank's reserve account at the New York Fed by $100 million.

Figure 27.4 shows the effects of these actions on the balance sheets of the Fed and the Manhattan Commercial Bank. Ownership of the securities passes from the commercial bank to the Fed, so the bank's securities decrease by $100 million and the Fed's securities increase by $100 million, as shown by the red-to-blue arrow running from the Manhattan Commercial Bank to the Fed. The Fed increases the Manhattan Commercial Bank's reserves by $100 million, as shown by the green arrow running from the Fed to the Manhattan Commercial Bank. This action increases the reserves of the banking system.

FIGURE 27.4

The Fed Buys Securities from a Commercial Bank

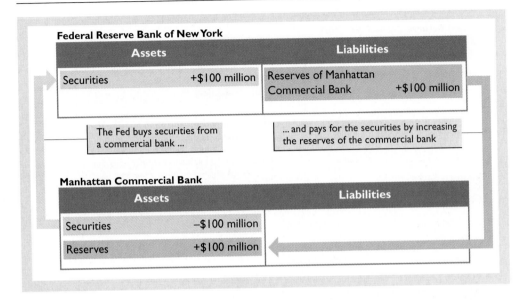

The commercial bank's total assets remain constant, but their composition changes. Its holdings of government securities decrease by $100 million, and its reserves increase by $100 million. The bank can use these additional reserves to make loans. When the bank makes loans, the quantity of money increases by the process that we described in the previous section.

We've just seen that when the Fed buys government securities from a bank, the bank's reserves increase. What happens if the Fed buys government securities from the public—say, from Goldman Sachs, a financial services company?

The Nonbank Public Sells   When the Fed buys $100 million of securities from Goldman Sachs, three things happen:

1. Goldman Sachs has $100 million less in securities, and the Fed has $100 million more in securities.

2. The Fed pays for the securities with a check for $100 million drawn on itself, which Goldman Sachs deposits in its account at the Manhattan Commercial Bank.

3. The Manhattan Commercial Bank collects payment of this check from the Fed, and the Manhattan Commercial Bank's reserves increase by $100 million.

Figure 27.5 shows the effects of these actions on the balance sheets of the Fed, Goldman Sachs, and the Manhattan Commercial Bank. Ownership of the securities passes from Goldman Sachs to the Fed, so Goldman Sachs's securities decrease by $100 million and the Fed's securities increase by $100 million (red-to-blue arrow). The Fed pays for the securities with a check payable to Goldman Sachs, which Goldman Sachs deposits in the Manhattan Commercial Bank. This payment increases Manhattan's reserves by $100 million (green arrow). It also increases Goldman Sachs's deposit at the Manhattan Commercial Bank by $100

■ **FIGURE 27.5**

The Fed Buys Securities from the Public

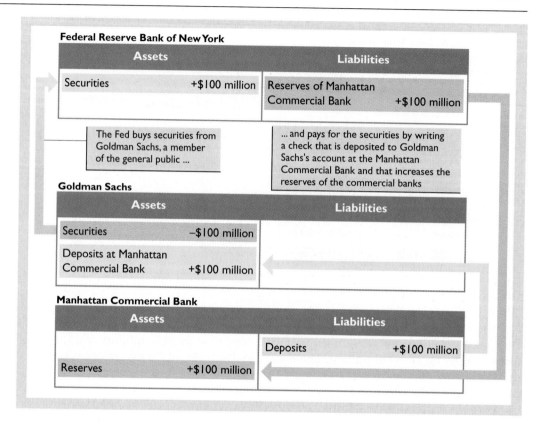

million (blue arrow). Just as when the Fed buys securities from a bank, this action increases the reserves of the banking system.

Goldman Sachs has the same total assets as before, but their composition has changed. It now has more money and fewer securities. The Manhattan Commercial Bank's reserves increase, and so do its deposits—both by $100 million. Because bank reserves and deposits have increased by the same amount, the bank has excess reserves, which it can use to make loans. When it makes loans, the quantity of money increases by the process that we described in the previous section.

We've worked through what happens when the Fed buys government securities from either a bank or the public. When the Fed sells securities, the transactions that we've just traced operate in reverse.

The Fed Sells Securities

If the Fed sells $100 million of U.S. government securities in the open market, most likely a person or business other than a bank buys them. (A bank would buy them only if it had excess reserves and couldn't find a better use of its funds.)

When the Fed sells $100 million of securities to Goldman Sachs, three things happen:

1. Goldman Sachs has $100 million more in securities, and the Fed has $100 million less in securities.

2. Goldman Sachs pays for the securities with a check for $100 million drawn on its deposit account at the Manhattan Commercial Bank.

3. The Fed collects payment of this check from the Manhattan Commercial Bank by decreasing its reserves by $100 million.

These actions decrease the reserves of the banking system. The Manhattan Commercial Bank is now short of reserves and must borrow in the federal funds market to meet its required reserve ratio.

The changes in the balance sheets of the Fed and the banks that we've just described are not the end of the story about the effects of an open market operation; they are just the beginning. A multiplier effect on the quantity of money now begins. To study this multiplier effect of an open market operation on the quantity of money, we build on the link between bank reserves and bank deposits that you studied in the previous section.

■ The Multiplier Effect of an Open Market Operation

An open market purchase that increases bank reserves also increases the *monetary base*. The increase in the monetary base equals the amount of the open market purchase, and initially, it equals the increase in bank reserves. To see why, recall that the *monetary base is the sum of Federal Reserve notes, coins, and banks' reserves at the Fed*. An open market purchase increases the banks' reserves at the Fed by the amount of the open market purchase. Nothing else changes, so the monetary base increases by the amount of the open market purchase.

If the Fed buys securities from the banks, the quantity of deposits does not change. If the Fed buys securities from the public, the quantity of deposits increases by the same amount as the increase in bank reserves. Either way, the banks have excess reserves that they now start to lend.

The following sequence of events now takes place:

- An open market purchase creates excess reserves.
- Banks lend excess reserves.
- Bank deposits increase.
- The quantity of money increases.
- New money is used to make payments.
- Some of the new money is held as currency—a currency drain.
- Some of the new money remains in deposits in banks.
- Banks' required reserves increase.
- Excess reserves decrease but remain positive.

This sequence is similar to the one you studied in the previous section of this chapter but with the addition of a currency drain. When a bank makes a loan, some of the loan remains in the banking system as deposits but some leaves the banks to be held as currency—called a **currency drain**. A currency drain doesn't change the monetary base. Bank reserves decrease, currency increases, and the monetary base remains the same. But the currency drain does change the amount of money that banks can create from a given increase in the monetary base because currency drains from their reserves and decreases the excess reserves.

The sequence described above repeats in a series of rounds, but each round begins with a smaller quantity of excess reserves than did the previous one. The process ends when excess reserves have been eliminated. Figure 27.6 illustrates and summarizes the sequence of events in one round of the process.

Currency drain
Funds loaned by banks that drain from the banks to be held as currency.

■ FIGURE 27.6

A Round in the Multiplier Process Following an Open Market Operation

❶ An open market purchase increases bank reserves and ❷ creates excess reserves. ❸ Banks lend the excess reserves, ❹ new deposits are created, and ❺ the quantity of money increases. ❻ New money is used to make payments. ❼ Households and firms receiving payments keep some on deposit in banks and some in the form of currency— ❽ a currency drain. The increase in bank deposits increases banks' reserves but also ❾ increases banks' required reserves. Required reserves increase by less than actual reserves, so the banks still have some excess reserves, though less than before. The process repeats until excess reserves have been eliminated.

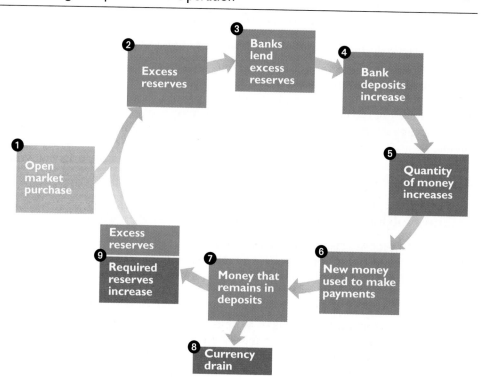

Figure 27.7 keeps track of the magnitudes of the increases in reserves, loans, deposits, currency, and money that result from an open market purchase of $100,000. In this figure, the required reserve ratio is 10 percent of deposits and the currency drain is 50 percent of deposits. We assume these numbers to keep the arithmetic simple.

The Fed buys $100,000 of securities from the banks. The banks' reserves increase by this amount, and the monetary base increases by $100,000. Deposits do not change, so banks have excess reserves of $100,000, and they lend those reserves. When the banks lend $100,000 of excess reserves, $66,667 remains in the banks as deposits and $33,333 drains off and is held outside the banks as currency. The quantity of money has now increased by $100,000—the increase in deposits plus the increase in currency holdings.

The increased bank deposits of $66,667 generate an increase in required reserves of 10 percent of that amount, which is $6,667. Actual reserves have increased by the same amount as the increase in deposits—$66,667. So the banks now have excess reserves of $60,000. At this stage, we have gone around the circle shown in Figure 27.6 once. The process that we've just described repeats but begins with excess reserves of $60,000. Figure 27.7 shows the next two rounds. At the end of the process, the quantity of money has increased by a multiple of the increase in the monetary base. In this case, the increase is $250,000, which is 2.5 times the increase in the monetary base.

An open market *sale* works similarly to an open market *purchase*, but the sale *decreases* the quantity of money. (Trace the process again but with the Fed *selling* and the banks or public *buying* securities.)

◼ FIGURE 27.7
The Multiplier Effect of an Open Market Operation

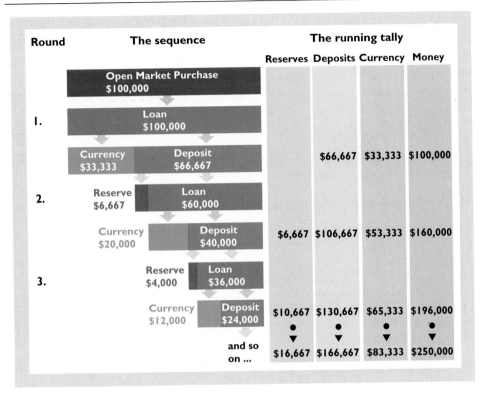

When the Fed provides the banks with $100,000 of additional reserves in an open market purchase, the banks lend those reserves. Of the amount loaned, $33,333 (33.33 percent) leaves the banks in a currency drain and $66,667 remains on deposit. With additional deposits, required reserves increase by $6,667 (10 percent required reserve ratio) and the banks lend $60,000. Of this amount, $20,000 leaves the banks in a currency drain and $40,000 remains on deposit. The process repeats until the banks have created enough deposits to eliminate their excess reserves. The additional $100,000 of reserves creates $250,000 of money.

◼ The Money Multiplier

The **money multiplier** is the number by which a change in the monetary base is multiplied to find the resulting change in the quantity of money. It is also the ratio of the change in the quantity of money to the change in the monetary base.

In the example we've just worked through, the money multiplier is 2.5 and the change in the monetary base is $100,000, and the quantity of money increases by $250,000.

The banks' required reserve ratio and the currency drain determine the size of the money multiplier. Call the required reserve ratio R and call the ratio of currency to deposits (the currency drain ratio) C. In our example, $R = 0.1$ and $C = 0.5$.

To see how the required reserve ratio and the currency drain determine the size of the money multiplier begin with the two facts that

Required reserves = $R \times$ Deposits, and Currency = $C \times$ Deposits.

The monetary base, MB, is the sum of required reserves and currency, so

$$MB = (R + C) \times \text{Deposits},$$

The quantity of money, M, is the sum of deposits and currency, so

$$M = \text{Deposits} + \text{Currency} = (1 + C) \times \text{Deposits}.$$

Now divide the quantity of money M by the monetary base, MB using the

Money multiplier
The number by which a change in the monetary base is multiplied to find the resulting change in the quantity of money.

fact that $M = (1 + C) \times$ Deposits and $MB = (R + C) \times$ Deposits to get

$$\frac{M}{MB} = \frac{(1 + C)}{(R + C)}$$

Now multiply both sides of the above equation by MB to get

$$M = \frac{(1 + C)}{(R + C)} \times MB$$

The quantity of money *changes* by the *change* in the monetary base multiplied by $(1 + C)/(R + C)$.

Using the numbers in our example, $R = 0.1$ and $C = 0.5$, so the money multiplier is $1.5/0.6 = 2.5$.

The larger the required reserve ratio and the larger the currency drain, the smaller is the money multiplier.

The Changing Money Multiplier

The money multiplier isn't a constant. You can see its value over the past forty years in *Eye on the U.S. Economy* on the next page. The money multiplier changes for two reasons: the currency drain changes and the banks' required reserve ratio changes.

The currency drain drifted upward gently before the 1990s but then surged after 1991. The main reason is that the U.S. dollar became much more widely used in other countries, and especially in the newly emerging market economies of Russia and Eastern Europe.

REALITY CHECK

Money Creation in YOUR Life

It might surprise you to realize just how big a role *you* play in the money creation process. Every time you charge something to your credit card, you help the bank that issued it to create money. The increase in your outstanding balance is a loan from the bank to you. The bank pays the seller right away. So the bank deposit of the seller and your outstanding balance increase together. Money has been created.

You contribute to the currency drain that limits the ability of your bank to create money when you visit the ATM and get some cash to pay for your late-night pizza.

Of course, your transactions are a tiny part of the total. But together, you and a few million other students like you play a big role in the money creation process.

The Money Multiplier

We can measure the money multiplier in the United States by using the following formula:

Money multiplier = Quantity of money ÷ Monetary base.

Because there are two main definitions of money, M1 and M2, there are two money multipliers: the M1 multiplier and the M2 multiplier.

Also, there are two measures of the currency drain and bank reserve ratios. Part (a) shows the currency drain measures: the ratio of currency to the deposits in M1 and the ratio of currency to the deposits in M2.

Notice the increase in the ratio of currency to M1 deposits, which arises mainly from a surge in holdings of U.S. currency abroad.

In part (b), you can see that the reserve ratios have fallen as required reserve ratios have been decreased. You can also see a spike in the reserve ratio in 2000 as the banks took precautions against a possible surge in demand for currency associated with the new millennium and the so-called Y2K problem. The reserve ratio increased sharply again in 2005.

In part (c), you can see the two money multipliers. The M2 multiplier increased through the 1980s because required reserves decreased. This multiplier decreased during the 1990s because the currency drain

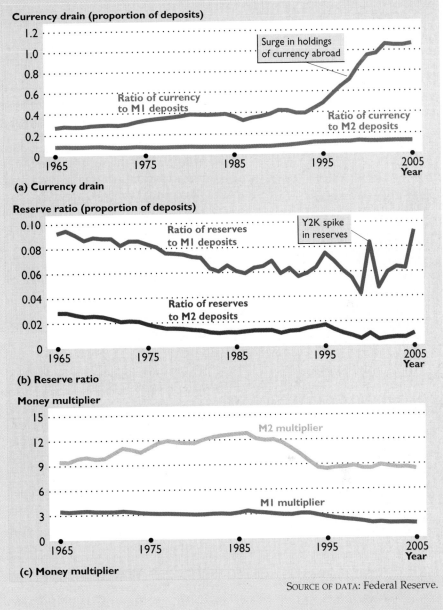

(a) Currency drain

(b) Reserve ratio

(c) Money multiplier

SOURCE OF DATA: Federal Reserve.

increased. In 2005, this multiplier was about 9.

The M1 multiplier was close to 3 from 1965 to the early 1990s and then

fell to a bit less than 2 as the currency drain increased.

The banks' reserve ratio has fallen because the required reserve ratio has fallen. But there have been other fluctuations in the reserve ratio. These fluctuations occur because the banks choose to hold excess reserves at levels that fluctuate. The banks are less eager to hold excess reserves when interest rates are high but more willing to hold such reserves when interest rates are low. Also, at times of financial uncertainty, such as the turn of the new century in 2000, they choose to hold excess reserves.

2 **Explain how the Fed influences the quantity of money.**

Practice Problems 27.2

1. What is the Fed's main policy tool?

2. What is the money multiplier? What determines its magnitude?

3. If the Fed makes an open market purchase of $1 million of securities,
   a. Who can sell the securities to the Fed in an open market operation? Does it matter from whom the Fed buys the securities?
   b. What initial changes occur in the economy if the Fed buys from a bank?
   c. What is the process by which the quantity of money changes?
   d. What factors determine how much the quantity of money changes?

Exercises 27.2

1. What is an open market operation? How do open market operations influence the monetary base?

2. Explain how the banking system creates money when the Fed conducts an open market operation.

3. If the Fed makes an open market sale of $1 million of securities,
   a. What initial changes occur in the economy?
   b. What is the process by which the quantity of money in the economy changes?
   c. By how much does the quantity of money change?
   d. What is the magnitude of the money multiplier?

Solutions to Practice Problems 27.2

1. The Fed's main policy tool is the open market operation.

2. The money multiplier is the number by which a change in the monetary base is multiplied to find the resulting change in the quantity of money. The currency drain and the banks' required reserve ratio determine its magnitude.

3a. The Fed buys securities from banks or the public. The Fed does not buy securities from the government. It does not matter from whom the Fed buys the securities. The change in the monetary base is the same.

3b. The monetary base increases by $1 million. Ownership of the securities passes from the bank to the Fed. As a result, the Fed's assets increase by $1 million. When the Fed pays for the securities, it increases the bank's deposit with the Fed by $1 million. The Fed's liabilities increase by $1 million. The bank's assets are the same, but their composition has changed. The bank has $1 million more in reserves and $1 million less in securities.

3c. The bank's reserves have increased by $1 million and its deposits have not changed, so it has excess reserves of $1 million. The bank makes loans and creates new deposits. The new deposits are new money.

3d. The required reserve ratio and the currency drain determine the increase in the quantity of money. The larger the required reserve ratio or the currency drain, the smaller is the increase in the quantity of money.

CHAPTER CHECKPOINT

Key Points

1 **Explain how banks create money by making loans.**

- Banks create money by making loans.
- Banks hold a proportion of their deposits as reserves to meet the *required reserve ratio*.
- Reserves that exceed the required reserve ratio are *excess reserves*, which banks loan.
- The quantity of reserves and the required reserve ratio limit the total quantity of deposits that the banks can create.
- The maximum quantity of deposits the banks can create equals the increase in bank reserves divided by the required reserve ratio.

2 **Explain how the Fed influences the quantity of money.**

- The Fed's main tool for influencing the quantity of money is the open market operation.
- When the Fed *buys* securities in an open market operation, it pays for them with newly created bank reserves. When the Fed *sells* securities in an open market operation, people pay for them with money and banks pay for them with reserves.
- An open market purchase increases the monetary base and creates the following sequence of events: Banks lend excess reserves; the quantity of money increases; new money is used to make payments; some of the new money is held as currency—a currency drain; some of the new money remains on deposit in banks; banks' required reserves increase; excess reserves decrease. This sequence repeats until excess reserves are eliminated.
- The money multiplier determines the amount of money that the banking system can create from a given increase in the monetary base.
- The money multiplier is determined by the banks' required reserve ratio and by the currency drain.
- The money multiplier changes because the required reserve ratio and the currency drain change. Also, the banks sometimes choose to hold excess reserves at a level that fluctuates.

Key Terms

Balance sheet, 674
Currency drain, 687

Money multiplier, 689

Exercises

1. If the banking system receives new deposits of $2 million, the required reserve ratio is 0.1, and there is no currency drain, calculate
   a. The bank's excess reserves as soon as the deposit is made.
   b. The maximum amount of loans that the banking system can make.
   c. The maximum amount of new money that the banking system can create.

2. If the banking system loses deposits of $3 million, the required reserve ratio is 0.1, and there is no currency drain, calculate
   a. The bank's excess reserves as soon as the deposit withdrawal occurs.
   b. The amount of loans that the banking system must call in.
   c. The amount of money that the banking system must destroy.

3. The required reserve ratio is 5 percent, and the currency drain ratio is 20 percent. If the Fed makes an open market purchase of $1 million of securities,
   a. What is the change in the monetary base?
   b. Which components of the monetary base change?
   c. By how much does the quantity of money change?
   d. How much of the new money is currency and how much is bank deposits?

4. Initially, the banking system has $2 trillion of deposits and no excess reserves. If the Fed lowers the required reserve ratio from 0.1 to 0.05, calculate the change in
   a. Reserves.
   b. Deposits.
   c. The quantity of money.

5. The First Student Bank has the following balance sheet (in millions of dollars).

Assets		Liabilities	
Reserves at the Fed	25	Demand deposits	90
Cash in ATMs	15	Savings deposits	110
Government securities	60		
Loans	100		

The required reserve ratio on all deposits is 5 percent.
   a. What, if any, are the bank's excess reserves?
   b. How much will the bank loan?
   c. If there is no currency drain and if all the funds loaned are deposited in the First Student Bank, what are the bank's excess reserves, if any, after the loans made in part b?
   d. If there is no currency drain and if all the funds loaned remain deposited in the First Student Bank, what is the quantity of loans and total deposits when the bank has no excess reserves?
   e. If the required reserve ratio is decreased to 2 percent and if there is no currency drain and all the funds loaned remain deposited in the First Student Bank, what is the quantity of loans and total deposits when the bank has no excess reserves?

6. The Second Student Bank has the following balance sheet (in millions of dollars).

Assets		Liabilities	
Reserves at the Fed	3	Demand deposits	90
Cash in ATMs	2	Savings deposits	110
Government securities	85		
Loans	110		

The required reserve ratio on all deposits is 5 percent.
   a. Does the bank have any excess reserves?
   b. Does the bank have a shortage of reserves?
   c. How much of the outstanding loans will the bank not renew?
   d. If there is no currency drain and if all the loans that are repaid are paid out of deposits in the Second Student Bank, what is the bank's shortage of reserves, if any, after the loans are repaid in part **c**?
   e. If there is no currency drain and if all the loans that are repaid come from deposits in the Second Student Bank, what is the quantity of loans and total deposits when the bank has no excess reserves?

7. If the Fed wants to decrease quantity of money, what type of open market operation might it undertake? Explain the process by which the quantity of money decreases.

8. Suppose that the currency drain ratio is 10 percent and the required reserve ratio is 1 percent. If the Fed sells $100,000 of securities on the open market, calculate the first round changes in
   a. Excess reserves.
   b. Deposits.
   c. Currency in circulation.

9. What can the Fed do to increase the quantity of money and keep the monetary base constant? Explain why the Fed would or would not do each of the following:
   a. Change the currency drain ratio.
   b. Change the required reserve ratio.
   c. Change the discount rate.
   d. Conduct an open market operation.

10. The commercial banks have the following balance sheet (in billions of dollars).

Assets		Liabilities	
Reserves	10	Deposits	210
Government securities	50		
Loans	150		

The required reserve ratio is 5 percent, there is no currency drain, and the Fed conducts an open market purchase of securities of $1 billion.
   a. What is the initial change in the reserves of the banks?
   b. By how much do loans increase?
   c. By how much do deposits increase?

Critical Thinking

11. An early goldsmith banker earned a profit (sometimes a large profit) simply by writing notes to certify that a person had deposited a certain amount of gold in his vault. By writing more notes than the amount of gold held, the goldsmith could lend the notes and charge interest on them.
    a. Did the goldsmith bankers make money out of thin air in a form of legal theft?
    b. Should the goldsmith bankers have been regulated to ensure that the amount of gold in their vaults equaled the value of the notes they created?
    c. What were the main benefits from the activities of the goldsmith bankers?

12. In the United States today, the Federal Reserve is the only bank that is permitted to create bank notes.
    a. Do you think that Citigroup and JP Morgan Chase should be permitted to issue their own private bank notes in competition with the Fed?
    b. Do you think the Fed should be the only bank that is permitted to issue e-cash?

13. Bank deposits are insured against the risk of bank failure. Can you think of any bad side effects of this arrangement?

Web Exercises

Use the links on MyEconLab to work the following exercises.

14. Visit the Web site of JP Morgan Chase and obtain the most recent balance sheet data for this bank.
    a. What is the total amount of deposits?
    b. What is the total amount of loans?
    c. What is the total amount of reserves held?
    d. What is the reserve ratio?
    e. Why can't you determine from the published balance sheet the deposits that are part of M1 and the deposits that are part of M2?

15. Visit the Web sites of JP Morgan Chase and Citigroup and obtain the most recent earnings data for these large banks.
    a. What are their profits during the most recent year?
    b. Explain how these banks earn such large profits.

16. Visit the Web site of the Federal Reserve and obtain the most recent data on the monetary base, M1, M2, and the composition of money and calculate for the most recent month
    a. The currency drain ratio (using both M1 and M2).
    b. The banks' reserve ratio (using both the M1 deposits and the M2 deposits).
    c. The money multiplier (for both M1 and M2).

17. Visit the Web site of the Federal Reserve and obtain the most recent information on "Factors Affecting Reserve Balances of Depository Institutions."
    a. Have the reserves of depository institutions increased or decreased?
    b. Has the Fed increased or decreased the amount that it has loaned to depository institutions?

Money, Interest, and Inflation

CHAPTER CHECKLIST

When you have completed your study of this chapter, you will be able to

1 Explain what determines the demand for money and how the demand for money and the supply of money determine the *nominal* interest rate.

2 Explain how in the long run, the quantity of money determines the price level and money growth brings inflation.

3 Identify the costs of inflation and the benefits of a stable value of money.

Greg McBride is a Fed watcher who shares what he sees with the readers of his Fed Outlook feature on bankrate.com. Greg is just one of hundreds of economists, financial analysts, and journalists whose lives reach fever pitch every six weeks or so when the FOMC meets to review its interest rate target. Why is Fed watching such a big sport? Why all the excitement? Because a small change in the Fed's interest rate target can bring a big and immediate change in bond and stock prices.

In this chapter, you'll learn how the Fed can influence the interest rate each day by changing the quantity of money. But you'll also see that in the long run, the Fed's ability to influence the interest rate is limited. It is the inflation rate—the rate at which the price level rises—not the interest rate, that the Fed's actions control in the long run. You'll see why inflation happens and how it can have a big influence on people's lives.

WHERE WE ARE AND WHERE WE'RE HEADING

Before we explore the effects of money on the interest rate and the inflation rate, let's take stock of what we've learned and preview where we are heading.

■ The Real Economy

Real factors that are independent of the price level determine potential GDP and the natural unemployment rate (Chapter 23). The demand for labor and supply of labor determine the quantity of labor employed and the real wage rate at full employment. The full-employment equilibrium quantity of labor and the production function determine potential GDP. At full employment, real GDP equals potential GDP and the unemployment rate equals the natural unemployment rate.

Investment demand and saving supply determine the amount of investment and saving and the real interest rate (Chapter 24). Investment and saving along with population growth, human capital growth, and technological change determine the growth rate of real GDP (Chapter 25).

■ The Money Economy

Money—the economy's means of payment—consists of currency and bank deposits (Chapter 26). Banks create deposits by making loans, and the Fed influences the quantity of money through its open market operations, which determine the monetary base and the federal funds rate—the interest rate on interbank loans (Chapter 27).

The effects of money on the economy, which we explore in this chapter, are complex, and to explain and understand them, we proceed in three steps. We take these steps in an order that might seem strange but that turns out to be the most effective.

Step one looks at the immediate effect of the Fed's actions. This effect is on the short-term nominal interest rate. The Fed raises and lowers the short-term nominal interest rate by changing the quantity of money.

Step two looks at the long-term effects of the Fed's actions. These effects are on the price level and the inflation rate. The Fed lowers or raises the price level by decreasing or increasing the quantity of money. And the Fed lowers or raises the inflation rate by slowing down or speeding up the rate at which the quantity of money grows. We take these two steps in the current chapter.

Step three provides a blow-by-blow explanation of how the Fed's actions ripple through the economy. The Fed's actions initially change the short-term interest rate. The effects then spread to change spending plans, real GDP, employment, and unemployment. In the long run, the real effects of the Fed's actions fade, leaving changes in only the price level and inflation rate.

We explore the ripple effects of the Fed's actions in Chapters 29 and 30, which pave the way for an examination of the ways in which policy can be used to contain inflation, sustain economic growth, and stabilize output and employment.

Some people approach a novel in the order in which we're going to study the effects of money on the economy: First, read the introduction, then the conclusion, and then the steps in between. Try it! It sometimes helps to know where you are going.

28.1 MONEY AND THE INTEREST RATE

To understand the Fed's short-run influence on the interest rate, we must understand what determines the demand for money, the supply of money, and the forces that bring equilibrium in the market for money. We'll begin by studying the demand for money.

■ The Demand for Money

The amount of money that households and firms choose to hold is the **quantity of money demanded**. What determines the quantity of money demanded? The answer is a benefit–opportunity cost calculation. The quantity of money that households and firms choose to hold is the quantity that balances the benefit of holding an additional dollar of money against the opportunity cost of doing so. But just what are the benefit and opportunity cost of holding money?

Quantity of money demanded
The amount of money that households and firms choose to hold.

Benefit of Holding Money

You've seen that money is the means of payment and that it serves as a medium of exchange, unit of account, and store of value (Chapter 26, pp. 648–649). You don't need any money to use it as a unit of account. You can keep financial records in dollars and cents even if you don't have any money. You don't need money to store your wealth. You can store it in the form of bonds, stocks, and mutual funds. Money and other financial assets are substitute stores of value. But you do need money to make payments and do transactions. These two features of money are the sources of benefit from holding money. The more money you hold, the easier it is for you to make payments and transactions.

The marginal benefit of holding money is the change in total benefit that results from holding one more dollar as money. The marginal benefit of holding money diminishes as the quantity of money held increases. If you hold only a few dollars in money, holding one more dollar brings large benefits—you can buy a cup of coffee, take a bus ride, or use a pay phone. If you hold enough money to make your normal weekly payments, holding one more dollar brings only a small benefit because you're not very likely to want to spend it. Holding even more money brings only a small additional benefit. You barely notice the difference in the benefit of having $1,000 versus $1,001 in your bank account.

To get the most out of your assets, you hold money only up to the point at which its marginal benefit equals its opportunity cost. But what is the opportunity cost of holding money?

Opportunity Cost of Holding Money

The opportunity cost of holding money is the interest rate forgone on an alternative asset. If you can earn 8 percent a year on a mutual fund account, then holding an additional $100 in money costs you $8 a year. Your opportunity cost of holding $100 in money is the goods and services worth $8 that you must forgo.

A fundamental principle of economics is that if the opportunity cost of something increases, people seek substitutes for it. Money is no exception. Other assets such as a mutual fund account are substitutes for money. And the higher the opportunity cost of holding money—the higher the interest income forgone by not holding other assets—the smaller is the quantity of money demanded.

Opportunity Cost: *Nominal* Interest Is a *Real* Cost

The opportunity cost of holding money is the nominal interest rate. In Chapter 22, (p. 562), you learned the distinction between the *nominal* interest rate and the *real* interest rate and that

$$\text{Nominal interest rate} = \text{Real interest rate} + \text{Inflation rate.}$$

We can use this equation to find the real interest rate for a given nominal interest rate and inflation rate. For example, if the nominal interest rate on a mutual fund account is 8 percent a year and the inflation rate is 2 percent a year, the real interest rate is 6 percent a year. Why isn't the real interest rate of 6 percent a year the opportunity cost of holding money? That is, why isn't the opportunity cost of holding $100 in money only $6 worth of goods and services forgone?

The answer is that if you hold $100 in money rather than in a mutual fund, your buying power decreases by $8, not by $6. With inflation running at 2 percent a year, on each $100 that you hold as money and that earns no interest, you lose $2 worth of buying power a year. On each $100 that you put into your mutual fund account, you gain $6 worth of buying power a year. So if you hold money rather than a mutual fund, you lose the buying power of $6 plus $2, or $8—equivalent to the nominal interest rate on the mutual fund, not the real interest rate.

Because the opportunity cost of holding money is the nominal interest rate on an alternative asset,

Other things remaining the same, the higher the nominal interest rate, the smaller is the quantity of money demanded.

This relationship describes the decision of an individual or firm about how much money to hold. It also describes money-holding decisions for the economy—the sum of the decisions of every individual and firm.

We summarize the influence of the nominal interest rate on money-holding decisions in a demand for money schedule and curve.

The Demand for Money Schedule and Curve

Demand for money
The relationship between the quantity of money demanded and the nominal interest rate, when all other influences on the amount of money that people wish to hold remain the same.

The **demand for money** is the relationship between the quantity of money demanded and the nominal interest rate, when all other influences on the amount of money that people wish to hold remain the same. We illustrate the demand for money with a demand for money schedule and a demand for money curve, such as those in Figure 28.1. If the interest rate is 5 percent a year, the quantity of money demanded is $1 trillion. The quantity of money demanded decreases to $0.98 trillion if the interest rate rises to 6 percent a year and increases to $1.02 trillion if the interest rate falls to 4 percent a year.

The demand for money curve is *MD*. When the interest rate rises, everything else remaining the same, the opportunity cost of holding money rises and the quantity of money demanded decreases—there is a movement up along the demand for money curve. When the interest rate falls, the opportunity cost of holding money falls and the quantity of money demanded increases—there is a movement down along the demand for money curve.

■ FIGURE 28.1

The Demand for Money

	Nominal interest rate (percent per year)	Quantity of money demanded (trillions of dollars)
A	6	0.98
B	5	1.00
C	4	1.02

Nominal interest rate (percent per year)

① Effect of a rise in the interest rate

A

B

② Effect of a fall in the interest rate

C

MD

Quantity of money (trillions of dollars)

The demand for money schedule is graphed as the demand for money curve, *MD*. Rows *A, B,* and *C* in the table correspond to points *A, B,* and *C* on the curve. The nominal interest rate is the opportunity cost of holding money.

① Other things remaining the same, an increase in the nominal interest rate decreases the quantity of money demanded, and **②** a decrease in the nominal interest rate increases the quantity of money demanded.

■ Changes in the Demand for Money

A change in the nominal interest rate brings a change in the quantity of money demanded and a movement along the demand for money curve. A change in any other influence on money holding changes the demand for money. The three main influences on the demand for money are

- The price level
- Real GDP
- Financial technology

The Price Level

The demand for money is proportional to the price level—an *x* percent rise in the price level brings an *x* percent increase in the quantity of money demanded at each nominal interest rate. The reason is that we hold money to make payments: If the price level changes, the quantity of dollars that we need to make payments changes in the same proportion.

Real GDP

The demand for money increases as real GDP increases. The reason is that expenditures and incomes increase when real GDP increases. So households and firms must hold larger average inventories of money to make the increased expenditures and income payments.

Financial Technology

Changes in financial technology change the demand for money. Most changes in financial technology come from advances in computing and record keeping. Some advances increase the quantity of money demanded, and some decrease it.

Daily interest checking deposits and automatic transfers between checking and savings deposits enable people to earn interest on money, lower the opportunity cost of holding money, and increase the demand for money. Automatic teller machines, debit cards, and smart cards, which have made money easier to obtain and use, have increased the marginal benefit of money and increased the demand for money.

Credit cards have made it easier for people to buy goods and services on credit and pay for them when their credit card account becomes due. This development has decreased the demand for money.

A change in any of the influences on money holdings that we've just reviewed other than the interest rate changes the demand for money and shifts the demand for money curve. A rise in the price level, an increase in real GDP, or an advance in financial technology that lowers the opportunity cost of holding money or makes money more useful increases the demand for money and shifts the demand curve rightward. A fall in the price level, a decrease in real GDP, or a technological advance that creates a substitute for money has the opposite effect.

■ The Supply of Money

Supply of money
The relationship between the quantity of money supplied and the nominal interest rate.

The quantity of money supplied is determined by the actions of the banking system and the Fed. On any given day, the quantity of money supplied is fixed. The **supply of money** is the relationship between the quantity of money supplied and the nominal interest rate. In Figure 28.2, the quantity of money supplied is $1 trillion regardless of the nominal interest rate. So the money supply curve is the vertical line *MS*.

■ The Nominal Interest Rate

People hold some of their financial wealth as money and some in the form of other financial assets. You have seen that the amount that people hold as money depends on the nominal interest rate that they can earn on other financial assets. Demand and supply determine the nominal interest rate. We can study the forces of demand and supply in either the market for financial assets or the market for money. Because the Fed influences the quantity of money, we focus on the market for money.

On a given day, the price level, real GDP, and the state of financial technology are fixed. Because these influences on the demand for money are fixed, the demand for money curve is given. The *MD* curve in Figure 28.2 is a demand for money curve.

The interest rate is the only influence on the quantity of money demanded that is free to fluctuate. And every day, the interest rate adjusts to make the quantity of money demanded equal the quantity of money supplied—to achieve money market equilibrium.

In Figure 28.2, the equilibrium interest rate is 5 percent a year. At any interest rate above 5 percent a year, the quantity of money demanded is less than the quantity of money supplied. At any interest rate below 5 percent a year, the quantity of money demanded exceeds the quantity of money supplied.

The Interest Rate and Bond Price Move in Opposite Directions   When the government issues a bond, it specifies the dollar amount of interest that it will pay each year on the bond. Suppose that the government issues a bond that pays $100 of interest a year. The interest *rate* that you receive on this bond depends on the price that you pay for it. If the price is $1,000, the interest rate is 10 percent a year—$100 is 10 percent of $1,000.

If the price of the bond *falls* to $500, the interest rate *rises* to 20 percent a year. The reason is that you still receive an interest payment of $100, but this amount is 20 percent of the $500 price of the bond. If the price of the bond *rises* to $2,000, the interest rate *falls* to 5 percent a year. Again, you still receive an interest payment of $100, but this amount is 5 percent of the $2,000 price of the bond.

Interest Rate Adjustment   If the interest rate is above its equilibrium level, people would like to hold less money than they are actually holding. So they try to get rid of money by buying other financial assets such as bonds. The demand for financial assets increases, the prices of these assets rise, and the interest rate falls. The interest rate keeps falling until the quantity of money that people want to hold increases to equal the quantity of money supplied.

Conversely, when the interest rate is below its equilibrium level, people are holding less money than they would like to hold. So they try to get more money by selling other financial assets. The demand for these financial assets decreases, the prices of these assets fall, and the interest rate rises. The interest rate keeps rising until the quantity of money that people want to hold decreases to equal the quantity of money supplied.

FIGURE 28.2

Money Market Equilibrium

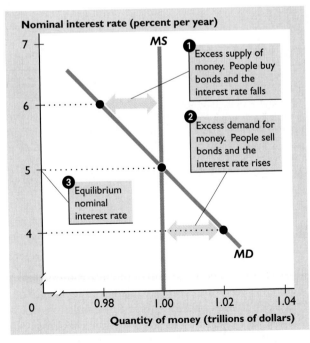

The supply of money curve is *MS*, and the demand for money curve is *MD*.

❶ If the interest rate is 6 percent a year, the quantity of money held exceeds the quantity demanded. People buy bonds, the price of a bond rises, and the interest rate falls.

❷ If the interest rate is 4 percent a year, the quantity of money held falls short of the quantity demanded. People sell bonds, the price of a bond falls, and the interest rate rises.

❸ If the interest rate is 5 percent a year, the quantity of money held equals the quantity demanded. The money market is in equilibrium.

EYE ON THE U.S. ECONOMY

Credit Cards and Money

Today, 80 percent of U.S. households own a credit card, and most of us use a credit card account as a substitute for money. When we buy goods or services, we use our credit card. And when the monthly bill arrives, most of us pay off some of the outstanding balance but not all of it. In 2005, 57 percent of credit card holders had an outstanding balance after making their most recent payment, and the average card balance exceeded $5,000.

But back in 1970, only 20 percent of U.S. households had a credit card.

How has the spread of credit cards affected the amount of money that people hold?

The answer is that the quantity of M1 money has decreased as a percentage of GDP. Part (a) of the figure shows that as the ownership of credit cards expanded from 20 percent in 1970 to 80 percent in 2005, the quantity of M1—basically, currency plus checking deposits—fell from a bit more than 20 percent of GDP to less than 12 percent.

The expansion of credit card ownership is a change in financial technol-

ogy that has led to a steady decrease in the demand for money.

Part (b) of the figure shows the decrease in the demand for money. Here, we graph the quantity of M1 as a percentage of GDP against the interest rate. You can see that as credit card use has increased, the demand for money has decreased and the demand for money curve has shifted leftward.

You can also see that when the interest rate decreased from 1981 to 1993, the quantity of money demanded increased.

(a) Changes in the use of credit cards and money

(b) Changes in the demand for M1

SOURCE OF DATA: Federal Reserve.

■ Changing the Interest Rate

To change the interest rate, the Fed changes the quantity of money. Figure 28.3 illustrates two changes. The demand for money curve is MD. If the Fed increases the quantity of money to $1.02 trillion, the supply of money curve shifts rightward from MS_0 to MS_1 and the interest rate falls to 4 percent a year. If the Fed decreases the quantity of money to $0.98 trillion, the supply of money curve shifts leftward from MS_0 to MS_2 and the interest rate rises to 6 percent a year.

FIGURE 28.3
Interest Rate Changes

The demand for money is *MD*, and initially, the supply of money is MS_0. The interest rate is 5 percent a year.

❶ The Fed increases the quantity of money, and the supply of money curve shifts rightward to MS_1. The interest rate falls to 4 percent a year.

❷ The Fed decreases the quantity of money, and the supply of money curve shifts leftward to MS_2. The interest rate rises to 6 percent a year.

REALITY CHECK

Money Holding and Fed Watching in YOUR Life

Do you pay off a smaller part of your credit card balance than you can afford to pay just to keep some money in the bank? You almost certainly do not. Why? Because the opportunity cost of holding that money would be too high. By paying off as much as you can afford to, you avoid a high interest rate on the outstanding balance. Your demand for money is sensitive to this opportunity cost.

Do you watch the Fed? Probably not. But you can learn to become an effective Fed watcher. And in the process, you will become much better informed about the state of the U.S. economy and the state of the economy in your region. Get into the habit of visiting the Fed's Web site at www.federalreserve.gov and look especially at the Beige Book in which you will learn what is happening in your region.

1 **Explain what determines the demand for money and how the demand for money and the supply of money determine the *nominal* interest rate.**

Practice Problems 28.1

FIGURE 1

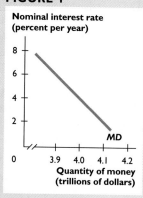

Nominal interest rate (percent per year)

Quantity of money (trillions of dollars)

1. Figure 1 shows the demand for money curve. The quantity of money is $4 trillion.
   a. What is the nominal interest rate?
   b. If real GDP increases, how will the interest rate change? Explain the process that brings about the change in the interest rate.
   c. If the Fed decreases the quantity of money to $3.9 trillion, will bond prices rise or fall? Why? What happens to the nominal interest rate?

2. Suppose that banks increase the fee they charge for credit cards, introduce a user fee on every credit card purchase, and increase the interest rate on outstanding credit card balances.
   a. How would the demand for money change?
   b. How would the nominal interest rate change?

Exercises 28.1

1. Figure 1 shows the demand for money curve. The quantity of money supplied is $3.9 trillion.
   a. What is the nominal interest rate?
   b. If real GDP decreases, how will the interest rate change? Explain what happens in the market for bonds as the market returns to equilibrium.
   c. If the Fed increases the quantity of money to $4.0 trillion, what is the change in the nominal interest rate? What happens to the price of bonds?

FIGURE 2

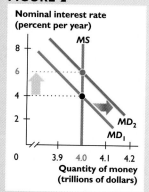

Nominal interest rate (percent per year)

Quantity of money (trillions of dollars)

2. Suppose that banks launch an aggressive marketing campaign to get everyone to use credit cards for every conceivable transaction. They offer prizes to new cardholders and slash the interest rate on outstanding credit card balances.
   a. How would the demand for money change?
   b. How would the nominal interest rate change?

Solutions to Practice Problems 28.1

1a. The interest rate is 4 percent a year, at the intersection of MD_1 and MS (Figure 2).

FIGURE 3

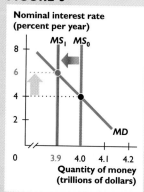

Nominal interest rate (percent per year)

Quantity of money (trillions of dollars)

1b. The demand for money increases, and the demand for money curve shifts from MD_1 to MD_2. At an interest rate of 4 percent a year, people want to hold more money so they sell bonds. The price of a bond falls, and the interest rate rises (Figure 2).

1c. At an interest rate at 4 percent a year, people would like to hold $4 trillion. With only $3.9 trillion of money available, they sell bonds. The price of a bond falls, and the interest rate rises. The new equilibrium nominal interest rate is 6 percent a year (Figure 3).

2a. The demand for money would increase as people used their credit cards less and used money for more transactions.

2b. With an increase in the demand for money, the nominal interest rate would rise.

28.2 MONEY, THE PRICE LEVEL, AND INFLATION

Each day, the price level and real GDP are at levels that have resulted from previous decisions. When the Fed conducts an open market operation to change the quantity of money, the nominal interest rate is the only variable that is free to adjust to make the quantity of money demanded equal the quantity of money supplied. You've seen that if the Fed decreases the quantity of money, the interest rate rises, and if the Fed increases the quantity of money, the interest rate falls.

These changes in the nominal interest rate also change the real interest rate. The reason is that the inflation rate is slow to adjust. It does not change every time the Fed changes the quantity of money.

Changes in the real interest rate influence spending plans. If the real interest rate falls, firms borrow and invest more and households borrow and spend more on consumption goods, especially on big-ticket items such as homes and automobiles. Similarly, if the real interest rate rises, firms borrow and invest less and households borrow and spend less on consumption goods.

These changes in spending change production and prices. The details of the adjustment process are complex, and we explore them in the next two chapters. But the place where the adjustment process comes to rest is easier to describe. We're now going to explain the long-run outcome of a change in the quantity of money and a change in the growth rate of money.

■ The Money Market in the Long Run

The *long run* refers to the economy at full employment or when we smooth out the effects of the business cycle. Potential GDP, the current state of financial technology, the price level, and the nominal interest rate determine the quantity of money demanded at full employment. The actions of the Fed and the banking system determine the quantity of money supplied. In the short run, the nominal interest rate adjusts to bring equilibrium in the market for money, but in the long run, the price level does the adjusting. To see why, let's see what determines the other influences on the quantity of money demanded.

Potential GDP and Financial Technology

Potential GDP and the state of financial technology, two influences on the quantity of money demanded, are determined by real factors and are independent of the price level. You studied potential GDP in Chapter 23. It is the real GDP produced by the full-employment quantity of labor. This quantity is determined by the equilibrium real wage rate at which the quantity of labor demanded equals the quantity of labor supplied. Potential GDP is independent of the price level.

Financial technology is determined by the state of knowledge and the quantity of capital (computers, ATMs, and so on) that banks have installed. Like potential GDP, financial technology is independent of the price level.

The Nominal Interest Rate in the Long Run

In 2001, businesses in the United States could borrow at a nominal interest rate of around 7 percent a year. Businesses in Russia paid a nominal interest rate of 60 percent a year, and businesses in Turkey paid 80 percent a year. Although the U.S. nominal interest rate has never been as high as these two cases, U.S. businesses faced a nominal interest rate of 16 percent a year during the 1980s.

Nominal interest rates vary across countries and over time for many reasons, but the dominant one is differences in inflation rates. The equilibrium nominal interest rate equals the equilibrium real interest rate plus the inflation rate. That is, the nominal interest rate exceeds the real interest rate by the inflation rate.

You studied the global financial market, which determines investment, saving, and the equilibrium real interest rate in Chapter 24. The real interest rate, like potential GDP, is independent of the price level. It is also independent of the inflation rate in the long run.

But the nominal interest rate depends directly on the inflation rate. Borrowers are willing to pay a higher nominal interest rate when there is inflation because the real value of loans decreases over time. And lenders insist on receiving a higher nominal interest rate because the money with which they are repaid buys less than what the money they loaned would have bought.

An Example   Suppose that when there is no inflation, investment equals saving at a real interest rate of 3 percent a year. Walt Disney Corporation is willing to pay an interest rate of 3 percent a year to get the funds it needs to pay for its new theme parks. Sue (along with millions of others) is willing to save and lend Disney the amount it needs for its theme parks at a real interest rate of 3 percent a year.

Now imagine that the inflation rate is steady at 2 percent a year. All dollar amounts, including theme park profits and car prices, are rising by 2 percent a year. If Disney was willing to pay an interest rate of 3 percent a year when there was no inflation, it is now willing to pay 5 percent a year. Its profits are rising by 2 percent a year, so it is really paying only 3 percent a year. Similarly, if Sue was willing to lend at 3 percent a year when there was no inflation, she is now willing to lend only if the interest rate is 5 percent a year. The price of the car that Sue is planning to buy is rising by 2 percent a year, so she is really getting an interest rate of only 3 percent a year.

Because borrowers are willing to pay the higher rate and lenders are willing to lend only if they receive the higher rate when inflation is present, the nominal interest rate increases by an amount equal to the inflation rate.

We'll explain how the inflation rate is determined later in this chapter.

Money Market Equilibrium in the Long Run

In the long run, money market equilibrium determines the price level. All the other factors that influence the amount of money that people plan to hold are determined outside the money market.

Figure 28.4 shows long-run money market equilibrium. The position of the demand for money curve in part (a) depends on real GDP and the price level. But in the long run, real GDP equals potential GDP, so the demand for money curve depends only on the price level. The figure shows three possible short-run situations. First, if the price level is 100, the demand for money is MD_0 and the equilibrium nominal interest rate is 5 percent a year. Second, if the price level is 102, the demand for money is MD_1 and the equilibrium nominal interest rate is 6 percent a year. Finally, if the price level is 98, the demand for money is MD_2 and the equilibrium nominal interest rate is 4 percent a year.

Only one of these short-run situations describes the long run. Which one? Part (b) provides the answer. Saving and investment decisions determine the long-run equilibrium real interest rate, which we'll assume to be 3 percent a year. The nominal interest rate is the real interest rate plus the inflation rate. We'll assume that

FIGURE 28.4
Long-Run Equilibrium

(a) Three short-run situations

(b) Money market equilibrium in the long run

❶ The demand for money depends on the price level, so ❷ the equilibrium nominal interest rate also depends on the price level.

❸ The long-run equilibrium real interest rate (determined in the global financial market) plus ❹ the inflation rate determines the

❺ long-run equilibrium nominal interest rate.

❻ The price level adjusts to 100 to achieve money market equilibrium at the long-run equilibrium interest rate.

the inflation rate is 2 percent a year. So the long-run equilibrium nominal interest rate is 5 percent a year. Only one of the *possible* equilibrium situations shown in part (a) is consistent with the long-run equilibrium nominal interest rate. It is the situation in which the price level is 100, the demand for money is MD_0, and the nominal interest rate is 5 percent a year.

You will see how this long-run equilibrium comes about by considering what happens if the Fed changes the quantity of money.

■ A Change in the Quantity of Money

Suppose that the quantity of money is initially $1 trillion and the Fed then increases it by 2 percent to $1.02 trillion. In the short run, the greater quantity of money lowers the nominal interest rate. With a lower interest rate, aggregate demand increases and the price level rises. Eventually, a new long-run equilibrium is reached at which the price level has increased in proportion to the increase in the quantity of money.

Because the quantity of money increased by 2 percent from $1 trillion to $1.02 trillion, the price level rises by 2 percent from 100 to 102.

Figure 28.5 illustrates these events. Initially, the supply of money curve is MS_0, the demand for money curve is MD_0, the nominal interest rate is at its long-run equilibrium level of 5 percent a year, and the price level that lies behind MD_0 is 100.

The quantity of money then increases, and the supply of money curve shifts rightward to MS_1. Initially, the price level remains at 100, so the demand for money curve remains at MD_0. The nominal interest rate falls below its long-run equilibrium level to 4 percent a year. The lower interest rate brings increased spending, which eventually raises the price level to 102. The demand for money increases as the price level rises, and the interest rate rises. Eventually, the economy is back at its long-run equilibrium interest rate but at a higher price level.

You've just seen a key proposition about money and the price level.

In the long run and other things remaining the same, a given percentage change in the quantity of money brings an equal percentage change in the price level.

The Price Level in a Baby-Sitting Club

It is hard to visualize a long-run equilibrium and even harder to visualize and compare two long-run equilibrium situations. So an example of a simpler situation might help.

In an isolated neighborhood, there are no teenagers but lots of young children and parents can't find any babysitters. So they form a club and sit for each other. The deal is that each time a parent sits for someone else, he or she receives a token that can be used to buy one sit from another member of the club. The organizer

---

■ **FIGURE 28.5**

A Change in the Price Level

❶ The quantity of money increases by 2 percent from $1 trillion to $1.02 trillion, and the supply of money curve shifts from MS_0 to MS_1.

❷ In the short run, the interest rate falls to 4 percent a year.

❸ In the long run, the price level rises by 2 percent from 100 to 102, the demand for money curve shifts from MD_0 to MD_1, and the nominal interest rate returns to its long-run equilibrium level.

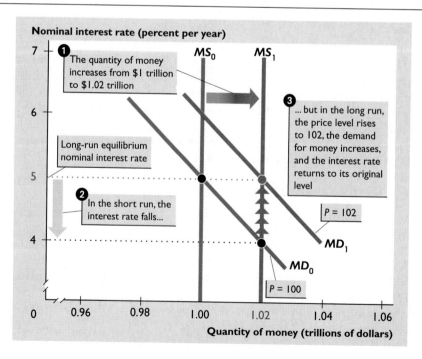

notices that the club is inactive. Every member has a few unspent tokens, but they spend them infrequently. To make the club more active, the organizer decides to issue every member one token for each token that is currently held, so the supply of tokens doubles.

With more tokens to spend, parents start to plan more evenings out. Suddenly, the phones are ringing as parents seek babysitters. Every member of the club wants a sitter. But there are no more sitters than before. After making a few calls and finding no sitters available, anxious parents who really do need a sitter start to offer a higher price: two tokens per session. That does the trick. At the higher price, the quantity of baby-sitting services demanded decreases and the quantity supplied increases. Equilibrium is restored. Nothing real has changed, but the quantity of tokens and the price level have doubled.

Think of the equilibrium quantity of baby-sitting services as potential GDP, the quantity of tokens as the quantity of money, and the price of a baby-sitting session as the price level. You can then see how a given percentage change in the quantity of money at full employment brings an equal percentage change in the price level.

■ The Quantity Theory of Money

The proposition that when real GDP equals potential GDP, an increase in the quantity of money brings an equal percentage increase in the price level is called the **quantity theory of money**. We've derived this proposition by looking at equilibrium in the money market in the long run. Another way of seeing the relationship between the quantity of money and the price level uses the concepts of *the velocity of circulation* and *the equation of exchange*. We're now going to explore this alternative approach. We're then going to see how ongoing money growth brings inflation and see what determines the inflation rate in the long run.

Quantity theory of money
The proposition that when real GDP equals potential GDP, an increase in the quantity of money brings an equal percentage increase in the price level.

The Velocity of Circulation and Equation of Exchange

The **velocity of circulation** is the number of times in a year that the average dollar of money gets used to buy final goods and services. The value of final goods and services is nominal GDP, which is real GDP, Y, multiplied by the price level, P. If we call the quantity of money M, then the velocity of circulation is determined by the equation:

$$V = (P \times Y) \div M.$$

In this equation, P is the GDP deflator divided by 100. For example, if the GDP deflator is 125, the price level is 1.25. If the price level is 1.25, real GDP is $8 trillion, and the quantity of money is $2 trillion, then the velocity of circulation is

$$V = (1.25 \times \$8 \text{ trillion}) \div \$2 \text{ trillion, or}$$

$$V = 5.$$

That is, with $2 trillion of money, the average dollar gets used 5 times, so $2 trillion $\times$ 5 = $10 trillion of goods and services are bought.

The **equation of exchange** states that the quantity of money, M, multiplied by the velocity of circulation, V, equals the price level P, multiplied by real GDP, Y. That is,

$$M \times V = P \times Y.$$

Velocity of circulation
The number of times in a year that the average dollar of money gets used to buy final goods and services.

Equation of exchange
An equation that states that the quantity of money multiplied by the velocity of circulation equals the price level multiplied by real GDP.

The equation of exchange is *always* true because it is implied by the definition of the velocity of circulation. That is, if you multiply both sides of the equation on page 711 that defines the velocity of circulation by M, you get the equation of exchange.

Using the above numbers—a price level of 1.25, real GDP of $8 trillion, the quantity of money of $2 trillion, and the velocity of circulation of 5—you can see that

$$M \times V = \$2 \text{ trillion} \times 5 = \$10 \text{ trillion,}$$

and

$$P \times Y = 1.25 \times \$8 \text{ trillion} = \$10 \text{ trillion.}$$

So,

$$M \times V = P \times Y = \$10 \text{ trillion.}$$

The Quantity Theory Prediction

We can rearrange the equation of exchange to isolate the price level on the left side. To do so, divide both sides of the equation of exchange by real GDP to obtain

$$P = M \times V \div Y.$$

On the left side is the price level. And on the right side are all the things that influence the price level. But this equation is still just an implication of the definition of the velocity of circulation. To turn the equation into a theory of what determines the price level, we use two other facts: (1) At full employment, real GDP equals potential GDP, which is determined only by real factors and not by the quantity of money; and (2) the velocity of circulation is relatively stable and does not change when the quantity of money changes.

So if M increases with V and Y constant, P must increase, and the percentage increase in P equals the percentage increase in M.

We can use the above numbers to illustrate this prediction. Real GDP is $8 trillion, the quantity of money is $2 trillion, and the velocity of circulation is 5. Put these values into the equation:

$$P = M \times V \div Y$$

to obtain

$$P = \$2 \text{ trillion} \times 5 \div \$8 \text{ trillion} = 1.25.$$

Now increase the quantity of money from $2 trillion to $2.4 trillion. The percentage increase in the quantity of money is

$$(\$2.4 \text{ trillion} - \$2 \text{ trillion}) \times 100 \div \$2 \text{ trillion} = 20 \text{ percent.}$$

Now find the new price level. It is

$$P = \$2.4 \text{ trillion} \times 5 \div \$8 \text{ trillion} = 1.50.$$

The price level rises from 1.25 to 1.50. The percentage increase in the price level is

$$(1.50 - 1.25) \times 100 \div 1.25 = 20 \text{ percent.}$$

The price level and the quantity of money increase by the same 20 percent.

■ Inflation and the Quantity Theory of Money

The equation of exchange tells us about the price *level*, the quantity of money, the level of real GDP and the level of the velocity of circulation. We can turn the equation into one that tells us about *rates of change* or *growth rates*. We want to make this conversion because the inflation rate is the rate of change in the price level, and we want to know what determines the inflation rate.

In rates of change or growth rates,

Money growth + Velocity growth = Inflation rate + Real GDP growth,

which means that

Inflation rate = Money growth + Velocity growth − Real GDP growth.

Figure 28.6 illustrates three cases. In each case, the velocity growth rate is 1 percent a year and the real GDP growth rate is 3 percent a year. If the quantity of money grows at a rate of 2 percent a year, there is no inflation. That is,

Inflation rate = 2 percent a year + 1 percent a year − 3 percent a year = 0.

With the quantity of money growing at 4 percent a year, the inflation rate is 2 percent a year. That is,

Inflation rate = 4 percent a year + 1 percent a year − 3 percent a year = 2.

And with the quantity of money growing at 10 percent a year, the inflation rate is 8 percent a year. That is,

Inflation rate = 10 percent a year + 1 percent a year − 3 percent a year = 8.

■ **FIGURE 28.6**
Money Growth and Inflation

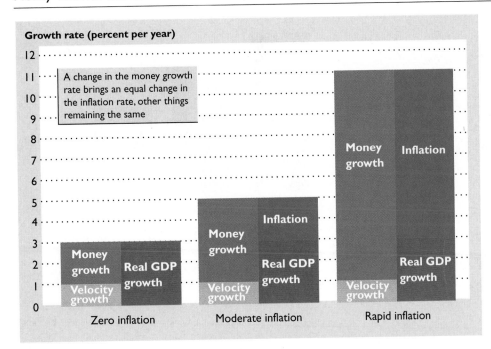

The velocity of circulation grows at 1 percent a year (the orange block), and real GDP grows at 3 percent a year (the red block). The inflation rate is determined by money growth.

If the quantity of money grows at 2 percent a year, the inflation rate is zero.

If the quantity of money grows at 4 percent a year, the inflation rate is a moderate 2 percent a year.

But if the quantity of money grows at 10 percent a year, the inflation rate is a rapid 8 percent a year.

Changes in the Inflation Rate

Figure 28.6 illustrates three different inflation rates—zero, moderate, and rapid—with a given growth rate of real GDP and velocity. But are the real GDP growth rate and rate of change of velocity independent of the money growth rate? Do they remain the same when the money growth rate changes?

The answer is that the inflation rate does influence velocity and real GDP, so the link between money growth and inflation is not as precise as that shown in Figure 28.6.

Velocity increases when the inflation rate speeds up. But this increase does not persist. Once velocity has increased in response to a higher inflation rate, it remains constant at its new level. You can see in *Eye on the U.S. Economy* below that velocity growth has been zero for most of the past 40 years and only during the 1990s contributed slightly to the inflation rate.

A faster inflation reduces potential GDP and slows real GDP growth (for reasons that we explore in the final section of this chapter). But for low inflation rates, these effects are small and are dominated by the main direct effect of money growth on the inflation rate.

Again, you can see in *Eye on the U.S. Economy* below that changes in the growth rate of real GDP have been small in comparison to the changes in the growth rate of money and the inflation rate.

So it is changes in the money growth rate that bring changes in the inflation rate. This fact is at its clearest when money growth and inflation are rapid.

EYE ON THE U.S. ECONOMY

The Quantity Theory of Money in Action

During the 1960s, M2 velocity was constant, real GDP grew at 4.4 percent a year, the quantity of M2 grew at 6.7 percent a year, and the inflation rate was 2.3 percent a year.

During the 1970s, M2 growth climbed, real GDP growth shrank, and the inflation rate increased to 6.6 percent a year. During the 1980s and 1990s, M2 growth slowed and so did inflation. But during the 1990s, an

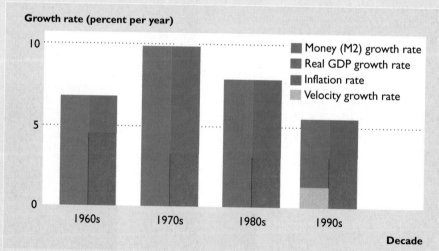

SOURCE OF DATA: Federal Reserve.

increase in the velocity of circulation of M2 kept the inflation rate higher than it would otherwise have been by almost 2 percent a year.

■ Hyperinflation

Truly rapid inflation, when the inflation rate exceeds 50 percent *a month,* is called **hyperinflation**. Hyperinflation occurs when a government's expenditures exceed the sum of what it can collect in tax revenue and borrow. In such a situation, the government prints money and the quantity of money increases at an extraordinarily rapid rate. This phenomenon is rare but not unknown (see *Eye on the Past* below). The highest inflation rates in the world today, in the African nations of Angola and Zimbabwe, exceed 100 percent a year but are not considered hyperinflation.

Hyperinflation
Inflation at a rate that exceeds 50 percent *a month.*

EYE ON THE PAST

Hyperinflation in Germany in the 1920s

An international treaty signed in 1919 required Germany to pay large amounts as compensation for war damage to other countries in Europe. To meet its obligations, Germany started to print money. The German money supply increased by 24 percent in 1921, by 220 percent in 1922, and by 43 *billion* percent in 1923!

Not surprisingly, the price level increased rapidly. The figure shows you how rapidly. In November 1923, when the hyperinflation reached its peak, the price level was more than doubling every day. Wages were paid twice a day, and people spent their morning's wages at lunchtime to avoid the loss in the value of money that the afternoon would bring.

In 1923, bank notes were more valuable as fire kindling than as money, and the sight of people burning Reichmarks (the name of Germany's money at that time) was a common one.

SOURCE OF DATA: Phillip Cagan, "The Monetary Dynamics of Hyperinflation," in Milton Friedman (editor), *Studies in the Quantity Theory of Money,* University of Chicago Press, 1956.

2 **Explain how in the long run, the quantity of money determines the price level and money growth brings inflation.**

Practice Problems 28.2

1. In 1999, the Canadian economy was at full employment. Real GDP was $886 billion, the nominal interest rate was around 6 percent per year, the inflation rate was 2 percent a year, the price level was 1.1, and the velocity of circulation was constant at 10.
   a. Calculate the real interest rate.
   b. If the real interest rate remains unchanged when the inflation rate increases to 4 percent a year, explain how the nominal interest rate changes.
   c. What was the quantity of money in Canada?

2. If the quantity of money grows at a rate of 10 percent a year and potential GDP grows at 3 percent a year, what is the inflation rate in the long run?

Exercises 28.2

1. In 2002, the United Kingdom was at full employment. Nominal GDP was £850 billion, the real interest rate was 5 percent per year, the inflation rate was 6 percent a year, and the price level was 120.
   a. Calculate the nominal interest rate.
   b. If the real interest rate remains unchanged when the inflation rate in the long run decreases to 3 percent a year, explain how the nominal interest rate changes.

2. In 2003, the United Kingdom was at full employment. Nominal GDP was £900 billion, the nominal interest rate was 8 percent per year, the price level was 130, and the velocity of circulation was constant at 2. What was the quantity of money in the United Kingdom?

3. In exercise 2, if the velocity of circulation remains at 2, money grows at 8 percent a year, and real GDP grows at 5 percent a year in the long run, what is the inflation rate in the long run?

Solutions to Practice Problems 28.2

1a. The real interest rate equals the nominal interest rate minus the inflation rate. That is, the real interest rate equals 6 percent a year minus 2 percent a year, which equals 4 percent a year.

1b. The nominal interest rate rises from 6 percent a year to 8 percent a year.

1c. Velocity of circulation (V) = Nominal GDP $(P \times Y)$ ÷ Quantity of money (M). Rewrite this equation as: $M = (P \times Y) \div V$.
$(P \times Y)$ = $886 billion $\times$ 1.1, or $975 billion, so M = $975 billion ÷ 10, or $97.5 billion.

2. With velocity constant, velocity growth is zero. So the inflation rate in the long run equals the money growth rate minus the real GDP growth rate, which is 10 percent a year minus 3 percent a year, or 7 percent a year.

28.3 THE COST OF INFLATION

Inflation decreases potential GDP, slows economic growth, and consumes leisure time. These outcomes occur for four reasons that we classify as the four costs of inflation:

- Tax costs
- Shoe-leather costs
- Confusion costs
- Uncertainty costs

■ Tax Costs

We've seen that inflation occurs when the quantity of money grows more rapidly than real GDP. But why would we ever want to make this happen? Why don't we keep the quantity of money growing at the same pace as real GDP grows? One part of the answer is that the government gets revenue from inflation.

Inflation Is a Tax

Inflation is a tax on holding money. To see how the inflation tax gets paid, suppose that the Coca-Cola Company keeps $100,000 in money on the average. With inflation at 10 percent a year, that money will buy only $90,000 of goods and services after one year. So Coca-Cola loses $10,000 a year—it pays $10,000 a year in inflation tax.

You've seen how Coca-Cola *pays* the inflation tax. But how does the government get *revenue* from it? The answer is by selling government securities that end up being held by the Federal Reserve. When the government issues securities, it must pay interest on them. But paying interest to the Fed costs the government nothing because it owns the Fed and gets the Fed's profits. So when the government issues securities that end up at the Fed, the government gets the value of those securities to spend. But when the Fed buys government securities, the quantity of money grows and money growth brings inflation.

So inflation is a tax. If this were the end of the story, the inflation tax would not be a problem. It would be just one more way for the government to collect revenue—an alternative to the income tax or the sales tax. Inflation would transfer resources from households and businesses to the government, but it would not be a cost to society. Some would pay and others would benefit, and the two actions would cancel each other out.

Inflation Tax, Saving, and Investment

The inflation tax is bigger than the tax on money holding, and it interacts with the income tax to lower saving and investment. The core of the problem is that inflation increases the nominal interest rate, and because income taxes are paid on nominal interest income, the true income tax rate rises with inflation. Let's consider an example.

Suppose that the real interest rate is 4 percent a year and the income tax rate is 50 percent. With no inflation, the nominal interest rate is also 4 percent a year and 50 percent of this rate is taxed. The real after-tax interest rate is 2 percent a year (50 percent of 4 percent). Now suppose the inflation rate is 4 percent a year, so the nominal interest rate is 8 percent a year. The after-tax nominal rate is 4 percent a year (50 percent of 8 percent). Now subtract the 4 percent inflation rate from this amount, and you see that the after-tax real interest rate is zero! The true income tax rate is 100 percent.

The higher the inflation rate, the higher is the true income tax rate on income from capital. And the higher the tax rate, the higher is the interest rate paid by borrowers and the lower is the after-tax interest rate received by lenders.

With a low after-tax real interest rate, the incentive to save is weakened and the supply of saving decreases. With a high cost of borrowing, the amount of investment decreases. And with a fall in saving and investment, the pace of capital accumulation slows and so does the long-term growth rate of real GDP.

■ Shoe-Leather Costs

The "shoe-leather costs" of inflation are costs that arise from an increase in the velocity of circulation of money and an increase in the amount of running around that people do to try to avoid incurring losses from the falling value of money.

When money loses value at a rapid anticipated rate, it does not function well as a store of value and people try to avoid holding it. They spend their incomes as soon as they receive them, and firms pay out incomes—wages and dividends—as soon as they receive revenue from their sales. The velocity of circulation increases.

During the 1990s when inflation in Brazil was around 80 percent a year, people would end a taxi ride at the ATM closest to their destination, get some cash, pay the driver, and finish their journey on foot. The driver would deposit the cash in his bank account before looking for the next customer.

During the 1920s when inflation in Germany exceeded 50 percent a month—hyperinflation—wages were paid and spent twice in a single day!

Imagine the inconvenience of spending most of your time figuring out how to keep your money holdings close to zero.

One way of keeping money holdings low is to find other means of payment such as tokens, commodities, or even barter. All of these are less efficient than money as a means of payment. For example, in Israel during the 1980s, when inflation reached 1,000 percent a year, the U.S. dollar started to replace the increasingly worthless shekel. Consequently, people had to keep track of the exchange rate between the shekel and the dollar hour by hour and had to engage in many additional and costly transactions in the foreign exchange market.

■ Confusion Costs

We make economic decisions by comparing marginal cost and marginal benefit. Marginal cost is a real cost—an opportunity forgone. Marginal benefit is a real benefit—a willingness to forgo an opportunity. Although costs and benefits are real, we use money as our unit of account and standard of value to calculate them. Money is our measuring rod of value. Borrowers and lenders, workers and employers, all make agreements in terms of money. Inflation makes the value of money change, so it changes the units on our measuring rod.

Does it matter that our units of value keep changing? Some economists think it matters a lot. Others think it matters only a little.

Economists who think it matters a lot point to the obvious benefits of stable units of measurement in other areas of life. For example, suppose that we had not invented an accurate time-keeping technology and clocks and watches gained 5 to 15 minutes a day. Imagine the hassle you would have arriving at class on time or catching the start of the ball game. For another example, suppose that a tailor used an elastic tape measure. You would end up with a jacket that was either too tight or too loose, depending on how tightly the tape was stretched.

For a third example, recall the crash of the Mars Climate Orbiter.

> "Mars Climate Orbiter . . . failed to achieve Mars orbit because of a navigation error. . . . Spacecraft operating data needed for navigation were provided . . . in English units rather than the specified metric units. This was the direct cause of the failure." (Mars Program Independent Assessment Team Summary Report, March 14, 2000)

If rocket scientists can't make correct calculations that use just two units of measurement, what chance do ordinary people and business decision makers have of making correct calculations that involve money when its value keeps changing?

These examples of confusion and error that can arise from units of measurement don't automatically mean that a changing value of money is a big problem. But they raise the possibility that it might be.

■ Uncertainty Costs

A high inflation rate brings increased uncertainty about the long-term inflation rate. Will inflation remain high for a long time or will price stability be restored? This increased uncertainty makes long-term planning difficult and gives people a shorter-term focus. Investment falls, and so the economic growth rate slows.

But this increased uncertainty also misallocates resources. Instead of concentrating on the activities at which they have a comparative advantage, people find it more profitable to search for ways of avoiding the losses that inflation inflicts. As a result, inventive talent that might otherwise work on productive innovations works on finding ways of profiting from the inflation instead.

Uncertainty about inflation makes the economy behave a bit like a casino in which some people gain and some lose and no one can predict where the gains and losses will fall. Gains and losses occur because of unpredictable changes in the value of money. In a period of rapid, unpredictable inflation, resources get diverted from productive activities to forecasting inflation. It becomes more profitable to forecast the inflation rate correctly than to invent a new product. Doctors, lawyers, accountants, farmers—just about everyone—can make themselves better off, not by specializing in the profession for which they have been trained but by spending more of their time dabbling as amateur economists and inflation forecasters and managing their investment portfolios.

From a social perspective, this diversion of talent resulting from uncertainty about inflation is like throwing scarce resources onto the garbage heap. This waste of resources is a cost of inflation.

■ How Big Is the Cost of Inflation?

The cost of inflation depends on its rate and its predictability. The higher the rate, the greater is the cost. And the more unpredictable the rate, the greater is the cost. Peter Howitt of Brown University, building on work by Robert Barro of Harvard University, has estimated that if inflation is lowered from 3 percent a year to zero, the growth rate of real GDP will rise by between 0.06 and 0.09 percentage points a year. These numbers might seem small. But they are growth rates. After 30 years, real GDP would be 2.3 percent higher and the accumulated value of all the additional future output would be worth 85 percent of current GDP, or $10.5 trillion!

In hyperinflation, the costs are much greater. Hyperinflation is rare, but there have been some spectacular examples of it. Several European countries experienced hyperinflation during the 1920s after World War I and again during the 1940s after World War II. But hyperinflation is more than just a historical curiosity. It occurs in today's world. In 1994, the African nation of Zaire had a hyperinflation that peaked at a monthly inflation rate of 76 percent. Also in 1994, Brazil almost reached the hyperinflation stratosphere with a monthly inflation rate of 40 percent. A cup of coffee that cost 15 cruzeiros in 1980 cost 22 billion cruzeiros in 1994. And Russia has had a near hyperinflation experience in recent years.

CHECKPOINT 28.3

3 **Identify the costs of inflation and the benefits of a stable value of money.**

Practice Problem 28.3

1. Suppose that you have $1,000 in your savings account and the bank pays an interest rate of 5 percent a year. The inflation rate is 3 percent a year. The government taxes the interest that you earn on your deposit at 20 percent.
   a. Calculate the nominal after-tax interest rate that you earn.
   b. Calculate the real after-tax interest rate that you earn.

Exercise 28.3

1. Sally has a credit card balance of $4,000. The credit card company charges a nominal interest rate of 18 percent a year on unpaid balances. The inflation rate is 3 percent a year.
   a. Calculate the real interest rate that Sally pays the credit card company.
   b. If the inflation rate falls to 2 percent a year and the nominal interest rate remains the same, calculate the real interest rate that Sally pays.

Solution to Practice Problem 28.3

1a. You earn $50 of interest and the government takes $10 of the interest in tax, so the interest income you earn after tax is $40. The nominal after-tax interest rate is 4 percent a year.

1b. The real after-tax interest rate equals the nominal after-tax interest rate minus the inflation rate, which is 1 percent a year.

CHAPTER CHECKPOINT

Key Points

1 **Explain what determines the demand for money and how the demand for money and the supply of money determine the *nominal* interest rate.**

- The demand for money is the relationship between the quantity of money demanded and the nominal interest rate, other things remaining the same—the higher the nominal interest rate, other things remaining the same, the smaller is the quantity of money demanded.
- Increases in real GDP increase the demand for money. Some advances in financial technology increase the demand for money, and some advances decrease it.
- Each day, the price level, real GDP, and financial technology are given and money market equilibrium determines the nominal interest rate.
- To lower the interest rate, the Fed increases the supply of money. To raise the interest rate, the Fed decreases the supply of money.

2 **Explain how in the long run, the quantity of money determines the price level and money growth brings inflation.**

- In the long run, real GDP equals potential GDP and the real interest rate is the level that makes the quantity of investment demanded equal the quantity of saving supplied in the global financial market.
- The nominal interest rate in the long run equals the equilibrium real interest rate plus the inflation rate.
- Money market equilibrium in the long run determines the price level.
- An increase in the quantity of money, other things remaining the same, increases the price level by the same percentage.
- The inflation rate in the long run equals the growth rate of the quantity of money minus the growth rate of potential GDP.
- The equation of exchange and the velocity of circulation provide an alternative way of viewing the relationship between the quantity of money and the price level (and money growth and inflation).

3 **Identify the costs of inflation and the benefits of a stable value of money.**

- Inflation has four costs: tax costs, shoe-leather costs, confusion costs, and uncertainty costs.
- The higher the inflation rate, the greater are these four costs.

Key Terms

Demand for money, 700
Equation of exchange, 711
Hyperinflation, 715

Quantity of money demanded, 699
Quantity theory of money, 711
Supply of money, 702

Velocity of circulation, 711

Exercises

1. Review the factors that influence the quantity of money that people plan to hold and
   a. Draw a graph to illustrate the demand for money curve.
   b. Show the new demand for money curve that results from an increase in real GDP.
   c. Illustrate on your graph the effects of a change in the interest rate.
   d. Show the effects of an increase in the number of families that have a credit card.
   e. Explain how the spread of ATMs has influenced the demand for money.

2. The Fed decreases the quantity of money. Explain the effects of this action in the short run and the long run on
   a. The quantity of money demanded.
   b. The nominal interest rate.
   c. The real interest rate.
   d. Real GDP.
   e. The price level.

3. The Fed conducts an open market purchase of securities. [Hint: Check back with Chapter 27 if you need a reminder about the effects of an open market operation.] Explain the effects of this action in the short run and the long run on
   a. The quantity of money.
   b. The quantity of money demanded.
   c. The nominal interest rate.
   d. The real interest rate.
   e. Real GDP.
   f. The price level.

4. In 2000, the United States was at full employment. The quantity of money was growing at 8.3 percent a year, the nominal interest rate was 9.5 percent a year, real GDP grew at 5 percent a year, and the inflation rate was 3.1 percent a year.
   a. Calculate the real interest rate.
   b. Use the information given along with the quantity theory of money to see whether the velocity of circulation was constant. If it was not constant, how did it change? And if it changed, why might it have changed?

5. Suppose the government passes a new law that sets a limit on the interest rate that credit card companies can charge on overdue balances. As a result, the nominal interest rate charged by credit card companies falls from 15 percent a year to 7 percent a year. If the average income tax rate is 30 percent, explain how the real after-tax interest rate on overdue credit card balances changes.

6. Draw a graph of the money market to illustrate equilibrium in both the short run and the long run. If the growth rate of the quantity of money increases,
   a. Explain what happens to the real interest rate and the nominal interest rate in the short run.
   b. Explain what happens to the real interest rate and the nominal interest rate in the long run.
   c. Explain why the short-run effects are different from the long-run effects.

7. What is the quantity theory of money?

8. Define the velocity of circulation and explain how it is measured.

9. If the quantity of money is $3 trillion, real GDP is $10 trillion, the price level is 0.9, the real interest rate is 2 percent a year, and the nominal interest rate is 7 percent a year,
   a. What is the velocity of circulation?
   b. What is the value of $M \times V$?
   c. What is the value of nominal GDP?

10. If the velocity of circulation is constant, real GDP is growing at 3 percent a year, the real interest rate is 2 percent a year, and the nominal interest rate is 7 percent a year,
    a. What is the inflation rate?
    b. What is the growth rate of money?
    c. What is the growth rate of nominal GDP?

11. If the velocity of circulation is growing at a rate of 1 percent a year, the real interest rate is 2 percent a year, the nominal interest rate is 7 percent a year, and the growth rate of real GDP is 3 percent a year,
    a. What is the inflation rate?
    b. What is the growth rate of money?
    c. What is the growth rate of nominal GDP?

12. List the costs of inflation and provide an example of each type of cost.

Critical Thinking

13. Explain what the costs of inflation were for Brazilians when inflation hit 40 percent a month in Brazil.

14. Explain why businesses paid workers twice a day during the hyperinflation in Germany after World War I and why workers spent their incomes as soon as they were paid.

15. With the spread of credit cards, debit cards, and e-cash, people will want to hold less and less money. Eventually, no one will want to hold any money and the Federal Reserve will have no role. Critically evaluate this view.

16. The Federal Reserve could easily eliminate inflation by making the quantity of money grow at a rate equal to the growth rate of real GDP minus the growth rate of the velocity of circulation. Do you think the Fed should pursue this objective? Explain why or why not.

17. The Federal Reserve could hold the interest rate constant by making the quantity of money adjust to match the quantity of money demanded at the chosen interest rate. Do you think the Fed should pursue this objective? Explain why or why not.

18. Do you think the Federal Reserve could simultaneously pursue a fixed interest rate and a money growth rate equal to the growth rate of real GDP minus the growth rate of the velocity of circulation? Explain why or why not.

Web Exercises

Use the links on MyEconLab to work the following exercises.

19. Visit the Web sites of the Federal Reserve and the Bureau of Economic Analysis and obtain the latest data on the quantity of M1 and M2, real GDP, and the price level.
    a. Calculate the inflation rate, the growth rate of the two money aggregates, and the growth rate of real GDP.
    b. Use the information you calculated in part **a** to determine whether the velocity of circulation was constant. If it was not constant, how did it change? If it changed, why might it have changed?
    c. Given the information that you obtained in part **a,** do you think the Fed is trying to slow inflation, speed up inflation, or neither? If neither, what do you think the Fed is trying to do?

20. Visit the European Central Bank Web site.
    a. Obtain data on money supply growth rates and inflation rates for the euro area.
    b. Is the money supply in the euro area growing faster or slower than in the United States?
    c. Would you expect inflation in the euro area to be higher, lower, or about the same as in the United States? Explain why.

21. Visit the International Monetary Fund's World Economic Outlook database Web site.
    a. Obtain data on money supply growth rates and inflation rates for Advanced Economies and the Developing Economies.
    b. Use a spreadsheet program (Excel or Lotus 1-2-3) to make a scatter diagram of the data placing money growth on the *x*-axis and inflation on the *y*-axis.
    c. Do these data support or contradict the quantity theory of money?

AS-AD and the Business Cycle

CHAPTER CHECKLIST

When you have completed your study of this chapter, you will be able to

1 Provide a technical definition of recession and describe the history of the U.S. business cycle and the global business cycle.

2 Define and explain the influences on aggregate supply.

3 Define and explain the influences on aggregate demand.

4 Explain how fluctuations in aggregate demand and aggregate supply create the business cycle.

What kind of economy will you face when you graduate? Will production and jobs be expanding rapidly in a booming economy? Or will production and jobs be shrinking in a stagnating economy? You know that both booming and stagnating conditions happen, and you've seen both in the period since 2000. Between 2000 and 2002, real GDP barely changed and unemployment soared. But after 2002, real GDP surged and unemployment fell.

In this chapter, you're going to review what economists know about the sources of economic fluctuations. You're going to study the aggregate supply–aggregate demand, or *AS-AD,* model. The purpose of this model is to explain, predict, and hopefully better control the business cycle—the recessions and expansions that alternate through our economic history.

We begin with some definitions and a bit of business-cycle history.

29.1 BUSINESS-CYCLE DEFINITIONS AND FACTS

We defined the *business cycle* in Chapter 20 (p. 513) as a periodic but irregular up-and-down movement in production and jobs. A business cycle has two phases, expansion and recession, and two turning points, a peak and a trough. An expansion runs from a trough to a peak, and a recession runs from a peak to a trough.

Over the business cycle, real GDP fluctuates around trend. When real GDP is below trend, resources are *under*used—some labor is unemployed and capital is underemployed. When real GDP is above trend, resources are *over*used—people work longer hours than they are willing to put up with in the long run, capital is worked so intensively that it is not maintained in prime condition, delivery times lengthen, bottlenecks occur, and backorders increase.

■ Dating Business-Cycle Turning Points

The task of identifying and dating business-cycle phases and turning points is performed not by the U.S. government, but by a private research organization, the National Bureau of Economic Research (NBER). The NBER's Business Cycle Dating Committee determines the month in which a cycle peak or trough occurred. In November 2001, the committee announced that a business-cycle peak had occurred in March 2001. By coincidence, November 2001 was eventually identified (in July 2003) as the month of the trough and the end of recession.

Recession
A decrease in real GDP that lasts for at least two quarters (six months) or a period of significant decline in total output, income, employment, and trade, usually lasting from six months to a year, and marked by widespread contractions in many sectors of the economy.

To date the business-cycle turning points, the NBER needs a definition of recession. A standard definition of **recession** is a decrease in real GDP that lasts for at least two quarters (six months). The NBER uses a broader definition. It defines a recession as "a period of significant decline in total output, income, employment, and trade, usually lasting from six months to a year, and marked by widespread contractions in many sectors of the economy."

In this definition of recession, total output and income are the same thing as real GDP. You've seen that employment fluctuations closely match fluctuations in real GDP. Because real GDP measures production in all sectors of the economy, a decrease in real GDP means that many sectors of the economy are experiencing falling production. So although the NBER looks beyond real GDP to date the turning points precisely, a two-quarter decrease in real GDP is a good practical indicator of recession and gives almost the same dating as the NBER's method.

■ U.S. Business-Cycle History

The NBER has identified 33 complete cycles starting from a trough in December 1854. In 2001, we entered the 34th expansion. (*Eye on the U.S. Economy* on p. 728 examines the details of the 2001 recession and subsequent onset of expansion.)

Over all 33 complete cycles, the average length of an expansion is 35 months, the average length of a recession is 18 months, and the average time from trough to trough is 53 months. So over the 152 years since 1854, the U.S. economy has been in recession for about one third of the time and in expansion for about two thirds of the time.

The 152-year averages hide big changes that have occurred in the length of a cycle and the relative length of the recession and expansion phases. Figure 29.1 shows these changes by dividing U.S. business-cycle history into three periods: 1854–1919 (before and during World War I), 1919–1945 (between the two World Wars and through World War II), and 1945–2005 (the post–World War II years).

FIGURE 29.1
Recession, Expansion, and Cycle Length: A Summary

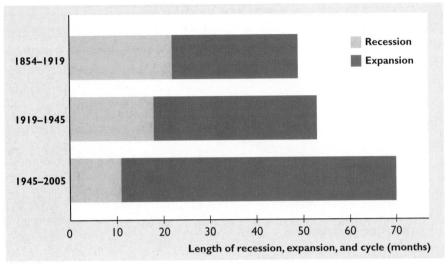

During the nineteenth century and through World War I, recessions were almost as long as expansions. During the twentieth century, recessions shortened, expansions lengthened, and complete cycles lengthened.

SOURCE OF DATA: National Bureau of Economic Research.

The figure shows that before 1919, recessions lasted for 22 months and expansions for 27 months on the average. So during this period, recession was almost as common an experience as expansion.

During the years between the wars and through World War II, the average recession shortened to 18 months and the average expansion lengthened to 35 months. (It is a coincidence that these durations are the same as the overall averages for the entire period since 1854.) One recession during this period, the Great Depression, was enormous and lasted for 43 months.

During the years since World War II, the average recession has shortened to 11 months and the average expansion has lengthened to 59 months. The longest ever expansion is the one that began in March 1991 and ended in March 2001.

One of the main reasons for the trend toward longer expansions and shorter recessions is the advance in economic theory that enables governments and central banks to better control aggregate economic performance.

Recent Cycles

The last completed cycle began at a trough of March 1991 and ended at a trough of November 2001. The economy expanded from March 1991 until March 2001, the longest (120 months) in U.S. history. The previous record expansion ran from February 1961 to December 1969 (106 months).

Figure 29.2 shows three features of the recent cycles: real GDP fluctuations around potential GDP, the unemployment rate, and the inflation rate. The dates in the three parts of the figure are aligned above each other so that you can see the relationship between the three variables. The two most recent recessions are highlighted in all three parts.

In part (a), you can see that real GDP fell from a peak in mid-1990 to a trough in the first quarter of 1991, and it fell from a peak at the end of 2000 to a trough in

■ **FIGURE 29.2**

Recent U.S. Cycles

The two most recent recessions (highlighted in all three parts) began in mid-1990 and in the first quarter of 2001. The expansion that followed the 1990–1991 recession was the longest in U.S. history.

When real GDP decreases in a recession in part (a), the unemployment rate increases in part (b), and a little later, the inflation rate decreases in part (c). When real GDP increases toward potential GDP, the unemployment rate falls toward the natural unemployment rate. When real GDP increases above potential GDP, the unemployment rate falls below the natural unemployment rate and the inflation rate rises.

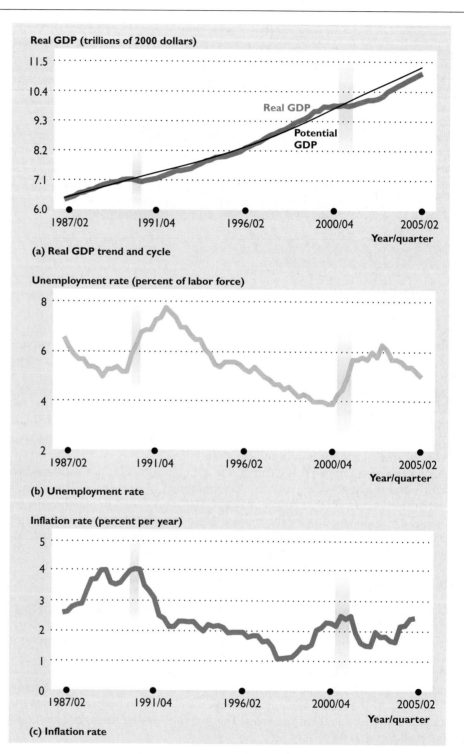

(a) Real GDP trend and cycle

(b) Unemployment rate

(c) Inflation rate

SOURCES OF DATA: Bureau of Economic Analysis, Bureau of Labor Statistics, and Congressional Budget Office.

the third quarter of 2001. In a recession, real GDP moves from above potential GDP to below potential GDP. From the trough, real GDP begins its long expansion. In the expansion of the 1990s, real GDP reached potential GDP in 1998 and then moved above potential GDP.

In part (b), you can see that the unemployment rate increased during the recession. It kept increasing after the recession was over but then began a long and steady decline. At its peak, the unemployment rate exceeded the natural unemployment rate. The natural unemployment rate decreased during the 1990s (see Chapter 32, pp. 822–823), but at its lowest level, in 2000, the unemployment rate was below the natural unemployment rate.

In part (c), the inflation rate reached a peak during the 1990 recession and then fell steadily until 1998. It then began to increase as real GDP moved above potential GDP. So the business cycle is not confined to the real economy. The money economy cycles alongside the real economy. The inflation rate decreases when real GDP is below potential GDP and increases when real GDP is above potential GDP.

CHECKPOINT 29.1

1 Provide a technical definition of recession and describe the history of the U.S. business cycle and the global business cycle.

Practice Problem 29.1

1. Table 1 shows real GDP in Canada from the first quarter of 1989 to the fourth quarter of 1993.
   a. In which quarter was Canada at a business-cycle peak?
   b. In which quarter was Canada at a business-cycle trough?
   c. Did Canada experience a recession during these years?
   d. In what periods did Canada experience an expansion?

Exercise 29.1

1. Table 2 shows real GDP in Mexico from the first quarter of 1994 to the last quarter of 1996.
   a. In which quarters was Mexico at a business-cycle peak?
   b. In which quarters was Mexico at a business-cycle trough?
   c. Did Mexico experience a recession during these years?
   d. In what years did Mexico experience an expansion?

Solution to Practice Problem 29.1

1a. Canada was at a business-cycle peak in the first quarter of 1990.

1b. Canada was at a business-cycle trough in the first quarter of 1991.

1c. Yes, the recession ran from the first quarter of 1990 to the first quarter of 1991.

1d. Expansions ran from the first quarter of 1989 to the first quarter of 1990 and from the first quarter of 1991 to the fourth quarter of 1993.

TABLE 1

Billions of 1996 dollars

Year	Quarter			
	1	2	3	4
1989	700	703	705	706
1990	711	709	705	698
1991	689	691	694	696
1992	696	697	699	702
1993	708	712	716	722

TABLE 2

Trillions of 1993 pesos

Year	Quarter			
	1	2	3	4
1994	1.25	1.19	1.29	1.27
1995	1.21	1.16	1.28	1.27
1996	1.27	1.29	1.25	1.37

The National Bureau Calls a Recession

The NBER's Business Cycle Dating Committee announced in November 2001 that a peak in business activity had occurred in the U.S. economy in March 2001. So, according to the NBER committee, the expansion that began in March 1991 ended in March 2001 and a recession began.

To identify the date of the cycle peak, the NBER committee looked at industrial production, employment, real income, and wholesale and retail sales. But they paid most attention to employment.

Part (a) of the figure shows that employment peaked in March 2001. The other factors considered by the NBER didn't peak in March but didn't contradict the employment numbers, so the committee was clear that March was the peak month.

The NBER committee gives relatively little weight to real GDP because it is measured only quarterly and is subject to ongoing revisions. Nonetheless, it is interesting to see what real GDP tells us. And long enough after the event, the real GDP revisions are complete, so the numbers do provide a good indicator of the overall level of economic activity.

Part (b) of the figure shows that through 2000, real GDP exceeded potential GDP. Real GDP was shrinking during the first quarter of 2001, *before* the NBER says that recession began. In June 2001, real GDP was close to potential GDP, and after June, real GDP fell to below potential GDP.

In July 2003, the NBER committee announced that a new expansion had begun in November 2001. This timing lines up much better with real GDP than with employment. Part (b) shows that the real GDP trough occurred between the third and fourth quarters of 2001, after which the economy was expanding.

But the employment trough in part (a) didn't occur until April 2002. This lagging of employment behind real GDP is normal and occurs in all expansions.

Employment (millions)

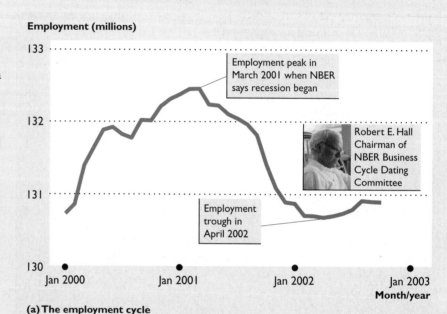

(a) The employment cycle

Real GDP (trillions of 2000 dollars)

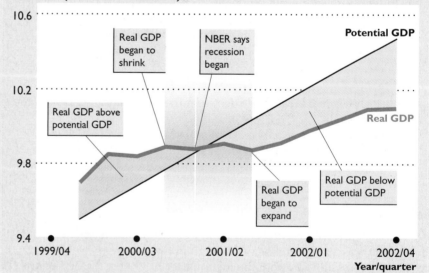

(b) The real GDP cycle

SOURCES OF DATA: Bureau of Labor Statistics, Bureau of Economic Analysis, and Congressional Budget Office.

The Global Business Cycle

Every economy has a business cycle. And business cycles travel from one economy to another. But the timing of recessions and expansions is not the same across all economies.

In part (a) of the figure, you can compare the business cycles of the United States, Europe, and Japan. These economies account for 50 percent of the global economy.

The graph shows the deviation of real GDP from potential GDP—the output gap—for these three economies.

You can see that the business cycles in these economies differ in two ways: the severity of recessions and timing.

The U.S. recession of the early 1980s was the deepest and was much more severe than the recessions experienced by Europe and Japan.

The business cycle in the United States appears to lead that of Europe, reaching its peak and trough a year or so before the same event in Europe.

Since the early 1990s, the business cycle of Japan has taken its own downward course, and for almost a decade, Japan's real GDP has been below potential GDP—a negative output gap.

Part (b) of the figure shows the cycle of the world economy. We don't know the output gap for the world as a whole because no one has attempted to measure it. But we do have estimates of the growth rate of world real GDP. That is what part (b) plots.

The first thing that jumps out of this graph is the fact that for the world as a whole, there has been no recession during the years shown here: 1980–2005. Even when the world economy is growing slowly, as it was in the early 1980s and early 1990s, real GDP continues to grow.

The second striking fact is that the Asian economies are driving the global economy. A financial crisis in 1997 brought a temporary drop in growth, but the 2000s saw extremely strong growth in China and India.

Output gap (percent deviation from potential GDP)

(a) Cycle in richest economies

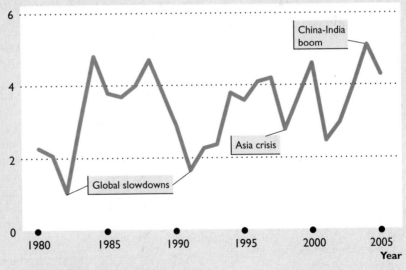

Real GDP growth (percent per year)

(b) Cycle in global economy

SOURCE OF DATA: World Economic Outlook Data Base, the International Monetary Fund, April 2005.

29.2 AGGREGATE SUPPLY

Real GDP depends on the quantities of

- Labor employed
- Capital, human capital, and the state of technology
- Land and natural resources
- Entrepreneurial talent

You saw in Chapter 23 how real GDP is determined at full employment. The quantities of capital and human capital, the state of technology, and the amount of entrepreneurial talent are fixed. Labor market equilibrium determines the quantity of labor employed, which is equal to the quantity of labor demanded and the quantity of labor supplied at the equilibrium real wage rate. The quantity of real GDP at full employment is *potential GDP*.

Over the business cycle, real GDP fluctuates around potential GDP because the quantity of labor employed fluctuates around its full employment level. The aggregate supply–aggregate demand model explains these fluctuations.

We begin on the supply side with the basics of aggregate supply.

■ Aggregate Supply Basics

Aggregate supply
The relationship between the quantity of real GDP supplied and the price level when all other influences on production plans remain the same.

Aggregate supply is the relationship between the quantity of real GDP supplied and the price level when all other influences on production plans remain the same. This relationship can be described as follows:

Other things remaining the same, the higher the price level, the greater is the quantity of real GDP supplied, and the lower the price level, the smaller is the quantity of real GDP supplied.

Figure 29.3 illustrates aggregate supply as an aggregate supply schedule and aggregate supply curve. The aggregate supply schedule lists the quantities of real GDP supplied at each price level, and the upward-sloping *AS* curve graphs these points.

The figure also shows potential GDP: $10 trillion in the figure. When the price level is 110, the quantity of real GDP supplied is $10 trillion, which equals potential GDP (at point *C* on the *AS* curve).

Along the aggregate supply curve, the only influence on production plans that changes is the price level. A rise in the price level brings an increase in the quantity of real GDP supplied and a movement up along the aggregate supply curve; a fall in the price level brings a decrease in the quantity of real GDP supplied and a movement down along the aggregate supply curve.

Among the other influences on production plans that remain constant along the *AS* curve are

- The money wage rate
- The money prices of other resources

In contrast, along the potential GDP line, when the price level changes, the money wage rate and the money prices of other resources change by the same percentage as the change in the price level to keep the real wage rate (and other real prices) at the full-employment equilibrium level.

FIGURE 29.3

Aggregate Supply Schedule and Aggregate Supply Curve

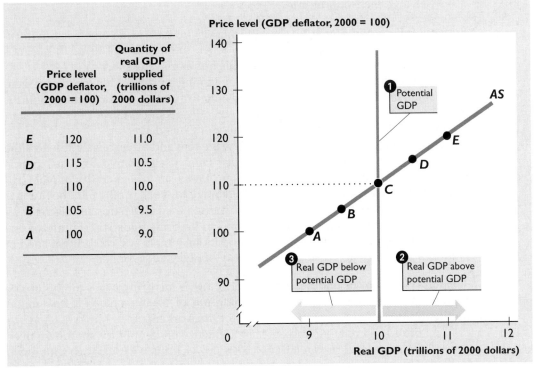

Price level (GDP deflator, 2000 = 100)	Quantity of real GDP supplied (trillions of 2000 dollars)
E	120	11.0
D	115	10.5
C	110	10.0
B	105	9.5
A	100	9.0

The aggregate supply schedule and aggregate supply curve, AS, show the relationship between the quantity of real GDP supplied and the price level when all other influences on production plans remain the same. Each point A through E on the AS curve corresponds to the row identified by the same letter in the schedule.

❶ Potential GDP is $10 trillion, and when the price level is 110, real GDP equals potential GDP.

❷ If the price level is above 110, real GDP exceeds potential GDP.

❸ If the price level is below 110, real GDP is less than potential GDP.

Why the AS Curve Slopes Upward

Why does the quantity of real GDP supplied increase when the price level rises and decrease when the price level falls? The answer is that a movement along the AS curve brings a change in the real wage rate (and changes in the real cost of other resources whose money prices are fixed). If the price level rises, the real wage rate falls, and if the price level falls, the real wage rate rises.

Think about a concrete example. Suppose Microsoft has a contract with its programmers to pay them $200 an hour. Microsoft sells copies of Windows to computer makers (such as Dell Computer Corporation) for $100 a copy. The real wage rate of a programmer is 2 copies of Windows. That is, Microsoft must sell 2 copies of Windows to buy one hour of programming labor. Now suppose the price of a copy of Windows falls to $50. The real wage rate of a programmer has increased to 4 copies of Windows—Microsoft must now sell 4 copies of the program to buy one hour of programming labor.

If the price of a copy of Windows increased, the real wage rate of a programmer would fall. For example, if the price increased to $200 a copy, the real wage rate would be one copy of Windows—Microsoft would need to sell only one copy of the software to buy one hour of programmer time.

A change in the real wage rate means that the cost of labor changes relative to the revenue that an hour of labor can produce, and it changes a firm's profit. A rise in the real wage rate cuts into a firm's profit, and a fall in the real wage rate boosts a firm's profit. Firms respond to a change in the real wage rate and their profit in one of three possible ways:

- Go out of business or start up in business.
- Shut down temporarily or restart production.
- Change their output rate.

Business Failure and Startup   New businesses are born and some existing businesses die every day. Real GDP changes when the number of firms in business changes. And the price level influences this number in the short run.

People create businesses in the hope of earning a profit. When profits are generally high, more firms start up, fewer existing firms fail, and the number of firms increases. When profits are squeezed or when losses arise, fewer new firms start up, more existing firms fail, and the number of firms decreases.

The price level relative to the money wage rate and other costs influences the number of firms in business. If the price level rises relative to costs, profits increase, the number of firms in business increases, and the quantity of real GDP supplied increases. If the price level falls relative to costs, profits fall, the number of firms in business decreases, and the quantity of real GDP supplied decreases.

In a severe recession, business failure can be contagious. The failure of one firm puts pressure on both its suppliers and its customers and can bring a flood of failures and a large decrease in the quantity of real GDP supplied.

Temporary Shutdowns and Restarts   A firm that is incurring a loss might foresee a profit in the future. So rather than going out of business, such a firm might decide to shut down temporarily and lay off its workers.

The price level relative to costs is an influence on temporary shutdown decisions. If the price level rises relative to costs, fewer firms will decide to shut down temporarily; so more firms operate and the quantity of real GDP supplied increases. If the price level falls relative to costs, a larger number of firms find that they cannot earn enough revenue to pay the wage bill and so temporarily shut down. The quantity of real GDP supplied decreases.

Changes in Output Rate   The price level relative to costs influences even those firms that remain profitable and keep producing. You know that to produce more output, a firm must hire more labor. It is profitable to hire more labor if the additional labor brings in more revenue than it costs. If the price level rises and the money wage rate doesn't change, an extra hour of labor that was previously unprofitable becomes profitable. So when the price level rises and the money wage rate doesn't change, the quantity of labor demanded and production increase. For the economy as a whole, the quantity of real GDP supplied increases.

Production at a Pepsi Plant

At a bottling plant, Pepsi produces the quantity of cola that maximizes profit. The production plant is fixed, but Pepsi can increase production by hiring more labor and working the plant harder. But each additional hour of labor hired produces fewer additional bottles of cola than the previous hour produces. So Pepsi increases the quantity of labor hired and increases production only if the real wage rate falls. But if the price of cola rises and the money wage rate and other costs don't change, the real wage rate *does* fall. Similarly, if the price of cola falls and the money wage rate and other costs don't change, the real wage rate *rises*. In this situation, Pepsi decreases the quantity of labor demanded and decreases production.

What is true for Pepsi bottlers is true for the producers of all goods and services. So when the price level rises and the money wage rate and other resource prices remain constant, the quantity of labor demanded increases and the quantity of real GDP supplied increases.

■ Changes in Aggregate Supply

You saw in Figure 29.3 that a change in the price level changes the quantity of real GDP supplied and brings a movement along the aggregate supply curve. But it does not change aggregate supply.

Aggregate supply changes when any influence on production plans other than the price level changes. In particular, aggregate supply changes when

- Potential GDP changes.
- The money wage rate changes.
- The money prices of other resources change.

Changes in Potential GDP

Anything that changes potential GDP changes aggregate supply and shifts the aggregate supply curve. Figure 29.4 illustrates. You can think of point C as an anchor point. The AS curve and potential GDP line are anchored at this point, and when potential GDP changes, aggregate supply changes along with it. Point C shifts to point C', and the AS curve and potential GDP line shift rightward together. When potential GDP increases from \$10 trillion to \$11 trillion, the AS curve shifts from AS_0 to AS_1.

FIGURE 29.4

An Increase in Potential GDP

❶ An increase in potential GDP increases aggregate supply. ❷ The aggregate supply curve shifts rightward from AS_0 to AS_1.

Changes in Money Wage Rate and Other Resource Prices

A change in the money wage rate or in the money price of another resource changes aggregate supply because it changes firms' costs. The higher the money wage rate or the price of another resource, the higher are firms' costs and the smaller is the quantity that firms are willing to supply at each price level. So an increase in the money wage rate or the price of another resource decreases aggregate supply.

Suppose that the money wage rate is $33 an hour and the price level is 110. Then the real wage rate is $30 an hour ($33 × 100 ÷ 110 = $30). If the full-employment equilibrium real wage rate is $30 an hour, the economy is at full employment and real GDP equals potential GDP. In Figure 29.5, the economy is at point C on the aggregate supply curve AS_0. The money wage rate is $33 an hour at all points on AS_0.

Now suppose the money wage rate rises to $36 an hour but the full-employment equilibrium real wage rate remains at $30 an hour. Real GDP now equals potential GDP when the price level is 120, at point D on the aggregate supply curve AS_2. (If the money wage rate is $36 an hour and the price level is 120, the real wage rate is $36 × 100 ÷ 120 = $30 an hour.) The money wage rate is $36 an hour at all points on AS_2. The rise in the money wage rate *decreases* aggregate supply and shifts the aggregate supply curve leftward from AS_0 to AS_2.

A change in the money wage rate does not change potential GDP. The reason is that potential GDP depends only on the economy's real ability to produce and on the full-employment quantity of labor, which occurs at the equilibrium *real* wage rate. The equilibrium real wage rate can occur at any money wage rate.

■ **FIGURE 29.5**

A Change in the Money Wage Rate

A rise in the money wage rate decreases aggregate supply. The aggregate supply curve shifts leftward from AS_0 to AS_2. A rise in the money wage rate does not change potential GDP.

CHECKPOINT 29.2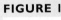

2 **Define and explain the influences on aggregate supply.**

Practice Problem 29.2

1. In May 2000, armed men took over the Parliament in Fiji and held the Prime Minister and other people as hostages. This action led to many other events. Explain the effect of each of the following events on Fiji's aggregate supply.
    a. Downtown Suva (the capital of Fiji) was heavily looted, and businesses were destroyed.
    b. Dock workers in Australia refused to handle cargo to and from Fiji, including raw material going to Fiji's garment industry.
    c. The number of tourists fell, and many hotels closed.
    d. As unemployment increased, the workweek in Fiji was shortened.
    e. The fresh tuna industry in Fiji boomed with increased sales to Japan and the United States.
    f. Suppose that workers in Fiji demanded higher wages and got them.

Exercise 29.2

1. Many events have followed the ending of apartheid in South Africa. Explain the effect of each of the following events on South Africa's aggregate supply.
    a. Businesses around the world have established branches in South Africa.
    b. More South Africans have access to education.
    c. Trade sanctions ended.
    d. Unemployment decreased.
    e. Tourism increased, and many new hotels were built.
    f. AIDS became more prevalent.

Solution to Practice Problem 29.2

1a. As businesses closed, real GDP supplied at the current price level decreased. The *AS* curve shifted leftward (Figure 1).

1b. As Fiji's garment industry ran out of raw materials, production in the garment industry decreased and the quantity of real GDP supplied at the current price level decreased. The *AS* curve shifted leftward (Figure 1).

1c. As many hotels closed, the quantity of tourist services supplied decreased and the quantity of real GDP supplied at the current price level decreased. The *AS* curve shifted leftward (Figure 1).

1d. As employers cut the workweek and shared jobs among workers, production decreased and the *AS* curve shifted leftward (Figure 1).

1e. As the tuna industry continued to expand, production increased. In isolation, its effect shifted the *AS* curve rightward (Figure 2).

1f. As the wage rate increased, businesses that became unprofitable closed and real GDP produced at the current price level decreased. The *AS* curve shifted leftward (Figure 1).

FIGURE 1

FIGURE 2

29.3 AGGREGATE DEMAND

The *quantity of real GDP demanded* (*Y*) is the total amount of final goods and services produced in the United States that people, businesses, governments, and foreigners plan to buy. This quantity is the sum of the real consumption expenditure (*C*), investment (*I*), government expenditure on goods and services (*G*), and exports (*X*) minus imports (*M*). That is,

$$Y = C + I + G + X - M.$$

Many factors influence expenditure plans; to study aggregate demand, we divide them into two groups: the price level and everything else. We'll first consider the influence of the price level on expenditure plans and then consider the other influences.

■ Aggregate Demand Basics

Aggregate demand
The relationship between the quantity of real GDP demanded and the price level when all other influences on expenditure plans remain the same.

Aggregate demand is the relationship between the quantity of real GDP demanded and the price level when all other influences on expenditure plans remain the same. This relationship can be described as follows:

Other things remaining the same, the higher the price level, the smaller is the quantity of real GDP demanded, and the lower the price level, the greater is the quantity of real GDP demanded.

Figure 29.6 illustrates aggregate demand by using an aggregate demand schedule and aggregate demand curve. The aggregate demand schedule lists the quantities of real GDP demanded at each price level, and the downward-sloping *AD* curve graphs these points.

Along the aggregate demand curve, the only influence on expenditure plans that changes is the price level. A rise in the price level decreases the quantity of real GDP demanded and brings a movement up along the aggregate demand curve; a fall in the price level increases the quantity of real GDP demanded and brings a movement down along the aggregate demand curve.

The price level influences the quantity of real GDP demanded because a change in the price level brings changes in

- The buying power of money
- The real interest rate
- The real prices of exports and imports

The Buying Power of Money

A rise in the price level lowers the buying power of money and decreases the quantity of real GDP demanded. To see why, think about the buying plans in two economies—Russia and Japan—where the price level has changed a lot in recent years.

Anna lives in Moscow, Russia. She has worked hard all summer and has saved 20,000 rubles (the ruble is the currency of Russia), which she plans to spend attending graduate school when she has earned her economics degree. So Anna's money holding is 20,000 rubles. Anna has a part-time job, and her income from this job pays her expenses. The price level in Russia rises by 100 percent. Anna needs 40,000 rubles to buy what 20,000 rubles once bought. To make up some of

FIGURE 29.6

Aggregate Demand Schedule and Aggregate Demand Curve

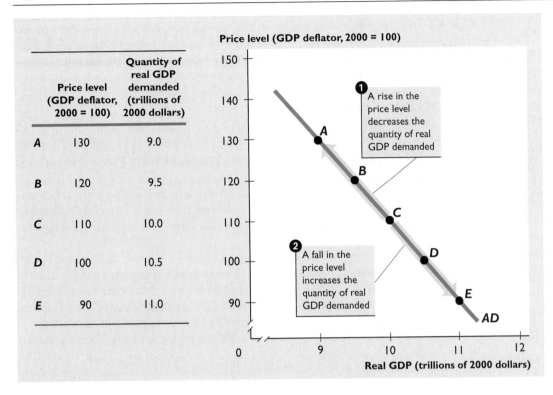

	Price level (GDP deflator, 2000 = 100)	Quantity of real GDP demanded (trillions of 2000 dollars)
A	130	9.0
B	120	9.5
C	110	10.0
D	100	10.5
E	90	11.0

The aggregate demand schedule and aggregate demand curve, *AD*, show the relationship between the quantity of real GDP demanded and the price level when all other influences on expenditure plans remain the same. Each point *A* through *E* on the *AD* curve corresponds to the row identified by the same letter in the schedule.

The quantity of real GDP demanded ❶ decreases when the price level rises and ❷ increases when the price level falls.

the fall in the buying power of her money, Anna slashes her spending.

Similarly, a fall in the price level, other things remaining the same, brings an increase in the quantity of real GDP demanded. To see why, think about the buying plans of Mika, who lives in Tokyo, Japan. She too has worked hard all summer and has saved 200,000 yen (the yen is the currency of Japan), which she plans to spend attending school next year. The price level in Japan falls by 10 percent; now Mika needs only 180,000 yen to buy what 200,000 yen once bought. With a rise in what her money buys, Mika decides to buy a DVD player.

The Real Interest Rate

When the price level rises, the real interest rate rises. You saw in Chapter 28 (p. 699) that an increase in the price level increases the amount of money that people want to hold—increases the demand for money. When the demand for money increases, the nominal interest rate rises. In the short run, the inflation rate does not change, so a rise in the nominal interest rate brings a rise in the real interest rate. Faced with a higher real interest rate, businesses and people delay plans to buy new capital and consumer durable goods and cut back on spending. So the rise in the price level decreases the quantity of real GDP demanded.

Anna and Mika Again   Think about Anna and Mika again. Both of them want to buy a computer. In Moscow, a rise in the price level increases the demand for money and raises the real interest rate. At a real interest rate of 5 percent a year,

Anna was willing to borrow to buy the new computer. But at a real interest rate of 10 percent a year, she decides that the payments would be too high, so she delays buying it. The rise in the price level decreases the quantity of real GDP demanded.

In Tokyo, a fall in the price level lowers the real interest rate. At a real interest rate of 5 percent a year, Mika was willing to borrow to buy a low-performance computer. But at a real interest rate of close to zero, she decides to buy a fancier computer that costs more: The fall in the price level increases the quantity of real GDP demanded.

The Real Prices of Exports and Imports

When the U.S. price level rises and other things remain the same, the prices in other countries do not change. So a rise in the U.S. price level makes U.S.-made goods and services more expensive relative to foreign-made goods and services. This change in real prices encourages people to spend less on U.S.-made items and more on foreign-made items. For example, if the U.S. price level rises relative to the foreign price level, foreigners buy fewer U.S.-made cars (U.S. exports decrease) and Americans buy more foreign-made cars (U.S. imports increase).

Anna's and Mika's Imports In Moscow, Anna is buying some new shoes. With a sharp rise in the Russian price level, the Russian-made shoes that she planned to buy are too expensive, so she buys a less expensive pair imported from Brazil. In Tokyo, Mika is buying a CD player. With the fall in the Japanese price level, a Sony CD player made in Japan looks like a better buy than one made in Taiwan.

In the long run, when the price level changes by more in one country than in other countries, the exchange rate changes. The exchange rate change neutralizes the price level change, so this international price effect on buying plans is a short-run effect only. But in the short run, it is a powerful effect.

■ Changes in Aggregate Demand

A change in any factor that influences expenditure plans other than the price level brings a change in aggregate demand. When aggregate demand increases, the aggregate demand curve shifts rightward, which Figure 29.7 illustrates as the rightward shift of the AD curve from AD_0 to AD_1. When aggregate demand decreases, the aggregate demand curve shifts leftward, which Figure 29.7 illustrates as the leftward shift of the AD curve from AD_0 to AD_2. The factors that change aggregate demand are

- Expectations about the future
- Fiscal policy and monetary policy
- The state of the world economy

Expectations

An increase in expected future income increases the amount of consumption goods (especially big-ticket items such as cars) that people plan to buy now and increases aggregate demand.

An increase in expected future inflation increases aggregate demand because people decide to buy more goods and services now before their prices rise.

An increase in expected future profit increases the investment that firms plan to undertake now and increases aggregate demand.

▮ FIGURE 29.7

Change in Aggregate Demand

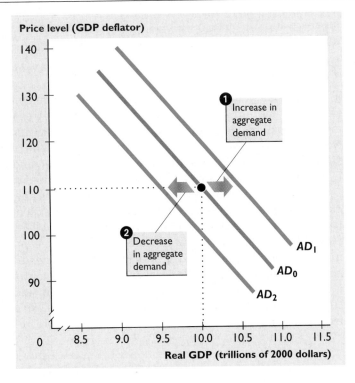

① Aggregate demand *increases if*

- Expected future income, inflation, or profits increase.
- The government or the Federal Reserve takes steps that increase planned expenditure.
- The exchange rate falls or the global economy expands.

② Aggregate demand *decreases if*

- Expected future income, inflation, or profits decrease.
- The government or the Federal Reserve takes steps that decrease planned expenditure.
- The exchange rate rises or the global economy contracts.

Fiscal Policy and Monetary Policy

We study the effects of policy actions on aggregate demand in Chapter 31. Here, we'll just briefly note that the government can influence aggregate demand by setting and changing taxes, transfer payments, and government expenditure on goods and services. And the Federal Reserve can influence aggregate demand by changing the quantity of money and the interest rate.

A tax cut or an increase in either transfer payments or government expenditure on goods and services increases aggregate demand. A cut in the interest rate or an increase in the quantity of money increases aggregate demand.

The World Economy

Two main influences that the world economy has on aggregate demand are the foreign exchange rate and foreign income. The foreign exchange rate is the amount of a foreign currency that you can buy with a U.S. dollar. Other things remaining the same, a rise in the foreign exchange rate decreases aggregate demand.

To see how the foreign exchange rate influences aggregate demand, suppose that $1 exchanges for 100 Japanese yen. A Fujitsu phone made in Japan costs 12,500 yen, and an equivalent Motorola phone made in the United States costs $110. In U.S. dollars, the Fujitsu phone costs $125, so people around the world buy the cheaper U.S. phone. Now suppose the exchange rate rises to 125 yen per dollar. At 125 yen per dollar, the Fujitsu phone costs $100 and is now cheaper than the Motorola phone. People will switch from the U.S. phone to the Japanese phone.

U.S. exports will decrease and U.S. imports will increase, so U.S. aggregate demand will decrease.

An increase in foreign income increases U.S. exports and increases U.S. aggregate demand. For example, an increase in income in Japan and Germany increases Japanese and German consumers' and producers' planned expenditures on U.S.-made goods and services.

■ The Aggregate Demand Multiplier

The aggregate demand multiplier is an effect that magnifies changes in expenditure plans and brings potentially large fluctuations in aggregate demand. When any influence on aggregate demand changes expenditure plans, the change in expenditure changes income; and the change in income induces a change in consumption expenditure. The increase in aggregate demand is the initial increase in expenditure plus the induced increase in consumption expenditure.

Suppose that an increase in expenditure induces an increase in consumption expenditure that is 1.5 times the initial increase in expenditure. Figure 29.8 illustrates the change in aggregate demand that occurs when investment increases by $0.4 trillion. Initially, the aggregate demand curve is AD_0. Investment then increases by $0.4 trillion ($\Delta I$) and the purple curve $AD_0 + \Delta I$ now describes aggregate spending plans at each price level. An increase in income induces an increase in consumption expenditure of $0.6 trillion, and the aggregate demand curve shifts rightward to AD_1. Chapter 30 (pp. 766–770) explains the expenditure multiplier in detail.

FIGURE 29.8
The Aggregate Demand Multiplier

① An increase in investment increases aggregate demand and increases income. **②** The increase in income induces an increase in consumption expenditure, so **③** aggregate demand increases by more than the initial increase in investment.

CHECKPOINT 29.3

3 **Define and explain the influences on aggregate demand.**

Practice Problem 29.3

1. Mexico has signed free trade agreements with many countries, including the United States, Canada, and the European Union. Explain the effect of each of the following events on Mexico's aggregate demand in the short run.
   a. The government of Mexico cuts taxes.
   b. The United States and Canada experienced strong economic growth.
   c. The European Union goes into a recession.
   d. The Mexican government sets new environmental standards that require factories to upgrade their production facilities.
   e. Mexico adopts an expansionary monetary policy and increases the quantity of money.

Exercise 29.3

1. Explain the effect on Japan's aggregate demand in the short run of each of the following events, one at a time.
   a. The price level in Japan rises.
   b. The rest of Asia goes into recession.
   c. The Asian economies experience very strong growth.
   d. The yen strengthens against the U.S. dollar.
   e. Japan adopts an expansionary fiscal policy and cuts taxes.

Solution to Practice Problem 29.3

1a. A tax cut in Mexico increases disposable income, which increases Mexico's aggregate demand. The *AD* curve shifts rightward (Figure 1).

1b. Strong economic growth in Canada and the United States increases the demand for Mexican-produced goods and services, which increases aggregate demand in Mexico. The *AD* curve shifts rightward (Figure 1).

1c. A recession in the European Union decreases European demand for goods and services. Some of these goods and services are produced in Mexico. So Mexico's exports decrease, and its aggregate demand decreases. The *AD* curve shifts leftward (Figure 2).

1d. As Mexican factories upgrade their production facilities, investment in Mexico increases. Aggregate demand in Mexico increases, and the *AD* curve shifts rightward (Figure 1).

1e. An increase in the quantity of money increases aggregate demand, and the *AD* curve shifts rightward (Figure 1).

FIGURE 1

FIGURE 2

29.4 UNDERSTANDING THE BUSINESS CYCLE

Macroeconomic equilibrium
When the quantity of real GDP demanded equals the quantity of real GDP supplied at the point of intersection of the AD curve and the AS curve.

Aggregate supply and aggregate demand determine real GDP and the price level. **Macroeconomic equilibrium** occurs when the quantity of real GDP demanded equals the quantity of real GDP supplied at the point of intersection of the *AD* curve and the *AS* curve. Figure 29.9(a) shows such an equilibrium at a price level of 110 and real GDP of $10 trillion.

To see why this position is the equilibrium, think about what happens if the price level is something other than 110. Suppose that the price level is 120 and that real GDP is $11 trillion (point *E* on the *AS* curve). The quantity of real GDP demanded is less than $11 trillion, so firms are unable to sell all their output. Unwanted inventories pile up, and firms cut production and prices until they can sell all their output, which occurs only when real GDP is $10 trillion and the price level is 110.

Now suppose the price level is 100 and real GDP is $9 trillion (point *A* on the *AS* curve). The quantity of real GDP demanded exceeds $9 trillion, so firms are unable to meet the demand for their output. Inventories decrease, and customers clamor for goods and services. So firms increase production and raise prices until firms can meet demand, which occurs only when real GDP is $10 trillion and the price level is 110.

■ **FIGURE 29.9**

Macroeconomic Equilibrium

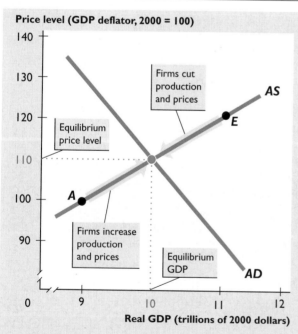

(a) Macroeconomic equilibrium

Macroeconomic equilibrium occurs at the intersection of the *AD* and *AS* curves. Macroeconomic equilibrium might be below full employment, at full employment, or above full employment.

(b) Three types of macroeconomic equilibrium

❶ Below full-employment equilibrium
❷ Full-employment equilibrium
❸ Above full-employment equilibrium

In macroeconomic equilibrium, the economy might be at full employment or above or below full employment. Figure 29.9(b) shows these three possibilities. **Full-employment equilibrium**—equilibrium real GDP equals potential GDP— occurs where AD_0 intersects the aggregate supply curve AS. Fluctuations in aggregate demand bring fluctuations in real GDP around potential GDP. If aggregate demand increases to AD_1, firms increase production and raise prices until they can meet the higher demand. Real GDP increases to $10.5 trillion and exceeds potential GDP in an **above full-employment equilibrium**. If aggregate demand decreases to AD_2, firms decrease production and cut prices until they can sell all their output. Real GDP decreases to $9.5 trillion and is less than potential GDP in a **below full-employment equilibrium**.

Full-employment equilibrium
When equilibrium real GDP equals potential GDP.

Above full-employment equilibrium
When equilibrium real GDP exceeds potential GDP.

Below full-employment equilibrium
When potential GDP exceeds equilibrium real GDP.

■ Aggregate Demand Fluctuations

Fluctuations in aggregate demand are one of the sources of the business cycle. To focus on the aggregate demand cycle, suppose that potential GDP and the full-employment price level remain constant. And suppose that aggregate demand fluctuates between AD_1 and AD_2 in Figure 29.9(b). The result of these fluctuations is the cycle in real GDP around potential GDP that Figure 29.10 shows.

In year 1, aggregate demand is AD_0. The economy is at full employment with real GDP at $10 trillion. Then, in year 2, aggregate demand increases to AD_1. As aggregate demand increases, real GDP increases to $10.5 trillion at point D in Figure 29.9(b) and at a business cycle peak in Figure 29.10. In year 3, aggregate demand decreases to AD_0. Real GDP now falls to $10 trillion, and the economy is back at full employment. Aggregate demand decreases further in year 4 to AD_2. Real GDP now decreases to $9.5 trillion, and the economy is in recession. Finally, in year 5, aggregate demand increases to AD_0 and real GDP increases again to $10 trillion, the full employment level.

The sources of the fluctuations in aggregate demand could be any of the factors that we reviewed: Changes in expectations about the future, changes in fiscal policy and monetary policy, and changes in the world economy.

FIGURE 29.10

An Aggregate Demand Cycle

myeconlab

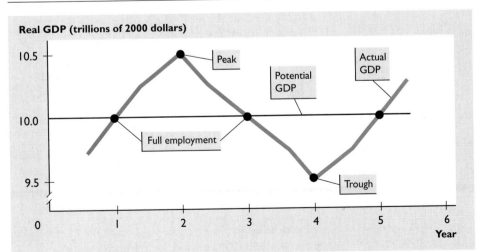

Fluctuations in aggregate demand bring fluctuations in real GDP around potential GDP.

In year 1, real GDP equals potential GDP. The economy is at full employment, such as at point C in Figure 29.9(b). In year 2, at a business cycle peak, real GDP exceeds potential GDP. The economy is operating above full employment, such as at point D in Figure 29.9(b). In year 3, there is full employment again. In year 4, at a business cycle trough, real GDP is below potential GDP. The economy is operating below full employment, such as at point B in Figure 29.9(b).

■ Aggregate Supply Fluctuations

Aggregate supply can fluctuate for two types of reasons. First, potential GDP grows at an uneven pace. During a period of rapid technological change and capital accumulation, potential GDP grows rapidly and above its long-term trend. The second half of the 1990s experienced this type of expansion.

Second, a change in the money price of a major resource, such as crude oil, might change. Oil is used so widely throughout the economy that a large change in its price affects almost every firm and impacts the aggregate economy.

Figure 29.11 shows how large changes in the price of oil can bring recession and expansion. In part (a), the aggregate demand curve is AD and initially, the aggregate supply curve is AS_0. Equilibrium real GDP is $10 trillion, which equals potential GDP, and the price level is 110. Then the price of oil rises. Faced with higher energy and transportation costs, firms decrease production. Aggregate supply decreases, and the aggregate supply curve shifts leftward to AS_1. The price level rises to 115, and real GDP decreases to $9.75 trillion. Because real GDP decreases, the economy experiences recession. Because the price level increases, the economy experiences inflation. A combination of recession and inflation, called **stagflation**, actually occurred in the United States and the global economy in the mid-1970s and early 1980s. But events like this are infrequent.

Stagflation
A combination of recession (falling real GDP) and inflation (rising price level).

■ **FIGURE 29.11**
An Oil Price Cycle

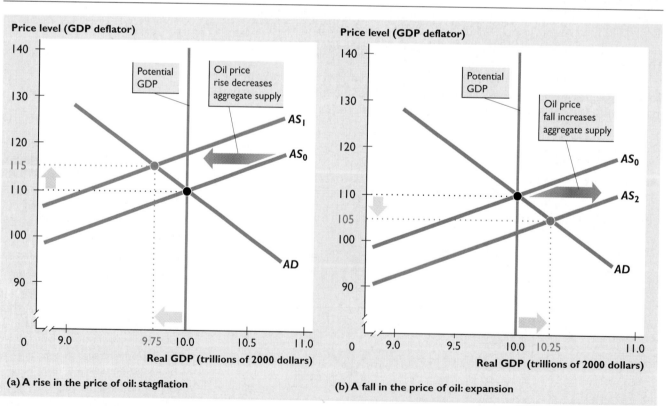

(a) A rise in the price of oil: stagflation

(b) A fall in the price of oil: expansion

In part (a), a decrease in aggregate supply shifts the AS curve leftward to AS_1. Real GDP decreases, and the price level rises.

In part (b), an increase in aggregate supply shifts the AS curve rightward to AS_2. Real GDP increases, and the price level falls.

In Figure 29.11(b), starting from the same full-employment equilibrium as before, the price of oil falls. With lower energy and transportation costs, firms increase production and the aggregate supply curve shifts rightward to AS_2. The price level falls to 105, and real GDP increases to $10.25 trillion. The economy experiences expansion and moves above full employment, but the price level falls. Similar events occurred in the United States and global economies during the mid-1980s, bringing strong economic expansion. The price level didn't fall, but inflation slowed, so the price level was lower than it otherwise would have been.

E Y E ON THE P A S T

Oil Price Cycles in the U.S. and Global Economies

In 1970, a barrel of crude oil cost around $3.50—a bit more than $12 in 2000 dollars (see the figure). Most of the world's crude oil came from a handful of nations mainly located in the Persian Gulf region, and the large producer nations were (and still are) members of an international cartel known as OPEC—the Organization of Petroleum Exporting Countries. (A cartel is an organization that seeks to control the supply and the price of a commodity and is illegal in the United States.)

In September 1973, OPEC cut the production of crude oil and raised its price to $10 a barrel—about $30 in 2000 dollars. This near tripling of the price of crude oil sent the United States, Europe, Japan, and the developing nations into recession.

Through the rest of the 1970s, the price of oil drifted upward slightly. Then, in 1980, OPEC delivered its second jolt to the global economy by again cutting production and then raising the price to $37 a barrel—almost $70 in 2000 dollars.

The global economy experienced another recession. But this recession

was much more severe than that of the mid-1970s because the oil price shock was accompanied by a large decrease in aggregate demand that resulted from the Fed's monetary policy.

With the very high price of oil, it did not take long for OPEC to be joined by many other producers. Canada and the United States intensified exploration and increased North American oil production. Britain and Norway developed oil resources in

the North Sea. And Mexico stepped up its production.

As these additional supplies came onstream, the price of oil tumbled. By 1998, it had fallen to $14 a barrel and this price fall aided the expansion of the U.S. and global economies during the 1980s and 1990s.

Strong Asian demand for oil increased its price in the 2000s. By 2005, the price of oil had surged to almost $60 a barrel. Will this high oil price bring recession again?

SOURCES OF DATA: *International Financial Statistics*, International Monetary Fund and Bureau of Economic Analysis.

■ Adjustment Toward Full Employment

When the economy is away from full employment, forces begin to operate that move it back toward full employment. In Figure 29.12(a), aggregate supply is AS_0 and an increase in aggregate demand from AD_0 to AD_1 moves real GDP above full employment. There is now an **inflationary gap**—a gap that brings a rising price level. Workers have experienced a fall in the buying power of their wages, and firms' profits have increased. Workers demand higher wages, and firms, anxious to maintain their employment and output levels in the face of a labor shortage, meet those demands. As the money wage rate rises, aggregate supply decreases and the aggregate supply curve shifts leftward. Eventually, it will reach AS_1, where real GDP is back at potential GDP.

In Figure 29.12(b), aggregate supply is AS_1 and a decrease in aggregate demand from AD_1 to AD_2 moves real GDP below full employment. There is a **recessionary gap**—a gap that brings a falling price level. The people who are lucky enough to have jobs see the buying power of their wages rise and firms' profits shrink. In these circumstances, and with a labor surplus, the money wage rate gradually falls and the aggregate supply curve gradually shifts rightward. Eventually, it reaches AS_2, where real GDP is back at potential GDP.

Inflationary gap
A gap that exists when real GDP exceeds potential GDP and that brings a rising price level.

Recessionary gap
A gap that exists when potential GDP exceeds real GDP and that brings a falling price level.

■ **FIGURE 29.12**

Adjustments Toward Full Employment

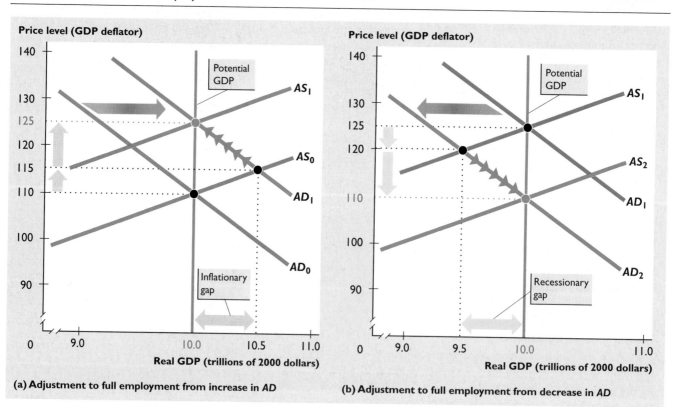

(a) Adjustment to full employment from increase in _AD_

(b) Adjustment to full employment from decrease in _AD_

In part (a), real GDP exceeds potential GDP—an inflationary gap. The money wage rate rises, aggregate supply decreases, real GDP decreases, and the price level rises.

In part (b), potential GDP exceeds real GDP—a recessionary gap. The money wage rate falls, aggregate supply increases, real GDP increases, and the price level falls.

Real GDP Growth, Inflation, and the Business Cycle

Each dot in the figure, which represents a year between 1970 and 2005, was generated by aggregate demand and aggregate supply.

The dots move rightward, which shows increasing real GDP or economic growth. The dots move upward, which shows a rising price level or inflation.

But the dots move rightward and upward in waves and occasionally move leftward. These patterns show the business cycle and the recessions.

Sometimes the economy is at full employment, as it was in 1970, and sometimes there is an output gap as in 2005.

SOURCES OF DATA: Bureau of Labor Statistics, Bureau of Economic Analysis, and Congressional Budget Office.

REALITY CHECK

AS-AD in YOUR Life

Consider the U.S. economy right now. Using all the knowledge that you have accumulated over the term (and by watching or reading the current news), can you determine whether real GDP is currently above, below, or at potential GDP?

Talk to your friends in class about where they see the economy right now. Is there a consensus?

What do you see as the main pressures on AS and AD right now? Do you think that real GDP will expand more quickly or more slowly over the coming months? Do you think the gap between real GDP and potential GDP will widen or narrow?

4 **Explain how fluctuations in aggregate demand and aggregate supply create the business cycle.**

Practice Problem 29.4

1. In the U.S. economy, real GDP equals potential GDP. Then the following events occur one at a time:
   - A deep recession hits the world economy.
   - The world oil price rises by a large amount.
   - U.S. businesses expect future profits to fall.
   a. Explain the effect of each event on aggregate demand and aggregate supply in the United States.
   b. Explain the effect of each event separately on the U.S. real GDP and price level.
   c. Explain the combined effect of these events on the U.S. real GDP and price level.
   d. Which event, if any, brings stagflation?

Exercise 29.4

1. In the Canadian economy, real GDP equals potential GDP. Then the following events occur one at a time:
   - The world economy goes into a strong expansion.
   - World oil price tumbles.
   - Canadian businesses expect future profits to rise.
   a. Explain the effect of each event on aggregate demand and aggregate supply in Canada.
   b. Explain the effect of each event separately on Canadian real GDP and price level.
   c. Explain the combined effect of these events on Canadian real GDP and price level.

FIGURE 1

Price level

Potential GDP

AS

110
105

AD_1 AD_0

0   9.5 10.0

Real GDP
(trillions of 2000 dollars)

FIGURE 2

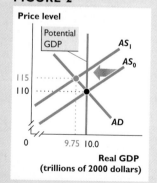

Price level

Potential GDP

AS_1
AS_0

115
110

AD

0   9.75 10.0

Real GDP
(trillions of 2000 dollars)

Solution to Practice Problem 29.4

1a. A deep recession in the world economy decreases U.S. aggregate demand. A rise in the world oil price decreases U.S. aggregate supply. A fall in expected future profits decreases U.S. aggregate demand.

1b. A deep recession in the world economy decreases U.S. aggregate demand. The AD curve shifts leftward. U.S. real GDP decreases, and the price level falls (Figure 1). A rise in the world oil price decreases U.S. aggregate supply. The AS curve shifts leftward. U.S. real GDP decreases, and the price level rises (Figure 2). A fall in expected future profits decreases U.S. aggregate demand. The AD curve shifts leftward. U.S. real GDP decreases, and the price level falls (Figure 1).

1c. All three events decrease U.S. real GDP. The deep world recession and the fall in expected future profits decrease the price level. The rise in the world oil price increases the price level. So the combined effect is ambiguous.

1d. The oil price increase brings stagflation because it decreases aggregate supply, lowers equilibrium real GDP, and raises the price level.

CHAPTER CHECKPOINT

Key Points

1 **Provide a technical definition of recession and describe the history of the U.S. business cycle and the global business cycle.**

- A recession is a decrease in real GDP that lasts for at least two quarters.
- U.S. recessions have been getting shorter, and expansions have been getting longer.

2 **Define and explain the influences on aggregate supply.**

- Aggregate supply is the relationship between the quantity of real GDP supplied and the price level when all other influences on production plans remain the same.
- The *AS* curve slopes upward because with a given money wage rate, a rise in the price level lowers the real wage rate, increases the quantity of labor demanded, and increases the quantity of real GDP supplied.
- A change in potential GDP, a change in the money wage rate, or a change in the money price of other resources changes aggregate supply.

3 **Define and explain the influences on aggregate demand.**

- Aggregate demand is the relationship between the quantity of real GDP demanded and the price level when all other influences on expenditure plans remain the same.
- The *AD* curve slopes downward because a rise in the price level decreases the buying power of money, raises the real interest rate, and raises the real price of domestic goods compared with foreign goods, and decreases the quantity of real GDP demanded.
- A change in expected future income, inflation, and profits, a change in fiscal policy and monetary policy, and a change in the foreign exchange rate and foreign real GDP change aggregate demand—the aggregate demand curve shifts.

4 **Explain how fluctuations in aggregate demand and aggregate supply create the business cycle.**

- Aggregate demand and aggregate supply determine real GDP and the price level.
- Business cycles occur because aggregate demand and aggregate supply fluctuate.
- Away from full employment, gradual adjustment of the money wage rate moves real GDP toward potential GDP.

Key Terms

Above full-employment equilibrium, 745
Aggregate demand, 738
Aggregate supply, 732

Below full-employment equilibrium, 745
Full-employment equilibrium, 745
Inflationary gap, 748
Macroeconomic equilibrium, 744

Recession, 726
Recessionary gap, 748
Stagflation, 746

Exercises

FIGURE 1

Real GDP (billions of 1990 Deutsche marks)

2,650

2,600

2,550

2,500

91/1   92/1   93/1   94/1

Year/quarter

1. Figure 1 shows real GDP in Germany from the first quarter of 1991 to the last quarter of 1994.
   a. In which quarter was Germany at a business-cycle peak?
   b. In which quarter was Germany at a business-cycle trough?
   c. Did Germany experience a recession during these years?
   d. In what years did Germany experience an expansion?

2. Over the course of the most recent U.S. business cycles, real GDP and the unemployment rate fluctuated in opposite directions. (See p. 728.)
   a. Did real GDP reach a peak at the same time that the unemployment rate reached its lowest level?
   b. Did real GDP reach a trough at the same time that the unemployment rate reached its highest level?
   c. Which of these two indicators begins to signal recession first?
   d. Which of these two indicators begins to signal expansion first?

3. Over the course of the most recent U.S. business cycles, real GDP and the inflation rate fluctuated together. (See p. 728.)
   a. Did real GDP reach a peak at the same time that the inflation rate reached its peak?
   b. Did real GDP reach a trough at the same time that the inflation rate reached its trough?
   c. Which of these two indicators begins to signal recession first?
   d. Which of these two indicators begins to signal expansion first?

4. At the beginning of 2001, the United States was at full employment.
   a. Suppose that in 2001, major union wage settlements pushed the money wage rate upward by 10 percent and that all other influences on aggregate supply remained the same. Explain the effect of the rise in the money wage rate on aggregate supply.
   b. Suppose that in 2001, the price level increased and all other influences on aggregate supply remained the same. Explain the effect of the rise in the price level on aggregate supply.
   c. Over time, potential GDP grows. Explain the effect of the increase in potential GDP on aggregate supply.

5. In 2010, the United States is at full employment. Then in 2011,
   a. The Fed cuts the quantity of money, and all other influences on aggregate demand remain the same. Explain the effect of the cut in the quantity of money on aggregate demand in the short run.
   b. The federal government cuts taxes, and all other influences on aggregate demand remain the same. Explain the effect of the tax cut on aggregate demand in the short run.
   c. The world economy goes into recession. Explain the effect of the world recession on U.S. aggregate demand in the short run.
   d. The U.S. price level rises faster than the price level in the world economy. Explain the effect of U.S. inflation on U.S. aggregate demand in the short run.

6. In 2003, the Japanese economy is at a below full-employment equilibrium.
   a. Compare the amount of unemployment in Japan with Japan's natural unemployment.
   b. Compare Japan's real GDP with its potential GDP.
   c. What policies could Japan adopt to restore full employment?
   d. Would any of the policies in part c create inflation? Explain.

7. Table 1 sets out an economy's aggregate demand and aggregate supply schedules.
   a. Plot the aggregate demand curve.
   b. Plot the aggregate supply curve.
   c. What is the macroeconomic equilibrium?
   d. If potential GDP is $800 billion, what is the type of macroeconomic equilibrium?

8. Use the information provided in Table 1 together with the information that potential GDP is $800 billion to draw an *AS-AD* graph of the economy and then
   a. Show the effect of a rise in the world oil price on your *AS-AD* graph. Does it change aggregate supply or aggregate demand and in which direction does it change?
   b. Following the increase in the world price of oil, what is the new short-run equilibrium?
   c. What is the adjustment process that now begins to restore full employment? Do you expect that process to work slowly or rapidly? Why?

9. Use the information provided in Table 1 together with the information that potential GDP is $800 billion to draw an *AS-AD* graph of the economy and then
   a. Show the effect of a rise in the quantity of money on your *AS-AD* graph. Does it change aggregate supply or aggregate demand and in which direction does it change?
   b. Following the increase in the quantity of money, what is the new short-run equilibrium?
   c. What is the adjustment process that now begins to restore full employment? Do you expect that process to work slowly or rapidly? Why?

10. Use the information provided in Table 1 together with the fact that potential GDP is $800 billion to draw an *AS-AD* graph of the economy and then
    a. Show the effect of a global recession on your *AS-AD* graph. Does the global recession change aggregate supply or aggregate demand, and in what direction?
    b. Following the onset of the global recession, what is the new short-run equilibrium?
    c. What is the adjustment process that now begins to restore full employment? Do you expect that process to work slowly or rapidly? Why?

11. For each of the events you analyzed in exercises 8 to 10, explain what happens to the unemployment rate and the real wage rate
    a. In the move to the initial short-run equilibrium.
    b. In the adjustment toward the new long-run equilibrium.

TABLE I

Price level (GDP deflator)	Real GDP demanded	Real GDP supplied
	(billions of 2000 dollars)	
90	900	600
100	850	700
110	800	800
120	750	900
130	700	1,000

Critical Thinking

12. Review the NBER committee's task of identifying the correct date for the onset of recession in 2001.
   a. Do you think the committee got the date of the onset of recession right?
   b. Do you think the committee was correct in November 2002 to wait for more evidence before declaring the recession over?
   c. Do you think the government rather than the NBER should determine the dates of recessions and expansions?

13. Because fluctuations in the world oil price make our economy fluctuate, someone suggests that we should vary the tax rate on oil, lowering the tax when the world oil price rises and increasing the tax when the world oil price falls, to stabilize the oil price in the U.S. market.
   a. How do you think such an action would influence aggregate demand?
   b. How do you think such an action would influence aggregate supply?
   c. Lay out the arguments for and against such a policy.

14. Recessions have been getting shorter, and expansions have been getting longer.
   a. When did the change in average length of recessions and expansions occur?
   b. Can you think of some reasons why this change in the business cycle might have occurred?
   c. What do you think of the view that policy actions designed to stabilize aggregate demand are responsible for this change in the business cycle?

Web Exercises

Use the links on MyEconLab to work the following exercises.

15. Visit the Web site of the National Bureau of Economic Research and read the announcements of November 2001, November 2002, and July 2003.
   a. What factors did the NBER committee consider to determine the onset of the 2001 recession?
   b. Did the NBER committee look at real GDP? Why or why not?
   c. Why did the NBER committee have a hard time determining when the 2001–2002 recession ended?
   d. On the day on which you are working this exercise, in which phase of the business cycle is the U.S. economy?

16. Visit the Web site of the Economic Cycle Research Institute and obtain information on the dates of recessions and expansions in three countries other than the United States that interest you.
   a. Compare the dates of recessions and expansions in the countries you've chosen with those in the United States.
   b. Compare the recessions in the three countries you've chosen and the United States.
   c. In which country do you think aggregate demand fluctuates most?
   d. The Economic Cycle Research Institute uses two definitions of the business cycle, one that is the same as the NBER definition and one called a "growth rate cycle." What is the difference between these two definitions? Which definition gives the higher frequency of recession?

Aggregate Expenditure

CHAPTER CHECKLIST

When you have completed your study of this chapter, you will be able to

1 Distinguish between autonomous expenditure and induced expenditure and explain how real GDP influences expenditure plans.

2 Explain how real GDP adjusts to achieve equilibrium expenditure.

3 Describe and explain the expenditure multiplier.

4 Derive the *AD* curve from equilibrium expenditure.

Keith Millner is a senior vice president at Nationwide Financial Services. He told Amey Stone, an economic journalist who writes for *BusinessWeek,* that he thinks the baby boomers—people born in the early 1950s and who are now approaching retirement—need to save more. He says that these people are spending too much and while that's good for the economy in the short term, it's risky from an individual perspective.

It is easy to see why saving too little is risky. A person ends up with too little on which to live in retirement. But how can spending too much be good for the economy in the short term? What do you think Mr. Millner means?

This chapter helps you to see why spending too much can be good for the economy in the short term. The chapter continues your exploration of the business cycle by studying the aggregate expenditure model—a model of the forces that make aggregate demand fluctuate.

A QUICK REVIEW AND PREVIEW

Before we begin our exploration of the aggregate expenditure model, let's take stock of what we've learned and preview where we are heading.

■ The Economy at Full Employment

At full employment, real GDP equals potential GDP and the unemployment rate equals the natural unemployment rate. Potential GDP and the natural unemployment rate are determined by *real* factors and are independent of the price level.

The quantity of money and potential GDP determine the price level. Changes in the quantity of money change the price level, but they have no effect on potential GDP.

This description of the forces that determine real GDP and the price level applies only to the full-employment economy. Away from potential GDP, real and monetary factors interact to determine real GDP and the price level. But potential GDP is like an anchor around which the economy fluctuates in the business cycle.

■ Departures from Full Employment

Our economy is like a boat on the ocean. The forward movement of the boat is like economic growth that brings a rising standard of living. The rocking and rolling of the boat as it is battered by waves and winds is like the alternation of the economy between recessionary gap and inflationary gap over the business cycle. The boat's navigation system that constantly pulls it back to its course is like the forces of aggregate demand and aggregate supply and the price and wage adjustments that pull the economy toward full employment.

To understand the business cycle, we use the aggregate supply and aggregate demand or *AS-AD* model explained in Chapter 29. Aggregate supply and aggregate demand determine equilibrium real GDP and the price level. And fluctuations in aggregate supply and aggregate demand bring fluctuations around full employment.

In this chapter, you're going to learn more about the forces that bring fluctuations to aggregate demand.

■ Fixed Price Level

The interaction of aggregate demand and aggregate supply determine equilibrium real GDP and the price level simultaneously. But the forces that we want to isolate and put in clear view are hard to see if we consider the *simultaneous* adjustment of real GDP and the price level. So in the aggregate expenditure model, the price level is fixed. The model explains what determines the quantity of real GDP demanded and changes in that quantity *at a given price level*.

The aggregate expenditure model was originally designed to explain what happens in an economy in deep recession when firms can't cut their prices any further but can increase production without raising their prices, so the price level is actually fixed. But you can also think about this model as telling us about the forces that determine the quantity of real GDP demanded at any given price level.

30.1 EXPENDITURE PLANS AND REAL GDP

You've seen from the circular flows of income and expenditure (Chapter 20, p. 500) that aggregate expenditure equals the sum of

- Consumption expenditure, C
- Investment, I
- Government expenditure on goods and services, G
- Net exports, NX

That is,

$$\text{Aggregate expenditure} = C + I + G + NX.$$

■ Planned and Unplanned Expenditures

Motorola decides to produce 11 million cell phones in 2005. The factors of production that it hires to produce these phones cost $550 million. So the incomes generated and the value of production is $550 million. Households, other firms, governments, and people in the rest of the world make their expenditure plans. Suppose they decide to buy 9 million Motorola phones. Their total expenditure on phones is $450 million. Motorola plans to sell 10 million phones and add 1 million to its inventory. (Firms need inventories to smooth out short-term fluctuations in production and sales.) But at the end of the year Motorola is left with 2 million phones in inventory. Valuing this inventory at the cost of production, Motorola has invested $100 million in an inventory of phones. Total expenditure on phones, including Motorola's investment in inventories, equals the value of phones produced and equals the incomes paid to produce the phones. But *planned* expenditure on phones is less than the value of the phones produced because Motorola planned to invest only $50 million in new inventory.

This account of a year in the life of Motorola can be extended to the economy as a whole. Aggregate expenditure equals aggregate income and real GDP. But aggregate *planned* expenditure might not equal real GDP because firms can end up with larger or smaller inventories than they had planned. Firms make their production plans, the aggregate value of which is real GDP. They pay incomes that equal the value of production, so aggregate income equals real GDP. Households and governments make their planned purchases of goods and services, and net exports are as planned. Firms make their planned purchases of new buildings, plant, and equipment and their *planned* inventory changes. The total of all these spending plans is **aggregate planned expenditure**.

If aggregate planned expenditure equals real GDP, the change in firms' inventories is the planned change. But if aggregate planned expenditure exceeds real GDP, firms' inventories are smaller than planned; and if aggregate planned expenditure is less than real GDP, firms' inventories are larger than planned. Notice that *actual* expenditure, which equals *planned* expenditure plus the *unplanned* change in firms' inventories, always equals real GDP and aggregate income.

Unplanned changes in firms' inventories lead to changes in production and incomes. If unwanted inventories have piled up, firms decrease production, which decreases real GDP. If inventories have fallen below their target levels, firms increase production, which increases real GDP.

Aggregate planned expenditure
Planned consumption expenditure plus planned investment plus planned government expenditure plus planned exports minus planned imports.

■ Autonomous Expenditure and Induced Expenditure

Continuing the story of Motorola, when the firm decreases production in 2006, the incomes of its workers and suppliers of other factors of production decrease. If most firms share Motorola's experience, aggregate income falls, and with lower incomes, people decrease their expenditures on all types of goods and services—including cell phones. So in 2006, Motorola sells even fewer phones than it sold in 2005. Where does this process end?

To begin to answer this question, we must again extend the Motorola story to the economy as a whole. Just as lower incomes bring a decrease in expenditure on cell phones, so lower *aggregate* income—lower real GDP—brings a decrease in expenditure on a wide range of goods and services. We divide aggregate expenditure into two components: autonomous expenditure and induced expenditure. **Autonomous expenditure** is the part of aggregate expenditure that does not respond to changes in real GDP. It equals investment plus government expenditure on goods and services, plus exports, plus the components of consumption expenditure and imports that are not influenced by real GDP. **Induced expenditure** is the part of aggregate expenditure that changes in response to a change in real GDP. It equals consumption expenditure minus imports (excluding the elements of consumption and imports that are part of autonomous expenditure).

Your next task is to learn more about the influence of real GDP on induced expenditure. We start with its influence on consumption expenditure.

■ The Consumption Function

The **consumption function** is the relationship between consumption expenditure and disposable income, other things remaining the same. *Disposable income* is aggregate income—GDP—minus net taxes. (Net taxes are taxes paid to the government minus transfer payments received from the government.)

Households must either spend their disposable income on consumption or save it. A decision to spend a dollar on consumption is a decision not to save a dollar. The consumption decision and the saving decision is one decision.

Consumption Plans

For households and the economy as a whole, as disposable income increases, planned consumption expenditure increases. But the increase in planned consumption is less than the increase in disposable income. The table in Figure 30.1 shows a consumption schedule. It lists the consumption expenditure that people plan to undertake at each level of disposable income.

Figure 30.1 shows a consumption function based on the consumption schedule. Along the consumption function, the points labeled *A* through *F* correspond to the rows of the table. For example, point *E* shows that when disposable income is $8 trillion, consumption expenditure is $7.5 trillion. Along the consumption function, as disposable income increases, consumption expenditure increases.

At point *A* on the consumption function, consumption expenditure is $1.5 trillion even though disposable income is zero. This consumption expenditure is called *autonomous consumption,* and it is the amount of consumption expenditure that would take place in the short run, even if people had no current income. This consumption expenditure would be financed either by spending past savings or by borrowing.

Autonomous expenditure
The components of aggregate expenditure that do not change when real GDP changes.

Induced expenditure
The components of aggregate expenditure that change when real GDP changes.

Consumption function
The relationship between consumption expenditure and disposable income, other things remaining the same.

FIGURE 30.1

The Consumption Function

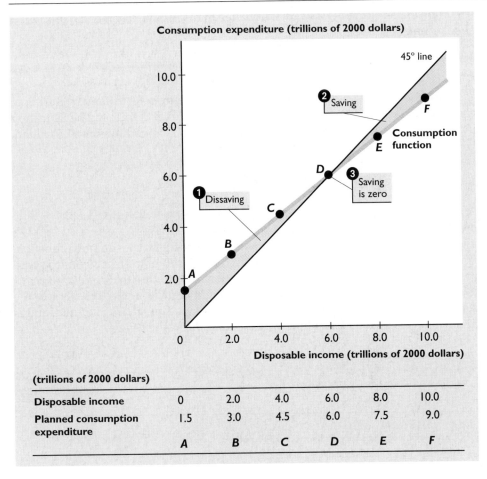

The table shows consumption expenditure (and saving) plans at various levels of disposable income. The figure graphs these data as the consumption function. The figure also shows a 45° line along which consumption expenditure equals disposable income.

❶ When the consumption function is above the 45° line, saving is negative (dissaving occurs).

❷ When the consumption function is below the 45° line, saving is positive.

❸ At the point where the consumption function intersects the 45° line, all disposable income is consumed and saving is zero.

(trillions of 2000 dollars)						
Disposable income	0	2.0	4.0	6.0	8.0	10.0
Planned consumption expenditure	1.5	3.0	4.5	6.0	7.5	9.0
	A	B	C	D	E	F

Figure 30.1 also shows a 45° line. Because the scale on the x-axis measures disposable income and the scale on the y-axis measures consumption expenditure, and because the two scales are equal, along the 45° line consumption expenditure equals disposable income. So the 45° line serves as a reference line for comparing consumption expenditure and disposable income. Between A and D, consumption expenditure exceeds disposable income; between D and F, disposable income exceeds consumption expenditure; and at point D, consumption expenditure equals disposable income.

You can see saving in Figure 30.1. When consumption expenditure exceeds disposable income (and the consumption function is above the 45° line), saving is negative—called *dissaving*. When consumption expenditure is less than disposable income (the consumption function is below the 45° line), saving is positive. And when consumption expenditure equals disposable income (the consumption function intersects the 45° line), saving is zero.

When consumption expenditure exceeds disposable income, past savings are used to pay for current consumption. Such a situation cannot last forever, but it can and does occur if disposable income falls temporarily.

Marginal Propensity to Consume

Marginal propensity to consume

The fraction of a change in disposable income that is spent on consumption—the change in consumption expenditure divided by the change in disposable income that brought it about.

The **marginal propensity to consume** (MPC) is the fraction of a change in disposable income that is spent on consumption. It is calculated as the change in consumption expenditure divided by the change in disposable income that brought it about. That is,

$$MPC = \frac{\text{Change in consumption expenditure}}{\text{Change in disposable income}}.$$

Suppose that when disposable income increases from $6 trillion to $8 trillion, consumption expenditure increases from $6 trillion to $7.5 trillion. The $2 trillion increase in disposable income increases consumption expenditure by $1.5 trillion. Using these numbers in the formula to calculate the MPC,

$$MPC = \frac{\$1.5 \text{ trillion}}{\$2.0 \text{ trillion}} = 0.75.$$

The marginal propensity to consume tells us that when disposable income increases by $1, consumption expenditure increases by 75¢.

Figure 30.2 shows that the MPC equals the slope of the consumption function. A $2 trillion increase in disposable income from $4 trillion to $6 trillion is the base of the red triangle. The increase in consumption expenditure that results from this increase in income is $1.5 trillion and is the height of the triangle. The slope of the consumption function is given by the formula "slope equals rise over run" and is $1.5 trillion divided by $2 trillion, which equals 0.75—the MPC.

▨ **FIGURE 30.2**

Marginal Propensity to Consume

The marginal propensity to consume, MPC, is equal to the change in consumption expenditure divided by the change in disposable income, other things remaining the same. The slope of the consumption function measures the MPC.

In the figure, ❶ a $2 trillion change in disposable income brings ❷ a $1.5 trillion change in consumption expenditure, so ❸ the MPC equals $1.5 trillion ÷ $2.0 trillion = 0.75.

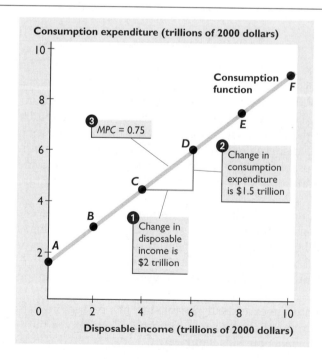

Other Influences on Consumption

Chapter 24 lists the factors that influence saving plans (see p. 602), and these same factors influence planned consumption expenditure. They are

- Disposable income
- Real interest rate
- The buying power of net assets
- Expected future disposable income

A change in disposable income leads to a change in consumption expenditure and a movement along the consumption function. A change in any of the other influences *shifts* the consumption function. For example, when the real interest rate falls or when the buying power of money or expected future income increases, consumption expenditure increases. Figure 30.3 shows the effects of these changes on the consumption function, which shifts upward from CF_0 to CF_1. Such a shift occurs during the expansion phase of the business cycle if a stock market boom increases the buying power of net assets and expected future income increases. A shift such as this occurred during the strong expansion of the late 1990s.

When the real interest rate rises or when the buying power of net assets or expected future income decreases, consumption expenditure decreases. Figure 30.3 also shows the effects of these changes on the consumption function, which shifts downward from CF_0 to CF_2. Such a shift occurs during a recession if a stock market crash decreases the buying power of net assets and expected future income decreases. A shift such as this occurred during the Great Depression of the 1930s.

FIGURE 30.3

Shifts in the Consumption Function

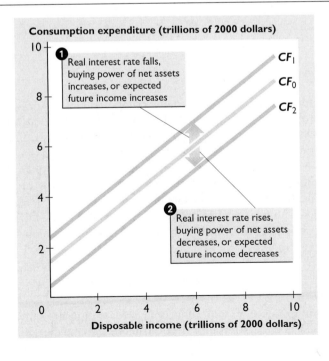

❶ A fall in the real interest rate or an increase in either the buying power of net assets or expected future income increases consumption expenditure and shifts the consumption function upward from CF_0 to CF_1.

❷ A rise in the real interest rate or a decrease in either the buying power of net assets or expected future income decreases consumption expenditure and shifts the consumption function downward from CF_0 to CF_2.

The U.S. Consumption Function

Each blue dot in the figure represents consumption expenditure and disposable income in the United States for a year between 1960 and 2005 (labeled at five-year intervals).

The line labeled CF_0 is an estimate of the U.S. consumption function during the 1960s and the line labeled CF_1 is an estimate of the U.S. consumption function during the 2000s.

The slope of the consumption function—the marginal propensity to consume—is 0.87, which means that a $1 increase in disposable income brings an 87¢ increase in consumption expenditure.

The consumption function shifted upward as influences on consumption expenditure other than disposable income changed. Of these other influences, rising expected future income and the rising wealth brought about by a rising stock market were the most important.

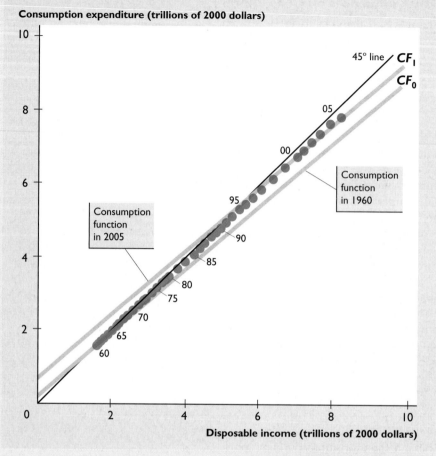

SOURCE: Bureau of Economic Analysis.

■ Imports and GDP

Imports are the other major component of induced expenditure. Many factors influence U.S. imports, but in the short run, one factor dominates: U.S. real GDP. Other things remaining the same, an increase in U.S. real GDP brings an increase in U.S. imports. The reason for this influence is that an increase in real GDP is also an increase in income. As incomes increase, people increase their expenditures on most goods and services. Because many goods and services are imported, an increase in incomes brings an increase in imports.

The relationship between imports and real GDP is described by the **marginal propensity to import**, which is the fraction of an increase in real GDP that is spent on imports.

$$\text{Marginal propensity to import} = \frac{\text{Change in imports}}{\text{Change in real GDP}}.$$

For example, if, with other things remaining the same, a $2 trillion increase in real GDP increases imports by $0.3 trillion, then the marginal propensity to import is 0.15.

Marginal propensity to import
The fraction of an increase in real GDP that is spent on imports—the change in imports divided by the change in real GDP.

CHECKPOINT 30.1

> **1** Distinguish between autonomous expenditure and induced expenditure and explain how real GDP influences expenditure plans.

Practice Problems 30.1

1. If the marginal propensity to consume is 0.8 and if disposable income increases by $0.5 trillion, by how much will consumption expenditure change?
2. If Americans decrease the fraction of each dollar of disposable income they spend on consumption, how will the U.S. consumption function change?
3. If Americans decide to decrease consumption expenditure by a fixed number of dollars, how will the U.S. consumption function change?
4. Suppose that expected future disposable income increases. Explain how this change in expectation will influence the consumption function.
5. Figure 1 shows the Canadian consumption function. What is the marginal propensity to consume and autonomous consumption in Canada?

FIGURE 1

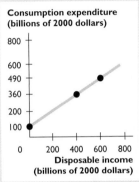

Exercises 30.1

1. The marginal propensity to consume in Japan is less than that in the United States, and for any amount of real GDP, Americans spend more on consumption than do the Japanese. Compare the consumption functions in Japan and the United States.
2. As China becomes richer, we expect that the marginal propensity to consume in China will decrease. What effect will this decrease have on the consumption function in China?
3. Suppose that the real interest rate in Japan rises. Explain how this change will influence the Japanese consumption function.
4. In 2002, autonomous consumption in the United Kingdom was £150 billion and the marginal propensity to consume was 0.9. Plot the U.K. consumption function.
5. The marginal propensity to import is higher in Singapore than it is in the United States. The growth rate of real GDP in Singapore exceeds that in the United States. Which country's imports grow more quickly and why?

Solutions to Practice Problems 30.1

1. Consumption expenditure will increase by $0.4 trillion, which is 0.8 multiplied by the change in disposable income of $0.5 trillion.
2. The marginal propensity to consume will decrease, so the slope of the consumption function will become less steep.
3. Autonomous consumption decreases, so the consumption function shifts downward.
4. Consumption expenditure will increase, and the consumption function will shift upward.
5. When disposable income increases by $200 billion, consumption expenditure increases by $130 billion. The *MPC* is $130 billion ÷ $200 billion = 0.65. Autonomous consumption (consumption expenditure that is independent of disposable income) equals the y-axis intercept and is $100 billion (Figure 2).

FIGURE 2

30.2 EQUILIBRIUM EXPENDITURE

You are now going to discover how, with a fixed price level, aggregate expenditure plans interact to determine real GDP. First we will study the relationship between aggregate planned expenditure and real GDP. Then we'll study the forces that make aggregate planned expenditure and actual expenditure equal.

An aggregate expenditure schedule and an aggregate expenditure curve describe the relationship between aggregate planned expenditure and real GDP.

■ Aggregate Planned Expenditure and Real GDP

You've seen that consumption expenditure increases when disposable income increases. Disposable income equals aggregate income—real GDP—minus net taxes, so disposable income and consumption expenditure increase when real GDP increases. We use this link between consumption expenditure and real GDP to determine equilibrium expenditure.

The table in Figure 30.4 sets out an aggregate expenditure schedule together with the components of aggregate planned expenditure. All the variables are measured in real (constant dollar) values. To calculate aggregate planned expenditure at a given real GDP, we add the various components together.

The first column of the table shows real GDP, and the second column shows the consumption expenditure generated by each level of real GDP. A $3 trillion increase in real GDP generates a $2.25 trillion increase in consumption expenditure—the *MPC* is 0.75. The next three columns show investment, government expenditure on goods and services, and exports. These items do not depend on real GDP. They are autonomous expenditure. Investment is $2 trillion, government expenditure is $1 trillion, and exports are $1.5 trillion.

The next column shows imports, which increase as real GDP increases. A $3 trillion increase in real GDP generates a $0.75 trillion increase in imports. The marginal propensity to import is 0.25.

The final column shows aggregate planned expenditure—the sum of planned consumption expenditure, investment, government expenditure on goods and services, and exports minus imports.

Figure 30.4 plots an aggregate expenditure curve. Real GDP is shown on the *x*-axis, and aggregate planned expenditure is shown on the *y*-axis. The aggregate expenditure curve is the red line *AE*. Points *A* through *F* on that curve correspond to the rows of the table. The *AE* curve is a graph of aggregate planned expenditure (the last column) plotted against real GDP (the first column).

Figure 30.4 also shows the components of aggregate expenditure. The horizontal lines in the figure show the constant components of aggregate expenditure—investment (*I*), government expenditure on goods and services (*G*), and exports (*X*). The line labeled *C* + *I* + *G* + *X* adds consumption expenditure to the constant components.

Finally, to construct the *AE* curve, subtract imports (*M*) from the *C* + *I* + *G* + *X* line. Aggregate expenditure is expenditure on U.S.-made goods and services. But *C* + *I* + *G* + *X* includes expenditure on imported goods and services. For example, if a student buys a Honda motorbike that is made in Japan, the student's expenditure is part of *C*, but it is not an expenditure on a U.S.-produced good. To find the expenditure on U.S.-produced goods, we subtract the value of the imported motorbike.

■ FIGURE 30.4
Aggregate Expenditure

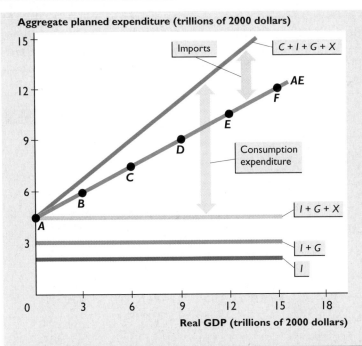

The aggregate expenditure schedule shows the relationship between aggregate planned expenditure and real GDP. For example, in row *B* of the table, when real GDP is $3 trillion, aggregate planned expenditure is $6 trillion ($2.25 + $2 + $1 + $1.5 − $0.75). As real GDP increases, aggregate planned expenditure increases.

This relationship is graphed as the aggregate expenditure curve *AE*. The components of aggregate expenditure that increase with real GDP are consumption expenditure and imports. The other components—investment, government expenditure, and exports—do not vary with real GDP.

	Real GDP (Y)	Consumption expenditure (C)	Investment (I)	Government expenditure (G)	Exports (X)	Imports (M)	Aggregate planned expenditure (AE = C + I + G + X − M)
				(trillions of 2000 dollars)			
A	0	0	2.00	1.00	1.50	0	4.50
B	3.00	2.25	2.00	1.00	1.50	0.75	6.00
C	6.00	4.50	2.00	1.00	1.50	1.50	7.50
D	9.00	6.75	2.00	1.00	1.50	2.25	9.00
E	12.00	9.00	2.00	1.00	1.50	3.00	10.50
F	15.00	11.25	2.00	1.00	1.50	3.75	12.00

Figure 30.4 shows that aggregate planned expenditure increases as real GDP increases. But notice that for each $1 increase in real GDP, aggregate planned expenditure increases by less than $1. For example, when real GDP increases from $9 trillion to $12 trillion (row *D* to row *E* of the table), aggregate planned expenditure increases from $9 trillion to $10.5 trillion. A $3 trillion increase in real GDP brings a $1.5 trillion increase in aggregate planned expenditure. So a $1 increase in real GDP brings a 50¢ increase in aggregate planned expenditure. This feature of the *AE* curve is important and plays a big role in determining equilibrium expenditure and the effect of a change in autonomous expenditure.

The *AE* curve summarizes the relationship between aggregate planned expenditure and real GDP. But what determines the point on the *AE* curve at which the economy operates? What determines actual aggregate expenditure?

■ Equilibrium Expenditure

Equilibrium expenditure
The level of aggregate expenditure
that occurs when aggregate planned
expenditure equals real GDP.

Equilibrium expenditure occurs when aggregate *planned* expenditure equals real GDP. In Figure 30.5(a) aggregate planned expenditure equals real GDP at all the points on the 45° line. Equilibrium occurs where the *AE* curve intersects the 45° line at point *D* with real GDP at $9 trillion. If real GDP is less than $9 trillion, aggregate planned expenditure exceeds real GDP; and if real GDP exceeds $9 trillion, aggregate planned expenditure is less than real GDP.

■ **FIGURE 30.5**
Equilibrium Expenditure

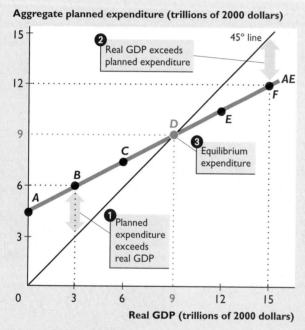

(a) Equilibrium expenditure

	Real GDP	Aggregate planned expenditure	Unplanned inventory change
		(trillions of 2000 dollars)	
A	0	4.5	−4.5
B	3.0	6.0	−3.0
C	6.0	7.5	−1.5
D	9.0	9.0	0.0
E	12.0	10.5	1.5
F	15.0	12.0	3.0

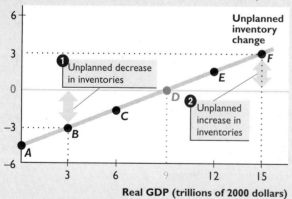

(b) Unplanned inventory change

The table shows expenditure plans and unplanned changes in inventories at different levels of real GDP. Part (a) illustrates equilibrium expenditure, and part (b) shows the unplanned inventory changes that bring changes in real GDP.

❶ When aggregate planned expenditure exceeds real GDP, an unplanned decrease in inventories occurs. Firms increase production, and real GDP increases.

❷ When real GDP exceeds aggregate planned expenditure, an unplanned increase in inventories occurs. Firms decrease production, and real GDP decreases.

❸ When aggregate planned expenditure equals real GDP, there are no unplanned inventory changes and real GDP remains at its equilibrium level.

■ Convergence to Equilibrium

At equilibrium expenditure, production plans and spending plans agree, and there is no reason for production or spending to change. But when aggregate planned expenditure and actual aggregate expenditure are unequal, production plans and spending plans are misaligned, and a process of convergence toward equilibrium expenditure occurs. Throughout this convergence process, real GDP adjusts.

What are the forces that move aggregate expenditure toward equilibrium? To answer this question, we look at a situation in which aggregate expenditure is away from equilibrium. Suppose that in Figure 30.5, real GDP is $3 trillion. With real GDP at $3 trillion, actual aggregate expenditure is also $3 trillion. But aggregate planned expenditure is $6 trillion (point *B* in Figure 30.5a). Aggregate planned expenditure exceeds actual expenditure. When people spend $6 trillion and firms produce goods and services worth $3 trillion, firms' inventories decrease by $3 trillion (point *B* in Figure 30.5b). Because the change in inventories is part of investment, the decrease in inventories decreases actual investment. So actual investment is $3 trillion less than planned investment.

Real GDP doesn't remain at $3 trillion for long. Firms have inventory targets based on their sales. When inventories fall below target, firms increase production. Suppose that they increase production by $3 trillion. Real GDP increases by $3 trillion to $6 trillion. At this real GDP, aggregate planned expenditure rises to $7.5 trillion (point *C* in Figure 30.5a). The unplanned decrease in inventories is now $1.5 trillion, so firms increase production yet again. Suppose that they increase production by another $3 trillion to $9 trillion. At this real GDP, aggregate planned expenditure rises to $9 trillion (point *D* in Figure 30.5a). The unplanned inventory change is zero, and firms have no reason to change production. Real GDP and aggregate expenditure are in equilibrium.

You can do a thought experiment similar to the one we've just done but starting with a level of real GDP greater than equilibrium expenditure. In this case, planned expenditure is less than actual expenditure, inventories pile up, and firms cut production. Real GDP decreases, and it will continue to decrease until it reaches its equilibrium level of $9 trillion.

Back at Motorola

You can now answer the question about Motorola that we left dangling earlier in this chapter. Recall that faced with unwanted inventories, Motorola and most other firms cut production in 2006. So Motorola sells even fewer phones in 2006 than in 2005. We asked: Where does this process end? It ends when equilibrium expenditure is reached. The economy arrives at equilibrium expenditure because a $1 increase in real GDP brings a less than $1 increase in aggregate planned expenditure (and a $1 decrease in real GDP brings a less than $1 decrease in aggregate planned expenditure).

Alternatively, if aggregate planned expenditure exceeds real GDP, firms increase production and real GDP increases. Aggregate planned expenditure increases, but real GDP increases by more than planned expenditure, so eventually the gap between planned expenditure and actual expenditure closes. Similarly, when aggregate planned expenditure is less than real GDP, firms cut production and real GDP decreases. Aggregate planned expenditure decreases, but real GDP decreases by more than planned expenditure, so again, eventually, the gap between planned expenditure and actual expenditure is closed.

Say's Law and Keynes' Principle of Effective Demand

During the Industrial Revolution, which began around 1760 and lasted for 70 years, technological change was rapid. People have talked about the "new economy" of the 1990s. But the 1990s was just another phase of a process that began in the truly new economy of the late 1700s. The pace of change in economic life during those years was unprecedented. Never before had old jobs been destroyed and new jobs created on such a scale. In this environment of rapid economic change, people began to wonder whether the economy could create enough jobs and a high enough level of demand to ensure that people would buy all the things that the new industrial economy could produce.

A French economist, Jean-Baptiste Say, provided the assurance that people were looking for. Born in 1767 (he was 9 years old when Adam Smith's *Wealth of Nations* was published—see Chapter 1, p. 10), Say suffered the wrath of Napoleon for his conservative call for smaller and leaner government and was the most famous economist of his era. His book *A Treatise on Political Economy (Traité d'économie politique)*, published in 1803, became the best-selling university economics textbook in both Europe and America.

In this book, Say reasoned that *supply creates its own demand*—an idea that came to be called *Say's Law*.

You've seen Say's Law at work in the full-employment economy. The real wage rate adjusts to ensure that the quantity of labor demanded equals the quantity of labor supplied and real GDP equals potential GDP. The real interest rate adjusts to ensure that the quantity of investment demanded equals the quantity of saving supplied. Because saving equals income minus consumption expenditure, the equilibrium real interest rate ensures that consumption expenditure plus investment exactly equals potential GDP.

Say's Law came under attack at various times during the nineteenth century. But it came under an onslaught during the Great Depression of the 1930s. With a quarter of the labor force unemployed and real GDP at around three quarters of potential GDP, it seemed like a stretch to argue that supply creates its own demand. But there was no simple principle or slogan with which to replace Say's Law.

In the midst of the Great Depression, in 1936, a British economist, John Maynard Keynes, provided the catchphrase that the world was looking for: *effective demand*.

Born in England in 1883, Keynes was one of the outstanding people of the twentieth century. He was a prolific writer on economic issues, represented Britain at the Versailles peace conference at the end of World War I, and played a prominent role in creating the International Monetary Fund, which monitors the global macroeconomy today.

Keynes revolutionized macroeconomic thinking by turning Say's Law on its head. Supply does *not* create its own demand, and *effective demand* determines real GDP. If businesses fail to spend on new capital the amount that people plan to save, equilibrium expenditure will be less than potential GDP. Prices and wages are sticky, and resources can become unemployed and remain unemployed indefinitely.

The aggregate expenditure model that you're studying in this chapter is the modern distillation of Keynes' idea.

Jean-Baptiste Say

John Maynard Keynes

CHECKPOINT 30.2

2   **Explain how real GDP adjusts to achieve equilibrium expenditure.**

Practice Problem 30.2

1. Table 1 is a spreadsheet that gives the components of real GDP in billions of
    dollars.
    a. Calculate aggregate planned expenditure when real GDP is $200 billion.
    b. Calculate aggregate planned expenditure when real GDP is $600 billion.
    c. Calculate equilibrium expenditure.
    d. If real GDP is $200 billion, explain the process that moves the economy
    toward equilibrium expenditure.
    e. If real GDP is $600 billion, explain the process that moves the economy
    toward equilibrium expenditure.

TABLE I

	A	B	C	D	E	F	G
1		Y	C	I	G	X	M
2	A	100	110	50	60	60	15
3	B	200	170	50	60	60	30
4	C	300	230	50	60	60	45
5	D	400	290	50	60	60	60
6	E	500	350	50	60	60	75
7	F	600	410	50	60	60	90

Exercise 30.2

1. Figure 1 shows aggregate planned expenditure.
    a. What is aggregate planned expenditure when real GDP is $8 billion?
    b. What is aggregate planned expenditure when real GDP is $2 billion?
    c. What is equilibrium expenditure?
    d. If real GDP is $8 billion, explain the process that moves the economy
    toward equilibrium expenditure.
    e. If real GDP is $2 billion, explain the process that moves the economy
    toward equilibrium expenditure.

FIGURE I

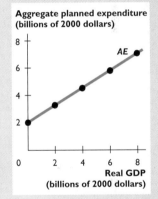

Solution to Practice Problem 30.2

1a. Aggregate planned expenditure equals $C + G + I + X - M$. When real
GDP is $200 billion, aggregate planned expenditure (in billions) equals
$170 + $50 + $60 + $60 - $30, which equals $310 billion (row B of
Table 1).

1b. Aggregate planned expenditure equals $C + G + I + X - M$. When real
GDP is $600 billion, aggregate planned expenditure (in billions) equals
$410 + $50 + $60 + $60 - $90, which equals $490 billion (row F of
Table 1).

1c. Equilibrium expenditure occurs when aggregate planned expenditure equals
real GDP. Equilibrium expenditure is $400 billion (row D of Table 1).

1d. If real GDP is $200 billion, aggregate planned expenditure is $310 billion.
Aggregate planned expenditure exceeds real GDP, so firms' inventories
decrease. Expenditure plans are not fulfilled. Firms increase production to
restore their inventories, and real GDP increases. As long as aggregate
planned expenditure exceeds real GDP, firms will increase production to
restore their inventories to their target level and real GDP will increase.

1e. If real GDP is $600 billion, aggregate planned expenditure is $490 billion.
Aggregate planned expenditure is less than real GDP, so firms' inventories
increase. Firms cut production and try to reduce their inventories. Real GDP
decreases. As long as aggregate planned expenditure is less than real GDP,
firms' inventories will increase. Firms will cut production and try to reduce
their inventories to their target level. Real GDP decreases.

30.3 THE EXPENDITURE MULTIPLIER

Multiplier

The amount by which a change in any component of autonomous expenditure is magnified or multiplied to determine the change that it generates in equilibrium expenditure and real GDP.

When investment increases, aggregate expenditure and real GDP also increase. But the increase in real GDP is larger than the increase in investment. The **multiplier** is the amount by which a change in investment (or any other component of autonomous expenditure) is magnified or multiplied to determine the change that it generates in equilibrium expenditure and real GDP.

■ The Basic Idea of the Multiplier

The growth of the Internet during the 1990s brought a large increase in investment in personal computers, servers, fiber-optic cables, satellites, and other communication and computing equipment. These investment expenditures increased aggregate expenditure and real GDP.

The increase in real GDP increased disposable income. The increase in disposable income increased consumption expenditure. And the increased consumption expenditure added even more to aggregate expenditure. Real GDP and disposable income increased further, and so did consumption expenditure.

The initial increase in investment brought an increase in aggregate expenditure that exceeded the increase in investment because it induced an increase in consumption expenditure.

The multiplier determines the magnitude of the increase in aggregate expenditure that results from an increase in investment or another component of autonomous expenditure.

Consumption expenditure decisions, imports, and income taxes that open a gap between disposable income and real GDP all influence the multiplier. But we can understand the basic idea of the multiplier more clearly if we temporarily ignore the effects of imports and income taxes and focus on the role of consumption expenditure.

Figure 30.6 illustrates the multiplier. The table shows an initial aggregate expenditure schedule, and the initial AE curve is AE_0. With this AE schedule and curve, equilibrium expenditure and real GDP are $9 trillion. You can see this equilibrium in row B of the table and where the curve AE_0 intersects the 45° line at point B in the figure.

Now suppose that investment increases by $0.5 trillion. What happens to equilibrium expenditure? Figure 30.6 shows the answer. When this increase in investment is added to the initial aggregate planned expenditure, aggregate planned expenditure increases by $0.5 trillion at each level of real GDP. The new AE curve is AE_1. The new equilibrium expenditure, highlighted in the table (row D'), occurs where AE_1 intersects the 45° line and is $11 trillion (point D'). At this real GDP, aggregate planned expenditure equals real GDP. The increase in equilibrium expenditure ($2 trillion) is larger than the increase in investment that brought it about ($0.5 trillion).

We've just analyzed the effects of an *increase* in investment. The same analysis applies to a *decrease* in investment. If initially the AE curve is AE_1, equilibrium expenditure and real GDP are $11 trillion. A decrease in investment of $0.5 trillion shifts the AE curve downward by $0.5 trillion from AE_1 to AE_0. Equilibrium expenditure decreases from $11 trillion to $9 trillion. The decrease in equilibrium expenditure ($2 trillion) is larger than the decrease in investment that brought it about ($0.5 trillion).

FIGURE 30.6
The Multiplier

Real GDP (Y)	Aggregate planned expenditure				
	Original (AE₀)		New (AE₁)		
(trillions of 2000 dollars)					
8.00	A	8.25	A'	8.75	
9.00	B	9.00	B'	9.50	
10.00	C	9.75	C'	10.25	
11.00	D	10.50	D'	11.00	
12.00	E	11.25	E'	11.75	

1 A \$0.5 trillion increase in investment shifts the *AE* curve upward by \$0.5 trillion from *AE₀* to *AE₁*.

2 Equilibrium expenditure increases by \$2 trillion from \$9 trillion to \$11 trillion.

3 The increase in equilibrium expenditure is 4 times the increase in autonomous expenditure, so the multiplier is 4.

■ The Size of the Multiplier

The multiplier is the amount by which a change in autonomous expenditure is multiplied to determine the change in equilibrium expenditure that it generates. To calculate the multiplier, we divide the change in equilibrium expenditure by the change in autonomous expenditure that generated it. That is,

$$\text{Multiplier} = \frac{\text{Change in equilibrium expenditure}}{\text{Change in autonomous expenditure}}.$$

The change in equilibrium expenditure also equals the change in real GDP, which we'll call ΔY. In Figure 30.6, the change in autonomous expenditure is a change in investment, which we'll call ΔI. The multiplier is

$$\text{Multiplier} = \frac{\Delta Y}{\Delta I}.$$

In Figure 30.6, equilibrium expenditure increases by \$2 trillion ($\Delta Y = \$2$ trillion) and investment increases by \$0.5 trillion ($\Delta I = \$0.5$ trillion), so the multiplier is

$$\text{Multiplier} = \frac{\Delta Y}{\Delta I} = \frac{\$2 \text{ trillion}}{\$0.5 \text{ trillion}} = 4.$$

The multiplier is 4—real GDP changes by 4 times the change in investment.

Why is the multiplier greater than 1? It is because an increase in autonomous expenditure induces further increases in aggregate expenditure—induced expenditure increases. If General Motors spends \$10 million on a new car assembly line, aggregate expenditure and real GDP immediately increase by \$10 million.

Engineers and construction workers now have more income, and they spend part of the extra income on cars, microwave ovens, vacations, and a host of other goods and services. Real GDP now increases by the initial $10 million plus the extra consumption expenditure induced by the $10 million increase in income. The producers of cars, microwave ovens, vacations, and other goods now have increased incomes, and they in turn spend part of the increase in their incomes on consumption goods and services. Additional income induces additional expenditure, which creates additional income.

■ The Multiplier and the *MPC*

Ignoring imports and income taxes, the magnitude of the multiplier depends only on the marginal propensity to consume. To see why, let's do a calculation. The change in real GDP (ΔY) equals the change in consumption expenditure (ΔC) plus the change in investment (ΔI). That is,

$$\Delta Y = \Delta C + \Delta I.$$

But with no income taxes, the change in consumption expenditure is determined by the change in real GDP and the marginal propensity to consume. It is

$$\Delta C = MPC \times \Delta Y.$$

Now substitute $MPC \times \Delta Y$ for ΔC in the previous equation:

$$\Delta Y = MPC \times \Delta Y + \Delta I.$$

Now solve for ΔY as

$$(1 - MPC) \times \Delta Y = \Delta I,$$

and rearrange the equation:

$$\Delta Y = \frac{1}{(1 - MPC)} \Delta I.$$

Finally, divide both sides of the previous equation by ΔI to give

$$\text{Multiplier} = \frac{\Delta Y}{\Delta I} = \frac{1}{(1 - MPC)}.$$

In Figure 30.6, the *MPC* is 0.75. So if we use the numbers in this figure,

$$\text{Multiplier} = \frac{\Delta Y}{\Delta I} = \frac{1}{(1 - 0.75)} = \frac{1}{0.25} = 4.$$

The greater the marginal propensity to consume, the larger is the multiplier. For example, if the marginal propensity to consume is 0.9, the multiplier is 10. Let's now look at the influence of imports and income taxes.

■ The Multiplier, Imports, and Income Taxes

The size of the multiplier depends not only on consumption decisions but also on imports and income taxes. Imports make the multiplier smaller than it otherwise would be. To see why, think about what happens following an increase in investment. The increase in investment increases real GDP, which in turn increases consumption expenditure. But part of the increase in expenditure is on imported goods and services, not U.S.-produced goods and services. Only expenditure on

U.S.-produced goods and services increases U.S. real GDP. The larger the marginal propensity to import, the smaller is the change in U.S. real GDP that results from a change in autonomous expenditure.

Income taxes also make the multiplier smaller than it otherwise would be. Again, think about what happens following an increase in investment. The increase in investment increases real GDP. But with increased incomes, income tax payments increase and disposable income increases by less than the increase in real GDP. Because disposable income influences consumption expenditure, the increase in consumption expenditure is less than it would be if income tax payments had not changed.

The marginal tax rate determines the extent to which income tax payments change when real GDP changes. The **marginal tax rate** is the fraction of a change in real GDP that is paid in income taxes. The larger the marginal tax rate, the smaller are the changes in disposable income and real GDP that result from a given change in autonomous expenditure.

The marginal propensity to import and the marginal tax rate together with the marginal propensity to consume determine the multiplier. And their combined influence determines the slope of the AE curve. The general formula for the multiplier is

$$\text{Multiplier} = \frac{\Delta Y}{\Delta I} = \frac{1}{(1 - \text{Slope of } AE \text{ curve})}.$$

Figure 30.7 compares two situations. In Figure 30.7(a), there are no imports and no taxes. The slope of the AE curve equals the MPC, which is 0.75, so the multiplier is 4 (as we calculated above). In Figure 30.7(b), imports and income taxes decrease

Marginal tax rate
The fraction of a change in real GDP that is paid in income taxes—the change in tax payments divided by the change in real GDP.

■ **FIGURE 30.7**

The Multiplier and the Slope of the AE Curve

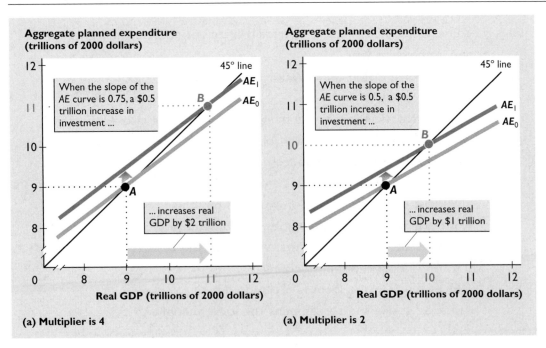

(a) Multiplier is 4

(a) Multiplier is 2

In part (a), with no imports and income taxes, the slope of the AE curve equals the marginal propensity to consume, which in this example is 0.75. The multiplier is 4.

In part (b), with imports and income taxes, the slope of the AE curve is less than the marginal propensity to consume. In this example, the slope of the AE curve is 0.5 and the multiplier is 2.

the slope of the *AE* curve to 0.5. So in this case,

$$\text{Multiplier} = \frac{\Delta Y}{\Delta I} = \frac{1}{(1 - 0.5)} = 2.$$

Over time, the value of the multiplier changes as the marginal tax rate, the marginal propensity to consume, and the marginal propensity to import change. These ongoing changes make the multiplier hard to predict.

■ Business-Cycle Turning Points

An expansion is triggered by an increase in autonomous expenditure. At the moment the economy turns the corner into expansion, aggregate planned expenditure exceeds real GDP. In this situation, firms see their inventories taking an unplanned dive. The expansion now begins. To meet their inventory targets, firms increase production, and real GDP begins to increase. This initial increase in real GDP brings higher incomes, and the higher incomes stimulate consumption expenditure. The multiplier process kicks in, and the expansion picks up speed.

The process works in reverse at a business cycle peak. A recession is triggered by a decrease in autonomous expenditure. At the moment the economy turns the corner into recession, real GDP exceeds aggregate planned expenditure. In this situation, firms see unplanned inventories piling up. The recession now begins. To reduce their inventories, firms cut production, and real GDP begins to decrease. This initial decrease in real GDP brings lower incomes. People cut their consumption expenditure. The multiplier process reinforces the initial cut in autonomous expenditure, and the recession takes hold.

REALITY CHECK

Multipliers in YOUR Life

You can see multipliers in your daily life if you look in the right places and in the right way.

Look for a major construction project that is going on near your home or school.

What supplies do you see being delivered to the site? How many workers do you estimate have jobs on the site? Where do the supplies and the workers come from? Whose income is higher because of the purchase of these supplies and jobs of the construction workers?

Where do the construction workers buy their coffee and lunch? Are their purchases creating jobs for students and others in local coffee shops and fast-food outlets? Where do the construction workers and suppliers spend their incomes?

How much of the income created goes to pay taxes or buy imported goods and so dampens the local multiplier?

CHECKPOINT 30.3

3 **Describe and explain the expenditure multiplier.**

Practice Problems 30.3

1. An economy has no imports or taxes, the *MPC* is 0.80, and real GDP is $150 billion. Businesses increase investment by $5 billion.
    a. Calculate the multiplier.
    b. Calculate the change in real GDP.
    c. Calculate the new level of real GDP.
    d. Explain why real GDP increases by more than $5 billion.

2. An economy has no imports or taxes. An increase in autonomous expenditure of $2 trillion increases equilibrium expenditure by $8 trillion.
    a. Calculate the multiplier.
    b. Calculate the marginal propensity to consume.
    c. What happens to the multiplier if an income tax is introduced in this economy?

Exercises 30.3

1. An economy has no imports or taxes. The marginal propensity to consume is 0.60, and real GDP is $100 billion. Businesses decrease investment by $10 billion.
    a. Calculate the multiplier.
    b. Calculate the change in real GDP.
    c. Calculate the new level of real GDP.
    d. Explain why real GDP decreases by more than $10 billion.

2. An economy has no imports or taxes. The multiplier is 1.25, and autonomous expenditure increases by $2 trillion.
    a. Calculate the change in real GDP.
    b. Calculate the marginal propensity to consume.
    c. If the government decides to open the country up to international trade, explain how international trade influences the multiplier.

Solutions to Practice Problems 30.3

1a. The multiplier equals $1/(1 - MPC)$. *MPC* is 0.8, so the multiplier is 5.
1b. Real GDP increases by $25 billion. The increase in investment increases real GDP by the multiplier (5) times the change in investment ($5 billion).
1c. Real GDP increases from $150 billion to $175 billion.
1d. Real GDP increases by more than $5 billion because the increase in investment induces an increase in consumption expenditure.

2a. The multiplier is the increase in equilibrium expenditure ($8 trillion) divided by the increase in autonomous expenditure ($2 trillion). The multiplier is 4.
2b. The marginal propensity to consume is 0.75. The multiplier $= 1/(1 - MPC)$. So $4 = 1/(1 - MPC)$, and *MPC* is 0.75.
2c. If the government introduces an income tax, the slope of the *AE* curve becomes smaller and the multiplier becomes smaller.

30.4 THE *AD* CURVE AND EQUILIBRIUM EXPENDITURE

In this chapter, we've studied the aggregate expenditure model, in which firms change production when sales and inventories change but they don't change their prices. The aggregate expenditure model determines equilibrium expenditure and real GDP at a given price level. In Chapter 29, we studied the simultaneous determination of real GDP and the price level using the *AS-AD* model. The aggregate demand curve and equilibrium expenditure are related, and this section shows you how.

■ Deriving the *AD* Curve from Equilibrium Expenditure

The *AE* curve is the relationship between aggregate planned expenditure and real GDP when all other influences on expenditure plans remain the same. A movement along the *AE* curve arises from a change in real GDP.

The *AD* curve is the relationship between the quantity of real GDP demanded and the price level when all other influences on expenditure plans remain the same. A movement along the *AD* curve arises from a change in the price level.

Equilibrium expenditure depends on the price level. When the price level rises, other things remaining the same, aggregate planned expenditure decreases and equilibrium expenditure decreases. And when the price level falls, other things remaining the same, aggregate planned expenditure increases and equilibrium expenditure increases. The reason is that a change in the price level changes the buying power of money, the real interest rate, and the real prices of exports and imports (see Chapter 29, pp. 738–740).

When the price level rises, each of these effects decreases aggregate planned expenditure at each level of real GDP. So the *AE* curve shifts downward. A fall in the price level has the opposite effect. When the price level falls, the *AE* curve shifts upward.

Figure 30.8(a) shows the shifts of the *AE* curve. When the price level is 110, the *AE* curve intersects the 45° line at point *B*. Equilibrium expenditure is $10 trillion. If the price level rises to 130, the *AE* curve shifts downward and equilibrium expenditure is $9 trillion at point *A*. If the price level falls to 90, the *AE* curve shifts upward and equilibrium expenditure is $11 trillion at point *C*.

The price level changes that shift the *AE* curve and change equilibrium expenditure bring movements along the *AD* curve. Figure 30.8(b) shows these movements. At a price level of 110, the quantity of real GDP demanded is $10 trillion—point *B* on the *AD* curve. If the price level rises to 130, the quantity of real GDP demanded decreases to $9 trillion at point *A*. If the price level falls to 90, the quantity of real GDP demanded increases to $11 trillion at point *C*.

The two parts of Figure 30.8 are connected and illustrate the relationship between the *AE* curve and the *AD* curve. Each point of equilibrium expenditure corresponds to a point on the *AD* curve. The equilibrium expenditure points *A*, *B*, and *C* (part a) correspond to the points *A*, *B*, and *C* on the *AD* curve (part b).

FIGURE 30.8

Equilibrium Expenditure and Aggregate Demand

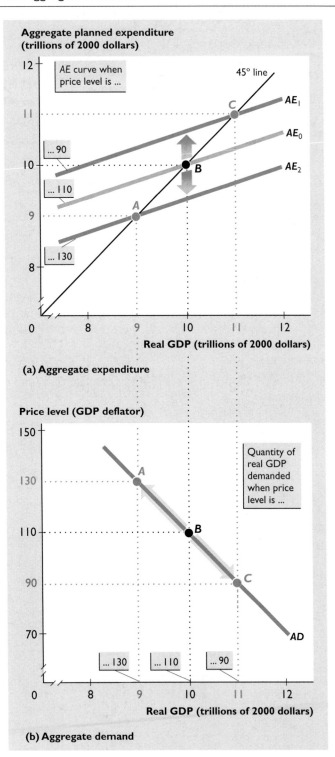

(a) Aggregate expenditure

(b) Aggregate demand

A change in the price level shifts the *AE* curve and results in a movement along the *AD* curve. When the price level is 110, equilibrium expenditure is $10 trillion at point *B*.

When the price level rises to130, equilibrium expenditure decreases to $9 trillion at point *A*. When the price level falls to 90, equilibrium expenditure increases to $11 trillion at point *C*.

Points *A*, *B*, and *C* on the *AD* curve in part (b) correspond to the equilibrium expenditure points *A*, *B*, and *C* in part (a).

4 **Derive the *AD* curve from equilibrium expenditure.**

Practice Problem 30.4

1. An economy has the following aggregate expenditure schedules:

Real GDP (trillions of 2000 dollars)	Aggregate planned expenditure in trillions of 2000 dollars when the price level is		
	110	100	90
0	1.0	1.5	2.0
1	1.5	2.0	2.5
2	2.0	2.5	3.0
3	2.5	3.0	3.5
4	3.0	3.5	4.0
5	3.5	4.0	4.5
6	4.0	4.5	5.0

a. Make a graph to show three *AE* curves.
b. Find equilibrium expenditure at each price level.
c. Construct the aggregate demand schedule and plot the aggregate demand curve.

Exercise 30.4

1. In the economy described in the practice problem, autonomous expenditure increases by $0.5 trillion.
   a. Make a graph to show three new *AE* curves.
   b. Find equilibrium expenditure at each price level.
   c. Construct the aggregate demand schedule and plot the aggregate demand curve.
   d. What is the magnitude of the multiplier?

Solution to Practice Problem 30.4

1a. Figure 1 shows the three AE curves.
1b. Figure 1 shows the three equilibrium levels of aggregate expenditure. When the price level is 90, equilibrium expenditure is $4 trillion. When the price level is 100, equilibrium expenditure is $3 trillion. When the price level is 110, equilibrium expenditure is $2 trillion.
1c. The table below shows the aggregate demand schedule, and Figure 2 shows the aggregate demand curve.

Price level	Quantity of real GDP demanded (trillions of 2000 dollars)
90	4
100	3
110	2

FIGURE I

FIGURE 2

CHAPTER CHECKPOINT

Key Points

1 Distinguish between autonomous expenditure and induced expenditure and explain how real GDP influences expenditure plans.

- Investment plus government expenditure on goods and services plus exports, which real GDP does *not* influence directly, plus the components of consumption expenditure and imports that are not influenced by real GDP is called autonomous expenditure.
- The components of consumption expenditure and imports, which real GDP influence, are called induced expenditure.
- Consumption expenditure varies with disposable income and real GDP and depends on the marginal propensity to consume.
- Imports vary with real GDP and depend on the marginal propensity to import.

2 Explain how real GDP adjusts to achieve equilibrium expenditure.

- Actual aggregate expenditure equals real GDP and differs from planned expenditure when firms have unplanned inventory changes.
- If aggregate planned expenditure exceeds real GDP, firms increase production and real GDP increases. If real GDP exceeds aggregate planned expenditure, firms decrease production and real GDP decreases.
- Real GDP changes until aggregate planned expenditure equals real GDP.

3 Describe and explain the expenditure multiplier.

- When autonomous expenditure changes, equilibrium expenditure changes by a larger amount: There is a multiplier.
- The multiplier is greater than 1 because a change in autonomous expenditure changes induced expenditure.
- The larger the marginal propensity to consume, the larger is the multiplier.
- Income taxes and imports make the multiplier smaller.

4 Derive the *AD* curve from equilibrium expenditure.

- The *AD* curve is the relationship between the quantity of real GDP demanded and the price level when all other influences on expenditure plans remain the same.
- The quantity of real GDP demanded on the *AD* curve is the equilibrium real GDP when aggregate planned expenditure equals real GDP.

Key Terms

Aggregate planned expenditure, 757
Autonomous expenditure, 758
Consumption function, 758

Equilibrium expenditure, 766
Induced expenditure, 758
Marginal propensity to consume, 760

Marginal propensity to import, 762
Marginal tax rate, 773
Multiplier, 770

myeconlab   # Exercises

1. The table shows disposable income and saving in the global economy.

Disposable income (trillions of dollars)	0	10	20	30	40	50
Saving (trillions of dollars)	−5	−3	−1	1	3	5

   a. Calculate consumption expenditure at each level of disposable income.
   b. Over what range of disposable income is there dissaving?
   c. Estimate the level of disposable income at which saving is zero.
   d. Calculate the marginal propensity to consume.
   e. If the buying power of net assets increased by $10 trillion, in which direction would the consumption function that you've found change?

2. The table shows some values of real GDP, Y, consumption expenditure, C, investment, I, government expenditure on goods and services, G, exports, X, imports, M, and aggregate planned expenditure, AE, in millions of dollars in an economy in which taxes are constant.

				Planned expenditure		
Y	C	I	G	X	M	AE
0	2.0	1.75	1.0	1.25	0.0	6.0
2	Q	1.75	1.0	1.25	0.4	6.8
4	4.4	R	1.0	1.25	0.8	7.6
6	5.6	1.75	S	1.25	1.2	8.4
8	6.8	1.75	1.0	T	1.6	9.2
10	8.0	1.75	1.0	1.25	U	10.0
12	9.2	1.75	1.0	1.25	2.4	V

   a. Find the value of Q, R, S, T, U, and V.
   b. Make a graph of the components of aggregate planned expenditure similar to Figure 30.4.
   c. Calculate the marginal propensity to consume.
   d. Calculate the marginal propensity to import.
   e. Find equilibrium expenditure.

3. In the economy described in exercise 2, investment crashes to $0.55 trillion but nothing else changes.
   a. What now is equilibrium expenditure?
   b. What is the multiplier?

4. In an economy with no exports or imports, autonomous consumption is $1 trillion, the marginal propensity to consume is 0.8, investment is $5 trillion, and government expenditure is $4 trillion. Taxes are $4 trillion and do not vary with real GDP.
   a. Calculate disposable income when real GDP is $30 trillion.
   b. Calculate consumption expenditure when real GDP is $30 trillion.
   c. Calculate aggregate planned expenditure when real GDP is $30 trillion.
   d. Calculate equilibrium expenditure.

e. If real GDP is $30 trillion, explain the process that takes the economy to equilibrium expenditure.

f. If real GDP is $40 trillion, explain the process that takes the economy to equilibrium expenditure.

5. In exercise 4, investment increases by $0.5 trillion. Calculate
   a. The size of the shift of the *AE* curve.
   b. The size of the multiplier.
   c. The change in equilibrium expenditure.

6. The Mexican government has just cut the marginal income tax rate. Explain how this cut will change
   a. Consumption expenditure in Mexico.
   b. Equilibrium expenditure in Mexico.
   c. The multiplier in Mexico.

7. In the global economy, when the price level is 100, aggregate planned expenditure would be $10 trillion if real GDP were zero; when the price level is 90, aggregate planned expenditure would be $11 trillion if real GDP were zero; and when the price level is 110, aggregate planned expenditure would be $9 trillion if real GDP were zero. For each $1 increase in real GDP, aggregate planned expenditure increases by 75¢, and this relationship between expenditure plans and real GDP is the same at every price level.
   a. Calculate aggregate planned expenditure when the price level is 100 at real GDP levels of $35 trillion, $40 trillion, and $45 trillion.
   b. Calculate aggregate planned expenditure when the price level is 110 at real GDP levels of $35 trillion, $40 trillion, and $45 trillion.
   c. Calculate aggregate planned expenditure when the price level is 90 at real GDP levels of $35 trillion, $40 trillion, and $45 trillion.
   d. Calculate equilibrium expenditure at price levels of 90, 100, and 110.
   e. Make graphs of the *AE* curves at price levels of 90, 100, and 110 and the *AD* curve.

8. In exercise 7, global investment increases by $1 trillion.
   a. Calculate aggregate planned expenditure when the price level is 100 at real GDP levels of $35 trillion, $40 trillion, and $45 trillion.
   b. Calculate aggregate planned expenditure when the price level is 110 at real GDP levels of $35 trillion, $40 trillion, and $45 trillion.
   c. Calculate aggregate planned expenditure when the price level is 90 at real GDP levels of $35 trillion, $40 trillion, and $45 trillion.
   d. Calculate equilibrium expenditure at price levels of 90, 100, and 110.
   e. Make graphs of the new *AE* curve at price levels of 90, 100, and 110 and the *AD* curve.

9. Compare the *AD* curve of exercise 7 with that of exercise 8.
   a. Does the *AD* curve shift leftward or rightward? Explain the direction of the shift.
   b. Does the *AD* curve shift by the same $1 trillion increase in investment, by more than that amount, or by less than that amount? Explain the magnitude of the shift.

Critical Thinking

10. It is 2000 and the Japanese economy is in a recession. Economists suggested that the Japanese government increase its expenditure on goods and services but not change taxes. Explain how such a policy change would influence equilibrium expenditure. Would such a policy change help to turn the economy from recession to expansion?

11. It is 2010, and real GDP in the U.S. economy is decreasing. Consumption and other components of aggregate expenditure are also decreasing. Explain how these events will influence
    a. The U.S. consumption function.
    b. The U.S. aggregate expenditure curve.
    c. Equilibrium expenditure in the United States.
    d. Autonomous expenditure in Mexico and Canada.
    e. The consumption functions of Mexico and Canada.
    f. The aggregate expenditure curves of Mexico and Canada.
    g. Equilibrium expenditure in Mexico and Canada.

12. Throughout the 1990s, the economy of Russia was in a prolonged recession—a depression. Use the aggregate expenditure model to illustrate the state of the Russian economy during its depression. Then explain how the following events might have influenced aggregate expenditure and equilibrium expenditure.
    a. The booming U.S. economy.
    b. Tax increases in Russia.
    c. Cuts in government expenditure on goods and services in Russia.

 ## Web Exercises

Use the links on MyEconLab to work the following exercises.

13. Visit the Bureau of Economic Analysis Web site and obtain annual data on real GDP, real consumption expenditure, real investment, real government expenditure on goods and services, real exports, and real imports since 1990.
    a. Load the data into a spreadsheet.
    b. Calculate the annual growth rates of each expenditure item.
    c. Make a graph of the annual growth rates of each expenditure item.
    d. Which component of aggregate expenditure fluctuates most and which fluctuates least?
    e. Which components of aggregate expenditure appear to have fluctuations that move in a similar way to the fluctuations in real GDP?
    f. Which components of aggregate expenditure appear to have fluctuations that are independent of real GDP?
    g. Which components of aggregate expenditure appear to be autonomous and which appear to be induced?

14. Use the data on real GDP and real consumption expenditure that you obtained in exercise 13.
    a. Make a graph to show consumption as a function of real GDP.
    b. Make an estimate of the marginal propensity to consume.
    c. Does the consumption function seem to have shifted? In which direction has it shifted? Can you think of reasons why it might have shifted?

Fiscal and Monetary Policy Effects

CHAPTER CHECKLIST

When you have completed your study of this chapter, you will be able to

1 Describe the federal budget process and explain the effects of fiscal policy.

2 Describe the Federal Reserve's monetary policy process and explain the effects of monetary policy.

The federal government is spending $425 billion a year more than it is collecting in taxes. At the end of 2005, the government's debt was close to $16,000 for every person in the United States. What are the effects of government spending, taxes, and a government budget deficit on the economy?

Every six weeks or so, the Federal Open Market Committee (FOMC) meets at the Fed's Washington, D.C., headquarters. The eyes of Wall Street and the nation's financial managers focus on this event, looking for signs of changes in the interest rate. What are the effects of the Fed's actions on the economy?

In this chapter, we build on what you have learned about aggregate demand and aggregate supply, aggregate expenditures, and money to explore the tools used by the federal government and the Federal Reserve to influence aggregate demand and counteract the forces that push the economy away from full employment. Our focus in this chapter is on the effects of these tools. The next two chapters examine questions about priorities and strategies in using these tools.

31.1 THE FEDERAL BUDGET AND FISCAL POLICY

Fiscal policy
The use of the federal budget to encourage sustained economic growth and smooth the business cycle.

Fiscal policy is the use of the federal budget to encourage sustained economic growth and smooth the business cycle. We begin our study of fiscal policy by describing the federal budget and the process that creates it.

■ The Federal Budget

Federal budget
An annual statement of the expenditures and tax receipts of the government of the United States.

The **federal budget** is an annual statement of the expenditures and tax receipts of the government of the United States. The government's surplus or deficit is equal to its tax receipts minus its expenditures. That is,

$$\text{Budget surplus } (+)/\text{deficit } (-) = \text{Tax receipts} - \text{Expenditures.}$$

Budget surplus
The budget balance when tax receipts exceed expenditures.

The government has a **budget surplus** if tax receipts exceed expenditures, a **budget deficit** if expenditures exceed tax receipts, and a **balanced budget** if tax receipts equal expenditures. The government budget balance is also equal to government saving (net taxes minus expenditure) that you met in Chapter 24 (p. 608).

Budget deficit
The budget balance when expenditures exceed tax receipts.

The government borrows to finance a budget deficit and repays its debt when it has a surplus. The amount of debt outstanding that arises from past budget deficits is called *national debt*. (*Eye on the Past* on p. 786 shows the history of the U.S. budget deficit and debt.)

Balanced budget
The budget balance when tax receipts equal expenditures.

A Personal Analogy   The government's budget and debt are like your budget and debt, only bigger. If you take a student loan each year to go to school, you have a budget deficit and a growing debt. If after graduating and getting a job, you repay some of your loan each year, you have a budget surplus and a shrinking debt.

Budget Time Line

The President and Congress make the federal budget on the time line shown in Figure 31.1. The President proposes and approves the budget, but Congress makes the tough decisions on spending and taxes. The House of Representatives and the Senate develop their ideas in their respective budget committees, and conferences between the two houses resolve differences and draft the bills that become the Budget Act. Fiscal year 2007 is the year that begins on October 1, 2006, and ends on September 30, 2007.

Types of Fiscal Policy

Fiscal policy can be either

- Discretionary or
- Automatic

Discretionary fiscal policy
A fiscal policy action that is initiated by an act of Congress.

Discretionary Fiscal Policy   A fiscal action that is initiated by an act of Congress is called **discretionary fiscal policy**. It requires a change in a spending program or in a tax law. For example, an increase in defense spending or a cut in the income tax rate is a discretionary fiscal policy.

Automatic fiscal policy
A fiscal policy action that is triggered by the state of the economy.

Automatic Fiscal Policy   A fiscal action that is triggered by the state of the economy is called **automatic fiscal policy**. For example, an increase in unemployment induces an increase in payments to the unemployed. A fall in incomes induces a decrease in tax receipts.

FIGURE 31.1

The Federal Budget Time Line for Fiscal 2007

Jan. 1, 06
Feb. 2, 06 — The President submits a budget proposal to Congress.

Congress debates, amends, and enacts the budget.
The President signs the budget act into law.

Oct. 1, 06 — Fiscal 2007 begins.
Supplementary budget laws may be passed.

State of the economy influences expenditures,
tax revenues, and the budget balance.

Sept.. 30, 07 — Fiscal 2007 ends.

Accounts for Fiscal 2007 are prepared.
Expenditures, tax revenues, and the
budget balance are reported.

The federal budget process begins with the President's proposals in February. Congress debates and amends these proposals and enacts a budget before the start of the fiscal year on October 1. The President signs the Budget Act into law. Throughout the fiscal year, Congress might pass supplementary budget laws. The budget outcome is calculated after the end of the fiscal year.

EYE ON THE GLOBAL ECONOMY

The U.S. Budget in Global Perspective

Summing the budgets of all the governments in the world, the IMF estimates that budgets were in deficit by 3.4 percent of world GDP in 2002.

Japan had one of the biggest deficits at more than 7 percent of GDP. But the developing countries of Asia, which include China and India, had large deficits.

Canada was the only major advanced economy with a surplus in 2002.

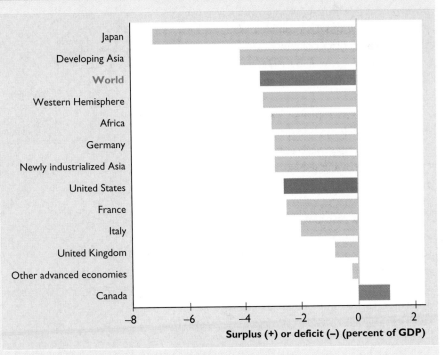

SOURCE OF DATA: International Monetary Fund, *World Economic Outlook*, September 2002.

EYE ON THE PAST

Federal Receipts, Expenditures, Deficit, and Debt

In 1940, in the first year of World War II, the federal government collected 6.5 cents out of every dollar earned in taxes. It spent 9.3 cents out of every dollar earned. By 1943, at the depth of the most terrible war in history, the government was spending 40 cents per dollar earned and collecting 12 cents in taxes. The government deficit in 1943 and 1944 was almost 30 percent of GDP.

The result of these enormous deficits was a mushrooming government debt that came close to hitting 100 percent of GDP.

During the 1950s and 1960s, the government's debt-to-GDP ratio (debt as a percentage of GDP) tumbled as small budget deficits combined with rapid real GDP growth. By 1974, the debt-to-GDP ratio had fallen to a low of 18.3 percent.

Budget deficits returned during the 1980s as the defense budget swelled and some tax rates were cut. The result was a growing debt-to-GDP ratio that climbed to almost 50 percent by 1995.

Expenditure restraint combined with renewed rapid real GDP growth lowered the debt-to-GDP ratio briefly during the 1990s, but the surge in expenditures to cope with the war against terrorism and further tax cuts swelled the debt-to-GDP ratio again.

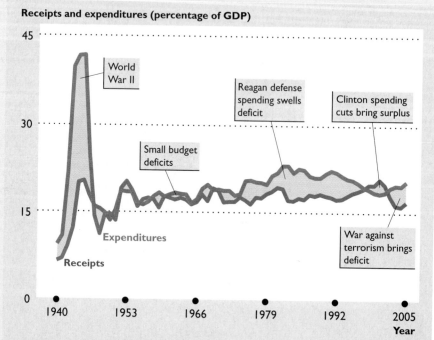

(a) Receipts, expenditures, and deficits

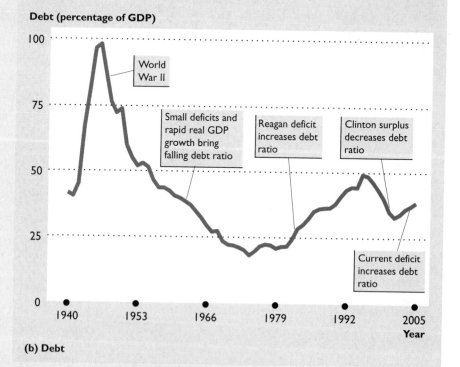

(b) Debt

SOURCE OF DATA: Office of Management and Budget, Historical Tables, Budget of the U.S. Government, Fiscal Year 2006.

■ Discretionary Fiscal Policy: Demand-Side Effects

Discretionary fiscal policy influences both aggregate demand and aggregate supply. We'll look first at the demand-side effects. Changes in government expenditure and changes in taxes have multiplier effects on aggregate demand similar to the multiplier that you studied in Chapters 29 and 30.

The Government Expenditure Multiplier

The **government expenditure multiplier** is the magnification effect of a change in government expenditure on goods and services on aggregate demand. Government expenditure is a component of aggregate expenditure, so when government expenditure changes, aggregate demand changes. Real GDP changes and induces a change in consumption expenditure, which brings a further change in aggregate expenditure. A multiplier process like the one described in Chapter 30 (pp. 770-774) ensues.

Government expenditure multiplier
The magnification effect of a change in government expenditure on goods and services on aggregate demand.

A Homeland Security Multiplier   The terrorist attacks of September 11, 2001, brought a reappraisal of the nation's homeland security requirements and an increase in government expenditure. This increase in purchases initially increased the incomes of producers of airport and border security equipment and security workers. Better-off security workers increased their consumption expenditures. With rising revenues, other businesses in all parts of the nation boomed and expanded their payrolls. A second round of increased consumption expenditures increased incomes yet further. The increase in security expenditures and its multiplier effect helped to end the 2001 recession.

The Tax Multiplier

The **tax multiplier** is the magnification effect of a change in taxes on aggregate demand. A *decrease* in taxes *increases* disposable income, which increases consumption expenditure. A decrease in taxes works like an increase in government expenditure. But the magnitude of the tax multiplier is smaller than the government expenditure multiplier. The reason is that a $1 tax cut generates *less than* $1 of additional expenditure. The marginal propensity to consume determines the increase in expenditure induced by a tax cut. For example, if the marginal propensity to consume is 0.75, then a $1 tax cut increases consumption expenditure by only 75 cents. In this case, the tax multiplier is 0.75 times the magnitude of the government expenditure multiplier.

Tax multiplier
The magnification effect of a change in taxes on aggregate demand.

A Bush Tax Cut Multiplier   Congress enacted the Bush tax cut package that lowered taxes in 2002. These tax cuts had a multiplier effect. With more disposable income, people increased consumption expenditure. This spending increased other people's incomes, which spurred yet more consumption expenditure. Like the increase in security expenditures, the tax cut and its multiplier effect helped to end the 2001 recession.

The Balanced Budget Multiplier

The **balanced budget multiplier** is the magnification effect on aggregate demand of a *simultaneous* change in government expenditure and taxes that leaves the budget balance unchanged. The balanced budget multiplier is positive because a $1 increase in government expenditure injects a dollar more into aggregate demand while a $1 tax rise takes less than $1 from aggregate demand. So when both government expenditure and taxes increase by $1, aggregate demand increases.

Balanced budget multiplier
The magnification effect on aggregate demand of a *simultaneous* change in government expenditure and taxes that leaves the budget balance unchanged.

Discretionary Fiscal Stabilization

Expansionary fiscal policy
Discretionary fiscal policy designed to increase aggregate demand—a discretionary increase in government expenditure or a discretionary tax cut.

If real GDP is below potential GDP, **expansionary fiscal policy** might be used in an attempt to restore full employment. The government might increase its expenditure on goods and services, cut taxes, or do some of both. These actions would increase aggregate demand. If they were timed correctly and were of the correct magnitude, they could restore full employment. Figure 31.2 shows how.

In Figure 31.2(a), potential GDP is $10 trillion. Real GDP is $9 trillion, and the price level is 105. There is a $1 trillion *recessionary gap* (see Chapter 29, p. 748).

To eliminate the recessionary gap and restore full employment, the government takes a discretionary fiscal policy action. An increase in government expenditure or a tax cut increases aggregate expenditure by Δ*E*. If this were the only change in spending plans, the *AD* curve would become $AD_0 + \Delta E$ in Figure 31.2(b). But the increase in government expenditure or the tax cut sets off a multiplier process, which increases consumption expenditure. As the multiplier process plays out, aggregate demand increases and the *AD* curve shifts rightward to AD_1.

With no change in the price level, the economy would move from the initial equilibrium point *A* to point *B* on AD_1. But the increase in aggregate demand combined with the upward-sloping aggregate supply curve brings a rise in the price level. So the economy moves to a new equilibrium at point *C*. The price level rises to 110, and real GDP increases to $10 trillion. Full employment is restored.

■ **FIGURE 31.2**
Expansionary Fiscal Policy

(a) Below full-employment equilibrium

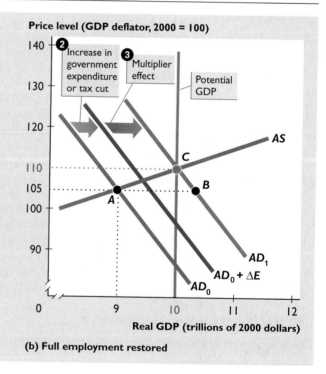

(b) Full employment restored

Potential GDP is $10 trillion, real GDP is $9 trillion, and **❶** there is a $1 trillion recessionary gap. **❷** An increase in government expenditure or a tax cut increases expenditure by Δ*E*.

❸ The multiplier increases induced expenditure. The *AD* curve shifts rightward to AD_1, the price level rises to 110, real GDP increases to $10 trillion, and the recessionary gap is eliminated.

If an inflationary gap exists, **contractionary fiscal policy** can be used to decrease aggregate demand, restore full employment, and eliminate inflationary pressure. In this case, the government decreases its expenditure on goods and services, raises taxes, or does some of both. These two actions decrease aggregate demand, decrease real GDP, and lower the price level. Figure 31.3 illustrates these effects.

In Figure 31.3(a), potential GDP is $10 trillion and equilibrium occurs at a real GDP of $11 trillion and a price level of 115. There is a $1 trillion *inflationary gap.*

To eliminate the inflationary gap and restore full employment, the government takes a discretionary fiscal policy action. A decrease in government expenditure or a rise in taxes decreases aggregate expenditure by ΔE. If this were the only change in spending plans, the *AD* curve would become $AD_0 - \Delta E$. But the initial decrease in aggregate expenditure sets off a multiplier process, which decreases consumption expenditure. As the multiplier process plays out, aggregate demand decreases and the *AD* curve shifts leftward to AD_1.

With no change in the price level, the economy would move from the initial equilibrium point *A* to point *B* on AD_1 in Figure 31.3(b). But the decrease in aggregate demand combined with the upward-sloping *AS* curve brings a fall in the price level. So the economy moves to a new equilibrium at point *C*. The price level falls to 110, and real GDP decreases to $10 trillion. The inflationary gap has been eliminated, inflation has been avoided, and the economy is back at full employment.

Contractionary fiscal policy
Discretionary fiscal policy designed to decrease aggregate demand—a discretionary decrease in government expenditure or a discretionary tax increase.

FIGURE 31.3
Contractionary Fiscal Policy

(a) Above full-employment equilibrium

(b) Full employment restored

Potential GDP is $10 trillion, real GDP is $11 trillion, and ❶ there is a $1 trillion inflationary gap. ❷ A decrease in government expenditure or a tax increase decreases expenditure by ΔE.

❸ The multiplier decreases induced expenditure. The *AD* curve shifts leftward to AD_1, the price level falls to 110, real GDP decreases to $10 trillion, and the inflationary gap is eliminated.

■ Discretionary Fiscal Policy: Supply-Side Effects

Both government expenditure and taxes influence aggregate supply, and we now look at the supply-side effects of fiscal policy.

Supply-Side Effects of Government Expenditure

Government provides services such as law and order, public education, and public health that increase production possibilities. For example, one of the reasons why we are more productive than are the citizens of the poor developing countries is that we are better educated and healthier than they are. Government also provides social infrastructure capital such as highways, bridges, tunnels, and dams that increase our production possibilities.

Government services and capital could be overprovided to the point at which they no longer increase production possibilities. But it is unlikely that we have reached such a point.

An *increase* in government expenditure that increases the quantities of productive services and capital increases potential GDP and increases aggregate supply.

The construction of the Hoover Dam during the 1930s and the interstate highway system that was begun during the 1950s are two of the most spectacular examples of an increase in productive government expenditures. The Hoover Dam increased the production of electricity, improved water management, and brought expanded recreation facilities. The interstate highway system improved transportation services, increased the productivity of truck drivers and other road users, and provided the foundation for the development of suburban shopping malls and entertainment centers.

Supply-Side Effects of Taxes

To pay for the productive services and capital that the government provides, it collects taxes. All taxes create disincentives to work, save, and provide entrepreneurial services.

Taxes on labor income decrease the supply of labor. And a smaller supply of labor means a higher equilibrium real wage rate and a smaller equilibrium quantity of labor employed. With a smaller quantity of labor employed, potential GDP and aggregate supply are smaller than they would otherwise be.

Taxes on the income from capital decrease saving and decrease the supply of capital. A smaller supply of capital means a higher equilibrium real interest rate and a smaller equilibrium quantity of investment and capital employed. With a smaller quantity of capital, potential GDP and aggregate supply are smaller than they would otherwise be.

Taxes on the incomes of entrepreneurs weaken the incentive to take risks and create new businesses. With a smaller number of firms, the quantities of labor and capital employed are lower and potential GDP and aggregate supply are smaller than they would otherwise be.

An *increase* in taxes strengthens the disincentive effects that we've just described. It decreases the supply of labor, capital, and entrepreneurial services; decreases potential GDP; and decreases aggregate supply. And a tax cut has the opposite effects. It strengthens the incentives to work, save, and provide entrepreneurial services. So a tax cut increases potential GDP and increases aggregate supply.

Scale of Government Supply-Side Effects

If both government expenditure and taxes increase, the scale of government grows. More productive government expenditure increases potential GDP, but higher taxes to pay for the expenditure decreases potential GDP. So an increase in the scale of government might increase or decrease potential GDP and aggregate supply depending on which effect is stronger. Some economists (and politicians) believe that a larger scale of government increases potential GDP and aggregate supply despite the weakened incentives from higher tax rates. Others believe that the incentive effects are so powerful that smaller government is more productive and brings a greater potential GDP and aggregate supply.

Supply-Side Effects on Potential GDP

Figure 31.4 illustrates the effects of fiscal policy on potential GDP. Initially, the production function is PF_0, the full employment quantity of labor is 200 billion hours, and potential GDP is $10 trillion (see Chapter 23, pp. 573–579).

A tax cut strengthens the incentive to work, which increases the supply of labor and increases the equilibrium level of employment at full employment. In Figure 31.4, employment increases to 210 billion hours a year. The tax cut also strengthens the incentive to save and invest, which increases the quantity of capital. With more capital per worker, labor productivity increases and the production function shifts upward to PF_1.

At the increased level of employment and on the new higher production function, potential GDP is $11 trillion. An increase in potential GDP increases aggregate supply, which also increases actual real GDP.

■ **FIGURE 31.4**

The Effects of Fiscal Policy on Aggregate Supply

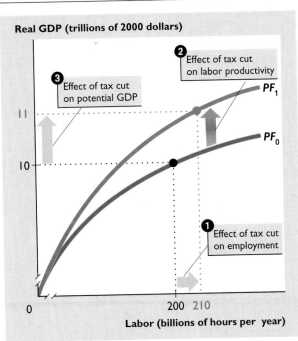

❶ A tax cut strengthens the incentive to work, increases the supply of labor, and increases employment.

❷ A tax cut strengthens the incentive to save and invest, which increases the quantity of capital and increases labor productivity.

❸ The combined effect of a tax cut on employment and labor productivity increases potential GDP.

■ Combined Demand-Side and Supply-Side Effects

You've seen that an expansionary fiscal policy increases aggregate demand and aggregate supply. What is the combined demand-side and supply-side effect? Because both aggregate demand and aggregate supply increase, we know that equilibrium real GDP increases. But the price level might rise, fall, or remain the same.

Figure 31.5 illustrates this last, neutral case. An expansionary fiscal policy increases aggregate demand and shifts the AD curve rightward from AD_0 to AD_1. The same fiscal actions increase aggregate supply and shifts the AS curve rightward from AS_0 to AS_1. The increase in aggregate supply equals the increase in aggregate demand in this example. The combination of the increase in aggregate demand and equal increase in aggregate supply increases real GDP and leaves the price level unchanged.

If an expansionary fiscal policy increases aggregate supply by more than it increases aggregate demand, real GDP still increases but the price level falls. (Draw a figure like Figure 31.5 to show this case.) Similarly, if the increase in aggregate supply were smaller than the increase in aggregate demand, again real GDP would increase but the price level would rise. (Draw another figure like Figure 31.5 to show this case.)

Some economists believe that the supply-side effects might be so powerful that a tax cut would end up *increasing* tax revenue. This outcome occurs if real GDP increases by a larger percentage than the percentage cut in tax rates so that when the lower tax rate is applied to the larger income, the total amount of tax revenue increases. There are no examples of this situation actually occurring.

■ **FIGURE 31.5**

The Combined Demand-Side and Supply-Side Effects of Expansionary Fiscal Policy

❶ A tax cut increases disposable income, which increases aggregate demand and shifts the AD curve from AD_0 to AD_1. A tax cut also strengthens the incentives to work, save, and invest, which increases aggregate supply and shifts the AS curve rightward from AS_0 to AS_1.

❷ Because both aggregate demand and aggregate supply increase, real GDP increases.

The price level might rise, fall, or (as shown here) remain constant depending on which effect, the demand-side effect or the supply-side effect, is larger.

The 2003 Dividend Tax Cut

Business profits are taxed twice: by the corporate income tax and by individual income taxes. In 2000, the Federal tax rate on business profit paid as dividends to a stockholder who paid the top income tax rate was 60.75 percent. State income taxes increase the total further. A tax on the income from capital at such a high rate has a damaging effect on investment and economic growth.

The Jobs and Growth Tax Relief Reconciliation Act of 2003 lowered this double tax by reducing income tax rates on dividends and capital gains.

One effect of this change was an increase in dividend payments. For example, Microsoft earns large profits, and previously it piled up cash reserves and paid no dividend. After the cut in the income tax on dividends, Microsoft began to pay dividends. So did many other firms. Increased dividend payments move

funds to investments that have the highest available rates of return and bring faster economic growth.

The figure shows the strong performance of the U.S. economy in 2005 and projection for 2006. Aggregate demand increased from AD_0 to AD_1 and aggregate supply increased from AS_0 to AS_1.

We don't know how much the dividend tax cut contributed to these increases in aggregate demand and aggregate supply, but they certainly played a role.

The result of the combined changes was rapid real GDP growth, moderate inflation, and the elimination of the output gap.

■ Limitations of Discretionary Fiscal Policy

Fiscal stabilization policy looks easy. Calculate the output gap and the multiplier, and determine the direction and size of the change in government expenditure or taxes that will eliminate the gap. In reality, discretionary fiscal policy is seriously hampered by three factors:

- Law-making time lag
- Estimating potential GDP
- Economic forecasting

Law-Making Time Lag

The law-making time lag is the amount of time it takes Congress to pass the laws needed to change taxes or spending. This process takes time because each member of Congress has a different idea about what is the best tax or spending program to change, so long debates and committee meetings are needed to reconcile conflicting views. The economy might benefit from fiscal stimulation today, but by the time Congress acts, a different fiscal medicine might be needed.

Estimating Potential GDP

It is not easy to tell whether real GDP is below, above, or at potential GDP. So a discretionary fiscal action might move real GDP *away* from potential GDP instead of toward it. This problem is a serious one because too much fiscal stimulation brings inflation and too little might bring recession.

Economic Forecasting

Fiscal policy changes take a long time to enact in Congress and yet more time to become effective. So fiscal policy must target forecasts of where the economy will be in the future. Economic forecasting has improved enormously in recent years, but it remains inexact and subject to error. So for a second reason, discretionary fiscal action might move real GDP *away* from potential GDP and create the very problems it seeks to correct.

■ Automatic Fiscal Policy

Automatic fiscal policy is a consequence of tax receipts and expenditures that fluctuate with real GDP. These features of fiscal policy are called **automatic stabilizers** because they work to stabilize real GDP without explicit action by the government. Their name is borrowed from engineering and conjures up images of devices that keep airplanes and ships steady in turbulent air and seas.

Automatic stabilizers
Features of fiscal policy that stabilize real GDP without explicit action by the government.

Induced Taxes

On the receipts side of the budget, tax laws define tax *rates*, not tax *dollars*. Tax dollars paid depend on tax rates and incomes. But incomes vary with real GDP, so tax receipts depend on real GDP. Taxes that vary with real GDP are called **induced taxes**. When real GDP increases in an expansion, wages and profits rise, so the taxes on these incomes—induced taxes—rise. When real GDP decreases in a recession, wages and profits fall, so the induced taxes on these incomes fall.

Induced taxes
Taxes that vary with real GDP.

Needs-Tested Spending

On the expenditure side of the budget, the government creates programs that pay benefits to suitably qualified people and businesses. The spending on such programs is called **needs-tested spending**, and it results in transfer payments that depend on the economic state of individual citizens and businesses. When the economy is in a recession, unemployment is high and the number of people experiencing economic hardship increases, but needs-tested spending on unemployment benefits and food stamps also increases. When the economy expands, unemployment falls, the number of people experiencing economic hardship decreases, and needs-tested spending decreases.

Needs-tested spending
Spending on programs that entitle suitably qualified people and businesses to receive benefits—benefits that vary with need and with the state of the economy.

Induced taxes and needs-tested spending decrease the multiplier effects of changes in autonomous expenditure (such as investment and exports). So they moderate both expansions and recessions and make real GDP more stable. They achieve this outcome by weakening the link between real GDP and disposable income and so reduce the effect of a change in real GDP on consumption expenditure. When real GDP increases, induced taxes increase and needs-tested spending decreases, so disposable income does not increase by as much as the increase in real GDP. As a result, consumption expenditure does not increase by as much as it otherwise would have done and the multiplier effect is reduced.

CHECKPOINT 31.1

1   **Describe the federal budget process and explain the effects of fiscal policy.**

Practice Problems 31.1

1. Classify each of the following as discretionary fiscal policy or automatic fiscal policy or neither.
    a. A decrease in tax receipts in a recession
    b. Additional expenditure to upgrade highways
    c. An increase in the public education budget
    d. A purchase of $1 billion of medicines to treat AIDS sufferers in Africa
    e. A cut in funding for NASA during an expansion

2. Explain the change in aggregate demand when
    a. Government expenditure increases by $100 billion, which the government spends on national defense.
    b. Taxes are increased by $100 billion.
    c. Parts **a** and **b** occur simultaneously.

Exercises 31.1

1. Classify each of the following as discretionary fiscal policy or automatic fiscal policy or neither.
    a. The imposition of huge fines on tobacco companies
    b. A cut in the gas tax
    c. A cut in cross-border (custom) taxes
    d. The cost of refurnishing the White House basement
    e. An increase in payments to unemployed people

2. Illustrate, using an *AS-AD* graph, the effects of
    a. A $100 billion decrease in government expenditure.
    b. A $100 billion decrease in taxes.
    c. Parts **a** and **b** occurring simultaneously.

Solutions to Practice Problems 31.1

1a. A decrease in tax receipts in a recession is an automatic fiscal policy.
1b. Expenditure to upgrade highways is a discretionary fiscal policy.
1c. An increase in the public education budget is discretionary fiscal policy.
1d. A purchase of $1 billion of medicines is a discretionary fiscal policy.
1e. A cut in funding for NASA is a discretionary fiscal policy.

2a. Aggregate demand increases by more than $100 billion because the increase in government expenditure has a multiplier effect that increases induced expenditure.
2b. Aggregate demand decreases by more than $100 billion because the tax increase has a multiplier effect that decreases induced expenditure.
2c. Aggregate demand increases because the increase in part **a** is larger than the decrease in part **b**.

31.2 THE FEDERAL RESERVE AND MONETARY POLICY

You've now seen how fiscal stabilization policy works, and you've seen that it has some pretty severe limitations. Automatic stabilizers help, but discretionary actions are very hard to get right. Fortunately, fiscal policy isn't the only tool available for seeking to stabilize the business cycle. Monetary policy is also available. We're now going to see how monetary policy works and how the Fed's actions ripple through the economy to influence real GDP and the price level.

■ The Monetary Policy Process

The Fed makes monetary policy in a process that has three main elements:

- Monitoring economic conditions
- Meetings of the Federal Open Market Committee (FOMC)
- Monetary Policy Report to Congress

Monitoring Economic Conditions

Beige Book
A report that summarizes current economic conditions in each Federal Reserve district and each sector of the economy.

Each Federal Reserve Bank constantly gathers information on its district by talking with business leaders, economists, market experts, and others. The Fed brings the results together in the **Beige Book**, which is published eight times a year. The Beige Book serves as a background document for the members of the Federal Open Market Committee.

The Beige Book is a public document that is easily accessible on the Fed's Web site and is a good source of current information for businesses and anyone who wants to be well informed about the current state of the economy.

Meetings of the Federal Open Market Committee (FOMC)

The FOMC, which meets eight times a year, makes the monetary policy decisions. The FOMC's first and fourth meetings of the year run for two days (the other six meetings run for one day) and are opportunities for the committee to assess the longer-term outlook as well as the current period's open market operations.

After each meeting, the FOMC announces its decisions and describes its view of the likelihood that its goals of price stability and sustainable economic growth will be achieved. The FOMC publishes the minutes of its meetings after they have been confirmed as a correct record of the meeting at the next scheduled meeting. For example, the minutes of the first meeting of the year are published after the second meeting of the year.

Full transcripts of FOMC meetings are published with a five-year time lag. This delay enables the members of the FOMC to have a frank exchange of views without worrying about how their discussions might be interpreted by the traders in financial markets. The eventual publication of the transcripts permits a detailed public scrutiny of the FOMC's decision-making process.

Monetary Policy Report to Congress

Twice a year, in February and July, the Fed prepares a Monetary Policy Report to Congress, and the Fed chairman testifies before the House of Representatives Committee on Financial Services. The report and the chairman's testimony review the monetary policy and economic developments of the past year and the economic outlook for the coming year.

■ Influencing the Interest Rate

When the FOMC announces a policy change, its press release talks about the federal funds rate, the interest rate at which banks borrow reserves from each other, or the discount rate, the interest rate at which banks borrow reserves from the Fed. The press release does not talk about the quantity of money or the size of the open market operations it plans to conduct. This focus on interest rates makes it appear as though the Fed determines interest rates rather than the quantity of money. But this impression is misleading for two reasons: a long-run reason and a short-run reason.

In the Long Run

In the long run, saving supply and investment demand determine the real interest rate in global financial markets (see Chapter 24, pp. 599–605). The inflation rate, along with the real interest rate, determines the nominal interest rate (Chapter 28, p. 700). The inflation rate in the long run is determined by the growth rate of the quantity of money that results from the Fed's actions.

So in the long run, the Fed *influences* the nominal interest rate by the effects of its policies on the inflation rate. But it does not directly control the nominal interest rate, and it has no control over the real interest rate.

In the Short Run

In the short run, the Fed influences both the nominal interest rate and the real interest rate. To change the nominal interest rate, the Fed undertakes an open market operation that changes the quantity of money. It is by changing the quantity of money that the Fed achieves its target for the federal funds rate. The expected inflation rate doesn't change every time the Fed changes the nominal interest rate. So an open market operation changes the real interest rate in the short run.

The Fed Raises Its Interest Rate Target

Suppose that the Fed fears inflation and decides that it must take action to decrease aggregate demand. The FOMC announces that it will raise its short-term interest rate target. How does the Fed achieve its goal of a higher interest rate?

The FOMC instructs the New York Fed to sell securities in the open market. This action mops up bank reserves. Some banks are short of reserves and seek to borrow reserves from other banks. The federal funds rate rises. With fewer reserves, the banks make a smaller quantity of new loans each day until the quantity of loans outstanding has fallen to a level that is consistent with the new lower level of reserves. The quantity of money decreases.

The demand for money determines the quantity of money that will achieve the FOMC's interest rate target. The Fed could, if it chose, fix the quantity of money and let the interest rate adjust to its equilibrium level. Or the Fed can, and does, fix the interest rate and adjust the quantity of money to the level that makes the chosen interest rate the equilibrium rate.

Suppose, for example, that the short-term nominal interest rate is 5 percent a year and the FOMC decides that it needs to rise to 6 percent a year. Figure 31.6(a) illustrates what the Fed must do. The demand for money is *MD*, so when the interest rate is 5 percent a year, the quantity of money is $1 trillion. The Fed conducts an

■ FIGURE 31.6

Interest Rate Changes

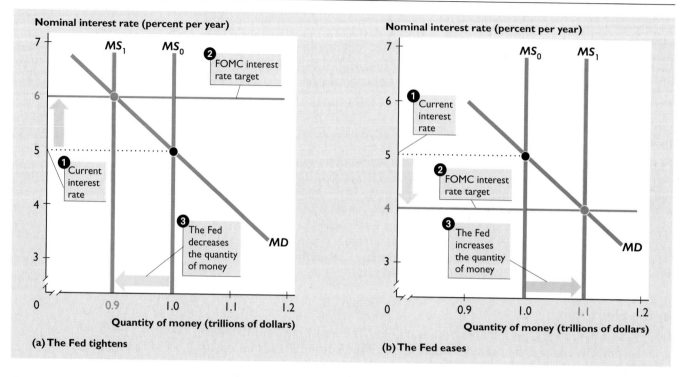

(a) The Fed tightens

(b) The Fed eases

1 The current interest rate is 5 percent a year, and **2** the FOMC's target is 6 percent a year. To raise the interest rate to the target, the Fed must sell securities in the open market and **3** decrease the quantity of money to $0.9 trillion.

1 The current interest rate is 5 percent a year, and **2** the FOMC's target is 4 percent a year. To lower the interest rate to the target, the Fed must buy securities in the open market and **3** increase the quantity of money to $1.1 trillion.

open market sale on a sufficiently large scale to decrease the quantity of money from $1 trillion to $0.9 trillion. When the quantity of money is $0.9 trillion, the nominal interest rate is 6 percent a year, the FOMC's target level.

The Fed Lowers Its Interest Rate Target

If the Fed fears recession, it acts to increase aggregate demand. The FOMC announces that it has lowered its short-term interest rate target. To achieve a lower interest rate, the FOMC instructs the New York Fed to buy securities in the open market. This action increases bank reserves. Flush with reserves, banks now seek to lend reserves to other banks. The federal funds rate falls. With more reserves, the banks increase their lending and the quantity of money increases.

Again, the demand for money determines the change in the quantity of money that achieves the Fed's interest rate target. Suppose the FOMC wants to lower the interest rate from 5 percent a year to 4 percent a year. Figure 31.6(b) shows what it must do. When the interest rate is 5 percent a year, the quantity of money is $1 trillion. The Fed conducts an open market purchase on a sufficiently large scale to increase the quantity of money from $1 trillion to $1.1 trillion. When the quantity of money is $1.1 trillion, the nominal interest rate is 4 percent a year, the FOMC's target level.

■ The Ripple Effects of the Fed's Actions

Suppose that the Fed increases the interest rate. What happens next?

Three main events follow:

- Investment and consumption expenditure decrease.
- The dollar rises, and net exports decrease.
- A multiplier process induces a further decrease in consumption expenditure and aggregate demand decreases.

Investment and Consumption Expenditure

The interest rate influences investment and consumption expenditure. When the Fed increases the nominal interest rate, the real interest rate rises temporarily, and investment and expenditure on consumer durables decrease. The reason is that the interest rate is the *opportunity cost* of the funds used to finance investment and the purchase of big-ticket consumer items. So when the opportunity costs of buying capital and consumer goods rise, the quantities bought and expenditures on these items decrease.

The Dollar and Net Exports

A rise in the interest rate, other things remaining the same, means that the U.S. interest rate rises relative to the interest rates in other countries. Some people will want to move funds into the United States from other countries to take advantage of the higher interest rate they can now earn on their U.S. bank deposits and bonds. When money is moved into the United States, people buy dollars and sell other currencies, such as Japanese yen or British pounds. With more dollars demanded, the price of the dollar rises on the foreign exchange market.

The higher price of the dollar means that foreigners must now pay more for U.S.-made goods and services. So the quantity demanded and the expenditure on U.S.-made items decrease. U.S. exports decrease. Similarly, the higher price of the dollar means that Americans now pay less for foreign-made goods and services. So the quantity demanded and the expenditure on foreign-made items increase. U.S. imports increase. So U.S. net exports decrease.

The Multiplier Process

Because investment, consumption expenditure, and net exports are all interest-sensitive components of expenditure, a rise in the interest rate brings a decrease in aggregate expenditure.

You already know the rest of the story, because it is the same as that of the fiscal policy multipliers. The decrease in expenditure decreases income, and the decrease in income induces a decrease in consumption expenditure. The decreased consumption expenditure lowers aggregate expenditure. Real GDP and disposable income decrease further, and so does consumption expenditure. Real GDP growth slows, and the inflation rate slows.

If the Fed lowers the interest rate, the events that we've just described occur in the opposite directions, so real GDP growth and the inflation rate speed up.

Figure 31.7 summarizes the process that we've just described. It begins with the Fed's open market operations that change the quantity of money and interest rate and ends with the effects on real GDP and the price level.

FIGURE 31.7

Ripple Effects of the Fed's Actions

The Fed's open market operations change the quantity of money and the interest rate. Expenditure plans eventually change, and so does aggregate demand. Eventually, the Fed's open market operation has ripple effects that change real GDP and the price level.

(a) The Fed tightens

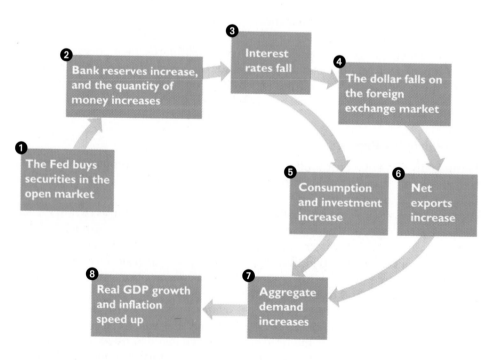

(b) The Fed eases

Monetary Stabilization in the *AS-AD* Model

We've described the broad outline of how the Fed's actions influence the economy. Let's now see how monetary policy might be used to stabilize real GDP.

The Fed Tightens to Fight Inflation

Figure 31.8(a) shows investment demand. Think of investment demand as representing all the interest-sensitive components of aggregate expenditure. Also, assume that there is no inflation so the interest rate is the real interest rate as well as nominal interest rate. Initially, the interest rate is 5 percent a year and the quantity of investment is $2 trillion. At this level of investment, aggregate demand is AD_0 in Figure 31.8(b). The aggregate supply curve is AS, so equilibrium real GDP is $11 trillion, which exceeds potential GDP. There is an inflationary gap.

The Fed now conducts an open market sale that increases the interest rate to 6 percent a year. The quantity of investment demand decreases to $1.5 trillion. If this were the only change in aggregate expenditure, aggregate demand would be $AD_0 - \Delta I$. But the multiplier decreases aggregate expenditure further, and the aggregate demand curve shifts leftward to AD_1.

The Fed's actions have eliminated an inflation threat and brought real GDP to equal potential GDP.

FIGURE 31.8

Monetary Stabilization: Avoiding Inflation

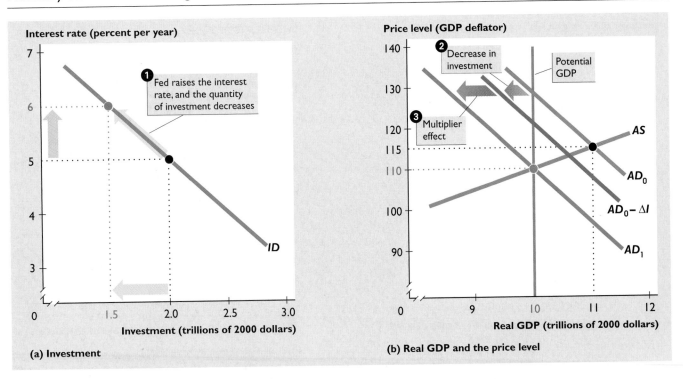

(a) Investment

(b) Real GDP and the price level

Real GDP exceeds potential GDP in part (b). To avoid inflation, ❶ the Fed raises the interest rate in part (a). ❷ Expenditure decreases by Δ*I*, and ❸ the multiplier induces additional expenditure cuts. The aggregate demand curve shifts leftward to AD_1. Real GDP decreases to potential GDP, and inflation is avoided.

The Fed Eases to Fight Recession

In Figure 31.9(a), the interest rate is 5 percent a year, and the quantity of investment demanded is $2 trillion. In Figure 31.9(b), aggregate demand is AD_0, aggregate supply is AS, and equilibrium real GDP is $9 trillion, which is less than potential GDP. There is a recessionary gap.

The Fed now conducts an open market purchase that lowers the interest rate to 4 percent a year. The quantity of investment increases to $2.5 trillion. Other interest-sensitive expenditure items (not shown in the figure) also increase. If this were the only change, aggregate demand would increase to $AD_0 + \Delta I$.

The multiplier increases aggregate expenditure further and the aggregate demand curve shifts to AD_1. The Fed's actions have eliminated a recession and brought real GDP to equal potential GDP at $10 trillion and the price level to 110.

The Size of the Multiplier Effect

The size of the multiplier effect of monetary policy depends on the sensitivity of expenditure plans to the interest rate. The larger the effect of a change in the interest rate on aggregate expenditure, the greater is the multiplier effect and the smaller is the change in the interest rate that achieves the Fed's objective.

FIGURE 31.9

Monetary Stabilization: Avoiding Recession

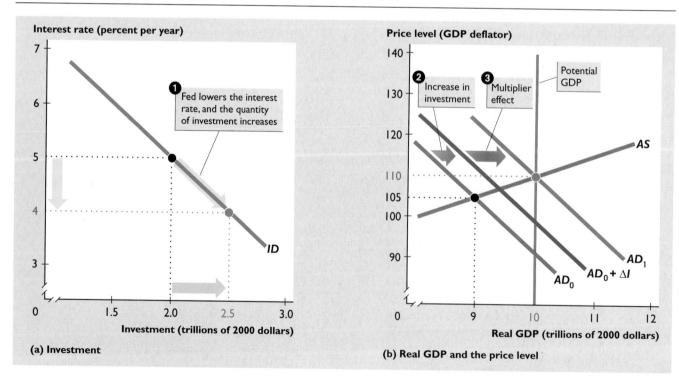

(a) Investment

(b) Real GDP and the price level

Real GDP is less than potential GDP (part b). To avoid recession, ❶ the Fed lowers the interest rate (part a). ❷ Expenditure increases by ΔI, and ❸ the multiplier induces additional expenditure. The aggregate demand curve shifts rightward to AD_1. Real GDP increases to potential GDP, and recession is avoided.

■ Limitations of Monetary Stabilization Policy

Monetary policy has an advantage over fiscal policy because it cuts out the law-making time lags. The FOMC meets eight times a year and can conduct telephone meetings between its scheduled meetings if the need arises. And the actual actions that change the quantity of money are daily actions taken by the New York Fed operating under the guidelines decided by the FOMC. So monetary policy is a continuous policy process and is not subject to the long decision lag and the need to create a broad political consensus that confronts fiscal policy.

But monetary policy shares the other two limitations of fiscal policy: Estimating potential GDP is hard, and economic forecasting is error-prone. Monetary policy suffers an additional limitation: Its effects are indirect and depend on how private decisions respond to a change in the interest rate. These responses are themselves hard to forecast and vary from one situation to another in unpredictable ways. A related problem is that the time lags in the operation of monetary policy are longer than those for fiscal policy. So the forecasting horizon must be longer.

In this chapter, we've described the fiscal and monetary policy processes and explained the effects of stabilization policies on real GDP and the price level. In the next two chapters, we study policy tradeoffs and alternative policy strategies.

REALITY CHECK

Fiscal Policy and Monetary Policy in YOUR Life

Consider the U.S. economy right now. Using all the knowledge that you have accumulated during your course and by reading or watching the current news, try to determine whether the U.S. economy is at full employment or has a recessionary or inflationary gap. In light of the current state of the U.S. economy, what type of fiscal policy and monetary policy would you recommend?

Consider recent changes in fiscal policy or monetary policy that you have seen reported in the media. What do you think these changes say about the federal government's and the Federal Reserve's views of the state of the economy?

Thinking further about recent changes in fiscal policy and monetary policy, how do you expect these changes to affect you? How might your spending, saving, and labor supply decisions change? Using your own responses to fiscal and monetary policy changes as an example, are these policy changes influencing aggregate demand, aggregate supply, or both? How do you think they will change real GDP?

2 Describe the Federal Reserve's monetary policy process and explain the effects of monetary policy.

Practice Problems 31.2

1. If the Fed cuts the quantity of money, explain how each of the following items changes.
   a. Businesses' purchases of new capital equipment
   b. Households' purchases of new cars and houses
   c. Foreigners' purchases of U.S.-made goods and services
   d. Americans' purchases of Canadian-made goods and services

2. What is the multiplier effect of monetary policy? How does it work? How does the size of the expenditure multiplier influence the size of the multiplier effect of monetary policy?

Exercises 31.2

1. If the Fed lowers the interest rate, explain how each of the following items changes.
   a. U.S exports
   b. U.S. imports
   c. Investment
   d. The value of the dollar on the foreign exchange market

2. Explain the process by which the Fed's monetary policy influences aggregate demand in the United States.

3. Compare the effectiveness of monetary policy and fiscal policy for stabilizing U.S. real GDP and employment.

Solutions to Practice Problems 31.2

1a. When the Fed cuts the quantity of money, the interest rate rises and businesses delay their purchases of new capital equipment.

1b. Households will delay their purchases of new cars and houses.

1c. As the U.S. interest rate rises and foreign interest rates remain the same, the dollar strengthens. U.S.-made goods and services become relatively more expensive for foreigners to buy. Foreigners' purchases of U.S.-made goods and services decrease.

1d. As the dollar strengthens, Canadian-made goods become cheaper for Americans to buy. Americans' purchases of Canadian-produced goods increase.

2. When the Fed increases the quantity of money, interest rates fall and the foreign exchange value of the dollar falls. As interest rates fall, aggregate expenditure increases because investment, consumption expenditure, and net exports increase. The multiplier effect of monetary policy is the change in aggregate demand that results from a change in the interest rate. When the interest rate changes, part of autonomous expenditure changes and the expenditure multiplier determines the change in aggregate demand. The larger the expenditure multiplier, the larger is the multiplier effect of monetary policy.

CHAPTER CHECKPOINT

Key Points

1 **Describe the federal budget process and explain the effects of fiscal policy.**

- The federal budget is an annual statement of the expenditures, tax receipts, and surplus or deficit of the government of the United States.
- Fiscal policy is the use of the federal budget to finance the federal government and to stabilize the economy.
- Fiscal policy can be either discretionary or automatic.
- Changes in government expenditure and changes in taxes have multiplier effects on aggregate demand and can be used to try to keep real GDP at potential GDP.
- In practice, law-making time lags, the difficulty of estimating potential GDP, and the limitations of economic forecasting seriously hamper discretionary fiscal policy.
- Automatic stabilizers arise because tax receipts and expenditures fluctuate with real GDP.

2 **Describe the Federal Reserve's monetary policy process and explain the effects of monetary policy.**

- The Fed makes monetary policy in an open and transparent process that involves three main elements: the Beige Book, meetings of the Federal Open Market Committee, and the Monetary Policy Report to Congress.
- When the FOMC announces a policy change, it is in terms of the interest rate, not the quantity of money.
- In the long run, the Fed influences the nominal interest rate but it has no control over the real interest rate.
- In the short run, the Fed can determine the nominal interest rate, but to do so, it must undertake open market operations that change the quantity of money.
- When the Fed changes the interest rate, the effects ripple through the economy by changing aggregate demand.
- The size of the multiplier effect of monetary policy depends on the sensitivity of expenditure plans to the interest rate.
- Monetary policy has no law-making time lag, but its effects are indirect and depend on how the interest rate influences private decisions.

Key Terms

Automatic fiscal policy, 784
Automatic stabilizers, 794
Balanced budget, 784
Balanced budget multiplier, 787
Beige Book, 796
Budget deficit, 784

Budget surplus, 784
Contractionary fiscal policy, 789
Discretionary fiscal policy, 784
Expansionary fiscal policy, 788
Federal budget, 784

Fiscal policy, 784
Government expenditure multiplier, 787
Induced taxes, 794
Needs-tested spending, 794
Tax multiplier, 787

Exercises

1. Sort the following items into those that are discretionary fiscal policy actions, those that are automatic fiscal policy actions, and those that are not fiscal policy.
   a. An increase in expenditure on homeland security
   b. An increase in unemployment benefits paid during the 2001 recession
   c. The Bush tax cuts
   d. An open market operation
   e. The fall in taxes paid by corporations because their profits fell in 2001
   f. Increased expenditures on national defense arising from the war against terrorism
   g. A rise in the federal funds rate
   h. An increase in Medicaid expenditure brought about by a flu epidemic
   i. The changes in farm subsidies arising from the 2002 Farm Bill
   j. A fall in customs revenue that resulted from a decrease in U.S. imports

2. Suppose that the U.S. government increases its expenditure on highways and bridges by $100 billion in 2006. Explain the effect that this expenditure would have on
   a. Autonomous expenditure.
   b. Aggregate demand.
   c. Real GDP.
   d. Needs-tested spending.
   e. The government's budget surplus.

3. Suppose that Congress passes additional tax cuts that total $100 billion in 2007. Explain the effect that this tax cut would have on
   a. Consumption expenditure before any change in real GDP occurs.
   b. Consumption expenditure induced by a change in real GDP.
   c. Aggregate demand.
   d. Real GDP.
   e. The government's budget surplus.

4. The income tax rate is higher in Sweden than it is in the United States. Also, Sweden has more generous payments to the unemployed and others who fall on hard economic times. And the percentage of expenditure on imported goods and services is much larger in Sweden than in the United States. Which country, Sweden or the United States, do you think is likely to have
   a. The larger government expenditure multiplier?
   b. The larger tax multiplier?
   c. The more effective automatic stabilizers?
   d. The greater fluctuations in real GDP over the business cycle?
   e. The greater fluctuations in the government budget balance over the business cycle?
   f. The larger supply-side effects of fiscal policy?

5. Describe the supply-side effects of fiscal policy and explain how a tax cut or an increase in government expenditure might influence
   a. Potential GDP.
   b. Aggregate supply.
   c. Equilibrium real GDP and the price level.
   Use an aggregate supply–aggregate demand graph to illustrate the effects you've described.

6. Suppose that the Fed sees an expansion slowing and forecasts a recession in the near future. What change in its monetary policy would lessen the effect of the recession? Use appropriate graphs to explain and illustrate the effect of the Fed's actions on
   a. Interest rates.
   b. The quantity of money.
   c. Investment.
   d. The foreign exchange value of the dollar.
   e. Net exports.
   f. Aggregate demand.
   g. Real GDP and the price level.

7. Suppose that the Fed sees the current expansion gaining too much steam and forecasts an increase in inflation in the near future. What change in its monetary policy would lessen the likelihood of inflation? Use appropriate graphs to explain and illustrate the effect of the Fed's actions on
   a. Interest rates.
   b. The quantity of money.
   c. Investment.
   d. The foreign exchange value of the dollar.
   e. Net exports.
   f. Aggregate demand.
   g. Real GDP and the price level.

8. Explain why monetary policy is used more often than fiscal policy to stabilize the economy.

9. Explain the effect of a decrease in the quantity of money on aggregate demand. What determines how big the change in aggregate demand will be?

10. If the U.S. government wanted to increase investment, would it encourage the Fed to change its monetary policy or would the government change its fiscal policy? Explain why. What effect would the policy change have on the price level?

11. If the U.S. government wanted to increase exports, would it encourage the Fed to change its monetary policy or would the government change its fiscal policy? Explain why. What effect would the policy change have on the composition of aggregate expenditure?

Critical Thinking

12. Suppose that Bill Frist (Republican) and Tom Daschle (Democrat) are debating the effects of fiscal policy on real GDP and the price level. Bill Frist says that a tax cut will increase real GDP and keep the price level stable. Tom Daschle says that the tax cut will only line the pockets of the rich and have no effects on output or the price level.
    a. Using the aggregate supply–aggregate demand model, provide an explanation of what Bill Frist says will happen.
    b. Using the aggregate supply–aggregate demand model, provide an explanation of what Tom Daschle says will happen.
    c. Highlight the differences in assumptions about how the economy works and sketch a research project that could settle the debate.

13. Review the main limitations of discretionary fiscal policy and contrast those limitations with the benefits of automatic fiscal policy.

14. In the U.S. recession of 2001, government expenditure increased and taxes were cut. Explain how the government's actions
    a. Changed aggregate demand.
    b. Changed the budget surplus and outstanding government debt.

15. Describe and critically evaluate the effects of the actions taken by the Federal Reserve and the federal government during 2002 to stimulate the U.S. economy and lift it from recession.

Web Exercises

Use the links on MyEconLab to work the following exercises.

16. Visit the Office of Management and Budget Web site and review the history of the budget surplus/deficit and the national debt. What events have led to the greatest increases in the national debt? In which periods has the debt been paid down? Looking at the history of the U.S. federal budget, do you think the current plan to pay off the national debt will be carried out? Why or why not?

17. Visit the Federal Reserve's Web site and review the current state of the U.S. economy using the latest issue of the Beige Book. In light of what you discover about real GDP, inflation, and the unemployment rate, set out your policy recommendations to
    a. The FOMC.
    b. Congress.

18. Visit the IMF World Economic Outlook Web site to review the current state of the global economy. [If you are working this exercise after 2005, change the 2005 in this URL to the current year and if it is before October change 02 to 01.] In light of what you discover about real GDP growth and inflation, set out your policy advice to the governments of the major countries.

The Short-Run Policy Tradeoff

CHAPTER CHECKLIST

When you have completed your study of this chapter, you will be able to

1 Describe the short-run tradeoff between inflation and unemployment.

2 Distinguish between the short-run and the long-run Phillips curves and describe the shifting tradeoff between inflation and unemployment.

3 Explain how the Fed can influence the expected inflation rate and how expected inflation influences the short-run tradeoff.

"It's the economy, stupid!" James Carville, one of Bill Clinton's advisers, wrote these four words on a whiteboard for Clinton to see every time he prepared a speech.

You know that as a voter, you care a lot about the economy. Polling shows that you're not alone. The economy can win or lose an election.

We care about our standard of living and cost of living—about unemployment that takes our jobs and inflation that erodes the buying power of what we earn.

We want low unemployment and low inflation. But can we have both at the same time? Or do we face a tradeoff between them?

If we do face a tradeoff, what is it like? Is it permanent or temporary? Must we pay a high cost in terms of unemployment for a small gain in lower inflation? Or can we get a big drop in inflation at a small unemployment cost?

This chapter answers these questions.

32.1 THE SHORT-RUN PHILLIPS CURVE

Short-run Phillips curve
A curve that shows the relationship between the inflation rate and the unemployment rate when the natural unemployment rate and the expected inflation rate remain constant.

The **short-run Phillips curve** is a curve that shows the relationship between the inflation rate and the unemployment rate when the natural unemployment rate and the expected inflation rate remain constant.

Figure 32.1 illustrates the short-run Phillips curve. Here, the natural unemployment rate is 6 percent and the expected inflation rate is 3 percent a year. At full employment, the unemployment rate equals the natural unemployment rate and the inflation rate equals the expected inflation rate at point *B*. This point is the anchor point for the short-run Phillips curve.

In an expansion, the unemployment rate decreases and the inflation rate rises. For example, the economy might move to a point such as *A,* where the unemployment rate is 5 percent and the inflation rate is 4 percent a year.

In a recession, the unemployment rate increases and the inflation rate falls. For example, the economy might move to a point such as *C,* where the unemployment rate is 7 percent and the inflation rate is 2 percent a year.

The short-run Phillips curve presents a *tradeoff* between inflation and unemployment because, along a given curve, a lower unemployment rate can be achieved only by paying the cost of a higher inflation rate, and a lower inflation rate can be achieved only by paying the cost of a higher unemployment rate. For example, in Figure 32.1, a decrease in the unemployment rate from 6 percent to 5 percent costs a 1-percentage point increase in the inflation rate from 3 percent a year to 4 percent a year.

■ **FIGURE 32.1**

A Short-Run Phillips Curve

1 If the natural unemployment rate is 6 percent, and **2** the expected inflation rate is 3 percent a year, then **3** point *B* is at full employment on a short-run Phillips curve.

4 The short-run Phillips curve (*SRPC*) shows the tradeoff between inflation and unemployment at the given natural unemployment rate and expected inflation rate.

A higher unemployment rate brings a lower inflation rate, and a lower unemployment rate brings a higher inflation rate.

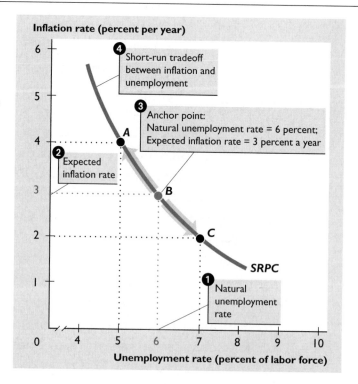

■ Aggregate Supply and the Short-Run Phillips Curve

The short-run Phillips curve is another way of looking at the upward-sloping aggregate supply curve that you learned about in Chapter 29—see pp. 732–735.

Both the short-run Phillips curve and the aggregate supply curve arise because the money wage rate is sticky in the short run.

Along an aggregate supply curve, the money wage rate is fixed. So when the price level rises, the *real wage rate* falls. And a fall in the real wage rate increases the quantity of labor employed and increases the quantity of real GDP supplied.

The events that we've just described also play out along a short-run Phillips curve. The rise in the price level means that the inflation rate has (perhaps temporarily) increased. The increase in the quantity of labor employed means a decrease in the number unemployed and a fall in the unemployment rate.

So a movement along an aggregate supply curve is equivalent to a movement along a short-run Phillips curve. Let's explore these connections between the aggregate supply curve and the short-run Phillips curve a bit more closely.

Unemployment and Real GDP

In a given period, with a fixed amount of capital and a given state of technology, real GDP depends on the quantity of labor employed. At full employment, the quantity of real GDP is *potential GDP* and the unemployment rate is the natural unemployment rate. If real GDP exceeds potential GDP, employment exceeds its full-employment level and the unemployment rate falls below the natural unemployment rate. Similarly, if real GDP is less than potential GDP, employment is less than its full-employment level and the unemployment rate rises above the natural unemployment rate.

The quantitative relationship between the unemployment rate and real GDP was first estimated by economist Arthur M. Okun and is called **Okun's Law**. Okun's Law states that for each percentage point that the unemployment rate is above the natural unemployment rate, real GDP is 2 percentage points below potential GDP. For example, if the natural unemployment rate is 6 percent and potential GDP is $10 trillion, then when the actual unemployment rate is 7 percent, real GDP is $9.8 trillion—98 percent of potential GDP, or 2 percentage points below potential GDP. And when the actual unemployment rate is 5 percent, real GDP is $10.2 trillion—102 percent of potential GDP, or 2 percentage points above potential GDP. Table 32.1 summarizes this relationship.

Okun's Law
For each percentage point that the unemployment rate is above the natural unemployment rate, real GDP is 2 percentage points below potential GDP.

TABLE 32.1

	Unemployment rate (percent)	Real GDP (trillions of 2000 dollars)
A	5	10.2
B	6	10.0
C	7	9.8

Inflation and the Price Level

The inflation rate is defined as the percentage change in the price level. So starting from last period's price level, the higher the inflation rate, the higher is the current period's price level. Suppose that last year, the price level was 100. If in the current year, the inflation rate is 2 percent, the price level rises to 102; if the inflation rate is 3 percent, the price level rises to 103; and if the inflation rate is 4 percent, the price level rises to 104.

With these relationships between the unemployment rate and real GDP and between the inflation rate and the price level, we can establish the connection between the short-run Phillips curve and the aggregate supply curve. Figure 32.2 shows this connection.

First suppose that in the current year, real GDP equals potential GDP and the unemployment rate equals the natural unemployment rate. In Figure 32.2, real

GDP is $10 trillion and the unemployment rate is 6 percent. The economy is at point *B* on the short-run Phillips curve in part (a) and point *B* on the aggregate supply curve in part (b). The inflation rate is 3 percent a year (its expected rate) in part (a), and the price level is 103 (also its expected level) in part (b).

Next suppose that instead of being at full employment, the economy is above full employment with real GDP of $10.2 trillion at point *A* on the aggregate supply curve in part (b). In this case, the unemployment rate is 5 percent at point *A* in part (a). The inflation rate is 4 percent a year (higher than expected) in part (a), and the price level is 104 (also higher than expected) in part (b).

Finally, suppose that the economy is below full employment with real GDP of $9.8 trillion at point *C* on the aggregate supply curve in part (b). In this case, the unemployment rate is 7 percent at point *C* in part (a). The inflation rate is 2 percent a year (lower than expected) in part (a), and the price level is 102 (also lower than expected) in part (b).

FIGURE 32.2

The Short-Run Phillips Curve and the Aggregate Supply Curve

(a) The short-run Phillips curve

(b) The aggregate supply curve

Point *A* on the Phillips curve corresponds to point *A* on the aggregate supply curve: The unemployment rate is 5 percent and the inflation rate is 4 percent a year (in part a), and real GDP is $10.2 trillion and the price level is 104 (in part b).

Point *B* on the Phillips curve corresponds to point *B* on the aggregate supply curve: The unemployment rate is 6 percent and the inflation rate is 3 percent a year (in part a), and real GDP is $10 trillion and the price level is 103 (in part b).

Point *C* on the Phillips curve corresponds to point *C* on the aggregate supply curve: The unemployment rate is 7 percent and the inflation rate is 2 percent a year (in part a), and real GDP is $9.8 trillion and the price level is 102 (in part b).

Aggregate Demand Fluctuations

A decrease in aggregate demand that brings a movement along the aggregate supply curve from point *B* to point *C* lowers the price level and decreases real GDP. That same decrease in aggregate demand brings a movement along the Phillips curve from point *B* to point *C*..

Similarly, an increase in aggregate demand that brings a movement along the aggregate supply curve from point *B* to point *A* raises the price level and increases real GDP relative to what they would have been. That same increase in aggregate demand brings a movement along the Phillips curve from point *B* to point *A*.

EYE ON THE GLOBAL ECONOMY

Inflation and Unemployment

The Phillips curve is so named because New Zealand economist A. W. (Bill) Phillips discovered the relationship in about 100 years of unemployment and wage inflation data for the United Kingdom.

The figure shows data on inflation and unemployment in the United Kingdom over most of the twentieth century—1900 to 1997. The data reveal no neat, tight tradeoff. The short-run tradeoff shifts around a great deal.

The highest inflation rate did not occur at the lowest unemployment rate. And the lowest inflation rate did

not occur at the highest unemployment rates. But the lowest unemployment rate in 1917 did bring a high inflation rate. And the highest unemployment rate during the Great Depression of the 1930s brought a gently falling price level.

A. W. (Bill) Phillips

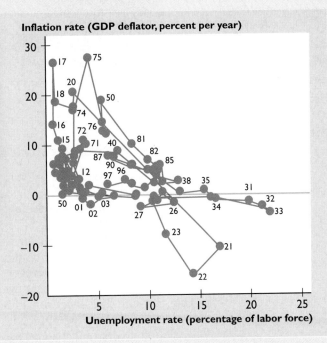

SOURCE: Michael Parkin, "Unemployment, Inflation, and Monetary Policy," *Canadian Journal of Economics*, November 1998.

EYE ON THE PAST

The U.S. Phillips Curve

Phillips made his discovery in 1958, two years before the election of John F. Kennedy as President of the United States. Very soon thereafter, two young American economists, Paul A. Samuelson and Robert M. Solow, both at MIT and eager to help the new Kennedy administration to pursue a low-unemployment strategy, looked for a Phillips curve in the U.S. data. The figure shows what they found: The red line joining the blue dots shows no recognizable relationship between inflation and unemployment for the 20 or so years that they studied.

Giving more weight to the 1950s experience and viewing the 1930s and 1940s as special because of the Great Depression and World War II, Samuelson and Solow proposed the U.S. Phillips curve shown in the figure. They believed that the U.S. Phillips curve provided support for the then growing view that the new Kennedy

SOURCE OF DATA: Paul A. Samuelson, and Robert M. Solow, "Problem of Achieving and Maintaining a Stable Price Level, Analytical Aspects of Anti-Inflation Policy." *American Economic Review*, 50(2), May 1960.

administration could pursue a low unemployment policy with only a moderate rise in the inflation rate.

As the 1960s unfolded, the Samuelson-Solow Phillips curve began to look like a permanent tradeoff

between inflation and unemployment. But in the late 1960s and early 1970s, the relationship disappeared in the face of rising inflation expectations.

■ Why Bother with the Phillips Curve?

You've seen that the short-run Phillips curve is another way of looking at the aggregate supply curve. And you might be wondering, why bother with the short-run Phillips curve? Isn't the aggregate supply curve adequate for describing the short-run tradeoff?

There are two reasons for using the Phillips curve. First, it focuses directly on two policy targets: the inflation rate and the unemployment rate. Second, the aggregate supply curve shifts whenever the money wage rate or potential GDP changes. Such changes occur every day. So the aggregate supply curve is not a stable tradeoff. The short-run Phillips curve isn't a stable tradeoff either, but it is more stable than the aggregate supply curve. It shifts only when the natural unemployment rate changes or when the expected inflation rate changes.

CHECKPOINT 32.1

1 **Describe the short-run tradeoff between inflation and unemployment.**

Practice Problem 32.1

1. Table 1 describes five possible situations that might arise in 2006, depending on the level of aggregate demand in that year. Potential GDP is $10 trillion, and the natural unemployment rate is 5 percent.
   a. Calculate the inflation rate for each possible outcome.
   b. Use Okun's Law to find the real GDP associated with each unemployment rate in Table 1.
   c. What is the expected inflation rate in 2006?
   d. What is the expected price level in 2006?
   e. Plot the short-run Phillips curve for 2006.
   f. Plot the aggregate supply curve for 2006.
   g. Mark the points A, B, C, D, and E on each curve that correspond to the data provided in Table 1 and the data that you have calculated.

TABLE 1

	Price level (2005 = 100)	Unemployment rate (percentage)
A	102.5	9
B	105.0	6
C	106.0	5
D	107.5	4
E	110.0	3

Exercises 32.1

1. In the economy in the practice problem, the outcome in 2006 turned out to be row B of Table 1. Table 2 shows five possible outcomes for 2007 depending on the level of aggregate demand in that year. Potential GDP has grown to $10.5 trillion, but the natural unemployment rate has remained at 5 percent.
   a. Plot the short-run Phillips curve for 2007.
   b. Use Okun's Law to find the real GDP associated with each unemployment rate in Table 2.
   c. What is the expected inflation rate in 2007?
   d. What is the expected price level in 2007?
   e. Plot the aggregate supply curve for 2007.
   f. Mark the points A, B, C, D, and E on each curve that correspond to the data provided in Table 2 and the data you have calculated.

TABLE 2

	Price level (2005 = 100)	Unemployment rate (percentage)
A	108	9
B	113	6
C	115	5
D	118	4
E	123	3

2. Compare the short-run Phillips curves and aggregate supply curves of 2006 with those of 2007. Thinking about the definitions of the short-run Phillips curve and the aggregate supply curve, what might have changed between the two years to make the curves shift?

Solution to Practice Problem 32.1

1a. and **1b.** The inflation rate equals the price level minus 100; real GDP equals potential GDP minus x percent of potential GDP, where $x = 2 \times$ (unemployment rate – natural unemployment rate)—Okun's Law.
1c. The expected inflation rate in 2006 is 6 percent a year.
1d. The expected price level in 2006 is 106.
1e. Figure 1 shows the short-run Phillips curve for 2006.
1f. Figure 2 shows the aggregate supply curve for 2006.
1g. The points are A, B, C, D, and E in Figures 1 and 2.

FIGURE 1

FIGURE 2

32.2 SHORT-RUN AND LONG-RUN PHILLIPS CURVES

The short-run Phillips curve is the *short-run tradeoff* between inflation and unemployment when aggregate demand changes and the natural unemployment rate and expected inflation rate remain the same. Over time, these two factors do not remain the same. And you've seen in the data that the actual fluctuations in inflation and unemployment do not fall along a neat Phillips curve.

Changes in the expected inflation rate influence the short-run tradeoff most. And changes in expected inflation create a long-run Phillips curve. Let's look at the properties of the long-run Phillips curve.

■ The Long-Run Phillips Curve

Long-run Phillips curve
The vertical line that shows the relationship between inflation and unemployment when the economy is at full employment.

The **long-run Phillips curve** shows the relationship between inflation and unemployment when the economy is at full employment. You learned in Chapter 23 that at full employment, the unemployment rate is the *natural unemployment rate.* So on the long-run Phillips curve, there is only one possible unemployment rate: the natural unemployment rate.

In contrast, the inflation rate can take on any value at full employment. You learned in Chapter 28 (pp. 711–714) that at full employment, for a given real GDP growth rate, the greater the money growth rate, the greater is the inflation rate.

This description of the economy in the long run tells us the properties of the long-run Phillips curve. The long-run Phillips curve is a vertical line located at the natural unemployment rate. In Figure 32.3, it is the vertical line *LRPC*. The long-run Phillips curve tells us that any inflation rate is possible at the natural unemployment rate.

■ FIGURE 32.3
The Long-Run Phillips Curve

The long-run Phillips curve is a vertical line at the natural unemployment rate. In the long run, there is no unemployment-inflation tradeoff.

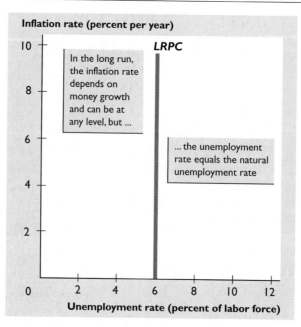

No Long-Run Tradeoff

There is no long-run tradeoff between unemployment and inflation. In the long run, any inflation rate can occur but only one unemployment rate—the natural unemployment rate—is available. You can think of the long-run Phillips curve as another way of looking at the potential GDP line in the *AS-AD* model. Let's examine this parallel.

■ Long-Run Adjustment in the *AS-AD* Model

The *AS-AD* model explains both the short-run and long-run effects of a change in aggregate demand. Figure 32.4 shows the long-run effect. Last year, aggregate demand was AD_0 and aggregate supply was AS_0. The price level was 100, and real GDP was $10 trillion—potential GDP. (To simplify the story, suppose there is no economic growth, so potential GDP remains at $10 trillion.)

Case 1: In the current year, aggregate demand increases from AD_0 to AD_1. The money wage rate rises to keep the real wage rate at its full-employment level. So the aggregate supply shifts from AS_0 to AS_1. The price level rises to 103—the inflation rate is 3 percent—and real GDP remains at potential GDP.

Case 2: In the current year, aggregate demand increases from AD_0 to AD_2. The money wage rate rises to keep the real wage rate at its full-employment level. So the aggregate supply shifts from AS_0 to AS_2. The price level rises to 107—the inflation rate is 7 percent—and real GDP remains at potential GDP.

In the *AS-AD* model, any price level is possible in the long run, but only one level of real GDP can occur: potential GDP.

FIGURE 32.4

Long-Run Adjustment in the *AS-AD* Model

Last year, aggregate demand was AD_0, aggregate supply was AS_0, the price level was 100, and real GDP was $10 trillion (at full employment).

❶ If aggregate demand increases to AD_1 and aggregate supply changes to AS_1, the price level rises by 3 percent to 103.

❷ But if aggregate demand increases to AD_2 and aggregate supply changes to AS_2, the price level rises by 7 percent to 107.

In both cases, real GDP remains at $10 trillion, and because the economy is at full employment, unemployment remains at the natural unemployment rate.

■ Expected Inflation

Full employment occurs when the *AD* and *AS* curves intersect at potential GDP. We're going to see that at full employment, the inflation rate equals the expected inflation rate. The **expected inflation rate** is the inflation rate that people forecast and use to set the money wage rate and other money prices.

Expected inflation rate
The inflation rate that people forecast and use to set the money wage rate and other money prices.

Suppose there is full employment and McDonald's servers earn $7 an hour. With no inflation, a money wage rate of $7 an hour keeps the market for servers in equilibrium. But with 10 percent inflation, a constant money wage rate means a falling real wage rate and a shortage of servers. Now, a 10 percent rise in the money wage rate to $7.70 is needed to keep the market for servers in equilibrium. If McDonald's and everyone else expect 10 percent inflation, the money wage rate will rise by 10 percent to prevent a labor shortage from arising.

If expectations about the inflation rate turn out to be correct, the price level rises by the 10 percent expected and the real wage rate remains constant at its full-employment equilibrium level. Real GDP remains at potential GDP, and unemployment remains at the natural unemployment rate.

Because the actual inflation rate equals the expected inflation rate at full employment, we can interpret the long-run Phillips curve as the relationship between inflation and unemployment when the inflation rate equals the expected inflation rate.

Figure 32.5 shows short-run Phillips curves for two expected inflation rates. A short-run Phillips curve shows the tradeoff between inflation and unemployment at *a particular expected inflation rate*. When the expected inflation rate changes, the

---

■ FIGURE 32.5

Short-Run and Long-Run Phillips Curves

If the natural unemployment rate is 6 percent, the long-run Phillips curve is *LRPC*. ❶ If the expected inflation rate is 3 percent a year, the short-run Phillips curve is *SRPC₀*. ❷ If the expected inflation rate is 7 percent a year, the short-run Phillips curve is *SRPC₁*.

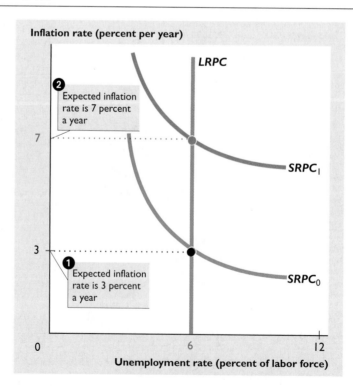

short-run Phillips curve shifts to intersect the long-run Phillips curve at the new expected inflation rate.

In Figure 32.5, when the expected inflation rate is 3 percent a year, the short-run Phillips curve is $SRPC_0$, and when the expected inflation rate is 7 percent a year, the short-run Phillips curve is $SRPC_1$.

The Natural Rate Hypothesis

The **natural rate hypothesis** is the proposition that when the money growth rate changes (and the aggregate demand growth rate changes), the unemployment rate changes *temporarily* and eventually returns to the natural unemployment rate.

Figure 32.6 illustrates the natural rate hypothesis. Initially, aggregate demand growth generates inflation at 3 percent a year and the economy is at full employment, at point *A*. Then aggregate demand grows more rapidly, at a rate that will eventually generate inflation at 7 percent a year. But in the short run, with a sticky money wage rate, the increase in aggregate demand brings an increase in real GDP and a decrease in the unemployment rate. The inflation rate increases to 5 percent a year, and the economy moves from point *A* to point *B*. Eventually, the higher inflation rate is expected and the money wage rate increases. As the expected inflation rate increases from 3 percent to 7 percent a year, the short-run Phillips curve shifts upward from $SRPC_0$ to $SRPC_1$. Inflation speeds up, real GDP moves back to its full-employment level, and the unemployment rate returns to the natural unemployment rate. In Figure 32.6, the economy moves from point *B* to point *C*.

Natural rate hypothesis
The proposition that when the money growth rate changes, the unemployment rate changes *temporarily* and eventually returns to the natural unemployment rate.

FIGURE 32.6
The Natural Rate Hypothesis

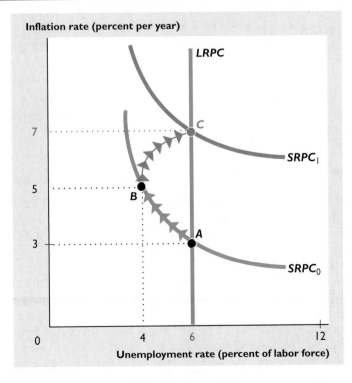

The inflation rate is 3 percent a year, and the economy is at full employment, at point *A*. Then the inflation rate increases.

In the short run, the money wage rate is sticky and the increase in inflation brings a decrease in the unemployment rate—a movement along $SRPC_0$ to point *B*.

Eventually, the higher inflation rate is expected, the money wage rate rises, and the short-run Phillips curve shifts upward gradually to $SRPC_1$. At the higher expected inflation rate, unemployment returns to the natural unemployment rate—the natural rate hypothesis. The economy is at point *C*.

EYE ON THE PAST

A Live Test of the Natural Rate Hypothesis

The figure describes the U.S. economy from 1960 to 1971 and shows that the natural rate hypothesis describes these years well.

The natural unemployment rate was around 6 percent, so the long-run Phillips curve, *LRPC*, was located at that unemployment rate.

At the beginning of the period, the inflation rate and the expected inflation rate were around 1 percent a year. So the short-run Phillips curve was $SRPC_0$.

Through 1966, the expected inflation rate remained at 1 percent a year but the actual inflation rate edged upward and the unemployment rate decreased below the natural unemployment rate. The economy moved up along $SRPC_0$ from point *A* to point *B*.

Then, from 1967 through 1969, the inflation rate increased and so did the expected inflation rate. By 1969, the economy had moved to point *C*. By 1970, the expected inflation rate was

SOURCE OF DATA: Bureau of Labor Statistics and Bureau of Economic Analysis.

around 5 percent a year and the short-run Phillips curve had shifted upward to $SRPC_1$. As the higher inflation rate came to be expected, the unemployment rate increased; by 1971, it had returned to the natural unemployment rate and the economy had moved to point *D*.

Notice the similarity between the actual events of this period and the natural rate hypothesis in Figure 32.6.

Interestingly, Edmund S. Phelps of Columbia University and Milton Friedman of the University of Chicago suggested the natural rate hypothesis *before* these events occurred.

■ Changes in the Natural Unemployment Rate

If the natural unemployment rate changes, both the long-run Phillips curve and the short-run Phillips curve shift. When the natural unemployment rate increases, both the long-run Phillips curve and the short-run Phillips curve shift rightward; and when the natural unemployment rate decreases, both the long-run Phillips curve and the short-run Phillips curve shift leftward.

Figure 32.7 illustrates these changes. When the natural unemployment rate is 6 percent, the long-run Phillips curve is $LRPC_0$. If the expected inflation rate is 3 percent a year, the short-run Phillips curve is $SRPC_0$. An increase in the natural unemployment rate, with no change in the expected inflation rate, shifts the two Phillips curves rightward to $LRPC_1$ and $SRPC_1$. And a decrease in the natural unemployment rate, with no change in the expected inflation rate, shifts the two Phillips curves leftward to $LRPC_2$ and $SRPC_2$.

■ FIGURE 32.7

Changes in the Natural Unemployment Rate

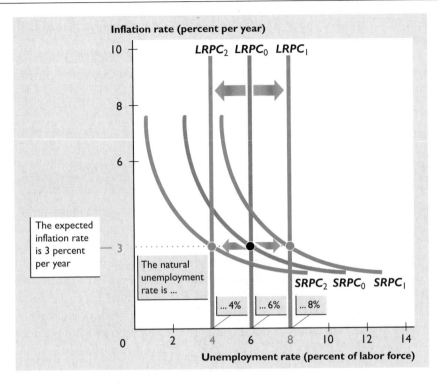

The natural unemployment rate is 6 percent, and the long-run Phillips curve is $LRPC_0$. The expected inflation rate is 3 percent a year, and the short-run Phillips curve is $SRPC_0$.

An increase in the natural unemployment rate shifts the two Phillips curves rightward to $LRPC_1$ and $SRPC_1$.

A decrease in the natural unemployment rate shifts the two Phillips curves leftward to $LRPC_2$ and $SRPC_2$.

■ Does the Natural Unemployment Rate Change?

You learned in Chapter 21 (pp. 539–541) that economists don't agree about the size of the natural unemployment rate or the extent to which it fluctuates. The majority view is that the natural unemployment rate changes slowly or barely at all and is around 6 percent, the actual average unemployment rate since 1960.

An increasing number of economists question the constant natural rate view and believe that changes in frictional and structural unemployment bring changes in the natural unemployment rate. It seems likely that the natural unemployment rate fell to perhaps as low as 4 percent in 2000 and then increased to perhaps 5 or 6 percent in 2002. But economists do not yet have a definite way of measuring the natural unemployment rate, so estimating it remains tricky and controversial.

You learned about the factors that determine the natural unemployment rate in Chapter 23 (pp. 582–587). Those factors divide into two groups: influences on job search and influences on job rationing. Job search is influenced by demographic change, unemployment compensation, and structural change. And job rationing arises from efficiency wages, the minimum wage, and union wages.

No one is sure how important these factors are in changing the natural unemployment rate. But to the extent that they do have an influence, they probably increased the natural unemployment rate during the 1970s. A bulge in the birth rate (known as the "baby boom") that occurred after World War II in the late 1940s and early 1950s brought a bulge in the number of young people entering the labor force during the late 1960s and early 1970s. This bulge in the number of new entrants increased the amount of job search and probably increased the natural unemployment rate.

Structural change during the 1970s and 1980s, much of it a response to massive hikes in the world price of oil, probably increased the natural unemployment rate further during the later 1970s and early 1980s.

EYE ON THE U.S. ECONOMY

The Shifting Short-Run Tradeoff

The short-run tradeoff between inflation and unemployment becomes less favorable—more inflation and more unemployment—if either the expected inflation rate or the natural unemployment rate increases.

The short-run tradeoff becomes more favorable—less inflation and less unemployment—if either the expected inflation rate or the natural unemployment rate decreases.

When the tradeoff becomes less favorable, the short-run Phillips curve shifts rightward and upward. When the tradeoff becomes more favorable, the short-run Phillips curve shifts leftward and downward.

The short-run tradeoff is fixed when the natural unemployment rate and the expected inflation rate don't change.

The figures describe the shifting tradeoff in the United States.

(a) An improving tradeoff: 1981–1986

(b) A fixed tradeoff: 1986–1993

As the baby boom generation approached middle age, during the 1980s and 1990s, the number of new labor market entrants decreased and the natural unemployment rate probably decreased too.

Also, during the 1990s, rapid technological change brought an increase in productivity and an increase in the demand for labor that made job search faster and lowered the natural unemployment rate yet further. During the 2000s, the natural unemployment rate returned to its long-run average level.

The description of the changing natural rate that we've just provided is consistent with the data and consistent with the shifting short-run tradeoff between inflation and unemployment. But it remains speculation rather than solid knowledge.

Between 1981 and 1986, the natural unemployment rate was around 6 percent and the expected inflation rate decreased. The long-run Phillips curve was $LRPC_0$, and the short-run Phillips curve shifted downward from $SRPC_0$ to $SRPC_1$. The tradeoff improved.

Between 1986 and 1993, the expected inflation rate was constant at 3 percent a year and the natural unemployment rate was constant at 6 percent. The Phillips curves remained at $LRPC_0$ and $SRPC_1$. The tradeoff was unchanging.

Between 1993 and 2000, both the natural unemployment rate and the expected inflation rate decreased. The long-run Phillips curve shifted from $LRPC_0$ to $LRPC_1$ and the short-run curve shifted from $SRPC_1$ and $SRPC_2$. The tradeoff improved again.

Finally, between 2000 and 2005, the natural unemployment rate returned to 6 percent but the expected inflation rate remained constant. The Phillips curves shifted to $LRPC_0$ and $SRPC_3$. The tradeoff worsened again.

(c) An improving tradeoff: 1993–2000

(d) A worsening tradeoff: 2000–2005

SOURCE OF DATA: Bureau of Labor Statistics and Bureau of Economic Analysis.

2 **Distinguish between the short-run and the long-run Phillips curves and describe the shifting tradeoff between inflation and unemployment.**

Practice Problems 32.2

FIGURE 1

Inflation rate (% per year)

1. Figure 1 shows a short-run Phillips curve and a long-run Phillips curve.
   a. Label the curves to identify the long-run curve and the short-run curve.
   b. What is the expected inflation rate?
   c. What is the natural unemployment rate?
   d. If the expected inflation rate increases to 7.5 percent a year, show the new short-run and long-run Phillips curves.
   e. If the natural unemployment rate increases to 8 percent, show the new short-run and long-run Phillips curves.

2. In the economy illustrated in Figure 1, aggregate demand starts to grow more rapidly, and eventually, the inflation rate rises to 10 percent a year. Explain how unemployment and inflation in this economy change.

Exercises 32.2

1a. Draw a graph to show the short-run Phillips curve and long-run Phillips curve in an economy in which the natural unemployment rate is 7 percent and the expected inflation rate is 4 percent a year.

1b. If the expected inflation rate changes to 3 percent a year, show the new short-run and long-run Phillips curves.

FIGURE 2

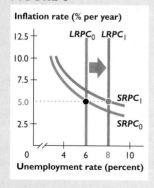

Inflation rate (% per year)

1c. If the natural unemployment rate becomes 6 percent, show the new short-run and long-run Phillips curves.

2. In exercise 1, aggregate demand starts to grow more slowly, and eventually the inflation rate falls to 2 percent a year. Explain how unemployment and inflation in this economy change.

Solutions to Practice Problems 32.2

1a. The long-run Phillips curve is the vertical curve, *LRPC*, and the short-run Phillips curve is the downward-sloping curve, $SRPC_0$ (Figure 2).

1b. The expected inflation rate is 5 percent a year. The expected inflation rate is the inflation rate at which *LRPC* and $SRPC_0$ intersect.

1c. The natural unemployment rate is 6 percent. The *LRPC* is vertical at the natural unemployment rate.

FIGURE 3

1d. The short-run Phillips curve shifts upward, but the long-run Phillips curve does not change (Figure 2).

1e. Both the short-run and long-run Phillips curves shift rightward (Figure 3).

FIGURE 4

Inflation rate (% per year)

2. Figure 4 shows that as expectations change, the inflation rate rises to 10 percent a year and unemployment returns to the natural unemployment rate.

32.3 EXPECTED INFLATION

You've seen that expected inflation plays a big role in determining the position of the short-run tradeoff. When the expected inflation rate is low, as it was in 2000, the tradeoff is more favorable than when the expected inflation rate is high, as it was in 1980. The effect of expected inflation on the short-run tradeoff raises two questions:

- What determines the expected inflation rate?
- What can policy do to lower expected inflation?

■ What Determines the Expected Inflation Rate?

The *expected inflation rate* is the inflation rate that people forecast and use to set the money wage rate and other money prices. To forecast the inflation rate, people use the same basic method that they use to forecast other variables that affect their lives.

Data make up the first ingredient in forecasting—data about the past behavior of the phenomenon that we want to forecast. When people laid heavy bets that Tiger Woods would win the British Open in 2005, they based their forecast on the performance of Tiger and the other golfers in the months leading up to that event.

Science is the second ingredient in forecasting—the specific science that seeks to understand the phenomenon that we wish to forecast. If we want to know whether it is likely to rain tomorrow, we turn to the science of meteorology. Science is not a substitute for data. It is knowledge that tells people how to interpret data.

So to forecast inflation, people use data about past inflation and other relevant variables and the science of economics, which seeks to understand the forces that cause inflation.

You already know the relevant economics: the *AS-AD* model. You know that the money growth rate determines the growth of aggregate demand in the long run. And you know that the trend growth rate of real GDP is the growth rate of aggregate supply in the long run. So the trend money growth rate minus the trend real GDP growth rate determines the trend inflation rate.

The inflation rate fluctuates around its trend as the state of the economy changes over the business cycle. In an expansion, the inflation rate rises above trend, and in a recession, the inflation rate falls below trend as aggregate demand fluctuates to bring movements along the aggregate supply curve. And you know that the money growth rate is one of the influences on these aggregate demand fluctuations.

The Fed determines the money growth rate, so the major ingredient in a forecast of inflation is a forecast of the Fed's actions. Professional Fed watchers and economic forecasters use these ideas along with a lot of data and elaborate statistical models of the economy to forecast the inflation rate.

When all the relevant data and economic science are used to forecast inflation, the resulting forecast is called a **rational expectation**. The rational expectation of the inflation rate is a forecast based on the Fed's forecasted monetary policy along with forecasts of the other forces that influence aggregate demand and aggregate supply. But the dominant factor is the Fed's monetary policy.

Rational expectation
The inflation forecast resulting from use of all the relevant data and economic science.

■ What Can Policy Do to Lower Expected Inflation?

If the Fed wants to lower the inflation rate, it can pursue two alternative lines of attack:

- A surprise inflation reduction
- A credible announced inflation reduction

A Surprise Inflation Reduction

In Figure 32.8, the economy is at full employment with inflation raging and expected to rage at 10 percent a year. Unemployment is at its natural rate, which is 6 percent. The economy is on its long-run Phillips curve, *LRPC*, and its short-run Phillips curve, $SRPC_0$ at point *A*.

No one is expecting the Fed to change its policy but the Fed does change its policy and starts to slow inflation to a target rate of 3 percent a year. The Fed raises interest rates and slows money growth. With no change in expected inflation, money wage rates continue to rise by the same amount as before but aggregate demand growth slows. The unemployment rate rises, and the inflation rate falls along $SRPC_0$. Gradually, the expected inflation rate falls and the short-run Phillips curve shifts downward toward $SRPC_1$. The Fed slows inflation but at the cost of recession. The economy follows the path of the red arrows—and unemployment remains above its natural rate until, eventually, the economy arrives at point *B*.

FIGURE 32.8

Slowing Inflation

The economy is at point *A*. The natural unemployment rate is 6 percent, and inflation is 10 percent a year.

An unexpected slowdown in aggregate demand growth slows inflation and increases the unemployment rate as the economy slides down along $SRPC_0$. Eventually, the expected inflation rate falls and the short-run Phillips curve shifts to $SRPC_1$. The unemployment rate remains above 6 percent through the adjustment to point *B*.

A credible, announced slowdown in aggregate demand growth lowers the expected inflation rate and shifts the short-run Phillips curve downward to $SRPC_1$. Inflation slows to 3 percent a year, and unemployment remains at 6 percent as the economy moves along the *LRPC* curve to point *B*.

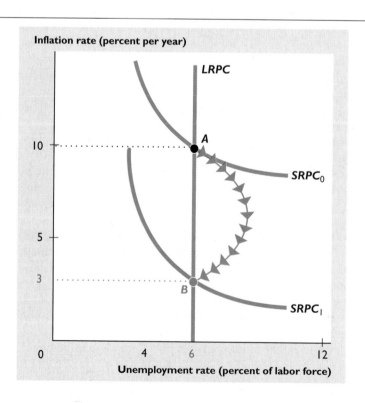

A Credible Announced Inflation Reduction

Suppose that instead of unexpectedly slowing inflation, the Fed announces its intention to bring the inflation rate down. Ahead of its action, the Fed convinces everyone that it has a credible plan, so its announcement is believed.

Because people believe that the Fed will lower the inflation rate, the expected inflation rate falls. And because the expected inflation rate falls, the rate of increase in the money wage rate slows.

The lower expected inflation rate shifts the short-run Phillips curve downward to $SRPC_1$, and the inflation rate falls to 3 percent a year, while the unemployment rate remains at the natural rate of 6 percent.

This announced inflation reduction lowers the inflation rate but with no accompanying loss of output or increase in unemployment. The economy moves directly from A to B in Figure 32.8.

Inflation Reduction in Practice

It was back in 1981 that the Fed was last faced with a high inflation rate. And to slow it, we paid a high price. The Fed's policy action was unexpected. Money wage rates had been set too high for the path that the Fed followed. The consequence was recession—a decrease in real GDP and increased unemployment. We followed a path like the red arrows in Figure 32.8. Whether policy can lower inflation without a deep recession is a controversial question. We'll return to it in the next chapter, where we review policy debates.

REALITY CHECK

The Short-Run Tradeoff in YOUR Life

Consider the *change* in the U.S. unemployment rate and inflation rate over the past year. Did they change in the same direction or in opposite directions? Can you interpret the change as a movement along a short-run Phillips curve or a shifting short-run Phillips curve? Can you think of reasons why the the short-run Phillips curve might have shifted? Did the natural unemployment rate change? Did the expected inflation rate change?

Thinking about your own expectations, did *you* expect the inflation rate to increase, decrease, or remain the same last year? Do you think what you expected is the same as what people on the average expected?

Thinking further about the change in unemployment and inflation, how do you think these changes should affect the policy decisions of the federal government and the Federal Reserve?

3 Explain how the Fed can influence the expected inflation rate and how expected inflation influences the short-run tradeoff.

Practice Problem 32.3

FIGURE 1

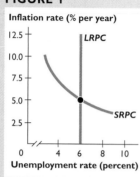

1. Figure 1 shows the short-run and long-run Phillips curves. The current inflation rate is 5 percent a year.
   a. Inflation is expected to remain at 5 percent next year. If the Fed slows the money growth rate, explain the effect of the Fed's action on inflation and unemployment next year.
   b. If the Fed announces that it will slow the money growth rate so that inflation will fall to 2.5 percent a year and everyone believes the Fed, explain the effect of the Fed's action on inflation and unemployment next year.
   c. Inflation is expected to remain at 5 percent next year. If the Fed slows the money growth rate such that inflation will fall to 2.5 percent a year and keeps it there for many years, explain the effect of the Fed's action on inflation and unemployment.

Exercise 32.3

1. In Figure 1, the current inflation rate is 5 percent a year.
   a. If the Fed announces that it will increase the money growth rate so that the inflation rate will rise to 6 percent a year and everyone believes the Fed, explain the effect of the Fed's action on inflation and unemployment next year.

FIGURE 2

   b. Inflation is expected to remain at 5 percent next year. If the Fed speeds up the money growth rate, explain the effect of the Fed's action on inflation and unemployment next year.
   c. In part **b**, if the Fed keeps the money growth rate constant for many years, explain the effect of the Fed's action on inflation and unemployment.

Solution to Practice Problem 32.3

1a. The inflation rate will fall below 5 percent a year and the unemployment rate will rise above 6 percent as the economy moves down along its short-run Phillips curve (see Figure 2).

FIGURE 3

1b. The inflation rate falls to 2.5 percent a year, and unemployment remains at 6 percent. If people believe the Fed's announcement, expected inflation will fall to 2.5 percent a year. The short-run Phillips curve will shift downward to $SRPC_1$ (Figure 3).

1c. Initially, inflation falls below 5 percent a year and unemployment rises above 6 percent. The longer the Fed maintains the slower money growth rate, the more people will start to expect lower inflation and the short-run Phillips curve will start to shift downward. The unemployment rate will start to decrease. Eventually, inflation is 2.5 percent a year and the unemployment rate returns to 6 percent (Figure 4).

FIGURE 4

CHAPTER CHECKPOINT

Key Points

1   Describe the short-run tradeoff between inflation and unemployment.

- The short-run Phillips curve is the downward-sloping relationship between the inflation rate and the unemployment rate when all other influences on these two variables remain the same.
- The short-run Phillips curve presents a *tradeoff* between inflation and unemployment.
- The short-run Phillips curve is another way of looking at the aggregate supply curve.

2   Distinguish between the short-run and long-run Phillips curves and describe the shifting tradeoff between inflation and unemployment.

- The long-run Phillips curve shows the relationship between inflation and unemployment when the unemployment rate equals the natural unemployment rate and the inflation rate equals the expected inflation rate.
- The long-run Phillips curve is vertical at the *natural unemployment rate,* and there is no long-run tradeoff between unemployment and inflation.
- When the expected inflation rate changes, the short-run Phillips curve shifts to intersect the long-run Phillips curve at the new expected inflation rate.
- When the money growth rate changes, the unemployment rate changes temporarily and eventually returns to the natural unemployment rate—the natural rate hypothesis.
- Changes in the natural unemployment rate shift both the *SRPC* and the *LRPC.*

3   Explain how the Fed can influence the expected inflation rate and how expected inflation influences the short-run tradeoff.

- The rational expectation of the inflation rate is based on the forecasted actions of the Fed's monetary policy and the other forces that influence aggregate demand and aggregate supply.
- A change in the expected inflation rate changes the short-run tradeoff gradually because the money wage rate responds only gradually to a change in the expected inflation rate.
- To lower the expected inflation rate, the Fed must take actions that will slow the actual inflation rate.

Key Terms

Expected inflation rate, 818
Long-run Phillips curve, 816
Natural rate hypothesis, 819

Okun's Law, 811
Rational expectation, 825
Short-run Phillips curve, 810

Exercises

1. Table 1 describes four possible situations that might arise in 2006, depending on the level of aggregate demand in that year.

TABLE 1

	Price level (2005 = 100)	Real GDP (trillions of 2005 dollars)	Unemployment rate (percent of labor force)
A	102	11.0	9
B	104	11.1	7
C	106	11.2	5
D	108	11.3	4
E	110	11.4	3

   a. Plot the Phillips curve and the aggregate supply curve for 2006.
   b. Mark the points A, B, C, D, and E on each curve that correspond to the data provided in the table.

2. In the economy in exercise 1, the outcome in 2006 turned out to be row C of Table 1. Four possible outcomes for 2007 are shown in Table 2.

TABLE 2

	Price level (2005 = 100)	Real GDP (trillions of 2005 dollars)	Unemployment rate (percent of labor force)
A	108	11.1	9
B	110	11.2	7
C	112	11.3	5
D	114	11.4	4
E	116	11.5	3

   a. Plot the Phillips curve and the aggregate supply curve for 2007.
   b. Mark the points A, B, C, D, and E on each curve that correspond to the data provided in the table.
   c. Compare the Phillips curves and aggregate supply curves of 2007 with those of 2006.

3. Refer to the data in exercise 1.
   a. The natural unemployment rate is 6 percent in 2005. What is the expected inflation rate?
   b. If the natural unemployment rate increases to 7 percent in 2006, explain how the short-run and long-run tradeoffs change.
   c. If the natural unemployment rate remains at 6 percent in 2006 but the expected inflation rate is 4 percent a year, explain how the short-run and long-run tradeoffs change.

4. What is Okun's Law? Does the economy described in Tables 1 and 2 above behave in accordance with Okun's Law?

5. What is the relationship between the long-run Phillips curve and potential GDP and between the short-run Phillips curve and the aggregate supply curve?

6. The inflation rate is 5 percent a year, and the quantity of money is growing at a pace that will maintain that inflation rate. The natural unemployment rate is 6 percent, and the current unemployment rate is 4 percent.

a. In what direction will the unemployment rate change?

b. How will the short-run Phillips curve shift?

c. How will the long-run Phillips curve shift?

d. How will the *AS* and *AD* curves shift as the events you've described in parts **a, b,** and **c** unfold?

7. The inflation rate is 5 percent a year, and the quantity of money is growing at a pace that will maintain that inflation rate. The natural unemployment rate is 6 percent, and the current unemployment rate is 8 percent.

a. In what direction will the unemployment rate change?

b. How will the short-run Phillips curve shift?

c. How will the long-run Phillips curve shift?

d. How will the *AS* and *AD* curves shift as the events you've described in parts **a, b,** and **c** unfold?

8. The inflation rate is 6 percent a year, the unemployment rate is 4 percent, and the economy is at full employment. The Fed declares that it wants to slow the inflation rate to 3 percent a year and that it intends to slow the money growth rate to keep the inflation rate at 3 percent a year for the foreseeable future. People believe the Fed.

a. Explain how unemployment and inflation change in the short run, and use the short-run Phillips curve and *AS* curve to illustrate your explanation.

b. Explain how unemployment and inflation change in the long run, and use the short-run and long-run Phillips curves and the *AS* curve to illustrate your explanation.

9. The inflation rate is 6 percent a year, the unemployment rate is 4 percent, and the economy is at full employment. Without warning and to everyone's astonishment, the Fed slows the money growth rate to keep inflation at 3 percent a year.

a. Explain how unemployment and inflation change in the short run, and use the short-run Phillips curve and *AS* curve to illustrate your explanation.

b. Compare and contrast the situation in exercise 9 with that in exercise 8.

10. The Reserve Bank of New Zealand signed an agreement with the New Zealand government in which the Bank agreed to maintain inflation inside a low target range. Failure to achieve the target would result in the governor of the Bank (the equivalent of the chairman of the Fed) losing his job.

a. Explain how this arrangement might have influenced New Zealand's short-run Phillips curve.

b. Explain how this arrangement might have influenced New Zealand's long-run Phillips curve.

11. Brazil, Chile, Bolivia, and Uruguay have repeatedly permitted inflation to rise to levels unheard of in the United States.

a. Explain how a history of rapid inflation might influence the short-run Phillips curves in these countries.

b. Explain how a history of rapid inflation might influence the long-run Phillips curves in these countries.

Critical Thinking

12. In light of the fact that whenever the inflation rate is lowered, the unemployment rate increases, do you think it is ever worth lowering inflation? Would it be better to simply live with the inflation rate we've currently got?

13. In light of the fact that whenever the inflation rate is lowered, the unemployment rate increases, do you think we should ever permit the inflation rate to rise to an unacceptable level? Would it be better to nip an increase in inflation in the bud even if it meant a small and brief recession?

14. Looking at the data on inflation and unemployment, it is very difficult to see any sign of a short-run tradeoff.
    a. Explain why it is difficult to see the short-run tradeoff.
    b. Does the fact that the short-run tradeoff is hard to see in the data mean that we can ignore it? Why or why not?

15. "The Phillips curve adds nothing to the *AS-AD* model." Argue against this proposition.

 ## Web Exercises

Use the links on MyEconLab to work the following exercises.

16. Visit the Web site of the Bureau of Labor Statistics and obtain data on the unemployment rate and the inflation rate for the past 20 years.
    a. In a spreadsheet, make a scatter diagram of the two variables, placing the unemployment rate on the *x*-axis.
    b. Interpret the data in terms of shifting short-run and long-run Phillips curves.
    c. In any periods in which you think the natural unemployment rate was falling, can you think of some of the reasons for the fall?
    d. In any periods in which you think the natural unemployment rate was rising, can you think of some of the reasons for the rise?
    e. In any periods in which you think the expected inflation rate was falling, can you think of some of the reasons for the fall?
    f. In any periods in which you think the expected inflation rate was rising, can you think of some of the reasons for the rise?

17. Visit the Web site of the *Economic Report of the President* and obtain data on the unemployment rate and the inflation rate for the major industrial countries for the past 20 years.
    a. In a spreadsheet, make scatter diagrams of the two variables for each country, placing the unemployment rate on the *x*-axis.
    b. Interpret the data in terms of short-run and long-run Phillips curves.
    c. In which of the countries for which you have data do you think the natural unemployment rate is highest? Can you explain why?
    d. In which of the countries for which you have data do you think the natural unemployment rate is lowest? Can you explain why?
    e. In which of the countries for which you have data do you think the expected inflation rate is highest? Can you explain why?
    f. In which of the countries for which you have data do you think the expected inflation rate is lowest? Can you explain why?

Fiscal and Monetary Policy Debates

CHAPTER CHECKLIST

When you have completed your study of this chapter, you will be able to

1 Discuss whether fiscal policy or monetary policy is the better stabilization tool.

2 Explain the rules-versus-discretion debate and compare Keynesian and monetarist policy rules.

3 Assess whether policy should target the inflation rate rather than real GDP.

Maestro: Greenspan's Fed and the American Boom is the title of a biography of Alan Greenspan, Fed chairman from 1987 through 2005, written by *Washington Post* editor Bob Woodward.

Greenspan is portrayed as a "maestro" for two reasons. First, he is a Julliard-trained jazz saxophone player. But second, and more profoundly, he is seen by many as the maestro conductor of a well-tuned economic orchestra.

Should monetary stabilization be left to the discretion of a maestro? Or should the government lay down rules for policy makers to follow? Should we try to keep the economy at full employment and not worry too much about inflation? Or should we target inflation and not worry too much about employment? This chapter studies some hard questions about fiscal and monetary policy. Surprisingly, economists are agreed on most of the answers. But some debates remain, as you're about to discover.

33.1 FISCAL POLICY VERSUS MONETARY POLICY

Which tool does the better job of stabilizing short-run economic fluctuations: fiscal policy or monetary policy? This question has been debated for many decades and was at the core of a controversy that raged during the 1960s. That old debate has been settled, but the lessons that we learn from it are important and remain relevant today. We will examine the fiscal policy versus monetary policy debate by considering its three aspects:

- Policy effects
- Goal conflicts
- Timing and flexibility

■ Policy Effects

Which policy action has the larger and more predictable effect on aggregate demand: a change in government expenditure or a change in the supply of money? The answer to this question was once controversial, and the question lay at the heart of the original 1960s debate.

Investment demand (Chapter 24, pp. 599–601) and the demand for money Chapter 28, pp. 699–702) determine the effects of monetary policy and fiscal policy. Let's look first at the effects of monetary policy.

The Effects of Monetary Policy

The two steps in the transmission of monetary policy are

Step 1 A change in the supply of money influences the interest rate, and

Step 2 A change in the interest rate influences investment and other interest-sensitive components of aggregate expenditure.

The demand for money and investment demand determine whether monetary policy has a powerful or a weak effect. Look first at step 1.

Step 1 Whether a given increase in the supply of money lowers the interest rate by a lot or a little depends on the sensitivity of the demand for money to the interest rate. Suppose that the quantity of money demanded is relatively insensitive to the interest rate, so a change in the interest rate brings a small change in the quantity of money demanded. Then, when the supply of money increases by a given amount, the decrease in the interest rate is large. In contrast, suppose that the quantity of money demanded is highly sensitive to the interest rate, so even a small change in the interest rate brings a large change in the quantity of money demanded. Then, when the supply of money increases by a given amount, the decrease in the interest rate is small.

Look next at step 2.

Step 2 Whether a given decrease in the interest rate increases aggregate expenditure by a lot or a little depends on the sensitivity of investment and other components of aggregate expenditure to the interest rate. If aggregate expenditure is highly sensitive to the interest rate, then a given change in the interest rate brings a large change in aggregate expenditure. If aggregate expenditure is insensitive to the interest rate, then a given change in the interest rate brings a small change in aggregate expenditure.

Figure 33.1 illustrates the two cases. In part (a), an increase in the supply of money from MS_0 to MS_1 brings a large fall in the interest rate and a large increase in investment. In contrast, in part (b), the same increase in the supply of money brings a small fall in the interest rate and a small increase in investment.

FIGURE 33.1

The Effectiveness of Monetary Policy

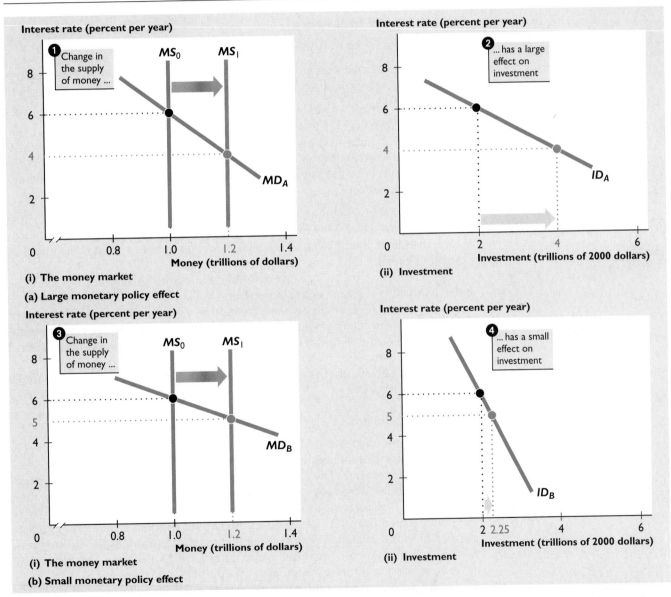

(a) Large monetary policy effect

(b) Small monetary policy effect

In part (a), ❶ when the supply of money increases and the supply of money curve shifts from MS_0 to MS_1, the interest rate falls from 6 percent to 4 percent a year and ❷ investment increases from $2 trillion to $4 trillion along the investment demand curve ID_A.

In part (b), ❸ the same change in the supply of money lowers the interest rate from 6 percent to 5 percent a year and ❹ increases investment from $2 trillion to $2.25 trillion. Monetary policy is more powerful in the conditions shown in part (a).

The Predictability of Monetary Policy   The two steps in the transmission of monetary policy determine the predictability of monetary policy.

At step 1, for a given change in the supply of money to have a predictable effect on the interest rate, the demand for money must be predictable.

At step 2, for a given change in the interest rate to have a predictable effect on investment and aggregate expenditure, the investment demand must be predictable.

So the more predictable the demand for money and investment demand, the more predictable is the effect of monetary policy.

Let's now look at the effects of fiscal policy.

The Effects of Fiscal Policy

The three steps in the transmission of fiscal policy are

Step 1 An increase in government expenditure or a tax cut increases aggregate expenditure and increases aggregate demand with a multiplier.

Step 2 A change in real GDP changes the demand for money, which changes the interest rate.

Step 3 A change in the interest rate changes investment and other interest-sensitive components of aggregate expenditure, which counteract the effects of the initial increase in aggregate expenditure—a crowding-out effect.

If a given change in the demand for money has a large effect on the interest rate and if a given change in the interest rate has a large effect on aggregate expenditure, then the crowding-out effect is large and fiscal policy has a weak effect on aggregate demand.

The conditions that we've just described that make fiscal policy weak are the ones that make monetary policy powerful.

If a given change in the demand for money has a small effect on the interest rate and if a given change in the interest rate has a small effect on aggregate expenditure, then the crowding-out effect is small and fiscal policy has a powerful effect on aggregate demand.

These conditions that make fiscal policy powerful are the ones that make monetary policy weak.

Extreme Conditions

At one extreme, monetary policy is all-powerful and fiscal policy is completely ineffective. This extreme occurs if the quantity of money demanded is independent of the interest rate. The demand for money curve is vertical. In such a situation, the amount of money that people want to hold depends only on their expenditure. For a given supply of money, there is only one equilibrium level of aggregate expenditure. So a change in the supply of money changes aggregate expenditure. But a change in government expenditure changes the interest rate, which in turn changes expenditure and completely crowds out the increase in government expenditure. So aggregate expenditure is unchanged.

At the other extreme, monetary policy is completely ineffective and fiscal policy is all-powerful. This extreme occurs if the quantity of money demanded is infinitely sensitive to the interest rate. The demand for money curve is horizontal at a particular interest rate. At that interest rate, people are willing to hold any quantity of money. This situation is called a **liquidity trap**. In a liquidity trap, a change in the supply of money changes the quantity of money held but has no effect on the interest rate and so it has no effect on aggregate expenditure. But a change in government expenditure leaves the interest rate unchanged, so there is no crowding out and fiscal policy has a large multiplier effect on aggregate expenditure.

Liquidity trap
An interest rate at which people are willing to hold any quantity of money.

Reality

The extreme conditions were once thought to apply to real economies. Keynesian economists (see p. 843) believed that a liquidity trap rendered monetary policy useless and fiscal policy all-powerful. Monetarist economists (see p. 842) believed the opposite. We now know, as a result of an enormous amount of research using data for all the major economies, that neither extreme occurs in real economies. Some people have suggested that Japan was in a liquidity trap in the late 1990s and early 2000s. But this suggestion is not supported by evidence. Either fiscal policy or monetary policy can be used to manipulate aggregate demand.

■ Goal Conflicts

You've seen that both fiscal policy and monetary policy influence aggregate demand, so either policy can be used in the attempt to stabilize aggregate demand, real GDP, and the price level.

But stabilization policy actions have side effects—effects on factors other than the stabilization goals. These side effects can create a conflict between stabilization and some other goals. It turns out that goal conflict is more serious for fiscal policy than for monetary policy.

Fiscal Policy Goal Conflicts

Fiscal policy has three goals: to provide public goods and services, to redistribute income, and to stabilize aggregate demand. These goals can come into conflict.

One aspect of the government's budget that does not create conflict is its *automatic stabilizer* effect. We described these features in Chapter 31 (p. 794). The income tax and needs-tested spending programs, such as unemployment benefits, that automatically adjust expenditure and tax receipts in response to the state of the economy help to achieve the government's goals of redistributing income and improving economic stability.

In contrast, *discretionary* fiscal actions—actions that require changes in spending or taxes to be legislated—create goal conflicts. The main source of conflict is the very large number of spending programs and tax arrangements in place and the difficulty (impossibility perhaps) of changing all of them to balance the costs and benefits of one against the costs and benefits of others.

For example, suppose that fiscal stimulation is called for in a recession. Should the government spend more on the space program, national defense, the environment, or education? Or should it cut the income tax? And whose income tax should it cut? Or should it cut the excise tax on alcohol, tobacco, or gasoline? The government must make a very large number of detailed decisions about what to produce more of, whom to benefit, which industries to benefit, and which regions to benefit.

If the government wants to meet its goals in the provision of public goods and services and achieve its income redistribution goals, fiscal policy must be freed up from the additional task of helping to stabilize the economy.

Monetary Policy Goal Conflicts

Monetary policy has three main goals: price level stability, real GDP stability, and stability of the financial system. There is less conflict among these goals than among those of fiscal policy.

First, stability of the financial system and aggregate demand stability go together. Each contributes to the other. So there is no conflict here.

Second, stability of real GDP and stability of the price level are both served by stabilizing aggregate demand. There is a conflict about how much weight to place on price level stability versus real GDP stability. But this conflict is also present for fiscal policy. So fiscal policy does not outperform monetary policy in this area.

■ Timing and Flexibility

The ability to forecast the near future state of the economy and act at the appropriate time to counteract any unwanted recession or inflation is a crucial part of a successful stabilization policy. The timing of policy actions is vitally important. How do fiscal policy and monetary policy stack up on this dimension?

Inflexible Fiscal Policy

Fiscal policy is political. Lawmakers must debate and make deals for months before they are ready to vote on and change a spending program or a tax code. And the issues that matter most in this process do not include the forecast of aggregate demand over the next 18 months.

Worse, the election cycle dominates fiscal policy making, and only by coincidence are the business cycle and the election cycle aligned. So fiscal policy is inflexible and incapable of the rapid-fire response that is often called for to keep aggregate demand growing smoothly.

Flexible Monetary Policy

In contrast, stabilization is the purpose of monetary policy. The Fed and its policy committee, the FOMC, were created to enable policy actions to be taken quickly and on the basis of a careful, professional evaluation of the current and likely future state of the economy. And every day, the financial markets are watched for signs that policy needs to be tweaked to keep the economy on track.

Monetary policy *effects* are long and drawn out, but actions can be taken quickly.

■ And the Winner Is?

There is no clear winner. Automatic fiscal stabilizers do an important part of the job of maintaining macroeconomic stability. Discretionary fiscal policy is sometimes a vital part of the policy mix, especially if the economy is in a deep recession or in a seriously overheated condition. But for dealing with normal fluctuations, monetary policy is the preferred stabilization tool because it is more flexible in its timing.

What should monetary policy try to achieve? Should it try to maintain full employment? Or should it try to stabilize the inflation rate (or price level) rather than real GDP and employment? We study these questions in the next section.

CHECKPOINT 33.1

I **Discuss whether fiscal policy or monetary policy is the better stabilization tool.**

Practice Problems 33.1

1. The Fed decreases the quantity of money.
   a. Use a graph like Figure 33.1 to work out the effects of the Fed's policy on the interest rate, the quantity of money demanded, and investment.
   b. Explain the effects of the Fed's policy on aggregate expenditure and aggregate demand.
   c. Explain the conditions that make the Fed's policy more effective.

2. If a change in the supply of money leads to a large change in the interest rate and investment is very sensitive to the interest rate, would a contractionary fiscal policy be an effective policy? Explain why or why not.

Exercises 33.1

1. If the government adopts a contractionary fiscal policy, explain
   a. The effects of the government's policy on the interest rate, the quantity of money demanded, and investment.
   b. The effects of the government's policy on aggregate expenditure and aggregate demand.
   c. The conditions that make the government's policy more effective.

2. If a change in the supply of money leads to a small change in the interest rate and investment is not very sensitive to the interest rate, would an expansionary fiscal policy be an effective policy? Explain why or why not.

3. Explain why monetary policy is a better tool than fiscal policy for stabilizing aggregate demand.

Solutions to Practice Problems 33.1

1a. When the Fed decreases the quantity of money, **1** the supply of money decreases and **2** the interest rate rises. The quantity of money demanded decreases and **3** investment decreases (Figure 1).

1b. The decrease in investment decreases aggregate expenditure. Aggregate demand decreases.

1c. The Fed's policy is more effective when the change in aggregate demand is larger. The change in aggregate demand will be larger, the bigger is the change in investment resulting from a given change in the interest rate. And the change in the interest rate will be larger, the less sensitive is the demand for money to the interest rate. Figure 33.1(a) illustrates these conditions.

2. A contractionary fiscal policy decreases aggregate demand and decreases real GDP. The decrease in real GDP decreases the demand for money, and the interest rate falls by a large amount. With investment highly sensitive to the interest rate, investment increases by a large amount. The increase in investment works against the decrease in government expenditure and limits the effectiveness of the fiscal policy action.

FIGURE I

(a) Money market

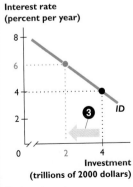

(b) Investment

33.2 RULES VERSUS DISCRETION

We've seen that monetary policy is more suited to macroeconomic stabilization than is fiscal policy. But *how* should the Fed conduct its monetary policy? Should the Fed be free to use its own discretion, or should it be constrained to follow rules? And if it should follow rules, what kind of rules?

There is little disagreement with the view that Congress should formulate the broad goals for the Fed to pursue. But there is debate about how closely the Fed should be directed in the detailed policy objectives and the means of achieving them. Three broad approaches to the Fed's monetary policy are

- Discretionary policy
- Fixed-rule policy
- Feedback-rule policy

■ Discretionary Policy

Discretionary monetary policy
Monetary policy that is based on the judgments of policy makers about the current needs of the economy.

Discretionary monetary policy is monetary policy that is based on the judgments of the policy makers about the current needs of the economy. Discretionary monetary policy is setting the discount rate and determining open market operations by the Fed on the basis of the expert opinion of the members of the FOMC and their advisors.

Examples of discretionary policy occur every minute on our highways. Each driver uses discretionary policy in deciding how fast to go and how close to other vehicles to travel.

An example of discretionary monetary policy occurred during 1998 in the face of a sagging Asian economy. During this "Asia Crisis," the Fed cut interest rates several times to maintain economic growth. The Fed might have delayed cutting interest rates until it was sure that lower interest rates were needed and then cut them in larger increments. The Fed used discretion based on lessons it had learned from earlier expansions.

■ Fixed-Rule Policies

Fixed-rule policy
A policy that is pursued independently of the state of the economy.

A **fixed-rule policy** specifies an action to be pursued independently of the state of the economy. A stop sign is an everyday-life example of a fixed rule. It says, "Stop regardless of the state of the road ahead, even if no other vehicle is trying to use the road." One fixed-rule policy, proposed by Nobel Prize–winning economist Milton Friedman, is to keep the quantity of money growing at a constant rate year in and year out, regardless of the state of the economy, to make the average inflation rate zero. Fixed rules are rarely followed in practice, but they have some merits in principle that we'll examine later in this chapter.

■ Feedback-Rule Policies

Feedback-rule policy
A policy that specifies how policy actions respond to changes in the state of the economy.

A **feedback-rule policy** specifies how policy actions respond to changes in the state of the economy. A yield sign is an everyday feedback rule. It says, "Stop if another vehicle is attempting to use the road ahead, but otherwise, proceed." A feedback rule for monetary policy is one that changes the quantity of money or the interest rate in response to the state of the economy. Some feedback rules guide the actions of policy makers. For example, the Fed's FOMC used a feedback rule when it kept pushing interest rates ever higher through 1999 and 2000 in response to persistently falling unemployment and strong real GDP growth. And it continued to use the same feedback rule but in the reverse direction when it lowered interest rates during 2002.

We'll study the effects of stabilization policy rules by comparing the performance of real GDP and the price level under a fixed rule and a feedback rule. Because fluctuations can result from demand shocks or supply shocks, we need to consider these two cases. We'll begin with demand shocks.

■ Stabilizing Aggregate Demand Shocks

Figure 33.2 illustrates an economy that starts out at full employment and has no inflation. The aggregate demand curve is AD_0, and the aggregate supply curve is AS. The price level is 110, and real GDP is $10 trillion, which is also potential GDP.

Investment decreases because of a wave of pessimism about future profits, and aggregate demand decreases. The aggregate demand curve shifts leftward, to AD_1 in Figure 33.2. Aggregate demand curve AD_1 intersects the aggregate supply curve, AS, at a price level of 107 and real GDP of $9.8 trillion. The economy is in a recession. Real GDP is less than potential GDP, and unemployment is above the natural unemployment rate.

At some later time, when profit prospects improve and firms increase investment, the aggregate demand curve will return from AD_1 to AD_0. In the meantime, while aggregate demand is depressed at AD_1, the course of real GDP and the price level depend on the stabilization policy that is pursued. We'll work out how the economy responds under a fixed rule and under a feedback rule.

■ FIGURE 33.2

A Decrease in Aggregate Demand Brings Recession

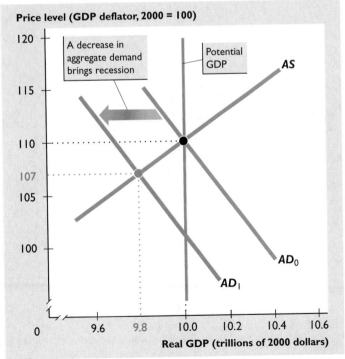

Initially, the economy is at full employment. The price level is 110 and real GDP equals potential GDP at $10 trillion.

A decrease in aggregate demand shifts the aggregate demand curve leftward from AD_0 to AD_1. The economy goes into recession. Real GDP decreases to $9.8 trillion, and the price level falls to 107.

Monetarist
An economist who believes that fluctuations in the quantity of money are the main source of economic fluctuations and who advocates that the quantity of money grow at a constant rate.

Fixed Rule: Monetarism

A **monetarist** is an economist who believes that fluctuations in the quantity of money are the main source of economic fluctuations and who advocates that the quantity of money grow at a constant rate. The fixed rule that we'll study here is one in which the quantity of money remains constant.

Figure 33.3(a) illustrates the response of the economy under this rule. A decrease in aggregate demand brings recession as the economy moves from A to B. With a recessionary gap and unemployment above the natural unemployment rate, the money wage rate gradually falls. Aggregate supply increases toward AS_1 to take the economy from B to C and back to full employment.

Eventually, aggregate demand returns to its original level, and the aggregate demand curve shifts rightward to AD_0. Real GDP now expands in a move from C to D. With an inflationary gap and unemployment below the natural unemployment rate, the money wage rate gradually rises. Aggregate supply decreases toward AS_0 to take the economy from D to A and to full employment once more.

With a fixed-rule monetary policy, fluctuations in aggregate demand bring fluctuations in real GDP around potential GDP. Let's contrast the performance of the economy under a fixed rule with that under a feedback rule.

FIGURE 33.3

Stabilization Policies: Aggregate Demand Shocks

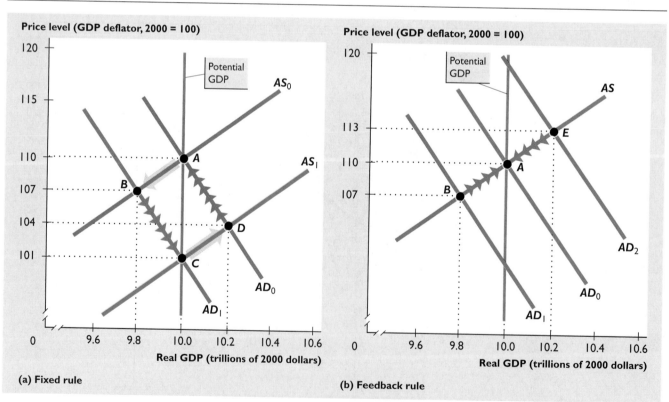

(a) Fixed rule

(b) Feedback rule

A fixed-rule policy leaves real GDP and the price level to fluctuate from A to B, to C, to D and back to A in part (a).

A feedback-rule policy tries to restore full employment as quickly as possible in part (b).

Feedback Rule: Keynesian Activism

A **Keynesian activist** is an economist who believes that fluctuations in investment are the main source of economic fluctuations and who advocates interest rate cuts when real GDP falls below potential GDP and interest rate hikes when real GDP exceeds potential GDP.

Figure 33.3(b) illustrates the response of the economy under this feedback-rule policy. When aggregate demand decreases to AD_1, the economy is at point B. There is a recessionary gap to which the Fed reacts by increasing the quantity of money and cutting the interest rate. This policy action increases aggregate demand, but only gradually. So the aggregate demand curve moves toward AD_0. As it does so, real GDP increases and the price level rises. Eventually, the economy is back at point A, its starting point before the recession.

When profit prospects improve and firms increase investment, aggregate demand increases from AD_0 to AD_2, and the economy moves to point E. This expansion brings an inflationary gap to which the Fed reacts. The Fed now decreases the quantity of money and raises the interest rate. This policy action gradually decreases aggregate demand, and the aggregate demand curve moves leftward toward AD_0. As it does so, real GDP decreases and the price level falls. Again, the economy returns to point A, its starting point before the expansion.

The Two Rules Compared

Under a fixed-rule policy, a decrease in aggregate demand puts real GDP below potential GDP, where it remains until either a fall in the money wage rate or a subsequent increase in aggregate demand restores full employment. Similarly, an increase in aggregate demand puts real GDP above potential GDP, where it remains until either a rise in the money wage rate or a subsequent decrease in aggregate demand restores full employment.

Under a feedback-rule policy, the economy is pulled out of a recessionary gap or an inflationary gap by a policy action. There is no need to wait for an adjustment in the money wage rate—which everyone agrees takes a long time—for full employment to be restored.

Real GDP decreases and increases by the same amounts under the two policies, but real GDP stays below potential GDP and above potential GDP for longer with a fixed rule than it does with the feedback rule.

Are Feedback Rules Better?

Isn't it obvious that a feedback rule is better than a fixed rule? Can't the Fed use feedback rules to keep the economy close to full employment with a stable price level? Of course, unforecasted events—such as a collapse in business confidence—will hit the economy from time to time. But by responding with a change in the quantity of money and the interest rate, can't the Fed minimize the damage from such a shock?

Despite the apparent superiority of a feedback rule, many economists remain convinced that a fixed rule stabilizes aggregate demand more effectively than does a feedback rule. These economists assert that fixed rules are better than feedback rules because

- Potential GDP is not known.
- Policy lags are longer than the forecast horizon.
- Feedback-rule policies are less predictable than fixed-rule policies.

Keynesian activist
An economist who believes that fluctuations in investment are the main source of economic fluctuations and who advocates interest rate cuts when real GDP falls below potential GDP and interest rate hikes when real GDP exceeds potential GDP.

Let's look at these assertions.

Knowledge of Potential GDP   To decide whether a feedback-rule policy needs to stimulate or retard aggregate demand, it is necessary to determine whether real GDP is currently above or below potential GDP. But potential GDP is not known with certainty. It depends on a large number of factors, one of which is the level of employment when unemployment is at the natural unemployment rate. But with uncertainty and disagreement about how the labor market works, we can only estimate the natural unemployment rate. As a result, there is often uncertainty about the direction in which a feedback policy should be pushing the level of aggregate demand.

Policy Lags and the Forecast Horizon   The effects of policy actions taken today are spread out over the following two years or even more. But no one is able to forecast accurately that far ahead. The forecast horizon—the distance into the future that forecasters can see—is less than a year. Further, the Fed can't predict the precise timing and magnitude of the effects of its policy actions. So feedback-rule policies that react to today's economy might be inappropriate for the state of the economy at that uncertain future date when the policy's effects are felt.

Predictability of Policies   To make decisions about long-term contracts for employment (wage contracts) and for borrowing and lending, people must anticipate the future course of the price level—the future inflation rate. To forecast the inflation rate, it is necessary to forecast aggregate demand. And to forecast aggregate demand, it is necessary to forecast the Fed's policy actions.

If the Fed sticks to a rock-steady, fixed rule for money growth rate, then policy is predictable and it does not contribute to unexpected fluctuations in aggregate demand.

In contrast, if the Fed pursues a feedback rule, there is more scope for the policy actions to be unpredictable. The main reason is that feedback rules are not written down for all to see. Rather, they have to be inferred from the Fed's behavior. So with a feedback-rule policy, it is necessary to predict the variables to which the Fed reacts and the extent to which it reacts. Consequently, a feedback rule for monetary policy can create more unpredictable fluctuations in aggregate demand than a fixed rule can.

We reviewed three reasons why feedback-rule policies might not be more effective than fixed-rule policies in controlling aggregate demand. But there is a fourth reason why some economists prefer fixed rules: Not all shocks to the economy are on the demand side. Advocates of feedback rules generally believe that most fluctuations do come from aggregate demand. Some advocates of fixed rules believe that aggregate supply fluctuations are the dominant ones. Let's now see how aggregate supply fluctuations affect the economy under a fixed rule and under a feedback rule. We will also see why those economists who believe that aggregate supply fluctuations are the dominant ones also favor a fixed rule rather than a feedback rule.

■ Stabilizing Aggregate Supply Shocks

Everyone agrees that the economy is sometimes hit by an aggregate supply shock. There is disagreement about how frequent and important these supply shocks are. But there is no disagreement about the effect on aggregate supply of a change in the world oil price. In 1974, when the world oil price increased from $2 a barrel to $10 a barrel, the global economy experienced a severe negative supply shock. A further negative supply shock occurred in 1980 and 1981 when the world oil price jumped first to $26 a barrel and then to $32 a barrel. Positive supply shocks occurred during the 1980s as the world oil price fell back to around $13 a barrel. Price hikes to more than $60 a barrel in 2005 delivered another negative shock to aggregate supply.

To see the effects of supply shocks and the policy to stabilize them, we'll again start out at full employment with no inflation. Figure 33.4 illustrates an economy with aggregate demand curve AD and aggregate supply curve AS_0. The price level is 110, and real GDP is $10 trillion, which is also potential GDP.

The world oil price jumps and aggregate supply decreases. The aggregate supply curve shifts leftward, to AS_1 in Figure 33.4. The aggregate supply curve, AS_1, intersects the aggregate demand curve, AD, at a price level of 113 and real GDP of $9.9 trillion. The economy is in a recession. Real GDP is less than potential GDP, and unemployment is above the natural unemployment rate.

At some later time, when world oil production increases, the world price of oil will fall to its original level and aggregate supply will return from AS_1 to AS_0. In the meantime, while aggregate supply is at AS_1, the course of real GDP and the price level depend on the stabilization policy that is pursued. We'll again work out how the economy responds under a fixed rule and under a feedback rule.

FIGURE 33.4

A Decrease in Aggregate Supply Brings Recession

Initially, the economy is at full employment. The price level is 110 and real GDP equals potential GDP at $10 trillion.

A decrease in aggregate supply shifts the aggregate supply curve leftward from AS_0 to AS_1. The economy goes into recession. Real GDP decreases to $9.9 trillion, and the price level rises to 113.

Fixed Rule

Under a fixed-rule policy, the decrease in aggregate supply has no effect on aggregate demand. Real GDP decreases in a recession as the economy moves from point A to point B in Figure 33.5(a). With a recessionary gap and unemployment above the natural unemployment rate, the money wage rate gradually falls. The falling money wage rate increases aggregate supply and shifts the aggregate supply curve from AS_1 toward AS_0. Real GDP gradually returns to potential GDP as the economy moves from point B back to point A.

Feedback Rule

Under a Keynesian activist feedback rule, when the economy is at point B in Figure 33.5(b), the Fed reacts to the recessionary gap by increasing the quantity of money and cutting the interest rate. This policy action gradually increases aggregate demand and shifts the aggregate demand curve from AD_0 toward AD_1. Real GDP increases toward potential GDP but at a higher price level, as the economy moves from point B to point C. The feedback rule we just studied aims to return real GDP to potential GDP. But it is also possible to have a feedback rule that aims to return the price level to the initial price. We study this topic in the next section.

FIGURE 33.5

Stabilization Policies: Aggregate Supply Shocks

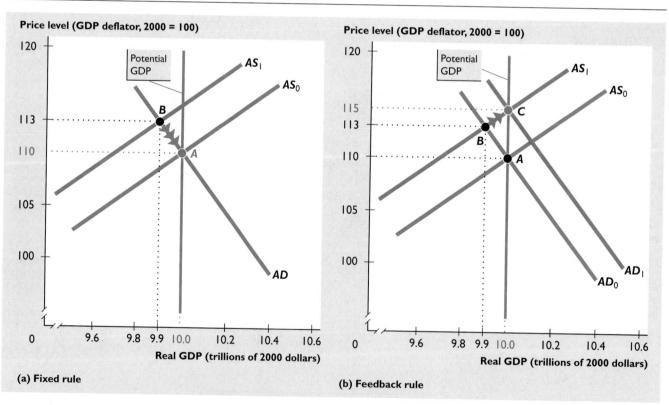

(a) Fixed rule

(b) Feedback rule

A fixed-rule policy leaves real GDP and the price level to gradually return from B to A as the money wage rate falls in part (a).

A feedback-rule policy tries to restore full employment as quickly as possible, moving from B to C in part (b).

CHECKPOINT 33.2

2 **Explain the rules-versus-discretion debate and compare Keynesian and monetarist policy rules.**

Practice Problem 33.2

1. The economy shown in Figure 1 is initially on aggregate demand curve AD_0 and aggregate supply curve AS. Then aggregate demand decreases, and the aggregate demand curve shifts leftward to AD_1.
   a. What are the initial equilibrium real GDP and price level?
   b. If the decrease in aggregate demand is temporary and the Fed adopts a fixed-rule policy, what happens to real GDP and the price level?
   c. If the decrease in aggregate demand is temporary and the Fed adopts a feedback-rule policy, what happens to real GDP and the price level?
   d. If the decrease in aggregate demand is permanent and the Fed adopts a fixed-rule policy, what happens to real GDP and the price level?

FIGURE 1

Exercises 33.2

1. The economy shown in Figure 2 is initially on aggregate demand curve AD_0 and aggregate supply curve AS. Then aggregate demand increases, and the aggregate demand curve shifts rightward to AD_2. What happens to real GDP and the price level if the increase in aggregate demand is
   a. Temporary and the Fed adopts a fixed-rule policy?
   b. Temporary and the Fed adopts a feedback-rule policy?
   c. Permanent and the Fed adopts a fixed-rule policy?
   d. Permanent and the Fed adopts a feedback-rule policy?

2. Compare the price level fluctuations if the Fed adopts a feedback-rule policy or a fixed-rule policy in response to a positive aggregate supply shock.

FIGURE 2

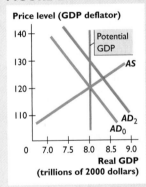

Solution to Practice Problem 33.2

1a. Initially, ❶ real GDP is $8 trillion, and the price level is 120 (Figure 3).

1b. ❷ Real GDP decreases to $7.8 trillion, and the price level falls to 118. If the shock is temporary, then the aggregate demand curve will shift rightward to AD_0, real GDP will return to $8 trillion, and the price level will rise to 120 (Figure 3).

1c. ❶ Real GDP remains at $8 trillion, and the price level remains at 120. The Fed will increase the quantity of money to keep the aggregate demand curve at AD_0. As the shock goes away, the Fed will decrease the quantity of money to keep the aggregate demand curve at AD_0 (Figure 3).

1d. ❶ Real GDP decreases to $7.8 trillion, and the price level falls to 118 (Figure 4). Unemployment exceeds the natural unemployment rate, so after some time, the money wage rate will start to fall. ❷ Real GDP will increase to $8 trillion, and the price level will fall to 115 (Figure 4).

FIGURE 3

FIGURE 4

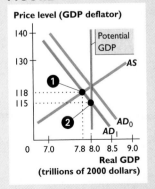

33.3 ALTERNATIVE POLICY TARGETS

Shocks to aggregate demand and aggregate supply bring fluctuations in real GDP and the price level (and inflation rate). We've just examined stabilization policies that target real GDP and aim to keep it as close as possible to potential GDP. But should policy target real GDP or inflation?

■ Real GDP Versus Inflation

When real GDP fluctuates around potential GDP, the unemployment rate also fluctuates around its natural rate. So targeting real GDP is equivalent to targeting the unemployment rate. Aiming to keep real GDP equal to potential GDP is the same as aiming to keep the unemployment rate equal to the natural unemployment rate.

When real GDP is below potential GDP, the economy is in a recessionary gap, output is lost, and jobs are hard to find. So if monetary policy can close a recessionary gap, people become better off.

When real GDP is above potential GDP, the economy is in an inflationary gap, resources are overworked, and inefficient plant breakdowns and bottlenecks arise. Also, inflation increases, which brings its own costs. So if monetary policy can close an inflationary gap, people become better off.

If aggregate demand shocks were the only source of economic fluctuations, the choice of a target for monetary policy would be easy: Stabilize aggregate demand. By doing so, real GDP would remain close to potential GDP, and the inflation rate would be as stable as possible.

But aggregate supply shocks also bring economic fluctuations. And this fact poses a problem for monetary policy. How should monetary policy try to influence aggregate demand when aggregate supply changes?

Two extreme targets for monetary policy are

- Real GDP
- The price level

Real GDP Target

If monetary policy targets real GDP, it seeks to neutralize the effects of aggregate supply shocks on real GDP. That is, an increase in aggregate supply is met by a decrease in aggregate demand; and a decrease in aggregate supply is countered by an increase in aggregate demand.

Figure 33.6(a) illustrates real GDP targeting. The blue band is the real GDP target. If aggregate supply is AS_0, monetary policy aims to place the aggregate demand curve (not shown) through point A. Here, real GDP is on target at $10 trillion and the price level is 110.

If aggregate supply increases to AS_1, monetary policy aims to *decrease* aggregate demand and place the aggregate demand curve through point B. Here, real GDP remains on target at $10 trillion but the price level falls to 107—deflation. If aggregate supply decreases to AS_2, monetary policy aims to *increase* aggregate demand and place the aggregate demand curve through point C. Again, real GDP remains on target at $10 trillion, but the price level now rises to 113—inflation.

You can see that in the face of shocks to aggregate supply, stabilizing real GDP means destabilizing the price level and inflation rate.

FIGURE 33.6

Alternative Monetary Policy Targets

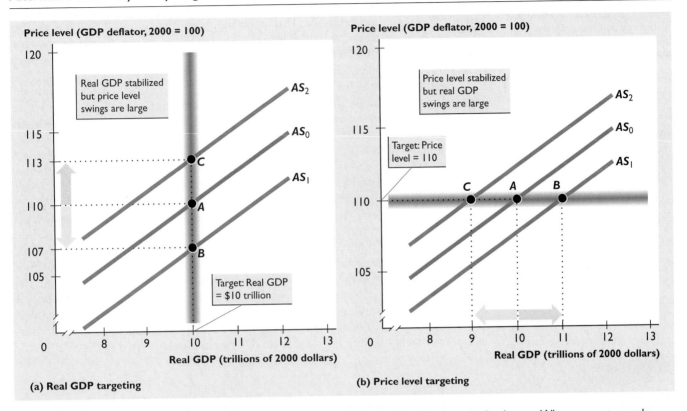

(a) Real GDP targeting

(b) Price level targeting

The blue band is the real GDP target. When aggregate supply increases from AS_0 to AS_1 or decreases from AS_0 to AS_2, monetary policy aims to change aggregate demand to keep real GDP on target at $10 trillion.

The blue band is the price level target. When aggregate supply increases from AS_0 to AS_1 or decreases from AS_0 to AS_2, monetary policy aims to change aggregate demand to keep the price level on target at 110.

Price Level Target

If monetary policy targets the price level, an increase in aggregate supply is met by an *increase* in aggregate demand; a decrease in aggregate supply is countered by a *decrease* in aggregate demand.

Figure 33.6(b) shows the outcome if monetary policy targets the price level. The blue band is now the price level target. If aggregate supply is AS_0, monetary policy aims to place the aggregate demand curve (not shown) through point A. Here, the price level is on target at 110 and real GDP is $10 trillion.

If aggregate supply increases to AS_1, monetary policy aims to *increase* aggregate demand and place the aggregate demand curve through point B. Here, the price level remains on target at 110 but real GDP increases to $11 trillion.

If aggregate supply decreases to AS_2, monetary policy aims to *decrease* aggregate demand and place the aggregate demand curve through point C. Again, the price level remains on target at 110 but real GDP decreases to $9 trillion.

You can see that in the face of shocks to aggregate supply, stabilizing the price level means destabilizing real GDP.

■ Inflation Targeting

Inflation targeting
A monetary policy framework that combines an announced target range for the inflation rate with the publication of the central bank's economic forecasts and analysis.

Inflation targeting is a monetary policy framework that combines an announced target range for the inflation rate with the publication of the central bank's economic forecasts and analysis. This approach was first adopted in 1988 by the Reserve Bank of New Zealand. Since then, it has come into widespread use (see *Eye on the Global Economy* below) and is considered by most economists who specialize in monetary policy analysis to be the best-practice monetary policy.

Despite its name, inflation targeting is not strict targeting of the inflation rate (or price level). Rather, it is an attempt to stabilize output and employment while maintaining an unwavering commitment to keeping inflation firmly inside an announced target range.

The main idea behind inflation targeting is that by announcing a target and openly explaining the reasons for each policy action, a central bank can better maintain low and stable inflation, which not only enhances economic efficiency and promotes economic growth but also anchors inflation expectations. When inflation expectations are stable, the money wage rate and aggregate supply fluctuate less, which in turn makes it easier to stabilize output and inflation.

Should the Fed join the inflation-targeting central banks? Many economists think such a move would improve U.S. monetary policy. It is noteworthy that none of the nations that have adopted inflation targets have abandoned the approach. They see it as working well. If the Fed did adopt inflation targeting, it would quantify its inflation target and regularly publish its forecasts and analysis of the economic outlook. It might also go public on the weights (relative importance) it attaches to inflation and real GDP fluctuations.

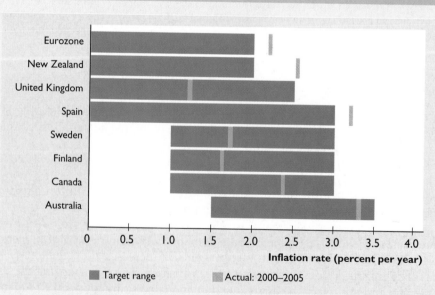

EYE ON THE GLOBAL ECONOMY

Inflation Targeting Around the World

Seven advanced economies and the Euro area have inflation targets (green bars) designed to anchor inflation expectations. Most inflation targets have been achieved (orange), which makes it easier for the central bank to stabilize both the inflation rate and real GDP.

SOURCES OF DATA: National central banks and World Economic Outlook database, April 2005.

EYE ON THE U.S. ECONOMY

The Fed's Targeting and the Taylor Rule

The Fed's objective is to maintain low inflation because that is the best contribution that it can make to achieving sustained long-term growth of real GDP. But the Fed also tries to minimize deviations of real GDP from potential GDP.

John Taylor, an economics professor at Stanford University and formerly Undersecretary of the Treasury for International Affairs in the George W. Bush administration, has proposed a feedback-rule policy that would deliver a better performance than what the Fed has achieved.

The Taylor rule adjusts the federal funds rate according to whether the inflation rate exceeds its target and whether real GDP exceeds potential GDP and places equal weights on inflation and real GDP.

John B. Taylor

SOURCES OF DATA: Federal Reserve Board and Federal Reserve Bank of St Louis.

The figure shows that the Fed has made the federal funds rate fluctuate more than it would if the Taylor rule were followed and that the interest rate was too low from 2001 to 2005.

REALITY CHECK

Policy Debates in YOUR Life

You have recently witnessed a change of guard at the Fed. In 2006, Ben Bernanke succeeded Alan Greenspan as Fed chairman. Chairman Greenspan was credited with keeping inflation in check and avoiding serious recession. Will Chairman Bernanke be as successful? Before his appointment as Fed chairman, Ben Bernanke said that he wanted the United States to set an inflation target. What do you think is best for the United States? Should the Fed announce an inflation target as Ben Bernanke and many other economists have suggested? Follow the debate in the media about the effects that Ben Bernanke might have or that commentators hope he will have on Fed policy.

3 Assess whether policy should target the inflation rate rather than real GDP.

Practice Problems 33.3

1. When a positive aggregate supply shock occurs, the Fed reacts by adjusting its monetary policy. Explain the effect of the Fed's action on real GDP and the price level if the Fed targets
   a. The price level.
   b. Real GDP.

2. The inflation rate is 3 percent a year and potential GDP is $12 trillion. Aggregate supply decreases, and the Fed decides that it wants to keep the inflation rate between 1 percent and 5 percent a year and real GDP within the range $11.9 trillion to $12.1 trillion.
   a. Is the Fed placing more weight on inflation or on real GDP?
   b. What actions will the Fed take?

Exercises 33.3

1. When a negative aggregate supply shock occurs, the Fed reacts by adjusting its monetary policy. Explain the effect of the Fed's action on real GDP and the price level if the Fed targets
   a. Real GDP.
   b. The price level.

2. The inflation rate is 4 percent a year, and potential GDP is $11 trillion. Faced with a world recession, the Fed decides that it wants to keep the inflation rate between 4 percent and 5 percent a year and real GDP at $11 trillion.
   a. Is the Fed placing more weight on inflation or on real GDP?
   b. What actions will the Fed take?

Solutions to Practice Problems 33.3

1a. If the Fed targets the price level, the price level will remain steady, and real GDP will increase.
1b. If the Fed targets real GDP and adjusts the quantity of money to remove any output gap, real GDP remains at potential GDP, and the price level falls.

2a. The Fed is placing more weight on real GDP. A deviation from potential GDP of $12 trillion by $0.1 trillion is less than a 1 percent deviation. The Fed is willing to tolerate a much larger spread in inflation.
2b. When aggregate supply decreases, the Fed will cut the interest rate to increase aggregate demand and keep real GDP inside its target range.

CHAPTER CHECKPOINT

Key Points

1 **Discuss whether fiscal policy or monetary policy is the better stabilization tool.**

- The demand for money and investment demand determine the effects of monetary policy and fiscal policy on aggregate demand. Both policy tools affect aggregate demand.

- Monetary policy has less conflict among its goals than does fiscal policy and is the more flexible.

- Monetary policy and automatic fiscal policy are the preferred tools for stabilizing aggregate demand in normal times.

2 **Explain the rules-versus-discretion debate and compare Keynesian and monetarist policy rules.**

- In the face of a shock to aggregate demand or aggregate supply, a fixed-rule policy takes no action. Real GDP and the price level fluctuate.

- In the face of a shock to aggregate demand or aggregate supply, a feedback-rule policy takes offsetting action. An ideal feedback rule keeps the economy at full employment, with a stable price level.

- Some economists say that a feedback rule creates fluctuations because it requires greater knowledge of the economy than we have, operates with time lags that extend beyond the forecast horizon, and introduces unpredictability about policy reactions.

3 **Assess whether policy should target the inflation rate rather than real GDP.**

- If monetary policy targets real GDP, aggregate demand and aggregate supply change in opposite directions, and price level fluctuations increase.

- If monetary policy targets the price level, aggregate supply and aggregate demand change in the same direction.

- Stabilizing real GDP destabilizes the price level and destabilizes the expected price level, so it makes aggregate supply *less* stable. So price level targeting might deliver more stable real GDP than real GDP targeting.

- Inflation targeting attempts to stabilize real GDP and keep inflation inside an announced target range.

Key Terms

Discretionary monetary policy, 840
Feedback-rule policy, 840
Fixed-rule policy, 840

Inflation targeting, 850
Keynesian activist, 843
Liquidity trap, 837

Monetarist, 842

(X) myeconlab **Exercises**

1. Describe the steps in the transmission of monetary policy and fiscal policy and explain why the conditions that make monetary policy highly effective make fiscal policy ineffective and the conditions that make fiscal policy highly effective make monetary policy ineffective.

2. Draw graphs to illustrate the conditions under which
   a. Fiscal policy is highly effective and monetary policy is ineffective.
   b. Monetary policy is highly effective and fiscal policy is ineffective.
   c. Monetary policy and fiscal policy are equally effective.

3. For the Fed to stabilize aggregate demand, what does the Fed have to be able to accurately predict?

4. What are the goals of discretionary fiscal policy? Why does discretionary fiscal policy create goal conflicts? Why does monetary policy not have the goal conflicts of discretionary fiscal policy?

5. Why is monetary policy more flexible than fiscal policy?

6. Define and distinguish among discretionary monetary policy, a fixed-rule policy, and a feedback-rule policy. Provide examples of each type of policy.

7. As the U.S. economy went into recession in 2001, the Fed repeatedly lowered the federal funds interest rate.
   a. Would you describe the Fed's actions as a feedback-rule policy or a fixed-rule policy?
   b. What do you predict the effects of the Fed's policies would be on real GDP and the price level?

8. Coinciding with the U.S. economy entering recession in 2001, Congress passed some tax cuts and voted to increase expenditure on homeland security.
   a. Would you describe the Congress's actions as a feedback-rule policy, a fixed-rule policy, or neither?
   b. What do you predict the effects of Congress's actions would be on real GDP and the price level?

9. Explain why a Keynesian activist feedback rule for monetary policy could create more fluctuations in aggregate demand than a monetarist fixed-rule policy creates.

10. Which type of monetary or fiscal stabilization policy requires accurate knowledge of the value of potential GDP? Explain why.
    a. A feedback-rule policy that targets real GDP.
    b. A fixed-rule policy that targets real GDP.
    c. A feedback-rule policy that targets the price level.
    d. A fixed-rule policy that targets the price level.

11. The U.S. economy is at full employment when it is hit by a positive aggregate supply shock. Explain how the U.S. price level and real GDP will change in the short run and the long run if the Fed adopts

   a. A feedback-rule policy that targets real GDP.
   b. A feedback-rule policy that targets the price level.
   c. A fixed-rule policy.

12. The U.S. economy is at full employment when it is hit by a negative aggregate supply shock. Explain how the U.S. price level and real GDP will change in the short run and the long run if the Fed adopts
   a. A feedback-rule policy that targets real GDP.
   b. A feedback-rule policy that targets the price level.
   c. A fixed-rule policy.

13. The U.S. economy is at full employment when it is hit by a positive aggregate demand shock. Explain how the U.S. price level and real GDP will change in the short run and the long run if the Fed adopts
   a. A feedback-rule policy that targets real GDP.
   b. A feedback-rule policy that targets the price level.
   c. A fixed-rule policy.

14. The U.S. economy is at full employment when it is hit by a negative aggregate demand shock. Explain how the U.S. price level and real GDP will change in the short run and the long run if the Fed adopts
   a. A feedback-rule policy that targets real GDP.
   b. A feedback-rule policy that targets the price level.
   c. A fixed-rule policy.

15. In a deep recession, the Fed, Congress, and the White House are discussing ways of restoring full employment. The President wants to stimulate aggregate demand but to do so in a way that will give the best chance of boosting investment and long-term economic growth. Explain which of the following actions would best meet the President's objectives and which would present the greatest obstacles to those objectives.
   a. A tax cut.
   b. An increase in government expenditure.
   c. An increase in the quantity of money and a cut in the federal funds rate.

16. What are the arguments for and against monetary policy targeting
   a. Real GDP?
   b. The price level?
   c. The inflation rate?

17. Inflation is rising toward 5 percent a year, and the Fed, Congress, and the White House are discussing ways of containing inflation without damaging employment and output. The President wants to cut aggregate demand but to do so in a way that will give the best chance of keeping investment high to encourage long-term economic growth. Explain which of the following actions would best meet the President's objectives and which would present the greatest obstacles to those objectives.
   a. A tax increase.
   b. A decrease in government expenditure.
   c. A decrease in the quantity of money and an increase in the federal funds rate.

Critical Thinking

18. All things considered, do you think the Fed should stabilize the economy with no help from fiscal policy or do you think fiscal policy should seek to stabilize the economy and the Fed should concentrate on keeping inflation low?

19. Do you think it likely that a Keynesian activist feedback rule for monetary policy would create more fluctuations in aggregate demand than a monetarist fixed rule would? Why or why not?

20. Describe and evaluate the Taylor rule for monetary policy.
    a. Why do you think the Fed doesn't follow this rule?
    b. Why do you think the Fed makes the federal funds rate fluctuate by more than it would if the Taylor rule were followed?
    c. Do you think the Fed places more weight on real GDP fluctuations or more weight on the inflation rate than the equal weights of the Taylor rule?

Web Exercises

Use the links on MyEconLab to work the following exercises.

21. Visit the Web sites of the Bank of Canada and Statistics Canada. Find the Canadian price level, inflation rate, and target inflation rate for the current year.
    a. What is the Bank of Canada's target for the inflation rate?
    b. If the Bank of Canada achieves its target, show on a graph the path of the Canadian price level.
    c. What might force the Bank of Canada to abandon its inflation target?

22. Visit the Web site of the International Monetary Fund (IMF). When the economies of Indonesia, Korea, Thailand, Malaysia, and the Philippines entered into recession in 1997, the IMF made loans but only on condition that the recipients of the loans increase interest rates, raise taxes, and cut government expenditures.
    a. Would you describe the IMF prescription as a feedback-rule policy or a fixed-rule policy?
    b. What do you predict the immediate effects of the IMF policies would be on real GDP and the price level?

23. Visit the Web site of the Bureau of Economic Analysis and obtain data on real GDP since 1990. Then visit the Web site of the Congressional Budget Office and obtain data on its estimates of potential GDP.
    a. Use a spreadsheet program to calculate the size of the recessionary and inflationary gap each quarter since 1990.
    b. In which periods do you think policy was seeking to stimulate aggregate demand and in which periods was policy seeking to restrain aggregate demand?

24. Visit the Web site of the Federal Reserve and obtain data on the federal funds rate since 1990. Compare and comment on the movements in the federal funds rate in relation to the predictions you made in part **b** of exercise 23.

International Trade

CHAPTER CHECKLIST

When you have completed your study of this chapter, you will be able to

1 Describe the patterns and trends in international trade.

2 Explain why nations engage in international trade and why trade benefits all nations.

3 Explain how trade barriers reduce international trade.

4 Explain the arguments used to justify trade barriers and show why these arguments are incorrect but also why some barriers are hard to remove.

We live in a global economy, but wages in most nations are lower than wages in the United States. How can we compete with countries that pay their workers a fraction of U.S. wages?

Would it be better if we isolated our economy from the rest of the world? Or are there some gains from trading with other nations that are worth the macroeconomic disturbances and international competition that they bring?

In this chapter, you are going to learn about international trade. You will discover how all nations can gain by specializing in producing the goods and services in which they have a comparative advantage and trading with other countries. You will discover that all countries can compete, no matter how high their wages are. And you'll learn why, despite the fact that international trade brings benefits to all countries, they nevertheless restrict trade.

34.1 TRADE PATTERNS AND TRENDS

The goods and services that we buy from people in other countries are called *imports*. The goods and services that we sell to people in other countries are called *exports*. What are the most important things that we import and export?

■ U.S. Exports and Imports

Most people would probably guess that a rich nation such as the United States imports raw materials and exports manufactured goods. Although that is one feature of U.S. international trade, it is not its most important feature. The vast bulk of U.S. exports and imports are manufactured goods and services. We sell to other countries automobiles, airplanes, supercomputers, scientific equipment, and financial, insurance, and education services. And we buy from other countries DVD players, T-shirts, and technical and professional services. See *Eye on the Global Economy* (p. 859) for the relative importance of broad categories of U.S. international trade.

Trade in Goods

In 2004, manufactured goods accounted for 54 percent of U.S. exports and for 66 percent of U.S. imports. Minerals and fuels accounted for 2 percent of U.S. exports and for 12 percent of U.S. imports, and agricultural products accounted for only 5 percent of U.S. exports and 3 percent of U.S. imports. The largest U.S. export *and* import item in 2004 (and for many years) was automobiles and auto parts.

But goods accounted for only 70 percent of U.S. exports and 83 percent of U.S. imports in 2004. The rest of U.S. international trade was in services.

Trade in Services

You might be wondering how a country can export and import services. Here are some examples.

If you take a vacation in France and travel there on an Air France flight from New York, the United States imports transportation services from France. The money you spend in France on hotel bills and restaurant meals is also classified as a U.S. import of services. Similarly, the vacation taken by a French student in the United States counts as a U.S. export of services to France.

When we import TV sets from South Korea, the owner of the ship that transports them might be Greek and the company that insures them might be British. The payments that we make for the transportation and insurance are U.S. imports of services. Similarly, when a U.S. shipping company transports California wine to Tokyo, the transportation cost is a U.S. export of a service to Japan. U.S. international trade in these types of services is large and growing.

■ The Outsourcing Trend

In 1960, we exported 5 percent of total output and imported 4 percent of the goods and services that we bought. By 2005, these percentages had jumped to 10.5 for exports and 16 for imports. Some of the increase arises from what has come to be called *offshore outsourcing*—buying a good or services from a lower-cost overseas supplier. This activity has received a lot of public attention as jobs have been lost in services such as data processing, computer programming, customer support, and telemarketing to providers in places as far afield as India and Ireland.

The Major Items That We Trade with Other Nations

The figure shows the U.S. volume of trade and balance of trade for the 20 largest traded items in 2004. If a bar has more red (imports) than blue (exports), the United States has a trade deficit in that item.

The largest traded item is automobiles and parts. Other private services (education and technical services are examples), fuels, consumer durables (TV sets, DVD players, and kitchen equipment are examples) travel, computers, and aircraft and parts are also large traded items. Notice that other private services and travel are larger than most goods.

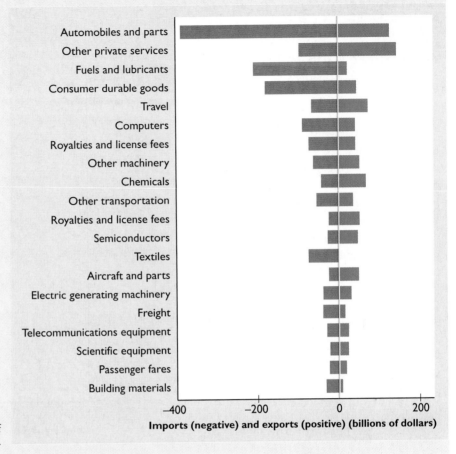

Imports (negative) and exports (positive) (billions of dollars)

SOURCE OF DATA: Bureau of Economic Analysis.

◼ Trading Partners and Trade Agreements

The United States has trading links with every part of the world and is a member of the World Trade Organization (or WTO), an organization that seeks to promote free international trade. The United States has also negotiated trade agreements with several individual countries and with some regional groups of countries.

U.S. Trading Partners

Canada is the United States' biggest trading partner. Mexico and China are the next biggest and almost equal. Our other large trading partners are Japan, Germany, and the United Kingdom. But we also have significant volumes of trade with the other rapidly expanding Asian economies such as South Korea, Taiwan, Singapore, and Hong Kong. *Eye on the Global Economy* on p. 860 shows the data for our 17 largest trading partners.

Trade Agreements

Trade agreements are treaties between two countries (called bilateral agreements) or among a number of countries (called multilateral agreements) designed to promote greater trade and economic cooperation, and sometimes, additionally, to promote political and social goals. The United States has entered into bilateral trade agreements with Australia, Bahrain, Chile, Israel, Jordon, Morocco, Oman,

The Major U.S. Trading Partners and Volumes of Trade

The figure shows the U.S. volume of trade and balance of trade with its 17 largest trading partners in 2004. If a bar has more red (imports) than blue (exports), the United States has a trade deficit with that country.

Canada is the major trading partner of the United States by a big margin. Mexico comes next. China overtook Japan in 2003 to take the third place. Of the newly industrialized countries of Asia, South Korea and Taiwan have much more trade with the United States than do Singapore and Hong Kong. Trade with Germany and the United Kingdom is large.

SOURCE OF DATA: Bureau of Economic Analysis.

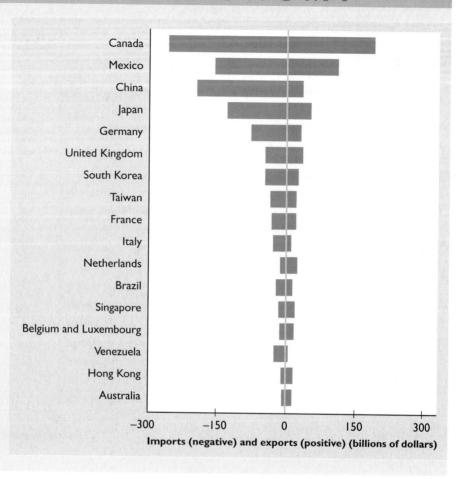

Imports (negative) and exports (positive) (billions of dollars)

Singapore, and Thailand. And the United States is a member of three multilateral regional groups that arise from the North American Free Trade Agreement, the Central American Free Trade Agreement, and Asia-Pacific Economic Cooperation. A larger Free Trade Area of the Americas is a possible future development.

North American Free Trade Agreement (NAFTA)   NAFTA is an agreement among the United States, Canada, and Mexico to make trade among the three countries easier and freer. This agreement came into effect in 1994. During the years since then, trade among these three nations has expanded rapidly.

Central American Free Trade Agreement (CAFTA)   CAFTA is a comprehensive trade agreement between Costa Rica, the Dominican Republic, El Salvador, Guatemala, Honduras, Nicaragua, and the United States. The agreement has both trade and political goals, the latter to promote freedom and democracy in Central America.

Asia-Pacific Economic Cooperation (APEC)   APEC is a group of 21 nations that border the Pacific Ocean. The largest of these are the United States, China, and Japan, but other significant members are Australia, Canada, Indonesia, and the dynamic new industrial Asian economies. The APEC nations conduct 50 percent of world trade.

Free Trade Area of the Americas (FTAA)   The American continents consist of 35 nations, and the governments of the 34 democracies (which exclude Cuba) have begun a Free Trade Area of the Americas process. The objective of this process is to achieve free international trade among all the nations of the Americas.

■ Balance of Trade and International Borrowing

The value of exports minus the value of imports is called the **balance of trade**. In 2005, the United States imported more than it exported. When a country imports more than it exports, it has a trade deficit and pays by borrowing from foreigners or selling some of its assets. When a country exports more than it imports, it has a trade surplus and lends to other countries or buys more foreign assets to enable the rest of the world to pay its trade deficit.

Balance of trade
The value of exports minus the value of imports.

CHECKPOINT 34.1

1   **Describe the patterns and trends in international trade.**

Practice Problem 34.1

1.   Use the spreadsheet on MyEconLab to answer the following questions:
   a. In 1990, what percentage of Canadian production was exported to the United States and what percentage of total goods and services bought by Canadians was imported from the United States?
   b. In 2005, what percentage of Canadian production was exported to the United States and what percentage of total goods and services bought by Canadians was imported from the United States?

Exercise 34.1

1.   Use the spreadsheet on MyEconLab to answer the following questions:
   a. In 1990, what percentage of Mexican production was exported to the United States and what percentage of total goods and services bought by Mexicans was imported from the United States?
   b. In 2005, what percentage of Mexican production was exported to the United States and what percentage of total goods and services bought by Mexicans was imported from the United States?

Solution to Practice Problem 34.1

1a. In 1990, Canada exported 19 percent of total production to the United States and imported 19 percent of total goods and services purchased from the United States.
1b. In 2005, Canada exported to the United States 28 percent of total production and imported from the United States 24 percent of goods and services purchased.

Comparative advantage is the fundamental force that generates international trade. And comparative advantage arises from differences in opportunity costs. You met this idea in Chapter 3 (pp. 81–82), but we're now going to put some flesh on the bones of the basic idea. We'll begin by looking at an item that we export.

■ Why the United States Exports Airplanes

Boeing produces many more airplanes each year than airlines in the United States buy. Most of Boeing's production goes to airlines in other parts of the world. The United States is an exporter of airplanes. Why?

The answer is that the United States has a comparative advantage in the production of airplanes. The opportunity cost of producing an airplane is lower in the United States than in most other countries. So buyers can obtain airplanes from Boeing for a lower price than the price at which they could buy them from other potential suppliers. And Boeing can sell airplanes to foreigners for a higher price than it could obtain from an additional U.S. buyer.

So both countries gain. The foreign buyer gains from lower-priced airplanes. And Boeing's stockholders, managers, and workers gain from higher-priced airplanes. A win-win situation!

Figure 34.1 illustrates the effects of international trade in airplanes. The demand curve *D* shows the demand for airplanes in the United States. This curve tells us the quantity of airplanes that U.S. airlines are willing to buy at various prices. The demand curve also tells us the most that an additional airplane is worth to a U.S. airline at each quantity.

The supply curve *S* shows the supply of airplanes in the United States. This curve tells us the quantity of airplanes that U.S. aircraft makers are willing to sell at various prices. The supply curve also tells us the opportunity cost of producing an additional airplane at each quantity.

No Trade

First, let's see what happens in the market for airplanes if there is no international trade. Figure 34.1(a) shows the situation. The airplane market is in equilibrium when 400 airplanes are produced by U.S. aircraft makers and bought by U.S. airlines. The price is $80 million an airplane.

Trade

Second, let's see what happens in the market for airplanes if international trade takes place. Figure 34.1(b) shows the situation. The price of an airplane is determined in the world market, not the U.S. domestic market. Suppose that world demand and world supply determine a world equilibrium price of $100 million per airplane. In Figure 34.1(b), the world price line shows this price.

The U.S. demand curve, *D*, tells us that at $100 million an airplane, U.S. airlines buy 300 airplanes a year. The U.S. supply curve, *S*, tells us that at $100 million per airplane, U.S. aircraft makers produce 800 airplanes a year. So domestic production at 800 a year exceeds domestic purchases of 300 a year.

The quantity produced in the United States minus the quantity purchased by U.S. airlines is the quantity of U.S. exports, which is 500 airplanes a year.

FIGURE 34.1

An Export

(a) With no international trade

(b) With international trade

With no international trade in airplanes, **1** equilibrium at the intersection of the domestic demand and supply curves determines **2** the price at $80 million an airplane and **3** the quantity at 400 airplanes a year.

With international trade, world demand and supply determine **1** the world price, which is $100 million an airplane. **2** Domestic purchases decrease to 300 a year, and **3** domestic production increases to 800 a year; **4** 500 airplanes a year are exported.

Comparative Advantage

You can see that U.S. aircraft makers have a comparative advantage in producing airplanes by comparing the U.S. supply curve and the world price line. At the equilibrium quantity of 800 airplanes a year, the world opportunity cost of producing an airplane is $100 million. But the U.S. supply curve tells us that only the 800th airplane has an opportunity cost of $100 million. Each of the other 799 airplanes has an opportunity cost of less than $100 million.

■ Why the United States Imports T-Shirts

Americans spend more than twice as much on clothing as the value of U.S. apparel production. That is, more than half of the clothing that we buy is manufactured in other countries and imported into the United States. Why?

The answer is that the rest of the world (mainly Asia) has a comparative advantage in the production of clothes. The opportunity cost of producing a T-shirt is lower in Asia than in the United States. So buyers can obtain T-shirts from Asia for a lower price than the price at which they could buy them from U.S. garment makers. And Asian garment makers can sell T-shirts to Americans for a higher price than they could obtain from an additional Asian buyer.

So again, both countries gain. The U.S. buyer gains from lower-priced T-shirts, and Asian garment makers gain from higher-priced T-shirts. Another win-win situation!

Figure 34.2 illustrates the effects of international trade in T-shirts. Again, the demand curve *D* and the supply curve *S* show the demand and supply in the U.S. domestic market only.

The demand curve tells us the quantity of T-shirts that Americans are willing to buy at various prices. The demand curve also tells us the most that an additional T-shirt is worth to an American at each quantity.

The supply curve tells us the quantity of T-shirts that U.S. garment makers are willing to sell at various prices. The supply curve also tells us the opportunity cost of producing an additional T-shirt in the United States at each quantity.

No Trade

Again, we'll first look at a market with no international trade, shown in Figure 34.2(a). The T-shirt market is in equilibrium when 20 million shirts are produced by U.S. garment makers and bought by Americans. The price is $8 a shirt.

FIGURE 34.2

An Import

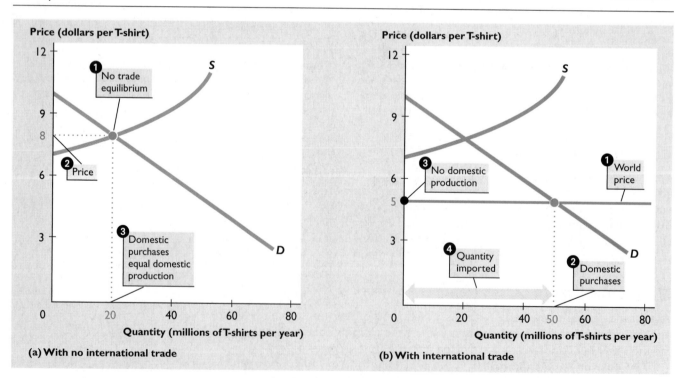

(a) With no international trade

(b) With international trade

With no international trade in T-shirts, ❶ equilibrium at the intersection of the domestic demand and supply curves determines ❷ the price at $8 a shirt and ❸ the quantity at 20 million shirts a year.

With international trade, world demand and supply determine the ❶ world price, which is $5 a shirt. ❷ Domestic purchases increase to 50 million shirts a year, and ❸ domestic production decreases to zero. ❹ The entire 50 million shirts a year are imported.

Trade

Figure 34.2(b) shows what happens in the market for T-shirts if international trade takes place. Now the price of a T-shirt is determined in the world market, not the U.S. domestic market. Suppose that world demand and world supply determine a world equilibrium price of $5 a shirt. In Figure 34.2(b), the world price line shows this price.

The U.S demand curve, *D*, tells us that at $5 a shirt, Americans buy 50 million shirts a year. The U.S. supply curve, *S*, tells us that at $5 a shirt, U.S. garment makers produce no T-shirts. So there is no domestic production, and domestic purchases are 50 million T-shirts a year. The entire quantity of T-shirts purchased in the United States is the quantity imported.

Comparative Advantage

Now you can see that Asian garment makers have a comparative advantage in producing T-shirts by comparing the U.S. supply curve and the world price line. At the equilibrium quantity of 50 million T-shirts a year, the world opportunity cost of producing a T-shirt is $5. But the U.S. supply curve tells us that no U.S. garment maker has such a low opportunity cost, not even at smaller outputs. So Asian garment makers have a comparative advantage in producing T-shirts.

■ Gains from Trade and the *PPF*

The demand and supply model that you've just studied makes it clear why we export some goods and import others. But it doesn't show directly the gains from international trade. Another way of looking at comparative advantage uses the production possibilities frontier (*PPF*) that you learned about in Chapter 3. This approach shows the gains from trade in a powerful way, as you're about to discover.

Let's explore comparative advantage using the production possibilities approach.

Production Possibilities in the United States and China

To focus on the essential idea, we'll assume that the United States can produce only two goods: airplanes and T-shirts. China can also produce only these same two goods. But production possibilities and opportunity costs are different in the two countries.

Table 34.1 shows U.S. production possibilities. If the United States uses all of its resources to produce airplanes, its output is 10 airplanes per year and no T-shirts. If it uses all of its resources to produce T-shirts, its output is 100 million T-shirts a year and no airplanes. We'll assume that the U.S. opportunity cost of producing an airplane is constant. To produce 10 airplanes, the United States must forgo 100 million T-shirts, which means that to produce 1 airplane, the United States must forgo 10 million T-shirts. That is,

The U.S. opportunity cost of producing 1 airplane is 10 million T-shirts.

Table 34.2 shows China's production possibilities. If China uses all of its resources to make airplanes, it can produce 2 airplanes a year and no T-shirts. And if it uses all of its resources to make T-shirts, it can produce 100 million T-shirts a year and no airplanes. We'll assume that China's opportunity cost of producing an

TABLE 34.1 U.S. PRODUCTION POSSIBILITIES

Item	Quantity per year
Airplane	10
T-shirt	100,000,000

TABLE 34.2 CHINA'S PRODUCTION POSSIBILITIES

Item	Quantity per year
Airplane	2
T-shirt	100,000,000

airplane is constant. To produce 2 airplanes, China must forgo 100 million T-shirts, which means that to produce 1 airplane, China must forgo 50 million T-shirts. That is,

China's opportunity cost of producing 1 airplane is 50 million T-shirts.

Figure 34.3(a) illustrates the production possibilities for the United States, and Figure 34.3(b) shows the production possibilities for China. The assumption that the opportunity costs are constant means that the two *PPFs* are linear.

We are assuming that the opportunity costs are constant so that we can illustrate the gains from trade in the simplest and cleanest way. We could assume that opportunity cost increases (as it does in Chapter 3) and we would reach the same conclusion that we'll reach here, but the story would be more complicated and the point wouldn't jump out as clearly as it does with constant opportunity costs.

Along the U.S. *PPF*, 1 airplane costs 10 million T-shirts. And along China's *PPF*, 1 airplane costs 50 million T-shirts. You can check these opportunity costs by calculating the slopes of the two *PPFs*: −10 for the U.S. *PPF* and −50 for China's *PPF*.

FIGURE 34.3
Production Possibilities in the United States and China

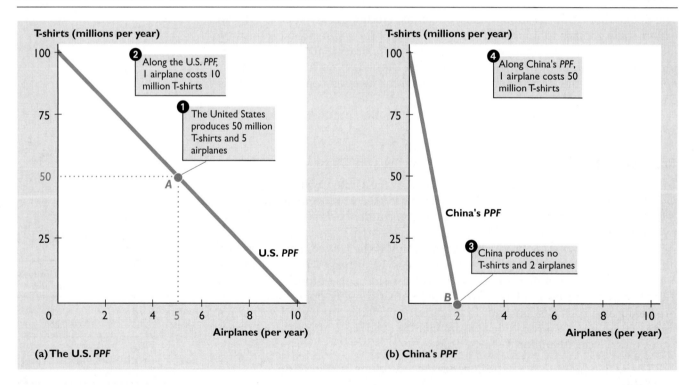

(a) The U.S. *PPF*

(b) China's *PPF*

❶ The United States produces at point *A* on its *PPF* (part a).
❷ The opportunity cost of an airplane is 10 million T-shirts.
❸ China produces at point *B* on its *PPF* (part b). ❹ The opportunity cost of an airplane is 50 million T-shirts.

The opportunity cost of an airplane is lower in the United States than in China, so the United States has a comparative advantage in producing airplanes. The opportunity cost of a T-shirt is lower in China than in the United States, so China has a comparative advantage in producing T-shirts.

No Trade

With no international trade, we'll suppose that the United States produces 5 airplanes and 50 million T-shirts at point *A* on its *PPF*. And we'll suppose that China produces 2 airplanes and no T-shirts at point *B* on its *PPF*.

Comparative Advantage

In which of the two goods does China have a comparative advantage? Recall that comparative advantage is a situation in which one nation's opportunity cost of producing a good is lower than another nation's opportunity cost of producing that same good. China has a comparative advantage in producing T-shirts. The opportunity cost of a T-shirt is 1/50,000,000 of an airplane in China and 1/10,000,000 of an airplane in the United States.

You can see China's comparative advantage by looking at the *PPFs* for China and the United States in Figure 34.3. China's *PPF* is steeper than the U.S. *PPF*. To produce an additional 1 million T-shirts, China must give up fewer airplanes than does the United States. So China's opportunity cost of a T-shirt is less than the U.S. opportunity cost of a T-shirt. This means that China has a comparative advantage in producing T-shirts.

The United States has a comparative advantage in producing airplanes. In Figure 34.3, the U.S. *PPF* is less steep than China's *PPF*. This means that the United States must give up fewer T-shirts to produce an additional airplane than does China. The U.S. opportunity cost of producing an airplane is 10 million T-shirts, which is less than China's 50 million T-shirts. So the United States has a comparative advantage in producing airplanes.

Because China has a comparative advantage in producing T-shirts and the United States has a comparative advantage in producing airplanes, both China and the United States can gain from specialization and trade. China specializes in T-shirts, and the United States specializes in airplanes.

The Gains Available from Trade

If the United States, which has a comparative advantage in producing airplanes, allocates all of its resources to that activity, it can produce 10 airplanes a year. If China, which has a comparative advantage in producing T-shirts, allocates all of its resources to that activity, it can produce 100 million T-shirts a year. By specializing, the United States and China together can produce 10 airplanes and 100 million T-shirts. With no trade, their total production had been 7 airplanes (5 from the United States and 2 from China) and 50 million T-shirts (all produced by the United States). The production of airplanes can increase by 3 and the production of T-shirts can increase by 50 million.

So both countries can end up with more of both goods. But to achieve the gains from specialization, the United States and China must trade with each other.

Achieving the Gains from Trade

Suppose that the world market price of an airplane is $100 million and that the world market price of a T-shirt is $5. Then on the world market, 1 airplane costs 20 million T-shirts.

Recall that the United States can produce an airplane at a cost of 10 million T-shirts. So by selling airplanes for 20 million T-shirts, the United States can get more T-shirts per airplane than it can by producing T-shirts. So the United States produces as many airplanes as it can and sells some in exchange for T-shirts. The United States produces 10 airplanes and no T-shirts.

Recall that China can produce an airplane at a cost of 50 million T-shirts. So by buying airplanes for 20 million T-shirts, China can get an airplane for fewer T-shirts than it can by producing airplanes. So China produces as many T-shirts as it can and sells some of them in exchange for airplanes. China produces 100 million T-shirts and no airplanes.

The quantities that people buy depend on their preferences, which influence demand. Suppose that at the world market price of 20 million T-shirts per airplane, U.S. residents and firms want to buy 60 million T-shirts and 7 airplanes. They can do so by devoting all their resources to producing airplanes and then sell 3 of these airplanes to China in exchange for T-shirts. Americans end up with 60 million T-shirts and 7 airplanes (10 produced minus 3 sold)—a gain of 10 million T-shirts and 2 airplanes. China sells 60 million T-shirts and buys 3 airplanes. The Chinese end up with 40 million T-shirts (100 million produced minus 60 million sold) and 3 airplanes—a gain of 40 million T-shirts and 1 airplane.

Figure 34.4 shows these gains from trade. The United States moves from point *A* with no trade to point *A'* with trade. China moves from point *B* to point *B'*.

As a result of specialization and trade, both countries consume outside their production possibilities frontiers and both countries gain from trade.

FIGURE 34.4
The Gains from Trade

❶ If the United States specializes in airplanes, it produces 10 a year at point *P*.

❷ If China specializes in T-shirts, it produces 100 million T-shirts a year at point *Q*.

❸ If T-shirts and airplanes are traded at 20 million T-shirts per airplane, both countries can increase their consumption of both goods and consume at points *A'* and *B'*. The gains from trade are the increases in consumption of the two countries.

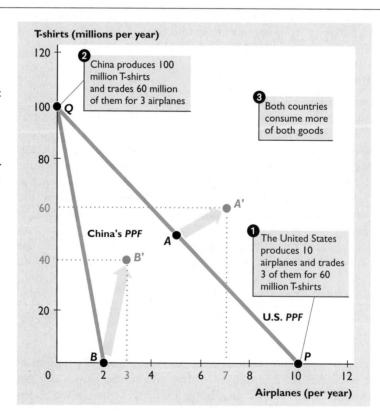

■ Offshoring and Outsourcing

If you have seen Lou Dobbs on the CNN evening news, you know that he is very concerned about what he calls "exporting America"—the phenomenon of jobs that were previously done in the United States now being done in some other country. Lou is worried about *offshoring*. What exactly is offshoring?

What Is Offshoring?

A firm in the United States can obtain the things that it sells in any of four ways:

1. Hire U.S. labor and produce in the United States.
2. Hire foreign labor and produce in other countries.
3. Buy finished goods, components, or services from other firms in the United States.
4. Buy finished goods, components, or services from other firms in other countries.

Activities 3 and 4 are **outsourcing**, and activities 2 and 4 are **offshoring**. Activity 4 is *offshore outsourcing*. Notice that offshoring includes activities that take place inside U.S. firms. If a U.S. firm opens its own facilities in another country, then it is offshoring.

Offshoring has been going on for hundreds of years. But the activity expanded rapidly and became a source of concern during the 1990s when it began to cover activities that went beyond manufacturing to include information technology services and general office services such as finance, accounting, and human resources management.

Outsourcing
A firm buying finished goods, components, or services from other firms.

Offshoring
A U.S. firm either producing in another country or outsourcing to a firm in another country.

Why Did Offshoring of Services Boom During the 1990s?

A dramatic fall in the cost of telecommunication generated the offshoring services boom of the 1990s. The gains from specialization and trade that you saw in the previous section must be large enough to make it worth incurring the costs of communication and transportation. If the cost of producing a T-shirt in China isn't lower than the cost in the United States by an amount that exceeds the cost of transporting a shirt from China to the United States, then it is more efficient to produce shirts in the United States and avoid the transportation costs.

If services are to be produced offshore, then the cost of delivering those services must be low enough to leave the buyer with an overall lower cost. Until the 1990s, the cost of communicating across large distances was too high to make the offshoring of business services efficient. But when satellites, fiber-optic cables, and computers cut the cost of a phone call between the United States and India to less than a dollar an hour, a huge base of offshore resources became competitive with similar resources in the United States.

What Are the Benefits of Offshoring?

Offshoring brings gains from trade that are identical to those of any other type of trade. We could easily change the names of the items traded from airplanes and T-shirts (the example in the previous section of this chapter) to banking services and call center services (or any other pair of services). A U.S. bank might export banking services to Indian firms, and Indians might provide call center services to U.S. firms. This type of trade would benefit both Americans and Indians provided the

United States has a comparative advantage in banking services and India has a comparative advantage in call center services.

Comparative advantages like these emerged during the 1990s. India has the world's largest educated English-speaking population and it is located at a time zone a half a day ahead of the United States, which facilitates 24×7 operations. When the cost of communicating with a worker in India was several dollars a minute, as it was before the 1990s, tapping these vast resources was just too costly. But at today's cost of a long-distance telephone call, resources in India can be used to produce services in the United States at a lower cost than those services can be produced by using resources located in the United States. And with the incomes that Indians earn from exporting services, they buy services (and goods) produced in the United States.

Why Is Offshoring a Concern?

Despite the obvious gain from specialization and trade that offshoring brings, many people believe that it also brings costs that swamp the gains. Why?

One reason is that jobs growth has slowed since 2001, which some people say is a consequence of offshoring stealing U.S. jobs in both manufacturing and services. The loss of manufacturing jobs to other countries has been going on for decades. But the U.S. service sector has always expanded by enough to create new jobs to replace the lost manufacturing jobs. Now that service jobs are also going overseas, the fear is that there will not be enough jobs for Americans.

This fear is misplaced. It is true that *some* service jobs are going overseas. But many service jobs are expanding. The United States imports call center services, but it exports education, health care, legal, and a host of other types of services. Jobs in these sectors are expanding and will continue to expand.

The numbers reinforce this view that the fear of job loss is misplaced. Exact numbers of jobs that have moved to lower-cost offshore locations are not known, and estimates vary. The best guess is that 200,000 jobs a year are going offshore. Some estimates are as high at 400,000 (and some are much lower). Assume that the 400,000 a year number is correct, and put it in perspective. Since 2000, each *month* on the average, 4.5 million people in the United States have been fired or quit their jobs, 4.6 million have started a new job, and the number of people employed has increased by 100,000. In 2005, 142 million Americans had jobs, the highest number in U.S. history. Set against these total job market numbers, the jobs going offshore are a drop in the ocean.

A second reason for concern about offshoring is that U.S. imports have grown faster than U.S. exports. You will learn in Chapter 35 what causes an overall deficit in our international trade and that offshoring is not one of the reasons.

Winners and Losers

Gains from trade do not bring gains for every single individual. Americans on the average gain from offshoring. But some lose. The losers are those who have invested in human capital to do a specific job that has now gone offshore.

Unemployment benefits provide short-term temporary relief for these displaced workers. But long-term solutions require retraining and the acquisition of new skills. Beyond providing short-term relief through unemployment benefits, there is a large role for government education and training policies to ensure that the labor force of the twenty-first century becomes increasingly flexible and capable of retooling to take on new jobs that today we can't foresee.

CHECKPOINT 34.2

2 **Explain why nations engage in international trade and why trade benefits all nations.**

Practice Problem 34.2

1. During most of the Cold War, the United States and Russia (then known as the Soviet Union) did not trade with each other. Both countries produced manufactured goods and farm produce. Suppose that in the last year of the Cold War, the United States could produce 100 million units of manufactured goods or 50 million units of farm produce and Russia could produce 30 million units of manufactured goods or 10 million units of farm produce.
    a. What was the U.S. opportunity cost of 1 unit of farm produce?
    b. What was the Russian opportunity cost of 1 unit of farm produce?
    c. Which country had a comparative advantage in producing farm produce?
    d. With the end of the Cold War and the opening up of trade between Russia and the United States, which good did the United States import from Russia?
    e. Did the United States gain from this trade? Explain why or why not.
    f. Did Russia gain from this trade? Explain why or why not.

Exercise 34.2

1. In 2005, the United States does not trade with Cuba. Suppose that the United States can produce 1,000 million units of manufactured goods or 500 million units of food. Suppose that Cuba can produce 2 million units of manufactured goods or 5 million units of food.
    a. What is the U.S. opportunity cost of 1 unit of food?
    b. What is the Cuban opportunity cost of 1 unit of food?
    c. Which country has a comparative advantage in producing food?
    d. Suppose that the United States opens up trade with Cuba. Which good will the United States import from Cuba?
    e. Will the United States gain from this trade? Explain why or why not.
    f. Will Cuba gain from this trade? Explain why or why not.

Solution to Practice Problem 34.2

1a. The U.S. opportunity cost of 1 unit of farm produce was 2 units of manufactured goods.

1b. The Russian opportunity cost of 1 unit of farm produce was 3 units of manufactured goods.

1c. The United States had a comparative advantage in producing farm produce because the U.S. opportunity cost of a unit of farm produce was less than the Russian opportunity cost of a unit of farm produce.

1d. The United States imported from Russia the good in which Russia had a comparative advantage. The United States imported manufactured goods.

1e. and 1f.   Both the United States and Russia gained because each country ended up with more of both goods. When countries produce the good in which they have a comparative advantage and trade, both countries gain.

34.3 INTERNATIONAL TRADE RESTRICTIONS

Governments use two main tools to restrict international trade and protect domestic industries from foreign competition. They are

- Tariffs
- Nontariff barriers

Tariff
A tax on a good that is imposed by the importing country when an imported good crosses its international boundary.

Nontariff barrier
Any action other than a tariff that restricts international trade.

A **tariff** is a tax on a good that is imposed by the importing country when an imported good crosses its international boundary. A **nontariff barrier** is any action other than a tariff that restricts international trade. Examples of nontariff barriers are quantitative restrictions and health and safety standards.

■ Tariffs

The temptation for governments to impose tariffs is a strong one. First, tariffs provide revenue to the government. Second, they enable the government to satisfy special interest groups in import-competing industries. But as we will see, free international trade brings enormous benefits that are reduced when tariffs are imposed. Let's see how.

E Y E ON THE P A S T

The History of U.S. Tariffs

U.S. tariffs today are modest in comparison with their historical levels. The figure shows the average tariff rate—total tariffs as a percentage of total imports. Tariffs peaked during the 1930s when Congress passed a law known as the Smoot-Hawley Act. The General Agreement on Tariffs and Trade (GATT), an international agreement to eliminate trade restrictions that was signed in 1947, resulted in a series of rounds of negotiations that have brought wide-spread tariff cuts. Today, the World Trade Organization (WTO) continues the work of GATT.

The United States is a party to the North American Free Trade Agreement (NAFTA), which became effective

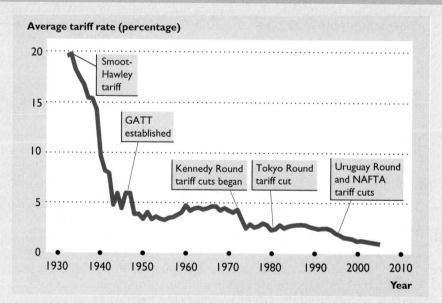

SOURCES OF DATA: The Budget for Fiscal Year 2006, Historical Tables, Table 2.5 and Bureau of Economic Analysis.

on January 1, 1994, and under which barriers to international trade between the United States, Canada, and Mexico will be virtually eliminated after a 15-year phasing-in period.

To analyze how tariffs work, let's return to the example of U.S. T-shirt imports. Figure 34.5 shows the market for T-shirts in the United States. Part (a) is the same as Figure 34.2(b) and shows the situation with free international trade. The United States produces no T-shirts and imports 50 million shirts a year at the world market price of $5 a shirt.

Now suppose that under pressure from U.S. garment makers, the U.S. government imposes a tariff on imported T-shirts. In particular, suppose that a tariff of 50 percent is imposed. What happens?

- The price of a T-shirt in the United States rises.
- The quantity of T-shirts bought in the United States decreases.
- The quantity of T-shirts produced in the United States increases.
- The quantity of T-shirts imported by the United States decreases.
- The U.S. government collects the tariff revenue.
- U.S. consumers lose.

FIGURE 34.5

The Effects of a Tariff

(a) Free trade

(b) A 50-percent tariff

With free trade (part a), ❶ the world price is $5 a T-shirt and ❷ the United States buys 50 million T-shirts. ❸ The United States produces no T-shirts and ❹ imports 50 million T-shirts.

In part (b), the United States imposes a tariff on imports of T-shirts. ❶ The domestic price equals ❷ the world price plus ❸ the tariff, so the tariff raises the price that Americans pay for a T-shirt.

❹ The quantity of T-shirts purchased by Americans decreases, ❺ the quantity produced in the United States increases, and ❻ the quantity imported decreases. The U.S. government collects tariff revenue shown by the purple rectangle.

Rise in Price of a T-Shirt

To buy a T-shirt, Americans must pay the world market price plus the tariff. So the price of a T-shirt rises by 50 percent to $7.50. Figure 34.5(b) shows the domestic price line, which lies 50 percent (or $2.50) above the world price line.

Decrease in Purchases

The higher price of a T-shirt brings a decrease in the quantity demanded, which Figure 34.5(b) shows as a movement along the demand curve for T-shirts from 50 million a year at $5 a shirt to 25 million a year at $7.50 a shirt.

Increase in Domestic Production

The higher price of a T-shirt stimulates domestic production, which increases from zero to 10 million shirts a year—a movement along the supply curve in Figure 34.5(b).

Decrease in Imports

T-shirt imports decrease by 35 million from 50 million to 15 million a year. Both the decrease in purchases and the increase in domestic production contribute to this decrease in imports.

Tariff Revenue

The government collects tariff revenue of $2.50 per shirt on the 15 million shirts imported each year, a total of $37.5 million, as shown by the purple rectangle.

U.S. Consumers Lose

A T-shirt costs only $5 to produce—the opportunity cost of that shirt is $5. But the American consumer pays $7.50 for a T-shirt. So the consumer pays $2.50 a shirt more than its opportunity cost. Consumers are willing to buy up to 50 million T-shirts a year at a price that equals the opportunity cost of a shirt. The tariff makes people pay more than the opportunity cost and deprives them of items they are willing to buy at a price that exceeds the opportunity cost.

Let's now look at the other tools for restricting trade: nontariff barriers.

■ Nontariff Barriers

Quota
A specified maximum amount of a good that may be imported in a given period of time.

A **quota**, which is a quantitative restriction on the import of a good that specifies the maximum amount of the good that may be imported in a given period, is a widely used nontariff barrier. The United States imposes quotas on many items, including sugar, tomatoes, bananas, and textiles.

How a Quota Works

Figure 34.6 shows how a quota works. Begin by identifying the situation with free international trade. The United States produces no T-shirts and imports 50 million shirts a year at the world market price of $5 a shirt.

Now suppose that the United States imposes a quota that restricts imports to 15 million T-shirts a year. The total of the imports permitted under the quota and the quantity produced in the United States is the market supply in the United States. This market supply curve is the one labeled *S + quota* in Figure 34.6.

FIGURE 34.6

The Effects of a Quota

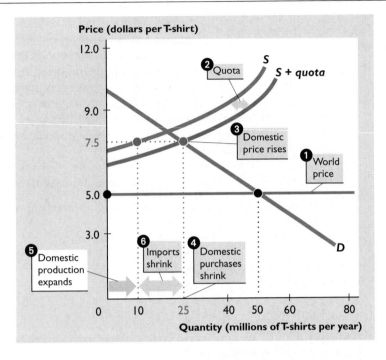

❶ The world price is $5 a T-shirt.
❷ A quota of 15 million shirts a year is added to the U.S. supply to give the market supply curve, S + *quota*.
❸ The equilibrium domestic price rises to $7.50 a shirt, and ❹ domestic purchases decrease. ❺ The United States produces 10 million shirts a year, and ❻ U.S. imports equal the quota of 15 million a year.

With this new supply curve, the U.S. price of a T-shirt is $7.50, the price that makes the quantity demanded by Americans equal the quantity supplied by U.S. producers plus imports. This quantity is 25 million shirts a year.

At a price of $7.50, U.S. garment makers produce 10 million shirts a year and U.S. imports equal the quota of 15 million a year.

We've made the outcome with a quota in Figure 34.6 the same as that with a tariff in Figure 34.5(b). But there is a difference between a tariff and a quota. In the case of a tariff, the U.S. government collects tariff revenue. In the case of a quota, there is no tariff revenue and the difference between the world price and the U.S. price goes to the person who has the right to import T-shirts under the import quota regulations.

Health, Safety, and Other Nontariff Barriers

Thousands of detailed health, safety, and other regulations restrict international trade. Here are just a few examples. All U.S. imports of food products are examined by the Food and Drug Administration to determine whether the imported food is "pure, wholesome, safe to eat, and produced under sanitary conditions." The discovery of BSE in just one U.S. cow in 2003 was enough to close down international trade in U.S. beef. The European Union has banned imports of most genetically modified foods, such as U.S.-produced soybeans and Canadian granola. Australia has banned the import of U.S. grapes to protect its domestic grapes from a virus that is present in California. Restrictions also apply to many nonfood items. Although regulations of the type we've just described are not designed to limit international trade, they have that effect.

3 **Explain how trade barriers reduce international trade.**

Practice Problems 34.3

1. Before 1995, the United States imposed tariffs on goods imported from Mexico and Mexico imposed tariffs on goods imported from the United States. In 1995, Mexico joined NAFTA. U.S. tariffs on imports from Mexico and Mexican tariffs on imports from the United States are gradually being removed. Explain how the removal of tariffs will change
   a. The price that U.S. consumers pay for goods imported from Mexico.
   b. The quantity of U.S. imports from Mexico.
   c. The quantity of U.S. exports to Mexico.
   d. The U.S. government's tariff revenue from trade with Mexico.

2. In 2000, the U.S. government placed a ban on potato imports from Canada. Explain how this ban influences
   a. The price that U.S. consumers pay for potatoes.
   b. The quantity of potatoes consumed in the United States.
   c. The price received by Canadian potato growers.
   d. The U.S. and Canadian gains from trade.

Exercises 34.3

1. In 2000, the U.S. Congress and Senate extended an arrangement that limits the tariffs on imports from China. If the United States imposed higher tariffs on imports from China, explain how a higher tariff on toys will change
   a. The price that U.S. consumers pay for toys imported from China.
   b. The quantity of U.S. imports of toys from China.
   c. The quantity of toys produced in the United States.
   d. The U.S. government's tariff revenue from trade in toys with China.
   e. The U.S. and Chinese gains from trade.

2. Australia has a comparative advantage in producing beef. Explain how a quota on U.S. imports of beef from Australia influences
   a. The price that U.S. consumers pay for beef.
   b. The quantity of beef produced in the United States.
   c. The U.S. and Australian gains from trade.

Solutions to Practice Problems 34.3

1a. The price that U.S. consumers pay for goods imported from Mexico will fall.
1b. The quantity of U.S. imports from Mexico will increase.
1c. The quantity of U.S. exports to Mexico will increase.
1d. The U.S. government's tariff revenue from trade with Mexico will fall to zero.

2a. The price that U.S. consumers pay for potatoes will rise.
2b. The quantity of potatoes consumed in the United States will fall.
2c. The price received by Canadian potato growers will fall.
2d. Both the U.S. and Canadian gains from trade will decrease.

34.4 THE CASE AGAINST PROTECTION

For as long as nations and international trade have existed, people have debated whether free international trade or protection from foreign competition is better for a country. The debate continues, but most economists believe that free trade promotes prosperity for all countries while protection reduces the potential gains from trade. We've seen the most powerful case for free trade: All countries benefit from their comparative advantage. But there is a broader range of issues in the free trade versus protection debate. Let's review these issues.

■ Three Traditional Arguments for Protection

Three traditional arguments for protection and restricting international trade are

- The national security argument
- The infant-industry argument
- The dumping argument

Let's look at each in turn.

The National Security Argument

The national security argument for protection is that a country must protect industries that produce defense equipment and armaments and those on which the defense industries rely for their raw materials and other intermediate inputs. This argument for protection can be taken too far.

First, it is an argument for international isolation, for in a time of war, there is no industry that does not contribute to national defense. Second, if the case is made for boosting the output of a strategic industry—say aerospace—it is more efficient to achieve this outcome with a subsidy financed out of taxes than with a tariff or quota. A subsidy would keep the industry operating at the scale that is judged appropriate, and free international trade would keep the prices faced by consumers at their world market levels.

The Infant-Industry Argument

The **infant-industry argument** for protection is that it is necessary to protect a new industry to enable it to grow into a mature industry that can compete in world markets. The argument is based on the idea of dynamic comparative advantage, which can arise from learning-by-doing.

Learning-by-doing is a powerful engine of productivity growth, and comparative advantage evolves and changes because of on-the-job experience. But these facts do not justify protection.

For example, there are huge productivity gains from learning-by-doing in the manufacture of aircraft. But almost all of these gains benefit the stockholders and workers of aircraft producers such as Boeing. Because the people making the decisions, bearing the risk, and doing the work are the ones who benefit, they take the dynamic gains into account when they decide on the scale of their activities. Only if some of the benefits spill over to other parts of the economy would government assistance be needed to achieve an efficient outcome.

The historical evidence is against the protection of infant industries. Countries in East Asia that have not given such protection have performed well. Countries that have protected infant industries, as India once did, have performed poorly.

Infant-industry argument
The argument that it is necessary to protect a new industry to enable it to grow into a mature industry that can compete in world markets.

The Dumping Argument

Dumping
When a foreign firm sells its exports at a lower price than its cost of production.

Dumping occurs when a foreign firm sells its exports at a lower price than its cost of production. A firm that wants to gain a global monopoly might use dumping. In this case, the foreign firm sells its output at a price below its cost to drive domestic firms out of business. When the domestic firms have gone, the foreign firm takes advantage of its monopoly position and charges a higher price for its product. Dumping is usually regarded as a justification for temporary tariffs and the WTO and NAFTA and CAFTA permit such tariffs. Consequently, anti-dumping tariffs have become important in today's world.

But there are powerful reasons to resist the dumping argument for protection. First, it is virtually impossible to detect dumping because it is hard to determine a firm's costs. As a result, the test for dumping is whether a firm's export price is below its domestic price. But this test is a weak one because it can be rational for a firm to charge a lower price in markets in which the quantity demanded is highly sensitive to price and a higher price in a market in which demand is less price-sensitive.

Second, it is hard to think of a good that is produced by a natural global monopoly. So even if all the domestic firms were driven out of business in some industry, it would always be possible to find several and usually many alternative foreign sources of supply and to buy at prices determined in competitive markets.

Third, if a good or service were a truly global natural monopoly, the best way to deal with it would be by regulation—just as in the case of domestic monopolies. Such regulation would require international cooperation.

The three arguments for protection that we've just examined have an element of credibility. The counterarguments are in general stronger, so these arguments do not make the case for protection. But they are not the only arguments that you might encounter. There are many others, five of which we'll now examine.

■ Five Newer Arguments for Protection

Five newer but commonly made arguments for restricting international trade are that protection

- Saves jobs
- Allows us to compete with cheap foreign labor
- Brings diversity and stability
- Penalizes lax environmental standards
- Protects national culture

Saves Jobs

The argument is that when we buy shoes from Brazil or shirts from Taiwan, U.S. workers lose their jobs. With no earnings and poor prospects, these workers become a drain on welfare and spend less, causing a ripple effect of further job losses. The proposed solution to this problem is to ban imports of cheap foreign goods and to protect U.S. jobs. The proposal is flawed for the following reasons.

First, free trade does cost some jobs, but it also creates other jobs. It brings about a global rationalization of labor and allocates labor resources to their highest-valued activities. Because of international trade in textiles, tens of thousands of workers in the United States have lost jobs because textile mills and other factories have closed. But tens of thousands of workers in other countries now have jobs because textile mills have opened there. And tens of thousands of U.S.

workers now have better-paying jobs than as textile workers because other export industries have expanded and created more jobs than have been destroyed.

Second, imports create jobs. They create jobs for retailers that sell imported goods and for firms that service those goods. They also create jobs by creating incomes in the rest of the world, some of which are spent on imports of U.S.-made goods and services.

Protection saves some particular jobs, but it does so at a high cost. For example, until 2005, textile jobs in the United States were protected by quotas imposed under an international agreement called the Multifiber Arrangement (or MFA). The U.S. International Trade Commission (ITC) estimated that because of quotas, 72,000 jobs existed in textiles that would otherwise disappear and annual clothing expenditure in the United States was $15.9 billion, or $160 per family, higher than it would be with free trade. In other words, the ITC estimated that each textile job saved costs consumers $221,000 a year. The end of the MFA led to the destruction of a large number of textile jobs in the United States and Europe in 2005.

Allows Us to Compete with Cheap Foreign Labor

With the removal of protective tariffs in U.S. trade with Mexico, some people said that jobs would be sucked into Mexico and that the United States would not be able to compete with its southern neighbor. Let's see what's wrong with this view.

The labor cost of a unit of output equals the wage rate divided by labor productivity. For example, if a U.S. auto worker earns $30 an hour and produces 15 units of output an hour, the average labor cost of a unit of output is $2. If a Mexican auto worker earns $3 an hour and produces 1 unit of output an hour, the average labor cost of a unit of output is $3. Other things remaining the same, the higher a worker's productivity, the higher is the worker's wage rate. High-wage workers have high productivity. Low-wage workers have low productivity.

Although high-wage U.S. workers are more productive, on the average, than lower-wage Mexican workers, there are differences across industries. U.S. labor is relatively more productive in some activities than in others. For example, the productivity of U.S. workers in producing movies, financial services, and customized computer chips is relatively higher than their productivity in the production of metals and some standardized machine parts. The activities in which U.S. workers are relatively more productive than their Mexican counterparts are those in which the United States has a comparative advantage. By engaging in free trade, increasing our production and exports of the goods and services in which we have a comparative advantage, and decreasing our production and increasing our imports of the goods and services in which our trading partners have a comparative advantage, we can make ourselves and the citizens of other countries better off.

Brings Diversity and Stability

A diversified investment portfolio is less risky than one that has all of its eggs in one basket. The same is true for an economy's production. A diversified economy fluctuates less than an economy that produces only one or two goods.

But big, rich, diversified economies like those of the United States, Japan, and Europe do not have this type of stability problem. Even a country such as Saudi Arabia that produces almost only one good (in this case, oil) can benefit from specializing in the activity at which it has a comparative advantage and then investing in a wide range of activities in other countries to bring greater stability to its income and consumption.

Penalizes Lax Environmental Standards

A new argument for protection is that many poorer countries, such as Mexico, do not have the same environmental standards that we have, and because they are willing to pollute and we are not, we cannot compete with them without tariffs. So if they want free trade with the richer and "greener" countries, they must clean up their environments to our standards.

This argument for trade restrictions is not entirely convincing. A poor country is less able than a rich one to devote resources to achieving high environmental standards. So if free trade helps a poor country to become richer, it will also help that country to develop the means to improve its environment. But there probably is a case for using the negotiation of free trade agreements such as NAFTA and CAFTA to hold member countries to higher environmental standards. There is an especially large payoff from using such bargaining to try to avoid irreversible damage to resources such as tropical rainforests.

Protects National Culture

The national culture argument for protection is not heard much in the United States, but it is a commonly heard argument in Canada and Europe.

The expressed fear is that free trade in books, magazines, movies, and television programs means U.S. domination and the end of local culture. So, the reasoning continues, it is necessary to protect domestic "culture" industries from free international trade to ensure the survival of a national cultural identity.

Protection of these industries is common and takes the form of nontariff barriers. For example, regulations often require local content on radio and television broadcasting and in magazines.

The cultural identity argument for protection is used most aggressively by writers, publishers, and broadcasters who want to limit foreign competition so that they can earn larger incomes. Many of the creators of so-called American cultural products are not Americans, but the talented citizens of other countries, ensuring the survival of their national cultural identities in Hollywood! Also, if national culture in Canada and Europe is in danger, it is not clear that preventing competition is the best way to restore it to health. Competition among cultures might be a source of strength.

So none of the five common arguments that we've just considered provide overwhelming support for protection. They all have flaws and leave the case for free international trade a strong one.

■ Why Is International Trade Restricted?

Why, despite all the arguments against protection, is international trade restricted? There are two key reasons:

- Tariff revenue
- Rent seeking

Tariff Revenue

Government revenue is costly to collect. In developed countries, such as the United States, well-organized tax collection systems exist that can generate billions of dollars of income tax and sales tax revenues. These tax collection systems are made possible by the fact that firms that must keep properly audited financial records do most economic transactions. Without such records, the revenue collection agencies (such as the Internal Revenue Service in the United States) would be severely hampered in their work. Even with audited financial accounts, some proportion of potential tax revenue is lost. Nonetheless, for industrialized countries, the income tax and sales taxes are the major sources of revenue and the tariff plays a very small role.

But governments in developing countries have a difficult time collecting taxes from their citizens. Much economic activity takes place in an informal economy with few financial records. So these countries collect only a small amount of revenue from income taxes and sales taxes. The one area in which economic transactions are well recorded and audited is international trade. So this activity is an attractive base for tax collection in these countries and is used much more extensively than it is in the developed countries.

EYE ON THE GLOBAL ECONOMY

Competing with Low-Wage Nations

New Balance athletic shoes are made in two ways:

(1) At a New Balance factory in Norridgewock, Maine, skilled workers who earn $14 an hour operate "see-and-sew" machines—$100,000 automated sewing machines guided by cameras. It costs $4 to make a pair of shoes in Maine.

(2) At a subcontractor's factory in China, low-skilled women in their teens and early twenties who earn 40 cents an hour operate ordinary sewing machines. It costs $1.30 to make a pair of shoes in China.

China and other Asian economies have a comparative advantage in making athletic shoes. Even though New Balance has invested heavily in equipment to make its U.S. work force much more productive than the Chinese work force, it costs three times as much to make a pair of shoes in Maine as it costs in China.

Given this cost difference, Nike and other makers of athletic shoes produce their entire output in Asia.

But New Balance produces 25 percent of its output in the United States and the rest in Asia.

Why is New Balance willing to pay three times as much to produce shoes in Maine?

First, the cost of production is a small part of the retail price.

Second, some people are willing to pay more for a product with a label that says "Made in the United States." If 25 percent of New Balance's customers are willing to pay just a few dollars more for a pair of "Made in the United States" shoes, New Balance profits by producing some shoes in Maine.

Rent Seeking

Rent seeking is lobbying and other political activity that seeks to capture the gains from trade. Free trade increases consumption possibilities on the average, but not everyone shares in the gain and some people even lose. Free trade brings benefits to some and imposes costs on others, with total benefits exceeding total costs. It is the uneven distribution of costs and benefits that is the principal source of impediment to achieving more liberal international trade.

Suppose that we had a tariff on T-shirts, as in the example that you studied earlier in this chapter. A few thousand (perhaps a few hundred) garment makers and their employees who must switch to some other activity would bear the cost of the United States moving to free trade. The millions of T-shirt buyers would reap the benefits of moving to free trade. The number of people who gain will, in general, be enormous in comparison with the number who lose. The gain per person will therefore be small. The loss per person to those who bear the loss will be large.

Because the loss that falls on those who bear it is large, it will pay those people to incur considerable expense to lobby against free trade. On the other hand, it will not pay those who gain to organize to achieve free trade. The gain from trade for any one individual is too small for that individual to spend much time or money on a political organization to lobby for free trade. The loss from free trade will be seen as being so great by those bearing that loss that they will find it profitable to join a political organization to prevent free trade. Each group is

When the United States and Canada negotiated the Canada-U.S. Free Trade Agreement (the predecessor of NAFTA), U.S. President Ronald Reagan (hand out-stretched on the right) and Canadian Prime Minister Brian Mulroney (maple-leafed figure on the left), were able to go only as far as their national self-interested rent seekers would allow them to go in dismantling tariffs and other barriers to free trade between the world's two largest trading partners.

Cartoon by Alan King, The Ottawa Citizen, Canwest News Service.

weighing benefits against costs and choosing the best action for themselves. But the anti-free-trade group will undertake a larger quantity of political lobbying than will the pro-free-trade group.

Compensating Losers

If, in total, the gains from free international trade exceed the losses, why don't those who gain compensate those who lose so that everyone is in favor of free trade? To some degree, such compensation does take place. When Congress approved the NAFTA deal with Canada and Mexico, it set up a $56 million fund to support and retrain workers who lost their jobs because of the new trade agreement. During the first six months of the operation of NAFTA, only 5,000 workers applied for benefits under this scheme.

It is difficult to identify and compensate the losers from free international trade. But if we don't make a better effort to do so, protectionism will remain a popular and permanent feature of our national economic and political life.

REALITY CHECK

International Trade in YOUR Life

International trade plays an extraordinarily large role in *your* life in three broad ways.

First, as a consumer, you benefit from the availability of a wide range of low-cost, high-quality goods and services that are produced in other countries. Look closely at the labels on the items you buy. Where was your computer made? Where were your shirt and your shoes made? Where are the fruits and vegetables that you buy, especially in winter, grown?

Second, as a producer (or as a potential producer if you don't yet have a job) you benefit from huge global markets for U.S. products. Your job prospects would be much dimmer if the firm for which you work didn't have global markets in which to sell its products. Even if you were to become a college professor, you would benefit if your school could sell its education services to foreign students.

Third, as a voter, you have a big stake in the politics of free trade versus protection. As a buyer, your self-interest is hurt by tariffs on imported goods. Each time you buy a $20 sweater, you contribute $5 to the government in tariff revenue. But as a worker, your self-interest might be hurt by offshoring and by freer access to U.S. markets for foreign producers. As a voter, you must decide what trade policy serves your self-interest and what best serves the social interest.

4 Explain the arguments used to justify trade barriers and show why these arguments are incorrect but also why some barriers are hard to remove.

Practice Problems 34.4

1. Japan sets quotas on imports of rice. California rice growers would like to export more rice to Japan. What are Japan's arguments for restricting imports of Californian rice? Are these arguments correct? Who loses from this restriction in trade?

2. The United States has, from time to time, limited imports of steel from Europe. What argument has the United States used to justify this quota? Who wins from this restriction? Who loses?

3. The United States maintains a quota on imports of sugar. What is the argument for this quota? Is this argument flawed? If so, explain why.

Exercises 34.4

1. Venezuelan president Hugo Chavez opposes the creation of a Free Trade Area of the Americas (FTAA). Why? Who does he think will gain and lose? Do you think he is correct?

2. The Summit of the Americas in November 2005, President George W. Bush made no progress in his bid to create the FTAA. What are the main obstacles to establishing the FTAA?

3. Hong Kong has never restricted trade. What gains has Hong Kong reaped by unilaterally adopting free trade with all nations? Is there any argument for restricted trade that might have benefited Hong Kong?

Solutions to Practice Problems 34.4

1. The main arguments are that Japanese rice is a better quality rice and that the quota limits competition faced by Japanese farmers. The arguments are not correct. If Japanese consumers do not like the quality of Californian rice, they will not buy it. The quota does limit competition but allows Japanese farmers to use their land less efficiently. The big losers are the Japanese consumers who pay about three times the U.S. price for rice.

2. The U.S. argument is that European producers dump steel on the U.S. market. With a quota, U.S. producers will face less competition in the market for steel and U.S. jobs will be saved. Workers in the steel industry and owners of steel companies will win at the expense of U.S. buyers of steel.

3. The argument is that the quota protects the jobs of U.S. workers. The argument is flawed because the United States does not have a comparative advantage in producing sugar and so a quota allows the U.S. sugar industry to be inefficient. With free trade in sugar, the U.S. sugar industry would exist but it would be much smaller and more efficient.

CHAPTER CHECKPOINT

Key Points

1 **Describe the patterns and trends in international trade.**

- Large flows of trade take place between countries; most trade is in manufactured goods exchanged among rich industrialized countries.
- Since 1960, the volume of U.S. trade has more than doubled and offshore outsourcing has expanded.
- The United States has trading links with every part of the world and is a member of several international organizations and treaties that seek to promote free international trade.

2 **Explain why nations engage in international trade and why trade benefits all nations.**

- When opportunity costs between countries diverge, comparative advantage enables countries to gain from international trade.
- By increasing production of goods in which it has a comparative advantage and then trading some of the increased output, a country can consume at points outside its production possibilities frontier.

3 **Explain how trade barriers reduce international trade.**

- Countries restrict international trade by imposing tariffs and quotas.
- Trade restrictions raise the domestic price of imported goods, lower the volume of imports, and reduce the total value of imports.

4 **Explain the arguments used to justify trade barriers and show why these arguments are incorrect but also why some barriers are hard to remove.**

- The arguments that protection is necessary for national security, for infant industries, and to prevent dumping are weak.
- Arguments that protection saves jobs, allows us to compete with cheap foreign labor, makes the economy diversified and stable, protects national culture, prevents rich countries from exploiting developing countries, and is needed to offset the costs of environmental policies are flawed.
- Trade is restricted because tariffs raise government revenue and because protection brings a small loss to a large number of people and a large gain per person to a small number of people.

Key Terms

Balance of trade, 861
Dumping, 878
Infant-industry argument, 877
Nontariff barrier, 872

Offshoring, 869
Outsourcing, 869
Quota, 874
Tariff, 872

Exercises

FIGURE 1

Cars (millions per year)

1. Suppose that with no international trade between the United States and Brazil, Figure 1 shows the U.S. production possibilities and the quantities of coffee and cars produced (point *A*). Figure 2 shows Brazil's production possibilities and the quantities of coffee and cars produced (point *B*).
   a. What is the opportunity cost of a bag of coffee in the United States?
   b. What is the opportunity cost of a bag of coffee in Brazil?
   c. Which country has a comparative advantage in producing coffee?
   d. Which country has a comparative advantage in producing cars?
   e. With free trade between Brazil and the United States, what does the United States import from Brazil and what does it export to Brazil? Explain your answer.
   f. Does Brazil gain from trade with the United States? Why or why not?

2. When free trade occurs in exercise 1, the world price of a bag of coffee is 1/25th of a car. If Brazil completely specializes in coffee and exports half of it to the United States,
   a. Show on Figure 2 the quantities of the two goods that Brazil consumes.
   b. Show on Figure 1 the quantities of the two goods that the United States consumes.

FIGURE 2

Cars (millions per year)

3. The table provides information about production possibilities in Kenya and Morocco.

	Kenya's production possibilities			
Item	**A**	**B**	**C**	**D**
Coffee (millions of bags per year)	0	2	4	6
Oranges (millions per year)	3	2	1	0

	Morocco's production possibilities			
Item	**A**	**B**	**C**	**D**
Coffee (millions of bags per year)	0	1	2	3
Oranges (millions per year)	6	4	2	0

   a. What is the opportunity cost of producing a bag of coffee in Kenya?
   b. What is the opportunity cost of producing a bag of coffee in Morocco?
   c. What is the opportunity cost of producing an orange in Kenya?
   d. What is the opportunity cost of producing an orange in Morocco?
   e. Suppose that Kenya and Morocco do not trade and that in each country, production and consumption are 2 million bags of coffee and 2 million oranges. Make a graph of the two *PPFs* and mark on them the point at which each country produces and consumes.

f. Now suppose that the two countries specialize and trade. What now are the total quantities of coffee and oranges produced?

g. If one bag of coffee exchanges for one orange on the world market, what are the volumes of exports and imports of Kenya and Morocco?

h. What are the consumption of coffee and oranges in Kenya and Morocco?

4. Look at the information provided in *Eye on the Global Economy* on p. 859.
   a. Select an item from the figure in which the United States has a comparative advantage.
   b. Select an item from the figure in which the rest of the world has a comparative advantage.
   c. Make some assumptions about prices and quantities and draw your own figures similar to Figure 34.1 and 34.2 to illustrate the situation in the markets for the two items you chose in parts **a** and **b**.
   d. Make some assumptions about opportunity costs and draw your own figures similar to the two parts of Figure 34.3 to illustrate the U.S. *PPF* and the rest-of-the-world *PPF* for the two items you chose in parts **a** and **b**.

5. Figure 3 shows the car market in Brazil when Brazil places no restriction on imports of cars. The world price of a car is $10,000. If the government of Brazil introduces a 20 percent tariff on car imports, what will be
   a. The price of a car in Brazil?
   b. The quantity of cars imported into Brazil?
   c. The quantity of cars produced in Brazil?
   d. The government's tariff revenue?

6. Suppose that in exercise 5, the Brazilian government introduces a quota of 50 million cars a year. Show on Figure 3
   a. The price of a car in Brazil.
   b. The quantity of cars imported into Brazil.
   c. The quantity of cars produced in Brazil.

7. If the tariff described in exercise 5 is imposed,
   a. Who will gain and who will lose?
   b. Why might a tariff be imposed?

8. If the quota described in exercise 6 is imposed,
   a. Who will gain and who will lose?
   b. Why might a quota be imposed?

FIGURE 3

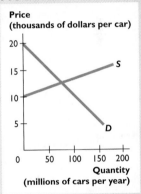

Critical Thinking

9. In the 1950s, Ford and General Motors established a small car-producing industry in Australia and argued for a high tariff on car imports. The tariff has remained through the years. In 2000, the tariff was cut from 22.5 percent to 15 percent. What might have been the argument for the high tariff? Is the tariff the best way to achieve the goals of the argument?

10. The Canadian government argues against free trade in magazines and movies. Why is the Canadian government concerned about the quantity of U.S. magazines and movies that Canadians see? What is wrong with the Canadian government's argument? Who in Canada gains from the government's argument?

11. The U.S. government imposes a quota on lamb imports from New Zealand and Australia. New Zealand and Australia have lobbied the U.S. government for an increase in the quota. What is the argument put forward by the New Zealand and Australian governments? What is the counterargument put forward by the U.S. government? Which argument is really an example of rent seeking?

12. In 1845, French economist Frédéric Bastiat wrote a satirical "petition of the candlemakers" in which he argued that competition from the sun was unfair to the makers of artificial lighting. He suggested that to level the playing field, boost the production of artificial light, and create much employment and economic activity, the government should pass a law ordering the shutting up of all windows, openings, and chinks through which sunlight may enter buildings.
    a. Explain why passing the law called for in Bastiat's petition would create inefficiency.
    b. Explain why the argument presented in Bastiat's petition is similar to that of people who argue for protection from foreign competition.

Web Exercises

Use the links on MyEconLab to work the following exercises.

13. Visit the Web site of the World Trade Organization (WTO).
    a. What is the WTO?
    b. Review the ten benefits of the WTO trading system listed on the Web site. Do you agree that these are benefits? Who benefits?
    c. Review the ten common misunderstandings about the WTO listed on the Web site. Do you agree that these are misunderstandings? Explain why or why not.

14. Visit the Agriculture Negotiations page of the WTO Web site.
    a. What are the problems facing international trade in agricultural products?
    b. How does the WTO plan to deal with these problems?
    c. If international trade in agricultural products becomes freer, do you expect U.S. farms to expand or contract? Why?

15. Visit the Global Trade Watch page on the Web site of the Public Citizen.
    a. What are the views expressed by Global Trade Watch?
    b. Are these views among the ten common misunderstandings about the WTO?
    c. Are the views of Global Trade Watch consistent with the ideas about the gains from international trade that you've studied in this chapter?
    d. Explain why you agree or disagree with the views of Global Trade Watch.

16. Visit the Web site of the U.S. International Trade Commission (USITC).
    a. What are the main functions and responsibilities of the USITC?
    b. How does the role of the USITC differ from that of the WTO?
    c. Review the page on effects of the proposed Free Trade Agreement between the United States and the Southern Africa Customs Union. Who do you think would gain from such an agreement and why?

International Finance

CHAPTER CHECKLIST

When you have completed your study of this chapter, you will be able to

1 Describe a country's balance of payments accounts and explain what determines the amount of international borrowing and lending.

2 Explain how the exchange rate is determined and why it fluctuates.

Every single year since 1982, the United States has spent more on imports than it has earned on exports. By the end of 2004, the accumulated deficit exceeded $4 trillion! How can a nation spend more than it earns? What determines the balance of international payments?

The world's four big currencies are the U.S. dollar, the Japanese yen, the British pound, and the European euro. Most of the world's international trade and finance are conducted in terms of these four currencies. But another currency—the Chinese yuan—is important for the United States. The values of most currencies fluctuate. For example, since 1998, the U.S. dollar has fluctuated between a high of 145 yen and a low of 103 yen. But our dollar bought the same 8.28 yuan every month from January 1998 through June 2005. Why is our dollar permitted to fluctuate against some currencies but is fixed against others? Is a fluctuating currency better or worse than a fixed one?

In this chapter, you are going to learn about international finance. You will discover how nations keep their international accounts and what determines the balance of payments and the value of the dollar.

35.1 FINANCING INTERNATIONAL TRADE

When Apple Computer, Inc. imports iPods that it manufactures in Taiwan, it pays for them using Taiwanese dollars. When a French construction company buys an earthmover from Caterpillar, Inc., it uses U.S. dollars. Whenever we buy things from another country, we pay in the currency of that country. It doesn't make any difference what the item being traded is; it might be a consumption good or a service or a capital good, a building, or even a firm.

We're going to study the markets in which different types of currency are bought and sold. But first we're going to look at the scale of international trading and borrowing and lending and at the way in which we keep our records of these transactions. These records are called the balance of payments accounts.

■ Balance of Payments Accounts

Balance of payments accounts
The accounts in which a nation records its international trading, borrowing, and lending.

A country's **balance of payments accounts** record its international trading, borrowing, and lending. There are in fact three balance of payments accounts:

- Current account
- Capital account
- Official settlements account

Current account
Record of international receipts and payments—current account balance equals exports minus imports, plus net interest and transfers received from abroad.

Capital account
Record of foreign investment in the United States minus U.S. investment abroad.

Official settlements account
Record of the change in U.S. official reserves.

U.S. official reserves
The government's holdings of foreign currency.

The **current account** records receipts from the sale of goods and services to other countries (exports), minus payments for goods and services bought from other countries (imports), plus the net amount of interest and transfers (such as foreign aid payments) received from and paid to other countries. The **capital account** records foreign investment in the United States minus U.S. investment abroad. The **official settlements account** records the change in official U.S. reserves. **U.S. official reserves** are the government's holdings of foreign currency. If U.S. official reserves increase, the official settlements account balance is negative. The reason is that holding foreign money is like investing abroad. U.S. investment abroad is a minus item in the capital account and in the official settlements account. (By the same reasoning, if official reserves decrease, the official settlements account balance is positive.)

The sum of the balances on the three accounts always equals zero. That is, to pay for our current account deficit, we must either borrow more from abroad than we lend abroad or use our official reserves to cover the shortfall.

Table 35.1 shows the U.S. balance of payments accounts in 2004. Items in the current account and capital account that provide foreign currency to the United States have a plus sign; items that cost the United States foreign currency have a minus sign. The table shows that in 2004, U.S. imports exceeded U.S. exports and the current account deficit was $668 billion. We paid for imports that exceeded the value of our exports by borrowing from the rest of the world. The capital account tells us by how much. We borrowed $1,440 billion (foreign investment in the United States) but made loans of $860 billion (U.S. investment abroad). So our measured net foreign borrowing was $580 billion. Measurement error (recorded in the balance of payments accounts as a statistical discrepancy) was $85 billion. Our official reserves decreased by $3 billion and are shown in Table 35.1 as a positive $3 billion, a convention that makes the three accounts sum to zero.

You might better understand the balance of payments accounts and the way in which they are linked if you think about the income and expenditure, borrowing and lending, and bank account of an individual.

The U.S. Balance of Payments

The numbers in Table 35.1 provide a snapshot of the U.S balance of payments in 2004. The figure puts this snapshot into perspective by showing how the balance of payments evolved from 1980 to 2004.

(Because the economy grows and the price level rises, changes in the dollar value of the balance of payments do not convey much information. To remove the influences of growth and inflation, the figure shows the balance of payments as a percentage of GDP.)

The capital account balance is almost a mirror image of the current account balance because the official settlements balance is very small in comparison with the balances on these other two accounts. A large cur-

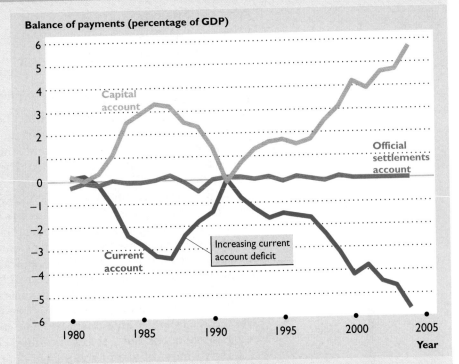

SOURCE OF DATA: Bureau of Economic Analysis.

rent account deficit (and capital account surplus) emerged during the 1980s but declined from 1987 to 1991. Throughout the 1990s and 2000s, the current account deficit increased.

■ TABLE 35.1

The U.S. Balance of Payments Accounts in 2004

Current account	(billions of dollars)
Exports of goods and services	+1,152
Imports of goods and services	−1,769
Net interest	30
Net transfers	−81
Current account balance	−668
Capital account	
Foreign investment in the United States	+1,440
U.S. investment abroad	−860
Statistical discrepancy	85
Capital account balance	+665
Official settlements account	
Official settlements account balance	3

SOURCE OF DATA: Bureau of Economic Analysis.

Personal Analogy

You have a set of personal balance of payments accounts that parallel those of a nation. You have a current account, a capital account, and a settlements account.

Your current account records your income from supplying the services of factors of production and your expenditure on goods and services. Consider, for example, Joanne. She worked in 2005 and earned an income of $25,000. Joanne has $10,000 worth of investments that earned her interest of $1,000. Joanne's current account shows an income of $26,000. Joanne spent $18,000 buying goods and services for consumption. She also bought a new house, which cost her $60,000. So Joanne's total expenditure was $78,000. The difference between her expenditure and her income is $52,000 ($78,000 minus $26,000).

To pay for expenditure of $52,000 in excess of her income, Joanne has to use the money that she has in the bank or she has to take out a loan. Suppose that Joanne took a mortgage of $50,000 to help buy her house. This mortgage was the only borrowing that Joanne did, so her capital account surplus was $50,000. With a current account deficit of $52,000 and a capital account surplus of $50,000, Joanne is still $2,000 short. She got that $2,000 from her own bank account. Her cash holdings decreased by $2,000. Joanne's settlements balance was $2,000.

Joanne's income from her work is like a country's income from its exports. Her income from her investments is like a country's interest from foreigners. Her purchases of goods and services, including her purchase of an apartment, are like a country's imports. Joanne's mortgage—borrowing from someone else—is like a country's borrowing from the rest of the world. The change in Joanne's bank account is like the change in a country's official reserves.

Check that the sum of Joanne's balances is zero. Her current account balance is −$52,000, her capital account balance is +$50,000, and her settlements account balance is +$2,000, so the sum of the three balances is zero.

■ Borrowers and Lenders, Debtors and Creditors

Net borrower
A country that is borrowing more from the rest of the world than it is lending to the rest of the world.

Net lender
A country that is lending more to the rest of the world than it is borrowing from the rest of the world.

Debtor nation
A country that during its entire history has borrowed more from the rest of the world than it has lent to the rest of the world.

Creditor nation
A country that during its entire history has invested more in the rest of the world than other countries have invested in it.

A country that is borrowing more from the rest of the world than it is lending to the rest of the world is called a **net borrower**. Similarly, a **net lender** is a country that is lending more to the rest of the world than it is borrowing from it.

The United States is a net borrower, but it is a relative newcomer to the ranks of net borrower nations. Throughout the 1960s and most of the 1970s, the United States was a net lender to the rest of the world. It had a surplus on its current account and a deficit on its capital account. It was not until 1983 that the United States became a significant net borrower from the rest of the world. Between 1983 and 1987, U.S. borrowing increased each year. Then it decreased and was briefly zero in 1991. After 1991, U.S. borrowing started to increase again. The average net foreign borrowing by the United States between 1983 and 2004 was $183 billion a year.

Most countries are net borrowers like the United States. But a small number of countries, including Japan and oil-rich Saudi Arabia, are net lenders.

A net borrower might be reducing its net assets held in the rest of the world, or it might be going deeper into debt. A nation's total stock of foreign investment determines whether the nation is a debtor or creditor. A **debtor nation** is a country that during its entire history has borrowed more from the rest of the world than it has lent to the rest of the world. It has a stock of outstanding debt to the rest of the world that exceeds the stock of its own claims on the rest of the world. A **creditor nation** is a country that during its entire history has invested more in the rest of the world than other countries have invested in it.

Flows and Stocks

At the heart of the distinction between a net borrower and a net lender on the one hand and between a debtor nation and a creditor nation on the other hand is the distinction between flows and stocks, which you have encountered many times in your study of macroeconomics. Borrowing and lending are flows—amounts borrowed or lent per unit of time. Debts are stocks—amounts owed at a point in time. The flow of borrowing and lending changes the stock of debt.

The United States was a debtor nation through the nineteenth century as we borrowed from Europe to finance our westward expansion, railroads, and industrialization. We paid off our debt and became a creditor nation for most of the twentieth century. But following a string of current account deficits, we became a debtor nation again in 1989.

Since 1989, the total stock of U.S. borrowing from the rest of the world has exceeded U.S. lending to the rest of the world. The largest debtor nations are the capital-hungry developing countries (as the United States was during the nineteenth century). The international debt of these countries grew from less than a third to more than a half of their gross domestic product during the 1980s and created what is called the "Third World debt crisis."

Should we be concerned that the United States is a net borrower? The answer to this question depends mainly on what the net borrower is doing with the borrowed money. If borrowing is financing investment that in turn is generating economic growth and higher income, borrowing is not a problem. If the borrowed money is being used to finance consumption, then higher interest payments are being incurred, and consequently, consumption will eventually have to be reduced. In this case, the more the borrowing and the longer it goes on, the greater is the reduction in consumption that will eventually be necessary. We'll see below whether the United States is borrowing for investment or for consumption.

■ Current Account Balance

What determines a country's current account balance and net foreign borrowing? You've seen in Table 35.1 that exports of goods and services (X) and imports of goods and services (M) are the largest items in the current account. We call exports minus imports net exports (NX). So net exports is the main component of the current account. We can define the current account balance (CAB) as

$$CAB = NX + \text{Net interest and transfers from abroad}$$

Fluctuations in net exports are the main source of fluctuations in the current account balance. Net interest and transfers from abroad are small and have trends but do not fluctuate much. So we can study the current account balance by looking at what determines net exports.

■ Net Exports

The government budget and private saving and investment determine net exports. To see how they determine net exports, we need to recall some of the things that we learned about the National Income Accounts in Chapter 20. Table 35.2 will refresh your memory and summarize some calculations.

■ **TABLE 35.2**

Net Exports, the Government Budget, Saving, and Investment

	Symbols and equations	United States in 2004 (billions of dollars)
(a) Variables		
Exports	X	1,174
Imports	M	1,798
Investment	I	1,928
Saving	S	1,716
Government expenditure on goods and services	G	2,216
Net taxes	NT	1,804
(b) Balances		
Net exports	$X - M$	$1,174 - 1,798 = -624$
Private sector balance	$S - I$	$1,716 - 1,928 = -212$
Government sector balance	$NT - G$	$1,804 - 2,216 = -412$
(c) Relation among balances		
National accounts	$Y = C + I + G + X - M = C + S + NT$	
Rearranging:	$X - M = S - I + NT - G$	
Net exports	$X - M$	-624
Equals:		
Private sector balance	$S - I$	-212
Plus:		
Government sector balance	$NT - G$	-412

SOURCE OF DATA: Bureau of Economic Analysis, 2005. (The National Income and Product Accounts measures of exports and imports are slightly different from the Balance of Payments Accounts measures in Table 35.1 on p. 505. The government sector includes state and local governments.)

Private sector balance
Saving minus investment.

Government sector balance
Net taxes minus government expenditure on goods and services.

Part (a) of Table 35.2 lists the national income variables with their symbols. Part (b) defines three balances. *Net exports* are exports of goods and services minus imports of goods and services.

The **private sector balance** is saving minus investment. If saving exceeds investment, a private sector surplus is lent to other sectors. If investment exceeds saving, borrowing from other sectors finances a private sector deficit.

The **government sector balance** is equal to net taxes minus government expenditure on goods and services. If that number is positive, a government sector surplus is lent to other sectors; if that number is negative, borrowing from other sectors must finance a government deficit. The government sector is the sum of the federal, state, and local governments.

Part (b) also shows the values of these balances for the United States in 2004. As you can see, net exports were $-\$624$ billion, a deficit. The private sector saved $1,716 billion and invested $1,928 billion, so it had a deficit of $212 billion. The government sector's revenue from net taxes was $1,804 billion, and its expenditures were $2,216 billion, so its balance was $-\$412$ billion, a deficit.

Part (c) of Table 35.2 shows the relationship among the three balances. From the national income accounts, we know that real GDP, Y, is the sum of consumption expenditure, C; investment, I; government expenditure on goods and services, G; and net exports, $X - M$. Real GDP also equals the sum of consumption expenditure; saving, S, and net taxes, NT. Rearranging these equations tells us that net exports equals $(S - I)$, the private sector balance, plus $(NT - G)$, the government sector balance. That is,

$$\text{Net exports} = (S - I) + (NT - G).$$

Should we be concerned that the United States is a net borrower? The answer is probably not. Our international borrowing finances the purchase of new capital goods. In 2004, businesses spent $1,928 billion on new buildings, plant, and equipment. Government spent $373 billion on defense equipment and public structures. All these purchases added to the nation's capital, and much of it increased productivity. Governments also purchased education and health care services, which increased human capital.

Our international borrowing is financing private and public investment, not consumption.

EYE ON THE GLOBAL ECONOMY

Current Account Balances Around the World

The U.S. current account deficit in 2004 is the major international payments deficit. No other country has a deficit remotely similar to that of the United States.

For every deficit, there must be a corresponding surplus. The figure shows that the U.S. deficit is reflected in a large number of small surpluses spread around the world. No single country or group of countries has a surplus to match the U.S. deficit.

Notice in particular how small China's surplus is. The other advanced nations were the ones with the largest surpluses in 2004. Other large surpluses are earned by the oil-exporting Middle East and by Japan and other industrialized Asian economies.

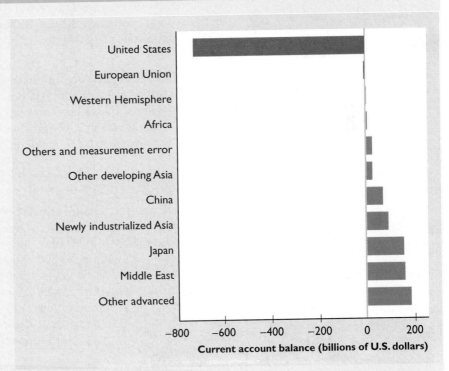

SOURCE OF DATA: International Monetary Fund, *World Economic Outlook*, April 2005.

1 Describe a country's balance of payments accounts and explain what determines the amount of international borrowing and lending.

Practice Problem 35.1

1. It is 2006, and the U.S. economy records the following transactions: Imports of goods and services, $2,000 billion; interest paid to the rest of the world, $500 billion; interest received from the rest of the world, $400 billion; decrease in U.S. official reserves, $10 billion; government sector balance, $200 billion; saving, $1,800 billion; investment, $2,000 billion; net transfers, zero.

   a. Calculate the current account balance, the capital account balance, the official settlements account balance, and exports of goods and services.
   b. Is the United States a debtor or a creditor nation in 2006?
   c. If government expenditures increase by $100 billion, what happens to the current account balance?

Exercise 35.1

1. It is 2007, and the U.S. economy records the following transactions: Exports of goods and services, $1,800 billion; interest payments to the rest of the world, $550 billion; interest received from the rest of the world, $350 billion; decrease in U.S. official reserves, $10 billion; government sector balance, $200 billion; saving, $1,800 billion; investment, $2,000 billion; net transfers are zero.

   a. Calculate the current account balance, the capital account balance, the official settlements account balance, and imports of goods and services.
   b. Has the United States become a larger or smaller debtor or creditor nation in 2007 than it was in 2006 (practice problem 35.1)?
   c. If net taxes increase by $100 billion, what happens to the capital account balance?

Solution to Practice Problem 35.1

1a. The current account balance equals net exports plus net interest from abroad (−$100 billion) plus net transfers (zero). Net exports equal the government sector balance ($200 billion) plus the private sector balance. The private sector balance equals saving ($1,800 billion) minus investment ($2,000 billion), which is −$200 billion. So net exports are zero, and the current account balance is −$100 billion. The capital account balance is the negative of the sum of the current account and official settlements account balances, which is $90 billion. The official settlements account balance is a *surplus* of $10 billion. Exports equal net exports (zero) plus imports ($2,000 billion), which equals $2,000 billion.

1b. The United States is a debtor nation in 2006 because it pays more in interest to the rest of the world than it receives in interest from the rest of the world.

1c. If government expenditures increase by $100 billion, the government sector balance decreases. Net exports decrease, and the current account deficit increases.

35.2 THE EXCHANGE RATE

When we buy foreign goods or invest in another country, we pay using that country's currency. When foreigners buy U.S.-made goods or invest in the United States, they pay in U.S. dollars. We get foreign currency, and foreigners get U.S. dollars in the foreign exchange market. The **foreign exchange market** is the market in which the currency of one country is exchanged for the currency of another. The foreign exchange market is not a place like a downtown flea market or produce market. It is made up of thousands of people: importers and exporters, banks, and specialist traders of foreign exchange, called foreign exchange brokers. The foreign exchange market opens on Monday morning in Hong Kong, which is still Sunday evening in New York. As the day advances, markets open in Singapore, Tokyo, Bahrain, Frankfurt, London, New York, Chicago, and San Francisco. As the U.S. West Coast markets close, Hong Kong is only an hour away from opening for the next business day. Dealers around the world are in continual contact, and on a typical day in 2005, $2 trillion changed hands.

The price at which one currency exchanges for another is called a **foreign exchange rate**. For example, in August 2005, one U.S. dollar bought 111 Japanese yen. The exchange rate was 111 yen per dollar. We can also express the exchange rate in terms of dollars (or cents) per yen, which in August 2005 was a bit less than 1 cent per yen.

Currency depreciation is the fall in the value of one currency in terms of another currency. For example, if the dollar falls from 100 yen to 80 yen, the dollar depreciates by 20 percent.

Foreign exchange market
The market in which the currency of one country is exchanged for the currency of another.

Foreign exchange rate
The price at which one currency exchanges for another.

Currency depreciation
The fall in the value of one currency in terms of another currency.

E Y E ON THE P A S T

The Dollar and the Yen Since 1980

From 1985 to 1995, the value of the dollar fell against the yen—the dollar depreciated. From 1995 to 1998, the value of the dollar rose against the yen—the dollar appreciated. Since 1998, the exchange rate between the dollar and the yen has been more stable and has fluctuated in a very narrow range.

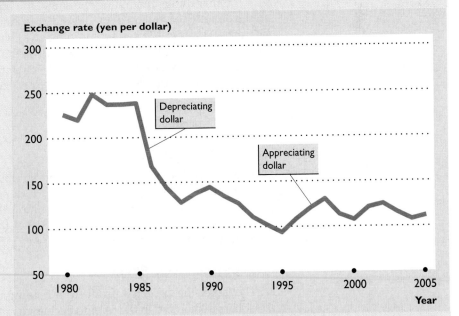

SOURCE OF DATA: PACIFIC FX Service, University of British Columbia.

Currency appreciation
The rise in the value of one currency in terms of another currency.

Currency appreciation is the rise in the value of one currency in terms of another currency. For example, if the dollar rises from 100 yen to 120 yen, the dollar appreciates by 20 percent. When the U.S. dollar appreciates against the yen, the yen depreciates against the dollar.

Why does the U.S. dollar fluctuate in value? Why does it sometimes depreciate and sometimes appreciate?

The exchange rate is a price. And like all prices, demand and supply determine the exchange rate. So to understand the forces that determine the exchange rate, we need to study demand and supply in the foreign exchange market. We'll begin by looking at the demand side of the market.

■ Demand in the Foreign Exchange Market

The quantity of U.S. dollars demanded in the foreign exchange market is the amount that traders plan to buy during a given time period at a given exchange rate. This quantity depends on many factors, but the main ones are

- The exchange rate
- Interest rates in the United States and other countries
- The expected future exchange rate

Let's look first at the relationship between the quantity of dollars demanded in the foreign exchange market and the exchange rate.

■ The Law of Demand for Foreign Exchange

People do not buy dollars because they enjoy them. The demand for dollars is a *derived demand*. People demand dollars so that they can buy U.S.-made goods and services (U.S. exports). They also demand dollars so that they can buy U.S. assets such as bank accounts, bonds, stocks, businesses, and real estate. Nevertheless, the law of demand applies to dollars just as it does to anything else that people value.

Other things remaining the same, the higher the exchange rate, the smaller is the quantity of dollars demanded. For example, if the price of the U.S. dollar rises from 100 yen to 120 yen but nothing else changes, the quantity of U.S. dollars that people plan to buy decreases. Why does the exchange rate influence the quantity of dollars demanded? There are two separate reasons, and they are related to the two sources of the derived demand for dollars. They are

- Exports effect
- Expected profit effect

Exports Effect

The larger the value of U.S. exports, the larger is the quantity of dollars demanded. But the value of U.S. exports depends on the exchange rate. The lower the exchange rate, other things remaining the same, the cheaper are U.S.-made goods and services to people in the rest of the world, the more the United States exports, and the greater is the quantity of U.S. dollars demanded to pay for them.

Expected Profit Effect

The larger the expected profit from holding dollars, the greater is the quantity of dollars demanded in the foreign exchange market. But expected profit depends on the exchange rate. The lower the exchange rate, other things remaining the same, the larger is the expected profit from holding dollars and the greater is the quantity of dollars demanded on the foreign exchange market.

FIGURE 35.1
The Demand for Dollars

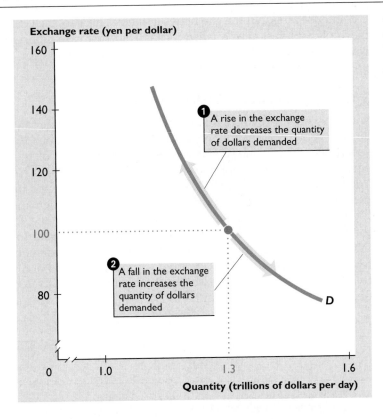

Other things remaining the same, the quantity of dollars that people plan to buy depends on the exchange rate.

1 If the exchange rate rises, the quantity of dollars demanded decreases and there is a movement up along the demand curve for dollars.

2 If the exchange rate falls, the quantity of dollars demanded increases and there is a movement down along the demand curve for dollars.

To understand this effect, suppose that you think the dollar will be worth 120 yen by the end of the month. If a dollar costs 115 yen today, you buy dollars. But a person who thinks that the dollar will be worth 115 yen at the end of the month does not buy dollars. Now suppose that the exchange rate falls to 110 yen per dollar. More people think that they can profit from buying dollars, so the quantity of dollars demanded increases.

Figure 35.1 shows the demand curve for U.S. dollars in the foreign exchange market. For the two reason we've just reviewed, when the foreign exchange rate rises, other things remaining the same, the quantity of dollars demanded decreases and there is a movement up along the demand curve, as shown by the arrow. When the exchange rate falls, other things remaining the same, the quantity of dollars demanded increases and there is a movement down along the demand curve, as shown by the arrow.

■ Changes in the Demand for Dollars

A change in any other influence on the quantity of U.S. dollars that people plan to buy in the foreign exchange market brings a change in the demand for dollars, and the demand curve for dollars shifts. These other influences are

- Interest rates in the United States and other countries
- The expected future exchange rate

Interest Rates in the United States and Other Countries

U.S. interest rate differential
The U.S. interest rate minus the foreign interest rate.

If you can borrow in another country and lend in the United States at a higher interest rate, you will make a profit. What matters is not the level of foreign and U.S. interest rates, but the gap between them. This gap, the U.S. interest rate minus the foreign interest rate, is called the **U.S. interest rate differential**. The larger the U.S. interest rate differential, the greater is the demand for U.S. assets and the greater is the demand for dollars.

The Expected Future Exchange Rate

Suppose you are Toyota's finance manager. The exchange rate is 100 yen per dollar, and you expect that by the end of the month, it will be 120 yen per dollar. You spend 100,000 yen today and buy $1,000. At the end of the month, the dollar equals 120 yen, as you predicted, and you sell the $1,000. You get 120,000 yen. You've made a profit of 20,000 yen. The higher the expected future exchange rate, the greater is the expected profit and the greater is the demand for dollars.

Figure 35.2 summarizes the influences on the demand for dollars. A rise in the U.S. interest rate differential or a rise in the expected future exchange rate increases the demand for dollars today and shifts the demand curve rightward from D_0 to D_1. A fall in the U.S. interest rate differential or a fall in the expected future exchange rate decreases the demand for dollars today and shifts the demand curve leftward from D_0 to D_2.

FIGURE 35.2

Changes in the Demand for Dollars

❶ The demand for dollars increases if:

■ The U.S. interest rate differential increases.
■ The expected future exchange rate rises.

❷ The demand for dollars decreases if:

■ The U.S. interest rate differential decreases.
■ The expected future exchange rate falls.

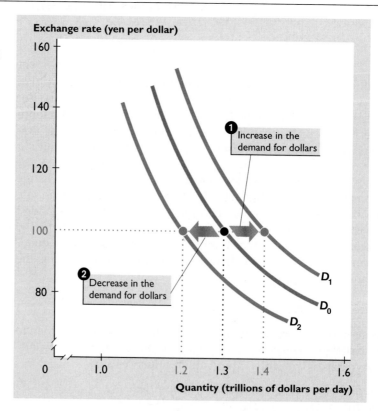

■ Supply in the Foreign Exchange Market

The quantity of U.S. dollars supplied in the foreign exchange market is the amount that traders plan to sell during a given time period at a given exchange rate. This quantity depends on many factors, but the main ones are

- The exchange rate
- Interest rates in the United States and other countries
- The expected future exchange rate

Does this list of factors seem familiar? It should: It is the same list as that for demand. The demand side and the supply side of the foreign exchange market are influenced by all the same factors. But the ways in which these three factors influence supply are the opposite of the ways in which they influence demand.

Let's look first at the relationship between the quantity of dollars supplied in the foreign exchange market and the exchange rate.

■ The Law of Supply of Foreign Exchange

Traders supply U.S. dollars in the foreign exchange market when people and businesses buy other currencies. And they buy other currencies so that they can buy foreign-made goods and services (U.S. imports). They also supply dollars and buy foreign currencies so that they can buy foreign assets such as bank accounts, bonds, stocks, businesses, and real estate. The law of supply applies to dollars just as it does to anything else that people plan to sell.

Other things remaining the same, the higher the exchange rate, the greater is the quantity of dollars supplied in the foreign exchange market. For example, if the price of the U.S. dollar rises from 100 yen to 120 yen but nothing else changes, the quantity of U.S. dollars that people plan to sell in the foreign exchange market increases. Why does the exchange rate influence the quantity of dollars supplied?

There are two reasons, and they parallel the two reasons on the demand side of the market. They are

- Imports effect
- Expected profit effect

Imports Effect

The larger the value of U.S. imports, the larger is the quantity of foreign currency demanded to pay for these imports. And when people buy foreign currency, they supply dollars. So the larger the value of U.S. imports, the greater is the quantity of dollars supplied on the foreign exchange market. But the value of U.S. imports depends on the exchange rate. The higher the exchange rate, other things remaining the same, the cheaper are foreign-made goods and services to Americans. So the more the United States imports, the greater is the quantity of U.S. dollars supplied on the foreign exchange market to pay for these imports.

Expected Profit Effect

The larger the expected profit from holding a foreign currency, the greater is the quantity of that currency demanded and the greater is the quantity of dollars supplied in the foreign exchange market. But the expected profit from holding a foreign currency depends on the exchange rate. The higher the exchange rate, other things remaining the same, the larger is the expected profit from selling dollars and the greater is the quantity of dollars supplied on the foreign exchange market.

FIGURE 35.3

The Supply of Dollars

Other things remaining the same, the quantity of dollars that people plan to sell depends on the exchange rate.

1 If the exchange rate rises, the quantity of dollars supplied increases and there is a movement up along the supply curve of dollars.

2 If the exchange rate falls, the quantity of dollars supplied decreases and there is a movement down along the supply curve of dollars.

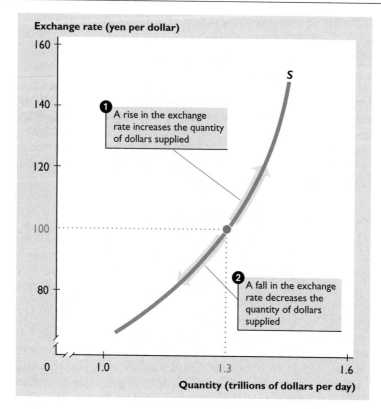

For the two reasons we've just reviewed, other things remaining the same, when the foreign exchange rate rises, the quantity of dollars supplied increases, and when the foreign exchange rate falls, the quantity of dollars supplied decreases. Figure 35.3 shows the supply curve of U.S. dollars in the foreign exchange market. In this figure, when the foreign exchange rate rises, other things remaining the same, there is an increase in the quantity of dollars supplied and a movement up along the supply curve, as shown by the arrow. When the exchange rate falls, other things remaining the same, there is a decrease in the quantity of dollars supplied and a movement down along the supply curve, as shown by the arrow.

■ Changes in the Supply of Dollars

A change in any other influence on the quantity of U.S. dollars that people plan to sell in the foreign exchange market brings a change in the supply of dollars, and the supply curve of dollars shifts. Supply either increases or decreases. These other influences on supply parallel the other influences on demand but have exactly the opposite effects. These influences are

- Interest rates in the United States and other countries
- The expected future exchange rate

Interest Rates in the United States and Other Countries

The larger the U.S. interest rate differential, the smaller is the demand for foreign assets and the smaller is the supply of dollars on the foreign exchange market.

The Expected Future Exchange Rate

Other things remaining the same, the higher the expected future exchange rate, the smaller is the supply of dollars. To see why, suppose that the dollar is trading at 100 yen per dollar today and you think that by the end of the month, the dollar will trade at 120 yen per dollar. You were planning on selling dollars today, but you decide to hold off and wait until the end of the month. If you supply dollars today, you get only 100 yen per dollar. But at the end of the month, if the dollar is worth 120 yen as you predict, you'll get 120 yen for each dollar you supply. You'll make a profit of 20 percent. So the higher the expected future exchange rate, other things remaining the same, the smaller is the expected profit from selling U.S. dollars today and the smaller is the supply of dollars today.

Figure 35.4 summarizes the above discussion of the influences on the supply of dollars. A rise in the U.S. interest rate differential or a rise in the expected future exchange rate decreases the supply of dollars today and shifts the supply curve leftward from S_0 to S_1. A fall in the U.S. interest rate differential or a fall in the expected future exchange rate increases the supply of dollars today and shifts the supply curve rightward from S_0 to S_2.

FIGURE 35.4

Changes in the Supply of Dollars

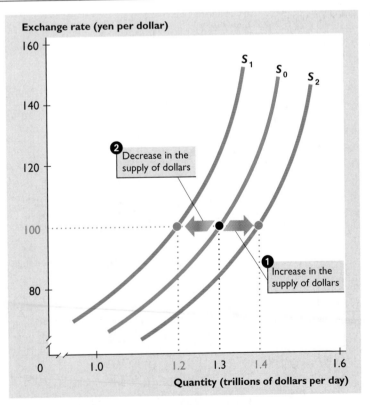

❶ The supply of dollars increases if:

- The U.S. interest rate differential decreases.
- The expected future exchange rate falls.

❷ The supply of dollars decreases if:

- The U.S. interest rate differential increases.
- The expected future exchange rate rises.

◼ Market Equilibrium

Figure 35.5 shows how demand and supply in the foreign exchange market determine the exchange rate. The demand curve is *D,* and the supply curve is *S.* Just as in all the other markets you've studied, the price (the exchange rate) acts as a regulator. If the exchange rate is too high, there is a surplus—the quantity supplied exceeds the quantity demanded. For example, in Figure 35.5, if the exchange rate is 120 yen per dollar, there is a surplus of dollars.

If the exchange rate is too low, there is a shortage—the quantity supplied is less than the quantity demanded. For example, in Figure 35.5, if the exchange rate is 80 yen per dollar, there is a shortage of dollars.

At the equilibrium exchange rate, there is neither a shortage nor a surplus. The quantity supplied equals the quantity demanded. In Figure 35.5, the equilibrium exchange rate is 100 yen per dollar. At this exchange rate, the quantity demanded equals the quantity supplied and is $1.3 trillion a day.

The foreign exchange market is constantly pulled to its equilibrium by the forces of supply and demand. Foreign exchange dealers are constantly looking for the best price they can get. If they are selling, they want the highest price available. If they are buying, they want the lowest price available. Information flows from dealer to dealer through the worldwide computer network, and the price adjusts second by second to keep buying plans and selling plans in balance. That is, price adjusts second by second to keep the market at its equilibrium.

◼ FIGURE 35.5
Equilibrium Exchange Rate

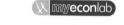

The demand curve for dollars is *D,* and the supply curve is *S.*

❶ If the exchange rate is 120 yen per dollar, there is a surplus of dollars and the exchange rate falls.

❷ If the exchange rate is 80 yen per dollar, there is a shortage of dollars and the exchange rate rises.

❸ If the exchange rate is 100 yen per dollar, there is neither a shortage nor a surplus of dollars and the exchange rate remains constant. The market is in equilibrium.

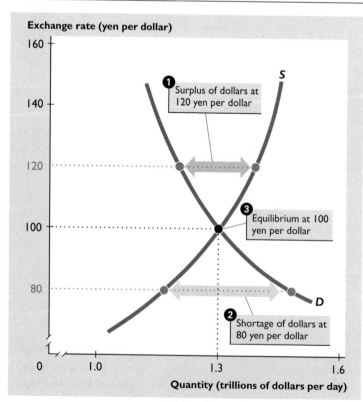

Changes in the Exchange Rate

A change in either the demand for dollars or the supply of dollars (or both) changes the exchange rate. Let's look at two episodes during the 1990s.

A Depreciating Dollar: 1994–1995

Between 1994 and the summer of 1995, the exchange rate fell from 100 yen to a low of 84 yen per dollar. Figure 35.6(a) explains this fall. In 1994, the demand and supply curves were those labeled D_{94} and S_{94}. The exchange rate was 100 yen per dollar. During 1994, traders expected the U.S. dollar to depreciate. They expected a lower exchange rate. As a result, the demand for dollars decreased and the supply of dollars increased. The demand curve shifted leftward to D_{95}, and the supply curve shifted rightward to S_{95}. The exchange rate fell to 84 yen per dollar.

An Appreciating Dollar: 1995–1998

Between 1995 and 1998, the dollar appreciated against the yen. It rose from 84 yen to 130 yen per dollar. Figure 35.6(b) explains why this happened. In 1995, the

---

FIGURE 35.6

Exchange Rate Fluctuations

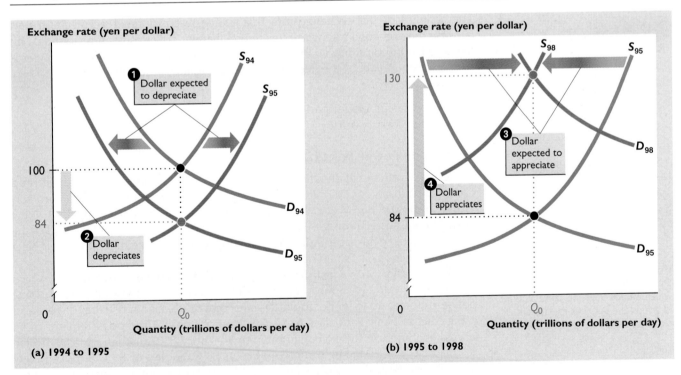

(a) 1994 to 1995

(b) 1995 to 1998

① The dollar is expected to depreciate, so the supply of dollars increases and the demand for dollars decreases.

② An excess supply of dollars brings a falling exchange rate.

③ The dollar is expected to appreciate so the supply of dollars decreases and the demand for dollars increases.

④ An excess demand for dollars brings a rising exchange rate.

demand and supply curves were those labeled D_{95} and S_{95}. The exchange rate was 84 yen per dollar—where the supply and demand curves intersect. During the next two years, Japan was in recession and the U.S. economy was expanding. Interest rates in Japan fell, and the yen was expected to depreciate. The demand for yen decreased, and the demand for dollars increased. The demand curve shifted from D_{95} to D_{98}. The supply of dollars decreased, and the supply curve shifted from S_{95} to S_{98}. These two shifts reinforced each other, and the exchange rate increased to 130 yen per dollar.

Why the Exchange Rate Is Volatile

You've seen that sometimes the dollar depreciates and at other times it appreciates. But the quantity of dollars traded each day barely changes. Why? Because in the foreign exchange market, supply and demand are not independent.

When we studied the demand for dollars and the supply of dollars, we saw that unlike other markets, the demand side and the supply side of the market have common influences. A change in the expected future exchange rate or a change in the U.S. interest rate differential changes *both* demand and supply, and they change in *opposite directions*. These common influences on both demand and supply explain why the exchange rate can be volatile at times, even though the quantity of dollars traded does not change.

Everyone in the market is potentially either a demander or a supplier. Each has a price above which he or she will sell and below which he or she will buy.

■ Exchange Rate Expectations

The changes in the exchange rate that we've just examined occurred in part because the exchange rate was expected to change. This explanation sounds a bit like a self-fulfilling forecast. But what makes expectations change? The answer is new information about the deeper forces that influence the value of money. There are two such forces:

- Purchasing power parity
- Interest rate parity

Purchasing Power Parity

Money is worth what it will buy. But two kinds of money, U.S. dollars and Canadian dollars, for example, might buy different amounts of goods and services. Suppose a Big Mac costs $4 (Canadian) in Toronto and $3 (U.S.) in New York. If the Canadian dollar exchange rate is $1.33 Canadian per U.S. dollar, the two monies have the same value. You can buy a Big Mac in either Toronto or New York for either $4 Canadian or $3 U.S.

Purchasing power parity
Equal value of money—a situation in which money buys the same amount of goods and services in different currencies.

The situation we've just described is called **purchasing power parity**, which means equal value of money. If purchasing power parity does not prevail, some powerful forces go to work. To understand these forces, suppose that the price of a Big Mac in New York rises to $4 U.S., but in Toronto the price remains at $4 Canadian. Suppose the exchange rate remains at $1.33 Canadian per U.S. dollar. In this case, a Big Mac in Toronto still costs $4 Canadian or $3 U.S. But in New York, it costs $4 U.S. or $5.32 Canadian. Money buys more in Canada than in the United States. Money is not of equal value in both countries.

If all (or most) prices have increased in the United States and not increased in Canada, then people will generally expect that the U.S. dollar exchange rate is going to fall. The demand for U.S. dollars decreases, and the supply of U.S. dollars increases. The U.S. dollar exchange rate falls, as expected. If the U.S. dollar falls to $1.00 Canadian and there are no further price changes, purchasing power parity is restored. A Big Mac now costs $4 in either U.S. dollars or Canadian dollars in both New York and Toronto.

If prices increase in Canada and other countries but remain constant in the United States, then people will generally expect that the value of the U.S. dollar on the foreign exchange market is too low and that the U.S. dollar exchange rate will rise. The demand for U.S. dollars increases, and the supply of U.S. dollars decreases. The U.S. dollar exchange rate rises, as expected.

Ultimately, the value of money is determined by prices. So the deeper forces that influence the exchange rate have tentacles that spread throughout the economy. If prices in the United States rise faster than those in other countries, the exchange rate falls. And if prices in the United States rise more slowly than those in other countries, the exchange rate rises.

EYE ON THE GLOBAL ECONOMY

Purchasing Power Parity

Purchasing power parity (PPP) is a long-run phenomenon. In the short run, deviations from PPP can be large.

The figure shows the range of deviations from PPP in November 2002. At that time, the Norwegian krone was overvalued by 45 percent and the Japanese yen was overvalued by 22 percent. The yen has been overvalued for most of the past 10 years. An overvalued currency is one that, according to PPP, will depreciate at some point in the future.

The most undervalued currency in November 2002 was the Polish zloty. An undervalued currency is one that, according to PPP, will appreciate at some time in the future. But PPP does not predict *when* a currency will depreciate or appreciate.

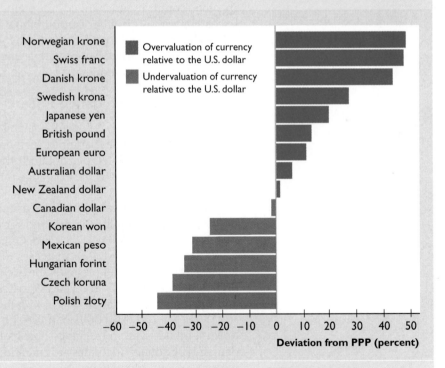

SOURCE OF DATA: PACIFIC FX Service, University of British Columbia, August 7, 2005.

Interest Rate Parity

Suppose a Canadian dollar bank deposit in a Toronto bank earns 5 percent a year and a U.S. dollar bank deposit in a New York bank earns 3 percent a year. Why does anyone deposit money in New York? Why doesn't all the money flow to Toronto? The answer is: Because of exchange rate expectations. Suppose people expect the Canadian dollar to depreciate by 2 percent a year. This 2 percent depreciation must be subtracted from the 5 percent interest to obtain the net return of 3 percent a year that an American can earn by depositing funds in a Toronto bank. The two returns are equal. This situation is one of **interest rate parity**—equal interest rates when exchange rate changes are taken into account.

Interest rate parity always prevails. Funds move to get the highest return available. If the Canadian dollar was higher than its interest rate parity level, the return expected in Toronto would be lower than in New York. In seconds, traders would sell the Canadian dollar, its exchange rate would fall, and the expected return from lending in Toronto would rise to equal that in New York.

Interest rate parity
Equal interest rates—a situation in which the interest rate in one currency equals the interest rate in another currency when exchange rate changes are taken into account.

■ Monetary Policy and the Exchange Rate

Monetary policy influences the interest rate (see Chapter 28, pp. 702–705). So monetary policy also influences the interest rate differential and the exchange rate. If the Fed increases the U.S. interest rate and other central banks keep interest rates in other countries unchanged, the value of the U.S. dollar rises on the foreign exchange market. If other central banks increase their interest rates and the Fed keeps the U.S. interest rate unchanged, the value of the U.S. dollar falls on the foreign exchange market. So exchange rates fluctuate in response to changes and expected changes in monetary policy in the United States and around the world.

■ Pegging the Exchange Rate

Some central banks try to avoid exchange rate fluctuations by pegging the value of their currency against another currency. Suppose the Fed wanted to keep the dollar pegged at 100 yen per dollar. If the exchange rate rose above 100 yen, the Fed would sell dollars. If the exchange rate fell below 100 yen, the Fed would buy dollars.

Figure 35.7 illustrates foreign exchange market intervention. The supply of dollars is S, and initially, the demand for dollars is D_0. The equilibrium exchange rate is 100 yen per dollar, which is also the Fed's target—the horizontal red line.

If the demand for dollars increases to D_1, the Fed increases the supply of dollars—sells dollars—and prevents the exchange rate from rising. If the demand for dollars decreases to D_2, the Fed decreases the supply of dollars—buys dollars—and prevents the exchange rate from falling.

When the Fed buys dollars, it uses its reserves of yen. And when the Fed sells dollars, it takes yen in exchange and its reserves of yen increase. As long as the demand for dollars fluctuates around and, on the average, remains at D_0, the Fed's reserves of yen fluctuate but neither run dry nor persistently increase.

But if the demand for dollars decreased permanently to D_2, to maintain the exchange rate at 100 yen per dollar, the Fed would have to buy dollars and sell yen every day. The Fed would soon run out of yen. And when it did, the dollar would sink. If the demand for dollars increased permanently to D_1, the Fed would have to sell dollars and buy yen every day. The Fed would be piling up unwanted yen and at some point would let the dollar rise.

FIGURE 35.7

Foreign Exchange Market Intervention

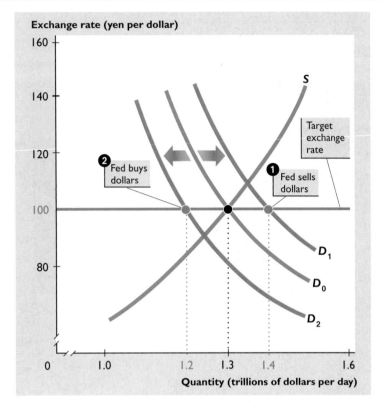

Initially, the demand for dollars is D_0, the supply of dollars is S, and the exchange rate is 100 yen per dollar. The Fed can intervene in the foreign exchange market to keep the exchange rate close to its target rate (100 yen in this example).

❶ If demand increases from D_0 to D_1, the Fed sells dollars to increase supply.

❷ If demand decreases from D_0 to D_2, the Fed buys dollars to decrease supply.

Persistent intervention on one side of the market cannot be sustained.

■ The People's Bank of China in the Foreign Exchange Market

Although the Fed could peg the value of the dollar, it chooses not to do so. But China's central bank, the People's Bank of China, does intervene to peg the value of its currency—the yuan. *Eye on the Global Economy* on page 911 shows the result of this intervention.

During much of the period that the yuan has been pegged to the U.S. dollar, China has piled up U.S dollar reserves. Figure 35.8(a) shows the numbers. You can see that in 2004 and 2005, China's reserves increased by $200 billion a year.

Figure 35.8(b), which shows the market for U.S. dollars priced in terms of the yuan, explains why China's reserves increased. The demand curve D and supply curve S intersect at 5 yuan per dollar. If the People's Bank of China took no actions in the foreign exchange market, this exchange rate would be the equilibrium rate. (This particular value is only an example. No one knows what the yuan-dollar exchange rate would be with no intervention.)

By intervening in the market and buying U.S. dollars, the People's Bank can peg the yuan at 8.28 yuan per dollar. But to do so, it must keep holding the dollars that it buys. In Figure 35.8(b), the People's Bank buys $200 billion a year.

Only by allowing the yuan to appreciate can China stop accumulating dollars. That is what the People's Bank decided to do in July 2005. But China continues to intervene in the foreign exchange market to manage the rate of appreciation of the yuan. Eventually, when China's foreign exchange market becomes more accustomed to a floating yuan, it is likely that the People's Bank will lessen its intervention and the value of the yuan will be determined by market forces.

FIGURE 35.8

China's Foreign Exchange Market Intervention

China has been piling up reserves of U.S. dollars since 2000. In 2004 and 2005, the build-up of reserves was very large. Part (a) shows the numbers.

Part (b) shows the market for the U.S. dollar in terms of the Chinese yuan. Note that a higher exchange rate (yuan per dollar) means a lower value of the yuan and a higher value of the dollar. The yuan appreciates when the number of yuan per dollar decreases.

❶ With demand curve *D* and supply curve *S*, the equilibrium exchange rate is 5 yuan per dollar. (The equilibrium value is not known, and the value assumed is only an example.)

❷ The People's Bank of China has a target exchange rate of 8.28 yuan per dollar. At this exchange rate, the yuan is *undervalued*.

❸ To keep the exchange rate pegged at its target level, the People's Bank of China must buy U.S. dollars in exchange for yuan, and China's reserves of dollars piles up.

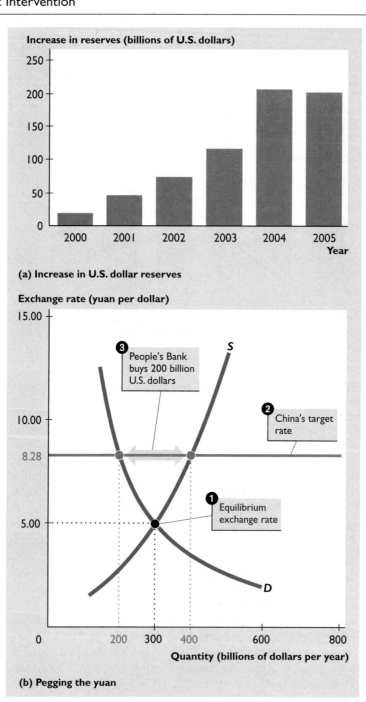

SOURCE OF DATA: The People's Bank of China.

The Fixed Yuan

THE PEOPLE'S BANK OF CHINA

Exchange rate (yuan per dollar)

China pegs the yuan to the US dollar

China devalues the yuan

Yuan on managed float

Jan 1992 Jan 1994 Jan 1996 Jan 1998 Jan 2000 Jan 2002 Jan 2004 Jan 2006

Month/year

The Chinese central bank, the People's Bank of China, has pegged the value of the yuan in terms of the U.S. dollar for more than 10 years.

The figure shows the value of the yuan (yuan per dollar) from the early 1990s to 2005.

The yuan was devalued in January 1994. It appreciated a bit during 1994 and 1995. But it was then pegged at 8.28 yuan per U.S. dollar, a value that was maintained for more than 10 years. In July 2005, the yuan began a managed float.

SOURCE OF DATA: PACIFIX FX Service, University of British Columbia.

REALITY CHECK

International Finance in YOUR Life

If you go to Europe for a vacation, you will need some euros. What is the best way to get euros? One way is to just take your cash card to use an ATM in Europe. You get euros from the cash machine, and your bank account in the United States gets charged for the cash you obtain.

When you get euros, the number of euros you request is multiplied by the exchange rate to determine how many dollars to take from your bank account.

You have just made a transaction in the foreign exchange market. You have exchanged dollars for euros.

The exchange rate that you paid was probably costly. Your bank took a commission for helping you get euros. Some banks charge as much as 5 percent. Check in advance. It might be better to buy euros from your bank before you leave on your trip.

2 Explain how the exchange rate is determined and why it fluctuates.

Practice Problem 35.2

1. Suppose that yesterday, the U.S. dollar was trading on the foreign exchange market at 100 yen per dollar. Today, the U.S. dollar is trading at 105 yen per dollar.
    a. Which of the two currencies (the dollar or the yen) has appreciated and which has depreciated today?
    b. List the events that could have caused today's change in the value of the U.S. dollar on the foreign exchange market.
    c. Did the events that you listed in part **b** change the demand for U.S. dollars, the supply of U.S. dollars, or both the demand for and supply of U.S. dollars?
    d. If the Fed had tried to stabilize the value of the U.S. dollar at 100 yen per dollar, what action would it have taken?
    e. In part **d,** what effect would the Fed's actions have had on U.S. official reserves?

Exercise 35.2

1. Suppose that yesterday, the Canadian dollar ($C) was trading on the foreign exchange market at $0.85 U.S. per $C. Today, the Canadian dollar is trading at $0.80 U.S. per $C.
    a. Which of the two currencies (the Canadian dollar or the U.S. dollar) has appreciated and which has depreciated today?
    b. List the events that could have caused today's change in the value of the Canadian dollar on the foreign exchange market.
    c. Did the events that you listed in part **b** increase or decrease the demand for Canadian dollars, the supply of Canadian dollars, or both the demand for and supply of Canadian dollars?
    d. If the Bank of Canada had tried to stabilize the value of the Canadian dollar at $0.85 U.S., what action would it have taken?
    e. In part **d,** what effect would the Bank of Canada's actions have had on Canadian official reserves?

Solution to Practice Problem 35.2

1a. Because the U.S. dollar costs a larger number of yen, the U.S. dollar has appreciated. The yen has depreciated because it buys fewer dollars.
1b. The main events might be an increase in the U.S. interest rate, a decrease in the Japanese interest rate, or a rise in the expected future exchange rate of the U.S. dollar.
1c. The events that you listed in part **b** change both the demand for and supply of dollars. They increase demand and decrease supply.
1d. To stabilize the value of the U.S. dollar, the Fed would have sold U.S. dollars to increase the supply of U.S. dollars in the foreign exchange market.
1e. When the Fed sells U.S. dollars, it buys foreign currency. U.S. official reserves would have increased.

CHAPTER CHECKPOINT

Key Points

1 Describe a country's balance of payments accounts and explain what determines the amount of international borrowing and lending.

- Foreign currency is used to finance international trade.
- A country's balance of payments accounts record its international transactions.
- Historically, the United States has been a net lender to the rest of the world, but in 1983, that situation changed and the United States became a net borrower, and in 1989 the United States became a debtor nation.
- Net exports are equal to the private sector balance plus the government sector balance.

2 Explain how the exchange rate is determined and why it fluctuates.

- Foreign currency is obtained in exchange for domestic currency in the foreign exchange market.
- The exchange rate is determined by demand and supply in the foreign exchange market.
- The lower the exchange rate, the greater is the quantity of dollars demanded. A change in the exchange rate brings a movement along the demand curve for dollars.
- Changes in the expected future exchange rate and the U.S. interest rate differential change the demand for dollars and shift the demand curve.
- The lower the exchange rate, the smaller is the quantity of dollars supplied. A change in the exchange rate brings a movement along the supply curve of dollars.
- Changes in the expected future exchange rate and the U.S. interest rate differential change the supply of dollars and shift the supply curve.
- Fluctuations in the exchange rate occur because fluctuations in the demand for and supply of dollars are not independent.
- A central bank can intervene in the foreign exchange market to smooth fluctuations in the exchange rate.

Key Terms

Balance of payments accounts, 890
Capital account, 890
Creditor nation, 892
Currency appreciation, 898
Currency depreciation, 897
Current account, 890

Debtor nation, 892
Foreign exchange market, 897
Foreign exchange rate, 897
Government sector balance, 894
Interest rate parity, 908
Net borrower, 892

Net lender, 892
Official settlements account, 890
Private sector balance, 894
Purchasing power parity, 906
U.S. interest rate differential, 900
U.S. official reserves, 890

⟨X myeconlab⟩ Exercises

1. The following data describe the economy of Antarctica in 2050:

Item	(billions of Antarctica dollars)
Imports of goods and services	150
Exports of goods and services	50
Net interest	−10
Net transfers	35
Foreign investment in Antarctica	125
Antarctica's investment abroad	55

   a. Calculate Antarctica's current account balance.
   b. Calculate Antarctica's capital account balance.
   c. Calculate the increase in Antarctica's official reserves.
   d. Is Antarctica a debtor nation or a creditor nation?
   e. Are Antarctica's international assets increasing or decreasing?
   f. Can you determine whether Antarctica is borrowing to finance investment or consumption? Why or why not?

2. The U.S. dollar appreciates, and the nation's official holdings of foreign currency increase. State which of the following events could have caused these changes to occur and why.
   a. The Fed intervened in the foreign exchange market and sold dollars.
   b. The Fed conducted an open market operation and sold bonds.
   c. People began to expect the dollar to appreciate.
   d. The U.S. interest rate differential narrowed.
   e. The U.S. current account went into deficit.

3. The U.S. dollar depreciates. State which of the following events could have caused the depreciation and why.
   a. The Fed intervened in the foreign exchange market and sold dollars.
   b. The Fed intervened in the foreign exchange market and bought dollars.
   c. People began to expect the dollar to depreciate.
   d. The U.S. interest rate differential increased.
   e. Foreign investment in the United States increased.

4. The euro appreciates. State which of the following events could have caused the appreciation and why.
   a. The ECB intervened in the foreign exchange market and sold euros.
   b. The Fed intervened in the foreign exchange market and bought dollars.
   c. People began to expect the euro to depreciate.
   d. The EU interest rate differential increased.
   e. The EU interest rate differential decreased.
   f. Profits increased in Europe, and foreign investment in European companies surged.

5. If Japan has a lower inflation rate than the United States and the difference in inflation rates persists for some years, will
   a. The dollar appreciate or depreciate against the yen?
   b. The yen appreciate or depreciate against the dollar?

c. Purchasing power parity be violated? Why or why not?

d. Interest rate parity hold? Why or why not?

e. U.S. interest rates be higher or lower than Japanese interest rates? Why or why not?

f. The inflation difference influence the expected future exchange rate? Why or why not?

g. The inflation difference influence the U.S. current account balance? Why or why not?

6. Suppose that the euro keeps rising and hits $2 U.S. At this point, the Fed decides to stop the euro from rising (stop the dollar from falling) by intervening in the foreign exchange market.

a. What actions might the Fed take in the foreign exchange market?

b. Could the Fed take the actions you described in part **a** forever if necessary?

c. Would the Fed's actions prevent interest rate parity from being achieved? Why or why not?

d. Are there any other actions that the Fed could take to raise the foreign exchange value of the dollar? Explain your answer.

Critical Thinking

7. Many people think that a current account deficit is a sign that a nation is not able to compete in international markets. Explain why this view is incorrect and describe the factors that create a current account deficit.

8. For most of the 1990s, Argentina pegged the value of its currency, the peso, to the U.S. dollar. 1 peso equaled 1 U.S. dollar. Then, at the end of 2001, the peso was allowed to find its own value on the foreign exchange market and it fell dramatically.

a. Why might it be difficult for Argentina to peg the value of its currency to the U.S. dollar?

b. Why, nonetheless, might it be a good idea for Argentina to peg the value of its currency to the U.S. dollar? What are the potential benefits to Argentina?

c. On balance, do you think a country such as Argentina should peg its currency to the U.S. dollar?

9. Now that Europe has replaced its national currencies (such as the French franc, German mark, and Italian lira) with a new single currency, the euro, some people say that North America should do the same. The suggestion is that the Mexican peso and Canadian dollar be scrapped and that the entire NAFTA area use the U.S. dollar for all transactions.

a. What are some of the differences between the European and North American situations that might mean that the European solution would not work in North America?

b. What are some of the similarities between the European and North American situations that might mean that the European solution *would* work in North America?

Web Exercises

Use the links on MyEconLab to work the following exercises.

10. Visit FRED, the Federal Reserve Economic Database, and find data on the exchange rate and international trade.
    a. When did the United States last have a current account surplus?
    b. Does the United States have a surplus or a deficit in trade in goods?
    c. Does the United States have a surplus or a deficit in trade in services?
    d. What has happened to foreign investment in the United States during the past 10 years?
    e. Do you think the U.S. balance of payments record is a matter for concern? Why or why not?

11. Visit the PACIFIC Exchange Rate Service and obtain data on the exchange rate of the U.S. dollar against two other currencies.
    a. Use the demand and supply model to explain the changes (or absence of changes) in the exchange rates.
    b. What specific events might have changed exchange rate expectations?
    c. What forces might have prevented the exchange rate from changing?
    d. What information would you need to have to determine whether the central bank intervened in the foreign exchange market to limit the change in the exchange rate?

Glossary

Ability-to-pay principle The proposition that people should pay taxes according to how easily they can bear the burden. (p. 210)

Above full-employment equilibrium When equilibrium real GDP exceeds potential GDP. (p. 745)

Absolute advantage When one person is more productive than another person in several or even all activities. (p. 82)

Aggregate demand The relationship between the quantity of real GDP demanded and the price level when all other influences on expenditure plans remain the same. (p. 738)

Aggregate hours The total number of hours worked by all the people employed, both full time and part time, during a year. (p. 527)

Aggregate planned expenditure Planned consumption expenditure plus planned investment plus planned government expenditure plus planned exports minus planned imports. (p. 757)

Aggregate supply The relationship between the quantity of real GDP supplied and the price level when all other influences on production plans remain the same. (p. 732)

Allocative efficiency A situation in which the quantities of goods and services produced are those that people value most highly—it is not possible to produce more of a good or service without giving up some of another good that people value more highly. (p. 72)

Antitrust law A law that regulates and prohibits certain kinds of market behavior, such as monopoly and monopolistic practices. (p. 434)

Automatic fiscal policy A fiscal policy action that is triggered by the state of the economy. (p. 784)

Automatic stabilizers Features of fiscal policy that stabilize real GDP without explicit action by the government. (p. 794)

Autonomous expenditure The components of aggregate expenditure that do not change when real GDP changes. (p. 758)

Average cost pricing rule A rule that sets price equal to average cost to enable the firm to cover its costs. (p. 427)

Average fixed cost Total fixed cost per unit of output. (p. 309)

Average product Total product divided by the quantity of an input. The average product of labor is total product divided by the quantity of labor employed. (p. 304)

Average tax rate The percentage of income that is paid in tax. (p. 201)

Average total cost Total cost per unit of output, which equals average fixed cost plus average variable cost. (p. 309)

Average variable cost Total variable cost per unit of output. (p. 309)

Balance of payments accounts The accounts in which a nation records its international trading, borrowing, and lending. (p. 890)

Balance of trade The value of exports minus the value of imports. (p. 861)

Balance sheet A statement that summarizes assets (amounts owned) and liabilities (amounts owed). (p. 674)

Balanced budget The budget balance when tax receipts equal expenditures. (p. 784)

Balanced budget multiplier The magnification effect on aggregate demand of a simultaneous change in government expenditure and taxes that leaves the budget balanced unchanged. (p. 787)

Barrier to entry A natural or legal constraint that protects a firm from competitors. (p. 350)

Barter The direct exchange of goods and services for other goods and services, which requires a double coincidence of wants. (p. 649)

Beige Book A report that summarizes current economic conditions in each Federal Reserve district and each sector of the economy. (p. 796)

Below full-employment equilibrium When potential GDP exceeds equilibrium real GDP. (p. 745)

Benefit The benefit of something is the gain or pleasure that it brings. (p. 11)

Benefits principle The proposition that people should pay taxes equal to the benefits they receive from public goods and services. (p. 210)

Big tradeoff A tradeoff between efficiency and fairness that recognizes the cost of making income transfers. (p. 162)

Black market An illegal market that operates alongside a government-regulated market. (p. 173)

Bond A promise to pay specified sums of money on specified dates; it is a debt for the issuer. (pp. 447, 597)

Bond market A financial market in which bonds issued by firms and governments are traded. (pp. 447, 597)

Budget deficit The budget balance when expenditures exceed tax receipts. (p. 784)

Budget line A line that describes the limits to consumption possibilities and that depends on a consumer's budget and the prices of goods and services. (p. 266)

Budget surplus The budget balance when tax receipts exceed expenditures. (p. 784)

Business cycle A periodic but irregular up-and-down movement of total production and other measures of economic activity. (p. 513)

Capital Tools, instruments, machines, buildings, and other items that have been produced in the past and that businesses now use to produce goods and services. (p. 38)

Capital account Record of foreign investment in the United States minus U.S. investment abroad. (p. 890)

Capital goods Goods that are bought by businesses to increase their productive resources. (p. 34)

Capture theory The theory that a regulated firm captures the regulator and makes a monopoly profit. (p. 425)

Cartel A group of firms acting together to limit output, raise price, and increase economic profit. (p. 402)

Central bank A public authority that provides banking services to banks and regulates financial institutions and markets. (p. 663)

Ceteris paribus Other things remaining the same (often abbreviated as *cet. par.*). (p. 15)

Change in demand A change in the quantity that people plan to buy when any influence on buying plans other than the price of the good changes. (p. 94)

Change in the quantity demanded A change in the quantity of a good that people plan to buy that results from a change in the price of the good. (p. 96)

Change in the quantity supplied A change in the quantity of a good that suppliers plan to sell that results from a change in the price of the good. (p. 103)

Change in supply A change in the quantity that suppliers plan to sell when any influence on selling plans other than the price of the good changes. (p. 101)

Circular flow model A model of the economy that shows the circular flow of expenditures and incomes that result from decision makers' choices and the way those choices interact to determine what, how, and for whom goods and services are produced. (p. 42)

Classical growth theory The theory that the clash between an exploding population and limited resources will eventually

bring economic growth to an end. (p. 629)

Classical macroeconomics A body of theory about how a market economy works and why it experiences economic growth and fluctuations. (p. 570)

Coase theorem The proposition that if property rights exist, only a small number of parties are involved, and transactions costs are low, then private transactions are efficient and the outcome is not affected by who is assigned the property right. (p. 224)

Command system A system that allocates resources by the order of someone in authority. (p. 144)

Commercial bank A firm that is chartered by the Comptroller of the Currency in the U.S. Treasury (or by a state agency) to accept deposits and make loans. (p. 656)

Commodity market A market in which raw materials are traded. (p. 448)

Common resource A resource, one unit of which, can be used only once but no one can be prevented from using what is available. (p. 243)

Comparative advantage The ability of a person to perform an activity or produce a good or service at a lower opportunity cost than someone else. (p. 81)

Complement A good that is consumed with another good. (p. 94)

Complement in production A good that is produced along with another good. (p. 101)

Constant returns to scale A condition in which, when a firm increases its plant size and labor employed by the same percentage, its output increases by the same percentage and its average total cost remains constant. (p. 316)

Consumer Price Index A measure of the average of the prices paid by urban consumers for a fixed market basket of consumption goods and services. (p. 548)

Consumer surplus The marginal benefit from a good or service minus the price paid for it, summed over the quantity consumed. (p. 149)

Consumption expenditure The expenditure by households on consumption goods and services. (p. 499)

Consumption function The relationship between consumption expenditure and disposable income, other things remaining the same. (p. 758)

Consumption goods and services Goods and services that are bought by individuals and used to provide personal enjoyment and contribute to a person's standard of living. (p. 34)

Contractionary fiscal policy Discretionary fiscal policy designed to decrease aggregate demand—a discretionary decrease in government expenditure or a discretionary tax increase. (p. 789)

Copyright A government-sanctioned exclusive right granted to the inventor of a good, service, or productive process to produce, use, and sell the invention for a given number of years. (p. 235)

Correlation The tendency for the values of two variables to move in a predictable and related way. (p. 16)

Cost of living index A measure of changes in the amount of money that people would need to spend to achieve a given standard of living. (p. 554)

Credit union A financial institution owned by a social or economic group such as a firm's employees, that accepts savings deposits and makes mostly consumer loans. (p. 658)

Creditor nation A country that during its entire history has invested more in the rest of the world than other countries have invested in it. (p. 892)

Cross elasticity of demand A measure of the responsiveness of the demand for a good to a change in the price of a substitute or complement when other things remain the same. (p. 135)

Cross-section graph A graph that shows the values of an economic variable for different groups in a population at a point in time. (p. 24)

Crowding-out effect The tendency for a government budget deficit to decrease investment. (p. 610)

Currency Notes (dollar bills) and coins. (p. 650)

Currency appreciation The rise in the value of one currency in terms of another currency. (p. 898)

Currency depreciation The fall in the value of one currency in terms of another currency. (p. 897)

Currency drain Funds loaned by banks that drain from the banks to be held as currency. (p. 687)

Current account Record of international receipts and payments—current account balance equals exports minus imports, plus net interest and transfers received from abroad. (p. 890)

Cyclical unemployment The fluctuating unemployment over the business cycle that increases during a recession and decreases during an expansion. (p. 538)

Deadweight loss The decrease in total surplus that results from an inefficient underproduction or overproduction. (p. 157)

Debtor nation A country that during its entire history has borrowed more from the rest of the world than it has lent to it. (p. 892)

Decreasing marginal returns When the marginal product of an additional worker is less than the marginal product of the previous worker. (p. 302)

Demand The relationship between the quantity demanded and the price of a good when all other influences on buying plans remain the same. (p. 91)

Demand curve A graph of the relationship between the quantity demanded of a good and its price when all the other influences on buying plans remain the same. (p. 92)

Demand for labor The relationship between the quantity of labor demanded and real wage rate when all other influences on firms' hiring plans remain the same. (p. 575)

Demand for money The relationship between the quantity of money demanded and the nominal interest rate, when all other influences on the amount of money that people wish to hold remain the same. (p. 700)

Demand schedule A list of the quantities demanded at each different price when all the other influences on buying plans remain the same. (p. 92)

Depreciation The decrease in the value of capital that results from its use and from obsolescence. (p. 506)

Deregulation The process of removing restrictions on prices, product standards and types, and entry conditions. (p. 424)

Derived demand The demand for a factor of production, which is derived from the demand for the goods and services it is used to produce. (p. 449)

Diminishing marginal rate of substitution The general tendency for the marginal rate of substitution to decrease as the consumer moves down along the indifference curve, increasing consumption of the good measured on the x-axis and decreasing consumption of the good measured on the y-axis. (p. 290)

Diminishing marginal utility The general tendency for marginal utility to decrease as the quantity of a good consumed increases. (p. 273)

Diminishing returns The tendency for each additional hour of labor employed to produce a successively smaller additional amount of real GDP. (p. 574)

Direct relationship A relationship between two variables that move in the same direction. (p. 26)

Discount rate The interest rate at which the Fed stands ready to lend reserves to commercial banks. (p. 665)

Discouraged worker A person who does not have a job, is available and willing to work, but has not made specific efforts to find a job within the previous four weeks. (p. 526)

Discretionary fiscal policy A fiscal policy action that is initiated by an act of Congress. (p. 784)

Discretionary monetary policy Monetary policy that is based on the judgments of policy makers about the current needs of the economy. (p. 840)

Diseconomies of scale A condition in which, when a firm increases its plant size and labor employed by the same percentage, its output increases by a smaller percentage and its average total cost increases. (p. 316)

Disposable income Income earned minus net taxes. (p. 602)

Disposable personal income Income received by households minus personal income taxes paid. (p. 507)

Dumping When a foreign firm sells its exports at a lower price than its cost of production. (p. 878)

Duopoly A market with only two firms. (p. 402)

Earnings sharing regulation A regulation that requires firms to make refunds to customers when profits rise above a target level. (p. 430)

Economic depreciation An opportunity cost of a firm using capital that it owns—measured as the change in the market value of capital over a given period. (p. 297)

Economic freedom A condition in which people are able to make personal choices, their private property is protected, and they are free to buy and sell in markets. (p. 639)

Economic growth The sustained expansion of production possibilities. (p. 79)

Economic growth rate The annual percentage change of real GDP. (p. 620)

Economic profit A firm's total revenue minus total cost. (p. 297)

Economic rent The income received by any factor of production over and above the amount required to induce a given quantity of the factor to be supplied. (p. 464)

Economics The social science that studies the choices that we make as we cope with scarcity and the incentives that influence and reconcile our choices. (p. 3)

Economies of scale A condition in which, when a firm increases its plant size and labor employed by the same percentage, its output increases by a larger percentage and its average total cost decreases. (p. 315)

Efficiency wage A real wage rate that is set above the full-employment equilibrium wage rate to induce greater work effort. (p. 585)

Efficient scale The quantity at which average total cost is a minimum. (p. 387)

Elastic demand When the percentage change in the quantity demanded exceeds the percentage change in price. (p. 120)

Elastic supply When the percentage change in the quantity supplied exceeds the percentage change in price. (p. 130)

Electronic cash (or **e-cash**) An electronic equivalent of paper notes and coins. (p. 652)

Electronic check (or **e-check**) An electronic equivalent of a paper check. (p. 652)

Entrepreneurship The human resource that organizes labor, land, and capital. (p. 39)

Equation of exchange An equation that states that the quantity of money multiplied by the velocity of circulation equals the price level multiplied by real GDP. (p. 711)

Equilibrium expenditure The level of aggregate expenditure that occurs when aggregate planned expenditure equals real GDP. (p. 766)

Equilibrium price The price at which the quantity demanded equals the quantity supplied. (p. 105)

Equilibrium quantity The quantity bought and sold at the equilibrium price. (p. 105)

Excess burden The amount by which the burden of a tax exceeds the tax revenue received by the government—the deadweight loss from a tax. (p. 196)

Excess capacity When the quantity that a firm produces is less than the quantity at which average total cost is a minimum. (p. 387)

Excess demand A situation in which the quantity demanded exceeds the quantity supplied. (p.105)

Excess reserves Bank reserves that exceed those needed to meet the required reserve ratio. (p. 657)

Excess supply A situation in which the quantity supplied exceeds the quantity demanded. (p. 105)

Excludable A good, service, or resource is excludable if it is possible to prevent someone from enjoying its benefits. (p. 242)

Expansionary fiscal policy Discretionary fiscal policy designed to increase aggregate demand—a discretionary increase in government expenditure or a discretionary tax cut. (p. 788)

Expected inflation rate The inflation rate that people forecast and use to set the money wage rate and other money prices. (p. 818)

Explicit cost A cost paid in money. (p. 297)

Exports of goods and services Goods and services that are produced in one country and sold in other countries; Items that firms in the United States produce and sell to the rest of the world. (pp. 34, 500)

Externality A cost or a benefit that arises from production that falls on someone other than the producer or a cost or benefit that arises from consumption that falls on someone other than the consumer. (p. 218)

Factor markets Markets in which factors of production are bought and sold. (p. 42)

Factor price The price of a factor of production. The wage rate is the price of labor, the interest rate is the price of capital, and rent is the price of land. (p. 446)

Factors of production The productive resources that are used to produce goods and services—land, labor, capital, and entrepreneurship. (p. 36)

Federal budget An annual statement of the expenditures, tax receipts, and surplus or deficit of the government of the United States. (p. 784)

Federal funds rate The interest rate on interbank loans (loans made in the federal funds market). (p. 657)

Federal Open Market Committee The Fed's main policy-making committee. (p. 664)

Federal Reserve System The central bank of the United States. (p. 663)

Feedback-rule policy A policy that specifies how policy actions respond to changes in the state of the economy. (p. 840)

Fiat money Objects that are money because the law decrees or orders them to be money. (p. 650)

Final good or service A good or service that is produced for its final user and not as a component of another good or service. (p. 498)

Financial capital The funds that firms use to buy and operate physical capital. (pp. 447, 594)

Financial markets The collection of people and firms who are lending and borrowing to finance the purchase of physical capital. (p. 447) The collection of households, firms, governments, banks, and other financial institutions that lend and borrow. (p. 596)

Firms The institutions that organize the production of goods and services. (p. 42)

Fiscal policy The use of the federal budget to encourage sustained economic growth and smooth the business cycle. (p. 784)

Fixed-rule policy A policy that is pursued independently of the state of the economy. (p. 840)

Foreign exchange market The market in which the currency of one country is exchanged for the currency of another. (p. 897)

Foreign exchange rate The price at which one currency exchanges for another. (p. 897)

Four-firm concentration ratio The percentage of the total revenue of an industry accounted for by the four largest firms in the industry. (p. 380)

Free lunch A gift—getting something without giving up something else. (p. 65)

Free rider A person who enjoys the benefits of a good or service without paying for it. (p. 245)

Frictional unemployment The unemployment that arises from normal labor turnover—from people entering and leaving the labor force and from the ongoing creation and destruction of jobs. (p. 537)

Full employment When there is no cyclical unemployment or, equivalently, when all the unemployment is frictional, structural, and seasonal. (p. 539)

Full-employment equilibrium When equilibrium real GDP equals potential GDP. (p. 745)

Full-time workers People who usually work 35 hours or more a week. (p. 526)

Functional distribution of income The distribution of income among the factors of production. (p. 40)

Game theory The tool that economists use to analyze strategic behavior—behavior that recognizes mutual interdependence and takes account of the expected behavior of others. (p. 411)

GDP deflator An average of current prices expressed as a percentage of base-year prices. (p. 510)

Goods and services The objects (goods) and the actions (services) that people value and produce to satisfy human wants. (p. 3)

Goods markets Markets in which goods and services are bought and sold. (p. 42)

Government expenditure multiplier The magnification effect of a change in government expenditure on goods and services on aggregate demand. (p. 787)

Government expenditure on goods and services The expenditure by all levels of government on goods and services. (p. 500)

Government goods and services Goods and services that are bought by governments. (p. 34)

Government sector balance Net taxes minus government expenditure on goods and services. (p. 894)

Great Depression A decade (the 1930s) of high unemployment and stagnant production throughout the world economy. (p. 570)

Gross domestic product (GDP) The market value of all the final goods and services produced within a country in a given time period. (p. 498)

Gross investment The total amount spent on new capital goods. (p. 594)

Gross national product (GNP) The market value of all the final goods and services produced anywhere in the world in a given time period by the factors of production supplied by the residents of the country. (p. 507)

Herfindahl-Hirschman Index The square of the percentage market share of each firm summed over the largest 50 firms (or summed over all the firms if there are fewer than 50) in a market. (p. 381)

Horizontal equity The requirement that taxpayers with the same ability to pay should pay the same taxes. (p. 210)

Households Individuals or groups of people living together. (p. 42)

Human capital The knowledge and skill that people obtain from education, on-the-job training, and work experience. (p. 37)

Hyperinflation Inflation at a rate that exceeds 50 percent a month. (p. 715)

Implicit cost An opportunity cost incurred by a firm when it uses a factor of production for which it does not make a direct money payment. (p. 297)

Imports of goods and services Items that households, firms, and governments in the United States buy from the rest of the world. (p. 500)

Incentive A reward or a penalty—a "carrot" or a "stick"—that encourages or discourages an action. (p. 13)

Income elasticity of demand A measure of the responsiveness of the demand for a good to a change in income when other things remain the same. (p. 136)

Increasing marginal returns When the marginal product of an additional worker exceeds the marginal product of the previous worker. (p. 302)

Indifference curve A line that shows combinations of goods among which a consumer is indifferent. (p. 289)

Individual transferable quota (ITQ) A production limit that is assigned to an individual, who is free to transfer the quota to someone else. (p. 259)

Induced expenditure The components of aggregate expenditure that change when real GDP changes. (p. 758)

Induced taxes Taxes that vary with real GDP. (p. 794)

Inelastic demand When the percentage change in the quantity demanded is less than the percentage change in price. (p. 120)

Inelastic supply When the percentage change in the quantity supplied is less than the percentage change in price. (p. 130)

Infant-industry argument The argument that it is necessary to protect a new industry to enable it to grow into a mature industry that can compete in world markets. (p. 877)

Inferior good A good for which demand decreases when income increases. (p. 95)

Inflationary gap A gap that exists when real GDP exceeds potential GDP and that brings a rising price level. (p. 748)

Inflation rate The percentage change in the price level from one year to the next. (p. 551)

Inflation targeting A monetary policy framework that combines an announced target range for the inflation rate with the publication of the central bank's economic forecasts and analysis. (p. 850)

Intellectual property rights The property rights of the creators of knowledge and other discoveries. (p. 235)

Interest Income paid for the use of capital. (p. 39)

Interest rate parity Equal interest rates—a situation in which the interest rate in one currency equals the interest rate in another currency when exchange rate changes are taken into account. (p. 908)

Intermediate good or service A good or service that is produced by one firm, bought by another firm, and used as a component of a final good or service. (p. 498)

Inverse relationship A relationship between two variables that move in opposite directions. (p. 27)

Investment The purchase of new capital goods(tools, instruments, machines, buildings, and other constructions) and additions to inventories. (p. 499)

Investment demand The relationship between the quantity of investment demanded and the real interest rate, other things remaining the same. (p. 599)

Involuntary part-time workers People who work 1 to 34 hours a week but who are looking for full-time work. (p. 526)

Job A contract between a firm and a household to provide labor services. (p. 446)

Job rationing A situation that arises when the real wage rate is above the full-employment equilibrium level. (p. 584)

Job search The activity of looking for an acceptable vacant job. (p. 583)

Keynesian activist An economist who believes that fluctuations in investment are the main source of economic fluctuations, and who advocates interest rate cuts when real GDP falls below potential GDP and interest rate hikes when real GDP exceeds potential GDP. (p. 843)

Keynesian macroeconomics A body of theory about how a market economy works that stresses its inherent instability and the need for active government intervention to achieve full employment and sustained economic growth. (p. 570)

Labor The work time and work effort that people devote to producing goods and services. (p. 37)

Labor force The number of people employed plus the number unemployed. (p. 524)

Labor force participation rate The percentage of the working-age population who are members of the labor force. (p. 526)

Labor market A collection of people and firms who are trading labor services. (p. 446)

Labor productivity The quantity of real GDP produced by one hour of labor. (p. 624)

Land The "gifts of nature," or natural resources, that we use to produce goods and services. (p. 36)

Law of decreasing returns As a firm uses more of a variable input, with a given quantity of fixed inputs, the marginal product of the variable input eventually decreases. (p. 304)

Law of demand Other things remaining the same, if the price of a good rises, the quantity demanded of that good decreases; and if the price of a good falls, the quantity demanded of that good increases. (p. 91)

Law of market forces When there is a shortage, the price rises; when there is a surplus, the price falls. (p. 105)

Law of supply Other things remaining the same, if the price of a good rises, the quantity supplied of that good increases; and if the price of a good falls, the quantity supplied that good decreases. (p. 98)

Legal monopoly A market in which competition and entry are restricted by the granting of a public franchise, government license, patent, or copyright. (p. 351)

Linear relationship A relationship that graphs as a straight line. (p. 26)

Liquid asset An asset that can be easily, and with certainty, converted into money—converted into the means of payment. (p. 660)

Liquidity trap An interest rate at which people are willing to hold any quantity of money. (p. 837)

Long run The time frame in which the quantities of all resources can be varied. (p. 300)

Long-run average cost curve A curve that shows the lowest average cost at which it is possible to produce each output when the firm has had sufficient time to change both its plant size and labor employed. (p. 316)

Long-run Phillips curve The vertical line that shows the relationship between inflation and unemployment when the economy is at full employment. (p. 816)

Lorenz curve A curve that graphs the cumulative percentage of income (or wealth) against the cumulative percentage of households. (p. 472)

Loss Income earned by an entrepreneur for running a business when that income is negative. (p.39)

M1 Currency held outside banks and traveler's checks plus checkable deposits owned by individuals and businesses. (p. 653)

M2 M1 plus savings deposits and small time deposits, money market funds, and other deposits. (p. 653)

Macroeconomic equilibrium When the quantity of real GDP demanded equals the quantity of real GDP supplied at the point of intersection of the *AD* curve and the *AS* curve. (p. 744)

Macroeconomics The study of the aggregate (or total) effects on the national economy and the global economy of the choices that individuals, businesses, and governments make. (p. 14)

Malthusian theory Another name for classical growth theory—named for Thomas Robert Malthus. (p. 629)

Margin A choice on the margin is a choice that is made by comparing *all* the relevant alternatives systematically and incrementally. (p. 12)

Marginal benefit The benefit that arises from a one-unit increase in an activity. The marginal benefit of something is measured by what you *are willing* to give up to get one additional unit of it. (p. 12)

Marginal cost The opportunity cost that arises from a one-unit increase in an activity. The marginal cost of something is what you *must* give up to get one more unit of it. (p. 12) The marginal cost of producing a good is the change in total cost that results from a one-unit increase in output. (p. 308)

Marginal cost pricing rule A rule that sets price equal to marginal cost to achieve an efficient output in a regulated industry. (p. 427)

Marginal external benefit The benefit from an additional unit of a good or service that people other than the consumer of the good or service enjoy. (p. 230)

Marginal external cost The cost of producing an additional unit of a good or service that falls on people other than the producer. (p. 220)

Marginal private benefit The benefit from an additional unit of a good or service that the consumer of that good or service receives. (p. 230)

Marginal private cost The cost of producing an additional unit of a good or service that is borne by the producer of that good or service. (p. 220)

Marginal product The change in total product that results from a one-unit increase in the quantity of labor employed. (p. 302)

Marginal propensity to consume The fraction of a change in disposable income that is spent on consumption—the change in consumption expenditure divided by the change in disposable income that brought it about. (p. 760)

Marginal propensity to import The fraction of an increase in real GDP that is spent on imports—

the change in imports divided by the change in real GDP. (p. 762)

Marginal rate of substitution The rate at which a person will give up good y (the good measured on the y-axis) to get more of good x (the good measured on the x-axis) and at the same time remain on the same indifference curve. (p. 290)

Marginal revenue The change in total revenue that results from a one-unit increase in the quantity sold. (p. 325)

Marginal social benefit The marginal benefit enjoyed by society—by the consumers of a good or service and by everyone else who benefits from it. It is the sum of marginal private benefit and marginal external benefit. (p. 230)

Marginal social cost The marginal cost incurred by the entire society—by the producer and by everyone else on whom the cost falls. It is the sum of marginal private cost and marginal external cost. (p. 220)

Marginal tax rate The percentage of an additional dollar of income that is paid in tax. (p. 201) The fraction of a change in real GDP that is paid in income taxes—the change in tax payments divided by the change in real GDP. (p. 773)

Marginal utility The change in total utility that results from a one-unit increase in the quantity of a good consumed. (p. 273)

Marginal utility per dollar The marginal utility from a good relative to the price paid for the good. (p. 277)

Market Any arrangement that brings buyers and sellers together and enables them to get information and do business with each other. (p. 42)

Market demand The sum of the demands of all buyers in a market. (p. 93)

Market equilibrium When buyers' and sellers' plans are in balance—the quantity demanded equals the quantity supplied. (p. 105)

Market income A household's income earned from the markets for factors of production and with no government redistribution. (p. 487)

Market supply The sum of the supplies of all the sellers in the market. (p. 100)

Markup The amount by which price exceeds marginal cost. (p. 387)

Means of payment A method of settling a debt. (p. 648)

Median voter theory The theory that governments pursue policies that make the median voter as well off as possible. (p. 490)

Medium of exchange An object that is generally accepted in return for goods and services. (p. 649)

Microeconomics The study of the choices that individuals and businesses make and the way these choices interact and are influenced by governments. (p. 14)

Minimum wage law A government regulation that makes hiring labor for less than a specified wage illegal. (p. 180)

Monetarist An economist who believes that fluctuations in the quantity of money are the main source of economic fluctuations, and who advocates that the quantity of money grow at a constant rate. (p. 842)

Monetary base The sum of coins, Federal Reserve notes, and banks' reserves at the Fed. (p. 666)

Monetary policy Adjusting the quantity of money in the economy. (p. 663)

Monetary system The Federal Reserve and the banks and other institutions that accept deposits and provide the services that enable people and businesses to make and receive payments. (p. 656)

Money Any commodity or token that is generally accepted as a means of payment. (p. 648)

Money income Market income plus money benefits paid by the government. (p. 488)

Money market fund A financial institution that obtains funds by selling shares and uses these funds to buy assets such as U.S. Treasury bills. (p. 658)

Money multiplier The number by which a change in the monetary base is multiplied to find the resulting change in the quantity of money. (p. 689)

Monopolistic competition A market in which a large number of firms compete by making similar but slightly different products. (p. 324)

Monopoly A market for a good or service that has no close substitutes and in which there is one supplier that is protected from competition by a barrier preventing the entry of new firms. (p. 324)

Multiplier The amount by which a change in any component of autonomous expenditure is magnified or multiplied to determine the change that it generates in equilibrium expenditure and real GDP. (p. 770)

Nash equilibrium An equilibrium in which each player takes the best possible action given the action of the other player. (p. 412)

National debt The total amount that the federal government has borrowed to make expenditures that exceed tax revenue—to run a government budget deficit. (p. 46)

Natural monopoly A monopoly that arises because one firm can meet the entire market demand at a lower average total cost than two or more firms could. (p. 350)

Natural rate hypothesis The proposition that when the money growth rate changes, the unemployment rate changes temporarily and eventually returns to the natural unemployment rate. (p. 819)

Natural unemployment rate The unemployment rate at full employment. (p. 539)

Needs-tested spending Spending on programs that entitle suitably qualified people and businesses to receive benefits—benefits that vary with need and with the state of the economy. (p. 794)

Negative externality A production or consumption activity that creates an external cost. (p. 218)

Negative income tax A tax and redistribution scheme that provides every household with a guaranteed minimum annual income and taxes all earned income above the guaranteed minimum at a fixed rate. (p. 491)

Negative relationship A relationship between two variables that move in opposite directions. (p. 27)

Neoclassical growth theory The theory that real GDP per person will increase as long as technology keeps advancing. (p. 632)

Net borrower A country that is borrowing more from the rest of the world than it is lending to the rest of the world. (p. 892)

Net domestic product at factor cost The sum of wages, interest, rent, and profit. (p. 505)

Net exports of goods and services The value of exports of goods and services minus the value of imports of goods and services. (p. 500)

Net investment The change in the quantity of capital—equals gross investment minus depreciation. (p. 594)

Net lender A country that is lending more to the rest of the world than it is borrowing from the rest of the world. (p. 892)

New growth theory The theory that our unlimited wants will lead us to ever greater productivity and perpetual economic growth. (p. 633)

New macroeconomics A body of theory about how the economy works that is based on the view that macro outcomes depend on micro choices—the choices of rational individuals and firms interacting in markets. (p. 571)

Nominal GDP The value of the final goods and services produced in a given year valued at the prices that prevailed in that same year. (p. 509)

Nominal interest rate The percentage return on a loan expressed in dollars. (p. 562)

Nominal wage rate The average hourly wage rate measured in current dollars. (p. 560)

Nonexcludable A good, service, or resource is nonexcludable if it is impossible to prevent someone from benefiting from it. (p. 242)

Nonrenewable natural resources Natural resources that can be used only once and that cannot be replaced once they have been used. (p. 463)

Nonrival A good, service, or resource is nonrival if its use by one person does not decrease the quantity available to someone else. (p. 242)

Nontariff barrier Any action other than a tariff that restricts international trade. (p. 872)

Normal good A good for which demand increases when income increases. (p. 95)

Normal profit The return to entrepreneurship. Normal profit is part of a firm's opportunity cost because it is the cost of not running another firm. (p. 297)

Official settlements account Record of the change in U.S. official reserves. (p. 890)

Offshoring A U.S. firm either producing in another country or outsourcing to a firm in another country. (p. 869)

Okun's Law For each percentage point that the unemployment rate is above the natural unemployment rate, there is a 2 percent gap between real GDP and potential GDP. (p. 811)

Oligopoly A market in which a small number of firms compete. (p. 324)

Open market operation The purchase or sale of government securities—U.S. Treasury bills and bonds—by the Federal Reserve in the open market. (p. 666)

Opportunity cost The opportunity cost of something is the best thing you must give up to get it. (p. 11)

Outsourcing A firm buying finished goods, components, or services from other firms. (p. 869)

Part-time workers People who usually work less than 35 hours a week. (p. 526)

Patent A government-sanctioned exclusive right granted to the inventor of a good, service, or productive process to produce, use, and sell the invention for a given number of years. (p. 235)

Payoff matrix A table that shows the payoffs for each player for every possible combination of actions by the players. (p. 412)

Perfect competition A market in which there are many firms, each selling an identical product; many buyers; no restrictions on the entry of new firms into the industry; no advantage to established firms; and buyers and sellers who are well informed about prices. (p. 324)

Perfect price discrimination Price discrimination that extracts the entire consumer surplus by charging the highest price that consumers are willing to pay for each unit. (p. 366)

Perfectly elastic demand When the quantity demanded changes by a very large percentage in response to an almost zero percentage change in price. (p. 120)

Perfectly elastic supply When the quantity supplied changes by a very large percentage in response to an almost zero percentage change in price. (p. 130)

Perfectly inelastic demand When the quantity demanded remains constant as the price changes. (p. 120)

Perfectly inelastic supply When the quantity supplied remains the same as the price changes. (p. 130)

Personal distribution of income The distribution of income among households. (p. 40)

Physical capital The tools, instruments, machines, buildings, and other items that have been produced in the past and that are used to produce goods and services. (p. 594)

Positive externality A production or consumption activity that creates an external benefit. (p. 218)

Positive relationship A relationship between two variables that move in the same direction. (p. 26)

Potential GDP The level of real GDP that the economy would produce if it were at full employment. (pp. 541, 573)

Poverty A state in which a household's income is too low to be able to buy the quantities of food, shelter, and clothing that are deemed necessary. (p. 477)

Predatory pricing Setting a low price to drive competitors out of business with the intention of setting a monopoly price when the competition has gone. (p. 437)

Present value The present value of a future sum of money is the amount that will earn enough interest to grow to that future sum. (p. 617)

Price cap A government regulation that places an upper limit on the price at which a particular good, service, or factor of production may be traded. (p. 172)

Price cap regulation A rule that specifies the highest price that a firm is permitted to set—a price ceiling. (p. 430)

Price ceiling A government regulation that places an upper limit on the price at which a particular good, service, or factor of production may be traded. (p. 172)

Price-discriminating monopoly A monopoly that is able to sell different units of a good or service for different prices. (p. 352)

Price elasticity of demand A measure of the responsiveness of the quantity demanded of a good to a change in its price when all other influences on buyers' plans remain the same. (p. 118)

Price elasticity of supply A measure of the responsiveness of the quantity supplied of a good changes to a change in its price when all other influences on sellers' plans remain the same. (p. 130)

Price floor A government regulation that places a lower limit on the price at which a particular good, service, of factor of production may be traded. (p. 179)

Price support A price floor in an agricultural market maintained by a government guarantee to buy any surplus output at that price. (p. 185)

Price taker A firm that cannot influence the price of the good or service that it produces. (p. 325)

Principle of minimum differentiation The tendency for competitors to make themselves identical to appeal to the maximum number of clients or voters. (p. 250)

Prisoners' dilemma A game between two prisoners that

shows why it is hard to cooperate, even when it would be beneficial to both players to do so. (p. 411)

Private good A good or service that can be consumed by only one person at a time and only by the person who has bought it or owns it. (p. 242)

Private sector balance Saving minus investment. (p. 894)

Producer surplus The price of a good minus the marginal cost of producing it, summed over the quantity produced. (p. 152)

Product differentiation Making a product that is slightly different from the products of competing firms. (p. 378)

Production efficiency A situation in which we cannot produce more of one good or service without producing less of something else—production is at a point on the PPF. (p. 64)

Production function A relationship that shows the maximum quantity of real GDP that can be produced as the quantity of labor employed changes and all other influences on production remain the same. (p. 574)

Production possibilities frontier The boundary between the combinations of goods and services that can be produced and the combinations that cannot be produced, given the available factors of production and the state of technology. (p. 62)

Profit Income earned by an entrepreneur for running a business. (p. 39)

Progressive tax A tax whose average rate increases as income increases. (p. 201)

Property rights Legally established titles to the ownership, use, and disposal of factors of production and goods and services that are enforceable in the courts. (pp. 223, 639)

Proportional tax A tax whose average rate is constant at all income levels. (p. 201)

Public good A good or service that can be consumed simultaneously by everyone and from which no one can be excluded. (p. 243)

Public interest theory The theory that regulation seeks an efficient use of resources. (p. 425)

Public provision The production of a good or service by a public authority that receives most of its revenue from the government. (p. 232)

Purchasing power parity Equal value of money—a situation in which money buys the same amount of goods and services in different currencies. (p. 906)

Quantity demanded The amount of any good, service, or resource that people are willing and able to buy during a specified period at a specified price. (p. 91)

Quantity of labor demanded The total labor hours that all the firms in the economy plan to hire during a given time period at a given real wage rate. (p. 575)

Quantity of labor supplied The number of labor hours that all the households in the economy plan to work during a given time period and at a given real wage rate. (p. 577)

Quantity of money demanded The amount of money that households and firms choose to hold. (p. 699)

Quantity supplied The amount of any good, service, or resource that people are willing and able to sell during a specified period at a specified price. (p. 98)

Quantity theory of money The proposition that when real GDP equals potential GDP, an increase in the quantity of money brings an equal percentage increase in the price level. (p. 711)

Quota A specified maximum amount of a good that may be imported in a given period of time. (p. 874)

Rate of return regulation A regulation that sets the price at a level that enables a regulated firm to earn a specified target percent return on its capital. (p. 428)

Rational choice A choice that uses the available resources to most effectively satisfy the wants of the person making the choice. (p. 10)

Rational expectation The inflation forecast resulting from use of all the relevant data and economic science. (p. 825)

Rational ignorance The decision not to acquire information because the marginal cost of doing so exceeds the marginal benefit. (p. 251)

Real GDP The value of the final goods and services produced in a given year expressed in the prices of a base year. (p. 509)

Real GDP per person Real GDP divided by the population. (pp. 513, 620)

Real interest rate The percentage return on a loan, calculated by using purchasing power—the nominal interest rate adjusted for the effects of inflation. (p. 562)

Real wage rate The average hourly wage rate measured in the dollars of a given reference base year. (p. 560)

Recession A decrease in real GDP that lasts for at least two quarters (six months) or a period of significant decline in total output, income, employment, and trade, usually lasting from six months to a year, and marked by widespread contractions in many sectors of the economy. (p. 726)

Recessionary gap A gap that exists when potential GDP exceeds real GDP and that brings a falling price level. (p. 748)

Reference base period A period for which the CPI is defined to equal 100. Currently, the reference base period is 1982–1984. (p. 548)

Regressive tax A tax whose average rate decreases as income increases. (p. 201)

Regulation Rules administered by a government agency to influence economic activity by determining prices, product standards and types, and the conditions under which new firms can enter an industry. (p. 424)

Relative price The price of one good in terms of another good—an opportunity cost. It equals the price of one good divided by the price of another good. (p. 270)

Renewable natural resources Natural resources that can be used repeatedly. (p. 463)

Rent Income paid for the use of land (p. 39)

Rent ceiling A regulation that makes it illegal to charge more than a specified rent for housing. (p. 172)

Rent seeking The act of obtaining special treatment by the government to create economic profit or to divert consumer surplus or producer surplus away from others. (p. 361)

Required reserve ratio The minimum percentage of deposits that banks and other financial institutions must hold in reserves. (p. 657)

Resale price maintenance An agreement between a manufacturer and a distributor on the price at which a product will be resold. (p. 435)

Reserves The currency in the bank's vaults plus the balance on its reserve account at a Federal Reserve Bank. (p. 657)

Rival A good, service, or resource is rival if its consumption by one person decreases the quantity available to someone else. (p. 242)

Rule of 70 The number of years it takes for the level of any variable to double is approximately 70 divided by the annual percentage growth rate of the variable. (p. 621)

Saving The amount of income that is not paid in taxes or spent on consumption goods and services—saving adds to wealth. (p. 596)

Savings and loan association A financial institution that accepts checkable deposits and savings deposits and that makes personal, commercial, and home purchase loans. (p. 658)

Savings bank A financial institution that accepts savings deposits and makes mostly consumer and home-purchase loans. (p. 658)

Saving supply The relationship between the quantity of saving supplied and the real interest rate, other things remaining the same. (p. 602)

Scarcity The condition that arises because wants exceed the ability of resources to satisfy them. (p. 2)

Scatter diagram A graph of the value of one variable against the value of another variable. (p. 24)

Search activity The time spent looking for someone with whom to do business. (p. 174)

Seasonal unemployment The unemployment that arises because of seasonal weather patterns. (p. 538)

Self-interest The choices that are best for the individual who makes them. (p. 4)

Shortage A situation in which the quantity demanded exceeds the quantity supplied. (p. 105)

Short run The time frame in which the quantities of some resources are fixed. In the short run, a firm can usually change the quantity of labor it uses but not its technology and quantity of capital. (p. 300)

Short-run Phillips curve A curve that shows the relationship between the inflation rate and the unemployment rate when the natural unemployment rate and the expected inflation rate remain constant. (p. 810)

Shutdown point The output and price at which the firm just covers its total variable cost. (p. 329)

Signal An action taken by an informed person (or firm) to send a message to uninformed people. (p. 394)

Single-price monopoly A monopoly that must sell each

unit of its output for the same price to all its customers. (p. 352)

Slope The change in the value of the variable measured on the y-axis divided by the change in the value of the variable measured on the x-axis. (p. 29)

Social interest The choices that are best for society as a whole. (p. 4)

Stagflation A combination of recession (falling real GDP) and inflation (rising price level). (p. 746)

Standard of living The level of consumption of goods and services that people enjoy, *on the average*; it is measured by average income per person. (p. 498)

Statistical discrepancy The discrepancy between the expenditure approach and the income approach estimates of GDP, calculated as the GDP expenditure total minus GDP income total. (p. 506)

Stock A certificate of ownership and claim to the profits that a firm makes. (p. 596)

Stock market A financial market in which shares in the stocks of companies are traded. (pp. 447, 597)

Store of value Any commodity or token that can be held and exchanged later for goods and services. (p. 649)

Strategies All the possible actions of each player in a game. (p. 412)

Structural unemployment The unemployment that arises when changes in technology or international competition change the skills needed to perform jobs or

change the locations of jobs. (p. 537)

Subsidy A payment by the government to producers to cover part of the cost of production. (pp. 185, 233)

Substitute A good that can be consumed in place of another good. (p. 94)

Substitute in production A good that can be produced in place of another good. (p. 101)

Sunk cost A previously incurred and irreversible cost. (p. 11)

Supply The relationship between the quantity supplied and the price of a good when all other influences on selling plans remain the same. (p. 98)

Supply curve A graph of the relationship between the quantity supplied of a good and its price when all the other influences on selling plans remain the same. (p. 99)

Supply of labor The relationship between the quantity of labor supplied and the real wage rate when all other influences on work plans remain the same. (p. 577)

Supply of money The relationship between the quantity of money supplied and the nominal interest rate. (p. 702)

Supply schedule A list of the quantities supplied at each different price when all the other influences on selling plans remain the same. (p. 99)

Surplus A situation in which the quantity supplied exceeds the quantity demanded. (p. 105)

Tariff A tax on a good that is imposed by the importing coun-

try when an imported good crosses its international boundary. (p. 872)

Taxable income Total income minus a personal exemption and a standard deduction (or other allowable deductions). (p. 200)

Tax incidence The division of the burden of a tax between the buyer and the seller. (p. 194)

Tax multiplier The magnification effect of a change in taxes on aggregate demand. (p. 787)

Time-series graph A graph that measures time on the x-axis and the variable or variables in which we are interested on the y-axis. (p. 24)

Total cost The cost of all the factors of production used by a firm. (p. 307)

Total fixed cost The cost of the firm's fixed factors of production—the cost of land, capital, and entrepreneurship. (p. 307)

Total product The total quantity of a good produced in a given period. (p. 301)

Total revenue The amount spent on a good and received by sellers and equals the price of the good multiplied by the quantity of the good sold. (p. 126)

Total revenue test A method of estimating the price elasticity of demand by observing the change in total revenue that results from a price change (with all other influences on the quantity sold remaining unchanged). (p. 127)

Total surplus The sum of consumer surplus and producer surplus. (p. 155)

Total utility The total benefit that a person gets from the consumption of a good or service. Total utility generally increases as the quantity consumed of a good increases. (p. 272)

Total variable cost The cost of the firm's variable factor of production—the cost of labor. (p. 307)

Tradeoff An exchange—giving up one thing to get something else. (p. 65)

Tragedy of the commons The absence of incentives to prevent the overuse and depletion of a commonly owned resource. (p. 254)

Transactions costs The opportunity costs of making trades in a market. (pp. 159, 224)

Trend A general tendency for the value of a variable to rise or fall. (p. 24)

Tying arrangement An agreement to sell one product only if the buyer agrees to buy another, different product. (p. 436)

Unemployment rate The percentage of the people in the labor force who are unemployed. (p. 525)

Union wage A wage rate that results from collective bargaining between a labor union and a firm. (p. 585)

Unit elastic demand When the percentage change in the quantity demanded equals the percentage change in price. (p. 120)

Unit elastic supply When the percentage change in the quantity supplied equals the percentage change in price. (p. 130)

Unit of account An agreed-upon measure for stating the prices of goods and services. (p. 649)

U.S. interest rate differential The U.S. interest rate minus the foreign interest rate. (p. 900)

U.S. official reserves The government's holdings of foreign currency. (p. 890)

Utilitarianism A principle that states that we should strive to achieve "the greatest happiness for the greatest number." (p. 162)

Utility The benefit or satisfaction that a person gets from the consumption of a good or service. (p. 272)

Utility-maximizing rule The rule that leads to the greatest total utility from all the goods and services consumed. The rule is: 1. Allocate the entire available budget. 2. Make the marginal

utility per dollar equal for all goods. (p. 276)

Value of marginal product The value to a firm of hiring one more unit of a factor of production, which equals price of a unit of output multiplied by the marginal product of the factor of production. (p. 449)

Velocity of circulation The number of times in a year that the average dollar of money gets used to buy final goods and services. (p. 711)

Vertical equity The requirement that taxpayers with a greater ability to pay bear a greater share of the taxes. (p. 211)

Voucher A token that the government provides to households that can be used to buy specified goods or services. (p. 234)

Wages Income paid for the services of labor. (p. 39)

Wealth The value of all the things that a person owns (p. 596)

Working-age population The total number of people aged 16 years and over who are not in jail, hospital, or some other form of institutional care or in the U.S. Armed Forces. (p. 524)

Index

Credits

Chapter 24: p. 611: Getty Images News.

Chapter 25: p. 626 top: © Minnesota Historical Society/CORBIS; p. 626 bottom: © Bob Rowan, Progressive Image/CORBIS.

Chapter 26: p. 665: Federal Reserve Board.

Chapter 27: p. 675: Copyright Scala/Art Resource, NY.

Chapter 28: p. 715: © Bettmann/CORBIS.

Chapter 30: p. 768 top: Bibliotheque Nationale, Paris, France/Giraudon-Bridgeman Art Libary; p. 768 bottom: © Bettmann/ CORBIS.

Chapter 32: p. 813: © MIT Museum.

Chapter 33: p. 851 top: Photo courtesy of Stanford University.

Chapter 34: p. 881 left: © Jason Grow; p. 881 right: David G. McIntyre/BLACK STAR.

Figures and Tables

Chapter 5: Some Price Elasticities of Demand, p. 125, Sources of Data: Ahsan Mansur and John Whalley, "Numerical Specification of Applied General Equilibrium Models: Estimation, Calibration, and Data," in *Applied General Equilibrium Analysis*, eds. Herbert E. Scarf and John B. Shoven (New York: Cambridge University Press, 1984), and Henri Theil, Ching-Fan Chung, and James L. Seale, Jr., Advances in Econometrics, Supplement I, 1989, International Evidence on Consumption Patterns (Greenwich, Conn.: JAI Press Inc., 1989). Reprinted with permission; Income Elasticities of Demand, p. 137, Sources of Data: Ahsan Mansur and John Whalley, "Numerical Specification of Applied General Equilibrium Models: Estimation, Calibration, and Data", in *Applied General Equilibrium Analysis*, eds. Herbert E. Scarf and John B. Shoven (New York: Cambridge University Press, 1984), and Henri Theil, Ching-Fan Chung, and James L. Seale, Jr., Advances in Econometrics, Supplement I, 1989, International Evidence on Consumption Patterns (Greenwich, Conn.: JAI Press Inc., 1989). Reprinted with permission.

The Addison-Wesley Series in Economics

Abel/Bernanke
Macroeconomics

Bade/Parkin
Foundations of Economics

Bierman/Fernandez
Game Theory with Economic Applications

Binger/Hoffman
Microeconomics with Calculus

Boyer
Principles of Transportation Economics

Branson
Macroeconomic Theory and Policy

Bruce
Public Finance and the American Economy

Byrns/Stone
Economics

Carlton/Perloff
Modern Industrial Organization

Caves/Frankel/Jones
World Trade and Payments: An Introduction

Chapman
Environmental Economics: Theory, Application, and Policy

Cooter/Ulen
Law and Economics

Downs
An Economic Theory of Democracy

Ehrenberg/Smith
Modern Labor Economics

Ekelund/Ressler/Tollison
Economics

Fusfeld
The Age of the Economist

Gerber
International Economics

Ghiara
Learning Economics

Gordon
Macroeconomics

Gregory
Essentials of Economics

Gregory/Stuart
Russian and Soviet Economic Performance and Structure

Hartwick/Olewiler
The Economics of Natural Resource Use

Hubbard
Money, the Financial System, and the Economy

Hughes/Cain
American Economic History

Husted/Melvin
International Economics

Jehle/Reny
Advanced Microeconomic Theory

Johnson-Lans
A Health Economics Primer

Klein
Mathematical Methods for Economics

Krugman/Obstfeld
International Economics

Laidler
The Demand for Money

Leeds/von Allmen/Schiming
Economics

Leeds/von Allmen
The Economics of Sports

Lipsey/Courant/Ragan
Economics

Melvin
International Money and Finance

Miller
Economics Today

Miller
Understanding Modern Economics

Miller/Benjamin
The Economics of Macro Issues

Miller/Benjamin/North
The Economics of Public Issues

Mills/Hamilton
Urban Economics

Mishkin
The Economics of Money, Banking, and Financial Markets

Parkin
Economics

Perloff
Microeconomics

Phelps
Health Economics

Riddell/Shackelford/Stamos/ Schneider
Economics: A Tool for Critically Understanding Society

Ritter/Silber/Udell
Principles of Money, Banking, and Financial Markets

Rohlf
Introduction to Economic Reasoning

Ruffin/Gregory
Principles of Economics

Sargent
Rational Expectations and Inflation

Scherer
Industry Structure, Strategy, and Public Policy

Stock/Watson
Introduction to Econometrics

Studenmund
Using Econometrics

Tietenberg
Environmental and Natural Resource Economics

Tietenberg
Environmental Economics and Policy

Todaro/Smith
Economic Development

Waldman
Microeconomics

Waldman/Jensen
Industrial Organization: Theory and Practice

Weil
Economic Growth

Williamson
Macroeconomics

Macroeconomic Data

These macroeconomic data series show some of the trends in GDP and its components, the price level, and other variables that provide information about changes in the standard of living and the cost of living—the central questions of macroeconomics. You will find these data in a spreadsheet that you can download from your MyEconLab Web site.

NATIONAL INCOME AND PRODUCT ACCOUNTS		1960	1961	1962	1963	1964	1965	1966	1967	1968	1969
EXPENDITURES APPROACH											
the sum of	1 Personal consumption expenditures	331.7	342.1	363.3	382.7	411.4	443.8	480.9	507.8	558.0	605.2
	2 Gross private domestic investment	78.9	78.2	88.1	93.8	102.1	118.2	131.3	128.6	141.2	156.4
	3 Government expenditures	111.6	119.5	130.1	136.4	143.2	151.5	171.8	192.7	209.4	221.5
	4 Exports	27.0	27.6	29.1	31.1	35.0	37.1	40.9	43.5	47.9	51.9
less	5 Imports	22.8	22.7	25.0	26.1	28.1	31.5	37.1	39.9	46.6	50.5
equals	6 Gross domestic product	526.4	544.7	585.6	617.7	663.6	719.1	787.8	832.6	910.0	984.6
INCOMES APPROACH											
plus	7 Compensation of employees	296.6	305.4	327.2	345.3	370.7	399.5	442.6	475.1	524.3	577.6
	8 Net operating surplus	131.8	137.6	150.6	159.6	172.4	190.9	204	207.2	220.5	226.5
equals	9 Net domestic product at factor cost	428.4	443	477.8	504.9	543.1	590.4	646.6	682.3	744.8	804.1
plus	10 Indirect taxes less subsidies	43.5	45	48.1	51.2	54.6	57.8	59.4	64.2	72.3	79.5
	11 Depreciation (capital consumption)	55.6	57.2	59.3	62.4	65	69.4	75.6	81.5	88.4	97.9
	12 GDP (income approach)	527.5	545.2	585.2	618.5	662.7	717.6	781.6	828	905.5	981.5
	13 Statistical discrepancy	−0.9	−0.6	0.4	−0.8	0.8	1.6	6.3	4.6	4.6	3.2
equals	14 GDP (expenditure approach)	526.4	544.7	585.6	617.7	663.6	719.1	787.8	832.6	910.0	984.6
	15 Real GDP (billions of 2000 dollars)	2,501.8	2,560.0	2,715.2	2,834.0	2,998.6	3,191.1	3,399.1	3,484.6	3,652.7	3,765.4
	16 Real GDP growth rate (percent per year)	2.5	2.3	6.1	4.4	5.8	6.4	6.5	2.5	4.8	3.1
OTHER DATA											
	17 Population (millions)	180.7	183.7	186.5	189.2	191.9	194.3	196.6	198.7	200.7	202.7
	18 Labor force (millions)	69.6	70.5	70.6	71.8	73.1	74.5	75.8	77.3	78.7	80.7
	19 Employment (millions)	65.8	65.7	66.7	67.8	69.3	71.1	72.9	74.4	75.9	77.9
	20 Unemployment (millions)	3.9	4.7	3.9	4.1	3.8	3.4	2.9	3.0	2.8	2.8
	21 Labor force participation rate (percent of working-age population)	59.4	59.3	58.8	58.7	58.7	58.9	59.2	59.6	59.6	60.1
	22 Unemployment rate (percent of labor force)	5.5	6.7	5.5	5.7	5.2	4.5	3.8	3.8	3.6	3.5
	23 Real GDP per person (2000 dollars per year)	13,847	13,936	14,556	14,976	15,627	16,423	17,293	17,536	18,199	18,578
	24 Growth rate of real GDP per person (percent per year)	0.9	0.6	4.4	2.9	4.3	5.1	5.3	1.4	3.8	2.1
	25 Quantity of money (M2, billions of dollars)	312.4	335.5	362.7	393.2	424.7	459.2	480.2	524.8	566.8	587.9
	26 GDP deflator (2000 = 100)	21.0	21.3	21.6	21.8	22.1	22.5	23.2	23.9	24.9	26.1
	27 GDP deflator inflation rate (percent per year)	1.4	1.1	1.4	1.1	1.5	1.8	2.8	3.1	4.3	5.0
	28 Consumer price index (1982–1984 = 100)	29.6	29.9	30.2	30.6	31	31.5	32.4	33.4	34.8	36.7
	29 CPI inflation rate (percent per year)	1.7	1.0	1.0	1.3	1.3	1.6	2.9	3.1	4.2	5.5
	30 Current account balance (billions of dollars)	2.8	3.8	3.4	4.4	6.8	5.4	3.0	2.6	0.6	0.4

1970	1971	1972	1973	1974	1975	1976	1977	1978	1979	1980	1981	1982
648.5	701.9	770.6	852.4	933.4	1,034.4	1,151.9	1,278.6	1,428.5	1,592.2	1,757.1	1,941.1	2,077.3
152.4	178.2	207.6	244.5	249.4	230.2	292.0	361.3	438.0	492.9	479.3	572.4	517.2
233.8	246.5	263.5	281.7	317.9	357.7	383.0	414.1	453.6	500.8	566.2	627.5	680.5
59.7	63.0	70.8	95.3	126.7	138.7	149.5	159.4	186.9	230.1	280.8	305.2	283.2
55.8	62.3	74.2	91.2	127.5	122.7	151.1	182.4	212.3	252.7	293.8	317.8	303.2
1,038.5	1,127.1	1,238.3	1,382.7	1,500.0	1,638.3	1,825.3	2,030.9	2,294.7	2,563.3	2,789.5	3,128.4	3,255.0
617.2	658.9	725.1	811.2	890.3	949.2	1059.4	1180.6	1336.2	1500.8	1651.9	1826	1926
220.6	245.7	276.1	311.4	314.6	352.7	394.1	445.3	507.4	544.4	562.3	658.9	675.4
837.8	904.6	1001.2	1122.6	1204.9	1301.9	1453.5	1625.9	1843.6	2045.2	2214.2	2484.9	2601.4
86.7	95.9	101.5	112.1	121.7	131	141.5	152.8	162.3	171.9	190.9	224.5	226.3
106.7	115	126.5	139.3	162.5	187.7	205.2	230	262.3	300.1	343	388.1	426.9
1031.2	1115.5	1229.2	1374	1489.1	1620.6	1800.2	2008.7	2268.2	2517.2	2748.1	3097.5	3254.6
7.3	11.6	9.1	8.6	10.9	17.7	25.1	22.3	26.6	46	41.4	30.9	0.3
1,038.5	1,127.1	1,238.3	1,382.7	1,500.0	1,638.3	1,825.3	2,030.9	2,294.7	2,563.3	2,789.5	3,128.4	3,255.0
3,771.9	3,898.6	4,105.0	4,341.5	4,319.6	4,311.2	4,540.9	4,750.5	5,015.0	5,173.4	5,161.7	5,291.7	5,189.3
0.2	3.4	5.3	5.8	−0.5	−0.2	5.3	4.6	5.6	3.2	−0.2	2.5	−1.9
205.1	207.7	209.9	211.9	213.9	216.0	218.0	220.2	222.6	225.1	227.7	230.0	232.2
82.8	84.4	87.0	89.4	91.9	93.8	96.2	99.0	102.3	105.0	106.9	108.7	110.2
78.7	79.4	82.2	85.1	86.8	85.8	88.8	92.0	96.0	98.8	99.3	100.4	99.5
4.1	5.0	4.9	4.4	5.2	7.9	7.4	7.0	6.2	6.1	7.6	8.3	10.7
60.4	60.2	60.4	60.8	61.3	61.2	61.6	62.3	63.2	63.7	63.8	63.9	64.0
4.9	5.9	5.6	4.9	5.6	8.5	7.7	7.1	6.1	5.8	7.1	7.6	9.7
18,395	18,774	19,557	20,488	20,199	19,962	20,826	21,570	22,531	22,987	22,666	23,011	22,350
−1.0	2.1	4.2	4.8	−1.4	−1.2	4.3	3.6	4.5	2.0	−1.4	1.5	−2.9
626.5	710.3	802.3	855.5	902.1	1016.2	1152	1270.3	1366	1473.7	1599.8	1755.4	1910.3
27.5	28.9	30.2	31.8	34.7	38.0	40.2	42.8	45.8	49.5	54.0	59.1	62.7
5.3	5.0	4.3	5.6	9.0	9.4	5.8	6.4	7.0	8.3	9.1	9.4	6.1
38.8	40.5	41.8	44.4	49.3	53.8	56.9	60.6	65.2	72.6	82.4	90.9	96.5
5.7	4.4	3.2	6.2	11.0	9.1	5.8	6.5	7.6	11.3	13.5	10.3	6.2
2.3	−1.4	−5.8	7.1	2.0	18.1	4.3	−14.3	−15.1	−0.3	2.3	5.0	−5.5

Macroeconomic Data

These macroeconomic data series show some of the trends in GDP and its components, the price level, and other variables that provide information about changes in the standard of living and the cost of living—the central questions of macroeconomics. You will find these data in a spreadsheet that you can download from your MyEconLab Web site.

		NATIONAL INCOME AND PRODUCT ACCOUNTS	1983	1984	1985	1986	1987	1988	1989	1990	1991	1992
		EXPENDITURES APPROACH										
the sum of	1	Personal consumption expenditures	2,290.6	2,503.3	2,720.3	2,899.7	3,100.2	3,353.6	3,598.5	3,839.9	3,986.1	4,235.3
	2	Gross private domestic investment	564.3	735.6	736.2	746.5	785.0	821.6	874.9	861.0	802.9	864.8
	3	Government expenditures	733.5	797.0	879.0	949.3	999.5	1,039.0	1,099.1	1,180.2	1,234.4	1,271.0
	4	Exports	277.0	302.4	302.0	320.5	363.9	444.1	503.3	552.4	596.8	635.3
less	5	Imports	328.6	405.1	417.2	453.3	509.1	554.5	591.5	630.3	624.3	668.6
equals	6	Gross domestic product	3,536.7	3,933.2	4,220.3	4,462.8	4,739.5	5,103.8	5,484.4	5,803.1	5,995.9	6,337.7
		INCOMES APPROACH										
	7	Compensation of employees	2042.8	2255.8	2424.9	2571.9	2751.6	2968.1	3146.5	3340.5	3448	3638.4
plus	8	Net operating surplus	761.9	920.9	984.7	1013.7	1086.6	1212.1	1281.8	1315.1	1319.3	1390.8
equals	9	Net domestic product at factor cost	2804.7	3176.7	3409.6	3585.6	3838.2	4180.2	4428.3	4655.6	4767.3	5029.2
	10	Indirect taxes less subsidies	242.5	269.2	287.2	298.9	317.7	345.5	372.1	398.7	430.2	453.9
plus	11	Depreciation (capital consumption)	443.8	472.6	506.7	531.3	561.9	597.6	644.3	682.5	725.9	751.9
	12	GDP (income approach)	3491	3918.5	4203.5	4415.8	4717.8	5123.3	5444.7	5736.8	5923.4	6235
	13	Statistical discrepancy	45.7	14.6	16.7	47	21.7	−19.5	39.7	66.2	72.5	102.7
equals	14	GDP (expenditure approach)	3,536.7	3,933.2	4,220.3	4,462.8	4,739.5	5,103.8	5,484.4	5,803.1	5,995.9	6,337.7
	15	Real GDP (billions of 2000 dollars)	5,423.8	5,813.6	6,053.7	6,263.6	6,475.1	6,742.7	6,981.4	7,112.5	7,100.5	7,336.6
	16	Real GDP growth rate (percent per year)	4.5	7.2	4.1	3.5	3.4	4.1	3.5	1.9	-0.2	3.3
		OTHER DATA										
	17	Population (millions)	234.3	236.3	238.5	240.7	242.8	245.0	247.3	250.1	253.5	256.9
	18	Labor force (millions)	111.6	113.5	115.5	117.8	119.9	121.7	123.9	125.8	126.3	128.1
	19	Employment (millions)	100.8	105.0	107.2	109.6	112.4	115.0	117.3	118.8	117.7	118.5
	20	Unemployment (millions)	10.7	8.5	8.3	8.2	7.4	6.7	6.5	7.0	8.6	9.6
	21	Labor force participation rate (percent of working-age population)	64.0	64.4	64.8	65.3	65.6	65.9	66.5	66.5	66.2	66.4
	22	Unemployment rate (percent of labor force)	9.6	7.5	7.2	7.0	6.2	5.5	5.3	5.6	6.8	7.5
	23	Real GDP per person (2000 dollars per year)	23,148	24,598	25,386	26,028	26,668	27,519	28,226	28,435	28,011	28,559
	24	Growth rate of real GDP per person (percent per year)	3.6	6.3	3.2	2.5	2.5	3.2	2.6	0.7	−1.5	2.0
	25	Quantity of money (M2, billions of dollars)	2126.5	2309.9	2495.7	2732.3	2831.4	2994.4	3158.4	3279.2	3379.1	3432.8
	26	GDP deflator (2000 = 100)	65.2	67.7	69.7	71.3	73.2	75.7	78.6	81.6	84.4	86.4
	27	GDP deflator inflation rate (percent per year)	4.0	3.8	3.0	2.2	2.7	3.4	3.8	3.9	3.5	2.3
	28	Consumer price index (1982–1984 = 100)	99.6	103.9	107.6	109.6	113.6	118.3	124	130.7	136.2	140.3
	29	CPI inflation rate (percent per year)	3.2	4.3	3.6	1.9	3.6	4.1	4.8	5.4	4.2	3.0
	30	Current account balance (billions of dollars)	−38.7	−94.3	−118.2	−147.2	−160.7	−121.2	−99.5	−79.0	2.9	−50.1